GERMAN TOYS
Der Universal-Spielwaren-Katalog 1924/1926

GERMAN TOYS

Der Universal-Spielwaren-Katalog 1924/1926

Reprinted from original German catalogs
with English,
German, and Spanish descriptions

Commentary by Dr. Manfred Bachmann

Published By

HOBBY HOUSE PRESS, INC.
Cumberland, Maryland 21502

Our reprint is based on two original copies (signatures SV 50a and 50c) owned by the Spielzeugmuseum, Sonneberg. The lender kindly consented to combining the two volumes into a single issue in original page sequence.

Translation of the commentary from the German by Charles Dukes

ISBN: 0-87588-251-X

Printed in the German Democratic Republic

Vorwort.

Der vorliegende Katalog zeigt Ihnen ein

GESAMTBILD DER DEUTSCHEN SPIELWAREN-INDUSTRIE

und unterscheidet sich von anderen bisher erschienenen Spielwarenkatalogen dadurch, daß er nicht das Angebot eines einzigen Spielwarenhändlers darstellt, sondern

NAMHAFTESTE SPIELWAREN-HERSTELLER

veranschaulichen darin ihre Erzeugnisse, und Sie kaufen daher nach diesem Katalog besonders vorteilhaft.

Wir empfehlen Ihnen diesen Katalog zur besonderen Beachtung, bewahren Sie denselben gut auf, er wird Ihnen ein dauerndes Nachschlagewerk sein und wird nach Bedarf durch Nachträge ergänzt werden.

Bei Bestellungen achten Sie bitte genau auf die Nummern und Bezeichnungen; die Preise befinden sich in beifolgendem Preisverzeichnis, das mit einem beachtenswerten Vorwort und Erklärung zur Benutzung versehen ist.

Preface.

The present catalogue gives you

A GENERAL VIEW OF THE GERMAN TOY INDUSTRY

and is distinguished from other toy catalogues that have hitherto appeared by the fact that it does not merely contain the goods offered by one toy dealer or manufacturer, but a selection of the best lines of more than hundred of the

LEADING GERMAN TOY MANUFACTURERS.

You therefore purchase from this catalogue most advantageously.

This catalogue is recommended to your special attention and care, for it will form a lasting and useful reference, especially as it will be completed by supplements according to requirements.

When ordering please note carefully the Nos. and designations; the prices are in the enclosed price list, which is furnished with a notworthy preface and an explanation how the list is to be used.

Prefacio.

El presente catálogo contiene un

SURTIDO COMPLETO

de todo lo que se produce en la

INDUSTRIA DE JUGUETES ALEMANA,

y se distingue de otros catálogos, que hasta ahora se han publicado, por no contener solamente los artículos de una sola casa sino el extracto de los mejores artículos de más de cien de las

FÁBRICAS DE JUGUETES MÁS RENOMBRADAS

de Alemania.

Cada artículo de este catálogo se ofrece pues del fabricante especial más competente.

Este catálogo se recomienda á su grata atención y le servirá de guía permanente, porque se completará continuadamente por suplementos importantes.

Pidiendose por este catálogo es necesario indicar bien exactamente todos los números y denominaciones.

Los precios se cotizan en la lista adjunta, en que se dan todos los detalles necesarios.

36/1722

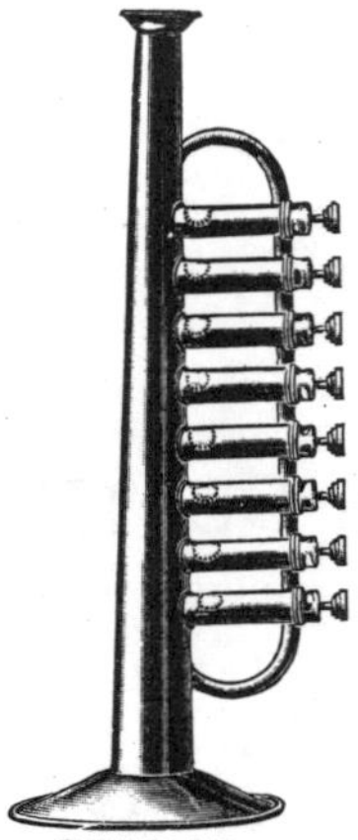

36/1814/8

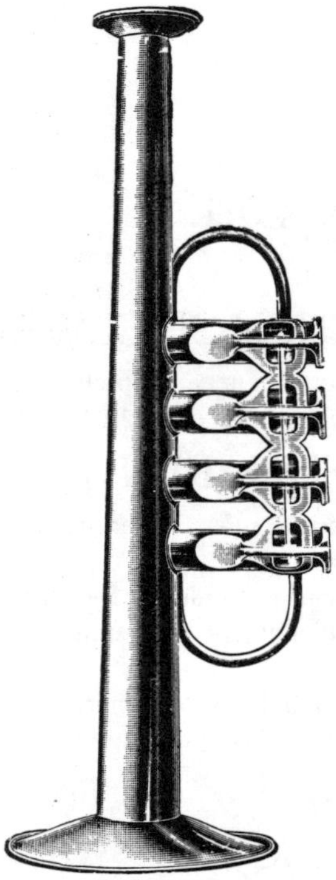

36/1003/4

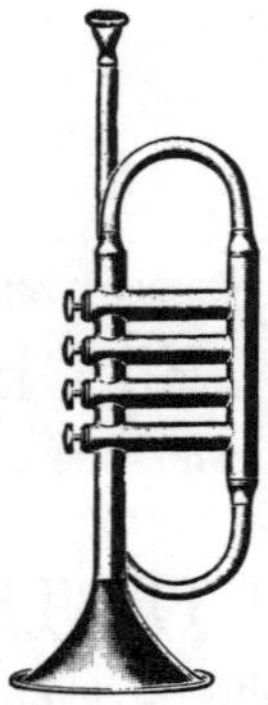

36/1816/4

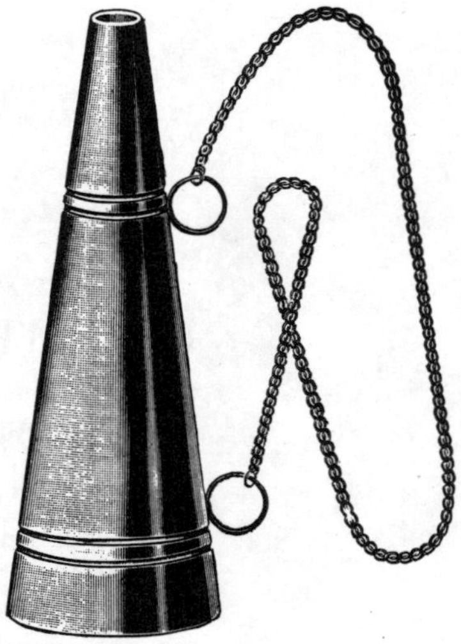

36/1862/3 K

36/1779

36/1721

36/1860/R

36/1633

36/1783

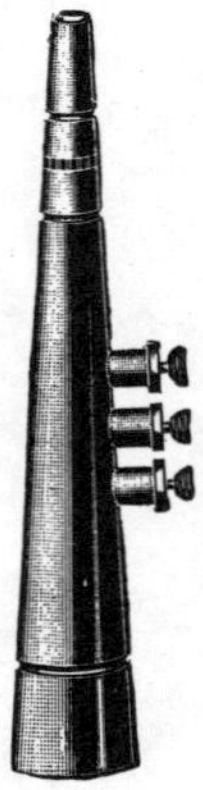

36/1823/3

Nr. **36**/1722 **Eintönige Hupe.**
Single tone horn.
Silbatos de lata de un solo tono.

„ **36**/1814/8 **Cornet aus Nickelblech.**
Cornet-a-piston of nickel.
Coınetas a pistón cubiertas de níquel.

„ **36**/1003/4 **Cornet aus Nickelblech.**
Cornet-a-piston of nickel.
Cornetas a pistón cubiertas de níquel.

„ **36**/1816/4 **Messing-Piston,** 4tönig.
Cornet-a-piston of brass, 4 tones.
Cornetas a pistón cubiertas de latón con 4 pistones.

Nr. **36**/1862/3K **Vernickeltes Autohorn,** 3tönig, mit Kette.
Auto-horn, nickelled, with 3 tones, with chain.
Corneta de automóvil de níquel con 3 pistones, con cadena.

„ **36**/1721 **Vernickeltes Autohorn.**
Auto-horn, nickelled.
Corneta de automóvil niquelada.

„ **36**/1860 R **Autohorn, Nickel,** 1 tönig.
Auto-horn, nickel, 1 tone.
Corneta de automóvil de níquel con 1 pistón.

„ **36**/1633 **Schreihahn aus farbigem Blech.**
Crowing-cocks, tin coloured.
Gallos para silbar, lata en colores.

Nr. **36**/1783 **Schreihahn aus farbigem Blech.**
Crowing-cocks, tin coloured.
Gallos para silbar, lata en colores.

„ **36**/1823/3 **Auto-Cornet, Nickel,** 3tönig.
Auto-cornet, nickel, 3 tones.
Cornetas a pistón cubiertas de níquel con 3 pistones.

36/1870/4

36/1762

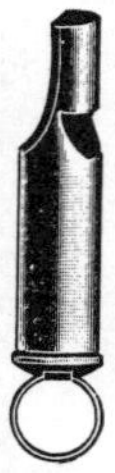

36/1757/6

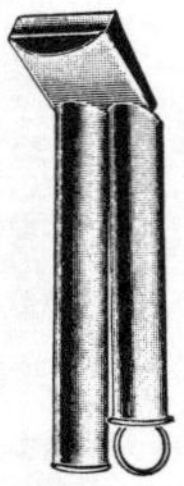

36/1070/2

36/1520/5

36/1693 K

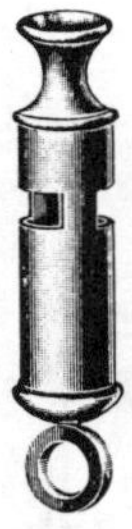

36/1728/2

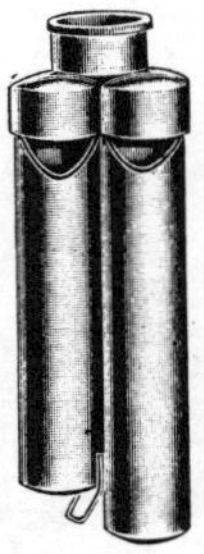

36/1744

36/1577

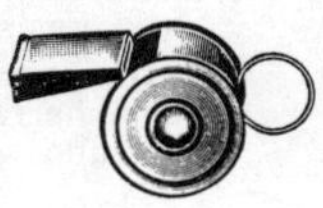

36/1741

36/1566

36/1755

36/1559

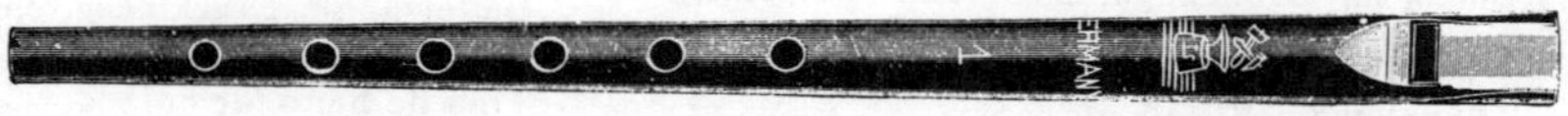

36/1503/1

36/1506/0

Nr. **36**/1762 **Vogelpfeife aus buntem Blech.**
Bird-call, tin, fancy colours.
Flauta de lata pintada.

„ **36**/1757/6 **Trillerpfeife, vernickelt.**
Trill-whistle, nickelled.
Silbato niquelado.

„ **36**/1070/2 **Doppelpfeife, vernickelt.**
Duplex whistle, nickelled.
Silbato doble, niquelado.

„ **36**/1520/5 **Trillerpfeife, vernickelt.**
Trill-whistle, nickelled.
Silbato niquelado.

„ **36**/1693 K **Trillerpfeife, vernickelt, mit Kette.**
Trill-whistle, nickelled, with chain.
Silbato niquelado, con cadena.

Nr. **36**/1728/2 **Doppelpfeife, Messing.**
Duplex whistle, brass.
Silbato doble, latón.

„ **36**/1744 **Fußballpfeife, Messing vernickelt.**
Football-whistle, brass, nickelled.
Silbato para el juego con bolas de pie.

„ **36**/1577 **Doppelpfeife, vernickelt.**
Duplex whistle, nickelled.
Silbato doble, lata niquelada.

„ **36**/1741 **Trillerpfeife, Weißblech.**
Trill-whistle, tin.
Silbato lata.

„ **36**/1566 **Vogelpfeife.**
Bird-call.
Silbato ruiseñor.

Nr. **36**/1755 **Trillerpfeife, Messing vernickelt.**
Trill-whistle, brass nickelled.
Silbato, laton niquelado.

„ **36**/1559 **Sirenenpfeife, vernickelt.**
Torpedo-whistle, nickelled.
Silbato de sirena, niquelado.

„ **36**/1503/1 **Flöte, vernickelt.**
Flute, nickelled.
Flauta de lata, niquelada.

„ **36**/1506/0 **Flagolett-Flöte, vernickelt.**
Flageolet, nickelled.
Flagolette niquelada.

„ **36**/1870/4 **Flöte, abgestimmt, aus schwarz lackiertem Blech mit Goldverzierung.**
Flute, tuned, black lacq. sheet metal, with gilt decoration.
Flauta, afinada de hoja de lata embarnizada en negro con decoración dorada.

Abbildungen in 1/2 natürlicher Größe. — Drawings in 1/2 natural size. — Ilustraciones en 1/2 del tamaño natural.

139/765

Badetische, weiß lackiert, mit Behang. sowie Badepuppe und Eimer.
Bathing-table, white varnished fitted out with bathing doll, pail, etc.
Mesa para baño, embarnizada en color blanco, con muñeca a bañar, cubo, etc.

	Länge	Breite	Höhe	Behang
Nr. **139**/765/1	85 mm	85 mm	145 mm	2 fach
„ **139**/765/3	95 „	95 „	170 „	2 „
„ **139**/765/4	115 „	115 „	185 „	3 „
„ **139** 765/5	125 „	125 „	210 „	3 „
„ **139**/765/6	135 „	135 „	250 „	4 „
„ **139**/765 7	150 „	150 „	270 „	4 „
„ **139**/765/8	170 „	170 „	290 „	5 „
„ **139**/765/9	200 „	200 „	315 „	5 „

Badeständer, rund, fein lackiert, mit Badepuppe und Eimer.
Wash-stand, round, elegantly varnished, with bathing doll and pail.
Estante para baño, redondo, bien embarnizado, con muñeca a bañar y cubo.

	Schüsseldurchmesser	Höhe
Nr. **139**/316/1	67 mm	105 mm
„ **139**/316/1½	80 „	110 „
„ **139** 316/2	97 „	130 „
„ **139**/316/2½	110 „	150 „

139/316/1½

139/316/5

Badeständer, rund, fein lackiert, mit Badepuppe und Eimer, sowie dreifachem Behang mit Badetuch.
Wash-stand, round, elegantly varnished, with bathing doll, bathing cloth, etc.
Estante para baño, redondo, bien embarnizado, con muñeca a bañar, cubo, tela, etc.

	Schüsseldurchmesser	Höhe
Nr. **139**/316/3	110 mm	140 mm
„ **139** 316/4	127 „	160 „
, **139**/316 5	143 „	175 „
„ **139**/316/6	160 „	195 „

139/317/13

Badeständer, oval, weiß lackiert, mit abnehmbarem rotem Schaff, mit Badepuppe und Eimer.
Wash-stand, oval, white varnished, with dismountable red basin, with bathing doll, and pail.
Estante para baño, óvalo, embarnizado en color blanco, con herrada roja separable, con muñeca a bañar y cubo.

	Länge	Breite	Höhe
Nr. **139** 317/12	105 mm	80 mm	160 mm
„ **139**/317/13	130 „	103 „	190 „
„ **139**/317/14	145 „	115 „	220 „

139/313/45

Badewanne, fein lackiert, auf hohen Füßen, mit Bildern, Wasserhahn, mit Badepuppe, Eimer und zweifachem Behang.
Bathing-tub, elegantly varnished, on high legs, with pictures, cock, with bathing doll, pail, etc.
Tina de baño. bien embarnizada, sobre altos pies, con figuras, con grifo de agua, con muñeca a bañar, con cubo, etc.

	Länge	Breite	Höhe
Nr. **139**/313 41	145 mm	70 mm	145 mm
„ **139**/313/42	162 „	80 „	150 „
„ **139**/313 43	178 „	92 „	170 „
„ **139**/313/44	195 „	105 „	190 „
„ **139** 313/45	218 „	115 „	215 „
„ **139**/313/46	240 „	132 „	230 „
„ **139** 313/47	265 „	148 „	255 „
„ **139**/313/48	335 „	185 „	315 „

Badewanne, Druckblech, ohne Füße, mit Badepuppe.
Bathing-tub, of pressed tin, without feet, with bathing doll.
Tina de baño, de hoja lata comprimida, sin pies, con muñeca a bañar.

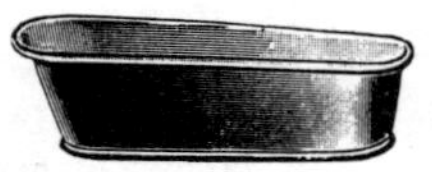

139/312/43

	Länge	Breite	Höhe
Nr. **139**/312/39	104 mm	56 mm	31 mm
„ **139**/312 40	117 „	61 „	35 „
„ **139** 312 41	145 „	70 „	42 „
„ **139**/312/42	162 „	80 „	44 „
„ **139**/312/43	178 „	92 „	47 „

139/315/44

Badewannen, fein lackiert, auf hohen Füßen, mit Goldstreifen und Wasserhahn, mit Badepuppe und Eimer.
Bathing-tub, elegantly varnished, on high legs, with gold stripes, with cock, with bathing doll, and pail.
Tinas de baño, bien embarnizado, sobre altos pies adornados con rayos dorados, con grifo de agua, con muñeca a bañar y cubo.

	Länge	Breite	Höhe
Nr. **139**/315/0	104 mm	56 mm	90 mm
„ **139**/315/38	104 „	56 „	105 „
„ **139**/315/39	104 „	56 „	110 „
„ **139** 315/40	117 „	61 „	120 „
„ **139**/315/41	145 „	70 „	145 „
„ **139**/315 42	162 „	80 „	150 „
„ **139**/315/43	178 „	92 „	170 „
„ **139**/315/44	195 „	105 „	190 „
„ **139**/315/45	218 „	115 „	215 „
„ **139** 315/46	240 „	132 „	230 „
„ **139**/315/47	265 „	148 „	255 „
„ **139**/315/48	335 „	185 „	315 „

139/315/0

Badewannen, ohne Füße, hochfein lackiert, mit Goldstreifen, Ausführung wie Serie 139/319, jedoch ohne Füße.
Bathing-tub, without feet, elegantly varnished, with gold stripes, finish the same as Serie 139/319, but without feet.
Tino de baño, sin pies, muy bien embarnizada y adornada de rayos dorados, la ejecución siendo la misma que la de la serie número 139/319, pero sin pies.

	Länge	Breite	Höhe
Nr. **139**/318 39	104 mm	56 mm	31 mm
„ **139** 318/40	117 „	61 „	35 „
„ **139**/318 41	145 „	70 „	42 „
„ **139**/318/42	162 „	80 „	44 „
„ **139** 318/43	178 „	92 „	47 „
„ **139** 318 44	195 „	105 „	65 „
„ **139**/318/45	218 „	115 „	75 „
„ **139** 318 46	240 ,	132 „	80 „
„ **139**/318/47	265 „	148 „	95 „
„ **139**/318/48	335 „	185 „	115 „

Länge = Length — Largo. Breite = Width — Ancho. Höhe = Height — Alto. Schüsseldurchmesser = Diameter of the basin — Diámetro de la fuente. Behang = Curtain - Colgadura.

139/319/44

Badewannen, fein lackiert, mit Goldstreifen auf Löwenfüßen, mit Badepuppe.

Bathing-tub, elegantly varnished, with gold stripes and lion feet, with bathing doll.

Tina de baño, bien embarnizada y adornada de rayos dorados, con pies de león, con muñeca a bañar.

	Länge	Breite	Höhe
Nr. **139**/319/39	104 mm	56 mm	45 mm
„ **139**/319/40	117 „	61 „	48 „
„ **139**/319/41	145 „	70 „	52 „
„ **139**/319/42	162 „	80 „	55 „
„ **139**/319/43	178 „	92 „	60 „
„ **139**/319/44	195 „	105 „	80 „
„ **139**/319/45	218 „	115 „	90 „
„ **139**/319/46	240 „	132 „	95 „
„ **139**/319/47	265 „	148 „	115 „
„ **139**/319/48	335 „	185 „	140 „

139/320/48

Badewannen, fein lackiert, mit Bildern, Goldstreifen, abnehmbar auf hohem Gestell, mit Wasserhahn, Badepuppe, Eimer und Behang.

Bathing tub, elegantly varnished, with pictures and gold stripes, dismountable on a high frame, with cock, bathing doll, pail, etc.

Tina de baño, bien embarnizada, con figuras y rayos dorados, separable, colocada sobre un estante alto, con grifo de agua, muñeca a bañar, cubo, etc.

	Länge	Breite	Höhe	Behang
Nr. **139**/320/42	162 mm	80 mm	155 mm	2 fach
„ **139**/320/43	178 „	92 „	175 „	2 „
„ **139**/320/44	195 „	105 „	205 „	2 „
„ **139**/320/45	218 „	115 „	235 „	2 „
„ **139**/320/46	240 „	132 „	245 „	4 „
„ **139**/320/47	265 „	148 „	275 „	4 „
„ **139**/320/48	335 „	185 „	315 „	4 „

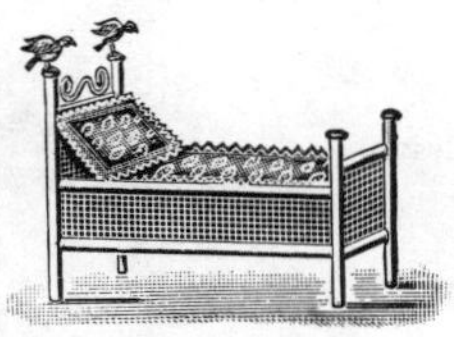

139/803/1

Betten, weiß lackiert, mit Adler, garniert.

Beds, white varnished, with eagle.

Camas, embarnizadas en color blanco, con águila, guarnecidas.

	Länge	Breite	Höhe
Nr. **139**/803/1	130 mm	70 mm	115 mm
„ **139**/803/2	150 „	85 „	130 „
„ **139**/803/3	170 „	95 „	140 „
„ **139**/803/4	195 „	107 „	160 „
„ **139**/803/5	215 „	117 „	175 „
„ **139**/803/6	235 „	130 „	190 „

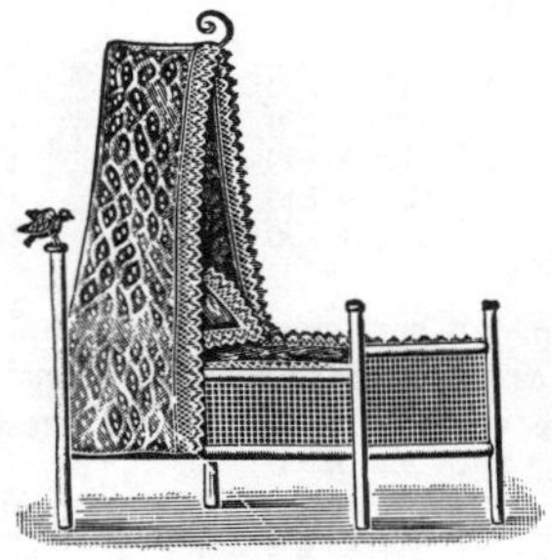

139/804/3

Betten, weiß lackiert, mit Adler, garniert und mit Himmel (Höhe ohne Himmel gemessen).

Beds, white varnished, with eagle, with canopy (height without canopy).

Camas, embarnizadas en color blanco, con águila, guarnecidas y con cielo (la altura medida sin el cielo).

	Länge	Breite	Höhe
Nr. **139**/804/1	130 mm	70 mm	115 mm
„ **139**/804/2	150 „	85 „	130 „
„ **139**/804/3	170 „	95 „	140 „
„ **139**/804/4	195 „	107 „	160 „
„ **139**/804/5	215 „	117 „	175 „
„ **139**/804/6	235 „	130 „	190 „

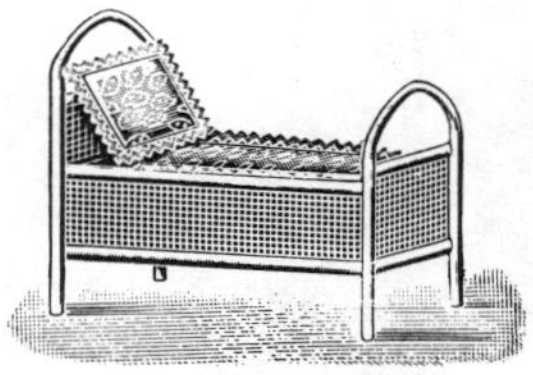

139/806/2

Betten, weiß lackiert, garniert.

Beds, white varnished.

Camas, embarnizadas en color blanco, guarnecidas.

	Länge	Breite	Höhe
Nr. **139**/806/1	130 mm	70 mm	105 mm
„ **139**/806/2	150 „	85 „	130 „
„ **139**/806/3	170 „	95 „	140 „
„ **139**/806/4	195 „	107 „	155 „
„ **139**/806/5	215 „	117 „	175 „
„ **139**/806/6	235 „	130 „	205 „

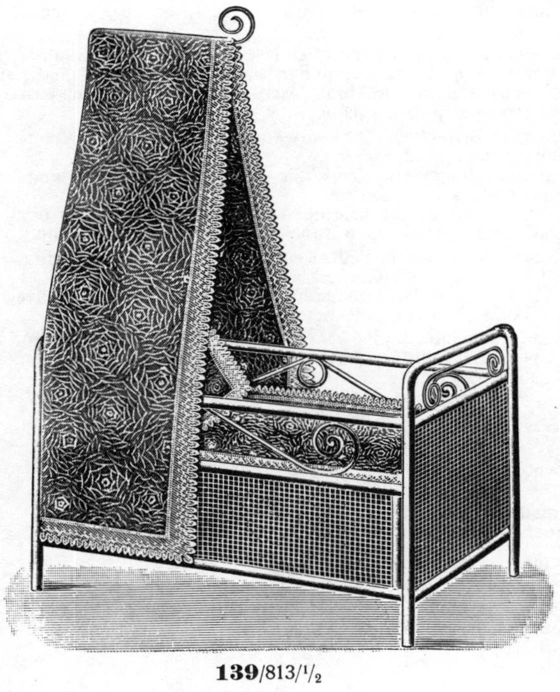

139/813/½

Betten, weiß lackiert, garniert, mit geschlossenem Himmel (Höhe ohne Himmel gemessen).

Beds, white varnished, with closed canopy (height without canopy).

Camas, embarnizadas en color blanco, guarnecidas, con cielo cerrado (la altura medida sin el cielo).

	Länge	Breite	Höhe
Nr. **139**/813/0	105 mm	65 mm	85 mm
„ **139**/813/1	125 „	70 „	95 „
„ **139**/813/1½	135 „	78 „	100 „
„ **139**/813/2	150 „	85 „	125 „
„ **139**/813/2½	170 „	95 „	130 „
„ **139**/813/3½	200 „	110 „	170 „
„ **139**/813/4½	230 „	125 „	180 „
„ **139**/813/5½	270 „	145 „	205 „
„ **139**/813/6½	295 „	160 „	215 „
„ **139**/813/7½	335 „	170 „	235 „
„ **139**/813/8½	380 „	190 „	260 „

139/807/5

Betten, weiß lackiert, garniert mit Himmel (Höhe ohne Himmel gemessen).

Beds, white varnished, with canopy (height without canopy).

Camas, embarnizadas en color blanco, guarnecidas, con cielo (la altura medida sin el cielo).

	Länge	Breite	Höhe
Nr. **139**/807/1	130 mm	70 mm	105 mm
„ **139**/807/2	150 „	85 „	130 „
„ **139**/807/3	170 „	95 „	140 „
„ **139**/807/4	195 „	107 „	155 „
„ **139**/807/5	215 „	117 „	175 „
„ **139**/807/6	235 „	130 „	205 „
„ **139**/807/7	280 „	142 „	190 „

Länge = Length — Largo. Breite = Width — Ancho. Höhe = Height — Alto.

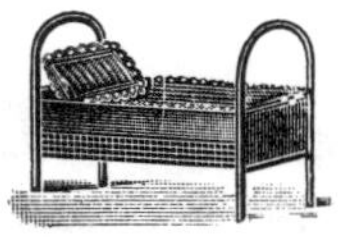

139/1006/11

Betten, lackiert, mit Garnitur.
Beds, varnished, with accessories.
Camas, embarnizadas, con guarnición.

	Länge	Breite	Höhe
Nr. **139**/1006/11	92 mm	57 mm	75 mm
„ **139**/1006/12	108 „	61 „	85 „
„ **139** 1006/13	118 „	70 „	100 „
„ **139**/1006/14	132 „	80 „	103 „

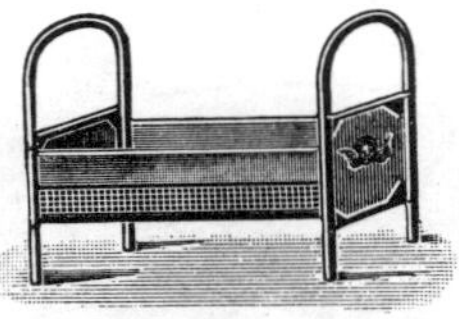

139/1009/14 L

Betten, leer, einfache Ausführung.
Beds, empty, simple style.
Camas, vacias, de elaboración sencilla.

	Länge	Breite	Höhe
Nr. **139**/1009/11 L	92 mm	57 mm	75 mm
„ **139**/1009/12 L	108 „	61 „	85 „
„ **139**/1009/13 L	118 „	70 „	100 „
„ **139**/1009/14 L	132 „	80 „	103 „

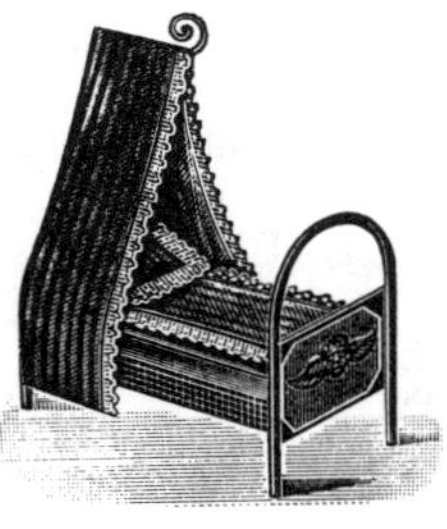

139/1007/13

Betten, lackiert, mit Garnitur und Himmel (Höhe ohne Himmel gemessen).
Beds, varnished, with accessories and canopy (height without canopy).
Camas, embarnizadas, con guarnición y con cielo (la altura medida sin el cielo).

	Länge	Breite	Höhe
Nr. **139**/1007/11	92 mm	57 mm	75 mm
„ **139**/1007/12	108 „	61 „	85 „
„ **139**/1007/13	118 „	70 „	100 „
„ **139**/1007/14	132 „	80 „	103 „

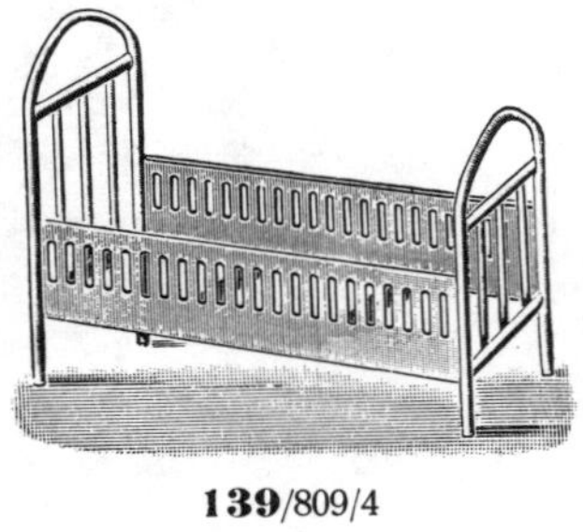

139/809/4

Betten, leer, fein lackiert.
Beds, empty, elegantly varnished.
Camas, vacias, bien embarnizadas.

	Länge	Breite	Höhe
Nr. **139**/809/1	130 mm	70 mm	105 mm
„ **139**/809/2	150 „	85 „	130 „
„ **139**/809/3	170 „	95 „	140 „
„ **139**/809/4	195 „	107 „	155 „
„ **139** 809/5	215 „	117 „	175 „
„ **139**/809/6	235 „	130 „	205 „

139/750/4

Brausebad, weiß lackiert, auf Löwenfüßen, Badepuppen, Handtuch und Eimer.
Shower bath, white varnished, on lion feet, bathing doll, towel and pail.
Baño de chorro, es decir una banca pequeña provista de una fuente pequeña para lavar bebés, embarnizada en color blanco, con pies de león, muñeca a bañar, toalla y cubo.

	Schaffdurchmesser	Höhe
Nr. **139**/750/2	97 mm	200 mm
„ **139**/750/3	110 „	240 „
„ **139**/750/4	127 „	260 „
„ **139**/750/5	143 „	280 „
„ **139**/750/6	160 „	300 „

Kehrgarnituren auf Karten, mit rotlackiertem Holzstiel, buntlackierter Schaufel.
Sweeping sets, on cards, with red varnished wooden handles, coloured varnished shovel.
Juegos para barrer, sobre cartón, con mango de madera embarnizado en color rojo y paleta embarnizada en varios colores.

	Kartengröße	Schaufelgröße	Besenlänge
Nr. **139**/75/20½	160 × 107 mm	72 × 65 mm	75 mm
„ **139**/75/21½	160 × 107 „	80 × 80 „	80 „
„ **139**/75 22½	185 × 130 „	90 × 85 „	80 „
„ **139**/75/23½	230 × 153 „	107 × 95 „	115 „
„ **139**/75/24½	230 × 153 „	110 × 110 „	140 „

139/75/23½

Besenständer, fein lackiert. — **Broom stands,** elegantly varnished. — **Estantes para escobas,** bien embarnizadas.

	Länge	Breite	Höhe	
Nr. **139**/910/0	65 mm Ø	—	150 mm	Mit Teppichbesen, Handbesen, Schaufel. With carpet broom, hand broom, shovel. Con escoba para alfombras, escoba pequeña.
„ **139**/910/1	85 „	„ 65 mm	160 „	Mit Teppichbesen, Handbesen, Schaufel. With carpet broom, hand broom, shovel. Con escoba para alfombras, escoba pequeña.
„ **139**/910/2	105 „	„ 80 „	180 „	Mit Teppichbesen, Handbesen, Schaufel, Eimer. With carpet broom, hand broom, shovel, pail. Con escoba para alfombras, escoba pequeña, cubo.
„ **139**/910/3	120 „	„ 90 „	220 „	Mit Teppichbesen, Bodenbesen, Handbesen, Schaufel und Eimer. With carpet broom, floor broom, hand broom, shovel and pail. Con escoba para alfombras, escoba para el suelo, escoba pequeña, paleta y cubo.
„ **139**/910/4	140 „	„ 105 „	245 „	Mit Teppichbesen, Bodenbesen, Schrubber, Handbesen, Schaufel und Eimer. With carpet broom, floor broom, scrubber, hand broom, shovel and pail. El mismo, con escoba para alfombras, escoba para el suelo, raedera, escoba pequeña, paleta y cubo.
„ **139**/910/5	140 „	„ 140 „	245 „	Mit Teppichbesen, Bodenbesen, Federwedel, Handbesen, Zylinderwischer, Schaufel und Eimer. With carpet broom, floor broom, feather duster, hand broom, lampchimney brush, shovel and pail. El mismo, con escoba para elfombras, escoba para el suelo, plumero, escoba pequeña, rodillo para limpiar, tubos de lámparas, paleta y cubo.
„ **139**/910/6	160 „	„ 160 „	275 „	Mit Teppichbesen, Bodenbesen, Federwedel, Handbesen, Ofenwischer, Ausklopfer, Schaufel, Eimer, Bank mit Schaff. With carpet broom, floor broom, feather duster, hand broom, stove cleaner, beater, shovel, pail, bench and small basin. El mismo, con escoba para alfombras, escoba para el suelo, plumero, escoba pequeña, rodillo para limpiar estufas, sacudidor, paleta, cubo, banca y herrada.

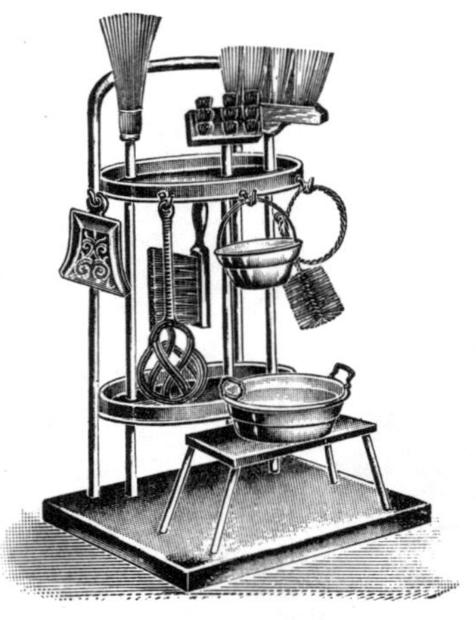

139/910/6

Kehrgarnituren auf Karten, mit schwarzlackiertem Holzstiel, vernickelter Schaufel.
Sweeping sets, on cards, black varnished wooden handles, nickelled shovel.
Juegos para barrer, sobre cartón, con mango de madera embarnizado en color negro y paleta niquelada.

	Kartengröße	Schaufelgröße	Besenlänge
Nr. **139** 76/20½	160 × 107 mm	72 × 65 mm	75 mm
„ **139**/76/21½	160 × 107 „	80 × 80 „	80 „
„ **139**/76 22½	185 × 130 „	90 × 85 „	80 „
„ **139**/79 23½	230 × 153 „	107 × 95 „	115 „
„ **139**/76/24½	230 × 153 „	110 × 110 „	140 „

Kehrgarnituren auf Karten, mit rotgebeiztem Holzstiel, vernickelter Schaufel.
Sweeping sets, on cards, with red stained wooden handles, nickelled shovel.
Juegos para barrer, sobre cartón, mango de madera trabajado con mordiente en color rojo y paleta niquelada.

	Kartengröße	Schaufelgröße	Besenlänge
Nr. **139**/77/20½	160 × 107 mm	72 × 65 mm	75 mm
„ **139**/77 21½	160 × 107 „	80 × 80 „	80 „
„ **139**/77 22½	185 × 130 „	90 × 85 „	80 „
„ **139** 77/23½	230 × 153 „	107 × 95 „	115 „
„ **139**/77/24½	230 × 153 „	110 × 110 „	140 „

139/9/2

Lampen, fein lackiert.
Lamps, elegantly varnished.
Lámparas, bien embarnizadas.

	Durchmesser	Höhe
Nr. **139**/9/1	45 mm	110 mm
„ **139**/9/2	60 „	140 „

Länge = Length — Largo. Breite = Width — Ancho. Höhe = Heigth — Alto. Kartengröße = Size of the card — Tamaño del carton. Schaufelgröße = Size of the shovel — Tamaño de la paleta. Besenlänge = Broom length — Largo de la escoba. Raddurchmesser = Diameter of wheel — Diametro de las ruedas. Glockendurchmesser = Diameter of bell — Diametro de las campanillas.

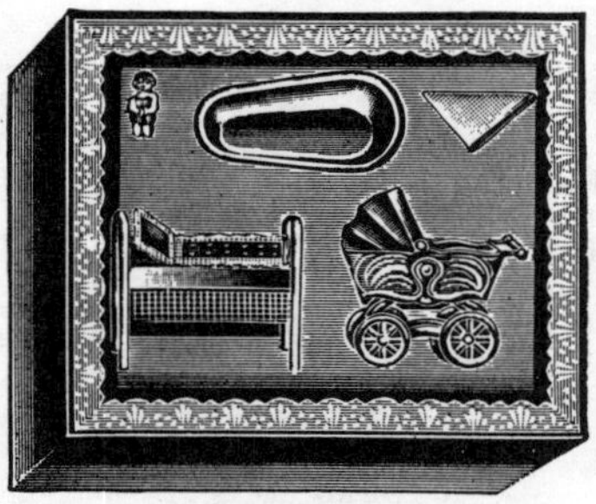

139/800/1

Puppengarnituren, in Kartons aufgenäht, in einfacher Ausführung.

Dolls set, fixed into cardboard boxes, simple execution.

Guarniciones para muñecas, cosidas sobre cartón, de elaboración sencilla.

Nr. **139**/800/1	Kartongröße	250 × 210 × 60 mm	Mit Badewanne, Puppenwagen, Bett. With bathing-tub, dolls go-cart, bed. Con tina de baño, coche para muñecas, cama.
„ **139**/800/2	„	285 × 250 × 60 „	Mit Badewanne, Puppenwagen, Bett und Waschtisch. With bathing-tub, dolls go-cart, bed and washing table. Con tina de baño, coche para muñecas, cama y lavadero.

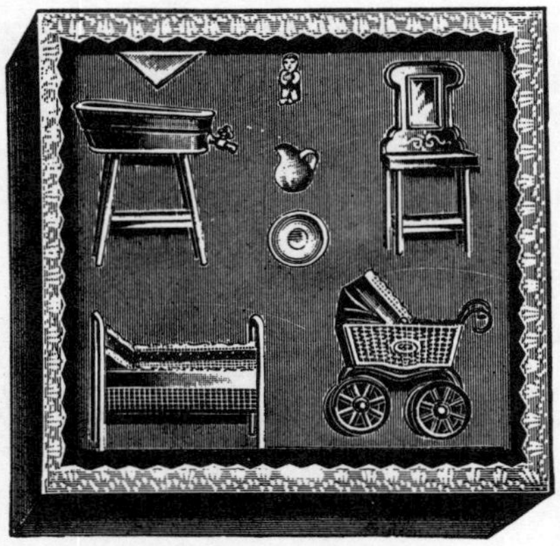

139/801/3

Puppengarnituren in hochfeiner lackierter Ausführung.

Dolls set, in very elegant varnished execution.

Guarniciones para muñecas, muy bien embarnizadas y de ejecución finísima.

Nr. **139**/801/1	Kartongröße	250 × 210 × 60 mm	Mit Badewanne, Puppenwagen und Bett. With bathing-tub, dolls go-cart and bed. Con tina de baño, coche para muñecas y cama.
„ **139**/801/2	„	305 × 270 × 60 „	Mit Badewanne, Puppenwagen und Waschtisch. With bathing-tub, dolls go-cart and washing table. Con tina de baño, coche para muñecas y lavadero.
„ **139**/801/3	„	305 × 305 × 65 „	Mit Badewanne, Puppenwagen, Bett und Waschtisch. With bathing-tub, dolls go-cart, bed and washing table. Con tina de baño, coche para muñecas, cama y lavadero.
„ **139**/801/4	„	350 × 345 × 80 „	
„ **139**/801/5	„	400 × 400 × 85 „	

139/843/0

Puppenwagen, weiß lackiert, mit beweglichem Dach.

Dolls go-cart, white varnished, with moveable shade.

Coches para muñecas, embarnizados en color blanco, con tejado móvil.

	Kastenlänge	Kastenbreite	Gesamthöhe (ohne Dach)
Nr. **139**/843/0	103 mm	43 mm	90 mm
„ **139**/843/9	85 „	37 „	80 „
„ **139**/843/10	97 „	43 „	95 „
„ **139**/843/12	122 „	59 „	110 „
„ **139**/843/14	140 „	65 „	130 „
„ **139**/843/16	160 „	75 „	140 „

139/50/3

Spardosen mit Schloß, fein lackiert.

Saving box with lock, elegantly varnished.

Cajas de ahorro con cerradura, bien embarnizadas

		Durchm.
Nr. **139**/50/1	Apfel-Apple-Manzana	80 mm
„ **139**/50/2	Birne-Pear-Pera	115×70 „
„ **139**/50/3	Mond-Moon-Luna	85 „

139/843/16

Puppenwagen, einfache Ausführung, mit beweglichem Dach.

Dolls go-cart, simple execution, with moveable shade.

Coches para muñecas, de elaboración sencilla, con tejado móvil.

	Kastenlänge	Kastenbreite	Gesamthöhe (ohne Dach)
Nr. **139**/844/0	70 mm	35 mm	55 mm
„ **139**/844/1	80 „	39 „	65 „

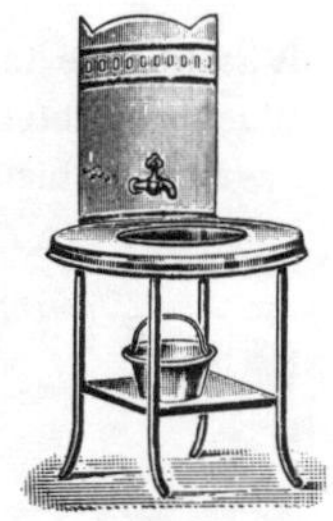

139/710/2

Waschtische, oval, weiß lackiert, mit Wasserhahn, Schüssel und Eimer.

Washing table, oval, white varnished, with cock, basin and pail.

Lavaderos, óvalos, embarnizados en color blanco, con grifo de agua, fuente y cubo.

	Länge	Breite	Höhe
Nr. **139**/710/1	85 mm	65 mm	155 mm
„ **139**/710/2	100 „	80 „	180 „
„ **139**/710/3	120 „	95 „	200 „

139/322/44

Duschwannen in hochfeiner lackierter Ausführung, mit Brause, Wasserhahn und Badewanne mit Badepuppe.

Tub for shower bathes in elegantly varnished execution, watercock, bathing tub with bathing doll.

Tinas para duchas, bien embarnizadas y de elaboración, boca de regadera, grifo de agua, colgadura, tina de baño y muñeca.

	Länge	Breite	Höhe
Nr. **139**/322/38	105 mm	75 mm	140 mm
„ **139**/322/39	105 „	75 „	135 „
„ **139**/322/40	120 „	80 „	150 „
„ **139**/322/41	140 „	85 „	170 „
„ **139**/322/42	150 „	105 „	185 „
„ **139**/322/43	165 „	115 „	200 „
„ **139**/322/44	185 „	125 „	215 „
„ **139**/322/45	205 „	140 „	240 „

139/711/10

Waschtische in einfacher Ausführung, mit Spiegel und Waschservice.
Washing tables of simple execution with mirror and washing service.
Lavaderos de elaboración sencilla, con espejo y servicio para lavar.

	Länge	Breite	Höhe	
Nr. **139**/711/1	60 mm	52 mm	125 mm	Mit viereckigem Spiegel, Krug und Schüssel. With square mirror, jug and basin. Con espejo cuadrado, cántaro y fuente.
„ **139**/711/10	67 „	55 „	145 „	Mit rundem Spiegel, Krug und Schüssel. With round mirror, jug and basin. Con espejo redondo, cántaro y fuente.
„ **139**/711/11	73 „	65 „	157 „	
„ **139**/711/12	80 „	74 „	175 „	Mit ovalem Spiegel, Krug und Schüssel. With oval mirror, jug and basin. Con espejo óvalo, cántaro y fuente.
„ **139**/711/13	90 „	78 „	180 „	
„ **139**/711/14	100 „	80 „	205 „	Mit ovalem Spiegel, Krug, Schüssel und Blecheimer. With oval mirror, jug, bassin and tin pail. Con espejo óvalo, cántaro, fuente y cubo de hoja lata.

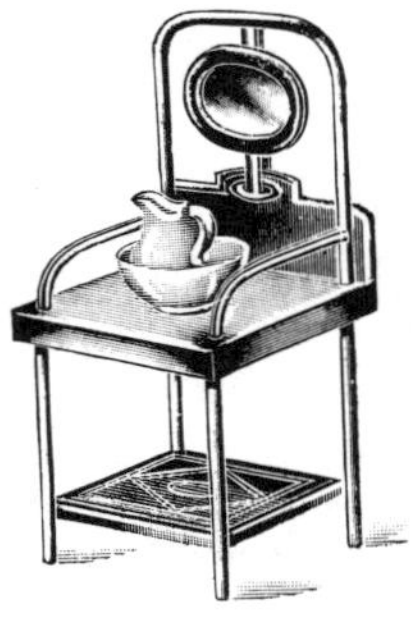

139/712/13

Waschtische, weiß lackiert, mit Spiegel und Waschservice.
Washing tables, white varnished, with mirror and washing service.
Lavaderos, embarnizados, en color blanco con espejo y servicio para lavar.

	Länge	Breite	Höhe	
Nr. **139**/712/10	67 mm	55 mm	145 mm	Mit rundem Spiegel, Krug und Schüssel. With round mirror, jug and basin. Con espejo redondo, cántaro y fuente.
„ **139**/712/11	73 „	65 „	157 „	
„ **139**/712/12	80 „	74 „	175 „	Mit ovalem Spiegel, Krug und Schüssel. With oval mirror, jug and basin. Con espejo óvalo, cántaro y fuente.
„ **139**/712/13	90 „	78 „	180 „	
„ **139**/712/14	100 „	80 „	205 „	Mit ovalem Spiegel, Krug, Schüssel und Blecheimer. With oval mirror, jug, basin, and tin pail. Con espejo óvalo, cántaro fuente y cubo de hoja lata.
„ **139**/712/16	125 „	100 „	230 „	

139/713/16

Waschtische, einfache Ausführung, ohne Spiegel, mit Waschservice.
Washing tables, simple form, without mirror, with wash service.
Lavaderos, elaboración sencille, sin espejo, con servicio para lavar.

	Länge	Breite	Höhe	
Nr. **139**/713/10	67 mm	55 mm	95 mm	Mit Schüssel und Krug. — With basin and jug. — Con fuente y cántaro.
„ **139**/713/11	73 „	65 „	105 „	
„ **139**/713/12	80 „	74 „	115 „	
„ **139**/713/13	90 „	78 „	130 „	
„ **139**/713/14	100 „	80 „	140 „	Mit Schüssel, Krug und Blecheimer. With basin, jug and tin pail. Con fuente, cántaro y cubo de hoja lata.
„ **139**/713/16	125 „	100 „	155 „	
„ **139**/713/17	130 „	107 „	170 „	

139/714/11

Waschtische in hochfeiner, lackierter Ausführung, Spiegel, Waschservice, Handtuch und Behang.
Washing tables, most elegant style, mirror, wash service, towel, etc.
Lavaderos, bien embarnizados y de elaboración finísima, con espejo, servicio para lavar, toalla, etc.

	Länge	Breite	Höhe	
Nr. **139**/714/1	60 mm	52 mm	125 mm	Viereckiger Spiegel, Krug und Schüssel. Square mirror, jug and basin. Espejo cuadrado, cántaro y fuente.
„ **139**/714/10	67 „	55 „	145 „	Ovaler Spiegel, Krug und Schüssel. Oval mirror, jug and basin. Espejo óvalo, cántaro y fuente.
„ **139**/714/11	73 „	65 „	157 „	Ovaler Spiegel, Krug, Schüssel und 2 Handtücher. Oval mirror, jug, basin and two towels. Espejo óvalo, cántaro, fuente y dos toallas.
„ **139**/714/12	80 „	74 „	175 „	
„ **139**/714/13	90 „	78 „	180 „	Viereckiger Spiegel, Krug, Schüssel, Eimer und 2 Handtücher. Square mirror, jug, basin, pail and two towels. Espejo cuadrado, cántaro, fuente, cubo y dos toallas.
„ **139**/714/14	100 „	80 „	205 „	
„ **139**/714/16	125 „	100 „	230 „	Vierekiger Spiegel, Krug, Schüssel, Eimer, 2 Handtücher und 2fachem Behang. Square mirror, jug, basin, pail, two towels and double curtain. Espejo cuadrado, cántaro, fuente, cubo, dos toallas y doble colgadura.
„ **139**/714/17	130 „	107 „	260 „	
„ **139**/714/18	155 „	125 „	295 „	
„ **139**/714/19	185 „	150 „	355 „	
„ **139**/714/20	225 „	175 „	410 „	

139/714/19

139/716/13

Waschtische, weiß lackiert, ohne Spiegel, mit Waschservice und Handtuch.
Washing tables, white varnished, without mirror, with washing service and towel.
Lavaderos, embarnizados en color blanco, sin espejo, con servicio para lavar y con toalla.

	Länge	Breite	Höhe	
Nr. **139**/716/10	67 mm	55 mm	95 mm	Mit Krug und Schüssel. With jug and basin. Con cantaro y fuente.
„ **139**/716/10½	67 „	55 „	95 „	Mit Krug, Schüssel und zwei Handtüchern. With jug, basin and two towels. Con cántaro, fuente y dos toallas.
„ **139**/716/11	73 „	65 „	105 „	
„ **139**/716/12	80 „	74 „	115 „	
„ **139**/716/13	90 „	78 „	130 „	
„ **139**/716/14	100 „	80 „	140 „	Mit Krug, Schüssel, Eimer und zwei Handtüchern. With jug and basin, pail, two towels. Con cántaro y fuente, cubo y dos toallas.
„ **139**/719/16	125 „	100 „	155 „	
„ **139**/716/17	130 „	107 „	170 „	

139/878/4

Roller, ohne Bespannung, mit lackierten Blechrädern und vernickelten Stahlglocken.
Rollers with varnished tin wheels, without horsing and with nickeled steel bells.
Vehículos, sin uñidura, con ruedas embarnizadas de hoja lata y campanillas de acero niqueladas.

	Raddurchmesser	Glockendurchmesser
Nr. **139**/878/0	60 mm	35 mm
„ **139**/878/1	67 „	35 „
„ **139**/878/2	80 „	35 „
„ **139**/878/3	92 „	40 „
„ **139**/878/4	110 „	45 „

Roller, ohne Bespannung, mit Druckblechrädern und vernickelten Stahlglocken.
Rollers, without horsing, with wheels of pressed tin and nickeled steel bells.
Vehículos, sin uñidura, con ruedas de hoja lata comprimida y campanillas de acero niqueladas.

	Raddurchmesser	Glockendurchmesser
Nr. **139**/879/0	60 mm	35 mm
„ **139**/879/1	67 „	35 „
„ **139**/879/2	80 „	35 „

139/879/0

139/878/16

Roller, ohne Bespannung, mit massiven lackierten Rädern und vernickelten Stahlglocken.
Rollers, without horsing, with solid varnished wheels and nickeled steel bells.
Vehículos, sin uñidura, con ruedas macizas y embarnizadas y con campanillas de acero niqueladas.

	Raddurchmesser	Glockendurchmesser
Nr. **139**/878/9	90 mm	40 mm
„ **139**/878/10½	105 „	45 „
„ **139**/878/12	120 „	50 „
„ **139**/878/13	130 „	50 „
„ **139**/878/14	140 „	55 „
„ **139**/878/16	160 „	60 „
„ **139**/878/17	170 „	65 „
„ **139**/878/19	190 „	70 „
„ **139**/878/21	210 „	75 „

139/880/19

139/881/19

Laufreifen, mit einfachem massiven Rad, Holzstab und vernickelten Stahlglocken.
Solid wheel, wooden rod and nickeled steel bells.
Cerco de carrera, con rueda sencilla y maciza, palo de madera y campanillas de acero niqueladas.

	Raddurchmesser	Glockendurchmesser
Nr. **139**/880/16	160 mm	40 mm
„ **139**/880/17	170 „	45 „
„ **139**/880/19	190 „	50 „
„ **139**/880/21	210 „	55 „

Laufreifen, mit massiven lackierten Doppelrädern, Holzstab und vernickelten Stahlglocken.
Solid varnished double wheels, with stick and nickeled steel bells.
Cerco de carrera, con dobles ruedas macizas y embarnizadas, palo de madera y campanillas de acero niqueladas.

	Raddurchmesser	Glockendurchmesser
Nr. **139**/881/9	90 mm	40 mm
„ **139**/881/10½	105 „	45 „
„ **139**/881/12	120 „	50 „
„ **139**/881/13	130 „	50 „
„ **139**/881/14	140 „	55 „
„ **139**/881/16	160 „	60 „
„ **139**/881/17	170 „	65 „
„ **139**/881/19	190 „	70 „
„ **139**/881/21	210 „	75 „

139/903/2

Roller, bespannt, einfache Ausführung, mit sortierten Papptieren und vernickelten Stahlglocken.
Roller, horsed, simple execution, with assorted animals of cardboard and nickeled steel bells.
Vehículo uñido, de elaboración sencilla, con animales surtidos y hechos de cartón, también con campanillas de acero niqueladas.

	Raddurchmesser	Glockendurchmesser	Länge
Nr. **139**/903/0	60 mm	35 mm	150 mm
„ **139**/903/1	67 „	35 „	175 „
„ **139**/903/2	80 „	35 „	195 „
„ **139**/903/3	92 „	40 „	200 „
„ **139**/903/4	110 „	45 „	230 „
„ **139**/903/9	90 „	40 „	200 „
„ **139**/903/10½	105 „	45 „	230 „

139/906/4

Roller, bespannt, mit lackierten Blechrädern, sortierten Papptieren und vernickelten Stahlglocken.
Roller, horsed, with varnished wheels of tin, assorted animals of cardboard and nickeled steel bells.
Vehículo uñido, con ruedas embarnizadas de hoja lata, con animales surtidos y hechos de cartón, también con campanillas de acero niqueladas.

	Raddurchmesser	Glockendurchmesser	Länge
Nr. **139**/906/0	60 mm	35 mm	150 mm
„ **139**/906/1	67 „	35 „	175 „
„ **139**/906/2	80 „	35 „	195 „
„ **139**/906/3	92 „	40 „	210 „
„ **139**/906/4	110 „	45 „	235 „

139/906/13

139/907/1

Roller, bespannt, mit lackierten Patenträdern, sortierten Papptieren, vernickelten Stahlglocken.

Roller, horsed, with varnished patent wheels, assorted animals of cardbord, nickeled steel bells.

Vehiculo, uñido, con ruedas patentadas y embarnizadas, con animales surtidos y hechos de cartón, también con campanillas de acero niqueladas.

Nr.	Raddurchmesser	Glockendurchmesser	Länge
Nr. **139**/996/9	90 mm	40 mm	210 mm
„ **139**/906/10½	105 „	45 „	230 „
„ **139**/906/12	120 „	50 „	260 „
„ **139**/906/13	130 „	50 „	280 „
„ **139**/906/14	140 „	55 „	335 „
„ **139**/906/16	160 „	60 „	350 „

Roller, bespannt, mit lackierten Blechrädern, mit überzogenen Stoffschafen, vernickelten Stahlglocken.

Roller, horsed, with varnished tin wheels, with cloth sheep, with steel bells.

Vehículo, uñido, con ruedas embarnizadas de hoja lata, con ovejas cubiertas de género y con campanillas de acero niqueladas.

Nr.	Raddurchmesser	Glockendurchmesser	Länge
Nr. **139**/907/0	60 mm	35 mm	160 mm
„ **139**/907/1	67 „	35 „	180 „
„ **139**/907/2	80 „	35 „	200 „
„ **139**/907/3	92 „	40 „	210 „
„ **139**/907/4	110 „	45 „	240 „

139/907/13

Roller, bespannt, mit lackierten massiven Patenträdern, sortierten Stofftieren, vernickelten Stahlglocken.

Roller, horsed, with varnished solid patent wheels, sorted cloth animals, nickeled steel bells.

Vehículo, uñido, con ruedas patentadas macizas y embarnizadas, con animales surtidos y cubiertos de género, también con campanillas de acero niqueladas.

Nr.	Raddurchmesser	Glockendurchmesser	Länge
Nr. **139**/907/9	90 mm	40 mm	210 mm
„ **139**/907/10½	105 „	45 „	230 „
„ **139**/907/12	120 „	50 „	255 „
„ **139**/907/13	130 „	50 „	280 „
„ **139**/907/14	140 „	55 „	320 „
„ **139**/907/16	160 „	60 „	345 „
„ **139**/907/17	170 „	65 „	375 „
„ **139**/907/19	190 „	70 „	420 „
„ **139**/907/21	210 „	75 „	460 „

139/907/21

139/908/17

Roller, bespannt, mit lackierten massiven Patenträdern, mit Plüschbären, vernickelten Stahlglocken.

Roller, horsed, with varnished solid patent wheels, with plush bears, nickeled steel bells.

Vehiculo, uñido, con ruedas patentadas macizas y embarnizadas, con osos de felpa y con campanillas de acero niqueladas.

Nr.	Raddurchmesser	Glockendurchmesser	Länge
Nr. **139**/908/10½	105 mm	45 mm	240 mm
„ **139**/908/12	120 „	50 „	255 „
„ **139**/908/13	130 „	50 „	280 „
„ **139**/908/14	140 „	55 „	330 „
„ **139**/908/16	160 „	60 „	345 „
„ **139**/908/17	170 „	65 „	380 „
„ **139**/908/19	190 „	70 „	440 „
„ **139**/908/21	210 „	75 „	460 „

139/932/12

Roller, bespannt, mit lackierten massiven Patenträdern, mit Karikaturhunden und -katzen, vernickelten Stahlglocken.

Roller, with varnished solid patent wheels and horsed with caricature dogs and cats, nickeled steel bells.

Vehículo, uñido, con ruedas patentadas macizas y embarnizadas, con caricaturas de petros y gatos, también con campanillas de acero niqueladas.

Nr.	Raddurchmesser	Glockendurchmesser	Länge
Nr. **139**/932/10½	105 mm	45 mm	220 mm
„ **139**/932/12	120 „	50 „	255 „
„ **139**/932/13	130 „	50 „	270 „
„ **139**/932/14	140 „	55 „	310 „
„ **139**/932/16	160 „	60 „	340 „
„ **139**/932/17	170 „	65 „	365 „
„ **139**/932/19	190 „	70 „	420 „
„ **139**/932/21	210 „	75 „	440 „

139/933/16

Roller, bespannt, mit lackierten massiven Patenträdern, mit Spitzhunden und vernickelten Stahlglocken.

Rollers, horsed, with varnished solid patent wheels, with dogs and nickeled steel bells.

Vehículo, uñido, con ruedas patentadas macizas y embarnizadas, con busquillos y con campanillas de acero niqueladas.

Nr.	Raddurchmesser	Glockendurchmesser	Länge
Nr. **139**/933/14	140 mm	55 mm	325 mm
„ **139**/933/16	160 „	60 „	350 „
„ **139**/933/17	170 „	65 „	375 „
„ **139**/933/19	190 „	70 „	410 „

139/935/19

Roller, bespannt, mit lackierten massiven Patenträdern, mit Pelzschafen und vernickelten Stahlglocken.

Rollers, horsed, with varnished solid patent wheels, with fur sheep and steel bells.

Vehículo, uñido, con ruedas patentadas macizas y embarnizadas, con ovejas de pelliza y con campanillas de acero niqueladas.

Nr.	Raddurchmesser	Glockendurchmesser	Länge
Nr. **139**/935/14	140 mm	55 mm	320 mm
„ **139**/935/16	160 „	60 „	350 „
„ **139**/935/17	170 „	65 „	380 „
„ **139**/935/19	190 „	70 „	420 „
„ **139**/935/21	210 „	75 „	450 „

139/936/21

Roller, bespannt, mit lackierten massiven Patenträdern, mit Fellspitz und vernickelten Stahlglocken.
Rollers, with varnished solid patent wheels, fur dog and nickeled steel bells.
Vehículo uñido, con ruedas patentadas macizas y embarnizadas, con bisquillos de pelliza y con campanillas de acero niqueladas.

	Raddurchmesser	Glockendurchmesser	Länge
Nr. **139**/936/17	170 mm	65 mm	370 mm
„ **139**/936/16	160 „	60 „	340 „
„ **139**/936/19	190 „	70 „	420 „
„ **139**/936/21	210 „	75 „	450 „

139/960/3

139/962/5

Fahrroller, mit zwei Glocken.
Rollers, with two bells.
Vehículos de carrera, con dos campanillas.

	Raddurchmesser	Glockendurchmesser
Nr. **139**/960/1	60 mm	40 und 45 mm
„ **139**/960/3	60 „	40 „ 45 „
„ **139**/960/5	60 „	40 „ 45 „

	Raddurchmesser	Glockendurchmesser
Nr. **139**/962/1	65 mm	50 und 55 mm
„ **139**/962/3	65 „	50 „ 55 „
„ **139**/962/5	65 „	50 „ 55 „

Teeseiher, mit gebeiztem Holzstiel.
Tea strainer, with wooden handle.
Coladero para té, con mango de madera trabajado con mordiente.

	Durchmesser
Nr. **139**/60/6	60 mm
„ **139**/60/6½	65 „
„ **139**/60/7	70 „
„ **139**/60/8	80 „

139/61/7

139/62/7

Teeseiher, mit lackiertem schwarzen oder gelben Holzstiel.
Tea strainer, with black or yellow varnished wooden handle.
Coladero para té, con mango de madera embarnizado negro ó amarillo.

	Durchmesser
Nr. **139**/61/6	60 mm
„ **139**/61/6½	65 „
„ **139**/61/7	70 „
„ **139**/61/8	80 „

Teeseiher, mit Drahtgriff und Blechhaken.
Tea strainer, with wire handle and tin hook.
Coladero para té, con mango de alambre y gancho de hojalata.

	Durchmesser
Nr. **139**/62/6	60 mm
„ **139**/62/6½	65 „
„ **139**/62/7	70 „
„ **139**/62/8	80 „

139/70/6

139/71/5

139/72/5

139/73/4

139/56/3

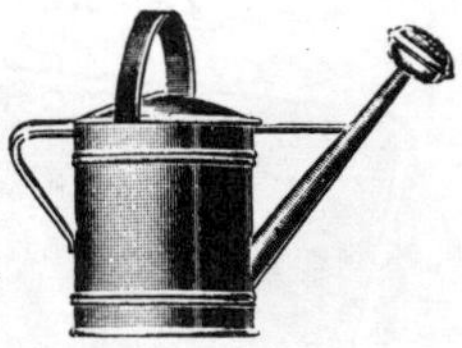

139/55/1

	Durchmesser	Höhe	
Nr. **139**/70/1	60 mm	55 mm	**Eimer,** Druckblech, mit Drahthenkel. **Pail** of pressed tin, with wire handle. **Cubo** de hoja comprimida, con mangos de alambre.
„ **139**/70/2	68 „	65 „	
„ **139**/70/3	83 „	77 „	
„ **139**/70/4	105 „	103 „	
„ **139**/70/5	118 „	115 „	
„ **139**/70/6	135 „	135 „	
„ **139**/71/2	68 „	65 „	**Eimer,** fein lackiert, mit zwei Goldstreifen, Drahthenkel. **Pail,** elegantly varnished, with two gold stripes, wire handle. **Cubo,** bien embarnizado y adornado de dos rayos dorados, con mango de alambre.
„ **139**/71/3	83 „	77 „	
„ **139**/71/4	105 „	103 „	
„ **139**/71/5	118 „	115 „	
„ **139**/71/6	135 „	135 „	
„ **139**/72/4	105 „	103 „	**Eimer,** hochfein weiß lackiert, mit zwei Bildern, Drahthenkel. **Pail,** very elegantly white varnished, with two pictures and wire handle. **Cubo,** muy bien embarnizado en color blanco, con dos dibujos y con mango de alambre.
„ **139**/72/5	118 „	115 „	
„ **139**/72/6	135 „	135 „	
„ **139**/73/2	68 „	65 „	**Eimer,** zweifarbig lackiert, m. Drahthenkel. **Pail,** varnished in two colours, with wire handle. **Cubo,** embarnizado en dos colores, con mango de alambre.
„ **139**/73/3	83 „	77 „	
„ **139**/73/4	105 „	103 „	
„ **139**/73/5	118 „	115 „	
„ **139**/73/6	135 „	135 „	

Gießkannen, hochfein lackiert. — **Watering pot,** very elegantly varnished.
Rociaderas, muy bien embarnizadas.

Nr. **139**/54/0	60 mm	80 mm	Einfarbig lackiert, sortierte Farben, mit zwei Goldstreifen. Varnished in one colour, assorted colours, with two gold stripes. Embarnizadas unicolores y adornadas de dos rayos dorados, las hay en colores surtidos.
„ **139**/55/1	80 „	90 „	
„ **139**/55/4	70 „	87 „	
„ **139**/55/2	80 „	90 „	Zweifarbig lackiert, mit zwei Goldstreifen. Varnished in two colours, with two gold stripes. Embarnizadas unicolores y adornadas de dos rayos dorados, las hay en colores surtidos.

	Durchmesser	Höhe	
Nr. **139**/55/3	80 mm	90 mm	Weiß lackiert, mit zwei Bildern und zwei Goldstreifen. White varnished, with two pictures and two gold stripes. Embarnizadas en color blanco y adornadas de dos dibujos y dos rayos dorados.
„ **139**/55/4	80 „	125 „	Einfarbig lackiert, sortierte Farben, mit zwei Goldstreifen. Varnished in one colour, assorted colours, with two gold stripes. Embarnizadas unicolores y adornadas de dos rayos dorados, las hay en colores surtidos.
„ **139**/55/5	80 „	125 „	Zweifarbig lackiert, mit zwei Goldstreifen. Varnished in two colours, with two gold stripes. Embarnizadas bicolores y adornadas de dos rayos dorados.
„ **139**/55/6	80 „	125 „	Weiß lackiert, mit zwei Bildern und zwei Goldstreifen. White varnished, with two pictures and two gold stripes. Embarnizadas en color blanco y adornadas de dos dibujos y dos rayos dorados.
„ **139**/56/1	103 „	125 „	Einfarbig lackiert, sortierte Farben, mit zwei Goldstreifen. Varnished in one colour, assorted colours, with two gold stripes. Embarnizadas unicolores y adornadas de dos rayos dorados, la hay en colores surtidos.
„ **139**/56/2	103 „	125 „	Zweifarbig lackiert, mit zwei Goldstreifen. Varnished in two colours, with two gold stripes. Embarnizadas bicolores y adornadas de dos rayos dorados.
„ **139**/56/3	103 „	125 „	Weiß lackiert, mit zwei Bildern und zwei Goldstreifen. White varnished, with two pictures and two gold stripes. Embarnizadas en color blanco y adornadas de dos dibujos y dos rayos dorados.

Sandsiebe, rund, mit Früchten, hochfein lackiert, mit 3, 4 und 5 Formen.

Sandsieves, round, with fruit forms, very elegantly varnished, with 3, 4 and 5 forms.

Cribas para arena, redondas y muy bien embarnizadas, con 3, 4 ó 5 moldes de fruta.

	Siebdurchmesser
Nr. **139**/615/1	170 mm
„ **139**/615/2	210 „
„ **139**/615/3	240 „
Nr. **139**/616/1	170 mm
„ **139**/616/2	210 „
„ **139**/616/3	240 „

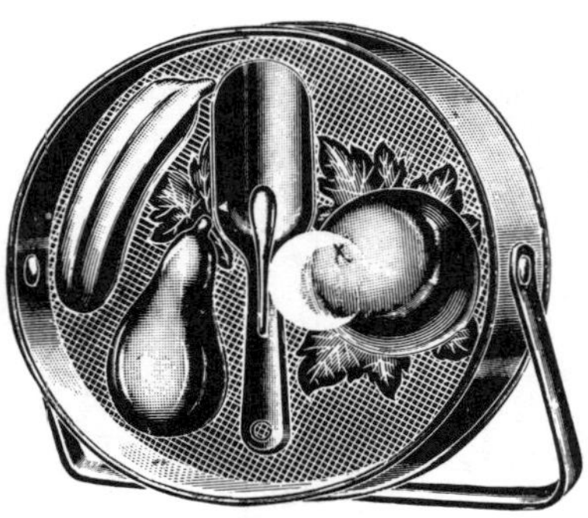

139/615/2

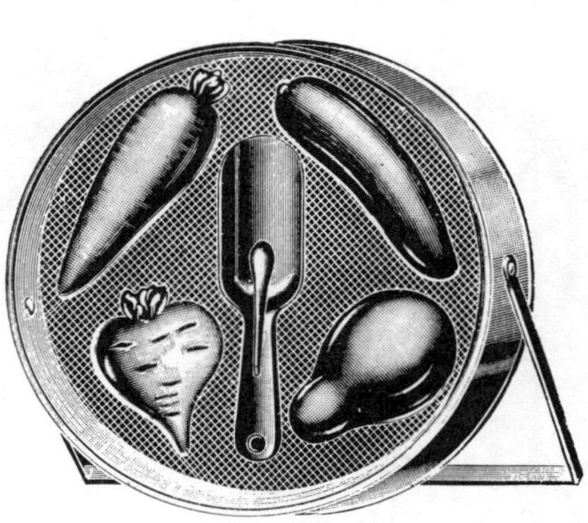

139/616/3

139/617/1

Sandsiebe, rund, Druckblech, mit 4, 5 und 6 Formen.

Sandsieves, round, of pressed tin, with 4, 5 and 6 forms

Cribas para arena, redondas, de hojalata comprimida, con 4, 5, ó 6 moldes.

	Siebdurchmesser
Nr. **139**/617/1	170 mm
„ **139**/617/2	210 „
„ **139**/617/3	240 „

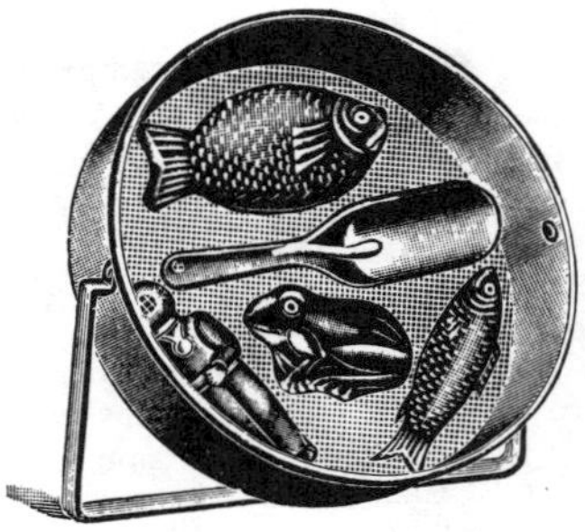

139/619/3

Sandsiebe, rund, mit verschiedenen hochfein lackierten Formen wie Fische, Taucher, Schiffe usw., mit 3, 4 und 5 Formen.

Sandsieves, round, with various very elegantly varnished forms such as fish, divers, ships etc., each with 3, 4 and 5 forms.

Cribas para arena, redondas, con varios moldes muy bien embarnizados que representan peces, somormujos, buques y otras cosas más, las hay con 3, 4 ó 5 moldes.

	Siebdurchmesser	
Nr. **139**/619/1	170 mm	mit 3 Formen
„ **139**/619/2	210 „	„ 4 „
„ **139**/619/3	240 „	„ 5 „

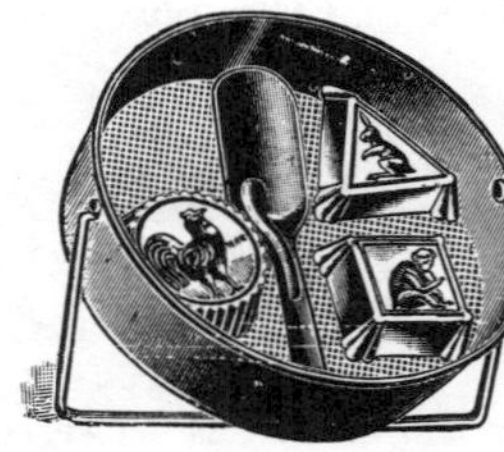

139/618/2

Sandsiebe, rund, mit hochfein lackierten weißen Tierformen, mit 3, 4 und 5 Formen.

Sandsieves, round, with very elegant white animal forms, with 3, 4 and 5 forms.

Cribas para arena, redondas, con moldes bien embarnizados en color blanco que representan animales, las hay con 3, 4 ó 5 moldes.

	Siebdurchmesser	
Nr. **139**/618/1	170 mm	mit 3 Formen
„ **139**/618/2	210 „	„ 4 „
„ **139**/618/3	240 „	„ 5 „

139/621/4

Sandspiele in Körben, mit Früchten, hochfein lackiert.

Toys for playing with sand, in baskets, with fruits, very elegantly varnished.

Juegos de arena, en canastos con frutas, muy bien embarnizados.

	Korblänge	Korbbreite
Nr. **139**/621/1	225 mm	150 mm
„ **139**/621/2	250 „	165 „
„ **139**/621/3	270 „	180 „
„ **139**/621/4	285 „	200 „
„ **139**/621/5	310 „	215 „
„ **139**/621/6	340 „	225 „
„ **139**/621/7	355 „	240 „

Sandspiele in Spitzenkartons aufgenäht, mit hochfein lackierten Gemüseformen.

Toys for playing with sand, in lace cardboard boxes, with very elegantly varnished vegetable forms.

Juegos de arena, cosidos en cartones con puntas, con moldes de legumbres muy bien embarnizados

	Kartonlänge	Kartonbreite
Nr. **139**/622/1	265 mm	195 mm
„ **139**/622/2	280 „	205 „
„ **139**/622/3	310 „	220 „
„ **139**/622/4	325 „	285 „
„ **139**/622/6	360 „	280 „

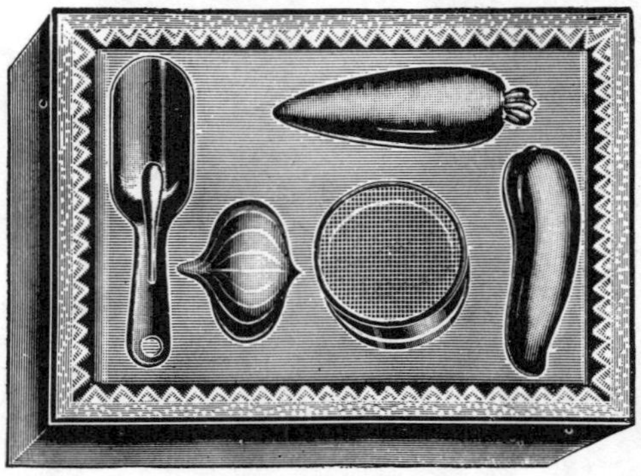

139/622/2

139/623/4

Sandspiele, in Kartons aufgenäht, mit hochfein lackierten Früchten.

Toys for playing with sand, in cardboard boxes, with very elegantly varnished fruit forms.

Juegos de arena, cosidos en cartones, con moldes muy bien embarnizados de frutas.

	Kartonlänge	Kartonbreite
Nr. **139**/623/1	250 mm	195 mm
„ **139**/623/2	280 „	195 „
„ **139**/623/3	320 „	215 „
„ **139**/623/4	325 „	230 „
„ **139**/623/5	360 „	245 „
„ **139**/623/6	360 „	280 „

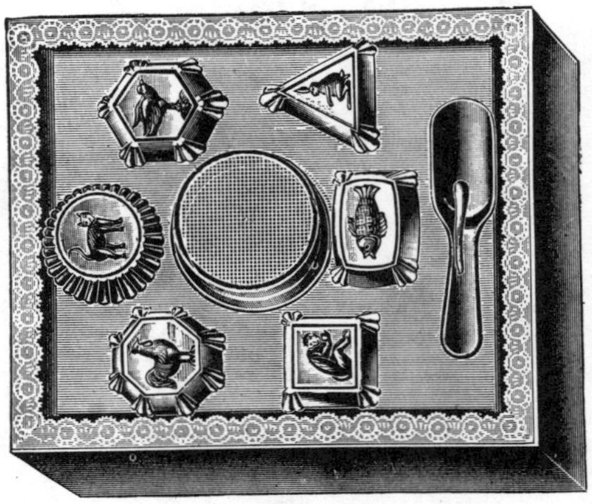

139/624/5

Sandspiele in Kartons aufgenäht, mit hochfein lackierten weißen Tierformen.

Toys for playing with sand, in cardboard boxes, with very elegantly varnished white animal forms.

Juegos de arena, cosidos en cartones, con moldes muy bien embarnizados en color blanco que representan animales.

	Kartonlänge	Kartonbreite
Nr. **139**/624/1	260 mm	190 mm
„ **139**/624/2	280 „	200 „
„ **139**/624/3	305 „	220 „
„ **139**/624/4	280 „	250 „
„ **139**/624/5	320 „	280 „

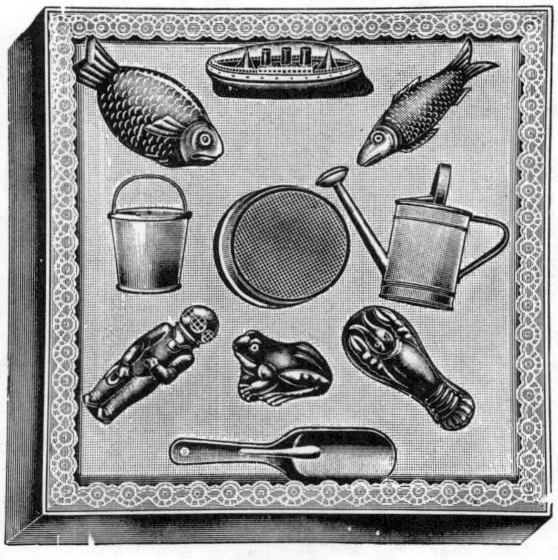

139/625/6

Sandspiele in Spitzenkartons aufgenäht, mit hochfein lackierten Formen wie Fische, Taucher.

Toys for playing with sand, in laced cardboard boxes, with very elegantly varnished forms such as fish, divers.

Juegos de arena, cosidos en cartones con puntas, con moldes muy bien embarnizados que representan peces, somormujos, etc.

	Kartonlänge	Kartonbreite
Nr. **139**/625/1	245 mm	210 mm
„ **139**/625/2	275 „	220 „
„ **139**/625/3	330 „	235 „
„ **139**/625/4	320 „	285 „
„ **139**/625/5	340 „	315 „
„ **139**/625/6	390 „	350 „

139/630/4

Sandspiele auf Karten genäht, einfache Ausführung.

Toys for playing with sand, stitched on in cardboard boxes, simple execution.

Juegos de arena, cosidos en cartones, de elaboración sencilla.

	Kartenlänge	Kartenbreite
Nr. **139**/630/1	185 mm	130 mm
„ **139**/630/2	230 „	150 „
„ **139**/630/3	230 „	185 „
„ **139**/630/3½	315 „	230 „
„ **139**/630/4	315 „	230 „
„ **139**/630/4½	340 „	240 „
„ **139**/630/5	440 „	245 „

139/633/3½

Sandspiele in Kartons aufgenäht, mit einfach lackierten Formen.

Toys for playing with sand, stitched on in cardboard boxes, with simple varnished forms.

Juegos de arena, cosidos en cartones, con sencillos moldes embarnizados.

	Kartonlänge	Kartonbreite
Nr. **139**/631/1	195 mm	135 mm
„ **139**/631/2	235 „	160 „
„ **139**/631/3	230 „	200 „
„ **139**/631/3½	285 „	205 „
„ **139**/631/4	320 „	235 „

	Kartonlänge	Kartonbreite
Nr. **139**/633/0	195 mm	135 mm
„ **139**/633/1	235 „	160 „
„ **139**/633/2	235 „	160 „
„ **139**/633/2½	235 „	160 „
„ **139**/633/3	230 „	200 „
„ **139**/633/3½	290 „	195 „

139/632/0

Sandspiele auf Karten genäht, einfach lackierte Formen.

Toys for playing with sand, stitched on to cardboard, simple varnished forms.

Juegos de arena, cosidos en cartones, con moldes muy bien embarnizados.

	Kartenlänge	Kartenbreite
Nr. **139**/632/0	185 mm	130 mm
„ **139**/632/1	230 „	150 „
„ **139**/632/2	230 „	150 „
„ **139**/632/2½	230 „	150 „
„ **139**/632/3	230 „	185 „
„ **139**/632/3½	280 „	185 „

139/634/4

Sandspiele auf Karten genäht, mit fein lackierten Formen.

Toys for playing in the sand, stitched on to cardboard, with elegantly varnished forms.

Juegos de arena, cosidos en cartones, con moldes muy bien embarnizados.

	Kartenlänge	Kartenbreite
Nr. **139**/634/1	185 mm	130 mm
„ **139**/634/2	230 „	150 „
„ **139**/634/3	230 „	185 „
„ **139**/634/3½	280 „	185 „
„ **139**/634/4	320 „	230 „

Sandspiele in Kartons genäht, mit fein lackierten Formen.

Toys for playing with sand, in cardboard boxes, with elegantly varnished forms.

Juegos de arena, cosidos en cartones, con moldes muy bien embarnizados.

	Kartonlänge	Kartonbreite
Nr. **139**/635/1	190 mm	140 mm
„ **139**/635/2	240 „	160 „
„ **139**/635/3	230 „	200 „
„ **139**/635/4	270 „	220 „
„ **139**/635/5	320 „	215 „
„ **139**/635/6	445 „	265 „
„ **139**/635/7	360 „	290 „
„ **139**/635/8	445 „	300 „
„ **139**/635/9	510 „	310 „

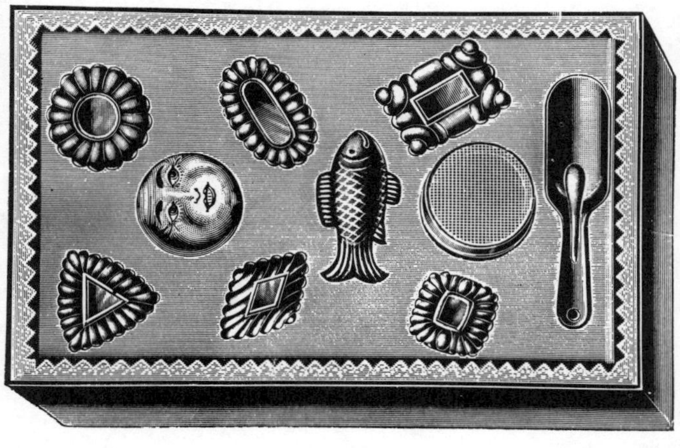

139/635/6

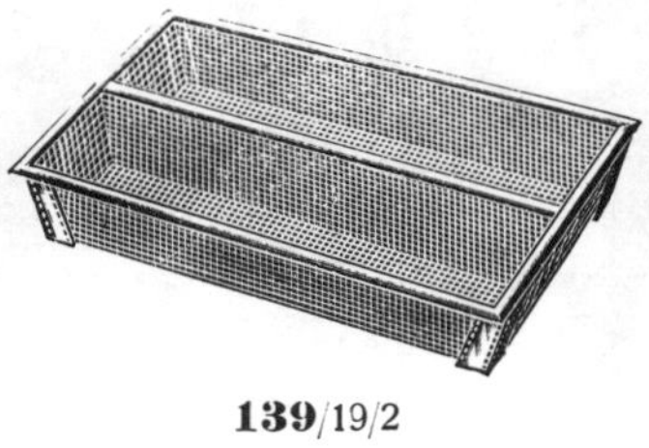

139/19/2

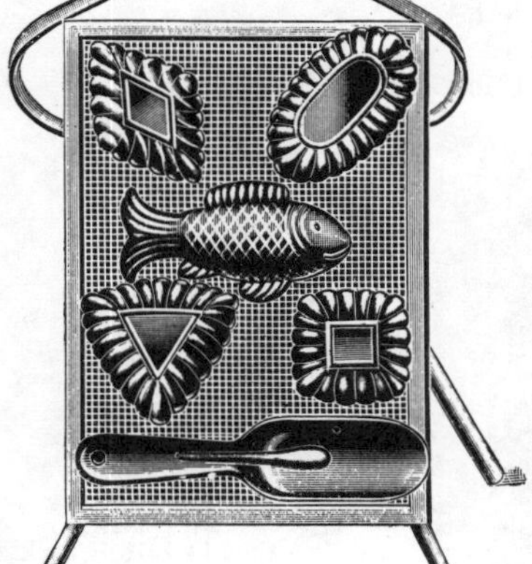

139/636/3

Sandspiele, auf Wurf, hochfeine Ausführung.

Toys for playing with sand, on sieves, elegant execution.

Juegos de areno, sobre criba, de elaboración finísima.

	Sieblänge	Siebbreite
Nr. **139**/636/1	165 mm	125 mm
„ **139**/636/1½	165 „	125 „
„ **139**/636/2	210 „	165 „
„ **139**/636/3	250 „	180 „
„ **149**/636/4	295 „	215 „

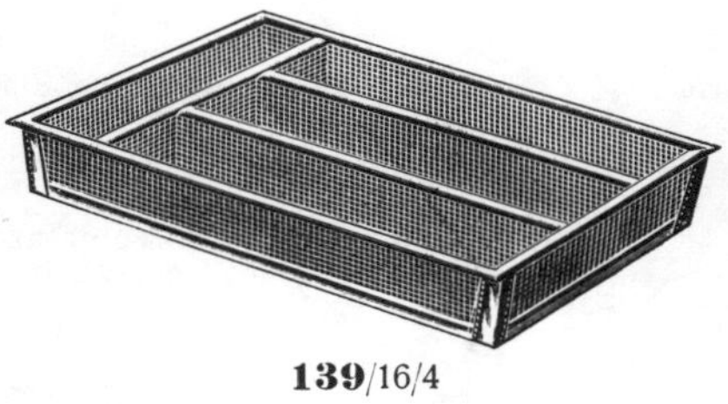

139/16/4

Messerkörbe mit blauem und grünem Gewebe, sort., verzinnte Blechstäbe, mit Schienen und Ecken.

Knife baskets with blue and green tissue, sorted, zinked tin rods, with supporting bands and corners.

Canastos para cuchillos, con tejidos de alambre azul o verde, varillas de hojalata, chapadas de cinc y con rieles y cantos.

	Länge	Breite	Höhe
Nr. **139**/15/3	290 mm	235 mm	50 mm
„ **139**/16/4	320 „	220 „	50 „
„ **139**/17/2	270 „	190 „	40 „
„ **139**/17/3	270 „	190 „	40 „
„ **139**/17/4	310 „	190 „	40 „
„ **139**/17/4 S	310 „	190 „	40 „
„ **139**/18/3	270 „	160 „	35 „
„ **139**/18/2	265 „	160 „	35 „
„ **139**/19/2	270 „	175 „	40 „

Kleine Abweichungen vorbehalten! — Small alterations to reserve! — Al excepción de pequeñas diferencias!

Serie 11/510 aus Schwarzblech, lac'iert.
out of black tin, varnished.
de hierro en hojas de color negro, barnizado.

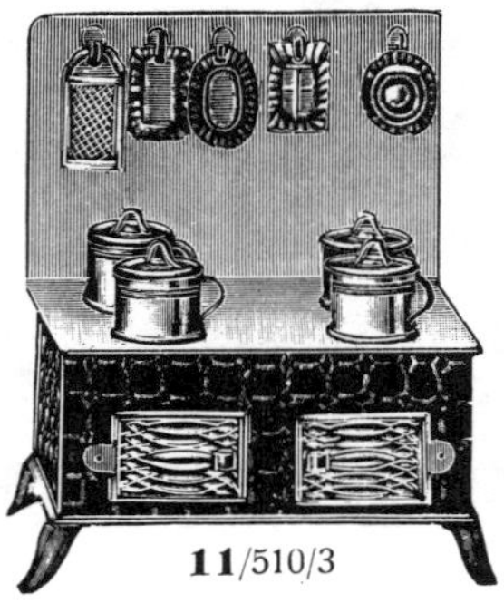

11/510/3

	11/510/0½	1	1½ L	1½	2	
Länge ..	9,7	11,7	14	14	14,8	cm
Breite...	7	8,5	9,1	9,1	10,3	„
Höhe ...	14	15,5	16,2	16,2	17,4	„
Geschirr	3	5	5	6	8	Stck
Packung	1	½	½	½	½	Dtz. in Papier

	2½	3a	3	4	5	6	
Länge...	16,4	17	17,9	20	22	24,2	cm
Breite...	11,6	11,6	12	12,5	14,3	15,5	„
Höhe . .	18,5	20	20,6	21	23,3	24,2	„
Geschirr	8	8	9	9	10	11	Stück
Packung	½	⅓	⅓	⅓	¼	⅙	Dtz. in Papier

Serie 11/520 aus Schwarzblech, lackiert.
out of black tin, varnished.
de hierro de hojas de color negro, barnizado.

11/520/4 L

	11/520/2/0	0	1	1½L	1½	2	2½	
Länge...	9,8	11,8	13,5	14	14	15	16	cm
Breite ..	7	8	9	9	9	10	11,5	„
Höhe .	5	5,5	6	6	6	6	6,5	„
Geschirr	1	2	2	2	3	4	4	Stck.
Packung	1	½	½	½	½	½	½	Dtz. in Papier

	3L	4L	5L	6L	7L	8-9L	
Länge .	17	18	22	24,1	25,5	28,6	cm
Breite ..	11	12	14,3	15,1	16,2	17,2	„
Höhe...	9,8	10,3	11,2	11,4	11.6	12,5	„
Geschirr	3	4	5	6	6	7	Stck.
Packung	⅓	⅓	⅓	¼	¼	1/12	Dtz. in Papier

Serie 11/664 aus Schwarzblech, schwarz lackiert, mit Weißblechbelag, stumpfe Töpfe.
of black tin, black varnished, with tin ornaments, blunt pots.
de hierro de hojas de color negro, barnizado negro, parte de hoja lata con ollas botas.

11/664/21/2

	11/664/3/0B	2/0	0	1	1½	2	2½	
Länge	12	12,5	14,5	15,8	17	18,2	19,5	cm
Breite	8,3	8,5	9,5	11,5	11	12,5	12,5	„
Höhe	8,3	9	9	9,5	9,5	10,5	10,5	„
Gesch.	3	3	3	3	4	4	5	Stck.
Packg.	½	½	½	½	½	⅓	⅓	Dtz. in Papier

	2½St	2½StK	3	4	5	6	
Länge	19,5	19,5	20,2	24	28,2	32,3	cm
Breite	12,5	12,5	15	15,5	18	21	„
Höhe	10,5	10,5	11,7	13,2	14	15	„
Gesch.	5	5	5	5	6	6	Stück
Packg.	¼	¼	¼	1/12	1/12	1/12	Dtz. in Papier

Serie 11/550 aus Schwarzblech, schwarz lackiert, mit Bratröhre.
of black tin, black varnished, with frying stove.
de hierro en hojas de color negro, barnizado negro, con hornilla.

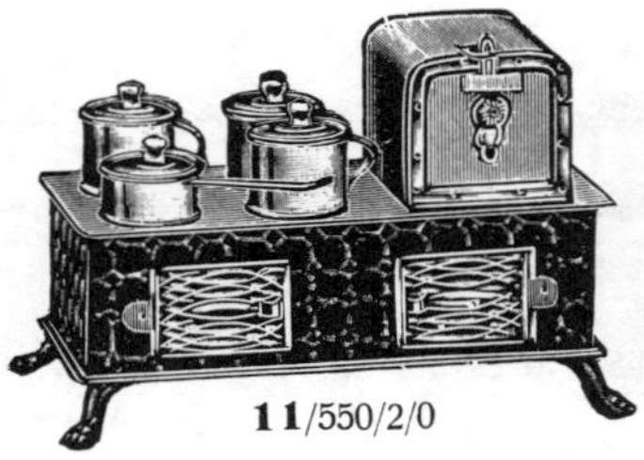

11/550/2/0

	11/550/3/0	2/0	0	1	
Länge...	16,8	22	23,5	27	cm
Breite...	11	11	14,5	14,5	„
Höhe ...	15	15,5	20	20	„
Geschirr	2	4	3	5	Stck.
Packung	⅙	⅙	⅙	⅙	Dtz. in Papier

Serie 11/636 aus Blaublech, mit Stahlplatte und ff. Bratröhre, Nickelgeschirr und Unterfeuerung.
of blue tin with steel plate and frying stove, nickel vessels, and firing from below.
de hierro de color azul con plancha de acero y hornilla de primera calidad, bateria de niquel, para encendar el fuego abajo.

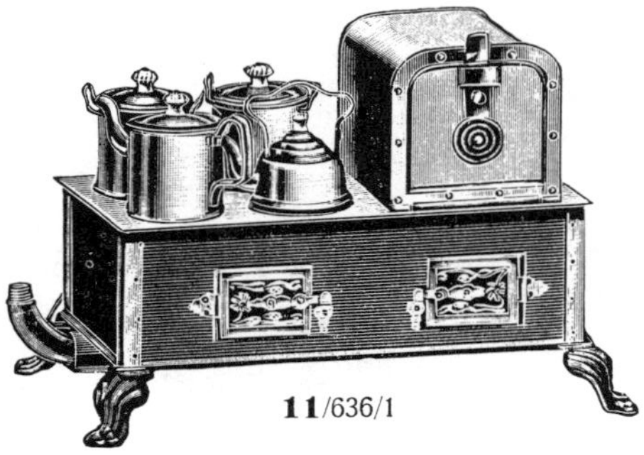

11/636/1

	11/636/0	1	
Länge...	23,5	27	cm
Breite...	14,5	14,5	„
Höhe ...	21,5	21,5	„
Geschirr	2	4	Stück
Packung	1/12	1/12	Dtz. in Karton

Serie 11/630Sp aus starkem Schwarzblech, mit Unterfeuerung und gutem Geschirr.
of strong black tin, with firing from below and good vessel.
de hierro en hojas, fuerte calidad, encender el fuego abajo, con batería de cocina buena.

11/630 Sp/3

	11.630Sp/4/0	3/0	2/0	0	1	
Länge .	13	14,5	16,5	18	17	cm
Breite ..	8,5	9	11	13	11	„
Höhe . .	9	10,3	10.5	11	10,8	„
Geschirr	3	3	4	3	3	Stck.
Packung	½	½	⅓	¼	1/12	Dtz. in Karton

	2	3	4	5	6	
Länge...	19,2	21,5	23,5	25,3	27,6	cm
Breite...	13	14,8	16	17,5	19,5	„
Höhe ..	11	11,5	13	14	14	„
Geschirr	3	4	4	5	5	Stck.
Packung	1/12	1/12	1/12	1/12	1/12	Dtz. in Karton

Serie 11/630 P aus Blaublech mit Belag, Stange, gußeisernen Füßen und Unterfeuerung.
of blue tin and ornaments, on cast iron feet and firing from below.
de hierro en hojas de color azul, barra, con pies de hierro colado, encender el fuego abajo.

11/630 P/4

	11/630P/1	2	3	4	5	6	
Länge...	20	22	24	26	28,5	32	cm
Breite...	12,5	14	16	17	18,5	21	„
Höhe ...	10,5	11	11	12,5	13	14	„
Geschirr	3	3	4	4	5	5	Stück
Packung	1/12	1/12	1/12	1/12	1/12	1/12	Dtz. in Karton

	7	8	9	10	11	12	
Länge..	34,5	37	39	40	42	48	cm
Breite...	22,5	24,5	25	27	28	29	„
Höhe ...	14,5	16	17,5	19,5	21	23	„
Geschirr	5	5	5	5	5	5	Stück
Packung	1/12	1/12	1/12	1/12	1/12	1/1·	Dtz. in Karton

Serie 11/817 aus Schwarzblech, lackiert.
of black tin, varnished.
de hierro en hojas de color azul, barnizado.

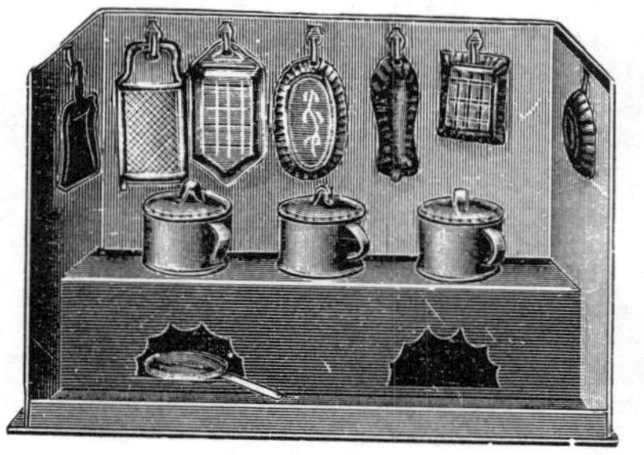

11/817/3

	11/817/1	2	2½	2¾	3	
Länge	18,5	20,7	23,8	25	26	cm
Breite	8	9,4	10,5	10,5	10,8	„
Höhe	11,3	12,2	14,7	15,8	17	„
Gesch.	8	9	10	10	11	St.
Packg.	½	½	½	⅙	⅙	Dtz. in Papier

	4	4½	5	6	
Länge	31,6	34,5	38,3	45,5	cm
Breite	12,7	14,5	15,7	17,3	„
Höhe	17,6	19	21,5	25,5	„
Gesch.	12	12	14	15	Stck.
Packg.	⅙	⅙	⅙	⅙	Dtz. in Papier

11/1920/5

Serie 11/1920 **aus starkem Schwarzblech,** mit polierter Stahlplatte, schrägen Füßen, Nickelgeschirr, mit Schiebelampe, ff. Qualität.
of strong black tin, with polished steel plate, sloping feet, nickel vessels and adjustable lamp, first-class quality.
de hierro en hojas fuerte calidad, con plancha de acero pulida, con pies oblicuos, con bateria de niquel de cocina, con lampara corrediza, primera calidad.

11/1920/1		2	3	4	5	6	
Länge	18,2	20,7	24,7	29,4	32,3	33	cm
Breite	15	16	19,7	22	23,5	26	„
Höhe	12,8	13,8	16,6	16,6	18,1	18,3	„
Geschirr	3	3	4	4	4	4	Stück
Packung	$^{1}/_{12}$	$^{1}/_{12}$	$^{1}/_{12}$	$^{1}/_{12}$	$^{1}/_{12}$	$^{1}/_{12}$	Dtzd. in Karton

11/1921/4

Serie 11/1921 **aus Blaublech,** mit polierter Stahlplatte, runder Stange, gußeisernen Füßen, Nickelgeschirr, Prägung, mit Schiebelampe, ff. Qualität.
of strong black tin, with polished steel plate, sloping feet, nickel vessels and adjustable lamp, first-class quality.
de hierro de color azul, con plancha de azero pulida, con barra redonda, pies de hierro colado, con bateria de niquel de cocina, con lampara corrediza, primera calidad.

11/1921/1		2	3	4	5	6	7	
Länge	24	27,8	30,5	35	36,5	41	43,3	cm
Breite	15	18,5	21,5	24,5	24,5	28,5	30,3	„
Höhe	12,8	13,5	15,4	17	19,8	21,1	23,7	„
Geschirr	3	4	4	5	5	5	5	Stück
Packung	$^{1}/_{12}$	$^{1}/_{12}$	$^{1}/_{12}$	$^{1}/_{12}$	$^{1}/_{12}$	$^{1}/_{12}$	$^{1}/_{12}$	Dtzd. in Karton

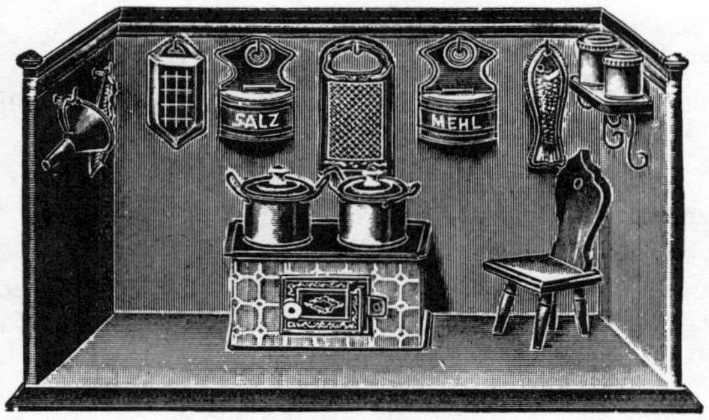

11/816/0

Serie 11/816 **bessere Ausführung, lackiert.**
better execution, varnished.
mejor ejecución, barnizado.

11/816/2/0E		2/0	2/0$^{1}/_{2}$	0	1	
Länge	33,5	33,5	36	39	43,5	cm
Breite	15	15	16	17	19,5	„
Höhe	20	20	20	21	23,5	„
Geschirr	9	12	13	14	15	Stück
Packung	$^{1}/_{6}$	$^{1}/_{6}$	$^{1}/_{6}$	$^{1}/_{12}$	$^{1}/_{12}$	Dtzd. i. Kart.

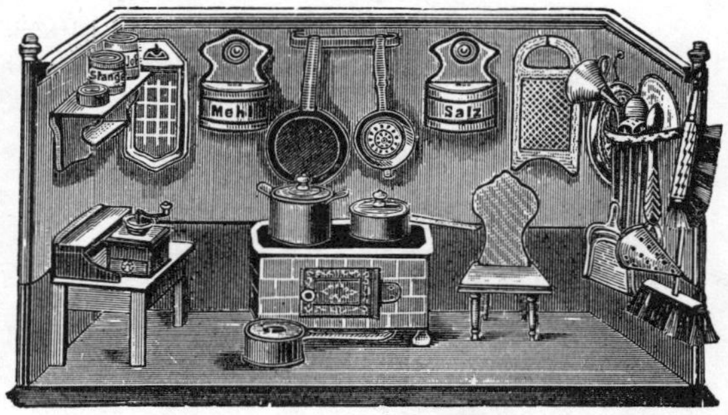

11/818/0

Serie 11/818 **ff. lackiert, mit Holzmöbeln.**
varnished, with wooden furnitures.
barnizado lo mejor, con muebles de madera.

11/818/2/0		0	1	2	3	4	
Länge	33,5	39	44	48	51,5	54	cm
Breite	15	17	20	22	23,5	26	„
Höhe	20	22	22,5	25	27	28	„
Geschirr	12	16	20	24	26	26	Stück
Packung	$^{1}/_{6}$	$^{1}/_{12}$	$^{1}/_{12}$	$^{1}/_{12}$	$^{1}/_{12}$	$^{1}/_{12}$	Dtzd. in Karton

11/360/8

Serie 11/360 teils stumpf, teils scharf, Weißblech, in roten Glacékartons.
partly blunt, partly sharp, of white tin, in red glaced cardboard boxes.
parte boto, parte cortante, hojalata, en cartones rojos "glacé".

11/360/4		5	6	7	8	9	10	
Kartonlänge	18	20,1	21,8	22,5	24,5	27,5	31,5	cm
Inhalt	8	9	12	13	14	16	19	Stück
Packung	1	1	1	1	1	$^{1}/_{2}$	$^{1}/_{2}$	Dutzend

Serie 11/390 **bunt,** auf Karten aufgenäht. — **Coloured,** sewn on cards. — **Cosidos,** sobre cartones.

11/390/5/0		4/0	3/0	2/0	0St	0	0$^{1}/_{2}$St	0$^{1}/_{2}$	1$^{1}/_{2}$	1	2	2$^{1}/_{4}$	2$^{1}/_{2}$	4$^{1}/_{2}$	4UE	4	
Länge	10	10	13,5	13,5	13,5	13,5	16	16	19,5	18,5	23	24,5	24,5	25,5	25,5	25,5	cm
Breite	8	8	9	9	9	9	11,4	11,4	14	11	14	16,5	16,5	22	22	22	„
Inhalt	4	4	4	5	6	6	6	6	6	9	10	10	10	13	13	12	Stück
Packung	12	12	6	6	6	6	6	6	6	2	1	1	1	1	1	1	Dtzd. i. Papier

11/390/4UE

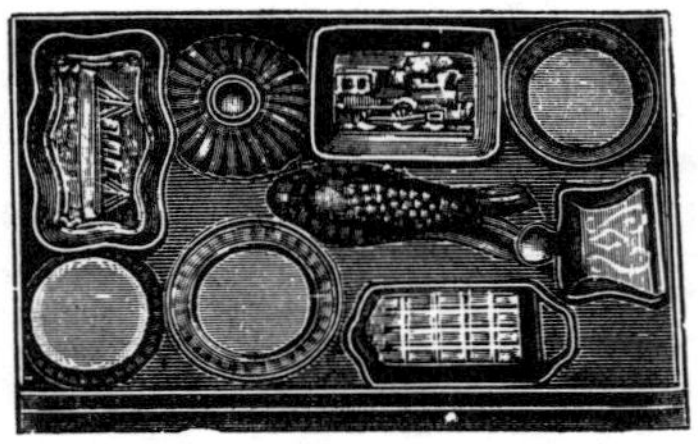

11/349/8

Serie 11/349 teils stumpf, teils scharf, lackiert, in bedruckten Pappkartons.
partly blunt, partly sharp, varnished, in printed cardboard boxes.
parte boto, parte cortante, barnizado, en cartones imprimidos.

11/349/4	5	6	7	8	9	10	
Kartonlänge	20,4	21,8	22,5	24,5	27,5	31,5	cm
Inhalt	8	8	8	9	12	14	Stück
Packung	1	1	1	1	½	½	Dutzend

11/348/0		1	2	3	4	5	6	7	8/9	
Kartonlänge	13	14	14,4	16,8	18	20,1	21,8	22,5	24,5	cm
Inhalt	8	10	10	13	13	13	13	14	15	Stück
Packung	3	1	1	1	1	1	1	1	1	Dutzend

11/348/6

11/1140/3

11/1860/0½

11/1136/4

11/1145/3½

11/1140/1		2	3	
Länge	6	7	8	cm
Breite	6	7	8	„
Höhe	7	7,5	9,5	„
Packung	1	1	1	Dutzend in Papier

11/1860/3/0	2/0	0	0½	1	2	3	3½	4	5	6	7	
Höhe	9	10	12,5	14	16	16,5	18,6	20,5	21	23,8	26,3	28,5 cm
Packung	2	2	1	1	1	1/12	1/12	1/12	1/12	1/12	1/12	1/12 Dutzend in Papier

11/1136/0		1	2	3	4	5	6	6½	7	
Breite	10,5	12	14	16,5	19	20	23	26	29,5	cm
Packung	3	2	1	1	1	1	½	½	½	Dutzend in Papier

11/1145/1		2	3	3½	4	5	6	7	8	
Breite	13	15,5	18	19	23,5	25,5	27,2	29	35	cm inkl. Henkel
Packung	½	½	½	½	¼	1/12	1/12	1/12	1/12	Dutzend in Papier

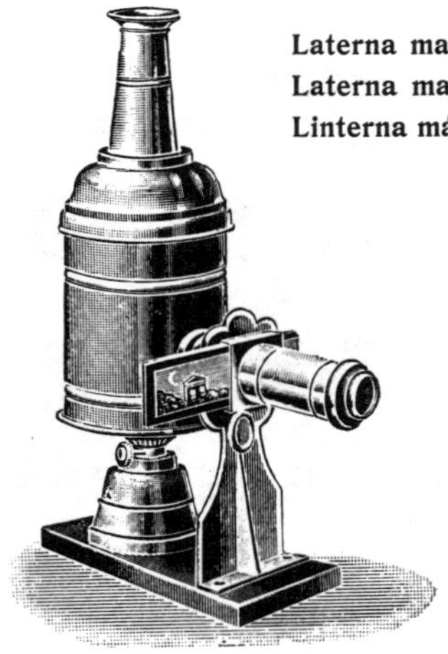

Laterna magica in schöner, solider Ausführung, auf Holzbrett, mit feinem schwarzgrauen Körper, vernickeltem Fuß und fein vernickeltem Dach.
Laterna magica in beautiful solid execution on wooden board, fine black grey body, nickeled foot and elegantly nickeled roof.
Linterna mágica de linda y sólida elaboración, montada sobre un tablero de madera, con cuerpo fino y de color negro gris, con pie niquelado y con tejado muy bien niquelado.

Nr.	Höhe
54/200	ca. 23 cm
54/202	„ 27 „
54/203	„ 28,5 „

Nr.	Höhe
54/2001 K	ca. 23 cm
54/2002 K	„ 26 „
54/2003 K	„ 28 „

Kinematographen in billiger, solider Ausführung, mit feinem schwarzgrauen Körper und fein vernickeltem Dach, mit einem Film 30 cm lang, endlos. Auf Wunsch können auch Laterna-magica-Bilder in beliebiger Anzahl dazu geliefert werden.

Cinematographs of cheap solid execution, fine black grey body and fine nickeled roof, with an endless film 30 cm long. If desired also laterna magica pictures in any desired number can be supplied.

Cinematógrafos de elaboración barata y sólida, que tien el cuerpo fino y de color negro gris, con una película infinita de 30 cm de largo. A pedido pueden suministrarse acompañados de una linterna mágica y de cualquier número de cuadros.

Musikroller und Musikwalzen.
Music roller and music rolls.
Rollos y cilindros de música.

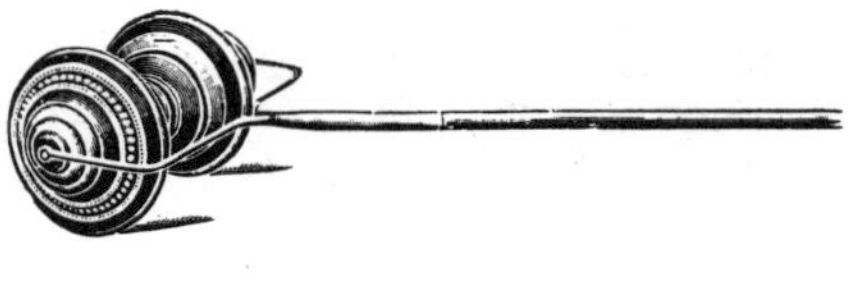

Nr.	Länge	Durchmesser	Breite
54/100	ca. 44 cm	ca. 7 cm	ca. 12 cm
54/100½	„ 44 „	„ 8 „	„ 13 „
54/120	„ 44 „	„ 8 „	„ 12 „

Musik- und Brummkreisel, mit schönen bunten Farben bemalt.
Music and growling top, painted in beautiful colours.
Peones que dando vueltas producen música o roncan, pintados en lindos y variados colores.

Nummer	Durchmesser	Höhe
54/30 Pfeife	ca. 7 cm	ca. 10½ cm
54/31 „	„ 7½ „	„ 12 „
54/32 „	„ 8¼ „	„ 12¼ „
54/33 „	„ 9¼ „	„ 13¾ „

Nummer	Durchmesser	Höhe
54/42 Musik	ca. 10½ cm	ca 15 cm
54/43 „	„ 11 „	„ 17 „
54/44 „	„ 12¼ „	„ 17¾ „
54/45 „	„ 12¾ „	„ 18¼ „
54/46 „	„ 15 „	„ 19½ „
54/47 „	„ 15½ „	„ 21 „
54/135 lithograph.	„ 12¼ „	„ 19¾ „

Mechanische Kreisel mit Pfeife oder Musik, mit schönen bunten Farben bemalt.
Mechanical tops with pipes or music, painted with beautiful colours.
Peones mecánicos que dando vueltas siban o produciendo música, pintados en lindos y variados colores.

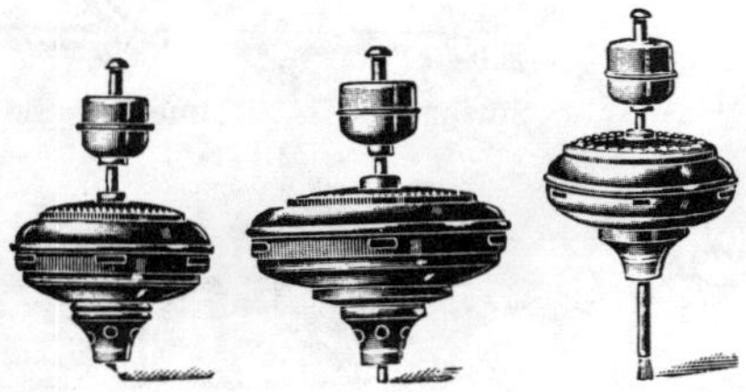

Nummer	Durchmesser	Höhe
54/70 Pfeife	ca. 6¼ cm	ca. 10 cm
54/71 „	„ 6¾ „	„ 10¾ „
54/72 „	„ 7 „	„ 11 „
54/70 B „ m. Bürste	„ 6¼ „	„ 13½ „

Nummer	Durchmesser	Höhe
54/85 Musik	ca. 8 cm	ca. 11¾ cm
54/86 „	„ 8½ „	„ 13¼ „
54/87 „	„ 10¼ „	„ 13½ „
54/85 B „ m. Bürste	„ 8 „	„ 15 „

Choral-Sing-Kreisel, hochfein vernickelt oder mit sehr schönen bunten Farben bemalt.
Choral singing top, elegantly nickeled or painted with beautiful colours.
Peones que dando vueltas cantan corales, muy bien niquelados o pintados en colores muy lindos.

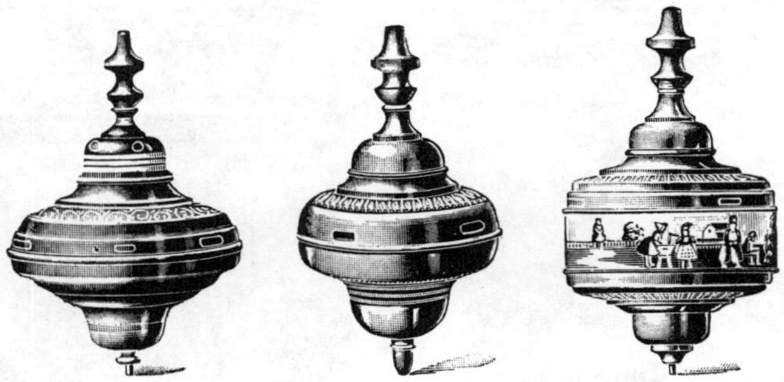

Nr.	Durchmesser	Höhe
54/55	ca. 11 cm	ca. 18 cm
54/56	„ 11½ „	„ 18½ „
54/58	„ 12¼ „	„ 19 „
54/59	„ 13½ „	„ 20¼ „

Nummer	Durchmesser	Höhe
54/136 N lithograph.	ca. 10¼ cm	ca. 20 cm
54/139 N „	„ 12¼ „	„ 20 „
54/850 automatisch selbsttätig wechselnd	ca. 11¼ cm	ca. 20½ „

Spiral-Stoß-Kreisel mit Pfeife oder Musik.
Spiral push top with pipes or music.
Peones que al darseles golpes se mueven en espirales, silbando o produciendo música.

Nummer	Durchmesser	Höhe
54/149 Pfeife	ca. 9¼ cm	ca. 13¾ cm
54/150 Musik	„ 10½ „	„ 16 „
54/351 Perpetuum mobile	„ 12½ „	„ 21 „
54/250 Eierstoß, Pfeife	„ 7 „	„ 13¾ „
54/251 „ Musik	„ 7½ „	„ 14½ „

Musikdosen, in den verschiedensten Ausführungen, bemalt, vernickelt, lithographiert, mit Trompete, Eiform usw.
Music boxes in varios shapes, painted, nickeled, lithographed, with trumpet, egg form, etc.
Cajas de música, de muy variada execución, pintadas o niqueladas, o con litografías, provistas de una trompeta, en forma de huevo, etc.

Nummer	Durchm.	Höhe
54/1	ca. 6½ cm	ca. 9 cm
54/2	„ 7½ „	„ 10½ „
54/3	„ 8½ „	„ 11½ „
54/7	„ 8 „	„ 12 „
54/8	„ 8¾ „	„ 12½ „

Nummer	Durchmesser	Höhe
54/9	ca. 9 cm	ca. 11¾ cm
54/10 lithographiert	„ 7¾ „	„ 9¼ „
54/11 mit Trompete	„ 9 „	„ 15 „
54/14 } extra fein vernick.	„ 8 „	„ 12 „
54/15 } mit Porzellank.	„ 8¾ „	„ 12¼ „
54/16 Eiform	„ 6½ „	„ 11 „

Durchmesser = Diameter — Diámetro. Höhe = Height — Altura.

Billige Blech-Spielwaren ohne Uhrwerk.
Cheap tin toys without clockwork.
Juguetes baratos de lata sin mecanismo.

2018/553

2018/594

Sortiment — Assortment — Surtido
2018/500 SE

Sortiment — Assortment — Surtido
2018/T

2018/541

2018/990/1

2018/565

2018/592

2018/950

2018/584

2018/979/1

2018/566

2018/961/1

2018/986/1

2018/965/1

2018/573

2018/973

2018/570

2018/571

2018/552/1

2018/957

2018/572

2018/537

2018/585

2018/586

2018/2

2018/4

2018/5

2018/587

Billige Blechspielwaren ohne Uhrwerk.
Cheap tin toys without clockwork.
Juguetes baratos de lata sin mecanismo de reloj.

Die Artikel mit der gleichen Packung können auch sortiert geliefert werden.
Goods packed in the same style can also be supplied assorted.
Artículos del mismo contenido pueden ser suministrardos assortidos.

2009/12. P. 4 Dtz.

2009/11. P. 4 Dtz.

2009/8. P. 4 Dtz.

2009/47. P. 4 Dtz.

2009/3. P. 6 Dtz.

2009/88. P. 4 Dtz.

2009/278. P. 4 Dtz.

2009/114. P. 4 Dtz.

2009/10. P. 2 Dtz.

2009/38. P. 4 Dtz.

2009/35. P. 2 Dtz.

2009/37. P. 2 Dtz.

2009/61. P. 2 Dtz.

2009/36. P. 2 Dtz.

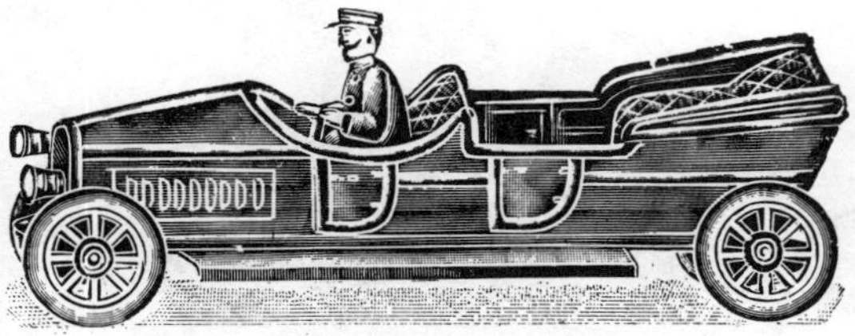
2009/159. P. 2 Dtz.

2009/71. P. 2 Dtz.

2009/1. P. 2 Dtz.

P. = Packung — Packing — Contenido

Billige Blechspielwaren mit und ohne Uhrwerk.
Cheap tin toys with or without clockwork.
Juguetes baratos de lata con y sin mecanismo de reloj.

Die Artikel mit der gleichen Packung können auch sortiert geliefert werden.
Goods packed in the same style can also be supplied assorted.
Artículos del mismo contenido pueden se entregar assortidos.

2009/132. P. 2 Dtz.

2009/133. P. 2 Dtz.

2009/134. P. 2 Dtz.

2009/135. P. 2 Dtz.

2009/153. P. 2 Dtz.

2009/144. P. 1 Dtz.

2009/60. P. 2 Dtz.

2009/57. P. 2 Dtz.

2009/16. P. 2 Dtz.

2009/77. P. 2 Dtz.

2009/97. P. 2 Dtz.

2009/109. P. 2 Dtz.

2009/89. P. 2 Dtz.

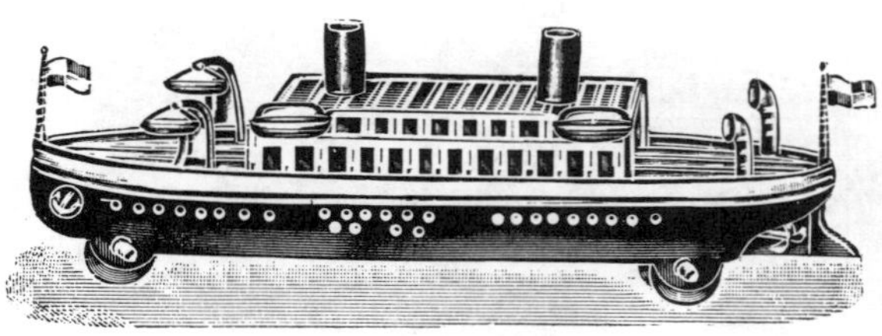

2009/65. P. 2 Dtz.

P. = Packung — Packing — Contenido.

2009/79. P. 1 Dtz.

Billige Blechspielwaren
mit und ohne Uhrwerk.

Cheap tin toys
with or without clockwork.

Juguetes baratos de lata
con y sin mecanismo de reloj.

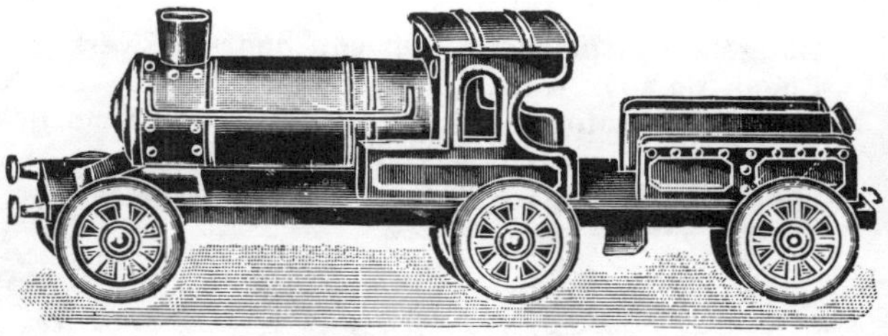

2009/128. P. 2 Dtz.

2009/46. P. 2 Dtz.

Die Artikel mit der gleichen Packung können auch sortiert geliefert werden.

Goods packed in the same style can also be supplied assorted.

Articulos del mismo contenido pueden se entregar assortidos.

2009/48. P. 2 Dtz.

2009/1010. P. 1 Dtz.

2009/146. P. $^1/_2$ Dtz.

2009/138. P. 1 Dtz.

2009/140. P. $^1/_2$ Dtz.

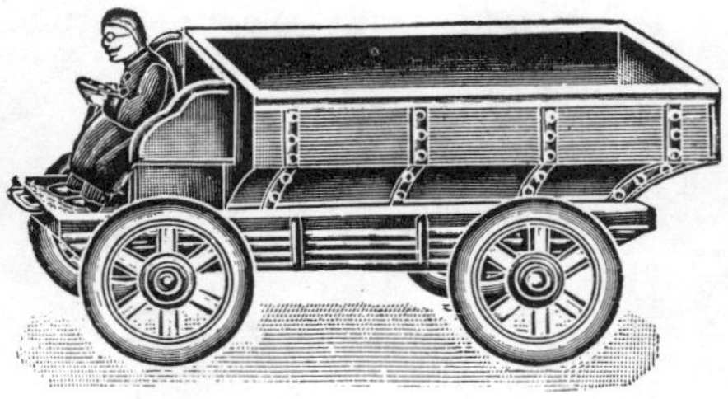

2009/107. P. $^1/_2$ Dtz.

2009/125. P. $^1/_2$ Dtz.

2009/25. P. 1 Dtz.

2009/54. P. 1 Dtz.

2009/150. P. $^1/_2$ Dtz.

P. = Packung — Packing — Contenido.

2009/92. P. $^1/_{12}$ Dtz.

Billige Blechspielwaren mit und ohne Uhrwerk.
Cheap tin toys with or without clockwork.
Juguetes baratos de lata con y sin mecanismo de reloj.

Die Artikel mit der gleichen Packung können auch sortiert geliefert werden.
Goods packed in the same style can also be supplied assorted.
Artículos del mismo contenido pueden se entregar assortidos.

2009/39. P. 2 Dtz.

2009/72. P. 2 Dtz.

2009/24. P. 2 Dtz.

2009/27. P. 2 Dtz.

2009/26. P. 2 Dtz.

2009/121. P. 2 Dtz.

2009/123. P. 2 Dtz.

2009/118. P. 2 Dtz.

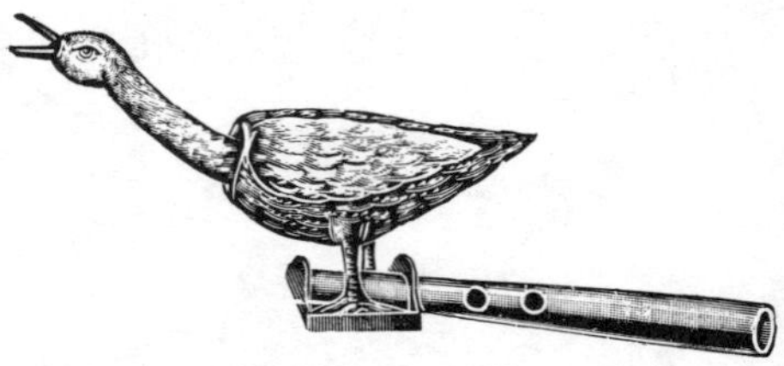

2009/59. P. 2 Dtz.

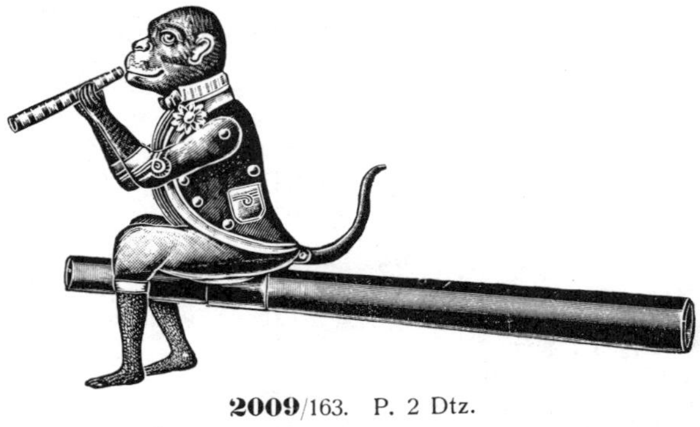

2009/163. P. 2 Dtz.

2009/164. P. 2 Dtz.

2009/86. P. 2 Dtz.

2009/70. P. 2 Dtz.

2009/69. P. 2 Dtz.

2009/67. P. 4 Dtz.

2009/68. P. 4 Dtz.

P. = Packung — Packing — Contenido

Billige Blechspielwaren mit und ohne Uhrwerk.
Cheap tin toys with or without clockwork.
Juguetes baratos de lata con y sin mecanismo de reloj.

Die Artikel mit der gleichen Packung können auch sortiert geliefert werden.
Goods packed in the same style can also be supplied assorted.
Artículos del mismo contenido pueden se entregar assortidos.

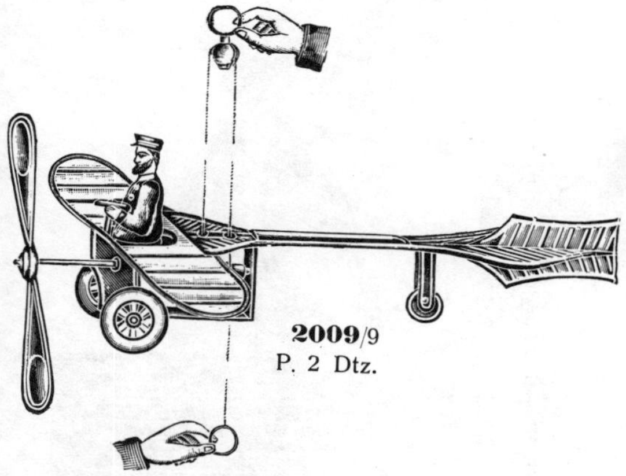

2009/9
P. 2 Dtz.

2009/91. P. 1 Dtz.
Sturzflieger

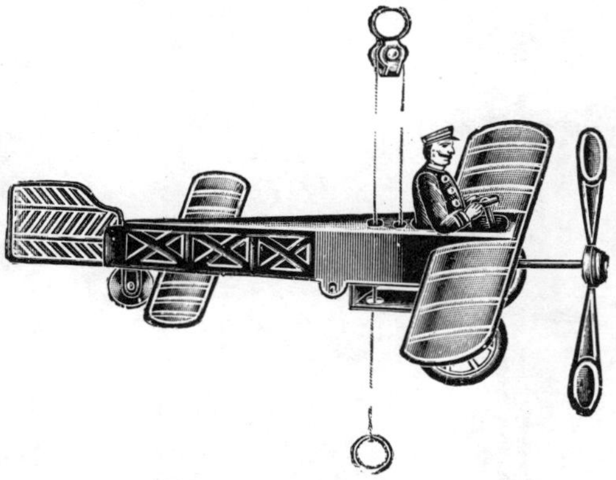

2009/4. P. 2 Dtz.

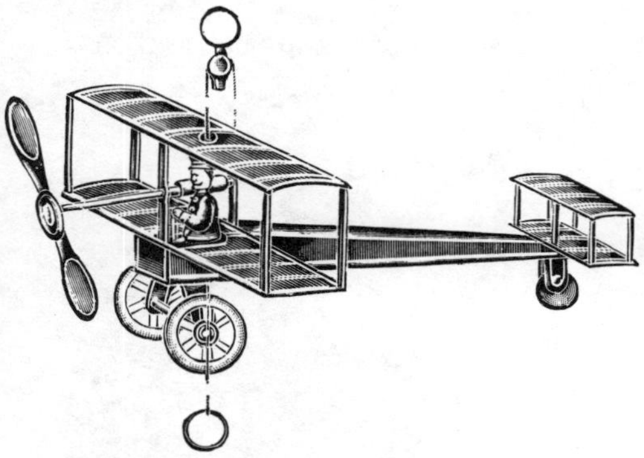

2009/6. P. 2 Dtz.

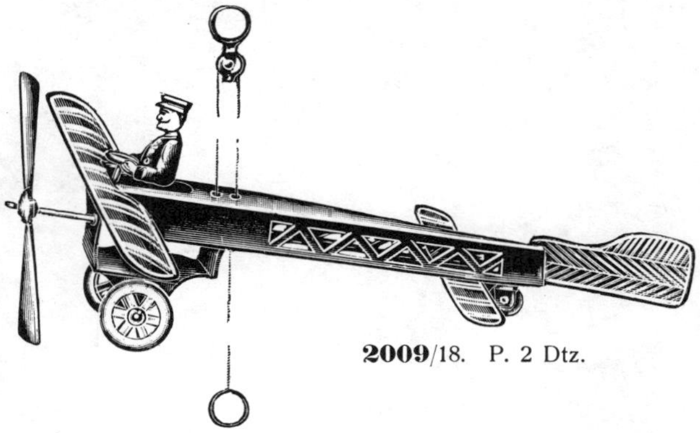

2009/18. P. 2 Dtz.

2009/112. P. 2 Dtz.

2009/120. P. 4 Dtz.

2009/126. P. 4 Dtz.

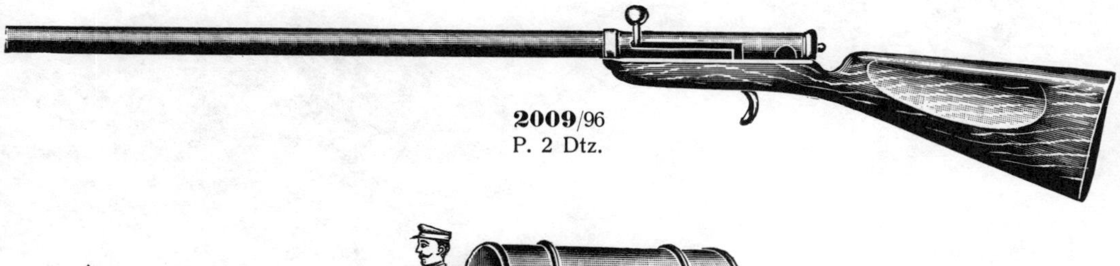

2009/96
P. 2 Dtz.

2009/5. P. 4 Dtz.

2009/127. P. 2 Dtz.

2009/131. P. 2 Dtz.

P. = Packung — Packing — Contenido

Billige Blechspielwaren mit und ohne Uhrwerk.
Cheap tin toys with or without clockwork.
Juguetes baratos de lata con y sin mecanismo de reloj.

Die Artikel mit der gleichen Packung können auch sortiert geliefert werden.

Goods packed in the same style can also be supplied assorted.

Artículos del mismo contenido pueden se entregar assortidos.

2009/33. P. 4 Dtz.

2009/34. P. 2 Dtz.

2009/81. P. 2 Dtz.

2009/63. P. 2 Dtz.

2009/44. P. 2 Dtz.

2009/43. P. 2 Dtz.

2009/74. P. 2 Dtz.

2009/58. P. 2 Dtz.

2009/130. P. 2 Dtz.

2009/31. P. 2 Dtz.

2009/19. P. 2 Dtz.

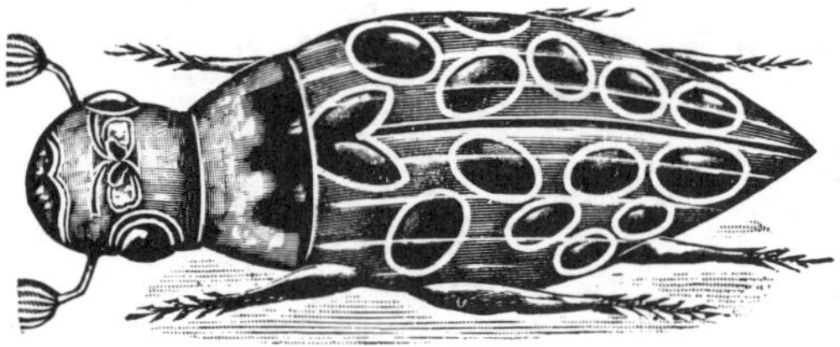
2009/29. P. 2 Dtz.

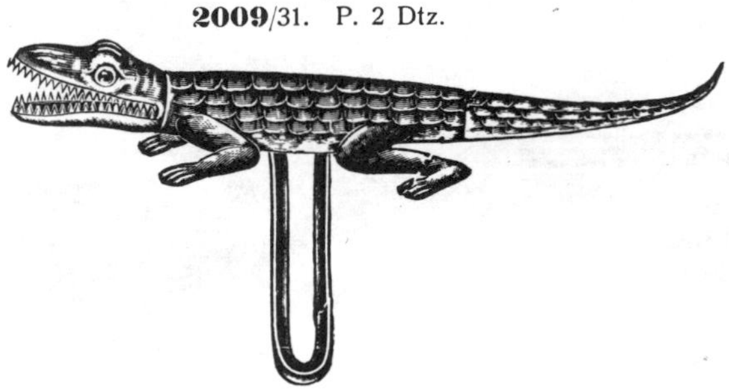
2009/84. P. 2 Dtz.

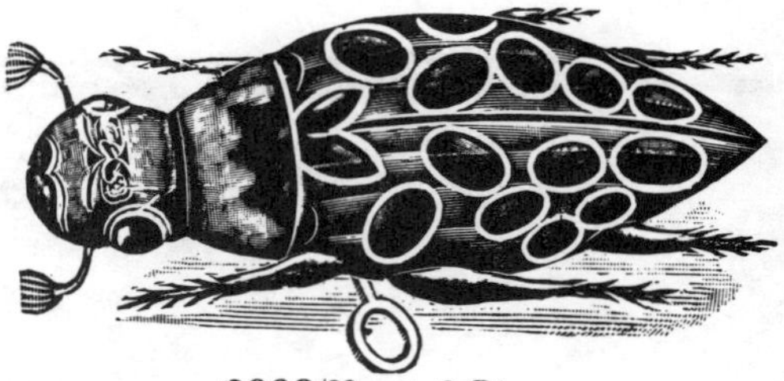
2009/20. P. 2 Dtz.

2009/85. P. 2 Dtz.

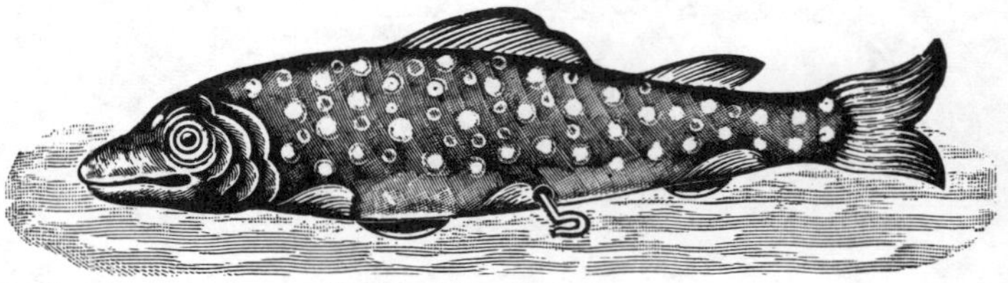
2009/156. P. 2 Dtz.

P. = Packung — Packing — Contenido.

Blechspielwaren mit und ohne Uhrwerk.
Tin toys with or without clockwork.
Juguetes de lata con y sin mecanismo de reloj.

Die Artikel mit der gleichen Packung können auch sortiert geliefert werden.
Goods packed in same style can also be supplied assorted.
Artículos del mismo contenido pueden se entregar assortidos.

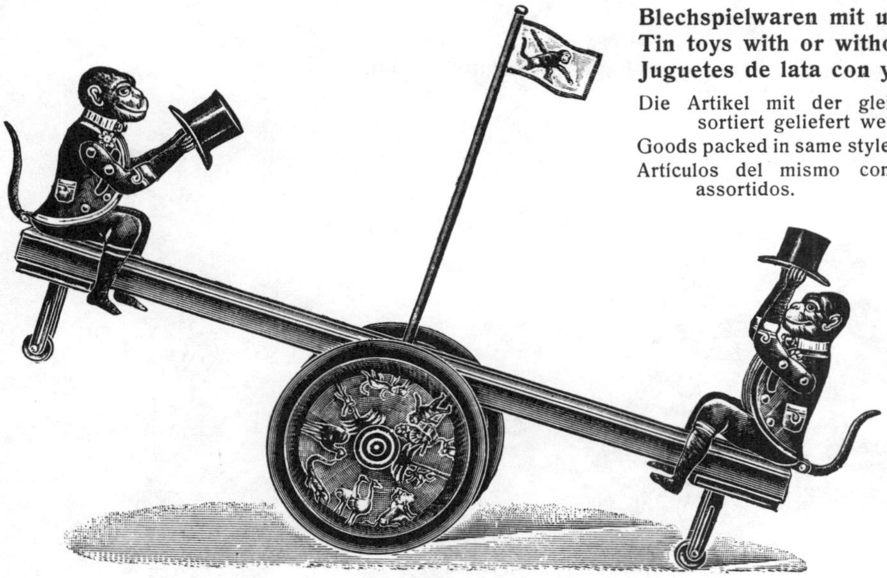

2009/232. P. 1/12 Dtz.

2009/274. P. 1 Dtz.

2009/194. P. 1/12 Dtz.

2009/216

2009/224

2009/89 P. 1 Stck.

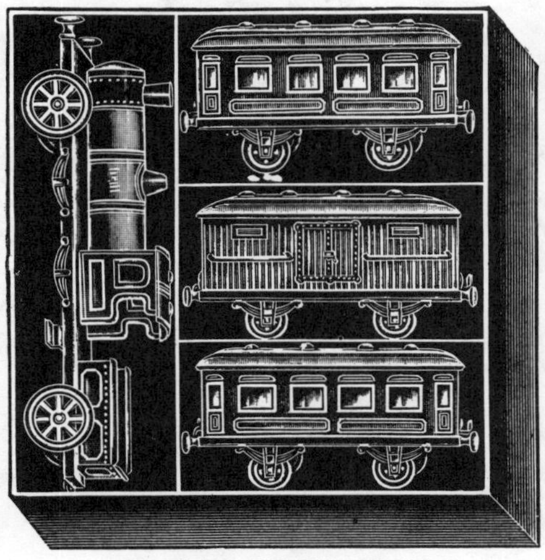

2009/202, 203, 204 und 205

2009/193

2009/254

P. = Packung — Packing — Contenido.

Billige Blechspielwaren. — Cheap tin toys. — Juguetes baratos de lata.

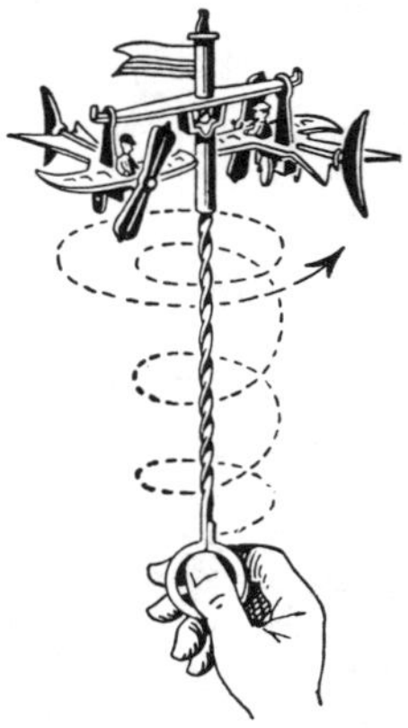

2014/4

2014/3

Mit Uhrwerk, vor- und rückwärts laufend.
With clockwork, reversing.
Con mecanismo de reloj, adelantando y retrocediendo.

2014/5

2014/13

2014/1

Mit Uhrwerk und Stimme.
With clockwork and voice.
Con mecanismo de reloj y voz.

2014/14

2014/15

2014/2

2014/11

2014/8

2014/6

2014/9

Billige Blechspielwaren. — Cheap tin toys. — Juguetes baratos de lata.

112/19

112/58

112/48

112/46

112/20

Mit Uhrwerk. — With clockwork. — Con mecanismo de reloj.

112/47

112/18

112/37

112/37 E W

112/39

Billardspieler mit Uhrwerk. — Billiard player with clockwork.

112/64

112/53

Billige Blechspielwaren. — Cheap tin toys. — Juguetes baratos de lata.

112/68

112/28

112/50

112/47

112/54

112/27

112/41

112/40

112/30

Russische Schaukeln, runde Karussells und Schwinger-Karussells.
Russian wheels, merry-go-rounds and swing-merry-go-rounds.
Columpios rusos, carrusels redondos y carrusels con volante.

41/403

		Höhe Height Altura	Durchmess. Diameter Diámetro	Packung Packing Contenido
41/401	2 Boote, boats, buques	10,5 cm	7 cm	1/2 Dtz.
41/402	3 Boote, boats, buques	13 ,,	8 ,,	1/2 ,,
41/403	3 Chaisen, chaises, sillas	18,5 ,,	12 ,,	1/12 ,,
41/404	3 Chaisen mit Musik, chaises with music, sillas con música	19,5 ,,	13 ,,	1/12 ,,
41/405	4 do.	22 ,,	14 ,,	1/12 ,,
41/406	4 Doppelchaisen mit Musik, double chaises with music, sillas doble con música	24 ,,	15,5 ,,	1/12 ,,
41/407	6 do.	26 ,,	19 ,,	1/12 ,,

41/413

41/411

		Höhe Height Altura	Durchmess. Diameter Diámetro	Packung Packing Contenido
41/410	2 Reiter, 2 Schwinger, 2 riders, 2 swings, 2 caballeros, 2 volantes	17 cm	11 cm	1/12 Dtz.
41/411	2 do., 3 do.	17 ,,	11 ,,	1/12 ,,
41/412	3 do., 3 do., mit Musik, with music, con música	19 ,,	12,5 ,,	1/12 ,,
41/413	do.	21,5 ,,	13,5 ,,	1/12 ,,
41/414	3 do., 4 do.	23 ,,	16 ,,	1/12 ,,
41/415	3 Reiter, 4 Doppelschwinger, mit Musik, 3 riders, 4 double swings, with music, 3 caballeros, 4 volantes doble, con música	26 ,,	18,5 ,,	1/12 ,,
	3 do., 4 do.	28 ,,	20,5 ,,	1/12 ,,
41/417	4 do., 6 do.	31,5 ,,	24,5 ,,	1/12 ,,

41/608

41/603

		Höhe Height Altura	Durchmess. Diameter Diámetro	Packung Packing Contenido
41/601	2 Figuren, figures, figuras	11 cm	8 cm	1/2 Dtz.
41/602	2 Reiter, riders, caballeros	15 ,,	9,5 ,,	1/2 ,,
41/603	3 Reiter, riders, caballeros	16 ,,	10 ,,	1/2 ,,
41/604	3 do., mit Musik, with music, con música	17 ,,	10 ,,	1/4 ,,
41/605	3 Reiter, riders, caballeros, 3 Säulen, columns, columnas, ohne Musik, without music, sin música	19 ,,	12 ,,	1/12 ,,
41/605/1M	do., mit Musik, with music, con música	19 ,,	12 ,,	1/12 ,,
41/606	3 Reiter, riders, caballeros, 4 Säulen, columns, columnas, mit Musik, with music, con música	24 ,,	15 ,,	1/12 ,,
41/608	4 do. 4 do.	28 ,,	19 ,,	1/12 ,,

41/903

		Höhe Height Altura	Durchmess. Diameter Diámetro	Packung Packing Contenido
41/901	3 Figuren, ohne Musik, 3 figures, without music, 3 figuras, sin música	15 cm	9 cm	1/2 Dtz.
41/902	do. mit Musik, with music, con música	16 ,,	10 ,,	1/2 ,,
41/903	3 Reiter, mit Musik 3 riders, with music 3 caballeros, con música	19 ,,	12 ,,	1/12 ,,
41/904	3 Reiter, 4 Säulen, mit Musik — 3 riders, 4 columns, with music, 3 caballeros, 4 columnas, con música	20,5 ,,	12 ,,	1/12 ,,
41/905	3 do. 4 do.	25 ,,	14,5 ,,	1/12 ,,
41/906	3 do. 4 do.	28 ,,	16,5 ,,	1/12 ,,
41/907	4 do. 4 do.	32 ,,	19 ,,	1/12 ,,

41/905

41/314

41/311

41/561

41/548

Schaukeln und Reckturner. — Swings, seesaws, gymnasts on a horizontal bar. — Columpios y gymnasticos en trapecio.

		Höhe - Height Altura	Länge - Length Longitud	Packung - Packing Contenido
41/551	Knabe mit Schaukel Boy with a swing Niño con columpia	18 cm	13 cm	1/2 Dtzd.
41/552	2 Clowns, schaukelnd, mit Musik 2 clowns, swinging, with music 2 payasos volantes con musica	20 „	29 „	1/12 „
41/561	Schaukel, mit 2 Figuren in 1 Chaise Swing with 2 figures in 1 chaise Columpia con 2 figuras in 1 silla	18 „	12,5 „	1/2 „
41/562	do. 4 do.	18,5 „	21 „	1/12 „
41/545	1 Äffchen am Reck 1 little monkey on a horiz. bar 1 monito en el trapecio	14 „	10 „	1/2 „
41/546	2 do.	16 „	12,5 „	1/2 „
41/547	2 Turner am Reck 2 gymnasts on a horiz. bar 2 gymnasticos en el trapecio	18 „	12,5 „	1/2 „
41/548	4 Turner am Reck 4 gymnasts on a horiz. bar 4 gymnasticos en el trapecio	18 „	20 „	1/12 „

		Höhe - Height Altura	Ø	Packung - Packing Contenido
41/311	4 Boote, boats, buques	16,5 cm	12 cm	1/2 Dtzd.
41/312	4 Schaukeln, swings, columpios	18,5 „	14 „	1/4 „
41/313	4 Chaisen, chaises, sillas	23 „	16 „	1/4 „
41/314	4 Chaisen mit Musik 4 chaises with music 4 sillas con música	26 „	20 „	1/12 „
41/315	4 Doppelchaisen mit Musik 4 double-chaises with music 4 sillas doble con música	30 „	24 „	1/12 „
41/316	6 do.	34 „	25 „	1/12 „

Mechanische Artikel. — Mechanical toys. — Juguetes con mecanismo.

		Höhe - Height Altura	Länge - Length Longitud	Packung - Packing Contenido
41/504	Nikolaus	17 cm	10 cm	1/2 Dtzd.
41/505	Hase, hare, conejo	18 „	10 „	1/2 „
41/506	Bär, bear, urso	17 „	9 5 „	1/2 „
41/507	Frosch, frog, rana	15,5 „	11 „	1/2 „
41/508	do., mit Mandoline do., with mandoline do., con mandoline	15,5 „	11 „	1/2 „
41/509	Clown, clown, payaso	15,5 „	11 „	1/2 „
41/510	Affe, monkey, mono	16 „	13 „	1/2 „
41/515	Strauß mit Reiter Ostrich with a rider on it Avestruz con caballero	13,5 „	13 „	1/2 „
41/516	Elefant mit Reiter Elefant with a rider on it Elefanto con caballero	13,5 „	11 „	1/2 „

Mechanische Artikel. — Mechanical toys. — Juguetes con mecanismo.

			Höhe - Height Altura	Länge - Length Longitud	Packung - Packing Contenido
41/517	Löwe mit Reiter Lion with a rider on it León con caballero		13,5 cm	13 cm	1/2 Dtzd.
41/520	Katze mit Maus Cat with mouse Gaton raton		9 „	18 „	1/2 „
41/565	do.		8 „	19 „	1/2 „
41/563	Hund mit Ball Dog with ball Perro con pelota		9 „	15 „	1/2 „
41/534	Knabe mit Pudel Boy with poodle Niño con perro		14 „	15 „	1/2 „
41/500	Adler mit festen Flügeln Eagle with firm wings Aguila con alas firmas		9 „	16 „	1/2 „
41/559	Adler mit beweglichen Flügeln Eagle with movable wings Aguila con alas movibles		4 „	14 „	1/2 „
41/501	Libelle mit festen Flügeln Dragon-fly with firm wings Libélula con alas firmas		4 „	14 „	1/2 „
41/560	Libelle mit beweglichen Flügeln Dragon-fly with movable wings Libélula con alas movibles		5 „	15 „	1/2 „
41/522	Huhn ohne Flügel Hen without wings Gallina sin alas	} auch sortiert zu liefern can also be delivered in assortment también para entregar en surtido	11 cm	12 cm	1/2 „
41/523	Ente ohne Flügel Duck without wings Pato sin alas	do. do. do.	5,5 „	14 „	1/2 „
41/524	Gans ohne Flügel Goose without wings Ganso sin alas	do. do. do.	8 „	16,5 „	1/2 „
41/553	Huhn mit festen Flügeln Hen with firm wings Gallina con alas firmas	do. do. do.	11 „	12 „	1/2 „
41/554	Ente mit festen Flügeln Duck with firm wings Pato con alas firmas	do. do. do.	11 „	15 „	1/2 „
41/558	Gans mit beweglichen Flügeln Goose with movable wings Ganso con alas movibles	do. do. do.	8 „	16 „	1/2 „
41/556	Huhn mit beweglichen Flügeln Hen with movable wings Gallina con alas movibles	do. do. do.	11 „	12 „	1/2 „
41/557	Ente mit beweglichen Flügeln Duck with movable wings Pato con alas movibles	do. do. do.	11 „	15 „	1/2 „
41/555	Gans mit festen Flügeln Goose with firm wings Ganso con alas firmas	do. do. do.	8 „	16 „	1/2 „
41/518	Ente mit Kind Duck with baby Pato con niño		12 „	13 „	1/2 „
41/550	3 Enten mit Kind 3 ducks with baby 3 gatos con niño		12 „	19 „	1/2 „

41/534

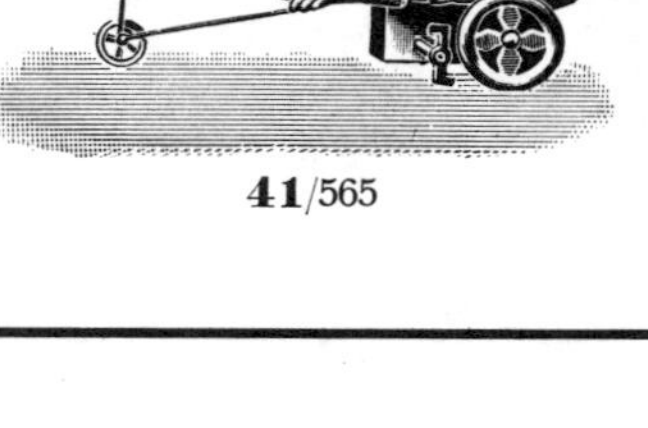

41/565

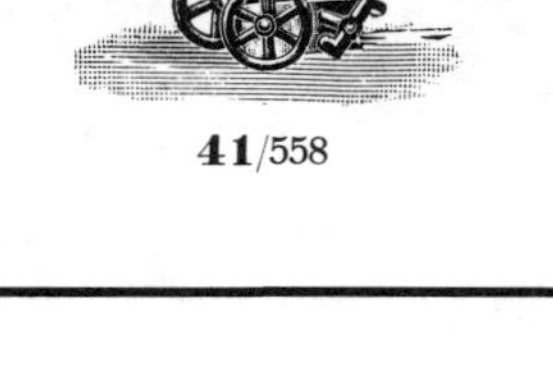

41/558

41/515

41/574

41/583

Mechanische Artikel.
Mechanical toys.
Juguetes con mecanismo.

Mechanische Figuren mit Musik. — Mechanical figures with music. — Figuras con mecanismo con música.

		Höhe Height Alto	Breite Breadth Ancho	Packung Packing Contenido
41/573	Affe mit Mandoline Monkey with mandoline Mono con mandoline	18 cm	12,5 cm	1/3 Dtzd.
41/574	Clown mit Mandoline Clown with mandoline Payaso con mandoline	17 „	12 „	1/3 „
41/575	Clown mit Baßgeige Clown with bass-viol Payaso con viola	21 „	11 „	1/4 „
41/580	Clown mit Musikroller Clown with music-roller Payaso con rodillos musicales	15,5 „	19,5 „	1/4 „
41/581	Affe mit Musikroller Monkey with music-roller Mono con rodillos musicales	15,5 „	19,5 „	1/4 „
41/582	Frosch mit Musikroller Frog with music-roller Rana con rodillos musicales	15,5 „	19,5 „	1/4 „
41/585	Zirkus mit Musik Circus with music Circo con música	15 „	18 „	1/4 „
41/586	Zirkus mit Musik Circus with music Circo con música	18 „	19,5 „	1/12 „

41/580

41/533

41/585

41/571

Mechanische Figuren mit Schirm. — Mechanical toys with umbrella. — Figuras con mecanismo con paragua.

		Höhe Height Alto	Breite Breadth Ancho	Packung Packing Contenido
41/530	Knabe, boy, niño	13,5 cm	12 cm	1/2 Dtzd.
41/531	Frosch, frog, rana	16 „	14 „	1/4 „
41/532	Affe, monkey, mono	16,5 „	15 „	1/4 „
41/533	Bär, bear, oso	17 „	14 „	1/4 „
41/570	Clown, clown, payaso	17,5 „	12 „	1/4 „
41/571	Bär, bear, oso	20 „	11,5 „	1/4 „
41/572b	Affe, monkey, mono	18,5 „	13,5 „	1/4 „
41/583	Schirmläufer, boy with two umbrellas, nino con dos paraguas	15 „	13 „	1/2 „

Mechanische Figuren mit Vor- und Rückwärtsbewegung und sonstige gute Nummern.
Mechanical figures, forward and backward moving, and other good articles.
Figuras con mecanismo con movimiento adelante y hacia atras y otros buenos artículos.

41/537

41/539

41/584

41/568

		Höhe Height Alto	Breite Breadth Ancho	Packung Packing Contenido
41/535	Clown mit Pudel, clown with poodle, payaso con perro	15 cm	15,5 cm	1/3 Dtzd.
41/536	Bär mit Führer, bear with a leader, oso con guia	16,5 „	15,5 „	1/3 „
41/537	Zwei Katzen mit Ball, two cats with ball, dos gatos con pelota	10 „	27 „	1/4 „
41/564	Zwei Hunde mit Ball, two dogs with ball, dos perros con pelato	11,5 „	30 „	1/12 „
41/584	Katze mit Maus, cat with mouse, gato con raton	9,5 „	25 „	1/2 „
41/538	Purzel-Frosch, tumpling frog, rana	10 „	12 „	1/2 „
41/539	Purzel-Bär, tumpling bear, oso	12 „	12 „	1/2 „
41/540	Purzel-Clown, tumpling clown, payoso	10 „	12 „	1/2 „
41/566	Clown mit Schellen, clown with bells, payaso con campanillos	16 „	13 „	1/12 „
41/567	Clown mit Reifen, clown in a hoop, payaso dentro di aro	17 „	Ø 6,5 „	1/12 „
41/568	Clown mit Kugel, clown with a bowl, payaso con bola	20,5 „	Ø 6 „	1/2 „
41/587	Zwei Geißböcke fahrend mit Knabe, boy with two goads, dos cabras con nino	13 „	16,5 „	1/2 „
41/588	Esel fahrend mit Clown, clown with two ass, dos asnos con payaso	13,5 „	18 „	1/2 „

41/567

Gaskochherde mit Aluminium-Geschirr und Lämpchen zum Brennen mit Spiritus.
Gas-cooking-stoves with best aluminium pottery and lamps to burn spirit in them.
Cacharros de gas con utensilios de aluminia y lamparas para quemar con espiritu.

41/702

	Länge Length Longitud	Breite Breadth Altitud	Höhe Height Altura	Packung Packing Contenido
41/700 Herd mit 1 Töpfchen Stove with a small pot Cacharro con 1 marmita	12,5 cm	8,5 cm	7 cm	1/2 Dtz.
41/701 Herd mit 2 Töpfchen Stove with 2 small pots Cacharro con 2 marmitas	16,5 „	8,5 „	7 „	1/2 „
41/702 Herd mit 1 Töpfchen und Stange Stove with 1 small pot and a rod Cacharro con 1 marmita y barra	12,5 „	8,5 „	7,5 „	1/2 „
41/703 = 701 mit Stange, with rod, con barra	16,5 „	8,5 „	8 „	1/2 „
41/704 — 702 auf einem Tisch on a table sobre la mesa	13,5 „	9 „	16,5 „	1/12 „
41/705 = 703 do.	17 „	9 „	17,5 „	1/12 „

41/704

Kochherde aus prima Material, mit prima Aluminium-Geschirr und Lampen zum Brennen von Spiritus.
Cooking-stoves of prima material, with best aluminium pottery and lamps to burn spirit in them.
Cacharros de la mejor materia, con los mejor utensilios de aluminia y lamparas para quemar con espiritu.

41/711

	Kochherde mit: Cooking-stoves with: Cacharros con:	Farbe Colour Color	Länge Length Longitud	Breite Breadth Altitud	Höhe Height Altura
41/710	1 Töpfchen, small pot. marmita, und 1 Pfanne, pan, sartén	blau, blue, azul	13,5 cm	8,5 cm	7,5 cm
41/711	2 Töpfchen, small pots, marmitas und 1 Pfanne, pan, sartén	do.	16,5 „	10,5 „	8,5 „
41/712	do.	do.	19 „	12,5 „	10 „
41/713	3 Töpfchen, small pots, marmitas und 1 Pfanne, pan, sartén	do.	21,5 „	14 „	13 „

41/722

	Kochherde mit: Cooking-stoves with: Cacharros con:	Farbe Colour Color	Länge Length Longitud	Breite Breadth Altitud	Höhe Height Altura
41/720	2 Töpfchen, small pots, marmitas,	grau, gray, gris	13,5 cm	8,5 cm	7,5 cm
41/721	do. und 1 Pfanne, pan, sartén	do.	16,5 „	10,5 „	8,5 „
41/722	4 Töpfchen, small pots, marmitas und 1 Pfanne, pan, sartén	do.	19 „	12,5 „	10 „
41/723	do.	do.	21,5 „	14 „	13 „

41/733

	Kochherde mit: Cooking-stoves with: Cacharros con:	Farbe Colour Color	Länge Length Longitud	Breite Breadth Altitud	Höhe Height Altura
41/730	2 Töpfchen, small pots, marmitas, und Stange, rod, barra	rotbraun, red-brown, rojo-oscura	15,5 cm	9,5 cm	7,5 cm
41/731	2 Töpfchen, small pots, marmitas und 1 Pfanne, pan, sartén und Stange, rod, barra	do.	18 „	11,5 „	8,5 „
41/732	4 Töpfchen, small pots, marmitas und 1 Pfanne, pan, sartén und Stange, rod, barra	do.	20,5 „	13 „	10 „
41/733	do.	do.	23,5 „	15 „	13 „

Packung: 1 Stück im Karton.
Packing: 1 piece in a box.
Contenido: 1 pieza en una caja.

Kochherde. — Cooking-stoves. — Cacharros.

41/740/750

		Farbe Colour Color	Länge Length Longitud	Breite Breadth Altitud	Höhe Height Altura	
41/740	mit 1 Töpfchen, 1 Pfanne	grün	13	7,5	15	cm
	with 1 small-pot, 1 pan	green	13	7,5	15	„
	con 1 marmita, 1 sartén	verde	13	7,5	15	„
41/741	mit 1 Töpfchen, 1 Pfanne	grün	15	10	17,5	„
	with 1 small-pot, 1 pan	green	15	10	17,5	„
	con 1 marmita, 1 sartén	verde	15	10	17,5	„
41/742	mit 2 Töpfchen, 1 Pfanne	grün	17	11	21,5	„
	with 2 small-pots, 1 pan	green	17	11	21,5	„
	con 2 marmitas, 1 sartén	verde	17	11	21,5	„
41/743	mit 3 Töpfchen, 1 Pfanne	grün	20,5	20,5	25	„
	with 3 small-pots, 1 pan	green	20,5	20,5	25	„
	con 3 marmitas, 1 sartén	verde	20,5	20,5	25	„

41/741/751

		Farbe Colour Color	Länge Length Longitud	Breite Breadth Altitud	Höhe Height Altura	
41/750	mit 1 Töpfchen, 1 Pfanne	grau	13	7,5	15	cm
	with 1 small-pot, 1 pan	gray	13	7,5	15	„
	con 1 marmita, 1 sartén	gris	13	7,5	15	„
41/751	mit 1 Töpfchen, 1 Pfanne	grau	15	10	17,5	„
	with 1 small-pot, 1 pan	gray	15	10	17,5	„
	con 1 marmita, 1 sartén	gris	15	10	17,5	„
41/752	mit 2 Töpfchen, 1 Pfanne	grau	17	11	21,5	„
	with 2 small-pots, 1 pan	gray	17	11	21,5	„
	con 2 marmitas, 1 sartén	gris	17	11	21,5	„
41/753	mit 3 Töpfchen, 1 Pfanne	grau	20,5	12,5	25	„
	with 3 small-pots, 1 pan	gray	20,5	12,5	25	„
	con 3 marmitas, 1 sartén	gris	20,5	12,5	25	„

41/742/752

		Farbe Colour Color	Länge Length Longitud	Breite Breadth Altitud	Höhe Height Altura	
41/760	mit Stange, 1 Töpfchen, 1 Pfanne	creme	13	7,5	15	cm
	with rod, 1 small-pot, 1 pan	„	13	7,5	15	„
	con barra, 1 marmita, 1 sartén	„	13	7,5	15	„
41/761	mit Stange, 1 Töpfchen, 1 Pfanne	„	15	10	17,5	„
	with rod, 1 small-pot, 1 pan	„	15	10	17,5	„
	con barra, 1 marmita, 1 sartén	„	15	10	17,5	„
41/762	mit Stange, 2 Töpfchen, 1 Pfanne	„	17	11	21,5	„
	with rod, 2 small-pots, 1 pan	„	17	11	21,5	„
	con barra, 2 marmitas, 1 sartén	„	17	11	21,5	„
41/763	mit Stange, 3 Töpfchen, 1 Pfanne	„	20,5	12,5	25	„
	with rod, 3 small-pots, 1 pan	„	20,5	12,5	25	„
	con barra, 3 marmitas, 1 sartén	„	20,5	12,5	25	„

Packung: 1 Stück im Karton.
Packing: 1 piece in a box.
Contenido: 1 pieza en una caja.

41/763

Mechanische Blechspielwaren. — Mechanical tin toys. — Juguetes con mecanismo de lata.

2015/15

2015/17

2015/12

2015/11

2015/13

2015/14

2015/24

2015/16

2015/25

2015/32

2015/21

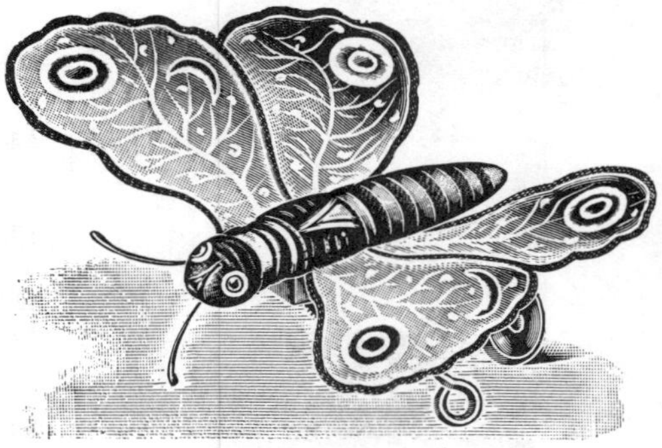

2015/27

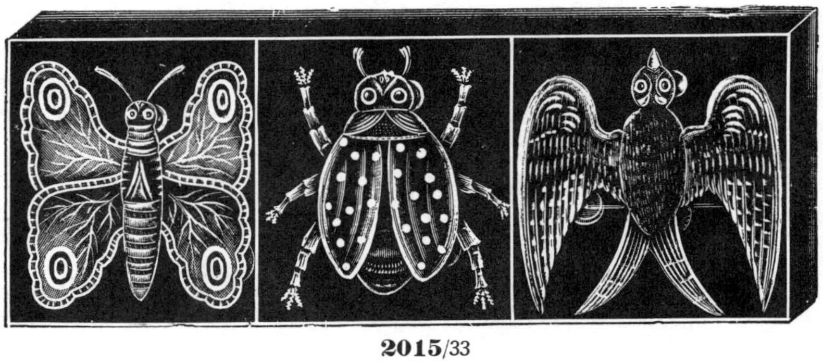

2015/33

2015/34

Mechanische Blechpielwaren. — Mechanical tin toys. — Juguetes con mecanismo de lata.

2015/2

2015/5

2015/1

2015/4

2015/28

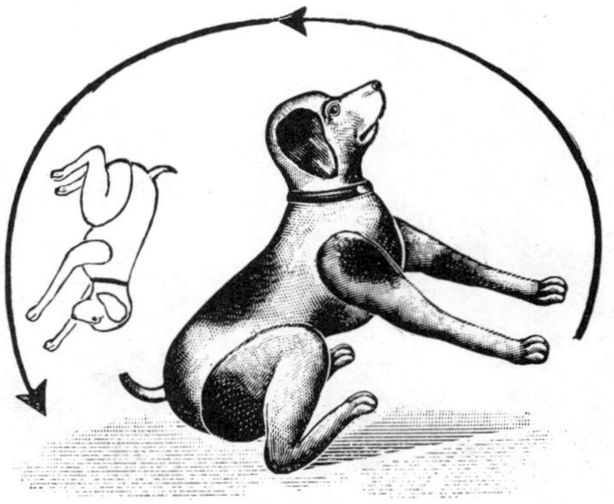

2015/3

2015/36

2015/29

2015/10

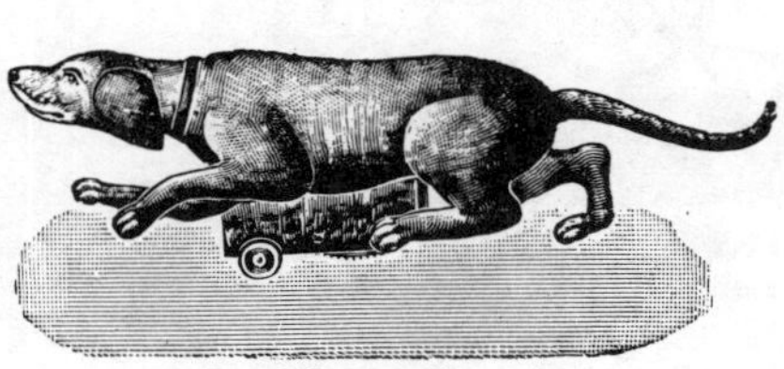

2015/22

2015/23

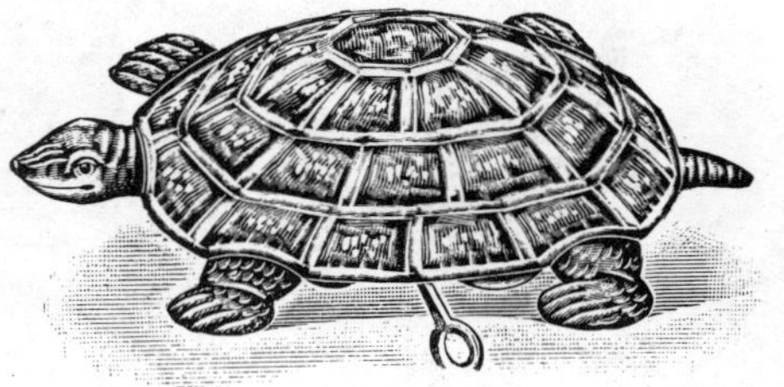

2015/20

Mechanische Blechspielwaren. — Mechanical tin toys. — Juguetes con mecanismo de lata.

2015/19

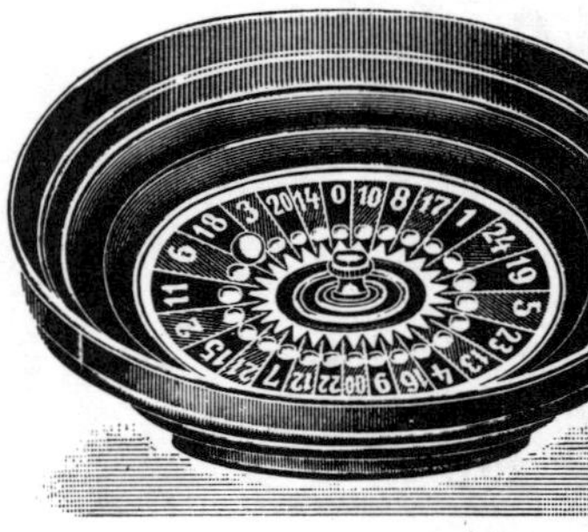

2015/37-38

2015/18

2015/30

2015/9

2015/35

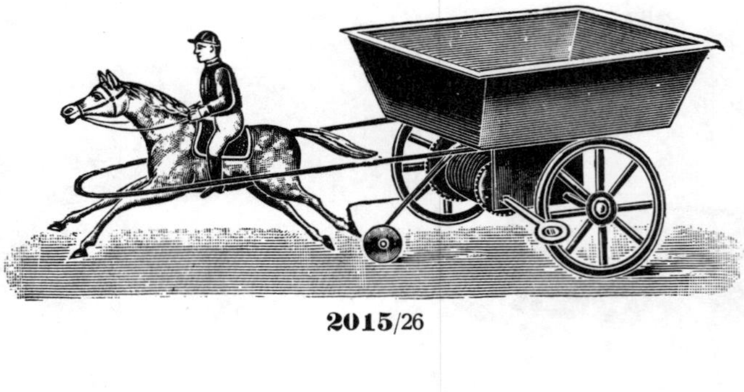

2015/26

Mechanische Blechspielwaren. — Mechanical tin toys. — Juguetes con mecanismo de lata.

2020/55

2020/50

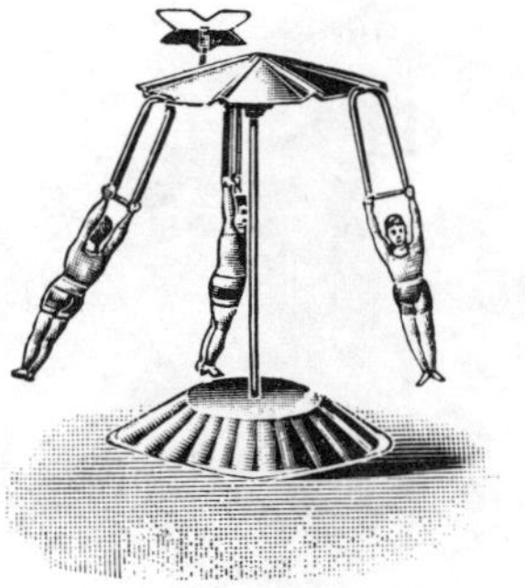

2020/52

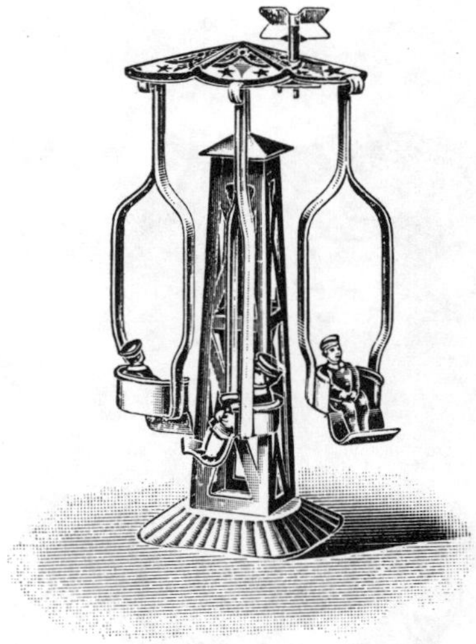

2020/57

2020/35

mit Musik,
with music,
con musica.

2020/62

2020/18

2020/13

2020/15

2020/14

2020/38

2020/24

Rechenkünstler mit Mechanik, gibt die richtige Lösung der Rechnung an.
Arithmetic artist with mechanic, indicates the exact result of the lesson.
Artiste de calculación con mecanismo, indica exactemente el resultato.

2020/39

Mechanische Blechspielwaren. — Mechanical tin toys. — Juguetes de lata con mecanismo.

2020/19

2020/37

2020/29

2020/27

2020/16

2020/31

2020/34

2020/20

2020/17

2020/32

2020/25

2020/1

2020/2

2020/7

2020/3

2020/12

Billige Blechspielwaren mit und ohne Uhrwerk. — Cheap tin toys with or without watchwork.
Juguetes baratos de lata con y sin mecanismo de reloj.

2005/1

2005/3

2005/2

2005/19

2005/16

2005/17

2005/5

2005/4

2005/11/12

Mit Musik. — With music. — Con música.

	Höhe Height Altura	Länge Length Longitud
Nr. **2005**/11	21,5 cm	12 cm
„ **2005**/12	25 „	17,5 „

2005/7

2005/6

2005/18

2005/9

2005/10

2005/20

2005/14

2005/21

Ebo-Toys.

Mechanical Toys. | Mechanische Blechspielwaren. | Juguetes mecánicos.

113/26. **Automobil.**
Covered Car. Automóvil cerrado.
19×9×9,5 cm 0,150 kg

Tourenwagen.
Touring Car. Automóvil abierto.
113/32 25,5×12,5×10,5 cm 0,300 kg
113/34 32 ×14,5×12,5 „ 0,425 „
113/36 36 ×16 ×13,5 „ 0,600 „

113/21. **Auto-Feuerleiter.**
Fire Escape. Automóvil con escalera.
21,5×10×14 cm 0,250 kg

113/3 **Lastauto.**
Motor Lorry. Automóvil para cargas.
18×9×9,5 cm 0,150 kg

113/57. **Lastauto.**
zum Kippen und Ausleeren.
Motor Lorry for tipping and emptying.
Automóvil para cargas.
27×12×10,5 0,300 kg

113/16. **Lokomotive.**
Locomotive. Locomotora.
23×9×9 cm 0,230 kg

113/14. **Clown-Auto.**
Comic Motor.
Automóvil con figura cómica.
18,5×14×11 cm 0,225 kg

113/22. **Pfau mit Stimme.**
Peacock with voice. Pavón con voce.
26×11×17 cm 0,135 kg

113/15. **Esel mit Wagen.**
Donkey and Cart. Carro con asno.
28×14×9 cm 0,220 kg

113/43. **Hennenwagen mit Stimme.**
Hen and Chicken Post.
Carro de gallina con voce.
24,5×10×9 cm 0,200 kg

113/12. **Laufende Ente.**
Moving Duck. Pato corriente.
15×8×11 cm 0,100 kg

113/1. **Pferd mit Wagen.**
Horse and Cart. Carro con caballo.
20×9×8 cm 0,125 kg

113/2. **Hüpfender Vogel.**
Hopping Bird. Pájaro brincador.
18×9×11 cm 0,080 kg

Packed each in box without label.
Weight and measures per piece without box.

Verpackung: Jedes Stück in Schachtel ohne Etikett.
Maße und Gewicht für das Stück ohne Schachtel.

Embalaje por pieza en cartón sin etiqueta.
Medidas y pesos por pieza sin cartón.

Blechspielwaren mit Uhrwerk. — Tin toys with or without clockwork.
Juguetes de lata con mecanismo de reloj.

2010/49

2010/56

2010/48

2010/2

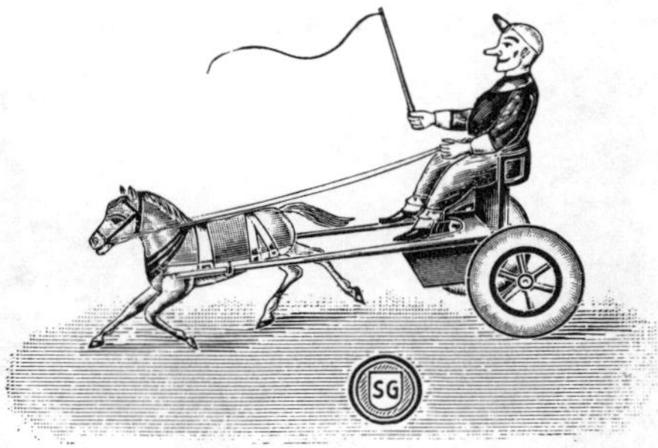

2010/6

2010/1

2010/15

2010/3

2010/9

2010/39

2010/62

2010/5

2010/63

2010/8

2010/4

Mechanische Blechspielwaren. — Mechanical tin toys. — Artículos de lata con mecanismo.

2010/43

2010/44

2010/45

2010/42

Nr. **2010**/40-45 Mit Uhrwerk, Revontinastimme, ff. Handlackierung.
With clockwork, Revontina voice, varnished by hand.
Con mecanismo de reloj, voz revontina, barnizado cuidadosamente á mano.

2010/17

2010/40

2010/61

2010/41

Nr. **2010**/7, 17. 18, 61 Mit Uhrwerk, in bester Ausführung und Lackierung.
With clockwork, of the best execution and varnishing.
Con mecanismo de reloj, de ejecución y embarnizadura superiores.

2010/7

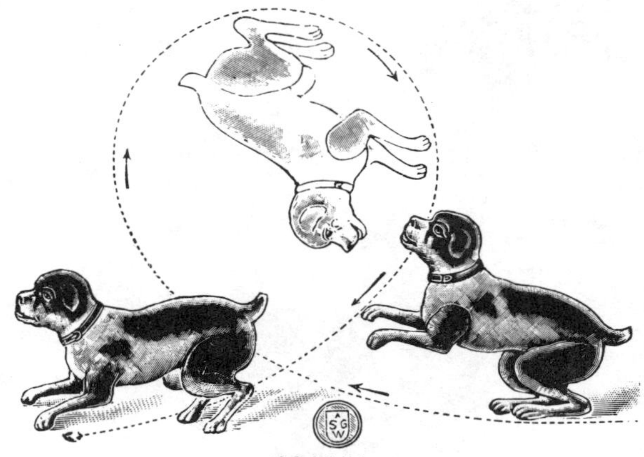

2010/11

2010/18

Nr. **2010**/11 „Saltomortale“. Der Hund schlägt wiederholt unter Brummen und Knurren einen vollständigen Salto.
„Saltomortale.“ The dog makes a complete salto thereby growling and snarling.
„Saltomortale“. El perro hace salto completo repetidamente, zumbando y gruñendo.

2010/20

2010/16

Nr. **2010**/20 Mit Uhrwerk, tanzend, ff. Handlackierung.
With clockwork, dancing, varnished by hand.
Con mecanismo de reloj, bailando, barnizado cuidadosamente á mano.

Nr. **2010**/16 -/10, -/19. Mit Uhrwerk, natürlich fortschreitender Bewegung und Stoffhose.
With clockwork, naturally walking movement and hare of cloth.
Con mecanismo de reloj, movimiento progresivo natural y pantalones de tela.

2010/10

2010/19

2010/14

2010/38

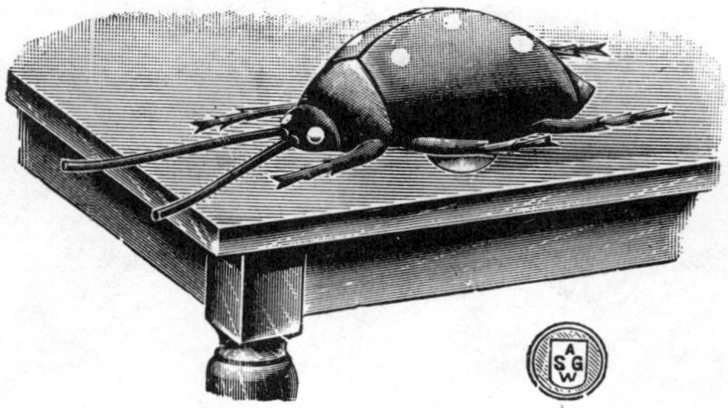

2010/12

Nr. **2010**/12 und 14 **Mechanische Artikel.** Kann infolge D. R. P.-Konstruktion nicht vom Tisch fallen.
Mechanical article. Because of its construction, patented in Germany, it can not fall from the table.
Artículo mecánico, no puede caer de la mesa según su construcción patentada, D. R. P.

Nr. **2010**/38 **Karussell,** mit Uhrwerk, Revontinastimme, ff. Handlackierung.
Merry-go-round with clockwork, Revontina voice, varnished by hand.
Carrusel con mecanismo de reloj, voz revontina, barnizado cuidadosamente á mano.

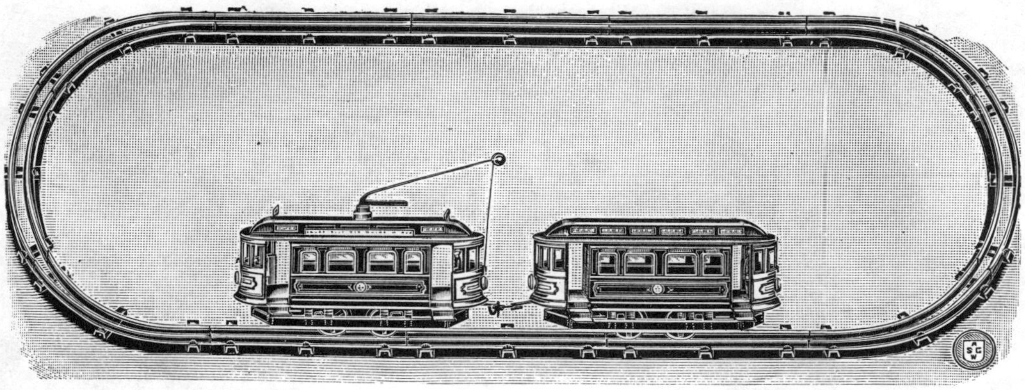

2010/21

Nr. **2010**/21 Mit automatisch hemmbarem Uhrwerk und Abstellvorrichtung.
With automatical clockwork and disengaging arrangement.
Con mecanismo de reloj que se para automáticamente y aparato de parar.

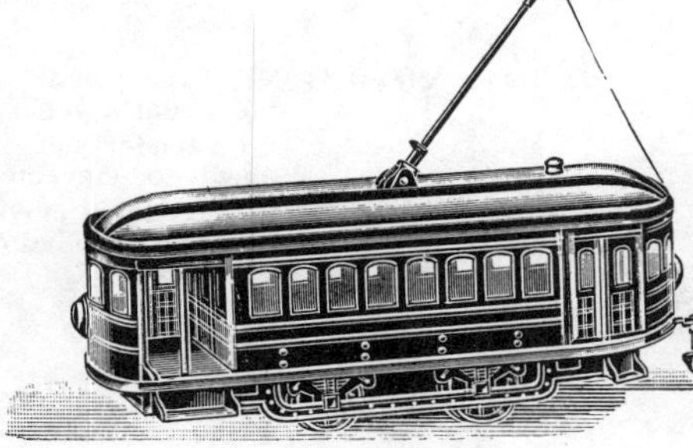

2010/25

2010/47

2010/26

Nr. **2010**/26 Mit Glasfenstern und Glocke.
With glass windows and bells.
Con ventanas de vidrio y campana.

Nr. **2010**/25 und 47 Mit Uhrwerk (amerikanische Fasson) und Glasfenstern.
With clockwork, American form and glass windows.
Con mecanismo de reloj, de estilo americano, y ventanas de vidrio.

2010/59

Nr. **2010**/59 Mit abnehmbarer Leiter und Schlauchkapsel, Glocke, Laterne und Rädern mit Gummi.
With dismountable ladder and hose capsule, bell, lantern and wheels with rubber.
Con escalera desmontable y cápsula de manguera, campana, linterna y ruedas con goma.

2010/57

Nr. **2010**/57 Mit Höhenstellung und Aufzugvorrichtung.
With hight adjustment and hoisting arrangement.
Con regulador de altura y aparato de montacargas.

2010/60

Nr. **2010**/60 Mit mechanischem Drehgestell und Aufzugvorrichtung, Laterne, Glocke und Rädern mit Gummi.
With mechanical turning frame and hoisting arrangement, lantern, bell and wheels with rubber.
Con boja mecánica y montacargas, linterna, campana y ruedas con goma.

2010/55

Nr. **2010**/55 Mit Spiralfederwerk, Glocke und imitierten Gummirädern.
With spring work, bell and imitated rubber wheels.
Con mecanismo de espiral, campana y ruedas de goma imitada.

2010/58

Nr. **2010**/58 Mit Spiralfederwerk, Laterne, Glocke und Rädern mit Gummi.
With spring work, lantern, bell and wheels with rubber.
Con mecanismo de espiral, linterna, campana y ruedas con goma.

2010/29

2010/33

Nr. **2010**/29 Mit Spiralfederwerk.
With spring work.
Con mecanismo de espiral.

2010/34

Nr. **2010**/33 Mit Tender und Zylinderbewegung.
With tender and cylinder movement.
Con ténder y movimiento de cilindros.

2010/30

Nr. **2010**/28/30/34 Mit Zylinderbewegung, Kuhfang und Glocke.
With cylinder movement and bell.
Con movimiento de cilindros, limpia-via (bajo en la parte delantera de la locomotora) y campana.

2010/28

2010/54

Nr. **2010**/54 **Neuheit! Zerleg- und konstruierbares Auto.** Es lassen sich aus dieser Nummer folgende Chassis-Arten konstruieren:

1. Offener Tourenwagen.
2. Halboffen m. Windschutzfenstern.
3. Geschlossen, Limousine.

Novelty: constructible and dismountable motor car. Of this No. the following kinds of cars can be constructed:

1. Open pleasure car.
2. Half open with wind screens.
3. Closed motor car.

¡Novedad! Automóvil que se puede desmontar y componer otra vez. Se puede construir de este número los estilos siguientes de chassis:

1. Coche de turismo abierto.
2. Medio-abierto con vidrio corta-viento.
3. Coche abrigado, limusina.

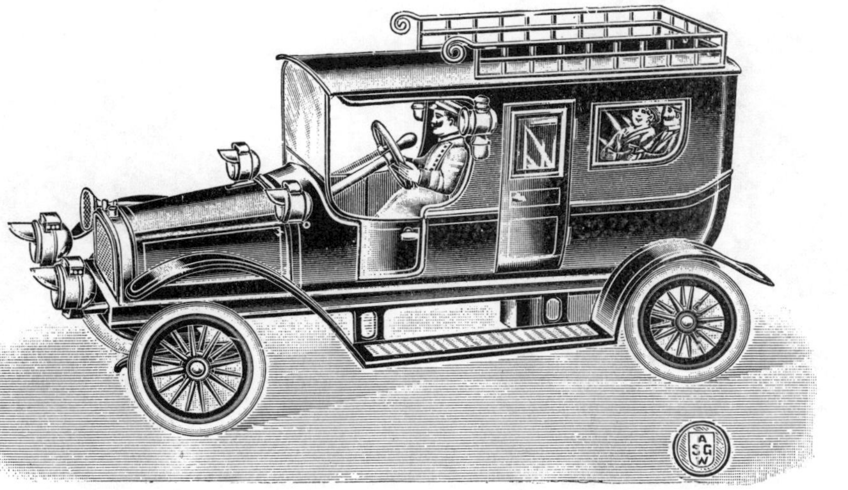

2010/53

Nr. **2010**/53 **Uhrwerk** mit Absteller und Gummibereifung.
Watchwork with disengager and rubber wheels.
Mecanismo de reloj con parada y bandajes de goma.

2010/51

Nr. **2010**/51 **Uhrwerk** mit Kurbelaufzug und Absteller.
Watchwork with crank hoist and disengager.
Mecanismo de reloj con manivela para dar cuerda y parada.

Nr. **2010**/52 **Uhrwerk** mit Absteller und Gummibereifung.
Watchwork with disengager and rubber wheels.
Mecanismo de reloj con parada y bandajes de goma.

2010/52

2010/46

Nr. **2010**/46 **Uhrwerk** mit Absteller, 4 verschieb- und herausnehmbaren Sitzen und 4 Laternen.
Watchwork with disengager, 4 lanterns and 4 seats which can be displaced and taken off.
Mecanismo de reloj con aparato de parar, 4 sillas cambiables y desmontables y 4 farols.

93/501
Herren-Dogcart, exzentrisch laufend.
Dogcart, eccentric wheels.
Coche inglés para Señores, con ruedas excentricas.
Länge / Length / Longitud = 18 cm

93/500
Damen-Dogcart, exzentrisch laufend.
Governess car, eccentric wheels.
Cabrioleta para Señoras, con ruedas excentricas.
Länge / Length / Longitud = 16½ cm

93/503
Auto Ruck-Ruck, exzentrisch laufend.
Three wheel run about, eccentric wheels.
Cycloneta con tres ruedas, con ruedas excentricas.
Länge / Length / Longitud = 16 cm

93/512
Auto mit Uhrwerk.
Motor car, clockwork
Automóvil de turismo, movimiento de muelles.
Länge / Length / Longitud = 15½ cm

93/507
Motor-Dreiradfahrer mit Uhrwerk.
Motor Side car, clockwork.
Motocicleta con side-car de muelles.
Länge / Length / Longitud = 16 cm

93/508
Motor-Dreiradfahrer mit Dame, mit Uhrwerk.
Motor cicle and Side car, clockwork.
Motocicleta con side-car y viajera de muelles.
Lenge / Length / Longitud = 16 cm

93/511
Renn-Auto mit Uhrwerk.
Racing car, clockwork.
Coche de corer, con mecánico de reloj.
Länge / Length / Longitud = 14 cm

93/519
Geschäfts-Auto mit Uhrwerk.
Delivery car, clockwork.
Coche de negocio, con mecánico de reloj.
Länge / Length / Longitud = 14 cm

93/515
Reise-Auto mit Uhrwerk.
Limousine, clockwork.
Coche de ciudad Automóvil, con mecánico de reloj.
Länge / Length / Longitud = 19 cm

93/504
Clownwagen, exzentrisch laufend.
Car for a clown, eccentric wheels.
Coche de payazo, con ruedas excentricas.
Länge / Length / Longitud = 12½ cm

93/526
Jagdwagen mit Uhrwerk.
Hunting waggonette, clockwork.
Dog-cart, movimiento de muelles.
Länge / Length / Longitud = 28½ cm

93/518
Geschäfts-Auto mit Uhrwerk.
Dilivery car, clockwork.
Coche de negocio, con mecánico de reloj.
Länge / Length / Longitud = 14 cm

93/524
Traber mit Uhrwerk.
Trotting-horse with clockwork.
Caballo trotador con reloj.
Länge / Length / Longitud = 23 cm

93/537
Milchwagen mit Esel, mit Uhrwerk.
Milk car with donkey with clockwork.
Carro de leche con burro, con mecanismo.
Länge / Length / Longitud = 21 cm

93/513
Auto mit Dame, mit Uhrwerk.
Motor car with lady, clockwork.
Automóvil de turismo con chofer y viajera, movimiento de muelles.
Länge / Length / Longitud = 15½ cm

Kleine Abweichungen vorbehalten. — Small alterations to reserve. — Al exceptión de pequeñas diferencias.

93/530
Amerikanische Autodroschke.
American Yellow taxi.
Limousina americana.
Länge / Length / Longitud = 19 cm

93/532
Straßenbahnwagen mit Uhrwerk.
Tramcar with clockwork.
Tramvia con mecánismo de reloj.
Länge / Length / Longitud = $17^1/_2$ cm

93/543
Rennauto mit Uhrwerk.
Racing car with clockwork.
Automóvil de carreras con reloj.
Länge / Length / Longitud = 17 cm

93/545
Limousine mit Uhrwerk.
Limousine with clockwork.
Limousine con reloj.
Länge / Length / Longitud = 17 cm

93/538
Damen-Dogcart mit springendem Pferd, exzentrisch. / **Governess car with a frisky horse,** eccentric wheels. / **Cabrioleta para Señoras, con caballo que salta,** con ruedas eccentricas.
Länge / Length / Longitud = $16^1/_2$ cm

93/539
Herren-Dogcart mit springendem Pferd, exzentrisch. / **Dogcart with a frisky horse,** eccentric wheels. / **Coche inglés para Señores, con caballo que salta,** con ruedas eccentricas,
Länge / Length / Longitud = 18 cm

93/542
Auto-Lastwagen mit Uhrwerk.
Camion with clockwork.
Camión con reloj.
Länge / Length / Longitud = 22 cm

93/540
Rennauto mit Uhrwerk.
Racing car with clockwork.
Auto de carrera con mecanismo.
Länge / Length / Longitud = $19^1/_2$ cm

93/541
Personen-Auto mit Uhrwerk.
Touring car with clockwork.
Automóvil de turismo con reloj.
Länge / Length / Longitud = $19^1/_2$ cm

93/527 — **Schiff** mit Uhrwerk. / **Steamer** with clockwork.
Vapor con mecánismo de reloj.
Länge / Length / Longitud = 23 cm

93/544/43/45
Autogarage mit einem Rennauto und einer Limousine, mit Uhrwerk. / **Garage** with automobil and limousine, with clockwork. / **Garage** para las automóviles, con un automóvil de carrera y un Limousine, con reloj.
Länge / Length / Longitud = $16^1/_2$ cm

93/528
Passagierdampfer mit Uhrwerk.
Passenger Steamer with clockwork.
Vapor, movimiento de muelles, con reloj.
Länge / Length / Longitud = 31 cm

Kleine Abweichungen vorbehalten. — Small alterations to reserve. — Al excepción de pequeñas diferencias.

42/150/4

42/151/5

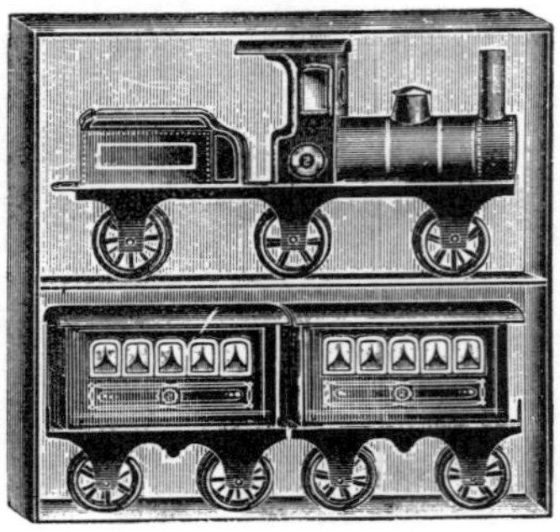

42/1900/4a

42/504/3

Mit Uhrwerk. — With watchwork.
Con mecanismo de reloj.

Nr. **42**/150/2 Lokomotive mit Tender.
Engine with tender.
Locomotora con tender.

„ **42**/150/3 Lokomotive mit Tender, 1 Personenwagen.
Engine with tender, 1 passenger-car.
Locomotora con tender, 1 vagón de viajeros.

„ **42**/150/4 Lokomotive mit Tender, 2 Personenwagen.
Engine with tender, 2 passenger-cars.
Locomotora con tender, 2 vagónes de viajeros.

„ **42**/150/5 Lokomotive mit Tender, 3 Personenwagen.
Engine with tender, 3 passenger-cars.
Locomotora con tender, 3 vagónes de viajeros.

„ **42**/150/6 Lokomotive mit Tender, 4 Personenwagen.
Engine with tender, 4 passenger-cars.
Locomotora con tender, 4 vagónes de viajeros.

„ **42**/150/7 Lokomotive mit Tender, 5 Personenwagen.
Engine with tender, 5 passenger-cars.
Locomotora con tender, 5 vagónes de viajeros.

„ **42**/150/8 Lokomotive mit Tender, 6 Personenwagen.
Engine with tender, 6 passenger-cars.
Locomotora con tender, 6 vagónes de viajeros.

„ **42**/151/4 Lokomotive mit Tender, 1 Personenwagen, 1 Güterwagen.
Engine with tender, 1 passenger-car, 1 goods waggon.
Locomotora con tender, 1 vagón de viajeros, 1 vagón de equipages.

„ **42**/152/6 Lokomotive mit Tender, 2 Personenwagen, 2 Güterwagen.
Engine with tender, 2 passenger-cars, 2 goods waggons.
Locomotora con tender, 2 vagónes de viajeros, 2 vagónes de equipages.

Nr. **42**/1900/2a½ Lokomotive und Tender auf 1 Brett.
Engine and tender on 1 board.
Locomotora y tender sobre 1 tabla.

„ **42**/1990/3a Lokomotive und Tender auf 1 Brett, 1 Personenwagen.
Engine and tender on 1 board, 1 passenger-car.
Locomotora y tender sobre 1 tabla, 1 vagón de viajeros.

„ **42**/1900/4a Lokomotive und Tender auf 1 Brett, 2 Personenwagen.
Engine and tender on 1 board, 2 passenger-cars.
Locomotora y tender sobre 1 tabla, 2 vagónes de viajeros.

„ **42**/1909/5a Lokomotive und Tender auf 1 Brett, 3 Personenwagen.
Engine and tender on 1 board, 3 passenger-cars.
Locomotora y tender sobre 1 tabla, 3 vagónes de viajeros.

„ **42**/1900/6a Lokomotive und Tender auf 1 Brett, 4 Personenwagen.
Engine and tender on 1 board, 4 passenger-cars.
Locomotora y tender sobre 1 tabla, 4 vagónes de viajeros.

„ **42**/1922/6a Lokomotive und Tender auf 1 Brett, 2 Personenwagen, 2 Güterwagen.
Engine and tender on 1 board, 2 passenger-cars, 2 goods-waggons.
Locomotora y tender sobre 1 tabla, 2 vagónes de viajeros, 2 vagónes de equipages.

„ **42**/504/3 Lokomotive, Tender, 1 Personenwagen, 4 runde schwarze Schienen.
Engine, tender, 1 passenger-car, 4 round black rails.
Locomotora, tender, 1 vagón de viajeros, 4 rieles negros redondos.

„ **42**/504/4 Lokomotive, Tender, 2 Personenwagen, 4 runde schwarze Schienen.
Engine, tender, 2 passenger-cars, 4 round black rails.
Locomotora, tender, 2 vagónes de viajeros, 4 rieles negros redondos.

„ **42**/508K/3R Lokomotive, Tender, 1 Personenwagen, 8 runde schwarze Schienen mit Kreuzung.
Engine, tender, 1 passenger-car, 8 round black rails with crossing.
Locomotora, tender, 1 vagón de viajeros, 8 rieles negros redondos con cruce.

„ **42**/508K/4R Lokomotive, Tender, 2 Personenwagen, 8 runde schwarze Schienen mit Kreuzung.
Engine, tender, 2 passenger-cars, 8 round black rails with crossing.
Locomotora, tender, 2 vagónes de viajeros, 8 rieles negros redondos con cruce.

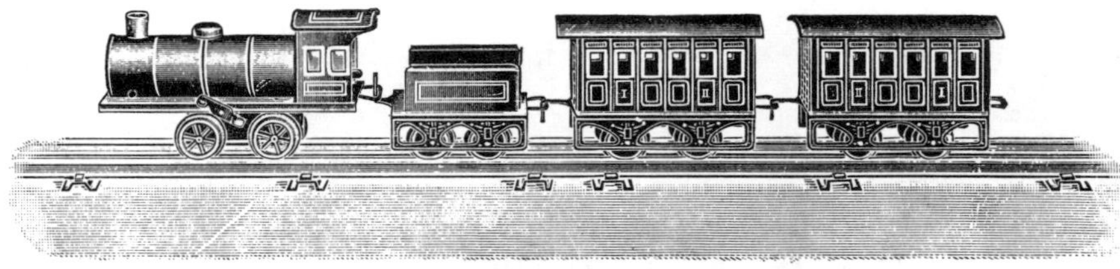

42/364/4. Mit Uhrwerk. — With watchwork. — con mecanismo de reloj.

Nr. **42**/364/3
Lokomotive, Tender, 1 Personenwagen, 4 runde schwarze Schienen.
Engine, tender, 1 passenger-car, 4 round black rails.
Locomotora, tender, 1 vagón de viajeros, 4 rieles negros redondos.

Nr. **42**/364/4
Lokomotive, Tender, 2 Personenwagen, 4 runde schwarze Schienen.
Engine, tender, 2 passenger-cars, 4 round black rails.
Locomotora, tender, 2 vagónes de viajeros, 4 rieles negros redondos.

Nr. **42**/364/3R
Lokomotive, Tender, 1 Personenwagen, 4 runde schwarze Schienen.
Engine, tender, 1 passenger-car, 4 round black rails.
Locomotora, tender, 1 vagón de viajeros, 4 rieles negros redondos.

Nr. **42**/364/4 R
Lokomotive, Tender, 2 Personenwagen, 4 runde schwarze Schienen.
Engine, tender, 2 passenger-cars, 4 round black rails.
Locomotora, tender, 2 vagónes de viajeros, 4 rieles negros redondos.

Nr. **42**/95/4/3 Lokomotive, Tender, 1 Personenwagen, 4 runde Schienen.
Engine, tender, 1 passenger-car, 4 round rails.
Locomotora, tender, 1 vagón de viajeros, 4 rieles redondos.

„ **42**/95/4/4 Lokomotive, Tender, 2 Personenwagen, 4 runde Schienen.
Engine, tender, 2 passenger-cars, 4 round rails.
Locomotora, tender, 2 vagónes de viajeros, 4 rieles redondos.

„ **42**/95/6/5 Lokomotive, Tender, 3 Personenwagen, 6 runde Schienen.
Engine, tender, 3 passenger-cars, 6 round rails.
Locomotora, tender, 3 vagónes de viajeros, 6 rieles redondos.

„ **42**/95/10K/3 Lokomotive, Tender, 1 Personenwagen, 10 Schienen u. Kreuzung.
Engine, tender, 1 passenger-car, 10 rails with crossing point.
Locomotora, tender, 1 vagón de viajeros, 10 rieles con cruce.

„ **42**/95/10K/4 Lokomotive, Tender, 2 Personenwagen, 10 Schienen u. Kreuzung.
Engine, tender, 2 passenger-cars, 10 rails with crossing point.
Locomotora, tender, 2 vagónes de viajeros, 10 rieles con cruce.

„ **42**/95/7W/3 Lokomotive, Tender, 1 Personenwagen, 7 Schienen u. 2 Weichen.
Engine, tender, 1 passenger-car, 7 rails and 2 switches.
Locomotora, tender, 1 vagón de viajeros, 7 rieles y 2 agujas.

„ **42**/95/7W/4 Lokomotive, Tender, 2 Personenwagen, 7 Schienen u. 2 Weichen.
Engine, tender, 2 passenger-cars, 7 rails and 2 switches.
Locomotora, tender, 2 vagónes de viajeros, 7 rieles y 2 agujas.

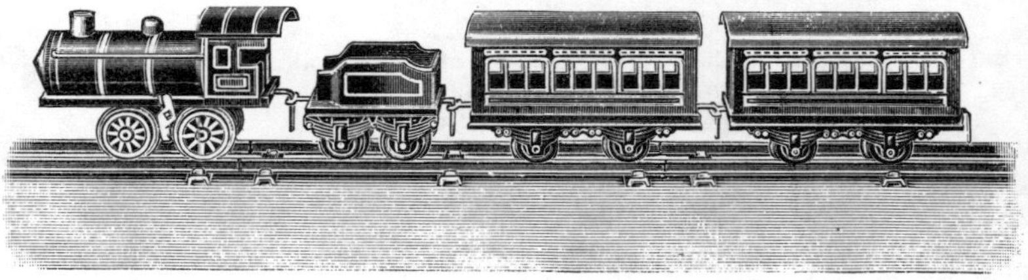

42/95/4/4. Mit Uhrwerk. — With watchwork. — Con mecanismo de reloj.

Nr. **42**/88/4/3
Lokomotive, Tender, 1 Personenwagen, 4 runde Schienen.
Engine, tender, 1 passenger-car, 4 round rails.
Locomotora, tender, 1 vagón de viajeros, 4 rieles redondos.

Nr. **42**/88/4/4
Lokomotive, Tender, 2 Personenwagen, 4 runde Schienen.
Engine, tender, 2 passenger-cars, 4 round rails.
Locomotora, tender, 2 vagónes de viajeros, 4 rieles redondos.

Nr. **42**/88/6/5
Lokomotive, Tender, 3 Personenwagen, 6 runde Schienen.
Engine, tender, 3 passenger-cars, 6 round rails.
Locomotora, tender, 3 vagónes de viajeros, 6 rieles redondos.

Nr. **42**/88/10K/3
Lokomotive, Tender, 1 Personenwagen, 10 Schienen mit Kreuzung.
Engine, tender, 1 passenger-car, 10 rails with crossing point.
Locomotora, tender, 1 vagón de viajeros, 10 rieles con cruce.

Nr. **42**/88/10K/4
Lokomotive, Tender, 2 Personenwagen, 10 Schienen mit Kreuzung.
Engine, tender, 2 passenger-cars, 10 rails with crossing point.
Locomotora, tender, 2 vagónes de viajeros, 10 rieles con cruce.

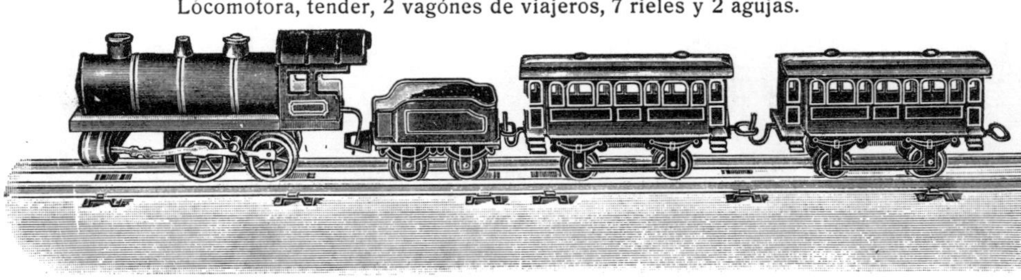

42/88/4/4. Mit Uhrwerk. — With watchwork. — Con mecanismo de reloj.

42/166/4. Mit Uhrwerk. — With clockwork. — Con mecanismo de reloj.

Nr. **42**/166/3 Lokomotive, Tender, 1 Personenwagen, 6 runde Schienen. Engine, tender, 1 passenger-car, 6 round rails Locomotora, tender, 1 vagón de viajeros, 6 rieles redondos.

„ **42**/166/4 Lokomotive, Tender, 2 Personenwagen, 6 runde Schienen. Engine, tender, 2 passenger-cars, 6 round rails. Locomotora, tender, 2 vagónes de viajeros, 6 rieles redondos.

„ **42**/166/5 Lokomotive, Tender, 3 Personenwagen, 6 runde Schienen. Engine, tender, 3 passenger-cars, 6 round rails. Locomotora, tender, 3 vagónes de viajeros, 6 rieles redondos.

„ **42**/160/10K/3 Lokomotive, Tender, 1 Personenwagen, 10 Schienen und Kreuzung. Engine, tender, 1 Passenger-car, 10 rails with crossing point. Locomotora, tender, 1 vagón de viajeros, 10 rieles con cruce.

„ **42**/160/10/K4 Lokomotive, Tender, 2 Personenwagen, 10 Schienen und Kreuzung. Engine, tender, 2 passenger-cars, 10 rails with crossing point. Locomotora, tender, 2 vagónes de viajeros, 10 rieles con cruce.

„ **42**/160/7W/3 Lokomotive, Tender, 1 Personenwagen, 7 Schienen und 2 Weichen. Engine, tender, 1 passenger-car, 7 rails and 2 switches. Locomotora, tender, 1 vagón de viajeros, 7 rieles y 2 agujas.

„ **42**/160/7W/4 Lokomotive, Tender, 2 Personenwagen, 7 Schienen und 2 Weichen. Engine, tender, 2 passenger-cars, 7 rails and 2 switches. Locomotora, tender, 2 vagónes de viajeros, 7 rieles y 2 agujas.

„ **42**/176/3 Lokomotive, Tender, 1 Personenwagen, 6 runde Schienen. Engine, tender, 1 passenger-car, 6 round rails. Locomotora, tender, 1 vagón de viajeros, 6 rieles redondos.

Nr. **42**/176/4 Lokomotive, Tender, 1 Personenwagen, 6 runde Schienen, 1 Gepäckwagen. Engine, tender, 1 passenger-car, 6 round rails, 1 baggage car. Locomotora, tender, 1 vagón de viajeros, 6 rieles redondos, 1 vagón de bagaje.

„ **42**/176/5 Lokomotive, Tender, 2 Personenwagen, 6 runde Schienen, 1 Gepäckwagen. Engine, tender, 2 passenger-cars, 6 round rails, 1 baggage car. Locomotora, tender, 2 vagónes de viajeros, 6 rieles redondos, 1 vagón de bagaje.

„ **42**/170/10K/3 Lokomotive, Tender, 1 Personenwagen, 10 Schienen mit Kreuzung. Engine, tender, 1 passenger-car, 10 rails with crossing point. Locomotora, tender, 1 vagón de viajeros, 10 rieles con cruce.

„ **42**/170/10K/4 Lokomotive, Tender, 1 Personenwagen, 10 Schienen mit Kreuzung, 1 Gepäckwagen. Engine, tender, 1 passenger-car, 10 rails with crossing point, 1 baggage car. Locomotora, tender, 1 vagón de viajeros, 10 rieles con cruce, 1 vagón de bagaje.

„ **42**/170/7W/3 Lokomotive, Tender, 1 Personenwagen, 7 Schienen und 2 Weichen. Engine, tender, 1 passenger-car, 7 rails and 2 switches. Locomotora, tender, 1 vagón de viajeros, 7 rieles y 2 agujas.

„ **42**/170/7W/4 Lokomotive, Tender, 1 Personenwagen, 7 Schienen und 2 Weichen, 1 Gepäckwagen. Engine, tender, 1 passenger-car, 7 rails and 2 switches, 1 baggage car. Locomotora, tender, 1 vagón de viajeros, 7 rieles y 2 agujas, 1 vagón de bagaje.

42/176/4. Mit Uhrwerk. — With clockwork. — Con mecanismo de reloj.

Automobile
mit Spiralfeder, ff. Lackierung.

Motor-cars
with spiral spring mechanism, finest varnished.

Automóviles
con resorte de espiral, muy bien embarnizado.

42/42/1R, 44/1R und 46/1R. Limousine.

42/47/1R. Limousine.

42/48. Offenes Auto. — Auto-car open. — Automóvil descubierto.

42/49. Limousine.

42/40/1R. Offenes Auto. — Auto-car open Automóvil descubierto.

2001/2

Scherenschleifer mit Uhrwerk
Scissors-grinder with clockwork
Afiladores de tijeras con mecanismo de reloj

2001/4

Nr. **2016**/18
Fußballspieler mit Uhrwerk
Football player with clockwork
Jugador con bolas de pie con mecanismo de reloj

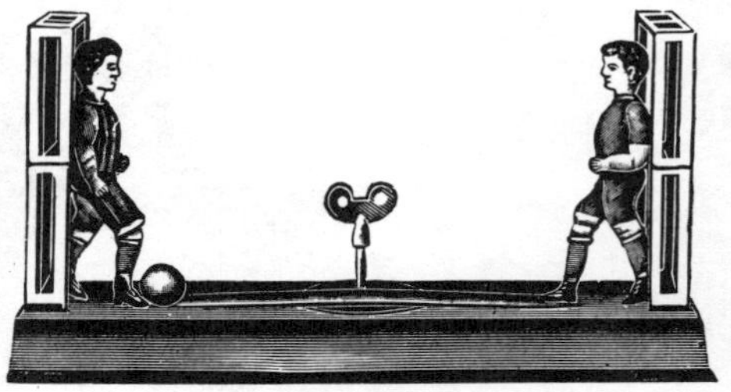

2016/18

Billige Blechspielwaren ohne Uhrwerk. — Cheap tin toys without clockwork. — Juguetes baratos sin mecanismo.

The Acrobatic Dog.
2016/1

2016/23

2016/31

2016/30

2016/27

2016/19

2016/15

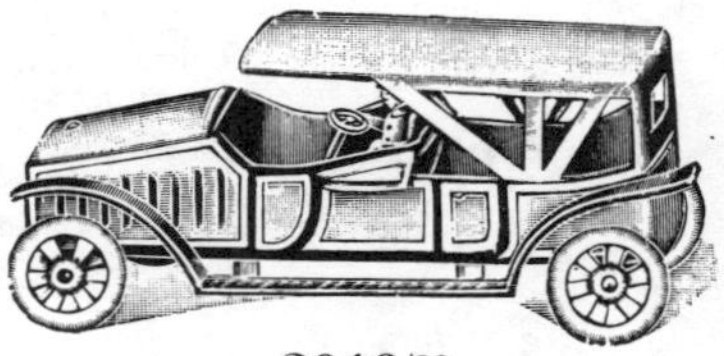

2016/29

2016/12

2016/13

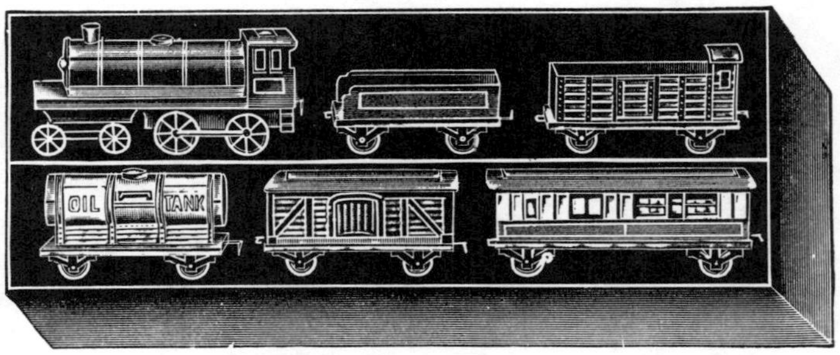

2016/33

2016/26

2016/25

2016/28

2007/3

2007/13

2007/8

2007/9

Billige Blechspielwaren mit und ohne Uhrwerk. — Cheap tin toys with or without clockwork. — Juguetes baratos con y sin mecanismo.

2007/1

2007/2

2007/5

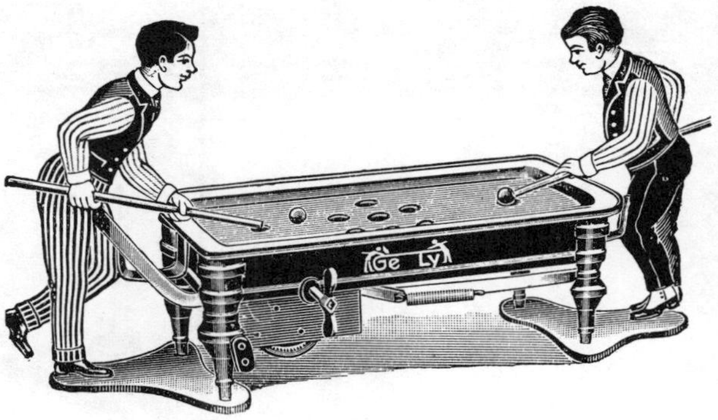

2007/7

Billardspieler mit Uhrwerk.
Billard player with clockwork.
Jugador a billar con mecanismo de reloj.

2007/12

2007/6

2007/10

2007/11

Eisenbahnen. — Railways. — Ferrocarriles.

2012/6

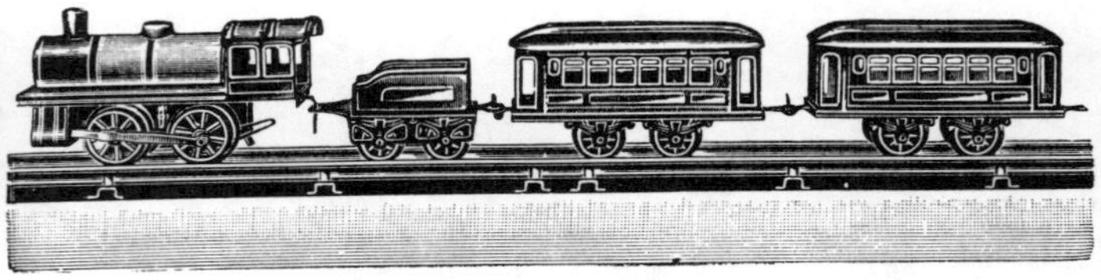

2012/4

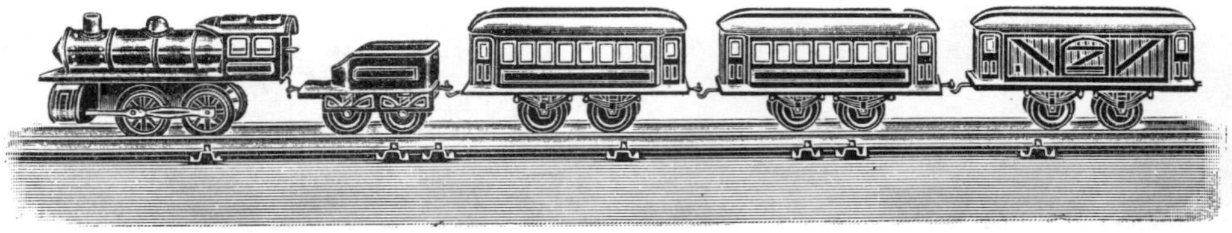

2012/5

2012/2

Nr. **2012**/2, 4, 5 und 6. Mit Uhrwerk, Regulator und Bremse.
With mechanism, regulated clockwork and brake.
Con mecanismo, regulador y freno.

2012/8

Nr. **2012**/8 und 9. Mit Uhrwerk und Bremse, vor- und rückwärts laufend.
With mechanism and brake, reversing.
Con mecanismo y freno, adelantando y retrocediendo.

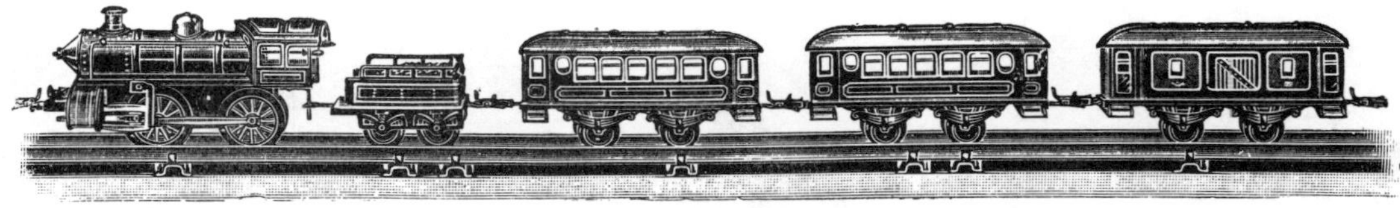

2012/9

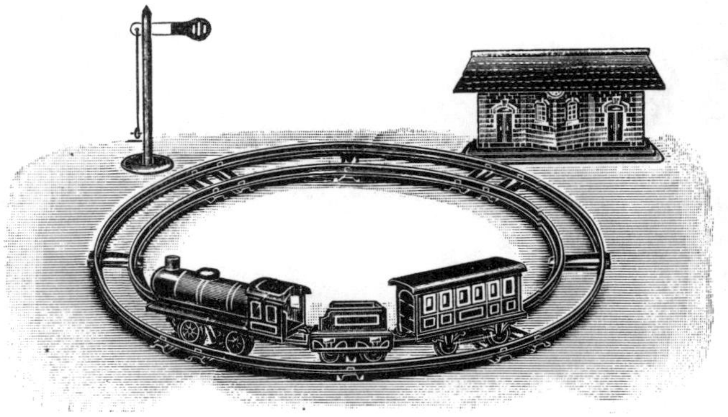

2012/32

Nr. **2012**/32. Mit Uhrwerk und Zubehör (Bahnhof und Signal).
With mechanism and accessories (station and signal.)
Con mechanismo y accesorios (Estación y señal).

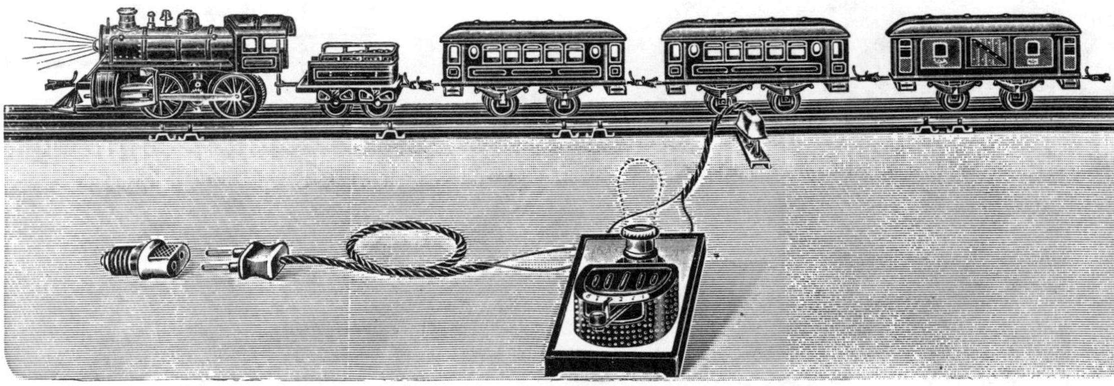

2012/11

Nr. **2012**/11. **Elektrische Bahn,** Lokomotive, Tender und 3 Wagen für Starkstrom (Gleich- und Wechselstrom) mit Universalwiderstand für Lichtleitungen 110—220 Volt, vor- und rückwärts laufend, Stirnlampe zum Ein- und Ausschalten.

Electric railways, engine, tender and 3 cars, for high current (direct and alternating current) wit reducer, for light circuits of 110—220 Volt, reversing head light can be turned an and off.

Ferrocarriles electricos, locomotora, tender y 3 vagones, para corriente fuerte (corriente continua y alternativa) con transformador universal, para electricidad de 110—220 Volt, adelantando y retrocidiendo. La lampara de delante puede estar encendida y apagada.

Dieselben Eisenbahnen können auch mit Kreuzung und Weichen geliefert werden. — The same railways can be also delivered with crossing point and switches.
Los mismos ferrocarriles se pueden también entregar con croze y con agujas.

Bahnhöfe und Bestandteile. — Stations and accessories. — Estaciones y accessorios.

2012/14

2012/25

2012/23

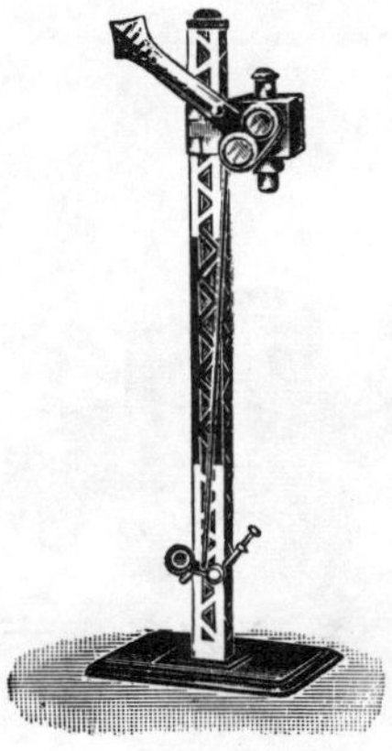

2012/28

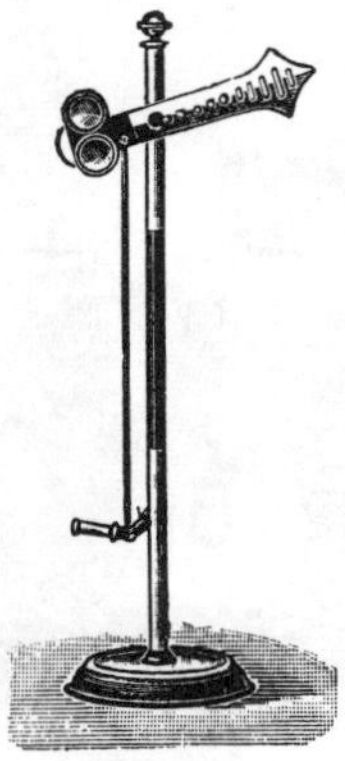

2012/27

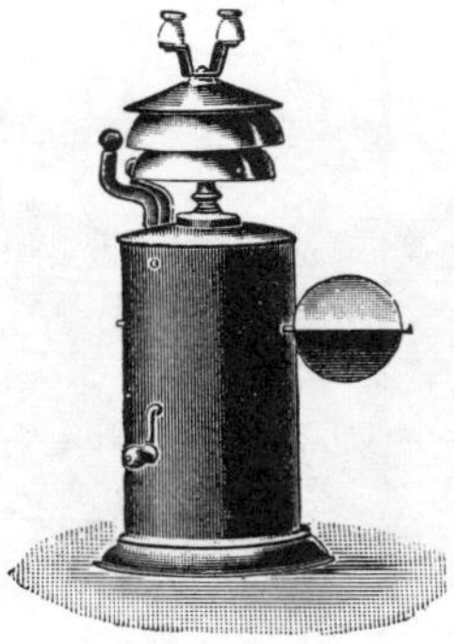

2012/22

2012/20

Automobile, Blech, mit Uhrwerk. **Motor Cars,** tin, with clockwork. **Automóviles,** de lata, con mecanismo.

2012/33/34

Länge / Length / Longitud = 20 cm
Breite / Breadth / Altitud = 9 „
Höhe / Height / Altura = $10^{1}/_{2}$ „

2012/36

Länge / Length / Longitud = 26 cm
Breite / Breadth / Altitud = 11 „
Höhe / Height / Altura = 13 „

2012/39
MitBremse, vor- und rückwärts laufend.
With brake, reversing.
Con freno, adelantado y retrocediendo.

Länge / Length / Longitud = 28 cm
Breite / Breadth / Altitud = 14 „
Höhe / Height / Altura = 15 „

2012/39

2012/39
kann auch in den Größen: Länge 35, Breite 14, Höhe 17 cm geliefert werden.
Can be also delivered in the: Length 35, Breadth 14, Height 17 cm.
Puede estar tambien suministrado en: Longitud 35, Altitud 14, Altura 17 cm.

14/980 **14**/R 980

14/990 **14**/R 990

14/1040 **14**/R 1040

14/E 1030 **14**/E 1041

Spurweite
Anchura de la vía
0: 35 mm
I: 48 „
Gauge
0: 1¹/₄ inch.
I: 1³/₄ „

14/EE 1020 **14**/EE 1021

14/H 1021

Uhrwerk-Lokomotiven.
Clockwork locomotives. — Locomotoras con aparatos de relojería.

Neueste Modelle in gediegenster Ausführung mit zugkräftigen Uhrwerken.

Latest models. Regulated clockworks. Correct in every detail.

Modelo novisimo con aparatos de relojeria de gran fuerza de tracción, ejecución más solida.

Nr.	Spurweite Gauge Anchura de la vía							Länge mit Tender Length with tender Largura con ténder cm	inches pulgadas
14/980	0	Lokomotive mit Tender, 2achsig, nur vorwärts fahrend, mit Bremse	Alles in feiner Chromolackierung	Locomotive with tender, 2 axles with brake	Finest chromolithography	Locomotora con ténder, 2 ejes con freno, no marchando que hacia adelante	Todo en fina cromo-embarnizadura	21	8¹/₂
14/R 980	0	**Vor- und rückwärts fahrend,** mit Bremse		With brake and **reversing gear**		Con freno, **marchando hacia adelante y hacia atrás**			
14/990	0	Lokomotive mit Tender, 2achsig, nur vorwärts fahrend, mit Bremse		Locomotive with tender, 2 axles with brake		Locomotora con ténder, 2 ejes con freno, no marchando que hacia adelante		25,5	10
14/R 990	0	**Vor- und rückwärts fahrend,** mit Bremse		With brake and **reversing gear**		Con freno, **marchando hacia adelante y hacia atrás**			
14/1040	0	Lokomotive mit Tender, 2achsig, nur vorwärts fahrend, mit Bremse		Locomotive with tender, 2 axles with brake		Locomotora con ténder, 2 ejes con freno, no marchando que hacia adelante		28	11
14/R 1040	0	**Vor- und rückwärts fahrend,** mit Bremse		With brake and **reversing gear**		Con freno, **marchando hacia adelante y hacia atrás**			
14/1041	I	Lokomotive mit Tender, 2achsig, nur vorwärts fahrend, mit Bremse		Locomotive with tender, 2 axles with brake		Locomotora con ténder, 2 ejes con freno, no marchando que hacia adelante		41	16¹/₈
14/R 1041	I	**Vor- und rückwärts fahrend,** mit Bremse		With brake and **reversing gear.**		Con freno, **marchando hacia adelante y hacia atrás**			
14/E 1030	0	Lokomotive mit Tender, 4achsig, **vor-und rückwärts fahrend,** mit Bremse		Locomotive with tender, 4 axles, bogie, with brake and reversing gear		Locomotora con ténder, 4 ejes con freno, marchando hacia adelante y hacia atrás		34	13³/₈
14/E 1041	I							41,5	16³/₈
14/EE 1020	0	Expreßzug-Lokomotive m. Tender, 4achsig, langsam und schnell fahrend, mit Bremse	Solide Handarbeit und feine Handlackierung	Four-coupled bogie Locomotive, type 4-4-0, with brake and reversing gear, speed regulation	Hand-made, beautifully japanned by hand	Locomotora para trenos expresos con ténder. 4 ejes con freno, marchando lentamente y rápidamente hacia adelante y hacia atrás	Solida obra de mano y fina laca de mano	37	14¹/₂
14/EE 1021	I							54,5	21¹/₂
14/H 1021	I	Schnellzug-Lokomotive m. Tender, 6achsig, vor- und rückwärts, langsam und schnell fahrend, mit Bremse. Nur für Schienen 1611 A (großer Radius)		Locomotive "Pacific", type 4-6-2, with brake, reversing gear and speed regulation To be used with large radius rails 1611 A		Locomotora para trenes rápidos con ténder, 6 ejes con freno, marchando lentamente y rápidamente hacia adelante y hacia atrás. Solamente para carriles 1611 A (gran radio)		74	29¹/₈

14/980/82/2 **14**/R 980/82/2

14/990/92/3 **14**/R 990/92/3

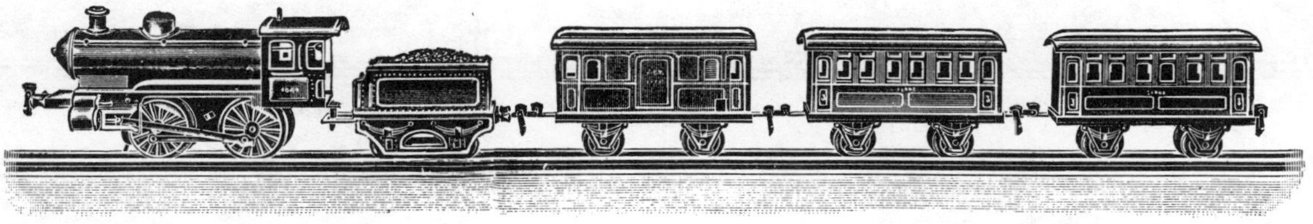

14/1040/92/3 **14**/R 1040/92/3 **14**/1041/92/3 **14**/R 1041/92/3

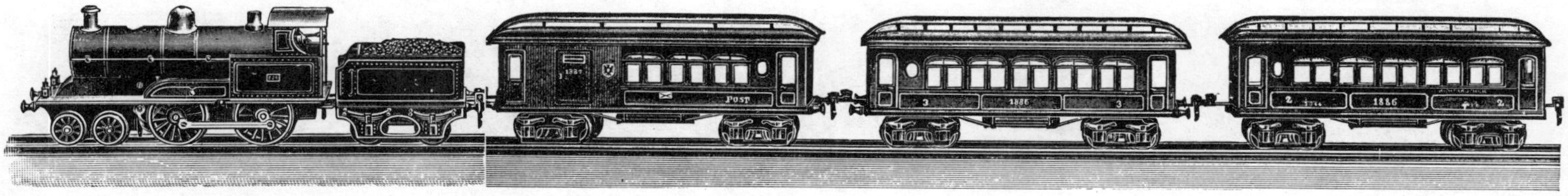

14/E 1030/86/3 **14**/E 1041/86/3

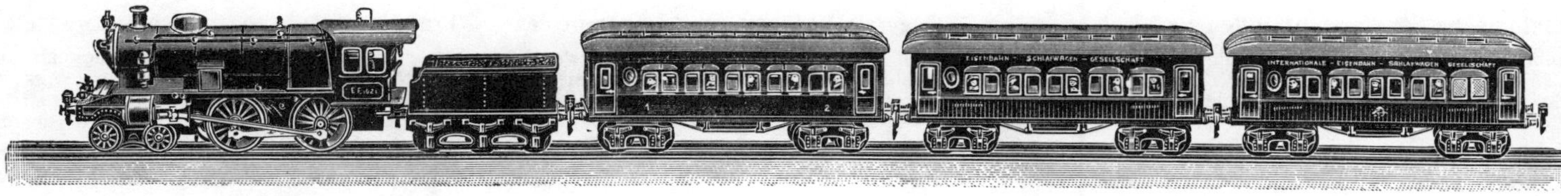

14/EE 1020/94/3 **14**/EE 1021/94/3

Uhrwerk-Eisenbahnen auf Schienen. — Clockwork Railways. — Ferrocarriles con aparatos de relojería sobre carriles.

Aufmachung in solidem Karton. — Sets in attractive cardboard boxes. — Puestos en una sólida caja de cartón.

Nr.	Spurweite Gauge Anchura de la vía							Zuglänge Length of train Largura del tren cm	inches pulgadas
14/980/82/2	0	Personenzug mit 2 Wagen, Schienenkreis, vorwärts fahrend, mit Bremse	Lokomotiven und Wagen in feiner Chromolackierung. Solide, kräftige Ausführung.	Clockwork Train with 2 cars. Circle set of rails. With brake, forward only	Locomotives and carriages finely chromolithographed. Solid strong construction.	Tren de viajeros con 2 vagones. Círculo de carriles, marchando hacia adelante. Freno	Locomotoras y vagones en fina cromo-embarnizadura. Ejecución sólida y robusta.	42	16 1/2
14/R 980/82/2	0	Vor- und rückwärts fahrend		With reversing gear		Marchando hacia adelante y hacia atrás			
14/990/92/3	0	Personenzug mit 3 Wagen, Schienenoval, vorwärts fahrend, mit Bremse		Clockwork Train with 3 cars. Oval set of rails. With brake, forward only		Tren de viajeros con 3 vagones. Carriles ovales, marchando hacia adelante. Freno		70	27 1/2
14/R 990/92/3	0	Vor- und rückwärts fahrend		With reversing gear		Marchando hacia adelante y hacia atrás			
14/1040/92/3	0	Personenzug mit 3 Wagen, Schienenoval, vorwärts fahrend, mit Bremse		Clockwork Train with 3 cars. Oval set of rails. With brake, forward only		Tren de viajeros con 3 vagones. Carriles ovales, marchando hacia adelante. Freno		72	28 3/8
14/R 1040/92/3	0	Vor- und rückwärts fahrend		With reversing gear		Marchando hacia adelante y hacia atrás			
14/1041/92/3	1	Personenzug mit 3 Wagen, Schienenoval, vorwärts fahrend, mit Bremse		Clockwork Train with 3 cars. Oval set of rails. With brake, forward only		Tren de viajeros con 3 vagones. Carriles ovales, marchando hacia adelante. Freno		106.5	42
14/R 1041/92/3	1	Vor- und rückwärts fahrend		With reversing gear		Marchando hacia adelante y hacia atrás			
14/E 1030/86/3	0	Expreßzug mit 3 D-Wagen, Schienenoval, vor- und rückwärts fahrend, mit Bremse		Clockwork Train with four-coupled bogie locomotive and carriages on bogies. Oval set of rails. Brake and reversing gear		Tren expreso con 3 vagones de corredor. Carriles ovales, marchando hacia adelante y hacia atrás. Con freno		93	36 5/8
14/E 1041/86/3	1							154	60 3/4
14/EE 1020/94/3	0	Expreßzug mit 3 D-Wagen, Personen-, Speise- und Schlafwagen mit feiner Innenausstattung, Türen zum öffnen. Schienenoval. Vor- und rückwärts, langsam und schnell fahrend, mit Bremse. **Solide Handarbeit und feine Handlackierung**		Clockwork Train with four-coupled bogie locomotive, 3 express cars with seats and passengers, doors to open. Oval set of rail. Brake, reversing gear and speed-regulation. **Magnificent model, finest hand-japanning**		Tren expreso con 3 vagones de corredor. Vagones restaurán y coches cama (wagons-lits) para viajeros con finísimo mueblaje interior. Puertas para abrir. Carriles ovales, marchando lentamente y rápidamente, hacia adelante y hacia atrás, con freno. **Sólida obra de mano y fina embarnizadura a mano**		98	38 1/2
14/EE 1021/94/3	1							154	60 3/4

14/R 3040/84/3 **14**/R 3041/84/3

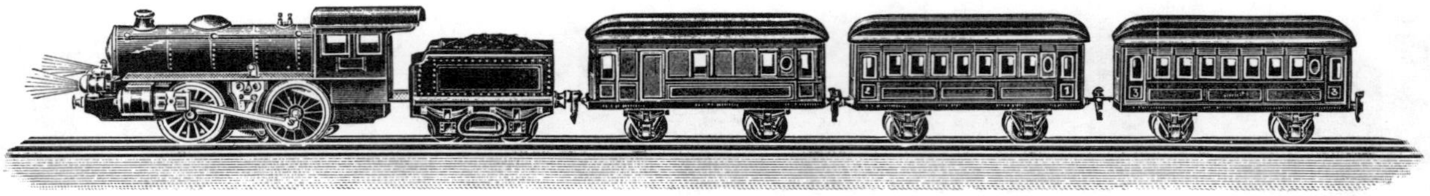

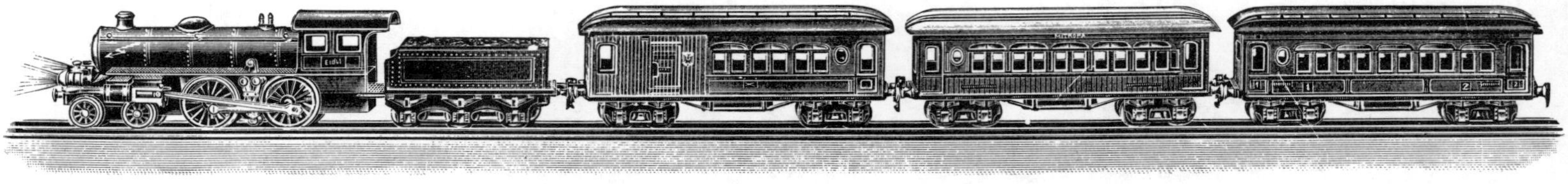

14/E 3040/86/3 **14**/E 3041/86/3

14/S 64/3020 **14**/S 64/3021 **14**/CE 64/3020 **14**/CE 64/3021

Elektrische Starkstrombahnen und Lokomotiven — Electric Railways and Locomotives — Tranvías eléctricos y locomotoras eléctricas

zum direkten Anschluß an Lichtleitungen von 110 bis 220 Volt, Gleich-, Wechsel- oder Drehstrom unter Zwischenschaltung eines Lampenwiderstandes mit Geschwindigkeitsregler.

high current 110—220 volts, for direct, alternating and three phase current, intercalation of resistance box with speed regulator.

para connexión directa con canalizaciones de luz de 110—220 voltios, corriente continua corrientes alternas o corrientes trifásicas intercalación de una resistencia de lámparas conectándola con el regulador de velocidad.

Nr.	Spurweite Gauge Anchura de la via				Länge — Length Largura cm	inches pulgadas
14/R 3040 **14**/R 3041	0 I	Elektrische Lokomotive, 2 achsig, vor- und rückwärts fahrend durch Handschaltung Spur 0: 1 Stirnlampe Spur I: 2 Stirnlampen und Steckanschluß für Wagenbeleuchtung	Electric Locomotive, 2 axles, reversing by hand Gauge 0: 1 headlight Gauge I: 2 headlights and sliding contact for lighting up cars	Locomotora eléctrica, con 2 ejes, marchando hacia adelante y hacia atrás, por medio de interrupción a mano vía 0: 1 lámpara frontal vía I: 2 lámparas frontales y unión por clavija para el alumbrado de los vagones	30,5 43,5	12 17
14 R 3040/84/3 **14** R 3041/84/3	0 I	Elektrischer Zug mit 3 D-Wagen, 2 achsig, Schienenoval, Widerstand, Anschlußkabel usw., vor- und rückwärts fahrend durch Handschaltung	Electric Railway with 3 carriages, 2 axles, oval set of rail including connecting-rail, wire, plug, and resistance, reversing by hand	Tren eléctrico con 3 vagones de corredor, 2 ejes, carr les ovales. Resistencia, cable de amarre, etc. Tren marchando hacia adelante y hacia atrás por medio de interrupción a mano	82,5 116,5	32 1/2 45 3/4
14/E 3040 **14**/E 3041	0 I	Elektrische Lokomotive, 4 achsig, vor- und rückwärts fahrend durch Handschaltung Spur 0: 1 Stirnlampe mit Steckanschluß für Wagenbeleuchtung Spur I: 2 Stirnlampen mit Steckanschluß für Wagenbeleuchtung	Electric Locomotive, type 4-4-0, reversing by hand Gauge 0: 1 headlight and sliding contact for lighting up carriages Gauge I: 2 headlights and sliding contact for lighting up carriages	Locomotora eléctrica con 4 ejes, marchando hacia adelante y hacia atrás, por medio de interrupción a mano vía 0: 1 lámpara frontal y unión por clavija para el alumbrado de vagones vía I: 2 lámparas frontales y unión de clavija para el alumbrado de vagones	35 50,5	13 3/4 20
14 E 3040/86/3 **14** E 3041/86/3	0 I	Elektrischer Zug mit 3 D-Wagen, 4 achsig, Schienenoval, Widerstand, Anschlußkabel usw., vor- und rückwärts fahrend durch Handschaltung	Electric Railway, fourcoupled bogie locomotive, 3 passenger cars on bogies, no seats, oval set of rail including connecting-rail, wire, plug, and resistance, reversing by hand	Tren eléctrico con 3 vagones de corredor, 4 ejes, carriles ovales. Resistencia, cable de amarre, etc. Tren marchando hacia adelante y hacia atrás por medio de interrupción a mano	93,5 154	37 60 1/2
		Alles in feiner Chromolackierung	*Locomotives and carriages finely chromolithographed*	*Todo en finísima cromo-embarnizadura*		
14 S 64/3020 **14** S 64/3021	0 I	Elektrische Vollbahn-Lokomotive, „Schweizer Typ", 4 achsig, auf Drehgestellen, vor- und rückwärts fahrend durch Handschaltung und automatisch vom Widerstand aus, 3 Stirnlampen und Anschluß für Wagenbeleuchtung	Electric Locomotive "Swiss" type on bogies, reversing by hand or from the regulating resistance, 3 headlights and sliding contact for lighting up carriages	Locomotora eléctrica para el ferrocarril principal, "tipo de Suiza", con 4 ejes sobre bogies. Locomotora marchando hacia adelante y hacia atrás por medio de interrupción a mano y automáticamente de la resistencia. 3 lámparas frontales y unión para el alumbrado de los vagones	30 45	11 3/4 17 3/4
14 CE 64/3020 **14** CE 64/3021	0 I	Schnellzug-Lokomotive, 5 achsig, vor- und rückwärts fahrend durch Handschaltung und automatisch vom Widerstand aus Spur 0: 1 Stirnlampe und Steckanschluß für Wagenbeleuchtung Spur I: 2 Stirnlampen und Steckanschluß für Wagenbeleuchtung	Electric Locomotive "Atlantic" type 4-4-2, reversing by hand or from the regulating resistance Gauge 0: 1 headlight and sliding contact for lighting up carriages Gauge I: 2 headlights and sliding contact for lighting up carriages	Locomotora para el tren rápido con 5 ejes, marchando hacia adelante y hacia atrás por interrupción a mano y automáticamente de la resistencia vía 0: 1 lámpara frontal y unión por clavija para el alumbrado de los vagones vía I: 2 lámparas frontales y unión por clavija para el alumbrado de los vagones	43 60	16 23 1/2
		Solide Handarbeit und feinste Handlackierung	*Very fine and powerful models. Carefully made, solid hand japanning*	*Sólida obra de mano y finísima embarnizadura a mano*		

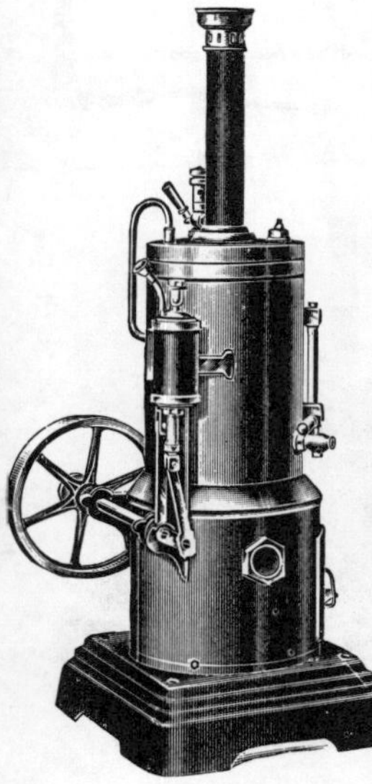

14/4107

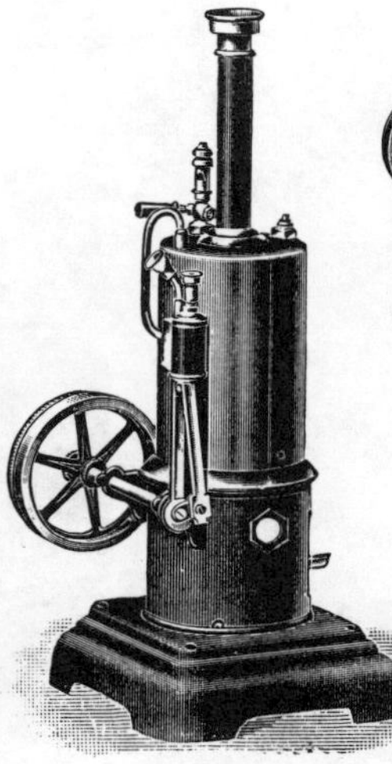

14/4106

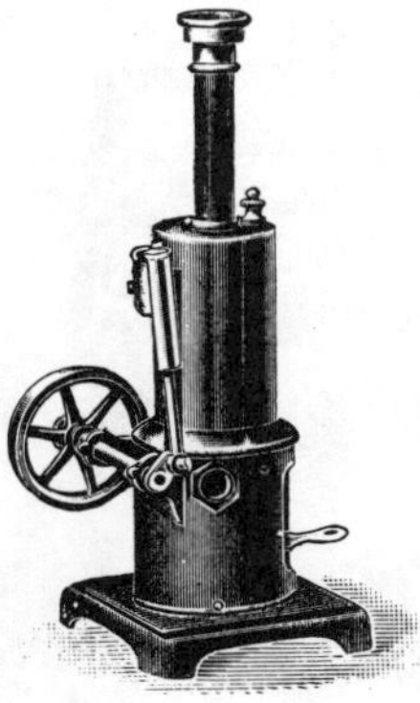

14/4104

14/4107/91

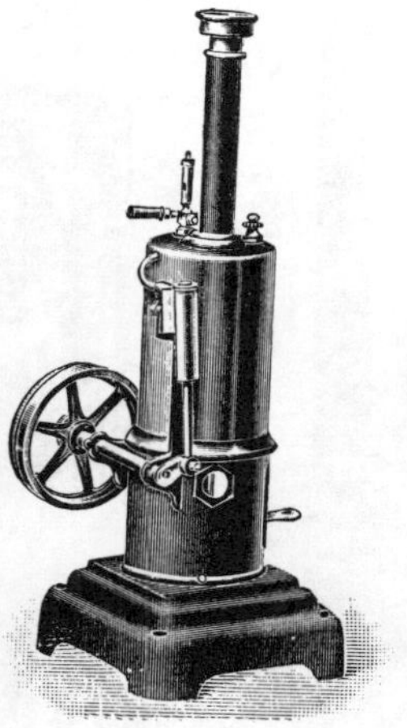

14/4105

14/4122

Dampfmaschinen.

Solide, kräftige Konstruktion. Messingkessel mit vernickelten Armaturen.

Vertical Steam Engines.

Good, reliable models. With finely nickelled fittings.

Máquinas de vapor.

Construcción sólida y robusta. Calderas de latón con guarniciones niqueladas.

Nr.	Größe Size Tamaño				Höhe — Height Altura cm	inches pulgadas
14/4104		Dampfmaschine mit oszillierendem Zylinder. Stahlblau patinierter und gezogener Messingkessel. Sicherheitsventil, Metallsockel fein lackiert	Steam Engine with oscillating cylinder. Oxydized brass boiler. Safety valve, japanned metal base	Máquina de vapor con cilindro oscilante. Caldera de latón pavonada (azul de acero) y estirada. Válvula de seguridad. Zócalo de metal embarnizado finísimamente	24	$10^1/_4$
14/4105	$5^1/_2$ $6^1/_2$	Dampfmaschinen wie zuvor, jedoch größer und mit Dampfpfeife	Steam Engines. same as above, but with steam whistle	Máquinas de vapor, como la precedente, pero de dimensiones más grandes y provistas de un silbato de vapor	30 32,5	$11^5/_8$ $12^1/_2$
14/4106	$5^1/_2$ $6^1/_2$	Dampfmaschine mit feststehendem Zylinder. Stahlblau patinierter oder fein polierter gezogener Messingkessel. Sicherheitsventil, Dampfpfeife. Metallsockel fein poliert	Steam Engines with slide valve cylinder. Polished or oxydized brass boiler. Safety valve, steam whistle. Metal base finely japanned	Máquina de vapor con cilindro fijo. Caldera de latón pavonada (azul de acero), estirada y pulida finísimamente. Válvula de seguridad. Silbato de vapor. Zócalo de metal pulido finísimamente	30 32,5	$11^5/_8$ $12^1/_2$
14/4107	$6^1/_2$ $7^1/_2$ $8^1/_2$	Dampfmaschinen wie zuvor, mit Wasserstandsanzeiger. Feuertür und Wasserablaßhahn. Solide Konstruktion	Steam Engines, same as above, but with water gauge, water outlet tap. Fire door. Solide construccion	Máquinas de vapor con indicador del nivel de agua, puerta del hogar y grifo de purgo. Construcción sólida	32 36,5 39	$12^1/_2$ $14^1/_4$ $15^3/_8$
14/4107/91	$6^1/_2$ $7^1/_2$ $8^1/_2$	Dampfmaschinen mit Dynamo und Schaltbrett. Direkte Kraftübertragung durch Transmissionsspirale. Zweckmäßig ausgeführte Kraftanlage	Steam Engines with dynamo and switchboard. With direct gear. Good effective plant	Máquinas de vapor con dinamo y cuadro de distribución. Directa transmisión de energía por una espiral de transmisión. Instalación de la máquina de vapor conveniente al objeto especial	28×13,5 28×14 30,5×14	$11\times5^1/_4$ $11\times5^1/_2$ $12\times5^1/_2$
14/4122	$7^1/_2$ 9 11	Dampfmaschinen mit doppeltwirkendem Zylinder. Stahlblau patinierter oder fein polierter gezogener Messingkessel. Sicherheitsventil, Dampfpfeife, Wasserstandsanzeiger. Richtiggehender Manometer. Speisepumpe. Metallfuß fein lackiert	Steam Engines with double action slide valve cylinder. Polished or oxydized brass boiler. Safety valve, steam whistle, water gauge, steam gauge governor, stop tap, water outlet tap, feeding pump. Finely japanned metal base	Máquinas de vapor con cilindro de doble efecto. Caldera de latón pavonada (azul de acero) o estirada y pulida finísimamente. Válvula de seguridad, silbato de vapor, indicador del nivel de agua. Manómetro funcionando precisamente. Bomba de alimentación. Embase de metal embarnizado finísimamente	40,5 44 52	$15^1/_4$ $17^1/_8$ 21

14/4251

14/4205

14/4254

14/4252

14/4335

14/4257

Betriebsmodelle.

Solide Ausführung, fein lackiert.

Working models.

Best workmanship. Fine finish.

Modelos de régimen.

Construcción sólida, embarnizada finísimamente.

14/4190

Nr.				Höhe — Height Altura cm	inch. - pulg.
14/4190/1	Ventilatoren	Ventilator	Ventiladores	8,5	$3^1/_8$
14/4190/2				13,5	$5^1/_2$
14/4205	Rübenmühle	Cutting machine	Molino para nabos	11	$4^1/_8$
14/4251/1	Schleifsteine	Grindstone	Piedras amoladeras	10	4
14/4251/2				13	$5^1/_8$
14/4252	Poliermaschine	Grinding and Polishing lathe	Máquina para pulir	10	4
14/4254/1	Kreissägen	Circular Saw	Sierras circulares	5,5	$2^3/_4$
14/4254/2				7	$3^1/_2$
14/4257	Gattersäge	Frame Saw	Sierra de marquetería	10,5	5
14/4265/1	Exzenterpressen	Eccentric Press	Prensas excéntricas	13	$5^1/_8$
14/4265/$1^1/_2$				15	6
14/4335	Hammerwerk	Model Power Hammer	Herrería (frágua)	6	$2^1/_8$

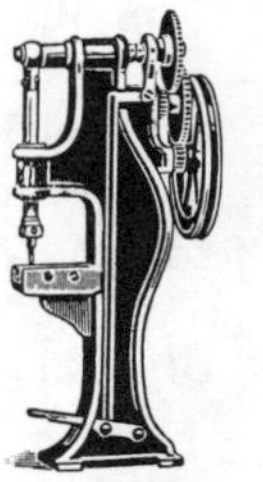

14/4265

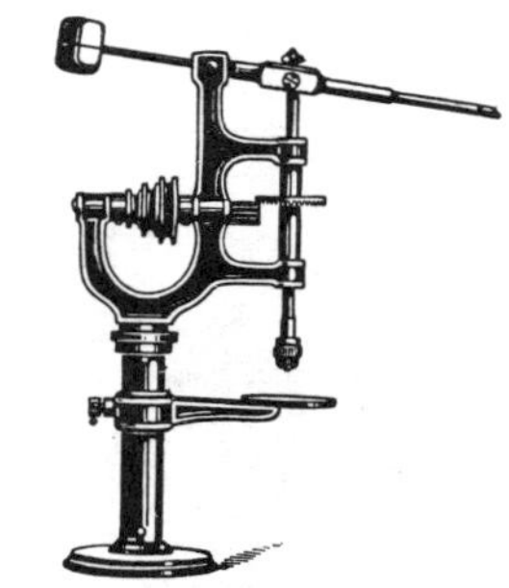

14/4263

14/4138

14/4271

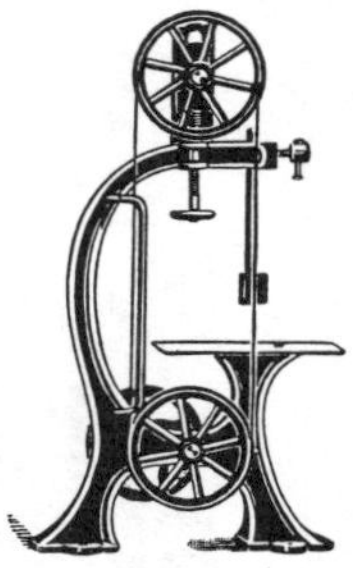

14/4255

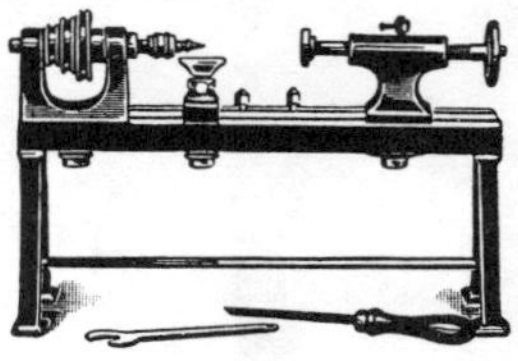

14/4260

14/4135

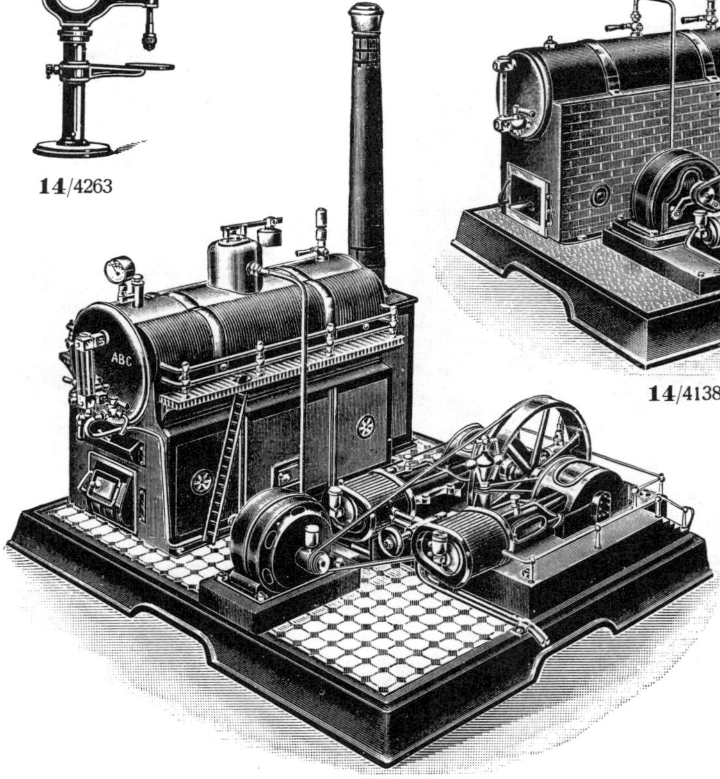

14/4161

14/4150

Dampfmaschinen, liegend.

Maschinen von äußerst kräftiger Bauart, ausgezeichneter Konstruktion und guter Leistung.

Steam Engines, horizontal.

Precise construction. Highest efficiency.

Máquinas de vapor horizontales.

Máquinas de una construcción extraordinariamente robusta y excelente y de buena potencia.

Nr.	Größe Size Tamaño				Gesamtgröße / Size Tamaño total cm	inches / pulgadas
14/4135	$4\frac{1}{2}$ $5\frac{1}{2}$	Dampfmaschinen mit oszillierendem Zylinder. Stahlblau patinierter Messingkessel. Sicherheitsventil und Dampfpfeife.	Steam Engines with oscillating cylinder. Oxydized brass boiler. Safety valve and steam whistle.	Máquinas de vapór con cilindro oscilante. Caldera de latón pavonada (azul de acero). Válvula de seguridad y silbato de vapor.	20×18×22,5 22,5×18,5×25	$8\times7\frac{1}{8}\times9$ $9\times7\frac{1}{2}\times10$
14/4138	5 $5\frac{1}{2}$ 7	Dampfmaschinen mit feststehendem Zylinder. Kessel aus Messing mit Flammrohr, blank geschliffen oder blau patiniert. Sicherheitsventil, Dampfpfeife, Wasserstandsanzeiger, Umsteuerung für beide Drehrichtungen. Metallsockel fein lackiert. Armaturen fein vernickelt.	Steam Engines with fixed, single acting cylinder. Horizontal boiler in polished or oxydized brass. Forward and backward movement according to the direction the flywheel is started. With safety valve, whistle, stop tap, water gauge, outlet tap. Fittings nickelplated. Japanned metal base.	Máquinas de vapor con cilindro fijo. Caldera de latón con tubo de hogar interior amolado y pulido o pavonado. Válvula de seguridad, silbato de vapor, indicador del nivel de agua, cambio de marcha para ambos sentidos de la rotación. Zócalo de metal pulido finisimamente. Guarniciones menudas.	24×22,5×33 28×27×35,5 30,5×30,5×40	$9\frac{1}{2}\times8\frac{7}{8}\times13$ $11\times10\frac{5}{8}\times14$ $12\times12\times15\frac{3}{4}$
14/4150	$5\frac{1}{2}$ 7 9	Dampfmaschinen wie zuvor, jedoch mit doppeltwirkendem Präzisionszylinder. Galerie zu beiden Seiten. Dampfdom mit Sicherheitsgewichtsventil. Dampfabsperrhahn. Speisepumpe. Massive Feuertür.	Steam Engines — same as above — but with double acting cylinder. Gallery on each side. Steam dome, feeding pump, governor.	Máquinas de vapor, como las precedentes, pero con cilindro de precisión de doble efecto. Galería (guarda-cuerpos) a ambos lados. Cúpula de vapor con válvula cargada de seguridad. Espita de interrupción de vapor. Bomba de alimentación. Puerta del hogar, maciza (solida).	35×28,5×35,5 34,5×32,5×42 50×42×50	$13\frac{3}{4}\times11\frac{1}{4}\times14$ $13\frac{1}{2}\times12\frac{3}{4}\times16\frac{1}{2}$ $19\frac{1}{2}\times16\frac{1}{2}\times19\frac{1}{2}$
14/4161	9 11	Dampfmaschinen wie zuvor, jedoch mit 2 doppeltwirkenden Hochdruckzylindern. Richtiggehender Manometer. In allen Teilen präzis gearbeitet und gut funktionierend.	Steam Engines — same as above — but with 2 fixed double acting high pressure cylinders. Steam gauge. Most powerful, technically perfect engine, uniform run.	Máquinas de vapor, como las precedentes, pero con 2 cilindros de alta presión de doble efecto. Manómetro funcionando con precisión. Todas las partes de la máquina construidas con precisión y funcionando bien.	51×42,5×51 53×46,5×54	$20\times16\frac{3}{4}\times20$ $20\frac{3}{4}\times18\frac{1}{2}\times21\frac{3}{4}$
14/4138/91	$5\frac{1}{2}$ 7	Dampfmaschinen mit Dynamo und Schaltbrett. Sonst Ausführung wie 14/4138.	Steam Engines with dynamo and switchboard. Same details as by 14/4138.	Máquinas de vapor con dinamo y cuadro de distribución. Construcción del resto como la de 14/4138.	28×27×35,5 30,5×30,5×40	$11\times10\frac{5}{8}\times14$ $12\times12\times15\frac{3}{4}$
14/4150/91	$5\frac{1}{2}$ 7 9	Dampfmaschinen mit Dynamo und Schaltbrett. Sonst Ausführung wie 14/4150.	Steam Engines with dynamo and switchboard. Same details as by 14/4150.	Máquinas de vapor con dinamo y cuadro de distribución. Construcción del resto como la de 14/4150.	35×28,5×35,5 34,5×32,5×42 50×42×50	$13\frac{3}{4}\times11\frac{1}{4}\times14$ $13\frac{1}{2}\times13\frac{3}{4}\times16\frac{1}{2}$ $19\frac{1}{2}\times16\frac{1}{2}\times19\frac{1}{2}$
14/4161/91 94	9 11	Dampfmaschinen mit Dynamo und Schaltbrett. Sonst Ausführung wie 14/4161.	Steam Engines with dynamo and switchboard. Same details as by 14/4161.	Máquinas de vapor con dinamo y cuadro de distribución. Construcción del resto como la de 14/4161.	51×42,5×51 53×46,5×54	$20\times16\frac{3}{4}\times20$ $20\frac{3}{4}\times18\frac{1}{2}\times21\frac{3}{4}$

Betriebsmodelle.

Besonders kräftige Ausführung.

Working models.

Strong and durable construction.

Modelos de régimen.

Construcción extraordinariamente robusta.

Nr.				Höhe — Height Altura cm	in. / pul.
Nr. **14**/4255/1	Bandsägen	Band Saw	Sierras rotativas	14	$5\frac{1}{2}$
$1\frac{1}{2}$				20	$7\frac{7}{8}$
2				23	9
„ **14**/4260/1	Drehbänke	Expanding Chuck	Tornos	8,5	$3\frac{3}{8}$
$1\frac{1}{2}$				11	$4\frac{3}{8}$
2				12,5	5
„ **14**/4263/1	Bohrmaschinen	Model Drill	Máquinas perforadoras	16	$6\frac{3}{8}$
$1\frac{1}{2}$				19	$7\frac{1}{2}$
2				23	$9\frac{1}{8}$
„ **14**/4271/1	Decoupiersägen	Power Fret Saw	Sierra extensible	14	$5\frac{1}{2}$

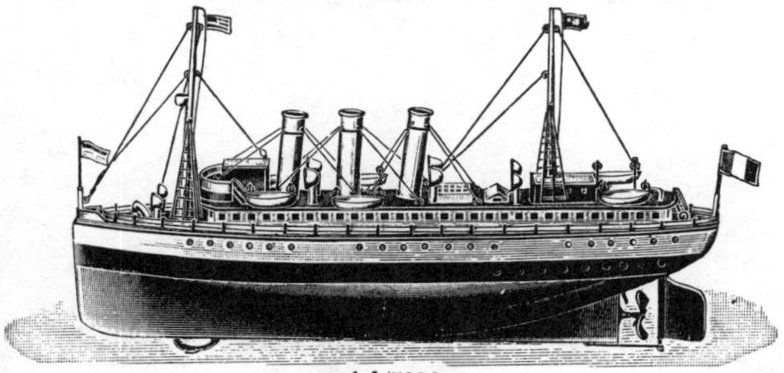

14/5026

14/5050

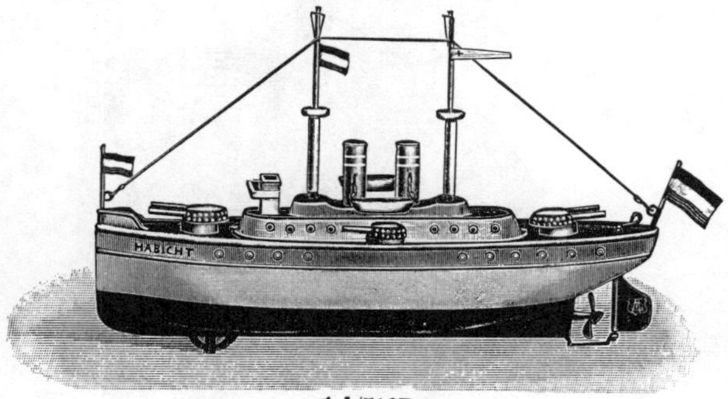

14/5107

14/5081

Uhrwerkschiffe.

Mit zugkräftigem Uhrwerk ausgerüstet. Gediegene Modelle. Feine Handlackierung.

Clockwork Steamers.

Fitted with regulated clockwork. Well constructed models. Best workmanship.

Buques con aparato de relojería.

Provistos de aparatos de relojería de gran fuerza de tracción. Modelos sólidos. Finísima embarnizadura a mano.

Nr.	Größe Size Tamaño				Rumpflänge Length of hull Largura del casco cm	inches pulgadas
14/5026	23	Passagierdampfer mit kräftigem Uhrwerk. Oberdeck abnehmbar	Passenger Steamer, strong clockwork. Upper deck detachable	Vapores para pasajeros con robusto aparato de relojería. Puente superior desmontable	23	9 1/8
	29				29	11 1/2
	33				33	13 1/8
	42				42	16 3/4
	47				47	18 3/4
14/5050	7	Ozeandampfer mit besonders starkem Uhrwerk. Größe 7: 2 Schornsteine, 1 Schraube „ 9: 3 „ 2 Schrauben	Ocean Liner with strong regulated clockwork. Size 7 with 2 funnels, 1 screw „ 9 „ 3 „ 2 screws	Vapores para el océano con aparato de relojería, extraordinariamente robusto. Tamaño 7: 2 chimeneas, 1 hélice „ 9: 3 „ 2 hélices	73	27 5/8
	9				98	35 1/2
14/5107	23	Kanonenboote, vorzüglich ausgerüstet. Oberdeck abnehmbar	Gunboat, well fitted. Upper deck detachable.	Cañoneras, equipadas excelentemente. Puente superior desmontable	23	9 1/8
	29				29	11 1/2
14/5081	41	Tauchboote. Extra großer Typ. Kräftiges, gut reguliertes Uhrwerk. Bewegliche Tiefruder an beiden Seiten. Wasserdicht abgeschlossen	Submarine. Large size, strong regulated clockwork, adjustable diving fins and rudder.	Buques inmergibles. Tipo de dimensiones extraordinariamente grandes. Aparato de relojería regulada bien. Timones móviles para immergir disluestos a los dos lados del buque. Cerrado impermeable al agua.	41	16 1/4
	57				57	22 1/2
	76				76	30

14/9081 G/1

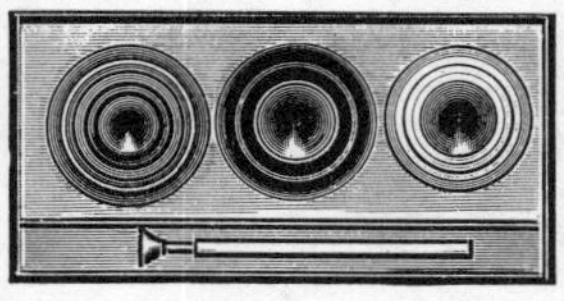

14/9059 G3

14/8986 G/6

14/8999 G/129

14/9084 G/3

Kreiselspiele.

Antrieb durch Stoßwirkung mittelst geeigneter Stöcke. Feine Ausführung. Hübsche Aufmachung in Kartons.

Spinning tops.

The tops are set into motion by patent driving sticks. Beautifully finished. Packed in attractive boxes.

Juegos de peonzas.

Impulsión por el efecto de choques usando bastones convenientes. Finísima ejecución. Embalados en bonitas cajitas de cartón.

Nr.				Kartongröße / Size of box Dimensiones de la cajita de cartón cm	Inch. / pulgadas
14/9059 G/2	Garnitur mit 2 Mignonkreiseln	Set of 2 Mignon plate tops	Juego de 2 peonzas "Mignon"	11×7,5	4 3/4×3
3	„ „ 3 „	„ „ 3 „ „ „	„ „ 3 „ „	20×7,5	7 7/8×3
4	„ „ 4 „	„ „ 4 „ „ „	„ „ 4 „ „	14,5×13,5	5 3/4×5 1/4
14/8986 G/3	Garnitur mit 3 Blumenkreiseln	Set of 3 Flower tops	Juego de 3 peonzas de flores	22×12	8 3/4×4 3/4
4	„ „ 4 „	„ „ 4 „ „	„ „ 4 „ „ „	25×14	9 7/8×5 1/2
6	„ „ 6 „	„ „ 6 „ „	„ „ 6 „ „ „	30×16	11 3/4×6 1/4
14/9081 G/2	Garnitur mit 2 Flugkreiseln, kleines Modell	Set of 2 Flying tops, small types	Juego de 2 peonzas voladoras } modelo pequeño	20×10,5	8 ×4 1/8
3	„ „ 3 „ „ „	„ „ 3 „ „ „ „	„ „ 3 „ „	25×10,5	9 7/8×4 1/8
4	„ „ 4 „ „ „	„ „ 4 „ „ „ „	„ „ 4 „ „	20×18,5	8 ×7 1/4
14/9084 G/2	Garnitur mit 2 Flugkreiseln, großes Modell	Set of 2 Flying tops, large types	Juego de 2 peonzas voladoras } modelo grande	28×15	11 ×6 1/4
3	„ „ 3 „ „ „	„ „ 3 „ „ „ „	„ „ 3 „ „	36,5×15	14 3/8×6 1/4
14/8999 G/129	Garnitur mit 1 Choralkreisel mit automatischem Akkordwechsel und 7 verschiedenartigen Blitzkreiseln	Set of 1 Musical Choral top, changing its tune automatically and 7 different kinds of Spinning tops	Juego de 1 peonza haciendo sonar 1 canto gregoriano y cambiando automáticamente el sonido y de 7 diferentes peonzas de relámpago	38×24	15 ×9 1/2

14/9612

14/9615

14/9614

Kinderkochherde

mit Sicherheitsspiritusheizung. Solide, kräftige Ausführung. Herdplatten fein geschliffen.

Children's Cooking Stoves

with Safety Spirit Lamps. Made of best material. Plates of polished sheet steel.

Hogares de cocina para niños

con lámpara de seguridad calentada por espíritu. Ejecución sólida y robusta.

Nr.	Größe Size Dimensiones				Herd — Stove — Hogar Länge Length Largura		Höhe Height Altura	
					cm	inches pulgadas	cm	inches pulgadas
14/9612	0	Kochherde mit 2 Weißblechgeschirren	Cooking Stoves with 2 pots	Hogares de cocina con 2 vasijas de hoja de lata	13	$5^{1}/_{8}$	8	$3^{1}/_{8}$
	1				15,5	$6^{1}/_{8}$	8	$3^{1}/_{8}$
	2				17,5	$6^{7}/_{8}$	10	4
14/9614	1	Kochherde mit 4 Weißblechgeschirren	Cooking Stoves with 4 pots	Hogares de cocina con 4 vasijas de hoja de lata	23	$8^{1}/_{4}$	11,5	$4^{1}/_{2}$
	2				25	$9^{3}/_{4}$	13	$5^{1}/_{4}$
	3				31	$12^{1}/_{4}$	14	$5^{1}/_{2}$
	4				34	$13^{1}/_{2}$	16	$6^{1}/_{4}$
14/9614 N oder K	2	Kochherde mit 4 Nickel- oder Kupfergeschirren und Nickelschutzstange	Cooking Stoves with 4 nickel or copper pots and nickel rail	Hogares de cocina con 4 vasijas de níquel y barra de protección de níquel	25	$9^{3}/_{4}$	13	$5^{1}/_{4}$
	3				31	$12^{1}/_{4}$	14	$5^{1}/_{2}$
	4				34	$13^{1}/_{2}$	16	$6^{1}/_{4}$
14/9615	2	Kochherde mit 4 Weißblechgeschirren und 1 Messingteekessel	Cooking Stoves with 4 pots and 1 brass tea kettle	Hogares de cocina con 4 vasijas de hoja de lata y 1 caldera de latón	31	$12^{1}/_{4}$	14	$5^{1}/_{2}$
	3				34	$13^{1}/_{2}$	16	$6^{1}/_{4}$
	4				37	$14^{1}/_{2}$	18	$7^{1}/_{4}$
	5				46	$18^{1}/_{4}$	27	$10^{5}/_{8}$
14/9615 N oder K	2	Kochherde mit 5 Nickel- oder Kupfergeschirren und Nickelschutzstange	Cooking Stoves with 5 nickel or copper pots and nickel rail	Hogares de cocina con 5 vasijas de níquel y barra de protección de níquel	31	$12^{1}/_{4}$	14	$5^{1}/_{2}$
	3				34	$13^{1}/_{2}$	16	$6^{1}/_{4}$
	4				37	$14^{1}/_{2}$	18	$7^{1}/_{4}$
	5				46	$18^{1}/_{4}$	27	$10^{5}/_{8}$

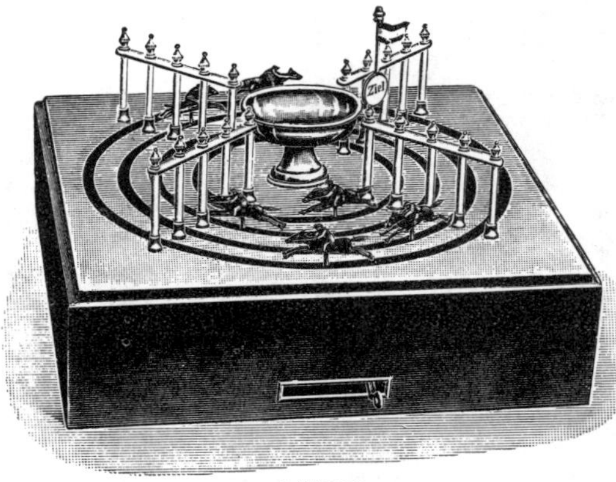

14/8892

14/8039

Pferde-Wettrennspiele — Kanonen.

Race Game — Cannons.

Juegos representando una corrida de caballos — Cañones.

Nr.					Größe	Size Dimensiones
					cm	inches, pulgadas
14/8892	1	Pferde-Wettrennspiel mit seitl. Hebelantrieb, in fein überzogen. Holzkasten — 1 Bahn 4 Pferde	Race Game in handsome covered wooden box. Excellent solid make — 1 track 4 horses	Juego representando una corrida de caballos con impulsión lateral por medio de una palanca, en una caja de madera con fina cubierta — 1 corredera 4 caballos	24×24×15	$9^{1}/_{2}\times9^{1}/_{2}\times6$
	2	2 Bahnen 4 „	2 tracks 4 „	2 correderas 4 „	30×30×17	$12\times12\times6^{3}/_{4}$
	3	3 „ 6 „	3 „ 6 „	3 „ 6 „	36×36×19	$14^{1}/_{4}\times13^{1}/_{4}\times7^{1}/_{2}$
	4	4 „ 8 „	4 „ 8 „	4 „ 8 „	42×42×21	$16^{1}/_{2}\times16^{1}/_{2}\times8^{1}/_{4}$
					Länge cm	Lenght, Largura inches, pulgadas
14/8039	1	Fidelio-Kanonen mit Amorcefeuerung und Gummigranaten. Solide Ausführung	Cannons. Ammunition: Amorces and rubber shells. Solíd construction	Cañones "Fidelio" tirados por cápsulas fulminantes y con granadas de caucho. Ejecución sólida	18	$7^{1}/_{8}$
	3				35	$13^{3}/_{4}$

MÄRKLIN

Metallbaukasten. — Construction games.
Cajas de construcciones metalicas.

Grundkasten **14**/2. — Märklin Outfit **14**/2.
Cajas principales **14**/2.

Grundkasten in elegant. stark. Kartonkasten.
Nr. **14**/0 1 2 3 4 5 6
Pracht-Ausrüstung, fein poliert. Holzkasten mit Schloß und Schlüssel. Nr. **14**/5H und **14**/6H. Inhalt wie bei vorstehenden Ausrüstungen Nr. **14**/5 und **14**/6.

Ergänzungskasten.
Grundkasten Nr. **14**/1—5 können durch Hinzunahme von Ergänzungskasten auf jede gewünschte Größe erweitert werden, z. B.: Grundkasten Nr. **14**/1 und Ergänzungskasten Nr. **14**/1a ergeb. den Grundkasten Nr. **14**/2. Grundkasten Nr. **14**/2 und Ergänzungskasten Nr. **14**/2a ergeb. den Grundkasten Nr. **14**/3. Grundkasten Nr. **14**/3 und Ergänzungskasten Nr. **14**/3a u. 4a ergeb. d. Grundkasten Nr. **14**/5.

Märklin Outfits.
In beautiful solid cardboard box.
Nr. **14**/0 1 2 3 4 5 6
Parlour Set, in an elegant wooden case with lock and key. No. **14**/5 H and No. **14**/6H. Contents as in the above Märklin Outfits Nos. **14**/5 and **14**/6.

Accessory Outfits.
When one already possesses one of the Main Outfits and desires to enlarge the same, the Supplementary Outfits furnish all the parts necessary for passing to the next largest Main Outfit, for instance: Supplementary Outfit No. **14**/1 a changes Main Outfit No. **14**/1 into Outfit No. **14**/2, Supplementary Outfit No. **14**/2a changes Main Outfit No. **14**/2 into Outfit No. **14**/3, Supplementary Outfit No. **14**/3a and 4a changes Main Outfit No. **14**/3 into Outfit No. **14**/5.

Cajas principales.
en cajita elegante de fuerte cartón.
No. **14**/0 1 2 3 4 5 6
Caja de lujo. En caja de madera de color nogal, bien pulida, con interior elegante, con cerradura y llave. No. **14**/5 H y **14**/6H. Contenido como las cajas No. **14**/5 y **14**/6.

Cajas complementarias.
El que tenga una de las cajas principales indicadas en la página que precede, y desee ampliarla, puede obtener de nosotros todas las piezas necesarias para pasar a la caja principal próxima mayor. Por ejemplo: La caja principal No. **14**/1 y caja suplementaria No. **14**/1 a forman la caja principal No. **14**/2a. La caja principal No. **14**/2 y caja suplementaria No. **14**/2 a forman la caja principal No. **14**/3. La caja principal No. **14**/3 y cajas suplementarias Nos. **14**/3 a y **14**/4 a forman la caja principal No. **14**/5.

14/201 und **14**/202.

Uhrwerk-Motor. — Clockwork Motor. Motor-reloj.

Nr. **14**/201.
Kleines Modell. Für Baukasten 0—2.
Small model. Suitable for Outfits 0—2.
Modelo chico. Para cajas de construcciones 0—2.

Nr. **14**/202.
Großes Modell. Für Baukasten 3—6.
Large size. Suitable for Outfits 3—6.
Modelo grande. Para cajas de construcciones 3—6.

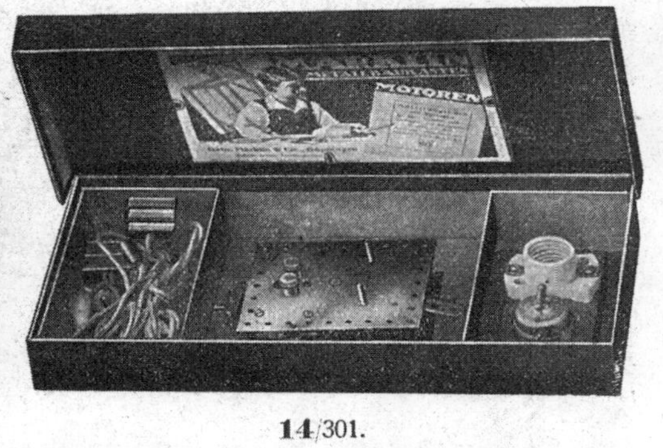

14/301.

Elektromotor. — Electric Motor. Electromotor.

Starkstrom — strong current
de corriente máxima
110—250 Volt.

In elegantem Karton. Als Ergänzung für alle Baukasten passend.
In beautiful cardboard box. A suitable complement to all Outfits.
En cajita elegante. Complemento adecuado para todas las cajas de construcción.

14/102 und **14**/104.

Zusatzkasten für Herstellung von Uhren.
Suplementary Outfit for constructing clocks.
Cajas complentarias para la construcción de relojes.

Nr. **14**/102.
Für den Bau von Uhren mit Uhrwerkbetrieb. (Der benötigte Uhrwerkmotor **14**/202 ist darin nicht enthalten.)
For building mechanically worked clocks. (The required clockwork motor **14**/202 is not contained)
Para la construcción de relojes con aparato de relojería. (El motor necesario **14**/202 con aparato de relojería no está contenido en esta.)

Nr. **14**/104.
Für den Bau von elektrischen Uhren und Elektromotoren.
For building Electric clocks and Electric motors.
Para la construcción de relojes eléctricos y electromotores.

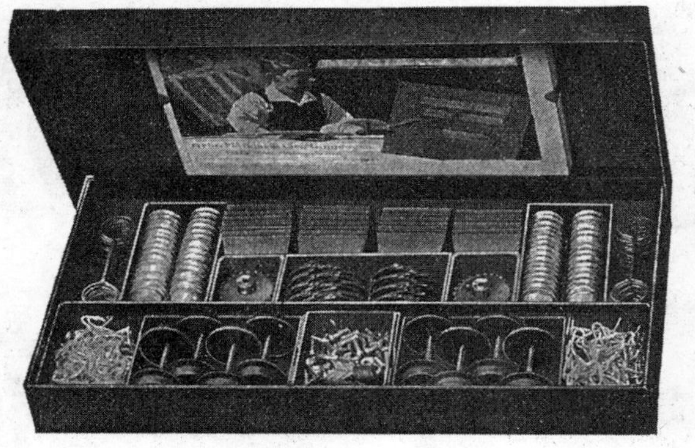

14/101/1 und **14**/101/2.

Zusatzkasten für Transportanlagen.
Supplementary Outfit for transportation plants.
Cajas complementarias para instalaciones de transporte.

Nr. **14**/101/1.
Zusatzkasten mit 197 Teilen für Baukasten **14**/1—3.
Supplementary Outfit with 197 parts for Outfits **14**/1—3.
Caja complementaria con 197 partes para cajas de construcción Nr. **14**/1—3.

Nr. **14**/101/2.
Zusatzkasten mit 391 Teilen für Baukasten **14**/3—6.
Supplementary Outfit with 391 parts for Outfits **14**/3—6.
Caja complementaria con 391 partes para cajas de construcción Nr. **14**/3—6.

14/401 und **14**/402.

Dampfmotoren. — Steam Engines. — Motores de vapor.

Die Dampfmotoren sind in allen Lagen verwendbar und können den Modellkonstruktionen überall leicht angepaßt werden.
The steam engines can be used in all positions and can be easily adapted to all models.
Los motores de vapor pueden aplicarse en todas las situaciones y se adaptan facilmente a los modelos de construcción.

No. **14**/401 Kleines Modell. Einfach wirkender Zylinder. Für Baukasten **14**/0—2.
Small size. Single stroke cylinder. Suitable for Outfits **14**/0—2.
Modelo chico. Cilindro de simple efecto. Para cajas de construcciones **14**/0—2.

No. **14**/402 Großes Modell. Doppelt wirkender Zylinder. Für Baukasten **14**/3—6.
Large size. Two-stroke cylinder. Suitable for Outfits **14**/3—6.
Modelo grande. Cilindro de efecto doble. Para cajas de construcciones.

Dampf-Lastzug
Steam Tractor with Trailers
Convoy de carga a vapor
mit Dampfmotor — with Steam Engine — con motor de vapor
Nr. **14**/401 und 2

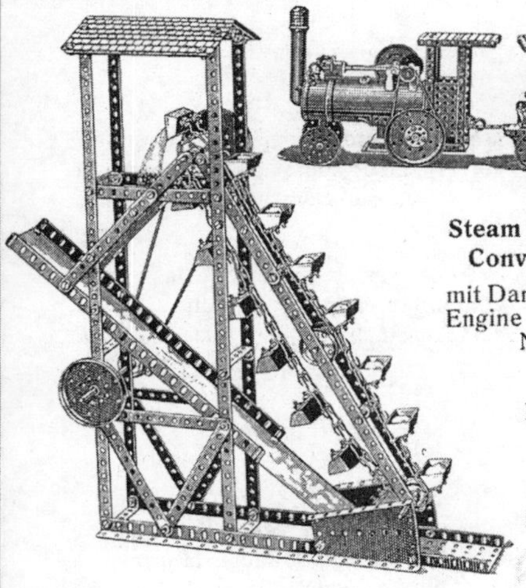

Becherwerk mit Rückführung, hergestellt mit Baukasten Nr. **14**/2 und Zusatzkasten für Transportanlagen Nr. **14**/101/1.
Dredger built with Outfit Nr. **14**/2 and Supplementary Outfit for transportation plants Nr. **14**/101/1.

Noria (elevador de canjilones) con disposición de conducción de retorno, construida por la caja de construcción No. **14**/2 y caja complementaria para instalaciones de transporte No. **14**/101/1.

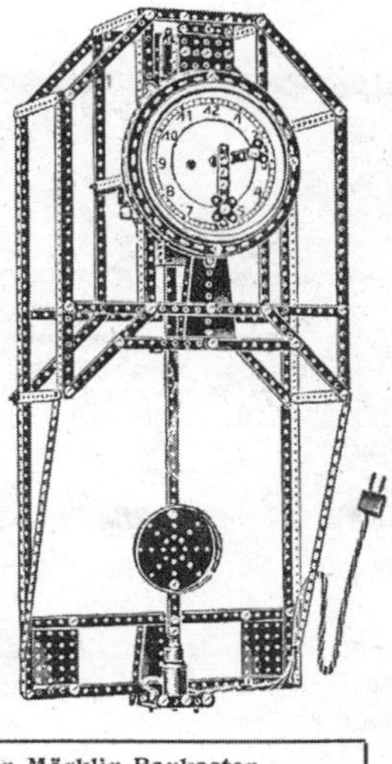

Man verlange Spezial-Liste von Märklin-Baukasten.
Ask for Special List of Märklin construction games.
Sirvase Vd. demandar nuestra lista especial de cajas de construcción "Märklin".

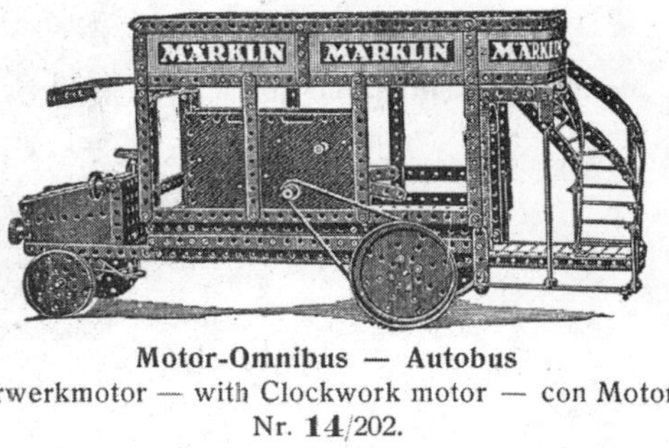

Motor-Omnibus — Autobus
mit Uhrwerkmotor — with Clockwork motor — con Motor reloj Nr. **14**/202.

Elektr. Wanduhr, hergestellt mit Baukasten Nr. **14**/4 und Zusatzkasten Nr. **14**/104.
Electric clock, made with Outfit Nr. **14**/4 and Supplementary Outfit Nr. **14**/104.
Reloj de pared, construido por la caja de construcción No. **14**/4 y caja complementaria No. **14**/104.

Länge 28³/₄ cm, feinste Lackierung, bestes Uhrwerk, doppelter Aufbau, 2 Salons, 2 Promenadedecks, Kommandobrücke, 3 Kamine, 2 Ventilatoren, 2 Strickleitermaste, Ankerwinde, Steuerruder, Flagge.

Length 28³/₄ cm, fine finish, best clockwork, 2 promenade decks, 2 saloons, conning bridge, 3 funnels, 2 ventilators, 2 masts with rope ladders, windable anchors, rudder, flag.

Longitud 28³/₄ cm, finamente barnizado, buen mecanismo, 2 paseos cubiertos, 2 salónes, 2 puentes-paseos, 2 pasarelas del comandante, 2 ventiladores, 2 mástiles con escalera de cuerda cabestante, timón, bandera.

116/876 Passagierdampfer. Passenger Steamer. Vapor de pasaje.

116/124 Vergnügungsdampfer. Pleasure boat. Vapor de recreo.

116/911/1 Torpedoboot. Torpedo boat. Torpedero.

116/1007 Kriegsschiff. Man of war. Barcos de guerra.

116/1403 Hafendampfer. Tug boat. Barcos de piloto.

*

Maße und Preise der **kompletten Serien,** sowie einige weitere Typen befinden sich in separater Preisliste.

*

Measures and prices of the **complete series,** also some other types are in separate price-list.

*

Proporciones y precios de las **series completas,** aún algunas otras barcos están en la lista de precios separata.

116/1206 Unterseeboot. Submarine. Submarino.

Das Boot taucht mehrmals nacheinander unter und kommt wieder an die Oberfläche des Wasserspiegels. Elegante, schlanke Bauart, 34 cm lang, Turm mit Kommandobrücke, Kapitän, Periskop, Steuer, Mast, 4 Lanzierrohre.

The boat dives several times and rises again to the surface of the water. — Length 34 cm, turret with conning bridge, captain, periscope, rudder, mast, 4 torpedo tubes.

El bote se sumerge repetidas veces, saliendo de nuevo á la superficie del agua. Tiene la forma de un pez elegante, último modelo. Longitud 34 cm, terre con pasarela des comandante, capitán, periscopio, mástil, timón, 4 tubos lanza-torpedos.

2000/219/1 = ca. 1/5 nat. Größe

Kinematographen, zugleich als **Laterna magica** verwendbar, auf kräftigem Metallsockel, mit gutem Mechanismus.
Cinematograph, can be used at the same time as **Laterna magica,** on strong metal socket, with good mechanism.
Cinematógrafos, sirviendo al mismo tiempo para **Linterna mágica,** sobre zócalo fuerte de metal, con buen mecanismo.

Nr. **2000**/219/1 Abgesetztes Objektiv 32 mm Durchmesser, beste Flachbrenner-Petroleumlampe mit Glaszylinder. Preis mit 2 langen bunten Filmen, 1 E. P.-Photofilm nebst 6 Laterna magica-Bildern, 3½ cm.

Objective 32 mm Ø, best flat burner petrol lamp with glass cylinder. Price with 2 long coloured films, 1 E. P. photo film and 6 Laterna magica pictures 3½ cm.

Objectivo contrapuesto de 32 mm de diámetro, mejor lámpara de petróleo con mecha llana y tubo de vidrio. Precio con 2 filmos largos, 1 filmo fotográfico E. P. y 6 dibujos de Linterna mágica de 3½ cm. p. p.

Nr. **2000**/219/1 E wie 2000/219/1, jedoch für elektrische Beleuchtung (ohne Birne), mit Kontakt und Kabel, fertig zum Anschluß. Preis mit Zugaben wie Nr. 2000/219/1.

as 2000/219/1 but for electrical illumination, with contact and cabel ready for connection. Price with above accessories.

como 2000/219/1, pero para alumbrado eléctrico (sin ampolla), con contacto y cable, pronto para conectar. Precio con accesorios como con No. 2000/219/1.

Kinematographen, zugleich als **Laterna magica** verwendbar, in vorzüglicher, neuer Ausführung, aus starkem Metall gefertigt und auf soliden Metallsockel montiert. Die Optik besteht aus 3 Linsen, das abgesetzte Objektiv hat Zahn und Trieb. Die Beleuchtung kann nur elektrisch erfolgen. Die obere Filmrolle ist mit einer Schutzkapsel versehen. Der Verschwinder befindet sich **vor** dem Objektiv. Der Apparat kann — neben seiner Verwendung als Laterna mágica — für reguläre Theaterfilme wie für endlose Filme und Photofilme verwendet werden.

Cinematographs, can be used at the same time as Laterna magica, in an excellent new style, manufactured of strong metal and mounted on a strong metal socket. The optic consists 3 lenses, the objektive having tooth and drive. The illumination can only be effected eletrically. The upper film roll is furnished with a protection case. The vanisher is in front of the objective. The apparatus can be used — besides its use as laterna magica — for regular theater films and photo films.

Cinematógrafos, sirviendo al mismo tiempo para Linterna mágica de ejecución superior y moderna. de metal fuerte y montados sobre zócalo metálico sólido. La óptica se compone de 3 lentes, el objectivo tiene diente y impulsión. El alumbrado se hace únicamente por electricidad. El carrete de filmo de encima tiene tapa de protección. La parada se encuenta antes del objectivo. El aparato puede emplearse — aparte de gastarlo como Linterna mágica — para filmos de teatro regulares así como para filmos sin fin y foto-filmos.

Nr. **2000**/221/1 E mit 12 Laterna magica-Bildern, 4 cm, nebst 1 Photofilm, 5 m lang, mit Kontakt und Kabel, fertig zum Anschluß (ohne Birne). Die Schutztrommel kann Filme bis zu 50 m Länge aufnehmen.

with 12 Laterna magica pictures, 4 cm, with 1 photo film, 5 m long, contact and cabel ready for connection. The protection drum can be used for films to a length of 50 m. Price packed in a solid cardboard box.

con 12 dibujos de Linterna mágica de 4 cm y 1 foto-filmo de 5 m de largo, con contacto y cable, pronto para conectar (sin ampolla). El tambor contiene filmos hasta 50 m de largo. Precio embalado en cartón sólido.

Nr. **2000**/223/1 E mit besserer Mechanik und automatischer Filmaufspulvorrichtung. Die Schutztrommel kann Filme bis zu 75 m Länge aufnehmen. Ausstattung mit 12 Laterna magica-Bildern, 4½ cm, und 1 Photofilm, 5 m lang, mit Kontakt und Kabel (ohne Birne), sonst wie Nr. 2000/221/1 E.

with better mechanic and automatical film spool arrangement. The protection drum can be used for films to a length of 75 m. Furnished with 12 Laterna magica pictures, 4½ cm, and 1 photo film, 5 m long, with contact and cabel, as 2000/221/1 E.

con mecanismo superior y arrollador de filmos automático. El tambor contiene filmos hasta 75 m de largo. Ejecución con 12 dibujos de Linterna mágica de 4½ cm y 1 foto-filmo de 5 m de largo, con contacto y cable (sin ampolla), por lo demás como No. 2000/221/1 E.

Nr. **2000**/224/1 E wie 2000/223/1, jedoch größer, mit Filmvoreilung zur besseren Schonung der Filme, mit 12 Laterna magica-Bildern, 5 cm, nebst 1 Photofilm, 5 m lang.

as 2000/223/1 but larger, with film hurryer for the better protection of the films, with 12 Laterna magica pictures, 5 cm, and 1 photo film, 5 m long.

como 2000/223/1, pero más grande, con anticipador de filmos para ahorrar los filmos, con 12 dibujos de Linterna mágica de 5 cm y 1 foto-filmo de 5 m de largo.

NB. Für vorstehende Apparate sind „Osram-Nitra-Projektionslampen" (ca. 60 Watt) besonders zu empfehlen!

NB. For above apparatusses the „Osram Nitra projektion lamp" (abt. 60 watt) can be recommended.

NOTA: ¡Para los aparatos mencionados se recomiendan especialmente las lámparas de proyección Osram-Nitra (de unos 60 vatios)!

2000/224/1 E

2000/229 E

Feine **Kinematographen**, zugleich **Laterna magica**, mit Film-Voreilung zur Schonung der Filme und selbsttätiger Filmaufspulung für lange Filme, Filmandrückrolle. Solider Metallsockel, zerlegbare Filmrolle. Abgesetzte feine Objektive.

Fine **cinemas**, at the same time **Laterna magica** with film hurryer for the protection of the film and automatical film spooling for long films, film pressing on roll. Solid metal socket, dismountable film roll. Fine objectives.

Cinematógrafos superiores, también **Linternas mágicas** con anticipador de filmo para ahorrar los filmos y carretes automáticos de filmo para filmos largos. Rollo de apretar filmos. Zócalo sólido de metal, rollo de filmo desmontable. Objectivos finos.

Nr. **2000**/225 E Ausstattung wie oben angeführt, alle Teile fein vernickelt, Objektiv 35 mm Durchmesser, mit Zahn und Trieb. Größe des Apparates mit Filmspule und Kamin 480 mm lang, 140 mm breit, 300 mm hoch, für elektrische Beleuchtung mit Kontakt und Kabel (ohne Birne). Preis mit einem 25 m langen Theaterfilm und 12 Filmbilderstreifen, 4 cm.

Execution as said above, all parts carefully nickeled, objective 35 mm Ø, with tooth and drive. Size of the apparatus with film spool and stove 480 mm long, 140 mm wide, 300 mm high, for electrical illumination with contact and cabel. Price with one 25 m theatre film and 12 film-picture-stripes, 4 cm.

Ejecución como arriba mencionado, todas las partes niqueladas, objectivo de 35 mm de diámetro, con diente y impulsión. Tamaño del aparato con carrete de filmo y chimenea 480 mm de largo, 140 mm de ancho, 300 mm de alto, para alumbrado eléctrico con contacto y cable (sin ampolla). Precio con 1 filmo de teatro de 25 m de largo y 12 cintas de dibujos de filmo de 4 cm.

Nr. **2000**/227 E, größer als 2000/225 E, alle Teile fein vernickelt, Objektiv 40 mm Durchmesser, mit Zahn und Trieb. Größe des Apparates mit Filmspule und Kamin 500 mm lang, 150 mm breit, 345 mm hoch, für elektrische Beleuchtung mit Kontakt und Kabel (ohne Birne). Preis mit einem 25 m langen Theaterfilm und 12 Filmbilderstreifen, 4½ cm.

larger than 2000/225 E, all parts carefully nickeled, objective 40 mm with tooth and drive. Size of the apparatus with film spool and stove 500 mm long, 150 mm wide, 345 mm high, for electrical illumination with contact and cabel. Price with one 25 m theatre film and 12 film-picture-stripes, 4½ cm.

más grande que 2000/225 E, todas partes bien niqueladas, objectivo de 40 mm de diámetro, con diente y impulsión. Tamaño el aparato con carrete de filmos y chimenea 500 mm de largo, 150 mm de ancho, 345 mm de alto, para alumbrado eléctrico con contacto y cable (sin ampolla). Precio con uno filmo de teatro de 25 m y 12 cintas de dibujos de filmo de 4½ cm.

Nr. **2000**/229 E, wie Abbildung, alle Teile fein vernickelt, Kondensator 55 mm, Objektiv 45 mm Durchmesser, mit Zahn und Trieb. Größe des Apparates mit Filmspule und Kamin 560 mm lang, 165 mm breit, 370 mm hoch, für elektrische Beleuchtung mit Kontakt und Kabel (ohne Birne). Preis mit einem 25 m langen Theaterfilm und 12 Filmbänderstreifen, 5 cm.

the same as illustration, all parts carefully nickeled, condensator 55 mm, objective 45 mm Ø, with tooth and drive. Size of the apparatus with film spool and stove 560 mm long, 165 mm wide, 370 mm high, for electrical illumination with contact and cabel. Price with one 25 m theatre film and 12 film-picture-stripes, 5 cm.

que ilustración, todas partes bien niqueladas, condensador de 55 mm, objectivo de 45 mm de diámetro, con diente y impulsión. Tamaño del aparato con carrete y chimenea 560 mm de largo, 165 mm de ancho, 370 mm de alto, para alumbrado eléctrico, con contacto y cable (sin ampolla). Precio con uno filmo de teatro de 25 m y 12 cintas de dibujos de filmo de 5 cm.

NB. Für vorstehende Apparate sind „Osram-Nitra-Projektioslampen“ (ca. 100 Watt) besonders zu empfehlen.

NB. For above apparatuses the "Osram Nitra lamp" (ca. 100 watt) can be recommended.

Nota: ¡Para los aparatos arriba mencionados se recomiendan especialmente lámparas de proyección "Osram Nitra" (de unos 100 vatios)!

Laterna magica, mit Petroleumbeleuchtung, von bester Wirkung, mit guter Optik (von 2000/116 beginnend mit 3 Linsen), Petroleumlampen mit Flachbrenner und Glaszylinder, sowie mit hübschen Glasbildern ausgestattet.

Laterna magica with petrol illumination of the best effect, with good optic (from No. 2000/116 beginning with 3 lenses), petrol lamps with flat burners and glass cylinders, furnished with pretty glass pictures.

Linternas mágicas con alumbrado de petróleo, de mejor efecto, con buena óptica (desde el No. 2000/116 con 3 lentes), lámparas de petróleo con mechero llano y tubo de vidrio, así como graciosos dibujos de vidrio.

Nr. **2000**/112	p. p.	3	Bilder / pictures / dibujos de	2,5 cm	Objektiv / Objective / Objectivo de	20	mm	Ø
„ **2000**/114	„	6	„	3	„	24	„	„
„ **2000**/116	„	6	„	3	„	24	„	„
„ **2000**/126	„	12	„	3	„	27	„	„
„ **2000**/128	„	12	„	3,5	„	32	„	„
„ **2000**/130	„	12	„	3,5	„	32	„	„
„ **2000**/132	„	12	„	4	„	35	„	„

2000/126 = 1/5 nat. Größe

Kinematographen, zugleich als **Laterna magica** verwendbar. Gute Optik. Solide Ausführung.

Cinematograph can be used at the same time as **Laterna magica.** Good optik; solid execution.

Cinematógrafos sirviendo también para **Linterna mágica.** Buena óptica — ejecución sólida.

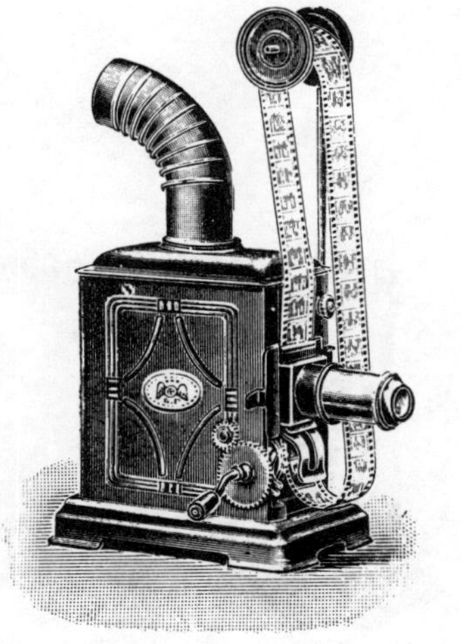

2000/213 = ca. $^{1}/_{4}$ natürlicher Größe.

Nr. **2000**/210 mit Filmstange, 2 Linsen, Objektiv 20 mm Durchmesser. Flachbrenner-Petroleumlampe mit Glaszylinder. Preis mit 1 Film und 2 Laterna-magica-Bildern, $2^{1}/_{2}$ cm.

with film rod, 2 lenses, objective 20 mm Ø, flat burner petrol lamp with glass cylinder. Price with 1 film and 2 laterna-magica-pictures, $2^{1}/_{2}$ cm.

barra de filmo, 2 lentes, objectivo de 20 mm de diámetro, lámpara de petróleo con mechero llano y tubo de vidrio. Precio con 1 filmo y 2 dibujos de linterna mágica de $2^{1}/_{2}$ cm.

„ **2000**/212 mit verstellbarer Filmstange, Metallsockel, 2 Linsen, Objektiv 24 mm Durchmesser, Flachbrenner-Petroleumlampe und Glaszylinder. Preis mit 1 Film und 3 Laterna-magica-Bildern, 3 cm.

with adjustable film rod, metal sockets, 2 lenses, objective 24 mm Ø, flat burner petrol lamp with glass cylinder. Price for 1 film and 3 laterna-magica-pictures, 3 cm.

con barra de filmo ajustable, zócalo metálico, 2 lentes, objectivo de 24 mm de diámetro, lámpara de petróleo con mechero llano y tubo de vidrio. Precio con 1 fi mo y 3 dibujos de linterna mágica de 3 cm.

„ **2000**/213 mit verstellbarer Filmstange und Rolle, 2 Linsen, Objektiv 27 mm urchmesser, Flachbrenner-Petroleumlampe mit Glaszylinder. Preis mit 1 bunten Film und 3 Laterna-magica-Bildern, 3 cm.

with adjustable film rod and roller, 2 lenses, objective 27 mm Ø, flat burner petrol lamp with glass cylinder. Price incl. 1 coloured film and 3 laterna-magica-pictures 3 cm.

con barra de filmo ajustable y rollo, 2 lentes, objectivo de 27 mm de diámetro, lámpara de petróleo con mechero llano y tubo de vidrio. Precio con 1 filmo de color y 3 dibujos de linterna mágica de 3 cm.

„ **2000**/213 E wie Nr. 2000/213, jedoch für elektrische Beleuchtung (ohne Birne), mit Kontakt und Kabel, fertig zum Anschluß.

as Nr. 2000/213, but for electrical illumination (without pear), with contact and cabel ready for connection.

como No. 2000/213, pero para alumbrado eléctrico (sin ampolla), con contacto y cable, pronto para conectar.

„ **2000**/214 mit Stativ vor dem Körper, verstellbarer Filmstange und Rolle, 2 Linsen, Objektiv 27 mm Durchmesser, Flachbrenner-Petroleumlampe mit Glaszylinder. Preis mit 2 bunten Filmen und 3 Laterna-magica-Bildern.

with stand in front of the machine, adjustable film rod and roller, 2 lenses, objective 27 mm Ø, flat burner petrol lamp with glass cylinder. Price with 2 coloured films and 3 laterna-magica-pictures.

con estator antes del cuerpo, barra de filmo ajustable y rollo, 2 lentes, objectivo de 27 mm de diámetro, lámpara de petróleo con mechero llano y tubo de vidrio. Precio con 2 filmos de color y 3 dibujos de linterna mágica.

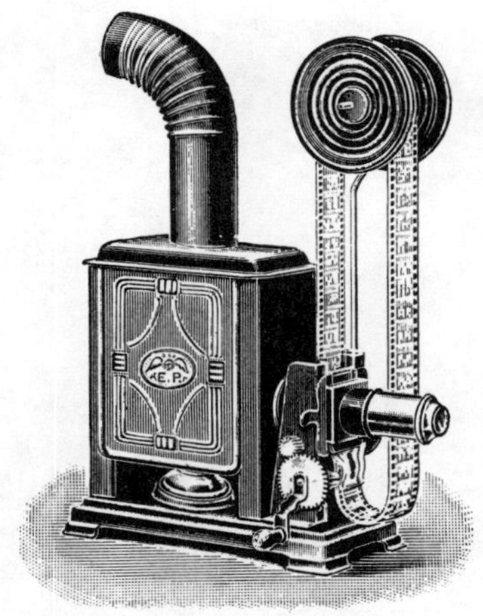

2000/216 = ca. $^{1}/_{4}$ natürlicher Größe.

„ **2000**/214 E wie Nr. 2000/214, jedoch für elektrische Beleuchtung (ohne Birne), mit Kontakt und Kabel, fertig zum Anschluß.

as Nr. 2000/214, but for electrical illumination (without pear), with contact and cabel ready for connection.

como No. 2000/214, pero para alumbrado eléctrico (sin ampolla), con contacto y cable, pronto para conectar.

„ **2000**/216 größer als Nr. 2000/214, mit 3 Linsen, Objektiv 27 mm Durchmesser, Flachbrenner-Petroleumlampe mit Glaszylinder. Preis mit 2 bunten Filmen und 3 Laterna-magica-Bildern, 3 cm.

larger than Nr. 2000/214, with 3 lenses, objective 27 mm Ø, flat burner petrol lamp with glass cylinder. Price with 2 coloured films and 3 laterna-magica-pictures, 3 cm.

más grande que el No. 2000/214, con 3 lentes, objectivo de 27 mm de diámetro, lámpara de petróleo con mechero llano y tubo de vidrio. Precio con 2 filmos de colores y 3 dibujos de linterna mágica de 3 cm.

„ **2000**/216 E wie Nr. 2000/216, jedoch für elektrische Beleuchtung (ohne Birne), mit Kontakt und Kabel, fertig zum Anschluß.

as Nr. 2000/216, but for electrical illumination (without pear), with contact and cabel, ready for connection.

como el No. 2000/216, pero para alumbrado eléctrico (sin ampolla), con contacto y cable, pronto para conectar.

„ **2000**/217 größer und feiner als Nr. 2000/216, mit Verschwinder, Preis mit 2 bunten Filmen und 6 Laterna-magica-Bildern, 3 cm.

larger and finer than Nr. 2000/216, with vanisher. Price with 2 coloured films and 6 laterna-magica-pictures, 3 cm.

más grande y fino que el No. 2000/216, con parada. Precio con 2 filmos de color y 6 dibujos de linterna mágica de 3 cm.

„ **2000**/217 E wie Nr. 2000/217, jedoch für elektrische Beleuchtung (ohne Birne), mit Kontakt und Kabel, fertig zum Anschluß.

as Nr. 2000/217, but for electrical illumination (without pear), with contact and cabel, ready for connection.

como el No. 2000/217, pero para alumbrado eléctrico (sin ampolla), con contacto y cable, pronto para conectar.

„ **2000**/218/1 Objektiv 32 mm Durchmesser, beste Flachbrenner-Petroleumlampe mit Glaszylinder. Preis mit 2 bunten Filmen und 6 Laterna-magica-Bildern, $3^{1}/_{2}$ cm breit.

Objective 32 mm Ø, best flat burner petrol lamp with glass cylinder. Price with 2 coloured films and 6 laterna-magica-pictures, $3^{1}/_{2}$ cm wide.

objectivo de 32 mm de diámetro. mejor lámpara de petróleo con mechero llano y tubo de vidrio. Precio con 2 filmos de color y 6 dibujos de linterna mágica de $3^{1}/_{2}$ cm de ancho.

„ **2000**/218/1 E wie vorstehend, für elektrische Beleuchtung (ohne Birne), mit Kontakt und Kabel fertig zum Anschluß. Preis mit Zugabe wie bei Nr. 2000/218/1.

as above, for electrical illumination (without pear), with contact and cabel, ready for connection. Price with 2 coloured films and 6 laterna-magica-pictures, $3^{1}/_{2}$ cm.

como arriba mencionado, para alumbrado eléctrico (sin ampolla), con contacto y cable, pronto para conectar. Precio con accesorios como con el No. 2000/218/1.

2000/218/1 = ca. $^{1}/_{5}$ natürlicher Größe.

Dampfmaschinen

mit oszillierenden Messing-Dampfzylindern. Stehend angeordnete Dampfkessel. Metallsockel.

Steam engine

with oszillated brass steam cylinder. Horizontal arranged steam boiler. Metal socket.

Máquinas de vapor

con cilindros de vapor de latón, oscilantes, caldera vertical, zócalo de metal.

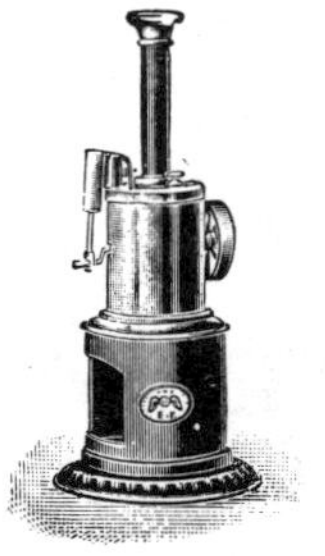

2000/300

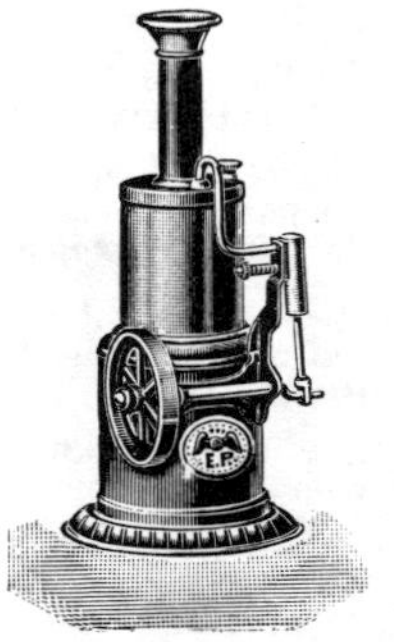

2000/305

2000/305/1

Nr. **2000**/300 Dampfmaschine, etwa 225 mm hoch, mit gelb verniertem Messingkessel und Wasserfüllschraube.
„ **2000**/301 wie Nr. 300, etwa 235 mm hoch, mit Sicherheitsventil und Dampfpfeife.
„ **2000**/303 Dampfmaschine, etwa 225 mm hoch, mit stahlblau patiniertem Messingdampfkessel, Zylinder an Metallbügel montiert, mit Wasserfüllschraube.
„ **2000**/305/1 wie Nr. 305, etwa 240 mm hoch, mit Sicherheitsventil und Dampfpfeife, Garnitur vernickelt.
„ **2000**/305/2 wie Nr. 305/1, etwa 255 mm hoch, mit Sicherheitsventil und Dampfpfeife.
„ **2000**/305/4 wie Nr. 305/2, etwa 270 mm hoch, mit Sicherheitsventil und Dampfpfeife.
„ **2000**/305/5 wie Nr. 305/4, etwa 295 mm hoch, mit Sicherheitsventil und Dampfpfeife.
„ **2000**/305/6 wie Nr. 305/5, etwa 315 mm hoch, mit Sicherheitsventil und Dampfpfeife.

Nr. **2000**/300 Steam engine, abt. 225 mm high, with yellow brass boiler and waterfilling screw.
„ **2000**/301 as Nr. 300, abt. 235 mm high, with safety valve and steam pipe.
„ **2000**/305 Steam engine, abt. 225 mm high, with steel blue patinated brass boiler, cylinder mounted on metal bow with water filling screw.
„ **2000**/305/1 as Nr. 305, abt. 240 mm high, with safety valve, set nickeled.
„ **2000**/305/2 as Nr. 305/1, abt. 255 mm high, with safety valve and steam pipe.
„ **2000**/305/4 as Nr. 305/2, abt. 270 mm high, with safety valve and steam pipe.
„ **2000**/305/5 as Nr. 305/4, abt. 295 mm high, with safety valve and steam pipe.
„ **2000**/305/6 as Nr. 305/5, abt. 315 mm high, with safety valve and steam pipe.

Nr. **2000**/300 Máquina de vapor, unos 225 mm de alto, caldera barnizada amarilla y tapón roscado de relleno.
„ **2000**/301 como Nr. 300, unos 235 mm de alto, con válvula de seguridad y silbato de vapor.
„ **2000**/305 Máquina de vapor, unos 225 mm de alto, con caldera de latón patinada azul de acero, cilindro montado sobre arco metálico, con tapón roscado de relleno.
„ **2000**/305/1 como Nr. 305, unos 240 mm de alto, con válvula de seguridad y silbato de vapor, garnitura niquilada.
„ **2000**/305/2 como Nr. 305/1, unos 255 mm de alto, con válvula de seguridad y silbato de vapor.
„ **2000**/305/4 como Nr. 305/2, unos 270 mm de alto, con válvula de seguridad y silbato de vapor.
„ **2000**/305/5 como Nr. 305/4, unos 295 mm de alto, con válvula de seguridad y silbato de vapor.
„ **2000**/305/6 como Nr. 305/5, unos 315 mm de alto, con válvula de seguridad y silbato de vapor.

Dampfmaschinen mit feststehenden Messing-Dampfzylindern, vor- und rückwärts laufend, ohne Umsteuerung. Die Dampfkessel sind stahlblau patiniert. Messing-Dampfzylinder an Metallbügel montiert. Metallsockel. Armaturen Messing, teils vernickelt.

Steam engines with stationary brass cylinder, working forward and backward without reversing gear. The brass boilers are steel blue patinated. Brass steam cylinder mounted on a metalbow. Metal socket. Armatures of brass, partly nickeled.

Máquinas de vapor con cilindros fijos de latón, con marcha hacia adelante y atrás, sin cambio. Las calderas de latón son patinadas de azul de acero. Cilindros de latón montados sobre arcos de metal. Zócalos metálicos. Armaturas de latón, á partes niqueladas.

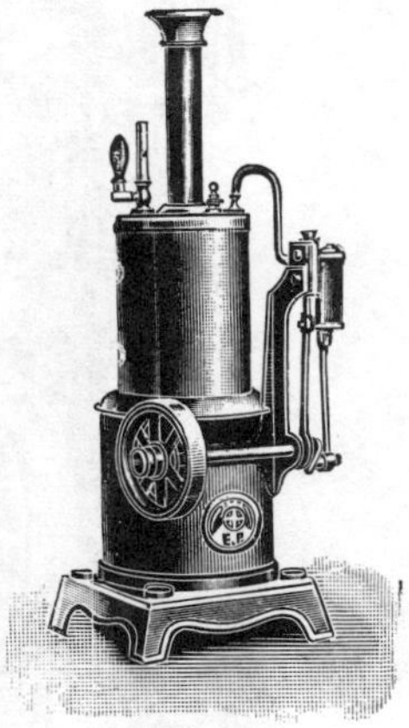

2000/310

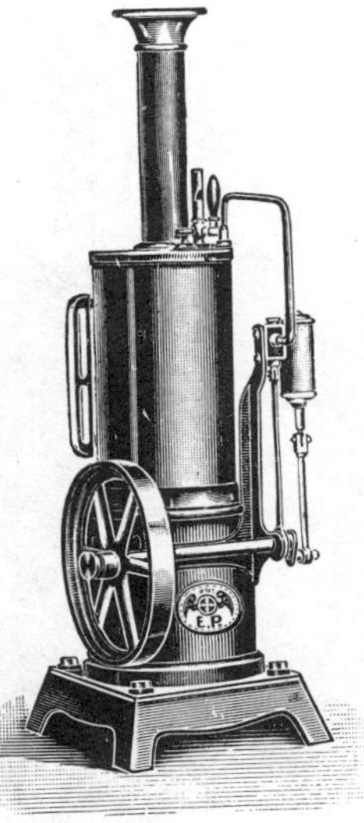

2000/315

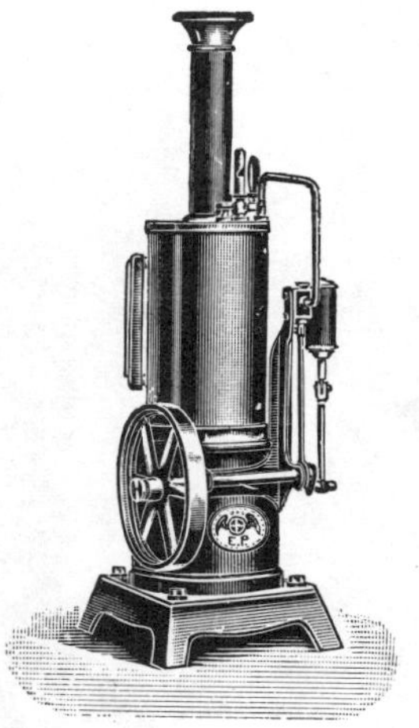

2000/312

Nr. **2000**/309 Dampfmaschine, etwa 250 mm hoch, mit Sicherheitsventil.
„ **2000**/310 Dampfmaschine, etwa 270 mm hoch, mit Sicherheitsventil, Wasserfüllschraube und Dampfpfeife.
„ **2000**/311 Dampfmaschine, etwa 300 mm hoch, mit Sicherheitsventil, Wasserfüllschraube und Dampfpfeife.
„ **2000**/312 Dampfmaschine, etwa 310 mm hoch, mit Sicherheitsventil, Wasserfüllschraube, Dampfpfeife und Wasserstandsanzeiger.
„ **2000**/314 Dampfmaschine, etwa 330 mm hoch, mit Wasserfüllschraube, Dampfpfeife, Wasserstandsanzeiger und E. P.-Manometer.
„ **2000**/315 Dampfmaschine, etwa 350 mm hoch, mit Wasserfüllschraube, Dampfpfeife, Wasserstandsanzeiger und E. P.-Manometer.
„ **2000**/317 Dampfmaschine, etwa 375 mm hoch, mit Wasserfüllschraube, Dampfpfeife, Wasserstandsanzeiger und E. P.-Manometer.
„ **2000**/319 Dampfmaschine, etwa 400 mm hoch, mit Wasserfüllschraube, Dampfpfeife, Wasserstandsanzeiger, Wasserablaßschraube und E. P.-Manometer.

Nr. **2000**/309 Steam engine, abt. 250 mm high, with safety valve.
„ **2000**/310 Steam engine, abt. 270 mm high, with safety valve, water filling screw and steam pipe.
„ **2000**/311 Steam engine, abt. 300 mm high, with safety valve, water filling screw and steam pipe.
„ **2000**/312 Steam engine, abt. 310 mm high, with safety valve, water filling screw and water level indicator.
„ **2000**/314 Steam engine, abt. 330 mm high, with water filling screw, steam pipe, water level indicator and manometer.
„ **2000**/315 Steam engine, abt. 350 mm high, with water filling screw, steam pipe, water level indicator and manometer.
„ **2000**/317 Steam engine, abt. 375 mm high, with water filling screw, steam pipe, water level indicator and manometer.
„ **2000**/319 Steam engine, abt. 400 mm high, with water filling screw, steam pipe, water level indicator, water discharge screw and manometer.

Nr. **2000**/309 Máquina de vapor, unos 250 mm de alto, con válvula de seguridad.
„ **2000**/310 Máquina de vapor, unos 270 mm de alto, con válvula de seguridad, tapón roscado de relleno y silbato de vapor.
„ **2000**/311 Máquina de vapor, unos 300 mm de alto, con válvula de seguridad, tapón roscado de relleno y silbato de vapor.
„ **2000**/312 Máquina de vapor, unos 310 mm de alto, con válvula de seguridad, tapón roscado de relleno, silbato de vapor y indicador del nivel de agua.
„ **2000**/314 Máquina de vapor, unos 330 mm de alto, con tapón roscado de relleno, silbato de vapor, indicador del nivel de agua y manómetro E. P.
„ **2000**/315 Máquina de vapor, unos 350 mm de alto, con tapón roscado de relleno, silbato de vapor, indicador del nivel de agua y manómetro E. P.
„ **2000**/317 Máquina de vapor, unos 375 mm de alto, con tapón roscado de relleno, silbato de vapor, indicador del nivel de agua y manómetro E. P.
„ **2000**/319 Máquina de vapor, unos 400 mm de alto, con tapón roscado de relleno, silbato de vapor, indicador del nivel de agua, tornillo de vaciado y manómetro E. P.

Dampfmaschinen in feinmechanischer Ausführung.

Mit feststehenden Messing-Dampfzylindern, mit Exzentersteuerung und geschlossenem Schieberkasten; vor- und rückwärts laufend, ohne Umsteuerung. Spiritusvergaserlampe. Räder, Bügel und Sockel aus kräftigem Eisenguß.

Steam engines in fine mechanical execution.

With stationary brass steam cylinder with eccentes steering and closed sliding box; working forward an backward, without reversing gear, spiritus carburettor lamp. Wheels, bows and socket of strong cast iron.

Máquinas de vapor de ejecución de precisión.

Con cilindros fijos de latón con distribución de excéntrico y caja de vapor encerrada, marcha hacia adelante y atrás, sin cambio, lámpara de carburación de alcohol. Ruedas, arcos y zócalos de hierro fuerte de fundición.

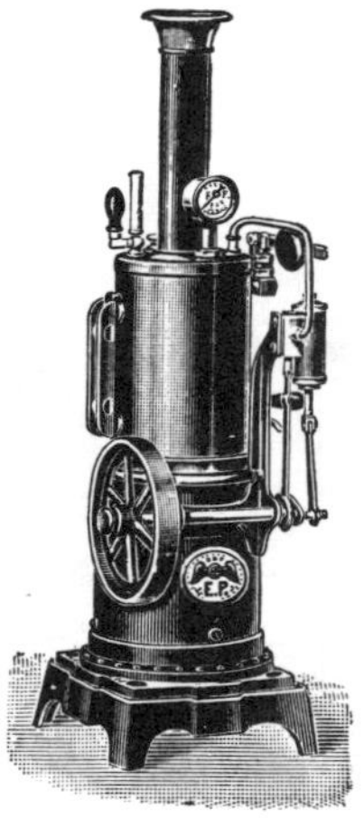

2000/324

2000/325

2000/326

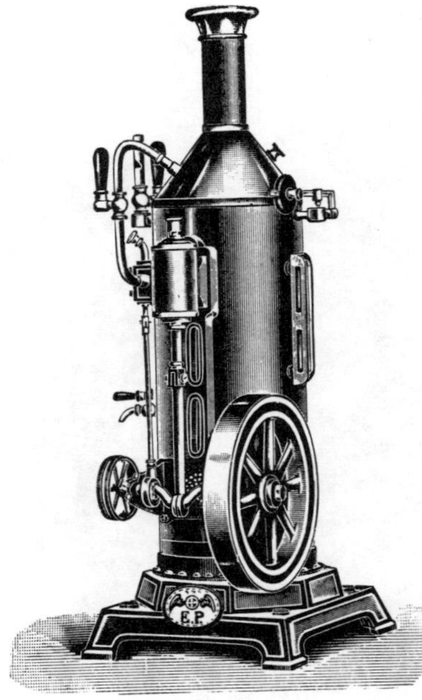

2000/336

Nr. **2000**/324 Dampfmaschine, etwa 320 mm hoch, mit Wasserfüllschraube, Manometer, Dampfpfeife, Wasserstandsanzeiger, Wasserablaßhahn, Oelvorrichtungen und Dampfabsperrhahn.

„ **2000**/325 Dampfmaschine, etwa 345 mm hoch, mit Wasserfüllschraube, Manometer, Dampfpfeife, Wasserstandsanzeiger, Wasserablaßhahn, Oelvorrichtungen und Dampfabsperrhahn.

„ **2000**/326 Dampfmaschine, etwa 375 mm hoch, mit Wasserfüllschraube, Manometer, Dampfpfeife, Wasserstandsanzeiger, Wasserablaßhahn, Oelvorrichtungen und Dampfabsperrhahn.

„ **2000**/334 Dampfmaschine, etwa 380 mm hoch, mit Wasserfüllschraube, Gewichtsventil, Manometer, Dampfpfeife, Wasserstandsanzeiger, Wasserablaßhahn, Selbstöler und Regulator, von kräftiger Wirkung.

„ **2000**/336 Hochfeine Dampfmaschine, etwa 415 mm hoch, mit Wasserfüllschraube, Gewichtsventil, Manometer, Dampfpfeife, Wasserstandsanzeiger, Wasserablaßhahn, Selbstöler und Regulator, von überaus kräftiger Wirkung.

Nr. **2000**/324 Steam engine, abt. 320 mm high, with water filling screw, manometer, water level indicator, water discharge cock, lubrication arrangement and steam locking cock.

„ **2000**/325 Steam engine, abt. 345 mm high, with water filling screw, manometer, steam pipe, water level indicator, water discharge cock, lubrication arrangement and steam locking cock.

„ **2000**/326 Steam engine, abt. 375 mm high, with water filling screw, manometer, steam pipe, water level indicator, water discharge cock, lubrication arrangement and steam locking cock.

„ **2000**/334 Steam engine, abt. 380 mm high, with water filling screw, weight valve, manometer, steam pipe, water level indicator, water discharge cock, automatical lubricator and regulator, strongly acting.

„ **2000**/336 Very elegant steam engine, abt. 415 mm high, with water filling screw, weight valve, manometer, steam pipe, water level indicator, water discharge cock, automatical lubricator and regulator, acting very strongly.

No., **2000**/324 Máquina de vapor, unos 320 mm de alto, con tornillo de relleno, manómetro, silbato de vapor, indicador del nivel de agua, grifo de descarga, engrasadores y robinete de aislamiento.

„ **2000**/325 Máquina de vapor, unos 345 mm de alto, con tornillo de relleno, manómetro, silbato de vapor, indicador del nivel de agua, grifo de descarga, engrasadores y robinete de aislamiento.

„ **2000**/326 Máquina de vapor, unos 375 mm de alto, con tornillo de relleno, manómetro, silbato de vapor, indicador del nivel de agua, grifo de descarga, engrasadores y robinete de aislamiento.

„ **2000**/334 Máquina de vapor, unos 380 mm de alto, con tornillo de relleno, válvula de peso, manómetro, silbato de vapor, indicador del nivel de agua, grifo de descarga, engrasador automático y regulador, my fuerte.

„ **2000**/336 Máquina de vapor, muy elegante, unos 415 mm de alto, con tornillo de relleno, válvula de peso, manómetro, silbato de vapor, indicador del nivel de agua, grifo de descarga, engrasador automático y regulador, de suma potencia.

Dampfmaschinen mit oszillierenden Messing-Dampfzylindern. Liegend angeordnete Dampfkessel.

Steam engine with oscillerating brass steam cylinder. With vertically arranged steam boiler.

Máquinas de vapor con cilindros de latón oscilantes. Calderas horizontales.

2000/360/1

2000/340/1

2000/342

2000/350

Nr. **2000**/360/1 Dampfmaschine, ca. 105×70×185 mm, auf Holzsockel montiert, mit gelb verniertem Messingkessel, oszillierendem Messingzylinder und Füllschraube.
„ **2000**/340/1 Dampfmaschine, etwa 175×130×200 mm, auf fein lackierten Metallsockel montiert, mit gelb verniertem Messingkessel, oszillierendem Messingzylinder und Füllschraube.
„ **2000**/342 Dampfmaschine, etwa 175×130×220 mm, auf fein lackierten Metallsockel montiert, Dampfkessel Messing stahlblau patiniert, mit oszillierendem Messingzylinder, Sicherheitsventil, Dampfpfeife und Ablaßschraube.
„ **2000**/344 Dampfmaschine, etwa 165×165×260 mm, auf fein lackierten Metallsockel montiert, Dampfkessel Messing stahlblau patiniert, mit oszillierendem Messingzylinder, Sicherheitsventil, Dampfpfeife und Ablaßschraube. Garnitur teils vernickelt.

Nr. **2000**/360/1 Steam engine, about 105×70×185 mm, mounted on a wooden socket, with yellow brass boiler, oszillerated brass cylinder and filling screw.
„ **2000**/340/1 Steam engine, about 175×130×200 mm, on a well varnished metal socket, with yellow brass boiler, oszillerated brass cylinder and filling screw.
„ **2000**/342 Steam engine, about 175×130×220 mm, mounted on a Ia. varnished metal socket, steel blue brass steam boiler, with oszillerated brass cylinder, safety valve and discharge screw.
„ **2000**/344 Steam engine, about 165×165×260 mm, mounted on a Ia. varnished metal socket, steel blue brass steam boiler, with oszillerated brass cylinder, safety valve, steam pipe and discharge screw.

No. **2000**/360/1 Máquina de vapor, unos 105×70×185 mm, montada sobre zócalo de madera, con caldera de latón barnizada amarilla, cilindro oscilante de latón y tornillo de relleno.
„ **2000**/340/1 Máquina de vapor, unos 175×130×200 mm, sobre zócalo metálico barnizado, con caldera de latón barnizada amarilla, cilindro de latón oscilante y tornillo de relleno.
„ **2000**/342 Máquina de vapor, unos 175×130×220 mm, montada sobre zócalo metálico barnizado, caldera de latón patinado azul de acero, con cilindro de latón oscilante, válvula de seguridad, silbato de vapor y tornillo de vaciado.
„ **2000**/344 Máquina de vapor, unos 165×165×260 mm, montada sobre zócalo barnizado metálico, caldera de latón patinado azul de acero, con cilindro de latón oscilante, válvula de seguridad, silbato de vapor y tornillo de vaciado. Garnitura á partes niquelada.

2000/356

Dampfmaschinen mit liegend angeordneten Messing-Dampfkesseln. Messingzylinder feststehend, vor- und rückwärts laufend ohne Umsteuerung. Sämtliche Armaturen aus Messing vernickelt. Fundamente: fein lackierte Metallsockel. Von Nr. **2000**/354 an mit Spiritusvergaserlampe.

Steam engine with vertically arranged brass steam boiler. Brass cylinder, fixed, running forward and backward without return steering, all armatures of nickeled steel. Foundation: Ia. varnished metal socket. From Nr. **2000**/354 with spiritus carburettor.

Máquinas de vapor con calderas de latón horizontales. Cilindros de latón fijos, marcha hacia adelante y atrás sin cambio. Todas las armaturas de latón niquelado. Fundaciones: zócalos metálicos barnizados. Desde el No. **2000**/354 con lámpara de carburación de alcohol.

Nr. **2000**/350 Dampfmaschine mit Sicherheitsventil, Dampfpfeife, Wasserfüllschraube, Größe der Maschine 180×180×275 mm.
„ **2000**/351 Dampfmaschine mit Gewichtsventil, Dampfpfeife, Wasserfüllschraube, Wasserablaßschraube, Größe der Maschine 190×190×290 mm.
„ **2000**/352 Dampfmaschine mit Manometer, Dampfpfeife, Wasserfüllschraube, Wasserablaßschraube, Wasserstandsanzeiger, Größe der Maschine 200×200×315 mm.
„ **2000**/354 Dampfmaschine mit Manometer, Dampfpfeife, Wasserfüllschraube, Wasserablaßschraube, Wasserstandsanzeiger, Größe der Maschine 215×215×340 mm.
„ **2000**/356 Dampfmaschine mit Manometer, Dampfpfeife, Gewichtsventil, Wasserfüllschraube, Wasserablaßschraube, Wasserstandsanzeiger, Größe der Maschine 230×230×365 mm.

Nr. **2000**/350 Steam engine with safety valve, steam pipe, water filling screw, size of the machine 180×180×275 mm.
„ **2000**/351 Steam engine with weight valve, steam pipe, water filling screw, water discharge screw, size of the machine 190×190×290 mm.
„ **2000**/352 Steam engine with manometer, steam pipe, water filling screw, water level indicator, size of the machine 200×200×315 mm.
„ **2000**/354 Steam engine with manometer, steam pipe, water filling screw, water discharge screw, water level indicator, size of the machine 215×215×340 mm.
„ **2000**/356 Steam engine with manometer, steam pipe, weight valve, water filling screw, water discharge screw, water level indicator, size of the machine 230×230×365 mm.

2000/354

No. **2000**/350 Máquina de vapor con válvula de seguridad, silbato de vapor, tornillo de relleno, tamaño de la máquina 180×180×275 mm.
„ **2000**/351 Máquina de vapor con válvula de peso, silbato de vapor, tornillo de relleno, tornillo de vaciado, tamaño de la máquina 190×190×290 mm.
„ **2000**/352 Máquina de vapor con manómetro, silbato de vapor, tornillo de relleno y de vaciado, indicador del nivel de agua, tamaño de la máquina 200×200×315 mm.
„ **2000**/354 Máquina de vapor con manómetro, silbato de vapor, tornillo de relleno y de vaciado, indicador del nivel de agua, tamaño de la máquina 215×215×340 mm.
„ **2000**/356 Máquina de vapor con manómetro, válvula de peso, silbato de vapor, tornillos de relleno y de vaciado, indicador del nivel de agua, tamaño de la máquina 230×230×365 mm.

Modelle für Dampfmaschinen. Attachments for engines. Modelos para máquinas.

143/2124/0

143/2044/0

143/2004/1

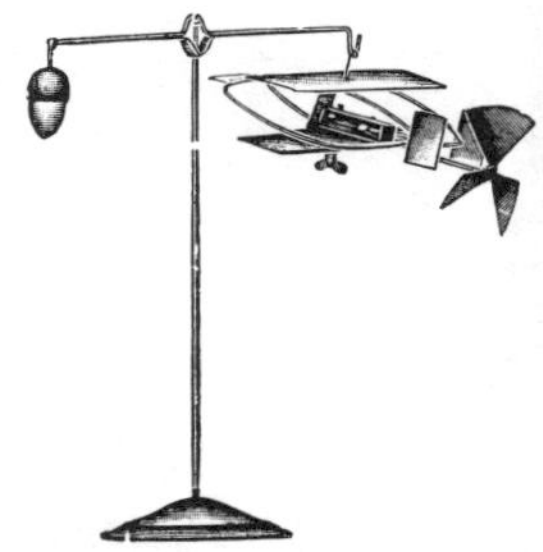
143/2130/2

143/10/2

143/184/0

143/61/0

143/1

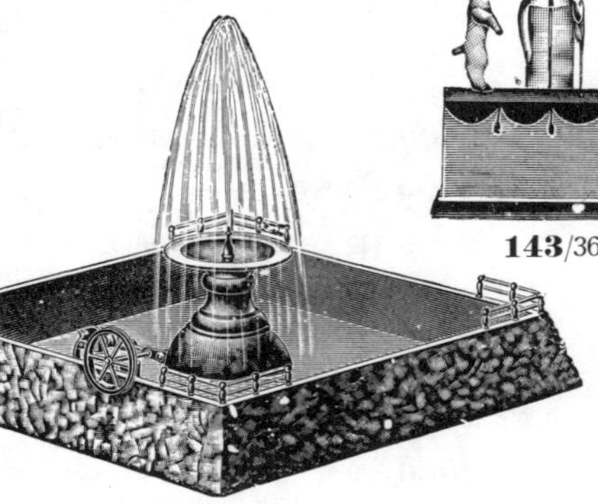
143/104/1

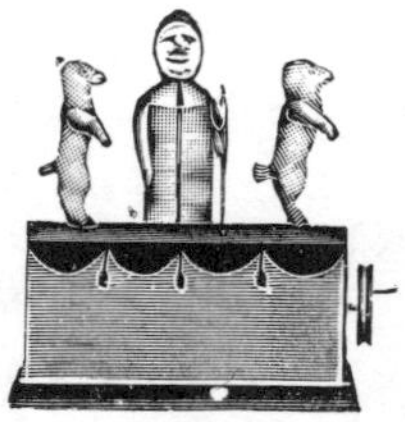
143/36/4

143/2046/1

143/121

143/86/1

143/57/0

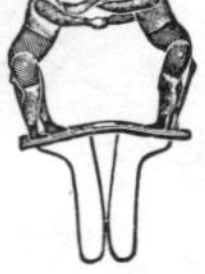
143/242

143/157 **143**/151 **143**/152

143/158

143/71

143/36/3

143/54/2

143/154 **143**/155 **143**/156

143/41/2

143/19/4

143/10/4

143/19/6

143/51/1

143/10/15

143/10/16

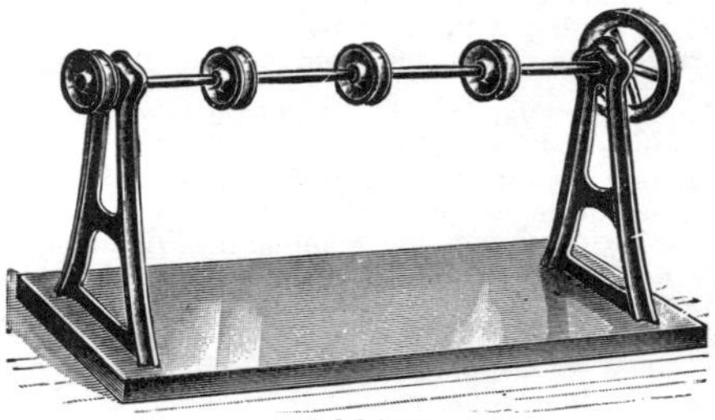
143/204

143/165

143/40/1

2021/1

Familienkino. Halbwatt-Modell I (wie vorstehende Abbildung).

Mit elektr. Motor sowie Handbetrieb, bestehend aus: Malteserkreuz-Mechanik komplett, mit Objektiv, Drehkurbel, Blende, Spirale, Lichtgehäuse, Kondensor, 3 m Leitungskabel mit Anschlußkontakt, Halbwattlampe 110 oder 220 Volt, 2 Stück feste Filmspulen à 400 m, 1 Stück zerlegbare Filmspule für 400 m, Eichenholzrahmen, Filmspulenträger mit eingebautem Filmumwickler. — Elektrischer Antriebsmotor, verwendbar für 110-220 Volt Gleich- oder Wechselstrom, mit Regulieranlasser und Leitungskabel.

Family cinomatograph. Half watt model I. (As illustrated above.)

With electrical motor, as well as hand drive, consisting of: Maltesa cross mechanic complete with, objective, turning crank, shade, spiral, light case, condenser, 3 m conducting cable with connection contact, half watt lamp 110 or 220 Volt, 2 fixed film spools, each of 400 m length, 1 decomposable film spool for 400 m, frame of oak, film spool support with build in film winder. — Electrical driving motor, useable for 110-220 Volt contineous or alternating current with regulation starter and conducting cable.

Cinematógrafo de familia. Modelo medio-vatio I (según dibujo que precede).

Con electro-motor y servicio á mano, componiendose de: Mecanismo de cruz de Malta completo, con objectivo, manivela, diafragma, espiral, caja de luz, condensador, 3 metros de línea de cable y contacto de unión, lámpara medio-vatio 110 ó 220 voltios, 2 piezas de carretes fijos de filmo de 400 metros cada uno, 1 pieza de carrete de filmo desmontable para 400 metros, cuadro de encina, soporte de carrete de filmo con aparato embutido de recubrir con filmos. — Electro-motor, sirviendo para 110-220 voltios, corriente continua ó alternativa con regulador de puesta en marcha y línea de cable.

2006/2

2006/3

2006/4

2006/5

Nr. **2006**/2 **Kino** auf solidem Metallfuß montiert, feine schwarze Lackierung, ist mit gutem Mechanismus, Petroleumlampe, Glaszylinder und Reflektor ausgestattet.
Cinomatograph, mounted on solid metal feet, fine black varnished, is with good mechanism, petrol lamp, glass cylinder and reflector.
Cinematógrafo, montado sobre zócalo sólido de metal, barnizado negro, provisto con mecanismo bueno, lámpara de petróleo, tubo de vidrio y reflector.

Nr. **2006**/3 **Kino,** auf solidem Metallfuß montiert, feine schwarze Lackierung, ist mit gutem Mechanismus, Petroleumlampe, Glaszylinder und Reflektor, kleinem Verschwinder und Filmrolle ausgestattet.
Cinomatograph, mounted on solid metal feet, fine black varnished, is furnished with a good mechanism, petrol lamp, glass cylinder, reflector, small vanisher, and film roll.
Cinematógrafo, montado sobre zócalo sólido de metal, barnizado negro, provisto con mecanismo bueno, lámpara de petróleo, tubo de vidrio y reflector, parada pequeña y rollo de filmo.

Nr. **2006**/4 **Kino,** auf solidem Metallfuß montiert, feine schwarze Lackierung, ist mit gutem Mechanismus, Petroleumlampe, Glaszylinder und Reflektor, großem Verschwinder und Filmrolle ausgestattet.
Cinomatograph, mounted on solid feet, fine black varnished, is furnished with a good mechanism, petrol lamp, glass cylinder and great vanisher, reflector and film roll.
Cinematógrafo, montado sobre zocalo sólido de metal, barnizado negro, provisto con mecanismo bueno, lámpara de petróleo, tubo de vidrio y reflector, parada pequeña y rollo de filmo.

Nr. **2006**/5 **Laterna magica,** fein lackiertes Blech, massiver Metallfuß, Flachbrenner-Petroleumlampe mit Glaszylinder, Reflektor, drei Glasbilder 3 cm und ein Objektiv 26 mm Ø.
Laterna magica, finely varnished tin, solid metal feet, flat burner petrol lamp with glass cylinder, reflector, three glass pictures 3 cm and objektive 26 mm Ø.
Linterna mágica, lata barnizada, zócalo macizo de metal, mechero llano, lámpara de petróleo y tubo de vidrio, reflector, 3 dibujos sobre vidrio 3 cm y un objectivo de 26 mm Ø.

Voltana-Experimente, das vielseitigste und lehrreichste Spielzeug der Gegenwart.
Voltana Experiments, the most manyfold and instructive toy of the present time.
Experimentos Voltana, el juguete más variado y instructivo del presente.

68/26

Die Voltana-Elektrisiermaschinen erzeugen Elektrizität in Form von Funken, die eine Länge bis zu $^2/_5$ des Scheibendurchmessers erreichen können, und zwar keine galvanische Elektrizität, wie solche den Elementen oder Akkumulatoren entnommen wird, sondern nach Art der Reibungselektrizität.

Die Voltana-Maschinen brauchen — selbst bei jahrelangem Gebrauch — niemals aufgefüllt oder aufgeladen zu werden. Nur durch einfaches Drehen mittelst der Hand liefern sie eine unerschöpfliche Menge Elektrizität, mit der sich Hunderte von Experimenten ausführen lassen.

The Voltana electrising machine produces electricity in the form of sparks which reach a length up to $^2/_5$ of the diameter of the disc, and this not from galvanic electricity as they are taken from the elements of accumulators but such as the friction electricity produces.

The Voltana Machine needs never — if even used for years — be filled up. Only by a simple turning by hand the instrument supplies an inexhaustible amount of electricity with which hundreds of experiments can be executed.

Las máquinas eléctricas Voltana producen electricidad bajo forma de chispas alcanzando una longitud hasta $^2/_5$ del diámetro del disco, y eso no es electricidad galvánica tal como se saca de elementos ó acumuladores, sino en el estilo de la electricidad de frotamiento.

No hay que rellenar ó recargar las máquinas Voltana — mismo al cabo de muchos años. Basta que las giren con la mano para sacar de ellas una cantidad inagotable de electricidad que se presta á la ejecución de muchos cientos de experimentos.

Voltana-Maschinen

besitzen zwei entgegengesetzt rotierende Hartgummischeiben, sie arbeiten ohne Polwechsel und haben Leidener Flaschen eigenartiger Anordnung (D.R.P.), um Funken verschiedener Stärke erzeugen zu können. Größe 68/26 liefert außer reinem Gleichstrom auch Wechselstrom (Hochfrequenz). Alle Metallteile sind fein vernickelt.

Nr. **68**/21 mit Scheibengröße von 21 cm auf Eisenfuß.
„ **68**/26 „ „ „ 26 cm „ Holzsockel.

Voltana machines

have two contrary running discs of hard rubber, they work without changing the pole and have Leidener bottles of a singular arrangement (German patent) to produce sparks of a different strength. Size 68/26 supplies continual current and alternating current (high frequency). All metal parts are carefully nickeled.

Nr. **68**/21 with a disc size of 21 cm on iron feet.
„ **68**/26 „ „ „ „ „ 26 cm on wooden socket.

Máquinas Voltana

tienen dos discos de ebonita rodando en el sentido opuesto los que obran sin alternación teniendo botellas de Leiden de disposición especial (patentada) á fin de producir chispas de fuerza variada. El tamaño Nr. 68/26 entrega fuera de corriente continua también corriente alternativa (de alta frecuencia). Todas las partes metálicas son cuidadosamente niqueladas.

Nr. **68**/21 con disco de 21 cm sobre zócalo de hierro.
„ **68**/26 „ „ „ 26 cm „ „ „ madera.

Experimentier-Kästen zu den Voltana-Maschinen.
Alle Apparate passen zu einem gemeinsamen isolierenden Stativ, auf welches sie beim Gebrauch aufgesetzt werden.

Experimenting boxes to the Voltana machines.
All apparatuses fit into a mutually insulated frame on which they are placed for use.

Cajas de experimentar para Máquinas Voltana.
Todos los aparatos se adaptan á un estator común aislando, sobre el cual se ponen para el uso.

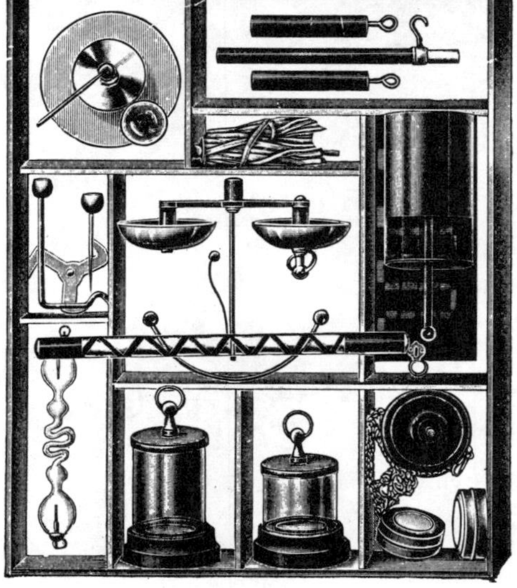

68/103

Nr. **68**/101 **Kollektion Elektron A.**

Inhalt: Universalstativ, Papierbüschel, Glockenspiel, Flugrad, Halter für Geißlerröhre und Blitztafel, Geißlerröhre, Blitztafel, Handhaben zum Elektrisieren, Leitungsketten, Glasstab und Hartgummistab für die Fundamentalversuche, Pendelhalter, Dose mit diversen Holunderkugeln, Holunderfigur, Leinen- und Seidenfäden und Kupferdraht zur Anfertigung von Pendeln usw.

Collection Electron A.

Universal frame, paper brush, bell play, fly wheel, holder for the Geissler tubes and lightning table, Geissler tubes, lightning table, handles for electrizising, conduit chains, glass rod and rod of hard rubber for the fundamental tests, pendel holder, tin with different elder balls, elder figures, linnen and silk threads and copper wire for the production of pendels.

Collección Electro A.

Contenido: Estator universal, mechon de papel, carillón, ruedo volante, tube de Geissler y tabla relámpago con soportes, mangos de electrizar, cadenas de conducir, barras de vidrio y ebonita para experimentos fundamentales, soporte de pendulo, cajas con diversas bolas de meollo de sabuco, figura de sabuco, hilos de lino, seda y cobre para fabricar pendulos, etc.

Nr. **68**/102 **Kollektion Elektron B.**

Inhalt: Blitzröhre, Kugeltanz, Apparat zur Luftreinigung, rotierender Kugellauf mit Glaskugel, Leydener Flasche, Glashöhe 9 cm und Entlader dazu mit Griff.

Collection Electron B.

Contents: Lightning tubes, ball dance, apparatus for cleaning air, rotating ball run with glass balls, Leydener bottle, glass height 9 cm and discharge thereto with handle.

Colleccíón Elektron B.

Contenido: Tubo de relámpago, baile de bolas, aparato para limpiar aire, corrida de bolas rotatoria con bola de vidrio, botella de Leyde de 9 cm de alto con descargador con puño.

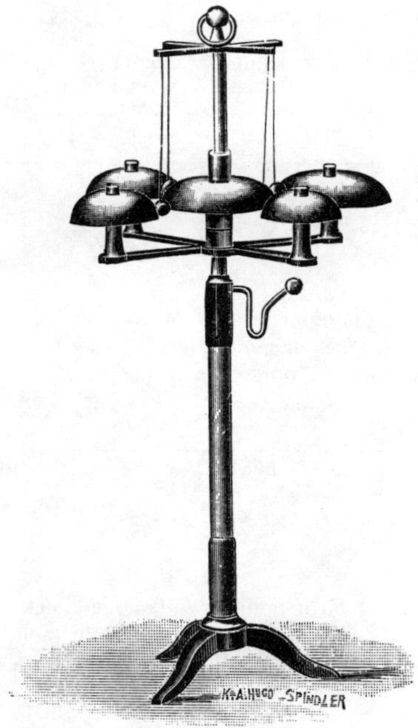

68/105/3

Glockenspiel.
Bell play.
Carillon.

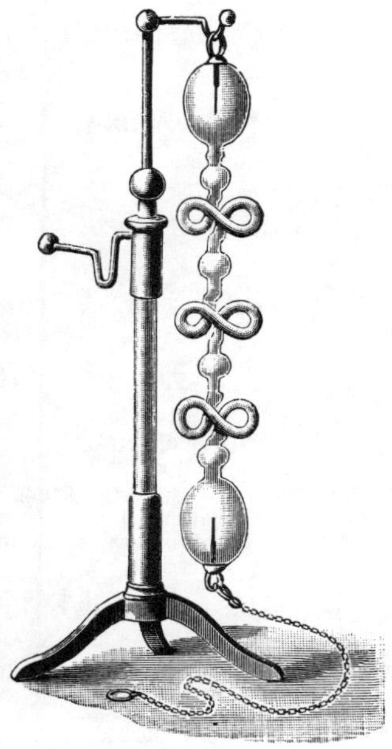

68/105/6

Geißler-Röhre nebst Halter.
Geissler tubes with holder.
Tube de Geissler con soporte.

Zwei Abbildungen von Skola-Apparaten in ca. 1/4 natürlicher Größe. Two illustrations of Skola-apparatuses of about 1/4 nat. sizes.

Dos ilustraciones de los aparatos Skola en un cuarto aproximativamente, del tamaño natural.

Die Skola-Apparate sind größer in der Ausführung als Simplex nach Abbildung 68/105/3 und 68/105/6.

The Skola apparatuses are larger than the Simplex apparatuses, according to illustration 68/105/3 and 68/105/6.

Los aparatos Skola son más grandes, respectando la ejecución, que los Simplex, según ilustración 68/105/3 y 68/105/6.

Nr. **68**/103 **Kollektion Simplex.**

Inhalt: Nr. 68/101 und 68/102 vereinigt in einem Kasten.

Collection Simplex.

Contents: Nr. 68/101 and 68/102 united in one box.

Colección Simplex.

Los Nos. 68/101 y 68/102 unidos en una caja.

Nr. **68**/104 **Kollektion Klein-Skola.**

Inhalt wie Nr. 68/101.

Collection Small Skola.

Contents the same as Nr. 68/101.

Colección Skola pequeña.

Contenido como en el Nr. 68/101.

Nr. **68**/105 **Kollektion Groß-Skola.**

Inhalt wie Nr. 68/103.

Collection Large Skola.

Contents the same as Nr. 68/103.

Colección Skola grande.

Contenido como en el No. 68/103.

Trompeten. — Trumpets. — Trompetas.

103/71/7

Blechtrompeten, bemalt, mit Blechmundstück.
Metal-plate trumpets, painted, with metal-plate mouthpiece.
Trompetas de chapa, pintadas, con boca de chapa.

Nr. **103**/71/1, 2 und 3 Glattes Blech, ohne Griff.
Plain metal-plate, without handle.
Chapa lisa, sin mango.

Nr. **103**/71/4, 5, 6, 7, 8 und 9 Dessiniertes Blech, mit Griff.
Platterned metal-plate, with handle.
Chapa con varas muestras, con mango.

Nr. **103**/71/1		2	3	4	5	6	7	8	9	
Länge — Length — Largura	5,5	7,5	8¾	10	11,5	15	17	19	21	cm
Trichterdurchmesser / Diameter of funnel / Diámetro del embudo	1,7	1,7	3	3,5	3,5	5,5	5,5	5,5	5,5	„

103/72/9

Blechtrompeten, dekoriertes Blech, Blechmundstück.
Metal-plate trumpets, decorated metal, metal-plate mouthpiece.
Trompetas de chapa, chapa decorada, boca de chapa.

Nr. **103**/72/1, 2 und 3 Ohne Griff.
Without handle.
Sin mango.

Nr. **103**/72/4, 5, 6, 7, 8 und 9 Mit Griff.
With handle.
Con mango.

Nr. **103**/72/1		2	3	4	5	6	7	8	9	
Länge — Length — Largura	5,5	7,5	8¾	10	11,5	15	17	19	21	cm
Trichterdurchmesser / Diameter of funnel / Diámetro del embudo	1,7	1,7	3	3,5	3,5	5,5	5,5	5,5	5,5	„

Blechtrompeten, bemalt, mit Griff und Porzellanmundstück.
Metal-plate trumpet, painted, with handle and porcelain mouthpiece.
Trompetas de chapa, pintadas, con mango y boca de porcelana.

Nr. **103**/73/5 und 6 Glattes Blech.
Plain metal.
Chapa lisa.

„ **103**/73/7, 8, 9 u. 10 Dessiniertes Blech.
Patterned metal.
Chapa con varas muestras.

Nr. **103**/73/5	6	7	8	9	10
Länge — Length — Largura	12	14,5	17	19	21	23 cm
Trichterdurchmesser / Diameter of funnel / Diámetro del embudo	3	3	5,5	5,5	5,5	6 „

103/73/10

Blechtrompeten, wie Nr. 103/73, jedoch dekoriertes Blech, wie Nr. 103/72, mit Griff und Porzellanmundstück.
Metal-plate trumpets, as Nr. 103/73, but with decorated metal as Nr. 103/72, with handle and porcelain mouthpiece.
Trompetas de chapa, tales que Nr. 103/73, pero de chapa decorada así como Nr. 103/72, con mango y boca de porcelana.

Nr. **103**/74/5		6	7	8	9	10
Länge — Length — Largura	12	14,5	17	19	21	23 cm
Trichterdurchmesser / Diameter of funnel / Diámetro del embudo	3	3	5,5	5,5	5,5	6 „

Nr. **103**/81
Blechtrompeten, in Ausführung wie Nr. 103/73/10, aber mit großem Mundstück und Porzellanspitze.
Metal-plate trumpets, style of Nr. 103/73/10, but with large mouthpiece and porcelain tip.
Trompetas de chapa, la misma ejecución que Nr. 103/73/10, pero con boca grande y punta de porcelana.

Nr. **103**/81/1		2	3	4
Länge — Length — Largura	23	25	28	35 cm
Trichterdurchmesser / Diameter of funnel / Diámetro del embudo	6	6	6	8 „

Nr. **103**/82
Blechtrompeten, wie Nr. 103/81, aber glattes, dekoriertes Blech.
Metal-plate trumpets, as Nr. 103/81, but plain decorated metal.
Trompetas de chapa, tales que Nr. 103/81, pero de chapa lisa y decorada.

Nr. **103**/82/1		2	3	4
Länge — Length — Largura	23	25	28	35 cm
Trichterdurchmesser / Diameter of funnel / Diámetro del embudo	6	6	6	8 „

103/75/1

Trompeten, Trompetenschlottern, Hupen. — Trumpets, Trumpetrattles, Hooters.
Trompetas, Chacoloteadores para trompetas, Rocinas.

Blechtrompeten, dekoriertes Blech, mit großem Blechmundstück, 1 Ton, Weißblechtrichter.
Metal-plate trumpets, decorated tin, with large metal-plate mouthpiece, 1 tone, tinplate funnel.
Trompetas de chapa, chapa decorada, con boca de chapa grande, 1 sonido, embudo de hoja lata.

Nr. **103**/75/1		2
Länge — Length — Largura	23	30 cm
Trichterdurchmesser / Diameter of funnel / Diámetro del embudo	6	6,5 „

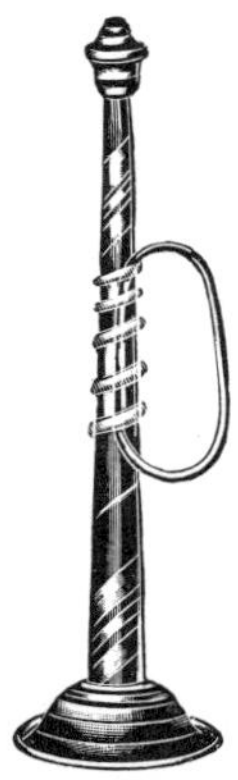

103/76/1

Blechtrompeten, dekoriert, großes Mundstück, Rohrbügel, Zinktrichter bemalt, Chenillewicklung.
Metal-plate trumpets, decorated, large mouthpiece, with handle, painted zinc funnel, chenille cord.
Trompetas de chapa, decoradas, boca grande, manija encorvada, embudo de cinc, pintado, envoltura de felpilla.

Nr. **103**/76/1 Einfacher Ton.
Single tone.
Un solo sinodo.

„ **103**/76/2 und 3 Vor- und Zurückstimme.
Push and pull tone.
Voz sonando hacia atrás y por adelante.

Nr. **103**/76/1		2	3
Länge — Length — Largura	24	25,5	31 cm
Trichterdurchmesser / Diameter of funnel / Diámetro del embudo	6,5	6,5	8 „

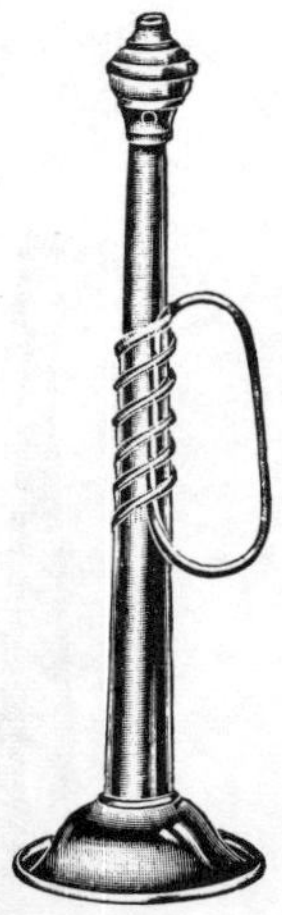

103/77/5 u.78/5

Trompeten. — Trumpets. — Trompetas.

Nickeltrompeten, Trichter innen blau bemalt.
Nickel trumpets, funnel painted blue inside.
Trompetas de niquel, interior del embudo pintado en azul.

Nr. **103**/77/1 u. 2 Einfach Ton, Blechgriff, Papier- und Wollschnurwicklung.
Single tone, metal-plate handle, wound round with paper and woollen cord.
Un solo sonido, mango de chapa, envoltura de cordones de lana y papel.

Nr. **103**/77/3, 4 u. 5 Vor- und Zurückton, Blechrohrbügel, Chenillewicklung.
Push and pull tone, metal-plate tube handle, chenille cord.
Voz sonando hacia atras y por adelante, manija de chapa encorvada, envoltura de felpilla.

	Nr. **103**/77/1	2	3	4	5
Länge — Length — Largura	17	19	20	25	29 cm
Trichterdurchmesser / Diameter of funnel / Diámetro del embudo	5	5,5	6	7	8 „

103/717 und 719

Nickeltrompeten, Vor- und Zurückton, Chenillewicklung, genau wie Nr. 103/77/3, 4, 5, aber Trichter innen und außen blank.
Nickel trumpets, push and pull tone, chenille cords, same as Nr. 103/77/3, 4 and 5, but funnel blank inside and out.
Trompetas de niquel, voz sonando hacia atras y por adelante, precisamente tales que No. 103/77/3, 4, 5, pero el interior y el exterior del embudo esta pulido.

	Nr. **103**/78/3	4	5
Länge — Length — Largura	20	25	29 cm
Trichterdurchmesser / Diameter of funnel / Diámetro del embudo	6	7	8 „

Trompetenschlottern, Zinkblech bemalt, mit Weißblechgriff, Doppelton.
Trumpet-rattles, zinc plate painted, with tinplate handle, double tone.
Chacoloteadores para trompetas, chapa de cinc pintada, con mango de hoja lata, sonido doble.

	Nr. **103**/717	**103**/719
Länge — Length — Largura	10,5	11 cm
Durchmesser — Diameter — Diámetro	4	5 „

103/714

Hupen aus gedrücktem, poliertem Zink, mit Ring und Doppelton.
Hooter, pressed polished zinc, with ring and double tone.
Rocinas de cinc comprimido y pulido con anillo y sonido doble.

	Nr. **103**/714
Länge — Length — Largura	7 cm
Durchmesser — Diameter — Diámetro	5,5 „

Trompetenschlottern. Posthörner. — Trumpet rottles. Post hornes. — Chacoloteadores para trompetas. Cornetas para postillon.

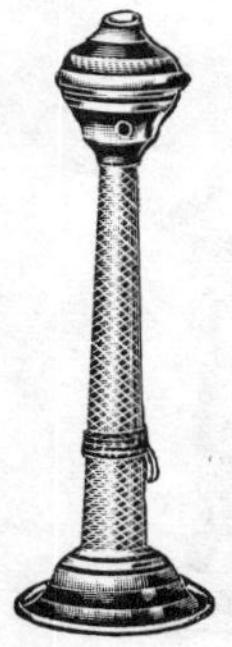

103/79/3

Trompetenschlottern, dessiniertes Blechrohr, Trichter und Schlotterkopf bemalt, Baumwollwicklung.
Trumpet-rattles, patterned metal-plate tube, funnel and rattle-head painted, corded with cotton.
Chacoloteadores para trompetas, tubo de chapa con varias muestras embudo y cabeza chacoloteador, envoltura de algodon.

Nr. **103**/79/1 Einfach Ton. Single tone. Un solo sonido.
Nr. **103**/2, 3 u. 4 Doppelton. Double tone. Sonido doble.

	Nr. **103**/79/1	2	3	4
Länge — Length — Largura	14	17	20	23 cm
Trichterdurchmesser / Diameter of funnel / Diámetro del embudo	5	5,5	6	6¾ „

Trompetenschlottern genau wie 103/79, aber in Nickelblech glatt, Trichter und Schlotter blank poliert, Baumwollwicklung.
Trumpet-rattles, precisely as 103/79, but in plain nickel metalplate, funnel and rattle polished blank, cotton wrapping.
Chacoloteadores para trompetas precisamente tales que 103/79, pero de lisa chapa de niquele, embudo y chacoloteador pulidos finisimamente, envoltura de algodon.

	Nr. **103**/80/1	2	3	4
Länge — Length — Largura	14	17	20	23 cm
Trichterdurchmesser / Diameter of funnel / Diámetro del embudo	5	5,5	6	6¾ „

103/9/3

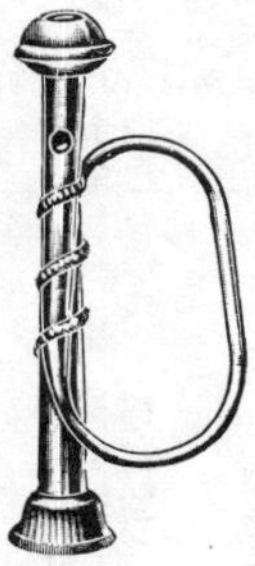

103/9/8

Posthörner, Weißblech mit Baumwollwicklung.
Posthornes, tinplate, with cotton cord.
Cornetas de postillon, de hoja lata con envoltura de algodon.

	Nr. **103**/9/1	2	3	4
Länge — Length — Largura	8	8,5	10,5	10,7 cm
Bogendurchmesser / Diameter of circle / Diámetro de la manija	3	3	4,8	4,8 „
Trichterdurchmesser / Diameter of funnel / Diametro del embudo	1,4	1,6	1,4	1,6 „
Wie Nr., as Nr., tales que No.	103/9/3	103/9/8	103/9/3	103/9/8

C-Trompeten. Blechnebelhörner. — C-trumpets. Metal-plate fog hornes. — Trompetas C. Bocinas de bruma.

103/28

C-Trompeten, Weißblech mit Baumwollwicklung.
C-trumpets, tinplate with cotton cord.
Trompetas C, de hoja lata con envoltura de algodon.

	Nr. **103**/9/5	6	7	8
Länge — Length — Largura	7	7,5	9,2	9,4 cm
Trichter wie / Funnel as / Embudo tales que	**103**/9/3	-/-/8	-/-/3	-/-/8

Blechnebelhörner mit Holzmundstück und Bleistimme.
Metal-plate fog hornes with wooden mouthpiece and lead voice.
Bocinas de bruma con boca de madera y voz de plomo.

	Nr. **103**/13/1	16/1	18/1	21/1	25/1	28/1	35/1	40/1	
Länge ca. — Length about — Largura cerca de	13	16	18	21	25	28	35	40	cm
Bemalt mit Ringen — Painted with rings — Pintadas con anillos	13	16	18	21	25	28	35	40	„

Dekoriertes Blech. — Decorated metal. — Chapa decorada.

103/28/1

Orchestrion. — Orchestrion. — Orquestrión.

Nr. **2028**/3 und 4

In liegender Form, spielt ebenfalls Choral, ausgeführt in feinem Blechkasten mit prächtigem Farbendruck.
Nr. 3 mit 16 Tönen ist 17 cm lang, 11 cm breit und 12,5 cm hoch.
„ 4 „ 20 „ „ 18,5 „ „ 12,5 „ „ „ 13 „ „

Horizontal style, playing a hymn tune, made up in good quality metal box, with spendid colour printing.
Nr. 3 with 16 notes is 17 cm long, 11 cm wide, 12,5 cm high.
„ 4 „ 20 „ „ 18,5 „ „ 12,5 „ „ 13 „ „

En forma horizontal, tocando cantos gregorianos, montado en una fina caja de chapa con cromotipografía magnifica.
No. 3 con 16 sonidos, largura 17 cm, anchura 11 cm, altura 12,5 cm.
„ 4 „ 20 „ „ 18,5 „ „ 12,5 „ „ 13 „

Trompeten. — Trumpets. — Trompetas.

1 2 4 5 8 9

Serie 1.

Nr.				
Nr.	**160**/15/5	Größe, size, tamaño	15×5,5	cm
„	**160**/17½/5	„ „ „	17,5×5,5	„
„	**160**/19/5	„ „ „	19×5,5	„
„	**160**/21/5	„ „ „	21×5,5	„

Serie 2.

Nr.	**160**/26/7	Größe, size, tamaño	25,5×7	cm
„	**160**/33/9	„ „ „	31×8,5	„
„	**160**/37/9	„ „ „	36,5×8,5	„
„	**160**/44/9	„ „ „	42,5×8,5	„
„	**160**/44/10T	„ „ „	42,5×10	„

Serie 3.

Nr.	**160**/19/9	Größe, size, tamaño	19×6	cm
„	**160**/23/7	„ „ „	22,5×7	„
„	**160**/25½/9	„ „ „	26×8,5	„
„	**160**/29/9	„ „ „	29×8,5	„
„	**160**/34/9	„ „ „	34×8,5	„

Serie 4.

Nr.	**160**/30/10	Größe, size, tamaño	29×10	cm
„	**160**/35/10	„ „ „	34×10	„
„	**160**/40/10	„ „ „	39×10	„

Serie 5.

Nr.	**160**/19/6 GS	Größe, size, tamaño	19×6	cm
„	**160**/23/7 GS	„ „ „	22,5×7	„
„	**160**/25½/9 GS	„ „ „	26×8,5	„
„	**160**/29/9 GS	„ „ „	29×8,5	„
„	**160**/34/9 GS	„ „ „	34×8,5	„

Serie 6.

Nr.	**160**/19/6 G	Größe, size, tamaño	19×6	cm
„	**160**/23/7 G	„ „ „	22,5×7	„
„	**160**/26/7 G	„ „ „	25,5×7	„
„	**160**/33/9 G	„ „ „	31×8,5	„

Serie 7.

Nr.	**160**/30/9	Größe, size, tamaño	28,5×8,5	cm
„	**160**/35/9	„ „ „	33,5×8,5	„
„	**160**/39/9	„ „ „	38,5×10	„

Serie 8.

Nr.	**160**/30/9 GS	Größe, size, tamaño	28,5×8,5	cm
„	**160**/35/9 GS	„ „ „	33,5×8,5	„
„	**160**/39/9 GS	„ „ „	38,5×10	„

Serie 9.

Nr.	**160**/18/5 Sch	Größe, size, tamaño	18,5×5,5	cm
„	**160**/23/7 Sch	„ „ „	22,5×7	„
„	**160**/34/9 Sch	„ „ „	33,5×8,5	„
„	**160**/27/9 Sch	„ „ „	27×8,5	„

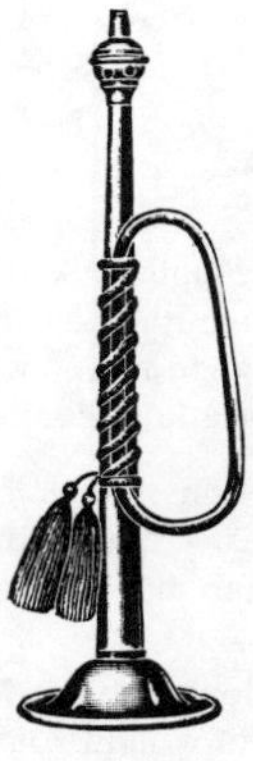

80/300

80/304

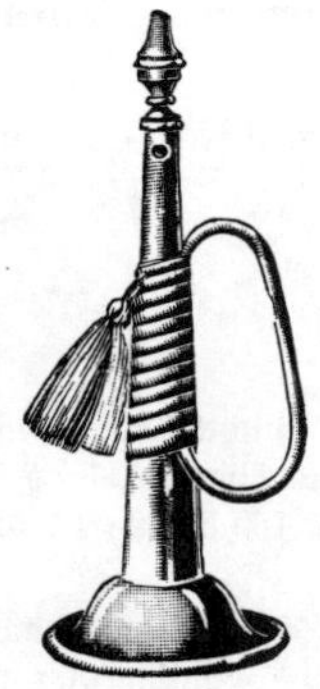

80/355

80/368

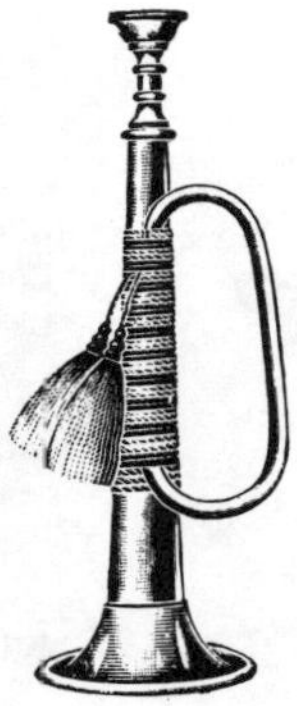

80/603

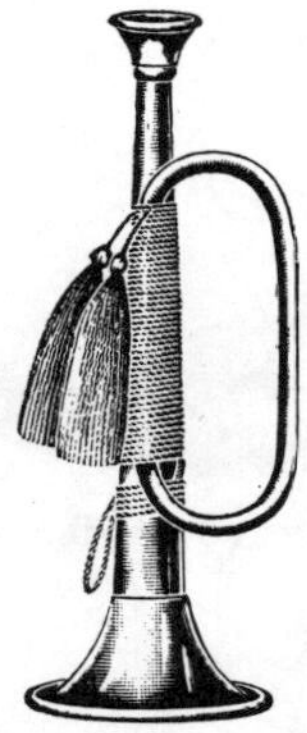

80/101

Mit lackiertem Trichter und einfacher Chenillenumwicklung.
Varnished funnel simple chenille wrapping.
Con embudo barnizado y envolvimiento sencillo de chenilla.

80/300/3	2	1
31	27	24 cm

Mit poliertem Trichter, Baumwollquaste, Chenillen- und Bortenumwicklung.
With polished funnel, cotton tassel, chenille and border wrapping.
Con embudo pulido, borla de algodon, envolvimiento de chenilla y galon.

80/304	305	329	330
28,5	31,5	36	40,5 cm

Mit poliertem Trichter, Chenillenschnüre und Goldumwicklung, Umhangschnur und Seidenquaste.
With polished funnel, chenille string and gold wrapping, hanging string and silk tassel.
Con embudo pulido, cuerdas chenilla y envolvimiento de oro, cuerdo de colgar y borla de seda.

80/355	353	352	351	311	302
40	32,5	31	26 5	22	19 5 cm

Mit poliertem Trichter, beste Ausführung, in Anbindung mit Seidenband und Seidenquaste.
With polished funnel, best work, with binding with silk ribbon and silk tassel.
Con embudo pulido, trabajo mejor a union concinta de seda y borla de seda.

80/374	372	371	370	369	368
40,5	36	31,5	27	23 5	22 cm

Mit poliertem Trichter, Anbindung in Grün mit Gold, Umhangschnur mit Seidenquaste.
With polished funnel, binding in green and gold, hanging string and silk tassel.
Embudo pulido, en union en verde cuerda de colcar y borla de seda.

80/606	605	604	603
36	31	25	20,5 cm

Mit poliertem Trichter, Anbindung in Rot, mit gleichfarbiger Vollquaste.
With polished tube, red cord and woolen banderol of same colour.
Embudo lustrado, con cordel rojo y borla de lana del mismo color.

80/103	102	101
31,5	27,5	23 cm

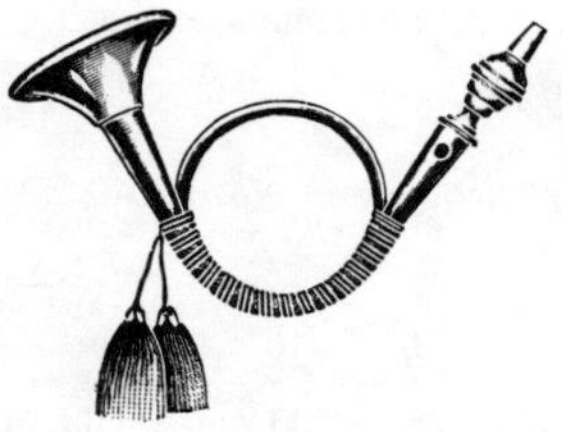

80/321

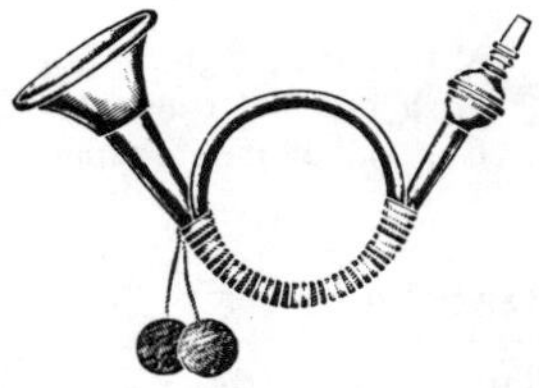

80/488

80/373

Mit poliertem Trichter, Beinmundstück, Chenillen- und Goldumwicklung, mit Seidenquaste.
With polished funnel, bone bit, chenille and gold wrapping with silk tassel.
Embudo polido, boca de hueso envolvimiento de chenilia y oro con borla de sela.

80/488	487	486	484	485
28	24	20	18	18 cm

Mit poliertem Trichter, beste Ausführung, in Umwicklung mit Seidenband und Seidenquaste.
With polished funnel, finest work wrapped with silk ribben and silk tassel.
Embudo pulido, trabajo mejor, envolvimiento de cinta de seda y borla.

80/376	375	373
31	29	25 cm

Mit poliertem Trichter, Chenillenschnur-Umwicklung, mit Baumwollquaste.
With polished funnel, chenille string wrapping with cotton tassel.
Embudo pulido, chenilla y envolvimiento de cuerda con borla de algodon.

80/321	320	318	317	316
36	32	28	26	23 cm

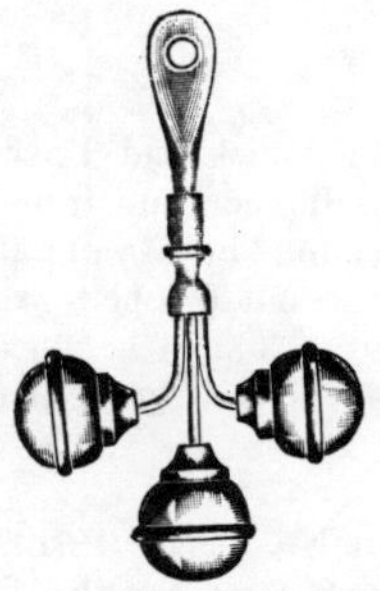

80/513

80/516

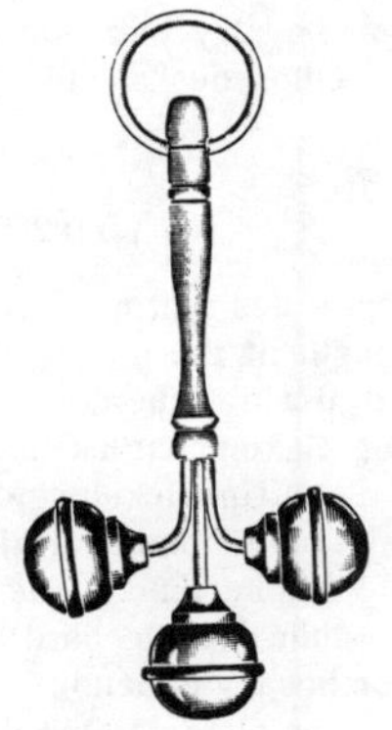

80/514

80/519

Schlottern aus Zelluloid, mit Beingriff und vernickelten Messingglocken, in Stückkartons.
Celluloid-rattles with bone handle and nickeled brass bells, each in a box.
Sonajeros de celuloid, mango de hueso con campanillas de laton niqueladas, en cajitas de 1 pieza.

Hörner. — Horns. — Cuernos.

Nr. **159**/520

Nr. **159**/420/6	7	**159**/520/7	8	9	10	11	12	13	14	
Länge des Horns: 11	13	14	16	17	20	25	29	31	34	inkl. Mundstück in cm.
Length of the horn:										incl. mouthpiece in cm.
Largura del cuerno:										incluyendo el bocal, expresada in centímetros.

Mit Zinkmundstück, gezackt. Nr. 159/420/6 und 7 Harmonikastimme, Nr. 159/520/7 – 14 Doppeltonstimme. Nr. 159/420/6 mit Öse, Nr. 159/420/7 trägt die Umwickelung eines roten Schnürchens, Nr. 159/520/7 und 8 die Umwickelung einer Chenille-Schnur, Nr. 159/520/9—14 die Umwickelung einer Chenille-Schnur mit anhängenden Seidenquasten.

With mouthpiece of cinc, teethed. Nr. 159/420/6 and 7 harmonica tune, Nr. 159/520/7 — 14 double tune, Nr. 159/420/6 with eye, Nr. 150/420/7 carries the winding of a red thin coard, Nr. 159/520/7 und 8 is wound round with a chenille coard, Nr. 159/520/9 — 14 the winding round of a chenille coard with suspended silk troddle.

Con bocal de zinc acuchillado. Los Nr. 159/420/6 y 7 con alma de harmonica, los Nr. 159/420/7 – 14 con alma de tuno doble, el Nr. 159/420/6 con corcheta, el Nr. 159/420/7 guarnecido con un cordoncillo rojo, los Nr. 159/520/7 y 8 guarnecidos con un cordoncillo de “chenille”, los Nr. 159/520/9—14 guarnecidos con un cordoncillo de “chenille” adornado con pendientes borlillas de seda.

Nr. **159**/100/200

	Nr. **159**/100/3	4	5	6	7	
Länge des Horns:	15	17	19	22	25 cm	inkl. Mundstück
Length of the horn:						incl. mouthpiece
Largura del cuerno:						incluyendo el bocal

Mit Hornmundstück und Zinktrichter. Die Umwickelung ist Chenille-Schnur.
With mouthpiece of horn and trumpet of zinc. For winding round a chenille cord is taken.
Con bocal de cuerno y pabellón de cinc, guarnecidos con un cordoncillo de “chenille”.

	Nr. **159**/200/3	4	5	6	7	
Länge des Horns:	15	17	20	22	25 cm	inkl. Mundstück und Trichter.
Length of the horn:						incl. mouthpiece and trumpet.
Largura del cuerno:						incluyendo el bocal y el pabellón.

Mit vermessingtem Trichter wie Nr. 159/100.
With brassed trumpet as in Nr. 159/100.
Con pabellones chapados de latón, lo mismo que el No. 159/100.

Nr. **159**/700

	Nr. **159**/700/3	5	6	6½	7	8	9	10	
Länge des Horns:	13	14	17	19	21	23	28	33 cm	inkl. Mundstück.
Length of the horn:									incl. mouthpiece.
Largura del cuerno:									incluyendo el bocal.

Mit Hornmundstück, Chenilleschnur, Nr. 159/700/6—10 mit anhängender Seidenquaste.
With mouthpiece of horn, chenille cord, Nr. 159/700/6—10 with suspended silk troddle.
Con bocal de cuerno y cordoncillo de “chenille”, los No. 159/700/6—10 también con pendientes borlillas de seda.

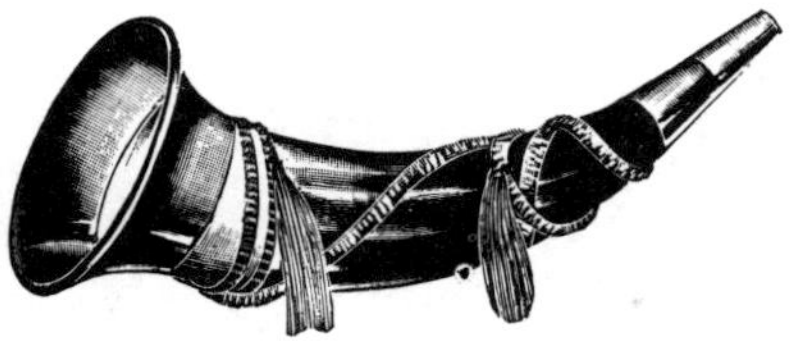

Nr. **159**/80

	Nr. **159**/80/1	2	3	4	5	
Länge des Horns:	15	17	19	21	25 cm	inkl. Mundstück und Trichter.
Length of the horn:						incl. mouthpiece and trumpet.
Largura del cuerno:						incluyendo el bocal y el pabellón.

Mit vermessingtem Mundstück, Trichter und doppeltöniger Holzstimme. Die Umwicklung besteht aus Chenilleschnur.
With brassed mouthpiece, trumpet and double tuned wooden voice. The winding round consists of a chenille cord.
Con bocal y pabellón chapados de latón, provistos de alma de madera de tono doble, guarnecidos de cordoncillos de “chenille”.

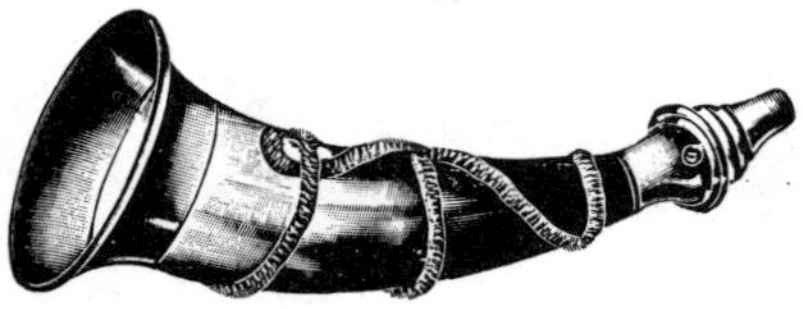

Nr. **159**/366

	Nr. **159**/266/3	**159**/366/1	3	4	4½	5	6	
Länge des Horns:	15	13	15	18	20	22	26 cm	inkl. Mundstück und Trichter.
Length of the horn:								incl. mouthpiece and trumpet.
Largura del cuerno:								incluyendo el bocal y el pabellón.

Mit Zinkmundstück und Zinktrichter, Nr. 159/266/3 mit Harmonikastimme, die Nr. 366/1—6 mit Doppeltonstimme. Die Umwickelung der Nr. 266/3—366/6 besteht aus rotem Schnürchen, die der Nr. 159/366/3 aus Chenilleschnur.

With mouthpiece of zink and trumpet of zink, Nr. 266/3 with harmonica tune, the siries 366/1 till 366/6 with double tune. The winding round of Nr. 266/3—366/1 consists of a thin red cord, that of Nr. 366/3—6 of a thin chenille cord.

Con bocal y pabellón hechos de cinc. El No. 159/266/3 con alma de armónica, las serins de No. 159/266/1—159/366/6 con alma de tono doble, los No. 159/266/3—159/366/1 guarnecidos con cordoncillos rojos y los No. 159/366/3—6 con cordoncillos de “chenille”.

Kinder-Klappwagen. — Childrens folding cars. — Coches plegables para niños.

23/2438
Gewicht — weight — peso 9,5 kg

23/2448½ S
Gewicht — weight — peso 11 kg

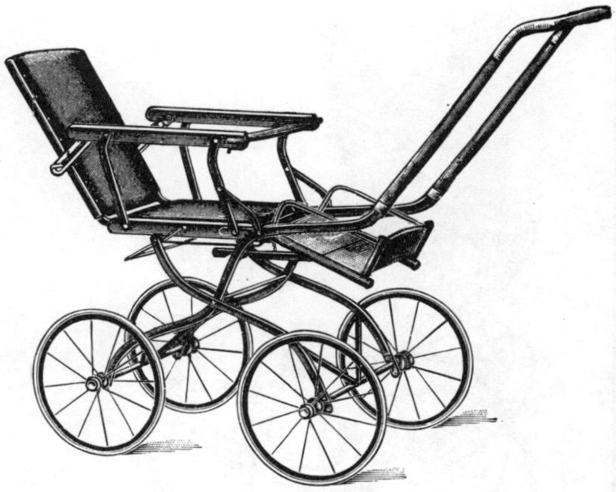

23/2448½
Gewicht — weight — peso 10 kg

Nr. **23**/2438, 2448½, 2448½ S — Mit Gummirädern, Nickelgriff, Holz gebeizt, Metallteile emailliert.
With rubber wheels, nickel handles, wood carroded, metal parts enamelled.
Con ruedas de cautchouc, con puños de niquel, las piezas de madera trabajadas con mordiente, las piezas de metal esmaltadas.

23/2469½ D
Gewicht — weight — peso 13 kg

Nr. **23**/2469½ D

Gummiräder, Nickelgriff, doppelter Ledertuchausschlag.

Rubber wheels, nickel handles, double leather cloth lining.

Con ruedas de cautchouc, puños de niquel, con doble guarnición de tela muy dura.

Nr. **23**/2475D

Gummiräder, Nickelgriff, doppelter Ledertuchausschlag, federndes Gestell.

Rubber wheels, nickel handles, double leather cloth lining, elastical frame.

Con ruedas de cautchouc, puños de niquel, con doble guarnición de tela muy dura, bastidor elastico.

23/2475 D
Gewicht — weight — peso 15 kg

23/2473 und 2474
Gewicht — weight — peso 15 kg

Nr. **23**/2473 Vollständig zusammenklappbar, doppelter Ledertuchausschlag, Nickelgriff, Gummiräder, schwarz.

Can be comoletely folded, double leather cloth lining, nickel handle, rubber wheels, black.

Completamente plegable, con dcble guarnición de tela muy dura, puños de niquel con ruedas de cautchouc, negro.

Nr. **23**/2474 Wie Nr. 23/2473, Tangentspeichenräder, Nabe vernickelt.

As Nr. 23/2473, tangent spoke wheels, nave nickeled.

Igual al número 23/2473, pero las ruedas provistas de rayos tangentes y el cubo niquelado.

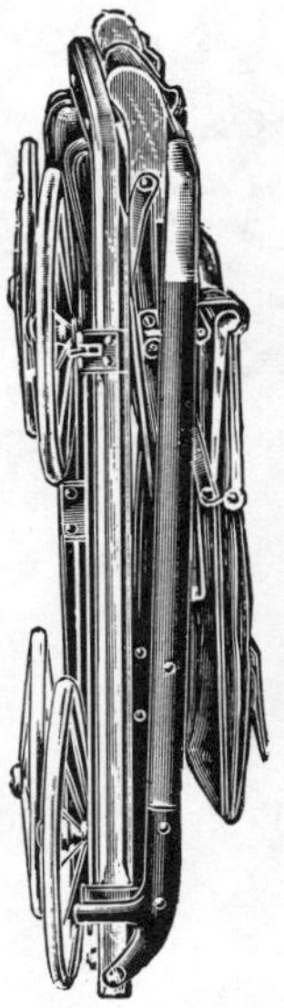

Nr. **23**/2473 und 2474
zusammengeklappt — foldet
plegable

Zierliche Kinderwagen. — Smart Perambulators. — Elegantes coches para niños.

23/2522

23/2539

23/2570

Nr. **23**/2522/2539. Weidenschienenkorb, gelb lackiert, Ledertuchausschlag, Gummiräder, Porzellangriff, Stahlbügelverdeck, Mullvorhänge. Gewicht 20 kg.

Basket of split willows, yellow varnished, leather cloth lining, porcelain handles, steel bow canopy, weight 20 kg.

Con cesta tejida de sauce, embarnizada amarilla, con guarnición de tela muy dura, con ruedas de cautchouc, con mango de porcelana, con cubierta que tiene refuerzos por varillas de acero, con cortinas de beatilla, peso 20 kg.

Nr. **23**/2570 Rohrkorb, Riemenhängefedergestell, Gummiräder, Porzellangriff, Ledertuchausschlag, Stahlbügelverdeck, Mullvorhänge. Gewicht 20 kg.

Willow basket, suspension spring frame with leather strap, porcelain handles, leather cloth lining, steel bow canopy, curtains, weight 20 kg.

Con cesta de caña, con bastidor de resortes con correas, con ruedas de cautchouc, con mango de porcelana, con guarnición de tela muy dura, con cubierta que tienen refuerzos por varillas de acero, peso 20 kg.

23/2541

23/2553

23/2554

Nr. **23**/2541/2553. Ledertuchausschlag, Gummiräder, Porzellangriff, Stahlbügelverdeck, Mullvorhänge. Gewicht 20 kg.

Leather cloth lining, rubber wheels, porcelain handles, steel bow canopy, curtains. Weight 20 kg.

Con guarnición de tela muy dura, con ruedas que tienen bandaje de caucho, con mango de porcelana, con cubierta que tienen refuerzos por varillas de acero, con cortinas de beatilla, peso 20 kg.

Nr. **23**/2554. Gewölbte Seitenteile, Riemenhängefedergestell, Gummiräder, Porzellangriff, Ledertuchpolsterung, gefüttertes Verdeck ohne Garnierung, Fußkasten verdeckt. Gewicht 23 kg.

Arshed side walls, suspension spring frames with leather strap, rubber wheels, porcelain handles, leather cloth lining, lined canopy without ornamenting, covered foot box, weight 23 kg.

Con liezas laterales encorvadas, con bastidor de resortes con correas, con ruedas de cautchouc, con mango de porcelana, con almohadilla de tela muy dura, con cubierta aforrada sin guarnición, con caja no visible para los pies, peso 23 kg.

Kinderwagen. — Perambulators. — Coches para niños.

23/5004

23/668

23/1448 V

Nr. **23**/5004 Schneckengestell, Gummiräder, Porzellangriff, Stoffvorhänge.
Worm frame, rubber wheels, porcelan handles, cloth curtains.
Con bastidor en formade caracol, con ruedas de cautchouc, con mango de porcelana, con cortinas de género
Gewicht, weight, peso 22 kg.

Nr. **23**/668 Hängegestell, Gummiräder, Porzellangriff, Mullvorhänge.
Suspension frame, rubber wheels, porcelan handles, curtains.
Con bastidor colgado, con ruedas de cautchouc, con mango de porcelana, con cortinas de beatilla.
Gewicht, weight, peso 25 kg.

Nr. **23**/1448 V Riemenfedergestell, Gummiräder, Porzellangriff, Spitzenvolant.
Spring frame with leather strap, rubber wheels, porcelan handles, lace volant.
Con bastidor de resortes con correas, con ruedas de cautchouc, con mango de porcelana, con orladura de puntillas.
Gewicht, weight, peso 29 kg.

23/652

23/656

Nr. **23**/652 Mit Seitenauflagen.
With edge strengthening.
Con aplicación lateral.

Nr. **23**/656 Ganz gewölbte Seitenteile.
Wholy arched outer walls.
Con piezas laterales completamente encorvadas.

Feinste Wagen, Riemenfedergestell, Ledertuchpolster, gefüttertes Stahlbügelverdeck, Porzellangriff, Fußkasten verdeckt.
Best car, spring frame with leather strap, leather cloth lining, lined steel bow conopy, porcelan handles, covered foot box.
Coches elegantisimas, con bastidor de resorte con correas, con almohadillas de tela muy dura, con cubierta aforada que tienen refuerzos por varillas de acero, con mango de porcelana, la caja para los pies no visible.

Gewicht, weight, peso 29 kg.

Kinderwagen. — Perambulators. — Coches para niños.

23/765

23/714

23/2615 H

Nr. **23**/765 Gewicht 19 kg. Weidenkorb gelb lackiert, Gestell schwarz emailliert, Stahlräder, Ledertuchausschlag, Stoffvorhänge.

Weight 19 kg. Willow basket yellow varnished, frame black enamelled, steel wheels, leather cloth lining, cloth curtains.

Peso 19 kg. Con cesta de sauce, embarnizada amarilla, el bastidor esmaltado negro, con ruedas de acero, con guarnición de tela muy dura, con cortinas de género.

Nr. **23**/714 u. 2615 Gewicht 19 kg. Weidenschienenkorb gelb lackiert, Stahlräder, Gestell schwarz emailliert, Ledertuchausschlag, Porzellangriffe am Dach, Stoffvorhänge.

Weight 19 kg. Basket of split willows yellow varnished, frame black enamelled, leather cloth lining, porcelan handles on the canopy, cloth curtains.

Peso 19 kg. Con cesta tejida de sauce embarnizada amarilla, con ruedas de acero, el bastidor esmaltado negro, con guarnición de tela muy dura, con mangos de porcelana en el tejado, con cortinas de género.

23/627 K

23/2674 K

23/635 LR

Nr. **23**/627 K u. 2674 K Gewicht 20 kg. Weidenschienenkorb gelb lackiert, Hängefedergestell, Gummiräder, Porzellangriff, Stahlbügelverdeck, Mullvorhänge.

Weight 20 kg. Basket of split willows yellow varnished, suspension spring frame, rubber wheels, porcelan handles, steel bow canopy, curtains.

Peso 20 kg. Con cesta tejida de sauce embarnizada amarilla, con bastidor de resortes colgados, con ruedas de cautchouc,con mango de porcelana, con cubierta que tienen refuerzos porvarillas de acero, con cortinas de beatilla.

Nr. **23**/635LR Gewicht 25 kg. Rohrkorb naturlackiert, geflochtener Wulstrand, Riemenfedergestell, Gummiräder, Porzellangriff, Mullvorhänge, Stahlbügelverdeck.

Weight 25 kg. Willow basket, entwined thickened edges, spring frame with leather strap, rubber wheels, porcelan handles, curtains, steel bow canopy.

Peso 25 kg. Con cesta de caña embarnizada en color natural, y que tiene un bord tejido en forma de rodete, con bastidor de resorte con correas, con ruedas que tienen bandaje de caucho, con mango de porcelana, con cortinas de beatilla, con cubierta que tiene refuerzos por varillas de acero.

Puppenwagen.
Dolls Perambulator. — Coches para muñecas.

23/997 B

23/1078

Nr. **23**/997 B
„ **23**/1078
Eisenräder, Stoffvorhang.
Iron wheels, cloth curtains.
Con reudas de hierro, con cortinas de género.

23/997 B	**23**/1078 B	C	D	
45	45	52	58	cm Länge, length, de largo
1,8	2	2,4	2,7	kg Gewicht, weight, de peso

Nr. **23**/1307 Stoffausschlag, Eisenräder, Stoffvorhang.
Cloth lining, iron wheels, cloth curtains.
Con guarnicion de género, con ruedas de hierro, con cortinas de género.

½	A	B	C	
42	47	53	60	cm Länge, length, de largo
2,1	2,5	3,2	3,8	kg Gewicht, weight, de peso

23/1307

23/1707 S

Nr. **23**/1707 S Bogengestell, Stoffausschlag, Stoffvorhang, Eisenräder.
Arched frame, cloth lining, cloth curtains, iron wheels.
Con bastidor en forma de arco, con guarnicíon de género, con cortinas de género, con ruedas de hierro.

A	B	C	
45	50	55	cm Länge, length, de largo
3,2	4,3	4,8	kg Gewicht, weight, de peso

Nr. **23**/2712 Bogengestell emailliert, Metallräder, Stoffausschlag.
Enamelled arched frame, metal wheels, cloth lining.
Con bastidor en forma de arco, esmaltado, con ruedas de metal, con guarnición de tela muy dura.

B	C	
50	55	cm Länge, length, de largo
4,3	5	kg Gewicht, weight, de peso

23/2712

23/2737 III

Nr. **23**/2737 III Hängegestell, emailliert, Metallräder, Ledertuchausschlag.
Enamelled suspension frame, metal wheels, leather cloth lining.
Con bastidor colgado, esmaltado, con ruedas de metal, con guarnición de tela muy dura.

C	D	
55	60	cm Länge, length, de largo
5	5,5	kg Gewicht, weight, de peso

Nr. **23**/1715 Bogengestell, Eisenräder, Stoffausschlag.
Arched frame, iron wheels, cloth lining.
Con bastidor en forma de arco, con ruedas de hierro, con guarnición de género.

A	B	C	
45	50	55	cm Länge, length, de largo
3,5	4	4,5	kg Gewicht, weight, de peso

23/1715

23/2392

Nr. **23**/2392 Bogengestell, Metallräder, Stoffausschlag.
Arched frame, metal wheels, cloth lining.
Con bastidor en forma de arco, con ruedas de metal, con guarnición de género.

B	C	D	
50	55	60	cm Länge, length, de largo
4	4,5	5	kg Gewicht, weight, de peso

Nr. **23**/2393 III Hängegestell, emailliert, Metallräder, Ledertuchausschlag.
Enamelled suspension frame, metal wheels, leather cloth lining.
Con bastidor colgado, esmaltado, con ruedas de metal, con guarnición de tela muy dura.

C	D	
55	60	cm Länge, length, de largo
4,5	5	kg Gewicht, weight, de peso

23/2393 III

23/2753

Nr. **23**/2753 Riemenfedergestell, Gummiräder, Porzellangriff, Stahlbügelklappverdeck gefüttert, Ledertuchpolster, Fußkasten verdeckt.
Spring frame with leather belt, rubber cloth lining, porcelain handles, steel bow folding canopy lined, leather cloth polstering, covered foot box.
Con batidor de resorte con correas, con ruedas que tienen bandaje de caucho, con mango de porcelana, con cubierta que tienen refuerzos por varillas de acero y está aforrado, con almohadillas de tela muy dura, la caja para los pies no visible.

D	E	
60	70	cm Länge, length, de largo
8	11	kg Gewicht, weight, de peso

23/3157 B

23/3164 B

23/354 B

23/3154 B

23/3033 B

23/3079

Kindergarnituren aus Hartholz, hell lackiert, mit Klosett.
Baby chairs of hard wood, light varnished, with lavatory.
Sillas para bebés y para niños, hechas de madera dura, embarnizadas en color claro, con bacín.

	Nr. **23**/3157 B	**23**/3164 B	**23**/354 B	**23**/3154 B	**23**/3033 B
Gewicht Weight Peso	6	6,5	7	8,5	8 kg

Nr. **23**/3079, **23**/3111.

Oberteil gepolstert, vernickelte Gummiräder, mit Klosett.
Upper part polstered, nickeled rubber wheels, with lavatory.
La parte superior colchonada, ruedas niqueladas de cautchouc, con bacín.

Nr. **23**/3079 Gewicht, weight, peso 9 kg. Nr. **23**/3111 Gewicht, weight, peso 10 kg.

23/3111

23/110

Nr. **23**/110, **23**/108.

Wiegenschaukel, Hartholz, hell lackiert.
Rocking chair, hard wood, light varnished.
Coonmecedor de madera dura, en barnizadas en color claro.

Nr. **23**/110 Gewicht, weight, peso 4 kg.
„ **23**/108 „ „ „ 8,5 „

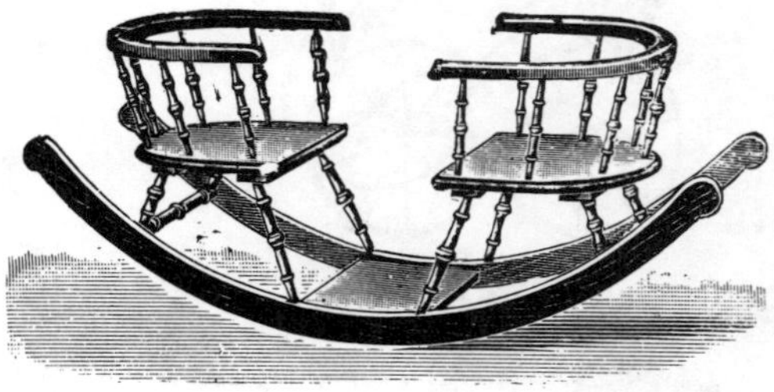

23/108

23/466

23/345 B

23/948

Kinderpult, verstellbar, Gewicht 23 kg, aus Hartholz, mattbraun oder Natureiche.

Children desk, adjustable, weight 23 kg, of hard wood, dead brown or natural oak.

Pupitre para niños, hecho de madera dura, en los colores moreno mate o roble natural, regulable, de 23 kg de peso.

Kinderlaufgitter aus Hartholz, hell lackiert, Gewicht 8 kg.

Square railing for teaching children to walk, of hard wood, light varnished, weight 8 kg.

Que están jaula para los chiquillos apreniendo a correr, hecha de madera dura, embarnizada en color claro, tiene 8 kg de peso.

Kinderroller aus Hartholz, hell lackiert, Räder mit Messinglager und Eisenreif, Gewicht 2 kg.

Children roller of hard wood, light varnished, brass bearing and iron tyres, weight 8 kg.

Tablero pequeno con rodillos y guia para ninos, hecho de madera dura, embarnizado en color claro, los rodillos o sea las ruedecitas con cojinetes de laton y cercos de hierro, tiene 2 kg de peso.

Straßenrenner. — Street Runners. — Bicicletas para carreras sobre carreteras.

23/966

Mit Kurbelantrieb, Holz hell lackiert.

With winch drive, wood light varnished.

Con accionamiento por manivela, la madera embarnizada en color claro.

Für Knaben von
For boys of
Para muchachos que tienen de

Nr.	Jahren, years, años	Gewicht, weight, peso
Nr. **23**/966	3—7	6,5 kg
„ **23**/967	4 8	8,5 „
„ **23**/967½	5—10	9,5 „
„ **23**/968 A	6—13	11 „

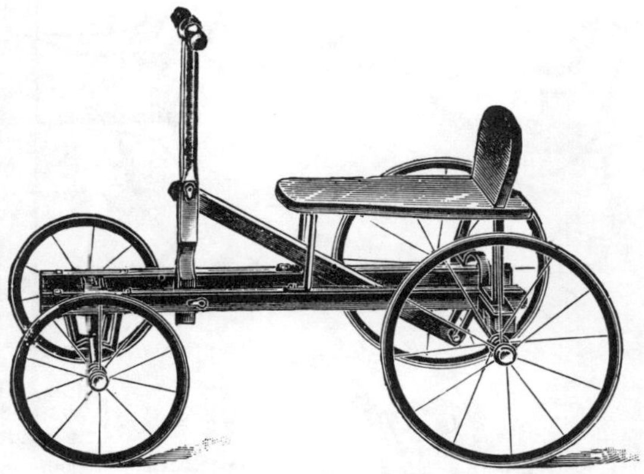

23/967, 967½ und 968 A

Nr. **23**/968 B Wie Nr. 23/968 A, mit 2 Sitzen für 2 Knaben von 6—13 Jahren. Gewicht 15 kg.
As Nr. 23/968 A, with 2 seats for 2 boys of 6—13 years. Weight 15 kg.
Igual al No. 23/968 A, con 2 asientos para 2 muchachos de 6—13 años de edad. Peso 15 kg.

Nr. **23**/962 und 963 A Mit Zahnradgetriebe, hell lackiert. — With tooth wheel drive, light varnished.
Con accionamiento por ruedas dentadas, la madera embarnizada en color claro.

23/962 und 963 A

Nr. **23**/962 Für Knaben von 4—8 Jahren. Gewicht 10 kg.
For boys of 4—8 years. Weight 10 kg.
Para muchachos que tienen de 4—8 años de edad. Peso 10 kg.

Nr. **23**/963 A Für Knaben von 5—10 Jahren, Gewicht 12 kg.
For boys of 5—10 years. Weight 12 kg.
Para muchachos que tienen de 5—10 años de edad. Peso 12 kg.

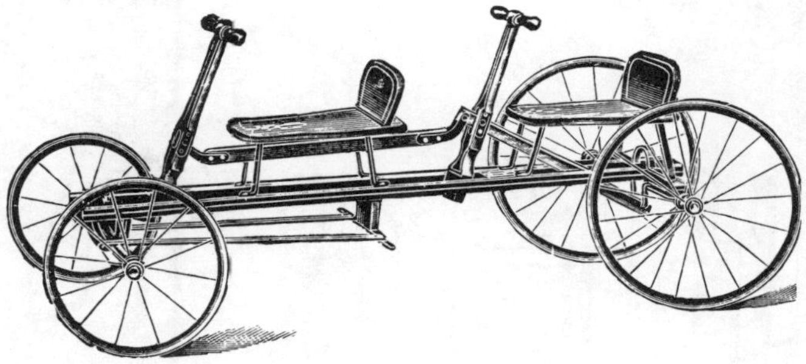

23/968 B

Knabendreiräder. — Boys tricycle. — Tricicletas para muchachos.

23/941

Nr. **23**/941 Mit verstellbarem Federsattel, fein lackiert, 59 cm hoch. Gewicht 8 kg.
With adjustable spring seat, elegantly varnished, 59 cm height. Weight 8 kg.
Con asiento elastico regulable, bien embarnizada, con 59 cm de altura y 8 kg de peso.

Nr. **23**/939 Einfache Art, fein lackiert.
Simple kind, elegantly varnished.
De construcción sencilla, bien embarnizada.

Nr. **23**/939 A Höhe 65 cm. Gewicht 7 kg.
Height 65 cm. Weight 7 kg.
Con 65 cm de altura y 7 kg de peso.

Nr. **23**/939 B Höhe 71 cm. Gewicht 7,5 kg.
Height 71 cm. Weight 7,5 kg.
Con 71 cm. de altura y 7,5 kg de peso.

Nr. **23**/939 C Höhe 81 cm. Gewicht 8 kg.
Height 81 cm. Weight 8 kg.
Con 81 cm de altura y 8 kg de peso.

23/939

Nr. **23**/950—952 Beste Ausführung, schwarz emailliert, Feder und Sattel verstellbar.
Best execution, black enamelled, spring and seat adjustable.
De la mejor elaboración, esmaltadas negras, los resortes y los asientos son regulables.

Nr. **23**/950 Mit Stahlrädern. — With steel wheels. — Con ruedas de acero.

Nr. **23**/951 Mit Gummirädern. — With rubber wheels. — Con ruedas de cautchouc.

Nr. **23**/952 Mit Tangentspeichenrädern, Kugellagerpedalen, halb vernickelt.

Größe	A	B	C
Für Beinlänge cm	45—52	52—57	58—62
Gewicht	10	11	13 kg

Nr. **23**/952 With tangent spoke wheels, ball bearing pedals, half nickeled.

Size	A	B	C
For length of legs cm	45—52	52—57	58—62
Weight	10	11	13 kg

No. **23**/952 Los hay en los tamaños y para las larguras de los piernas en centímetros, como sigue:

Tamaño	A	B	C
cm de largura	45—52	52—57	58—62
kg de peso	10	11	13 kg

23/950—952

Nr. **33**/922 Mit Fellpferd, Metallteile fein lackiert.
With horse covered with hide, metal parts, elegantly varnished.
Con caballo cubierto de pelliza, las piezas de metal, bien embarnizadas.

Nr. **23**/922 A Höhe 50 cm, Gewicht 11 kg.
Height 50 cm, weight 11 kg.
Con 50 cm de altura y 11 kg de peso.

Nr. **23**/922 B Höhe 55 cm, Gewicht 13 kg.
Height 50 cm, weight 13 kg.
Con 55 cm de altura y 13 kg de peso.

23/922

23/1876

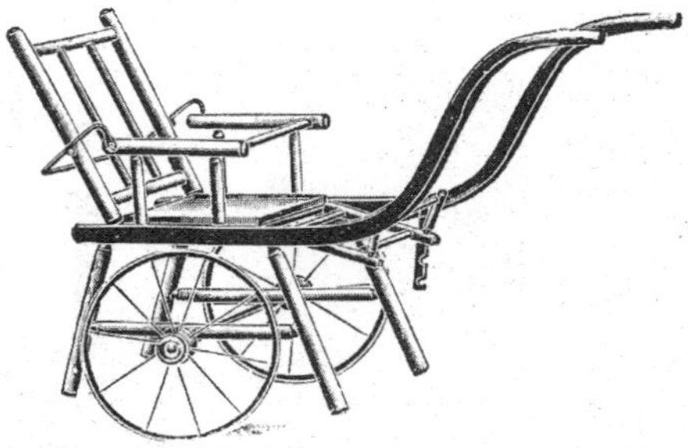

23/2812

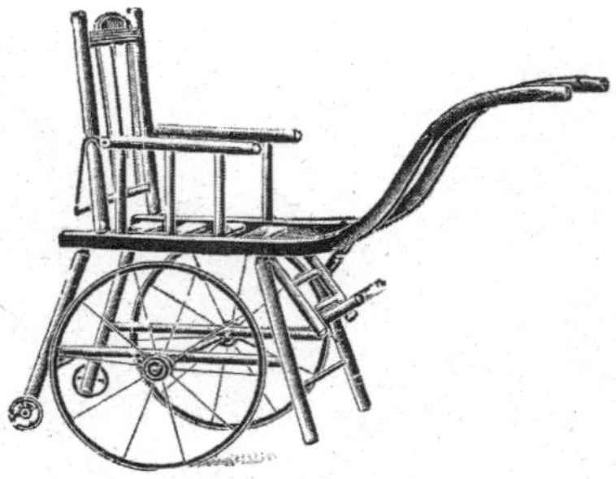

23/2811

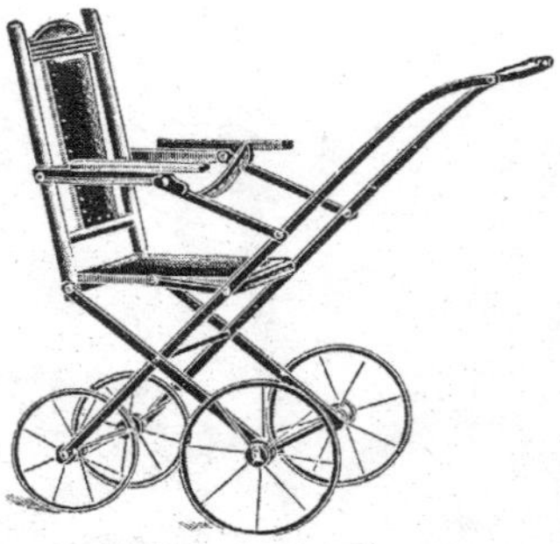

23/1914

Puppensportwagen. — Dolls Go Carts. — Coches de deporte para muñecas.

23/1919

Nr.		Gewicht — Weight — Peso
23/1876	Holz, farbig lackiert. Wood, coloured varnished. La madera embarnizada en colores diferentes.	1,5 Kg
„ **23**/2812		1,8 „
„ **23**/2811		2,5 „
„ **23**/1914	Zusammenklappbar, grün lackiert. Foldable, green varnished. Plegable, embarnizado verde.	2,4 „
„ **23**/1919	Zusammenklappbar, hell lackiert. Foldable, light varnished. Plegable, embarnizado en color claro.	4,0 „
„ **23**/1961½	Zusammenklappbar, Ledertuchausschlag, Stahlbügelverdeck, Nickelgriff. Foldable, leather lining, steel bow canopy, nickel handles. Plegable, con guarnición de tela muy dura, con cubierta que tiene refuerzos por varillas de acero, con mango de niquel.	6,0 „

23/1961½

„Lina"

23/4076

23/442

Puppenmöbel, Holz, hell lackiert.
Dolls Furnitures, wood, light varnished.
Muebles para muñecas, la madera embarnizada en color blanco.

Garnitur Set — Juego	Tischhöhe / Height of the table Altura de la mesa	Gewicht / Weight Peso
Lina A	26 cm	3 kg
Lina B	34 „	4 „

Nr.	Sitzhöhe / Height of the seat Altura del asiento	
23/4076	—	2 kg
23/ 442 A	15 cm	0,5 „
23/ 442 B	20 „	1 „

Kindermöbel. — Children Furnitures. — Muebles pàra niños.

23/304 B

23/3700 B

23/438½ B

23/292 B

23/392½ B

23/3649 B

Nr.		Gewicht / Weight Peso
23/ 304 B	Holz, hell lackiert. — Wood light varnished. La madera embarnizada en color blanco.	2,5 kg
23/3700 B		3,8 „
23/ 438½ B		5,7 „
23/ 292 B		1,2 „
23/ 392½ B	Holz, hell lackiert, mit Klosett. — Wood light varnished, lavatory. — La madera embarnizada en color claro, con orinal.	1,8 „
23/3649 B		3,0 „

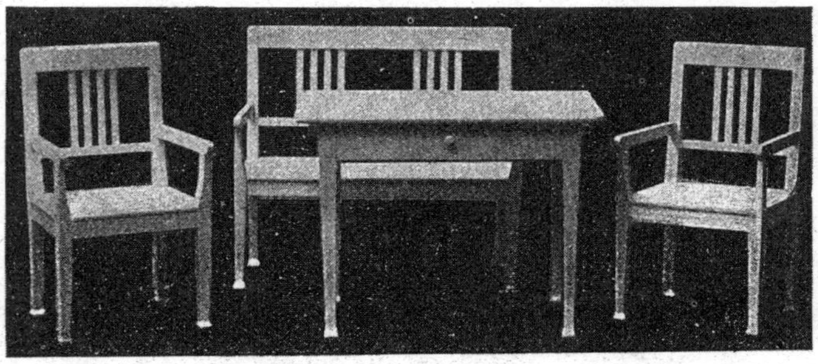

Garnitur — Set — Juego "LOTTE".

Weiß lackiert oder natureichen. — White varnished or natural oak.
Embarnizado en colores blanco ó roble natural.
Gewicht — Weight — Peso: 19,5 kg.

Garnitur — Set — Juego "ELSE".

Hell oder weiß lackiert. — Light or white varnished.
Embarnizado en colores claro ó blanco.
Gewicht — Weight — Peso: 19,5 kg.

Blechspielwaren mit Schwungradantrieb. — Patent Friction toys. — Juguetes de lata con volante.

2011/4/6 P = 1/2 Dtz.
2011/4/1 P = 1/12 „

2011/1 P = 1 Stck.
Tourenwagen mit Bremse, vor- und rückwärts fahrend; wird durch Andrehen der Kurbel in Bewegung gesetzt. — **Touring car with brake,** reversing; to be set in motion by turning the crank. — **Automóvil con freno,** marchando hacia adelante y hacia atras; se le pone en marcha haciendo dar vueltas a la manivela.

2011/3/6 P = 1/2 Dtz.
2011/3/1 P = 1/12 „

2011/6/6 P = 1/2 Dtz.
2011/6/1 P = 1/12 „

2011/5/12 P = 1 Dtz.
2011/5/1 P = 1/12 „
Maus und Ente mit Rollerantrieb.
Mouse and duck with friction movement.
Raton y pato con movimiento con volante.

2011/2 P = 1 Stck.
Limousine mit Bremse. Konstruktion wie Nr. 2011/1.
Limousine Car with brake. Construction as Nr. 2011/1.
Limousine con frene. Construcción como No. 2011/1.

2011/10/3 P = 1/4 Dtz.
2011/10/1 P = 1/12 „

2011/53
Nr. **2011**/53, 59 Mit 1 — 16 Wagen.
With 1 — 16 carriages.
Con 1 — 16 vagónes.

2011/42
Nr. **2011**/42, 45 Mit 1 — 14 Wagen.
With 1 — 14 carriages.
Con 1 — 14 vagónes.

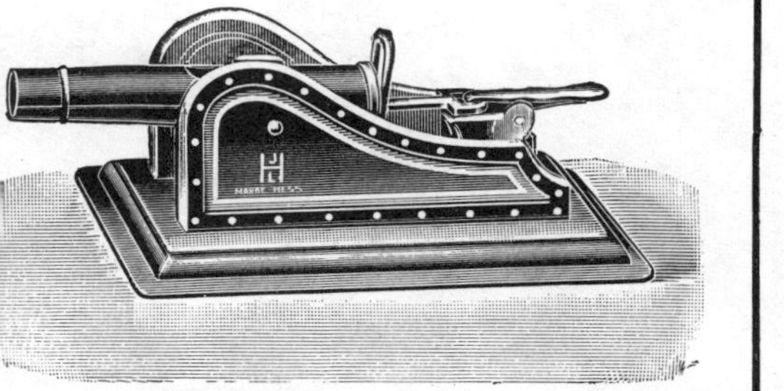

2011/9/3 P = 1/4 Dtz.
2011/9/1 P = 1/12 „
Kanonen zum Erbsenschießen.
Cannons for shooting with peas.
Canones para tirar con balines.

2011/59
Nr. **2011**/42, 45, 53, 59. Ohne Uhrwerk. — Without clockwork. — Sin mecanismo de reloj.

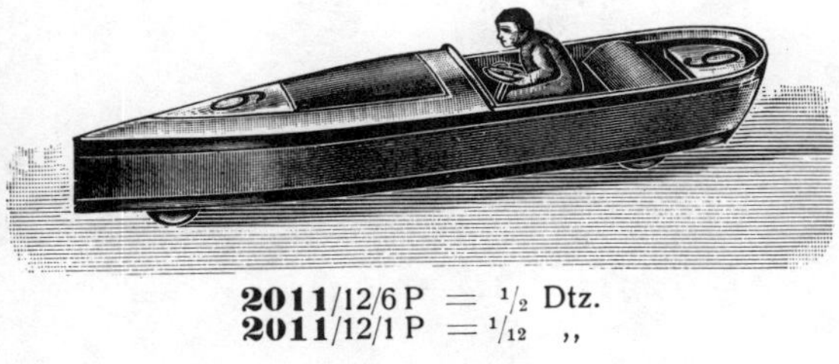

2011/12/6 P = 1/2 Dtz.
2011/12/1 P = 1/12 „

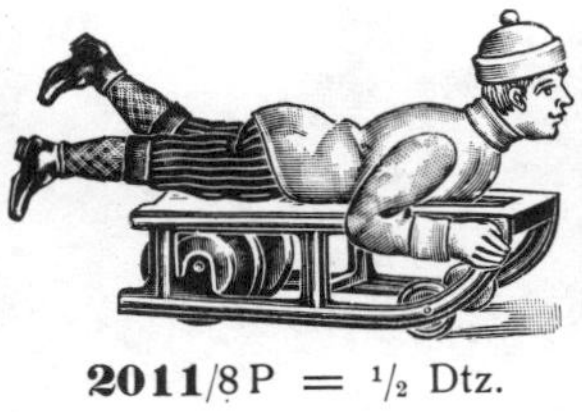

2011/8 P = 1/2 Dtz.

2011/66 Mit Uhrwerk. — With clockwork. — Con mecanismo.

2011/45

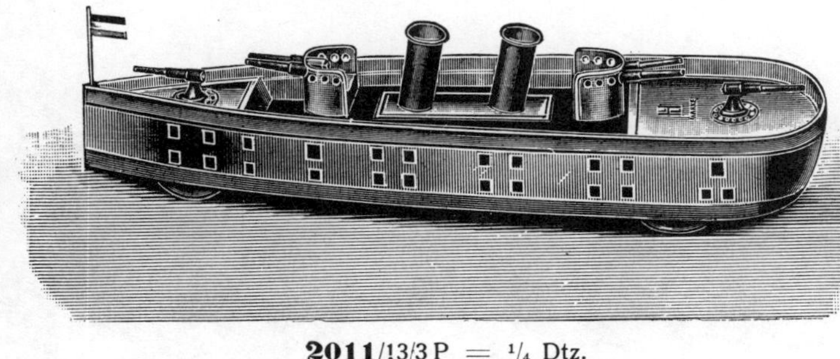

2011/13/3 P = 1/4 Dtz.
2011/13/1 P = 1/12 „

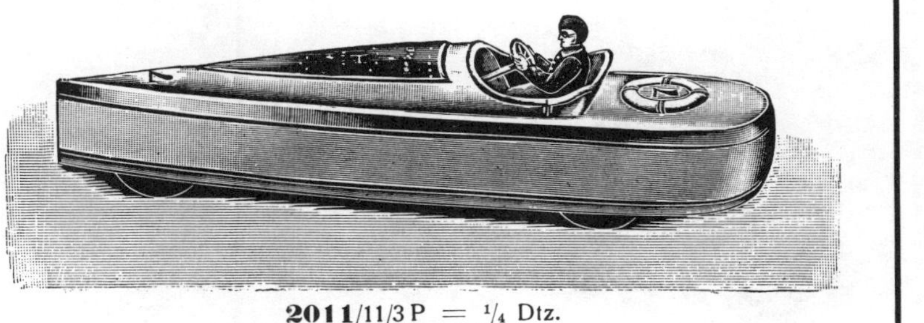

2011/11/3 P = 1/4 Dtz.
2011/11/1 P = 1/12 „

P = Verpackung. — Packing. — Embaque.

Dynamobile und Modelle. — Dynamobils and models. — Dynamóviles y modelos.

2011/31 P. = 1/12 Dtz.

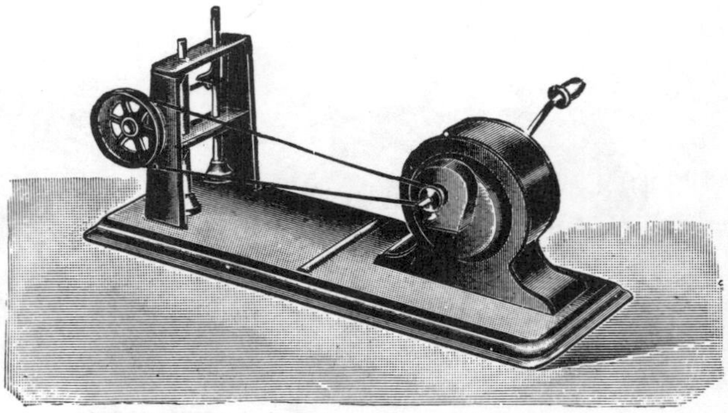

2011/24/3 P. = 1/4 Dtz. **2011**/24/1 P. = 1/12 Dtz.

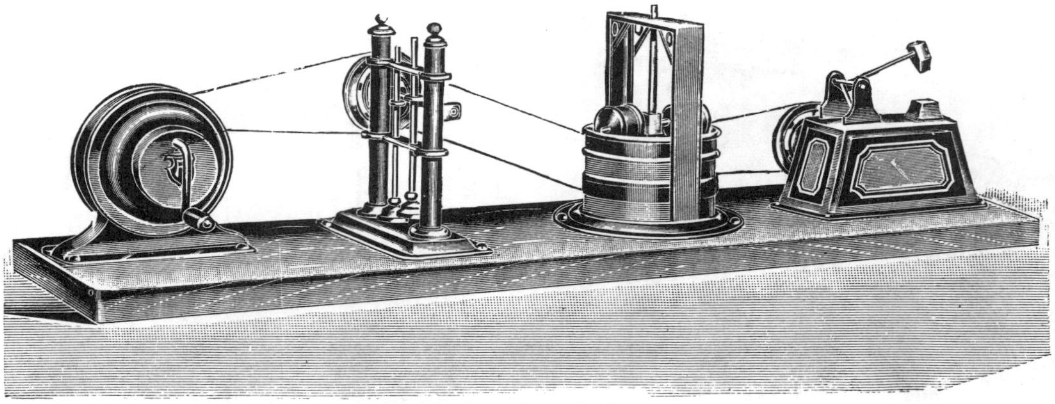

2011/34 P. = 1/12 Dtz.

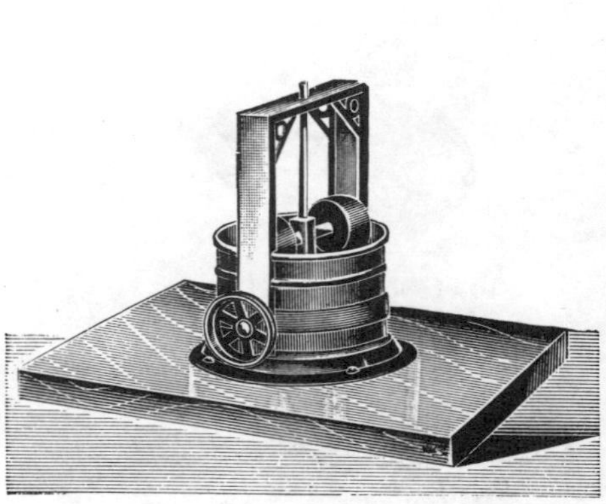

2011/37/3 P. = 1/4 Dtz. **2011**/37/1 P. = 1/12 Dtz.

2011/25/3 P. = 1/4 Dtz. **2011**/25/1 P. = 1/12 Dtz.

2011/40 P. = 1/3 Dtz.

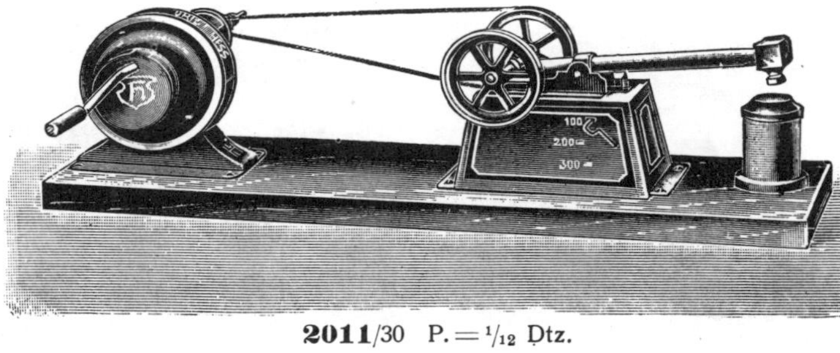

2011/30 P. = 1/12 Dtz.

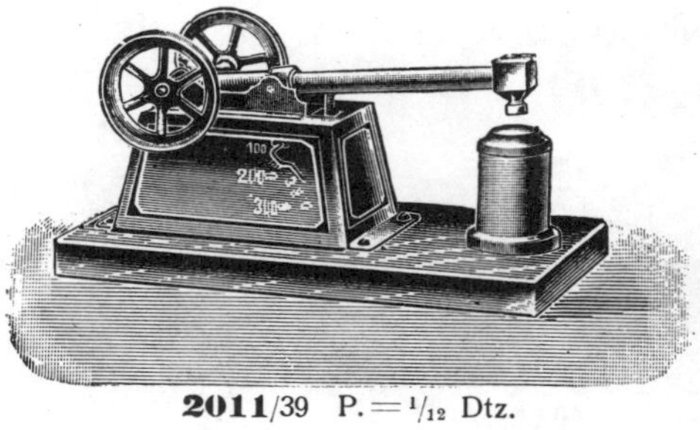

2011/39 P. = 1/12 Dtz.

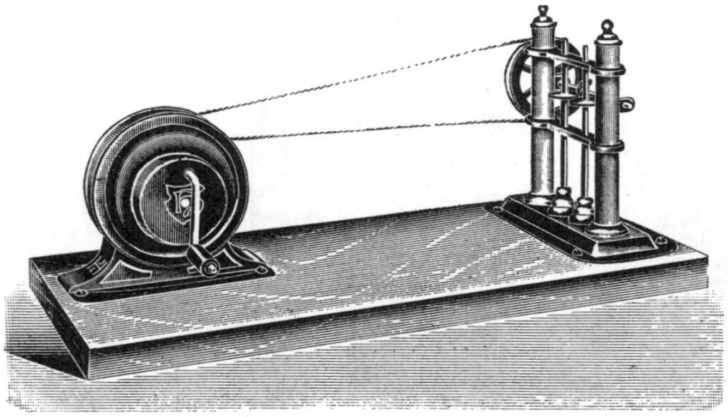

2011/27 P. = 1/12 Dtz.

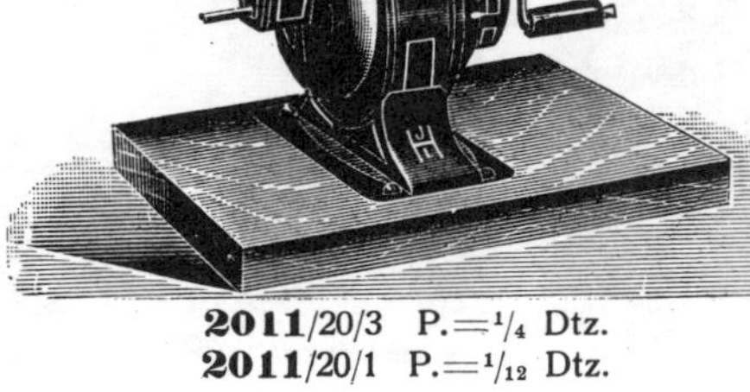

2011/20/3 P. = 1/4 Dtz.
2011/20/1 P. = 1/12 Dtz.

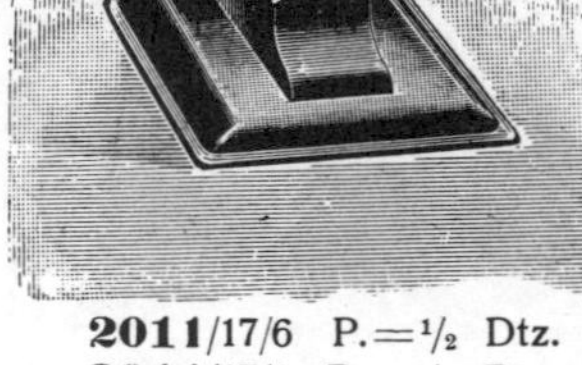

2011/17/6 P. = 1/2 Dtz.
2011/17/1 P. = 1/12 Dtz.

Ia. Emaille-Spielwaren. — Enamelled Toys. — Juguetes esmaltados para niños.

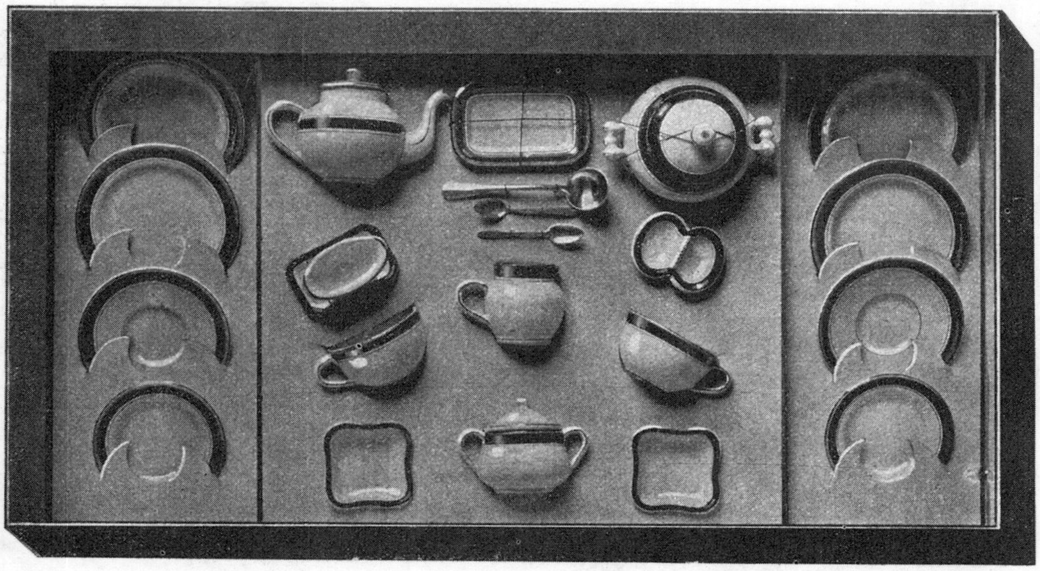

62/704/2/12

Hochelegante Speise-Teeservice, mit teils emaillierten, teils versilberten Geschirren in garnierten Kartons aufgenäht.

Highly elegant Dinner Tea sets, utensils partly enamelled, partly silvered, sewn into decorated cardboard boxes.

Vajilla muy fina, utensilios esmaltados ó plateada, cosidos en elegantes cajitas de cartón.

Nr. **62**/704/2	Mit 22 Teilen, Karton With 22 pieces, cardboard box Con 22 piezas, caja de cartón	69×37 cm
„ **62**/704/4	Mit 35 Teilen, Karton With 35 pieces, cardboard box Con 35 piezas, caja de cartón	82×51 „
„ **62**/705/2	Mit 25 Teilen, Karton With 25 pieces, cardboard box Con 25 piezas, caja de cartón	54×48 „
„ **62**/705/4	Mit 38 Teilen, Karton With 38 pieces, cardboard box Con 38 piezas, caja de cartón	74×63 „

Dekor — decoration — con decorado.

4 Streublumen — scattered flowers — flores esparcidas.

12 Kobalt — white with dark blue bordes (Limoges) — cobalto.

29 Zwiebel — white with Saxon pattern — blanco y „azul Saxe".

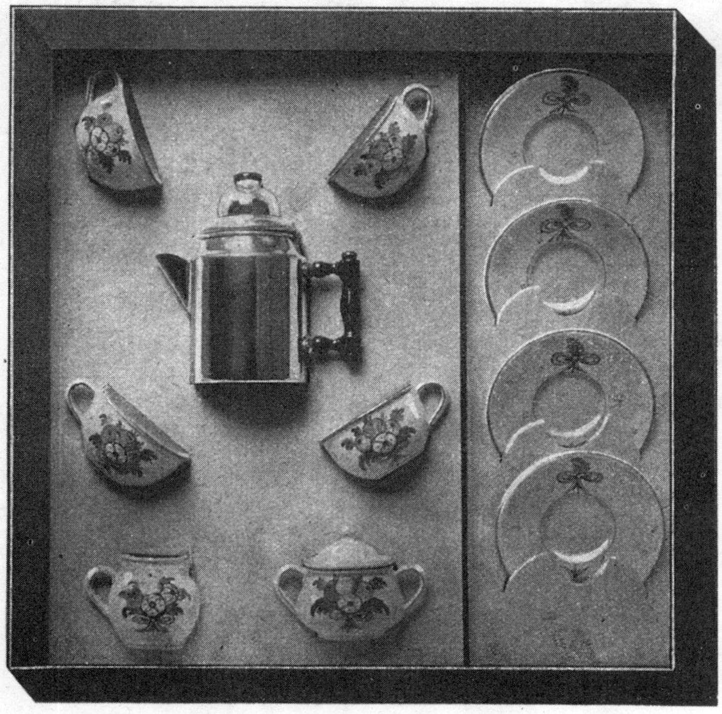

62/33/905/4

Teeservice, blau oder grau emailliert oder dekoriert, in überzogenem Karton eingeschnitten.

Tea sets, blue or grey enamelled or decorated, in lined card board box.

Servicios de té, esmaltados en azul ó gris o con decorados, cartados en cartón forrado.

Nr. **62**/0/2/900/8
Mit 4 Brottellern, 4 Tassen, Karton.
With 4 assietts, 4 cups, cardboard box.
Con 4 plato, 4 tazas, caja de cartón.

Nr. **62**/0/2/900/2
Mit 6 Brottellern, 6 Tassen, Karton.
With 6 assietts, 6 cups, cardboard box.
Con 6 plato, 6 tazas, caja de cartón.

62/12/900/4

Nr. **62**/0/2/4/12/29/900/1½	Mit With Con	2	Tassen Cups Tazas	Karton Cardboard box Caja de cartón	22 ×16 cm
„ **62**/0/2/4/12/29/900/2		2			28 ×21 „
„ **62**/0/2/4/12/29/900/3		3			29,5 ×24 „
„ **62**/0/2/4/12/29/900/4		4			30,5 ×25 „
„ **62**/0/2/4/12/29/900/6		6			38 ×30 „

Kaffeeservice. — Coffee Sets. — Servicios para café.

Nr. **62**/33/905/4	Mit — With — Con	4	Tassen — Cups — Tazas	13	teilig parts piezas	Karton	42 × 42 cm
„ **62**/33/905/6		6		17			47 × 43,5 „
„ **62**/34/905/4		4		13		Cardboard box	42 × 42 „
„ **62**/34/905/6		6		17			47 × 43,5 „
„ **62**/34/905/4		4		13		Caja de cartón	42 × 42 „
„ **62**/34/905/6		6		17			47 × 43,5 „

Baby-Frühstückservice, hellblau emailiert, eingenäht in überzogenem Karton, zum richtigen Gebrauch.
Baby Breakfast Service, light blue enamelled, sewn into lined cardboard box, for actual use.
Servicios de desayuno para bébés, esmaltados en azul claro, cosidos en carton forrado para uso efectivo.

Nr. **62**/2/322	Hellblau Light blue Azul	mit with 2 con	Geschirren Utensils Baterías	Karton Cardboard box Caja de cartón	39 × 24 cm

Nr. **62**/4/322	Streublumen	Scattered flowers	Con flores esparcidas
„ **62**/12/322	Kobalt	Cobalt	Con cobalto
„ **62**/17/322	Rosen	Roses	Con rosas
„ **62**/27/322	Kinderbilder	Children	Con niños
„ **62**/30/322	Blaue Blumen	With blue flowers	Con flores en azul
„ **62**/31/322	Kinderbilder	Children	Con niños

62/27/322

Ia. Emaille-Spielwaren. — Enamelled toys. — Juguetes esmaltados para niños.

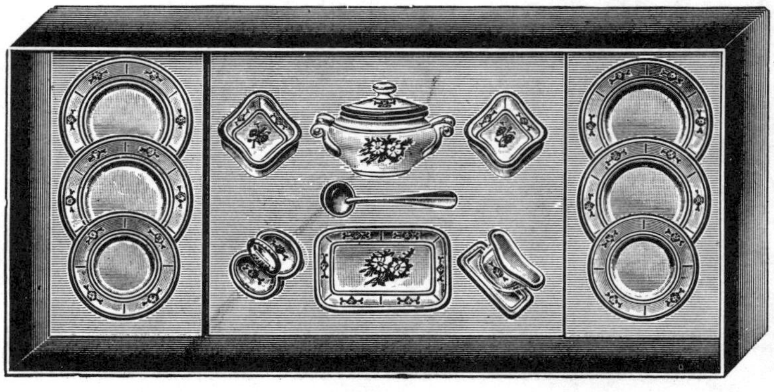

62/29/703/2

Speiseservice, in extra feiner Ausführung, fein weiß emailliert, mit hübschen Dekors.

Dinner-sets, of finest execution, white enamelled, with nice patterns in solid cardboard box.

Servicio de manjar, en ejecución extra, fina blanco esmaltado, con decoraciones graciosas en cartón solido.

Nr. **62**/ 4/703/ 2	2 Personen	13 teilig	Karton	63 × 26½ cm
„ **62** 12/703/ 2	2 persons	13 parts	Cardboard box	
„ **62**/29/703/ 2	2 personas	13 piezas	Cartón	
„ **62**/ 4/703/ 4	4 Personen	20 teilig	Karton	71 × 38 „
„ **62**/12/703/ 4	4 persons	20 parts	Cardboard box	
„ **62**/29/703/ 4	4 personas	20 piezas	Cartón	
„ **62**/ 4/703/ 8	8 Personen	34 teilig	Karton	89½ × 43½ „
„ **62**/12/703/ 8	8 persons	34 parts	Cardboard box	
„ **62**/29/703/ 8	8 personas	34 piezas	Cartón	
„ **62**/ 4/703/12	12 Personen	46 teilig	Karton	92 × 45½ „
„ **62**/12/703/12	12 persons,	46 parts	Cardboard box	
„ **62**/29/703/12	12 personas	46 piezas	Cartón	

Dekor: /4/ Streublümchen. /12/ Kobalt. /29/ Delft.
Decoration: /4/ Scattered flowers. /12/ Cobalt. /29/ Delft.
Condecorado: /4/ Flores escarpidas. /12/ Cobalto. /29/ Delft.

62/0 2/900/2

Teeservice, blau oder grau emailliert, in überzogenem Karton eingeschnitten.

Tea-set, blue or grey enamelled, in lined cardboard box.

Servicios de té, esmaltados en azul ó gris, cartados en cartón forrado.

Nr. **62**/0/2/900/1½	2	Tassen / Cups / Tazas	Karton / Cardboard box / Cartón	22 × 16 cm
„ **62**/0/2/900/2	2			28 × 21 „
„ **62**/0/2/900/3	3			29½ × 24 „
„ **62**/0/2/900/4	4			30½ × 25 „
„ **62**/0/2/900/6	6			38 × 30 „

Nr. **62**/0/2/900/8 Mit 4 Brottellern, 4 Tassen, Karton.
With 4 assietts, 4 cups, cardboard box.
Con 4 platos, 4 tazas, Cartón.

Nr. **62**/0/2/900/2 Mit 6 Brottellern, 6 Tassen, Karton.
With 6 assietts, 6 cups, cardboard box.
Con 6 platos, 6 tazas, Cartón.

62/699/2

Emaillierte Speiseservice, hellblau emailliert, in elegantem Karton aufgenäht.

Enamelled dinner-sets, light blue enamelled, sewn into elegant cardboard box.

Servicios de meso, esmaltados, azul claro esmaltados, cosidos en elegantes cajitas de cartón.

Nr. **62**/699/1	Karton / Cardboard box / Cartón	28½ × 20 cm	9	teilig / parts / piezas
„ **62**/699/2		31½ × 25 „	10	
„ **62**/699/3		35 × 29 „	10	
„ **62**/699/4		36 × 32 „	10	

62/1900

Teeservice, blau oder grau emailliert, lose im Karton, kleine Tasse.

Tea-set, blue or grey enamelled, loose in cardboard box, small cup.

Servicios de té, esmaltados en azul o gris sueltos en cartón, jicaras.

Nr. **62**/1900/1½	Mit / With / Con 2	Tassen / Cups / Tazas	Karton / Cardboard box / Cartón	19×13 cm
„ **62**/1900/2	2			
„ **62**/1900/3	3			
„ **62**/1900/4	4			
„ **62**/1900/5	6			

62/17/320/2

Toiletteservice, hellblau emailliert, eingenäht in starkem überzogenem Karton.

Toilet-articles, light-blue enamelled, sewn into strong cardboard box.

Servicios de tocador, esmaltados en azul claro, cosidos en cartón fuerte forrado.

Nr. **62**/2/320/1	Mit 5 Geschirren	Karton	27 × 25 cm
	With 5 utensils	Cardboard box	27 × 25 „
	Con 5 baterias	Cartón	27 × 25 „
Nr. **62**/2/320/2	Mit 5 Geschirren	Karton	34½ × 31½ „
	With 5 utensils	Cardboard box	34½ × 31½ „
	Con 5 baterias	Cartón	34½ × 31½ „

Dekoriert. — Decorated. — Condecorado.

Nr. **62**/17/320/1, /2	Rosen,	roses,	con rosas.
„ **62**/18/320/1, /2	Margareten,	daisies,	con margaritas.
„ **62**/19/320/1, /2	Goldwürfel,	gold-checkering,	con cubos de oro.

Einrichtungsgegenstände für Kinderküchen. — Kitchen Utensils for Toy Kitchens.
Utensilios para cocinas de niños.

62/511
Fisch, gebogen. — **Fish,** curved.
Pescado encorvado.
8 cm lang — in length — largo.

62/700/3/7

Kochherde mit Weißblechgeschirren. — **Cooking stoves** with white metal-vessels.
Hogares de cocina con baterías de cocina de hoja de lata.

62/513
Traube. — Grape. — Gajo.
7 cm lang — in length — largo.

62/557
Wasserkonsol. — Bracket. — Consolidados para agua.
8 cm hoch — in height — alto.

62/523

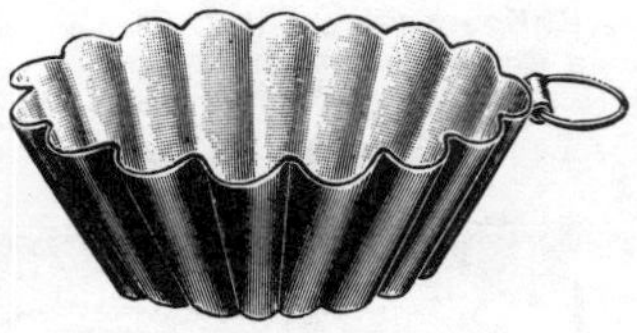

62/503
Rundform, konisch. — **Circular mould,** conical.
Forma redonda, cónica.

Nr. **62**/503/1	2
7	8 cm Durchmesser in diameter diámetro.

62/302

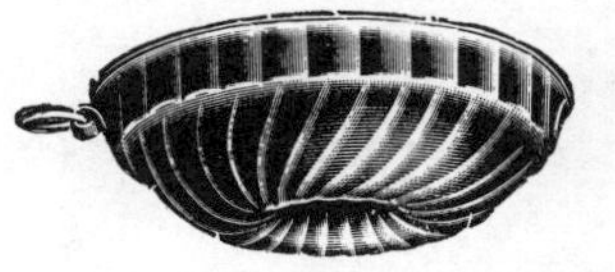

62/506
Buntform, mit Rohr. — **Round mould,** with tube.
Forma para tartas con tubo.

Nr. **62**/506/1	2	3	4
5,5	7	8,5	9,5 cm Durchmesser in diameter diámetro.

62/298/1

Emaillierte Kinderküchen-Sortimente, außen und innen neublau, in Karton aufgenäht, Ia. Qualität.
Enamelled toy kitchen assortments, outside and inside light blue, sewn in cardboard boxes, Ist quality.
Baterías de cocina esmaltadas para niñas, exterior azul claro, interior azul claro, piezas cosidas y empacadas en elegantes cajitas de carton, Ia. calidad.

Nr. **62**/298/1	Mit / With / Con	7	Geschirren / Utensils / Baterías	Karton / Cardboard box	23 ×16 cm
„ **62**/298/2		10			27,5×21 „
„ **62**/298/3		10			31 ×23 „
„ **62**/298/4		13			33 ×25 „
„ **62**/298/5		15			34 ×27 „
Nr. **62**/302/1	Mit / With / Con	13	Geschirren / Utensils / Baterías	Karton / Cardboard box	32×24,5 cm
„ **62**/302/2		11			34×28 „
„ **62**/302/3		12			37×31 „
„ **62**/302/4		12			38×31 „

Dekor. — Decoration. — Con decorado.

0	Grau	Grey	Gris	Gleicher Preis. Same Price. Precio igual.
2	Hellblau	Light blue	Azul	
4	Streublumen	Scattered flowers	Floros es parcidas	
12	Kobald	Cobalt	Cobalto	
21	Dunkelblau mit roten Blumen	Dark blue with pink flowers	En azul-oscuro con flores rojas	
28	Weiß mit blauen Blumen	White with blue flowers	Blanco con decorado en colores	
29	Zwiebelmuster	Bulb pattern	Blanco y azul Saxe	
33	Weiß antik mit Blumen	White with handpainted flowers	Blanco con decorado en colores	
34	Blau antik mit Blumen	Blue with handpainted flowers	Azul claro con decorado en colores	
35	Gelb antik mit Blumen	Yellow with handpainted flowers	Crema con decorado en colores	

Elegante Kinder-Spiel- und Gebrauchsservice in ff. Kartonaufmachung.
Elegant sets for children, for games or general use put up in best quality cartons.
Armamentos elegantes de juguetes y objetos de uso para niños en finisimas cajitas de cartón.

55/3000

Kinder-Kaffeeservice mit 6 Tassen.
Children Coffee Set with 6 cups.
Servicio de café para niños con 6 tazas.
Größe des Kartons: 33×27 cm

55/8000

Kinder-Kaffeeservice mit 6 Tassen.
Children Coffee Set with 6 cups.
Servicio de café para niños con 6 tazas.
Größe des Kartons: 26×20 cm.

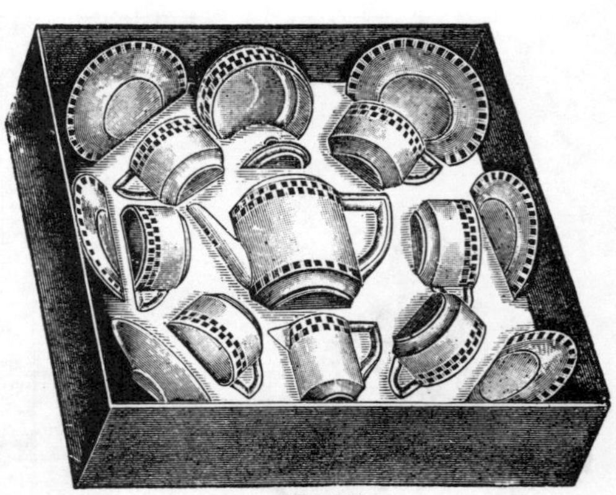

55/4000

Kinder-Teeservice mit 6 Tassen.
Children Tea Set with 6 cups.
Servicio de té para niños con 6 tazas.
Größe des Kartons: 33×27 cm.

55/1200

Kinder-Teeservice mit 6 Tassen.
Children Tea Set with 6 cups.
Servicio de té para niños con 6 tazas.
Größe des Kartons: 27×22 cm.

55/7000

Kinder-Tafelservice, 18teilig.
Children Dinner Set, 18 pieces.
Vajilla para niños, 18 piezas.
Größe des Kartons: 45×45 cm.

55/900

Kinder-Kaffeeservice mit 4 Tassen.
Children Coffee Set with 4 cups.
Servicio de café para niños con 4 tazas.
Größe des Kartons: 27×22 cm.

55/1057/1058

Kinder-Küchentisch, weiß lackiert, mit 24teil. Tafelservice besetzt.
Children Table, varnished white, with Dinner Set, 24 pieces
Mesa de cocina para niños, embarnizada en blanco, con vasilla de 24 piezas sobre ella
Nr. **55**/1057 Höhe: 55 cm. Breite: 37 cm.
„ **55**/1058 Höhe: 63 cm. Breite: 47 cm.

55/1072/1073

Puppen-Waschtisch, weiß lackiert, mit 5teil. Garnitur.
Toy Wash Stand, varnished white, with Wash Set, 5 pieces.
Lavadero para muñecas, embarnizado en blanco con guarnición de 5 piezas.
Nr. **55**/1072 Höhe: 24 cm.
„ **55**/1073 Höhe: 29 cm.

55/1048

Puppen-Waschtisch, weiß lackiert, mit 6teil. Garnitur.
Toy Wash Stand, varnished white, with Wash Set, 6 pieces.
Lavadero para muñecas, embarnizado en blanco con guarnición de 6 piezas.
Höhe: 36 cm.

55/2100

Puppen-Waschservice, 6teilig.
Toy Wash Set, 6 pieces.
Utensilios de lavadero para muñecas, 6 piezas.
Größe des Kartons: 32×24 cm.

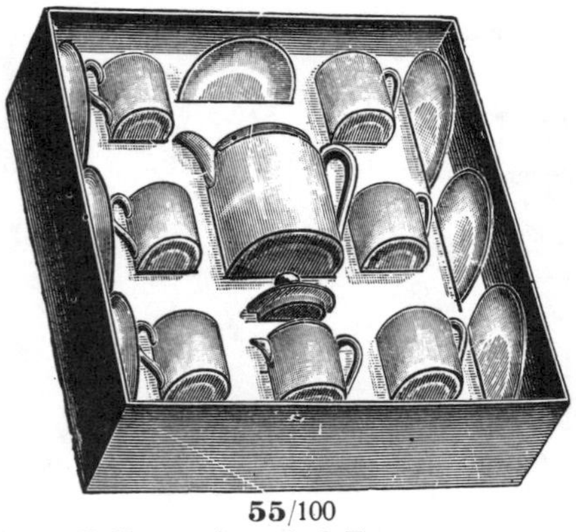

55/100

Kinder-Kaffeeservice mit 6 Tassen.
Children Coffee Set with 6 cups.
Servicio de café para niños con 6 tazas.
Größe des Kartons: 29×29 cm.

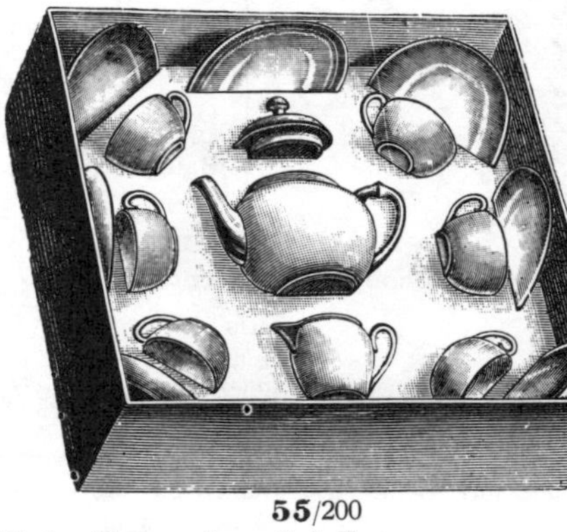

55/200

Kinder-Teeservice mit 6 Tassen.
Children Tea Set with 6 cups.
Servicio de té para niños con 6 tazas.
Größe des Kartons: 29×32 cm

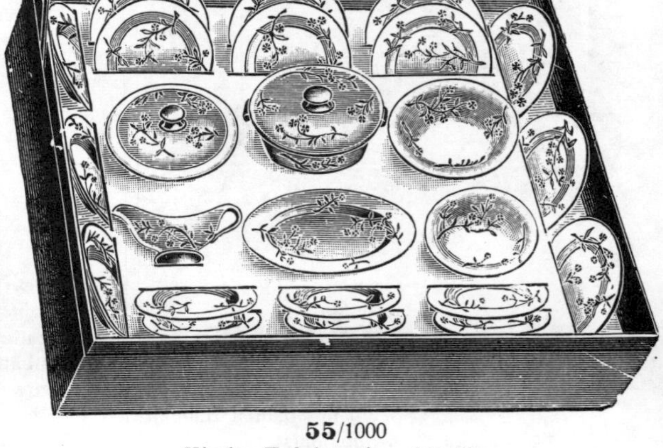

55/1000

Kinder-Tafelservice, 24teilig.
Children Dinner Set, 24 pieces.
Vajilla para niños, 24 piezas.
Größe des Kartons: 49×38 cm.

Größe des Kartons. — Size of the box. — Tamaño de la cajita de cartón. Höhe. — Height. — Altura. Breite. — Breadth. — Anchura

Aluminium-Kinderküchengarnituren in eleganten Kartons.
Set of kitchen-utensils in elegant cardboard boxes.
Baterías de cocina para niños elegante presentación en cajas fantasia.

71/77/3
Größe — Size — Tamaño 30½×30½×6 cm.

71/3021/14
Größe — Size — Tamaño 24½×24½×3 cm.

71/400/13
Größe — Size — Tamaño 30×30×6 cm.

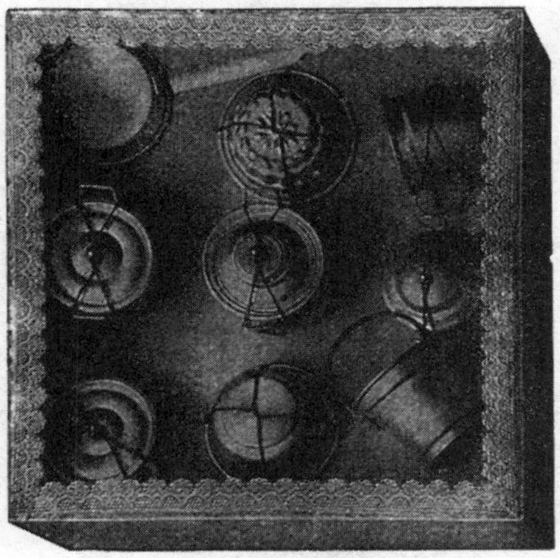

71/54/9
Größe — Size — Tamaño 33×33×8 cm.

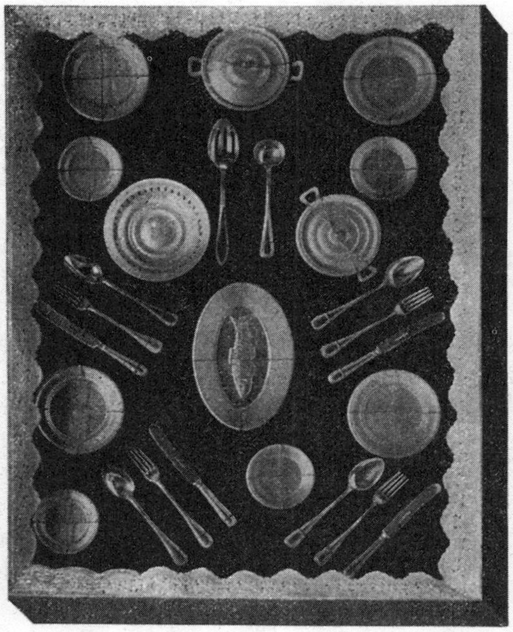

71/3070/26
Größe — Size — Tamaño 44×34×6 cm.

71/105/16
Größe — Size — Tamaño 28×28×3 cm.

71/3000/6
Größe — Size — Tamaño 17×20 cm.

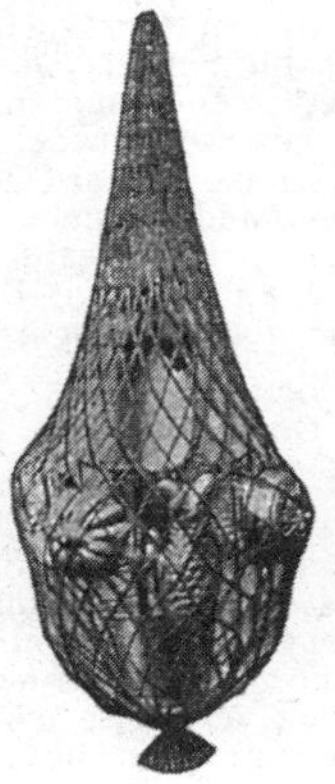

71/8/2

71/B67/6
Größe — Size — Tamaño 14×14 cm.

89/932

89/934

Schachspiele aus Bein. — Bone-Chessmen. — Ajedreces de hueso.

	Ausführung / Finish / Ejecución	Größe / Size / Tamaño	Höhe / Height / Altura: des Königs / of king / del rey (ca. cm)	des Bauern / of pawn / del peón (ca. cm)
Nr. **89**/932	Pariser Form Paris form Forma de Paris	0	$6^1/_2$	$2^1/_2$
		1	$7^1/_2$	$2^3/_4$
		2	8	3
		3	9	$3^1/_4$
„ **89**/934	Staunton-Form mit Tuchunterlage Staunton-Form with cloth Forma Staunton con paño	00	$5^3/_4$	$2^3/_4$
		0	$6^1/_2$	3
		1	7	$3^1/_4$
		2	8	$3^1/_2$
		3	$8^1/_2$	$3^3/_4$

Schachspiele aus Holz.
Chessmen wood. — Ajedreces de madera.

	Ausführung / Finish / Ejecución	Größe / Size / Tamaño	Höhe / Height / Altura: des Königs / of king / del rey (ca. cm)	des Bauern / of pawn / del peón (ca. cm)
Nr. **89**/4574	Staunton-Form mit Tuchunterlage	1	$6^1/_2$	$3^1/_4$
	Staunton-Form with cloth	2	7	$3^1/_2$
	Forma Staunton con paño	3	$7^1/_2$	$3^3/_4$
		4	8	$4^1/_4$

Reiseschach. — Travelling Chess. — Ajedrez de viaje.

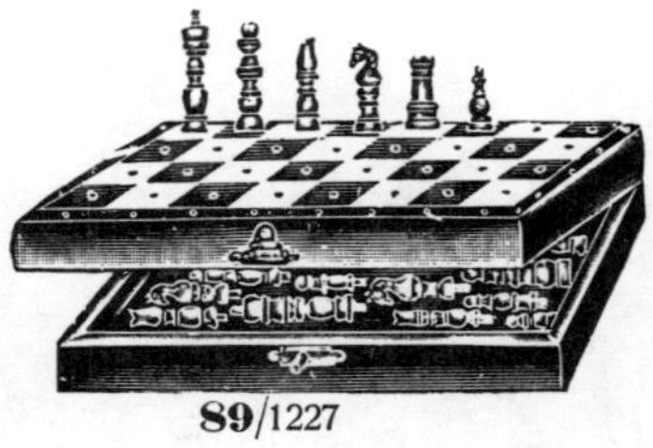

89/1227

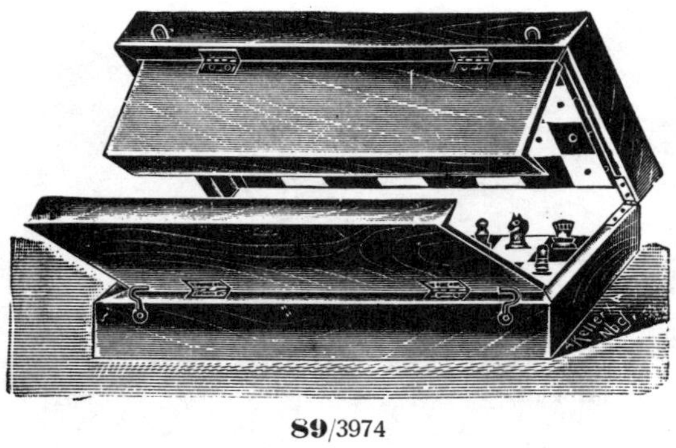

89/3974

	Ausführung / Finish / Ejecución	Größe / Size / Tamaño	Größe des geschloss. Kastens / Size of the closed Box / Tamaño de la cajita cerrada (cm)
Nr. **89**/1227	Mit Beinfiguren zum Einstecken With bone pegged men Con figuras de hueso	1	14/7
		2	$17/8^1/_2$
		3	20/10
„ **89**/2721	Mit feinen Buchsholzfiguren zum Einstecken With best box wood pegged men Con figuras de bujo barnizadas	1	14/7
		2	$17/8^1/_2$
		3	20/10
„ **89**/3974	Mit feinen Beinfiguren, fein polierter Kasten Best polished box with sidewings to interrupt the game at any time. Best bone men Cajita bien pulida con figuras en hueso fino y que se cierra de tal modo que se puede siempre interrumpir y volver á comenzar el juego		$18/8^1/_2$
„ **89**/2001	do. in größer, larger, más grande		23/11
„ **89**/4326	Portefeuille-Reiseschach aus Leder, mit einsteckbar. Celluloidfiguren Leather-Pocket-Chessboard with Celluloid men De cuero, las figuras de celuloid		$13^1/_2/9$
„ **89**/4326 Im.	Dasselbe Reiseschach, aber die Tasche aus Kaliko The same line but in imitation leather De cuero imitado.		$13^1/_2/9$
„ **89**/2408	Reisemagazin, polierter Holzkasten mit fourniertem Schach und Puffplan für Schach, Dame und Puff Pocket Compendium in best polished box with best Chess- and Backgamon Board in lid, Bone Chess and Draughtsmen Juego combinado, cajita pulida conteniendo Tablero, Damas Tric-Trac, todas las figuras de hueso		$15/8^1/_2$
„ **89**/4660	Mit Domino With Domino Con Domino		$15/8^1/_2$
„ **89**/4435/1	Reisemagazin, Inhalt: Schach und Dame, feine Beinfiguren zum Einstecken, Steinnuß-Damsteine Pocket Compendium in best polished box, pegged Bone Chessmen, D'men vegetable ivory Juego combinado, figuras de hueso		11/11

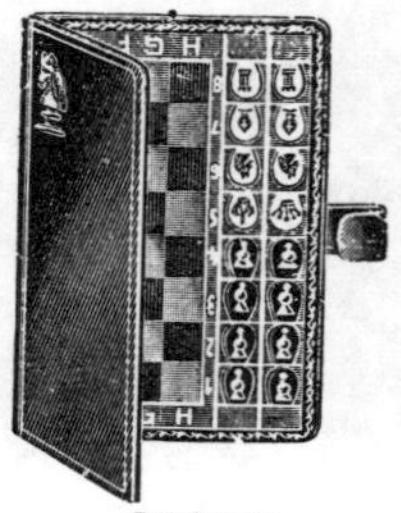

89/4326

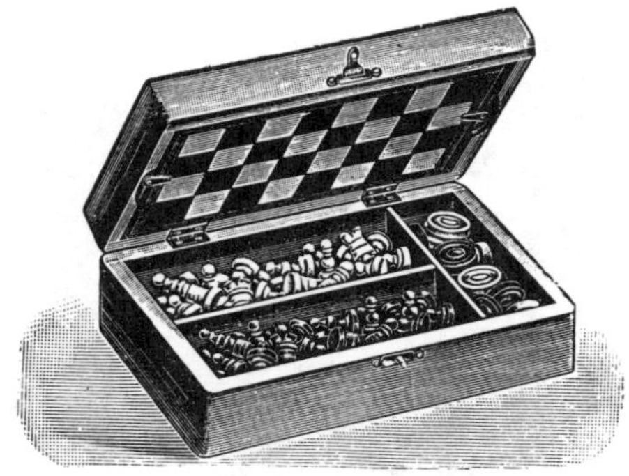

89/2408

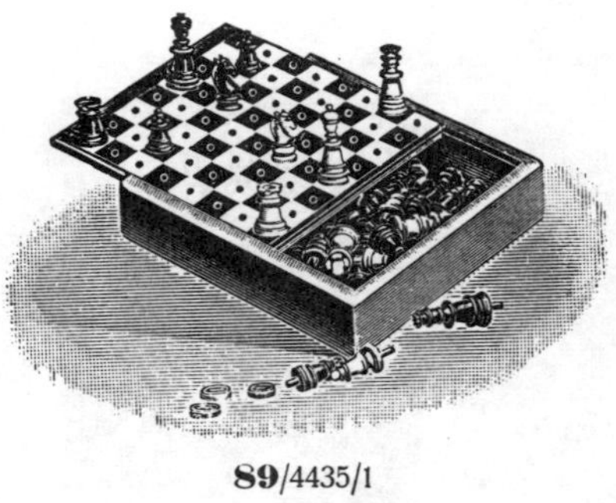

89/4435/1

89/2959 und 2960

89/2961

89/4250 und 4250 S

89/4174 und 4175

89/4395

Nr.		Größe — Size — Tamaño cm
Nr. **89**/2959	Nußbaumkasten mit Beschlag, eingelegtes Klappschach- und Mühlebrett. Inhalt 6 Spiele: Buchsschach, Buchsdamsteine, Beindomino, Würfelbecher mit Steinnußwürfel, Beindrehwürfel. Box nuttree, metal-mounted, 6 Games: Boxwood-Chess, Boxwood-Draughtsmen, Bone-Domino, Dice cup (leather), with Dice, Teetotum. Caja nogal, ornam. de metal, conteniendo 6 juegos: Ajedrez bujo, Peones de Damas bujo, Dómino hueso, Corneta cuero, con dádos de marfil vegetal, Dado para volver.	26×20×12
„ **89**/2960	Nußbaumkasten mit Beschlag, gleicher Inhalt wie vorstehend, mit besserer und größerer Füllung. The same as above larger and better. Lo mismo como arriba pero más grande y de mejor calidad.	28×20×12½
„ **89**/4175	Kasten hell Eiche poliert. Light oak box. Caja de roble claro.	29×24×14½
„ **89**/4174	Kasten dunkel Mahagoni poliert. Dark Mahogany. Caoba oscura.	29×24×14½
(4175 und 4174)	Beide gleichen Inhalts, und zwar 5 Spiele: Beinschach, Beindomino, Steinnuß-Damsteine, großer Lederwürfelbecher mit Steinnußwürfeln, eingelegtes Nußbaum-Schach- und Mühleklappbrett. Both containing: Bone-Chess, Bone-Domino, Draughtsmen, veget. Ivory, large Leather Dice cup with Dice, inlaid board with Chess and Mill. Contenido: Ajedrez, Dómino de hueso, Peones de Damas de marfil vegetal, Corneta de cuero, Dados para jugar, Tablero y Molino.	
„ **89**/2961	Nußbaumkasten dunkel, mit Beschlag, enthaltend eingelegtes Nußbaum-Schach- und Mühlebrett. Inhalt 7 Spiele: poliertes großes Buchsschach, Beindomino, polierte Buchsdamsteine, großer Lederwürfelbecher mit Steinnußwürfeln, 1 Satz Bostonmarken, Beindrehwürfel, 1 Satz Pokerwürfel. Nuttree-Box dark, metalmounted with best Chess and Millboard, containing 7 Games: Varnished Chess, Boxwood Draughtsmen, Bone-Domino, Leather Dice cup with Dice, 1 Set Counters, Teetotum, Poker Dice. Caja nogal oscuro con ornamentos de metal, contenido 7 juegos: Ajedrez bujo barnizado, Dómino de hueso, Peones de Damas bujo barnizado, Corneta de cuero para dados, 1 Guarnición de fichas, Dado para volver, Dados de Poker.	36×28×13
„ **89**/4395	Kasten, Truheform, dunkel Eiche. Inhalt: Buchsschach, Beindomino, polierte Buchsdamsteine, Roulette, Würfelbecher mit Würfel, Drehwürfel, Dominó, Satz Spielmarken, eingelegtes Schach- und Mühlebrett. Contents: Varnished Chessmen and Draughts, Roulette, Dice cup with Dice, Counters and Teetotum, Domino. Conteniendo: Ajedrez de bujo fino, Peones de damas barnizados, Corneta de cuero con Dados de marfil vegetal, 1 Guarnición de fichas, Dóminos, Dados.	30½×21×20
„ **89**/4250 S	Mahagonikasten, echt, hell, mit Nickelhenkel und eingelegtem Nußbaumklappschach- und Mühlebrett, alle Teile herausnehmbar. Inhalt 6 Spiele: feines poliertes Staunton-Buchsschach mit Bleiausguß, Beindomino, polierte Buchsdamsteine, feiner geprägter Würfelbecher mit Steinnußwurfeln, 1 Satz Pokerwürfel, 1 Satz Bostonmarken in eingerichtetem Holzkasten und dazu gehörigen Bostonkästchen. Real Mahogany Box, light, with nickelhandles, containing 6 Games: best Chessmen loaded and clothed, Bone-Domino, varnished Boxwood-Draughtsmen, embossed Leather Dice cup with Dice, Poker Dice, 1 Seet Counter. Caja de caoba verdadera clara con mangos niquelados, Tablero superfino, conteniendo 6 juegos: Ajedrez de bujo plomado y con paño, Dómino de hueso, Peones de damas barnizados, Corneta de cuero con Dados de marfil vegetal estampados, Dados para el Juego de Poker, 1 Guarnición de fichas.	35×26×12

Schachbretter. — Chess-Boards. — Tableros de Ajedrez.

Größe — Size — Tamaño					
1	2	3	4	5	6
22	27	32	37	41	43 cm

89/1272

Ausführung — Finish — Ejecución

Nr. **89**/1272
Furniert, ohne Mühle.
Inlaid, without millgame.
Sin molino.

„ **89**/1273
Furniert, gemalte Mühle.
Inlaid, painted mill.
Molino pintado.

„ **89**/1275
Halbfein, ohne Mühle.
Polished board, without mill.
Cuadros pulidos, sin molino.

Nr. **89**/1276
Halbfein, gemalte Mühle.
Polished board, painted mill.
Cuadros pulidos y molino pintado.

„ **89**/1280 E
Eiche, gezinkt, poliert, mit Mühle.
Oak wood, with mill.
De roble, con molino.

„ **89**/4588
Glas, ohne Mühle.
Glass, without mill.
Vidrio, sin molino.

Wachstuch-Schachdecken. — Oil cloth. — Tela encerada.

89/4135

Ausführung — Finish — Ejecución

Nr. **89**/4135 Imitiert Wachstuch.
Imitated oil cloth
Tela encerada imitada.

„ **89**/1284 Echt Wachstuch.
Real oil cloth.
Tela encerada verdadera.

	Größe — Size — Tamaño				
Nr. **89**/4135	19	26	33	36	40 cm
„ **89**/1284	32	40	48 cm		

Bein-Dominos. — Bone-Dominoes. — Juegos de Domino de hueso.

89/863

Größe der Steine. Size of the men. Tamaño de los dados.	
89/863/3	42/20
89/863/4	45/22
89/863/5	52/25
89/863/6	55/27
89/863/7	64/30
89/863/8	64/32

Mit 28 Steinen oder 6/6. — 28 men. — 28 dados.
Mit 36 Steinen oder 7/7. — 36 men. — 36 dados.
Mit 45 Steinen oder 8/8. — 45 men. — 45 dados.
Mit 55 Steinen oder 9/9. — 55 men. — 55 dados.

In fein polierten, gezinkten Hartholzschiebekästen.
In fine polished sliding boxes.
En cajitas pulidas finas.

Würfelbecher. — Leather Dice Cups. — Cornetas de cuero.

89/3458

Nr.	Höhe Length — Altura cm	Weite Bredth — Anch. cm
89/4386/1	5	4½
89/4386/2	6	5½
89/3458	8	6
89/535	8	7
89/534	9½	7½
89/1915	10	9

Rollbretter. — Chessboards rolling. — Tableros para Rodar.

89/1287

Größe — Size — Tamaño				
25	30	35	40	45 cm

Würfel. — Dice. — Dados.

89/476

Steinnuß-Würfel. — Dice vegetable ivory. — Dados de marfil vegetal.

Nr. **89**/476 12 14 16 18 20 mm

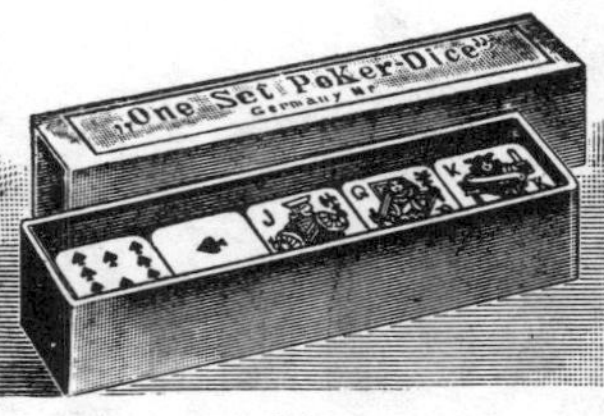

89/477

Nr. **89**/477 Poker-Würfel, 5 Stück im Satz, in Pappschiebschachtel mit Etikette.
Poker-Dice, 5 in set, in cardboard sliding box.
Poker-Dados, 5 piezas, cajata de carton.

89/1133

Nr. **89**/1133 Drehwürfel mit Buchstaben.
Teetotum with letters.
Dados para volver con letras.

Pokerkasten. — Poker Case with nickel handle. — Caja Poker.

89/4437

Größe — Size — Tamaño: 22×11,5 cm

Spielmarken. — Counters. — Fichas.

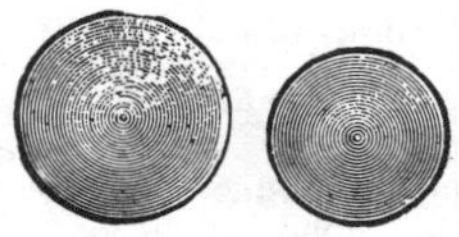

89/2616

	Durchmesser — Diameter — Diámetro			
Nr. **89**/2616	13	18	22	28 mm

Steinnuß. — Vegetable ivory. — Marfil vegetal.

In Rollen à 100 Stück, 4 Farben sortiert.
100 pieces wrapped in paper, assorted colours.
Envueltas en carpetas á la vez 100 piezas de diferentes colores.

89/2004

Poliert
Polished — Pulido

100 Stück per Satz, vierfarbig, im Karton.
100 assorted pieces in 4 colours, in box.
Conteniendo casa cajita 100 piezas en 4 colores.

Roulettes.

Für Kinder, Gesellschaften, Familien und Klubs.

For children, societies, families and clubs.

Para niños, sociedades, familias y clubs.

Präcisions-Roulettes

Superior make of high accuracy

Ruletas de calidad superior y de alta precisión

Fabrikmarke

Trade mark

Marca de fábricas

Nr. **44**/505 Offen, mit großer Messingscheibe.
Open, with large brass plate.
Abiertas, con lámina grande de latón.
10—34 cm Ø

„ **44**/507 Mit Holzstern, Messinggarnitur.
Superior make with rotating body of wood, mounted in brass.
Calidad superior con cilindro de madera, montadas en latón.
12—40 cm Ø

„ **44**/507 Mit Holzstern, Nickelgarnitur.
Superior make with rotating body of wood, mounted in nickel.
Calidad superior con cilindro de madera, montadas en niquel.
12—40 cm Ø

„ **44**/508 Mit Holzstern, feinem Knopf- und Messingfächer.
Superior make with rotating body of wood with elegant button, partitions of brass.
Calidad superior con cilindro de madera, con botón fino, particiones en latón.
14—40 cm Ø

„ **44**/509 Fein mit Holzstern, Messingfächer und angeschraubter Eisenplatte.
Superior make elegant finish, rotating body of wood, partitions of brass and with iron plate screwed to the bottom.
Calidad superior dejado lujoso con cilindro de madera, particiones en latón, con plancha de hierro atornillada al fondo.
18—40 cm Ø

„ **44**/509a Nußbaumholz mit Zinkstern und eingeschraubtem Eisenstift.
Superior make of nutwood with number disc of zinc and screwed on iron pivot.
Calidad superior de nogal con cilindro de zinc y con pivote de hierro atornillado.
20—80 cm Ø

„ **44**/511 Mahagoni oder Palisander mit Messingstern und starken Eisenstiften.
Mahogany or polisander wood, number disc of brass, strong iron pivot.
Calidad superior, caoba, ó palisandro pulimentadas, con cilindro de latón, y con pivote de hierro fuerte.
18—80 cm Ø

Nr. **44**/512 Fein schwarz poliert, hohe Fasson, mit Zinkstern und starken Eisenstiften.
Extra fine make black polish, high style, disc of zinc mounted in nickel, special strong iron plate.
Calidad superior dejado lujoso pulimentado en negro, estilo alto, cilindro de madera, montadas en niquel y con pivote de hierro fuerte.
18—80 cm Ø

„ **44**/560 Fein schwarz poliert, neue Fasson, Nr.-Scheibe aus einem Stück, genau wie in Monte-Carlo, Nickelgarnitur.
Elegant black polish, new style, number disc one piece as in Monte-Carlo, mounted in nickel.
Lujosamente pulimentado en negro, estilo nuevo, disco numeral de un sólo pedazo como en Monte-Carlo, montadas en niquel.
18—80 cm Ø

„ **44**/561 Fein schwarz poliert, neue Fasson, Zinkstern, Nr.-Scheibe, genau wie in Monte-Carlo.
Elegant black polish, new style, rotating body of zinc, division of number disc exactly as in Monte-Carlo.
Lujosamente pulimentado en negro, estilo nuevo, cilindro de zinc, disco numeral dividido exactamente como en Monte-Carlo.
18—80 cm Ø

„ **44**/562 Fein imit. Nußbaum, neue Fasson, massive Nr.-Scheibe, genau wie in Monte-Carlo, aus einem Stück, die in einem starken Messingring läuft, Messinggarnitur.
Superior make elegant imitation of walnut, new style, solid number disc, exactly the same as in Monte-Carlo, made all of one piece, and turning in a strong brass ring, mounted in brass.
Calidad superior muy lujoso imitación de nogal, estilo nuevo, disco numeral solido exactamente como en Monte-Carlo de un sólo pedazo y girando en un anillo fuerte de latón, montada en latón.
18—80 cm Ø

Nr. **44**/563 Genau wie Nr. 44/562, jedoch mit einer Libelle auf dem Zylinder und einstellbaren Metallfüßen.
Superior make same as Nr. 562 but with waterlevel fitted to cylinder standing on adjustable supports.
Calidad superior exactamente igual al núm 562 sin embargo con nivel de agua sobre el cilindro y montado sobre piés adjustables de metal.
18—80 cm Ø

Nr. **44**/564 Fein schwarz, neue Fasson, massive Nr.-Scheibe, genau wie in Monte-Carlo, aus einem Stück, die in einem vernickelten Messingring läuft, Nickelgarnitur.
Superior make elegant finish in black, new style, solid number disc, the same as in Monte-Carlo, made all in one piece and turning in a solid nickel plated brass ring, mounted in nickel.
Calidad superior, negro muy lujoso, estilo nuevo, disco numeral solido exactamente como en Monte-Carlo, hecha de un sólo pedazo y que gira en un anillo de latón niquelado, montado en niquel. 18—80 cm Ø

„ **44**/565 Genau wie Nr. 44/564, jedoch mit einer Libelle auf dem Zylinder und einstellbaren vernickelten Metallfüßen.
Superior make, the same as Nr. 564 but with water-level fitted to cylindre and standing on adjustable nickel plated supports.
Calidad superior igual al núm. 564 sin embargo con nivel de agua sobre el cylindro y montada sobre piés adjustables de metal niquelado.
18—80 cm Ø

„ **44**/566 Fein schwarz poliert, neue Fasson, Nr.-Scheibe aus einem Stück, genau wie in Monte-Carlo, Nickelgarnitur.
Elegant black polish, new style, number disc one piece as in Monte-Carlo, division number in niquel.
Lujosamente pulimentado en negro, estilo nuevo, disco numeral de un sólo pedazo como en Monte-Carlo, montadas en niquel. 18—80 cm Ø

„ **44**/567 Wie Nr. 44/566, Nr.-Scheibe mit grünem Tuch unterlegt.
Same as Nr. 566, division number with green cloth.
Mismo que Nr. 566, disco numeral sobre paño verde. 18—80 cm Ø

Roulette-Spielpläne auf grünem Wachstuch

Playing boards on oil cloth

Planos de ruleta sobre encerado

doppelt — double — doble

einfach — single — sencillo

Größe Size Tamaño cm	Mit roten u. schwarzen Zahlen / With red and black number / Con números rojos y negro: einfach / single / sencillo	doppelt / double / doble
44×37		
50×40		
65×47		
85×56		

Spieltisch

Playing table

Mesa de juego

95 × 68 cm

enthaltend — containing — conteniendo
1 Roulette — roulette — ruleta
1 Damespiel — draughtgame — juegos de damas
1 Schach — check — ajedreces
1 Puffspiel — "Puffgame" — juego de "Puff"
1 Domino — domino — juego de domino
1 Würfelbecher — leather dice cups — cornetas de cuero
Spielmarken — ships — fichas
1 grünes Kartenbrett —

44/520, 521, 522 und 530

Roulett — Roulette — Ruleta

ohne Deckel, mit dreifarbiger Nr.-Scheibe.

Without cover and with three coloured number disc.

Sin tapa, con disco numeral de tres colores.

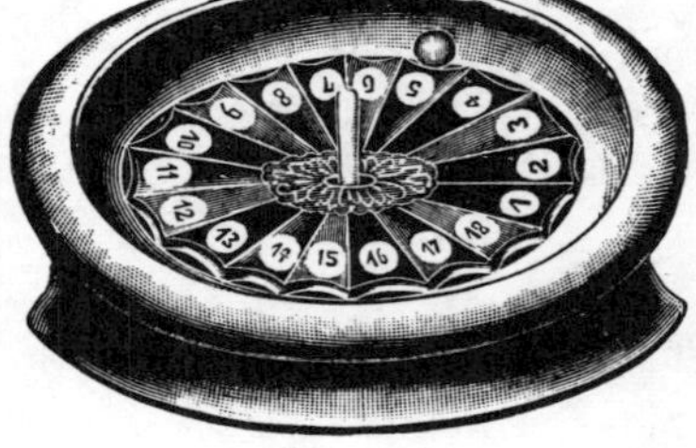

44/514

Roulett — Roulette — Ruleta

offen, ohne Deckel. — Open, without cover. Sin tapa.

Größe — Size — Tamaño

$8^1/_2$, 9, 10, 11, 12, 14, 17 cm

Roulett-Rechen — Roulette-rakes — Empujadores de dinero

45, 60, 75, 90 cm

Spielmagazin 0

Nr. **44**/0

Pol. Holzkasten, 25×27×7 cm, enthaltend: Roulett mit Plan, Domino, Holzschach, Damespiel.

Wooden box, polished, 25×27×7 cm, containing: roulette with plan, domino, wooden check, draughtgame.

Caja de madera pulida, 25×27×7 cm, conteniendo: ruleta con plano, juego de domino, ajedreces de madera, juego de damas.

Nr. **44**/1

Pappkasten, 42×25×8 cm. enthaltend: Roulett mit Plan, Holzschach, Domino, Damespiel.

Card-board box, 42×25×8 cm, containing: roulette with plan, domino, wooden check, draughtgame.

Cajita de cartón, 42×25×8 cm, conteniendo: ruleta con plano, juego de domino, ajedreces de madera, juego de damas.

Nr. **44**/1b

Kasten aus Holz, poliert, 42×25×8 cm, enthaltend: Roulett mit Plan, Domino, Holzschach, Damespiel.

Wooden box, polished, 42×25×8 cm, containing: roulette with plan, domino, wooden check, draughtgame.

Caja de madera pulida, 42×25×8 cm, conteniendo: ruleta con plano, juego de domino, ajedreces de madera, juego de damas.

Nr. **44**/3

Kasten aus Holz, fein poliert, mit Beschlag, 40×33×12 cm, enthaltend: Präzisions-Roulett, fein schwarz poliert, mit Metallscheibe, Spielplan, Beinschachspiel, Damespiel, Würfelbecher, Chips.

Wooden box, finely polished, mounted, 40×33×12 cm, containing: roulette, finely black polished, with metal disc, plan, bone-chessmen, draughtgame, leather dice cups, chips.

Caja de madera, muy bien pulida, con ornamentos, 40×33×12 cm, conteniendo: ruleta muy bien pulida en color negro, con disco de metal, plano, ajedreces de hueso, juego de damas, cornetas de cuero, fichas.

Kombiniertes Spielmagazin 3

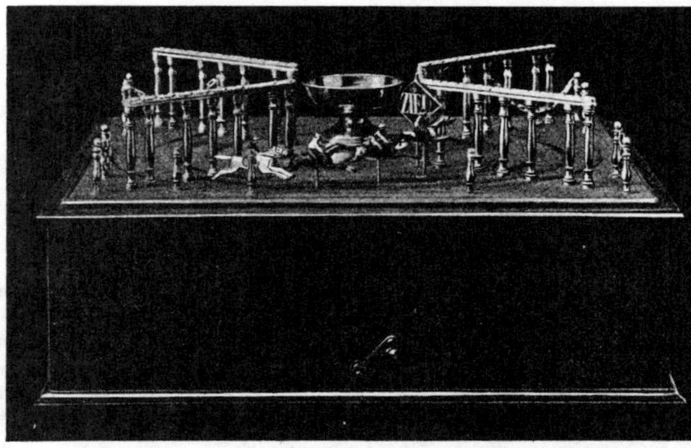

Pferdchenspiel — Horse race — Juego de caballos.

ca. 50×50×30 cm.

Mit 4 Pferden, feiner Holzkasten mit Deckel, erstklassige Ausstattung.

With 4 horses, fine wooden box with cover, best furnished.

Con 4 caballos, caja elegante de madera y de la primera calidad.

44/526 und 526/2

Nr. **44**/4

Kasten aus Holz, fein poliert, mit Beschlag, 40×33×12 cm, enthaltend: Präzisions-Roulett, fein schwarz poliert, mit Metallscheibe, Spielplan, Beinschachspiel, Damespiel, feines Bein-Domino, Würfelbecher, Chips.

Wooden box, finely polished, mounted, 40×33×12 cm, containing: roulette, finely black polished, with metal disc, plan, bone-chessmen, draughtgame, fine bone-domino, leather dice cups, chips.

Caja de madera, muy bien pulida, con ornamentos, 40×33×12 cm, conteniendo: ruleta muy bien pulida en color negro, con disco de metal, plano, ajedreces de hueso, domino de hueso de la primera calidad, juego de damas, cornetas de cuero, fichas.

Nr. **44**/5

Kasten aus Holz, fein Mahagoni, poliert, $39^1/_2$×28×12 cm, enthalt.: feines Staunton-Beinschach, Domino, Damespiel, Würfelbecher, Pokerwürfel.

Wooden box, fine Mahogany, polished, $39^1/_2$×28×12 cm, contain.: fine Staunton-bone-chessmen, domino, draughtgame, leather dice cups, poker-dice.

Caja de caoba, muy bien pulida, $39^1/_2$×28×12 cm, conteniendo: Staunton-ajedreces de hueso de la primera calidad, juego de domino, juegos de damas, cornetas de cuero, poker-dados.

10/68

Traber zum Fahren und Schaukeln. — **Trotter** on combination rockers. — **Caballos** en posición trotante sobre tabla y mecedor.

Nr. **10**/19P In Plüsch. — In plush. — De felpa.

„ **10**/19PC Plüsch-Zirkuspferd. — Plush-circus-horse. — Caballo de circo de felpa.

„ **10**/68 In prima Fell und extra fein gezäumt. — In selected skin, with extra fine bridle. — De piel escogida, con guarniciones muy ricas.

„ **10**/69 In extra feinem Fell, ausgesuchte Exemplare, extra rotes Luxusgeschirr mit Martingal und buntem Kopfschweif. — Choice horses with finest skin, most elegant red leather harness martingale and aigrette. — Caballos escogidos de piel muy fina, con guarniciones de lujo de cuero rojo, con gamarra y garzota.

Größe	9	10	11	12	•13	14	15
cm	52/43	58/47	64/50	72/55	78/60	95/71	104/76

10/18P

Pferde zum Fahren und Schaukeln. — **Combination rocking horses.** — **Caballos** sobre tabla y mecedor.

Nr. **10**/18F In Filz. — In felt. — De fieltro.

„ **10**/18P In Plüsch. — In plush. — De felpa.

„ **10**/38 In gutem Fell, mit Schnallenzaum und Zinngarnitur. — In skin, with bridle to be taken off. — De piel con brida para quitar.

„ **10**/48 In prima Fell, mit Doppelzügel und Nickelgarnitur. — In selected skin, with double reins and nickel-plated fittings. — De piel escogida, con riendas dobles y herraje niquelado.

Größe	$7^1/_2$	8	$8^1/_2$	9	10	11	12	13	14	15
cm	51/35	53/36	55/41	58/43	62/47	68/50	75/55	80/60	90/71	100/76

10/1115P

Elefanten. — Elephants. — Elefantes.

Nr. **10**/1115P In Plüsch, zum Fahren und Schaukeln. — In plush, on platform and rocker. — De felpa, sobre tabla y mecedor.

Größe	11	12	14
cm	58/83	63/92	76/106

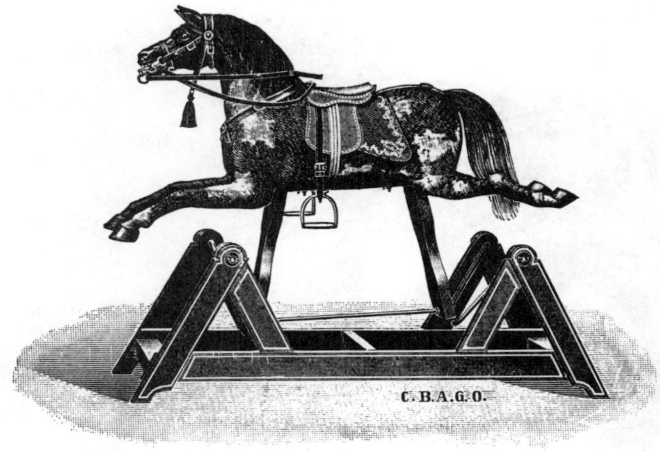

10/$59^1/_2$

Schwingende Pferde. — Swing horses. — Caballos balanceados.

Nr. **10**/59 In prima Fell mit Doppelzügel und Nickelgarnitur. — In selected skin, with double reins and nickel-plated fittings. — De piel escogida, con riendas dobles y herraje niquelado.

Größe	10	11	12	13	14	15
cm	62/46	65/50	72/56	82 65	93/75	100/85

Nr. **10**/59P In Plüsch. — In plush. — De felpa.

„ **10**/$59^1/_2$Sp. In Fell. — In skin. — De piel.

„ **10**/$59^1/_2$Sp.P. In Plüsch. — In plush. — De felpa.

Größe	8	$8^1/_2$	9	10	11	12	13	14
cm	42	44	48	51	54	57	60	66

10/910

Nr. **10**/910P In Plüsch. — In plush. — De felpa.

„ **10**/910 In Fell. — In skin. — De piel.

Größe	8	9	10	11	12
cm	42	48	51	54	60

10/35

Schaukelpferde. — Rocking horses. — Caballos mecedores.

Nr. **10**/15F In Filz. — In felt. — De fieltro.

„ **10**/15P In Plüsch. — In plush. — De felpa.

„ **10**/35 In gutem Fell, mit Schnallenzaum und Zinngarnitur. — In skin, with bridle to be taken off. — De piel, con brida para quitar.

„ **10**/45 In prima Fell, mit Doppelzügel und Nickelgarnitur. — In selected skin, with double reins and nickel-plated fittings. — De piel escogida, con riendas dobles y herraje niquelado.

Größe	$7^1/_2$	8	$8^1/_2$	9	10	11	12	13	14	15
cm	51/35	53/36	55/41	58/43	62/47	68/50	75/55	80/60	88/71	95/76

Größe = Size — Tamaño.

10/315

Percheron, mit starkem Arbeitsgeschirr.
Heavy draught-horse, with extra strong harness.
Caballo frisón con guarniciones muy fuertes.

Nr. **10**/315 In Fell. — In skin. — De piel.
„ **10**/315 P In Plüsch. — In plush. — De felpa.

Größe	0	1	2	3	4
cm	14/10	16/12	18/14	21/16	23/17

Größe	5	6	7	8
cm	27/19	30/22	36/27	41/31

10/305

Nr. **10**/305 Traber mit feinstem Fell und Ia Zäumung. — Trotter in fine skin and best fittings. — Caballo en posición trotante, de piel fina y con guarniciones de lujo.

Größe	1	2	3	4	5	6	7
cm	14/12	16/14	18/15	20/18	23/20	26/24	32/27

Größe	8	9	10	11	12	13
cm	37/31	53/42	60/45	68/54	78/63	85/83

10/10 P

Reitpferde. — Saddle horses.
Caballos de silla.

Nr. **10**/10 P In Plüsch. — In plush. — De felpa.
„ **10**/10 F In Filz. — In felt. — De fieltro.

Größe	0	½	¾	1	2	3
cm	14/10	16/11	17/12	19/13	22/15	23/16

Größe	3½	4	4½	5	5½	6
cm	24/18	26/19	29/21	31/22	32/23	34/24

Größe	6½	7	7½	8
cm	36/25	38/26	42/30	46/32

Nr. **10**/613 In gutem Fell, mit starkem Arbeitsgeschirr. — In fine skin, with strong harness. — De piel fina, con guarniciones fuertes para a trabajo.

„ **10**/614 In gutem Fell, mit schwarzem Chaisengeschirr. — In fine skin, with black driving harness. — En piel fina, con guarniciones negras para el coche.

„ **10**/313 In gutem Fell, mit starkem Arbeitsgeschirr. — In fine skin, with strong harness. — En piel fina, con guarniciones fuertes para el trabajo. } I. a.

„ **10**/314 In gutem Fell, mit schwarzem Chaisengeschirr. — In fine skin, with black driving harness. — En piel fina, con guarniciones negras para el coche. } I. a.

„ **10**/613 P In Plüsch. — In plush. — De felpa.
„ **10**/613 L Lackiert. — Varnished. — Pintado.
„ **10**/613 F In Filz. — In felt. — De fieltro.

Größe	4/0	3/0	2/0	0	1	2
cm	10,5/7,5	13/9	14/10	16/11	18/13	20/16
Größe	3	4	5	6	7	7½
cm	23/18	26/21	30/25	36/28	41/33	47/38

10/606

Reitpferde. — Saddle horses.
Caballos de silla.

Nr. **10**/606 In Fell. — In skin. — De piel.
„ **10**/853 Mit feinstem Fell und Ia Zäumung. — In fine skin and best fittings. — De piel fina y con guarniciones de lujo.
„ **10**/606 P In Plüsch. — In plush. — De felpa.
„ **10**/606 L Lackiert. — Varnished. — Pintado.
„ **10**/606 F In Filz. — In felt. — De fieltro.

Größe	4/0	3/0	2/0	0	1	2
cm	10,5/7,5	13/9	14/10	16/11	18/13	20/16
Größe	3	4	5	6	7	7½
cm	23/18	26/21	30/25	36/28	41/33	47/38

10/1553 F

Esel. — Donkeys. — Burros.

Nr. **10**/1553 F Filz, gesattelt. — Felt, with saddle. — Fieltro, con silla.
„ **10**/1553½ F Dieselben mit Stimme. — Same with voice. — Mismos con voz.
„ **10**/1560 F Filz, geschirrt. — Felt, with harness. — Fieltro, con guarniciones para el tiro.
„ **10**/1560½ F Dieselben mit Stimme. — Same with voice. — Mismos con voz.

Größe	1	2	3	4	5	6
cm	15/13	17/16	20/19	22/22	27/26	33/30

10/613

Geschirrte Pferde. — Harness horses.
Caballos de tiro.

10/001 P

Geschirrte Pferde. — Harness horses.
Caballos de tiro.

Nr. **10**/001 P In Plüsch. — In plush. — De felpa.
„ **10**/001 F In Filz. — In felt. — De fieltro.

Größe	0	½	¾	1	2	3
cm	14/10	16/11	17/12	19/13	22/15	23/16

Größe	3½	4	4½	5	5½	6
cm	24/13	26/19	29/21	31/22	32/23	34/24

Größe	6½	7	7½	8
cm	36/25	38/26	42/30	46/32

10/330

Ziegen. — Goats. — Cabras.

Nr. **10**/330 Fell, mit Stimme, gesattelt, von Größe Nr. 9/11. — In skin, with voice, with saddle in Nr. 9/11. — De piel, con voz y silla No. 9/11.
„ **10**/331 Fell, ohne Stimme, alle Größen gesattelt. — In skin, without voice, all Nrs. with saddle. — De piel, sin voc, con silla.
„ **10**/332 Fell, ohne Stimme, geschirrt. — In skin, without voice, with harness. — De piel, sin voz, con guarniciones para el tiro.
„ **10**/329 Fell, gesattelt, zum Fahren u. Schaukeln. — In skin, with saddle, on platform and rocker. — De piel, con silla, sobre tubla y mecedor.
„ **10**/1452 Fell, gesattelt, schwingend. — In skin, with saddle, swinging. — De piel, con silla, balanceandos.

Größe	1	2	3	4	5	6
cm	18/13	20/15	24/16	26/19	28/23	35/24

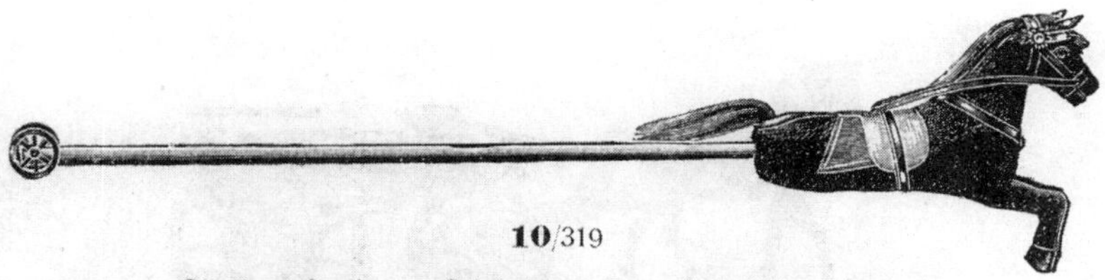

10/319

Steckenpferde. — Stick-horses. — Caballitos con palo.

Nr. **10**/319 Fell. — In skin. — De piel.
„ **10**/319 P Plüsch. — In plush. — De felpa.
„ **10**/319 F Filz. — In felt. — De fieltro.
„ **10**/435 Fell, ohne Beine. — In skin, without leds. — De piel, sin huesos.
„ **10**/435 P Dieselben in Plüsch. — Same in plush. — Los mismos en la felpa.
„ **10**/435 F Dieselben in Filz. — Same in felt. — Los mismos de fieltros.

Größe	2	3	4	5	6
cm	—/15	—/18	—/20	—/23	—/28

10/960

Schafe mit ff. langer Naturwolle. — Sheep, with long natural wool. Ovega, con lana natural y escogida.

Nr. **10**/337 Ohne Stimme. — Without voice. — Sin voz.
„ **10**/336 Mit Stimme. — With voice. - Con voz.
„ **10**/336½ Dieselben mit vergoldeten Hörnern. — Same with gold-colored horns. — Los mismos con cuernos de color de oro.

Lamm. — Lamb. — Cordero.

Nr. **10**/960 Mit Stimme. — With voice. — Con voz.
„ **10**/960½ Dieselben mit vergoldeten Hörnern. — Same with gold-colored horns. — Los mismos con cuernos de color de oro.

Größe	1	2	3	4	5	6	7	8	9	10
cm	20/19	23/22	26/26	29/29	33/33	38/38	41/42	45/52	58/66	61/77

10/123

Kippkarren aus ff. Naturhölzern. — **Tilt-carts** of fine natural wood.
Carros de revolteo de maderas finas.

Nr. **10**/124 Mit Fell-Percheron. — With heavy draught-horse (skin). — Con caballo frison de piel.
„ **10**/124 P Mit Plüsch-Percheron. — With heavy draught-horse (plush). — Con caballo frison de felpa.
„ **10**/123 Mit Fellpferd. — With skin-horse. — Con caballo de piel.
„ **10**/123 P Mit Plüschpferd. — With plush-horse. Con caballo de felpa.
„ **10**/123 F Mit Filzpferd. — With felt-horse. — Con caballo de fieltro.
„ **10**/123 L Mit gemaltem Pferd. — With painted horse. — Con caballo pintado.

Größe	2	3	4	5	6	7	7½
cm	45	52	60	65	70	76	88

10/1551

Nr. **10**/1551 Mit Fellpferd. — With skin-horse. — Con caballo de piel.
„ **10**/1551 P Mit Plüschpferd. — With plush-horse. — Con caballo de felpa.
„ **10**/1551 F Mit Filzpferd. — With felt-horse. — Con caballo de fieltro.
„ **10**/1551 L Mit lackiertem Pferd. — With painted horse. — Con caballo pintado.

Größe	1	3	5	7
cm	54	70	90	110

Sandwagen. — Sandwagons. — Carros.

10/664

Nr. **10**/664 Mit Fellpferd. With skin-horse. Con caballo de piel.
„ **10**/664 P Mit Plüschpferd. — With plush-horse. — Con caballo de felpa.
„ **10**/664 F Mit Filzpferd. — With felt-horse. — Con caballo de fieltro.
„ **10**/663 Mit 2 Fellpferden. — With 2 skin-horses. — Con 2 caballos de piel.

Nr. **10**/663 P Mit 2 Plüschpferden. — With 2 plush-horses. — Con 2 caballos de felpa.
„ **10**/663 F Mit 2 Filzpferden. — With 2 felt-horses. — Con 2 caballos de fieltro.
„ **10**/1428 F Mit Filzkuh. — With felt-cow. — Con vaca de fieltro.
„ **10**/1429 F Mit 2 gesprenkelten Filzkühen. — With 2 speckled felt-cows. — Con 2 vacas abigarradas de fieltro.

Größe	3	4	5	6
cm	58	63	75	82

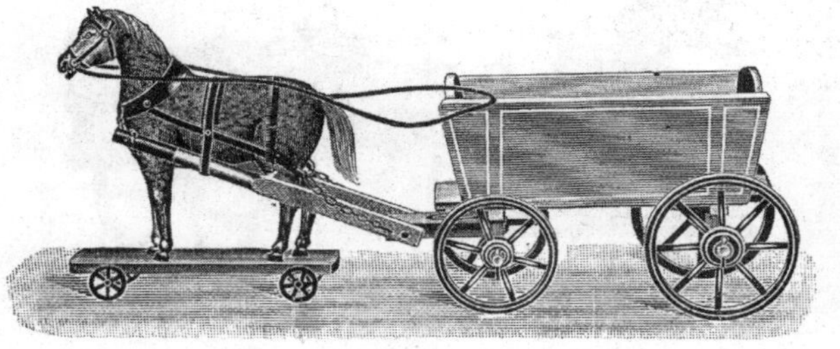

10/201 P

Nr. **10**/201 P Mit Plüschpferd. — With plush-horse. — Con caballo de felpa.
„ **10**/201 F Mit Filzpferd. — With felt-horse. — Con caballo de fieltro.
„ **10**/2011 P Mit 2 Plüschpferden. — With 2 plush-horses. — Con 2 caballos de felpa.
„ **10**/2011 F Mit 2 Filzpferden. — With 2 felt-horses. — Con 2 caballos de fieltro.
„ **10**/201 L Mit lackiertem Pferd. — With painted horse. — Con caballo pintado.
„ **10**/2011 L Mit 2 gemalten Pferden. — With 2 painted horses. — Con 2 caballos pintados.

Größe	0	1	2	3	4	5	6
cm	37	40	48	58	63	75	83

10/103

Nr. **10**/103 Mit Fellpferd. — With skin-horse. — Con caballo de piel.
Nr. **10**/103 P Mit Plüschpferd. — With plush-horse. — Con caballo de felpa.
Nr. **10**/103 F Mit Filzpferd. — With felt-horse. — Con caballo de fieltro.
Nr. **10**/103 L Mit lakkiertem Pferd. - With painted horse. - Con caballo pintado.

Nr. **10**/107 P Mit Plüschesel. — With plush-donkey. — Con burro de felpa.
„ **10**/107 F Mit Filzesel. — With felt-donkey. — Con burro de fieltro.
„ **10**/108 Mit Fellziege. — With skin-goat. — Con cabra de piel.
„ **10**/109 Mit Fellkuh. — With skin cow. — Con vaca de piel.
„ **10**/109 P Mit Plüschkuh. — With plush-cow. — Con vaca de felpa.
„ **10**/1338 Mit Fellhund. — With skin-hound. — Con perro de piel.

Größe	2/0	0	1	2	3	4	5	6	7	7½
cm	29	31	32	37	42	48	55	62	76	83

Nr. **10**/203 Mit Fellpferd. — With skin-horse. — Con caballo de piel.
„ **10**/2033 Mit 2 Filzpferden. — With 2 skin-horses. — Con 2 caballos de piel.
„ **10**/203 P Mit Plüschpferd. — With plush-horse. — Con caballo de felpa.
„ **10**/203 F Mit Fellpferd. — With felt-horse. — Con caballo de fieltro.
„ **10**/2033 P Mit 2 Plüschpferden. — With 2 plush-horses. — Con 2 caballos de felpa.
„ **10**/2033 F Mit 2 Filzpferden. — With 2 felt-horses. — Con 2 caballos de fieltro.
„ **10**/203 L Mit gemaltem Pferd. — With painted horse. — Con caballo pintado.
„ **10**/2033 L Mit 2 gemalten Pferden. — With 2 painted horses. — Con 2 caballos pintados.
„ **10**/208 Mit Fellziege. — With skin-goat. — Con cabra de piel.
„ **10**/2088 Mit 2 Fellziegen. — With 2 skin-goats. — Con 2 cabras de piel.
„ **10**/209 Mit Fellkuh. — With skin-cow. — Con vaca de piel.
„ **10**/2099 Mit 2 Fellkühen. — With 2 skin-cows. — Con 2 vacas de piel.
„ **10**/209 P Mit Plüschkuh. — With plush-cow. - Con vaca de felpa.
„ **10**/2099 P Mit 2 Plüschkühen. — With 2 plush-cows. — Con 2 vacas de felpa.

Größe	1	2	3	4	5	6	7	7½
cm	40	48	58	63	75	83	113	124

Größe = Size — Tamaño

10/1406

Nr. **10**/1406 P Mit Plüschpferd. — With plush-horse. — Con caballo de felpa.
„ **10**/1406 F Mit Filzpferd. — With felt-horse. — Con caballo de fieltro.
„ **10**/1406 L Mit lackiertem Pferd. — With painted horse. — Con caballo pintado.

Größe	4/0	3/0	2/0	0	1	2
cm	29	30	32	40	48	53

10/1064

Nr. **10**/1064 Mit Fellpferd. — With skin-horse. — Con caballo de piel.
„ **10**/1064 P Mit Plüschpferd. — With plush-horse. — Con caballo de felpa.
„ **10**/1064 F Mit Filzpferd. — With felt-horse. — Con caballo de fieltro.
„ **10**/1064 L Mit lackiertem Pferd. — With painted horse. — Con caballo pintado.

10/1045 P

Nr. **10**/1045 Mit Fellpferd. — With skin-horse. — Con caballo de piel.
„ **10**/1045 P Mit Plüschpferd. — With plush-horse. — Con caballo de felpa.
„ **10**/1045 F Mit Filzpferd. — With felt-horse. — Con caballo de fieltro.
„ **10**/1045 L Mit lackiertem Pferd. — With painted horse. — Con caballo pintado.

Größe	1	2	3	4	5	6	7
cm	39	43	47	53	63	73	83

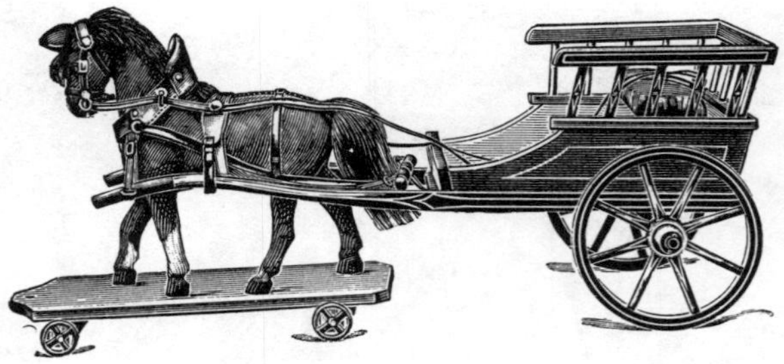

10/653

Nr. **10**/653 Mit Fellpferd. — With skin-horse. — Con caballo de piel.
„ **10**/653 P Mit Plüschpferd. — With plush-horse. — Con caballo de felpa.
„ **10**/653 F Mit Filzpferd. — With felt-horse. — Con caballo de fieltro.
„ **10**/653 L Mit lackiertem Pferd. — With painted horse. — Con caballo pintado.
„ **10**/658 Mit Fellziege. — With skin-goat. — Con cabra de piel.

Größe	2	3	4	5	6	7	8
ca. cm	47	53	60	70	80	88	100

Milchwagen. — Milk-wagons. — Carros de lechero.

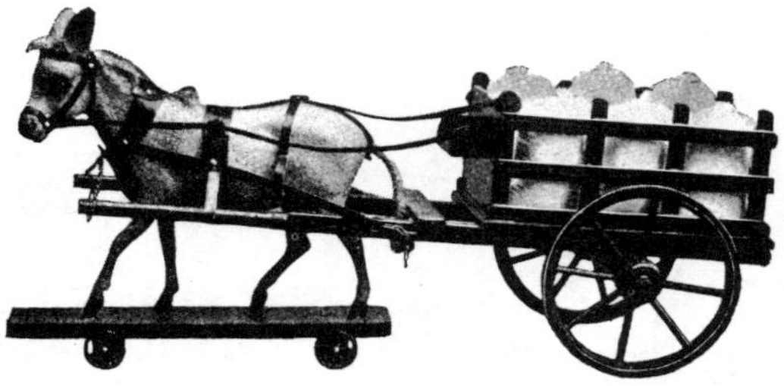

10/1556 E T

Nr. **10**/1556 E F Mit Filzesel. — With felt donkey. — Con burro de fieltro.
„ **10**/1556 P Mit Plüschpferd. — With plush-horse. — Con caballo de felpa.

Größe	2	3	4
cm	42	51	57

10/1234

Nr. **10**/1234 Mit Fellpferd. — With skin-horse. — Con caballo de piel.
„ **10**/1234 P Mit Plüschpferd. — With plush-horse. — Con caballo de felpa.
„ **10**/1234 F Mit Filzpferd. — With felt-horse. — Con caballo de fieltro.
„ **10**/1234 L Mit lackiertem Pferd. — With painted horse. — Con caballo pintado.

Größe	1	2	3
ca. cm	48	63	85

Müllerkarre, mit Säcken beladen. — **Miller's cart,** loaded with flower-bags. — **Carro del molinere,** cargado de costales.

10/551 P

10/597 P

Nr. **10**/551 P Mit Plüschpferd. — With plush-horse. — Con caballo de felpa.
„ **10**/551 F Mit Filzpferd. — With felt-horse. — Con caballo de fieltro.
„ **10**/551 L Mit lackiertem Pferd. — With painted horse. — Con caballo pintado.
„ **10**/557 P Mit Plüsch-Esel. — With plush-donkey. — Con burro de felpa.

Größe	0	1	2	3	4
cm	33	42	54	60	75

Rollwagen mit Kisten, Säcken, Fässern usw. beladen.
Trucks, loaded with cases, bags and barrels.
Camiones cargados de cajas, barriles y costales.

10/221 P

Nr. **10**/221 P Mit Plüschpferd. — With plush-horse. — Con caballo de felpa.

„ **10**/221 F Mit Filzpferd. — With felt-horse. — Con caballo de fieltro.

„ **10**/2211 P Mit 2 Plüschpferden. — With 2 plush-horses. — Con 2 caballos de felpa.

„ **10**/2211 F Mit 2 Filzpferden. — With 2 felt-horses. — Con 2 caballos de fieltro.

„ **10**/221 L Mit gemaltem Pferd. — With painted horse. — Con caballo pintado.

„ **10**/2211 L Mit 2 gemalten Pferden. — With 2 painted horses. — Con 2 caballos pintados.

Größe	0	1	2	3	4	5	6	7	7½
cm	38	40	53	62	72	82	90	100	130

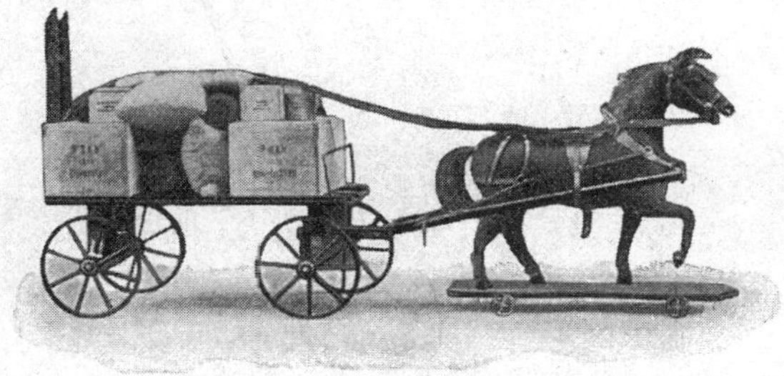

10/376

Aus Buchenholz. — Of beechen-wood. — De madera de haya.

Nr. **10**/376 Mit 1 Fell-Percheron. — With 1 heavy draught-horse (skin). — Con 1 caballo frison de piel.

„ **10**/375 Mit 2 Fell-Percherons. — With 2 heavy draught-horses (skin). — Con 2 caballos frisones de piel.

„ **10**/376 P Mit Plüsch-Percheron. — With heavy draught-horse (plush). — Con caballo frison de felpa.

„ **10**/375 P Mit 2 Plüsch-Percherons.— With 2 heavy draught-horses (plush). — Con 2 caballos frisones de felpa.

Größe	1	2	3	4	5	6	7
cm	48	58	68	80	86	100	108

10/9466

Wagen für Kinder zum Bespannen mit lebenden Ziegenböcken geeignet oder als Lastwagen zu benutzen.
Carriages for children, may be used with live goats.
Carruajes para niños, se pueden usar para cabras vivantes.

Länge ohne Deichsel ca. 125 cm. / Length without the pole ca. 125 cm. Largura sin timon ca. 125 cm.

Nr. **10**/9466 Wagen mit Zugstange für 2 Fellpferde. — Carriage with pole for 2 skin-horses. — Carruaje con mango para 2 caballos de piel.

„ **10**/9466/11 Zwei dazu passende Fellpferde. - 2 skin-horses just. - 2 caballos de piel justo.

10/1628

Menagerie. — Menagery. — Casa de fieras.

Nr. **10**/1628 F
100 cm

Rennwagen. — Racing-cart. — Carro de carreras.

10/5800

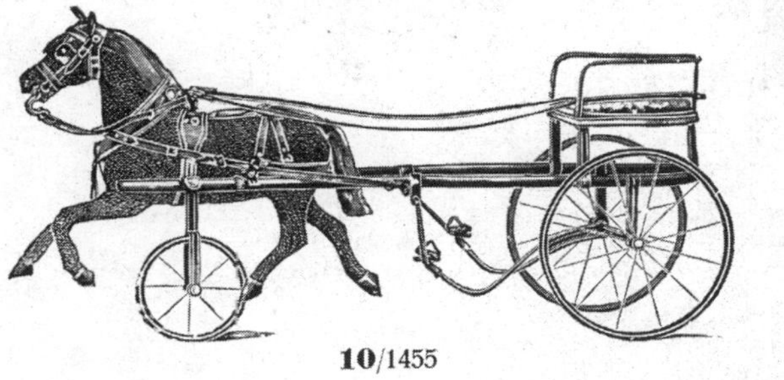

10/1455

Durch Treten der Pedale fortzubewegen und mit den Zügeln zu lenken.
Movable by treading the pedals, guidable by the reins.
Para mover por el movimiento de los pedalos, para dirigir por los riendas.

Nr. **10**/5800 Korbgeflecht, mit Fellpferd.
Basket-carriage, wi h skin-horse.
De mimbre, con caballo de piel.

„ **10**/5800 P Korbgeflecht, mit Plüschpferd.
Basket-carriage, with plush-horse.
De mimbre, con caballo de felpa.

Größe 140 cm

Nr. **10**/1455 Eisenkonstruktion, mit Fellpferd.
Iron-construction, with skin-horse.
Construcción de hierro, con caballo de piel.

„ **10**/1455 P Eisenkonstruktion, mit Plüschpferd.
Iron-construction, with plush-horse.
Construcción de hierro, con caballo de felpa.

Größe	8	10
cm	125	140

Größe = Size — Tamaño.

Cabriolets.

10/1353 P

10/1386

10/1800

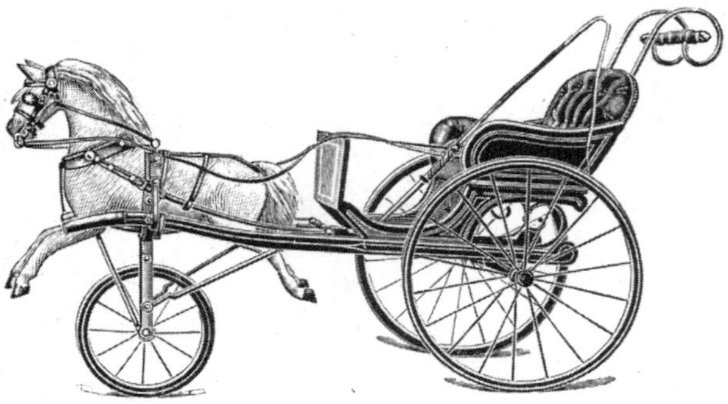

10/2500

Mit Plüschpferd.
With plush-horse.
Con caballo de felpa.

Nr. **10**/1800 P. = 120 cm
„ **10**/2500 P. = 145 cm
„ **10**/5000 P. = 155 cm

Mit Fellpferd
With skin-horse
Con caballo de piel.

Nr. **10**/1800 = 120 cm
„ **10**/2500 = 145 cm
„ **10**/5000 = 155 cm

10/5000

Nr. **10**/1353 P. Mit Plüschpferd. — With plush-horse. — Con caballo de felpa.

Größe	5	7	8
	85	103	127 cm

Nr. **10**/1386. Mit Fellschaf. — With skin-sheep. — Con ovega de piel.

Größe	5	6	7
	74	90	100 cm

10/1598
Mit Fellpferden. — With skin-hores. — Con cabellos de piel. ca. 102/94/103 cm

Nr. **10**/1464 Mit Fellpferd. — With skin-horse. — Con caballo de piel
„ **10**/1464 P Mit Plüschpferd. — With plush-horse. — Con caballo de felpa.
„ **10**/1464 F Mit Filzpferd. — With felt-horse. — Con caballo de fieltro.
„ **10**/1464 L Mit lackiertem Pferd. — With painted horse. — Con caballo pintado.

Größe	0	1	2	3	4
ca. cm	29/27	32/30	37/33	41/34	45/38

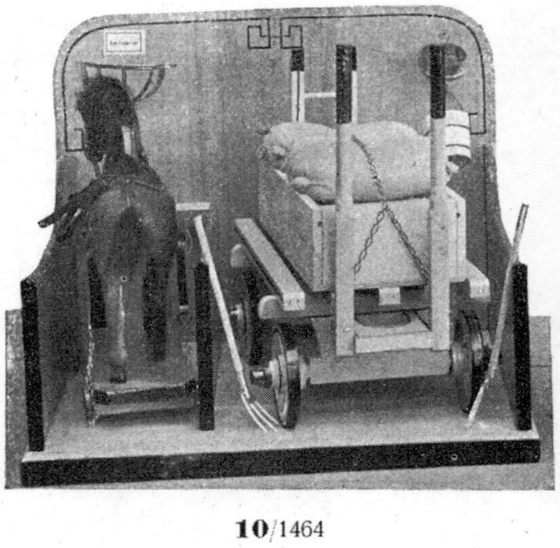

10/1464

Nr. **10**/1170 Mit Fellpferd. — With skin-horse. — Con caballo de piel.
„ **10**/1170 P Mit Plüschpferd. — With plush-horse. — Con caballo de felpa.
„ **10**/1170 F Mit Filzpferd. — With felt-horse. — Con caballo de fieltro.
„ **10**/1170 L Mit lackiertem Pferd. — With painted horse. — Con caballo pintado.

Größe	2/0	0	1	2	3	4	5
ca. cm	30/19	32/20	35/23	38/27	41/31	46/34	49/40

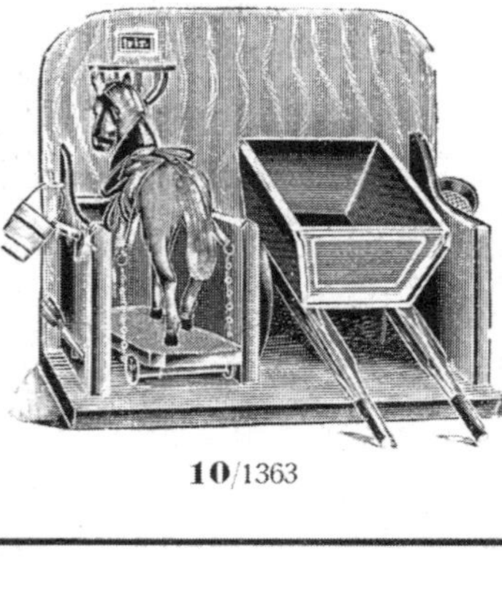

10/1363

Nr. **10**/1363 Mit Fellpferd. — With skin-horse. — Con caballo de piel.
„ **10**/1363 P Mit Plüschpferd. — With plush-horse. — Con caballo de felpa.
„ **10**/1363 F Mit Filzpferd. — With felt-horse. — Con caballo de fieltro.
„ **10**/1363 L Mit lackiertem Pferd. — With painted horse. — Con caballo de pintado.

Größe	3/0	2/0	0	1	2
ca. cm	24/23	25/24	27/27	29/29	31/33

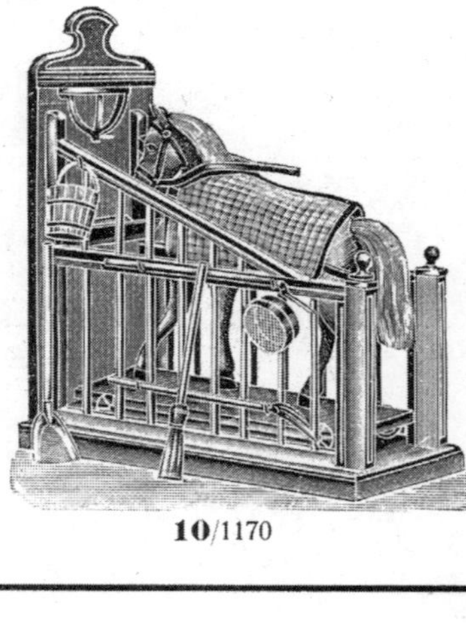

10/1170

Automobile,

sehr stabil gebaut und ff. lackiert, durch Treten der Pedale fortzubewegen und mittels Steuerrads zu lenken.

Automobiles,

very strong, best varnish, movable by treading the pedals, guidable by steering wheel.

Automóviles,

para mover por el movimiento de los pedalos, para dirigir por el rueda del timón. Muy fuertes, bien varnizados.

10/1642

10/400 M

Nr. **10**/1642 Für 1 Kind mittlerer Größe. For 1 child of middling tallness. Para 1 niño de tamaño mediano. } 95 cm

	Nr. **10**/300 N	400 M S	4400 M S
Länge, length, largo	ca. cm 120	220	220

10/106 **10**/105 **10**/125 **10**/126 **10**/125 **10**/105/3014 **10**/105/3013

10/185

Nr. **10**/106, 105, 125, 126, **10**/105/3014, 105/3013

Hochfein gekleidete Stehbabys
Standing babies, finely dressed
Babys derechos muy bien trajeadas. } 24 cm

Nr. **10**/184, 185

Stehbabys in allerfeinster Seidenkleidung
Standing babies, finest silk-dress
Babys derechos con vestido de seda primera } 27 — 72 cm

10/184

10/6033

Kinderklappstuhl. — Baby's high-chair.
Silla decora para niños.

Nr. **10**/6036 48 × 40 × 85 cm.

10/6062

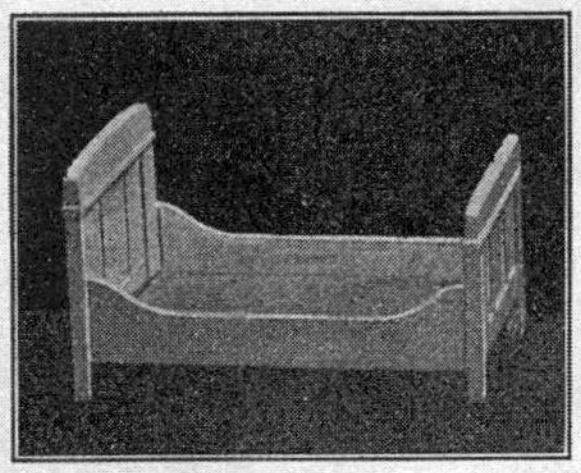

10/6063

Puppenbetten. — Doll's beds.
Camas para niños.

Größe	Länge — Length Longitud
1	60 cm
2	70 „
3	80 „

10/6084 — **10**/6085

Schultafeln.— Blackboard with easel.
Pizarra.

	Nr. **10**/6072/1	2	3	
Staffelei-Höhe Height of the easel Altura del caballete	100	125	150	cm
Tafelgröße Size of the black-board. — Tamaño de la pizarra	50 × 35	60 × 40	70 × 50	„

10/6072

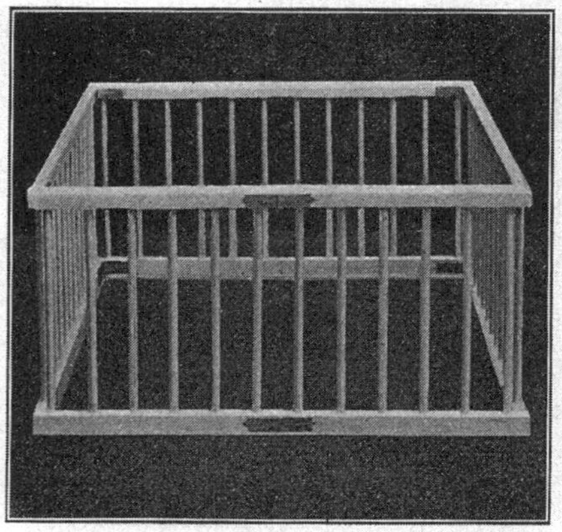

10/6073

100 × 100 cm

10/6021

Nr. **10**/6021/1 60 × 22 × 60 cm
„ **10**/6021/2 75 × 25 × 75 „

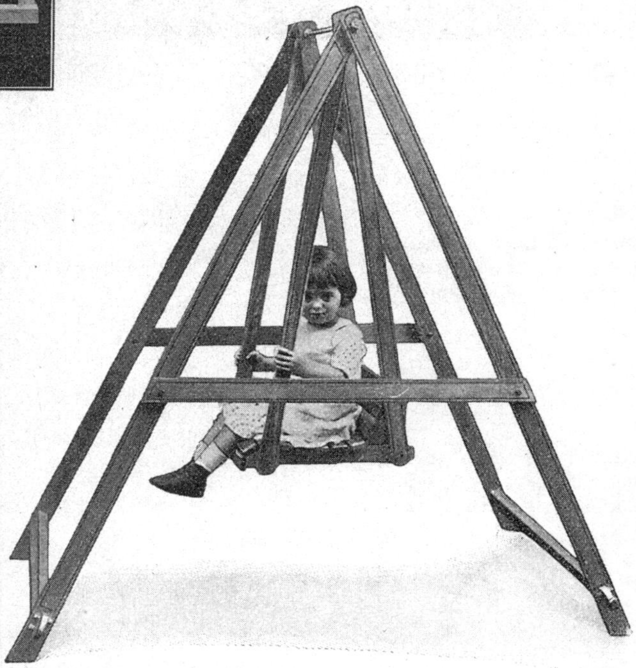

10/6074

Gartenschaukel. — Garden-swing. — Mecedero para jardínes.

180×160×90 cm.

10/6024

132×103×90 cm.

Reitpferde, Geschirrpferde, Schaukelpferde, Steckenpferde. — Saddle horses, harness horses, rocking horses, stick horses.
Caballos de silla, caballos de tiro, caballos mecedores, caballitos con palo.

53/200 und 200 E

53/707 G und 707 R

53/700 R und 700 G

Reitpferde, bemalt und lackiert. — **Saddle horses,** painted and varnished. — **Caballos de silla,** pintados y barnizados.

Nr. **53**/200 Mit Holzrädern. — With wooden wheels. — Con ruedas de madera. Nr. **53**/200 E Mit Eisenrädern. — With iron wheels. — Con ruedas de hierro.

Größe	2	3	4	5	6	7	8	9	10	11	12	13	14	15
cm	16/10	17½/12	17½/12	20/13½	21½/15½	23½/17	26½/19	30/21½	33/24	35/26½	38/29	44/32	48/36	53/40

Pferde, fein bemalt und lackiert. — **Horses,** finely painted and varnished. — **Caballos,** elegantemente pintados y barnizados.

Nr. **53**/700 R und 707 R Mit ff. Sattelung und Steigbügeln. — With finest saddle and stirrups. — Con silla y estribos de primera cualidad.

Nr. **53**/700 G und 707 G Mit ff. Geschirrung — Most finely harnessed. — Con arreos de primera cualidad.

Nr. **53**/700 R und 700 G Größe	00	0	1	2	3	4	5	6	7	8	9	10
cm	21/15	24/18	26/20	29/21	32/23	36/26	38/29	42/32	48/36	50/40	57/44	63/48

Nr. **53**/707 R und 707 G

Größe	0	1	2	3
cm	13	14	17	20

53/730

53/725

53/735

Schaukelpferde, fein bemalt und lackiert.
Rocking horses, finely painted and varnished.
Caballos mecedores, elegantemente pintados y barnizados.

Nr. **53** 725 Größe	1	2	3	4
cm	65/48	75/51	85/56	100/60
Nr. **53**/730 Größe	1	2	3	4
cm	67/44	72/48	80/51	85/56

Nr. **53**/735

Größe	1	2	3	4
cm	73/44	80/48	85/51	90/56

Steckenpferd, fein geschnitzter Kopf, fein geschirrt.
Stick horse, finely carved head, good harness.
Caballito con palo, cabeza de fina escultura, arreos muy bonitos.

53/715

Steckenpferd, fein geschnitzt, mit Ledertuchsattel.
Stick horse, finely carved, with leather cloth saddle gear.
Caballito con palo, fina escultura, con silla de paño de cuero.

Größe	1	2
Länge cm	17	20

53/720

Nr. **53**/720

Größe	1	2
Länge cm	17	20

53/220 und 225

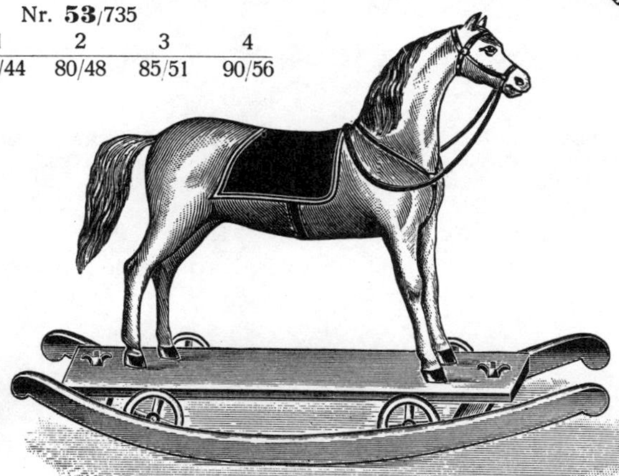
53/230 und 235

Schaukelpferde, bemalt und lackiert. -- **Rocking horses,** painted and varnished, **Caballos mecedores,** pintados y embarnizados.

Nr. **53**/220 und 225 Mit gemaltem Sattel. — With painted saddle. — Con silla pintado.

Nr. **53**/220 W und 225 W Mit Ledertuchsattelung, Steigbügeln und Zaumzeug. – With leather cloth saddle gear, stirrups and bridle. — Con silla de paño de cuero estribos y guarniciones.

Wiege aus gebogenem Hartholz. — Rockers of bent hardwood. — Mecedero de madero fuerte encorvada.

Größe	0	1	1½	2	5	6	7
cm	56/36	59/40	64/43	68/46	71/48	77/54	86/60

Schaukel-Fahrpferde, bemalt und lackiert. — **Combined rocking and riding horses,** painted and varnished. — **Caballos mecedores mobiles sobre ruedas y para mecerse,** pintados y embarnizados.

Nr. **53**/230W und 235W Mit Ledertuchsattelung, Steigbügeln und Zaumzeug. — With leather cloth saddle gear, stirrups and bridle. — Con silla de paño de cuero estribos y guarniciones.

Auf Brett mit Eisenrädern zum Abschrauben von der Wiege, bemalt und lackiert, Wiege aus gebogenem Hartholz. — On board with iron wheels, for unscrewing from the rockers, painted and varnished, rockers of bent hardwood. — Sobre una tabla con ruedas de hierro para destornilla del mecedero, pintada y embarnizada, mecedero de madera fuerte encorvada.

53/250/255

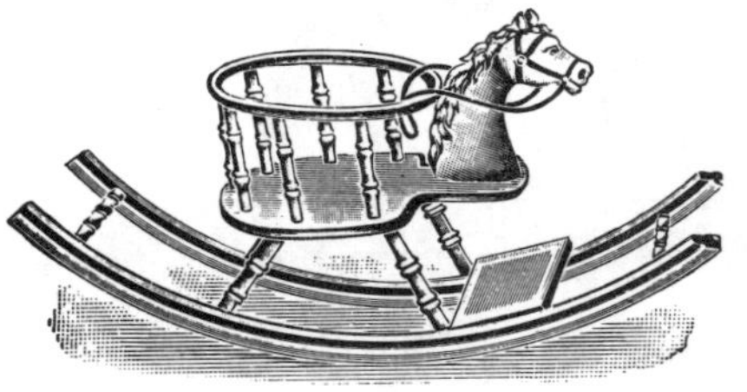

53/270 (260/265/266)

Schaukelstühle — Rocking chairs — Sillone paramecerse (mecedores).

Nr. **53**/250/255 Mit Doppelpferden, fein bemalt und lackiert.
With double horses, well painted and varnished.
Con dos caballitos, fina pintura y embarnizadura.

„ **53**/250 Sitz und Lehne ohne Polster.
Seat and back without upholstering.
Asiento y espaldo sin rehenchidura.

„ **53**/255 Mit gepolstertem Sitz und Lehne, fein geschnitzte Pferde.
With upholstered seat and back, finely carved horses.
Con asiento y espalda acolchados, caballos de fina escultura.

Mit geschnitztem Pferdekopf und Griff durch den Hals, Wiege aus gebogenem Hartholz.
With carved horse's head and handle through the neck, rockers of bent hardwood.
Con cabeza de caballo esculpida y mango al través del cuello, mecedero de madera fuerte encorvada.

„ **53**/260 Einfache Ausführung, gelb bemalt und lackiert.
Plain style, painted yellow and varnished.
Ejecución sencilla, pintada en amarillo y embarnizada.

„ **53**/265 Bessere Ausführung, mit gebrannten Sprossen, naturlackiert.
Better finish, with pyrogravure rungs, varnished natural colour.
Ejecución mejor, con escalones marcadas con un hierro caliente, embarnizadura natural.

„ **53**/266 Bessere Ausführung, mit Zaumzeug, gebrannten Sprossen, fein naturlackiert.
Better finish, with bridling, pyrogravure rungs, best varnished natural colour.
Ejecución mejor, con guarniciones, escalones marcadas con un hierro caliente, fina embarnizadura natural.

„ **53**/270 Feine Ausführung, mit Zaumzeug, gedrehten Sprossen, fein naturlackiert.
Best finish, with bridling, turned rungs, best varnished natural colour.
Fina ejecución, con guarniciones, escalones torneadas fina embarnizadura natural.

53/295

Nr. **53**/295 **Kastenwagen,** bemalt und lackiert, mit 1 Geschirrpferd.
Box cart, painted and varnished, with 1 harnessed horse.
Carro con caja, pintado y embarnizado, con 1 caballo con arreos.

Größe	1	2	3
cm	55	60	85

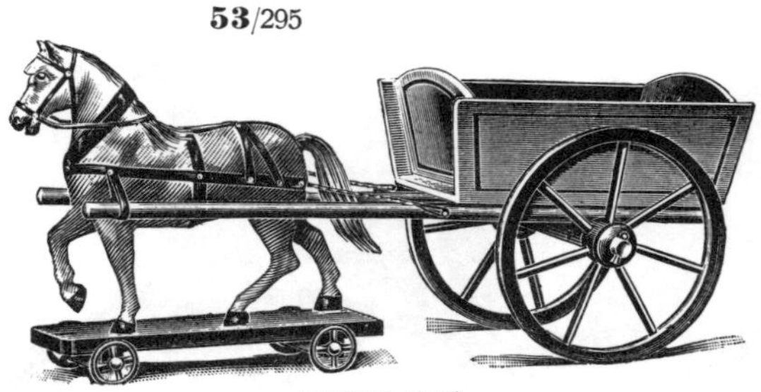

53/845 (345)

53/370 (870)

Nr. **53**/845 (345) **Sandkarren,** bemalt und lackiert.
Sand cart, painted and varnished.
Carretas para carretear arena, pintades y embarnizadas

Nr. **53**/370 (870) **Leiterwagen,** bemalt und lackiert.
Open-spar wagon, painted and varnished.
Carros con adrales, pintados y embarnizados.

Nr. **53**/845/870 Mit 1 Pferd. — With 1 horse. — Con 1 caballo. Nr. **53**/705.
„ **53**/345/370 „ 1 „ „ 1 „ „ 1 „ „ **53**/210.

Nr. **53**/840 (340) **Milchwagen,** fein bemalt und lackiert, mit Milchkannen beladen.
Milk cart, well painted and varnished, loaded with milk cans.
Carras de techero, pintados y embarnizados, cargados de vasijas de techero.

Größe	1	2
cm	46	54

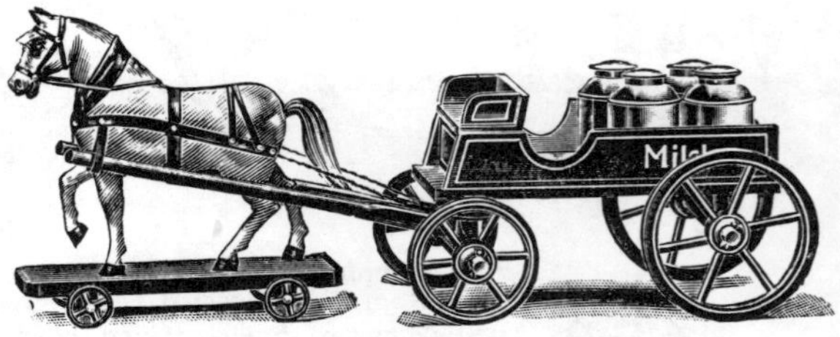

53/840 (340)

Nr. **53**/807 (307) **Rollwagen,** bemalt und lackiert, mit Kisten, Fässern und Säcken beladen.
Dray, painted and varnished, loaded with cases, casks and sacks.
Carruajes, pintados y embarnizados, cargados de cajas, barriles y sacos.

Größe	1	2	3	4
cm	47	57	75	85

Nr. **53**/300 (307/340) Mit 1 Pferd. — With 1 horse. — Con 1 caballo. Nr. **53**/210.
„ **53**/800 A (807/840) „ 1 „ „ 1 „ „ 1 „ „ **53**/705.

53/807 (307)

Nr. **53**/800 B (800 A, 300) **Frachtwagen,** bemalt und lackiert, mit Kisten, Fässern und Säcken beladen.
Goods wagon, painted and lacquered, loaded with cases, casks and sacks.
Carros de carga, pintados y embarnizados, cargados de cajas, barriles y sacos.

Größe	00	0	1	2	3	4	5	6	7	8
cm	38	44	55	65	75	85	55	65	75	85

Nr. **53**/800 B Mit 1 Pferd. — With 1 horse. — Con 1 caballo. Nr. **53**/710.

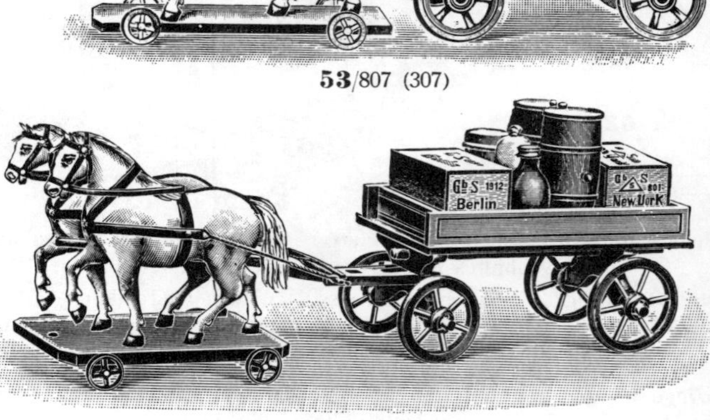

53/800 B (800 A, 300)

53/415

Schiebkarren mit Scheibenrand.
Wheelbarrow, with disc wheel.
Carretones con rueda discoide.

	Unbemalt. Unpainted. No pintada.		Bemalt und lackiert. Painted and varnished. Pintada y embarnizada.	
Größe -- Size Tamaño	1	2	1	2
cm	82	91	82	91

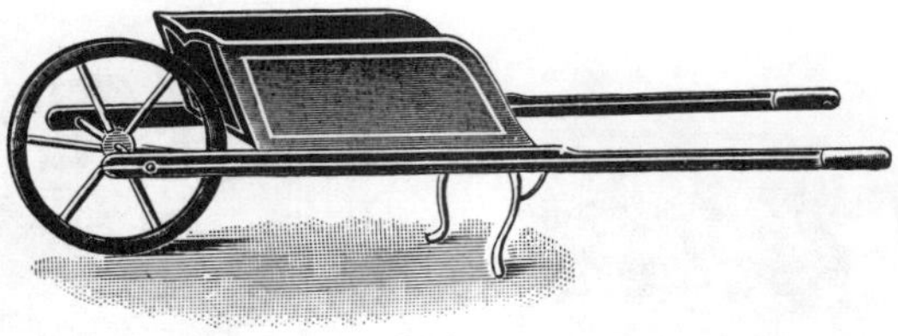

53/425

Schiebkarren mit Speichenrad und eisernen Stützen, fein bemalt und lackiert.
Wheelbarrow, with spoke wheel and iron stays, well painted and varnished.
Carretones con rueda con rayos y apoyos de hierro, fina pintura y embarnizadura.

Größe	1	2	3
Länge cm	85	95	110

53/430

Schiebkarren mit Speichenrad und eisernen Stützen, naturlackiert, feine solide Ausführung aus Buchenholz.
Wheelbarrow, with spoke wheel and iron stays, varnished natural colour, good quality and substantial style, of beechwood.
Carretones con rueda con rayos y apoyos de hierro, ejecución fina y sólida de haya.

Größe	1	2	3
Länge cm	91	100	115

53/285

Leiterwagen.
Open-spar wagon. — Carros con adrales.

Größe	1	2	5	6
cm	38	44	28	28

53/405

Nr. **53**/405
Kastenwagen, Größe 1—3, 7—9 unbemalt; Größe 4—6, 10—12 bemalt und lackiert.
Box cart, Nr. 1—3, 7—9 unpainted; Nr. 4—6, 10—12 painted and varnished.
Carro con cajo, No. 1—3, 7—9 no pintado; No. 4—6, 10—12 pintado y embarnizado.

Größe	1	2	3	4	5	6
cm	30	35	40	30	35	40

Mit Scheibenrädern. — With disc wheels. — Con ruedas discoides.

Größe	7	8	9	10	11	12
cm	30	35	40	30	35	40

Mit Speichenrädern. — With spoke wheels. — Con ruedas con rayos.

Nr. **53**/601-605
Pferdeställe, naturlackiert, mit 2 feingeschnitzt. Geschirrpferden und 1 beladenen Frachtwagen.

Nr.	601	602	603	604	605
Länge cm	40	50	46	50	58
Höhe „	27	27	31	36	40
Breite „	23	23	30	31	35
Gewicht kg	2,8	3,2	3,8	4,5	5,3

53/602

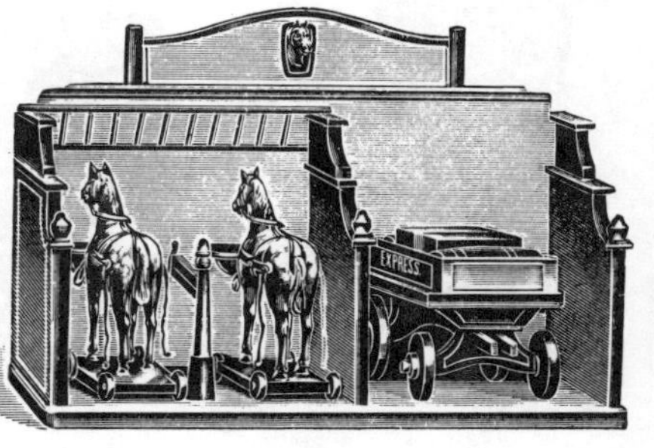

53/605

Nr. **53**/601/605 **Horse stables,** varnished natural colour, with two well carved harness horses and a loaded goods wagon.
Caballerizas (cuadras), embarnizadura natural, con dos caballos de fina escultura con arreos y con un carro de carga, cargado.

Nr. **53**/500 **Roller,** 3rädriges Rollfahrzeug. (Für Kinder von 2 bis 6 Jahren.)
Roller, 3 wheel dray. (For children of 2—6 years.)
Vehículo sobre rollo. (Para niños de 2—6 años.)

Größe — Size — Tamaño		1	2	3
Sitzhöhe und Länge / High of seat and length / Altura de silla y longitud	cm	25/45	28/50	33/59
Gewicht — Weight — Peso	kg	2,3	3	4

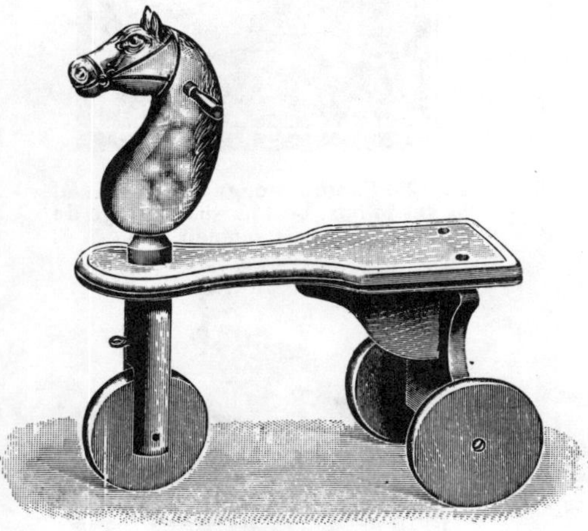

53/500

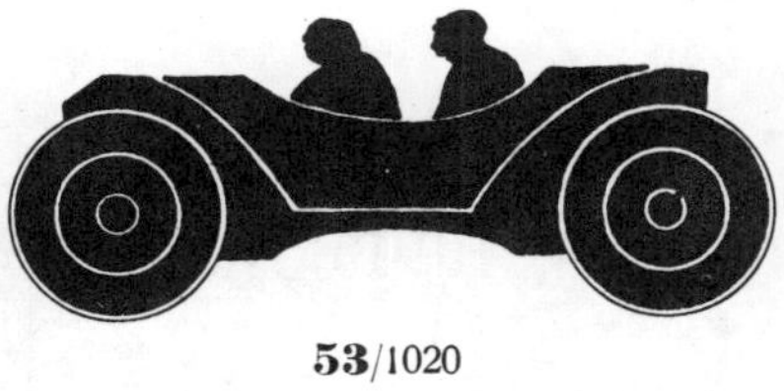

53/1020

53/1000/1001

Nr. **53**/1020 **Automobil** mit beweglichen Figuren. — Originelle Neuheit.
Motor car with moving figures. — Original novelty.
Automóvil con figuras móviles. — Novedad curiosa.

Nr. **53**/1000 **Automobil-Lastwagen** zum Ziehen, fein bemalt und lackiert.
Motor freight car for pulling, well painted and varnished.
Carromato automóvil para triar, fina pintura y embarnizadura.

Größe	1	2
Länge cm	25	35

Nr. **53**/1001 Desgl., mit Fässern beladen.
Ditto, loaded with casks
Idem, cargados de barriles.

Größe	1	2
Länge cm	25	35

17/89/3 **Spreng-Auto,** Blech. – **Water lorry,** tin painted. — **Automóvil regadero,** hojalata.

17/89/1 **Spreng-Auto,** Blech. – **Water lorry,** tin painted. — **Automóvil regadero,** hojalata.

17/19/2 **Menagerie-Auto,** Blech garniert. – **Menagerie Auto,** tin painted. — **Automóvil,** casa de fieras, hojalata.

17/19/1 A **Menagerie-Auto,** garniert mit Affen, Blech. — **Menagerie Auto,** tin, fitted with mokeys. — **Automóvil,** casa de fieras hojalata.

17/91/2 **Postauto** von Blech. — **Motor car,** tin painted. — **Automóvil de correo,** hojalata.

17/90/1 **Gepäckauto** von Blech. — **Motor lorry,** tin painted. — **Automóvil de bagaje,** hojalata.

17/85 **Puppenwagen.** – **Dolls pram,** strongly made. — **Coche para muñecas.**

17/1031/3 **Milchwagen** zum Ziehen. **Milch cart** to pull. — **Carretilla de leche** para tirar.

17/461 **Eimer,** Blech, fein bemalt. — **Tin pail.** — **Cubo,** hojalata.

17/461 gt **Eimer,** garniert. — **Tin pail,** fitted.–**Cubo,** guarn. hojalata.

17/9010 **Holzeimer,** feineAusführung.– **Wooden pail,** well made. — **Cubo,** madera.

17/2170 **Figurenkreisel.** — **Spinning top.** — **Péon con figura.**

17/2165 **Tellerkreisel.** — **Spinning top.** – **Peón platillo.**

17/1227 **Sandsieb,** fein lackiert. — **Sand sieve,** nicely painted. — **Criba de arena,** barnizado fino.

17/1270 **Sandformengarnitur,** mit fein bemalten Formen. — **Sand set,** nicely painted in box. — **Juego de arena,** en caja pintado fino.

17/13 **Badeanstalt,** mit Duschen. — **Swimming bath,** with showers. — **Baño publico,** con ducha.

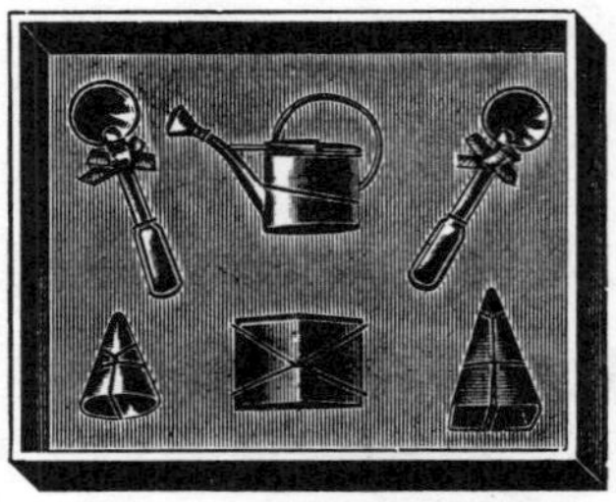

17/1257 **Sandformengarnitur.** – **Sand set** in box, best finish. – **Juego de arena,** en caja pintado fino.

17/12 **Badeanstalten,** fein lackiert, garniert mit Puppen, Wäsche usw. — **Swimming baths,** nicely painted, fitted with dolls washing, etc. — **Baño publico,** barnizado fino.

17/11/5 **Schwimmbad,** ganz feine Ausführung, mit Brause, Einzelbad, Restauration etc. — **Swimming bath,** highest finish, fitted. — **Nadadero,** ejecución muy fina, con ducha, baño separado, restaurant.

17/11 **Badeanstalt,** ganz feine Ausführung. – **Swimming bath,** best finish. — **Baño publico,** ejecución muy fina.

17/2125 **Geschirrwagen,** hübsch garniert. — **Crockery cart,** nicely fitted. — **Carretilla de vasijas,** bonito guarnizado.

17/2130 **Sommerspielwagen,** hübsch garniert. — **Play waggon,** nicely fitted. — **Carretilla de juguetes verano,** bonito guarnizado.

17/1230/3 **Seebadewagen,** sehr hübsch garniert. **Bathing-machine,** nicely fitted. — **Carretilla de baño de mar,** muy bonito guarnizado.

17/1028 **Milchkarren,** groß, fein lackiert. — **Milk-cart,** large, nicely painted. — **Carretón de leche,** grande, barnizado fino.

17/2140 **Gärtnerwagen,** sehr solide gearbeitet, mit Gartengarnitur, Korb usw. — **Gardener's barrow,** fitted, very well made. — **Carretón de jardín,** ejecución solida, con sesta.

17/2126 **Kippwagen** (Kasten zum Umkippen). — **Tip waggon,** fitted. — **Carretilla-chirrión.**

17/88 **Wasser- bzw. Sprengwagen,** zum Ziehen, 4rädrig, sehr solide gearbeitet. — **Water cart to pull,** 4 wheels, very well finished. — **Aguatero,** 4 ruedas, ejecución solido.

17/86 **Wasser- bzw. Sprengwagen,** zum Schieben, 2rädrig, sehr solide gearbeitet. — **Water cart to push,** 2 wheels strongly made. - **Aguatero,** 2 ruedas, ejecución solida.

17/1074 Extra solide **Gartenspritze.** — **Garden hose,** strongly made. — **Jeringa de jardín,** muy sólida.

17/1037 **Sandkarren** aus Blech und Eisen. — **Sand barrow,** tin and iron, very strong. — **Carretón de arena** de hojalata y hierro.

17/72/2 **Geschirrwagen,** hübsch garniert. — **Crockery cart,** nicely fitted. **Carretilla de vasijas,** bonito guarn.

17/18/5 **Menageriewagen,** garniert, mit Elefant. — **Menagerie,** fitted with animals, with elephant. — **Carretilla-casa** de fieres, guarnizado, con elefante.

17/74/4 **Geschirrwagen** zum Ziehen. — **Crockery cart** to pull, fitted. — **Carretilla de vasijas** para tirar.

17/74/6 **Geschirrwagen,** hübsch garniert und fein lackiert, mit Stoffdach. — **Crockery cart** with cloth-hood. — **Carretilla de vasijas,** bonito guarn., barnizado fino, con tejado de genero.

17/18 **Menageriewagen,** garniert. — **Menagerie to pull,** fitted. — **Carretilla-casa de fieras,** guarnizado.

17/7/2

Brunnen, viereckig.
Pump, squart.
Fuente, cuadrado.

17/2/4

Brunnen, oval.
Pump, oval.
Fuente, oval.

17/25

Schwanenteich.
Swan pond.
Estanque para cisnes.

17/1265/1

Ziehbrunnen.
Well.
Pozo.

17/1267

Ziehbrunnen, feine, moderne Ausführung.
Well, highest finish.
Pozo, ejecución fina y moderna.

17/1361

Botanisierbüchse, kurze Form.
Botany box, short form.
Caja para botanistas, forma corta.

17/1360

Botanisierbüchse, lange Form.
Botany box, long form.
Caja para botanistas, forma larga.

17/355/10

Butterbrottasche, mit origineller Bemalung.
Lunch basket, tin painted,
Bolsillo para merienda. coloración bonita.

17/1297

Feine moderne **Gießkanne.**
Sprinkling can, highest finish.
Regadera, forma moderna.

17/435

Gießkannen, rund.
Watercan, round.
Regadera, redonda.

17/976

Sandschaufel, Blech, lackiert.
Sand shovel, tin painted.
Pala de arena, hojalato barnizado.

Sandschaufel, Ahornholz.
Sand shovel, maple-wood.
Pala de arena, madera.

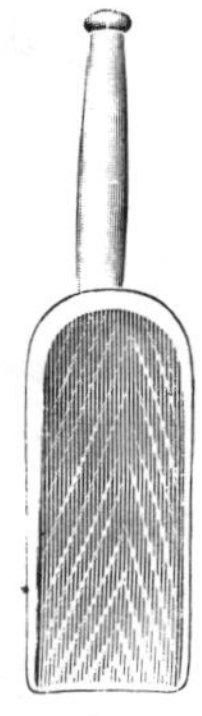

17/968

17/2070

Wurfscheibe mit Bällen.
Ball game with balls.
Tiro con pelotas.

17/2096/3

Neue Ringwurfscheibe.
New ring game.
Tiro con aros.

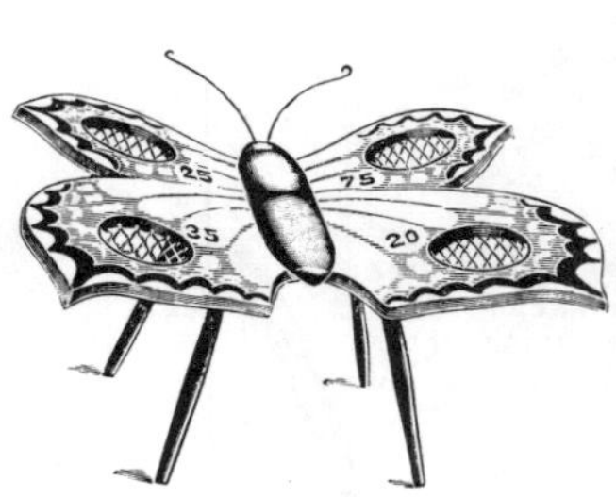

17/2074

Wurfscheibe, Schmetterling.
Ball game, "Butterfly".
Tiro, mariposa.

17/2076

Wurfscheibe, Neger.
Ball game, "Nigger".
Tiro, negro.

17/1088/7

Glockenwagen, fein lackiert.
Bell chime, nicely painted.
Carretilla de campanilla, barnizado fino.

17/1083

Laufreif mit Glocke. — **Hoop** with bell.
Aro con campanilla.

Nr. **17**/1088/5
Rollglocke, starke Ausführung.
Bell chime, very strongly made.
Carretilla de campanilla, ejecución muy fuerte.

17/1088/5

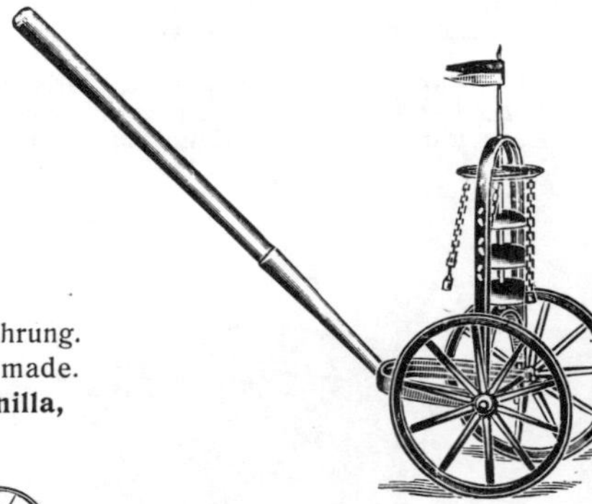

17/1085

Glockenwagen mit Stiel.
Bell chime with handle.
Carretilla de campanilla con mango.

17/39/1—2

Sandzug, Lokomotive, 2 Wagen. — **Train to pull,** engine, 2 waggons. **Tren de arena,** locomodora, 2 coches.

17/41/1—2

Personenzug, feine Ausführung, Lokomotive, 3 Wagen. — **Passenger train,** highest finish, engine, 3 waggons. — **Tren de viajeros,** ejecución fina, locomodora, 3 coches.

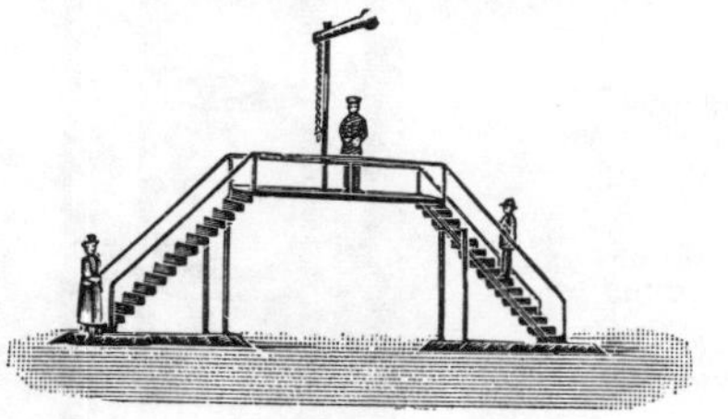

17/68/1—2

Bahnübergang. – Bridge. – Pasaje de ferrocarril.

17/54/1½—2

Bahnschranke. — Level crossing. — Barrera de ferrocarril.

17/1003

Klappstuhl, fein lackiert. — **Folding chair** with counting frame, nicely painted. — **Silla de muelles,** ramangadora con barnizado fino.

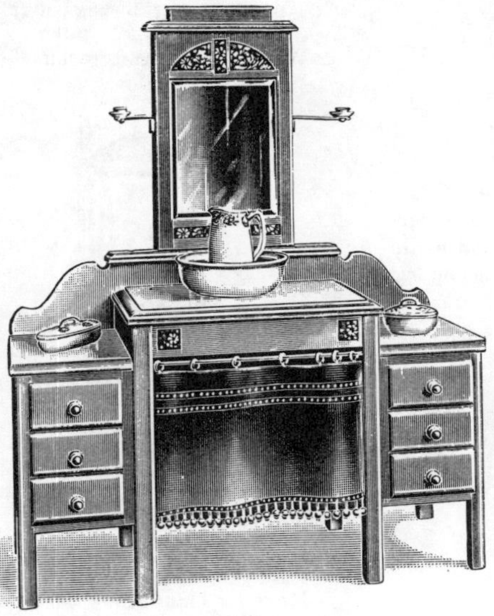

17/1414

Waschtisch, groß, weiß lackiert, mit Spiegel.
Wash stand, with mirror, large, white enamelled.
Lavabo, barnizado blanco, con espejo.

17/1013

Waschtisch.
Wash stand with mirror.
Lavabo con espejo.

17/1413

Waschtisch mit Spiegel.
Wash stand with mirror.
Lavabo con espejo.

17/1410/1

Toilettenstand m. verstell. Spiegeln
Toilet stand with mirror.
Tocador con espejos movibles.

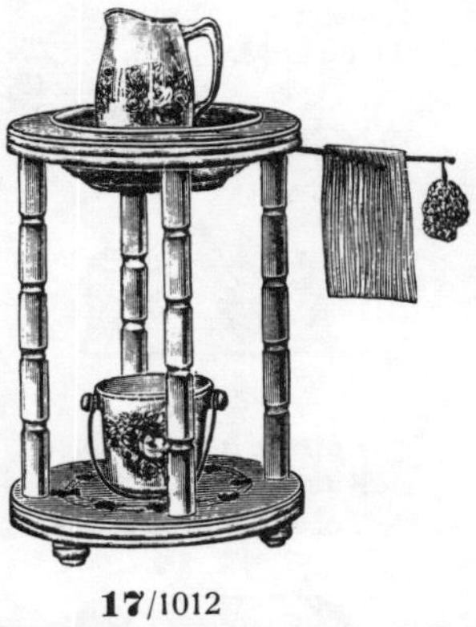

17/1012

Waschtisch, Holz, ganz moderne Form.
Wash stand, wood, white enamelled.
Lavabo, madera, forma moderna.

17/1412

Waschtisch, groß, fein lackiert, mit Spiegel.
Wash stand with mirror.
Lavabo, grande, barnizado fino, con espejo.

17/1014

Waschtisch, fein weiß lackiert.
Wash stand, white enamelled.
Lavabo, barnizado fino.

17/1015

Waschtisch, fein weiß lackiert.
Wash stand, white enamelled.
Lavabo, barnizado fino.

17/5004/5/1

Möbelgarnitur, bestehend aus 1 Tisch u. 2 Stuhlen. — **Set of furniture,** white enamelled, 1 table, 2 chairs. — **Juego de muebles,** compuesto de 1 mesa, 2 sillas.

17/1006

Möbelgarnitur, farbig lackiert, aufgenäht auf feinem Karton. – **Set of furniture,** white enamelled. — **Juego de muebles,** barnizado colorado y casido sobre cartón fino.

17/1004/5

Möbelgarnitur, mit rundem Tisch und runden Stühlen, Garnitur fein lackiert. **Set of furniture,** with round table and chairs. — **Juego de muebles,** con mesa redonda y sillas redondas, barnizado fino.

17/1007/0

Möbelgarnitur, best. aus 1 Tisch, 6 Stühlen, auf Karton. – **Set of furniture,** 1 table, 6 chairs. **Juego de muebles,** 1 mesa, 6 sillas, sobre cartón.

17/171
Waschständer mit Blechkübel.
Washing set with washing tub.
Juegos lavatorios.

17/402
Badeständer auf Bock, fein lackiert.
Doll's bath on stand, white enamelled.
Juegos lavatorios.

17/116

Nr. **17**/113
Besenständer, hochfein weiß lackiert.
Brush stand, finely white enamelled.
Porta-escobas, barnizado blanco muy fino.

Nr. **17**/116
Besenständer, naturlackiert, mit guten Besen.
Brush stand, varnished, with good brushes.
Porta-escobas, barnizado natural, con buenas escobas.

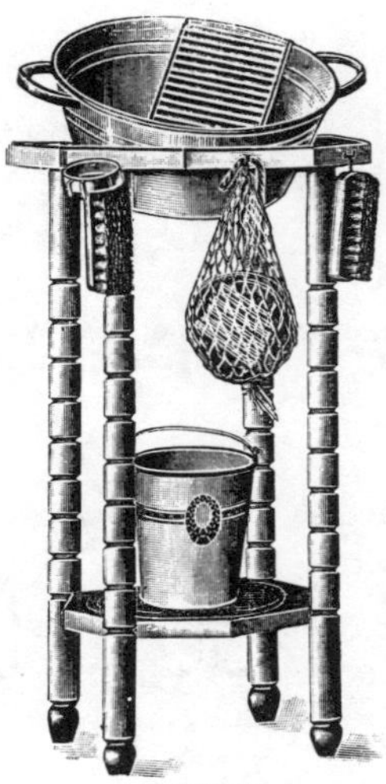

17/172
Waschständer mit Blechkübel, moderne Ausführung und feine Bemalung.
Washing set, white enamelled.
Juegos lavatorios.

17/415
Kaffeemühle.
Coffee machine.
Molinillo de café.

17/536/1
Küchenwage. — Scale.
Balanza de cocina.

17/325/2
Küchenlampe z. Brennen.
Lamp. — Lámpara de cocina para encender.

17/124
Dirndl-Schaukel.
Doll's swing, nicely painted.
Mecedor-moza.

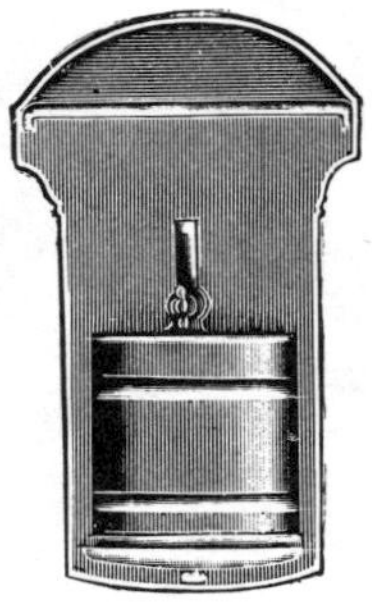

17/510/2
Handwaschgefäß, lack.
Washhand basin.
Vasija lava-manos, barnizado.

17/550
Mehlschaufel.
Flour scoop.
Paleta de harina.

17/660
Mandelreiber.
Almond mincer.
Pallador de almendras.

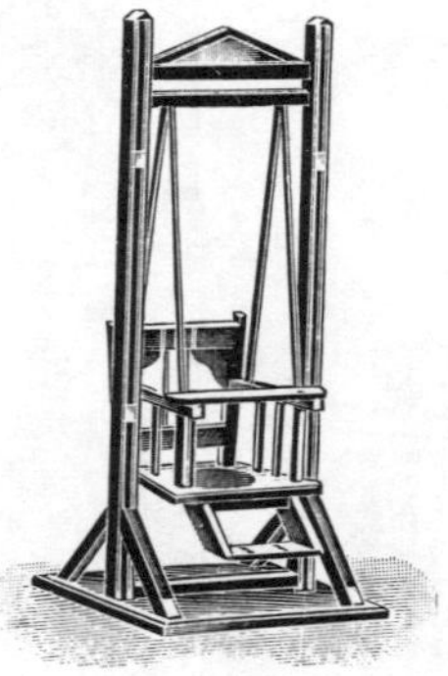

17/122
Puppenschaukel, farbig lackiert.
Doll's swing, painted in colours.
Mecedor-muñeca, barnizado colorado.

17/353
Brotkasten.
Bread box.
Cajita-pan.

17/354
Biskuitkasten.
Biscuit box.
Cajita-bizcochos.

Kaffee- u. Tee-dose.
Coffee and tea canister.
Caja de café.

17/413

17/911/1
Aufsatz mit 2 Töpfen.
Kitchen rack.
Tocado con 2 jarras.

17/9036/1
Wellholzhalter.
Rolling pin rack.
Porta-haz de leña.

17/911/2
Aufsatz mit 3 Töpfen.
Kitchen rack.
Tocado con 3 jarras.

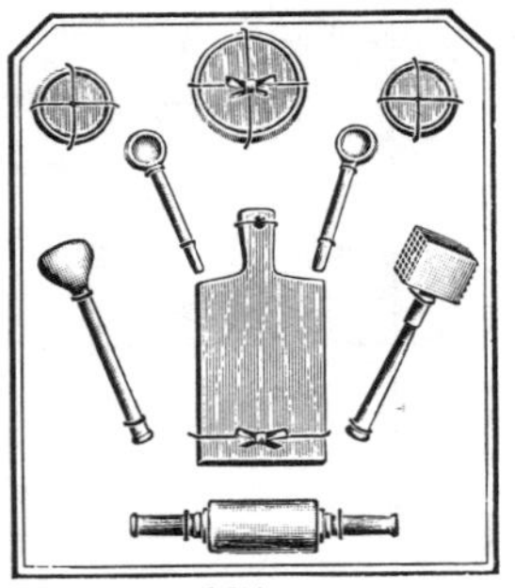

17/770
Küchengarnitur.
Cooking set, wood.
Juego de cocina.

17/6031
Biskuitdose, Glas, mit Doppelfassung.
Biscuit box.
Cajita-bizcochos, vidrio, doble engaste.

17/908
Parkettbohner (Blocker).
Polisher. — Encerador.

17/6034
Aufsatz, doppelt, mit 2 Glastellern.
Cake stand.
Tocado doble con 2 platos de vidrio.

17/936
Wellholz. — Rolling pin.
Haz de leña.

17/9036/2
Wellholzhalter mit Etagere.
Rolling pin rack.
Porta-haz de leña con consola.

17/6032
Dessertteller, Glas mit Henkel.
Fruit plate.
Plato-postre, vidrio con mango.

17/6035
Fruchtkorb, Glas.
Fruit basket.
Castillo-frutas, vidrio.

17/6033
Fruchtschale, Glas.
Fruit stand.
Platillo-frutas, vidrio.

17/6030
Fruchtschale.
Fruit stand.
Platillo-frutas.

17/911/3
Aufsatz mit 2 Dosen und Kaffeemühle.
Kitchen rack.
Tocado con 2 cajitas y molinillo de café.

17/348
Tischtelephon, groß.
Table telephone, large.
Teléfono, grande.

17/345/0
Telephon, zum Läuten.
Telephone.
Teléfono, para tocar.

17/345/2
Telephon, größer u. stärker.
Telephone, bigger and stronger.
Teléfono más grande y fuerte.

17/720
Bügeleisen mit Stahl.
Irons, best made.
Plancha con acero.

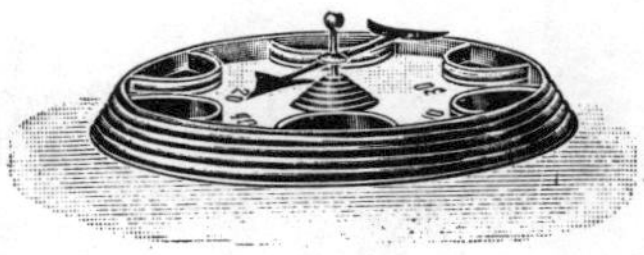

17/2088
Drehbrett, beliebtes Spiel für kleinere Kinder.
Game, very amusing.
Torno, juguete preferido por niños.

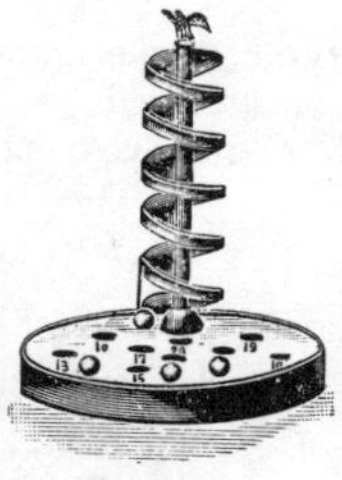

17/103/0—/1

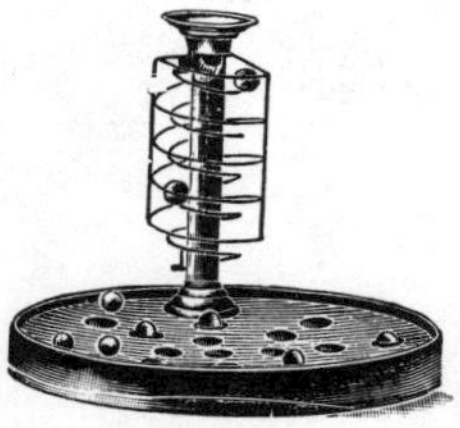

17/103/2

17/102/2½

Turmspiel, sehr beliebtes Gesellschaftsspiel für jung und alt (jedes Stück in Karton).
Tower game, very amusing, best value (each in a box).
Juego de torre, juego bien apreciado por adultos y niños (cada pieza en cartón).

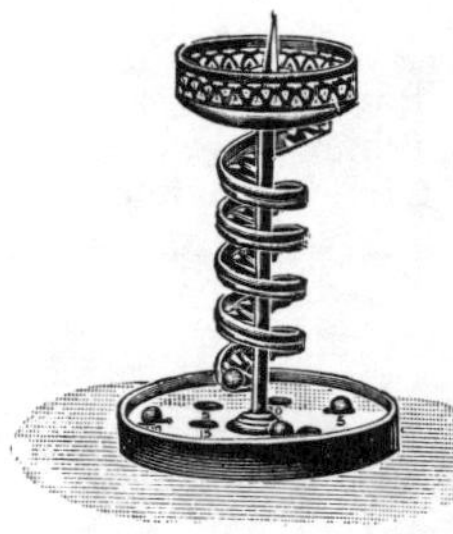

17/2045
Turm-Roulette.
Tower roulette.
Ruleta torre.

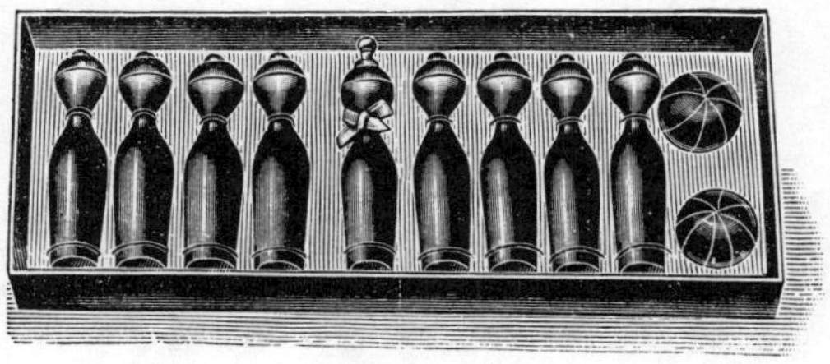

17/1961
Kegelspiel, in Karton aufgenäht, mit ganz feinpolierten Kegeln und Kugeln.
Skittles, wood, highly polished, in box.
Bolzo en cartón, superior y barnizado fino.

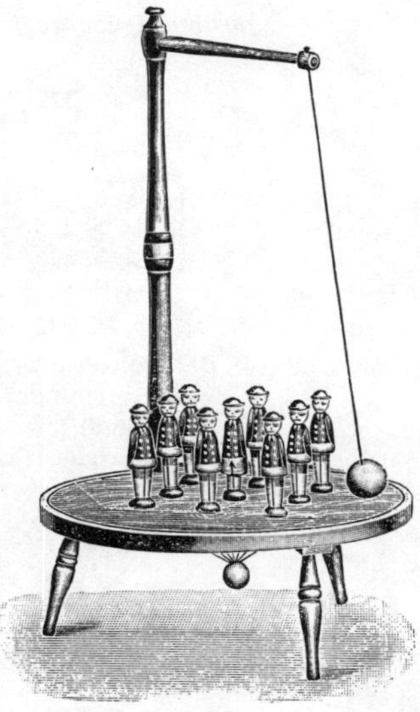

17/1921
Kegeltisch mit fein bemalten Bauernkegeln.
Skittles, nicely painted.
Juego de bolos, barnizado fino.

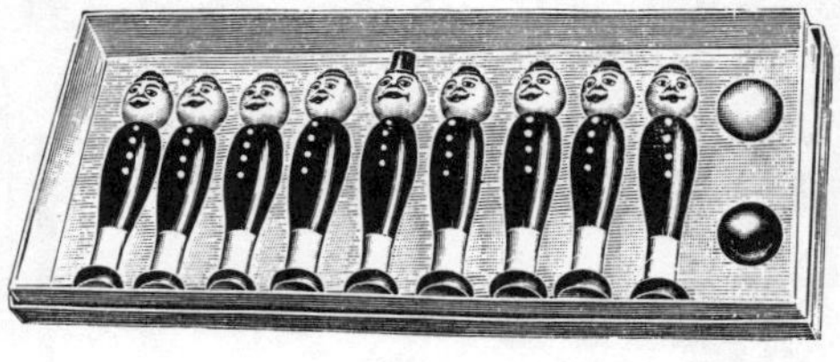

17/1960/6
Kegelspiel in hochfeinem Karton und schöner Lackierung.
Skittles, nicely painted, 6 different patterns.
Bolzo en carton, superior y barnizado fino.

17/100
Kegeltisch, fein poliert.
Skittles, highly polished.
Juego de bolos, barnizado superior.

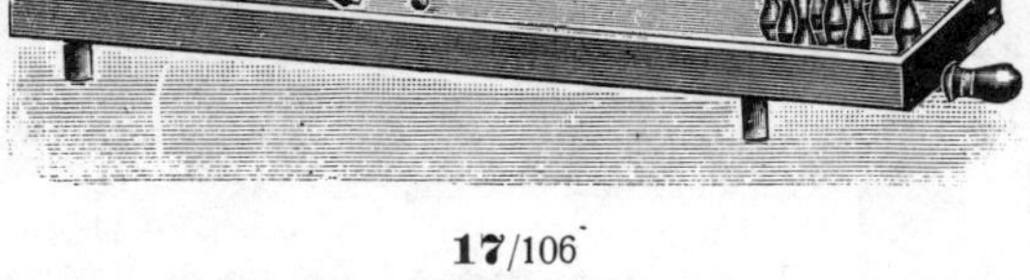

17/106
Kegelbahn, Holz.
Bowling place, green, wood.
Polzo, madera.

17/2022

17/2023

Schnellspiel mit Metallgarnitur in neuer feiner Aufmachung.
New flip game, 4 players. — **New flip game,** 6 players.
Juego de lance con guarnición de metal en ejucución nueva y fina.

17/63/5

Büfettwagen, groß.
Buffet, large, strongly made.
Carretilla-bufete, grande.

17/150/2

Marktstand mit Schirm, reichhaltig garniert.
Market stand, with umbrella.
Tiendo de mercado, copiosamente guarn.

17/64/2

Büfettwagen, groß, schön garniert.
Buffet, large, nicely fitted.
Carretilla-bufete, grande, bonito guarn.

17/240

Blumentisch, rund.
Flower stand, round.
Jardinera, redonda.

17/237

Blumentisch, mit Seitenaufsätzen.
Flower stand.
Jardinera.

17/63/0–3

Büfettwagen, feine Lackierung.
Buffet, nicely fitted.
Carretilla-bufete, barnizado fino.

17/241

Blumentisch.
Flower stand.
Jardinera.

17/238

Blumentisch, hübsch garniert, mit kleiner Gießkanne.
Flower stand with sprinkling can.
Jardinera con regadera.

17/239

Blumentisch mit Vogelkäfig.
Flower stand with birds cage.
Jardinera con pajarera.

17/202

Waschtisch.
Wash stand.
Lavabo.

17/150/6

Marktstand, groß, schönes Ausstellungsstück.
Market stand, large, splendid show piece.
Tienda de mercado, grande, propio para exposición.

17/230

Bettstelle mit Drahtgitter.
Bed stead.
Armadura de la cama.

17/232

Bettstelle mit Sprungfedermatratze.
Bed stead.
Armadura de la cama.

17/303

Blumentisch.
Flower stand.
Jardinera.

17/236

Blumentisch, rund
Flower stand, round.
Jardinera, redonda.

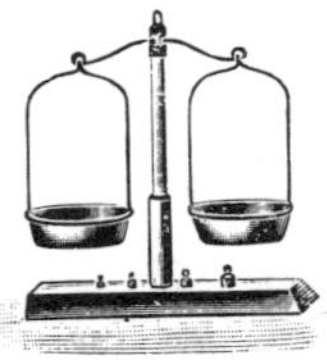

17/527

Ständerwage mit Messingschalen.
Scales.
Balanza.

17/270/2

Grammophon, sehr gangbarer Artikel.
Doll's Grammoph.
Gramophon por muñecas.

17/526

Tafelwage mit Messingschalen. — **Scales** for doll's shop. — **Balanza.**

17/162/1

Küche, hochfein lackiert, garniert ohne Herd.
Kitchen, wood, finely enamelled, fitted without stove.
Cocina, barnizado superior, guarn. sin fogón.

17/349

Telephonzelle für Kaufladen, enthaltend kleines Telephon.
Telephone box for doll's shop.
Locutorio para almacén, conteniendo pequeño teléfono.

17/555

Ladenkasse für Kaufladen.
Cash for shops.
Caja de almacén para almacén.

Große Verkaufstände, hochfein lackiert, zusammenlegbar und sehr raumsparend.

Grocery shop, high-class wood, highly japanned and foulding up.
Almacénes grandes, barnizados superior, á doblar.

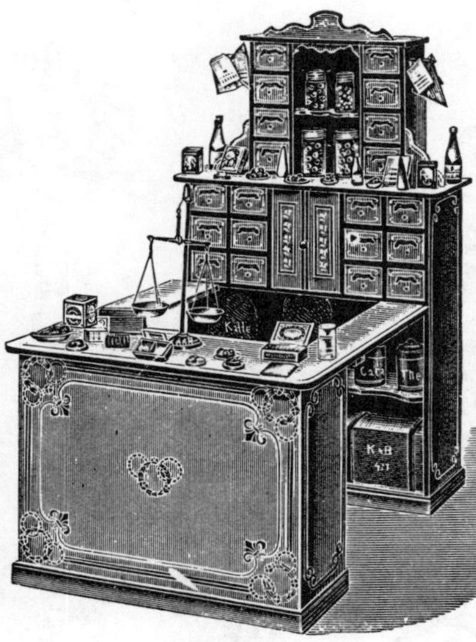

17/140/11

Verkaufstand, fein lackiert.
Grocery, large, highly finished, foulding up.
Tienda, grande, barnizado superior, guarn. fino, á doblar.

17/140/17

Verkaufstand, groß, hochfein lackiert und sehr reichhaltig garniert.
Grocery, large, highly finished, english inscriptions, foulding up.
Tienda, grande, barnizado superior y copiosamente guarn. y á doblar. Suscripciones españoles.

17/140

Ladentische (Theken), fein weiß lackiert.
Grocery counters, fitted white enamelled, english inscriptions.
Almacén, barnizado superior, guarn.

17/137/1—5

Kaufladen, tapeziert und weiß lackiert.
Grocery shop, nicely finished, english inscriptions.
Almacén, entapizado y barnizado blanco.

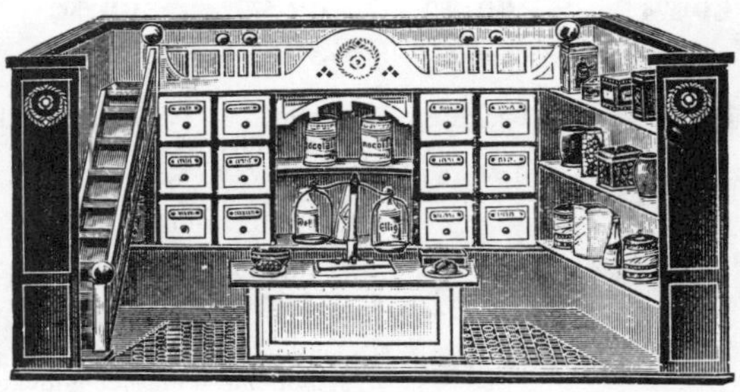

17/144/1—5

Kaufladen, hochfein lackiert.
Grocery shop, highly japanned, english inscriptions.
Almacén, barnizado superior, con suscripciones españoles.

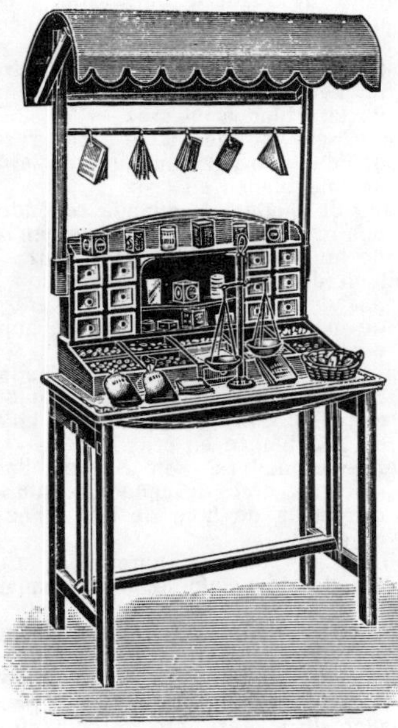

17/150/7½

Marktstand mit Dach, fein lackiert und zusammenlegbar.
Market stand, large, nicely fitted, foulding up.
Tienda de mercado con tejado, barnizado fino y á doblar.

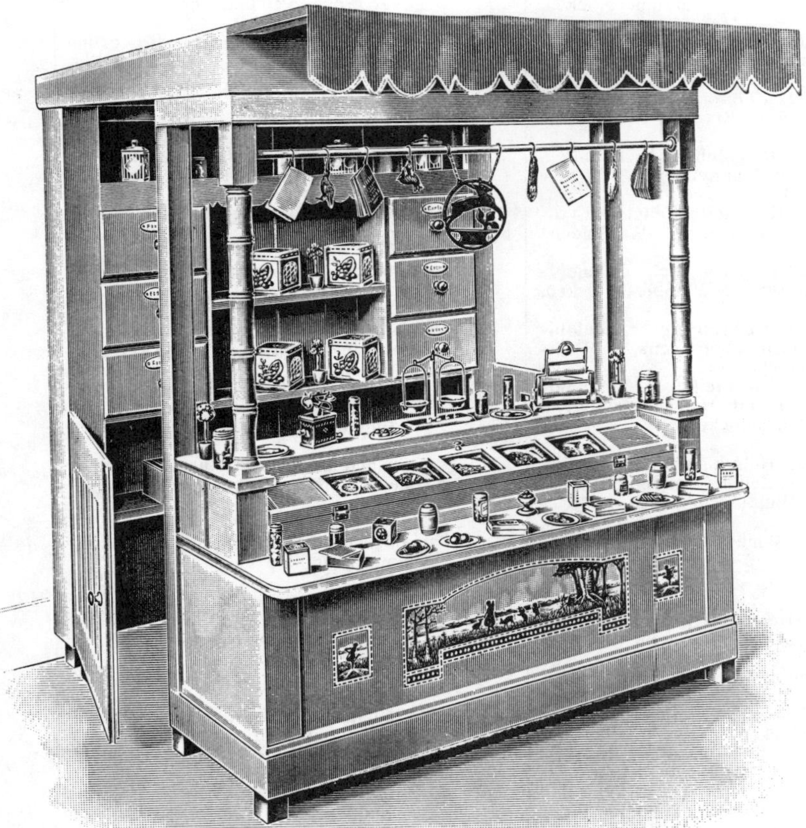

17/140/18

Kaufladen, groß, hübsch garniert, mit abnehmbarem Dach. — **Grocery,** large, nicely fitted (roof can be taken off). — **Almacén,** grande, bonito guarn., con tejado á quitar.

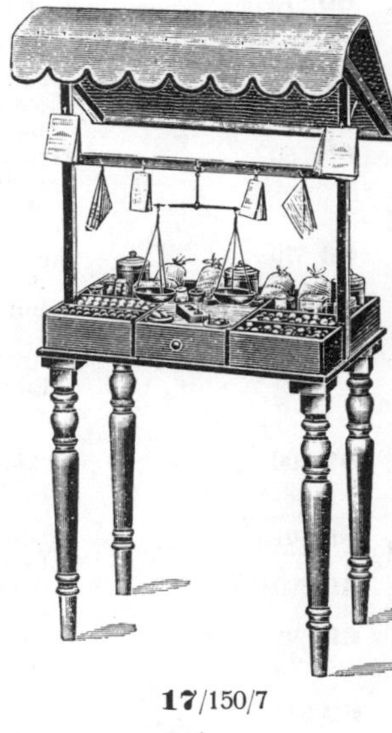

17/150/7

Marktstand, groß.
Market stand, large, nicely fitted, foulding up.
Tienda de mercado, grande, bonito guarn., á doblar.

Schlottern. — Rattles. — Sonajeros.

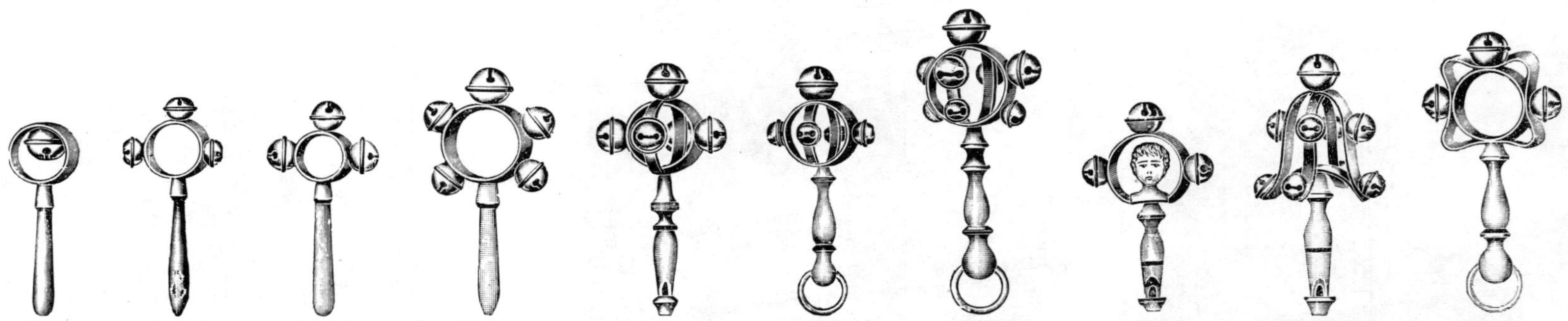

69/566 69/555 69/500 69/503 69/506 E 69/507 69/508 69/561 69/565 Pf 69/572

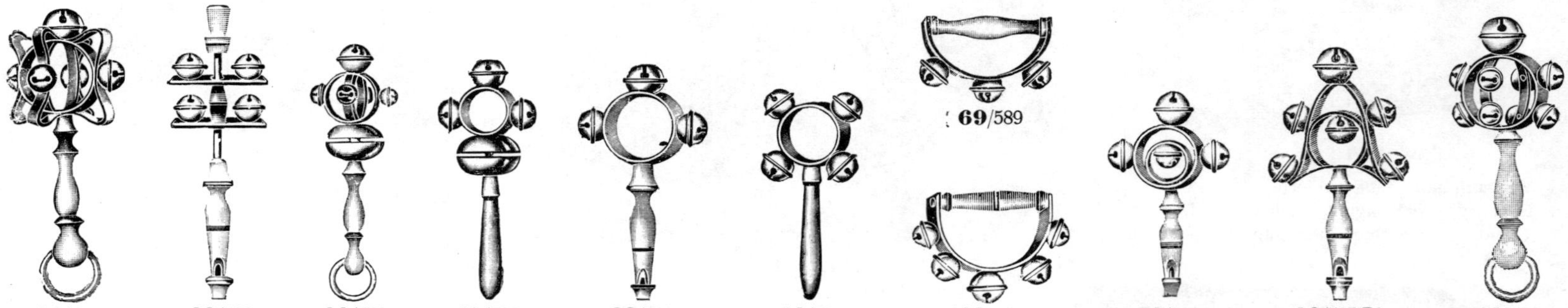

69/574 69/580 69/579 69/592 69/600 69/801 69/589 69/591 69/523 69/527 Pf. 69/530

Nr. **69**/566	Schlotter, Holzstiel, 1 Weißblechglocke im Zelluloidreifen.	Rattle, wood handles, 1 tinplate bell in celluloid hoop.	Sonajero, cabo de madera, con una campana de hoja de lata blanca en un arco de celuloido.
„ **69**/555	„ Holzstiel, Zelluloidreifen, 3 kleine Weißblechglocken.	„ wood handles, celluloid hoop, 3 small tinplate bells.	„ cabo de madera, arco de celuloido, 3 pequenas campanas de hoja de lata blanca.
„ **69**/500	„ Holzstiel, Zelluloidreifen, 3 größere Weißblechglocken.	„ wood handles, celluloid hoop, 3 larger tinplate bells.	„ cabo de madera, arco de celuloido, 3 grandes campanas de hoja de lata blanca.
„ **69**/503	„ Holzstiel, Zelluloidreifen, 5 verschiedene Weißblechglocken.	„ wood handles, celluloid hoop, 5 different tinplate bells.	„ cabo de madera, celuloido, 5 diferentes campanas de hoja de lata blanca.
„ **69**/506	„ lackierte Holzpfeife, Zelluloidreifen über Kreuz, 5 Weißblechglocken.	„ varnished wooden pipe, celluloid hoop over cross, 5 tinplate bells.	„ pifano de madera barnizada, con arco de celuloido y 5 campanas de hoja de lata blanca en cruz.
„ **69**/507	„ lackierter Holzringstiel, Zelluloidreifen über Kreuz, 5 Weißblechglocken.	„ varnished wooden ring handle, celluloid hoop over cross, 5 tinplate bells.	„ cabo redondo de madera, con arco de celuloido y 5 campanas de hoja de lata blanca en cruz.
„ **69**/508	„ lackierter Holzringstiel, Zelluloidreifen über Kreuz, 9 Weißblechglocken.	„ varnished wooden ring handle, celluloid hoop over cross, 9 tinplate bells.	„ cabo redondo de madera, con arco de celuloido y 9 campanas de hoja de lata blanca en cruz.
„ **69**/561	„ lackierte Holzpfeife, Nickelreifen, Zelluloid-Puppenkopf, 3 Nickelglocken.	„ varnished wooden pipe, nickel hoop, celluloid doll's head and 3 nickel bells.	„ pifano de madera barnizada, arco de níquel y cabeza de muneca, con 3 campanas de níquel.
„ **69**/565 Pf.	„ lackierte Holzpfeife, Zelluloid, Lyraform über Kreuz, 9 Weißblechglocken.	„ varnished wooden pipe, celluloid in form of lyre over cross, 9 tinplate bells.	„ pifano de madera barnizada, con lira de celuloido y 9 campanas de hoja de lata blanca en cruz.
„ **69**/572	„ lackierter Holzringstiel, Zelluloid-Rosenform, 3 Weißblechglocken.	„ varnished wooden ring handle, celluloid in form of rose, 3 tinplate bells.	„ cabo redondo de madera, con rosa de celuloido y 3 campanas de hoja de lata blanca en cruz.
„ **69**/574	„ lackierter Holzringstiel, Zelluloid-Rosenform über Kreuz, 5 Weißblechglocken.	„ varnished wooden ring handle, celluloid in form of rose over cross, 5 tinplate bells.	„ cabo de madera barnizada redondo, con rosa de celuloido y 5 campanas de hoja de lata blanca en cruz.
„ **69**/580	„ lackierte Holzpfeife, 2 Zelluloidspangen mit Holzmittelstück, 4 Weißblechglocken.	„ varnished wooden pipe, 2 celluloid spangles with wooden middle piece, 4 tinplate bells.	„ pifano de madera barnizada, con 2 pasadores de celuloido, con centro de madera y 4 campanas de hoja de lata blanca en cruz.
„ **69**/579	„ lackierter Holzringstiel, 2 massive Schalen, Zelluloidreifen üb. Kreuz, mit 5 Weißblechglocken.	„ varnished wooden ring handle, 2 solid shells, celluloid hoop, 5 tinplate bells.	„ cabo redondo de madera barnizada, con 2 escudillas macidas, arco de celuloido con 5 campanas de hoja de lata blanca en cruz.
„ **69**/592	„ Holzstiel, 2 massive Schalen, Zelluloidreifen, 3 Weißblechglocken.	„ wooden handle, 2 solid shells, celluloid hoop, 3 tinplate bells.	„ cabo de madera, con 2 escudillas macizas, arco de celuloido, con 3 campanas de hoja de lata blanca en cruz.
„ **69**/600	„ lackierte Holzpfeife, großer Zelluloidreifen, 3 Nickelglocken.	„ varnished wooden pipe, large celluloid hoop, 3 nickel bells.	„ pifano de madera barnizada, aro grande de celuloido, 3 campanas de níquel.
„ **69**/801	„ Ausführung wie Nr. 501, jedoch Leder statt Zelluloidreifen.	„ style as 501, but leather instead of celluloid hoop.	„ ejecución como no. 501 pero aro de cuero en vez de celuloido.
„ **69**/589	„ Holzgriff, Zelluloidreifen, 3 Weißblechglocken.	„ varnished wooden handle, celluloid hoop, 3 tinplate bells.	„ mango de madera, aro de celuloido, 3 campanas de hoja de lata blanca.
„ **69**/591	„ Holzgriff, Zelluloidreifen, 5 verschiedene Weißblechglocken.	„ varnished wooden handle, celluloid hoop, 5 different tinplate bells.	„ mango de madera, aro de celuloido, 5 diversas campanas de hoja de lata blanca.
„ **69**/523	„ lackierte Holzpfeife, Zelluloidreifen, 2 Messing-, 2 Nickelglocken.	„ varnished wooden pipe, celluloid hoop, 2 brass and 2 nickel bells.	„ pifano de madera, aro de celuloido, 2 campanas de latón y 2 de níquel.
„ **69**/527 Pf.	„ lackierte Holzpfeife, Zelluloid-Lyraform, 3 Messing-, 3 Nickelglocken.	„ varnished wooden pipe, celluloid in form of lyre, 3 brass and 3 nickel bells.	„ Pifano de madera, lira de celuloido, 3 campanas de latón y 3 de níquel.
„ **69**/530	„ Ausführung wie Nr. 508, jedoch 5 Messing- und 4 Nickelglocken.	„ style of 508, but 5 brass bells, and 4 nickel ones.	„ ejecución como de no. 508 pero con 5 campanas de latón y 4 de níquel.

Schlottern. — Rattles. — Sonajeros.

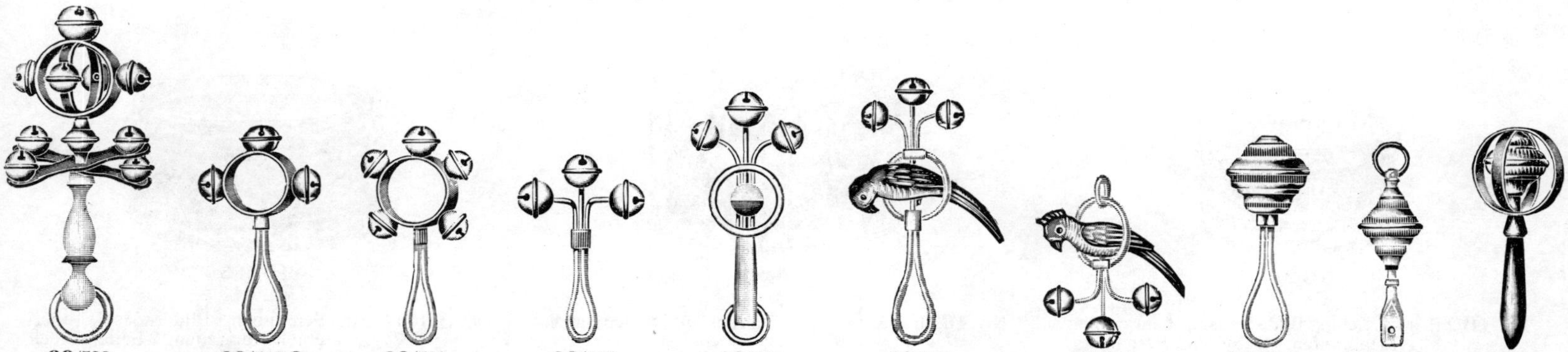

69/533 69/543 C 69/539 69/545 69/546 69/548 69/552 69/556 69/560 69/605

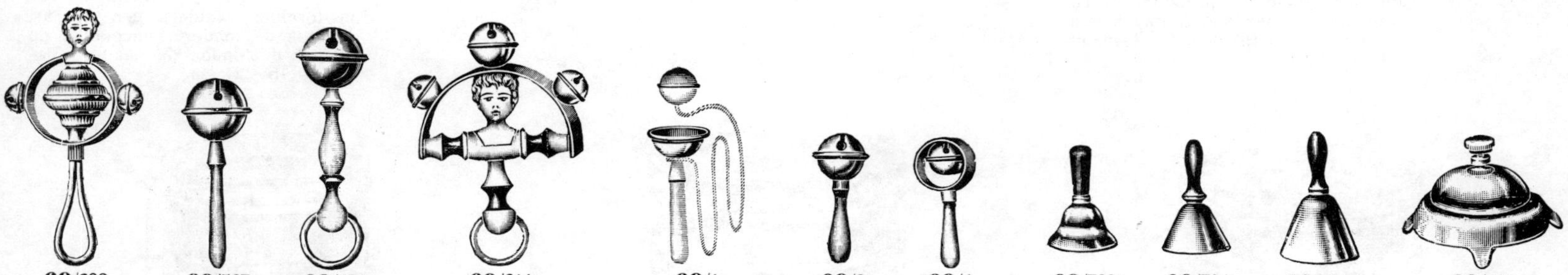

69/608 69/567 69/571 69/611 69/1 69/2 69/4 69/708 69/704 69/706 69/702

Nr. 69/533	Schlotter, Ausführung wie Nr. 511, jedoch 5 Messing- und 4 Nickelglocken.	Rattle, style of 511, but 5 brass bells and 4 nickel ones and one brass middle piece.	Sonajero, ejecución como no. 511 pero con 5 campanas de latón y 4 de níquel y centro de madera.
„ 69/543 C	„ Zelluloid-Gabelstiel, Zelluloidreifen, 3 Weißblechglocken.	„ celluloid fork handle, celluloid hoop, 3 tinplate bells.	„ horquilla de celuloido con 3 campanas de hoja de lata blanca.
„ 69/539	„ Zelluloid-Gabelstiel, großer Nickelreifen, 5 Nickelglocken.	„ celluloid fork handle, large nickel hoop, 5 nickel bells.	„ horquilla de celuloido con 5 campanas y grande aro de níquel.
„ 69/545	„ Zelluloid-Gabelstiel, 3 Fäden, 3 Weißblechglocken.	„ celluloid fork handle, 3 tinplate bells.	„ horquilla de celuloido con 3 cabos, 3 campanas de hoja de lata blanca.
„ 69/546	„ Zelluloidstiel mit Ballen, 3 Nickelglocken.	„ celluloid handles with balls, 3 nickel bells.	„ cabo de celuloido con bolas y 3 campanas de níquel.
„ 69/548	„ Zelluloidstiel mit buntem Zelluloidvogel, 3 Weißblechglocken.	„ celluloid handle, with coloured celluloid bird, 3 tinplate bells.	„ cabo de celuloido con pajaros de celuloido multicolores y 3 campanas de hoja de lata blanca.
„ 69/552	Gehänge, bunter Zelluloidvogel im Ring, 3 Messingglocken.	Coloured celluloid birds hung in ring, 3 brass bells.	„ pajaros multicolores pendientes en un arco con 3 campanas de latón.
„ 69/556	Aluminiumschlotter mit Zelluloidstiel.	Aluminium rattle, with celluloid handle.	„ de aluminio con cabo de celuloido.
„ 69/560	„ mit Beinstiel und Galalithring.	„ „ with leg handle and galalith ring.	„ de aluminio con cabo de hueso y arco de galalite.
„ 69/605	„ mit Holzstiel und Zelluloidreifen über Kreuz.	„ „ with wooden handle and celluloid hoop over cross.	„ de aluminio con cabo de madera y arco de celuloido en cruz.
„ 69/608	„ mit Zelluloidstiel und Puppenkopf, Zelluloidreifen mit 2 Glocken.	„ „ with celluloid handle and doll's head and cell. hoop with 2 bells.	„ de aluminio con cabo celuloido y cabeza de muñeca y arco celuloide con 2 campanas.
„ 69/567	Schlotter, Holzstiel, große Weißblechkugel.	Rattle, wooden handle, large tinplate ball.	„ cabo de madera con grande bola de hoja de lata blanca.
„ 69/571	„ lackierter Ringstiel, große Messingkugel.	„ varnished ring handle, large brass ball.	„ cabo redondo barnizado grande bola de latón.
„ 69/611	„ lackierter Kreuzstiel mit Ring und Puppenkopf, 2 Nickel- und 1 Messinglocke.	„ varnished cross handle with ring and doll's head, 2 nickel and 1 brass ball.	„ cabo en cruz barnizado con arco y cabeza de muñeca, 2 campanas de niquel, 1 de latón.
„ 69/1	Fangbecher, Holzstiel, lackierte Blechkugel.	Cup and ball, wood handle, varnished tinplate ball.	Cabo de madera con una copa y bola de hoja de lata barnizada.
„ 69/2	Puppenschlotter, Holzstiel, 1 Weißblechglocke.	Doll's rattle, wood handle, 1 tinplate bell.	Sonajero de muñeca con cabo de madera, 1 campana de hoja de lata blanca.
„ 69/4	„ Holzstiel, 1 Weißblechglocke im Zelluloidreifen.	„ „ wood handle, 1 tinplate bell in celluloid hoop.	„ de muñeca con cabo de madera, 1 campana de hoja de lata blanca, 1 aro celuloido.
„ 69/708	Tischglocke, Weißblech, lackierter Holzstiel.	Table bell, tinplate, varnished stand.	Campanilla de mesa de hoja de lata blanca con cabo de madera barnizada.
„ 69/704	„ massiv vernickelt, Holzstiel.	„ „ solid nickeled, wooden stand.	„ de mesa maciza niquelada con cabo de madera.
„ 69/706	„ „ „ „	„ „ solid nickeled, wooden stand.	„ de mesa maciza niquelada con cabo de madera.
„ 69/702	„ zum Drehen, massiv.	„ „ solid, to rotate.	„ de mesa maciza para manejarse.

Trommeln. — Drums. — Tambores.

16/2 H

Nr. **16**/2 H Mit Leine, Bilderkessel, überklebten Holzreifen, 2 Seiten Pergament. Größe 12—24 cm.

With cord, cylinder with pictures, wood rims pasted over, both ends parchment. Sizes 12 - 24 cm.

Con cuerda, caldera con figuras, cerco de madera encolado de papel, dos lados de pergamino. Tamaño 12 – 24 cm.

16/66

Nr. **16**/66 Mit Leine, Bilderkessel, 2 Seiten Blech. Größe 12—24 cm.

With cord, cylinder with pictures, 2 sides sheet metal. Sizes 12—24 cm.

Con cuerda, caldera con figuras, 2 lados de chapa. Tamaño 12 - 24 cm.

16/61 S

Nr. **16**/61 S Mit Schrauben, Bilderkessel, überklebten Holzreifen, 2 Seiten Blech. Größe 16 - 24 cm.

With adjusting screws, cylinder with pictures, wood rims pasted over, both ends sheet metal. Sizes 16 - 24 cm.

Con tornillos, caldera con figuras, cercos de madera, encolados de papel, dos lados de chapa. Tamaño 16 – 24 cm.

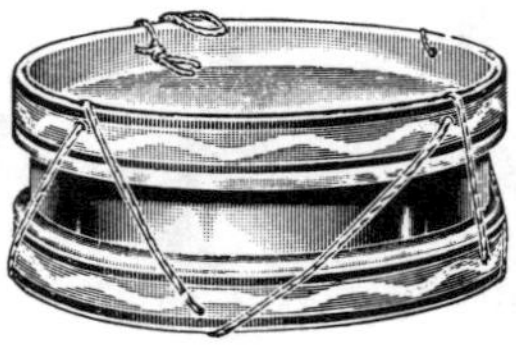

16/$1^1/_2$

Nr. **16**/$1^1/_2$ Mit Leine, Blechkessel, überklebten Holzreifen, eine Seite Fell, eine Seite Stoffpergament. Größe 18 - 32 cm.

With cord, sheet metal cylinder, wood rims pasted over, 1 end vellum, 1 end parchment. Sizes 18 32 cm.

Con cuerda, caldera de chapa, cercos de madera encolados de papel, un lado de piel, un lado de pergamino de estofa. Tamaño 18 - 32 cm.

16/$1^1/_2$ S

Nr. **16**/$1^1/_2$ S Mit Schrauben, Blechkessel, überklebten Holzreifen, eine Seite Fell, eine Seite Stoffpergament. Größe 18 - 32 cm.

With adjusting screws, sheet metal cylinder, wood rims past d over, 1 end vellum, 1 end parchment. Sizes 18—32 cm.

Con tornillos, caldera de chapa, cercos de madera encolados de papel, un lado de piel, un lado de pergamino de estofa. Tamaño 18 – 32 cm.

16/$1^3/_2$ Sp

Nr. **16**/$^3/_2$ Sp Mechanische Trommel. Auf dieser Trommel kann jedes Kind durch Drehen einer Scheibe einen taktmäßigen Marsch spielen, außerdem ist dieselbe mit den beigegebenen Stöcken wie eine gewöhnliche Trommel zu benutzen. Größe 18 - 24 cm.

Mechanical drums. On this drum any child can play amarch in proper tact by simply turning a disc, besides which it can be used like an ordinary drum with the drumsticks supplied with it. Sizes 18 – 24 cm.

Tambores con mecanismo. Dando vueltas a un disco, todo niño puede hacer sonar una marcha, fuera de esto, usando los palillos eccesorios, se puede manejarla de la misma manera que un tambor ordinario. Tamaño 18 – 24 cm.

Säbel. — Swords. — Sables.

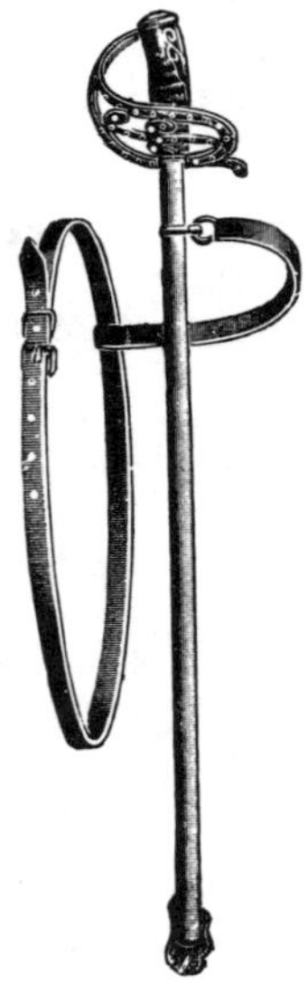

2004/1 und 2

Nr. **2004**/1 57 cm
„ **2004**/2 65 „

2004/3 und 4

Nr. **2004**/3 55 cm
„ **2004**/4 65 „

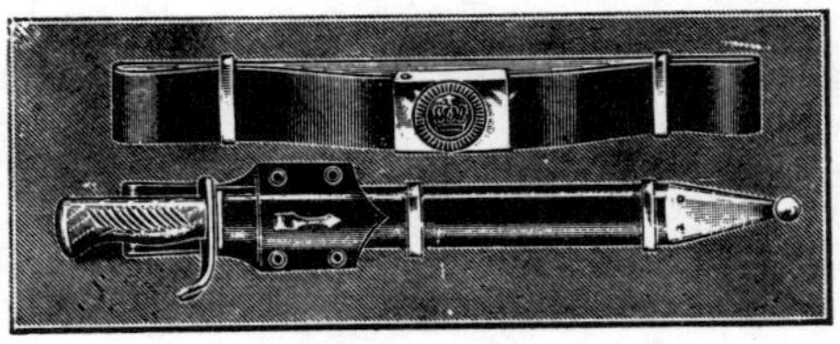

2004/11 und 12

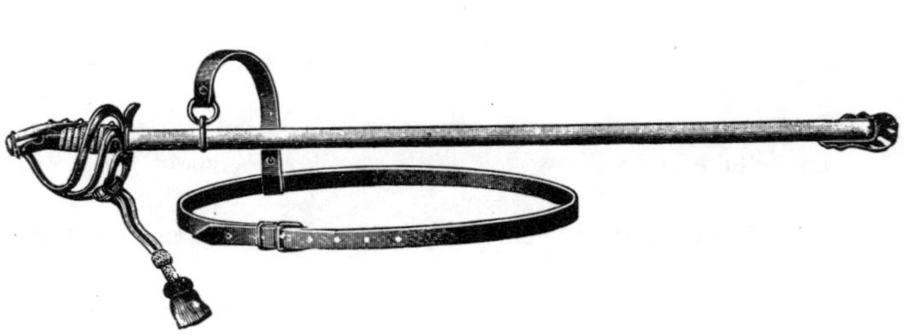

2004/9 und 10

Nr. **2004**/9 72 cm

Nr. **2004**/10 82 cm

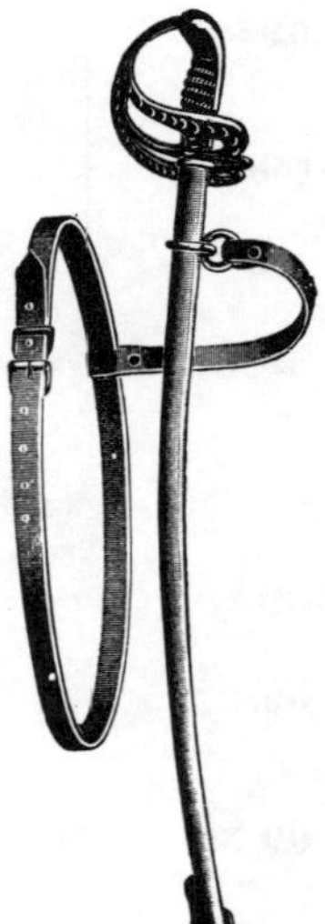

2004/5

Nr. **2004**/5 72 cm

Kinder-Pistolen. — Pistols for children. — Pistolas para niños.

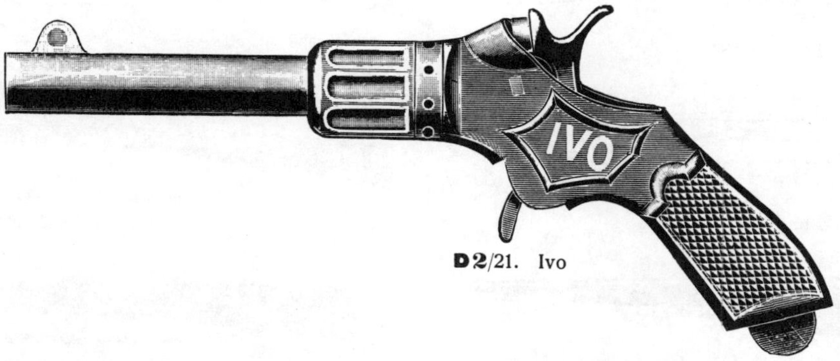

D2/21. Ivo

Amorces-Pistolen. — Percussion-cap pistols. — Pistolas tiradas por cápsulas fulminantes.

Länge — Length — Altura: 13 cm = $5^1/_4$ inches.

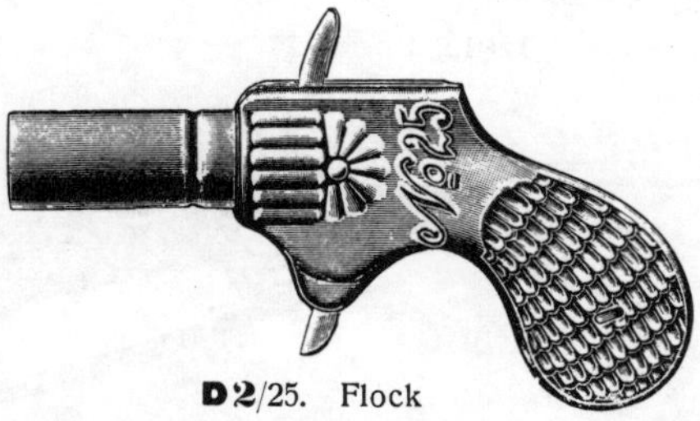

D2/25. Flock

Knallkorken- oder Schreckschuß-Pistolen. — Pop-guns or scare-shot pistols. Pistolas tirando con corchos dando un estallido y pistolas de alarma.

Nr. **D2**/25 Flock, im Ofen hochglanz schwarz lackiert.
Flock, in the heat black japanned.
Flock, embarnizadas y bruñidas en negro en el horno.

„ **D2**/$25^1/_2$ Flock, mit Nickelgriff und blauem Lauf.
Flock, with nickeled handle and blue barrel.
Flock, con mango de níquel y canon azul.

Länge — Length — Altura: 12 cm = $4^3/_4$ inches.

D2/26. Nora

Knallkorken- oder Schreckschuß-Pistolen. — Pop-guns or scare-shot pistols. Pistolas tirando con corchos dando un estallido y pistolas de alarma.

Nr. **D2**/26 Nora, im Ofen hochglanz schwarz lackiert.
Nora, in the heat black japanned.
Nora, embarnizadas y bruñidas en negro en el horno.

„ **D2**/$26^1/_2$ Nora, für Liliput-Munition.
Nora, for Liliput-ammunition.
Nora, para la munición Liliput.

Länge — Length — Altura: 13 cm = $5^1/_8$ inches.

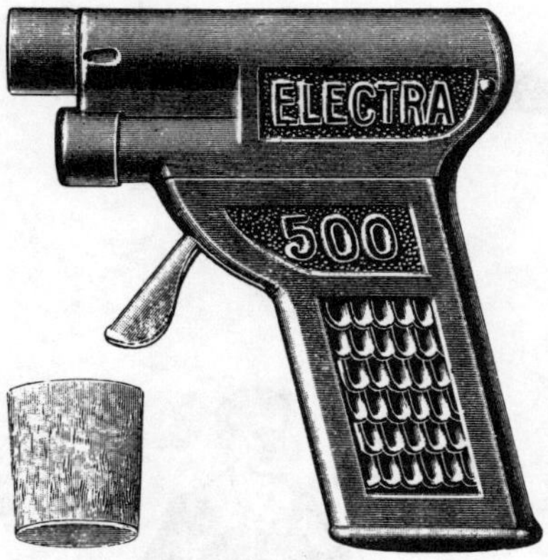

D2/500. Electra

Knallkorken- oder Schreckschuß-Pistolen. — Pop-guns or scare-shot pistols. Pistolas tirando con corchos dando un estallido y pistolas de alarma.

Nr. **D2**/500 Electra, im Ofen hochglanz schwarz lackiert.
Electra, in the heat black japanned.
Electra, embarnizadas y bruñidas en negro en el horno.

Länge — Length — Altura: 13 cm = $5^1/_2$ inches.

D2/575

100 Schuß Amorces-Repetier-Pistole. — Repeating pistols for paper percussion caps, 100 shot. — Pistola de repetición tirada por cápsulas fulminantes y arreglada por 100 tiros.

Länge — Length — Altura: $12^1/_2$ cm = 5 inches.

Knallflinten. — Pop guns.
Fusiles con corcho.

18/131, 132, 133 und 134

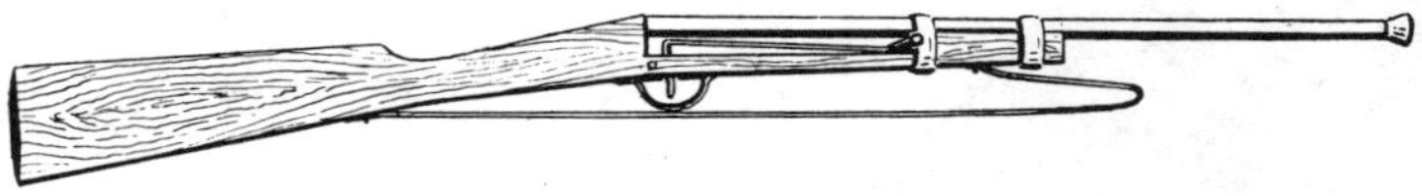

18/135, 836 und 658

18/659/1 und 659/2

18/588

18/867

18/175, 176/2 und 668

18/627, 628 und 629

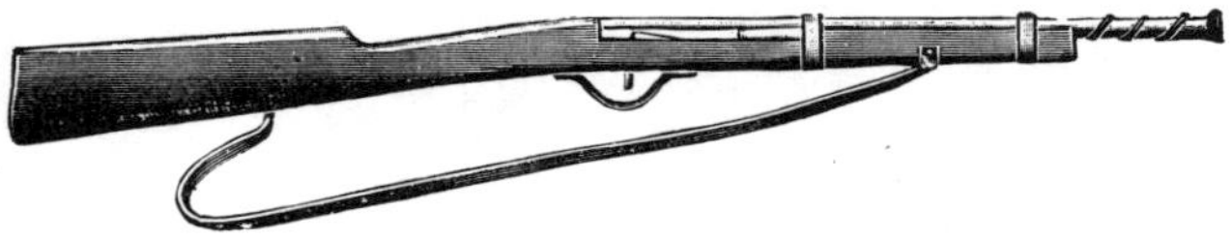

18/146/2 und 146/3

Perkussionsflinten. — Percussion guns.
Fusiles de percusión.

18/371

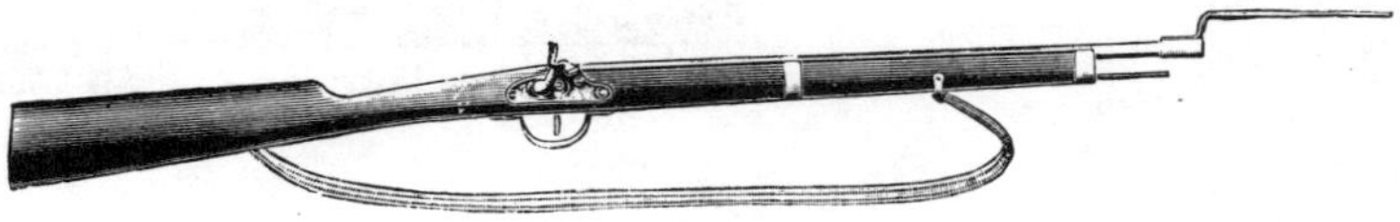

18/845 und 27

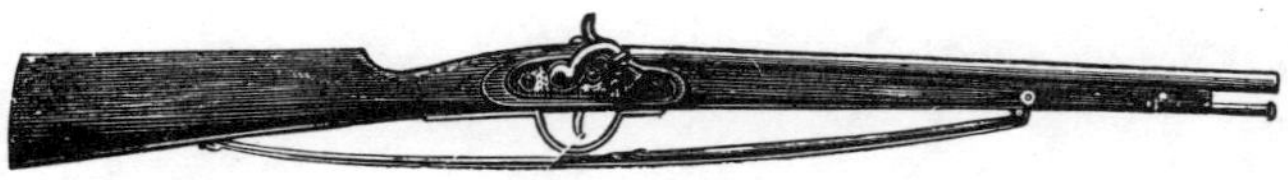

18/738 und 35

18/15, 16 und 17

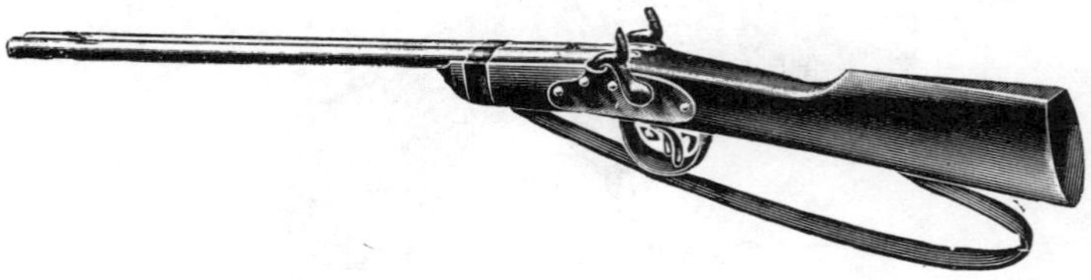

18/373, 374 und 70

18/703 und 716

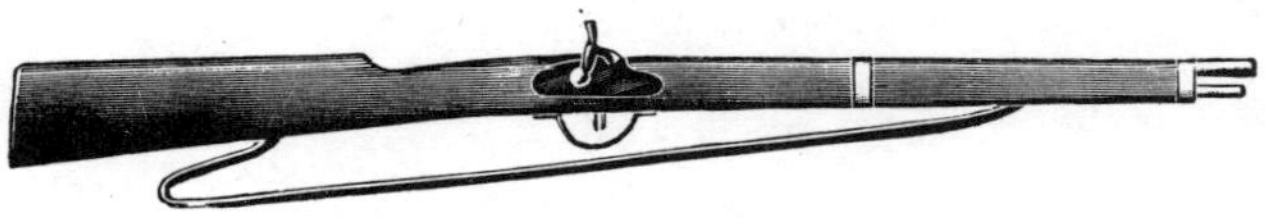

18/366, 581, 582, 48/1 und 48/2

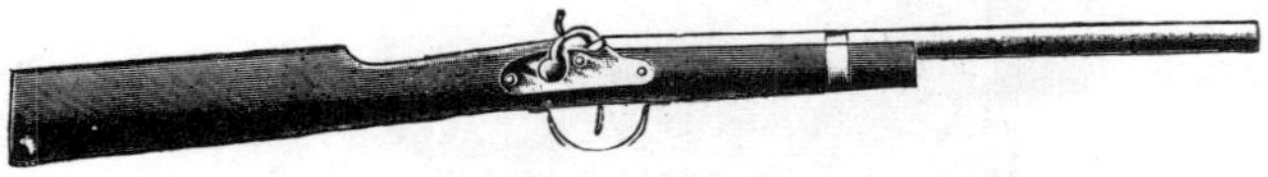

18/546 und 547

18/908/2

18/823, 826 und 828

18/914 und 918

Eureka-Gewehre und Pistolen.
Gefahrloser Schießsport mit Gummipfeil.

Eureka guns and pistols.
Shooting sport with rubber dart, free from danger.

Fusiles Eureka con pistolas.
Divertimiento de tiro no peligroso con flecha de caucho.

43/200

43/222

Nr. **43**/200 Eureka-Pistole aus Stahlblech, schwarz brüniert, mit 1 Pfeil, auf Scheibe 17×24 cm.
Eureka pistol, of sheet steel, black burnished, with 1 dart, on target 17×24 cm.
Pistola Eureka de chapa de acero, bruñida en negro, con 1 flecha, para blanco 17×24 cm.

„ **43**/201 Eureka-Pistole mit lackiertem Holzschaft und vernickeltem Lauf, 1 Pfeil, auf Scheibe 17×24 cm.
Eureka pistol, with varnished wooden stock and nickel plated barrel, 1 dart, on target 17×24 cm.
Pistola Eureka con caña de madera embarnizada y cañón niquelado, 1 flecha, para blanco 17×24 cm.

„ **43**/220 Eureka-Gewehr aus kräftigem Stahlblech mit hübsch lackiertem Schaft, 1 Pfeil, auf Scheibe 17×24 cm.
Eureka gun, of strong sheet steel, with nicely varnished stock, 1 dart, on target 17×24 cm.
Fusil Eureka de robusta chapa de acero con caña embarnizada bonitamente, 1 flecha, para blanco 17×24 cm.

„ **43**/222 Eureka-Gewehr wie Nr. 220, mit 1 Pfeil, auf Scheibe 19×59 cm.
Eureka gun, as Nr. 220, with 1 dart, on target 19×59 cm.
Fusil Eureka, tal que Nr. 220, con 1 flecha, para blanco 19×59 cm.

„ **43**/223 Eureka-Gewehr, größer und stärker als Nr. 220, mit vernickeltem Lauf uud hübsch lackiertem Schaft, 1 Pfeil, auf Scheibe 19×70 cm.
Eureka gun, larger and stronger than Nr. 220, with nickel plated barrel and nickely varnished stock, 1 dart, on target 19×70 cm.
Fusil Eureka, más grande y más robusto que él del Nr. 220, con cañón niquelado y caña embarnizada bonitamente, 1 flecha, para blanco 19×70 cm.

„ **43**/225 Eureka-Gewehr mit vernickeltem Lauf und hübscher vernickelter Schloßgarnitur, lackiertem Holzschaft, zusammen mit 1 Pfeil, auf Scheibe 19×70 cm.
Eureka gun with nickel plated barrel and nicely nickel plated lock fittings, varnished wooden stock, with 1 dart, on target 19×70 cm.
Fusil Eureka con cañón niquelado y bonita guarnición de llave niquelada, caña de madera embarnizada, 1 flecha, para blanco 19×70 cm.

„ **43**/230 Eureka-Gewehr mit vernickeltem Stahlblechlauf und fein mattiertem Nußbaumholzschaft sehr kräftig und solide konstruiert; elegante Ausführung, zusammen mit 2 Pfeilen, auf Scheibe 19×70 cm.
Eureka gun with nickel plated sheet steel barrel and superior dead finish walnut stock, very strongly and substantially constructed, elegant style, with 2 darts, on target 19×70 cm.
Fusil Eureka con niquelado cañón de chapa de acero y caña de nogal empañada finísimamente, muy robusto y construido solidamente; ejecución elegante, con 2 flechas, para blanco 19×70 cm.

43/230

Eureka-Pfeile für Pistolen und Gewehre passend. — Eureka darts, suiting both pistols and guns.
Las flechas Eureka aptas a las pistolas y los fusiles.

Diana-Luftgewehre.
Hervorragende Sport- und Übungsgewehre für die Jugend und für Erwachsene.

Diana air guns.
Splendid guns for sport or practice, for youths and adults.

Fusiles neumáticos Diana.
Excelentes fusiles de divertimiento y de ejercicio para jovenes y adultos.

43/1

Nr. **43**/1 **Diana-Luftgewehr,** Vorderlader aus kräftigem Stahlblech, hochfein vernickelt, mit mattiertem Holzschaft. Länge 80 cm, Gewicht 0,9 kg, Kaliber 4,5 mm.

Nr. **43**/1 **Diana air gun,** muzzle loader of strong sheet steel, best quality nickel plated, with dead-finish wooden stock. Length 80 cm, weight 0,9 kg, calibre 4,5 mm.

Nr. **43**/1 **Fusil neumático Diana,** fusil cargade por la boca, de robusta chapa de acero, niquelado finísimamente con empañada cana de madera. Largura 80 cm, peso 0,9 kg, calibre 4,5 mm.

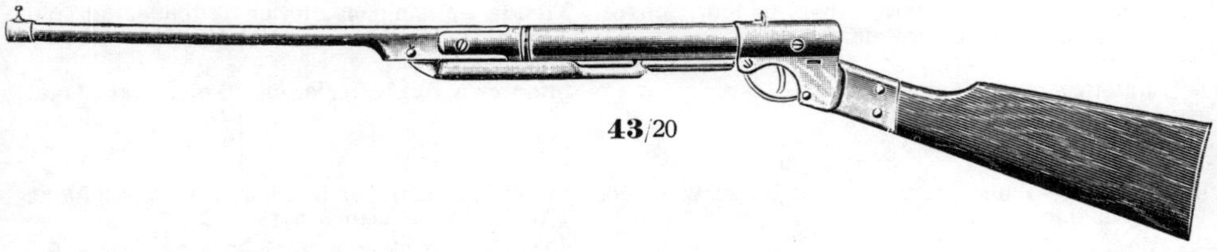

43/20

Nr. **43**/20 **Diana-Luftgewehr,** Laufspanner, Hinterlader, alle Teile aus kräftigem Stahlblech, hochfein vernickelt, Holzschaft mattiert. Länge 80 cm, Gewicht 1,2 kg, Kaliber 4,5 mm.

Nr. **43**/20 **Diana air gun,** with barrel cocking, breech loader, all parts of strong steel sheet, best quality nickel plated, dead-finish wooden stock. Length 80 cm, weight 1,2 kg, calibre 4,5 mm.

Nr. **43**/20 **Fusil neumático Diana,** fusil cargade por la colata, llave de cañón, todas partes de robusta chapa de acero, niquelado finísimamente, caña de madera empañada. Largura 80 cm, peso 1,2 kg, calibre 4,5 mm.

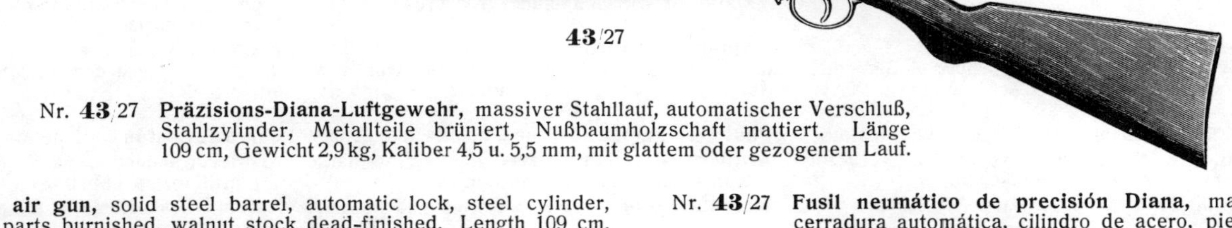

43/27

Nr. **43**/27 **Präzisions-Diana-Luftgewehr,** massiver Stahllauf, automatischer Verschluß, Stahlzylinder, Metallteile brüniert, Nußbaumholzschaft mattiert. Länge 109 cm, Gewicht 2,9 kg, Kaliber 4,5 u. 5,5 mm, mit glattem oder gezogenem Lauf.

Nr. **43**/27 **Diana air gun,** solid steel barrel, automatic lock, steel cylinder, metal parts burnished, walnut stock dead-finished. Length 109 cm, weight 2,9 kg, calibre 4,5 and 5,5 mm, smooth bore or rifled.

Nr. **43**/27 **Fusil neumático de precisión Diana,** macize cañón de acero, cerradura automática, cilindro de acero, piezas de metal bruñidas, caña de nogal empañada. Largura 109 cm, peso 2,9 kg, calibre 4,5 y 5,5 mm, cañón con interior liso o rayado.

126/1322/24 S 35 × 24 × 2,5 cm.

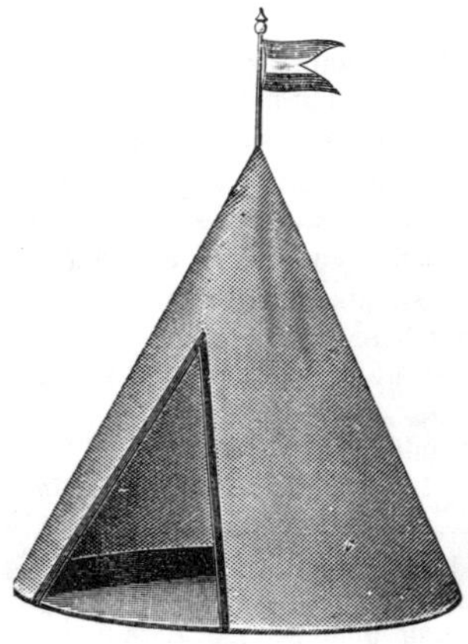

126/110

126/1374/1 33 × 30 × 3 cm.

Militärische Artikel. — Military articles. — Artículos militares.

126/2115/18 32×20×2,5 cm.

126/126/1 26 × 19 × 1,5 cm.

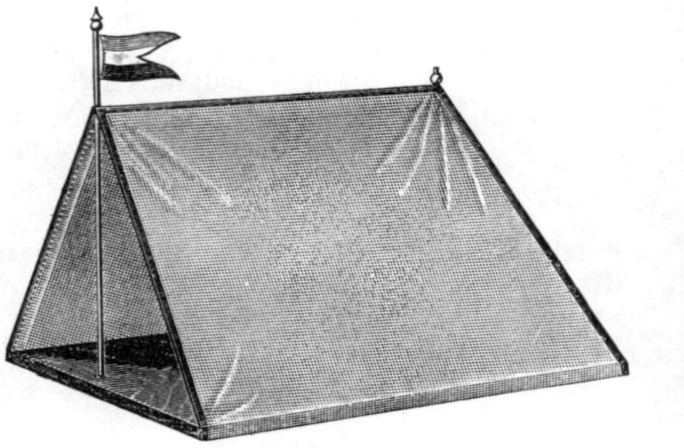

126/104

126/177/2 28×17×3,5 cm.

126/166/1 1/2 nat. Größe / size / tamaño.

126/1914 38 × 8 × 7 cm.

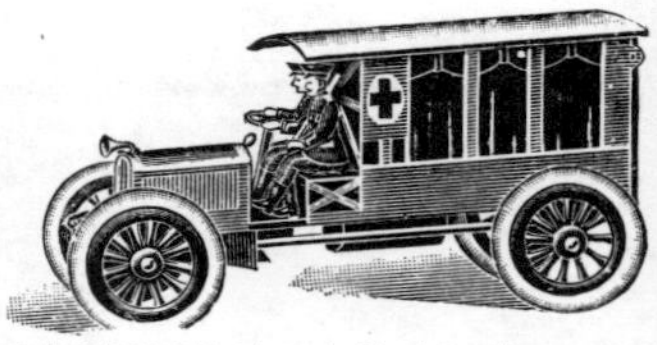

126/1933/1 1/2 nat. Gr./size/tamaño.

Nr. **126**/1322/12 S	**Infanterie,** stehend, kniend, liegend schießend und stürmend. Inhalt 12 Stück.	**Infantry,** standing, kneeling, lying shooting, and attacking. Contents 12 men.	**Infantería,** soldados en pie derecho, estando puestos, arrodillandose y tirando en estas posiciones y asaltando. Contenido 12 piezas.
„ **126**/1322/24 S	dto. Inhalt 24 Stück.	do. Contents 24 men.	do. Contenido 24 piezas.
„ **126**/110	**Zelt,** runde Form, khakifarbig, Größe 50-130 mm, mit Pappboden.	**Tent,** circular pattern, khaki colour. Sizes 50-130 mm with cardboard floor.	**Tienda** de campaña, forma redonda, de color "khaki". Tamaño 50-130 mm, con piso de cartón.
„ **126**/1374/0	**Infanterie und Kavallerie,** Inf. 6, Kav. 3 Stck.	**Infantry and cavalry,** 6 inf., 3 cav.	**Infantería y caballería,** inf. 6 piez., cab. 3 piez.
„ **126**/1374/1	do. „ 12, „ 6 „	do. 12 „ 6 „	do. „ 12 „ „ 6 „
„ **126**/1374/2	do. „ 16, „ 8 „	do. 16 „ 8 „	do. „ 16 „ „ 8 „
„ **126**/1374/3	do. „ 18, „ 9 „	do. 18 „ 9 „	do. „ 18 „ „ 9 „
„ **126**/2115/9	**Infanterie,** 6 Stck. im Marsch und **Kavallerie,** 3 Stck. im Schritt.	**Infantry,** 6 men, marching, and **Cavalry,** 3 men, walking pace.	**Infantería,** marchando 6 horas, y caballería caballeando a paso 3 horas.
„ **126**/2115/18	do. 12 bzw. 6 Stck.	do. 12 relatively 6.	do. 12 respectivamente 6 horas.
„ **126**/126/0	**Infanterie** mit 10 od. **Kavallerie** mit 5 St. Inhalt.	**Infantry,** contents 10, or **Cavalry,** contents 5.	**Infantería** con 10, o **caballería** con 5 piezas.
„ **126**/126/1	do. „ 18 „ „ „ 10 „ „	do. „ 18, „ „ „ 10.	do. „ 18, „ „ „ 10 „
„ **126**/126/1½	do. „ 27 „ „ „ 15 „ „	do. „ 27, „ „ „ 15.	do. „ 27, „ „ „ 15 „
„ **126**/126/2	do. „ 36 „ „ „ 20 „ „	do. „ 36, „ „ „ 20.	do. „ 36, „ „ „ 20 „
„ **126**/104	**Zelt,** rechteckige Form, khakifarbig, Höhe ca. 60-160 mm, Länge ca. 100-250 mm mit Holzboden. kann auch in weiß geliefert werden oder mit Sanitätskreuz.	**Tent,** rectangular pattern, khaki colour, heigh about 60-160 mm, length about 100-250 mm, with wooden floor. Can also be supplied in white, or with ambulance red cross.	**Tienda,** forma rectangular, de color "khaki". Altura cerca de 60-160 mm, largura cerca de 100-250 mm, con piso de madera. La tienda puede ser entregada también en blanco o con cruz sanitaria.
„ **126**/177/0	**Artillerie** zu Fuß oder zu Pferde.	**Artillery** on foot or on horseback.	**Artillería** a pie o a caballo.
„ **126**/177/1	do. mit 1 bespanntem Geschütz u. Bedienung.	do. with 1 gun and horse team and gun crew.	do. con 1 pieza con uñidura y artilleros.
„ **126**/177/2	do. „ 2 bespannt. Geschützen „ „	do. „ 2 guns „ „ teams „ „	do. „ 2 „ „ „ „
„ **126**/177/3	do. „ 2 „ „ 4 spänn. u. Bedien.	do. „ 2 „ „ 4 „ „ „ „	do. „ 2 „ „ „ (4 cab.) y artiller.
„ **126**/166/1	**Pontonwagen** mit 2 Pontons, Brettchen u. Balken.	**Pontoon wagon** with 2 pont., boards, and beams.	**Carro de pontón** con 2 pontones, tablitas y vigas.
„ **126**/1914	**Artillerie** im Schritt, Geschütz mit 4 Pferden und aufsitzender Mannschaft.	**Artillery** at walking pace, gun with 4 horse teams, and gun crew on horses.	**Artillería** andando a paso, pieza con 4 caballos y artilleros a caballo.
„ **126**/1933/1	**Sanitätsauto** mit Werk zum Aufziehen.	**Hospital motor car** with clockwork to wind up.	**Automóvil sanitario** con mecanismo de reloj para dar cuerda.

Maße und Preise der **kompletten Serien,** sowie einige weitere Typen befinden sich in separater Preisliste. — Measures and prices of the **complete series,** also some other types are in separate price-list. — Proporciones y precios de las **series completas,** aún algunas otras barcos estan en la lista de precios separata.

Nichtmilitärische Darstellungen und Puppenzimmerartikel.

Non military articles. Doll's room articles.

Representaciones no militares. Artículos para cuartos para muñecas.

Nr. **126**/1364/1 **Hühnerfütterung,** 20 Stück Inhalt.
„ **126**/1364/2 **Hühnerfütterung,** größere Ausführung, 42 Stück Inhalt.
„ **126**/1364/A **Viehweide** mit verschiedenen Tieren, 40 Stück Inhalt.

„ **126**/1364 1 **Feeding the poultry.** Contents 20.
„ **126**/1364/2 **Feeding the poultry,** larger make. Contents 42.
„ **126**/1364/A **Cattle meadow,** with various animals. Contents 40.

„ **126**/1364/1 **Cebamiento de gallinas,** contenido 20 piezas.
„ **126**/1364/2 **Cebamiento de gallinas,** ejecución más grande, contenido 42 piezas.
„ **126**/1364/A **Dehesa de ganado** con diferentes animales, contenido 40 piezas.

126/1364 b (26×25×2 cm)

126/543/1

126/1252/2

126/549

126/1265

126/1800

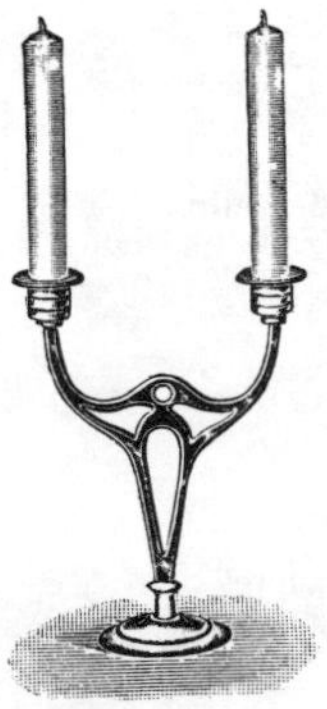
126/1074/2

126/1074/1

126/1739

126/1463/1

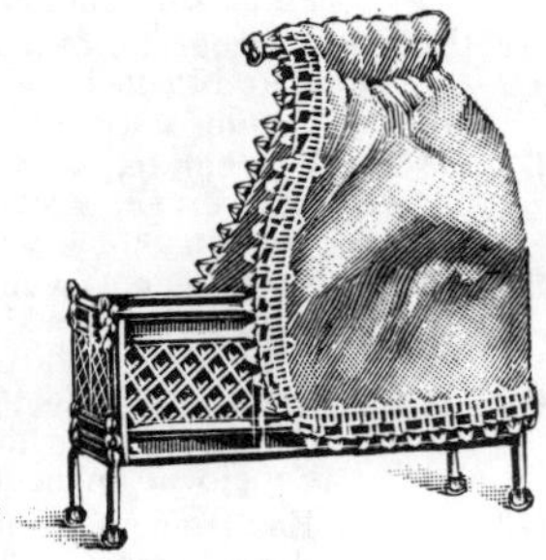
126/1010/1 g

126/1631/1

126/1700

Elektrisch brennbare Artikel. — Electrically combustible articles. Artículos combustiblos eléctricos.

126/828/1 E

126/51

126/23

126/66

126/22

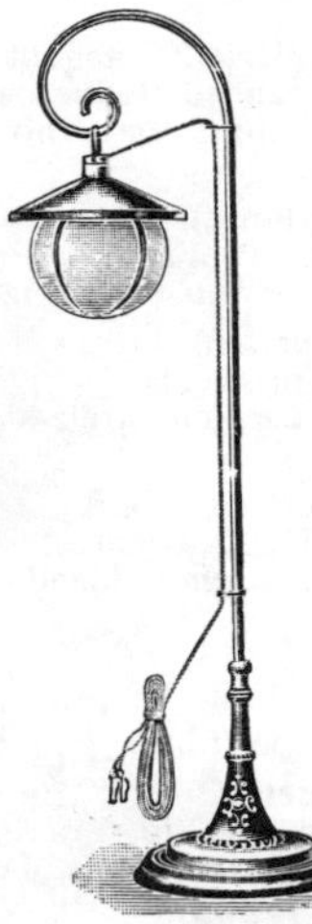
126/90/0

126/13

126/2

Feine Bürsten- und Besenwaren für Puppen und Kinder. — Fine brushes and brooms, for doll's houses and for children.
Finas mercancías de brozas y escobas, para muñecas y niños.

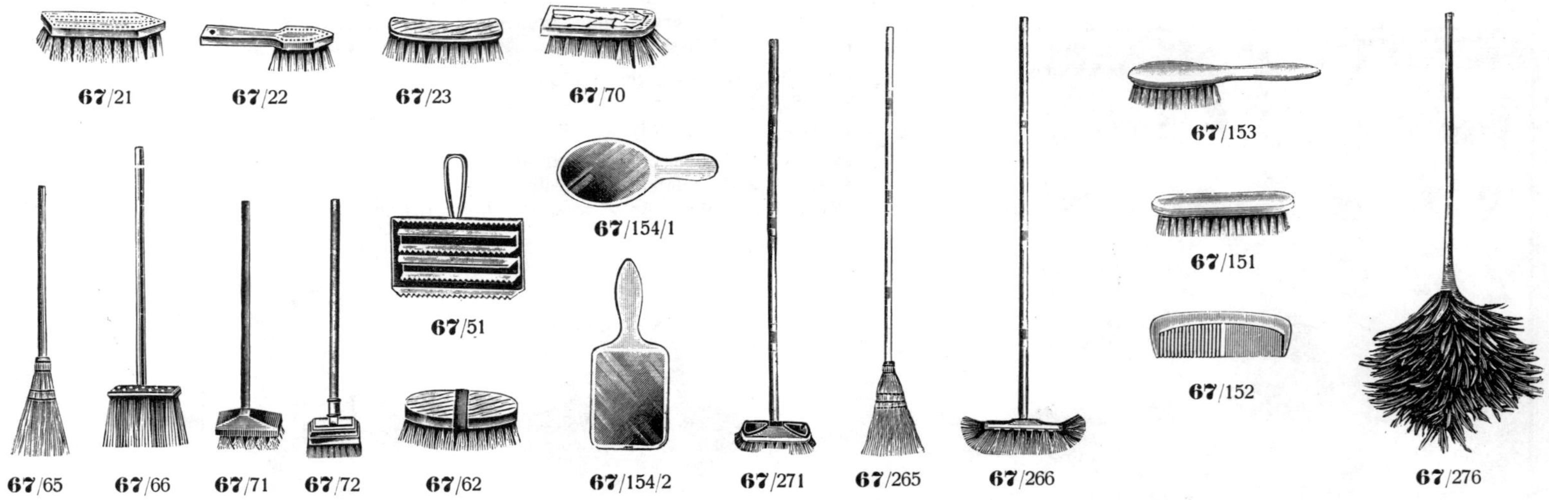

Nr.		
Nr. **67**/21/0	Abreibbürste (Fibre) Shoe dirt brushes (fibre) Broza para fregar (fibra)	5 cm
„ **67**/21/1	Abreibbürste Shoe dirt brushes (fibre) Broza para fregar (fibra)	8½ „
„ **67**/21/W 1	Abreibbürste, weiß lackiert Shoe dirt brushes (fibre), japanned white Broza para fregar (fibra), embarnizada en blanco	8½ „
„ **67**/22/0	Anstreichbürste (Haare) Shoe blacking brushes (hair) Broza para pintar (cabellos)	9 „
„ **67**/22/1	Anstreichbürste (Haare) Shoe blacking brushes (hair) Broza para pintar (cabellos)	9 „
„ **67**/22 W 1	Anstreichbürste, weiß lackiert. Shoe blacking brushes, japanned white. Broza para pintar, embarnizada en blanco	9 „
„ **67**/23/0	Glanzbürste (Haare) Shoe polishing brushes (hair) Brocha para pulir (cabellos)	5 „
„ **67**/23/1	Glanzbürste (Haare) Shoe polishing brushes (hair) Brocha para pulir (cabellos)	8½ „
„ **67**/23/W 1	Glanzbürste, weiß lackiert Shoe polishing brushes, japanned white Brocha para pulir, embarnizada en blanco	8½ „
„ **67**/51/0	Striegel Curry comb Almohaza	7 „
„ **67**/51/1	Striegel Curry comb Almohaza	7 „
„ **67**/62	Kardätsche Mane brush Broza para limpiar caballos	6 „
„ **67**/65/0	Teppichbesen (1 × abgenäht) Carpet broom (once sewn through) Broza para limpiar alfombras (pespuntada una vez)	20 „
„ **67**/65/1	Teppichbesen, lackiert (2 × abgenäht) Carpet broom, white japanned (twice sewn through) Escoba para limpiar alfombras, embarnizada (pespuntada dos vezes)	20 „
„ **67**/65 W 1	Teppichbesen, weiß lackiert (2 × abgenäht) Carpet broom, white japanned (twice sewn through) Escoba para limpiar alfombras, embarnizada en blanco (pespuntada tres vezes)	20 „
„ **67**/66/0	Staubbesen, unlackiert (Fibre) Dust broom, unvarnished (fibre) Escoba para despolvorear, no embarnizada (fibra)	19 „
„ **67**/66/1	Staubbesen, lackiert (Borsten) Dust broom, japanned (bristles) Escoba para despolvorear, embarnizada (sedas de puerco)	19 „
„ **67**/66/W 1	Staubbesen, weiß lackiert (Borsten) Dust broom, white japanned (bristles) Escoba para despolvorear, embarnizada en blanco (sedas de puerco)	19 „
„ **67**/70/0	Bodenbürste (Fibre) Scrubbing brush (fibre) Escoba para limpiar pisos (fibra)	6½ „
„ **67**/70/W 0	Bodenbürste, weiß lackiert Scrubbing brush, japanned white Escoba para limpiar pisos, embarnizada en blanco	6½ „
„ **67**/70/1	Bodenbürste, unlackiert (Fibre) Scrubbing brush, unvarnished (fibre) Escoba para limpiar pisos, no embarnizada (fibra)	9 „
Nr. **67**/70/W 1	Bodenbürste, weiß lackiert (fibre) Scrubbing brush, japanned white Escoba para limpiar pisos, embarnizada en blanco (fibra)	9 cm
„ **67**/71/0	Schrupper (Fibre) Long handle scrub brushes Lampazo (fibra)	18 „
„ **67**/71/1	Schrupper, lackiert (Fibre) Long handle scrub, brushes japanned Lampazo, embarnizada (fibra)	18 „
„ **67**/71/W 1	Schrupper, weiß lackiert (Fibre) Long handle scrub brushes, japanned withe Lampazo, embarnizada en blanco (fibra)	18 „
„ **67**/72	Parkettbohner Parquetry wax polishing brushes Encerador para pavimientos de madera ensamblada	20 „
„ **67**/151/B	Kleiderbürste, braun lackiert Clothes brushes, japanned brown Cepillo para los vestidos, embarnizada en pardo	9 „
„ **67**/151 W	Kleiderbürste, weiß lackiert Clothes brushes, japanned withe Cepillo para los vestidos, embarnizada en blanco	9 „
„ **67**/152	Kamm, weiß Celluloid Comb, white celluloid Peine de celluloido blanco	9 „
„ **67**/153 B	Haarbürste, braun lackiert Hair brush, brown varnished Cepillo para los cabellos, embarnizada en pardo	12 „
„ **67**/153 W	Haarbürste, weiß lackiert Hair brush, white varnished Cepillo para los cabellos, embarnizada en blanco	12 „
„ **67**/154/1	Handspiegel, weiß Celluloid Hand mirror, white celluloid Espejo de mano de celuloido blanco	10½ „
„ **67**/154/2	Handspiegel, weiß Celluloid Hand mirror, white celluloid Espejo de mano de celuloido blanco	12 „
„ **67**/155	Handspiegel, weiß Celluloid Hand mirror, white celluloid Espejo de mano de celuloido blanco	10½ „
„ **67**/265	Teppichbesen Carpet broom Escoba para limpiar alfombras	Größe/Size/Tamaño 2 3 4 Länge/Length/Largura 60 80 95 cm
„ **67**/265 W	Teppichbesen, weiß lackiert Carpet broom, japanned white Escoba para limpiar alfombras, embarnizada en blanco	Größe/Size/Tamaño 2 3 4 Länge/Length/Largura 60 80 95 cm
„ **67**/266	Staubbesen Dust brooms Escoba para despolvorear, embarnizada en blanco	Größe/Size/Tamaño 2 3 4 Länge/Length/Largura 60 80 95 cm
„ **67**/266 W	Staubbesen, weiß lackiert Dust brooms, japanned white Escoba para despolvorear, embarnizada en blanco	Größe/Size/Tamaño 2 3 4 Länge/Length/Largura 60 80 95 cm
„ **67**/271	Schrupper Long handle scrub Lampazo, embarnizada en blanco	Größe/Size/Tamaño 2 3 4 Länge/Length/Largura 60 80 95 cm
„ **67**/271 W	Schrupper, weiß lackiert Long handle scrub, japanned white Lampazo, embarnizada en blanco	Größe/Size/Tamaño 2 3 4 Länge/Length/Largura 60 80 95 cm
„ **67**/276	Federwedel, Holz Feather duster, wood Aventador de plumas de madera	Größe/Size/Tamaño 2 3 Länge/Length/Largura 47 65 cm
„ **67**/276	Federwedel, Rohr Feather duster, cane Aventador de tubo	Größe/Size/Tamaño 2 3 Länge/Length/Largura 47 65 cm

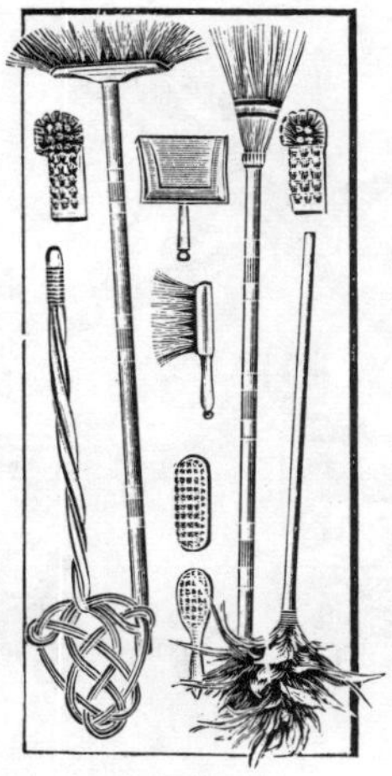

67/355/W

67/350

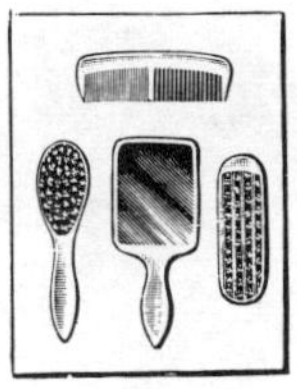

67/306/W

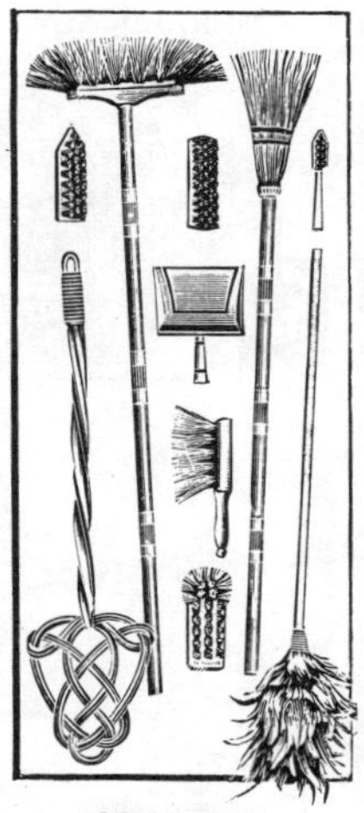

67/354/W2

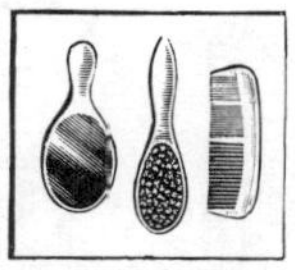

67/305/W

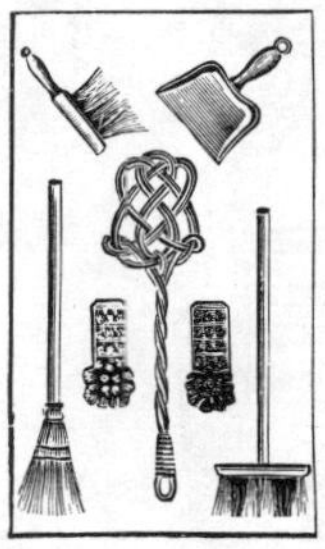

67/349

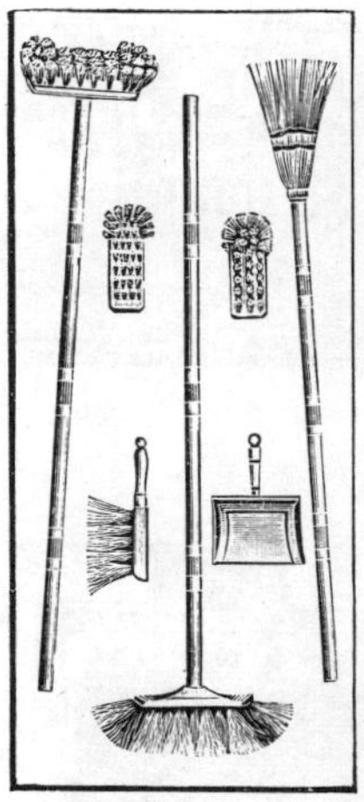

67/351/W2

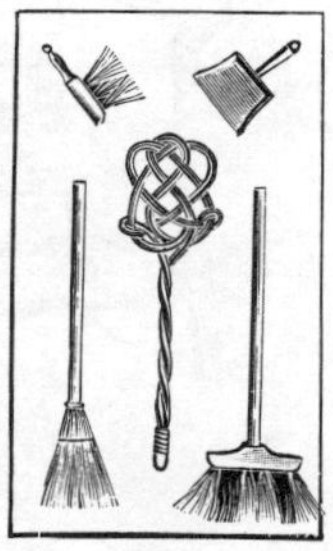

67/346

67/458

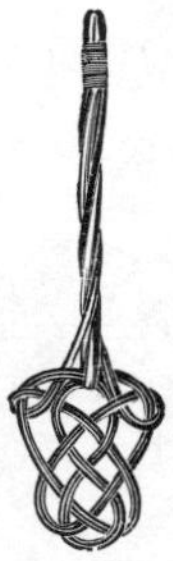

67/450

67/295/WG

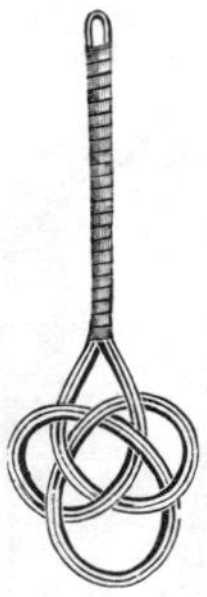

67/452

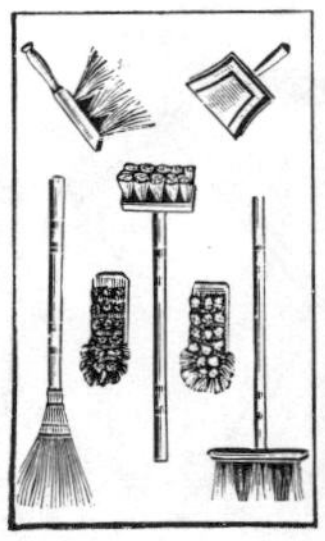

67/351/W1

Kehrgarnituren. — Sweeping sets. — Guarniciones para barrer.

Nr. **67**/295/G Staubschaufel mit Kehrwisch, unlackiert.
Dust pan with hand broom, unvarnished.
Pala para recoger el polvo con cepillo para barrer, no embarnizada.

„ **67**/295/WG Staubschaufel mit Kehrwisch, weiß lackiert.
The same, japanned white.
Pala para recoger el polvo con cepillo para barrer, embarnizada en blanco.

„ **67**/295/G	Größe/Size/Tamaño	0	$1^1/_2$	2	3	4	5	
	Länge/Length/Largura	$6^1/_2$	8	9	12	15	21	cm
„ **67**/295/WG	Größe/Size/Tamaño	0	$1^1/_2$	2	3	4	5	
	Länge/Length/Largura	$6^1/_2$	8	9	12	15	21	cm

Frisiergarnituren. — Hairdressing sets. — Guarniciones para peinar.

Nr. **67**/305/W Frisiergarnituren — Größe $14^1/_2 \times 15$ cm
Hairdressing sets
Guarniciones para peinar

„ **67**/306/W Frisiergarnituren — „ 16 × 22 „
Hairdressing sets
Guarniciones para peinar

Besengarnituren (auf Karten aufgenäht). — **Broom sets** (sewn on cards).
Guarniciones de escobas (cocidas sobre cartas).

Nr. **67**/346 5teilig, unlackiert — Größe 18×32 cm
5pieces, unvarnished
5partes, no embarnizada

„ **67**/349 7teilig, hellbraun lackiert — „ 18×32 „
7pieces, varnished light brown
7partes, embarnizada en pardo claro

„ **67**/350 4teilig, unlackiert — „ 16×32 „
4pieces, unvarnished
4partes, no embarnizada

„ **67**/351/1 7teilig, hellbraun lackiert — „ 18×32 „
7pieces, varnished light brown
7partes, embarnizada en pardo claro

„ **67**/351/W1 7teilig, weiß lackiert — „ 18×32 „
7pieces, japanned white
7partes, embarnizada en blanco

„ **67**/351/2 7teilig, unlackiert — „ 70×30 „
7pieces, unvarnished
7partes, no embarnizada

Nr. **67**/351/W2 7teilig, weiß lackiert — Größe 70×30 cm
7pieces, japanned white
7partes, embarnizada en blanco

„ **67**/351/3 9teilig, unlackiert — „ 84×35 „
9pieces, unvarnished
9partes, no embarnizada

„ **67**/351/W3 9teilig, weiß lackiert — „ 84×35 „
9pieces, japanned white
9partes, embarnizada en blanco

„ **67**/354/2 10teilig, unlackiert — „ 70×30 „
10pieces, unvarnished
10partes, no embarnizada

„ **67**/354/W2 10teilig, weiß lackiert — „ 70×30 „
10pieces, japanned white
10partes, embarnizada en blanco

„ **67**/354/3 11teilig, unlackiert — „ 84×35 „
11pieces, unvarnished
11partes, no embarnizada

„ **67**/354/W3 11teilig, weiß lackiert — „ 84×35 „
11pieces, japanned white
11partes, embarnizada en blanco

„ **67**/355 10teilig, unlackiert — „ 70×30 „
10pieces, unvarnished
10partes, no embarnizada

„ **67**/355/W 10teilig, weiß lackiert — „ 70×30 „
10pieces, japanned white
10partes, embarnizada en blanco

Rohrklopfer. — Cane carpet beaters. — Golpeadores de tubo.

Nr. **67**/450	2fädig, Länge 2strand 2hilos	20	25	30	35	40	45	cm
„ **67**/452	3fädig „ 3strand 3hilos	15	20	25	30	35		„
„ **67**/458	3fädig „ 3strand 3hilos	20	25	30	35	40	45	„

Holzspielwaren. — Wooden toys. — Juguetes de madera.

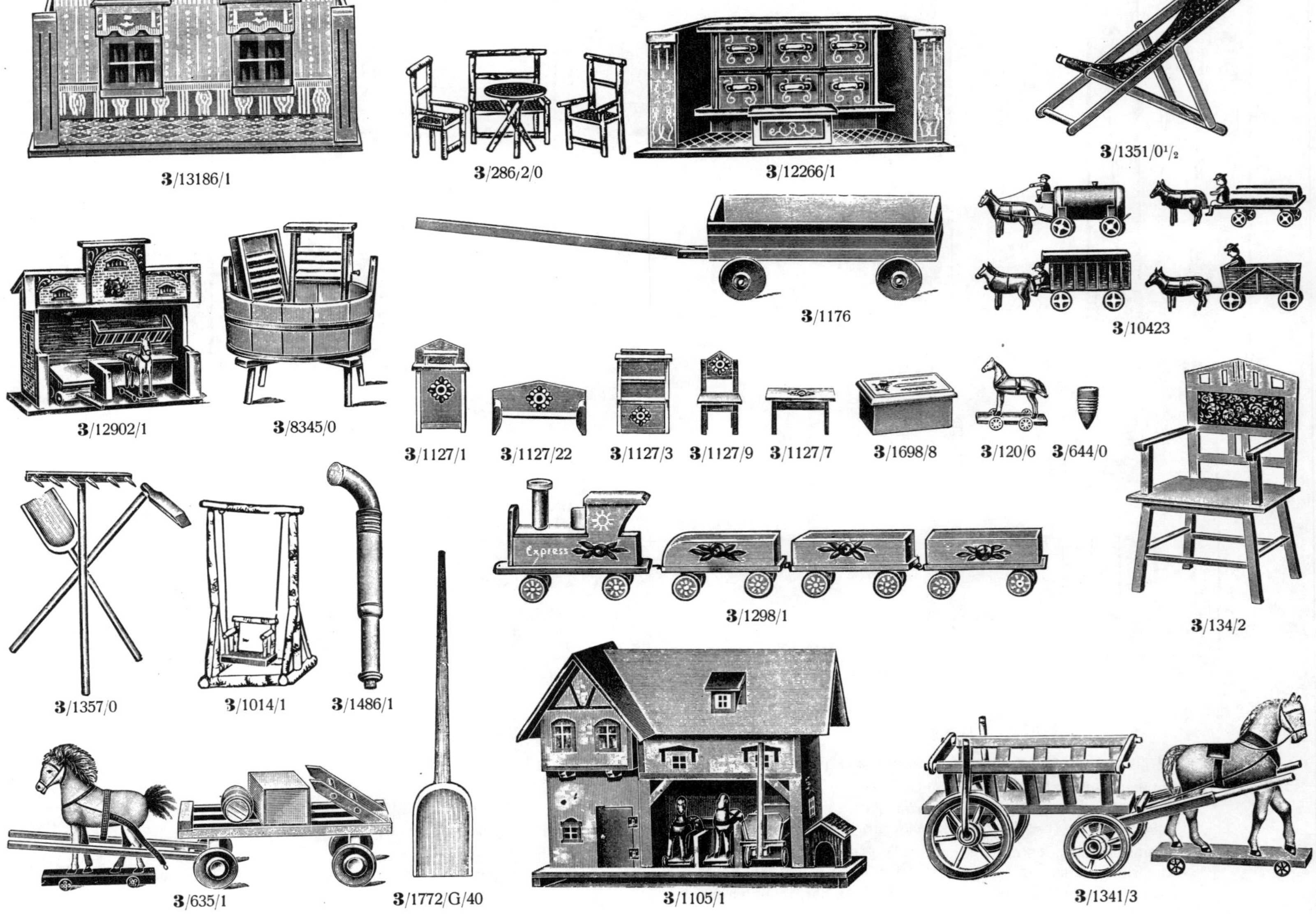

3/13186/1 · 3/286/2/0 · 3/12266/1 · 3/1351/0½ · 3/12902/1 · 3/8345/0 · 3/1176 · 3/10423 · 3/1127/1 · 3/1127/22 · 3/1127/3 · 3/1127/9 · 3/1127/7 · 3/1698/8 · 3/120/6 · 3/644/0 · 3/1357/0 · 3/1014/1 · 3/1486/1 · 3/1298/1 · 3/134/2 · 3/635/1 · 3/1772/G/40 · 3/1105/1 · 3/1341/3

Nr.		Länge Length Largura	Breite Width Anchura	Höhe Height Altura
3/13186/1	Stuben, rooms, cuartos	39	15,5	16,5 cm
3/13186/2		42	18,5	18 „
3/286/2/0	Gartenmöbel, Birke, im Karton Birch garden furniture, in cardboard box Muebles de jardín de madera de abedul en cajita de cartón	12,5	12	6,5 „
3/12266/1	Läden, lith., shops lith., tiendas lit.	37	14	14,5 „
3/12266/2		50	26	17 „
3/134/2	Stuhl, weiß Emaille White enamelled chair Silla, esmaltado blanco	16	14	28 „
3/1351/0½	Liegestühle mit Stoff Couches covered with cloth Sillas para descansarse, revestidas de estofa	21,5	8,5	— „
3/1351/0¾		29	10	— „
3/1351/1		35	11,5	— „
3/1351/2		41,5	13,5	— „
3/1351/3		46	15,5	— „
3/1351/4		51	17	— „
3/8345/0	Waschgeräte (Maße der Wanne) Washing-table set (size of basin) Utensilios de lavadero (dimensiones del cubeto)	19	13	11,5 „
3/8345/1	do.	24	16	14 „
3/1127/3	Möbel, einzeln, mit Blume, Küchenschrank Single pieces of furniture, plain wood, with flower, kitchen cupboard Muebles separados, no trabajados, con flor, dispensa	7	3	13,5 „
3/1127/22	do. mit Sofa, sofa, sofa	12,5	4	6,5 „
3/1127/9	do. mit Stuhl, chair, silla	6	4	9,5 „
3/1127/2	do. mit Vertikow, linen press, armario de lujo	7	3	11,5 „
3/1127/7	do. mit Tisch, table, mesa	9,5	7,5	7 „
3/1127/1	do. mit Kommode, chest of drawers, cómoda	9,5	7,5	7,5 „
3/644/0	Kreisel, ord., ordinary top, peones ordinarios	4,5	2,5	— „
3/6.4/1		5	2,8	— „
3/644/2		5,5	3,5	— „
3/644/3		6,2	3,6	— „
3/1772G/30	Schaufeln mit Griff Spades of beech with handle Palas con mango	30	—	— „
3/1772G/35		35	—	— „
3/1772G/40		40	—	— „
3/1772G/50		50	—	— „
3/1772G/60		60	—	— „
3/1772G/70		70	—	— „

Nr.		Länge Length Largura	Breite Width Anchura	Höhe Height Altura
3/1698/8	Sparkasten mit Vexier Money box with puzzle lock Cajita para conservar dinero ahorrado con decoraciones	10,5	7,5	5 cm
3/1357/5/0	Gartengeräte, Buche, 3teilig Beech garden implements, 3 pieces Utensilios de jardín de haya, 3 piezas	13	—	— „
3/1357/4/0		15	—	— „
3/1357/3/0		18	—	— „
3/1357/2/0		20	—	— „
3/1357/0		25	—	— „
3/1357/0½		30	—	— „
3/1357/0¾		33	—	— „
3/120/6	Stallpferd auf Brett Stable horse on stand Caballo en la cuadra sobre una tabla	8,5	3,5	8,5 „
3/10423	Min.-Wagen (1 Dtz. im Karton) Min. carriages (1 Dtz. in cardboard box) Coche en miniatura (1 doc. en la cajita de cartón)	19	14	5 „
3/1176	Kastenwagen, braun gebeizt (Kastenmaße) Enclosed lorrey, stained brown (size of body) Chirrión macerado en pardo (dimensiones de la cajita)	27	10,5	6 „
3/12902/1	Stall, lith., mit Pferd und Wagen Stable, lith., with horse and cart Cuadra lit. con caballo y coche	22	12,5	19 „
3/1486/1	Knallpistolen, poliert Pop-pistols, polished Pistoles de estrépido, pulidas	20	—	— „
3/1486/2		25	—	— „
3/1486/3		32	—	— „
3/1105/1	Stall, gemalt, mit 2 Pferden und Wagen Stable, painted, with 2 horses and cart Cuadra pintada con 2 caballos y coche	38	15	28 „
3/1298/1	Eisenbahn, Buche, mit Blumen, im Karton Railways, in beech, with flower, in cardboard box Ferrocarriles de haya con flores, en cajita de cartón	28	20	7 „
3/635/1	Rollwagen mit Pferd Lorrey with horse Carruaje con caballo	45	13,5	11 „
3/1341/3	Leiterwagen, opensided lorrey, carro con adreles	47	16	12 „
3/1014/1	Schaukeln, Birke, 1/6 Dtz. im Karton Birchwood swings, 1/6 Dtz. in cardboard box Columpios de abdul, 1/6 de la docena en cajita de cartón	24	13,5	13 „

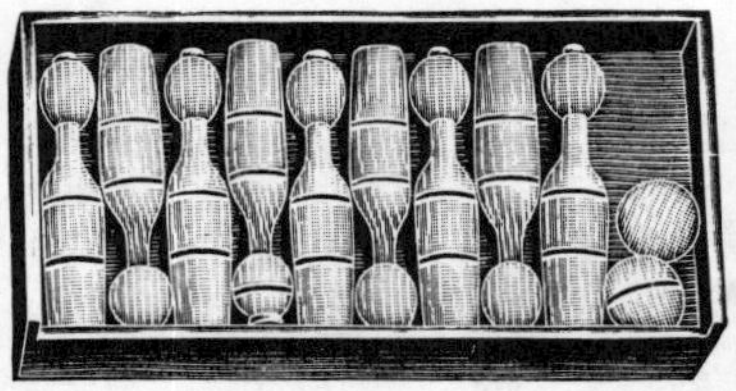

3/553 K/7

3/703/2

3/2567/7

3/1324

3/12568/28

3/292/1

3/1076/1

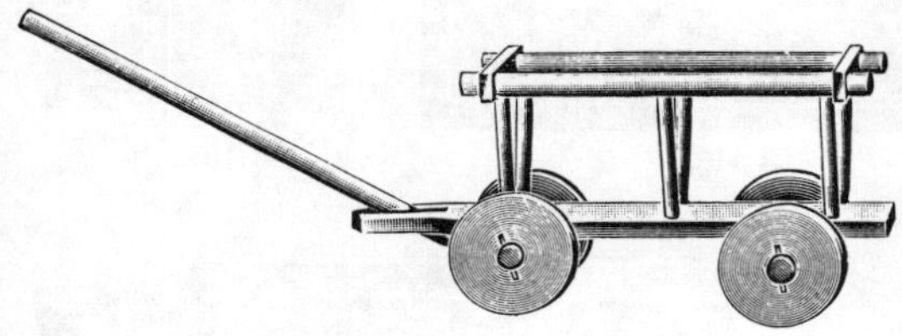

3/1290/0

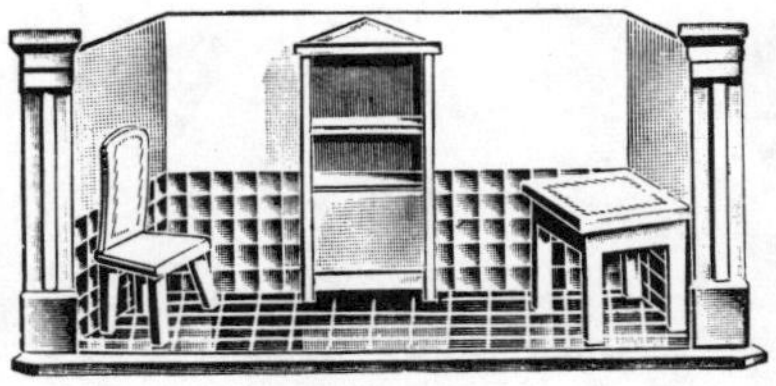

3/11086/1

3/1338

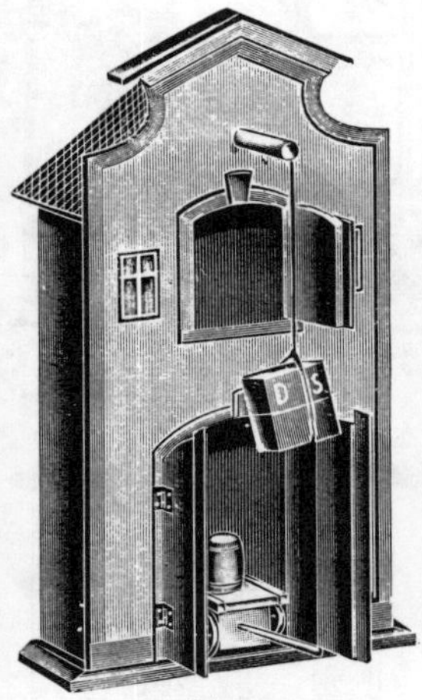

3/1344/0

3/13155/2

3/397/2

3/761/1

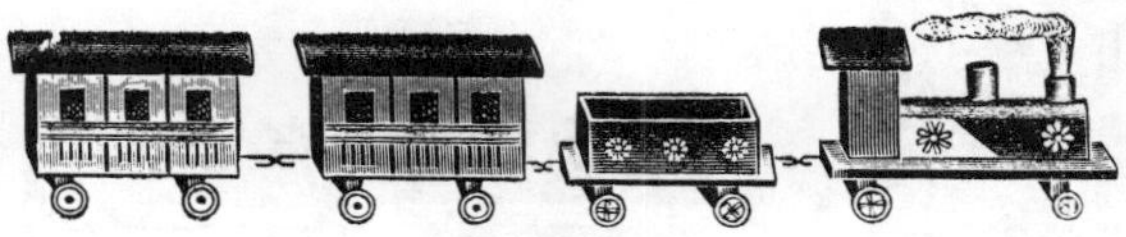

3/313/1

3/12478/38

3/1164 L/2

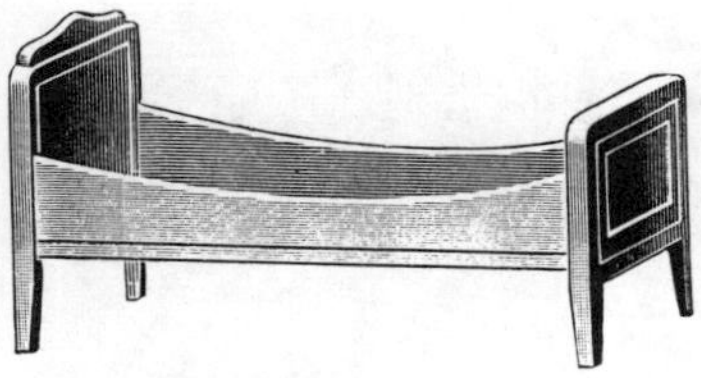

3/1245/3

3/681/0

3/107/0

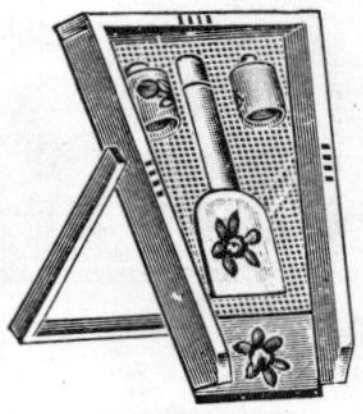

3/396/0

Nr.		Länge Length Largura	Breite Width Anchura	Höhe Height Altura	
3/1164L/1	Landgüter mit Tieren, im Karton.	33	21	5,5	cm
3/1164L/2	Farms with animals, in cardboard box	36	22,5	5,5	„
	Haciendas con animales, en cajita de cartón				
3/703/2	Häuser im Karton, 6 teilig	27	14,5	5,5	„
	Houses in cardboard box, 6 parts				
	Casas en cajita de cartón, conteniendo 6 piezas				
3/2567/7	Landgüter mit Tieren, im Karton	27	15,5	4	„
	Farms with animals, in cardboard box				
	Haciendas con animales. en cajita de cartón				
3/1324	Küchengarnituren, kitchen garniture, juego de molinillos	12,5	9,5	3,5	„
3/292/1	Gartenmöbel, im Karton	10	9,5	6,5	„
	Garden furniture, in cardboard box				
	Muebles de jardín en cajita de cartón				
3/1245/3	Betten, weiß lackiert	30	16	18	„
3/1245/4	White varnished bedsteads	35	18	19,5	„
3/1245/5	Camas embarnizadas en blanco	39,5	20	20	„
3/11086/1	Küche mit Möbel	37	14,5	16	„
3/11086/2	Kitchens with furniture	43,5	17	19	„
3/11086/3	Cocinas con muebles	50,5	20	23	„
3/11086/4		58	24	26	„
3/397/2		—	10	10	„
3/397/3		—	11,5	11,5	„
3/397/3½	Eimer mit Sandspielen, Brandmalerei	—	13	13	„
3/397/4	Pails with toys for playing with sand	—	14	14	„
3/397/5	Cubos con juegos para jugar con arena	—	16	15	„
3/397/6		—	18	17	„
3/397/7		—	20	19	„
3/1338	Küchenmöbel, gelb gebeizt, im Karton, kitchen furniture, stained yellow, in cardboard box, muebles de cocina, macerados en amarillo, en cajita de cartón	17	12	9	„
3/396/0	Durchwürfe mit Sandformen	20	—	—	„
3/396/1	Sieves with sand-forms	25	—	—	„
3/396/2	Zarzos para pasar arena con juegos para jugar	30	—	—	„
3/396/3	con arena	34	—	—	„
3/1344/3/0	Speicher	29	19	10	„
3/1344/2/0	Lofts	37	21	12	„
3/1344/0	Almacenes	43	23	13	„
3/313/1	Eisenbahnen, im Karton, railways in cardboard box, ferrocarriles en cajita de cartón	25	14	16	„

Nr.		Länge Length Largura	Breite Width Anchura	Höhe Height Altura	
3/313/2	Eisenbahnen, im Karton	25,5	16	6	cm
3/313/3	Railways, in cardboard box	28,5	16	7	„
3/313/4	Ferrocarriles, en cajita de cartón	29	19	7,5	„
3/553 K/4		23	10	3	„
3/553 K/5		24	12	3,5	„
3/553 K/6		26,5	13	3,5	„
3/553 K/7	Holzkegel, in Holzkiste	31	15	4	„
3/553 K/8	Skittles, plain wood, in small wooden box	35	16,5	5	„
3/553 K/9	Bolos no trabajados, en cajita de madera	37,5	18	5	„
3/553 K/10		42	20 5	5,5	„
3/553 K/11		32	24,5	11	„
3/553 K/12		35	27	13	„
3/12568/28	Dominos m. 28 Steinen, im Holzkasten, dominoes, 28 stones, in wooden box, juego del dominó con 28 dados planos, en caja de madera	17	5,5	3,5	„
3/1076/1	Wetterhäuser, im Karton, weather boxes, in cardboard box, higrómetros en cajita de cartón	18,5	13,5	8,5	„
3/1290/0	Leiterwagen, Buche, open lorreys of beechwood,	30	16	15	„
3/1290/1	carro con adreles, de haya	32	20	17	„
3/13155/2	Ställe, naturlackiert, stables, plain varnished, cuadras embarnizadas de laca natural	37,5	16	32	„
3/107/0		15	5,5	17	„
3/107/1		18	6	19	„
3/107/2	Pferde, geschirrt, aus Holz	20	6,5	21,5	„
3/107/3	Horses, in harness. of wood	24	8	26,5	„
3/107/4	Caballos enjaezados, de madera	25	10	28	„
3/107/5		30	10	33,5	„
3/107/6		35	12,5	34	„
3/107/7		39	14	36	„
3/681/0	Kastenwagen mit Eisenrädern (Maß des Kastens),	28	14	7	„
3/681/1	enclosed lorrey wi h iron wheels (dimensions	34	17	9	„
3/681/2	of body), chirriones con ruedas de hierro	37	20	11	„
3/681/3	(dimensiones de la cajita)	43	21	12	„
3/761/1	Kastenwagen mit Pferd, rot lackiert	42	10	9	„
	Enclosed lorrey with horse, red varnished				
	Chirriones con caballo, embarnizados en rojo				
3/12478/33	Tivolis, lith. mit braun gebeiztem Rand	33	15	3	„
3/12478/38	Tivolis, lith. border stained brown	38	17	3	„
3/12478/48	Juegos de tivoli, con borde macerado en pardo	48	19	3	„
3/12478/60		60	20	3	„

3/1850/0

3/13334/1

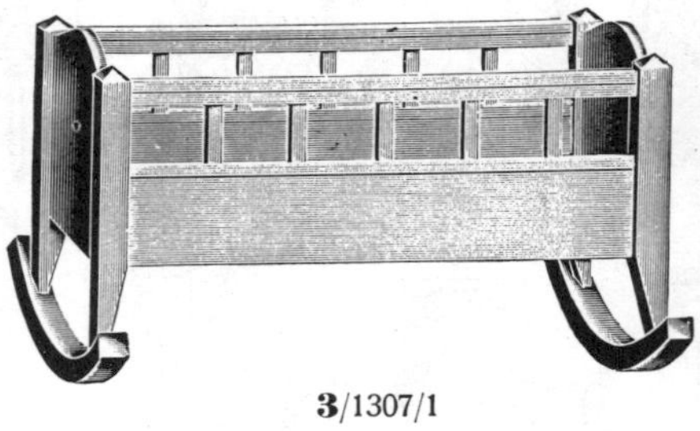

3/1307/1

3/1135/1

3/13333/1

3/12697/1

3/1081/0

3/991/3

3/39

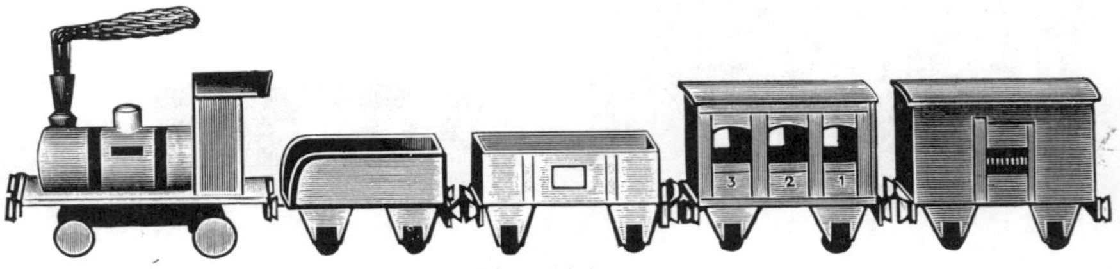

3/13335/2/0

3/13332/1

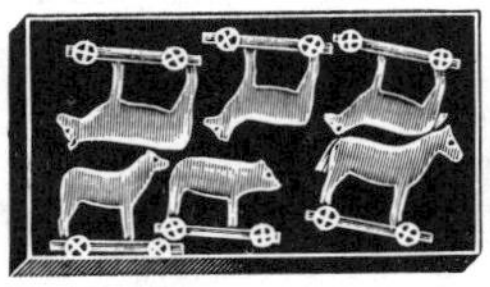

3/7159/0

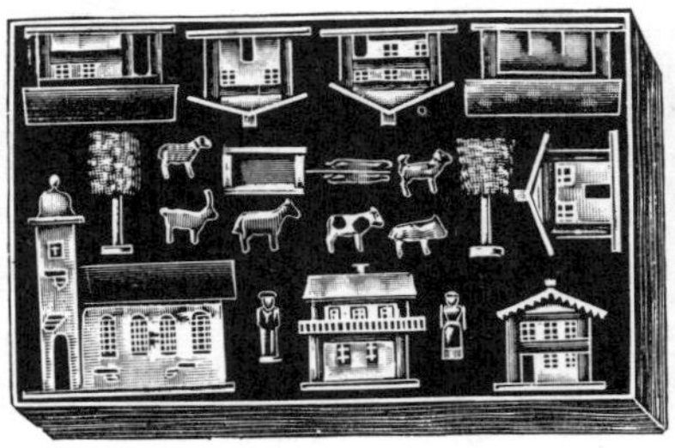

3/1134/2

3/1156/3

3/1112/3

3/1158/1

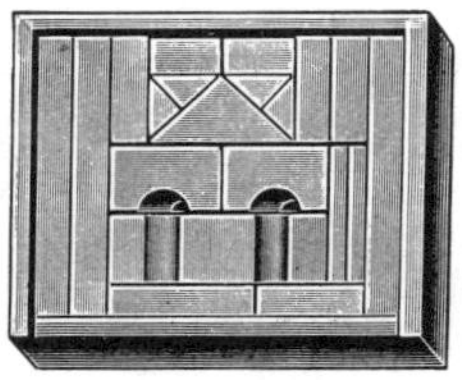

3/617/1

3/1258/29

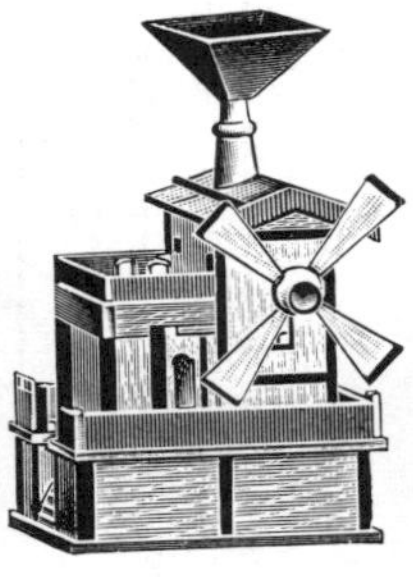

3/6584/0

3/398/1

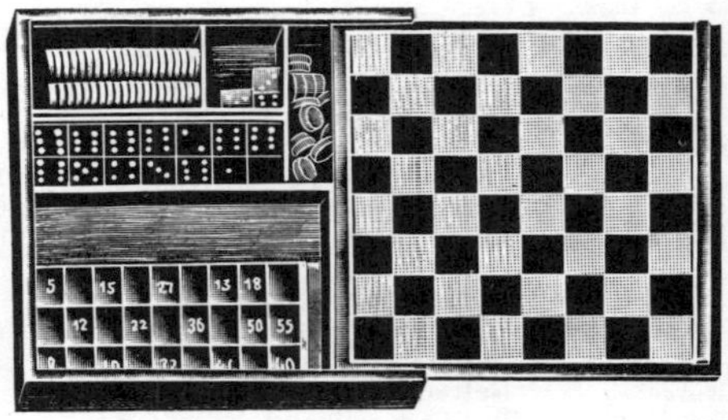

3/9076/1

3/1865/5

3/1863/0

3/1492/5

3/1034/0

3/1492/2

3/1492/0

3/127

3/1750/2

3/12823 K/9

3/1579/3

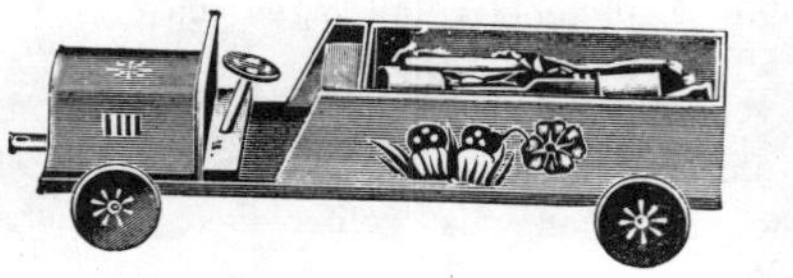

3/394/2

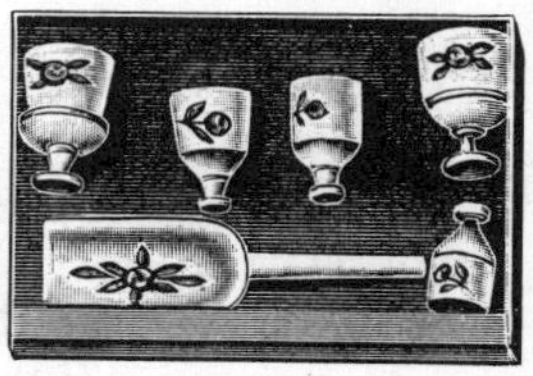

3/403/3

3/1750/4

3/1764/2

3/268/1

3/1750/3

Nr.		Länge, length, largura cm	Breite, width, anchura cm	Höhe, height, altura cm
3/1156/1	Landgüter im Karton	29	18	5,5
3/1156/2	Farms in cardboard box	33	21	6
3/1156/3	Haciendas en cajita de cartón	36	22,5	6,5
3/39	Villen, 6teilig, im Karton Villas, 6parts, i. cardboard box Quintas, 6 partes, en cajita de cartón	33,5	19	8
3/1134/1	Landgüter im Karton Farms in cardboard box	33	21	6
3/1134/2	Haciendas en cajita de cartón	36	22,5	6
3/1112/1	Menagerien	29	18	6,5
3/1112/2	Menageries	32	20	6,5
3/1112/3	Casas de fieras	36	22,5	6,5
3/7159/0	Weiße Tiere, auf Rädern, im Karton; animals, white, on wheels, in cardboard box; animales, blances, sobre ruedas, en cajita de cartón	22,5	12,5	3,5
3/158/1	Miniatur-Landgüter i. Karton; miniature farms in cardboard box; haciendas en miniatura en cajita de cartón	21	14	4
3/6584/0	Sandmühlen, Sand mills, molinos para moler arena	21,5	17	10
3/398/2/0	Körbe mit Sandspielen Baskets with toys for playing with sand Cestas con juegos para jugar con arena	10,5	7	5
3/398/0		12	8	6,5
3/398/0¾		15	10	8
3/398/1		18	12	8,5
3/398/1¾		21	14	9,5
3/398/2		24	16	10
3/1258/16	Baukasten, gotisch, Hartholz Building bricks of hard wood in box, gothic Caja de madera fuerte para construir edificios en estillo gótico	19	16,5	6
3/1258/18		23	16,5	6
3/1258/22		26	19	6
3/1258 24		26	21	6
3/1258/26		28	21	6
3/1258/27		30	21	6
3/1258/28		32,5	21	6
3/1258/29		30	23	6
3/617/3/0	Baukasten, Schweizer Weichholz Building bricks of soft wood in box, Swiss Caja de madera ligera para construir edificios en estillo suizo	13	14	5
3/617/2/0		13	16	5
3/617/0		16	14	5
3/617/1		19,5	16	5
3/617/2		23	16	5
3/617/2¾		27	18	5
3/617/3		28,5	19,5	5
3/617/4		30	21,5	5
3/617/5		34	21,5	5
3/9076/0	Spielmagazin, enthaltend Damebrett und Mühle, Lotto und Domino Collection of games, contg. draugh-board and mill, lotto and dominos Almacén de juegos, conteniendo: juego de las damas, el juego tres en raya y un juego de dominó	18,5	18,5	4
3/9076/1		24	24	5

Nr.		Länge, length, largura cm	Breite, width, anchura cm	Höhe, height, altura cm
3/135/1	Landgüter im Karton Farms in cardboard box Haciendas en cajita de cartón	32	20	7
3/135/2		36	22,5	7
3/135/3		42	26	9,5
3/135/4		46	30	9,5
3/12823 K/4	Kegel, Weichholz lackiert, mit bunten Ringen; skittles soft wood varnished, with coloured rings; bolos de madera ligera embarnizados con cercos de varios colores	24	12	3,5
3/12823 K/5		26,5	13	3,5
3/12823 K/6		31	15	4
3/12823 K/7		35	16,5	5
3/12823 K/8		37,5	18	5
3/12823 K/9		42	20,5	5,5
3/403/1	Sandspiele mit Brandmalerei, im Karton; toys for playing with sand in cardboard box; juegos para jugar con arena en cajita de cartón	18	11	4
3/403/2		20	13	4,5
3/403/3		24	16	5
3/394/2/0	Autos mit Sandspielen und Brandmalerei; automobiles with toys for playing with sand; automóviles con juegos para jugar con arena	24	—	—
3/394/0		28	—	—
3/394/1		32	—	—
3/394/2		38	—	—
3/394/2½		42	—	—
3/1579/1	Miniatur-Städte im Karton; miniature cities in cardboard box; ciudades en miniatura en cajita de cartón	16	10	2
3/1579/3		19	12	2
3/1579/4		21	14	2
3/1579/5		24	15,5	2
3/1850/2/0	Puppenhaus Dolls' house Casa para muñecas	19,5	16	28
3/1850/0		27	17	32
3/1850/1		31	19	42
3/1850/2		34,5	21	46
3/1850/3		37	23,5	53
3/12697/1	Klappstühle, Ahorn, im Karton; Sycamore folding chairs in cardboard box; sillas para plegar de acere en cajita de cartón	24	15	15,5
3/13334/1	Kleiderschränke, weiß m. Gold wardrobes, white with gold decoration; guardaropas en blanco con decoraciones doradas	22,5	9	32
3/13333/1	Küchenschränke, weiß mit Gold; kitchen cupboards with gold decoration; dispensas en blanco con decoraciones doradas	18,5	9	29
3/13332/1	Komoden, weiß mit Gold; Chests of drawers, white with gold decoration; Cómodas en blanco con decoraciones doradas	22	11	17,5
3/1307/1	Wiegen, weiß Cradles white Cunas blancas	38	19	22
3/1307/2		40,5	20,5	24
3/1307/3		43	22	25,5
3/1307/4		46	24	27
3/1307/5		49	26	29

Nr.		Länge, length, largura cm	Breite, width, anchura cm	Höhe, height, altura cm
3/1750/2	Städte und Tiere im Karton; towns and animals in cardboard box; ciudades y animales en cajita de cartón	33	21	5
3/1750/3		32	21	6,5
3/1750/4		43	31	10,5
3/991/1	Läden Shops Tiendas	41	20	19
3/991/2		48	22	22
3/991/3		53	24	24
3/991/4		61	27,5	37
3/13335/2/0	Eisenbahnen aus Holz im Karton; wooden railways in cardboard box; ferrocarriles de madera en cajita de cartón	38	22	7
3/13335/0		43	26,5	10
3/13335/1		48	29	14
3/13335/1½		54	33	16
3/13335/2		60	36	18
3/13335/3		66	40	20
3/1081/2/0	Postwagen mit Pferd, Postillion und Inhalt; mail carts with horse, postillion and contents; diligencia con caballo y postillón y contenido	31	12,5	15
3/1081/0		40	15	19
3/1081/1		48	16,5	21,5
3/1081/1½		53	20	24
3/1081/2		60	23	26,5
3/1081/3		65	24	30
3/1764/2	Landgut; Farm; Hacienda	29	18	5,8
3/268/1	Dörfer aus Holz im Karton; villages of wood in cardboard box; aldeas de madera en cajita de cartón	27	18	3
3/127	Landgut im Karton; country Residence in cardboard box; hacienda en cajita de cartón	50	34	8
3/1492/3/0	Archen, ord. gemalt Noah's arks, simple painted Arcas, ordinarias pintadas	13	4,5	6,5
3/1492/0		16	5,5	7,5
3/1492/1		19	6	8
3/1492/2		23	7	9,5
3/1492/3		24	7,5	10,5
3/1492/4		28,5	8,5	12
3/1492/5		31,5	9,5	13
3/1492/6		36	10,5	14.5
3/1492/7		38	11	16
3/1492/8		42	11,5	17,5
3/1865/5	Gondelarchen, fein gemalt und lackiert; gondola arks, finely painted and varnished; arcas finas en forma de una gondola, pintadas finísimamente y embarnizadas	41	10,5	18,5
3/1865/7		45	11,5	22
3/1865/9		50	13	27
3/1863/0	Räderarchen mit Galerie, lackiert; arks on wheels with galery, varnished; arcas sobre ruedas con galería embarnizadas	39	14	18
3/1034/0	Gondelarchen, fein gemalt, mit Einrichtung; gondola arks with fittings, finely painted; arcas en forma de una góndola, pintadas finísimamente con mueblaje.	48	13	29

Lineale, Federkästen und Sparkästen. — Rulers, pen boxes and saving boxes.
Reglas, cajas para plumas y cajas de ahorro.

12/499

12/523

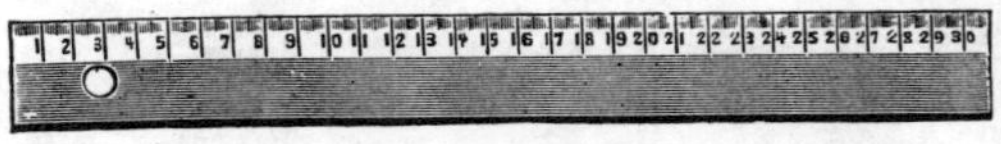

12/527

Nr. **12**/499	Lineal, obere Fläche, beide Kanten abgeschrägt, mit cm und Knopf, gelb gebeizt, in Längen von 20, 25 und 30 cm.	Rulers, both 'edges on the upper surface sloped, with cm and button, yellow corroded, in lengthes of 20, 25 and 30 cm.	Regla, la haz superior cortada de soslayo, con escala métrica y botón, trabajada con mordiente en color amarillo, de 20, 25, 30 cm de large.
„ **12**/500	Dasselbe Lineal, gelb lackiert,	The same ruler, yellow varnished.	La misma regla, embarnizada en color amarillo.
„ **12**/501	Dasselbe Lineal, naturpoliert.	The same ruler, natural polished.	La misma regla, pulida en color natural.
„ **12**/527	Lineal, roh Buche, mit Maß aus gelber Fase, 30—100 cm lang.	Ruler, raw beach, with measure, on yellow ground, 30—100 cm long.	Regla de madera cruda de haya, con escala métrica sobre base amarilla, de 30—100 cm de largo.
„ **12**/504	Dasselbe Lineal, gelb poliert.	The same ruler, yellow polished.	La misma regla, pulida en color amarillo.
„ **12**/523	Kantel, Buche, mit Maß, 10 mm, roh.	Square ruler, beach, with measure, 10 mm raw.	Regla cuadrada, de madera de haya, con escala métrica, de 10 milímetros de espesor cruda.
„ **12**/519a	Derselbe Kantel, 4 farbig gebeizt.	The same square ruler, corroded in 4 colours.	La misma regla, trabajada con mordiente en cuatro colores.
„ **12**/519	Derselbe Kantel, 4 farbig poliert.	The same square ruler, polished in 4 colours.	La misma regla, pulida en cuatro colores.

12/160

12/387

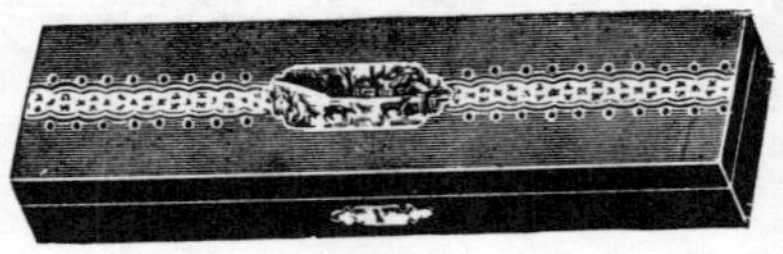

12/868

12/772

12/1039

12/87

Nr. **12**/160	Schloßfederkasten, Buche, Deckel poliert, Abzug, Seiten gebeizt.	Pen box with lock, dead beach, flour decoration, polished.	Caja para plumas, con cerradura, de madera de haya, la cubierta pulida, con metacromatipia, los lados trabajados con mordiente.
„ **12**/160	pol. Schloßfederkasten, auch die Seiten poliert.	Pen box with lock, sides also polished.	Caja para plumas, pulido.
„ **12**/387	Schloßfederkasten, gedämpft Buche, Friesel- und Blumenabzug, poliert.	Pen box with lock, dead beach, sides ground, lid polished.	Caja para plumas, con cerradura, de madera de haya, apagada, con metacromatipia, de friso y de flores, pulida.
„ **12**/868	Schloßfederkasten, gedämpft Buche, Streifenabzug, Deckel poliert.	Pen box with lock, dead beach, sides ground, lid polished.	La misma caja, con metacromatipia de rayos, la cubierta pulida.
„ **12**/87	Schnepperfederkasten, gedämpft Buche, Deckeleinlage, Abzugdeckel poliert.	Catch pen box with lock, dead beach, lid inlaid.	Caja para plumas, con pestillo, de madera de haya, apagada, la cubierta, pulida, con incrustación y metacromatipia.
„ **12**/88	Schloßfederkasten, gedämpft Buche, Deckeleinlage, Abzugdeckel poliert.	Pen box with lock, dead beach, sides polished.	La misma caja, con cerradura.
„ **12**/772	Schloßfederkasten, Buche, Deckel poliert, Pencil-Box-Abzug.	Pen box with lock, beach, lid polished.	Caja para plumas, con cerradura, de madera de haya, la cubierta pulida, con metacromatipia.
„ **12**/1039	Federkasten mit 2 Rolldeckeln, 2 farbig poliert.	Pen box with lock, 2 rolling lids, polished in colours.	Caja para plumas, con dos cubiertas a rollar pulidas en dos colores.

12/1092

12/1094

12/1021

Nr. **12**/1092	Federkasten, Deckel poliert, Abzug leer, 3,7×1,9 cm	Pen box, lid polished, sides plain, 3,7×1,9 cm.	Caja para plumas, la cubierta pulida, con metacromatipia, vacía, tamaño, 3,7×1,7 cm.
„ **12**/1021	Federkasten, Deckel poliert, Blumenabzug, 3 fach. 6,3×2,5 cm.	Pen box, lid polished, flour decoration, 3 departments, 6,3×2,5 cm.	Caja para plumas, la cubierta pulida, con metacromatipia, de flores, en tres partes, 6,3×2,5 cm.
„ **12**/1094	Federkasten, Deckel poliert, Fruchtabzug, 3 fach. 5,8×3,2 cm.	Pen box, lid polished, fruit decoration, 3 departments.	Caja para plumas, la cubierta pulida, con metacromatipia, en tres partes.

Lineale, Federkästen und Sparkästen. — Rulers, pen boxes and saving boxes. Reglas, cajas para plumas y cajas de ahorro.

12/1009

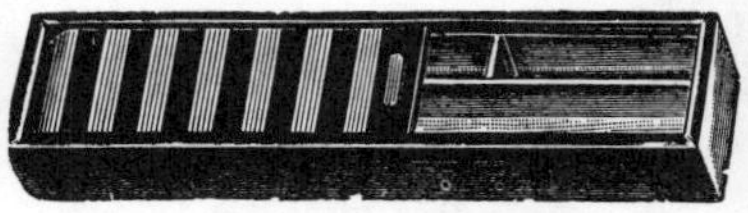

12/876

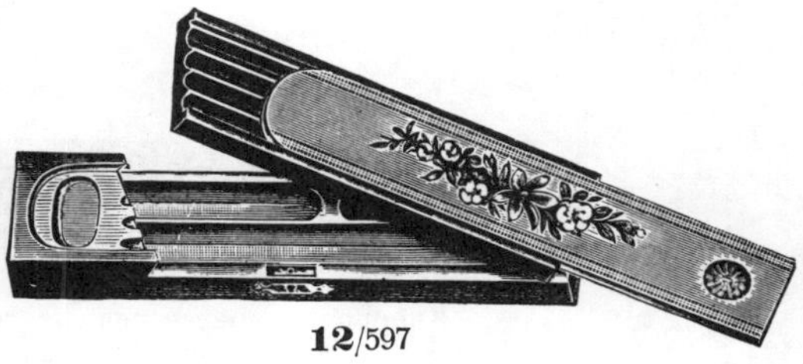

12/597

Nr. **12**/1022	Federkasten, Deckel poliert, Seiten poliert. 6,3×2,5 cm.	Pen box, lid polished, sides polished.	Caja para plumas, la cubierta pulida, los lados pulidos.
„ **12**/1013	Federkasten, Deckel poliert, kl. Abzug, 3fach. 4,3×1,7 cm.	Pen box, lid polished, small decoration, 3 departments.	Caja para plumas, la cubierta pulida, con pequeña metacromatipía, en tres partes.
„ **12**/1015	Federkasten, Deckel poliert, kl. Abzug, 3fach. 5,3×2,2 cm.	Pen box, lid polished, fruit decoration, 3 departments.	Caja para plumas, la cubierta pulida, con metacromatipía de frutas, en tres partes.
„ **12**/1262	Federkasten, Deckel poliert, Seiten poliert. 5,8×2,1 cm.	The same box, sides polished, as Nr. 12/1094	La misma caja, los lados pulidos, como No. 12/1094.
„ **12**/1009	Überschobener polierter Drehkasten, oben 4 Riefen, Gummil., Mitte 3fach, unten leer, 5,8×5 cm.	Polished turning pen box, upper box 4 departments, rubber, middle 3 departments, lower box empty.	Caja giratoria pulida, con cuatro ranuras, arriba goma, el centro en tres partes, la parte inferior vacía.
„ **12**/470	Derselbe Kasten, Abzug, Deckel poliert, 5,8×4,3 cm.	The same box, decorated lid, polished.	La misma caja con metacromatipía, la cubierta pulida.
„ **12**/473	Überschobener polierter Drehkasten, oben 3 Riefen, Mitte und unten leer, 4,4×5 cm.	Polished turning pen box, upper box 3 departments, middle empty, lower box empty.	Caja giratoria pulida, con tres ranuras, el centro vacío, la parte inferior vacía.
„ **12**/1307	Überschobener polierter Drehkasten, oben 4 Riefen, Mitte und unten leer, 4,5×4,9 cm.	Polished turning pen box, upper box 4 departments, middle empty and lower box empty.	Caja giratoria pulida, con cuatro ranuras arriba, el centro vacío, la parte inferior vacía.
„ **12**/597	Drehkasten, poliert, mit Schloß, oben 3 Riefen, unten leer, Gummil. 4,8×4,2 cm.	Turning pen box, polished, with lock, upper box 3 departments, below empty, rubber.	Caja giratoria pulída, con cerradura, con tres ranuras arriba, la parte inferior vacía, goma.
„ **12**/876	Rollfederkasten, Ha'tholzdeckel, 2farbig, Seiten poliert, gelb, 4,8×4,2 cm.	Roll pen box, hard wood, lid 2 colours, sides yellow polished.	Caja para plumas a rollar, de madera dura, la cubierta en dos colores, los lados pulidos en color amarillo.
„ **12**/871	Derselbe Kasten, Seiten gelb gebeizt, 4,8×4,2 cm.	Roll pen box, hard wood, lid 2 colours, yellow corroded.	Caja para plumas a rollar, de madera dura la cubierta en dos colores los lados trabajados con mordiente en color amarillo.
„ **12**/870	Derselbe Kasten, Weichholzdeckel, Seiten gelb gebeizt, 4,8×4,2 cm.	Roll pen box, soft wood, lid 2 colours, yellow corroded.	Caja para plumas a rollar, de madera blanda, la cubierta en dos colores, los lados trabajados con mordiente en color amarillo.
„ **12**/875	Derselbe Kasten, Seiten gelb poliert, 4,8×4,2 cm.	Roll pen box, soft wood, lid 2 colours, yellow polished.	Caja para plumas a rollar, de madera blanda, la cubierta en dos colores, los lados pulidos en color amarillo.

12/691

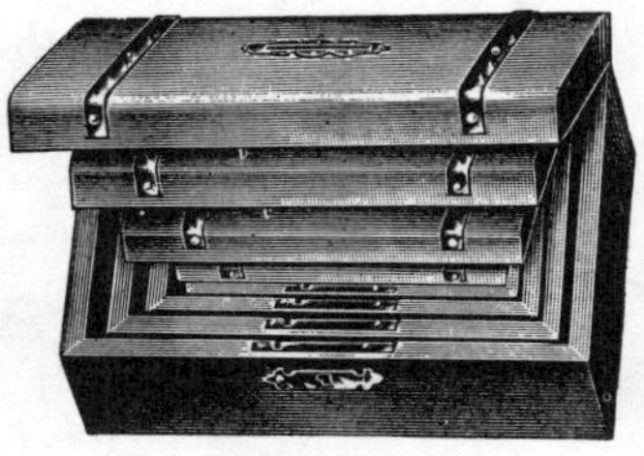

12/967

12/124

12/94

12/1 B

12/31 l

12/800 a

Nr. **12**/1 B	Sparkasten mit Schloß, gebeizt, Aufleimbild, Schlitz, 10,8×6×3,8 cm.	Saving box with lock, corroded, glued on picture, slit.	Caja de ahorro, con cerradura, trabajada con mordiente, con metacromatipía y con hendidura.
„ **12**/5	Derselbe Kasten, Weichholz, 11,2×6,3×4,8 cm.	Soft wood, the same box.	La misma caja, de madera blanda.
„ **12**/7	Derselbe Kasten, Weichholz, 13,2×7,8×4,8 cm.	Soft wood, the same box.	La misma caja, de madera blanda.
„ **12**/124	Weichholz-Sparkasten, Deckel poliert, mit Schrift, Seiten gebeizt, 10,5×6,3×4,8 cm.	Soft wood saving box, lid polished with inscription, sides corroded.	Caja de ahorro, de madera blanda, la cubierta pulida y con inscripción, los lados trabajados con mordiente.
„ **12**/125	Derselbe Kasten 11,4×6,2×4 cm.	The same box.	La misma caja.
„ **12**/127	Derselbe Kasten 13×7,3×4,5 cm.	The same box.	La misma caja.
„ **12**/94	Ged. Hartholz - Sparkasten, doppelter Deckel, poliert, Henkel, 12,5×7,6×5 cm.	Hard wood saving box, double lid, polished, handle.	Caha de ahorro, de madera dura, con doble cubierta, pulida, con mango.
„ **12**/92	Naturpolierter Hartholz - Sparkasten, doppelter Deckel mit Frieseinlagen, 16,2×7,8×6,1 cm.	Natural polished saving box, double lid, with inlaid frize.	Caja de ahorro, pulida en color natural, con doble cubierta y con incrustaciones de friso.
„ **12**/691	Nußbaumpol. Hartholz-Sparkasten, Deckel natur, schwarz-rot Lackrand, 4 Spangen, 12,3×7,4×5,3cm	Nut tree polished saving box, lid natural, black/red edge.	Caja de ahorro, pulida en color de nogal, la cubierta, en color negro natural con borde de barniz en color rojo, y con cuatro presillas.
„ **12**/800 a	Gelbpoliert. Hartholz-Sparkasten, Landschaftsbild, 4-Kleebl.-Beschlag, 11,2×7,2×5,7 cm.	Yellow polished saving box, landscape picture, 4 trios garnished.	Caja de ahorro, pulida en color amarillo, con metacromatipía de un paisaje, y con guarnición de cuatro hojas de trébol.

Holzschiffe. — Wooden boats. — Buques de madera.

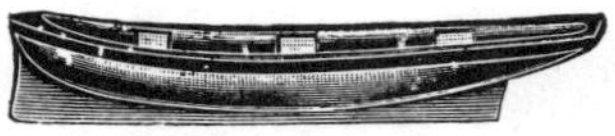

118/701

Kahnboote, poliert, bunt bemalt.
Boats, polished and in colours.
Botes muy pequeños, pulidos, pintados de varios colores. (10—25 cm)

118/699

Rettungsboote mit Matrosen, poliert und bunt bemalt.
Lifeboats with sailors, polished and in colours.
Lanchas de salvamento con marineros, pulidas y pintadas de varios colores. (10—40 cm)

118/150

Leichte Segelkähne, bunt bemalt, vorzüglich segelnd, geeignet zum Beladen.
Ligth sailing boats, in colours, excellent sailers, suitable for loading.
Ligeras barquillas a la vela, pintadas de varios colores, velejando de manera excelente, apropiandose a ser cargadas. (20– 40 cm)

118/756

Kutter mit Galerie, feine Ausführung.
Cutter with gallery poop, finely executed.
Cúter con galería, fina ejecución. (9—15 cm)

118/608

Segelschiffe mit 1 Mast, weiß lackiert, mit rotem Rand, halbhohl.
Sailing ships with 1 mast, white varnished, with red border, half hollow.
Navíos a la vela con 1 palo, embarnizados en blanco, borde rojo, mitada hueca. (21—50 cm)

118/752

Segelschiffe mit 2 Masten, 2 Rettungsbooten, blau bemalt, mit Silberrand.
Two-masted sailers with 2 lifeboats, blue with silver border.
Navíos a la vela con 2 palos, con 2 lanchas de salvamento, pintados en azul con bordo argentado. (30 – 40 cm)

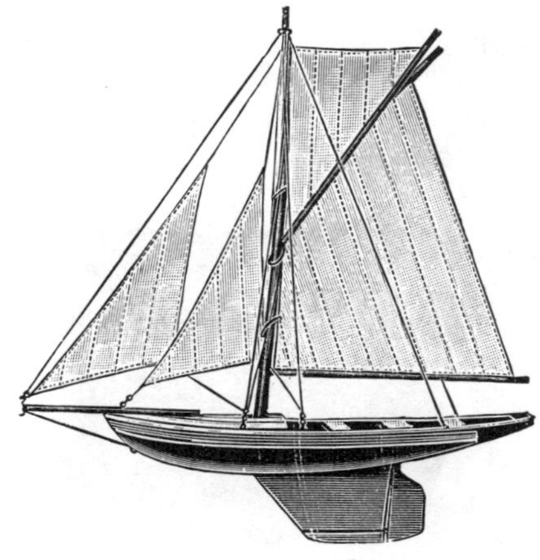

118/711

Kreuzerjacht mit Segeln, halbhohl, mit Sitzen.
Cruiser yacht with sails, half hollow, with seats.
Yate cruzador con velas, mitad hueca, con asientos. (40—80 cm)

118/305

Seekutter mit 2 Masten, hohl, mit Deck und Kajüte, große Takelage, fein bemalt.
Sea cutter with 2 masts, hollow, with deck and cabin, fully rigged, finely painted.
Cúter de mar con 2 palos, hueco, con cubierta y camarote, aparejo grande, pintado finísimamente. (21—120 cm)

118/606

Segelschiff mit 2 Masten, grün bemalt, mit blauem Rand.

Two-masted sailers, painted green with blue border.

Navíos a la vela con 2 palos, pintados en verde con borde azul. (21—50 cm)

118/165

Segelboote mit 2 Masten, feinste Ausführung, vorzüglicher Segler, zum Beladen geeignet.
Sailing boats with 2 masts, finest style, splendid sailer, adapted for loading.
Barcos a la vela con 2 palos, ejecución finísima, velejando de manera excelente, apropiandose a ser cargados. (35—72 cm)

Unzerbrechliche, doppelseitig feinbemalte, gepreßte Holztiere und Figuren.
Unbreakable, double-sided, fine painted wooden animals and figures.
Animales y figuras infrangibles de madera aprensada finamente pintados por los dos lados.

58/270

58/304

58/267

58/269

58/279

58/280

58/1007

58/285

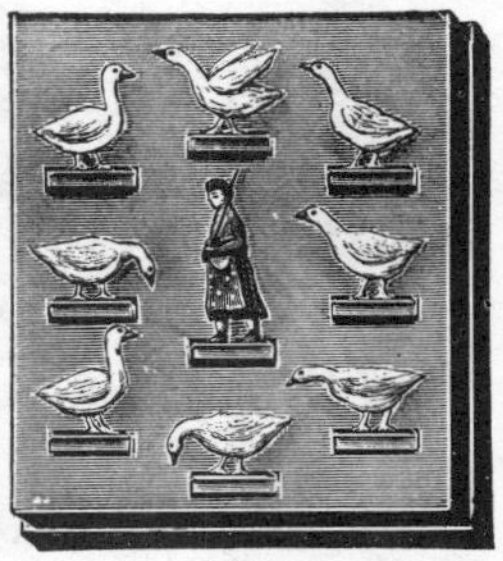

58/261

58/318/1

58/318

58/275

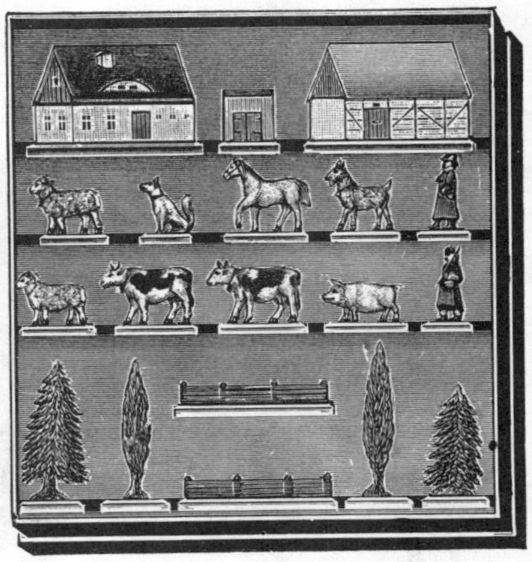

58/276

58/1027 D

58/297

58/288

58/264

Fahrtiere.
Animals on wheels.
Animales con ruedidas.

58/1055

58/1043

58/1044

58/1039

58/1040

Unzerbrechliche, doppelseitig feinbemalte, gepreßte Holztiere und Figuren.
Unbreakable, double-sided, fine painted wooden animals and figures.
Animales y figuras infrangibles de madera aprensada finamente pintados por los dos lados.

58/1079

58/Inf. 18

58/Cav. 9

58/1063

Gespanne. — Teams — Tiros.

58/1024

Wackelfiguren. — Tettering figures, fine painted. — Figuras de movimiento.

58/604

58/603

58/600

58/1069

58/1070

Fahrtiere. — Animals on wheels.
Animales con ruedidas.

58/1074

58/283/9

Kreisgehende Scheren. — Circulating scissors. — Tijeras de movimiento yendo en circulo.

58/291

58/1034

Weiße Sandformen, gedreht im Netz.
White Sandforms in nettwork.
Moldes de areña en red.

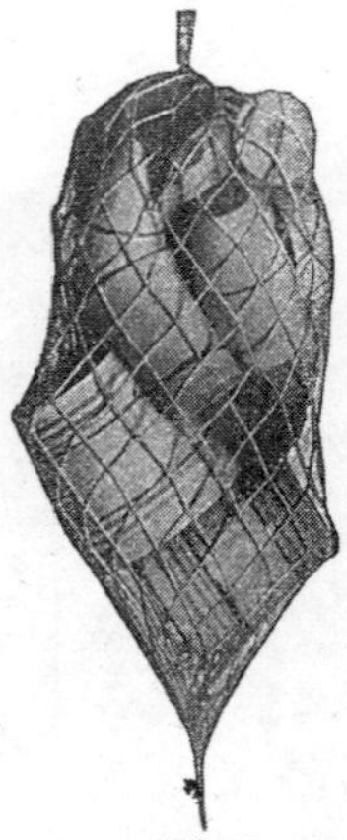

58/III

Filzpuppen mit gehärtetem Filzkopf. — Felt dolls, indestructible, harden felt head.
Muñecas de fieltro para tira con cabeza de fieltro endurecida.

58/I K

58/I M

58/F 50

58/451

Filzbälle.
Felt Balls.
Pelotas de fieltro.

58/5/4—15/6

Sommerballspiele. — Summerball plays.
Pelotas en el verano.

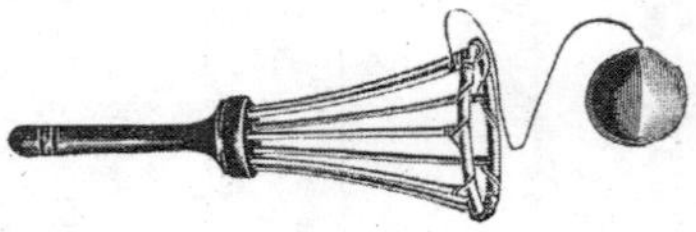

58/„Cilly"

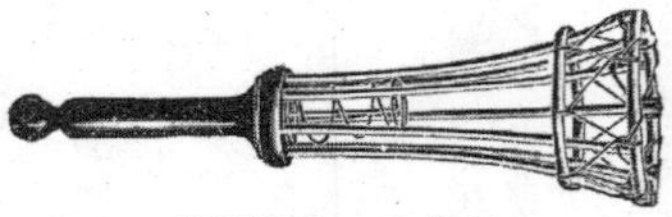

58/Pilot mit Ball

Fröbelsche Ausnäharbeiten und Beschäftigungen. — "Fröbel" Sewing Boxes and div. working.
Distracciones segun Fröbel.

58/5016

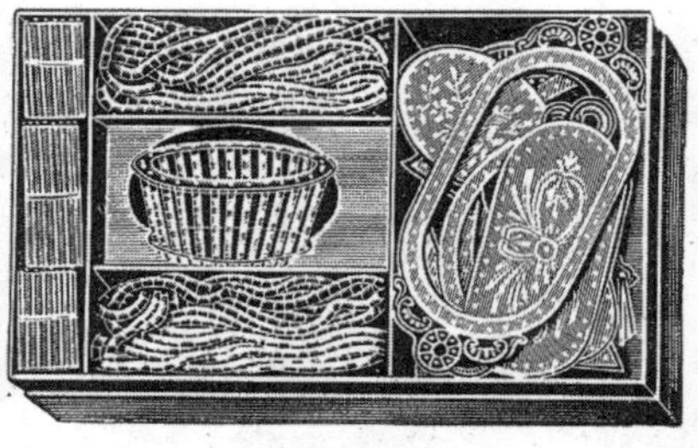

58/5011

58/5003

58/5012

58/5017

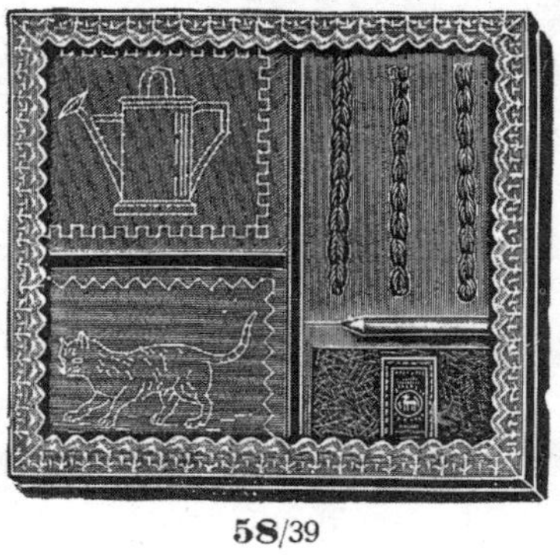

58/39

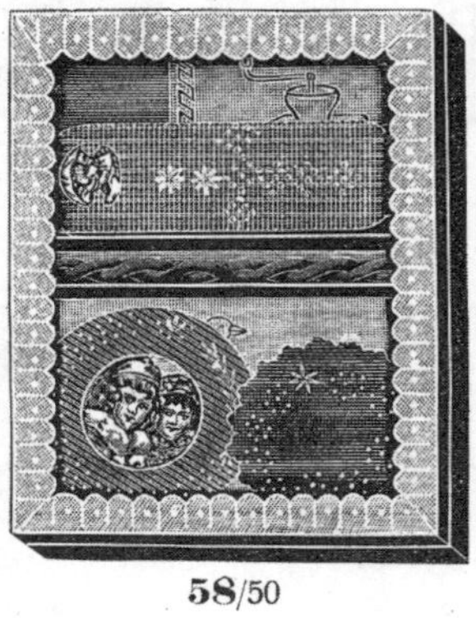

58/50

58/5001

Holzspielwaren. — Wooden toys. — Juguetes de madera.

Trade mark. Marca registrada.

Eingetragene Schutzmarke.

136/136 Sammelprospekt. — General catalogue. — Prospecto colector.

136/3
Affe. — Monkey. — Mono.
15 × 35 cm.

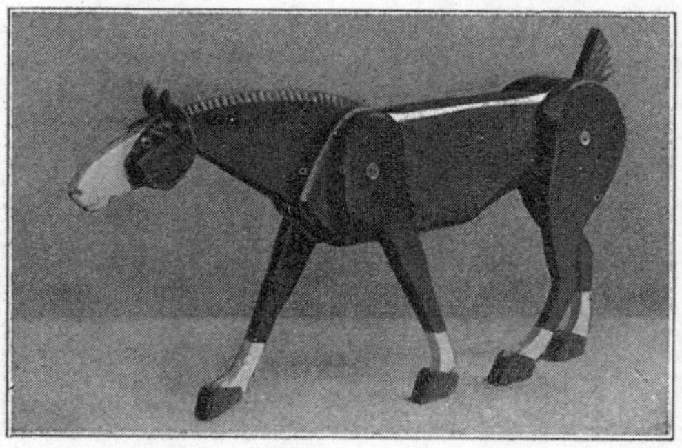

136/1 Pferd. — Horse. — Caballo.
24 × 50 cm.

136/2 Bär. — Bear. — Oso.
19 × 33 cm.

136/4
Elefant.
Elephant. — Elefante.
22 × 50 cm.

136/7 Stierkampf. — Bullfight. — Taurocidio.
$28^1/_2 \times 8^1/_2$ cm.

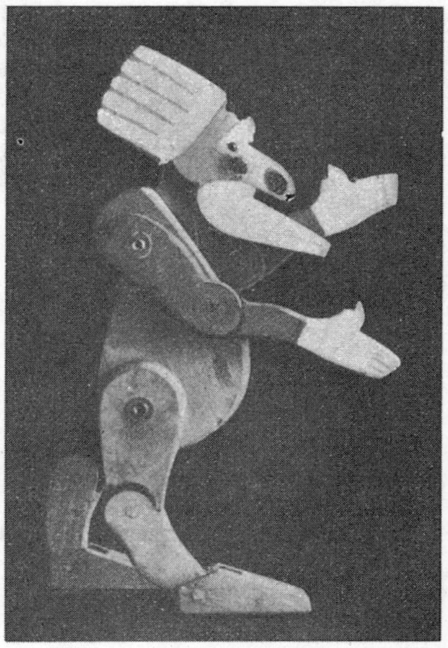

136/11 Zwerg. — Dwarf. — Enano.
25 × 13 cm.

Holzspielwaren. — Wooden toys. — Juguetes de madera.

136/136/10 (20×13 cm)
Eichhorn. — Acorn. — Ardilla.

136/13 (25×16 cm)
Clown.

136/12 (17×35 cm)
Esel. — Donkey. — Asno.

Moving rocking-horse, steerable.

	Height of saddle:
Nr. **136**/100/1	55 cm
„ **136**/100/2	45 „
„ **136**/100/3	35 „
	Length:
Nr. **136**/100/1	150 cm
„ **136**/100/2	142 „
„ **136**/100/3	135 „
	Breadth:
Nr. **136**/100/1	50 cm
„ **136**/100/2	45 „
„ **136**/100/3	40 „

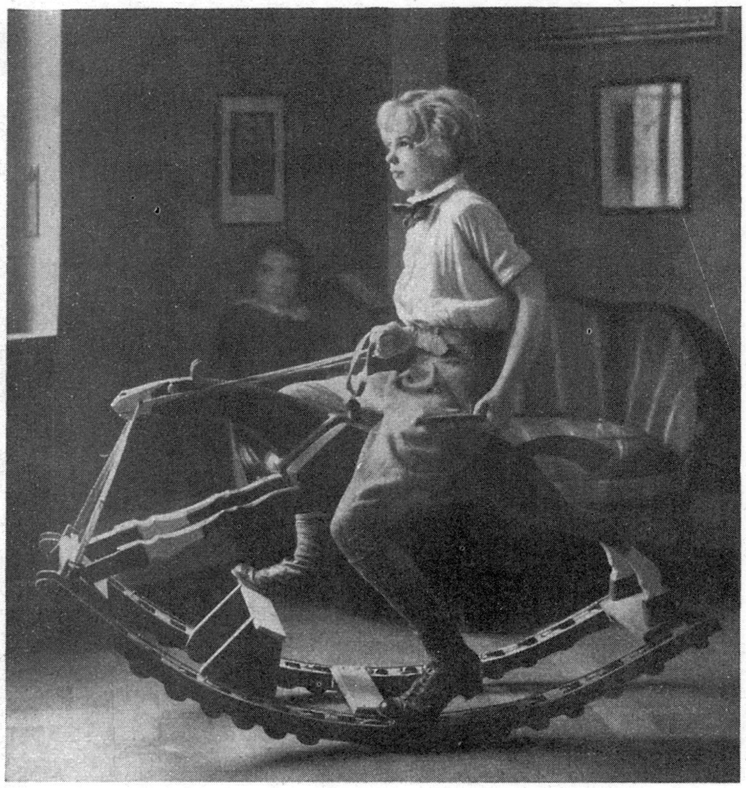

Caballo para mecerse, corriendo y dirigible.

	Altura de la silla:
Nr. **136**/100/1	55 cm
„ **136**/100/2	45 „
„ **136**/100/3	35 „
	Longura:
Nr. **136**/100/1	150 cm
„ **136**/100/2	142 „
„ **136**/100/3	135 „
	Anchura:
Nr. **136**/100/1	50 cm
„ **136**/100/2	45 „
„ **136**/100/3	40 „

136/100/1/2/3
Laufendes und lenkbares Schaukelpferd.

Nr. **136**/100/1	Länge 150 cm	Breite 50 cm	Sattelhöhe 55 cm
„ **136**/100/2	„ 142 „	„ 45 „	„ 45 „
„ **136**/100/3	„ 135 „	„ 40 „	„ 35 „

Außer den abgebildeten Nummern enthält die Kollektion:

Nr. **136**/5	Löwe.	Nr. **136**/17	Ziegenbock.
„ **136**/6	Panther.	„ **136**/18	Kamel.
„ **136**/8	Hund.	„ **136**/19	Giraffe.
„ **136**/9	Katze.	„ **136**/20	Gnu.
„ **136**/14	Stier.	„ **136**/21	Dackel.
„ **136**/15	Hase.	„ **136**/22	Nilpferd.
„ **136**/16	Nashorn.	„ **136**/23	Bongo.

Diese Tiere sind in allen Gliedern beweglich und werden in 2 Größen hergestellt.

In addition to the Nos. illustrated herein the collection includes:

Nr. **136**/5	Lion.	Nr. **136**/17	Billy-goat.
„ **136**/6	Panther.	„ **136**/18	Camel.
„ **136**/8	Dog.	„ **136**/19	Giraffe.
„ **136**/9	Cat.	„ **136**/20	Gnu.
„ **136**/14	Bull.	„ **136**/21	Crook-legged German terrier.
„ **136**/15	Hare.		
„ **136**/16	Rhinoceros.	„ **136**/22	Hippopotamus.
		Nr. **136**/23	Bongo.

All these animals have movable limbs and are supplied in two sizes.

Fuera de los números ilustrados la colección contiene:

No. **136**/5	León.	No. **136**/17	Macho cabrio
„ **136**/6	Pantera.	„ **136**/18	Camello.
„ **136**/8	Perro.	„ **136**/19	Jirafa.
„ **136**/9	Gatto.	„ **136**/20	Gnu.
„ **136**/14	Toro.	„ **136**/21	Zarcero.
„ **136**/15	Liebre.	„ **136**/22	Hipopótamo.
„ **136**/16	Rinoceronte.	„ **136**/23	Bongo.

Todas las coyunturas, de estos animales son móvibles, los últimos están construidos en 2 tamaños.

Puppenhäuser und -villen, vorn zum Öffnen, mit Möbeln, gemalt und lackiert.

Dolls houses and villas, front can be opened, with furniture, painted and varnished.

Casas para muñecas y quintas, lado delantero para abrir, con muebles, pintados y embarnizados.

7/5602 F (51×24×53,5 cm)

7/5619 F (27,5×19×30 cm)

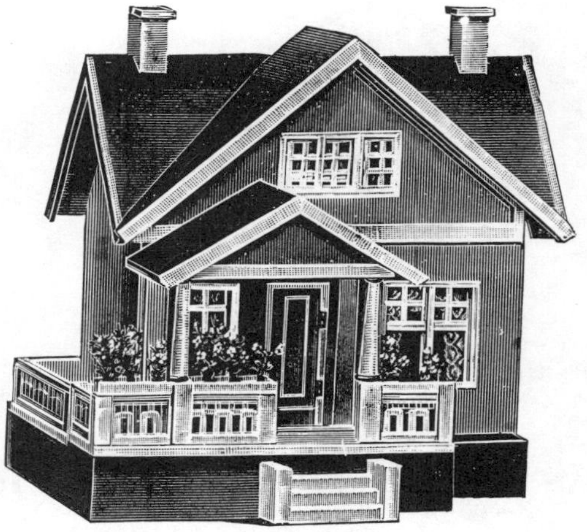

7/5992 F (39×25×39 cm)

7/5720

Verkaufsstände mit Jalousie u. Einrichtung, weiß lackiert.

Shop window stands, with blinds and equipment, white varnished.

Lonjas de venta con persiana y mueblaje, embarnizada en blanco.

7/5720 (33,5×10,5×37,5 cm)

7/6051 F (28,5×22×42,5 cm)

7/5983 (32×16,5×41 cm)

Nr. 7/5983 **Verkaufsstände** mit Schaufenstern und Schiebegitter, weiß lack., schwarz abgesetzt.

Shop stands, with window for display and sliding lattice, white varnished, set off with black.

Lonjas de venta con mostradores y enrejado corredizo, embarnizada en blanco, contraponiendo en negro.

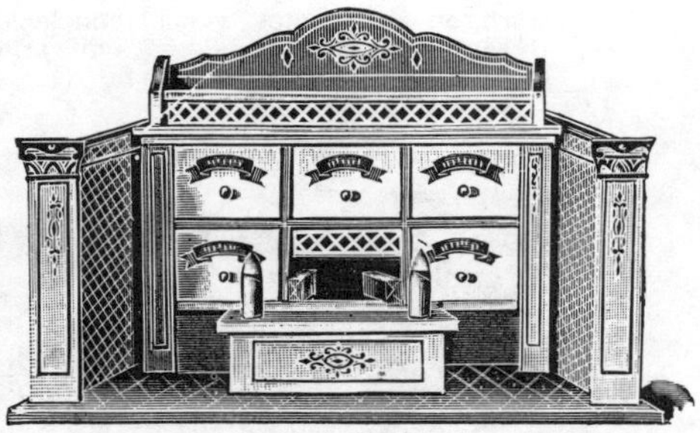

7/5624 (40×17×18 cm)

Nr. 7/5624 und 7/5914

Kaufläden, hell gemalt.
Shops, painted in light colour.
Tiendas, pintadas en color claro.

7/5914 (50,5×21,5×31 cm)

7/3290 (26,5×15×31 cm)

Theater mit Szenerie, Pappfiguren und Buch.
Theatre, with scenery, pasteboard figures and book
Teatro con escena, figuras de cartón y libro.

7/5109 (39×31×46 cm)

7/5259 (42×30×36 cm)

Festungen, gemalt und lackiert.
Fortresses, painted and varnished.
Fortalezas, pintadas y embarnizadas.

Siehe auch Schlußbemerkung auf Seite 141.

7/5542 26×14×29 cm

Pferdeställe mit Heuboden.
Stables for horses, with loft.
Cuadras con henil.

7/5934 42×25×49 cm

Pferdeställe mit Wohnung, Heuboden und Aufzug, gemalt und lackiert.
Stables for horses, with living-rooms attached, loft and lift, painted and varnished.
Cuadras con habitación, henil y elevador, pintadas y embarnizadas.

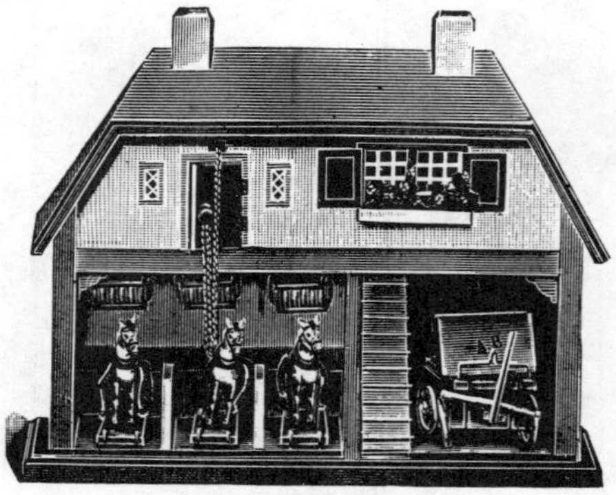

7/6061 45,5×19×34,5

Pferdeställe, gemalt und lackiert, mit Galerie.
Stables for horses, with gallery, painted and varnished.
Cuadras, pintadas y embarnizadas, con galería.

7/5976 30×22×51 cm

Speicher mit Aufzug.
Loft with lift.
Almacén con elevador.

7/6030 21×23×25 cm

Garagen für 1 Auto, gemalt und lackiert.
Garages for 1 taxi, painted and varnished.
Reservatorios para 1 automóvil, pintados y embarnizados.

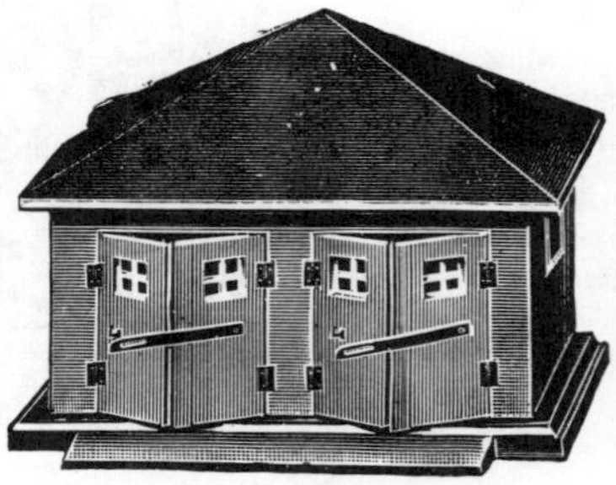

7/6035 36×23×26,5 cm

Garagen für 2 Autos, gemalt und lackiert.
Garages for 2 taxis, painted and varnished.
Reservatorios para 2 automóviles, pintados y embarnizados.

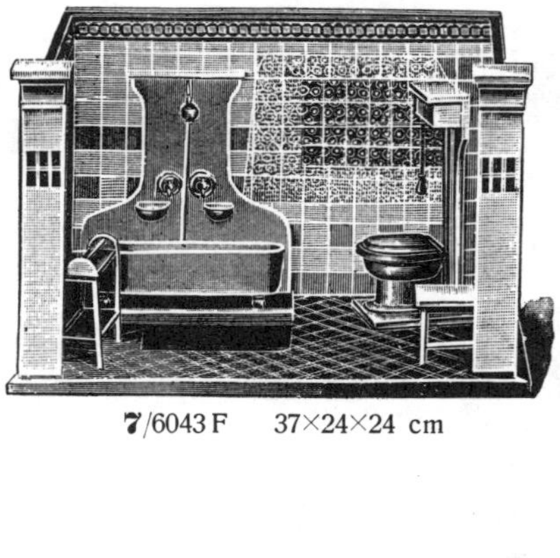

7/6043 F 37×24×24 cm

Nr. 7/6043 F, 7/6044 F
Badezimmer mit Einrichtung
Bath room, fully equipped.
Baño con mueblaje.

7/6044 F 44×31,5×29 cm

7/5924 37×30×23 cm

Nr. 7/5924, 7/5692
Küchen mit Ausbau und Fenster, komplett eingerichtet.
Kitchen with extension and windows, completely equipped.
Cocinas con saledizo y ventana, con todos los utensilios necesarios.

Siehe auch Schlußbemerkung von Seite 141.

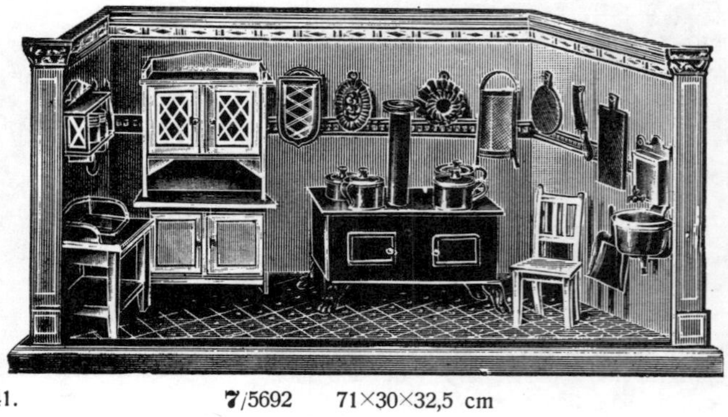

7/5692 71×30×32,5 cm

Puppenmöbel, in Kartons geheftet. — **Dolls furnitures**, fastened in cardboard boxes. — **Muebles para muñecas**, fijados en cajitas de cartón.

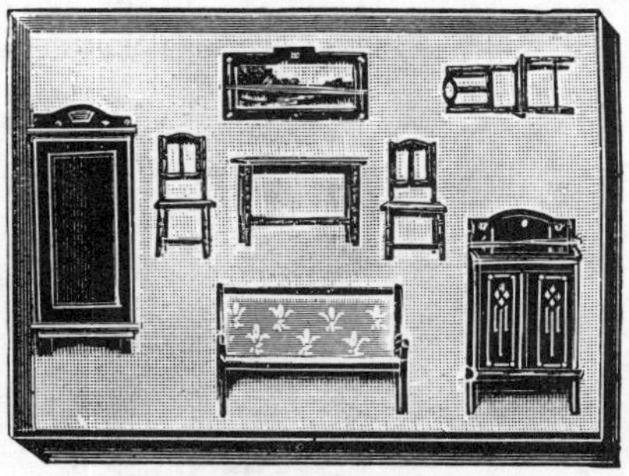

7/5029/3 (30×22×5 cm)

Salonmöbel, klein, Mahagoni.
Drawing room furniture, small, mahogany.
Muebles para el salón, pequeños, de caoba.

7/5426/105 (40×33×7 cm)

Salonmöbel, Mahagoni oder dunkel Eiche.
Drawing room furniture, mahogany or dark oak.
Muebles para el salón, de caoba o roble oscuro.

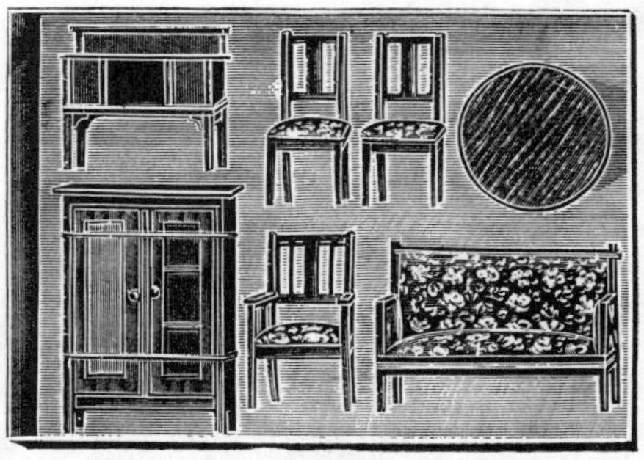

7/5911/205 (43×31×10 cm)

Salonmöbel, größer, Mahagoni oder dunkel Eiche.
Drawing room furniture, larger size, mahogany or dark oak.
Muebles para el salón, más grandes, de caoba o roble oscuro.

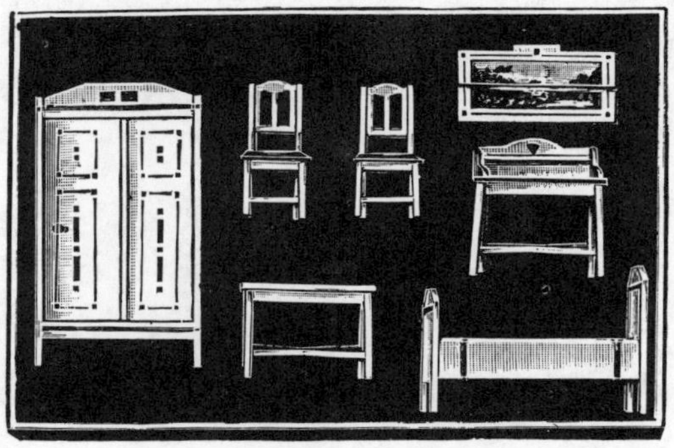

7/5039/3 (30×20×5,5 cm)

Nr. 7/5039/3
Schlafzimmermöbel, klein, weiß lackiert.
„ 7/5272/75
Schlafzimmermöbel, mittl. Größe, weiß lackiert.
„ 7/6021/50
Schlafzimmermöbel, groß, weiß lackiert.

7/5272/75 (44,5×29,5×9,5 cm)

Nr. 7/5039/3
Bedroom furniture, small, white enamel varnished.
„ 7/5272/75
Bedroom furniture, medium size, white enamel varnished.
„ 7/6021/50
Bedroom furniture, large size, white enamel varnished.

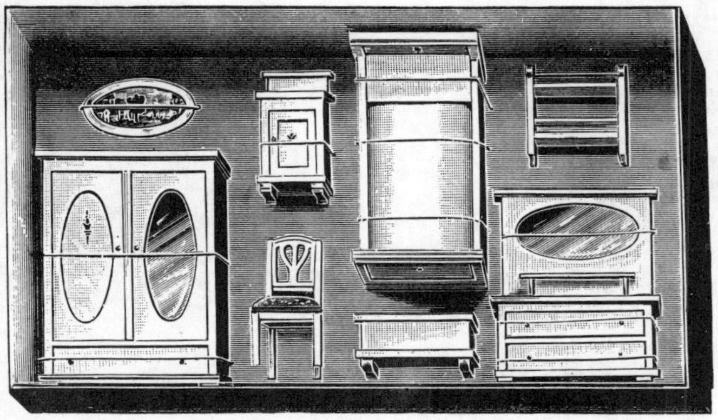

7/6021/50 (61×37×14 cm)

Nr. 7/5039/3
Muebles para el cuarto de dormir, pequeños, embarnizados en blanco.
„ 7/5272/75
Muebles para el cuarto de dormir, medio tamaño, embarnizados en blanco.
„ 7/6021/50
Muebles para el cuerto de dormir, grandes, embarnizados en blanco.

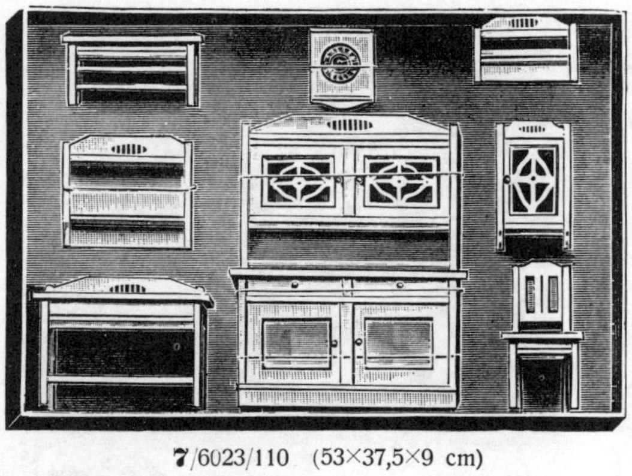

7/6023/110 (53×37,5×9 cm)

Küchenmöbel, weiß lackiert.
Kitchen furniture, white varnished.
Muebles para la cocina, embarnizados en blanco.

7/6075/25 (28×26×7,5 cm)

Badezimmermöbel, weiß lackiert.
Bath room furniture, white enamel varnished.
Muebles para el baño, embarnizados en blanco.

Die hier aufgenommenen Abbildungen zeigen Modelle, die in den verschiedenen Größen laut beifolgender Preisliste lieferbar sind, wobei die abgebildeten Nummern durch Fettdruck besonders kenntlich gemacht sind.

These illustrations depict models that can be supplied in the various sizes mentioned on enclosed Pricelist; the illustrated numbers being in heavy print.

Las ilustraciones mostradas aquí representan modelos entregables en diferentes tamaños según la adjunta lista de precios; los números ilustrados están marcados por letras gruesas.

Handgearbeitete, künstlerisch bemalte Holzspielwaren, wie Puppenhäuser, Puppenstuben, Wiegen, Betten und andere Puppenmöbel, garniert.
Hand-worked, artistically painted wooden toys, such as doll's houses, doll's rooms, cradles, beds, and other doll's furniture, fitted up and furnished.
Juguetes de madera artísticos, pintados, mano de obra, como casas para muñecas, cuartos para muñecas, cunas, camas y otras muebles para muñecas, guarnecidos.

Kl. 1

Kl. 1a

Kl. 2

Kl. 3

Kl. 4

Kl. 5

Die hier aufgenommenen Abbildungen sollen nur die Aufmachung und die Ausstattung sowie einzelne Formen zeigen; Einzelheiten sind aus der beifolgenden Preisliste zu entnehmen.
The illustrations shown here are intended only to show the get-up and the fitting-up, and also individual shapes; details may be obtained from the enclosed price list.
Las ilustraciones presentándose aquí no están destinadas a mostrar que la decoración y la guarnición del artículo así como algunas formas; en cuanto a detalles se puede ver todo lo necesario en la adjunta lista de precios.

Holzbaukasten. — Wooden building blocks. — Caja de construcción de madera.

30/1–19

Normal-Baukasten. Kasten von Weichholz und gelb gestrichen. Inhalt von weißem und braungedämpftem Buchenholz. Größenmaß der Bausteine $17^{1}/_{2}$ mm.

Normal box of bricks. Box of soft wood, painted yellow. Contents white and brown matted beech. Size of bricks $17^{1}/_{2}$ mm.

Caja de construcción normal. Caja de madera ligera y pintada en amarillo. Contenido de haya matizada en blanco y pardo. Dimensión de los cantos $17^{1}/_{2}$ mm.

30/58–70

Baukasten, Buche. Kasten von Weichholz und gelb gestrichen. Inhalt von weißem und braungedämpftem Buchenholz. Grundmaß der Bausteine 23 mm.

Box of bricks, beechwood. Box of soft wood, painted yellow. Contents white and brown matted beech. Base measurement of bricks 23 mm.

Caja de construcción — de haya. Caja de madera ligera y pintada en amarillo. Contenido de haya matizada en blanco y pardo. Dimensión fundamental de los cantos 23 mm.

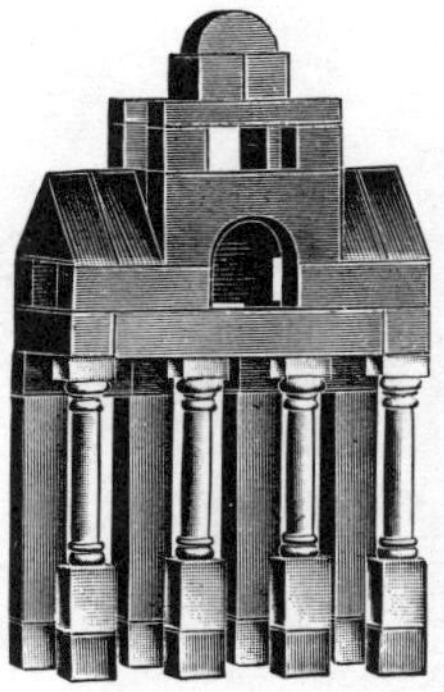

30/84–93

Baukasten, Buche (Teppich- oder Baby - Baukasten). Kasten von Weichholz und gelb gestrichen. Inhalt von weißem und braungedämpftem Buchenholz. Grundmaß der Bausteine 3 cm.

Box of bricks, beechwood (Carpet or Baby bricks). Box of soft wood, painted yellow. Contents white and brown matted beech. Base measurement of bricks 3 cm.

Caja de construcción — de haya (Caja de construcción sobre un tapiz ó caja de construcción para babies [niños]). Caja de madera ligera y pintada en amarillo. Contenido de haya matizada en blanco y pardo. Dimensión fundamental de los cantos 3 cm.

30/100–106

Baukasten „Orbis laboris“ oder „Das Bauen aus dem Kindergarten“. Kasten von Weichholz und gelb gestrichen. Inhalt von weißem, gedämpftem und buntgefärbtem Buchenholz. Tür- und Fensterbogen mit aufgedruckter Zeichnung.

Box of bricks "Orbis laboris", or "Building in the kindergarten". Box of soft wood and painted yellow. Contents white, matted, and coloured beech wood. Door and window arches with printed decoration.

Caja de construcción "Orbis laboris" ó "El construir en el escuela infantil". Caja de madera ligera y pintada en amarillo. Contenido de haya blanca, matizada y de varios colores. Medios puntos de las puertas y ventanas con dibujo imprimido sobre ellos.

30/129/0–132 f

Baukasten (gotischer Baustil). Kasten von Weichholz und gelb gestrichen. Inhalt von weißem und braungedämpftem Buchenholz. Tür- und Fensterspitzbogen m. aufgeprägtem Ornament. Grundmaß der Bausteine $17^{1}/_{2}$ mm.

Box of bricks (gothic style). Box of soft wood, painted yellow. Contents white and brown matted beech. Door and pointed window arches with embossed decoration. Base measurement of bricks $17^{1}/_{2}$ mm.

Caja de construcción (estilo arquitectural gótico). Caja de madera ligera y pintada en amarillo. Contenido de haya matizada en blanco y pardo. Ojivas de las puertas y ventanas con ornamentos imprimitos sobre. Dimensión fundamental de los cantos $17^{1}/_{2}$ mm.

30/154–157

Parkettspiel. Kasten von Weichholz und gelb gestrichen. Inhalt: Hartholztäfelchen, weiß und dunkelbraun gestrichen. (2 Lagen.)

Parquetry game. Box of soft wood, painted yellow. Contents: pieces of hard wood, white and dark brown. (2 layers.)

Juego de tablado. Caja de madera ligera y pintada en amarillo. Contenido: Tablillas de madera fuerte, pintadas en blanco y moreno. (2 series.)

30/210–223

Jubiläums - Baukasten 1900. Kasten von Weichholz und gelb gestrichen. Inhalt von weißem und braungedämpftem Buchenholz mit aufgeprägtem Ornament. Grundmaß der Bausteine $17^{1}/_{2}$ mm.

Jubileum box of bricks 1900. Box of soft wood, painted yellow. Contents white and brown matted beech with embossed ornamentation. Base measurement of bricks $17^{1}/_{2}$ mm.

Caja de construcción de jubileo de 1900. Caja de madera ligera y pintada en amarillo. Contenido de haya matizada en blanco y pardo con ornamentos imprimidos sobre. Dimensión fundamental de los cantos $17^{1}/_{2}$ mm.

30/172–175 a

Hammer und Nagel. Kasten bei den kleineren Ausgaben von Weichholz und gelb gestrichen; bei den größeren Nummern von Lärchenholz, gezinkt und geölt. Inhalt: Brettchen und Balken, Nagel, Hammer und Pfriemen.

Hammer and nails. Small boxes, of soft wood, painted yellow; larger sizes, of larch, galvanized and oiled. Contents: board, joist, nails, hammer and awl.

Martillo y clavo. Cajas de las ejecuciones más pequeñas de madera ligera y pintadas en amarillo; cajas de las ejecuciones más grandes de madero de alerce, endentadas y aceitadas. Contenido: Tabletas y vigas, clavos, martillos y punzones.

Nr. **30**/231–234 **Der praktische Wagenbauer.** Kasten der kleinen Ausgaben von Weichholz, gelb gestrichen, der großen Ausgaben von Lärchenholz, gezinkt und geölt. Inhalt: Holz- und Eisenteile.

30/231–234

The practical carriage builder. Small boxes, of soft wood, painted yellow; larger sizes, of larch, galvanized and oiled. Contents: wooden and iron parts.

El carretero práctico. Cajas de las ejecuciones más pequeñas de madera ligera, pintadas en amarillo; cajas de las ejecuciones más grandes de madero de alerce, endentadas y aceitadas. Contenido: Piezas de madera y de hierro.

Nr. **30**/257–265 **Fröbels Baukasten.** Kasten von Weichholz und gelb gestrichen. Grundmaß der Bausteine der kleinen Nummern $17^{1}/_{2}$ mm, der größten Nummern 25 mm. Inhalt von weißem, buntgefärbtem und braungedämpftem Buchenholz. Tür- und Fensterbogen mit aufgedruckter Zeichnung.

Fröbel box of bricks. Box of soft wood, painted yellow. Base measurements or bricks, smaller boxes $17^{1}/_{2}$ mm; larger ones, 25 mm. Contents: white, coloured, and brown matted beech. Door and window arches with printed decoration.

Caja de construcción de Fröbel. Caja de madera ligera y pintada en amarillo. Dimensión fundamental de los cantos de los pequeños números $17^{1}/_{2}$ mm la de los números más grandes 25 mm. Contenido: Haya blanca, pintada con varios colores y matizada en pardo. Ojivas de las puertas y ventanas con dibujo imprimido sobre.

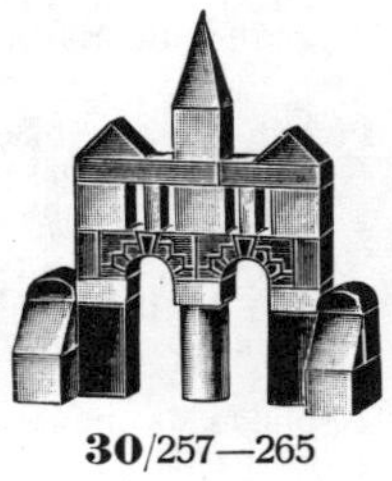

30/257–265

Holzbaukasten. — Wooden building blocks. — Caja de construcción de madera.

30/297 – 304

Schwarzwald (Häuserbaukasten), D. R. G. M. Nr. 461 228. Kasten von Weichholz und gelb gestrichen. Inhalt von weißem und buntgefärbtem Buchenholz mit Aufdruck. Grundmaß der Bausteine 2 cm.

Black Forest (House bricks), Patent 461 228. Box of soft wood, and painted yellow. Contents of white and coloured beech, with printing. Base measurement of bricks 2 cm.

Selva Negra (Caja para construir casas), muestra de uso privilegiada en Alemania (D. R. G. M.) No. 461 228. Caja de madera ligera y pintada en amarillo. Contenido: Haya blanca y pintada con varios colores. Dimensión fundamental de los cantos 2 cm.

30/288—295

Helvetia-Häuser (Schweizer Baukasten). Kasten von Weichholz und gelb gestrichen. Inhalt von weißem und buntgefärbtem Buchenholz mit Aufdruck. Grundmaß der Bausteine 2 cm.

Helvetia Houses (Swiss style). Box of soft wood, painted yellow. Contents of white and coloured beech, with printing. Base measurement of bricks 2 cm.

Casas de Helvecia (Caja de construcción suiza). Caja de madera ligera y pintada en amarillo. Contenido: Haya blanca y pintada con varios colores con impresión. Dimensión fundamental de los cantos 2 cm.

30/266—273

Miniatur - Baukasten. Kasten von Weichholz und gelb gestrichen. Inhalt von weißem und rotgefärbtem Buchenholz mit schwarzem Aufdruck. Grundmaß der Bausteine 2 cm.

Miniature box of bricks. Box of soft wood painted yellow. Contents of white and red beech, with black printing. Base measurement of bricks 2 cm.

Caja de construcción en miniatura. Caja de madera ligera y pintada en amarillo. Contenido: Haya blanca y pintada en rojo con impresión negra. Dimensión fundamental de los cantos 2 cm.

30/280—287

Burgen und Schlösser. Kasten von Weichholz und gelb gestrichen. Inhalt von weißem und buntgefärbtem Buchenholz mit schwarzem Aufdruck. Grundmaß der Bausteine 2 cm.

Burghs and castles. Box of soft wood painted yellow. Contents of white and coloured beech, with black printing. Base measurement of bricks 2 cm.

Castillos y palacios. Caja de madera ligera y pintada en amarillo. Contenido: Haya blanca y pintada con varios colores con impresión negra. Dimensión fundamental de los cantos 2 cm.

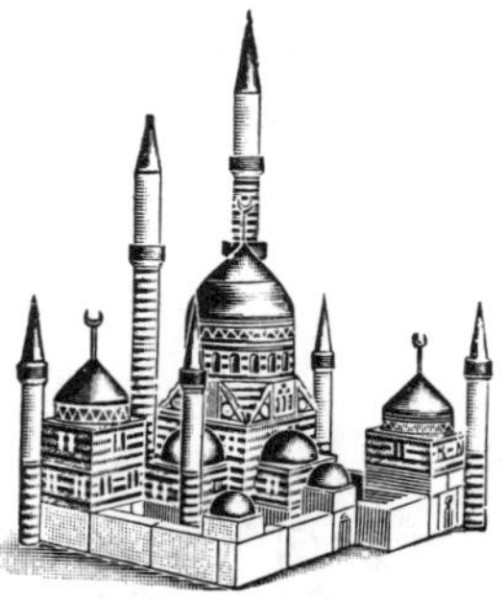

30/305—312

Orient (Baukasten nach orientalischem Stil). Kasten von Weichholz und gestrichen. Inhalt von weißem und buntgefärbtem Buchenholz mit Aufdruck. Grundmaß der Bausteine 2 cm.

Oriental box of bricks (Eastern style). Box of soft wood, painted. Contents of white and coloured beech, with printing. Base measurement of bricks 2 cm.

Oriente (Caja de construcción según el estilo arquitectural oriental). Caja de madera ligera y pintada. Contenido: Haya blanca y pintada con varios colores con impresión. Dimensión fundamental de los cantos 2 cm.

30/277

Der kleine Schwede. Gebrauchsmuster Nr. 327 278 (vom 10. Januar 1908). Eingetragen in die Warenzeichenrolle (v. 3. März 1908) unter Nr. 105 525. Schwedenholzschachtel, enthaltend weiße, bedruckte und rotgefärbte Steinchen sowie Vorlage.

The little Swede. Entered in the list of goods (3/3/1908) sub No. 105 525. Swedish match box, containing white printed and red stones, and pattern sheet.

El pequeño Sueco. Muestra de uso privilegiada No. 327 278 (del 10 Enero 1908). Registrada en la matrícula para marcas de fábrica (del 3 Marzo 1908) con el No. 105 525. Cajita de madera sueca, conteniendo cantos blancos, imprimidos y pintados en rojo así como un dibujo sirviendo de muestra.

30/313 und 320

Heimatliche Baukunst für Stadt und Land. Kasten von Weichholz und gestrichen. Inhalt von weißem und buntgefärbtem Buchenholz mit Aufdruck. Grundmaß der Bausteine 2 cm.

Home Architecture for town and country. Box of soft wood, painted. Contents of white and coloured bricks of beech, with printing. Base measurement of bricks 2 cm.

Arquitectura nativa para la ciudad y la campaña. Caja de madera ligera y pintada. Contenido: Haya blanca y pintada con varios colores con impresión. Dimensión fundamental de los cantos 2 cm.

30/321—328

Fachwerk - Baukasten. Kasten von Weichholz und gestrichen. Inhalt von weißem und buntgefärbtem Buchenholz mit Aufdruck. Grundmaß der Bausteine 2 cm.

Openwork building box. Box of soft wood painted. Contents of white and coloured beech, with printing. Base measurement of bricks 2 cm.

Caja de construcción de madera. Caja de madera ligera y pintada. Contenido: Haya blanca y pintada con varios colores con impresión. Dimensión fundamental de los cantos 2 cm.

30/225

Puzzle-Spiel. Kasten von Weichholz, farbig gestrichen. Inhalt: Braungedämpfte Hartholztäfelchen.

Puzzle Game. Box of soft wood, coloured. Contents: brown matted hard wood tablets.

Juego de burla (Juego "Puzzle"). Caja de madera ligera, pintada con varios colores. Contenido: Tablillas de madera fuerte matizadas en pardo.

30/278

Fröbels Baukasten. Gabe 3, Miniatur-Volksausgabe. Schwedenholzschachtel, enthaltend 8 farbige Holzwürfel und Vorlagen.

Fröbel box of bricks. Gift 3, Miniature popular specimen. Swedish match box, containing 8 coloured wooden dice and pattern sheets.

Caja de construcción de Fröbel. Gabe 3, edición popular en miniatura. Cajita de madera sueca, conteniendo 8 dados de madera y dicujos sirviendo de muestra.

30/279

Fröbels Baukasten. Gabe 4, Miniatur-Volksausgabe. Schwedenholzschachtel, enthaltend 8 farbige Längentafeln und Vorlagen.

Fröbel box of bricks. Gift 4, Miniature popular specimen. Swedish match box, containing 8 coloured oblong plates and model sheets.

Caja de construcción de Fröbel. Gabe 4, edición popular en miniatura. Cajita de madera sueca, conteniendo 8 tablas longitudinales y dibujos sirviendo de muestra.

30/337

Baukästchen. Kasten von Weichholz, gelb gestrichen. Inhalt: Verschiedene Hartholzbausteinchen. Grundmaß $17^1/_2$ mm.

Box of bricks. Box of soft wood, painted yellow. Contents various hard wood bricks. Base measurement of bricks $17^1/_2$ mm.

Cajitas de construcción. Cajita de madera ligera, pintada en amarillo. Contenido: Varios cantos de madera fuerte. Dimensión fundamental $17^1/_2$ mm.

Puppenmöbel. Marke: Gezapft und gefugt. — Dolls furniture. Brand: Tenoned and rabbened.
Muebles para muñecas. Marca: provista de gorrones y encajes.

39/338

39/348

Nr. **39**/295 Schlafzimmer, klein, hell, enthaltend: 2 Betten, 1 Kleiderschrank, 1 Waschtisch, 2 Nachttische, 2 Stühle.

Bedroom, small, light, containing: 2 beds, 1 wardrobe, 1 washstand, 2 bedside tables, 2 chairs.

Cuarto de dormir, pequeño, claro, conteniendo: 2 camas, 1 guardaropa (armario), 1 lavadero, 2 mesas de noche, 2 sillas.

„ **39**/295 a Desgl., größer, hell.

The same, larger, light.

Idem, más grande, claro.

„ **39**/303/I Klavier, ohne Musikwerk.

Piano without musical action.

Pianoforte, sin aparato de música.

„ **39**/303a/I Flügel, ohne Musikwerk.

Grand piano without musical action.

Piano de cola, sin aparato de música.

„ **39**/305 Salon, weiß oder gelb, enthaltend 1 Sofa mit Umbau, 1 Salonschrank, 1 Pfeilerspiegel, 1 Salontisch, 3 Plüschstühle.

Drawing room, white or yellow, containing: 1 sofa with adjoining cabinet work, drawing room cupboard, 1 pier glass, 1 drawing room table, 3 plush chairs.

Salón, blanco ó amarillo, conteniendo: 1 sofá con reconstrucción, 1 armario de salón, 1 trumé (espejo grande entre dos ventanas), 1 mesa de salón, 3 sillas de velludo (felpa).

„ **39**/305 a Desgl., groß, weiß oder gelb, enthaltend: 1 Sofa mit Umbau, 1 Salonschrank, 1 Pfeilerspiegel, 1 Salontisch, 1 Säule, 2 Plüschstühle, 2 Sessel, 2 Hocker.

The same, larger, white or yellow, containing: 1 sofa with adjoining cabinet work, drawing room cupboard, 1 pier glass, 1 drawing room table, 1 pillar, 2 plush chairs, 2 easy chairs, 2 stools.

Idem, grande, blanco ó amarillo, conteniendo: 1 sofá con reconstrucción, 1 armario de salón, 1 trúme, 1 mesa de salón, 1 columna, 2 sillas de velludo, 2 sillas, 2 haraganes.

„ **39**/306/I Baby-Bett, klein.

Baby's cot, small.

Cama para niños, pequeña.

„ **39**/309/I Wohnzimmer, braun oder schwarz, enthaltend: 1 Büfett, 2 Polsterstühle, 1 Sofa, 1 runden Tisch.

Sitting room, brown or black, containing: 1 sideboard, 2 upholstered chairs, 1 sofa, 1 round table.

Cuarto (aposento), pardo ó negro, conteniendo: 1 bufete, 2 sillas acolchadas, 1 sofá, 1 mesa redonda.

„ **39**/309/II Desgl., größer, braun oder schwarz, enthaltend: 1 Büchertisch, 1 runden Tisch, 1 Armstuhl, 3 Polsterstühle, 1 Bücherschrank.

Sitting room, brown or black, containing: 1 book table, 1 round table, 1 arm chair, 3 upholstered chairs, 1 bookcase.

Idem, más grande, pardo ó negro, conteniendo: 1 mesa para libros, 1 mesa redonda, 1 silla poltrona (silla de brazos), 3 sillas acolchadas, 1 plúteo (armario para libros).

Nr. **39**/309/III Desgl., größer, braun oder schwarz, enthaltend: 1 Büfett, 3 Polsterstühle, 1 Schaukelstuhl, 1 Bücherschrank, 1 runden Tisch.

The same, larger, brown or black, containing: 1 sideboard, 3 upholstered chairs, 1 rocking chair, 1 bookcase, 1 round table.

Idem, más grande, pardo ó negro, conteniendo: 1 bufete, 3 sillas acolchadas, 1 mecedor (silla para mecerse), 1 armario para libros, 1 mesa redonda.

„ **39**/309/IV Desgl., größer, braun oder schwarz, enthaltend: 1 Büchertisch, 1 runden Tisch, 1 Klubsessel, 2 Armstühle, 1 Schaukelstuhl, 1 Bücherschrank, 1 Sofabank.

The same, larger, brown or black, containing: 1 book table, 1 round table, 1 club-room easy chair, 2 arm chairs, 1 rocking chair, 1 bookcase, 1 settee.

Idem, más grande, pardo o negro, conteniendo: 1 mesa para libros, 1 mesa redonda, 1 sillón (silla de club), 2 sillas poltronas (sillas de brazos), 1 mecedor (silla para mecerse), 1 armario para libros, 1 banco de sofá.

„ **39**/309/V Desgl., größer, braun oder schwarz, enthaltend: 1 Büfett, 1 Sofabank, 2 Polsterstühle, 1 Klubsessel, 1 Schaukelstuhl, 1 Bücherschrank, 1 runden Tisch, 1 Büchertisch.

The same, larger, brown or black, containing: 1 sideboard, 1 settee, 2 upholstered chairs, 1 club-room easy chair, 1 rocking chair, 1 bookcase, 1 round table, 1 book table.

Idem, más grande, pardo ó negro, conteniendo: 1 bufete, 1 banco de sofá 2 sillas acolchadas, 1 sillón, (silla de club), 1 mecedor, 1 armario para libros, 1 mesa redonda, 1 mesa para libros.

„ **39**/314 Schlafzimmer, weiß, enthaltend: 2 Betten, 2 Nachttische, 1 Waschkommode mit Spiegel, 2 Stühle (ähnlich der Nr. 309).

Bedroom, white, containing: 2 beds, 2 bedside tables, 1 washstand-chest of drawers with mirror, 2 chairs (similar to Nr. 309).

Cuarto de dormir, blanco, conteniendo: 2 camas, 2 mesas de noche, 1 cómoda-lavadero con espejo, 2 sillas (somejante a No. 309).

„ **39**/315 Desgl., weiß, enthaltend, 2 Betten, 2 Nachttische, 1 Waschkommode mit Toilettenaufsatz, 1 Kleiderschrank, 2 Stühle, 1 Schaukelstuhl.

The same, white, containing: 2 beds, 2 bedside tables, 1 washstand-chest of drawers with toilet mirror and drawers, 1 wardrobe, 2 chairs, 1 rocking chair.

Idem, blanco, conteniendo: 2 camas, 2 mesas de noche, 1 cómoda-lavadero con tocador, 1 guardaropa, (armario), 2 sillas, 1 silla para mecerse (mecedor).

Puppenmöbel. Marke: Gezapft und gefugt. — Dolls furniture. Brand: Tenoned and rabbened. Muebles para muñecas. Marca: provista de gorrones y encajes.

Nr. **39**/316 Schlafzimmer, weiß, enthaltend: 2 Betten, 2 Nachttische, 1 Waschkommode mit Spiegel, 1 Kleiderschrank, 2 Stühle, 1 Handtuchhalter, 1 Chiffonier, 1 großer Toilettenspiegel, 1 Toilettentisch.

Bedroom, white, containing: 2 beds, 2 bedside tables, 1 washstand-chest of drawers with mirror, 1 wardrobe, 2 chairs, 1 towel rack, 1 chiffonier, 1 large toilet mirror, 1 toilet table.

Cuarto de dormir, blanco, conteniendo: 2 camas, 2 mesas de noche, 1 cómoda-lavadero, con espejo, 1 guardaropa, 2 sillas, 1 enjugador, 1 chiffonier, 1 gran espejo de tocador, 1 mesa de tocador.

„ **39**/310 Schlafzimmer, klein, weiß, enthaltend: 2 Betten, 1 Kleiderschrank, 1 Waschtisch, 2 Nachttischchen, 2 Stühle.

Bedroom, small, white, containing: 2 beds, 1 wardrobe, 1 washstand, 2 bedside tables, 2 chairs.

Cuarto de dormir, pequeño, blanco, conteniendo: 2 camas, 1 guardaropa, 1 lavadero (lavabo), 2 pequeñas mesas de noche, 2 sillas.

„ **39**/311 Desgl., groß, weiß, derselbe Inhalt wie 310, aber größer, weiß mit grau abgesetzt.

The same, large, white. The same contents as Nr. 310, but larger, white picked out with grey.

Idem, grande, blanco, el mismo contenido que él del No. 310, pero más grande, blanco y gris cambiando.

„ **39**/317 Gartenmöbel, weiß, bestehend aus einer Bank, zwei Armsesseln und einem runden Tisch.

Garden furniture, white, consisting of a benche, 2 arm chairs, 1 round table.

Muebles de jardín, blancos, compuestos de un banco, 2 sillas de brazes y 1 mesa redonda.

„ **39**/338 Speisezimmer, braun oder schwarz, enthaltend: 1 modernes, breites Büfett, 1 Ausziehtisch, 1 Büchertisch, 1 Sofabank, 1 Armstuhl, 4 Polsterstühle, 1 Spieltisch.

Dining room, brown or black, consisting of 1 modern, wide sideboard, 1 extension table, 1 book table, 1 settee, 1 arm chair, 4 upholstered chairs, 1 card table.

Comedor, pardo ó negro, conteniendo: 1 bufete ancho y moderno, 1 mesa para tirar (extender), 1 mesa para libros, 1 banco de sofá, 1 silla de brazos, 4 sillas acolchadas, 1 mesa de juego.

„ **39**/339 Schlafzimmer, hell, enthaltend: 1 dreiteiligen Wäscheschrank mit 6 Kästen und 2 großen Spiegelscheiben, 2 Betten, 2 Nachtschränkchen, 1 Waschtisch, 2 Polsterstühle.

Bedroom, light, containing: 1 three-part linen press with 6 lockers and 2 large mirrors, 2 beds, 2 bedside tables, 1 washstand, 2 upholstered chairs.

Cuarto de dormir, claro, conteniendo: 1 armario para la ropa blanca, compuesta de tres partes y conteniendo 6 cajas y teniendo 2 lunas de espejo (vidrios de cristal), 2 camas, 2 pequeños armarios de noche, 1 lavadero (lavabo), 2 sillas acolchadas.

„ **39**/328 Wasser-Klosett.
Water closet.
Letrina inglesa (W. C.)

„ **39**/329 Desgl.
Ditto.
Idem.

„ **39**/330 Waschtisch.
Washstand.
Lavadero (lavabo).

39/328/332

Nr. **39**/331 Badewanne.
Bath tub.
Cuba para baños (tina de baños).

„ **39**/332 Spülstein.
Sink.
Vertedero de aguas.

„ **39**/340 Weißer Badesessel.
White bathroom easy chair.
Silla blanca de baño.

„ **39**/341 Ovaler Waschtisch.
Oval washstand.
Lavadero (lavabo) oval.

„ **39**/348 Schlafzimmer, hell. Möbel für größere Puppenstuben, enthaltend: 2 Betten, 2 Nachttische, 2 Stühle, 1 Waschtisch mit Spiegel und weißer Marmorplatte.

Bedroom, light. Furniture for larger dolls houses, containing: 2 beds, 2 bedside tables, 2 chairs, 1 washstand with mirror and white marble top.

Cuerto de dormir, blanco. Mueblaje para cuartos de muñeca más grandes, conteniendo: 2 camas, 2 mesas de noche, 2 sillas, 1 lavadero (lavabo) con espejo y placa de mármol blanco.

„ **39**/348 w Desgl., weiß.
The same, white.
Idem, blanco.

„ **39**/348 a Desgl., größer, hell, enthaltend: 2 Betten, 2 Nachttische, 2 Stühle, 1 Waschtisch mit Spiegel und weißer Marmorplatte, 1 kombinierten Wäsche- und Kleiderschrank mit Spiegelscheibe.

The same, light, larger, containing: 2 beds, 2 bedside tables, 2 chairs, 1 washstand with mirror and white marbel top, 1 combined linen press and wardrobe with mirror.

Idem, más grande, claro, conteniendo: 2 camas, 2 mesas de nocho, 2 sillas, 1 lavadero con espejo y placa de mármol blanco, 1 armario combinado como guardaropa y armario para la ropa-blanca con luna de espejo.

„ **39**/348 a w Desgl., größer, weiß.
The same, larger, white.
Idem, más grande, blanco.

„ **39**/349 Speisezimmer, braun oder schwarz. Möbel Größe II, enthaltend: 4 Stühle, 1 Ausziehtisch, 1 Büfett, 1 Anrichte, sehr elegant und modern.

Dining room, brown or black. Furniture size II, containing: 4 chairs, 1 extension table, 1 sideboard, 1 dresser, very elegant and modern.

Comedor, pardo ó negro. Mueblaje tamaño II, conteniendo: 4 sillas, 1 mesa para extender (tirar), 1 bufete, 1 aparador elegantísimo y muy moderno.

„ **39**/385 Herrenzimmer, rot oder braun, enthaltend: 1 Chaiselongue, 1 modernen dreiteiligen Bücherschrank oder Büfett, 1 runden Tisch, 4 Stühle, 1 Standuhr.

Gentlemen's room, red or brown, containing: 1 chaiselongue, 1 modern threepart bookcase or sideboard, 1 round table, 4 chairs, 1 grandfather's clock.

Salón para señores, rojo ó pardo, conteniendo: 1 camilla para descansar (chaiselongue), 1 armario moderno para libros compuesto de tres partes ó bufete, 1 mesa redonda, 4 sillas, 1 gran reloj vertical sobre pies.

„ **39**/391 Speisezimmer, braun, enthaltend: 1 runden Tisch, 2 Armsessel, 2 Stühle, 1 modernes Büfett, 1 Uhr.

Dining room, brown, containing: 1 round table, 2 easy arm chairs, 2 chairs, 1 modern sideboard, 1 clock.

Comedor, pardo, conteniendo: 1 mesa redonda, 2 sillas de brazos, 2 sillas, 1 bufete (buffet) moderno, 1 reloj.

Feine Legespiele, Baukästen, Zusammensetzspiele. — High-class fretwork puzzles, sets of building blocks, Chinese puzzles.
Spezialität: Würfel, Würfelbecher, Halmafiguren und Damesteine. — Specialities: Dice, dice cupo, Halma pieces, draughts men.

Finos juegos para colocar alguna cosa, cajas de construcción, juegos para componer objetos.
Especialidades: Dados, cubiletes, figuras para el juego "Halma" y piezas para el juego de las damas.

39/188

39/299

39/222

39/223

39/276

Nr. **39**/134	Kuben-Mosaik	Cubs mosaics	Mosaico de cubos	145×145 mm
„ **39**/284	Riesen-Kuben-Mosaik	Giant cubs mosaics	Mosaico gigantesco de cubos	175×175 „
„ **39**/167	Platten-Mosaik	Plate mosaics	Mosaico de placas	203×203 „
„ **39**/187	Platten-Mosaik	Plate mosaics	Mosaico de placas	314×314 „
„ **39**/188 kl.	Landschafts-Mosaik	Landscape mosaics	Mosaico de paisajes	248×330 „
„ **39**/188 gr.	Landschafts-Mosaik	Landscape mosaics	Mosaico de paisajes	266×398 „
„ **39**/222	Perlen-Mosaik	Bead mosaics	Mosaico de perlas	193×179 „
„ **39**/223	Konstrukteur-Mosaik	Constructor mosaics	Mosaico para constructores	175×155 „
„ **39**/343	Konstrukteur-Mosaik	Constructor mosaics	Mosaico para constructores	330×283 „
„ **39**/229	Platten-Mosaik	Plate mosaics	Mosaico de placas	190×190 „
„ **39**/230	Platten-Mosaik	Plate mosaics	Mosaico de placas	265×265 „
„ **39**/233	Ring-Mosaik	Ring mosaics	Mosaico de anillos	190×190 „
„ **39**/234	Ring-Mosaik	Ring mosaics	Mosaico de anillos	260×260 „
„ **39**/240 kl.	Universal-Mosaik	Universal mosaics	Masaico universal	230×230 „
„ **39**/244	Ring-Mosaik	Ring mosaics	Mosaico de anillos	330×330 „
„ **39**/307	Stern-Mosaik	Star mosaics	Mosaico de estrellas	308×262 „
„ **39**/245	Platten-Mosaik	Plate mosaics	Mosaico de placas	150×150 „
„ **39**/245 a	Platten-Mosaik	Plate mosaics	Mosaico de placas	193×193 „
„ **39**/245 b	Platten-Mosaik	Plate mosaics	Mosaico de placas	217×217 „
„ **39**/277	Platten-Mosaik	Plate mosaics	Mosaico de placas	190×190 „
„ **39**/253	Städte-Baukasten	Town building blocks	Cajas de construcción para edificar ciudades	157×157 „
„ **39**/253 a	Städte-Baukasten	Town building blocks	Cajas de construcción para edificar ciudades	193×193 „
„ **39**/253 d	Städte-Baukasten	Town building blocks	Cajas de construcción para edificar ciudades	306×189 „
„ **39**/253 b	Städte-Baukasten	Town building blocks	Cajas de construcción para edificar ciudades	365×218 „
„ **39**/253 c	Städte-Baukasten	Town building blocks	Cajas de construcción para edificar ciudades	425×218 „
„ **39**/255 kl.	Landschafts-Mosaik	Landscape mosaics	Mosaico de paisajes	340×244 „
„ **39**/265	Puppen-Mosaik	Doll mosaics	Mosaico de muñecas	154×284 „
„ **39**/267 kl.	Baby-Baukasten	Baby building blocks	Gajas de construcción para niños	208×208 „
„ **39**/272	Mosaik-Künstler	The mosaic artist	Artista en mosaicos	222×222 „
„ **39**/268	Mosaik-Künstler	The mosaic artist	Artista en mosaicos	267×267 „
„ **39**/276	Sport-Mosaik	Sport mosaics	Mosaico de divertimiento	299×199 „
„ **39**/294	Platten-Mosaik	Plate mosaics	Mosaico de placas	150×250 „
„ **39**/298	Villa-Nova (Vill en-Baukasten)	Villa-nova (cottage building blocks)	Villa-Nova (Caja de construcción para edifica casas privadas)	260×190 „
„ **39**/299	Villa-Nova (Villen-Baukasten)	Villa-nova (cottage building blocks)	Villa-Nova (Caja de construcción para edificar casas privadas)	362×242 „
„ **39**/312	Platten-Mosaik	Plate mosaics	Mosaico de placas	250×250 „
„ **39**/350	Tier-Mosaik	Animal mosaics	Mosaico de animales	200×200 „
„ **39**/370	Auto-Baukasten (4 verschiedene Typen)	Motor car building blocks (4 different types)	Caja de construcción para construir automóviles (4 varias generos)	352×172 „
„ **39**/386 a	Eisenbahn-D-Zug (Lokomot. u. 3 Wag.) Länge 70 cm	Railway corridor train, Locomotive and 3 carriages. Length 29¹/₆″	Tren de corredor, locomotora y 3 vagones, largura: 70 cm	
„ **39**/386 b	Eisenbahn-D-Zug (Lokomot. u. 2 Wag.) Länge 57 cm	Railway corridor train, Locomotive and 2 carriages. Length 23²/₃″	Tren de corredor, locomotora y 2 vagones, largura: 57 cm	
„ **39**/387 a	Güterzug (Lokomotive und 3 Wagen) Länge 70 cm	Goods train, locomotive and 3 waggons Length 29¹/₆″	Tren de mercancias, locomotora y 3 vagones, largura: 70 cm	
„ **39**/387 b	Güterzug (Lokomotive und 2 Wagen) Länge 57 cm	Goods train, locomotive and 2 waggons Length 23²/₃″	Tren de mercancias, locomotora y 2 vagones, largura: 57 cm	
„ **39**/388	Holzschienen, passend zu Nr. 386 u. 387	Wooden rails, suitable for Nr. 386 & 387	Carriles de madera adecuados al No. 386 y 387	
„ **39**/389	Sandsteckspiel (Dorfbaukasten) Häusergröße 20×12 mm	Sand game (Village building blocks) Size of house: 20×12 mm	Juego para meter objetos en la arena (Caja de construcción para edificar pueblos, grandeza de las casas: 20×12 mm)	
„ **39**/390	Sandsteckspiel in größerer Ausgabe	Sand game, in greater execution	Juego para meter objetos en la arena, más grande	
„ **39**/282/10	Miniatur-Eisenbahn	Miniature railway	Tren en miniatura	
„ **39**/301	Miniatur-D-Zug	Miniature corridor train	Tren de corredor en miniatura	
	28 er Dominos, schwarz m. weiß. Augen	28's dominoes, black with white points	Dominós con 28 piezas, negras con ojos blancos	
	36 er Dominos, schwarz m. weiß. Augen	36's dominoes, black with white points	Dominós con 36 piezas, negras con ojos blancos	
	45 er Dominos, schwarz m. weiß. Augen	45's dominoes, black with white points	Dominós con 45 piezas, negras con ojos blancos	
	55 er Dominos, schwarz m. weiß. Augen	55's dominoes, black with white points	Dominós con 55 piezas, negras con ojos blancos	

Über Bein- und Holzwürfel, Spielmarken, Damesteine und Galalith-Dominos verlange man Spezialofferte!
Please apply for special quotations for bone and wood dice, chips, draughts men, and galalith dominoes.
Sírvase Vd. demandar ofertas especiales tocante a dados de hueso y de madera, fichas, piezas para el juego de las damas y dominós de galalith.

„Architectus“ Zusammensetz-Holzbaukasten. — „Architectus“ Wood-building-blocks. — „Architectus“ Caja de construcción de madera.

Der „Architectus“-Zusammensetz-Baukasten für Knaben und Mädchen in 5 Größen:

Nr. **137**/1 Größe: 18×18 cm, Höhe: 3 cm, Gewicht: 1/3 kg, enthält Modellbogen für folgende 12 Modelle: Einfacher Bilderrahmen, kleine Doppelleiter, Barren, einfache Schaukel, chin. Tor, Hocker, einfacher Stuhl, Speisezimmerstuhl, einfache Bank, Topfständer, Ehrenpforte, Windmesser und Signalscheibe.

Nr. **137**/2 Größe 24×29 cm, Höhe: 3 cm, Gewicht: 2/3 kg, enthält Modellbogen für folgende 30 Modelle: 12 Modelle wie Nr. 1, ferner: Handtuchständer, Palmkübel, Vogelschutzhüttchen, Gehlauf, Palmständer, Blumenkrippe, Topfständer, Sitzgondel, Klubsessel, Lehnsessel, Blumenampel, einfaches Schreibzeug, Säulentisch, Salontisch, Zimmertisch, einfache Bettstelle, Puppenbettstelle, Gartenlaube.

Nr. **137**/2 E Größe: 23×35 cm, Höhe: 3 cm, Gewicht: 4/5 kg, enthält Modellbogen für folgende 40 Modelle: 30 Modelle wie Nr. 2, ferner: Feuerwehrleiter, Schubkarren, Schleifstein, verstellbarer Liegesessel, Krahn, Leiterwagen, Rollwagen, Kleiner Wagen mit Bock, Eisenbahn-Güterwagen, Förderwagen.

Nr. **137**/3 Größe: 25×36 cm, Höhe 3 cm, Gewicht: 1 1/6 kg, enthält Modellbogen für folgende 45 Modelle: 30 Modelle wie Nr. 2, ferner: Bilderrahmen, Doppelschreibzeug, Klubsofa, Gartenbank, Obstspalier, Standuhr, altes Tor mit Zugbrücke, große Bettstelle, Wintergartenwand, Ballustrade, Postament, große Schaukel, Haus mit Balkon, Wartehäuschen, Turm.

Nr. **137**/3 E Größe 29×35 cm, Höhe: 3 cm, Gewicht: 1 1/2 kg, enthält Modellbogen für folgende 66 Modelle: 45 Modelle wie Nr. 3, ferner: Feuerwehrleiter, Schubkarren, Schleifstein, verstellbarer Liegesessel, Krahn, Leiterwagen, Rollwagen, kleiner Wagen mit Bock, Eisenbahn-Güterwagen, Förderwagen, Eisenbahn-Barrière, großer Lastwagen mit Verdeck und Bock, geschlossene Lieferantenwagen, Lift (80 cm hoch), aufziehbare Schiffbrücke, Lastautomobil, Straßenbahnwagen, Rutschbahn mit auf Schienen laufendem Rollwagen, großer Krahn, Pfahlrammer, Rollsessel.

The „Architectus“ game of building-blocks for boys and girls in 5 sizes viz:

Sizes: 18×18 cm, height: 3 cm, weight: 1/3 kg, contains model-drawings for the following 12 models: Simple picture frame, small double stepladder, double bars, simple swing, chinese gate, stool, simple chair, dining-room chair, simple bench, flowerpotstand, triumphal arch, winding-gage and signal disk.

Sizes: 24×29 cm, height: 3 cm, weight: 2/3 kg, contains model-drawings for the following 30 models: 12 models same as Nr. 1, further: towelrack, palm-pot, shelter for birds, go-cart, palmstand, flowerstand, potholder, chair in gondola form, club chair, easy chair, hanging flowerstand, simple inkstand, table with pillars, drawing-room table, sitting-room table, simple bedstead, dolls bedstead, arbour.

Sizes: 23×35 cm, hight: 3 cm, weight: 4/5 kg, contains model-drawings for the following 40 models: 30 models same as Nr. 2, further: firemen's ladders, wheelbarrow, grindstone, adjustable deck chair, crane, rack-waggon, express-waggon, small-waggon with driver's seat, railway van, truck.

Sizes: 25×36 cm, height: 3 cm, weight: 1 1/6 kg, contains model-drawings for the following 45 models: 30 models same as Nr. 2, further: picture frame, double inkstand, clubsofa, garden bench, fruit trellis, standing clock, ancient gate with drawbridge, large bedstead, screen for conservatory, balustrade, pedestal, large swing, house with balcony, waiting hut, tower.

Sizes: 29×35 cm, height: 3 cm, weight: 1 1/2 kg, contains model-drawings for the following 66 models: 45 models same as Nr. 3, further: firemen's ladders, wheelbarrow, grindstone adjustable deck chare, cran, rack-waggon, express-waggon, small-waggon with driver's seat, railway van, truck, railway bars, large van with cover and driver's seat, close delivery waggon, lift (80 cm high), movable pontoon-bridge, freight motor, tramway, slide with waggon running on rails, large crane, pile driver, easy-chair on castors.

La caja de construcción „Architectus“ para niños y niñas en 5 tamaños:

Tamaño: 18×18 cm, altura: 3 cm, peso: 1/3 kg, contiene los pliegos de modelo para los siguientes 12 modelos: sencillo marco de una pintura, pequeña escalera doble de mano, barra, sencillo mecedor, portezuela de la china, sillita, sencilla silla, silla para el comedor, sencillo banco, estante para flores, arco de triunfo, anemómetro y disco.

Tamaño: 24×29 cm, altura: 3 cm, peso: 2/3 kg, contiene los pliegos de modelo para los siguientes 30 modelos: 12 modelos igual a los No. 1, además: enjugador, cubeta para palmas, casita de protección para pájaritos, jardin para aprender andar, estante para palmas, mesita para flores, estante para cubetas, asiento, sillon de club, butaca, cubeta suspendida para flores, sencillo tintero, mesa de columnas, mesa de sala, mesa de habitación, sencilla cama, cama para muñecas, pabellón de emparrado.

Tamaño: 23×35 cm, altura: 3 cm, peso: 4/5 kg, contiene los pliegos de modelo para los siguientes 40 modelos: 30 modelos igual a los No. 2, adamás: escalera para bomberos, carro de mano, piedra de amolar, butaca móbil, grúa, carro con adrales, car uaje, pequeño carro con pescante, carro de ferrocarril para mercaderrias, carro de minos.

Tamaño: 25×36 cm, altura: 3 cm, peso: 1 1/6 kg, contiene los pliegos de modelo para los siguientes 45 modelos: 30 modelos igual a los No. 2, además: marco de una pintura, tintero doble, sofa de club, banco de jardin, enrejado para frutos, reloj estacionario, portezuela vieja con puente levadizo, cama grande, parde de invernadero balustrada, postamento, mecedor grande, casa con balcón, casita de espera, torre.

Tamaño: 29×35 cm, altura: 3 cm, peso: 1 1/2 kg, contiene los pliegos de modelo para los siguientes 66 modelos: 45 modelos igual a los No. 3, además: escalera para bomberos, carro de mano, piedra de amolar, butaca móvil, grúa, carro con adrales, carruaje, pequeño carruaje con pescante, carro de ferrocarril para mercaderias, carro de minas barra de ferrocarril, carruaje grande con techo y pescante, carruaje cerrado de proveedor, asensor (80 cm de alto), puente movil de barcas, automóvil de carga, carro de tramvia, resbaladero con carros andando sobre rieles, grúa grande, maza para empalizar, silla poltrona con ruedas.

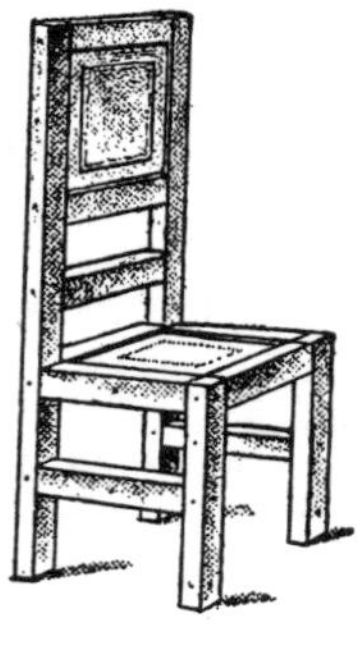

Konstruiert aus Nr. **137**/1
Constructed of Nr. **137**/1
Construido con la No. **137**/1

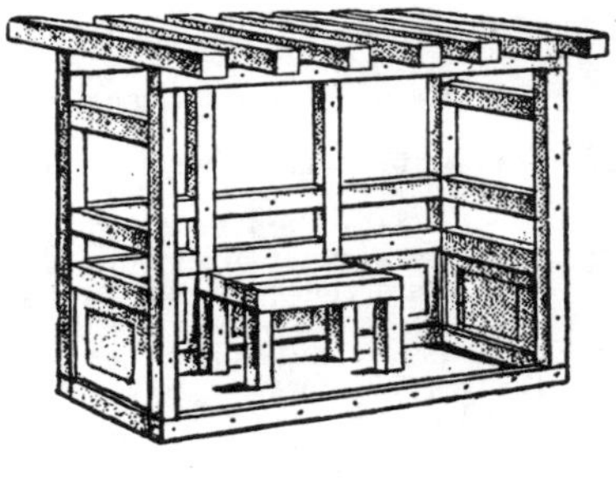

Konstruiert aus Nr. **137**/2
Constructed of Nr. **137**/2
Construido con la No. **137**/2

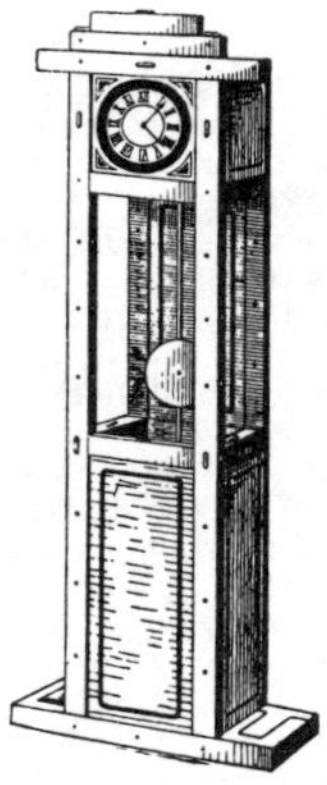

Konstruiert aus Nr. **137**/3
Constructed of Nr. **137**/3
Construido con la No. **137**/3

Konstruiert aus Nr. **137**/3 E
Constructed of Nr. **137**/3 E
Construido con la No. **137**/3 E

Einige Modelle, hergestellt mit „Architectus“-Baukasten.
Some samples, made with the „Architectus“-Box
Unos modelos, construidos con la caja de construcción „Architectus“.

Der Flitzer ist das Entzücken der Kinder. Er kann auch für Fahrten zur Schule, zu Besorgungen u. dgl. benutzt werden.

The Flitzer is the delight of all children, and can also be used to take them to school, to ran errands, and for any similar purposes.

El corredor "Flitzer" es el encanto de los ninos, se puede aprovecharlo tambien para meterse a la escuela, para efectuar comisiones y para cosas semejantes.

Der Flitzer eignet sich als Zweirad für Kinder von 6 bis 14 Jahren; als Dreirad für Kinder von 3 bis 14 Jahren.

TheFlitzer can be used as a bicycle by children of from 6 to 14 years of age; as a tricycle by children of from 3 to 14 years of age.

El corredor "Flitzer" puede ser empleado para servir de bicicleta para niños de 6—14 años; tricicleta para niños de 3—14 años.

Vorzüge des Flitzers: Ungefährliches Fahren, da Tretvorrichtung niedrig über der Erde und keine Kette vorhanden ist. **Unverwüstlich haltbar** durch Herstellung aus starkem Hartholz, bestem Guß und Reifen aus Vollgummi (Continental). Geringe Pflege und Schmierung.

Advantages of the "Flitzer": Travelling on it is not dangerous, as the treadling device is at a low height above the ground and there is no chain. **It is indestructible** because of its manufacture from strong hardwood, and best cast iron, with the tyres of solid rubber (Continental). Very little attention or lubrication necessary.

El manejo del corredor ne es peligroso, pues la disposición para pisar esta arreglado bajo encima del suelo y no hay cadena alguna. En consecuencia de su fabricación de robusta madera fuerte, del empleo de la mejor fundición y de bandajes macizos (Continental), **la duración del corredor es largisima.** No necesario que un minimum de mantenimiento y lubrificación.

Dreirad. — Three-wheels. — Tricicleta

Gewichte, Verpackung: Zweirad: 9,200 kg, Dreirad: 10,200 kg. Eine seemäßige Kiste (100×100×65 cm) faßt bei einem Nettogewicht von ca. 56 kg 12 Zweiräder oder 6 Dreiräder. Auf Wunsch auch starke Verschläge ohne unsere Garantie für guten Empfang.

Weights, Packages: Two-wheel: 9,200 kg, Three-wheel: 10,200 kg. A case for oversea transport, weighting nett about 56 kg (100×100×65 cm) contains: 12 two-wheel or 6 three-wheel "Flitzers". If desired the goods can be sent in strong crates, without responsibility on our part for safe arrival.

Pesos, embalaje: Bicicleta: 9,200 kg, Tricicleta: 10,200 kg. Cada máquina tenienda un peso de 56 kg más ó menos, se puede embalar en una caja (100×100×65 cm) 12 bicicletas o 6 tricicletas embaladas para salir al mar. A demanda se entregar también jaulas fuertes, pero sin garantía alguna de muestra parte por el buen recibo de la mercancía.

Zweirad. — Two-wheels. Bicicleta.

Farbkasten für Kinder und Schulen.
Paintboxes for Children and Schools.
Cajitas de colores para Niños y Escuelas.

24/30/15

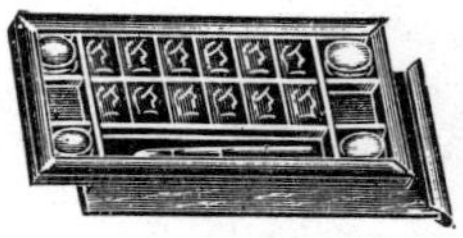

24/4/12

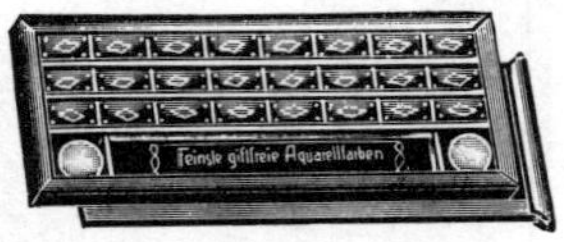

24/18/24

24/38/15

24/262

24/286

24/265

24/290

Farbkasten mit Schiebedeckel.

Nr. **24**/30/15
Kasten, 15 Farben Art I, 1 Pinsel.
Größe 12,5×8,5 cm.

Nr. **24**/4/12
Gelbgebeizter Kasten mit rot poliertem Rand, 12 Farben Art III, 4 Porzellan-Näpfchen, 1 Pinsel.
Größe 18×9,7 cm.

Nr. **24**/18/24
Braungebeizter Kasten mit dunkelgrün poliertem Rand, 24 Farben Art II, 2 Porzellan-Näpfchen, 1 Pinsel.
Größe 23×9,5 cm.

Nr. **24**/38/15
Gelbgebeizter Kasten mit schwarz poliertem Rand, 15 Farben Art XV, 15 Schüsselchen aus Porzellan, 1 Pinsel.
Größe 27×15 cm.

Farbkasten mit Klappdeckel.

Nr. **24**/262
Kasten aus Erle, hellmatt, mit Hakenverschluß, 16 Farben Art X, 1 Sepia, 1 Tusche, 2 Porzellan-Schälchen, 1 Pinsel.
Größe 21,8×13×3,5 cm.

Nr. **24**/286
Kasten aus Erle, hellmatt, mit Hakenverschluß, 21 Farben Art IV, 4 Porzellan-Schälchen, 1 Pinsel mit Stiel.
Größe 26×14×3,2 cm.

Nr. **24**/265
Kasten aus Erle, hellmatt, mit Schloß, 21 Farben Art XIII, 4 Porzellan-Näpfe, 1 Pinsel mit Stiel, Bild.
Größe 25,2×15×4 cm.

Nr. **24**/290
Kasten aus Erle, hellmatt, mit Hakenverschluß, 20 Farben Art VIII, 1 Sepia, 1 Tusche, 4 Porzellan-Näpfchen, 1 Pinsel mit Stiel.
Größe 28,5×19×3,4 cm.

Boxes with slide cover.

Box 15 colours of Nr. I, 1 brush.
Size 12,5×8,5 cm.

Box tinted yellow with red polished border, 12 colours of Nr. III, 4 porcelain dishes, 1 brush.
Size 18×9,7 cm.

Box tinted brown with dark green polished border, 24 colours of Nr. II, 2 porcelain dishes, 1 brush.
Size 23×9,5 cm.

Box tinted yellow with black polished border, 15 colours of Nr. XV, 15 dishes of porcelain, 1 brush.
Size 27×15 cm.

Paintboxes of hard wood with lid which can stand up.

Box of alder wood, matt with hook closure, 16 colours of Nr. X, 1 sepia, 1 China ink, 2 porcelain dishes, 1 brush.
Size 21,8×13×3,5 cm.

Box of alder wood, light matt, with lock, 21 colours of Nr. IV, 4 porcelain dishes, 1 brush with handle.
Size 26×14×3,2 cm.

Box of alder wood with lock, 21 colours of Nr. XIII, 4 porcelain dishes, 1 brush with handle.
Size 25,2×15×4 cm.

Box of alder wood, light matt, with hook closure, 20 colours of Nr. VIII, 1 sepia, 1 China ink, 4 porcelain dishes, 1 brush with handle.
Size 28,8×19×3,4 cm.

Cajitas con tapa corrediza.

Cajita, 15 colores clase I, 1 pincel.
Tamaño 15,5×8,5 cm.

Cajita pintado de amarillo con bordes rojos pulidos, 12 colores clase III, 4 conchitas de porcelana, 1 pincel.
Tamaño 18×9,7 cm.

Cajita pintada de pardo, bordes verde oscuro pulido, 24 colores clase II, 2 conchitas de porcelana, 1 pincel.
Tamaño 23×9,5 cm.

Cajita pintada de amarillo, con bordes pulidos de negro, 15 colores clase XV, 15 salseritos de porcelana, 1 pincel.
Tamaño 27×15 cm.

Cajas de colores de madera fuerte con tapa levadiza.

Cajita de madera de chopo mate claro, con cierre ganchito, 16 colores clase X, 1 sepia, 1 tinta de China, 2 salseritos de porcelana, 1 pincel.
Tamaño 21,8×13×3,5 cm.

Cajita de madera de chopo mate claro, cierre ganchito, 21 colores clase IV, 4 salseritos de porcelana, 1 pincel con mango.
Tamaño 26×14×3,2 cm.

Cajita de madera de chopo mate claro, con cerradura, 21 colores clase XIII, 4 conchitas de porcelana, 1 pincel con mango, diseno.
Tomaño 25,2×15×4 cm.

Cajita de madera de chopo, con cierre ganchito, 20 colores clase VIII, 1 sepia, 1 tinta de China, 4 conchitas de porcelana, 1 pincel con mango.
Tamaño 28,5×19×3,4 cm.

Farbkasten für Kinder und Schulen.
Paintboxes for Children and Schools.
Cajitas de colores para Niños y Escuelas.

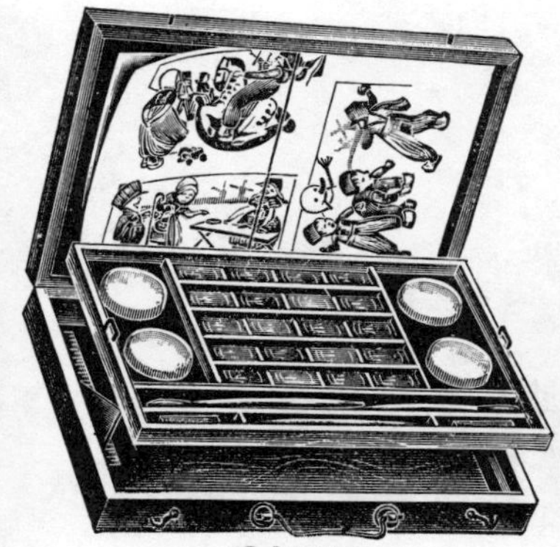

24/295

24/222

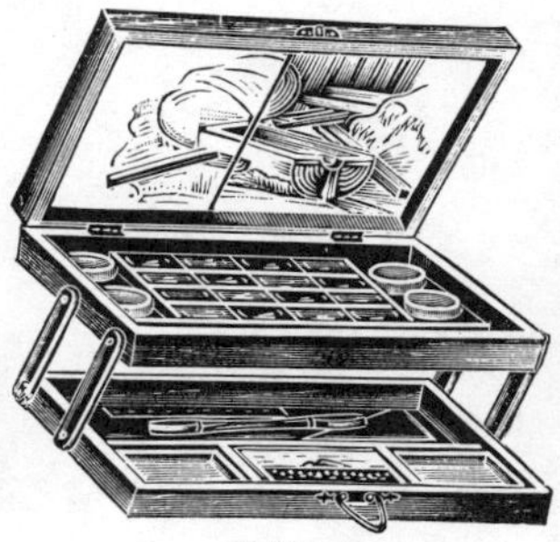

24/298

24/239

24/500/7

24/500/10

24/504/7

24/301/1

Farbkasten mit Klappdeckel.

Nr. **24**/295
Kasten aus Erle, hellmatt, mit Hakenverschluß und Griff, Einsatz zum Herausnehmen, 20 Farben Art VIII, 4 Porzellan-Näpfchen, 1 Sepia, 1 Tusche, 1 Lineal, 1 Bleistift, 1 Winkel, 1 Radiergummi.
Größe 28,5×18,5×4,2 cm.

Nr. **24**/222
Kasten aus Erle, hellmatt, mit Einsatz, Hakenverschluß und Griff an der Seite, 28 Farben Art IV, 4 Porzellan-Näpfchen mit Goldrand, 1 Etuis Pastellkreide, 3 Tuben (Weiß, Schwarz, Preuß. Blau), 1 Radiergummi, 1 Bleistift, 1 Zentimeter-Lineal, 2 Pinsel mit Stiel, 1 Winkel.
Größe 28,5×21,5×5,5 cm.

Nr. **24**/298
Scherenkasten zum Auseinanderziehen mit Schnappverschluß, 16 Farben Art VIII, 4 Goldrand-Porzellan-Näpfe, 1 Etui mit Ölkreide, 2 Porzellan-Paletten, 1 Zwinge, 1 Bleistift, 1 Zentimeter-Lineal, 1 Stielpinsel.
Größe 23×14,2×5 cm.

Nr. **24**/239
Kasten aus Erlenholz mit Kirschbaumdeckel, hellmatt, zum Auseinanderziehen, 6 Tuben Größe 1, 24 Farben Art IV, 1 Etui Pastellkreide, 4 Porzellan-Schälchen, 1 Radiergummi, 1 Zentimeter-Lineal, 1 Tusche, 1 Zwinge, 5 Reißbrettstifte auf Kork, 1 Winkel, 2 Pinsel mit Stiel.
Größe 24×13×5 cm.

Nr. **24**/301/1
Feiner hellmattierter Holzkasten aus Erlenholz, Deckel abgerundet, mit Schnäpperverschluß, innen schwarz lackiert, 6 Tuben Sorte 19, 1 Pinsel.
Größe 12×9×3 cm.

Blechtuschkasten.

Nr. **24**/500/7
Fein schwarz lackierter Blechkasten mit 7 Grundfarben Sorte 16, 1 Pinsel, 1 Vorschrift.
Größe 10×6,2×1,5 cm.

Nr. **24**/500/10
Fein schwarz lackierter Blechkasten mit 10 Farben Sorte 16, 1 Pinsel, 1 Vorschrift.
Größe 16,5×7,5×1,5 cm.

Nr. **24**/504/7
Feiner, außen schwarz, innen weiß lackierter Blechkasten mit 7 Tuben Sorte 20 (Grundfarben) und 1 Pinsel.
Größe 11,5×7×1,5 cm.

Boxes with slide cover.

Box of alder wood, light matt, with hook closure and handle, tray to take out, 20 colours of Nr. VIII, 4 porcelain dishes, 1 sepia, 1 China ink, 1 ruler, 1 pencil, 1 brush, 1 Indian rubber.
Size 28,5×18,5×4,2 cm.

Box of alder wood, light matt, with tray, closed by hooks, with handle on the side, 28 colours of Nr. IV, 4 porcelain dishes with gold rim, 1 case with pastil crayon, 3 tubes (white, black, Prussian blue), 1 Indian rubber, 1 pencil, 1 ruler, 2 brushes with handle, 1 triangle.
Size 28,5×21,5×5,5 cm.

Divided box as illustration, with spring lock, 16 colours Nr. VIII, 4 porcelain dishes with gold rim, 1 case with crayon, 2 porcelain palettes, 1 holder, 1 pencil, 1 ruler, 1 brush with handle.
Size 23×14,2×5 cm.

Box of alder wood with cherry wood lid, light matt, to be drawn out, 6 tubes size I, 24 colours of Nr. IV, 1 case with pastil crayon, 4 porcelain dishes, 1 Indian rubber, 1 cm ruler, 1 China ink, 1 holder, 5 drawing pins on cork, 1 triangle, 2 brushes with handle.
Size 24×13×5 cm.

Finely light matted box of alder wood, lid with rounded corners, inside black japanned, 6 tubes Nr. 19, 1 brush.
Size 12×9×3 cm.

Tin clip-boxes.

Finely japanned black tin boxes with seven prime colours, Nr. 16, 1 brush, 1 instruction.
Size 10×6,2×1,5 cm.

Finely black japanned box with 10 colours, Nr. 16, 1 brush, 1 instruction.
Size 16,5×7,5×1,5 cm.

Tin box, outside finely black, inside white japanned, with 7 tubes (prime colours), 1 brush.
Size 11,5×7×1,5 cm.

Cajas de colores de madera fuerte con tapa levadiza.

Cajita de madera de chopo, mate claro, con cierre ganchito y asa, con un encaje, 30 colores clase VIII, 4 conchitas de porcelana, 1 Sepia, 1 tinta de China, 1 pincel, 1 lapiz, 1 compas, 1 goma para borrar.
Tamaño 28,5×18,5×4,2 cm.

Cajita de madera de chopo, mate claro, con encaje, cierre ganchito, asa al lado, 28 colores clase IV, 4 conchitas de porcelana con filetes dorados, 1 estuche greda pastel, 3 tubitos (blanco, negro azul de Prusia), 1 goma para borrar, 1 lapiz, 1 regla cm, 2 pinceles con mango, 1 compás.
Tamaño 28,5×21,5×5,5 cm.

Cajoncito con cerradura de golpe, se puede estirar, 16 colores clase VIII, 4 conchas de porcelana con filete dorado, 1 estuche con greda oleada, 2 paletas de porcelana, 1 birola, 1 lapiz, 1 regla cm, 1 pincel con mango.
Tamaño 23×14,2×5 cm.

Cajita de madera pe chopo con tapa de madera cerezo, mate claro, se puede estirar, 6 tubos tamaño I, 24 colores clase IV, 1 estuche greda pastel, 4 conchitas de porcelana, 1 goma para borrar, 1 regla cm, 1 tinta de China, 1 birola, 5 chinches en un corcho, 1 compás, 2 pinceles con mango.
Tamaño 24×13×5 cm.

Caja de madera da arce, de tono fino mate, tapa redondeada con cierre a resorte, barnizada de negro por dentro, 6 tubitos clase 19, 1 pincel.
Tamaño 12×9×3 cm.

Caja de lata finamente.

Caja de lata barnizada finamente de negro, con 7 colores de aparejo clase 16, 1 pincel, 1 instrucción.
Tamaño 19×6,2×1,5 cm.

Caja de lata barnizada finamente de negro, con 10 colores, clase 16, 1 pincel, 1 instrucción.
Tamaño 10,5×7,5×1,5 cm.

Caja finamente barnizada de negro por fuera y de blanco por dentro con 7 tubitos clase 20 (colores de aparejo), 1 pincel.
Tamaño 11,5×7×1,5 cm.

Feine Holzspielwaren Erste Qualität Hübsch bunt bemalt.		Fine wooden toys First Quality Nicely coloured.	Juguetes de madera Primera calidad Elegantamente pintado.
Nr. **150**/99	Grüner Käfer.	Green beetle	$5^3/_5$ by $4^2/_5$ inches (Zoll)
„ **150**/100/I	Maikäfer, klein.	May buck, small	$5^3/_5$ „ $4^2/_5$ „
„ **150**/100/II	„ groß.	„ „ large	$6^4/_5$ „ $5^3/_5$ „
„ **150**/101/I	Sonnenkäfer klein.	Lady bird, small	$5^3/_5$ „ $4^2/_5$ „
„ **150**/101/II	„ groß.	„ „ large	$6^4/_5$ „ $5^3/_5$ „
„ **150**/102	Wespe.	Wasp	$6^4/_5$ „ 5 „
„ **150**/103	Libelle, rot.	Fly, red	$6^4/_5$ „ 5 „
„ **150**/103a	„ blau.	„ blue	$6^4/_5$ „ 5 „
„ **150**/104/IIg	Schmetterling, klein.	Butterfly, small	8 „ 12 „
„ **150**/104/IIb	„ „ verschieden.	„ „ different pattern	
„ **150**/104/IIIc	„ groß.	„ large	9 „ $13^3/_5$ „
„ **150**/104/IIIp	„ „ verschieden.	„ „ different pattern	
„ **150**/105	Libelle.	Dragon fly	$10^2/_5$ „ $11^3/_5$ „
„ **150**/106/I	Schildkröte, klein.	Turtle, small	8 „ 6 „
„ **150**/106/II	„ groß.	„ large	$9^1/_5$ „ $7^1/_5$ „
„ **150**/107	Hummel.	Humble bee	$6^2/_5$ „ $5^2/_5$ „
„ **150**/110	Frosch.	Frog	$7^3/_5$ „ $7^3/_5$ „
„ **150**/200/I	Elefant, klein.	Elephant, small	$7^3/_5$ „ 10 „
„ **150**/200/II	„ groß.	„ large	$11^1/_5$ „ $13^3/_5$ „
„ **150**/210/I	Schnecke mit Haus, klein.	Snail with its house, small	$8^4/_5$ „ 4 „
„ **150**/210/II	„ „ „ groß.	„ „ „ „ large	$12^4/_5$ „ 6 „
„ **150**/550	Chinesische Tee-Kulis.	Chinese tea coolies	$11^4/_5$ „ $15^4/_5$ „
„ **150**/575/I	Neger mit Krokodil, klein.	Nigger and crocodile, small	$16^4/_5$ „ $7^1/_5$ „
„ **150**/575/II	„ „ „ groß.	„ „ „ large	$19^1/_5$ „ $9^4/_5$ „
„ **150**/580/I	Krokodil, klein.	Crocodile, small	$12^4/_5$ „ $3^2/_5$ „
„ **150**/580/II	„ groß.	„ large	$16^2/_5$ „ 4 „
„ **150**/700	Straußenwagen.	Ostrich cart	$21^3/_5$ „ $15^2/_5$ „
„ **150**/701	Straußenreiter.	Ostrich rider	$15^2/_5$ „ 12 „
„ **150**/750/I	Affe auf Renner, klein.	Monkey on racer, small	13 „ $11^2/_5$ „
„ **150**/750/II	„ „ „ groß.	„ „ „ large	$16^2/_5$ „ $14^2/_5$ „
„ **150**/800	Auto in verschiedenen Farben, groß.	Auto in different colours, large	$22^2/_5$ „ $10^4/_5$ „
„ **150**/800/p	„ groß, mit Verdeck.	„ large with hoot	
„ **150**/801/III	„ mittelgroß.	„ medium size	$18^2/_5$ „ $9^1/_5$ „
„ **150**/801/IIIg	„ „ mit Geländer.	„ „ „ with railings	
„ **150**/801/IIIp	„ „ „ Verdeck	„ „ „ „ hood	
„ **150**/801/II	„ klein.	„ small	$16^2/_5$ „ $5^2/_5$ „
„ **150**/801/IIp	„ „ mit Verdeck.	„ „ with hood	

Bewegliche Holzspielsachen
Moveable Wooden Toys
Juguetes de Madera Movibles

150/575 *150/106/I* *150/700* *150/110* *150/200/II*

150/750/I *150/104/I* *150/550* *150/210/I* *150/240/I*

Erstklassig in Farbe und Ausführung
Quite First Class in Execution and Colour
Ejecución excelente

B·D·Co

Bewegliche Holzspielsachen
Moveable Wooden Toys
Juguetes de Madera Movibles

B·D·Co

150/810/II *150/701* *150/95* *150/810/I*

150/225 *150/107* *150/105* *150/101/II* *150/800*

Erstklassig in Farbe und Ausführung

Quite First Class in Execution and Colour

Ejecución excelente

Holzspielwaren.
Spiel- und Sportartikel für Sommer und Winter.

Wooden Toys.
Toys and Sport Articles for Summer and Winter.

Juguetes de Madera.
Juguetes y Artículos de Sport para Verano y Invierno.

8/250

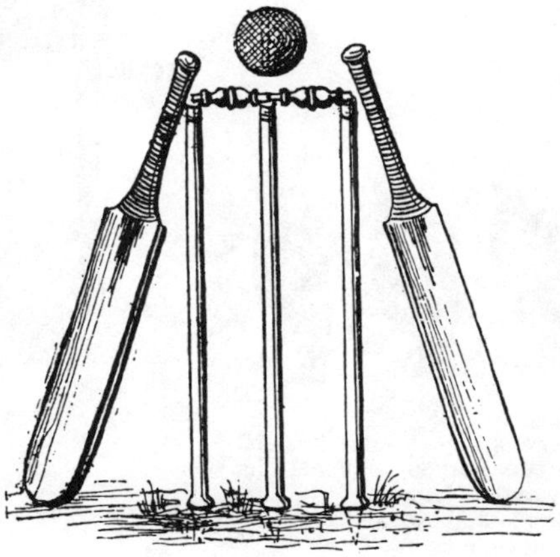

8/272

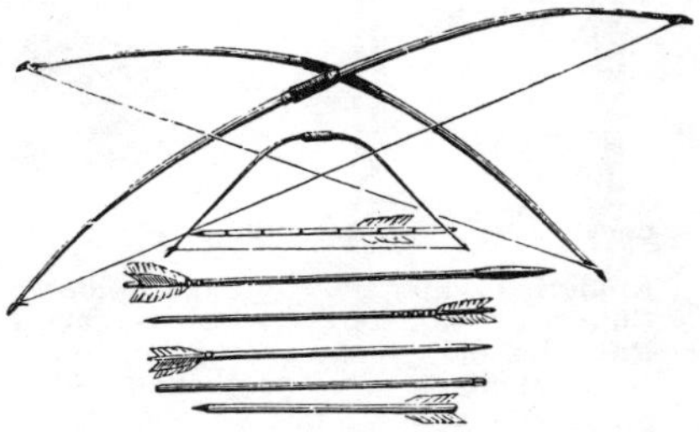

8/300 bis 8/302

Nr. 8/250 **Bastscheiben,** in verschiedenen Farben gemalt, mit Handpfeilen.
Bass Targets, painted in different colours, with darts.
Blancos, para el tiro de flechas de mano, colores vistosos con numeros.

„ 8/272 **Kricketspiele,** in Holzkasten, enthaltend 2 Schläger und 2 Tore.
Criquet Sets, made of best wood, containing 2 polished bats and 2 wickets.
Juego de Criquet, en caja de madera conteniendo 2 "bats" y 2 "wickets".

„ 8/300/302 **Bogen und Pfeile** in verschiedenen Größen und Ausführungen.
Bows and Arrows in different sizes and qualities.
Arcos y Flechas in varios tamaños y calidades para sport y para niños

„ 8/300 Aus bestem Eschenholz, eine Seite flach, eine Seite rund.
Of best ash wood, one side flat, one side round.
Del mejor fresno, un lado llano el otro curvado.

Nr. 8/300/1	2	3	
100	125	150	cm Länge, length, de largo

Nr. 8/301 Beide Seiten flach; both sides flat; ambos lados llanos.

Nr 8/301/0	1	2	3	4	
	60	75	90	125	150 cm Länge, length, de largo

„ 8/302 Besteht aus 2 flachen Eschenholzteilen, welche zusammengeleimt sind, sehr biegsam.
Consits of 2 flat ash wood parts, which are put together, very pliable.
Con 2 marcos de fresno, sobre puestos.

Nr. 8/302/1	2	3	
92	110	135	cm Länge, length, de largo

8/350

8/352/1

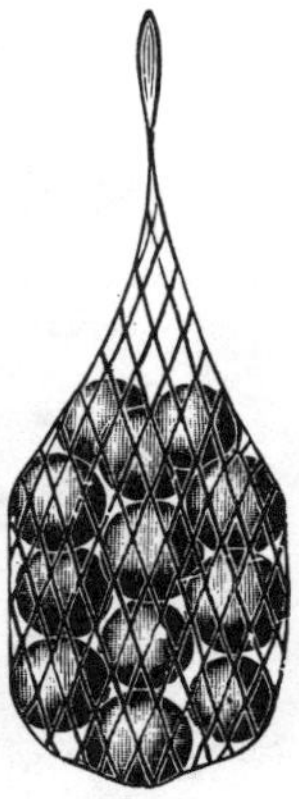

8/524

8/550

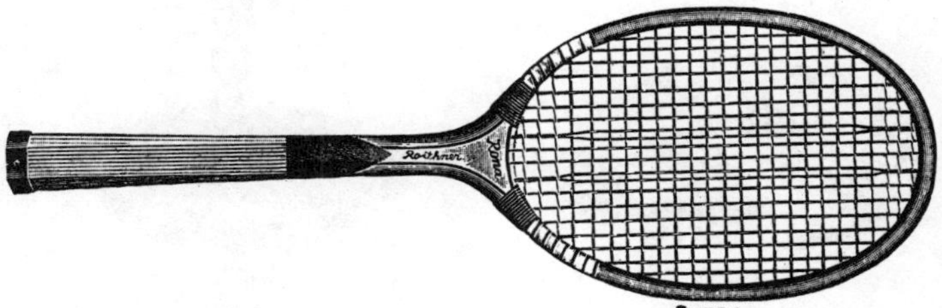

8/584

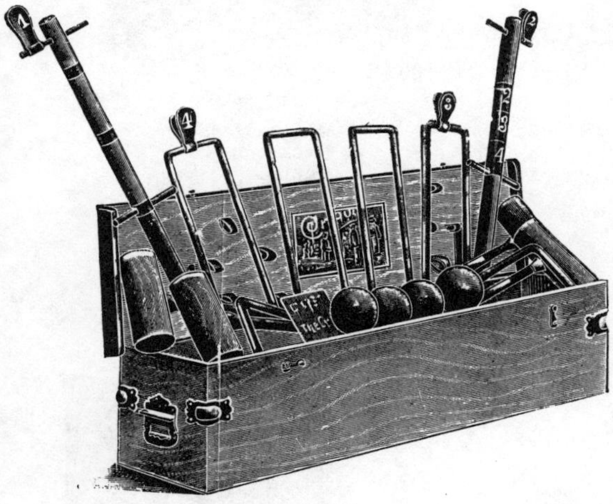

8/395

8/516/4

8/516/3

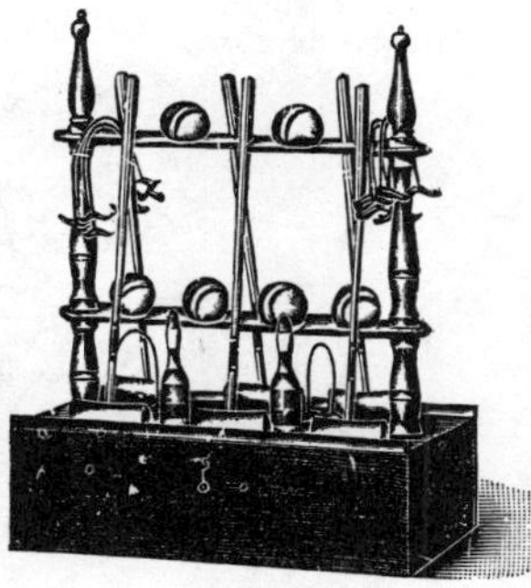

8/416

8/595/4

8/597/2

8/597/4

Nr. 8/350 u. 8/352/1 **Hockeystöcke** in verschiedenen Ausführungen.
Hockey Sticks, different sorts of best quality.
Palos para Hockey de Sport, del mejor fresno.

„ 8/395 **Sportkrocket** für Sport und für Kinder, in verschiedenen Größen.
Croquet Sets for Sport and for children in different sizes.
Croquets, juego de Sport y para niños.

„ 8/416 **Tischkrocket.**
Table Croquets.
Croquets de mesa.

„ 8/524 **Lawn-tennis-Ballnetze** aus farbigem Bindfaden.
Lawn-tennis Ball Nets of coloured cord.
Redes para Pelotas de Tennis, de cuerda de 2 colores.

„ 8/516/3 u. 4 **Racketpressen.**
Tennis Racket Presses.
Prensas para Raquetas.

Nr. 8/584 **Racket „Rona",** Tournierschläger.
Racket "Rona", Superior Sport Racket.
Raqueta "Rona", Raqueta para concurso.

„ 8/550 **Racket,** gute mittlere Qualität.
Tennis Racket, fine medium quality.
Raqueta de Tennis, de calidad fino mediano.

„ 8/595/4 **Tisch-Tennisschläger,** aus Eschenholz mit Darmsaiten.
Table-tennis Racket, of best ash wood with cat gut-stringing.
Raqueta para Tennis de Mesa, marcode fresno, con cuerdas de tripa.

„ 8/597/2 **Holzballschläger** für Tischtennis.
Battle dores for Table-tennis.
Palas de madera para Tennis de mesa.

„ 8/597/4 **Tisch-Tennisschläger** mit Korkauflage.
Battle dores with cork on both sides.
Palas para Tennis de mesa, cubierto con corcto.

Holzspielwaren und Spiele. — Wooden Toys and Games. — Juguetes y Juegos de Madera.

8/920 **8**/921

Kinderballschläger.
Children's raquets.
Raquetas para juego de volante.

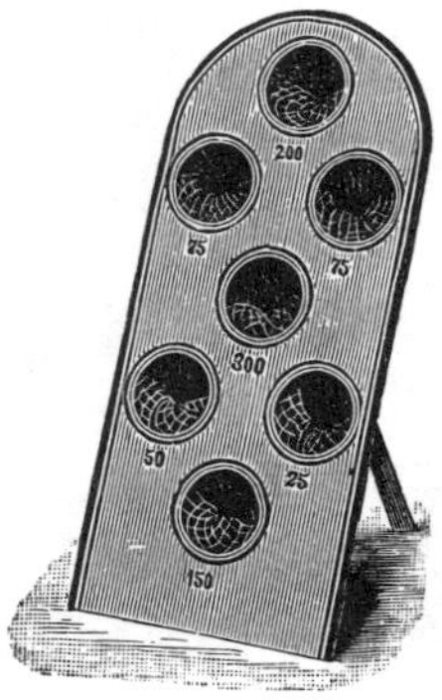

8/932/1

Ballscheiben, bunt bemalt.
Ball targets, nicely painted.
Juegos al Blanco, pintado color.

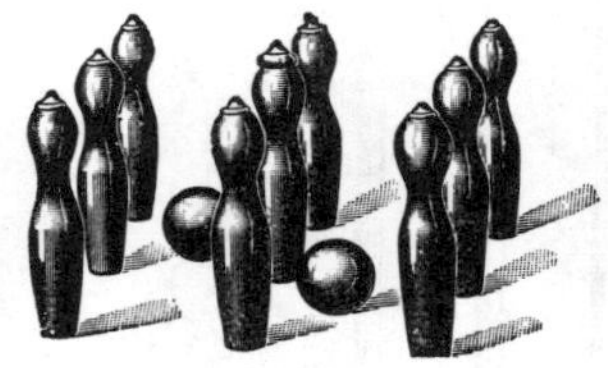

8/1000

Kegelspiele, in Holzkästen.
Skittle games, polished in wooden boxes.
Juegos de bolos, barnizados en caja de madera.

8/963

Billard.
Billiards.
Billareo.

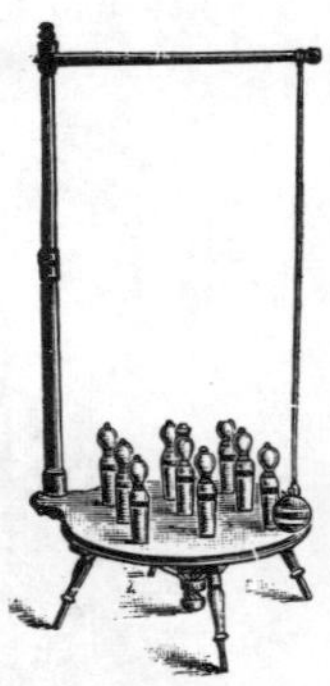

8/1022/1023

Baumelkegel.
Swing skittles.
Juegos de lanzar la bocha.

8/1100/16 **8**/1101/2

Kinderschaukeln, schön poliert.
Baby swings, nicely polished.
Columpios para niños, barnizados.

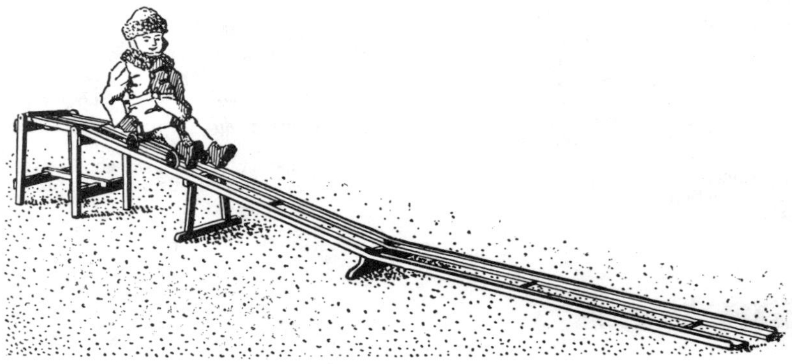

8/1112/3

Kinderrutschbahn.
Switch backs.
Resbalador.

8/1104/1 und 1½

Pferdekopfschaukeln, lackiert oder weiß gestrichen.
Horse rockers, varnished or painted white.
Caballo hamaca, barnizado y pintado blanco.

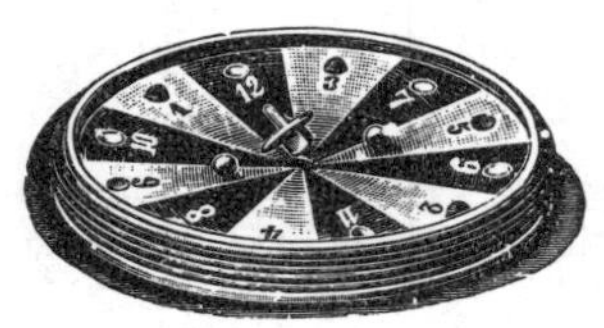

8/1162

Roulettespiel.
Game roulette.
Juego de ruleta.

8/1172

Turmspiel.
Tower game.
Juego de torre.

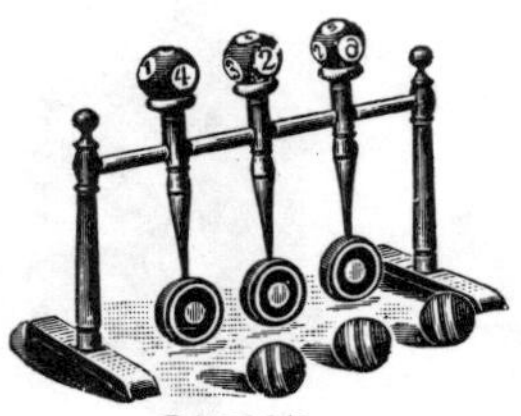

8/1206/2

Balanze-Würfelkugelspiel.
Balance and dic game.
Bochas de balancin.

8/2080/4

Ringwerfen.
Deck quoits.
Quoits.

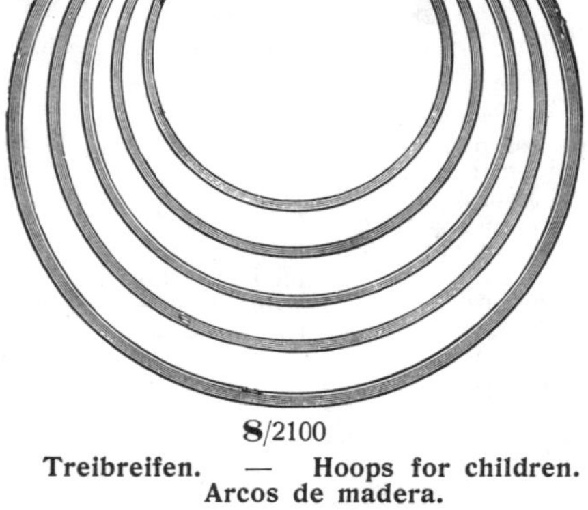

8/2100

Treibreifen. — **Hoops for children.**
Arcos de madera.

8/2240

Automobil für Kinder. — **Motor cars** for children.
Automóvil para niños.

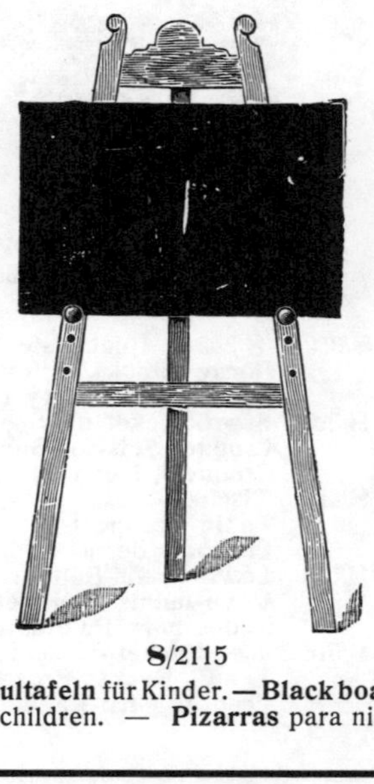

8/2115

Schultafeln für Kinder. — **Black boards** for children. — **Pizarras** para niños.

Holzspielwaren. — Wooden toys. — Juguetes de madera.

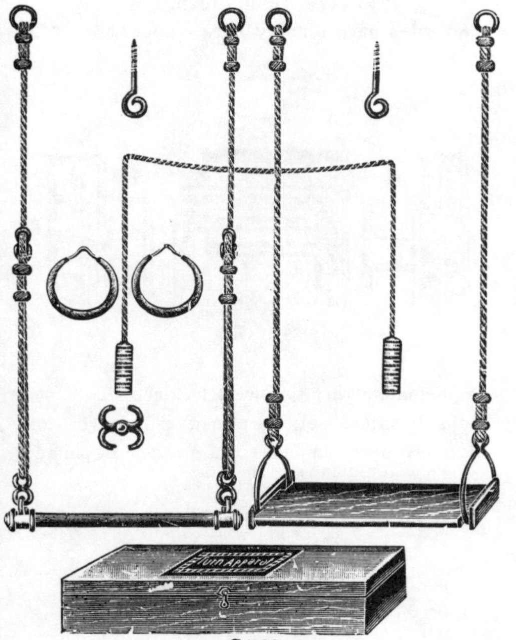

S/700

Komplette Turnapparate im Kasten.
Complete gymnastic sets in box.
Aparatos para gimnasia en caja de madera.

Hell oder dunkel lackiert.

Light or dark varnished.

S/735

Claras y oscuras barnizadas.

Turnkeulen. — Indian Clubs. — Clavos.

Nr. S/735/1	36 × 6,5	cm	450 g
„ S/735/2	40 × 7,5	„	675 „
„ S/735/3	44 × 8	„	900 „
„ S/735/4	48 × 9	„	1350 „
„ S/735/5	52 × 9,5	„	1800 „
„ S/735/6	56 × 10	„	2250 „

Turngeräte. — Gymnastic Apparatus. — Aparatas para gimnasia.

S/792

Als Turngerüst.
As combined gymnasium.
Como aparatos para gimnasia.

Nr. S/792
Kombiniertes Turngerüst, vollständig zerlegbar, bestehend aus: Barren, Reck, Leitern, Kletterstangen und -tauen, Schwebereck und Ringen. Höhe verstellbar von 250 - 300 cm.

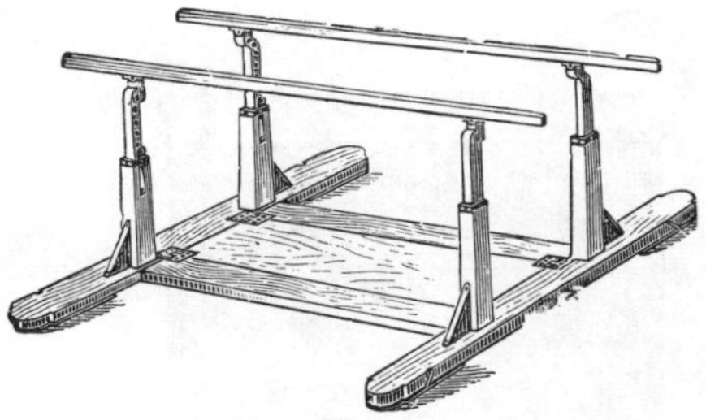

S/792

Als Barren. — As parallel bar. — Como barras.

Nr. S/792
Combined gymnasium, perfectly portable, composed of: Parallel bars, horizontal bar, climbing ladders, climbing-poles and -rapes, trapeze and swing rings. The gymnasium is adjustable in height from 250 - 300 cm.

No. S/792
Aparatos para gimnasia, desmontable, facil a transportar, muy solido, compuesto de Barras, barras horizontales, escalera derecha o vertical, escalera al costado, palo y cuerda para trepar, trapecio y argollas. El marco puede ser modificado de 250 - 300 cm de alto.

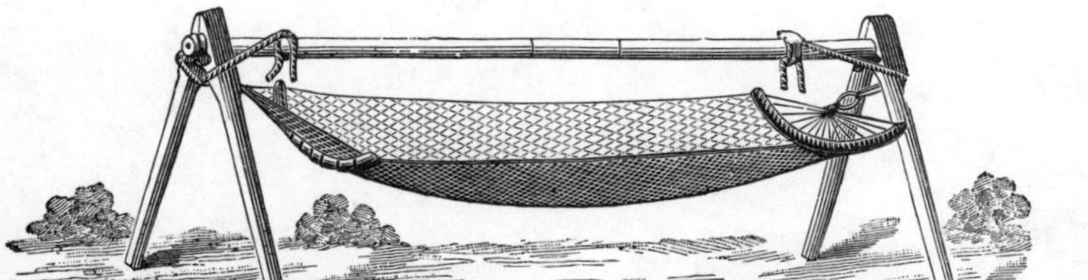

S/860/1-8 S/861/1-8

Hängematten. — Hammocks. — Hamacas.

Nr. S/860/1	Aus Ia. Bindfaden 3 Draht 4, filiert,	285	cm lang
„ S/860/2	„ „ 3 „ 3, „	285	„ „
„ S/860/3	„ „ „ 3 „ $2^1/_4$, „	285	„ „
„ S/860/4	„ „ „ 3 „ $2^1/_4$, „	300	„ „
„ S/860/5	„ „ „ 3 „ 6, „ mit dopp. Geflecht,	285	„ „
„ S/860/6	„ „ weißer, starker Aloeschnur, „	285	„ „
„ S/860/7	„ „ „ „ „ geflochten (ohne Knoten),	285	„ „
„ S/860/8	„ „ „ „ „ „ „ „ mit buntem Rand.	285	„ „

„ S/861/1 bis 8 Dieselben Hängematten wie S/860, aber mit eingeflochtenem Holzbügel.
Auf Wunsch können die Hängematten auch mit durchgehender Seitenschnur geliefert werden. Zu jeder Hängematte gehören 2 feste Anbindestricke von je 2 m Länge.
„ S/866 Holzspreizen mit Einschnitt zum Auseinanderhalten der Hängematten, hell lackiert, etwa 55 cm lang.

Nr. S/860/1	Of first class 3 twine 4, netted	285 cm long
„ S/860/2	„ „ „ 3 „ 3, „	285 „ „
„ S/860/3	„ „ „ 3 „ $2^1/_4$, „	285 „ „
„ S/860/4	„ „ „ 3 „ $2^1/_4$, „	300 „ „
„ S/860/5	„ „ „ 3 „ 6, with double network,	285 „ „
„ S/860/6	„ „ „ white, strong aloe cord, netted	285 „ „
„ S/860/7	„ „ „ „ „ „ „ plaited (without knots),	285 „ „
„ S/860/8	„ „ „ „ „ „ „ „ „ „ with coloured border	285 „ „

„ S/861/1 to 8 The same hammocks as S/860, but with wooden bow plaited in.
If desired the hammocks can also be supplied with side cord passing right through. With each hammock 2 strong cords for tying up, each 2 m long, are supplied.
„ S/866 Wooden spreaders with notch, for holding the hammocks wide open, clear varnished, about 55 cm long.

Nr. S/860/1	De hilo bramante 3 alambre 4, mallado	largura 285 cm
„ S/860/2	„ „ „ 3 „ 3, „	„ 285 „
„ S/860/3	„ „ „ 3 „ $2^1/_4$, „	„ 285 „
„ S/860/4	„ „ „ 3 „ $2^1/_4$, „	„ 300 ..
„ S/860/5	„ „ „ 3 „ 6, con mallas dobles	„ 285 „
„ S/860/6	de grueso cordon de áloe blanco, „	„ 285 „
„ S/860/7	„ „ „ „ „ „ con mallas (sin nudos),	„ 285 „
„ S/860/8	„ „ „ „ „ „ „ „ „ „ „ con borde de varios colores.	„ 285 „

„ S/861/1 hasta 8 Las mismas hamacas que aquellas de No. S/860, pero con cerco de madera trenzado en la red.
Si el cliente lo desea, las hamacas pueden ser entregadas con cordón lateral pasando por toda la red. A cada hamaca pertenecen 2 sogas sólidas para atarla, cada una de una largura de 2 metros.
„ S/866 Maderas extensoras con incisión para tener separadas las hamacas, embarnizadas en color claro, largura de 55 cm más o menos.

Holzspielwaren.
Kinder- und Puppenmöbel.

Wooden toys.
Children's and dolls furniture.

Juguetes de madera.
Muebles para niños y para muñecas.

S/1806 C

Puppenmöbelgarnitur, gelb oder weiß lackiert.
Dolls furniture set, varnished or painted white or yellow.
Muebles para muñecas, barnizados ó pintados en color blanco ó amarillo.

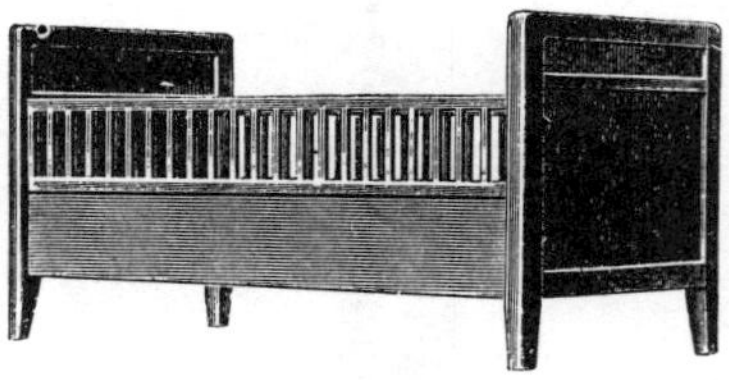

S/1905

Puppenbetten, weiß lackiert.
Dolls beds, painted white.
Camas para muñecas, pintado blanco.

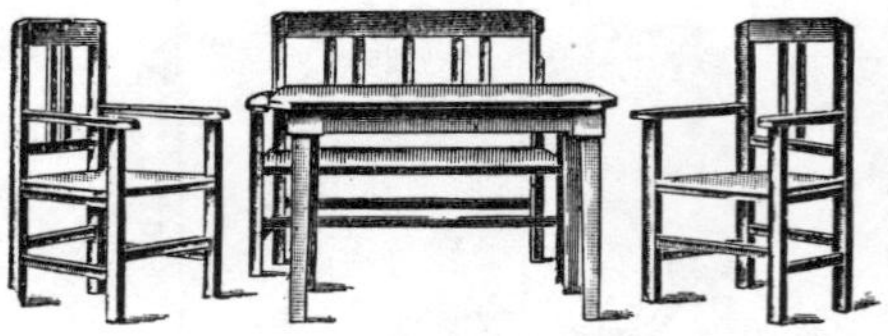

S/1817 C

Puppenmöbelgarnitur, weiß lackiert.
Dolls furniture set, varnished or paintet white.
Muebles para muñecas, barnizados ó pintados en color blanco ó amarillo.

S/2556

Schränke, weiß lackiert.
Wardrobes, painted white.
Armarios, pintados blanco.

S/2506

Kommoden, weiß lackiert.
Chest of drawers, painted white.
Cómodas, pintadas blanco.

S/2805

Waschtische, weiß lackiert, auch m. Spiegel lieferbar.
Wash stands, painted white, can be also delivered with looking glass.
Lavatorios, pintados blanco, pueden ser entregados con espejo.

S/2920

Kinderlaufgitter, hell oder dunkel lackiert.
Play grounds, bright or dark varnished.
Jaulas para bébés, barnizadas claro y oscuro.

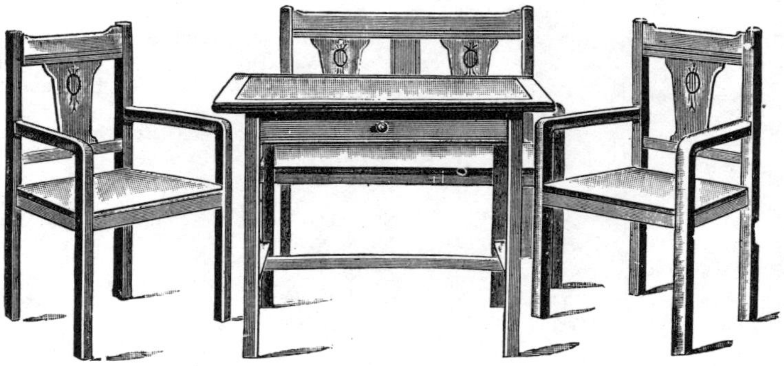

S/2980 C

Kindermöbelgarnitur, weiß lackiert.
Children's furniture set, painted white.
Muebles para niños, pintados blanco.

S/2927

Kinderlaufgitter, weiß lackiert u. gepolstert.
Play grounds, painted white and nicely upholstered.
Jaulas para bébés, pintadas blanco y tapizadas.

Stahlpianos für Kinder. — Pianos of steel for children. — Pianos con láminas de acero para niños.

75/9

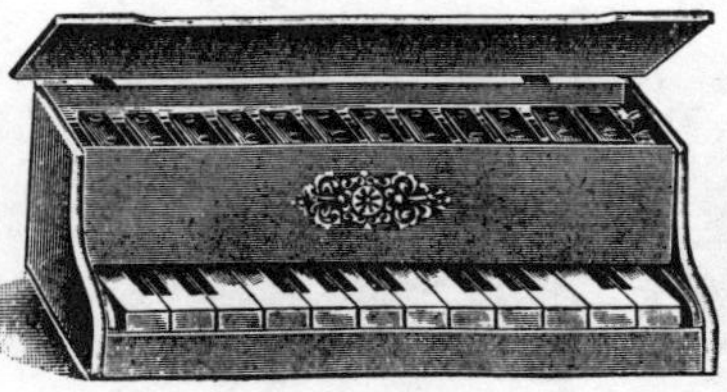

75/146

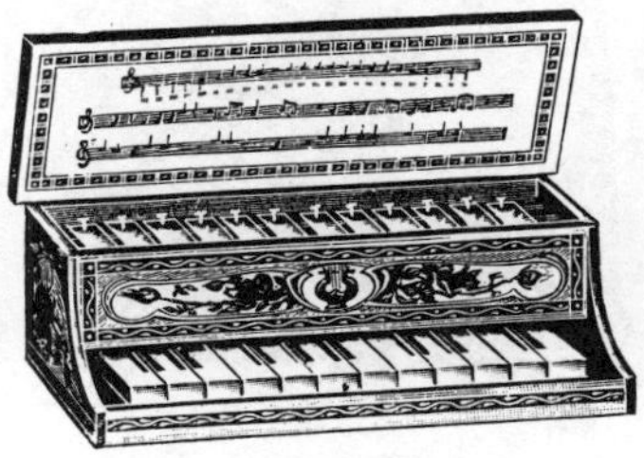

75/23

75/24

75/13

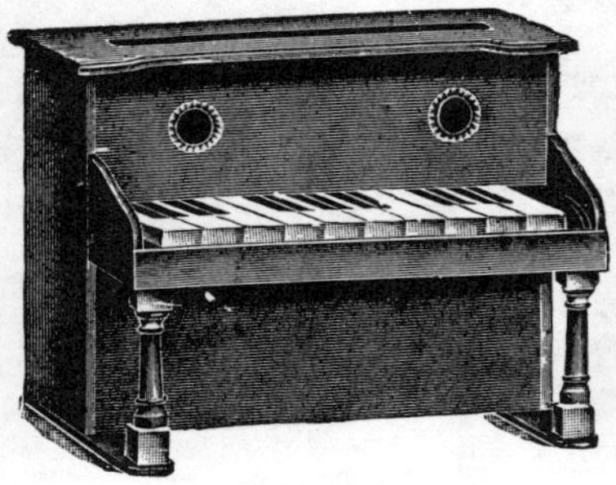

75/148

75/19

75/10

Nr. **75**/9 Stahlpiano, große flache, bunt lithographiert, Deckel geschlossen.
Steel-piano, large and plain, coloured printed, with cover shot.
Piano con láminas de acero, grande y llano, pintado, cobertera cenada.

Mit — With — Con	8	10	12	16	20	24	Tönen — Tones Tonos
Breite — Breadth Ancho	24	29,5	34	44,5	54	63,5	cm
Höhe — Height Alto	10	10	10	10	10	10	„
Tiefe — Depth Profundo	19	21	21	23,5	23,5	23,5	„

Nr. **75**/146 Stahlpiano, große flache, aus Eichenholz, lasiert, Deckel zum Öffnen.
Steel-piano, large and plain, of oak-wood, azured, cover for opening.
Piano con láminas de acero, grande y llano, de madera roble, azulado, cobertera para abrir.

Mit — With — Con	6	8	10	12	14	16	18	20	24	Tönen — Tones Tonos
Breite — Breadth Ancho	19	24	29,5	34	39	44,5	48	54	63	cm
Höhe — Height Alto	10	10	10	10	10	10	10	10	10	„
Tiefe — Depth Profundo	19	19	21	21	21	23,5	23,5	23,5	23,5	„

Nr. **75**/23 Stahlpiano, kleine flache, bunt lithographiert, Deckel zum Öffnen.
Steel-piano, little and plain, coloured printed, cover for opening.
Piano con láminas de acero, pequeño, llano, pintado, cobertera para abrir.

Mit — With — Con	6	8	10	12	14	16	Tönen — Tones Tonos
Breite — Breadth Ancho	17	21	25,5	30	34	39	cm
Höhe — Height Alto	8	8	9	9	9	9	„
Tiefe — Depth Profundo	14,5	14,5	16,5	16,5	16,5	18,5	„

Nr. **75**/24 Stahlpiano, große flache, bunt lithographiert, Deckel zum Öffnen.
Steel-piano, large and plain, coloured printed, cover for opening.
Piano con láminas de acero, grande y llano, pintado, cobertera para abrir.

Mit — With — Con	8	10	12	16	20	24	Tönen — Tones Tonos
Breite — Breadth Ancho	24	29,5	34	44,5	54	63,5	cm
Höhe — Height Alto	10	10	10	10	10	10	„
Tiefe — Depth Profundo	19	21	21	23,5	23,5	23,5	„

Nr. **75**/13 Stahlpiano, große hohe, bunt lithographiert.
Steel-cottage piano, large and tall, coloured printed.
Piano vertical, grande y alto, pintado.

Mit — With — Con	8	10	12	16	20	Tönen — Tones Tonos
Breite — Breadth Ancho	24,5	29,5	34	45	55	cm
Höhe — Height Alto	20	20	22	24	28	„
Tiefe — Depth Profundo	17	17	18,5	20	21	„

Nr. **75**/148 Stahlpiano, kleine hohe, aus Eichenholz, lasiert.
Steel-cottage piano, little and high, of oak wood, azured.
Piano vertical de acero, pequeño y alto, de madera roble, azulada.

Mit — With — Con	6	8	10	12	14	16	20	Tönen — Tones Tonos
Breite — Breadth Ancho	17	21,5	25 5	29,5	34	37,5	46	cm
Höhe — Height Alto	16	16	19	19	19	19	22	„
Tiefe — Depth Profundo	14,5	14,5	16,5	16,5	16,5	16,5	20	„

Nr. **75**/19 Stahlpiano, kleine hohe, bunt lithographiert.
Steel-cottage piano, little and tall, coloured printed.
Piano vertical de acero, pequeño y alto, pintado.

Mit — With — Con	6	8	10	12	Tönen — Tones Tonos
Breite — Breadth Ancho	17	21	26	30	cm
Höhe — Height Alto	6	16	18	18	„
Tiefe — Depth Profundo	14,5	14,5	16	16	„

Nr. **75**/10 Stahlpiano, kleine flache, bunt lithographiert, Deckel geschlossen.
Steel-piano, little and plain, coloured printed, with cover shot.
Piano con láminas de acero, pequeño y llano, pintado, cobertera cenada.

Mit — With — Con	5	6	8	9	10	12	14	16	Tönen — Tones Tonos
Breite — Breadth Ancho	14,5	17	21	23	25,5	30	34	39	cm
Höhe — Height Alto	8	8	8	8	9	9	9	9	„
Tiefe — Depth Profundo	14,5	14,5	14,5	14,5	16,5	16,5	16,5	18,5	„

75/154

75/149

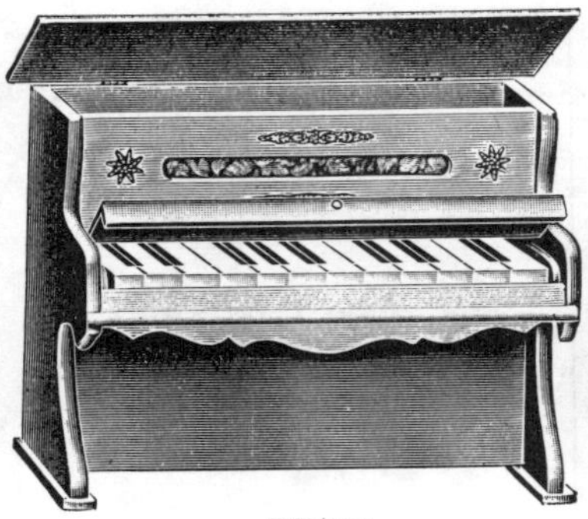

75/154 a

75/152

75/159

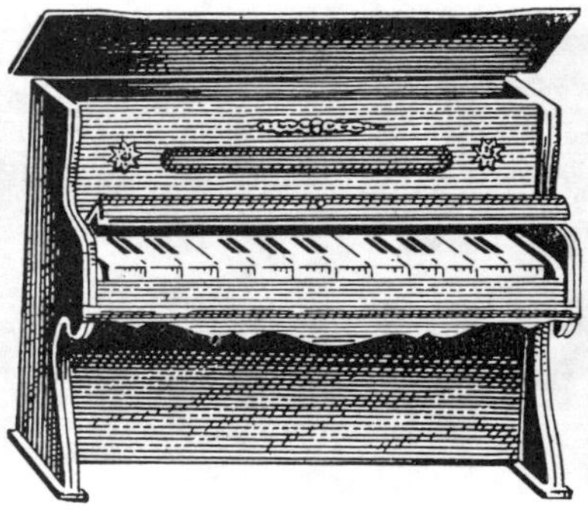

75/158

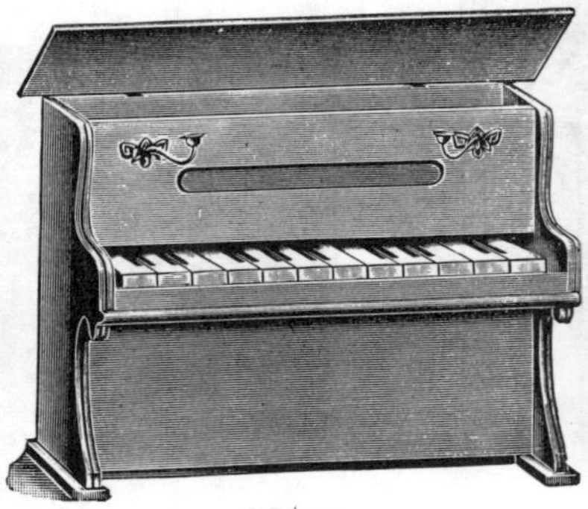

75/157

75/154 b

Nr. **75**/154 Stahlpianos, große hohe, aus Eichenholz, lasiert, mit Messingleuchter, Deckel zum Öffnen.

Steel-cottage piano, large and high, of oak wood, azured, with brass-candlesticks, cover for opening.

Piano vertical con laminas de acero, grando alto, de madera roble, azulada, con candeleros de laton, cobertera para abrir.

Mit — With — Con	8	10	12	16	20	24	Tönen — Tones Tonos
Breite — Breadth Ancho	25	30	35	45,5	55	65	cm
Höhe — Height Alto	22	24	25,5	28	28	28	„
Tiefe — Depth Profundo	18	18	19,5	20	22	22	„

Nr. **75**/149 Hohe Stahlpianos, aus Eichenholz, lasiert, Deckel zum Öffnen.

High steel-cottage piano, of oak wood, azured, cover for opening.

Piano vertical alto de acero, de madera roble, azulado, cobertera para abrir.

Mit — With — Con	8	10	12	16	20	Tönen — Tones Tonos
Breite — Breadth Ancho	32	27	31	39,5	47,5	cm
Höhe — Height Alto	17	19,5	19,5	19,5	21,5	„
Tiefe — Depth Profundo	14,5	16,5	16,5	18	19,5	„

Nr. **75**/154a Stahlpianos, große hohe, aus Eichenholz, lasiert, mit Tastenverdeck, Deckel zum Öffnen.

Steel-cottage piano, large and high, of oak-wood, azured, with key-keeper, cover for opening.

Piano vertical con laminas de acero, grande alto, de madera roble, azulado, con cobre-teclas, cobertera para abrir.

Mit — With — Con	8	10	12	16	20	24	Tönen — Tones Tonos
Breite — Breath Ancho	25	30	35	45,5	55	65	cm
Höhe — Height Alto	22	24	25,5	28	28	28	„
Tiefe — Depth Profundo	18,5	18,5	20	20,5	23,5	23,5	„

Nr. **75**/152 Stahlpianos, kleine flache, aus Buchenholz, lasiert.

Steel-piano, little and plain, of beech wood, azured.

Piano con laminas de acero, pequeño y llano, de madera azulada.

Mit — With — Con	6	8	10	12	14	16	Tönen — Tones Tonos
Breite — Breath Ancho	17	21	25,5	30	34	39	cm
Höhe — Height Alto	8	8	9	9	9	9	„
Tiefe — Depth Profundo	14,5	14,5	16,5	16,5	16,5	18,5	„

Nr. **75**/159 Hohe Stahlpianinos, weiß lackiert, mit Handmalerei und Tastenverdeck.

High steel-cottage piano, white varnished, hand-painted and with key-keeper.

Piano vertical con laminas de acero, embarnizado en color blanco, con cobre teclas.

Mit — With — Con	8	10	12	16	20	Tönen — Tones Tonos
Breite — Breath Ancho	25	30	35	45,5	55	cm
Höhe — Height Alto	22	24	25,5	28	28	„
Tiefe — Depth Profundo	18,5	18,5	20	20,5	23,5	„

Nr. **75**/158 Stahlpianinos, große hohe, weiß lackiert, mit Tastenverdeck und Verzierung, Deckel zum Öffnen.

Steel-cottage piano, large and high, white varnished, with key-keeper and ornaments, cover for opening.

Piano vertical con laminas de acero, grande alto, barnizado en color blanco con cobre teclas y ornamentos, cobertera para abrir.

Mit — With — Con	8	10	12	16	20	24	Tönen — Tones Tonos
Breite — Breath Ancho	25	30	35	45,5	55	65	cm
Höhe — Height Alto	22	24	25,5	28	28	28	„
Tiefe — Depth Profundo	18,5	18,5	20	20,5	23,5	23,5	„

Nr. **75**/157 Stahlpianos, große hohe, weiß lackiert, mit Gold abgesetzt, mit Messingleuchter, Deckel zum Öffnen.

Steel-cottage piano, large and high, white varnished, raised with gold, with brass-candlesticks, cover for opening.

Piano vertical con laminas de acero, grande alto, barnizado en color blanco, realzado con oro, con candeleros de laton, cobertera para abrir.

Mit — With — Con	8	10	12	16	20	24	Tönen — Tones Tonos
Breite — Breath Ancho	25	30	35	45,5	55	65	cm
Höhe — Height Alto	22	24	25,5	28	28	28	„
Tiefe — Depth Profundo	18	18	19,5	20	22	22	„

Nr. **75**/154B Stahlpianinos, große hohe, aus Eichenholz, lasiert, mit Messingleuchter, Deckel zum Öffnen.

Steel-cottage piano, large and high, of oak wood, with brass-candlesticks, cover for opening.

Piano vertical con laminas de acero, grande alto, de madera roble, azulado, con cadeleros de laton, cobertera para abrir.

Mit — With — Con	8	10	12	16	20	24	Tönen — Tones Tonos
Breite — Breath Ancho	25	30	35	45,5	55	65	cm
Höhe — Height Alto	22	24	25,5	28	28	28	„
Tiefe — Depth Profundo	18,5	18,5	20	20,5	23,5	23,5	„

75/178

75/176

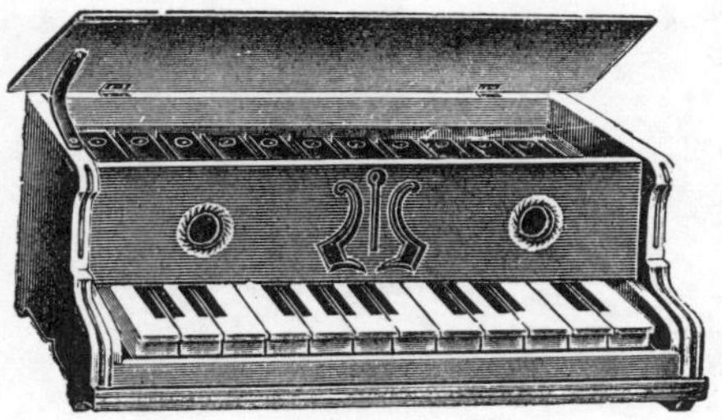

75/184

75/177

Nr. **75**/178 Stahlpianinos, mit ganzen und halben Tönen, mit Sessel, weiß lackiert, mit Gold abgesetzt.
Steel-cottage pianos, with whole and semi tones, with chair, white varnished, raised with gold.
Pianos vertical, con láminas de acero, con tonos medios y enteros, con tabourete, barnizado blanco, realzado con oro.

Mit — With — Con	24 und 17	Tönen — Tones — Tonos
Breite — Breadth — Ancho	67	cm
Höhe — Height — Alto	73	„
Tiefe — Depth — Profundo	37	„

Nr. **75**/176 Stahlpianinos, große hohe, aus Eichenholz, lasiert.
Steel-cottage pianos, large and high, of oak wood, azured.
Pianos vertical con láminas de acero, grande y alto, de madera roble, azulado.

Mit — With — Con	12	16	20	Tönen — Tones — Tonos
Breite — Breadth — Ancho	37	46	55,5	cm
Höhe — Height — Alto	36	40	40	„
Tiefe — Depth — Profundo	19	24	24	„

Nr. **75**/184 Stahlpianos, flache, aus Eichenholz, lasiert, Deckel zum Öffnen.
Steel-pianos, plain, of oak-wood, azured, cover for opening.
Pianos con láminas de acero, llano, de madera roble, azulado, cobertera para abrir.

Mit — With — Con	8	10	12	16	20	Tönen — Tones — Tonos
Breite — Breadth — Ancho	22,5	26	30,5	39	47	cm
Höhe — Height — Alto	10,5	11,5	11,5	11,5	12,5	„
Tiefe — Depth — Profundo	14,5	16	16	17,5	19,5	„

Nr. **75**/177 Stahlpianinos, mit Sessel, weiß lackiert, mit Gold abgesetzt.
Steel-cottage pianos, with chair, white varnished, raised with gold.
Pianos vertical con láminas de acero, con taburete, barnizado en color, blanco, realzado con oro.

Mit — With — Con	20	24	Tönen — Tones — Tonos
Breite — Breadth — Ancho	55	65	cm
Höhe — Height — Alto	54	54	„
Tiefe — Depth — Profundo	26	26	„

Puppenbetten

garniert und ungarniert

Nr. **20**/115u/	30 cm
„ **20**/115u/1	35 „
„ **20**/115u/2	38 „
„ **20**/115u/3	42 „
„ **20**/115u/4	45 „
„ **20**/115u/5	48 „
„ **20**/115u/6	53 „
„ **20**/115u/7	60 „

Nr. **20**/80/	30 cm
„ **20**/80/1	35 „
„ **20**/80/2	38 „
„ **20**/80/3	42 „
„ **20**/80/4	45 „
„ **20**/80/5	48 „
„ **20**/80/6	53 „
„ **20**/80/7	60 „

Nr. **20**/400/0	35 cm
„ **20**/400/1	40 „
„ **20**/400/2	47 „
„ **20**/400/3	52 „
„ **20**/400/4	62 „
„ **20**/400/5	72 „
„ **20**/400/6	82 „
„ **20**/400/7	92 „
„ **20**/400/8	102 „

Nr. **20**/500/3	52 cm
„ **20**/500/4	62 „
„ **20**/500/5	72 „
„ **20**/500/6	82 „
„ **20**/500/7	92 „
„ **20**/500/8	102 „

Nr. **20**/200/00	30 cm
„ **20** 200/0	35 „
„ **20**/200/$^{1}/_{2}$	38 „
„ **20**/200/1	40 „
„ **20**/200/2	47 „
„ **20**/200/3	52 „
„ **20**/200/4	62 „
„ **20**/200/5	72 „
„ **20**/200/6	82 „
„ **20**/200/7	92 „
„ **20**/200/8	102 „

Nr. **20**/200u/00	30 cm
„ **20**/200u/0	35 „
„ **20**/200u/$^{1}/_{2}$	38 „
„ **20**/200u/1	40 „
„ **20**/200u/2	47 „
„ **20**/200u/3	52 „
„ **20**/200u/4	62 „
„ **20**/200u/5	72 „

Maße und Serien
zu nebenstehenden Abbildungen.

Dolls bedsteads

with and without outfit

Nr. **20**/200u/6	82 cm
„ **20**/200u/7	92 „
„ **20**/200u/8	102 „

Nr. **20**/300/0	35 cm
„ **20**/300/1	40 „
„ **20**/300/2	47 „
„ **20**/300/3	52 „
„ **20**/300/4	62 „
„ **20**/300/5	72 „
„ **20**/300/6	82 „
„ **20**/300/7	92 „
„ **20**/300/8	102 „

Nr. **20**/300U/0	35 cm
„ **20**/300U/1	40 „
„ **20**/300U/2	47 „
„ **20**/300U/3	52 „
„ **20**/300U/4	62 „
„ **20**/300U/5	72 „
„ **20**/300U/6	82 „
„ **20**/300U/7	92 „
„ **20**/300U/8	102 „

Nr. **20**/700/1	40 cm
„ **20**/700/2	47 „
„ **20**/700/3	52 „
„ **20**/700/4	62 „
„ **20**/700/5	72 „
„ **20**/700 6	82 „
„ **20**/700/7	92 „
„ **20**/700/8	102 „

Nr. **20**/700u/1	40 cm
„ **20**/700u/2	47 „
„ **20**/700u/3	52 „
„ **20**/700u/4	62 „
„ **20**/700u/5	72 „
„ **20**/700u/6	82 „
„ **20**/700u/7	92 „
„ **20**/700u/8	102 „

Nr. **20**/130/3/0	15 cm
„ **20**/130/2/0	20 „
„ **20**/130/0	25 „
„ **20**/130/-	30 „
„ **20**/130/1	35 „
„ **20**/130/2	42 „
„ **20**/130/3	52 „
„ **20**/130/4	62 „
„ **20**/130/5	72 „

Nr. **20**/129/3/0	15 cm
„ **20**/129/2/0	20 „
„ **20**/129/0	25 „

Measure and series
to the following pictures.

Camas para muñecas

con y sin guarnición

No. **20**/130u/3/0	15 cm
„ **20**/130u/2/0	20 „
„ **20**/130u/0	25 „

No. **20**/130/-	30 cm
„ **20**/130/1	35 „
„ **20**/130/2	42 „
„ **20**/130/3	52 „
„ **20**/130/4	62 „
„ **20**/130/5	72 „

No. **20**/94/00	8 cm
„ **20**/94/G	10 „
„ **20**/94	$11^{1}/_{2}$ „
„ **20**/94/1	12 „
„ **20**/94/2	15 „
„ **20**/94/3	$17^{1}/_{2}$ „
„ **20**/94/4	20 „
„ **20**/94/5	22 „
„ **20**/94/6	25 „
„ **20**/94/$6^{1}/_{2}$	27 „
„ **20**/94/7	30 „
„ **20**/94/8	35 „
„ **20**/94/9	38 „
„ **20**/94/10	42 „

No. **20**/101	8 cm
„ **20**/102	10 „
„ **20**/103	$11^{1}/_{2}$ „
„ **20**/104	13 „
„ **20**/105	15 „
„ **20**/107	16 „
„ **20**/108	18 „
„ **20**/109	19 „
„ **20**/110	23 „
„ **20**/111	25 „

No. **20**/101u	8 cm
„ **20**/102u	10 „
„ **20**/103u	$11^{1}/_{2}$ „
„ **20**/104u	13 „
„ **20**/105u	15 „
„ **20**/107u	16 „
„ **20**/108u	18 „
„ **20**/109u	19 „
„ **20**/110u	23 „
„ **20**/111u	25 „

No. **20**/149/6	23 cm
„ **20**/149/7	28 „
„ **20**/149/8	45 „
„ **20**/149/9	46 „

Dimensiones y serias
para la representaciones sucesivo.

29/1740

Landhaussiedlung. — Country house settlement.
Colonia de casas de campo.

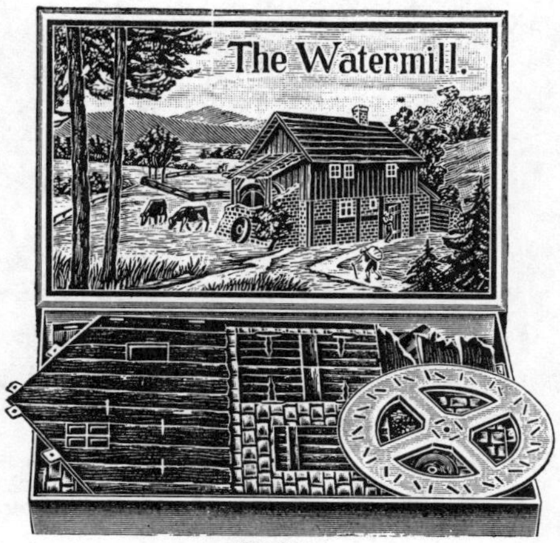

29/1534

Die Wassermühle. — The watermill.
El molino de agua.

29/1666

Zoologischer Garten. — The zoological garden.
Jardín zoológico.

29/3320

Ausschneide- und Aufklebearbeiten.
Cutting out and pasting on work.
Labores de cortar y pegar.

29/1260

Durchzeichnen und Ausmalen.
Tracing and colouring.
Calcar y pintar.

29/1270

Schablonenmalerei mit Farbstiften.
Stencil painting.
Pintura a dechados.

29/1766

Silhouetten-Schneiden.
The silhouette cutter.
Cortar siluetas.

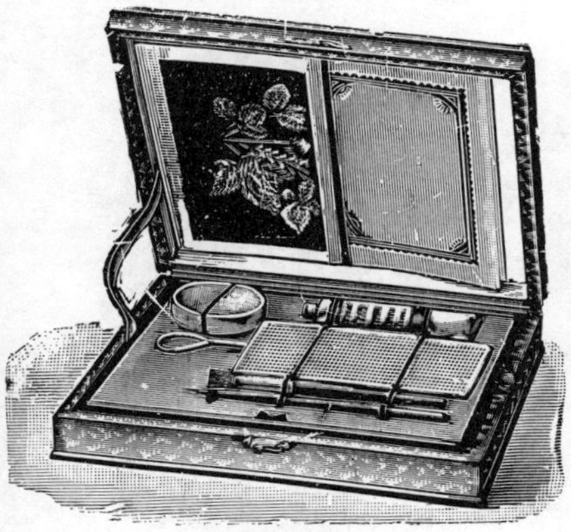

29/1019

Spritzmalerei
Sprinkle pictures.
Aparato para pinturas al jaspeado.

29/1267

Anfänge des Zeichnens.
The rudiments of drawing.
Principios del dibujo.

29/1010

Das Zeichnen mit Papierschablonen.
Drawing school.
Curso de dibujo y pintura.

29/1268

Silhouetten-Malen und -Ausschneiden.
Painting and cutting silhouettes.
Como se pintar y como se cortar siluetas.

29/1251

Schnellmaler.
The lightning artist
Pintor rápido.

29/1257

Schnellmaler.
The lightning artist.
Pintor rápido.

29/1189

Schnellmaler.
The lightning artist.
Pintor rápido.

29/1246

Schnellmaler.
The lightning artist.
Pintor rápido.

29/1233

Schnellmaler.
The lightning artist.
Pintor rápido.

29/1241

Malen und Zeichnen mit Metallschablonen.
Colouring and sketching with metal stencils.
Pintar y dibujar en patrones metálicos.

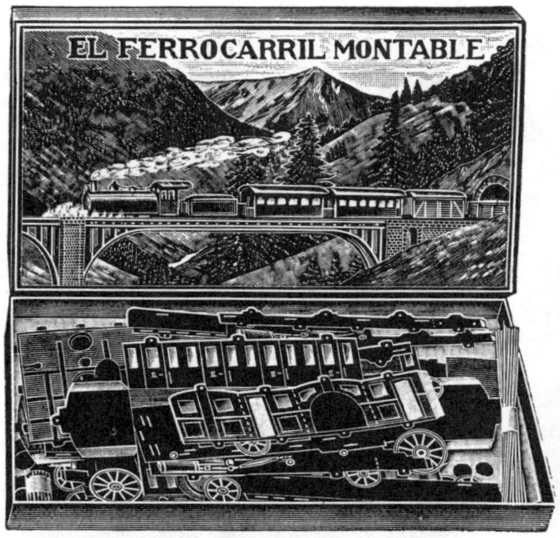

29/1762 **Eisenbahn** zum Zusammensetzen.
Train for construction.
El ferrocarril, montable.

29/1684 **Wildpark.**
Hunting party.
El parque de caza.

29/1660 **Russische Schaukel.**
The big wheel.
Columpio ruso.

29/1618 **Aufstellhäuser.**
The little house builder.
Casas transformables.

29/1564 **Beim Wagenbauer.**
The coach builder.
El carrotero.

29/1707 **Stäbchen-Klebearbeit.**
The little architect.
Labores de palitos encolados.

29/1523 **Papierblumen.**
Paper flowers.
Flores de papel.

29/1603 **Hammer und Nagel.**
Hammer and nails.
Martillo y clavo.

29/1155 **Der Farmer.**
The farmer.
El hacendado.

29/1669

29/1669 **Modell-Segelyacht.**
How to build a model sailing yacht.
Yates modelos.

29/1714 **Künstl. Ausschneide- u. Aufklebebilder.**
Artistic Patchwork pictures.
Figuras de recortar y pegar.

29/1604 Hammer und Nagel.
Hammer and nails. — Martillo y claro.

29/3304 Perlbilder zum Ausnähen. — Bead work.
Figuras de perlas.

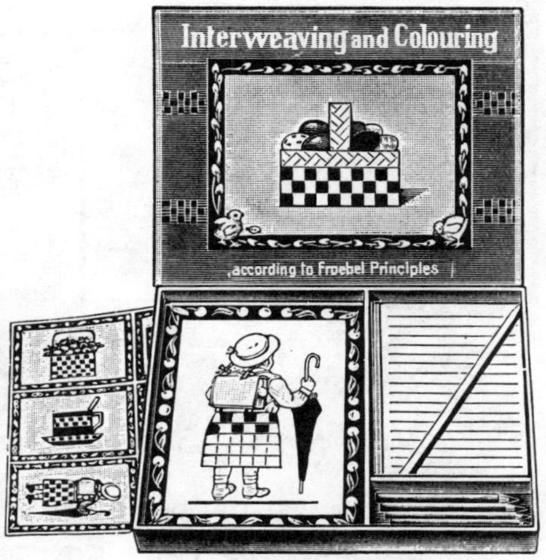

29/331 Flechten und Ausmalen.
Interweaving and colouring.
Tejer y pintar.

29/1655 Papierblumen.
Paper flowers. — Flores de papel.

29/3285 Ausnähbilder.
Models for embroidering.
Figuras para bordar.

29/3216 Bilderflechten.
Fairy pictures. — Tejer figuras.

29/3168 Ausstech- und Ausnähbilder.
Coloured embroidery cards.
Cuadros para picar y bordar.

29/3239 Flechtschule.
Paper plaiting.
Trenzar ó tejer.

29/1522 Papierblumen.
Paper flowers. — Flores de papel.

29/3217 Kanevasbilder.
The little canevas embroiderer.
Cuardros de cañamazo para bordar.

29/2205 Schattenspiele.
Shadow theatre. — Juegos de sombras.

29/1071

29/3274 Ausnähbilder.
Models for embroidering.
Figuras para bordar.

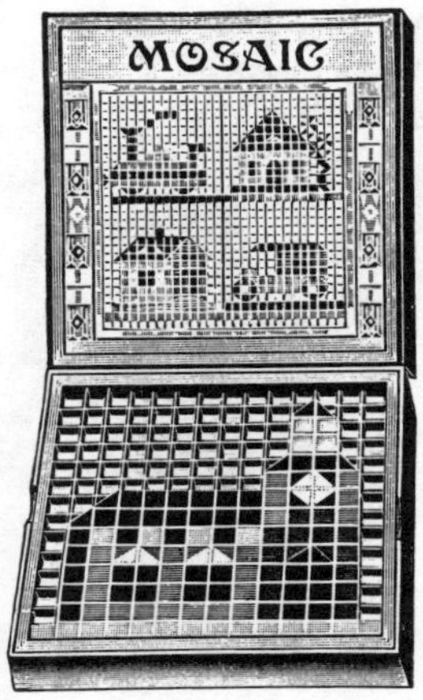

29/1741

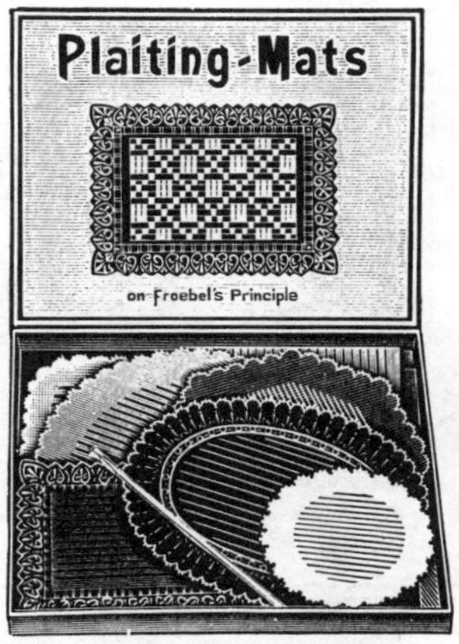

29/3194 Deckenflechten.
Playting mats.
Trenzar ó tejer carpetas.

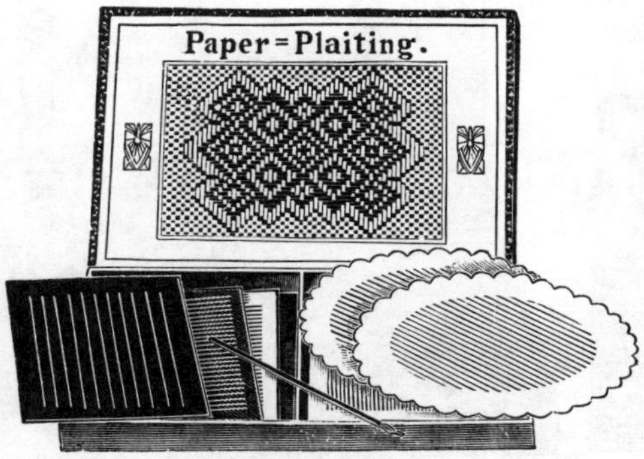

29/3204 Flechtschule.
Paper plaiting.
Trenzar ó tejer.

29/1634

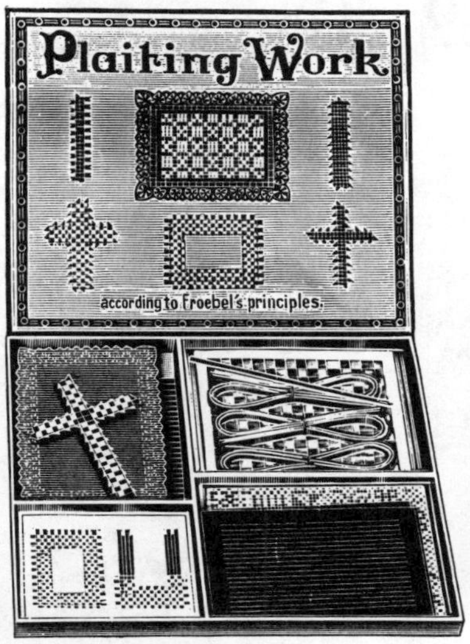

29/3293 Flechtarbeiten.
Plaiting work.
Labores y operationes de tejer.

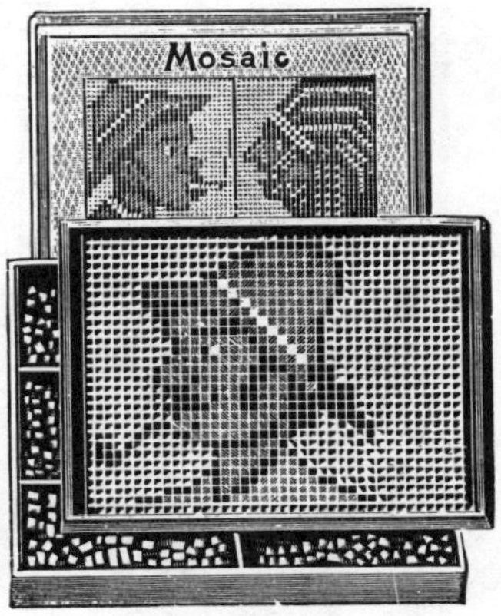

29/1670

29/3326 Tocka-Nähkunst.
Tocka outline sewing on linen.
Tocka. El arte de coser.

29/3249 Körbchen-Arbeiten.
The little basket maker.
La pequeña cestera.

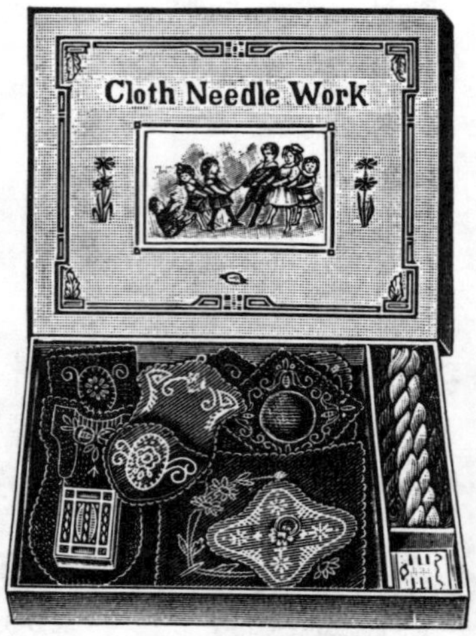

29/3231 Tuch-Ausnäharbeiten.
Cloth needle work.
Labores de costura de paño.

29/3177 Ausnähen und Ausmalen.
Embroidering and colouring.
Bordar y pintar.

29/3248 Gold-Körbchen.
Gold baskets.
Cestitos de oro.

29/3312 Körbchen-Arbeiten.
The little basket plaiter.
Labores de cesteria.

29/3256 Puppenmöbel-Flechten.
Doll's-house furniture.
Tejer mueblos de muñecas.

29/3697 Gold-Körbchen.
Gold baskets.
Cestitos de oro.

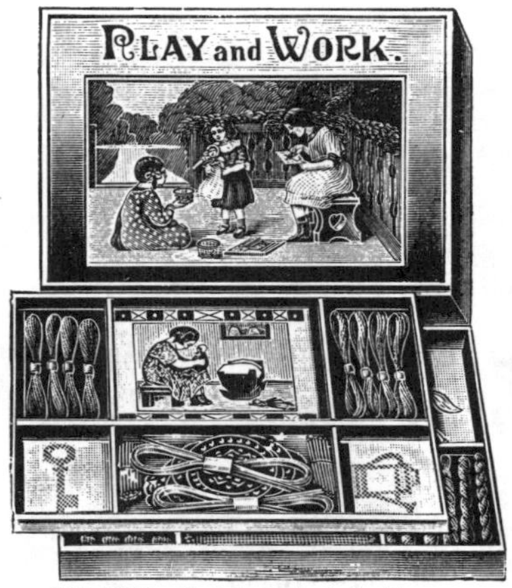

29/3289 Spiel und Arbeit.
Play and work.
Juego y trabajo.

29/3324 Tocka-Nähkunst.
Tocka outline sewing on linen.
Tocka. El arte de coser.

29/3313 Körbchen-Arbeiten mit Perlen und Kartonflechtstreifen.
The little basket plaiter.
Labores de cesteria.

29/3296 Perlkörbchen.
Bead baskets.
Cestitos de perlas.

29/3267

Nr. **29**/3267
Stickerei auf Kanevas.
The canevas embroiderer.
Bordados de cañamazo.

Nr. **29**/3236
Körbchen-Flechten.
Basket work.
Tejer cestitos.

29/3236

29/3259 Perlwebeapparat.
Bead weaving loom.
Aparato para tejer perlas.

29/3300 Perlkörbchen.
The bead basket worker.
Cestitos de perlas.

29/2338
Segelregatta
Yacht regatta.
Regata de yates.

29/3279
Zierkorb-Flechten.
Basket making of peddig reed.
Trenzar ó tejer cestitos de odorno de junco.

29/2337
Auto-Preisfahrt.
Motor races.
Carrera de automóvil.

29/2325
In der Tiefe des Meeres.
In the depth of the sea.
En el fondo del mar.

29/3175
Körbchen-Flechten.
The little basket weaver.
Tejer cestitos.

29/2227
Magnetisches Angelspiel.
Magnetic fish pond.
Juego magnético de anzuelo.

29/2345
Affenzirkus.
The ape circus.
El circo de los monos.

29/2299
Lustiges Einmaleins.
The arithmetical lotto.
Alegre tabla de multiplicar.

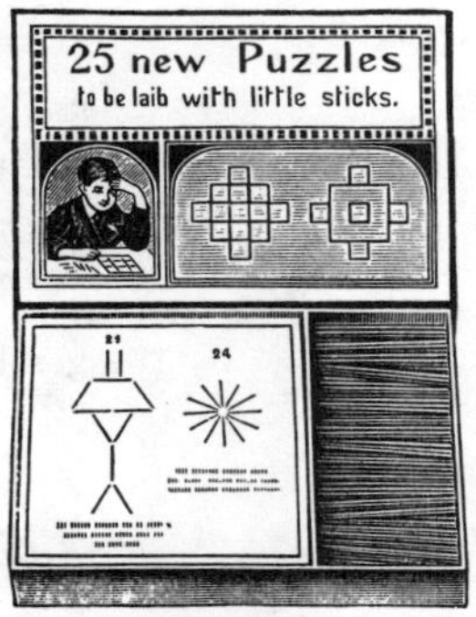

29/2235
Stäbchen-Geduldspiel.
25 new puzzles.
Rompecabezas de barritas.

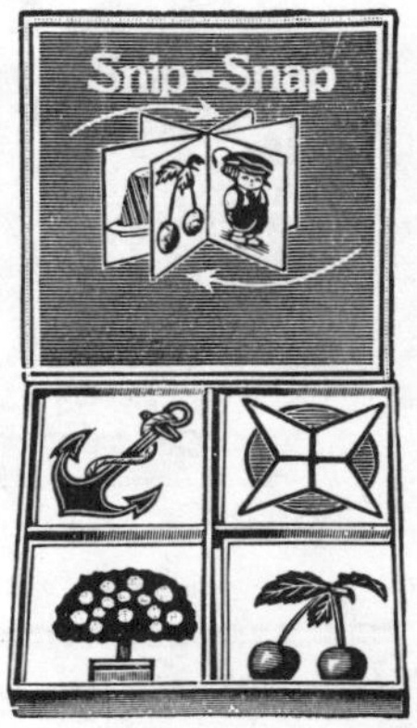

29/2303
Schnipp-Schnapp.
Snip-Snap.
Bim-Bam.

29/2004
15er-Spiel
Chinese puzzle.
Juego de parciencia.

29/2170
Die wunderbare 26.
The wonderful 26.
El maravilloso 26.

29/2343
Tierquartett.
Zoological quartet.
Cuarteto de animales.

29/2283
Überall 15.
Everywhere 15.
En todas partes el 15.

29/2344
Tierlotto. — Zoological lotto.
Lotería de animales.

29/2314
Bilderlotto. — Picture lotto.
Lotería de figures.

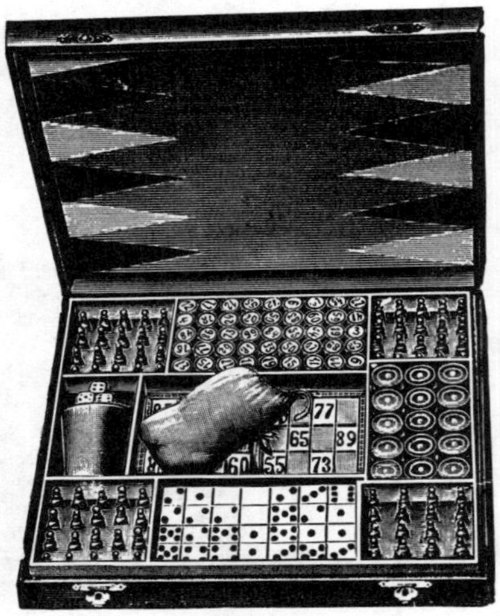

29/2224
Spielmagazin.
Compendium of games.
Almacén de juego.

29/2323
Wie lerne ich spielend Französisch?
French lessons at play time?
¿Como aprendo francés jugando?

29/2306
Das Gänsespiel. — The Goose game.
El juego de gansos.

29/2132 Halma.

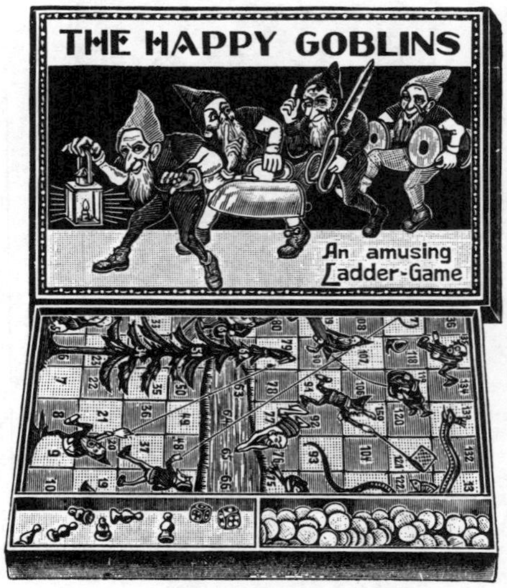

29/2320
Die Heinzelmännchen. — The happy goblins.
Los duendes trabajadores.

29/2328
Die geschickten Clowns. — The skilful clowns.
Los pajasos habiles.

29/2269 Lotto. — Lotería.

29/2349
Im Fahrstuhl. — The hotel game.
De abajo arriba y de arriba abajo en el ascensor.

29/2310
Wettrennen. — The steeple chase.
Carrera de caballos.

29/2297 Die Post von einst und jetzt.
The post of the past and at present.
El correo de antes y de ahora.

„Complex“

der neueste Steinbaukasten, liefert das Material zum Bauen von Gebäuden, allerlei Toren, Tempeln, Burgen, Domen und Türmen von märchenhaftem Reiz, monumentaler Schlichtheit, in geschmackvollen Farben.

Drei verschiedene sortierte Serien:
- A) 6 Kasten, für kleine Kinder, Steine in verschiedenen Farben.
- B) 10 Kasten, für ältere Kinder, gelbliche Steine und grüne Säulen für orientalische Bauten.
- C) 10 Kasten, für ältere Kinder, rote Steine für Bauten in romanischem Stil.

"Complex"

Stone building blocks, latest novelty, furnish the material for the construction of all sorts of buildings, gates, temples, castles, cathedrals and towers of encanting charm, monumental simplicity in tastefull colors.

Three series of different assortments:
- A) 6 boxes for small children, blocks of different tints.
- B) 10 boxes for older children, yellowish blocks and green pillars for buildings of an oriental character.
- C) 10 boxes for older children, red blocks for buildings of the romantic style.

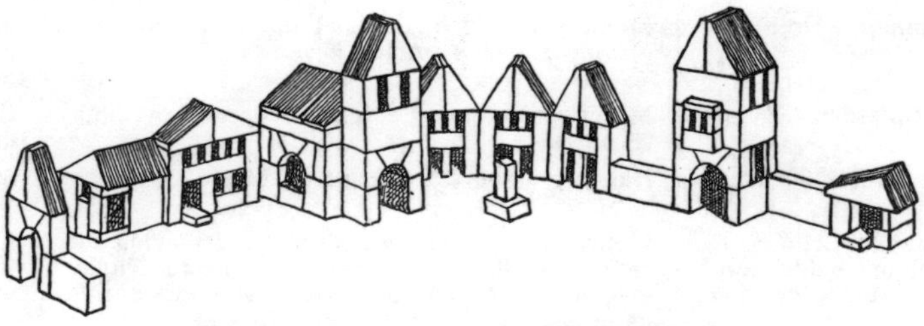

Erbaut mit Kasten — Constructed with box
Construido con la caja
157/A 34

"Complex"

Piedras de construcción, última novedad, con las cuales se puede construir edificios de todas clases, puertas, templos, castillos, catedrales y torres de fabuloso encanto, simplicidad monumental en gustosos colores.

Tres series diferentemente surtidas:
- A) 6 cajitas, para niños pequeños, piedras de varias tintas.
- B) 10 cajitas para niños de major edad, piedras amarillentes con columnas verdes para construcciones orientales.
- C) 10 cajitas para niños de major edad, piedras coloradas para construcciones en estilo romano.

Der „Complex“-Steinbaukasten kann in folgenden Sortimenten verkauft werden:

Serie	Nr.	Steinlagen im Kasten	Größe des Kastens cm	Für Kinder im Alter
157/A	1	1	12,5×20	unter 5
157/A	2	1	„	„
157/A	12	2	„	von 5—7
157/A	3	1	„	„
157/A	4	1	„	„
157/A	34	2	„	„
157/B	1	1	„	über 7
157/B	2	1	„	„
157/B	12	2	„	„
157/B	3	2	„	„
157/B	4	2	„	„
157/B	d	1	„	„
157/B	dd	2	„	„
157/B	123	2	20×25	„
157/B	12d	1	23,75×31,25	„
157/B	123dd	2	„	„
157/C	1	1	12,5×20	„
157/C	2	1	„	„
157/C	12	2	„	„
157/C	3	2	„	„
157/C	4	2	„	„
157/C	d	1	„	„
157/C	dd	2	„	„
157/C	123	2	20×25	„
157/C	12d	1	23,75×31,25	„
157/C	123dd	2	„	„
				Jahren

Die Nummern geben den Inhalt der verschiedenen Kasten an, indem sie zeigen, welche kleineren Kasten sie enthalten.
Der Kasten Nr. 157/A 34 z. B. enthält die Steine der Kasten: 157/A 3 und 157/A 4 und Kasten 157/C 12d die Steine der Kasten: 157/C 1, 157/C 2 und 157/C d.

The "Complex" building blocks are sold in the following assortments:

Series	Nr.	Layers of blocks in box	size of box inches	For the age of
157/A	1	1	5″×8″	less than 5
157/A	2	1	„	„
157/A	12	2	„	5—7
157/A	3	1	„	„
157/A	4	1	„	„
157/A	34	2	„	„
157/B	1	1	„	more than 7
157/B	2	1	„	„
157/B	12	2	„	„
157/B	3	2	„	„
157/B	4	2	„	„
157/B	d	1	„	„
157/B	dd	2	„	„
157/B	123	2	8″×10″	„
157/B	12d	1	8″×13¼″	„
157/B	123dd	2	„	„
157/C	1	1	5″×8″	„
157/C	2	1	„	„
157/C	12	2	„	„
157/C	3	2	„	„
157/C	4	2	„	„
157/C	d	1	„	„
157/C	dd	2	„	„
157/C	123	2	8″×10″	„
157/C	12d	1	8″×13¼″	„
157/C	123dd	2	„	„
				years

The numbers indicate the contents of the different boxes by showing which kinds of smaller boxes they contain. Box Nr. 157/A 34 e. g. contains the blocks of the boxes 157/A 3 and 157/A 4; and box 157/C 12d comprises the boxes 157/C 1, 157/C 2, and 157/C d.

Las piedras de construcción "Complex" se venden en los surtidos siguientes:

Series	No.	Capas de piedras en la caja	tamaño de la caja cm	Para el edad de
157/A	1	1	12,5×20	ménos de 5
157/A	2	1	„	„
157/A	12	2	„	5—7
157/A	3	1	„	„
157/A	4	1	„	„
157/A	34	2	„	„
157/B	1	1	„	más de 7
157/B	2	1	„	„
157/B	12	2	„	„
157/B	3	2	„	„
157/B	4	2	„	„
157/B	d	1	„	„
157/B	dd	2	„	„
157/B	123	2	20×25	„
157/B	12d	1	23,75×31,25	„
157/B	123dd	2	„	„
157/C	1	1	12,5×20	„
157/C	2	1	„	„
157/C	12	2	„	„
157/C	3	2	„	„
157/C	4	2	„	„
157/C	d	1	„	„
157/C	dd	2	„	„
157/C	123	2	20×25	„
157/C	12d	1	23,75×31,25	„
157/C	123dd	2	„	„
				años

Los números compuestos indican el condenido de las diferentes cajas, demostrando cuales de las cajas pequeñas están juntadas en ellas. Por ejemplo, caja 157/A 34 contiene las piedras de las cajas 157/A 3 y 157/A 4, y caja 157/C 12d las de las cajas 157/C 1, 157/C 2 y 157/C d.

Erbaut mit Kasten — Constructed with box
Construido con la caja
157/B 123

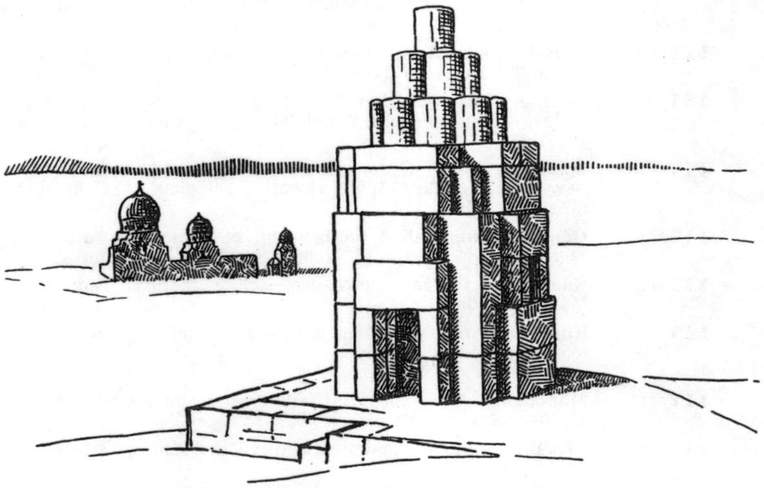

Erbaut mit Kasten — Constructed with box
Construido con la caja
157/B 12

Nr.	Mechanische Artikel mit Schweizer Musikspieldosen zum Drehen.	Mechanical toys for turning round, with Swiss musical box inside.	Artículos mecánicos con cajas de música suizas para girar.
Nr. **117**/2286	**Clowns**, musizierend, Auf-, Nieder- und Drehbewegung, Zelluloidköpfe. Musik 36 Töne.	**Musical Clowns**, Moving up, down, and round. Celluloid heads. 36 notes.	**Bufones** (clowns) haciendo música, movimiento de arriba abajo y de abajo arriba. Cabezas de celuloide. Música: 36 sonidos.
„ **117**/1088	**Harlekinpaar** mit Schellen, Arm- und Kopfbewegung, Porzellanköpfe. Musik 36 Töne.	**Couple of Harlequins**, with bells; motion of arms and heads. Porcelain heads. 36 notes.	**Un par de arlequinos** con cascabeles, movimiento de brazo y cabeza. Cabezas de porcelana. Música: 36 sonidos.
„ **117**/4675	**Plüschaffe** als Turko gekleidet, Drehorgel spielend. Musik 28 Töne.	**Monkey of plush**, dressed up as a Turk and playing a barrel organ. 28 notes.	**Mono de felpa** en uniforme de un "Turko" (soldado francés), girando un organo de mano. Música: 28 sonidos.
„ **117**/1322	**Karussell**, 4 Reiter auf Stoffpferden. Musik 28 Töne.	**Merry-go-round**, 4 riders on horses of cloth. 28 notes.	**Corrida de carruajes**, 4 jinetes sobre caballos de estofa. Música: 28 sonidos.
„ **117**/10142	**Tanzsalon** mit Spiegeleffekt. Musik 36 Töne.	**Dancing room**, with mirror effect. 36 notes.	**Salón de baile**, con efecto de espejo. Música: 36 sonidos.
„ **117**/2252	**2 Harlekinsknaben**, einer sitzend Cello spielend, einer stehend mit Violine, beide Kopf bewegend, hochfein gekleidet. Musik 28 Töne.	**2 Boy Harlequins**, one sitting and playing the cello; the other standing and playing the violin; elegantly dressed, both moving their heads. 28 notes.	**2 muchachos de arlequino**, uno de ellos sentado, y tocando el violón, el otro en pie derecho y tocando el violín. Música: 28 sonidos.
„ **117**/4677	**Frühlingstanz**, 3 Mädchen den Maibaum umtanzend. Musik 36 Töne.	**Spring Dance**; 3 girls dancing round the Maypole. 36 notes.	**Baile de primavera**, 3 muchachas danzan al rededor del abedal. Música: 36 sonidos.
„ **117**/9732	**Landschaft** mit beweglichen Figuren. Musik 36 Töne.	**Landscape** with moving figures. 36 notes.	**Paisaje** con figuras móviles. Música: 36 sonidos.
„ **117**/4695	**Windmühle** mit tanzender Schäferin. Musik 18 Töne.	**Windmill**, with dancing shepherdess. 18 notes.	**Molino de viento** con pastora danzando. Música: 18 sonidos.
„ **117**/4678	**Baby** mit Zelluloidkopf, fein in Kunstseide gekleidet, mit beweglichem Kopf, Armen und Beinen. Musik 18 Töne.	**Baby**, celluloid head, finely dressed in artificial silk, movable arms, legs and head. 18 notes.	**Bebe** (niño pequeño) con cabeza de celuloide, vestido finamente en seda artifical, con cabeza, brazos y piernas móviles. Música: 18 sonidos.
„ **117**/570	**Harlekin**, Porzellankopf, Kopf und Arme beweglich. Musik 18 Töne.	**Harlequin**, porcelain head, movable head and arms. 18 notes.	**Arlequino**, cabeza de porcelana, cabeza y brazos móviles. Música: 18 sonidos.
„ **117**/5250	**Knabe und Mädchen**, fein gekleidet, Zelluloidköpfe. Musik 28 Töne.	**Boy and girl**, well dressed, celluloid heads. 28 notes.	**Muchacho y muchacha**, vestidos finamente, cabezas de celuloide. Música: 28 sonidos.
„ **117**/575	**Tänzerin**, fein gekleidet, Zelluloidkopf. Musik 18 Töne.	**Dancer**, elegantly dressed, celluloid head. 18 notes.	**Bailadora**, vestida finamente, cabeza de celuloide, Música: 18 sonidos.
„ **117**/2280	**4 Kinder**, hübsch gekleidet, Ringelreihen tanzend, Porzellanköpfe. Musik 28 Töne.	**4 children**, nicely dressed, dancing in a circle, porcelain heads. 28 notes.	**4 niños**, vestidos finamente, danzando, cabezas de porcelana.
„ **117**/2244	**Hochfeine Kindergruppe**, 2 Kinder musizierend, 3 Kinder tanzend, Zelluloid- und Porzellanköpfe. Musik 36 Töne.	**Distinguished group of children**, 2 playing music, 3 dancing; celluloid or porcelain heads. 36 notes.	**Finísimo grupo de niños**, 2 niños haciendo música, 3 niños danzando, cabezas de celuloide y de porcelana.
„ **117**/1320	**Karussell** mit nach außen fliegenden Schaukeln. Musik 28 Töne.	**Merry-go-round**, with swings moving outwards. 28 notes.	**Corrida de carruajes**, con mecederos volando hacia fuera. Música: 28 sonidos.
„ **117**/2247	**Schafweide**, 1 Knabe Flöte spielend, 1 Mädchen tanzend, Porzellanköpfe, holländische Kostüme, 3 Schäfchen. Musik 28 Töne.	**Sheep pasture**, 1 youth playing the flute, 1 maiden dancing. Dutch costumes; porcelain heads; 3 little sheep. 28 notes.	**Pasto de ovejas**, 1 muchacho tocando la flauta, 1 muchacha danzando, cabezas de porcelana, trajes holandeses, 3 ovejas pequeñas. Música: 28 sonidos.
„ **117**/6075	**Feine Kindergruppe**, 1 Pärchen tanzend, 1 Knabe Ziehharmonika (Akkordion) spielend, Porzellanköpfe. Musik 36 Töne.	**Elegant group of children**, one couple dancing; 1 boy with accordion, porcelain heads. 36 notes.	**Fino grupo de niños**, 1 par danzando, 1 muchacho tocando el accordeón, cabezas de porcelana. Música: 36 sonidos.
„ **117**/2248	**Bauerntanz**, 3 Dirndel tanzend, 2 Knaben musizierend. Musik 36 Töne.	**Rustic dance**. 3 country girls dancing, 2 youths playing. 36 notes.	**Baile de campesinos**, 3 muchachas danzando, 2 muchachos haciendo música. Música: 36 sonidos.
„ **117**/3464	**Landschaft** mit beweglichen Figuren. Musik 28 Töne.	**Landscape** with moving figures. 28 notes.	**Paisaje** con figuras móviles. Música: 28 sonidos.
„ **117**/4694	do. „ 18 „	do. 18 notes.	do. „ 18 „
„ **117**/4664	do. „ 18 „	do. 18 notes.	do. „ 18 „
„ **117**/4690	do. fliegender Kuckuck mit Kuckuckstimme. Musik 18 Töne.	do. flying cuckoo uttering sound of cuckoo. 18 notes.	do., cúculo volante, con voz. „ 18 „

Nr.	Mechanische Artikel zum Fahren mit Schweizer Musikwerken.	Mechanical toys for moving about, with Swiss musical box inside.	Artículos mecánicos para acarrear con instrumentos de música suizos.
„ **117**/413	**3 Mädchen**, hochfein gekleidet, beweglich, Zelluloidköpfe. Musik 18 Töne.	**3 girls**, elegantly dressed, movable, celluloid heads. 18 notes.	**3 muchachas** vestidas finísimamente, móviles. Cabezas de celuloide. Música: 18 sonidos.
„ **117**/555	**Beckenschläger**, sitzend, Arme und Beine bewegend, Zelluloidkopf. Musik 18 Töne.	**Cymbal player**, seated, moving arms and legs. Celluloid head. 18 notes.	**Arlequino** sentado tocando los platillos, moviendo brazos y piernas. Cabeza de celuloide. Música 18 sonidos.
„ **117**/556	**Schellenbaumträger**, sitzend, beweglich, Zelluloidkopf. Musik 18 Töne.	**Figure** holding set of bells, seated, movable. Celluloid head. 18 notes.	**Portador** del ahoval, sentado móvil. Cabeza de celuloide. Música 18 sonidos.
„ **117**/30	**Wandervögel**, Mädchen und Junge, fein gekleidet, Laute spielend, Zelluloidköpfe. Musik 18 Töne.	**Wandering couple**, maiden and youth, elegantly dressed, playing the lute. Celluloid heads. 18 notes.	**Jovenes peregrinando**, la muchacha y el muchacho vestidos finamente tocan el laúd. Cabezas de celuloide. Música: 18 sonidos.
„ **117**/40	**Mädchen** mit 2 Kindern Pferdchen spielend, beweglich, Zelluloidköpfe. Hochfein gekleidet. Musik 18 Töne.	**Girl** playing horses with 2 children, movable. Celluloid heads. Very elegantly dressed. 18 notes.	**Muchacha** con 2 niños representando caballos, móviles. Cabezas de celuloide. Vestidos finísimos. Música: 18 sonidos.
„ **117**/28	**Gänsemädchen** mit 4 Stoffgänsen, beweglich, Zelluloidkopf. Musik 18 Töne.	**Goose girl**, with 4 geese made of material, movable. Celluloide. 18 notes.	**Pastora de ocas** con 4 ocas de estofa, móviles. Cabeza de celuloide. Música 18 sonidos.
„ **117**/436	**Knabe** mit Gänsen, beweglich, Zelluloidkopf. Musik 18 Töne.	**Boy with geese**, movable.. Celluloid head. 18 notes.	**Muchacho con ocas**, móviles. Cabeza de celuloide. Música: 18 sonidos.
„ **117**/34	**Knabe** mit Krimmerschäfchen, beweglich, Zelluloidkopf. Musik 18 Töne.	**Boy** with curly haired sheep, movable. Celluloid head. 18 notes.	**Muchacho** con pequeñas ovejas de lana de corderos de Crimea, móviles. Cabeza de celuloide. Música: 18 sonidos.
„ **117**/36	**Mädchen**, fein gekleidet, Zelluloidkopf, mit 2 Plüschkücken. Musik 18 Töne.	**Girl**, finely dressed, with 2 plush chickens. 18 notes.	**Muchacha**, vestida finamente, cabeza de celuloide, con 2 polluelos de felpa. Música 18 sonidos.
„ **117**/37	**2 Knaben** mit Zelluloidköpfen, beweglich. Musik 18 Töne.	**2 boys**, movable. Celluloid heads. 18 notes.	**2 muchachos** con cabezas de celuloide, móviles. Música: 18 sonidos.
„ **117**/428	**Clown** als Schellenschläger, 2 Knaben auf Scheibe sitzend, kreiselnd, Zelluloidkopf. Musik 18 Töne.	**Clown**, jingling bells; 2 boys on a disc that turns round. Celluloid head. 18 notes.	**Bufón** (clown) tocando el pandero, 2 muchachos sentados sobre un disco y juegando de la peonza. Cabeza de celuloide. Música: 18 sonidos.

Beschreibungen zu nebenstehenden Abbildungen. — Descriptions to the following pictures. — Descripciones para la representaciones sucesivo.

Fortsetzung Seite 168 d. — Continuation page 168 d. — Continuación página 168 d.

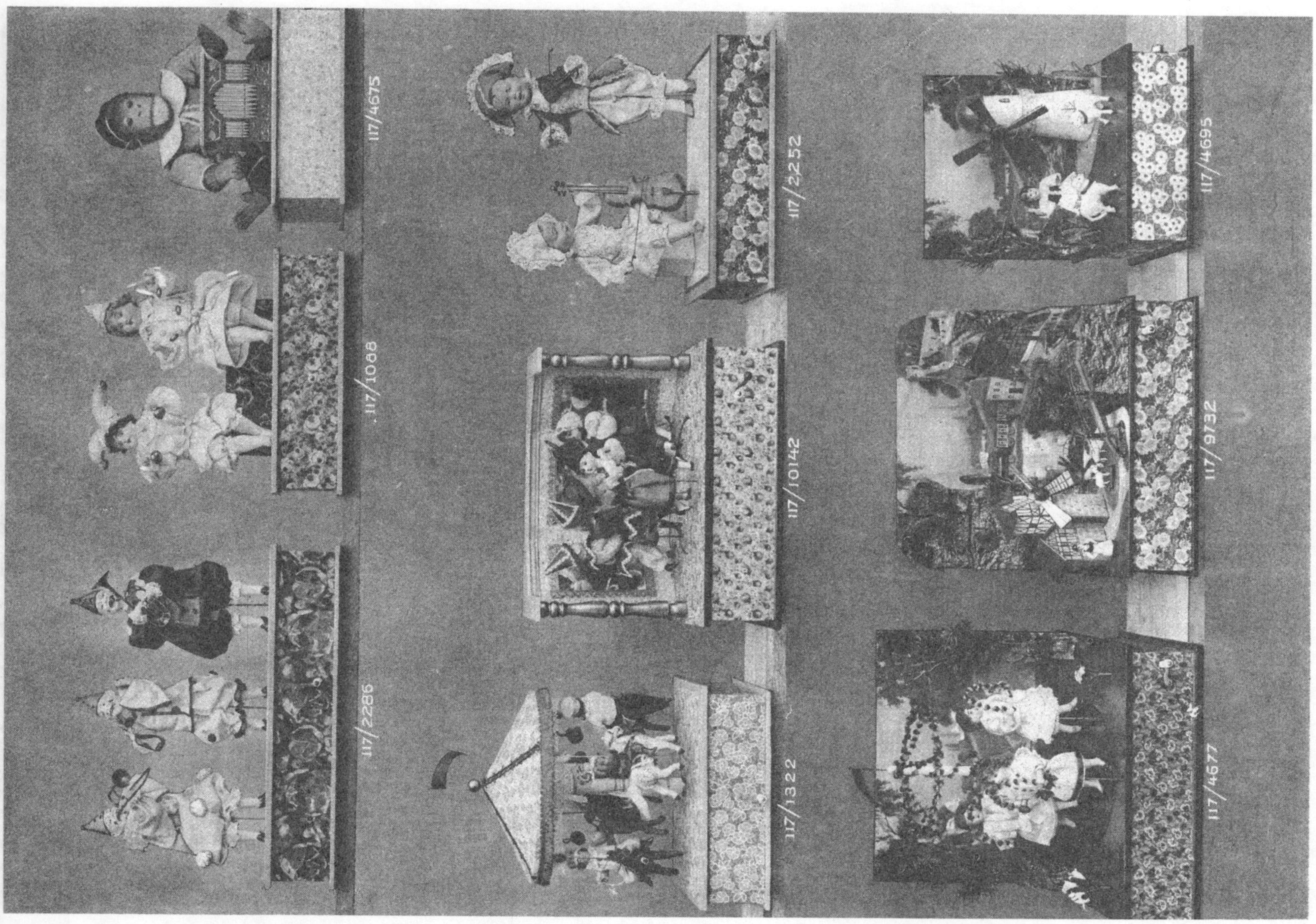
117/2286
.117/1068
117/4675
117/1322
117/10142
117/2252
117/4677
117/9732
117/4695

117/4678
117/570
117/5250
117/575
117/2280
117/2244
117/1320
117/2247
117/6075
117/2248

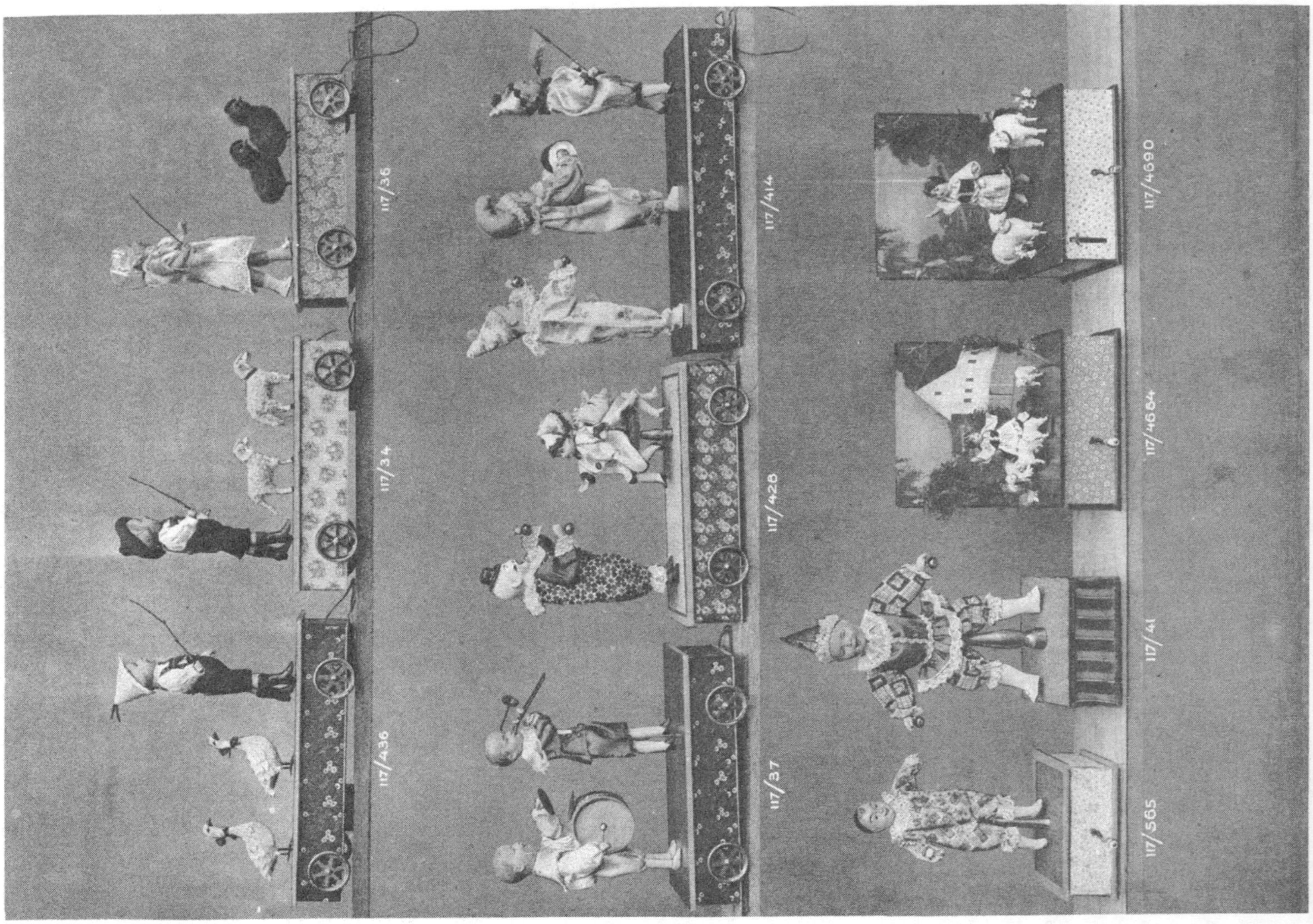
117/436
117/34
117/36
117/37
117/428
117/414
117/565
117/41
117/4684
117/4690

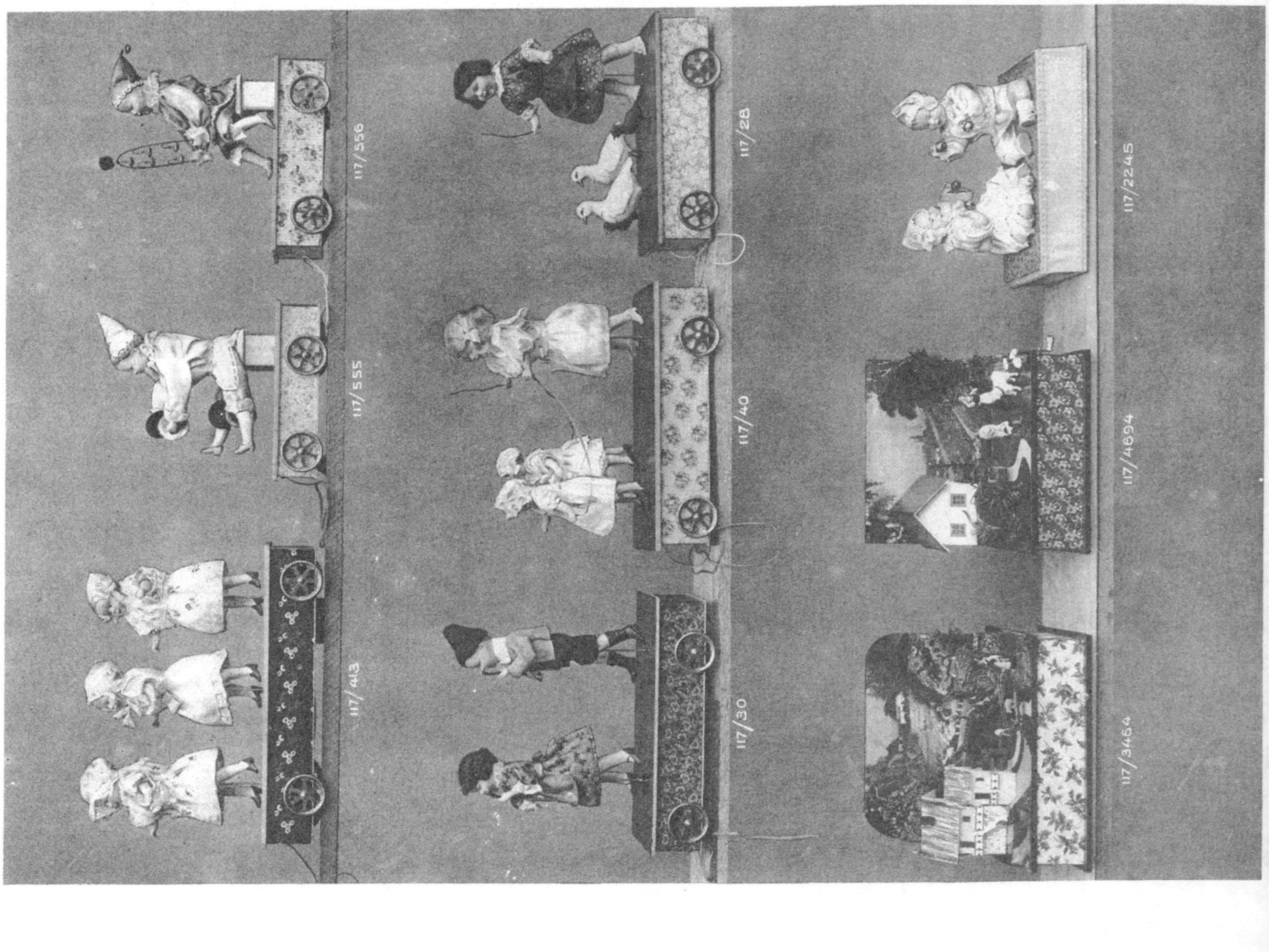
117/413
117/555
117/556
117/30
117/40
117/28
117/3464
117/4694
117/2245

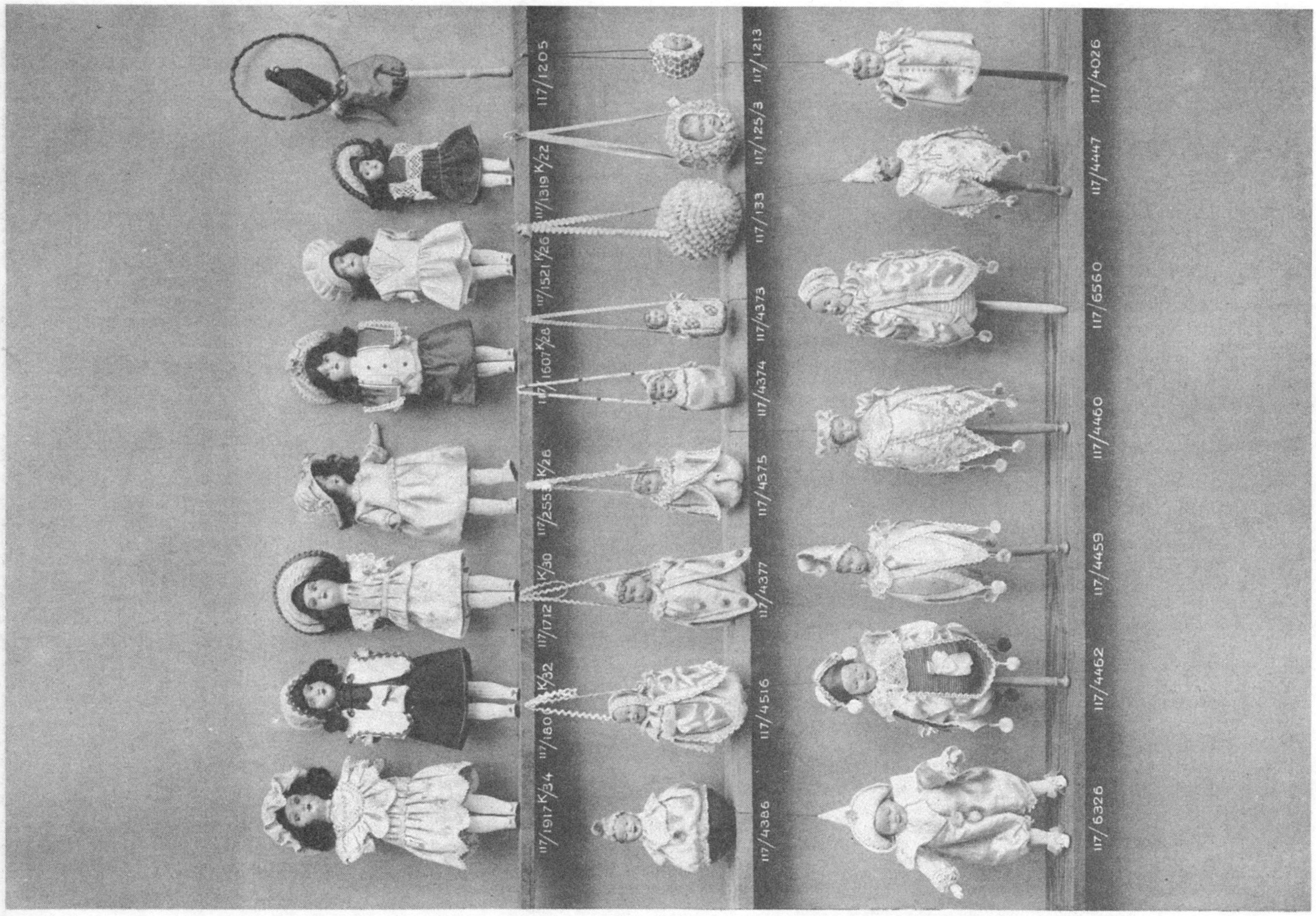
117/1917 K/34
117/180 K/32
117/1712 K/30
117/2553 K/26
117/1607 K/28
117/1521 K/26
117/1319 K/22
117/1205
117/4386
117/4516
117/4377
117/4375
117/4374
117/4373
117/133
117/125/3
117/1213
117/6326
117/4462
117/4459
117/4460
117/6560
117/4447
117/4026

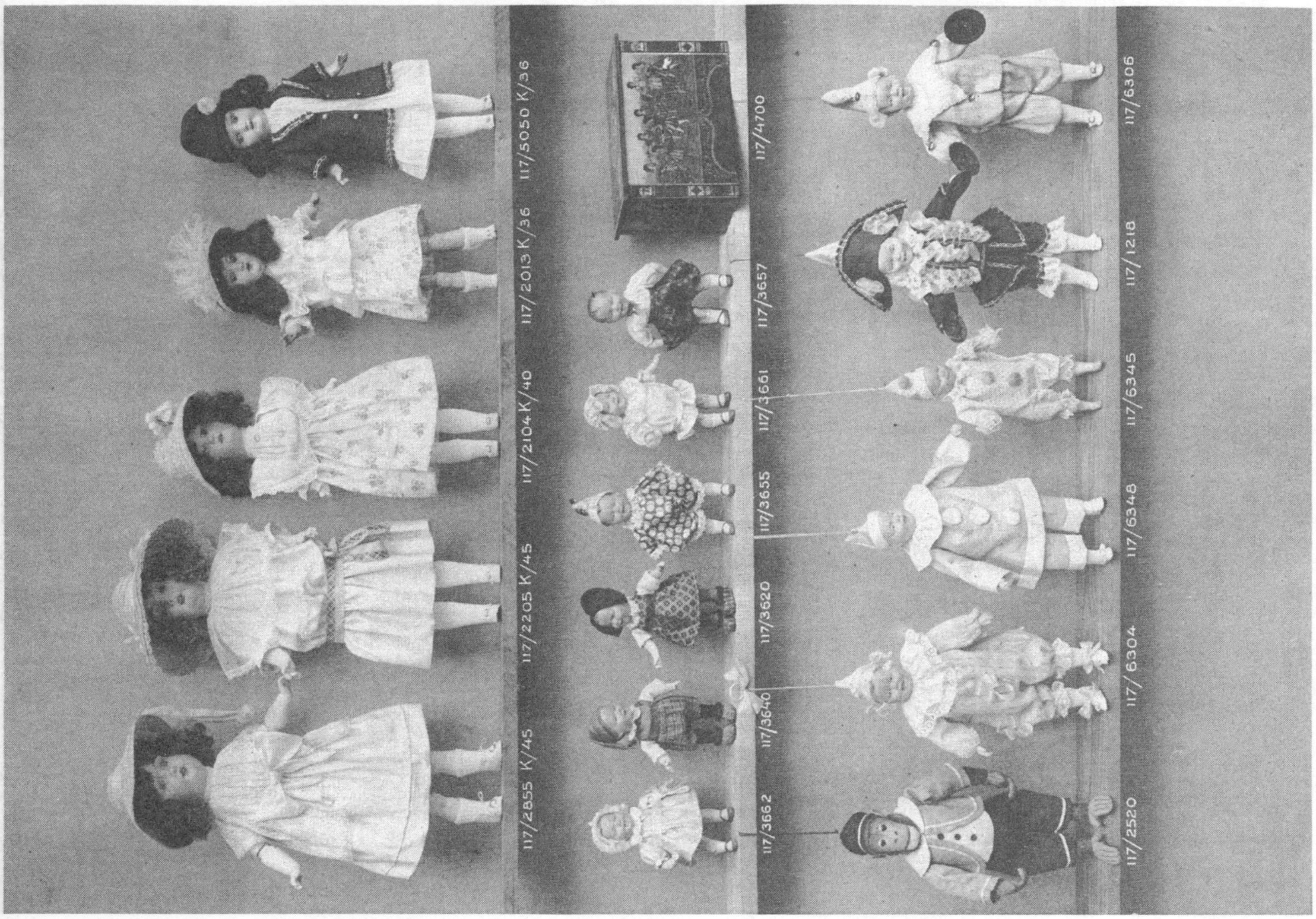
117/2855 K/45
117/2205 K/45
117/2104 K/40
117/2013 K/36
117/5050 K/36
117/3662
117/3640
117/3620
117/3655
117/3661
117/3657
117/4700
117/2520
117/6304
117/6348
117/6345
117/1218
117/6306

Nr.	Deutsch	English	Español
Nr. **117**/414	**3 Clowns** als Schellenschläger, Beckenschläger und Fahnenträger, Zelluloidköpfe, alles beweglich. Musik 18 Töne.	**3 Clowns** jingling bells, cymbal player and banner carrier. Celluloid heads. All movable. 18 notes.	**3 bufones** (clowns), uno de ellos tocando el pandero, el altro los platillos y el tercero representando un porta-estandarte. Cabezas de celuloide. Todos móvil. Música: 18 sonidos.
„ **117**/2245	**2 feingekleidete Babys,** mit Schellen, auf Postament sitzend, durch Niederdrücken beweglich, Zelluloidköpfe. Musik 18 Töne.	**2 elegantly dressed Babies,** with bells, seated on a pedestal; movable on being pressed. Celluloid heads. 18 notes.	**2 bebes** (niños pequeños), vestidos finamente, con cascabeles, sentados sobre un zócalo, los cuales se puede mover deprimiéndolos. Cabezas de celuloide. Música: 18 sonidos.
„ **117**/41	**Feingekleideter Clown** als Hampelmann und Schellenschläger, durch Niederdrücken beweglich, Zelluloidkopf. Musik 18 Töne.	**Well dressed Clown** as tomfool and cymbal player, movable on being pressed. Celluloid head. 18 notes.	**Bufón**(clown), vestido finamente y representando un Juan de las Viñas tocado el pandero, el cual sea puede mover deprimiéndole. Cabeza de celuloide. Música: 18 sonidos.
„ **117**/565	**Clown** tanzend, Zelluloidkopf, zum Drehen. Musik 18 Töne.	**Dancing Clown,** to turn round. Celluloid head. 18 notes.	**Bufón** (clown), danzando, cabeza de celuloide, para girar. Música 18 sonidos.
„ **117**/4700	**Kinderleierkasten,** fein mit bunten Bildern überzogen, lackiert. Musik 18 Töne.	**Child's barrel organ,** covered with elegant pictures, varnished. 18 notes.	**Organillo de cilindro,** revestido de finas pinturas de varios colores, embarnizado. Música: 18 sonidos.
„ **117**/4701	do. „ 28 „	do. 28 „	do. 28 „
„ **117**/4702	do. „ 28 „ 2 Arien.	do. 28 „ 2 tunes.	do. 28 „ 2 arias.
„ **117**/4703	do. „ 36 „ 3 „	do. 36 „ 3 „	do. 36 „ 3 „
„ **117**/6304	**Clown,** hochfein gekleidet, mit Musik, durch Drücken auf Brust oder Ziehen am Faden musizierend, Zelluloidkopf. Musik 18 Töne.	**Clown,** very elegantly dressed, musical on pressing on chest or on pulling string. Celluloid head. 18 notes.	**Bufón** (clown), vestido finísimamente y haciendo música, si se apreta su pecho tira un filo. Cabeza de celuloido. Música: 18 sonidos.
„ **117**/6306	**Beckenschläger,** fein gekleidet, Zelluloidkopf. Musik 18 Töne.	**Cymbal player,** finely dressed Celluloid head. 18 notes.	**Tocador de platillos,** vestido finamente. Cabeza de celuloide. Música: 18 sonidos.
„ **117**/1218	**Beckenschläger,** fein gekleidet, mit Harmonikastimme, Zelluloidkopf.	do. harmonica voice.	do. con tono de armónica.
„ **117**/6345	**Clown,** fein gekleidet, Zelluloidkopf, mit Glockentonstimme.	**Clown** well dressed. Celluloid head, with bell voice.	**Bufón** (clown), vestido finamente, cabeza de celuloide, con sonido de campana.
„ **117**/6348	**Pierrot,** fein gekleidet, Zelluloidkopf, mit Glockentonstimme.	**Pierrot,** finely got up. Celluloid head.	**Pierrot** (burlador), vestido finamente, cabeza de celuloide, con sonido de campana.
„ **117**/2520	**Plüschaffee,** gekleidet, mit Glockentonstimme.	**Ape** in plush very finely dressed, with bell voice.	**Mono de felpa,** vestido con sonido de campana.
„ **117**/3662	**Kinder,** hochfein gekleidet, Zelluloidköpfe, mit Stimme zum Niederdrücken (sehr drollig).	**Children,** very elegantly dressed. Celluloid head, with voice on pressing (very comical).	**Niños** vestidos finísimamente, cabezas de celuloide. Hablando, cuando ser deprimidos (muy chuscos).
„ **117**/3620	do.	do.	do.
„ **117**/3655	do.	do.	do.
„ **117**/3661	do.	do.	do.
„ **117**/3657	do.	do.	do.
„ **117**/1205	**Stoffpapagei** im Ring, mit Stimme am Griff.	**Parrot,** of material, in ring; with voice in the handle.	**Papagayo de estofa,** en un anillo, con voz al mango.
„ **117**/4386	**Stehauffigur** in Kunstseide gekleidet, Zelluloidkopf, Stimme.	**Figure,** standing up, dressed in artificial silk. Celluloid head. Voice.	**Dominguillo,** vestido en seda artificial, cabeza de celuloide, voz.
„ **117**/4385	„ kleiner, in Baumwolle gekleidet, Zelluloidkopf, Stimme.	do. „ in cotton.	do. vestido en algodón, más pequeño.
„ **117**/4516 „ **117**/4377 „ **117**/4375 „ **117**/4374 „ **117**/4373	**Baby-Hängefiguren,** fein gekleidet, Zelluloidköpfe, teils mit Glockenton, teils mit Stimme.	**Babies,** hanging figures, finely dressed, celluloid heads. Some with bell sound, some with voice	**Figuras de bebes** (niños pequeños) **para suspender,** vestidos finamente, cabezas de celuloide, algunas con sonido de campana y otras con voz.
„ **117**/133	**Wollball** mit Schweizer Musikwerk zum Drücken.	**Wool Ball,** with Swiss musical box, for pressing.	**Bola de lana** con instrumento de música suizo para comprimir.
„ **117**/124/2	do. „ Druckstimme.	do. with voice on pressing.	do. con voz para comprimir.
„ **117**/124/3	do. „ „	do.	do.
„ **117**/124/4	do. „ „	dd.	do.
„ **117**/125/3	**Babygehänge** mit Zelluloidmaske, Wollhäkelnetz und Stimme.	**Baby group of hanging figures,** with celluloid masks, with wool net and voice.	**Bebe** (niño pequeño) **para suspender,** con máscara de celuloide, red abrochada de lana y voz.
„ **117**/125/2	do.	do.	do.
„ **117**/125/1	do.	do.	do.
„ **117**/1213	**Babygehänge** mit Stoff überzogen, Zelluloidmaske und Stimme.	**Baby group of hanging figures,** covered with material. Celluloid masks and voice.	**Bebe** (niño pequeño) **para suspender,** revestido de estofa, con máscara de celuloide y voz.
„ **117**/6326	**Clown,** fein in Kunstseide gekleidet, mit Zelluloidkopf und Stimme.	**Clown,** finely got up in artificial silk, with celluloid head, and voice.	**Bufón** (clown), vestido finamente en seda artificial con cabeza de celuloide y voz.
„ **117**/4462	**Schwenkpuppe,** hochfein in Seide gekleidet, Zelluloidkopf. Schweizer Musikwerk 28 Töne, 2 Arien.	**Swinging Doll,** elegantly got up in silk. Celluloid head. Swiss musical box with 28 notes, 2 tunes.	**Muñeca para menear,** vestida finísimamente en seda, cabeza de celuloide. Instrumento de música suizo 28 sonidos, 2 arias.
„ **117**/4460	do. in Atlas, „ 28 „ 1 Arie.	do. in satin, 28 notes, 1 tune.	do. en raso, 28 sonidos, 1 aria.
„ **117**/4459	do. „ Kunstseide, „ 28 „ 1 „	do. in artificial silk, 28 notes, 1 tune.	do. en seda artificial, 28 sonidos, 1 aria.
„ **117**/4447	do. hübsch gekleidet, „ 18 „	do. elegantly dressed, 18 notes.	do. vestida de manera bonita, 18 sonidos.
„ **117**/4425	do. „ „ 12 „	do. 12 notes.	do. 12 sonidos.
„ **117**/6560	**Schwenkpuppe,** hochfein in Kunstseide gekleidet, Zelluloidkopf, mit Glockentonstimme.	**Swinging Doll,** elegantly dressed, in artificial silk, with bell voice. Celluloid head.	**Muñeca para menear,** vestida finísimamente en seda artificial, cabeza de celuloide, con voz de campana.
„ **117**/6559	do. Wie Nr. 2560 jedoch kleiner, in einfacherer Ausführung, mit Glockentonstimme.	Same as 6560, but smaller, in simpler style, with bell voice.	Tal que Nr. 6560, pero más pequeña y ejecución más sencilla, con voz de campana.
„ **117**/6561	do.	do.	do.
„ **117**/4026 „ **117**/4028 „ **117**/4029	**Griffpuppen** mit Zelluloidkopf, hübsch gekleidet, mit Pfeif- und Harmonikastimme.	**Dolls on handles,** celluloid head, nicely dressed, with whistle and concertina voice.	Muñecas de grifo vestidas de manera bonita con cabeza de celuloide, con voz para silbar y voz de armónica.

Puppen.	Dolls.	Muñecas.
Gekleidete Steifgelenkpuppen von 20 bis 50 cm in mittlerem und besserem Genre.	**Dressed Dolls** with rigid limbs, from 20—50 cm, medium and better styles.	**Muñecas** vestidas con coyunturas anquilosadas, de 20 hasta 50 cm, ejecución mediana y mejor.
Gekleidete Doppelgelenkpuppen von 22 bis 60 cm in mittlerem und besserem Genre.	do. double limbs, from 22—60 cm	do. con coyunturas dobles, de 22 hasta 60 cm.

Spiele. — Games. — Juegos.

99/6103

Nr. **99**/6103	Kasperltheater Punch and Judy Teatro de polichinela	30,7×22,7×2,2 cm
„ **99**/6104	Kasperltheater Punch and Judy Teatro de polichinela	31×22,5×3 „
„ **99**/XI	Pyramiden-Kubus. Pyramide-blocks. Pirámides cúbicas.	

Nr. **99**/7231

Glocke und Hammer Bell and hammer Campana y martillo	28×21×2,4 cm

Nr. **99**/7235	34×25 ×2,7 cm
„ **99**/7237	32×23,5×4,3 „
„ **99**/7238	33×24 ×6 „

99/XI

99/7231

Nr. **99**/4534 „ **99**/5354 „ **99**/5273	ABC-Spiel ABC game Juego de ABC	18,5×18,5×2,5 cm 24 ×24 ×3,5 „ 3 ×24 ×3,2 „
Nr. **99**/302 „ **99**/7241 „ **99**/7245 „ **99**/7247	Gänsespiel Game of geese Juego nuevo de gansos	25 ×18 ×2 cm 30,5×21,3×2,3 „ 38 ×26 ×3,2 „ 34,5×24,5×3,5 „
Nr. **99**/326 „ **99**/4608 „ **99**/5035 „ **99**/4561 „ **99**/5453	Flechten Paper plaiting Trenzar	25 ×18 ×2 cm 30 ×18,5×2,5 „ 34 ×23,4×2,5 „ 37,8×23,5×3,8 „ 42,2×28,5×3,5 „
Nr. **99**/381 „ **99**/6096 „ **99**/6098 „ **99**/6096/1 „ **99**/6097 „ **99**/6136	Schnipp-Schnapp! Snap! ¡Zis-Zas!	25 ×18 ×2 cm 27,9×20,7×2,3 „ 33,5×25,2×2,7 „ 11,4× 8,7×2,7 „ 12 × 9,5×4,5 „ 35 ×24,5×3,4 „

99/4534

99/7241

99/4608

99/6096

Nr. **99**/317 „ **99**/7221 „ **99**/7225 „ **99**/7227 „ **99**/7229	Das lustige Einmaleins. Comic multiplication. Tabla de multiplicación muy chistosa.	24,5×19 ×2 cm 27,5×20,5×2,2 „ 33,4×25 ×2,8 „ 32,4×23,6×3,9 „ 35,9×29,8×3,5 „

99/7221

Spiele. — Games. — Juegos.

99/7711

99/4552

99/4532

99/6114

99/6108

Nr.		
Nr. **99**/7711	Der Briefträger	30,5×21,3×2,3
„ **99**/7715	The postman	37,7×26,0×3,2
„ **99**/7717	El cartero	38,4×27,0×3,7
Nr. **99**/316		25 ×18 ×2,0
„ **99**/6540	Schwarzer Peter	27,8×20,7×2,4
„ **99**/6541	Black Peter	33,5×25,2×2,6
„ **99**/6542	Juego de Florentini ó el mozo dupado	11 × 7,2×2,5
„ **99**/6543		11,7× 8,1×2,7
Nr. **99**/3422		27,8×20,7×2,2
„ **99**/4552	Korbflechten	27,8×20,7×2,2
„ **99**/5451	Basket plaiting	33,9×23,5×2,5
„ **99**/5034	Hacer cestas	33,9×23,5×2,5
„ **99**/4560		37,6×23,5×3,6
„ **99**/5453		41,0×26,1×3,9
Nr. **99**/7361	Der kleine Silhouettenschneider	28 ×21 ×2,4
	The little Silhouette artist	
„ **99**/7365	El artista de siluetas	33,9×23,5×2,5
Nr. **99**/4532		30 ×18,5×2,5
„ **99**/5030		34 ×23,4×2,5
„ **99**/5023	Zeichenkunst	37,8×23,5×3,8
„ **99**/5192	Drawing Teacher	37,8×23,5×3,8
„ **99**/5190	Arte del dibujo	42,2×28,5×3,5
„ **99**/5028		41,0×26,3×3,5
„ **99**/5054		43,2×33,7×3,6
Nr. **99**/7821	Der kleine Architekt	27,5×20,9×2,4
„ **99**/7825	The young architect	33,0×25,3×2,8
„ **99**/7827	El pequeño arquitecto	34 ×25 ×4,3
Nr. **99**/325		19,7×19,7×2,0
„ **99**/6114	Kugelmosaik	27,3×21,0×2,5
„ **99**/6115	Ball mosaic game	30,0×23,2×3,0
„ **99**/5552	Mosáico de bolitas	39,8×27,2×3,0
„ **99**/5544		26,2×18,3×2,3
„ **99**/5559		30,0×23,2×3,0

Der kleine Zauberer. — The little conyurer — Cajas con hechizos.

Nr.		
Nr. **99**/11	5 teilig, pieces, partes	28,8×16,7×2,4
„ **99**/12	8 „ „ „	24,8×19,0×4,0
„ **99**/13	12 „ „ „	30,9×21,0×4,3
„ **99**/14	15 „ „ „	34,3×25,5×5,0
„ **99**/15	18 „ „ „	42,0×24,5×5,0
„ **99**/16	20 „ „ „	42,7×29,2×5,3
„ **99**/17	24 „ „ „	47,6×33,4×5,3

Nr.		
Nr. **99**/6108	Die Reise durch die Schweiz	30,5×21,3×2,3
„ **99**/6109	A journey through Switzerland	37,7×26 ×3,2
„ **99**/6110	El viaje á través de la Suiza	38,4×27 ×3,7
Nr. **99**/6116	Ankleidepuppen	28 ×20,7×2,2
„ **99**/6117	Dressing dolls	33,5×25,3×2,7
„ **99**/6118	Muñecas nuevas para vestir	34,5×24,6×3,8

99/6540

99/7361

99/7821

99/16

99/6116

99/7791

99/5933

Spiele	Games	Juguetes
in allen Sprachen.	in all languages.	en todas linguas.

Nr.	Spiel / Game / Juego	Größe / Size / Tamaño
Nr. **99**/7791	Schwupp di wupp Clown hop-la El salto del sombrero	28 × 21 × 2,4 cm
„ **99**/7795		33,8 × 25,7 × 2,8 „
Nr. **99**/5932	Fußballspiel Football game Juego de football	28 × 21 × 2,4 cm
„ **99**/5933		32,7 × 24 × 3,2 „
„ **99**/5910		do., bessere Ausführung. do., better execution. do., ejecución muy fino.
Nr. **99**/329	Eile mit Weile Ellsu Ludo	25 × 18 × 2 cm
„ **99**/4870		30,5 × 21,2 × 2,3 „
„ **99**/4942		37,7 × 26 × 3,2 „
„ **99**/4068		37 × 19,2 × 2,9 „
Nr. **99**/311	Neues Fußballspiel New Football game Nuevo juego de football	25 × 18 × 2 cm
„ **99**/7741		30,5 × 21,3 × 2,3 „
„ **99**/7745		37,7 × 26,0 × 3,2 „
„ **99**/7747		38,4 × 27,0 × 3,7 „
Nr. **99**/6248	Angelspiel, magnetisches Aquarium	26,6 × 20 × 2,4 cm
„ **99**/6249	Fish pond, magnetic fishing	32,4 × 27,5 × 2,5 „
„ **99**/6250	Aquario	35,3 × 31 × 2,6 „
Nr. **99**/6831	Im Walde In the forest En la selva	30,5 × 21,3 × 2,3 cm
„ **99**/6835		37,7 × 26 × 3,2 „
„ **99**/6837		38,4 × 27 × 3,7 „
Nr. **99**/7781	Ringwerfen Throwing the ring Juego de las anillas	28 × 20,9 × 2,3 cm
„ **99**/7785		33,7 × 25 × 2,5 „
Nr. **99**/4414	Der springende Frosch The jumping frog Saltos de las ranas	30,5 × 21,3 × 2,3 cm
„ **99**/4273		37,7 × 26 × 3,2 „
„ **99**/4239		37 × 19,2 × 2,9 „
Nr. **99**/304	Das lustige Leiterspiel Merry ladder game El juego alegre de la escalera	25 × 18 × 2 cm
„ **99**/5922		30,5 × 21,3 × 2,3 „
„ **99**/5923		37,7 × 26 × 3,2 „
„ **99**/5924		38,4 × 27 × 3,7 „
Nr. **99**/313	Bilderlotto Picture lotto Nueva lotería de cuadros	25 × 18 × 2 cm
„ **99**/7601		28 × 21 × 2,4 „
„ **99**/7605		33,7 × 25 × 2,8 „
„ **99**/7607		35,2 × 25,3 × 4 „
„ **99**/7191		28 × 21 × 2,4 „
„ **99**/7195		33,7 × 25 × 2,8 „
„ **99**/7197		35,2 × 25,3 × 4 „
„ **99**/7198		36,7 × 26,6 × 3 „
„ **99**/5132		37,2 × 29,2 × 3,5 „
„ **99**/6337		42,7 × 28,2 × 3,4 „

99/4870

99/7741

99/6831

99/6248

99/7781

99/4414

99/7191

99/5922

Bilderbücher	**English juvenile books**	**Libros de estampas**
in allen Sprachen	in all languages	en todas las hablas
auch ohne Text	also without text	también sin texto

Deutsche Bilderbücher in allen Preislagen, ca. 200 Sorten. Französische Bilderbücher ca. 80 Sorten. Ohne Schrift, für alle Länder, ca. 30 Sorten.

	Serie	Größe	Beschreibung	Inhalt	Gewicht
Papierbücher:	Nr. **100**/1948c	16 ×12½ cm	kindlich	7 bunte und 6 schwarze Bilder	30 g
	„ **100**/1071c	19½×17 „	kindlich	9 bunte Bilder	38 „
	„ **100**/1515	25½×19½ „	Tiere	8 „ „	100 „
	„ **100**/1883	25½×19½ „	Verwandlungsbücher	15 „ „	85 „
	„ **100**/2213	33 ×24½ „	Anschauungsbilder	31 „ „	270 „
Pappenbücher, ca. 25 Sorten:	„ **100**/1400	12 × 8½ „	kindlich	7 „ „	40 „
	„ **100**/2519	17 ×14 „	Tiere	9 „ „	125 „
	„ **100**/2184	24½×17 „	Tiere	9 „ „	150 „
	„ **100**/3520	22½×16 „	Tiere	9 „ „	190 „
	„ **100**/3401	26 ×19 „	Tiere	11 „ „	280 „
	„ **100**/3892	32 ×23½ „	Anschauungsbilder	11 „ „	400 „
Panoramabücher, (Leporello) ca. 15 Sorten:	„ **100**/2253	16½×12 „	Tiere und kindlich	15 „ „	100 „
	„ **100**/4556	19½×16 „	kindlich	9 „ „	115 „
	„ **100**/3594	22½×20 „	Tiere	11 „ „	220 „
	„ **100**/2969	19½×16½ „	kindlich	20 „ „	280 „
	„ **100**/4346	22 ×16¾ „	Anschauungsbilder	24 „ „	380 „
Malbücher, ca. 50 Sorten:	„ **100**/2063	16 ×11 „	Gegenstände	6 bunte und 6 schwarze Bilder	10 „
	„ **100**/2577	16 ×13½ „	kindlich	5 „ „ 4 „ „	38 „
	„ **100**/2579	21 ×15½ „	einfache Malbilder	7 „ „ 8 „ „	60 „
	„ **100**/6581	24½×18 „	Tiere	5 „ „ 4 „ „	90 „
	„ **100**/1129	29 ×23 „	Bauernhof (zum Malen, Ausschneiden und Aufstellen)	5 „ „ 5 „ „	170 „

Series		Size	Description	Contents	Weight
Nr. **100**/100	assorted in 4 sorts	18½×22 cm	Fairy Tales, Animals and Children's Scenes	2 col. pictures, 6 black pictures, varnished cover	20 g
„ **100**/200	assorted in 4 sorts	30 ×20 „	„ „ „ „ „ „	2 „ „ 6 „ „ „ „	60 „
„ **100**/300	assorted in 4 sorts	33 ×24 „	„ „ „ „ „ „	2 „ „ 6 „ „ „ „	80 „
„ **100**/2719	assorted in 4 sorts	27 ×20½ „	Animals and Children's Scenes	4 „ „ 4 „ „ double cover varnish.	55 „
„ **100**/2246	assorted in 3 sorts	29 ×20 „	„ „ „ „	5 „ „ 5 „ „ „ „ „	70 „
„ **100**/823c		29 ×22 „	Robinson	5 „ „ 7 „ „	95 „
„ **100**/1775		29 ×22 „	Animals	5 „ „ 7 „ „	95 „
„ **100**/2195		29 ×22 „	Happy Yinks	5 „ „ 7 „ „	95 „
„ **100**/1707		32 ×23½ „	Fairy Tales	12 full colour pictures, 2 black pictures	250 „
„ **100**/2205		32 ×23½ „	Playtime	12 „ „ „ 2 „ „	250 „
„ **100**/740		23 ×18 „	Moving Picture Book, assorted		170 „
„ **100**/1127		29 ×23½ „	3 books for cutting out and painting		170 „
„ **100**/1128		29 ×23½ „	3 „ „ „ „ „ „		170 „
„ **100**/1129		29 ×23½ „	3 „ „ „ „ „ „		170 „

Bilderbücher

in allen Sprachen
auch ohne Text

English juvenile books

in all languages
also without text

Libros de estampas

en todas las hablas
también sin texto

Serie	Título	Tamaño	Contenido	Descripción	Peso
No. **100**/909	Silabario de historia natural	$11^1/_2$×18 cm	18 páginas con colores y con un solo color	libro muy instructivo para los niños	30 g
„ **100**/1711	Dulce y amargo	17 ×25 „	10 páginas con colores y con un solo color	imagines infantiles	55 „
„ **100**/1361	A. B. C. del nene	22 ×28 „	14 páginas con colores y con un solo color	imagines infantiles	100 „
„ **100**/1458	Animales domésticos	19 ×25 „	7 imagenes dobles de animales en colores	imagines infantiles	100 „
„ **100**/1565/6	Animales domésticos	24 ×33 „	8 páginas de colores	imagines de animales, muy bien hechas	120 „
„ **100**/1707	Arca de Noé	24 ×33 „	12 páginas de colores		150 „
„ **100**/1287	El alfabeto del campo	22 ×28 „	26 páginas con colores y con un solo color	libro finamente adornado	210 „
„ **100**/1341	El alfabeto del campo	22 ×28 „	26 páginas con colores y con un solo color	libro finamente adornado	210 „
„ **100**/1343/43	Gran colacción de fieras	24 ×34 „	24 páginas de colores	todo el libro es en colores y con cubierta de cartón	300 „

Libros con movimiento:

Serie	Título	Tamaño	Contenido	Descripción	Peso
No. **100**/2569	De viage	18 ×23 cm	4 imagenes con movimiento	rico texto de colores	120 g
„ **100**/1812	La favorita de la abuela	19 ×26 „	4 imagenes con movimiento	rico texto de colores	140 „
„ **100**/903	¡Adelante caballeros!	19 ×26 „	4 imagenes con movimiento	con cubierta de cartón duro	170 „
„ **100**/1883	El libro de las transformaciones	19 ×$25^1/_2$ „	16 páginas de colores, pudiendo hacerse muchas imagenes diferentes	libro de transformación muy divertido	85 „

Außerdem können Bilderbücher in allen Sprachen in jeder beliebigen Preislage geliefert werden. — Besides, picture books can be delivered in all languages at any prices.
Además libros de estampas pueden ser mandados en todas las hablas y á todos los precios.

Fröbel-Modelierspiele,
Unterhaltungs- und Gesellschaftsspiele.

Froebel modelling games,
round games, and parlour games.

Juegos para modelar de Froebel,
juegos de entretenimiento y de compañía,

Nr. **66**/2b Froebel modelling game, containing about 300 g modelling material in 8 colours, 4 copies, 1 modelling stick, 1 slate with small model, 1 game of spilikins.

„ **66**/3b Froebel modelling game, containing about 400 g modelling material in 6 colours, 4 copies, 1 frontis-piece, 1 modelling stick, 1 slate with small model.

Every box contains a complete set, see Nr. **66**/2b; about 40 varios sizes and styles.

In case of need please apply for special catalogue, stating the Nr. **66**.

66/2b

No. **66**/2b Juego para modelar de Froebel conteniendo cerca de 300 g de la masa para modelar en 8 colores, 4 muestras, 1 palo para modelar, 1 hoja de pizarra con un modelo pequeño, 1 juego de palitos.

„ **66**/3b Juego para modelar de Froebel, conteniendo cerca de 400 g de la masa para modelar en 6 colores, 4 muestras, 1 pintura de título, 1 palo para modelar, 1 hoja de pizarra con un modelo pequeño.

Cada caja contiene una guarnición completa, véase No. **66**/2b, cerca de 40 diferentes tamaños y ejecuciones.

Cuando Vd. tiene necesidad de estos artículos, sirvase demandar el catálogo especial indicando el No. **66**.

Nr. **66**/2b Fröbel-Modelierspiel, enthaltend ca. 300 g Modeliermasse in 8 Farben, 4 Vorlagen, 1 Modelierholz, 1 Schiefertafel mit kleinem Modell, 1 Stäbchenspiel.

„ **66**/3b Fröbel-Modelierspiel, enthaltend ca. 400 g Modelliermasse in 6 Farben, 4 Vorlagen, 1 Titelbild, 1 Modellierholz, 1 Schiefertafel mit kleinem Modell.

Jeder Kasten enthält eine komplette Garnitur, siehe Nr. **66**/2b; ca. 40 verschiedene Größen und Ausführungen.

Bei Bedarf verlange man Spezialkatalog unter Angabe der Nr. **66**.

Puppenschulen. — Doll schools. — Escuelas para muñecas.

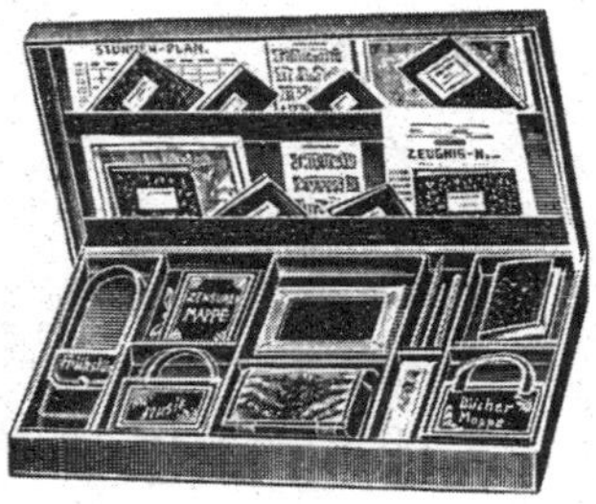

81/1070/5

81/1070/3

Inhalt: Sämtliche Schulbedarfsartikel.
Contents: All articles for school requirements.
Contenido: Todos los artículos para la escuela.

	Nr. **81**/1070/3	5	7	9
Größe der Kartons / Size of boxes / Tamaño de las cajitas	16×26	21×38	32×46	38×56 cm

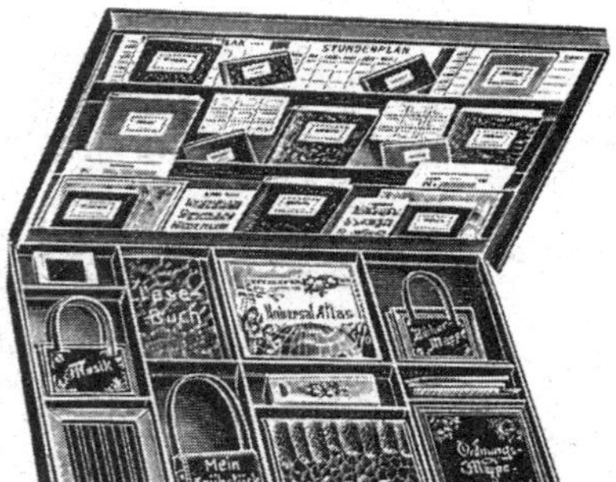

81/1070/7

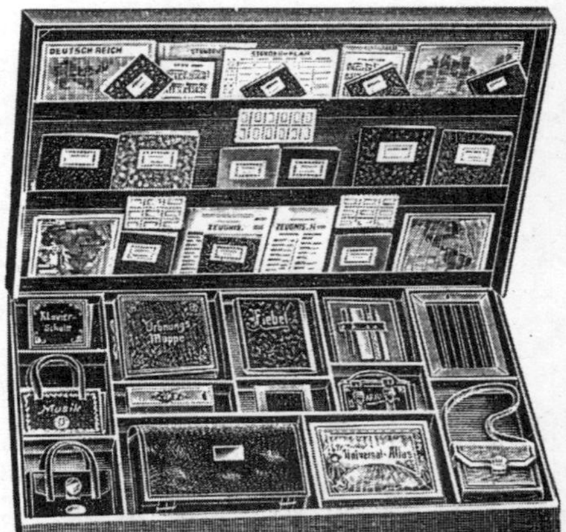

81/1070/9

Kinderdruckereien. — Printing outfits for children. — Imprentas para niños.

38/100

38/117

38/120

Nr. **38**/100 **Famos-Druckerei** mit Zubehör und 86 Gummilettern. — **Famos printing outfit,** contains 86 rubber types, typeholder, etc. — **Imprenta famos,** contiene 86 letras de goma, componedor.

Nr. **38**/117 **Famos-Druckerei** mit 140 Gummilettern, große und kleine Buchstaben, und Zubehör. — **Famos printing outfit,** contains 140 rubber types, small and capital letters, typeholders, etc. — **Imprenta famos,** contiene 140 letras de goma, minúsculas y mayúsculas, componedor, etc.

Nr. **38**/120 **Famos-Druckerei** mit 226 Gummilettern, mit Ovalstempel und Verzierungsstempel. — **Famos printing outfit** with 226 rubber types, oval typeholder for oval sets, typeholder with ornaments, etc. — **Imprenta famos,** contiene 226 letras de goma, componedores ovales y adornados, etc.

Nr. **38**/121 **Famos-Druckerei** mit 360 Gummilettern, verschiedenen Verzierungsstempeln und reichhaltigem Zubehör.
Famos printing outfit contains 360 rubber types, several typeholders, etc.
Imprenta famos ampliamente surtido, contiene 360 letras de goma, diferentes componedores.

Bilderstempelspiele, Sortimentkasten, enthaltend eine Anzahl Stempel mit Figuren, so daß man Bilder herstellen kann. Aus der großen Auswahl ist hervorzuheben:

Stempelspiel	Nr. **38**/40	Haustiere
„	„ **38**/41	„
„	„ **38**/42	Waldtiere
„	„ **38**/43	Wilde Tiere
„	„ **38**/44	„ „
„	„ **38**/60	Zirkus Bumbum
„	„ **38**/255	Fußballsport

Stamping toys. These boxes contain a certain number of stamps with figures, so that on can produce pictures as shown by the annexed diminished electro. Particular attention is called to the following numbers of the rich assortment:

Stamping toy	Nr. **38**/40	Domestic animals
„ „	„ **38**/41	„ „
„ „	„ **38**/42	Animals of the forest
„ „	„ **38**/43	Wild animals
„ „	„ **38**/44	„ „
„ „	„ **38**/60	Circus Bumbum
„ „	„ **38**/255	Football

Juegos de sellos con cuadros. Estas cajas contienen algunas sellos con imagenes, con las quales se pueden hacer cuadros como demuestra el cliché reducido. Del grand assortimente se recomiendan:

Juego de sello	No. **38**/40	Animales domésticos
„ „ „	„ **38**/41	„ „
„ „ „	„ **38**/42	„ de los bosques
„ „ „	„ **38**/43	„ ferocez
„ „ „	„ **38**/44	„ „
„ „ „	„ **38**/60	Arena Bumbum
„ „ „	„ **38**/255	Football

Nr. **38**/903 **Spielwaren-Neuheit: Der kleine Kaufmann.** In elegantem Karton, 31×38 cm groß, mit Scheckheften, Druckmaterial, Kontobüchern, Postwertzeichen usw.
Latest Novelty: The little Merchant. An elegant box of 31×38 cm, contains cheque book, stamping material, account books, postage stamps, etc.
¡Nuevo! El pequeño comerciante. Tomaño de la elejante caja 31×38 cm, contiene: cheques, libros para el pequeño tenedor de libros, marcas de correo, etc.

„ **38**/904 Wie oben, einfachere Ausführung.
Same as before, however simplier executed.
Idem, ejecución mas sencilla.

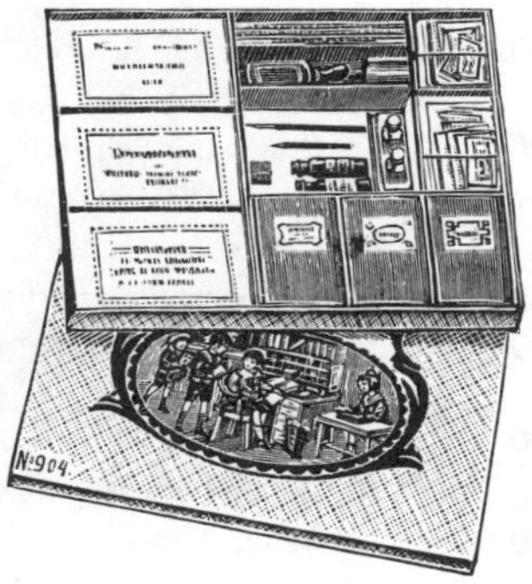

38/903

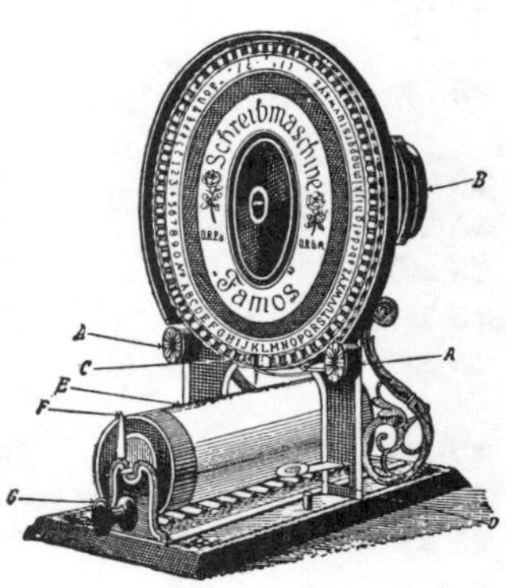

38/905

Der kleine Armbrustschütze. Ein ebenso originelles wie neuartiges Spiel in Verbindung mit einer Armbrustpistole und einer mechanischen Schießfront.
The little crossbow-shooter. Quite a new game consisting of a crossbow pistol and a mechanical target.
El pequeño Ballestero. Un juego tanto original como nuevo con una pistola de ballesta y un terrero mecánico.

Nr. **38**/905 **Kinderschreibmaschine „Famos"** schreibt große und kleine Buchstaben und liefert bei richtiger Handhabung eine Schrift gleich dieser Vorlage: `Kinderschreibmaschine »Famos«.`
Typewriter "Famos" for children writes small and capital letters and gives, when properly managed, characters like specimen hereafter.
Máquina de escribir para niños „Famos". Escribe letras mayúsculas y minúsculas y produce con correcto manejo en escrito como este modelo.

38/932

Nr. **38**/932

Hervorragende Spielwaren-Neuheit! Geniatus-Bauspiele. Dieses neue Bauspiel enthält Holzstäbchen in verschiedenen Längen und aus farbigem oder Weißblech gestanzte, verschiedenartig gebogene Verbinder. Mit diesen einfachen Hilfsmitteln ist das Kind imstande, Puppenmöbel, Häuser, Türme, Karussells und unzählige andere Gegenstände herzustellen. Dabei ist ein so hergestellter Gegenstand nicht nur für das Auge, sondern kann auch benutzt werden, besonders als Spielzeug für die Puppenstube. Jedes Spiel enthält eine Anzahl Vorlagen, es können deshalb mit diesem Spiel nicht nur diese Gegenstände, sondern noch viele andere hergestellt werden. Die Geniatus-Spiele werden sicher den Beifall jedes Kinderfreundes finden, weil hier ein Beschäftigungsspiel geboten wird, welches das Kind nicht nur unterhält, sondern auch zum Denken anregt und ihm eine dauernde Freude an dem selbstgeschaffenen Gegenstand schenkt. Durch großzügige maschinelle Einrichtung wird das Spiel so wohlfeil hergestellt, daß es trotz seiner Vorzüge zu den billigsten Spielen gehört, die auf dem Markte sind.

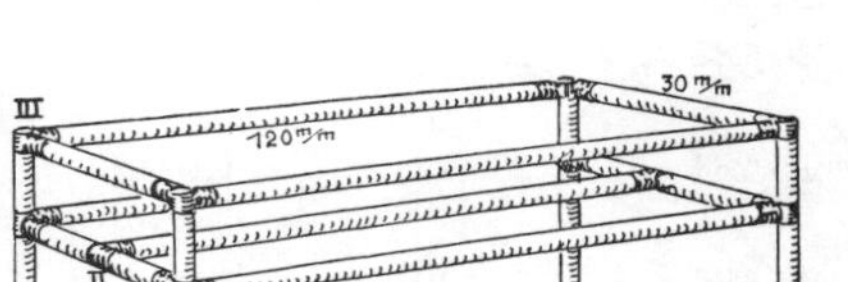

38/11

Construction game "Geniatus". This new game consists of wooden sticks of various lengths and different shaped metal joints. With these simple means the child is able to construct: furniture for dolls, houses, swings, turrets and innumerable other articles. Such an article is not only to be looked at, but it can also be used especially as a toy for the baby house. Each box contains a page of models; not only these but also many others can be constructed with such a box. The construction game "Geniatus" will certainly find the approval of every friend of children, because there is offered a game that does not only undertain the child, but is compels also to think. Although this game offers many advantages it belongs to one of the cheapest games.

"Geniatus" — Juguete de construcción. ¡La ultima novedad! El nuevo juguete es compuesto de palitos de larguras diferentes y con piezas de hojadelata curvadas para las coöexiones. Con este juguete tan sencillo se construyen casas y muebles para muñecas, torres y muchos otros modeles. Objetos construidos con el "Geniatus", no seran solamente como se dice mirane y no me toques ya que el niño los puede utilizar con otros juegos. Cada cajita contiene debujos de los diferentes objetos que se pueden construir. El "Geniatus" juguete hallara ciertamente la aprobación de cualquier amigo de niños porche aqui es ofrecido un juguete que no diverte solamente el niño, pero este juguete sirve aun para dessarrillar la inteligencia del niño. A pesar de las ventajas que ofrece este juguete es el más barato sobre el mercado.

Spielwaren mit Uhrwerk, gekleidet. — Dressed toys with clockworks. — Juguetes vistidos con mecanismos de reloj.

Nr.	Größe in cm Size in centimeters Tamaños en centimetros	Rein Nettogewicht per Dutzend ohne Kartons ungefähr Netweight per dozen approximative Aproximo peso neto de la docena sin cajitas de cartón	Beschreibung	Description	Descripción
25/156	20×9	1200 g	Matrosin, laufend.	Sailor girl, walking.	Marinera, andando.
25/169	20×9	1200 „	Rotkäppchen, laufend.	Red-riding-hood, walking.	Caperucita encarnada, andando.
25/184	16×11	1000 „	Tirolerknabe und -mädel, tanzend.	Tyrolerboy and girl, dancing.	Muchachos tiroleses, bailando.
25/185	16×11	1020 „	Hänsel und Gretel, tanzend.	Red-riding-hood and boy, „	Hansel y Gretel, „
25/187	16×11	1020 „	Sportpaar, tanzend.	Boy and girl in sport dress, „	Deportistas, pareja, „
25/189	16×11	1800 „	Bärenführer und Bär, tanzend.	Bear-leader and bear, „	Domador de osos y oso, „
25/190	16×11	1000 „	Matrosenknabe und -mädel, tanzend.	Sailor boy and girl, „	Muchacho marinero y muchacha, bailando.
25/199	15×15	1200 „	Stallmeister mit Pferd, im Kreise laufend.	Ringmaster with horse, moving in a circle.	Caballerizo con caballo marchando en círculo.
25/201	22×9	1200 „	Amme, laufend.	Nurse, walking.	Nodriza, andando.
25/214	18×28	2000 „	Jockei auf Gig mit Pferd.	Jockey on Gig with horse.	Jockey en gig con caballo.
25/217	16×20	1400 „	Jockei auf Pferd, natürlich reitend.	Jockey on horseback, when riding the figur is moving up and down.	Jockey sobre caballo, caballeando naturalmente.
25/219	20×9	1200 „	Gärtnerin, laufend.	Gardener lady, walking.	Jardinera, andando.
25/220	15×15	1200 „	Stierkämpfer mit Stier, im Kreise laufend.	Bullfighter, moving in a circle.	Torero con toro marchando en círculo.
25/223	16×20	1400 „	Parforcereiter, natürlich reitend.	Huntsman on horseback, when riding the figur is moving up and down.	Jinete sobre caballo, caballeando naturalmente.
25/230	19×23	1320 „	Dienstmann, Karre fahrend.	Porter pushing a car.	Mozo de cuerda con carro.
25/235	16×20	1400 „	Husar auf Pferd, natürlich reitend.	Hussar on horseback, when riding the figur is moving up and down.	Húsaro sobre caballo, caballeando naturalmente.
25/240	17×20	1500 „	Clown auf Schwein, „ „	Clown on pig, when riding the figur is moving up and down.	Payaso sobre cerdo, caballeando naturalmente.
25/241	18×17	1320 „	Clown mit Schwein, im Kreise laufend.	Clown with pig moving in a circle.	Payaso c. cerdo marchando en círculo.
25/242	16×11	960 „	Pirettenpaar, tanzend.	Boy and girl as harlequins, dancing.	Parejo de piretas, bailando.
25/250	23×15	1740 „	Holländerpaar, „	Dutchman and woman, dancing.	Holandeses, pareja, „
25/251	23×15	1690 „	Tirolerpaar, tanzend.	Tyrolerboy and girl, „	Muchachos tiroleses, „
25/253	16×20	1400 „	Stierfechter auf Pferd, natürlich reitend.	Bullfighter on horseback, when riding the figur is moving up and down.	Torero sobre caballo, caballeando naturalmente.
25/254	18×24	1500 „	Milchfrau, Karre mit Kanne fahrend.	Milk maid pushing a car.	Lechera con carro y jarra.
25/255	16×11	960 „	Holländerpaar, tanzend.	Dutchman and woman, dancing.	Holandeses, pareja, bailando.
25/257	22×10	1560 „	Baby, natürlich laufend.	Baby, naturally walking.	Bébé, andando.
25/258	15×15	1320 „	3 Kinder, Ringelreihen tanzend.	Ring around roses.	3 niños jugando y bailando.
25/265	22×10	1680 „	Max, laufend.	Max, walking.	Max, andando.
25/266	22×10	1680 „	Moritz, „	Moritz, „	Moritz, „
25/268	17×25	1800 „	Ziegengespann.	Goat pulling a car.	Cabra tirando un carro.
25/271	21×10	1500 „	Rotkäppchen, natürlich laufend.	Red-riding-hood, walking.	Caperucita encarnada, andando.
25/274	16×20	1400 „	Reiter auf Pferd, natürlich reitend.	Cowboy on horseback, riding.	Jinete sobre su caballo.
25/280	22×10	1500 „	Holländerin, natürlich laufend.	Dutchwoman, natur. walking.	Holándesa, andando.
25/281	22×10	1500 „	Holländer, „ „	Dutchman, „ „	Holándes, „
25/282	20×22	1200 „	Holländerin, Karre mit Korb fahrend.	Dutchwoman pushing a car with basket.	Holándesa tirando de un carro con cesta.
25/283	20×22	1200 „	Holländer, „ „ „ „	Dutchman „ „ „ „ „	Holándes tirando de un carro con cesta.
25/286	20×10	1200 „	Köchin, laufend.	Cook, walking.	Cocinera, andando.
25/314	25×10	1680 „	Clown, natürlich laufend.	Clown, naturally walking.	Payaso, „
25/326	20×10	1500 „	Puppe in Filzkleid, natürlich laufend.	Doll in feltdress, walking.	Muñeca c. vestico de fieltro, andando.
25/327	22×10	1560 „	Schusterjunge, natürlich laufend.	Shoemaker's-boy, „	Zapatero, andando.
25/330	25×11	1900 „	Teddybär, natürlich laufend.	Teddy-bear, walking.	Oso, andando.
25/332	22×10	1600 „	Neger, natürlich laufend.	Nigger, walking.	Negrito, „
25/334	35×43	5600 „	Zirkus (Clown mit Pferd).	Circus (Clown with horse).	Circo (Clown con caballo).
25/335	21×11	1020 „	Purzelclown.	Clown, tumbling.	Clown, dando vueltas.
25/337	22×21	1500 „	Jockei auf Pferd, natürlich reitend.	Jockey on horseback, when riding the figur is moving up and down.	Jockey sobre caballo, caballeando naturalmente.
25/338	20×10	1200 „	Gekleidete Puppe, laufend.	Dressed Doll, walking.	Muñeca vestida, andando.
25/339	20×10	1200 „	Puppe mit weißem Batistkleid, laufend.	Doll in white batist dress, walking.	Muñeca con vestido blanco de batista, andando.
25/340	23×10	1700 „	Matrose, natürlich laufend.	Sailor, naturally walking.	Marinero, andando.

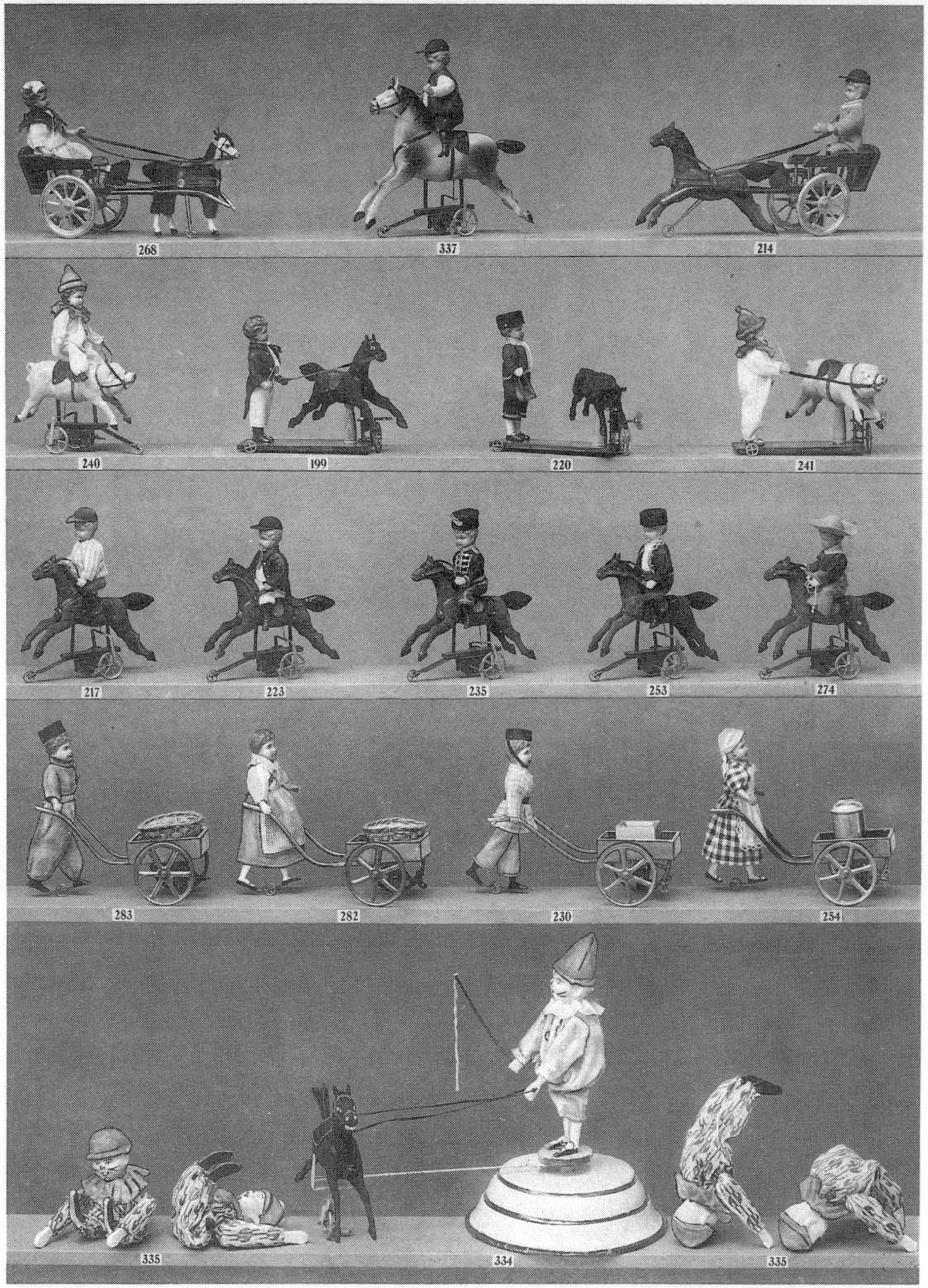

Kollektion Nr. 25

Werkzeugsortimente für Haushalt, Dilettanten, Knaben und Kinder zusammengestellt.
Tool sets for houshold, amateurs, boys and children arranged.
Surtidos de herramientas, para uso domestice, para muchachos, para niños.

In Schränken, zirka 30 Ausführungen, von 9 bis 47 Stück Inhalt.

Auf Wandbrettern, zirka 12 Ausführungen, von 5 bis 10 Stück Inhalt.

In Kästen, zirka 70 Ausführungen, von 5 bis 26 Stück Inhalt.

Auf Karten, zirka 50 Ausführungen.

In chests, about 30 different types, containing from 9 to 47 tools.

On boards, about 12 different types, containing from 5 to 10 tools.

In boxes, about 70 different types, containing from 5 to 26 tools.

On cards, about 50 different types.

En armarios, en 30 varios surtidos, conteniendo 9 hasta 47 piezas.

Sobre tablas, en 12 varios surtidos, conteniendo 5 hasta 10 piezas.

En Cajas, 70 varios surtidos, conteniendo 5 hasta 26 piezas.

Sobre cartanes, en 50 varios surtidos.

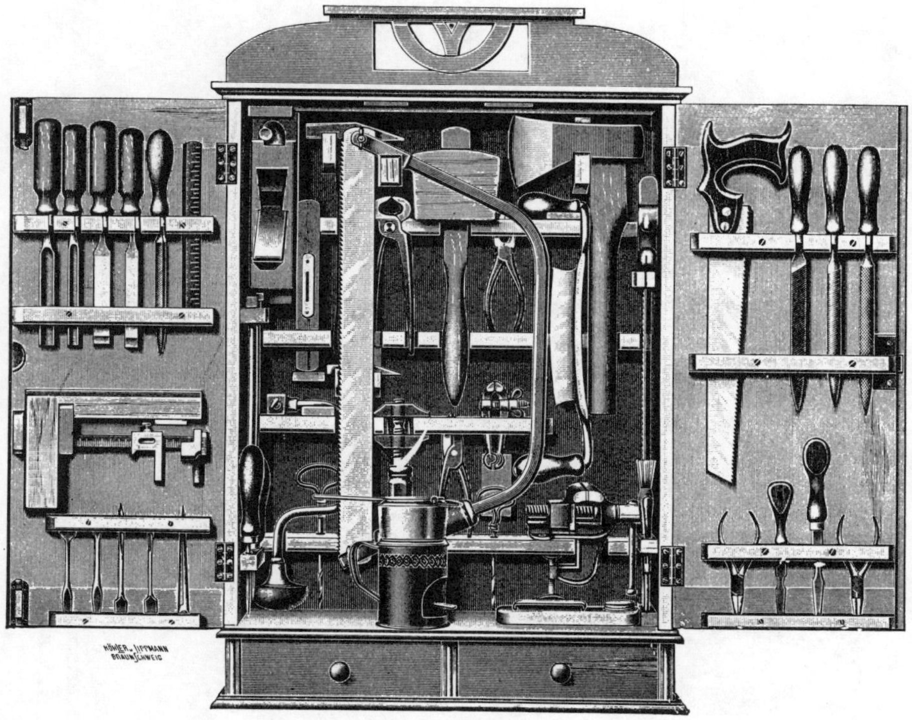

64/152/12

79 cm hoch, 52 cm breit, 19 cm tief, Gewicht ca. 19,5 kg, 47 Stück Inhalt.

About 31″ high, 20,5″ wide, 7,5″ deep, weight ca. 19,5, containing 47 pieces.

79 cm de altura, 52 cm de ancho, 19 cm de hondura, peso ca. 19,5 kg, con 47 piezas de contenido.

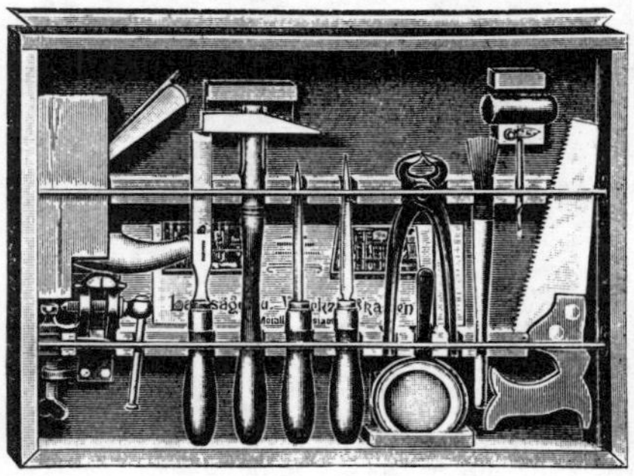

64/164/0

Im Gebrauch besonders bewährt! Werkzeugkasten mit Metallhalterstäben D R. G. M. 15 verschiedene Ausführungen. 40 cm lang, 30 cm breit, 7 cm hoch. Gewicht 2,6 kg. 12 Stück Inhalt.

Very handy in use! Tool boxes with metall fastenings. Trade mark registered. 15 different assortments. 15¾″ long, 11¾″ deep, 2¾″ high. Weight 2,6 kg, containing 12 tools.

¡Muy practico en usarse! Cajas de herramientas fijadas per medio de una barilla de hierro. Marca registrada. 15 verios surtidos. 40 cm de larga, 30 cm de ancho, 7 cm de altura. Peso 2,6 kg, con 12 piezas de contenido.

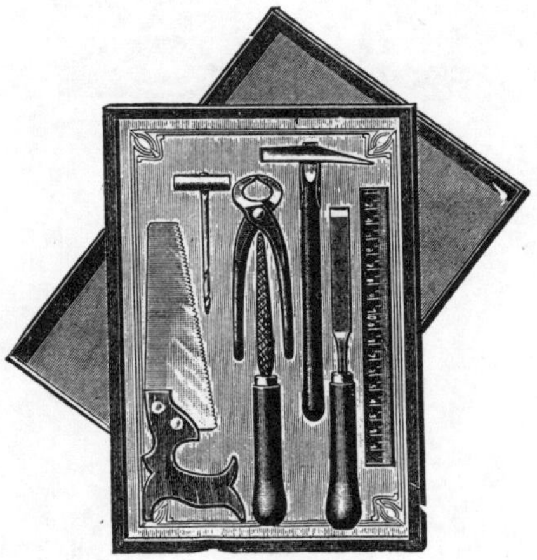

64/60/1 C

Gute Werkzeuge für Kinder, auf Karton im Holzrahmenkasten, 7 Stück Inhalt, 32 cm lang, 21,5 cm breit, 4 cm hoch, Gewicht 8,2 kg.

Good tools for children, on cards in wooden framed cardboard boxes, containing, 7 pieces, 12,5″ long, 8,5″ deep, 1,5″ high, weight 8,2 kg.

Herramientas finas para niños sobre cartones en caja de cartón con marco de madera con 7 piezas de contenido, 32 cm de larga, 21,5 cm de ancho, 4 cm de altura, peso 8,2 kg.

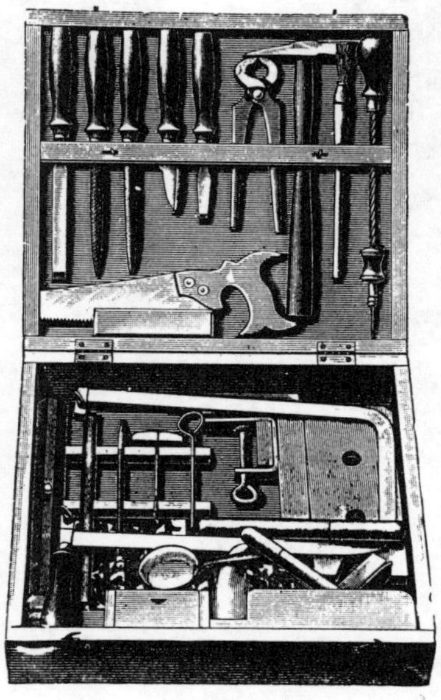

64/183/4

Laubsäge- und Werkzeugkasten, kombiniert, 7 verschiedene Ausführungen, 25 Stück Inhalt. 33 cm lang, 30 cm breit, 9,5 cm hoch, Gewicht 3,5 kg.

Fretwork and toolbox combined, 7 different assortments, containing 25 tools. 13″ long, 11¾″ deep, 3¾″ high, weight 3,5 kg.

Cajas de herramientas y con utilos de marqueteria, 7 varios surtidos, con 25 piezas de contenido. 33 cm de larga, 30 cm de ancho, 9,5 cm de altura, peso 3,5 kg.

Laubsägewerkzeuge — Fretworkers outfit — Herramientas de marqueteria

zusammengestellt
in Schränken, 4 Ausführungen;
auf Wandbrettern, in Kästen, ca. 50 Ausführungen;
auf Karten, ca. 30 Ausführungen.

arranged
in chests, 4 different types;
on boards, in boxes, about 50 types;
on cards, about 30 types.

para uso
en armarios, en 4 varios surtidos;
sobre tablas, en cajas, en 50 surtidos;
sobre cartones en 30 surtidos.

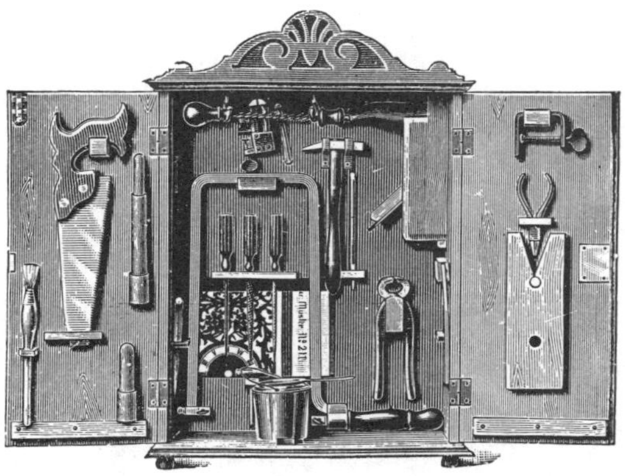

64/116/5

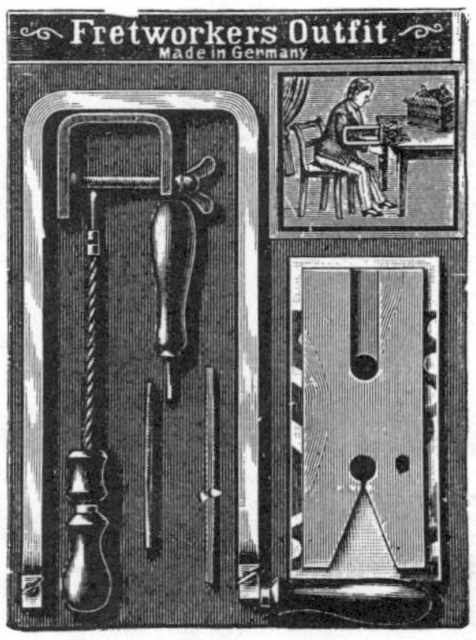

64/111 E/4

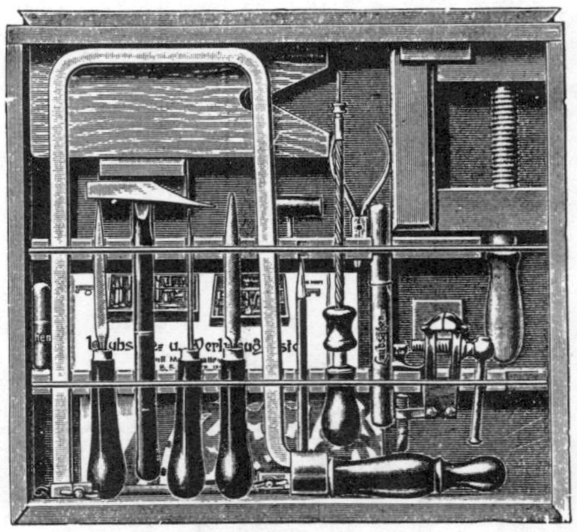

64/114 E/23

Nr. **64**/116/5
60 cm hoch, 38 cm breit, 14 cm tief, Gewicht 8 kg, 24 Stück Inhalt.
23,5″ high, 15″ wide, 5,5″ deep, weight 8 kg, containing 24 pieces.
60 cm de altura, 38 cm de ancho, 14 cm de hondura, peso 8 kg, con 24 piezas de contenido.

Nr. **64**/111 E/4
38 cm lang, 27 cm breit, Gewicht 7,600 kg, Inhalt 7 Stück.
$15^{1}/_{4}$″ long, $10^{3}/_{4}$″ wide, weight 7,600, containing 7 tools.
38 cm de larga, 27 cm de ancho, peso 7,600 kg, con 7 piezas de contenido.

Nr. **64**/114 E/23
Laubsägekasten mit Metallhaltestäben, mit sehr guten Werkzeugen, 22 Stück Inhalt, 39 cm lang, 36 cm breit, 6,5 cm hoch, Gewicht 2,750 kg.
Fretsaw-toolbox with tools of high quality, containing 22 tools, weight 2,750 kg, 15,5″ long, 14,5″ wide, 2,5″ high.
Caja con utiles de marqueteria con herramientas de primera calidad, con 22 piezas contenido, peso 2,750 kg, 39 cm de larga, 36 cm de ancho, 6,5 cm de altura.

64/185/4

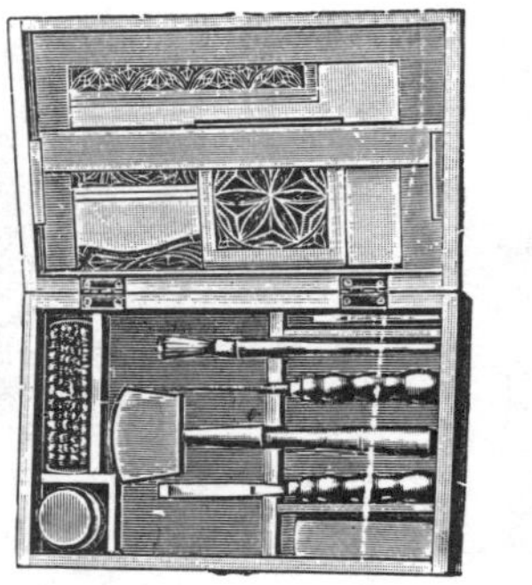

64/149/4

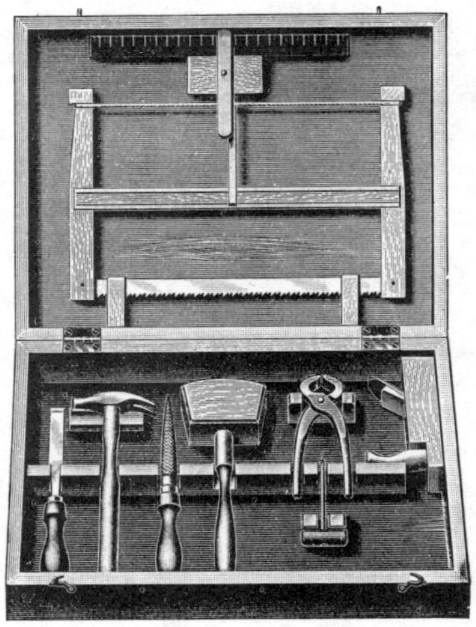

64/87

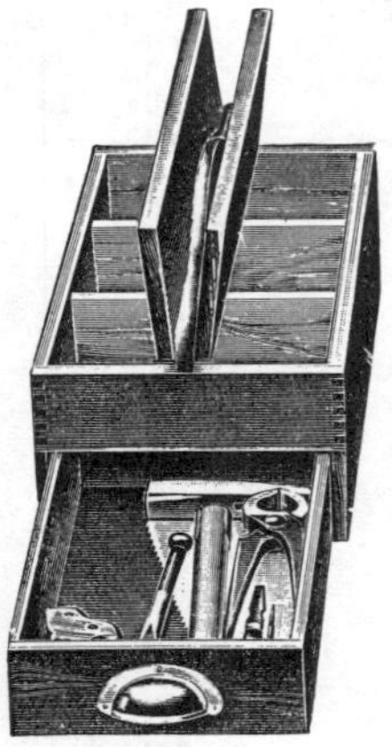

64/151/4

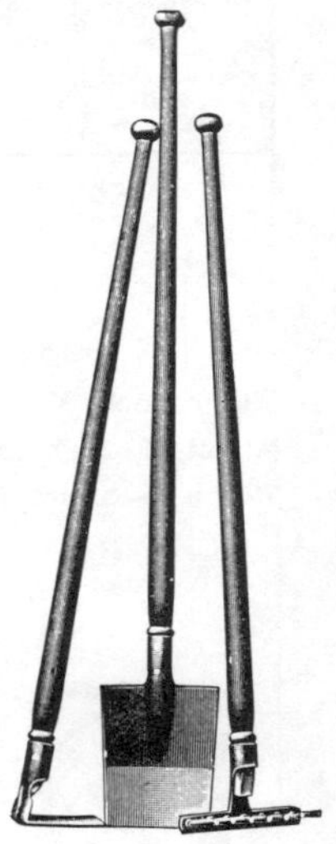

64/170/13

Nr. **64**/185/4
Buchbinderkasten ür Knaben und Dilettanten, 22 Stück Inhalt, Gewicht 1,700 kg, 29 cm lang, 22 cm breit, 7,5 cm hoch.
Bookbinding outfit for boys and amateurs, containing 22 tools, weight 1,700 kg, 11,5″ long, 8,5″ deep, 3″ high.
Cajas de encuardenas para niños con 22 piezas de contenido, peso 1,700 kg, 29 cm de larga, 22 cm de ancho, 7,5 cm de altura.

Nr. **64**/149/4
Werkzeuge für Kerbschnittarbeiten in Kästen und auf Karten, 30 cm lang, 19 cm breit, 6 cm hoch, Gewicht 1,500 kg, Inhalt 9 Stück.
Tools for woodcarving in boxes and on cards, $11^{3}/_{4}$″ long, 7,5″ deep, 2,5″ high, containing 9 tools, weight 1,500 kg.
Herramientas para trobojos de tajo y de zucquero en cajas y sobre cartones, 30 cm de larga, 19 cm de ancho, 6 cm de altura, peso 1,500 kg con 9 piezas de contenido.

Nr. **64**/87
Werkzeugkasten für Knaben, 35 cm lang, 27 cm breit, 6 cm tief, Gewicht 2,2 kg, Inhalt 9 Stück.
Toolbox for boys, 14″ long, 11″ wide, 2,5″ high, containing 9 tools, weight 2,2 kg.
Cajas de herramientas para muchachos, 35 cm de larga, 27 cm de ancho, 6 cm de altura, con 9 piezas de contenido, peso 2,2 kg.

Nr. **64**/151/4
Haushaltswerkzeugkasten mit sehr guten Werkzeugen, Inhalt 6 Stück, 38 cm lang, 22 cm breit, 15 cm hoch, Gewicht 3,900 kg.
Household-toolbox with first-class tools, containing 6 tools, 15″ long, $8^{3}/_{4}$″ wide, 6″ high, weight 3,900 kg.
Cajas de herramientas para uso demestico, con herramientas de primera calidad con 6 piezas de contenido, 38 cm de largo, 22 cm de ancho, 15 cm de altura, peso 3,900 kg.

Nr. **64**/170/13
Gartengeräte für Kinder in ca. 30 verschiedenen Ausführungen.
Gardening outfit for children in about 30 different assortments.
Utiles de jardinero para niños en 30 varios surtidos.

Spielzeug-Nähmaschinen. — Toy sewing machines. — Máquinas de coser para niños.

26/0

Größe / Size / Tamaño	$12{,}5 \times 9 \times 7{,}5$ cm $5 \times 4 \times 3$ inches
Gewicht / Weight / Peso	$^{3}/_{4}$ pound 0.375 kg

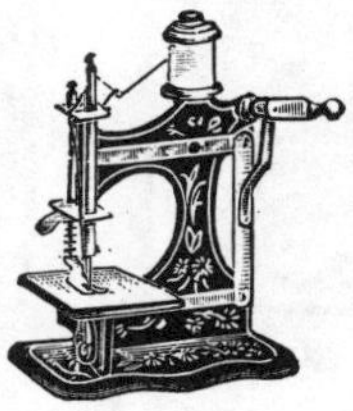

26/1

Größe / Size / Tamaño	$15 \times 11^{1}/_{4} \times 6^{1}/_{4}$ cm $6 \times 4^{1}/_{2} \times 2^{1}/_{2}$ inches
Gewicht / Weight / Peso	1 pound 0,450 kg

26/4

Größe / Size / Tamaño	$13^{3}/_{4} \times 13^{3}/_{4} \times 8^{3}/_{4}$ cm $5^{1}/_{2} \times 5^{1}/_{2} \times 3^{1}/_{2}$ inches
Gewicht / Weight / Peso	1 poud 0.450 kg

26/5

Größe / Size / Tamaño	$16^{1}/_{4} \times 16^{1}/_{4} \times 8^{3}/_{4}$ cm $6^{1}/_{2} \times 6^{1}/_{2} \times 3^{1}/_{2}$ inches
Gewicht / Weight / Peso	$1^{1}/_{2}$ pounds 0.675 kg

26/2

Größe / Size / Tamaño	20×20 cm 8×8 inches
Gewicht / Weight / Peso	2 pounds 0.900 kg

26/14

Größe / Size / Tamaño	20×20 cm 8×8 inches
Gewicht / Weight / Peso	2 pounds 0.900 kg

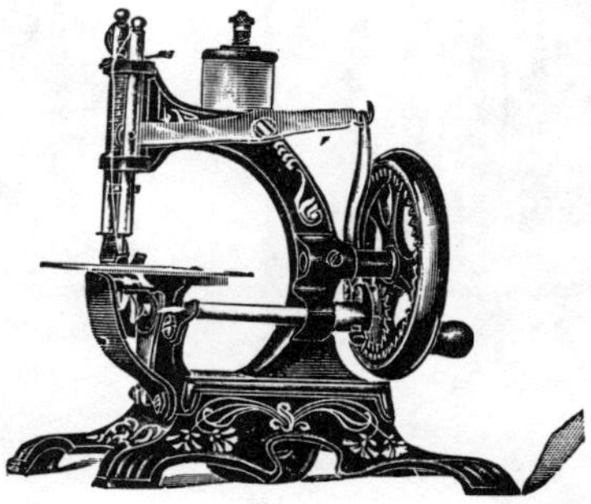

26/20

Größe / Size / Tamaño	$17^{1}/_{2} \times 13^{1}/_{4} \times 10$ cm $7 \times 5^{1}/_{2} \times 4$ inches
Gewicht / Weight / Peso	$2^{1}/_{2}$ pounds 1.125 kg

26/15

Größe / Size / Tamaño	$18^{3}/_{4} \times 12^{1}/_{2} \times 17^{1}/_{2}$ cm $7^{1}/_{2} \times 5 \times 7$ inches
Gewicht / Weight / Peso	$4^{1}/_{2}$ pounds 1.125 kg

26/12

Größe / Size / Tamaño	$28 \times 20 \times 15$ cm $11 \times 8 \times 6$ inches
Gewicht / Weight / Peso	8 pounds 3.600 kg

Nr. **26**/12 Als Zubehör wird mitgeliefert:
1 Ölkanne
1 Schraubenzieher
1 Messvorrichtung
1 Säumer
3 Nadeln

Die Maschine macht 4 Stiche bei jeder Umdrehung des Antriebrades. Wegen der Schnelligkeit des Nähens wird der Saum sehr regelmäßig, sauber und fest.

Die Maschine näht Stiche in jeder Länge, von der kürzesten bis zur längsten.

The following attachments are enclosed:
one oil can
one screw-driver
one gauge
one hemmer
three needles

It makes 4 stitches at each turn of the driving wheel. In consequence of the rapidity the same gets very regular, neat, and tight.

Sews any length of stitch from the shortest to the longest.

Se entregará las siguientes accesorias:
1 aceitera
1 destornillador
1 disposición para medir
1 disposición para hacer ribetes
1 agujas

Con cada revolución de la rueda de impulsión, la máquina cose 4 puntos.

La velocidad del coser efectua que el ribete es muy regular, aseado y firme.

La máquina puede coser puntos de toda largura, desde de los más cortos hasta los más largos.

Kinder-Werkzeuggarnituren. — Toy tool sets. — Surtidos de herramientas para miños.

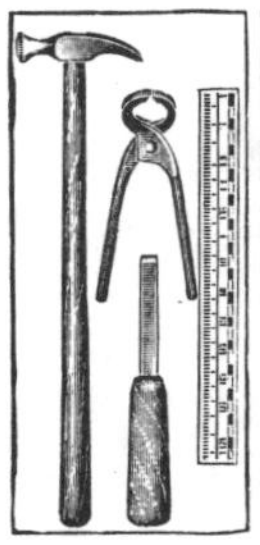

92/1 21×9 cm

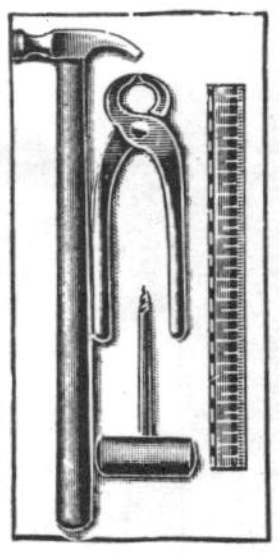

92/2 21×9 cm

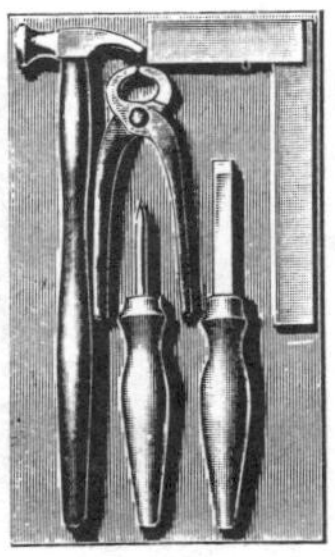

92/3 21×12 cm

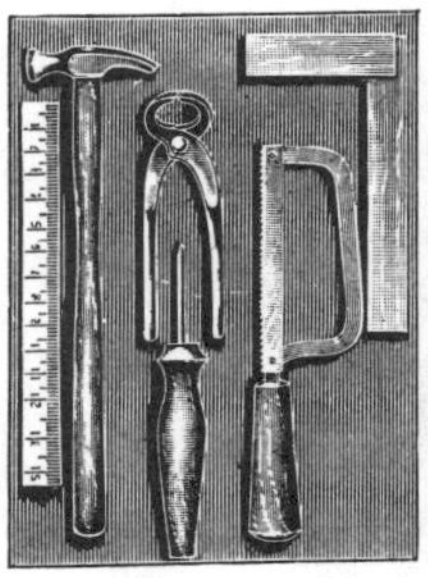

92/4 22×16 cm

Gelb gebeizte Hefte, auf Karten genäht.
Yellow stained handles, sewed on cards.
Mangos embarnizados, en amarillo sobre cartones.

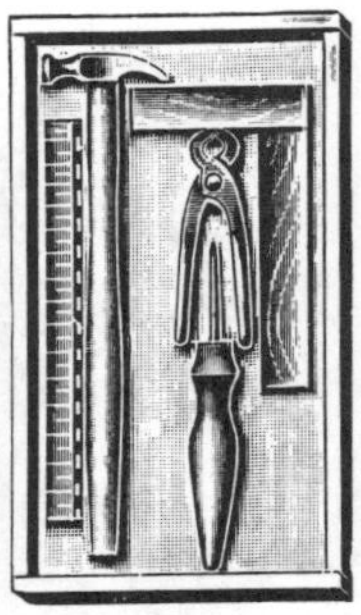

92/5 23×13 cm

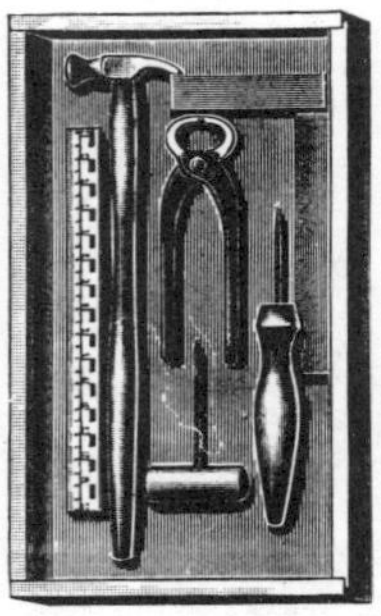

92/6 23½×14 cm

92/7 25×16 cm

Auf Karten genäht, in Holzkasten mit Schiebedeckel.
Sewed on cards, in wood boxes with sliding covers.
Sobre cartones, en cajas de madera con tapadera resbaladiza.

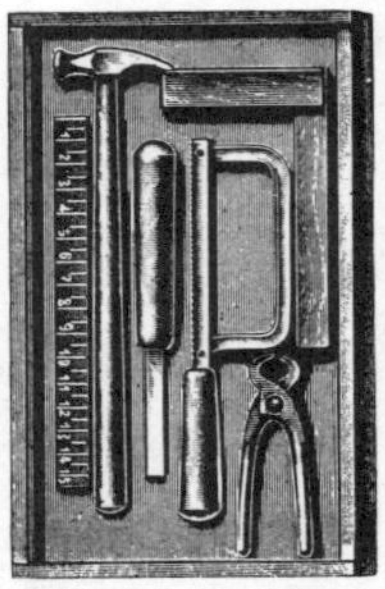

92/8 23½×14 cm

Rot lackierte Hefte.
Red varnished handles.
Mangos lacrados en rojo.

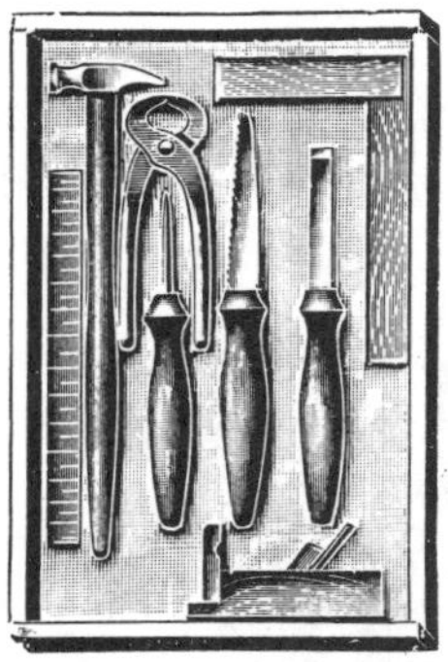

92/9 25×16 cm

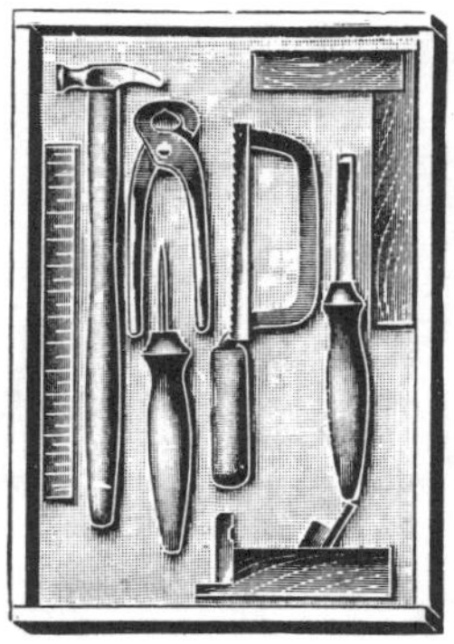

92/10 27×17 cm

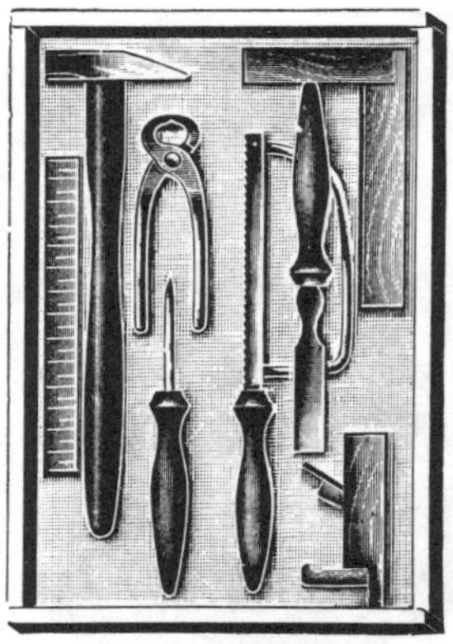

92/11 29×19 cm

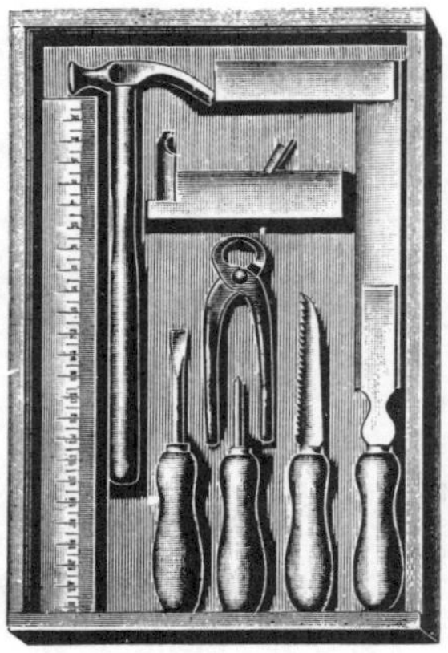

92/12 30×20 cm

Auf Karten genäht, in Holzkasten mit Schiebedeckel.
Sewed on cards, in wood boxes with sliding rovers.
Sobre cartones, en cajas de madera con tapadera resbaladiza

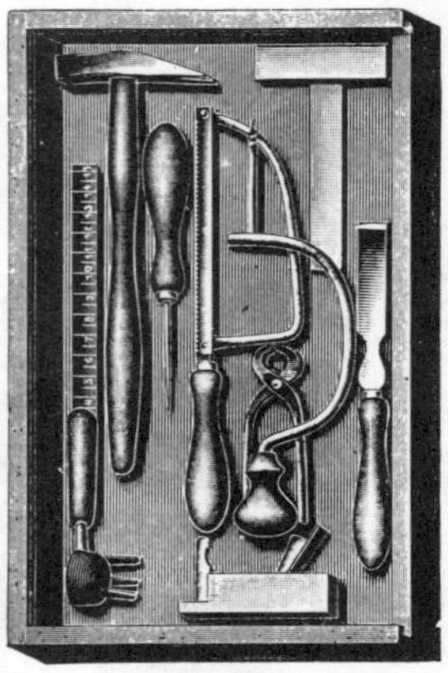

92/13 30×20 cm

Gelb lackierte Hefte.
Yellow varnished handles.
Mangos lacrados en amarillo.

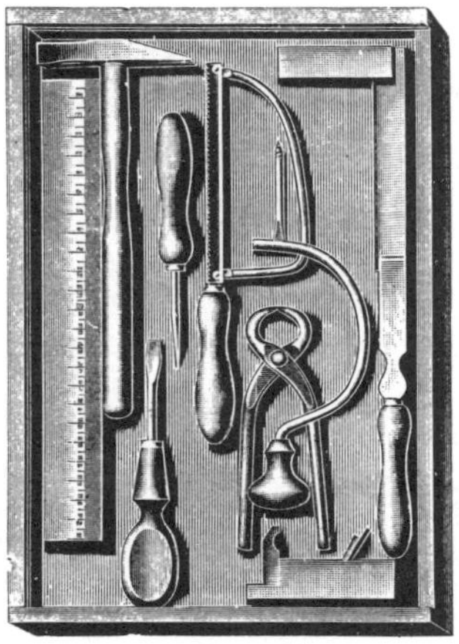

92/14 33×22 cm

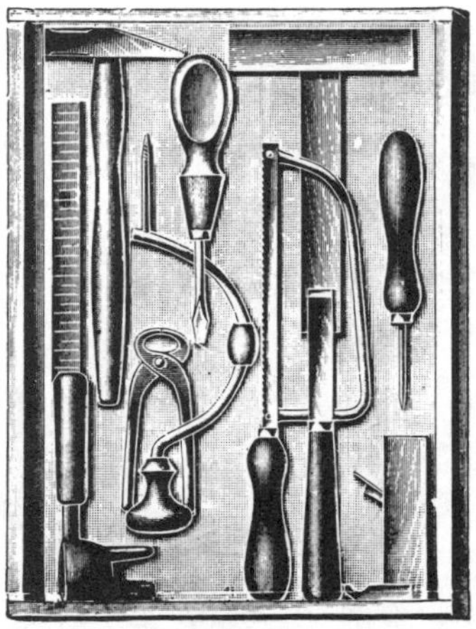

92/15 33×22 cm

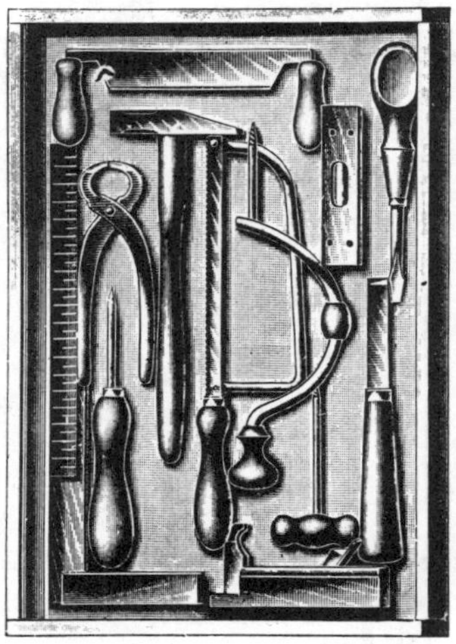

92/16 36×24 cm

Auf Karten genäht, in Holzkasten mit Schiebedeckel, gelb lackierte Hefte.
Sewed on cards, in wood boxes with sliding covers, yellow varnished handles.
Sobre cartones, en cajas de madera con tapadera resbaladiza, mangos lacrados en amarillo.

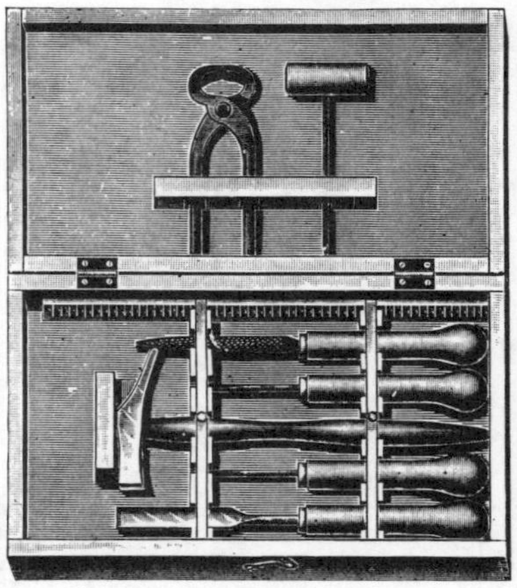

92/17 28½×17½ cm

In gelb lackiertem Klappdeckelkasten, gelb lackierte Hefte.
In yellow varnished well finished wood box, yellow varnished handles.
En caje con cubierta plecable lacrade en amarillo, mangos lacrados en amarillo.

Laubsägegarnituren für Kinder. — Toy fretwork outfit sets. — Surtidos de utiles de marqueteria para niños.

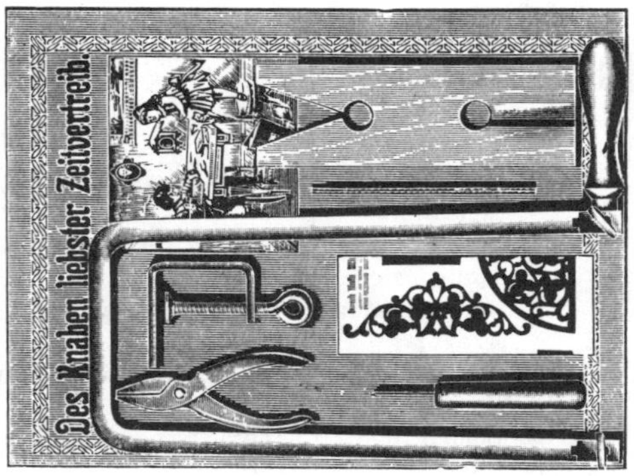

92/18 34×27 cm

Auf Karten genäht. — Sewed on cards.
Sobre cartones.

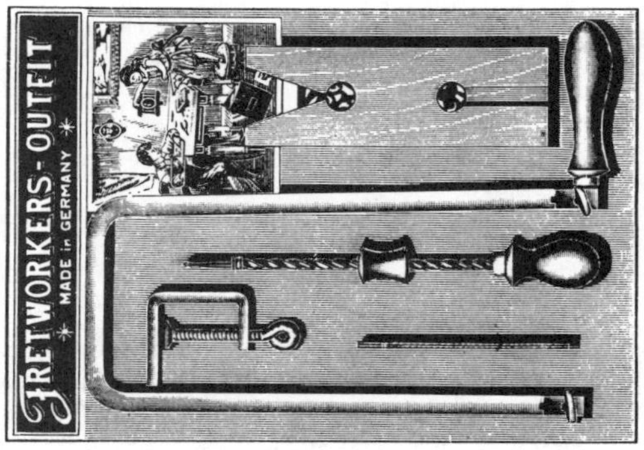

92/19 38×27 cm

Auf Karten genäht. — Sewed on cards.
Sobre cartones.

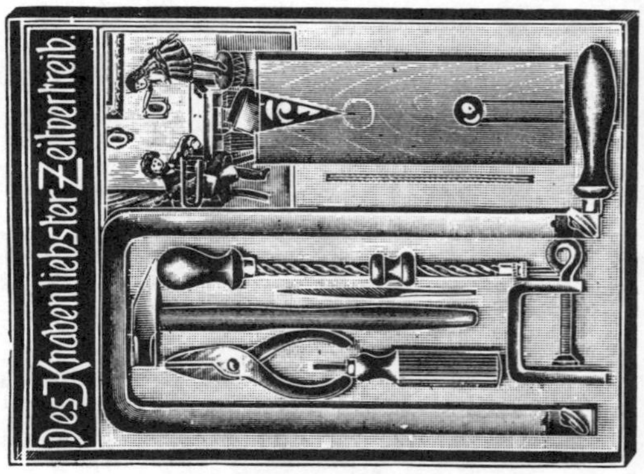

92/20 38×27 cm

Auf Karten genäht, in Stückkartons.—Sewed on cards, each card in a cardboard box. — Sobre cartones, toda en caja dє cartón.

Spielwaren mit Stimme. — Toys with voice. — Juguetes con voz.

Serie **109**/302

Zehn verschiedene amerikanische Figuren mit Stimme, auf Brett und Rädern, prima handgemalt, Größe ca. 26×20 cm, Packung 1/6 Dtz. im Karton.

Ten different American Figures that speak, on a board and with wheels; superior painting, size abt. 26×20 cm, packed 1/6 doz. in cardboard box.

Diez diferentes figuras americanas con voz, sobre tabla con ruedas; finamente pintadas a mano, dimensiones ca. 26×20 cm, empaque: cartones de a 1/6 doc.

Serie **109**/400

Zehn verschiedene Holztiere mit Stimme, wie Kuh, Katze, Elefant, Schaf, Ziege, Schwein, Eisbär, Hund, Esel, und Pferd, auf Brett mit Rädern, fein handgemalt, Größe ca. 24×16 cm, Packung 1/6 Dtz. im Karton.

Ten different voiced wooden animals, such as the cow, elephant, cat, sheep, goat, pig, polar bear, dog, donkey and horse, on a board and with wheels, finely painted by hand, size abt. 24×16 cm, packed 1/6 doz. in cardboard box.

Diez diferentes animales de madera con voz, como vaca, gato, elefante, oveja, cabra, cerdo, oso blanco, perro, burro y caballo, sobre tabla con ruedas, finamente pintados a mano, dimensiones ca. 24×16 cm, empaque: cartones de a 1/6 doc.

Serie **109**/433

Sechs verschiedene doppelte Figuren mit Stimme, wie Schweinetreiber, Schneeschuhläufer und Hund, Gänsemädchen, Ente mit Kücken, Mädchen mit 3 Hühnchen, Knabe mit Gans auf Brett mit Rädern, prima handgemalt, Größe ca. 27×20 cm, Packung 1/6 Dtz. im Karton.

Six different speaking double figures, such as pig driver, skirunner and dog, girl with geese, duck with ducklings, girl with 3 chickens, boy with a goose, on a board and with wheels, superior hand painted, size abt. 27×20 cm, packed 1/6 doz. in cardboard box.

Seis diferentes figuras dobles con voz, como porquero, eskiista con perro, pastorcilla de gansos, pato con pollito, niña con tres pollos, muchacho con ganso, en tabla con ruedas, finamente pintadas a mano, dimensiones ca. 27×20 cm, empaque: cartones de a 1/6 doc.

Serie **109**/500

Zehn verschiedene Holztiere in feinster Handbemalung, mit Naturstimme, wie Kuh, Katze, Elefant, Ziege, Hund, Schaf, Schwein, Esel, Eisbär und Pferd, auf Brett mit Rädern, Größe ca. 40×27 cm, Packung 1/6 Dtz. im Karton.

Ten different wooden animals, finest hand painting, with natural cries, such as a cow, cat, elephant, goat, dog, sheep, donkey, pig, polar bear and horse, on board with wheels, size abt. 40×27 cm packed 1/6 doz. in cardboard box.

Diez diferentes animales de madera, muy finamente pintados a mano, con voz natural, coma vaca, gato, elefante, cabra, perro, oveja, cerdo, burro, oso blanco y caballo, sobre tabla con ruedas, dimensiones ca. 40×27 cm, empaque: cartones de a 1/6 doc.

Serie **109**/446

Zwölf verschiedene Holztiere mit Stimme, wie Kuh, Katze, Elefant, Schaf, Ziege, Schwein, Eisbär, Hund, Esel, Pferd, Ente und Hase, auf Brett und Rädern, fein handgemalt, Größe 20×14 cm, Packung 1/6 Dtz. im Karton.

Twelve different voiced wooden animals, such as a cow, cat, elephant, sheep, goat, pig, polar bear, dog, donkey, horse, duck and hare, on a board with wheels, finely painted by hand, size abt. 20×14 cm, packed 1/6 doz. in cardboard box.

Doce diferentes animales de madera con voz, como gato, vaca, elefante, oveja, cabra, cerdo, oso blanco, perro, burro, caballo, pato y liebre, sobre tabla con ruedas, finamente pintados a mano, dimensiones 26×14 cm, empaque: cartones de a 1/6 doc.

Serie **109**/473

Acht verschiedene Tiere in feiner plastischer und naturgetreuer Ausführung, aus Pappe und Papiermaché, in Oelfarbe handgemalt, mit Naturstimme, wie Kuh, Katze, Elefant, Ziege, Schwein, Hund, Esel und Pferd, auf Brett mit Rädern, Größe ca. 24×16 cm, Packung 1/6 Dtz. im Karton.

Eight different animals plastically portrayed and true to nature, finely executed in pasteboard and papier-mache, hand painted in oils, with natural cries, such as a cow, cat, elephant, goat, pig, dog, donkey and horse, on a board with wheels, size abt. 24×16 cm, packet 1/6 doz. in cardboard box.

Ocho diferentes animales en ejecución fina, plástica y muy realística, de cartón y papel majado, pintados a mano con pintura al óleo, con voz natural, los animales son vaca, gato, elefante, cabra, cerdo, perro, burro y caballo, sobre tabla con ruedas, demensiones ca. 24×16 cm, empaque: cartones de a 1/6 doc.

Nr. **109**/491
Sechs verschiedene Holztiere mit Stimme, auf Brett mit Rädern, in der Ausführung wie Serie **109**/400 oder 446, Größe ca. 15×12 cm, Packung 1/6 Dtz. im Karton.

Nr. **109**/491
Six different wooden animals, voiced, on a board with wheels, same style as series **109**/400 or 446, size abt. 15×12 cm, packed 1/6 doz. in cardboard box.

Nr. **109**/491
Seis diferentes animales de madera con voz, sobre tabla con ruedas, en la misma ejecución que las series **109**/400 ó 446, demensiones ca. 15×12 cm, empaque: cartones de a 1/6 doc.

Gespanne. — Teams. — Tiros.

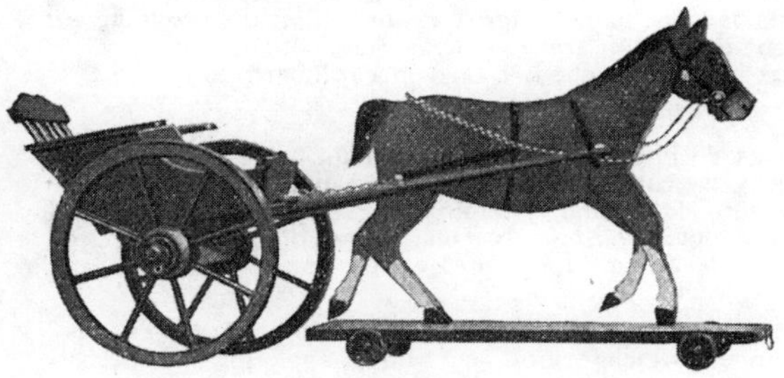

109/441

Nr. **109**/441 Kabriolett und Pferd mit Stimme, auf Brett mit Rädern, in feinster Handbemalung, Größe ca. 45 cm lang, Packung 1/3 Dtz. im Karton.

Cabriolet and neighing horse, on board with wheels, in finest hand painting, size abt. 45 cm long, packet 1/3 doz. in cardboard box.

Cabriolé y caballo von voz, sobre tabla con ruedas, muy finamente pintado a mano, longitud ca. 45 cm, empaque: cartones de a 1/3 doc.

„ **109**/441/5 Leiterwagen mit 2 Pferden mit Stimme, auf Brett mit Rädern, feinste Handbemalung, Größe ca 60 cm lang, Packung 1/12 Dtz. im Karton.

Open lorrey, with two neighing horses, on board with wheels, finest hand painting, size abt. 60 cm long, packed 1/12 doz. in cardboard box.

Carromato con dos caballos con voz, sobre tabla con ruedas, muy finamente pintado a mano, longitud ca. 60 cm, empaque: cartones de a 1/12 doc.

Nr. **109**/441/7 Kleiner Sandwagen mit Pferd, Esel oder Ziege, mit Stimme, auf Brett mit Rädern, Größe ca. 25 cm, Packung 1/3 Dtz. im Karton.

Small sand-cart, with a horse, donkey or goat, voiced, on a board wheels, size abt. 25 cm, Packed 1/3 doz. in cardboard.

Carro arenero con caballo, burro ó cabra con voz, cobre tabla con ruedas, longitud ca. 25 cm, empaque: cartones de a 1/3 doc.

Spielwaren mit Stimme. — Toys with voice. Juguetes con voz.

109/439

Nr. **109**/439 Holzfiguren mit Harmonikastimme, zum Stehen, wie Holländer-Knabe und -Mädchen, Clown, Zwerg usw., prima handgemalt. Größe ca. 30 cm hoch. Packung 1/6 Dtz. im Karton.

Nr. **109**/439 Wooden figures with harmonica voice, to stand up, such as Dutch boy and girl, clown, dwarf, etc.; first-class painted. Size about 30 cm high. Packed 1/6 dozen in cardboard box.

No. **109**/439 Figuras de madera con voz de armónica, sin tabla, como niño y niña holandeses, payaso, enano, etc. Empaque: cartónes de a 1/6 docena.

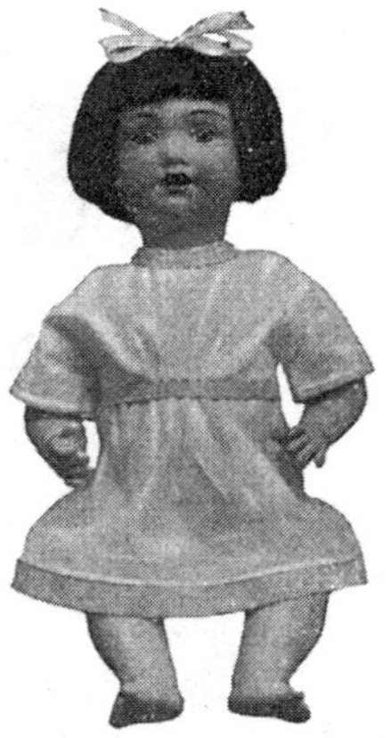

109/1003

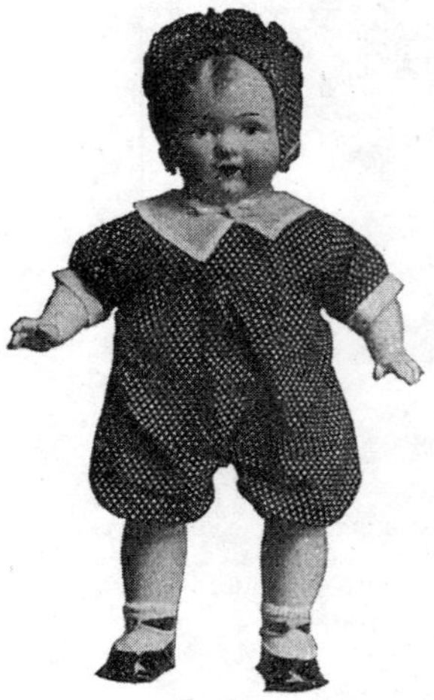

109/1011

Nr. **109**/1003 Sitzbabies „Lotte“ mit Kopfdruckstimme, feiner Perücke, Batisthemd, Porzellankopf und Kugelaugen. Größe 26, 29, 32, 35, 41, 44, 47, 53, 58 cm. Packung 1/12 Dtz. im Karton. — Dieselben, ohne Kopfstimme, mit selbsttätiger Mamastimme. Größe 35, 41, 44, 47, 53, 58 cm. Packung 1/12 Dtz. im Karton.

Seated babies "Lotte", crying out on pressing head, finest wig, cambric chemise, porcelain head and ball eyes. Size 26, 29, 32, 35, 41, 44, 47, 53, 58 cm. Packed 1/12 doz. in cardboard box. — The same, without head-voice, but crying "mama" automatically. Size 35, 41, 44, 47, 53, 58 cm. Packed in 1/12 doz. in cardboard box.

Bebé sedente "Lotte" con voz de cabeza, fina peluca, camisa de batista, cabeza de porcelana y ojos de bola. Tamaño 26, 29, 32, 35, 41, 44, 47, 53, 58 cm. Empaque en cartones de a 1/12 doc. — Los mismos bebés, sin voz de cabeza, pero con voz de "mamá" automática. Tamaño 35, 41, 44, 47, 53, 58 cm. Embaque: cartones de 1/12 doc.

Nr. **109**/1006 Doppelgelenkpuppen „Lotte“ mit Kopfdruckstimme, feiner Waltershäuser Perücke, Porzellankopf und Kugelaugen mit Wimpern, Batisthemd. Größe 34, 40, 46, 50, 55, 60, 66, 70, 75 cm. Packung 1/12 Dtz. im Karton. — Dieselben, aber ohne Kopfdruckstimme, mit selbsttätiger Mamastimme. Packung 1/12 Dtz. im Karton. Größe 50, 55, 60, 66, 70, 75 cm.

Double-jointed dolls "Lotty" with head-voice, fine Waltershaus wig, porcelain head and ball eyes with lashes; cambric chemise. Size 34, 40, 46, 50, 55, 60, 66, 70, 75 cm. Packed 1/12 doz. in cardboard box. — The same, but without head-voice, automatically crying "mama". Packed 1/12 doz. in cardboard box. Size 50, 55, 60, 66, 70, 75 cm.

Muñeca de doble articulación "Lotte" con voz de cabeza, fina peluca Waltershausen, cabeza de porcelana, ojos de bola con pestañas, camisa de batista. Tamaño 34, 40, 46, 50, 55, 60, 66, 70, 75 cm. Embaque: cartones de a 1/12 doz. — Las mismas muñecas, pero sin voz de cabeza, con voz de "mamá" automática. Empaque: cartones de a 1/12 doc. Tamaño 50, 55, 60, 66, 70, 75 cm.

Nr. **109**/1011 Laufpuppen, weichgestopft, mit Pappkopf und selbsttätiger Mamastimme. Größe 40 cm. Packung 1/3 Dtz.
„ 46 „ „ 1/3 „
„ 52 „ „ 1/12 „

Walking dolls, with soft stuffing, pastboard head and automatic cry of "mama". Size 40 cm. Packed 1/3 doz. in cardb. box.
„ 46 „ „ 1/3 „ „ „ „
„ 52 „ „ 1/12 „ „ „ „

Muñecas corredoras, con relleno blando, con cabeza de cartón y voz de "mamá" automática.
Tamaño 40 cm. Empaque: cartón de a 1/3 doc.
„ 46 „ „ „ „ „ 1/3 „
„ 52 „ „ „ „ „ 1/12 „

Nr. **109**/1015 Laufpuppen, weichgestopft, mit Pappbabykopf und „Mama“- und „Papa“-Stimme, deren Laut beim abwechselnden Heben und Senken des linken oder rechten Armes ertönt. Genre wie Serie 1011. Größe 40 cm. Packung 1/3 Dtz.
„ 46 „ „ 1/3 „
„ 52 „ „ 1/12 „

Walking dolls, with soft stuffing, pastboard baby head, crying "mama" or "papa" alternately on lifting and dropping the right or the left arm. Style as Series 1011.
Size 40 cm. Packed 1/3 doz. in cardboard box.
„ 46 „ „ 1/3 „ „ „ „
„ 52 „ „ 1/12 „ „ „ „

Muñecas corredoras, con relleno blando, con cabeza de bebé hecha de cartón, con voces de "mamá" y de "papá", que suenan al levantar y bajar el brazo izquierdo resp. el brazo derecho. Género como Serie 1011.
Tamaño 40 cm. Empaque: cartón de a 1/3 doz.
„ 46 „ „ „ „ „ 1/3 „
„ 52 „ „ „ „ „ 1/12 „

Nr. **109**/1010 Laufpuppen, weichgestopft, mit Babypappkopf und selbsttätiger „Mama“-Stimme, in feiner Kleidung, in Knabe und Mädchen sortiert. Größe 60 cm.

Walking dolls, with soft stuffing, and pastboard baby head, with automatic cry of "mama", finely dressed, boys and girls assorted. Size 60 cm.

Muñecas corredoras con relleno blando, con cabeza de bebé hecha de cartón, con voz de "mamá" automática, finamente vestida, niños y niñas surtidos. Tamaño 60 cm.

33/606

33/91

33/428

33/633

33/428

33/431

33/605

33/612

Fell-, Leder-, Plüsch- und Stofftiere aller Art mit Stimme.
Animals of skin, leather, plush and stuffed felt of all sorts with voice.
Animales de piel, cuero, felpa y pano de todas clases con voz.

Nr. **33**/606/	1	2	3	4	5	6
Größe/Size/Tamaño	15×10	19×12	24×16	28×21	33×25	36×31 cm

Nr. **33**/605/ Größe/Size/Tamaño							
	1	2	$2^1/_2$	3	$3^1/_2$	4	$4^1/_2$
	17×13	18×14	20×15	22×17	25×18	28×20	30×22 cm
	5	6	7	8	9	10	11
	34×24	36×27	41×31	47×34	55×46	64×46	90×58 cm

Nr. **33**/602/	1	2	3	4	5	6
Größe/Size/Tamaño	16×16	19×19	23×22	26×24	28×25	30×28 cm

Nr. **33**/604	
Größe/Size/Tamaño	39×30 cm

Nr. **33**/421/	1	2
Größe/Size/Tamaño	30×25	50×38 cm

Nr. **33**/631/ Größe/Size/Tamaño								
	4/0	3/0	2/0	0	1	2	$2^1/_2$	3
	13×13	15×15	17×17	19×19	20×20	22×22	24×24	26×26 cm
	4	5	$5^1/_2$	6	7	8	9	
	28×28	31×31	37×35	40×37	45×41	49×45	53×51 cm	

Nr. **33**/671/	0	1	$1^1/_2$	2	$2^1/_2$	3	4
Größe/Size/Tamaño	13	15	17	19	21	23	27 cm

Nr. **33**/433/	1	2	3
Größe/Size/Tamaño	13×11	14×12	17×14 cm

Nr. **33**/422/	1	2	3	4
Größe/Size/Tamaño	16	20	24	27 cm

Nr. **33**/201/	5	6	7	8
Größe/Size/Tamaño	22	26	28	32 cm

Nr. **33**/670/	1	$1^1/_2$	2	$2^1/_2$	3
Größe/Size/Tamaño	13×13	15×15	17×17	21×21	25×23 cm

Nr. **33**/614/	0	1	2	3	4	5	6	7	8	9
Größe/Size/Tamaño	14×13	16×14	17×16	19×18	21×19	23×22	29×25	30×27	32×29	35×32 cm

Nr. **33**/630/	0	1	2
Größe/Size/Tamaño	14×10	20×11	25×13 cm

Nr. **33**/608/	1	2	3	4	5
Größe/Size/Tamaño	19×17	23×19	28×24	33×25	36×30 cm

Nr. **33**/600/	0	1	2	3	4	5
Größe/Size/Tomaño	16×13	20×15	22×16	25×17	29×21	32×22 cm

Nr. **33**/613/	0	1	2	3	4	5	6	7	8	9
Größe/Size/Tamaño	16×13	20×14	21×15	22×16	24×17	32×20	38×22	40×25	43×26	48×29 cm

Nr. **33**/603/	1	2	3
Größe/Size/Tamaño	26×24	33×29	36×32 cm

Nr. **33**/609/	1	2	3	4
Größe/Size/Tamaño	13×11	14×13	17×16	42×33 cm

Nr. **33**/612/	1	2	3
Größe/Size/Tamaño	22×19	28×22	32×25 cm

Nr. **33**/431/	0	1	2	3	4	5	6

Nr. **33**/607/	1	2	3	4	5	6	7	8
Größe/Size/Tamaño	13×11	18×14	23×16	24×19	31×20	37×23	42×28	49×32 cm

Nr. **33**/428/	0	1	2	$2^1/_2$	3
Größe/Size/Tamaño	11×10	13×11	16×14	18×15	19×16 cm

Nr. **33**/633/	0	1	2	3	4	5
Größe/Size/Tamaño	9×9	11×11	15×13	20×18	23×21	27×23 cm

Nr. **33**/91/	1	2	3	4	5
Größe/Size/Tamaño	26×24	24×15	28×16	34×19	40×24 cm

33/602

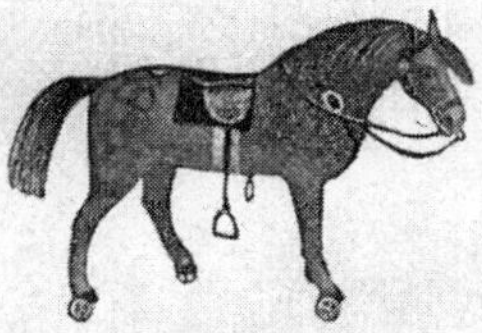

33/604

33/421

33/631

33/671

33/433

33/609

33/603

33/613

33/600

33/608

33/630

33/422

33/201

33/607

33/670

33/614

Serie **37**/320/104 Babys mit Trikotanzug, Porzellankopf, Schlafaugen.
Babies sockinet suit, bisc. head, moving eyes.
Bebes, vestido de tricot, cabeza de porcelana, ojos movibles.

„ **37**/320 Babys mit Hemd, Porzellankopf, Schlafaugen.
Babies with shirt, bisc. head, moving eyes.
Bebes von camisa, cabeza de porcelana, ojos movibles.

„ **37**/325 Fein gekleidete Sitzbabys, Kleider aus Seidentrikot, Porzellankopf, Schlafaugen.
Sitting babies, fine silk stockinet dress, bisc. head, moving eyes.
Bebes asentados vestidos finos de tricot de seda, cabeza de porcelana, ojos movibles.

„ **37**/322 Fein gekleidete Sitzbabys, Kleider aus Baumwollstoffen.
Sitting babies, cotton dress.
Bebes asentados vestidos de algodón.

„ **37**/403/1 Fein gekleidete Steifgelenkpuppen, Schlafaugen, Frisur.
Stiff jointed dolls, dressed, with moving eyes, with wig.
Muñecas con articulación simple, con ojos movibles y con peluca.

„ **37**/402/1 Fein gekleidete Doppelgelenkpuppen, Schlafaugen, Frisur.
Fine dressed double jointed dolls, with moving eyes and wig.
Muñecas con articulación doble, vestidos finos, ojos movibles, peluca.

„ **37**/104 Celluloid-Babys mit Trikotanzug, Schlafaugen und Frisur.
Celluloid-Babies with stockinet suit, moving eyes, wig.
Bebes de celuloide con vestido de tricot, ojos movibles, peluca.

„ **37**/103a Celluloid-Babys mit Trikotanzug (Badeanzug), gemalte Augen und gemaltes Haar.
Celluloid - Babies with stockinet bathing-suit, painted eyes, painted hair.
Bebes de celuloide con tricot de bano, ojos pintados, pelo pintado.
Feine Waltershäuser Perücken.
Fine Waltershausen wigs.
Pelucas muy finas, tipo de Waltershausen.

„ **37**/458 Pelzaffen an Spirale.
Fur-monkey on spiral cord.
Mono de piel al cordon espiral.

„ **37**/200 Feine Doppelgelenkpuppen im Hemd, Schlafaugen, Porzellankopf.
Fine double jointed dolls with shirt, bisc. head, moving eyes.
Muñecas con articulación doble con camisa, cabeza de porcelana, ojos movibles.

„ **37**/202 Feine Waltershäuser Doppelgelenkpuppen mit Hemd, Schlafaugen mit Wimpern.
Fine double jointed dolls with shirt, Waltershausen style, with moving eyes and eye lashes.
Muñecas finas con articulación doble, tipo de Waltershausen, con camisa con ojos movibles y pestanas.

„ **37**/371 Imitierte Lederbälge ohne Kopf, Einfachgelenk.
Imitation kid bodies, without head, stiff jointed.
Cuerpos de muñecas cuero imit. sin cabeza, articulación simple.

„ **37**/361 Imitierte Lederbälge ohne Kopf, Doppelgelenk.
Imitation kid bodies, without head, double jointed.
Cuerpos de muñecas cuero imit. sin cabeza, articulación doble.

„ **37**/370 Imitierte Lederpuppen mit Porzellankopf, Frisur, Schlafaugen, Einfachgelenk.
Imitation kid dolls with bisc. head, wig moving eyes, stiff jointed.
Muñecas con cuerpos de cuero imit., peluca, ojos movibles, articulación simple.

„ **37**/360 Imitierte Lederpuppen mit Porzellankopf, Frisur, Schlafaugen, Doppelgelenk.
Imitation kid dolls with bisc. head, wig moving eyes, double jointed.
Muñecas con cuerpos de cuero, imit., peluca, ojos movibles, articulación doble.

„ **37**/359/1 Haargestopfte Gangelpuppen, Papiermachékopf, Frisur.
Hair stuffed dolls, pink body, with papier mâché head and wig.
Muñecas con cuerpo de pink relleno, con cabeza de papel mâché y con peluca.

„ **37**/310 Hemdpuppe mit Papiermachékopf, Frisur, gemalte Augen.
Dolls with shirt, papier mâché head, painted eyes, wig.
Muñecas con camisa, cabeza de papel mâché, ojos pintados, peluca.

„ **37**/309 Handpuppen mit Papiermachékopf, gemalte Haare, gemalte Augen.
Dolls with shirt, papier mâché head, painted hair, painted eyes.
Muñecas con camisa, cabeza de papel mâché, ojos pintados, pelo pintado.

„ **37**/401/3 Gekleidete Kewpies.
Kewpies dressed.
Kewpies vestidos.

Serie **37**/636 Celluloid-Puppenköpfe mit Waltershäuser Frisur, Schlafaugen.
Celluloid, dolls heads with Waltershausen wig, moving eyes.
Cabezas de celuloide para muñecas, con peluca tipo de Waltershausen, ojos movibles.

„ **37**/605 Celluloid-Puppenköpfe mit Frisur und Schlafaugen.
Celluloid dolls heads with wig, moving eyes.
Cabezas de celuloide para muñecas con peluca, ojos movibles.

„ **37**/370/636W Porzellan-Brustköpfe mit Waltershäuser Lockenfrisur, Schlafaugen, Wimpern.
Biscuit shoulder heads with Waltershausen curled wig, moving eyes, eye lashes.
Cabezas de porcelana con anadida de pecho, peluca rizada tipo de Waltershausen, ojos movibles pestanas.

„ **37**/370/605 Porzellan-Brustköpfe mit Lockenfrisur, Schlafaugen.
Biscuit shoulder heads with curled wig, moving eyes.
Cabezas de porcelana con anadida de pecho, peluca rizada, ojos movibles.

„ **37**/370/641 Porzellan-Brustköpfe mit Schneckenfrisur, Schlafaugen.
Biscuit shoulder heads with german wig. moving eyes.
Cabezas de porcelana con anadida de pecho, peluca alemana y ojos movibles.

„ **37**/390/636W Porzellan-Kurbelköpfe mit Waltershäuser Frisur, Schlafaugen, Wimpern.
Biscuit sockets heads with Waltershausen wig, moving eyes, eye lashes.
Cabezas de porcelana con anadida de cuello, con peluca de Waltershausen, ojos movibles, pestanas.

„ **37**/470 Bären aus Plüsch, auf Rädern.
Bears on wheels.
Osos sobre ruedas.

„ **37**/471 Teddybären aus Plüsch, kurzhaariger Plüsch.
Teddy bears of plush, short haired.
Osos de felpa "Teddy", pelo corto.

„ **37**/472 Teddybären aus Plüsch, langhaariger Plüsch.
Teddy bears of plush, long haired.
Osos de felpa "Teddy", pelo largo.

„ **37**/473 Stofftiere sortiert, Hund, Hase, Katze, bewegliche Glieder.
Stuff animals assorted, dogg, hair, cat, moving legs.
Animales de tela surtidos, perro, liebro, gato, miembros movibles.

„ **37**/461 Katzen aus Papiermaché mit Stoff überzogen, auf Brett.
Papier mâché cats, stuff covered, on board.
Gatos de papel mâché, cubiertos de tela, sobre tablita.

Nr. **37**/459 Kühe, auf Brett mit Stoff überzogen.
Cows, stuff covered on board.
Vacas cubiertas de tela, sobre tablita.

„ **37**/450/1 Clowns aus Filz, gestopft, mit Celluloidgesicht.
Stuffed felt clown, with celluloid face.
Clowns de fieltro, con mascara de celuloide.

„ **37**/450/4 Mantelpuppen aus Filz, gestopft, mit Celluloidgesicht.
Soft stuff dolls of felt, with celluloid face.
Muñecas de fieltro de relleno, con mascara de celuloide

„ **37**/450/2 Clowns aus Filz, gestopft, mit Celluloidgesicht.
Stuffed felt clowns, with celluloid face.
Muñecas de fieltro de relleno, con mascara de celuloide.

„ **37**/450/3 Clown aus Filz, gestopft, mit Papiermachékopf.
Stuffed felt clown, with papier mâché head.
Muñecas de fieltro de relleno, con cabeza de papel mâché.

„ **37**/450/5 Filzpuppen, gestopft, mit Papiermachékopf.
Stuffed felt dolls, with papier mâché head.
Muñecas de fieltro, con cabeza de papel mâché.

„ **37**/453/1 Fellziegen auf Brett, mit Stimme.
Skin goats on board, with voice.
Cabras de piel sobre tablita, con voz.

„ **37**/452 Schafe freistehend.
Sheeps without board.
Ovejas sin tablita.

„ **37**/452/1 Schafe auf Brett.
Sheeps without on board.
Ovejas sin sobre tablita.

„ **37**/454 Fellhasen auf Bogen.
Skin hares on rockers.
Liebros sobre balancin.

„ **37**/460 Esel auf Brett, mit Zugstimme.
Donkey on board, with voice.
Burro, sobre tablita.

Celluloid
Celluloid
Cell. 636/14
Cell. 605/11

S T E I F F

SPIELWAREN

Schutzmarke — Knopf im Ohr

Weltberühmte Qualitätsmarke!

Steiff-Spiel- und Reittiere aus Filz, Plüsch, Samt usw. sind weichgestopft und unzerbrechlich aus nur besten Rohmaterial von langjährig geschulten Arbeitern hergestellt.

Das elektrisch geschweißte Eisengerippe hält ihnen dauernd die schöne Form und gibt ihnen hohe Tragfähigkeit. Fahrtiere haben farbige Holzrollen mit Stahlbüchsen, wodurch ein erstaunlich leichtes und elegantes Fahren erreicht wird.

Die Charakter- und Karikaturpuppen sind ebenfalls unverwüstlich, haben beweglichen Kopf und Glieder sowie ausziehbare Kleider.

Steiff-Roloplan ist bewährter Drachenflieger, leicht zu handhaben und zerlegbar.

Steiff-Holzspielwaren sind aus bestem Hartholz hergestellt und farbenprächtig bemalt. Steiff-„Skiro“ ist der Qualitätsroller für schonungslose Dauerbeanspruchung.

Steiff-Spielwaren sind im Verhältnis zu ihrer Größe leicht im Gewicht und dennoch stabil, daher hervorragende Exportartikel.

Alle Tiere haben eine Stimme; -,2 automatische-, Zug- oder Brummstimme, bei Puppen Mamastimme; -,1 Druckbalgstimme

TOYS

Trade Mark — Button in Ear

World famous make!

Steiff-Toys have always been leading and famed for their natural and beautiful shapes and their wonderful quality. Skilled workmanship only can produce such unequalled toys. They are soft stuffed and unbreakable, the very best raw-material being used.

The metal frames are electrically welded thus retaining the shapes and indestructible strength, nicely painted wood-wheels with metal nave box run smooth and noiseless.

Character and Comic dolls are most unique, they are fully jointed, they dress and undress.

Steiff-Roloplan-Kite is the winner of many flying contests, collapsible and easy to carry.

Steiff-Wood-Toys are made only of best hard wood, their natural and beautiful colouring and lifelike movements have rendered them most enjoyable toys and splendid sellers.

Steiff-Skiro, the scooter, is built for intensest wear, runs on roller bearings.

Steiff-Toys are light in weight as compared with their high value, they are most suitabe for shipping.

Each animal with voice; -,2 automatic animal voice, in regard to dolls "mama"-voice; -,1 "cuddle-me" animal voice.

JUGUETES

Marca de Fábrica — Boton en la oreja

La marca de calidad!

Los juguetes Steiff son rellenos e irrompibles. Para la fabricación de estos juguetes se emplean unicamente primeras materias de primera calidad, como fieltro, felpa etc. segun las caracteristicas de los animales. Su confección está confiada á obreros de gran pericia en este trabajo, adquirida en la practica de muchos años. La armadura electricamente soldada da á los animales, particularmente á las cabalgaduras, una solidez sorprendente.

Las muñecas caracteristicas, tan apreciadas, son también indestructibles. Los vestidos pueden quitarse y los cabellos pueden mojarse.

El roloplan "Steiff" es el cometa premiado en muchos concursos. Los juguetes de madera son fabricados de la mejor madera dura, y magnificamente pintados. Los artículos de sport se distinguen por su extraordinaria solidez y por la marcha ligerisma de las ruedas en coijnetes.

Los juguetes Steiff son legeros en proporción al tamaño, peró todavia son solidos, y de aquí tienen las calidades para la exportación.

Todos los animales tienen voz; -,2 voz automatica, en muñecos voz de mamá; -,1 voz de fuelle.

Abbildungen 1/8 nat. Größe. — Electros 1/8 nat. size.

28/10/1122 ex

Nr. **28**/10
Aff. — Ape. — Mono.
Filz, braun.
Felt, brown.
Fieltro, marron.
Nr. 28/10/1117 ex & 28/10/1122 ex (17 & 22 cm)

28/10/9/5322

Nr. **28**/10
Schimpanse. Chimpanzee. Chimpancé.
Mohairplüsch, braun.
Fine plush, brown.
Felpa mohair, marron.
Nr. 28/9/5314—28/9/5328 (14—28 cm)

28/10/325

Schimpanse Chimpanzee Chimpansé
als Selbstfahrer, on speedaway, ciclista.
Filz, rot. Felt red. Feltro, encarnado.
Record-Peter
Nr. 28/10/120—28/10/125
Mohairplüsch, braun. Fine plush, brown. Felpa mohair, marron.
Record-Peter
Nr. 28/10/320—28/10/325

28/12/1228

Nr. **28**/12
Bär. — Bear. — Oso.
Kurzplüsch, braun.
Plush, brown.
Fieltro peludo, marron
Nr. 28/12/1217 — 28/12/1260,2 (17—60 cm)

28/12/1350,2

Nr. **28**/12. **Bär. — Bear. — Oso.**
Mohairplüsch, braun — Fine plush, brown — Felpa mohair, marron
Nr. 28/12/1317—28/12/1380,2 (17—80 cm)

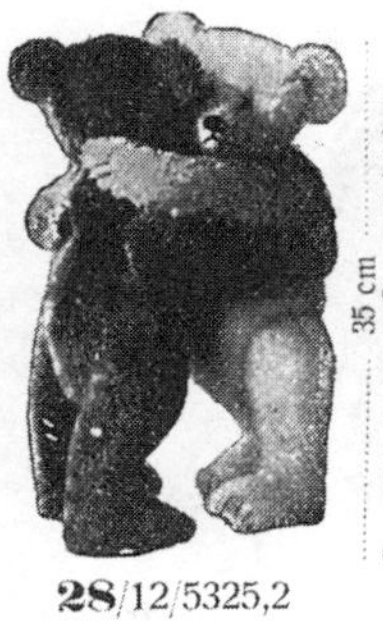

28/12/5325,2

Nr. **28**/12
Teddy.
Mohairplüsch, weiß od. blond.
Fine plush, white or light brown.
Felpa mohair, blanco ó rubio.
Nr. 28/12/5307—28/12/5313 (Höhe stehend, size standing, derecho 10—18 cm)
weiß, blond oder braun, white, light or darkbrown, blanco, rubio ó marron.
Nr. 28/12/5315—28/12/5380,2 (Höhe stehend, size standing, derecho 22—115 cm)

28/12/1328,01

Nr. **28**/12
Zottel-Bär. — Shaggy Bear. — Oso velloso.
Langhaariger Mohairplüsch, braun.
Longhair fine plush, brown.
Pelo largo felpa mohair, marron.
Nr. 28/12/1322,01—28/12/1328,01. (22—28 cm)

Alle hier nicht abgebildeten Tiere finden Sie in der Preisliste aufgeführt. — All articles not shown here, you will find in the according price list. Todos los animales non contenidos aqui, son ilustrados en la lista de precios.

28/20/1328

Nr. **28**/20
Elefant.
Mohairplüsch, grau.
Fine plush, grey.
Felpa mohair, gris.
Nr. 28/20/1328 — 28/20/1380,2
(28—80 cm.)

Nr. **28**/22 **Ente. — Duck. — Pato.**
Auf Exzenterrädern.
On eccentric wheels.
Sobre ruedas excéntricas.
Filz, bunt.
Felt, coloured.
Fieltro, varios colores.
Nr. 28/22/2106 ex — 28/22/2117,4 ex.

28/22/2114,4,2 ex

28/22/6314,2 ex

Mohairplüsch, gelb.
Fine plush, yellow.
Felpa mohair, amarillo.
Nr. 28/22/6310,2 ex — 28/22/6314,2 ex.

Entkett. — Ducktrain. — Familia de patos.
Nr. 28/22/10/6/3
28/22/10/6/6

28/22/10/6/3

Nr. **28**/24
Esel. — Donkey. — Burro.

28/24/1135

Filz, grau.
Felt, grey.
Fieltro, gris.
Nr. 28/24/1114 —28/24/1180,2

28/28/1322 ex

Nr. **28**/28
Fuchs. — Fox. Zorra.
Mohairplüsch, rotbraun.
Fine plush, red-brown.
Felpa mohair, rojo.
Nr. 28/28/1314 ex —28/28/1322 ex.

28/30/6317,2 ex

Nr. **28**/30
Gans. — Goose. Oca.
Mohairplüsch, grau.
Mohair plush, grey.
Felpa mohair, gris.
Nr. 28/30/6317,2 ex.

28/32/1150

Nr. **28**/32
Giraffe. — Jirafa.
Filz, natürlich gefleckt.
Felt, natural colour.
Fieltro, color natural.
Nr. 28/32/1128 — 28/32/11100.
(28—100 cm)

28/34/1128

Nr. **28**/34
Hahn. — Cock. — Gallo.
Filz, bunt.
Felt, coloured.
Fieltro, varios colores.
Nr. 28/34/1112 — 28/34/1128.

28/35/1117 ex

Nr. **28**/35
Henne. — Hen. Gallina.
Auf Exzenterrädern.
On eccentric wheels.
Sobre ruedas excéntricas.
Nr. 28/35/1117 ex.

28/35/6308

Nr. **28**/35
Kücke. — Chicken. — Pollito.
Mohairplüsch, gelb. — Mohair plush, yellow. — Felpa mohair, amarillo.
Nr. 28/35/6308.

Nr. **28**/36 **Hase. — Hare. — Conejo.**
Filz, braun. — Felt, brown.
Fieltro, color canela.

28/36/1114 ex

Auf Exzenterrädern.
On excentric wheels.
Sobre ruedas excéntricas.
Nr. 28/36/1112 ex — 28/36/1122 ex.

28/36/2110

Nr. 28/36/2108 — 28/36/2112.

28/36/4414

Mohairplüsch, weiß.
Mohair plush, white.
Felpa mohair, blanco.
Nr. 28/36/3310 — 28/36/3317.

Samt. — Velvet. Terciopelo.
Nr. 28/36/4410 und 28/36/4414.

28/36/3317

Hunde. — Dogs. — Perros.

28/14/1335,2

Nr. **28**/14 **Bernhardiner. — St. Bernardine dog. Perro Bernardino.**
Mohairplüsch, weiß/braun. — Mohair plush, white/brown. — Felpa mohair, blanco/marron.
Nr. 28/14/1317 — 28/14/1380,2. (17–80 cm.)

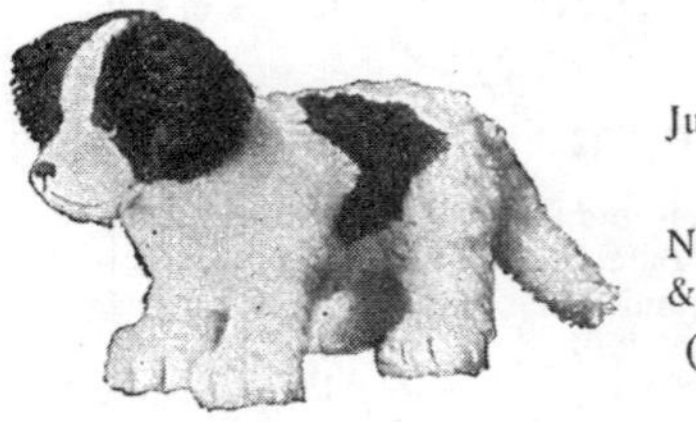

28/14/6322,01

Jung. — Young.
Joven.
Nr. 28/14/6317,01 & 28/14/6322,01.
(17 & 22 cm.)

Nr. **28**/17
King Charles.
Langhaar. Mohairplüsch, schwarz/weiß.
Longhair mohair plush, white/black.
Felpa mohair, blanco/negro.
Nr. 28/17/5317 — 28/17/5328.

28/17/5322

Nr. **28**/18
Dachshund. Perro-Basset.
Filz, braun.
Felt, brown.
Fieltro, marron.
Nummer 28/18/1117ex— 28/18/1122 ex.
(17—22 cm.)

28/18/1122 ex

28/26/1335

Nr. **28**/26 **Foxterrier.**
Mohairplüsch, weiß gefleckt. — Mohair plush, white striped. — Felpa mohair, blanco.
Nr. 28/26/1322 — 28/26/1350,2. Nr. 28/26/3317 — 28/26/3335. Nr. 28/26/6317,0—28/26/6322,0

28/26/3335

28/26/6322,0

28/40/1335

28/40/3322

Nr. 28/40

Irish Terrier.

Mohairplüsch, hellbraun
Fine plush, lightbrown.
Felpa mohair, rubio.

Nr. 28/40/1328 — 28/40/1350,2
28/40/3317 — 28/40/3322.

28/55/3328, 1

Nr. 28/55

Pintscher. — Pincher. Perro Pintscher.

Langhaariger Mohairplüsch, braun.
Long hair Mohair plush, brown.
Pelo largo Felpa mohair, marron.

Nr. 28/55/3328,1.

28/66/1328

Nr. 28/66

Spitzhund. — Pomeranian. — Perro Lulu.

Mohairplüsch, weiß.
Fine plush, white.
Felpa mohair, blanco.

Nr. 28/66/1317 — 28/66/1343,2

28/42/1143

Nr. 28/42 **Kamel. — Camel. — Camello.**
Filz, braun. — Felt, brown. — Fieltro, marron.
Nr. 28/42/1122 — 28/42/1180.

28/48/5322

Nr. 28/48

Löwe.— Lion.— Leon.

Mohairplüsch, hellbraun.
Fine Plush, lightbrown.
Felpa mohair, color natural.

Nr 28/5322.

28/44/1122 ex

Nr. 28/44

Katz. — Cat. — Gato.

Auf Exzenterrädern.
On eccentric wheels.
Sobre ruedas excentricas.
Filz, hellbraun oder grau.
Felt, lightbrown or grey.
Fieltro canela o gris.

Nr. 28/44/1112 ex — 28/44/1122 ex.

28/44/2317

Mohairplüsch, weiß.
Fine Plush, white.
Felpa mohair, blanco.

Nr. 28/44/2312 — 28/44/2322.

28/44/5322,2

Gegliedert und gestromelt.
Jointed and striped. — Articulado y listado.
Nr. 28/44/5322 — 28/44/5343,2.

28/46/1335

28/46/6522, 0

Nr. 28/46

Lamm. — Lamb. Cordero.

Lammplüsch, weiß.
Lambskin, white.
Felpa lama, blanco.
Nr. 28/46/1512,0 — 28/46/1580,2.

jung — young — joven
Nr. 28/46/6522,0 — 28/46/6528,0.

28/52/1343, 2

Nr. 28/52 **Ochs. — Ox. — Buey.**

Mohairplüsch, braun-weiß.
Fine Plush, brown-white.
Felpa mohair, marron-blanco.
Nr. 28/52/1335 — 28/52/1380,2.

28/56/1350

Nr. 28/56 **Pferd. — Horse. — Caballo.**
Mohairplüsch, braun. — Fine plush, brown.
Felpa mohair, marron.
Nr. 28/56/1350 — 28/56/1370.

28/64/1335

28/64/1328,01

Nr. 28/64 **Schwein. — Pig. — Cerdo.**
Mohairplüsch, rosa. — Fine plush, pink.
Felpa mohair rosa.
Nr. 28/64/1317 — 28/64/1350,2.

Mit Quietschstimme. — With grunting voice.
Cerdo gruñidor.
Nr. 28/64/1328,01.

28/74/1343,2

Nr. 28/74

Ziege. — Goat. Cabra.

Mohairplüsch, weiß.
Fine Plush, white.
Felpa mohair, blanco.

Nr. 28/74/1343,2 — 28/74/1350,2.

Gespanne. Animals with carts. Animales con carros.

Holzpferd mit Wagen.
Wooden horse with cart.
Carro y caballo de madera.

Nr. 28/1814/3810 — 28/1823/3815.

28/1820/3813

28/80

Nr. **28**/80

Kleine Tiere.
Small animals.
Animales pequeños.

Hase.— Hare.— Conejo.
Esel.—Donkey.—Burro.

28/79/Chimp. 317

28 75/Pato
6308,0

Nr. **28**/75

Kleine Tiere als Gehänge.
Small animals on elastic.
Animales pequeños con gordon de goma.

Ente. — Duck.
Pato.

Nr. **28**/79

Kasperltiere. — Punchy animals.
Figuras titeres.

Mohairplüsch. — Fine plush. — Felpa mohair.
Schimpanse. — Chimpanzee. — Chimpansé.

28/19/Charles 317

Nr. **28**/82

Rekordfiguren.
Speedaway toys.
Figuras record.

Rec. Radler 20
Rec. Puck 20

28/82/Rec. Radler 20

28/82/Rec. Puck 20

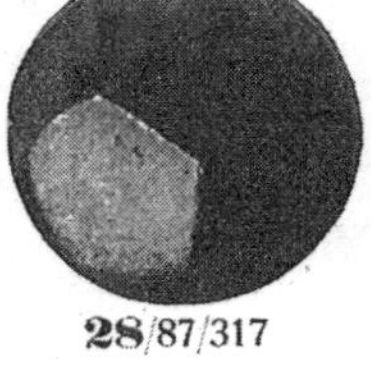

28/87/317

28/77/4134

Nr. **28**/87

Ball. — Pelota.

Mohairplüsch, 6farbig.
Multicoloured.
Felpa mohair, 6 colores

Nr.28/87/310
28/87/317

Nr. **28**/77

Eierwärmer. — Egg cosey. — Cubre-huevos.

Nr. 28/77/4134 — 28/77/3436

28/77a/7735 — **28**/77a/7734

Nr. **28**/77a

Topfanfasser.
Handle cover.
Cubre asa

Nr. 28/77a/7734, 28/77a/7735.

28/88/Trio 20

Nr. **28**/88

Karikaturpuppen.
Comic dolls.
Muñecas caricaturas.

Filz; Kopf und Glieder beweglich.—Felt; head, arms, legs jointed. Fieltro; testa, brazos, gambas articulado.

Nr. 28/88/Fu 35	Nr. 28/88/Max 30	Nr. 28/88/Fu 35
„ 28/88/Ga 50	„ 28/88/Moritz 30	„ 28/88/Fub 35
„ 28/88/Ho 35	„ 28/88/Clon 28—100	„ 28/88/Strolch 35
„ 28/88/Dach 35	„ 28/88/August 43	„ 28/88 Stru 30
„ 28/88/Bu 28		„ 28/88 Puck 20—30
„ 28/88/Trio 20		

28/88/Clon 20

28/88/Puck 30

28/90/Erich 35 — **28**/90/Berta 35

28/90

Charakterpuppen.
Character dolls.
Muñecas caracteristicas.

Unzerbrechlich, Kleider aus gut. Stoffen, ausziehbar, Kopf und Glieder beweglich.
Unbreakable, costumes take off; head, arms, legs jointed.
Irrompibles, vestidos pueden quitarse, testa brazos y gambas articulado.

Nr. 28/90/Erich 28—50,2	Nr. 28/90/Xaver 35
„ 28/90/Berta 28—50,2	„ 28/90/Toni 35

28/95/Toni 35, Xaver 35

Nr. **28**/95

Künstlerpuppen Steiff-Schlopsnies.
Steiff-Schlopsnies dolls.
Muñecas artisticas Steiff-Schlopsnies.

Größe 40 cm
Height 40 cm
Altura 40 cm

28/95 Vera Peter Theo Viktor

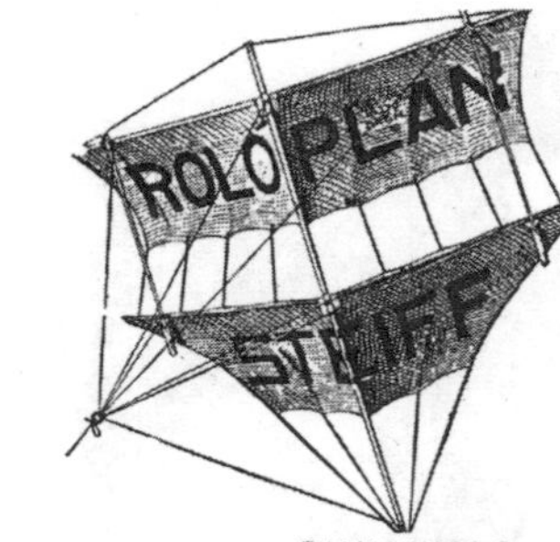

28/125/180/2

Nr. **28**/125

Roloplan, der beste Stoffdrachen, zusammenlegbar.
Roloplan, best cloth-kite in existence. Collapsable.
Roloplan, el mejor cometa de tela, plegable.

Nr. 28/125/80/2 — 28/125/360/2

hierzu — hereto — además

Schnurhaspel mit Schnur. — Winder with twine.
Devanadera con cordon.

Nr. **28**/130

Holztiere. — Wooden toys. — Animales de madera.

28/130 **28**/130/Velo Ele

Spatz.— Sparrow.— Gor: ion.

Pferd. — Horse. — Caballo.

Nr. **28**/130/1814 Nr. **28**/130/1823

Nr. **28**/138

Kindersporträder.
Children sporting articles.
Patines para niños.

Nr. **28**/138/Skiro 7876
„ **28**/138/Skiroco 7885
„ **28**/138/Skirit 7875
„ **28**/138/Bubirad 7830

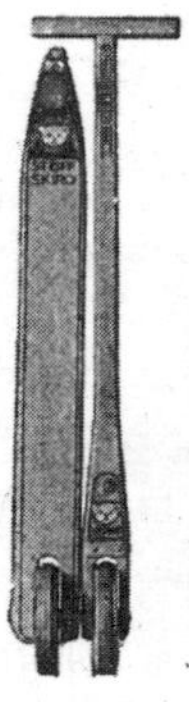

Skiro; zerlegt, jointed, rajo.

28/138/Skiro 7876

Musikspielwaren. — Musical toys. — Juguetes de música.

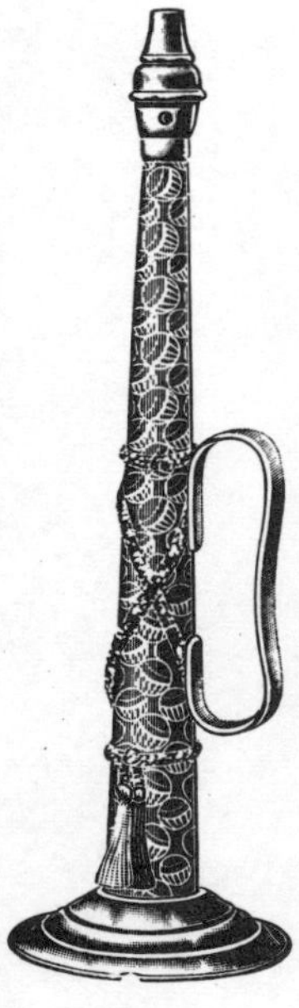

151/1
Größe/Size/Tamaño: 5½ × 9 cm

151/2a
4,8 × 7 cm

151/3
6 × 10 cm

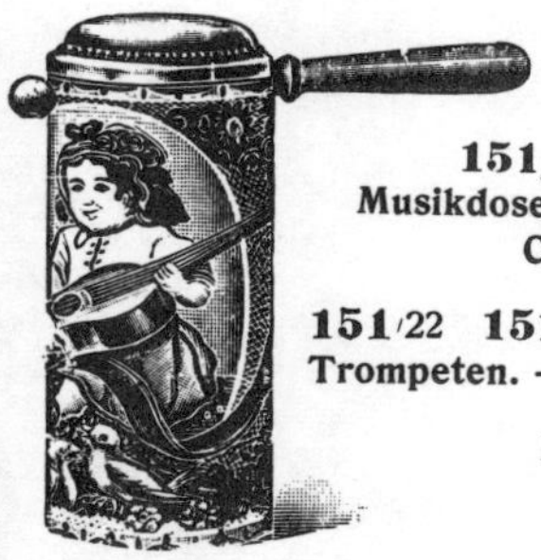

151/1 **151**/2a **151**/3
Musikdosen. — Musical boxes. — Caja para girar.

151/22 **151**/20a **151**/20H **151**/22H
Trompeten. — Trumpets. — Trompetas.

151/51 **151**/52
Revotina.

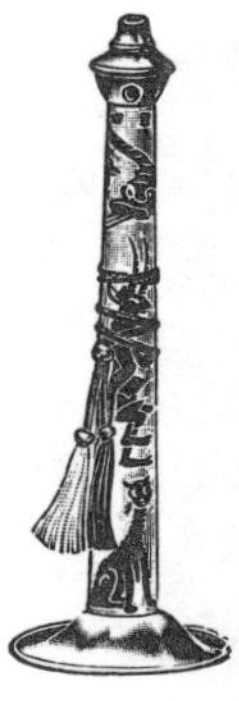
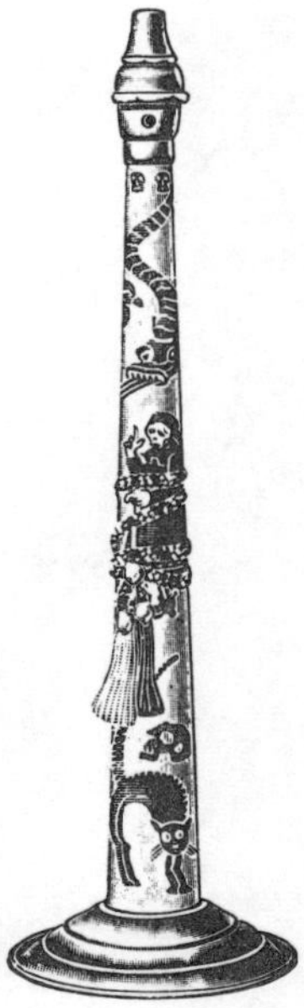

151/22 **151**/20a **151**/51 **151**/52 **151**/20H **151**/22H

Nr.			
Nr. **151**/22	Bunt, mit Griff, Länge 33 cm, Trichterdurchmesser 10 cm. Material: halb Pappe, halb Zink. Verpack. dtzw.	Gay colour, with handle, length 33 cm, diameter of mouth 10 cm. Material: half cardboard, half zinc. Packing in dozens.	Con mango. Largura 33 cm, diámetro de la boca 10 cm; material: mitad cartón, mitad zinc; embalaje a docenas.
„ **151**/22H	Halloween, ohne Griff, Länge 33 cm, Trichterdurchmesser 10 cm, Material: halb Pappe, halb Zink. Verpack. dtzw.	Halloween, without handle, length 33 cm, diameter of mouth 10 cm. Material: half cardboard, half zinc. Packing in dozens.	Halloween, sin mango. Largura 33 cm, diámetro de la boca 10 cm; material: mitad cartón, mitad zinc; embalaje a docenas.
„ **151**/20H	Halloween, ohne Griff, Länge 18 cm, Trichterdurchmesser 10 cm, Material: halb Pappe, halb Zink, Verpack. 4 dtzw.	Halloween, without handle, length 18 cm, diameter of mouth 6 cm. Material: half cardboard, half zinc. Packing in 4 dozens.	Halloween, sin mango. Largura 18 cm, diámetro de la boca 6 cm; material: mitad cartón, mitad zinc; embalaje a 4 docenas.
„ **151**/20a	Bunt, ohne Griff, Länge 24 cm, Trichterdurchm. 10 cm, Material: halb Pappe, halb Zink. Verpackung 2 dutzendw.	Gay colours, without handle, length 24 cm, diameter, of mouth 10 cm. Material: half cardboard, half zinc. Packing in 2 dozens.	De varios colores, sin mango. Largura 24 cm, diámetro de la boca 10 cm, material: mitad cartón, mitad zinc; embalaje a 2 docenas.
„ **151**/1	Zum Öffnen. Material halb und halb, Verpackung dutzendweise.	Can be opened. Material: half and half. Packing in dozens.	Para abrir, la mitad de todo material. Embalaje a docenas.
„ **151**/2a	Zinkdeckel. Material halb und halb, Verpackung dutzendweise.	Zink cover. Material: half and half. Packing in dozens.	Cubierta de zinc, material: la mitad de todo material. Embalaje a docenas.
„ **151**/3	Zum Öffnen. Material halb und halb, Verpackung dutzendweise.	Can be opened. Material: half and half. Packing in dozens.	Para abrir, la mitad de todo material, embalaje a docenas.
„ **151**/51	8 Ton, Material halb und halb, Verpackung dutzendweise.	8 tones. Packing in dozens. Material: half and half.	8 sonidos. Embalaje: a docenas; la mitad de todo material.
„ **151**/52	8 Ton, Material halb und halb, Verpackung dutzendweise.	8 tones. Packing in dozens. Material: half and half.	8 sonidos. Embalaje: a docenas; la mitad de todo material.

Kinder-Aluminium-Service.
In Kartons. Wirkungsvolle Aufmachung.

Children's aluminium services.
In cardboard box, effective style.

Servicios de aluminio para niños.
En cajita de cartón, ejecución haciendo gran efecto.

2022/68

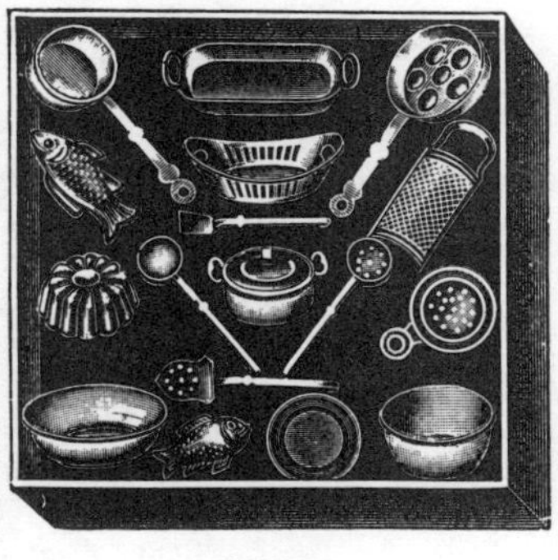

2022/70

2022/71

2022/69

2022/34

Aluminium-Teeservice. — Aluminium tea services. — Servicios de aluminio para el té.

2022/68 Mit, with, con	2	3	4	6	Tassen, cubs, tazas.
	7	9	11	15	Teile, pieces, piezas.
2022/34 Mit, with, con	2	3	4	6	Tassen, cubs, tazas.
	7	9	11	15	Teile, pieces, piezas.
2022/69			4	6	Tassen, cubs, tazas.
			11	15	Teile, pieces, piezas.

Kinder-Küchengarnituren, Blech lackiert. — Children's kitchen sets, sheet metal japanned. — Utensilios de cocina para niños, hoja de lata embarnizada.

2022/70 Weiße Lackierung, blau abgetönt. — White japanning, shaded blue. — Embarnizadura blanca, matizada en azul.
In 10, 14, 18, 20 Teilen, pieces, piezas.

2022/71 Blaue Lackierung. — Blue japanning. — Embarnizadura azul.
In 9, 11, 12, 14, 17 Teilen, pieces, piezas.

„Schuco"- -Patent

Mit nach allen Seiten selbsttätig beweglichem Kopf.

With authomatic movements of the head towards all sides.

Con cabeza móvil automáticamente hacia todos lados.

"Schuco-Monkey" Nr. 2/32	"Schuco"-Bear Nr. 10/50	"Acrobato"-Clown Nr. 220	"Schuco"-Chimpanzee Nr. 5/36
„ Mono „ 2/32	„ Oso „ 10/50	„ Arlequin „ 220	„ Chimpancé „ 5/36
„ Elephant „ 29/35	„ Elephant „ 29/60		„ Bear „ 9/35
„ Elefante „ 29/35	„ Elefante „ 29/60		„ Oso „ 9/35
			„ Bear „ 19/50
			„ Oso „ 19/50

„Schuco", das lebendige Spielzeug,

ist drollig wie ein junges Tier, entzückt jung und alt. Naturgetreu hebt und senkt „Schuco" den Kopf, guckt rechts und links oder rundum. Diese drolligsten Effekte werden durch einfaches Bewegen des Schwanzes erreicht.

"Schuco" the Living Toy

is as comical as a baby animal and furnishes amusement for young and old. It looks up or down in the cutest way and turns its head to the right or left. These cute movements are caused by a slight turn of the tail.

"Schuco" el juguete viviente,

es gracioso, como un animal joven, encanta a jóvenes y a viejos. "Schuco" alza y baja la cabeza con naturalidad, mira a la derecha y a la izquierda y a su alrededor. Todos esos graciosos efectos, alcánzanse por medio de un simple movimiente del rabo.

"Acrobato"

Turnt vor- und rückwärts, am Trapez und als Purzelfigur.

Ohne Feder! Unverwüstlich! Ohne Schlüssel! Keine Uhrwerk-Mängel!

Working forward and backward, on the trapeze, and tumbling. Without spring. Indestructible! Without key.

Da volteretas adelante y atrás y sobre el trapecio. Sin muelle. Sin llave.

Kompletter Katalog mit Neuheiten steht auf Wunsch zur Verfügung.

Complete Catalogue with Novelties sent at request.

A demanda, un catálogo completo con novedades está a la disposición del cliente.

Nr. 2/10	Lederpuppen (echtes Leder) mit Stimme im Kopf, Porzellankopf mit beweglichen Augen.	Kid dolls (real leather), with head voice, china head, movable eyes.	Muñecas de cuero (cuero genuino) con voz y cabeza de porcelana, con ojos móviles.
„ 2/11	Lederpuppen (echtes Leder), Porzellankopf, Kugelaugen mit Wimpern.	Kid dolls (real leather), china head, ball-joint eyes, and eyelashes.	Muñecas de cuero (cuero genuino), cabeza de porcelana, ojos esféricos con pestañas.
„ 2/12	Imitation-Lederpuppen mit Porzellankopf, beweglichen Augen.	Imitation kid dolls, china head, movable eyes.	Muñecas de cuero imitado con cabeza de porcelana y ojos móviles.
„ 2/13	Rosa Leinwandbälge, mit Haaren gestopft, mit Metallkopf, beweglichen Augen.	Dolls with pink linen, skin stuffed with hair, metal head, movable eyes.	Cuerpos de muñecas de lienzo de color de rosa (rellenados de pelo).
„ 2/14	dito, mit Porzellankopf, beweglichen Augen.	ditto, with china head, movable eyes.	Con cabeza de porcelana y ojos móviles.
„ 2/15	dito, mit Metallkopf, gemaltem Haar und Augen.	ditto, with metal head, painted hear and eyes.	Con cabeza de metal, cabellos y ojos pintados.
„ 2/16	Steifgelenk-Täuflinge mit Hemd und Porzellankopf, beweglichen Augen.	Stiff jointed dolls, dressed for baptism in shirt, china head, movable eyes.	Ahijados en camisa con coyunturas tiesas, con cabeza de porcelana y ojos móviles.
„ 2/17	dito.	Stiff jointed dolls, dressed for baptism in shirt, china head.	idem.
„ 2/18	dito.	ditto.	idem.
„ 2/19	dito, feine Ausführung.	ditto, best finish.	idem, fina ejecución.
„ 2/20	dito, mit Porzellankopf, festen Glasaugen.	ditto, china head, fixed glass eyes.	idem, con cabeza de porcelana y fijos ojos de vidrio.
„ 2/21	dito, mit Pappkopf, gemaltem Haar und Augen.	ditto, pasteboard head, painted hair and eyes.	idem, con cabeza de cartón, cabellos y ojos pintados.
„ 2/22/21	Gestopfte Puppen mit Pappkopf, mit Stimme, in Batisthemd.	Stuffed dolls with pasteboard head, with voice, with cambric shirt.	Muñecas emborradas en camisa de batista, con cabeza de cartón y voz.
„ 2/23	Gestopfte Puppen mit Batisthemd, mit Pappkopf, gemaltem Haar und Augen.	Stuffed dolls with cambric shirt, with pasteboard head, painted hair and eyes.	Muñecas emborradas en camisa de batista, con cabeza de cartón y cabellos y ojos pintados.
„ 2/24	Nankingpuppen mit Porzellankopf.	Nankeen dolls with china head.	Muñecas de nanquín con cabeza de porcelana.
„ 2/25	Sitzbaby, gekleidet, mit Porzellankopf, beweglichen Augen.	Sitting baby doll, dressed, china head, movable eyes.	Bebe (niño pequeño) sentado, vestido, con cabeza de porcelana y ojos móviles.
„ 2/26	dito.	ditto.	idem.
„ 2/27	dito.	ditto.	idem.
„ 2/28	dito, in Wollsweater.	ditto, in wool sweater.	idem, en sweater de lana.
„ 2/29	dito, mit Batisthemd.	ditto, with cambric shirt.	idem, en camisa de batista.
„ 2/30	dito.	ditto.	idem.
„ 2/31	Sitzbaby aus Holz, mit Zelluloidkopf, gemaltem Haar und Augen, mit Batisthemd.	Sitting baby doll of wood, celluloid head, with cambric shirt, painted hair and eyes.	Bebe (niño pequeño) de madera, sentado en camisa de batista, con cabellos y ojos pintados y cabeza de celuloide.
„ 2/32	Sitzbaby mit Batisthemd, mit Porzellankopf, beweglichen Schielaugen.	Sitting baby doll with cambric shirt, with china head, movable eyes (squinting).	Bebe sentado en camisa de batista con cabeza de porcelana y ojos bizcos móviles.
„ 2/33	Sitzbaby mit Batisthemd, mit Porzellankopf, beweglichen Augen.	ditto.	Bebe sentado en camisa de batista con cabeza de porcelana y ojos móviles.
„ 2/34	dito, mit Papiermachékopf, gemaltem Haar und Augen.	ditto, with papermaché head, painted hair and eyes.	idem, con cabeza de papier maché y cabellos y ojos pintados.
„ 2/35	Stehbaby, mit Batisthemd, mit Pappkopf, gemaltem Haar und Augen.	Standing baby doll, with cambric shirt, with pasteboard head, painted hair and eyes.	Bebe sentado en camisa de batista con cabeza de cartón y cabellos y ojos pintados.
„ 2/36/44	Gestopfte Puppen, gekleidet, mit unzerbrechlichem Kopf, gemaltem Haar und Augen.	Stuffed dolls, dressed, with unbreakable head, painted hair and eyes.	Muñecas emborradas, vestidas, con cabeza infrangible y cabellos y ojos pintados.
„ 2/37	dito, mit Mamastimme.	ditto, with mama-voice.	idem, con voz de la mamá.
„ 2/38/38	dito, mit Porzellankopf, beweglichen Augen, mit Mamastimme.	ditto, with china head, movable eyes, mama-voice.	idem, con cabeza de porcelana, ojos móviles y voz de la mamá.
„ 2/39	Stehbaby, gekleidet, mit Mantel, mit Porzellankopf, beweglichen Augen.	Standing baby doll, dressed, with cloak, china head, movable eyes.	Bebe en pie derecho, vestido, con capotillo, con cabeza de porcelana y ojos móviles.
„ 2/40	Doppelgelenk-Täuflinge mit Handgelenk, feinste Ausführung, mit Batisthemd, mit Porzellankopf, Perücke, beweglichen Augen.	Double jointed doll, dressed for baptism, jointed wrist, best finish, with cambric shirt, china head, wig, movable eyes.	Ahijadas con coyuntura doble, con puño, en camisa de batista, con cabeza de porcelana, peluca y ojos móviles, ejecución finísima.
„ 2/41	dito, mittlere Ausführung.	ditto, medium quality finish.	idem, ejecución mediana.
„ 2/42	dito, billige Ausführung.	ditto, cheap quality finish.	idem, ejecución barata.
„ 2/43	Waschbare Täuflinge, gestopft, mit Batisthemd, mit Frisur, festen Glasaugen.	Washable dolls, dressed for baptism, stuffed, with cambric shirt, with coiffure, fixed glass eyes.	Ahijadas para lavar, emborradas, con peinado, en camisa de batista, con fijos ojos de vidrio.
„ 2/44	Modell-Täuflinge, gestopft, mit Batisthemd, mit Frisur, festen Glasaugen.	Model dolls, dressed for baptism, stuffed, with cambric shirt, with coiffure, fixed glass eyes.	Ahijadas de modelo en camisa de batista, emborradas, con peinado y fijos ojos de vidrio.
„ 2/45	Waschbare Täuflinge, gestopft, mit Batisthemd, mit Frisur, festen Glasaugen, mit Papa- und Mamastimme durch Zug.	Washable dolls, dressed as above, stuffed, with cambric shirt, with coiffure, fixed glass eyes, with papa- and mama-voice.	Ahijadas para lavar, la misma ejecución que arriba, pero con voz del papá y de la mamá, las cuales voces se hace sonar tirando un filo.
„ 2/46	Waschbare Täuflinge, gestopft, mit Batisthemd, mit Frisur, festen Glasaugen, billige Ausführung.	Washable dolls, dressed for baptism, stuffed, with cambric shirt, with coiffure, fixed glass eyes, cheap quality finish.	Ahijadas para lavar, emborradas, en camisa de batista, con peinado y fijos ojos de vidrio.
„ 2/47/30	Stehbaby, gegossen, gemalte Schielaugen, gekleidet, mit Frisur.	Standing baby, of papier maché, painted squinting eyes, dressed, with coiffure.	Bebe en pie derecho, fundida, vestida, con ojos bizcos pintados y peinado.
„ 2/48/30	dito.	ditto.	idem.
„ 2/49/30	dito.	ditto.	idem.
„ 2/50/25	dito, mit Federausputz.	ditto, with feather ornaments.	idem, con adorno de plumas.
„ 2/51	dito, mit Seidenrock mit Pelz besetzt.	ditto, with silk skirt, trimmed with fur.	idem, con saya (vestido) de seda adornada con pieles.
„ 2/52	Steckkissen mit Baby.	Baby carrying cushion with baby doll.	Cojinito con bebe (niño pequeño).
„ 2/53	Baby mit Tragkleid.	Baby dolls in long clothes.	Bebe en vestido para llevar.
„ 2/54	Stehbaby, gekleidet, sechserlei sortiert, Porzellankopf, Kugel-Schielaugen.	Standing baby doll, dressed, assorted 6 kinds, china head, ball-socked eyes, squinting.	Bebe en pie derecho, vestida, en 6 surtidos, con cabeza de porcelana y bizcos ojos esféricos.
„ 2/55	Steifgelenkpuppen, gekleidet, feinste Ausführung, Porzellankopf, bewegliche Augen.	Stiff jointed dolls, dressed, best finsh, china head, movable eyes.	Muñecas con coyuntura tiesa, vestidas, cesto de porcelana, con ojos móviles, ejecución finísima.
„ 2/56/19	dito.	ditto.	idem.
„ 2/57	dito.	ditto.	idem.
„ 2/58	Steifgelenkpuppen, ganz in Pelz gekleidet, Porzellankopf, bewegliche Augen.	Stiff jointed dolls, dressed entirely in furs, china head, movable eyes.	Muñecas con coyuntura tiesa, cada una vestida enteramente en pieles, con cabeza de porcelana y ojos móviles.
„ 2/59	Steifgelenkpuppen, gekleidet, dreierlei sortiert, mit Porzellankopf, beweglichen Augen, bessere Ausführung.	Stiff jointed dolls, dressed, assorted 3 kinds, china head, movable eyes, superior finish.	Muñecas con coyuntura tiesa, vestidas, con cabeza de porcelana y ojos móviles, en 3 surtidos, ejecución mejor.
„ 2/60	dito.	ditto.	idem.
„ 2/61	dito.	ditto.	idem.
„ 2/62	dito.	ditto.	idem.
„ 2/63	dito.	ditto.	idem.

Nr. 2/64	Steifgelenkpuppen, gekleidet, dreierlei sortiert, mit Porzellankopf, beweglichen Augen, billige Ausführung.	Stiff jointed dolls, dressed, assorted 3 kinds, with china head, movable eyes, cheap quality finish.	Muñecas con coyuntura tiesa, con cabeza de porcelana y ojos móviles, en 3 surtidos, ejecución barata.
„ 2/65	dito.	ditto.	idem.
„ 2/66	dito.	ditto.	idem.
„ 2/67/28	dito, Rotkäppchen.	ditto, red ridding hood.	idem, caperuza roja.
„ 2/68	dito.	ditto.	idem, en 3 surtidos.
„ 2/69	dito, mit festen Glasaugen.	ditto, with fixed glass eyes.	idem, con fijos ojos de vidrio.
„ 2/70	Doppelgelenkpuppen, gekleidet, dreierlei sortiert, Porzellankopf, bewegliche Augen.	Double jointed dolls, dressed, assorted 3 kinds, china head, movable eyes.	Muñecas con coyuntura doble, vestidas, con cabeza de porcelana y ojos móviles, en 3 surtidos.
„ 2/71/54	dito, mit Seidenkleid.	ditto, in silk dress.	idem, en vestido de seda.
„ 2/72	dito, in sortierten Kleidern.	ditto, in assorted dresses.	idem, en vestidos surtidos.
„ 2/73	dito.	ditto.	idem.
„ 2/74/43	dito, in Samtkleid.	ditto, in velved dress.	idem, en vestido de terciopelo.
„ 2/75	Doppelgelenkpuppen, gekleidet, mit Mantel und Muff, mit Porzellankopf, beweglichen Augen.	Double jointed dolls, dressed with cloak and muff, china head, movable eyes.	Muñecas con coyuntura doble, vestidas, con capotillo y regalillo, con cabeza de porcelana y ojos móviles.
„ 2/76	dito, in dreierlei sortierten Kleidern.	ditto, in 3 assorted dresses.	idem, en vestidos de 3 surtidos.
„ 2/77	dito, in buntem Batistkleid, mit Stickereischürzen.	ditto, in coloured cambric dress, with embroidered apron.	idem, en vestido de batista de varios colores con delantales bordados.
„ 2/78	dito, in sortierten Kleidern.	ditto. in assorted dresses.	idem, en vestidos surtidos.
„ 2/80	2 Figuren, fein gekleidet, beweglich, auf Kasten mit Musik.	2 figures, well dressed, moving on box with music.	2 figuras vestidas finamente, móviles sobre una caja, con música.
„ 2/81	Knaben, fein gekleidet, beweglich, auf Kasten mit Musik.	Boys, well dressed, moving on box with music.	Muchachos vestidos finamente, móviles sobre una caja, con música.
„ 2/82	Drehfiguren, fein gekleidet, Porzellankopf, mit Musik.	Turning figures, well dressed, china head, with music.	Figuras girables, vestidas finamente, con cabeza de porcelana, con música.
„ 2/83	Quietscher, fein gekleidet, Porzellankopf, mit Stimme.	Squeaking figures, well dressed, china head, with voice.	Figuras chillando, vestidas finamente, con cabeza de porcelana y voz.
„ 2/84	Schlottern, fein gekleidet, mit Zelluloidkopf, mit Glockenstimme.	Shambling figures, well dressed, celluloid head, clear voice.	Figuras bambaneándose, vestidas finamente, con cabeza de celuloide y voz de campana.
„ 2/85	Quietscher, gekleidet, mit Papiermachékopf, mit Stimme.	Squeaking figures, dressed, papier mâché head, with voice.	Figuras chillando, vestidas, con cabeza de papier mâché y con voz.
„ 2/86	Stürzenschläger, fein gekleidet, mit Porzellankopf, mit Stimme.	Somersaulters, well dressed, china head, with voice.	Figura de un golpeador de planillos, vestidas finamente, con cabeza de porcelana.
„ 2/87	dito, mit Zelluloidgesicht, mit Stimme.	ditto, with celluloid face, with voice.	idem, con cara de celuloide y voz.
„ 2/88	dito, gekleidet, mit Papiermachékopf, mit Stimme.	ditto, dressed, papier mâché head, with voice.	idem, con cabeza de papier mâché y voz.
„ 2/89	Clown, fein gekleidet, stehend, mit Steigstimme.	Clown, well dressed, standing, with hig voice.	Bufones (clowns) en pie derecho, vestidos finamente, con voz creciendo.
„ 2/90	Stehender Clown, gekleidet, mit Zelluloidgesicht, mit vielen Stimmen.	Standing clown, dressed, with celluloid face, with various voices.	Bufones (clowns) en pie derecho, vestidos, con cara de celuloide y con muchas voces.
„ 2/91	Neger, fein gekleidet, mit Porzellankopf, sitzend auf Stoff-Giraffe mit Rädern.	Nigger, well dressed, china head, sitting on cloth giraffe on wheels.	Negro sentado sobre una jirafa de estofa con ruedas, vestido finamente, con cabeza de porcelana.
„ 2/92	dito, auf Esel.	ditto, on donkey.	Negro sentado sobre un burro de estofa con ruedas, vestido finamente, con cabeza de porcelana.
„ 2/93	dito, auf Elefant.	ditto, on elephant.	idem, sentado sobre un elefante de estofa.
„ 2/94	Knabe, fein gekleidet, mit Porzellankopf, sitzend auf Pelzziege.	Boy well dressed, china head, sitting on skin goat.	Muchacho sentado sobre una cabra de piel, vestido finamente, con cabeza de porcelana.
„ 2/95	dito, auf Esel mit Nickkopf.	ditto, on monkey with nodding head.	idem, sentado sobre un burro de estofa cabeceando, montado sobre ruedas.
„ 2/96	Pelzaffe, sitzend auf Dreirad.	Fur monkey, sitting on tricycle.	Mono de piel sentado sobre un tricicleta.
„ 2/97	Fahrfiguren, fein gekleidet, beweglich, auf Brett fahrend.	Figures, well dressed, movable on board on wheels.	Figuras móviles, vestidas finamente, andando sobre una tabla con ruedas.
„ 2/98	dito.	ditto.	idem.
„ 2/99	Fahrfiguren, Mädchen, fein gekleidet, mit Stoffschäfchen auf Brett fahrend.	Figures, girls, well dressed, with cloth sheep, movable on board on wheels.	idem, muchachas, vestidas finamente, con ovejas pequeñas de estofa, andando sobre una tabla con ruedas.
„ 2/100	Fahrfiguren, Knabe, gekleidet, mit Geige.	Figures, boy, dressed, with violin.	idem, muchacho móvil, vestido, con violín, andando sobre una tabla con ruedas.
„ 2/101	dito.	ditto.	idem.
„ 2/102	Knabe und Mädchen, fein gekleidet, auf Wagen mit 2 Stoffpferden mit Rädern.	Boy and girl, well dressed, on carriage with 2 cloth horses with wheels.	Muchacho y muchacha, vestidos finamente, en un coche con 2 caballos de estofa sobre ruedas.
„ 2/103	Figur, fein gekleidet, auf 4 Papppferden, beweglich, auf Rädergestell.	Figure, well dressed, on 4 paste board horses, movable on wheel carriage.	Figura vestida finamente, sobre 4 caballos de cartón, móvil sobre una plataforma con ruedas.
„ 2/104	Clown, fein gekleidet, reitend auf Papppferd, beweglich auf Rädergestell.	Clown, well dressed, riding on paste board horse, moving on wheel carriage.	Bufón (clown), vestido finamente, andando a un caballo de cartón móvil sobre una plataforma con ruedas.
„ 2/105/3	Sportwagen mit Puppe, fein gekleidet, mit Porzellankopf, beweglich, mit Stimme.	Sporting carriage with doll well dressed, china head, movable, with voice.	Coche de deporte con muñeca, vestida finamente, con móvil cabeza de porcelana, con voz.
„ 2/106/1	dito.	ditto.	idem.
„ 2/107/0	dito.	ditto.	idem.
„ 2/108	Knabe, gekleidet, mit Wagen mit beweglichem Papppferd.	Boy, dressed, on carriage with movable paste board horse.	Muchacho, vestido, en coche con móvil caballo de cartón.
„ 2/109	Clown, fein gekleidet, mit Papiermachékopf an Gummi.	Clown, well dressed, with papier mâché head on rubber.	Bufón (clown), vestido finamente, con cabeza de papier mâché.
„ 2/110	Papiermachéfigur, gemalt, mit Doppelbewegung.	Papier mâché figure, painted, with 2 movements.	Figura de papier maché, pintada, con movimiento doble.
„ 2/111	dito, mit beweglichem Kopf.	dito, with movable head.	Figura de papier mâché, pintada, con cabeza móvil.
„ 2/112	dito.	ditto.	idem.
„ 2/113	Papiermachéfigur, gemalt, mit beweglichem Kopf.	Papier mâché figure, painted, with movable head.	idem.
„ 2/114	Tiere, sechserlei sortiert, gemalt auf Balg, mit Stimme.	Animals, assorted 6 kinds, painted on bellows stand, with voice.	Animales pintados con piel, con voz, en 6 surtidos.
„ 2/115	Hahn in Pelz und Federn, bunt, auf Holzgestell, mit Stimme.	Rooster in skin and feathers, coloured, on wooden stand, with voice.	Gallo con piel y plumas de varios colores, montado sobre una plataforma de madera, con voz.
„ 2/116	Kuckuck, bunt, auf Balg, mit Stimme.	Cuckoo, coloured on bellow stand, with voice.	Cúculo de varios colores con piel, con voz.
„ 2/117	Geflügel, dreierlei (Hahn, Henne und Ente), befiedert, mit Stimme.	Poultry, 3 kinds (cock, hen and duck), feathered, with voice.	Volatería (gallo, gallina y ánade) con plumas, con voz, en 3 surtidos.
„ 2/118	Stoffkanarienvogel mit Pfeife.	Cloth canary with whistle.	Canario de estofa con silbato.

2/80
2/81
2/82/6
2/83/5
2/84/1½
2/85
2/86
2/87/3
2/88/1
2/89
2/90/1
2/91
2/92
2/93
2/94/1
2/95
2/96/1
2/97
2/98
2/99
2/100
2/101
2/102
2/103
2/104
2/105/3
2/106/1
2/107/0
2/108
2/109
2/110
2/111
2/112
2/113
2/114/3
2/115
2/116
2/117
2/118
2/119
2/120
2/121/3
2/122/2
2/123
2/124
2/125
2/126
2/127
2/128/4
2/129/3
2/130/29
2/131/26
2/132/1
2/133/1
2/134/1
2/135/1
2/136/1
2/137/2
2/138/30
2/139/30
2/140/2
2/141
2/142/25
2/143/1
2/144/1
2/145/2
2/146/2
2/147
2/148
2/149
2/150
2/151
2/152
2/153/2
2/154
2/155/2
2/156/1
2/157
2/158
2/159
2/160
2/161
2/162
2/163
2/164
2/165
2/166
2/167
2/168
2/169/1

2/170/1
2/171/0
2/172
2/173
2/174
2/175
2/176/34
2/177/35
2/178/2½
2/179/1
2/180/1
2/180/2
2/180/3
2/180/4
2/180/5
2/180/6
2/181/3
2/182/4
2/183/1
2/184/1
2/185/3
2/186
2/187
2/188/1
2/189/3
2/190
2/191
2/192
2/193/3
2/194
2/195/3
2/196/0
2/197/3
2/198/3
2/199/2
2/200/2
2/201/1
2/202/1
2/203/3
2/204
2/205
2/206
2/207/1
2/208/2
2/209/1
2/210/2
2/211/3
2/212/1
2/213/1
2/214
2/215/1
2/216/5
2/217/1
2/218
2/219/5
2/220/3
2/221/3
2/222/2
2/223/1½
2/224/4
2/225/0
2/226/3
2/227/7
2/228/2
2/229/7
2/230/1
2/231/2½
2/232/5
2/233/2
2/234/1
2/235/1
2/236/3

2/10/43
2/11/40
2/12/34
2/13/36
2/14/34
2/15/32
2/16/35
2/17/27
2/18/24
2/19/16
2/20/16
2/21/24
2/22/21
2/23/18
2/24/20
2/25/36
2/26/34
2/27/31
2/28/30
2/29/40
2/30/30
2/31/26
2/32/27
2/33/20
2/34/18
2/35/16
2/36/44
2/37/45
2/38/38
2/39/40
2/40/44
2/41/40
2/42/33
2/43/48
2/44/43
2/45/36
2/46/32
2/47/30
2/48/30
2/49/30
2/50/25
2/51/20
2/52/18
2/53/16
2/54/22
2/55/21
2/56/19
2/57/20
2/58/19
2/59/46
2/60/39
2/61/36
2/62/28
2/63/24
2/64/43
2/65/38
2/66/34
2/67/28
2/68/26
2/69/20
2/70/53
2/71/54
2/72/50
2/73/44
2/74/43
2/75/40
2/76/37
2/77/29
2/78/30

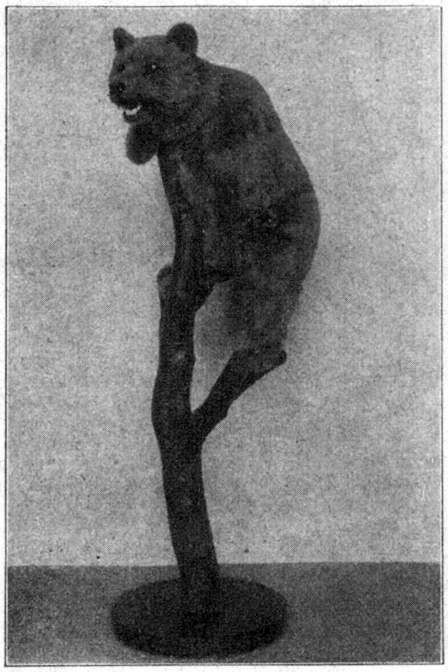

2/7007/1, 2, 3

2/6823, 6824

2/7100

2/6144/5, 8, 10

2/6703

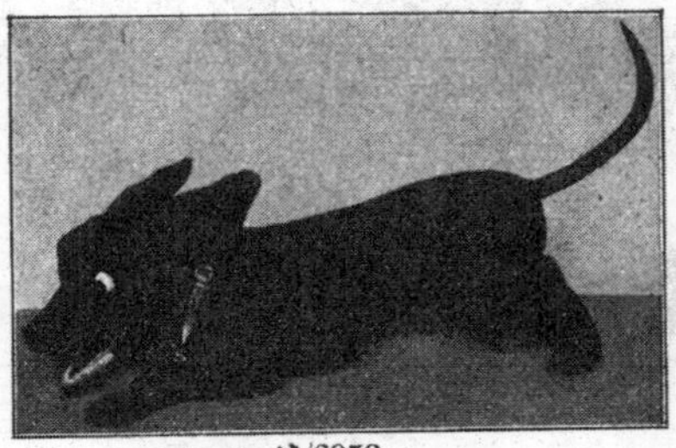

2/6053

2/7170/7, 8, 9, 10, 11, 12

2/6051

2/7107

2/6176

2/6711

2/6025/5, 10

2/6014

2/6159

Beschreibungen Seite 192h. Description page 192h. Descripciones pagina 192h.

2/6219/6, 7, 8, 9, 10, 12, 20

2/6117

2/6711, 2/6230

Nr.			
Nr. 2/119	Ente, bunt, sitzend auf Balg, mit Stimme.	Duck, coloured, sitting on belows stand, with voice.	Automóvil de madera con cane de estofa, con voz.
„ 2/120	Holzauto mit Stoffhund mit Stimme.	Wooden motor car, with cloth dog, with voice.	Coche de madera con oveja de algodón basto montada sobre una plataforma.
„ 2/121/3	Holzwagen mit Watteschaf auf Brett.	Wooden cart with wadding sheep on board.	Anade de varios colores, sentado, con piel, con voz.
„ 2/122/2	Watteschaf im Holzpferch.	Wadding sheep in wooden fold.	Oveja de algodón basto en una majada de madera.
„ 2/123	Holztiere, sechserlei, gemalt, auf Brett mit Rädern.	Wooden animals, assorted 6 kinds, painted, on board with wheels.	Animales de madera, 6 diferentes, pintados, montados sobre una tabla con ruedas.
„ 2/124	Papphähne, bunt, auf Holzgestell.	Pasteboard roosten, coloured, on wooden stand.	Gallos de cartón de varios colores, montados sobre una plataforma de madera.
„ 2/125	Holzschere mit 6 Gänsen und Mädchen.	Wooden shears with 6 geese and girl.	Tirejas de madera con 6 gansos y muchachas.
„ 2/126	Papagei, bunt, am Holzgestell.	Parrot, coloured, on wooden stand.	Papagayo de varios colores, montado sobre una plataforma de madera.
„ 2/127	Papptrompete mit Stimme.	Pasteboard trumpet with voice.	Trompeta de cartón con voz.
„ 2/128	Holzratschen.	Wooden rattles.	Carracas de madera.
„ 2/129	Filzclown, gestopft.	Felt clown, stuffed.	Bufón (clown) de fieltro, emborrado.
„ 2/130	Filzneger (Golliwog), gestopft, mit Stimme.	Felt golliwog, stuffed, with voice.	Negro de fieltro (Golliwog), emborrado, con voz.
„ 2/131	Filzpuppen, sortierte Farben, mit Zelluloidgesicht, gestopft, mit Stimme.	Felt dolls, assorted colours, with celluloid face, stuffed, with voice.	Muñecas de fieltro en colores surtidos, con cara de celuloide, emborradas, con voz.
„ 2/132	dito, gestopft, mit Pappkopf, klappernd.	ditto, stuffed, with pasteboard head, clicking.	idem, haciendo triquitraque, emborradas, con cabeza de cartón.
„ 2/133	Filzclown, gestopft, mit Zelluloidgesicht.	Felt clown, stuffed, with celluloid face.	Bufón (clown) de fieltro, emborrado, con cara de celuloide.
„ 2/134	Filzclown, gestopft, mit Papiermachékopf, mit Stimme.	Felt clown, stuffed, with papier mâché head with voice.	Bufón (clown) de fieltro, emborrado, con cabeza de papier maché y voz.
„ 2/135	Stoff-Elefanten mit Decke, gestopft, auf Rädern.	Cloth elephant with blanket, stuffed, on wheels.	Elefantes de estofa con cubierta, emborrados, sobre ruedas.
„ 2/136	Stofftiere, zweierlei, gestopft, auf Rädern.	Cloth animals, assorted 2 kinds, stuffed, on wheels.	Animales de estofa, 2 diferentes, emborrados, sobre ruedas.
„ 2/137	Stofftiere, dreierlei (Hase, Hund und Katze), gestopft, mit Stimme.	Cloth animals, assorted 3 kinds (hare, dog and cat), stuffed, with voice.	Animales de estofa, 3 diferentes (liebre, perro y gato), emborrados, con voz.
„ 2/138	Seidenplüsch-Teddybären, gestopft, mit Stimme.	Silk plush teddy bears, stuffed, with voice.	Osos "Teddy" de felpa de seda, emborrados, con voz.
„ 2/139	Seidenplüschaffen, gestopft, mit Stimme.	Silk plush monkeys, stuffed, with voice.	Mono de felpa de seda, emborrados, con voz.
„ 2/140	Plüschaffe, braun, gestopft, sitzend, mit Stimme.	Plush monkey, brown, stuffed, sitting, with voice.	Mono de felpa de seda, color pardo, emborrado, sentado, con voz.
„ 2/141	Stoff-Bi-Ba-Bo-Affe mit Mütze.	Cloth Bi-Ba-Bo-monkey with cap.	Mono "Bi-Ba-Bo" de estofa, con gorra.
„ 2/142	Papp-Nebelhörner mit Stimme.	Pasteboard foghorns, with voice.	Sirenas de cartón con voz.
„ 2/143	Holzhaus mit Weihnachtsmann mit Stimme.	Wooden house with father X-mas, with voice.	Casa de madera con el anciano de la Nochebuena regalando los niños (Padre de Navidad), con voz.
„ 2/144	Holzkäfig mit Hahn mit Stimme.	Roosten in wooden cage, with voice.	Jaula de madera con gallo con voz.
„ 2/145	Holzhundehütte mit Hund, beweglich, mit Stimme.	Dog in wooden kennel, movable, with voice.	Perrera de madera con perro móvil con voz.
„ 2/146	Theater mit 2 beweglichen Figuren, mit Stimme.	Theatre with 2 movable figures, with voice.	Teatro con 2 figuras móviles con voz.
„ 2/147	Holzspringkistchen mit Golliwog, mit Stimme.	Wooden Jack-in-the-box, with golliwog, with voice.	Cajita abriéndose saltando, de madera, con Golliwog, con voz.
„ 2/148	dito mit Käfer mit Spiralbeinen.	ditto, with beetle, with spiral spring legs.	idem, con escarabajo con piernas espirales.
„ 2/149	dito mit Stoffschäfchen.	Wooden Jack-in-the-box, with cloth sheep.	Cajita abriéndose saltando, con pequeñas ovejas de estofa.
„ 2/150	dito mit sortierten, gemalten Figuren.	ditto, with assorted painted figures.	idem, con figuras pintadas, en surtidos.
„ 2/151	Clown, gekleidet, auf Händen, auf Akkordeon.	Clown, dressed, standing on his hands, on accordeon.	Bufón (clown) vestido, levantado sobre sus manos sobre un acordeón.

Nr.	Deutsch	English	Español
Nr. 2/152	Holzwagen mit Holzhahn, fahrend, mit Uhrwerk.	Wooden cart with wooden roosten, going by clockwork.	Coche de madera con gallo de madera, sobre ruedas, con mecanismo de reloj.
„ 2/153	Pelzkatze, hüpfend, mit Uhrwerk.	Fur cat, jumping, with clockwork.	Gato de piel brincando, con mecanismo de reloj.
„ 2/154	Clown, Gaukler, tanzend.	Clown, juggler, dancing.	Bufón chocarrero (clown) danzando.
„ 2/155	Pelz-Purzelaffen mit Uhrwerk.	Fur monkey, turning comersaults by clockwork.	Monos tumbando de cabeza, de piel, con mecanismo de reloj.
„ 2/156	Holz-Gelenkeidechsen mit Uhrwerk.	Wooden jointed lizard, with clockwork.	Lagartos de madera con coyuntura, con mecanismo de reloj.
„ 2/157	Mädchen, fein gekleidet, auf Schaukel, mit Stimme.	Girl, well dressed, on swing, with voice.	Muchachas vestidas finamente sobre un mecedero, con voz.
„ 2/158	Baby, fein gekleidet, mit Porzellankopf, laufend, mit Stimme, mit Uhrwerk.	Baby, well dressed, with china head, walking by clockwork, with voice.	Bebe (niño pequeño) vestido finamente, con cabeza de porcelana, andando, con voz y mecanismo de reloj.
„ 2/159	Puppe, fein gekleidet, mit Zelluloidkopf, im Sportwagen, laufend, mit Uhrwerk.	Doll, well dressed, with celluloid head, with sporting carriage, going by clockwork.	Muñeca vestida finamente, con cabeza de celuloide en coche de deporte, andando, con mecanismo de reloj.
„ 2/160	Puppe, gekleidet, mit Papiermachékopf, tanzend, mit Uhrwerk.	Doll, dressed, with papier mâché head, dancing by clockwork.	Muñeca vestida, con cabeza de papier maché, danzando, con mecanismo de reloj.
„ 2/161	Clown, gekleidet, sitzend auf Dreirad, mit Uhrwerk.	Clown, dressed, sitting on tricycle, with clockwork.	Bufón (clown) sentado sobre un tricicleta, con mecanismo de reloj.
„ 2/162	Weihnachtsmann, rot gekleidet, laufend, mit Uhrwerk.	Father Christmas, dressed in red, walking by clockwork.	Anciano de la Nochebuena regalando los niños (Padre de Navidad), vestido en rojo, andando, con mecanismo de reloj.
„ 2/163	Clown, gekleidet, auf Händen laufend, mit Uhrwerk.	Clown, dressed, walking on his hands by clockwork.	Bufón (clown) vestido, andando sobre sus manos, con mecanismo de reloj.
„ 2/164	Seidenplüschkatze, liegend, mit Stimme, fahrend, mit Uhrwerk.	Silk plush cat, lying, with voice, moving by clockwork.	Gato de felpa de seda, extendido a lo largo, con voz, sobre ruedas, con mecanismo de reloj.
„ 2/165	Geflügel, dreierlei (Hahn, Henne, Ente), fahrend, mit Uhrwerk.	Poultry, assorted 3 kinds (cock, hen and duck), going by clockwork.	Volatería, 3 especies (gallo, gallina y ánade), sobre ruedas, con mecanismo de reloj.
„ 2/166	Geflügel, dreierlei (Hühnchen, Ente, Papagei), in Stoff, fahrend, mit Uhrwerk.	Poultry, 3 kinds (chicken, duck and parrot), of cloth, going by clockwork.	Volatería, 3 especies (polluelo, ánade, papagayo, de estofa, sobre ruedas, con macanismo de reloj.
„ 2/167	Geflügel, zweierlei (Fasan und Papagei), befiedert, fahrend, mit Uhrwerk.	Poultry, assorted 2 kinds (pheasant and parrot), feathered, going by clockwork.	Volatería, 2 especies (faisán y papagayo) con plumas, sobre ruedas, con mecanismo de reloj.
„ 2/168	Schildkröte, gemalt, fahrend, mit Uhrwerk.	Tortoise, painted, going by clockwork.	Tortuga pintada, sobre ruedas, con mecanismo de reloj.
„ 2/169	Frosch, in Stoff, grün, hüpfend, mit Uhrwerk.	Cloth frog, green, jumping by clockwork.	Rana de estofa, verde, salteando, con mecanismo de reloj.
„ 2/170/1	Zirkusgruppe, im Karton, 29×29 cm.	Circus groupe, in cardboard box 29 × 29 cm.	Grupo de un circo en cajita de cárton 29 × 29 cm, una docena en una cajita de cartón.
„ 2/170/2	dito, 39 × 39 cm.	ditto, 39 × 39 cm.	idem, 39 × 39 cm.
„ 2/170/3	dito, 45 × 45 cm.	ditto, 45 × 45 cm.	idem, 45 × 45 cm.
„ 2/171	Stoff-Viehweiden feine Ausführung.	Cloth cattle pastures, best finish.	Dehesas de ganado de estofa, fina ejecución, contenido cajita de cartón.
„ 2/172	Fell-Ziegenweiden, feine Ausführung, im Karton.	Skin goat pastures, best finish, in cardboard box.	Pastos de cabras de piel, fina ejecución, contenido cajita de cartón.
„ 2/173	Stoff-Schafweiden, im Karton.	Cloth sheep pastures, in carapoard box.	Pastos con ovejas de estofa en cajita de cartón.
„ 2/174	Watte-Schafweiden, im Karton.	Wadding sheep pastures, in cardboard box.	idem de algodón basto en cajita de cartón, una docena en una cajita de cartón.
„ 2/175	Zwölferlei Speisen auf Teller, in Karton.	Foodstuffs, ass'd 12 kinds, on plates, in carton.	12 diferentes comidas sobre platos en cajita de cartón.
„ 2/176	Holzgeigen.	Wooden violins.	Violines de madera.
„ 2/177	Holzguitarren.	Wooden guitars.	Guitarras de madera.
„ 2/178	Stoffkissen, gestopft, mit vielen Stimmen.	Cloth cushion, stuffed, with various voices.	Cojines de estofa emborrados, con muchas voces.
„ 2/179	Papagei, bunt, balancierend auf Gestell.	Parrot, coloured, balancing on wooden stand.	Papagayo de varios colores, balanceando sobre una plataforma.
„ 2/180	Strümpfe, gefüllt mit Spielwaren.	Stockings, filled with toys.	Medias llenadas de juguetes.
„ 2/181	Clown-Stehauf, in Stoff, gestopft.	Tambler clown, cloth, stuffed.	Bufón (clown) representando un dominguillo de estofa, emborrado.
„ 2/182	dito, gemalt.	ditto, painted.	idem, pintado.
„ 2/183	Dreierlei Clowns, gemalt, stehend auf Kugel, als Stehauf.	Clowns, ass'd 3 kinds, painted, standing on ball as tumbler.	3 bufones (clowns) diferentes, en pie derecho sobre un globo y representando un dominguillo.
„ 2/184	Papp-Stehauf-Figuren, sortiert, gemalt.	Pastebourd tumbler figures, ass'd, painted.	Figuras de cárton representando un dominguillo, pintadas, en surtidos.
„ 2/185	Clown-Stehauf, gemalt, mit 2 Rädern fahrend.	Tumbler clown, painted, going on 2 wheels.	Bufón (clown) representando un dominguillo, pintado, andando sobre 2 ruedas.
„ 2/186	Holzkarren mit Holzfigur, mit Karikaturhund.	Wooden cart with wooden figure and caricatur doy.	Caja de madera con figura de madera, con un perro representando una caricatura.
„ 2/187	Holzelefant mit Neger als Reiter, auf Brett, mit Rädern.	Wooden elephant with nigger on his back, on board, with wheels.	Elefante de madera con negro montado sobre el animal, montado sobre una tabla con ruedas.
„ 2/188	Wagen, bespannt mit Holzpferd, mit Brett.	Cart, with wooden horse on board.	Coche, al cual está uncido un caballo de madera montado sobre una tabla.
„ 2/189	Planwagen, bespannt mit Filzesel, auf Rädern.	Tilt wagon, with felt donkey, on wheels.	Carro entoldado, al cual está uncido un burro de fieltro sobre ruedas.
„ 2/190	Holzpferd, beweglicher Kopf, auf Brett, mit Rädern.	Wooden horse, movable head, on board, with wheels.	Caballo de madera con cabeza móvil montado sobre una tabla con ruedas.
„ 2/191	Holzbär, gemalt, auf Brett, mit Rädern.	Wooden bear, painted, on board, with wheels.	Oso de madera pintado, montado sobre una tabla con ruedas.

Nr. 2/192	Holztiere, sortiert, gemalt, mit Reiter.	Wooden animals, assorted, painted, with rider.	Animales de madera, pintados conjinete, en surtidos.
„ 2/193	Holzwagen mit Holzpferd, auf Brett, mit Rädern.	Wooden horse and cart, on board, with wheels.	Coche de madera con caballo de madera, montado sobre una tabla con ruedas.
„ 2/194	dito.	ditto.	idem.
„ 2/195	Holzwagen mit Pappferd, auf Brett, mit Rädern.	Wooden card with pasteboard horse, on board, with wheels.	Coche de madera con caballo de cartón, montado sobre una tabla con ruedas.
„ 2/196	dito.	ditto.	idem.
„ 2/197	dito.	ditto.	idem.
„ 2/198	Pelzhund, weiß, auf Rädern.	Fur dog, white, on wheels.	Perro de piel, blanco, sobre ruedas.
„ 2/199	Pelzhund, weiß, sitzend, mit Rückenstimme.	Fur dog, white, sitting, with voice in back.	Perro de piel, blanco, sentado, con voz sobre su espalda.
„ 2/200	Pelzkatze, weiß, sitzend, mit Stimme.	Fur cat, white, sitting, with voice.	Gato de piel, blanco, sentado, con voz.
„ 2/201	Pelzkatze, weiß, liegend, mit Rückenstimme.	Fur cat, white, lying, voice in back.	Gato de piel, blanco, extendido a lo largo, con voz sobre su espalta.
„ 2/202	Stoffkatze, liegend, auf Brett mit Rädern, mit Stimme.	Cloth cat, lying, on board, with wheels, with voice.	Gato de estofa, extendido a lo largo, montado sobre una tabla con ruedas, con voz.
„ 2/203	Stoffhund auf Holzrollen, bewegliches Maul, mit Stimme.	Cloth dog, in wooden wheels, movable mouth, with voice.	Perro de estofa sobre rodillos de madera, con boca móvil y con voz.
„ 2/204	Stofftiere, zweierlei (Hund und Katze), sitzend, beweglicher Kopf, mit Stimme.	Cloth animals, assorted 2 kinds (dog and cat), sitting, movable head, with voice.	Animales de estofa, 2 especies (perro y gato), sentados, con cabeza móvil y con voz.
„ 2/205	Stoffhund, sitzend, mit Stimme.	Cloth dog, sitting, with voice.	Perro de estofa, sentado, con voz.
„ 2/206	Stoff-Karikaturente, sitzend, beweglicher Kopf, mit Stimme.	Cloth caricature duck, sitting, movable head, with voice.	Anade de estofa representando una caricatura, sentado, con cabeza móvil y con voz.
„ 2/207	Stofftiere, dreierlei (eine Katze und zwei Hunde), gestopft, mit Stimme.	Cloth animals, assorted 3 kinds (1 cat and 2 dogs), sitting, stuffed, with voice.	Animales de estofa, 3 especies (1 gato y 2 perros), sentados, emborrados, con voz.
„ 2/208	Pelzschafe auf Rädern, mit Kopfdruckstimme.	Fur sheeps, on wheels, voice operated by pressing head.	Ovejas de piel sobre ruedas, con voz si se comprime sobre la cabeza.
„ 2/209	Pelzziege auf Rädern, mit Kopfdruckstimme.	Fur goats, on wheels, voice operated by pressing head.	Cabra de piel sobre ruedas, con voz si se comprime sobre la cabeza.
„ 2/210	Stoffschaf, auf Rädern.	Cloth sheep, on wheels.	Oveja de estofa sobre ruedas.
„ 2/211	Pelzschaf, mit Kopfdruckstimme, auf Brett, mit Rädern.	Fur sheep, voice operated by pressing head, on board, with wheels.	Oveja de piel, montada sobre una tabla con ruedas, con voz si se comprime sobre la cabeza.
„ 2/212	Pelzpudel, mit Schwanzdruckstimme, auf Brett, mit Rädern.	Fur poodle voice operated by pressing tail, on board, with wheels.	Perro de aguas, montado sobre una tabla con ruedas, con voz si se comprime su rabo.
„ 2/213	Pelzziege, mit Schwanzdruckstimme, auf Brett, mit Rädern.	Fur goat, voice operated by pressing tail, on board, with wheels.	Cabra de piel, montada sobre una tabla con ruedas, con voz si se comprime su cola.
„ 2/214	Stoffschaf, auf Brett, mit Rädern.	Cloth sheep, on board, with wheels.	Oveja de estofa sobre ruedas.
„ 2/215	Pelzhase auf Bogen.	Fur hare on rockers.	Liebre de piel, montada sobre un arco.
„ 2/216	Pelzhase, aufrecht, mit Schwanzdruckstimme, beweglichen Ohren.	Fur hare, standing upright, voice operated by pressing tail, movable ears.	Liebre de piel, en pie derecho, con orejas móviles, con voz si se comprime su cola.
„ 2/217	Pelzhase, sitzend, mit Schwanzdruckstimme, beweglichen Ohren.	Fur hare, sitting, voice operated by pressing tail, movable ears.	Liebre de piel, sentada, con orejas móviles, con voz si se comprime su cola.
„ 2/218	Pelztiere, dreierlei (Hund, Katze und Hase), liegend, mit Stimme.	Fur animals, ass'd 3 kinds (dog, cat and hare), lying, with voice.	Animales de piel, 3 especies (perro, gato y liebre), extendidos a lo largo, con voz.
„ 2/219	Stoffbulldogge (Französisch), auf Rädern, feine Ausführung.	Cloth bull-dog (french), on wheels, best finish.	Alano dogo "Bull" (francés) sobre ruedas, fina ejecución.
„ 2/220	dito.	ditto.	idem (inglés) sobre ruedas, fina ejecución.
„ 2/221	Stofffoxterrier, auf Rädern, feine Ausführung.	Cloth fox-terrier, on wheels, best finish.	Foxterrier (perro inglés) de estofa sobre ruedas, fina ejecución.
„ 2/222	Stoffbernhardiner, auf Rädern, feine Ausführung.	Cloth St. Bernhard dog, on wheels, best finish.	Perro del monte San Bernardo sobre ruedas, fina ejecución.
„ 2/223	Stoffjagdhund, auf Rädern, feine Ausführung.	Cloth retriever, on wheels, best finish.	Perro del monte de estofa sobre ruedas, fina ejecución.
„ 2/224	Stoffelefant, auf Rädern, beweglicher Rüssel, mit Stimme.	Cloth elephant, on wheels, movable trunk, with voice.	Elefante de estofa con trompa móvil, montado sobre ruedas, con voz.
„ 2/225	Mohairplüschbär, auf Rädern, mit Stimme.	Mohair plush bear, on wheels, with voice.	Oso de felpa de mohair sobre ruedas, con voz.
„ 2/226	Plüschbär, braun, auf Rädern.	Plush bear, brown, on wheels.	Oso de felpa, pardo, sobre ruedas.
„ 2/227	Filzesel, gesattelt, auf Rädern.	Felt donkey, saddled, on wheels.	Burro de fieltro, ensillado, sobre ruedas.
„ 2/228	Stoffkuh, auf Rädern, mit Schwanzdruckstimme.	Cloth cow, on wheels, voice operated by pressing tail.	Vaca de estofa montada sobre ruedas, con voz si se comprime su cola.
„ 2/229	Filzpferd, gesattelt, auf Rädern.	Felt horse, saddled, on wheels.	Caballo de fieltro, ensillado, sobre ruedas.
„ 2/230	Stoffziegen, mit Decke, auf Rädern.	Cloth goat, with body cloth, on wheels.	Cabras de estofa con cubierta, sobre ruedas.
„ 2/231	Zirkuspferd, gesattelt, auf Rädern.	Circus horse, saddled, on board, with wheels.	Caballo de circo, ensillado, sobre ruedas.
„ 2/232	Plüschpferd, gesattelt, auf Brett, mit Rädern.	Plush horse, saddled, on board, with wheels.	Caballo de felpa, ensillado, montado sobre una tabla con ruedas.
„ 2/233	Filzkuh, auf Brett, mit Rädern, mit Stimme.	Felt cow, on board, with wheels, with voice.	Vaca de fieltro sobre una tabla con ruedas, con voz.
„ 2/234	Filzesel, gesattelt, auf Brett, mit Rädern, mit Stimme.	Felt donkey, saddled, on board, with wheels, with voice.	Burro de fieltro, ensillado, montado sobre una tabla con ruedas, con voz.
„ 2/235	Filzpferd, braun, gesattelt, auf Brett, mit Rädern.	Felt horse, brown, saddled, on board, with wheels.	Caballo de fieltro, pardo, ensillado, montado sobre una tabla con ruedas.
„ 2/236	Pappferd, gemalt, gesattelt, auf Brett, mit Rädern.	Pasteboard horse, painted, saddled, on board, with wheels.	Caballo de cartón, pintado, ensillado, montado sobre una tabla con ruedas.

Nr.	Sämtliche Uhrwerke gehen mehrere Stunden.	All clockwork articles run for several hours.	Todos los mecanismos de reloj funcionan varias horas.	Höhe Height Altura cm
2/6014	Plüsch-Affe, beweglich Kopf, Maul, Augen und Arm.	Plush monkey, movable head, mouth, eyes and arm.	Mono con felpa, cabeza, boca, ojos y brazo móviles.	60
2/6025/5	Plüsch-Bär, beweglicher Kopf.	Plush bear, movable head.	Oso con felpa, cabeza móvil.	32
2/6025/10	dito.	ditto.	idem.	40
2/6051	Stoff-Hund, beweglich Maul und Augen.	Cloth dog, movable mouth and eyes.	Perro, boca y ojos móviles.	28
2/6053	dito.	ditto.	idem.	25
2/6117	dito.	ditto.	idem.	36
2/6131	Stoff-Kamel mit 2 Affen, beweglich Kopf, Maul und Augen. 3 Uhrwerke.	Cloth camel with 2 monkeys, movable head, mouth and eyes, 3 clockworks.	Camello de estofa con 2 monos, cabeza, boca y ojos móviles, 3 mecanismos de reloj.	125
2/6230	dito.	ditto.	idem.	190
2/6144/5	Stoff-Katze mit Jungen, beweglich Kopf und Maul.	Cloth cat with kittens, movable head and mouth.	Gato de estofa con sus hijuelos, cabeza y boca móviles.	27
2/6144/8	dito.	ditto.	idem.	30
2/6144/10	dito.	ditto.	idem.	35
2/6159	Stoff-Hund mit Jungen, beweglich Kopf und Maul.	Cloth dog with pups, movable head and mouth.	Perro de estofa con sus hijuelos, cabeza y boca móviles.	30
2/6176	Stoff-Papagei auf Ständer, beweglich Kopf und Schnabel.	Cloth parrot on stand, movable head and beak.	Papagayo de estofa sobre un poste, cabeza y boca móviles.	80
2/6219/6	Weihnachtsmann, gekleidet, auf Esel, bewegl. Kopf.	Father Christmas, dressed, on donkey, movable head.	Padre de Navidad, sobre un asno, cabeza móvil.	27
2/6219/7	dito.	ditto.	idem.	34
2/6219/8	dito.	ditto.	idem.	38
2/6219/10	dito.	ditto.	idem.	41
2/6219/12	dito.	ditto.	idem.	48
2/6219/20	dito.	ditto.	idem.	80
2/6703	Figur, gekleidet, beweglich Kopf Maul und Augen.	Figure, dressed, movable head, mouth and eyes.	Figura, vestida, cabeza, boca y ojos móviles.	43
2/6711	2 Clowns, gekleidet, bewegliche Köpfe, 2 Uhrwerke.	2 clowns, dressed, movable heads, 2 clockworks.	2 clowns, vestidos, cabezas móviles, 2 mecanismos de reloj.	77
2/7007/1	Plüsch-Bär auf Ast, beweglich Maul und Kopf.	Plush bear on branch, movable head and mouth.	Oso de felpa sobre un ramo, cabeza y boca móviles.	68
2/7007/2	dito.	ditto.	idem.	90
2/7007/3	dito.	ditto.	idem.	110
2/7100	Figur, gekleidet, beweglicher Kopf.	Figure, dressed, movable head.	Figura vestida, cabeza móvil.	57
2/7107	dito.	ditto.	idem.	105
2/7170/7	Weihnachtsmann, rot gekleidet, beweglicher Kopf.	Father Christmas, dressed in red, movable head.	Padre de Navidad, vestido en rojo, cabeza móvil.	53
2/7170/8	dito.	ditto.	idem.	65
2/7170/9	dito.	ditto.	idem.	80
2/7170/10	dito.	ditto.	idem.	90
2/7170/11	dito.	ditto.	idem.	105
2/7170/12	dito.	ditto.	idem.	120
2/6823	Weihnachtsmann im Schlitten mit Renntier, beweglicher Kopf.	Father Christmas in sledge with reindeer, movable head.	Padre de Navidad en trineo con cícroo, cabeza móvil.	85×35
2/6824	dito.	ditto.	idem.	120×45

Zelluloidpuppen. — Celluloid dolls. — Muñecas de celuloide.

Serie „Baby 1922"

Serie „A. K."

Serie „A. M."

Serie „E."

Serie „Bäbs"

Serie „Bäbs"

Serie „Baby 1922".
Neues verbessertes Modell in tadelloser Ausführung mit beweglichen Armen und Beinen; 24 Größen von ca. 7½-55 cm, von Größe 24 einschließlich an aufwärts, mit beweglichem Kopf.
Verpackung: bis Größe 15 = 1 Dtz. im Karton.
„ „ 18 = ½ „ „ „
„ „ 26 = ¼ „ „ „
„ „ 55 = 1 Stck. „ „

Serie „A. K."
Knabe mit beweglichen Armen. 10 Größen von ca. 10-32 cm.

Serie „A. M."
Mädchen mit beweglichen Armen. 10 Größen von ca. 10-32 cm.

Serie „E."
Badepuppe mit festen Gliedern, gemalten Schuhen und Strümpfen. 7 Größen von ca. 7½-25½ cm.

Serie „Bäbs".
4 Größen von ca. 5-21 cm, von Größe 11 aufwärts mit beweglichen Armen, gemalten Schuhen und Strümpfen. Verpackung: Größe 5 = 6 Dtz. im Karton.

Series "Baby 1922".
This improved model in unexceptionable style, with movable arms and legs; 24 sizes, from abt. 7½-55 cm; those from 24 cm upwards, with movable head.
Packed: those up to 15 cm, in cardboard boxes of 1 doz.
„ „ „ 18 „ „ „ „ ½ „
„ „ „ 26 „ „ „ „ ¼ „
„ „ „ 55 „ „ „ „ 1 piece

Series "A. K."
Boy with movable arms. 10 sizes, from abt. 10-32 cm.

Series "A. M."
Girl with movable arms. 10 sizes, from abt. 10-32 cm.

Series "E."
Bathing dolls, with rigid limbs, painted shoes and stockings. 7 sizes, from abt. 7½-25½ cm.

Series "Bäbs".
4 sizes, from abt. 5-21 cm; from size 11 upwards, with movable arms, painted shoes and stockings. Packed: size 5 = 6 doz. per cardboard box.

Serie "Baby 1922".
Modelo nuevo y reformado, de ejecución intachable, con brazos y piernas movibles, 24 diferentes tamaños de 7½ hasta 55 cm, de 24 cm para arriba con cabeza movible.
Empaque: hasta el tamaño de 15 cm en cart. de a 1 doc.
„ „ „ „ 18 „ „ „ „ ½ „
„ „ „ „ 26 „ „ „ „ ¼ „
„ „ „ „ 55 „ „ „ „ 1/12 „

Serie "A. K."
Niño con brazos movibles. 10 tamaños de ca. 10-32 cm.

Serie "A. M."
Niña con brazoz movibles. 10 tamaños de ca. 10-32 cm.

Serie "E."
Muñecas de baño con miembros fijos, zapatos y medias pintadas. 7 tamaños de ca. 7½-25½ cm.

Serie "Bäbs".
4 tamaños de ca. 5-21 cm, del tamaño 11 para arriba con brazos movibles, zapatos y medias pintadas. Empaque: tamaño 5 en cartones de a 6 docenas.

Knaben und Mädchen, nackt. — **Boys and girls,** naked. — **Muchacho y niña,** desundos.

Bademädchen.—Bathing girls. — Niña de baño.

Clown. — Clown. Payaso.

Holländerin. — Dutch-woman. — Holandesa.

Hirtenknabe. — Shepherd boy. — Pastorcito.

Serie „Kowenko Spezial".
Mit beweglichen Armen (Patent-Drehkopf), ca. 15 cm.
Verpackung je ½ Dtz. im Karton.

Series "Kowenko Special".
With movable arms (Pat. head to turn round), abt. 15 cm.
Packed ½ doz. in a cardboard box.

Serie "Kowenko especial".
Con brazos movibles (cabeza giratoria pat.), ca. 15 cm.
Empaque: cartones de a ½ doc.

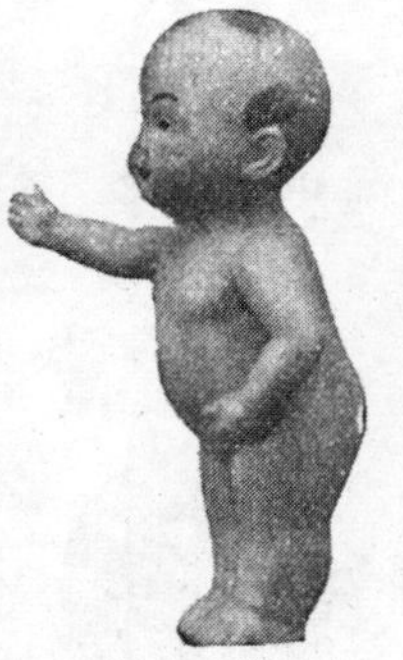
Serie „Pupsi"

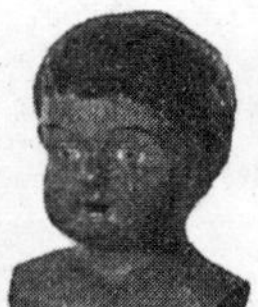
Serie „Brustblattköpfe"

Serie „Gesichtsmaske"

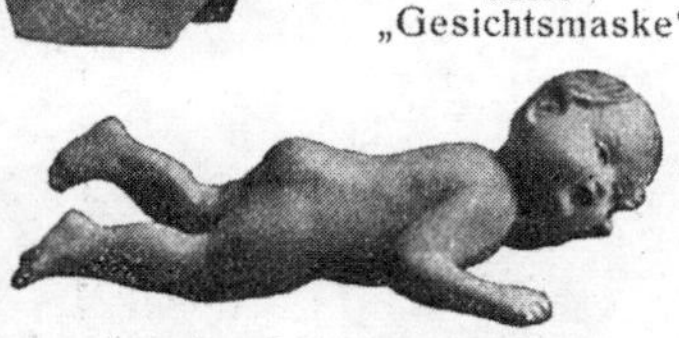
Serie „Schwimmbaby"

Serie „Sitzbaby"

Serie „Rococo"

Serie „Biedermeier"

Serie „Pupsi".
Mit beweglichen Armen, ca. 15 cm groß. Verpackung: ½ Dtz. im Karton.
Serie „Brustblattköpfe".
Gemaltes Haar, gemalte Augen, oder gemaltes Haar und Glasaugen. 11 Größen ca. 6½-14¾ cm, Größe 6½-9¾ = 1 Dtz. im Karton.
Serie „Gesichtsmaske".
10 Größen von 3½-18 cm. Verpackung: Größe 3½-6½ = 12 Dtz. im Karton.
Serie „Schwimmbaby".
Mit festen Gliedern, ca. 12 cm. Verpackung: 1 Dtz. im Karton.
Serie „Sitzbaby".
Mit festen Gliedern, ca. 4½ cm. Verpackung: 3 Dtz. im Karton.
Serie „Rococo". Serie „Biedermeier".
Sortierte Figuren mit beweglichen Armen und feiner Bemalung, ca. 18 cm. Verpackung: 3 Paar im Karton.

Series "Pupsi".
With movables arms, abt. 15 cm. Packed: ½ doz. in cardboard box.
Series "Brustblattköpfe".
Painted hair and eyes or painted hair and glass eyes. 11 sizes abt. 6½-14¾ cm. Sizes 6½-9¾ cm in boxes of 1 dozen.
Series "Gesichtsmaske".
10 sizes from 3½-18 cm. Packed: sizes 3½-6½ in cardboard boxes of 12 doz.
Series "Schwimmbaby".
With rigid limbs, abt. 12 cm. Packed: cardboard boxes of 1 doz.
Series "Sitzbaby".
With rigid limbs, abt. 4½ cm. Packed: 3 doz. in cardboard box.
Series "Rococo". Series "Biedermeier".
Assorted figures, with movable arms and finely painted, abt. 18 cm. Packed: 3 pairs in cardboard box.

Serie "Pupsi".
Con brazos movibles, tamaño ca. 15 cm. Empaque: cartones de a ½ docena.
Serie "Brustblattköpfe".
Cabello pintado y ojos pintados, o cabello pintado y ojos de vidrio. 11 tamaños de ca. 6½-14¾ cm. Empaque: tamaños 6½-9¾ cm en cartones de 1 docena
Serie "Gesichtsmaske".
10 tamaños de 3½-18 cm. Empaque: 3½-6½ cm en cartones de a 12 docenas.
Serie "Schwimmbaby".
Con miembros fijos, ca. 12 cm. Empaque: cartones de a 1 docena.
Serie "Sitzbaby".
Con miembros fijos, ca. 4½ cm. Empaque: cartones de a 3 docena.
Serie "Rococo". Serie "Biedermeier".
Figuras surtidas, finamente pintadas, con brazos movibles, tamaño ca. 18 cm. Empaque: 3 parejas en un cartón.

Zelluloid-Bälle und -Rasseln. — Celluloid balls and rattles. — Pelotas y sonajeras de celuloide.

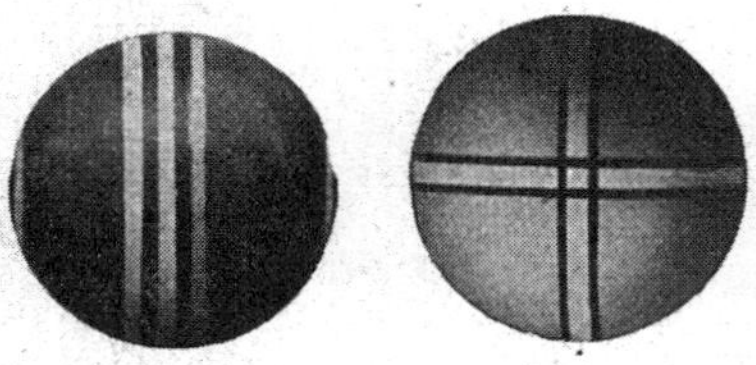

60/1018 — **60**/2036

In 12 Größen: von 1 1/2 bis 8 cm.	3 3/4 bis 10 cm.
In 12 sizes: 1 1/2 till 8 cm.	3 3/4 till 10 cm.
En 12 tamaños: 1 1/2 hasta 8 cm.	3 3/4 hasta 10 cm.

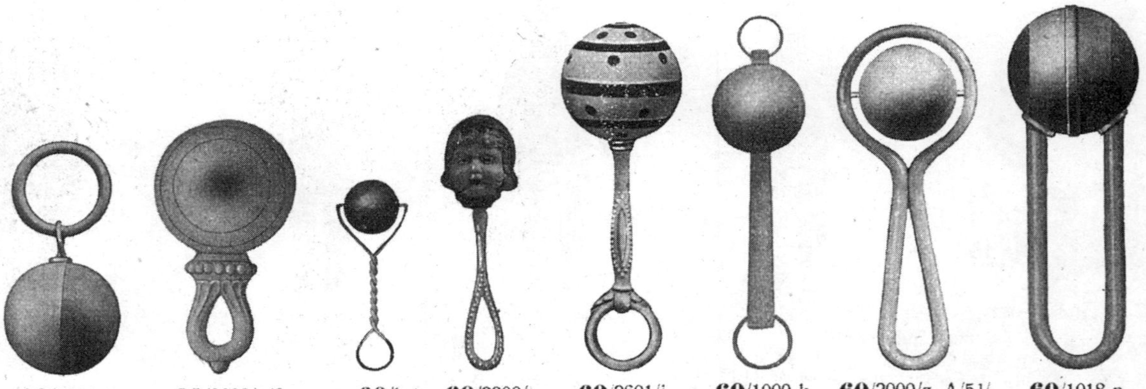

60/1011n P. 1 Dtz. — **60**/2002/v/6 — **60**/b P. 3 Dtz. — **60**/3300/e — **60**/2601/i — **60**/1000 k — **60**/2000/z. A/5 1/2 — **60**/1018 p

Nr. **60**/b Puppenrassel.
Doll's rattles.
Sonajeras para muñecas. P. 3 Dtz.

Nr. **60**/1000 k Mit Rohrstiel.
With hollow support.
Con mango de cana.

Nr. **60**/1018/p Mit Hufeisenstiel.
With horse-shoe support.
Con mango forma de herradura.

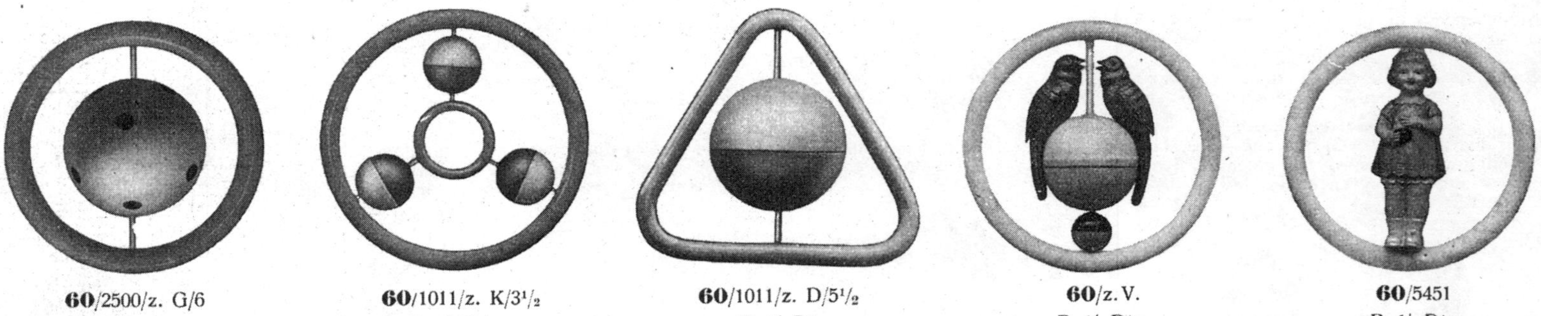

60/2500/z. G/6 P. 1/2 Dtz. — **60**/1011/z. K/3 1/2 P. 1/2 Dtz. — **60**/1011/z. D/5 1/2 P. 1/2 Dtz. — **60**/z. V. P. 1/2 Dtz. — **60**/5451 P. 1/2 Dtz.

P. = Packung, packing, embaque.

60/1011/b/4 1/2 — **60**/1011/d/5 1/2 — **60**/1013/e/5 — **60**/1017/c/5 1/2 — **60**/1026/e/5 — **60**/1029/c/5 1/2 — **60**/1030/d/5 1/2 — **60**/1032/e/5

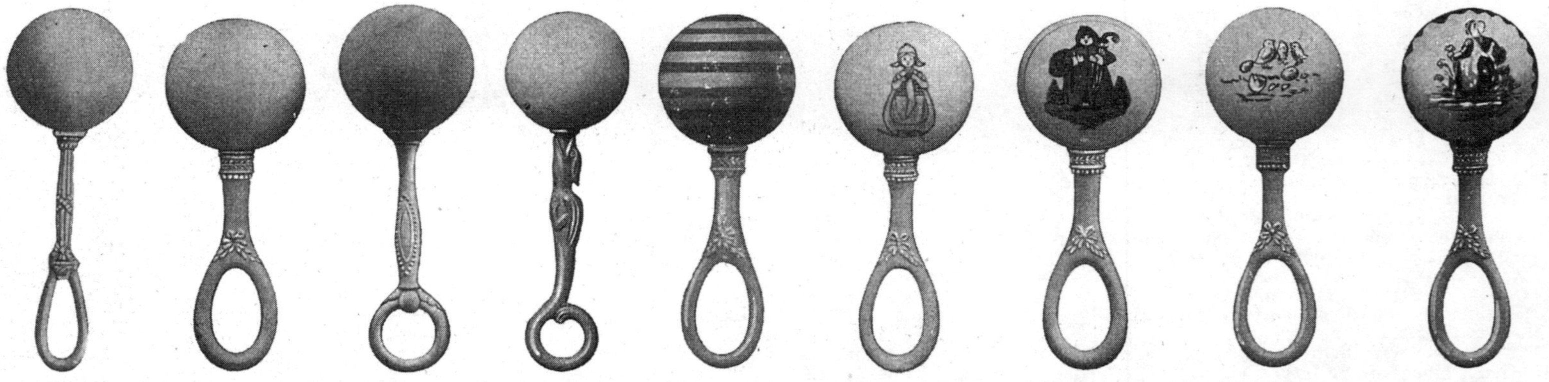

60/2000/f/5 — **60**/2000/g/6 — **60**/2000/i/6 — **60**/2000/t/5 — **60**/2020/g/6 — **60**/2035/g/6 — **60**/2040/g/6 — **60**/2081/g/6 — **60**/2083/g/6

Verpackung:
bis Ballgröße 4 1/2 = 1 Dtz.
„ 5, 5 1/2 und 6 = 1/2 „

Packing:
up to great of ball 4 1/2 = 1 doz.
„ „ „ 5, 5 1/2 and 6 = 1/2 „

Embaque:
hasta el tamaño de la pelota 4 1/2 = 1 doc.
„ „ „ „ 5, 5 1/2 y 6 = 1/2 „

Zelluloid-Rasseln, -Trompeten etc. — Celluloid rattles, trumpets, etc. — Sonajeras y trompetas de celuloide etc.

60/2033/e/5

60/2069/f/5

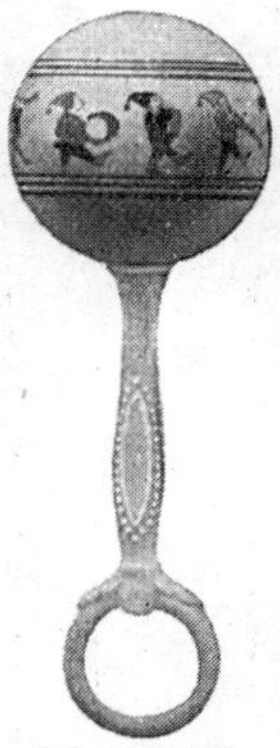
60/2060/i/6

60/2075/i/6

60/2077/i/6

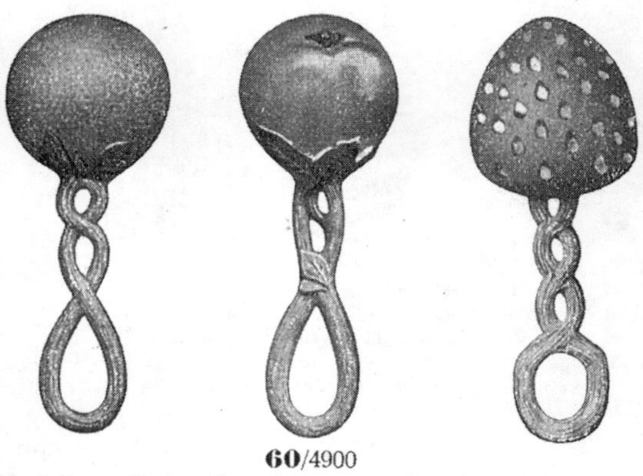
60/4900
(3 Modelle sortiert — 3 models assorted — 3 modelos surtidos)

60/4000

60/4064

60/4100

60/4200

60/4300

60/4163

60/B.K. 18/g

60/3000/e (Apfel – apple – manzano)
60/3100 (Birne — pear — pera)

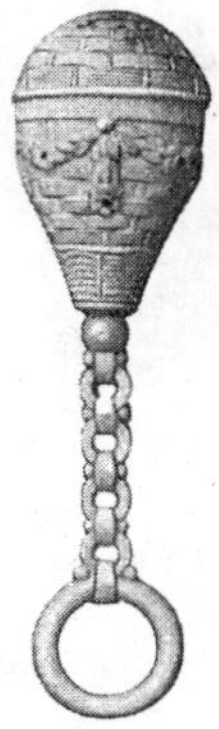
60/3400/h

60/3317/i

60/4600

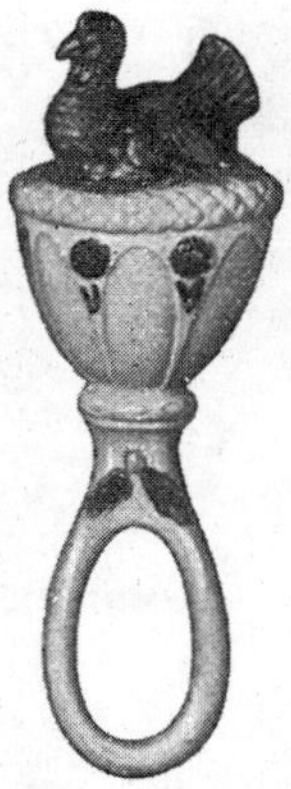
60/4650 (4 Modelle sortiert — 4 models assorted — 4 modelos surtidos

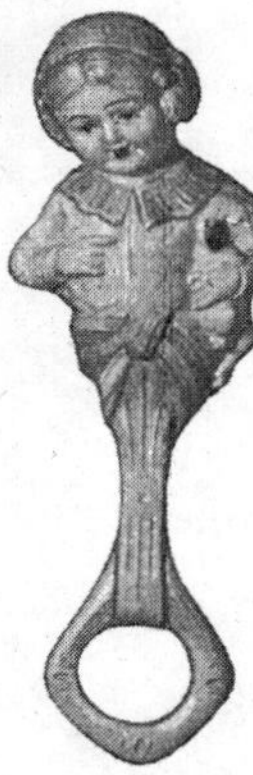
60/4901/M

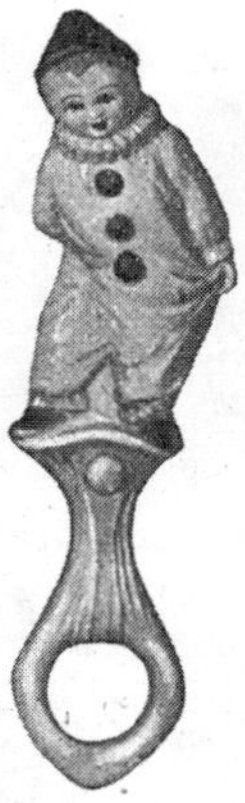
60/4901/K

60/4903

60/4904

60/4918/V

Verpackung: ½ Dtz. im Karton — Packing: ½ doz. in cardbox — Embalaje: ½ doc. en cajita de cartón.

Taucher — Diver — Buzo
in 3 Größen, sizes, tamaños
Nr. **60**/260 ca. 8½ cm
„ **60**/261 „ 13 „
„ **60**/262 „ 19 „
Verpackung — packing — embalaje
Nr. **60**/260 = ¼ Dtz.
„ **60**/261/2 = 1/12 Dtz.

Sort. **60**/4912, weiß — white — blanco
„ **60**/4913, leicht gemalt — lightly painted — ligerament pintado
„ **60**/4914, bunt gemalt — painted in various colours — multicolor
Packung, packing, embalaje: 1 doz. im Karton, cardbox, cajita de cartón

60/6600/II
in 3 Größen, sizes, tamaños
Nr. **60**/6600/I = 1 dz. } im Karton
„ **60**/6600/II/III = ½ „ } in cardbox
en cajita de cartón

Krokodilfalzer
in 4 Größen: **60**/8000/1 mit und ohne Bleistift
Crocodile Folder in 4 sizes, with or without pencil — Plegaderas cocodrilo en 4 tamaños, con o sin lápiz
60/8000/1 = 13 cm
60/8000/2 = 16 „
60/8000/3 = 19 „
60/8000/4 = 21 „

Die Trompeten können glatt, gerieft, weiß oder bunt geliefert werden.
The trumpets can be supplied plain, fluted, white or in colour.
Las trompetas se pueden suministrar lisas, estriadas, blancas o abigarradas.

60/6700/III
in 3 Größen, sizes, tamaños
Nr. **60**/6700/I = 1 dz. } im Karton
„ **60**/6700/II/III = ½ „ } in cardbox
en cajita de cartón

Stehauf-Figuren. — Figures that spring up erect. — Dominguillos.

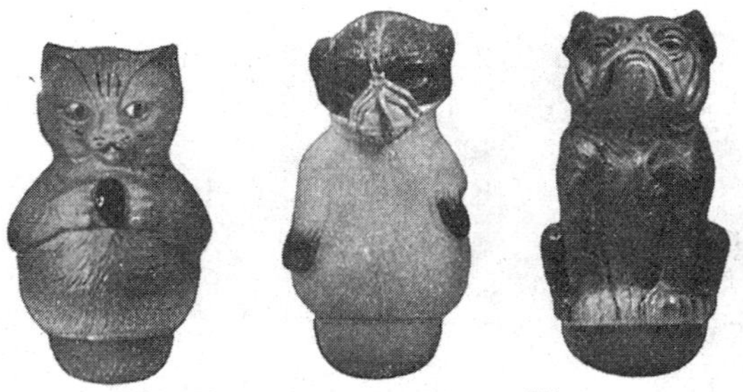

60/6200 ca. 4 cm, **60**/6300 ca. 5½ cm, **60**/6400 ca. 8½ cm.
3 Modelle sortiert in 3 Größen. — 3 models assorted in 3 sizes. — 3 modelos surtidos en 3 tamaños.
Verpackung: 3 Dtz. in Karton; packing: 3 doz. in cardbox; embaque: 3 doc. en cajita de cartón.

60/6000 ca. 4 cm, **60**/6100 ca. 5½ cm.
6 Modelle, sortiert in 2 Größen. — 6 models assorted in 2 sizes. 6 modelos surtidos en 2 tamaños.
Verpackung: je 1 Dtz. sortiert. — Packing: 1 doz. of each assorted. Embaque: 1 doc. de todos surtidos.

In 3 Größen; sizes; tamaños.
Nr. **60**/6050 ca. 10 cm P. 1 Dtz.
„ **60**/6051 „ 13 „ „ ½ „
„ **60**/6052 „ 17½ „ „ ½ „

Rasseltiere. — Animals Rattles. Animales con sonajeras.

60/6110
Sortiert, asssorted, surtido.
Größe, size, tamaño ca. 7 cm.
Verpackung, packing, embaque 1 Dtz.

60/500/x/I u. II.
4 Modelle in 2 Größen ca. 10 und 14 cm.
4 models in 2 sizes ca. 10 and 14 cm.
4 modelos en 2 tamaños ca. 10 en 14 cm.

Hängevögel. — Hanging birds. Aves colgantes.

6 Modelle als Rassel und Tischkartenhalter. — 6 models as rattles or as table card-holder. — 6 modelos como sonajera y sujetamanteles. — P. 1 Dtz.

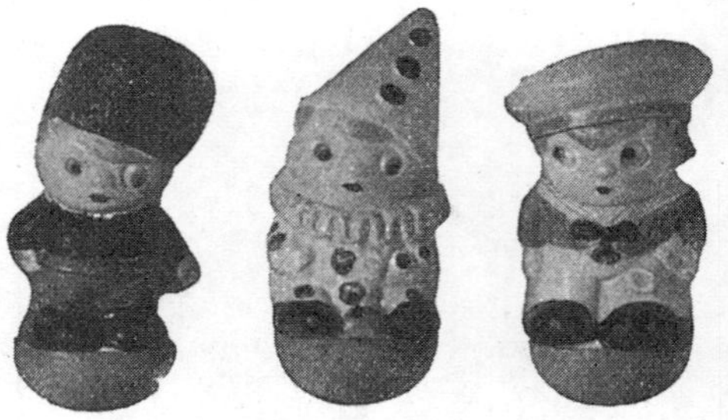

60/6030, 6031, 6032, 6033
3 Modelle sortiert in 4 Größen. — 3 models assorted in 4 sizes. — 3 modelos surtidos en 4 tamaños.
P. **60**/6030/32 1 Dtz. P. **60**/6033 ½ Dtz.

Haus- und wilde Tiere. — Domestic and wild animals. — Animales domesticos y fieras.

P. **60**/700/1–3 Haus- und wilde Tiere sortiert in gefächertem Karton.
Domestic and wild animals assorted in cardboard box with compartments.
Animales domesticos y fieras, surtidos en cartones con casillas.

P. **60**/700/4 Nur Haustiere in gefächertem Karton.
Domestic animals only in cardboard box with compartments.
Animales domesticos solo en cartones con casillas.

P. **60**/700/5 ½ Dutzend Haus- oder wilde Tiere in Karton.
½ doz. domestic or wild animals in cardboard box.
½ doc. animales domesticos ó fieras en cartones.

Geflügel. — Poultry. — Aves de corral.

12 Modelle, models, modelos.
2 Größen, sizes, tamaños.
Nr. **60**/250 Klein, small, pequeñas, ca. 4 cm.
„ **60**/251 Groß, larg, grandes, ca. 5½ cm.
P. 1 Dtz. in Karton, cardbox, cartones.

Schwimmtiere. — Animals that swim. — Animales nadadores.

Sortiment/Assortment/Surtido **60**/200/1¼, 1½, 1¾, 2, 2½, 2¾, 3, 3½, 4, 5, 5½ und 6.

P.	Größe / Size / Tamaño 1¼–2½ = 1 Dtz.	sortiert / assorted / surtidos	je 4 Schwäne und Enten und / 4 swans and ducks and / 4 cisnes y patos	je 2 Fische und Frösche im Karton. / 2 fishes and frogs in cardbox / 2 pescados y ranas en cartones.	
	do. 2¾–3½ = ½ „	do.	2 do.	1 do.	
	do. 4 = ½ „	do.	3 do.		
	do. 5½–6 = ⅓ „	do.	2 do.		

Charakter-Schwimmtiere. — Caricature swimming animals. — Animales nadadores caracteristicos.

3 Modelle, models, modelos.
Nr. **60**/213 Bunt. Vary-coloured. Multicolor.
„ **60**/212 Porzellan-Imitation. Imitation porcelain. Imitación de porcelana.
P. 1 Dtz.

5 Modelle, models, modelos.
2 verschiedene Bemalungen; various paintings; distintas pinturas.
Nr. **60**/212 Bunt, vary-coloured, multicolor.
„ **60**/216 Porzellan-Imitation. Imitation porcelain. Imitación de porcelana.
P. 1 Dtz.

Kragenknopf „Komet", prima Qualität, schwarz und weiß.
Collar stud "Komet", first-class quality, black and white.
Botón de cuello "Komet", Ia. calidad de una sola pieza, negros y blancos.
P. 1 Grs.

Fingerhüte in 6 Größen und verschiedenen Farben, wie weiß, blau, rosa, schwarz, braun und grün.
Thimbles in 6 sizes and in different colours, white, blue, pink, black, brown and green.
Dedales en 6 tamaños y de distintos colores, blanco, azul, rosa, negro, moreno y verde.
P. 3 Dtz. sortiert in Farben und Größen; in assorted sizes and colours; tamaños y colores surtidos.

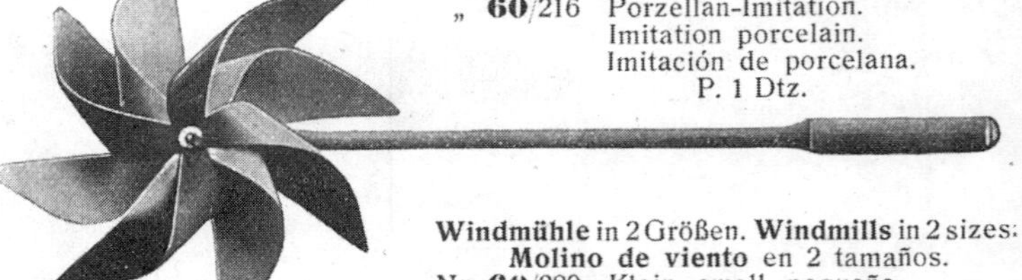

Windmühle in 2 Größen. **Windmills** in 2 sizes: **Molino de viento** en 2 tamaños.
Nr. **60**/280 Klein, small, pequeño.
„ **60**/281 Groß, large, grande. P. ½ Dtz.

P. = Packung. — Packing. — Empaque.

„TIPPLE-TOPPLE-TIERE"

Maché-Spielwaren. — Papier mache toys and animals. — Juguetes de papel comprimido.

Tipple-Topple.

Schutzmarke.
Trade mark.
Marca depósita.

Liliput **32**/5834/17

Liliput-Haustiersortiment.
Assortment of Liliputian domestic animals.
Surtido de animales domésticos liliputienses.

Liliput **32**/5864/14, **29**, 38, 64, 7, 8, 11

Holländersortiment (Liliput).
Liliput Dutch assortment.
Surtido holandés (Liliput).

Liliput **32**/5850/11, **16**,

Liliput-Eisenbahnfiguren-Sortiment.
Liliput railway figures assortment.
Liliput surtido de figuras de ferrocarril.

32/5232/28, **36**, 48, 60

Haustiersortiment.
Assortment of domestic animals.
Surtido de animales doméstico.

32/5039/14, **20**, 26

Geflügelsortiment.
Assortment of poultry.
Surtido de aves.

32/5037/6, 9, 12, **15**, 18, 24, 30

Haustiersortiment.
Assortment of domestic animals.
Surtido de animales doméstico.

32/5383/4, 6, 9, 10, **12**, 16, 20

32/5185/6, 9, 12, 16, **20**, 24, 28

32/5077/5, 6, 7, **9**, 12, 18

Haustiersortimente. — Assortments of domestic animals. — Surtidos de animales doméstico.

32/5219/2, 3, 4, **5**, 7

Pferdefamilie.
Droves of horses.
Yeguada caballos.

32/5220/2, 3, **4**, 5, 7

Rinderfamilie.
Droves if cattles.
Vaquerias.

Liliput **32**/5837/13

Liliput-Haustiersortiment.
Assortment of Liliputian domestic animals.
Surtido de animales domésticos liliputienses.

32/5073/7, 9, **13**
Kuhweiden
Pastures
Praderas

Tipple

Topple

Schutzmarke
Trade mark
Marca depósita

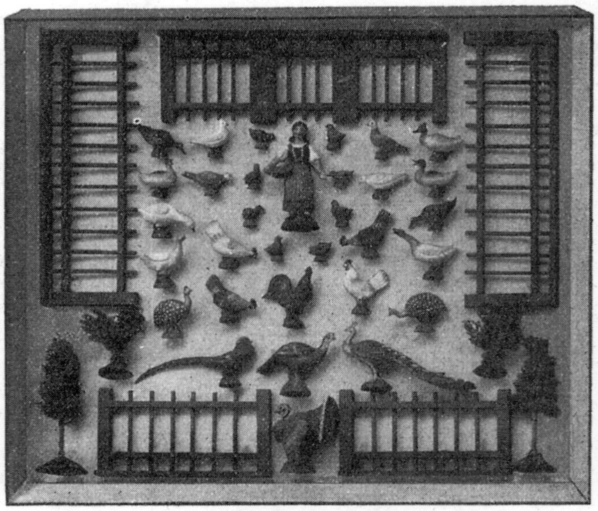

32/5040/14, 20, 26, **32**, 36
Geflügelsortiment
Assortment of poultry
Surtido de aves

32/5225/6, 8, 10, 12, **14**, 18, 28
Geflügelsortiment
Assortment of poultry
Surtido de aves

32/5285/7, **9**, 12, 16
Schäferei
Sheep fold
Aprisco

32/5066/06, 09, 012, 6, 9, **12**, 18
Schäferei — Sheep fold — Aprisco

Menagerietiersortimente. — Assortments of menagery animals. — Surtidos de animales de casa de fieras.

32/6062/4, 6, **9**, 12, 18

Liliput 32/5619/6, 9, 11, 14, 21

32/5654/6, 9, 12, **18**, 26

32/5215/5, 6, 9, **12**, 15, 18, 26

32/5495/**8**, 12, 16, 20

32/5398, 5399, 5400, 5401

Polartier-Sortiment.
Assortment of Polar animals.
Surtido de animales polares.

32/5257

Plastische Felsenkrippe.
Plastic rocky crib.
Portal en rocas plasticas.

Länge — length — largo: 44 cm = 17½ inches
Breite — breadth — ancho: 13 „ = 5¼ „
Höhe — height — alto: 27 „ = 10½ „

32/5230/5, 11, 14, 20

Krippenfiguren-Sortiment.
Assortment of figures for cribs.
Surtido de figures para portales de Belén.

32/5656/36

Menagerietier-Sortiment.
Assortment of menagery animals.
Surtido de animales de casa de fieras.

32/5931/6, 9, 12, 16, 20, 26

Tropische Jagd (Sortiment).
Shooting in the tropics (assortment).
Caza en los tropicos (surtido).

32/6063/7, 10

Indianer auf der Büffeljagd (Sortiment).
Indians shooting buffaloes (assortment).
Indios á la caza del bufalo (surtido).

32/5639/4, 6, 11

Indianersortiment.
Indians assortment.
Surtido d'Indianos.

Kugelgelenk-Babys „Hubsy“,

erstklassig gekleidet, in allen Dessins, Schlafaugen.

Jointed dolls "Hubsy",

high-class dressed dolls of all designs, sleeping eyes.

Bébés "Hubsy" con ariculacion a bolas,

vestidas con esmero, en todos los dibujos ojos movibles.

Modell **32**/2582

Seidenkleid, gestickt.
Silk dress, embroidered.
Traje de seda, bordado

Nr. **32**/2582 38, 42, 52, 58 cm.

Modell **32**/2584

Samtkleid mit gehäkeltem Aufputz.
Velvet dress with crotchet ornaments.
Traje de terciopelo con adornos de encajes.

Nr. **32**/2584 38, 42, 52, 58 cm

Modell **32**/2586

Samtkleid mit gehäkelten Sternen.
Velvet dress with crochet stars.
Traje de terciopelo con estrellas de encaje.

Nr. **32**/2586 38, 42, 52, 58 cm.

Modell **32**/2589

Seidenkleid mit Spitze und Goldband.
Silk dress with laces and gold ribbon.
Traje de seda con encaje y cinta de oro.

Nr. **32**/2589 38, 42, 52, 58 cm.

Unzerbrechliche, weichgestopfte „Hubsy Trikot-Puppen“

mit drehbarem Maché-Kopf, gemalten Augen und Perücke.

Soft stoffed body, unbreakable "Hubsy dolls"

with turning mâché head, painted eyes, wig.

Muñeca "Hubsy" de genero de punto é irrompible,

rellena de materia blanda con cabeza movible de cartón prensado, ojos pintados, peluca.

Modell **32**/2717

Baby-Kleidung, Häubchen, sortierte Farben.
Baby-dress, hood, assorted colours.
Vestuario de bébé, gorrita, colores surtidos.

Nr. **32**/2717/	0	2
Größe — Size — Tamaño	35	45 cm

Modell **32**/3076

Filzkopf, Seidentrikotkleid, sortierte Farben
Felt head, silk stockinette dress, assorted coloures.
Cabeza de fieltro, traje de genero de punto seda, colores surtidos.

Nr. **32**/3076/	1	2	3	4
Größe — Size — Tamañjo	40	45	55	68 cm

Nr. **32**/2717 Mit gemaltem Haar.
With painted hairs.
Con pelo pintado.

Nr. **32**/2717/	0	2
Größe — Size — Tamaño	35	45 cm

Modell **32**/2716

Baby-Kleidung, Hut, sortierte Farben.
Baby-dress, hat, assorted coloures.
Vestuario de bébé, sombrero, colores surtidos.

Nr. **32**/2716/	0	2
Größe — Size — Tamaño	35	45 cm

32/3061/0 Filzkleid mit Hühnermuster.
32/3061/2 Felt dress with pullet ornaments.
Vestido de fieltro con dibujos de pollos.

32/3070/0 Kreppkleid.—Tuchmantel.—
32/3070/2 Häubchen.
Crepe-dress. — Cloth mantelet.— Hood.
Vestido de crespon.–Abrigo de pano-gorrita.

32/3058/0 Flanellkleid. — Filzschürze.
32/3058/2 Haarschleife.
Flannel dress. — Felt apron. — Bow of hair.
Vestido de franela. — Delantal de fieltro. — Cinta para el pelo.

32/3061 32/3070 32/3070 32/3067 32/3110 32/3066
32/3058

Größe. — Size. — Tamaño: 0 = 35 cm.
„ „ „ 2 = 45 „

32/3067/0 Filzkleid, sortierte Farben.
32/3067/2 Felt dress, assorted colours.
Vestido de fieltro, colores surtidos.

32/3110/0 Filzkleid, sortierte Farben.
32/3110/2 Felt-dress, assorted colours.
Vestido de fieltro, colores surtidos.

32/3066/0 Filzkleid. — Häubchen. —
32/3066/2 Sortierte Farben.
Felt dress. — Hood. — Assorted colours.
Vestido de fieltro — Gorrita. — Colores surtidos.

32/2669

"Hubsy Clown" { **weichgestopft, unzerbrechlich. soft stuffed, unbreakable. de materia blanda y irrompible.**

Nr. 32/2669 Stoff, sortierte Farben.
Cloth, assorted colours.
Tejido, colores surtidos.

Größe — Size — Tamaño	1	2	3	4	
	40	45	55	68	cm

Nr. 32/2700 Seide, sortierte Farben.
Silk, assorted colours.
Seda, colores surtidos.

Größe — Size — Tamaño	1	2	3	4	
	40	45	55	68	cm

32/2700

Puppenkoffer, eingerichtet mit Puppe.
Dolls trousseaux, complete with doll.
Maletín, arreglado con muñeca.

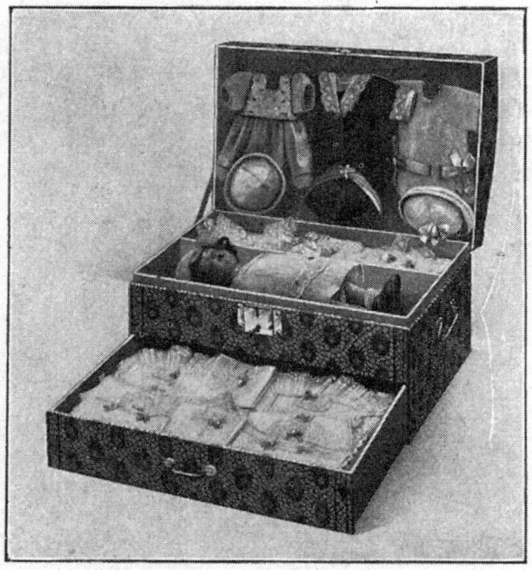

32/2499/4

Länge / Length / Largo 36 cm
Breite / Breadth / Ancho 26 „
Höhe / Height / Altura 21 „
Größe der Puppe / Size of the doll / Tamaño de la muñeca } 26 „

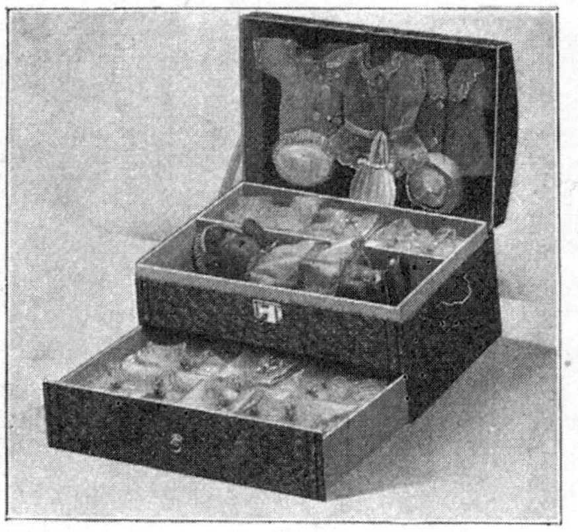

32/2499/3

Länge / Length / Largo 40 cm
Breite / Breadth / Ancho 26 „
Höhe / Height / Altura 23 „
Größe der Puppe / Size of the doll / Tamaño de la muñeca } 30 „

32/2499/5

Länge / Length / Largo 32 cm
Breite / Breadth / Ancho 19 „
Höhe / Height / Altura 20 „
Größe der Puppe / Size of the doll / Tamaño de la muñeca } 22 „

32/2765

Nr. **32**/2765 **Speisezimmer** mit elektrischer Stehlampe, erstklassige Tischlerarbeit.
Doll's dining room set, with electric standing lamp, high-class workmanship.
Comedor, con lampera de pie electrica, de trabajo de carpintería esmeradísimo.

32/2766

Nr. **32**/2766 **Kombinationskasten,** komplett eingerichtet mit Puppe, feinste Tischlerarbeit, das Puppenbett mit vollständiger Ausstattung ist im Innern des Kastens eingebaut. Länge 62 cm, Breite 24 cm, Höhe 70 cm. Größe der Puppe 38 cm.
Combination box, complete with doll and outfittings, finest workmanship, doll's bed with a complete suite will be found in the interior of the box. Length 62 cm, breath 24 cm, height 70 cm. Size of the doll 38 cm.
Caja combinadas con dotacion completa y muñeca, finísimo trabajo de carpintería, la cama para la muñeca provista de un ajuar completo esta colocada fijamente en el interior de la caja. Largura 62 cm, anchura 24 cm, altura 70 cm. Tamaño de la muñeca 38 cm.

32/2513

Nr. **32**/2513 **Schlafzimmer,** weiß emailliert, mit elektrischer Stehlampe und kompletter Ausstattung, feinste Tischlerarbeit, mit Puppe.
Doll's bedroom set, white enamelled, with electric standing lamp and complete outfit, excellent workmanship, with doll.
Dormitorio, en blanco esmaltado con lampera de pie electrica y dotacion completa, de trabajo de carpintería esmeradísimo, con muñeca.

Holzspielwaren. — Wooden toys. — Juguetes de madera.

2008/1 — 3

2008/4 — 7

Kegelspiele, lackiert, in den Farben weiß, blau, rot, grün und violett, bestehend aus 9 Kegeln und 2 Kugeln, im Karton verpackt.
Set of skittles, varnished, in white, blue, red, green, or violet: 9 pins and 2 bowls, packed in cardboard box.
Juego de bolos, barnizada, de colores blanco, azul, rojo, verde, y violeta, compuesto de 9 bolos y 2 pelotas, empacado en un caja de cartón.

Springseile, 17 cm Grifflänge, 2,10 m durchgehende Hanfschnur, im Stückkarton.
Skipping ropes, 17 cm handles, made of hemp cord 2,10 m long pasing through the handles, each rope in cardboard box.
Soga de saltar, 17 cm mango 2,10 m largo generalmente de cordón de cañamo en un pedazo de cartón.

Nr. **2008**/— In den Farben weiß, blau, rot und violett.
In white, blue, red, or violet.
De colores blanco, azul, rojo, y violetta.

Nr. **2008**/— In den Farben weiß mit blau, weiß mit rot, weiß mit rosa, weiß mit violett schattiert.
In white and blue, white and red, white and pink, white and violet.
Matizado de colores blanco con azul, blanco con rosa, blanco con rojo, blanco con violeta.

Springseile, 12 cm Grifflänge, 1,80 m eingeleimte Hanfschnur, im 1/2 Dtz. Karton.
Skipping ropes, 12 cm handles, made of hemp cord and glued into the handles in cardboard boxes of 1/2 dozen ropes. Rope 1,80 m long.
Soga de saltar, 12 cm mango, 1,80 m largo en cordón de cañamo encolado en caja de 1/2 docena.

Nr. **2008**/— In den Farben weiß, blau, rosa und violett.
In white, blue, red, or violet.
De colores blanco, azul, rojo y violeta.

Nr. **2008**/— In den Farben weiß mit blau, weiß mit rot, weiß mit rosa, weiß mit violett schattiert.
In white and blue, white and red, white and pink, and white and violet.
Matizado de colores blanco con azul, blanco con rosa, blanco con rojoy blanco con violeta.

Anerkannt unübertroffene Nachbildungen von Speisen, Desserts usw. auf Tellern und Platten, in Puppengröße, für Küchen und Kaufläden, in Glas und Porzellan auf Karton. Tafelaufsätze, garniert. Kaufladenartikel.

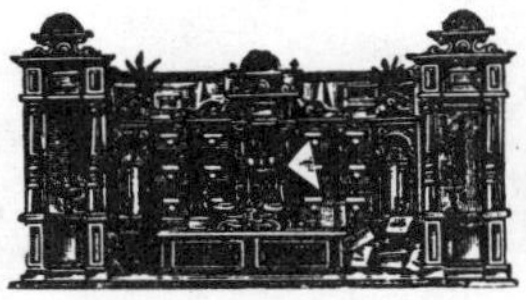

World's best make in dolls dinner and luncheon sets, dolls food on plates and dishes fittings for grocery stores. Leading standard lines in dinner-favors. Unequalled in artificial fashion and excellent finish.

Imitaciones reconocidos como sin igual de: comidas, postres, etc., en platos y fuentes de tamaño muñecas para cocinas y almacenes sobre porcelana, vidrio y cartón, cubiertas guarnecidas, artículos de almacén.

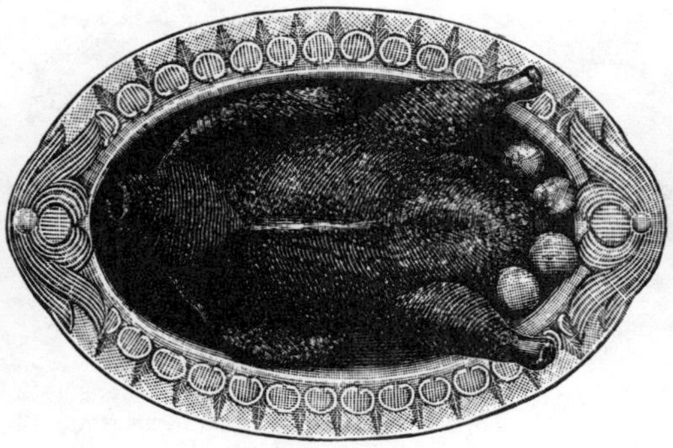

84/2524

Kartonplatte, 12fach sortiert. 6 cm.
Cardboard plate, ass. by 12. 6 cm.
Comidas en plato de cartón, en 12 surtidos. 6 cm.

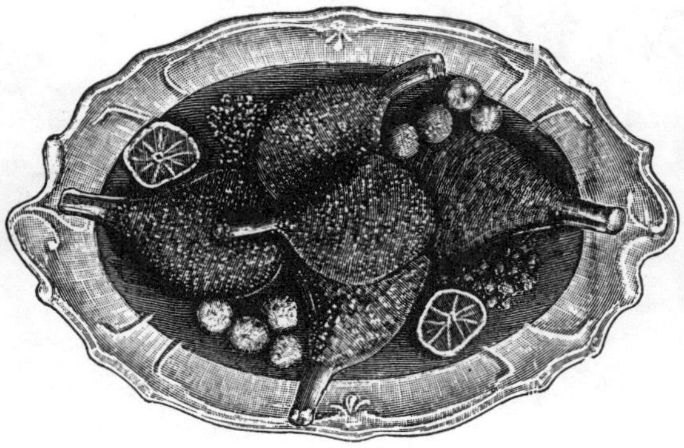

84/2512

Porzellanplatte, 12fach sortiert. 10 cm.
China plate, ass. by 12. 10 cm.
Plato de porcelana, en 12 surtidos. 10 cm.

84/814

Silberkartonplatte, sehr reich. 12fach sort. 8 ½ cm.
Silverplate cardboard, very rich, ass. by 12. 8 ½ cm.
Plato de cartón plateado, guarnecido rico, en 12 surtidos. 8 ½ cm.

84/861

Geburtstagskuchen, mit 6 Lichtern. 8 cm.
Birthday cake, with 6 real candles. 8 cm.
Torta para cumpleaños, con 6 velas. 8 cm.

84/2505

Porzellanteller, 12fach sort. Auflagen. 6 cm.
Lunch and cake on china, ass. by 12. 6 cm.
Postres surtidos sobre porcelana 12. 6 cm.

84/2010

Silberkartonplatte, mit sort. Auflagen. 6 cm.
Cardboard silverplate, ass. meat and fish. 6 cm.
Plato de cartón plateado con guarnición surtida. 6 cm.

84/2208

Glasaufsatz, Konfekt, 6fach sortiert. 6 ½ cm.
Glass stand, sweets, ass. by 6. 6 ½ cm.
Cubierta de vidrio pasteles, en 6 surtidos. 6 ½ cm.

48/2521

Fisch- und Fleischgerichte einfacher Ausführung. 5 cm.
Meat and fish on standard plate. 5 cm.
Manjares de pescado y carne. 5 cm.

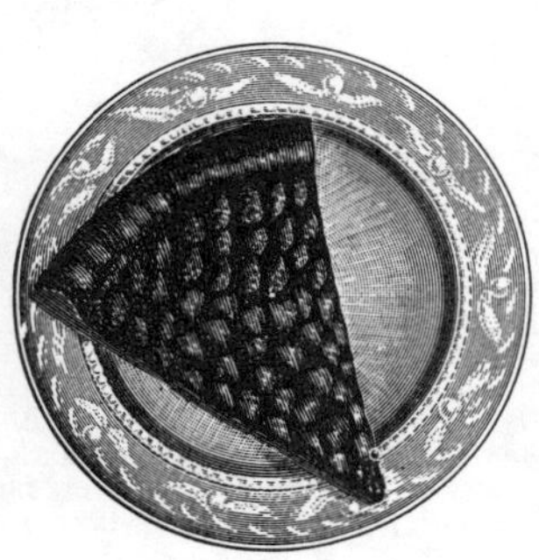

48/2522

Einfacher Dessertteller, 12fach sort. 5 cm.
Standard dessert plate, ass. by 12. 5 cm.
Platillos de postres, ejecución sencilla, en 12 surtidos. 5 cm.

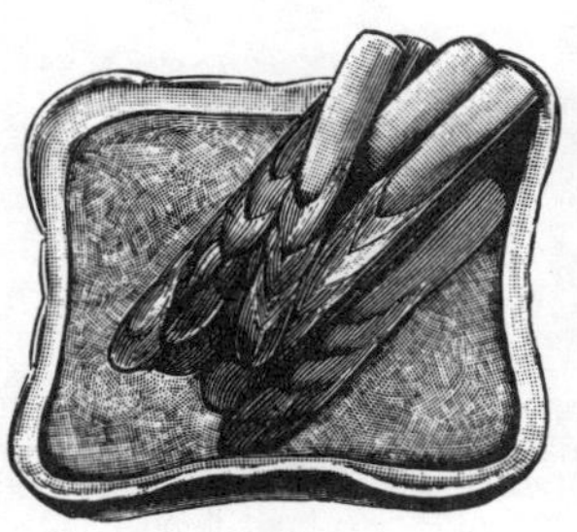

84/2525

Gemüseschüssel, Porzellan, sortiert. 5 cm.
Ass. Vegetables in a china dish. 5 cm.
Fuente para legumbres, porcelana, surtidos. 5 cm.

84/2549

Frühstücksteller, Porzellan, sortiert. 6 ½ cm.
Ass. luncheon china. 6 ½ cm.
Platillos desayuno, porcelana, surtidos. 6 ½ cm.

Spankörbe, gefüllt mit Früchten und Gemüsen in 20 verschiedenen Sorten und Arten, beste Ausführungen, auch mit Brot und Gebäck aller Art.

Filled Baskets, fruit and vegetables, 20 different kinds and sorts, bread, pastry and confectionery.

Cestillas de astilla, rellenados de frutas y legumbres, también con pan y cochura de toda clase.

84/915

Handgriffkorb mit je 8 großen Früchten gefüllt.
Large baskets, 8 selected pieces of fruit.
Cesta con mango con 8 grandes frutas.

84/806

Farbiger Korb mit Obst.
Colored basket fruit only.
Cesta colorado con frutas.

84/805

Gemüsekorb, sortiert
Vegetables, assorted
Cesta legumbre, plana.

84/908

Obst- und Gemüsekorb
12fach sortiert
Fruit and vegetables, ass. by 12
Frutas y legumbres, surtidos 12

Marktbuden und Verkaufsstände.
Groceries.
Lonjas de mercero, tiendas.

84/4082	Spezereihandlung	ca. 18 × 15 × 26 cm
	Grocery store	ca. 18 × 15 × 26 „
	Especería	ca. 18 × 15 × 26 „
84/4081	Marktbude als Gemüse und Obststand, garniert mit Körbchen	ca. cm 24×17×29
	Green grocery	24×17×29
	Lonja como tienda de legumbres y frutas	24×17×29
84/4080	Verkaufstand als Delikateßhandlung, garn.	ca. cm 36×24×38
	Food grocery store	36×24×38
	Especeria	36×24×28

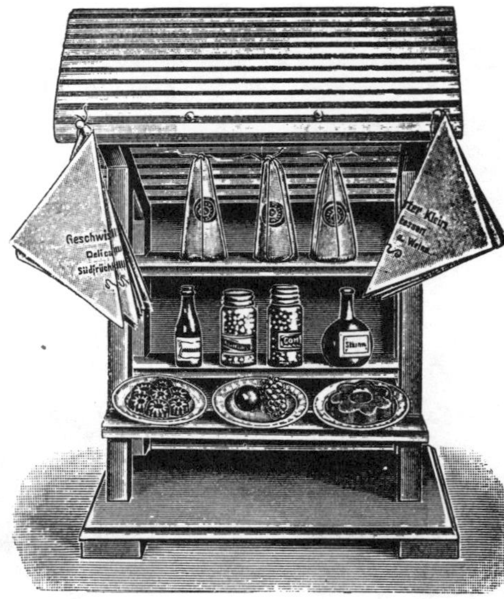

84/4082

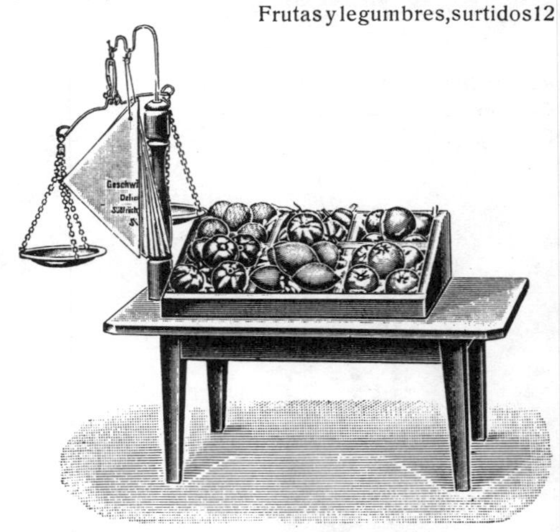

84/4085

Obst- und Gemüseverkaufstand.
Marked table fruit.
Tiendas con frutas y legumbres.

84/4084	mit 4 Fächern	ca. $12^1/_2$×20 cm
84/4085	„ 6 „	ca. 14 ×20 „

Für Kotillon und Karneval: Anhängetierchen mit Nadel.
For Cotillon and Carnival purpose: Most funny Insects, beatles, mice, etc. on pins.
Para Cotillón y Carnaval: Animalitos a prenderse con alfiler.

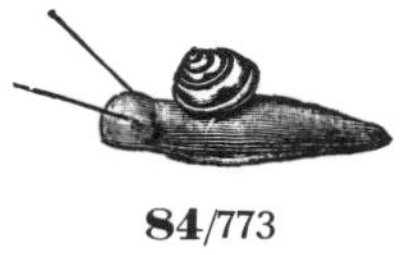

84/773

Schnecke
Snail
Caracol

84/767

Eidechse
Lizard
Lagardo

84/756

Maus, grau, weiss
Mouse, gray and white
Ratón

84/769

Raupe
Caterpiller
Gusano

84/790

Frosch
Frog
Rana

84/779

Maikäfer
Cockchafer
Abejorro

Die hier abgebildeten Nummern sind nur ein kleiner Ausschnitt aus meinem ungemein reichhaltigen Sortiment: für jedes Land, für jeden Geschmack. **Post-Mustersendungen** — je ein Originalkarton pro Nummer von $ **15** an aufwärts (für $ 50 läßt sich ein umfassendes Sortiment zeigen) — sind täglich sofort zu Diensten.

Aus jederzeit **großen** Lägern kommen Musterorders wie größere Verschiffungen in allerkürzester Zeit — oft wenige Tage nach Eingang der Order — zum Versand.

Die beiliegende Preisliste zeigt auch nur die allergangbarsten Nummern; die in der Liste **fett** gedruckten Nummern sind vorstehend **abgebildet.**

Specimen as illustrated are but a modest cut out of a very large and delightful assortment containing specialities for every country for every taste. Sample lots — just 1 box each number from $ 15 upwards by parcels post (for about $ 50 a decent assortment can be shown) — are quickly at your disposal. At every time I keep very large **stocks** of each number and sample orders as well as large shipments use to be effected in a few days time. — The annexed price-list will show you even the most current numbers, all proved good sellers — numbers specially marked there are the illustrated specimen. Run out your sample order please, which no doubt will be followed by regular request of larger shipments.

Los numeros aqui figurados representan solamente una pequeña prueba de mi surtimiento muy abundante, para cada pais, para cada gusto. **Remesas como ensayo** por correo — cada vez un cartón original correspondiente al número desde $ 15 en adelante — están a disposición diaria. Por $ 50 se presanta ya un surtimiento abundante.

Ordenes con muestras se expiden de siempre **grandes** almacenes y se efectuan embarques importantes dentro de poco tiempo, por lo general pocos dias despues de la entrada de la órden.

La adjunta lista de precios indica solamente los números más corrientes, los números con impreso grueso están figurados al lado.

Künstler-Dekorationspuppen. — Artistically got up dolls for decorative purposes. — Artísticas muñecas de decoración.

Aus haltbarer Spezial-Wachskomposition.
Vornehmster Dekorationsschmuck für elegante Wohn- und Geschäftsräume sowie Schaufenster usw.

Made of a special durable wax composition.
Elegant decorative ornaments for refined sitting-rooms or offices, shop windows, etc.

De una durable composición especial de cera.
La decoración más destinguida para habitaciones y casas de comercio, asícomo para mostradores, etc.

145/21 F. M.

145/12

145/16

145/13

145/23

145/9

145/22

Supplied in 50 superb different models, can be sent to **all** countries.

Lieferbar in 50 verschiedenen Modellen.
Versandfähig nach **allen** Weltteilen.

Entregables en 50 differentes modelos magníficos.
Prontas a ser expedidas a **todas** las partes del mundo.

Puppengarnituren.
Koll. **59**

Dolls sets.
Coll. **59**

Guarniciones para muñecas.
Coll. **59**

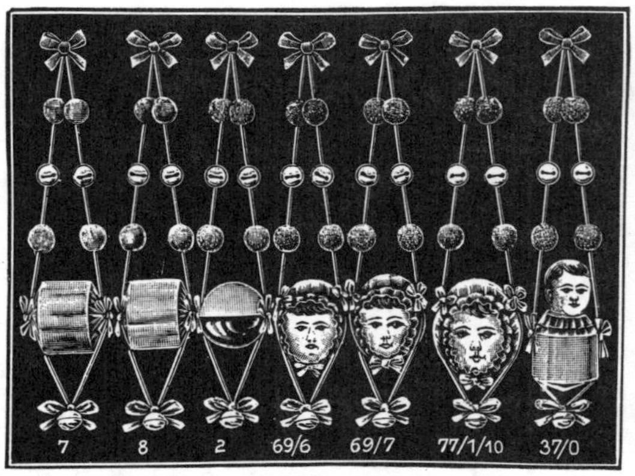

59/—

Wiegengehänge.
Cradle hangings.
Colgantes con voz para muñecas.

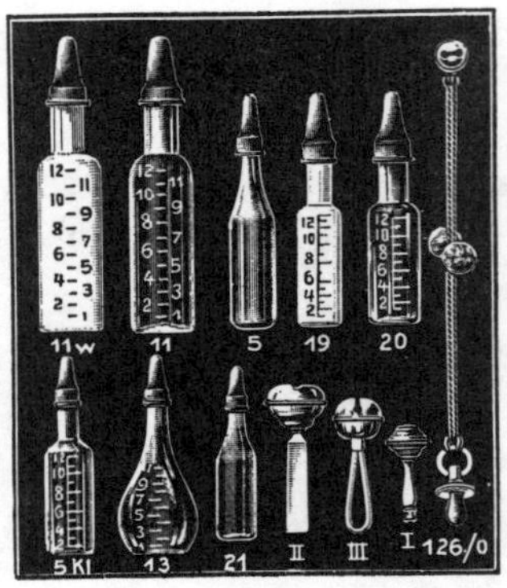

59/—

Puppenflaschen, unüberzogen.
Dolls sucking bottles.
Biberones de vidrio para muñecas.

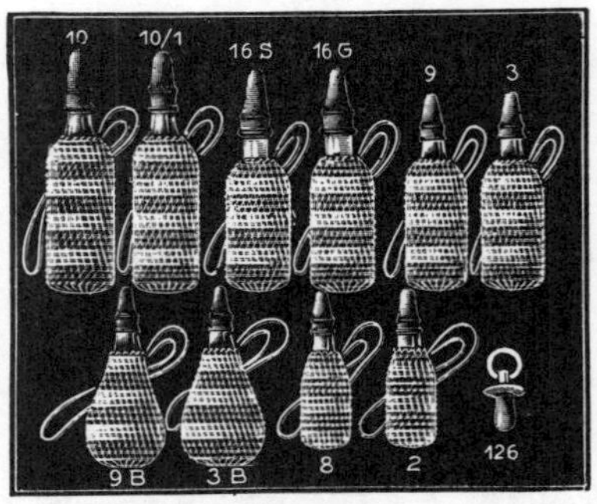

59/—

Puppenflaschen, überzogen.
Dolls sucking bottles, in nets.
Biberones recubiertos de tejedo para muñecas.

59/—

59/—

59/—

59/—

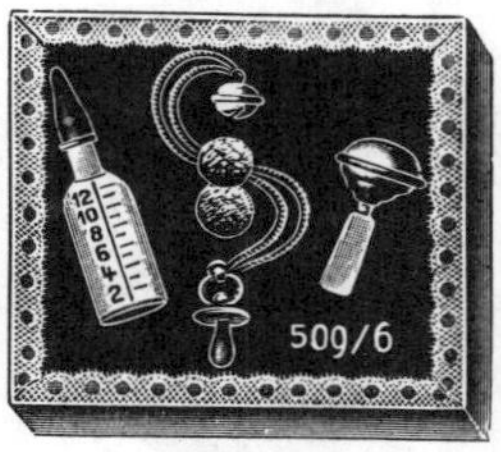

59/—

59/—

59/—

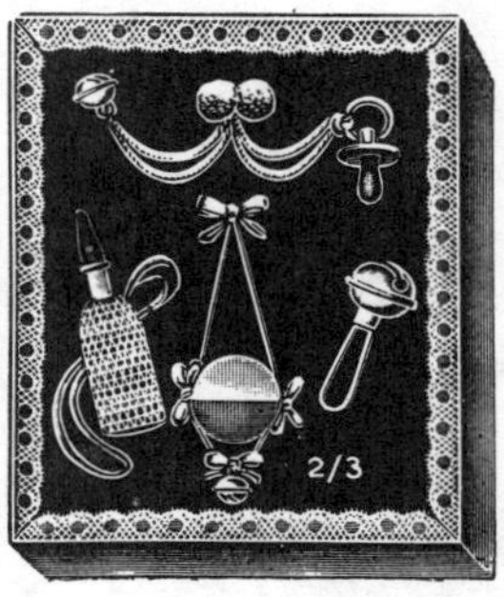

59/—

59/—

Puppengarnituren: Puppenflaschen, Puppensauger, Puppenschlottern bzw. Wiegengehänge.
Dolls sets: Dolls sucking bottles, sucking tubes, dolls rattles, or cradle hangings.
Guarniciones para muñecas: Biberones de vidrio, chupadores, sonajeros para muñecas, ó colgantes con voz para muñecas.

59/—

Puppenausstattungen.
Dolls furniture.
Equipos para muñecas.

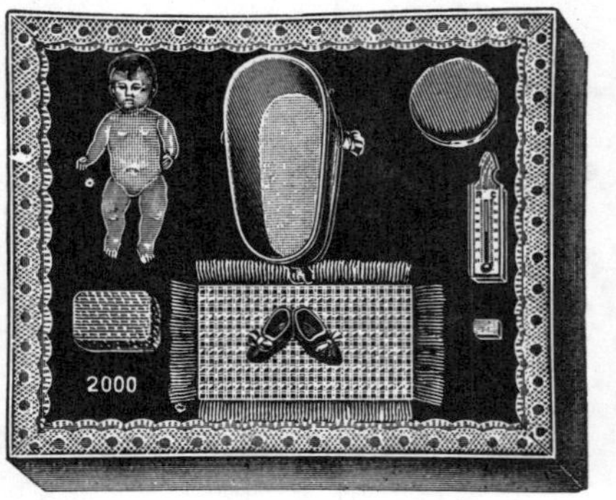

59/—

Puppen-Badegarnituren.
Dolls bath sets.
Guarniciones de baño para muñecas.

Bei Auftragserteilung ist die am Kopfe angeführte Kollektionsnummer **59** unbedingt vor die jeweilige Artikelnummer zu setzen.
When placing an order the coll. Nr. **59** specified at the head hereof must definitely be stated before the Nr. of the individual article in question.
Dandola órden, es indispensable meter la collección No. **59** indicada arriba ante el número del artículo en questión.

Rote Gummipuppen und -tiere. — Dolls and animals of red indian rubber. — Muñecas y animales de goma roja.

133/101

133/102

133/103

133/104

133/105

133/106

133/201

133/202

133/203

133/204

133/205

133/206

133/T 126

133/T 26

133/T 23

133/T 24

133/T 25

133/T 27

133/T 23

133/T 24

133/T 25

133/T 27

1/3 der natürlichen Größe. 1/3 of nat. sizes. 1/3 del tamaño natural.

Gekleidete Puppen in einfacher bis feinster Ausführung.
Dressed dolls in plain up to finest make.
Muñecas vestidas, ejecución de la sencilla hasta la más fina.

Tafel I. Gekleidete Gelenkpuppen mit Biskuit-Porzellanköpfen und festen Augen, Originalkarton mit 6 Stück in verschiedenen Farben sortiert. Die Artikel werden auch in Stückpackung und von 20 cm an mit Schlafaugen geliefert. Die Körper bestehen aus geprägter Pappe, die Glieder aus Papiermaché, mit gemalten Schuhen und Strümpfen und natürlichem Haar.

Plate I. *Dressed joint-dolls with biscuit-porcelain heads and fixed eyes, original cardboard box with 6 dolls assorted in different colours. The dolls are also delivered packed singly and, from 20 cm upwards, with sleeping eyes. The bodies are made of pressed cardboard and the limbs of papier mâché, with painted shoes and stockings; they have natural hair.*

Hoja I. Muñecas vestidas con coyuntura, cabezas de biscuit porcelana y ojos firmes, cartón con 6 piezas escogidas en diferentes colores. Los artículos se entregan también embalado cada una solo y desde 20 cm con ojos para dormir. Los cuerpos se componen de cartón estampado, los miembros de papelmachée con botas y medias pintadas, pelo natural.

Tafel II. Gekleidete Gelenkpuppen mit Biskuit-Porzellanköpfen, Schlafaugen und natürlichen Frisuren. Die Körper sind aus geprägter Pappe, die Glieder aus Papiermaché, natürliche Schuhe und Strümpfe. Die Kleider werden in verschiedenen Farben sortiert geliefert und ist jedes Stück in einem Spitzenkarton.

Plate II. *Dressed joint-dolls with biscuit-porcelain heads, sleeping eyes and natural hair coiffure. The bodies are of pressed cardboard, the limbs of papier mâché, real shoes and stockings. Dresses are assorted in different colours and each doll is packed in lace-trimmed cardboard box.*

Hoja II. Muñecas vestidas con coyuntura, cabezas de biscuit porcelana, ojos para dormir y pelo natural. Los cuerpos son de cartón estampado, los miembros de papelmachée, botas y medias, los vestidos escogidos de diferentes colores cada uno empaquetado en un cartón con encaje.

Tafel III und IV. Gekleidete Doppel-Gelenkpuppen mit Biskuit-Porzellanköpfen, Schlafaugen und guten Mohairfrisuren. Die Körper sind aus geprägter Pappe, die Glieder aus Holz und Papiermaché. Die Kleider werden in duftigen Farben geliefert und ist jedes Stück in einem Spitzenkarton verpackt.

Plate III and IV. *Dressed full-jointed dolls with biscuit-porcelain heads and sleeping eyes and good mohair coiffures. The bodies are of pressed cardboard and the limbs of wood or papier mâché. The dresses are in delicate colours and each doll is packed in lace-trimmed cardboard box.*

Hoja III y IV. Muñecas vestidas, doble coyuntura, cabeza de biscuit porcelana, ojos para dormir y peinado de mohair bueno. Los cuerpos son de cartón estampado, los miembros de madera y papelmachée. Los vestidos de colores finos, cada uno empaquetado en un cartón con encaje.

Tafel V. Fein gekleidete Doppel-Gelenkpuppen mit Biskuit-Porzellankopf, Schlafaugen und Wimpern, mit feinsten Mohairperücken. Beste Qualität in feinster Ausführung mit besonderem Handgelenk.

Plate V. *Elegantly dressed double-jointed dolls with biscuit-porcelain heads, sleeping eyes with lashes and finest mohair coiffure. Best quality with jointed wrists.*

Hoja V. Muñecas vestidas elegantisimamente con doble coyuntura, cabeza de biscuit porcelana, ojos para dormir, con pestañas y peinadas de mohair finisimo. La mejor calidad y ejecución finísima con puño de la mano.

4/2625/50 Seidenkleid. — *Silk dress.* — Vestido de seda.

4/2610/50 Kleid aus gesticktem Batist. — *Dress of embroidered muslin.* — Vestido de batista bordada.

4/2689/50 Pierrot im Seidenkleid. — *Piérrot in silk dress.* — Piérrot con vestido de seda.

4/2688/50 Kreponkleid. — *Crépon dress.* — Vestido de crespón.

4/2694/55 Gehäkeltes Wollkleid. — *Crocheted woollen dress.* — Vestido hecho de chrochet de lana.

4/2624/55 Samtkleid. — *Velvet dress.* — Vestido de terciopelo.

4/2695/55 Musselinkleid. — *Muslin dress.* — Vestido de muselina.

4/2437/60 Seidenbatistkleid. — *Dress of silk muslin.* — Vestido de batista de seda.

4/2700/60 Musselinkleid. — *Muslin dress.* — Vestido de muselina.

4/2698/60 Kleid aus feinem, bedrucktem Batist. — *Dress of finest printed muslin.* — Vestido de batista colorada.

4/2701/65 Voilekleid. — *Dress of voile.* — Vestido de voile.

4/2702/65 Kleid aus duftigem, geblümtem Batist. — *Dress of delicate art muslin.* — Vestido de batista fina floreada.

4/2703/65 Seidenkleid. — *Silk dress.* — Vestido de seda.

4/2390/70 Rotkäppchen. — *Little red riding hood.* — Vestido gorrita roja.

4/2544/75 Kleid aus duftigem, geblümtem Batist. — *Dress of delicate art muslin.* — Vestido de batista fina floreada.

4/2715/80 Seidenbatistkleid mit Tüllüberwurf. — *Dress of silk muslin with tulle tunic.* — Vestido de batista de seda con tul encima.

4/2710/90 Voilekleid mit reichem Spitzenüberwurf. — *Dress of voile with rich lace tunic.* — Vestido de voile con rico adorno de encaje.

4/2711/100 Seidenkleid mit Spitzenüberwurf. — *Silk dress with lace tunic.* — Vestido de seda con encaje fino.

I.
4/10060/12 4/10076/12 4/10087/12 4/10087/12 4/10088/12 4/10089/12 4/10092/12 4/10093/12 4/10094/12 4/10095/12 4/10096/12 4/10097/12 4/10098/12 4/10099/12
4/5619/15 4/5621/15 4/5624/15 4/5628/15 4/5694/15 4/5695/15 4/5696/15 4/5697/15 4/5698/15 4/5700/15 4/5701/15 4/5702/15
4/5634/18 4/5703/18 4/5636/18 4/5639/18 4/5705/18 4/5706/18 4/5707/18 4/5708/18 4/5709/18 4/5770/18
4/5473/20 4/5644/20 4/5646/20 4/5711/20 4/5712/20 4/5713/20 4/5714/20 4/5715/20 4/5716/20 4/5717/20 4/5723/20 4/5724/20
4/5540/22 4/5649/22 4/5718/22 4/5719/22 4/5720/22 4/5721/22 4/5722/22 4/5395/22 4/5504/22
4/5655/25 4/5725/25 4/5726/25 4/5727/25 4/5728/25 4/5729/25 4/5730/25 4/5731/25 4/5732/25 4/5733/25 4/5734/25

II.
4/1005/22
4/1007/22
4/1008/22
4/1009/22
4/1010/22
4/1011/22
4/5667/28 J
4/5667/28 M
4/5735/28
4/5738/28
4/5739/28
4/5504/30
4/5669/30
4/5671/30
4/5673/30
4/5723/30
4/5724/30
4/5740/30
4/5741/30
4/5742/30
4/5743/30
4/5744/33
4/5746/33
4/5747/33
4/5395/35
4/5687/35
4/5689/35
4/5752/38
4/5757/38
4/5758/38
4/5753/40
4/5759/40
4/5760/40
4/5763/42
4/5764/42
4/5691/45
4/5765/45
4/5767/45

III.
4/2645/25
4/2646/25
4/2647/25
4/2648/25
4/2649/25
4/2579/28
4/2650/28
4/2651/28
4/2652/28
4/2653/28
4/2530/31
4/2580/31
4/2591/31
4/2656/31
4/2657/31
4/2658/31
4/2472/33
4/2588/33
4/2659/33
4/2660/33
4/2661/33
4/2662/33
4/2773/33
4/2428/35
4/2663/35
4/2665/35
4/2666/35
4/2667/35
4/2668/35
4/2669/35

IV.
4/2508/38
4/2598/38
4/2599/38
4/2670/38
4/2671/38
4/2672/38
4/2673/38
4/2430/40
4/2602/40
4/2636/40
4/2674/40
4/2675/40
4/2676/40
4/2677/40
4/2516/42
4/2530/42
4/2678/42
4/2679/42
4/2680/42
4/2681/42
4/2682/42
4/2428/45
4/2683/45
4/2684/45
4/2685/45
4/2686/45
4/2687/45
4/2712/45

V.
4/2625/50
4/2610/50
4/2689/50
4/2688/50
4/2694/55
4/2624/55
4/2695/55
4/2437/60
4/2700/60
4/2698/60
4/2701/65
4/2702/65
4/2703/65
4/2390/70
4/2544/75
4/2715/80
4/2710/90
4/2711/100

Künstler-Spielpuppen.
Naturgetreu — Weichgestopft — Unzerbrechlich — Abwaschbar.
Qualitäts-Erzeugnisse. — Sorgfältige Handarbeit.

Artistic dolls.
Life like — Soft stuffing — Unbreakable — Washable.
First-class production — Careful hand-work.

Muñecas artísticas.
Natural — Relleno blando — Inquebrantable — Deslavable.
Producte de primera calidad — Trabajo cuidadoso a mano.

Trikotstoffpuppen.
Größen: 30—60 cm. Körper und Glieder sind weichgeformt und in jede beliebige Stellung zu bringen.

Tricotstuff dolls
Height: 30—60 cm. Body and limbs are soft and any kind of posture can be given.

Muñecas de tejidos de malla.
Tamaño: 30—60 cm. Cuerpo y miembros son blandos y se les puede dar cualquiera postura.

Grotesken.
Größe: 22 cm. Hochoriginell und in allen Teilen beweglich.

Grotesques.
Height: 22 cm. Very original and movable in all its parts.

Grutescos.
Tamaño: 22 cm. Muy original y movible en todas sus partes.

Stehpuppen.
Größe: 40 cm. Schön und farbenprächtig ausgestattet.

Standing dolls.
Height: 40 cm. Beautiful and of magnificent colours.

Muñecas en pie.
Tamaño: 40 cm. Hermosas y de colores esplendidos.

Illustrierter Katalog auf Wunsch. — Illustrated catalogues will be sent if desired. — A deseo se manda el catalogo ilustrado.

Muk-Puppe.
Die Künstler - Charakterpuppe.

Muk-Doll.
The artistical doll.

Muñecas Muk.
La muñeca artística.

153/21/III **153**/34 III

153/V/b

153/37/IV **153**/31/III

Kunst- und Modepuppen aus Filz, in 5 Größen, können mit und ohne Mamastimme geliefert werden.

Art and fashion dolls, of felt, in 5 sizes, can be supplied with or without voice, saying "Mama".

Muñecas artísticas y muñecas de moda de fieltro en 5 tamaños pueden ser entregadas con la voz de la mamá y sin tal.

Stoffpuppen, unzerbrechlich und abwaschbar, aus wasserdichtem Nessel. — Cloth dolls, unbreakable, of waterproof grass cloth. — Infrangibles muñecas de estofa, que se puede lavar, de albengala (lienzo de ortigas) impermeable.

27/IB15 „Bärbel"

27/IA55

27/IB73

27/IB74

27/IB68

Nr. **27**/IA Puppe I Serie A in besonders wohlfeilem Kleidchen.
„ **27**/IB Puppe I Serie B in schönem, einfachem Kinderkleidchen.
„ **27**/IC Puppe I Serie C in reicher ausgearbeitetem Kleidchen.
„ **27**/ID Puppe I Serie D in Kleidchen mit besonders mühevoller Ausarbeitung.

Die Puppe I ist 43 cm groß und kann innerhalb der 4 Serien A, B, C und D in einem reichhaltigen Farbensortiment geliefert werden.

Nr. **27**/IA Doll I series A, in specially cheap frocks.
„ **27**/IB Doll I series B, in pretty, simple frocks.
„ **27**/IC Doll I series C, in richly worked frocks.
„ **27**/ID Doll I series D, in frocks with specially elaborate work.

The doll I is 43 cm tall and can be supplied in an ample assortment of colours within the 4 series A, B, C, and D.

Nr. **27**/IA Muñeca I serie A en un vestido particularmente barato.
„ **27**/IB Muñeca I serie B en un sencillo vestido hermoso para niños.
„ **27**/IC Muñeca I serie C en un vestido de ejecución muy decorativa.
„ **27**/ID Muñeca I serie D en un vestido hecho de mucha diligencia.

La muñeca I tiene un tamaño de 43 cm y las 4 series A, B, C y D pueden ser entregadas en abondantes surtidos de varios colores.

27/IA54

27/IC65

27/IIB 1, 2, 3

Käthe Kruse

Stoffpuppen, unzerbrechlich und abwaschbar, aus wasserdichtem Nessel. — Cloth dolls, unbreakable, of waterproof grass cloth. — Infrangibles muñecas de estofa, que se puede lavar, de albengala (lienzo de ortigas) impermeable.

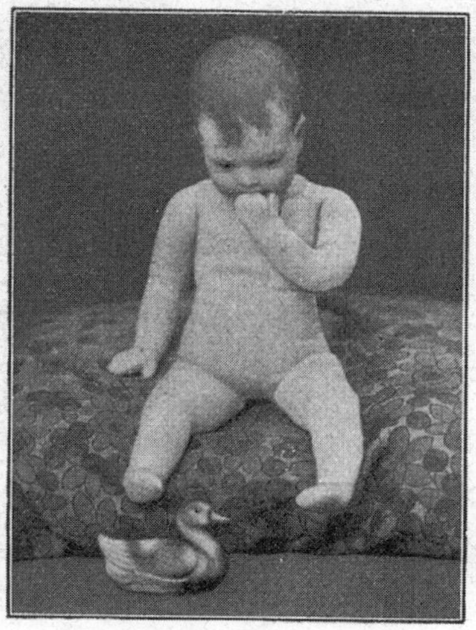

27/II A

27/II A

The little dangle limbs, 33 cm tall
prettiest as a naked baby, Nr. **27**/II
in little shirt „ **27**/II 1a
in swaddling clothes „ **27**/II 1b
Clothed, in crocheted free play pants „ **27**/II A
in plain frock „ **27**/II B
more richly fitted out:
in long clothes, in walking frock, as foundling „ **27**/II C
on carrying cushion „ **27**/II D

27/II C. 3

La muñeca meneando "Bambaleador" altura 33 cm,
bellísima como **muñeca desnuda,** Nr. **27**/II
en la camisa „ **27**/II 1a
en calzonillos de pañales „ **27**/II 1b
Vestida en calzones abrochados para patalear „ **27**/II A
en vestido más sencillo „ **27**/II B
ejecución más decorativa:
en vestido para llevar el niño, en vestido para correr, como niño desamparado „ **27**/II C
en el cojinito „ **27**/II D

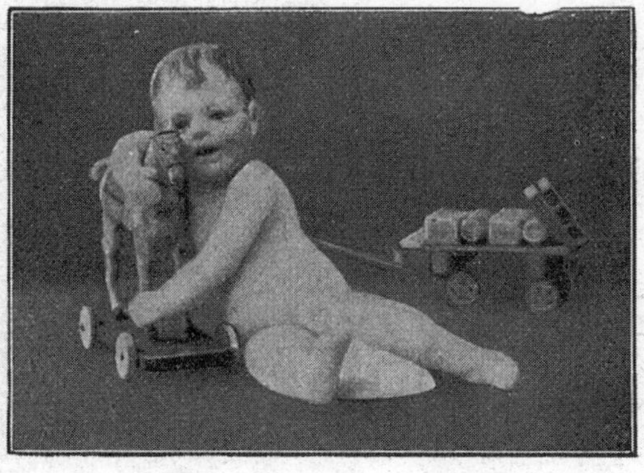

27/II A

27/II A

Das Schlenkerchen, 33 cm hoch,
am schönsten als **Nackedei,** Nr. **27**/II
im Hemdchen „ **27**/II 1a
im Windelhöschen „ **27**/II 1b
Gekleidet, in gehäkeltem Strampelhöschen „ **27**/II A
in schlichtem Kleidchen „ **27**/II B

Reicher ausgestattet:
im Tragkleidchen, im Laufkleidchen, als Findelkind Nr. **27**/II C
im Steckkissen „ **27**/II D

The famous **CASADORA-Patents** | *Die originellen* ***CASADORA-Patente*** | Los **Patentes CASADORA** originales

Lebende CASADORA-Puppen

mit **natürlicher Stimme** und **beweglichen Augen.**

Nach Einführung der rechten Hand in den Puppenkörper **erwacht die Puppe** und **bewegt Arme und Kopf, Augen und Wimpern**

mit verblüffender Natürlichkeit,

sobald man die Finger langsam hin und her bewegt.

Gediegene weiße Stoffausstattung mit Stickerei in hellblau oder rosa, mit Saugflasche. Feiner Charakterkopf mit Glasaugen und Wimpern.

31/200—203K

Muñecas vivientes "CASADORA"

con la **voz natural** y los **ojos movibles.**

Introduciendo la mano derecha en el cuerpo de la muñeca, **la muñeca se despierta y mueve brazos y cabeza, ojos y pestañas**

de una manera muy natural

cuando se agita lentamente los dedos.

Equipo blanco de algodón de primera, con bordado en azul claro o rosa. Cabeza de bebé artística con ojos de vidrio y pestañas.

Living CASADORA-Dolls

with natural voice and moving eyes.

By putting your right hand into the body of doll and moving then your fingers to and fro the dolly awakes and moves arms and head, eyes and lashes

in a startling naturalness.

White cloth equipment of best quality with embroideries of lustre yarn in light blue or pink; sucking bottle. Artistic character head with glass eyes and lashes.

Nr. **31**/	200 K	200 M	201 K	201 M	202 K	202 M	203 K	203 M
Länge / Length / Longitud	52	52	46	46	42	42	36	36 cm
	20½	20½	18	18	16½	16½	14	14 inches

desgl. als **Attrappe** — *do. as a filling doll* — id. como **bombonera**

Nr. **31**/303 K	36 cm	14 inches
„ **31**/303 M	36 „	14 „

CASADORA-Laufpuppen

mit automatischer Mamastimme.

Weich gestopft!

Unverwüstlich!

Laufen, an den Händen oder Armen geführt, in hochorigineller Weise.

Erstklassige Ausführung.

Nr. **31**/900 K und 900 M Moderne Babykleidung aus bestem Material zum An- und Ausziehen, mit Schuhen und Strümpfen; Charakterkopf und Glieder aus Kunstmasse, ff. bemalt.

Nr. **31**/901 K und 901 M Desgl., mit Schlafaugen und Wimpern, feine Mohairperücke.

31/900 M und 901 M

Muñecas que marchan "CASADORA"

con voz automática de mamá.

¡Rellenadas con material blando!

¡Casi indestructible!

Marchan de una manera muy original cuando se las guia por las manos ó brazos.

Fabricación de primera clase.

No. **31**/900 K y 900 M Vestido moderno de bebé de primera para poner y quitar con medias y zapatos; cabeza caracterizada y miembros de composición finamente pintados.

No. **31**/901 K y 901 M Idem, con ojos movibles y pestañas, peluca fina de mohair.

Walking and Talking Dolls "CASADORA"

Soft stuffed! *Almost indestructible!*

Walk in a quite original manner when lead by the hands or arms.

High class make.

Nr. 31/900K and 900M Up-to-date baby dress of best material to be put on and off, with shoes and stockings; character head and limbs of composition finely painted.

Nr. 31/901K and 901M Ditto, with sleeping eyes and lashes, fine mohair wig.

Nr. **31**/900 K	40	50	58 cm
	16	20	23 inches

Nr. **31**/900 M	40	50	58 cm
	16	20	23 inches

Nr. **31**/901 K	40	50	58 cm
	16	20	23 inches

Nr. **31**/901 M	40	50	58 cm
	16	20	23 inches

Aufmachungen in weißen Stückkartons. — *Each piece made up in a white cardboard box.* — Presentaciones en cajas blancas de cartón de á una.

Erklärung der Zeichen — *Explication of the signs* — Explicación de los signos: **K** = Knabe — *Boy* — Muchacho, **M** = Mädchen — *Girl* — Muchacha.

The famous
CASADORA-Patents

Die originellen
CASADORA-Patente

Los
Patentes CASADORA
originales

CASADORA-Schelm-Babys.

Schreien beim Kämmen und Bürsten der Haare.

Bewegen die Augen unabhängig von den Lidern nach allen Seiten und in jeder Stellung, begleitet von langsamen, ganz natürlichen Bewegungen der Wimpern.

Die Augenbewegungen erfolgen:

1. **automatisch,** in der bekannten Weise.
2. **mechanisch,** in liegender Stellung durch einfaches Ziehen an der Saugflasche oder Schlotter.

Qualitätsausführung.

Elegante Ober- und Unterkleidung zum An- und Ausziehen. Feiner Charakterkopf mit Ia. Mohairperücke.

31/700 M **31**/600 M **31**/700 K

Bebés traviesos "CASADORA"

Gritan cuando se peinan ó cepillan los cabellos.

Mueven los ojos independiente de los párpados por todas las partes en cualquier posición, acompañados de lentos movimientos todo naturales de las pestañas.

Los ojos y párpados funcionan:

1. **automáticamente** en el modo usual.
2. **mecánicamente** tirando al biberón ó sonajero cuando se acuesta la muñeca.

Calidad Superior.

Vestidos de bebé y ropa inferior elegantes para poner y quitar. Cabeza caracterizada con peluca fina de mohair.

CASADORA-Wonder-Babies.

Cry when combing or brushing the hair.

Move the eyes independently of the lids to all directions and in any position accompanied with slow life-like movements of the eye lashes.

The eyes and lids work:

1. *automatically in the costumary manner.*
2. *mechanically by simply pulling the bottle or rattle when laid down.*

SUPERIOR QUALITY.

Fashionable baby-dresses and elegant under-clothes all to be put on and off. Character-head with fine mohair.

Gelenk-Sitzbabys, weiß gekleidet.
Jointed sitting babies, dressed white.
Bebés sedentarios articulados, vestidos en blanco.

Nr. **31**/600 K	34	38 cm		Nr. **31**/600 M	34	38 cm
	13½	15 inches			13½	15 inches

Desgleichen, mit langem Kleid.
Dito, with long garment.
Idem, con vestido largo.

Nr. **31**/602 K	34	38 cm		Nr. **31**/602 M	34	38 cm
	13½	15 inches			13½	15 inches

Desgleichen, ungekleidet, mit Hemd.
Dito, undressed, with shirt.
Idem, sin vestido, en camisa.

Nr. **31**/601	34	38 cm
	13½	15 inches

Gelenk-Stehbabys, gekleidet.
Jointed standing babies, dressed.
Bebés de pié articulados, vestidos.

Nr. **31**/700 K	36	40 cm		Nr. **31**/700 M	36	40 cm
	14	16 inches			14	16 inches

Desgleichen, ungekleidet, mit Hemd.
Dito, undressed, with shirt.
Idem, sin vestido, en camisa.

Nr. **31**/701 K	36	40 cm
	14	16 inches

Desgleichen, ungekleidet, mit Hemdhose.
Dito, undressed, with combination.
Idem, sin vestido, en camisa-combinatión.

Nr. **13**/701 M	36	40 cm
	14	16 inches

Aufmachungen in weißen Stückkartons. — *Each piece made up in a white cardboard box.* — Präsentaciones en cajas blancas de cartón de á una.

Man verlange illustrierte Sonderliste über sämtliche CASADORA-Puppen und Spielwaren.

Please ask for special catalogue showing all kinds of CASADORA-Dolls and toys.

Pídase catálogo especial de todas las muñecas y juguetes "CASADORA".

Erklärung der Zeichen — *Explication of the signs* — Explicación de los signos: **K** = Knabe — *Boy* — Muchacho, **M** = Mädchen — *Girl* — Muchacha.

Puppen
aus gestopften Körpern und Zelluloidkopf, gemaltem Haar und Augen, deshalb unzerbrechlich. Größe 29 — 50 cm. Man verlange Spezialkatalog unter Nr. 149.

Dolls
stuffed body and celluloid head, painted hair and eyes, and consequently unbreakable. Sizes 29 — 50 cm. Please apply for special catalogue Nr. 149.

Muñecas
de cuerpos zurvidos, con cabeza de celuloide, cabellos y ojos pintados, por consiguiente infrangibles. Tamaño 29 – 50 cm. Sírvase Vd. demandar el catálogo especial No. 149.

149/311

149/419

149/410

149/320

149/312

149/164

149/117

149/165

149/309

149/308

149/403

Strasser-Puppe

vereinigt drei Vorzüge:

Höchste künstlerische Schönheit, größte Naturwahrheit, solideste Fabrikationsarbeit.

Merkmale der Strasser-Puppen:

Der unzerbrechliche, drehbare Kopf (D. R. P. a.) mit dem waschbaren, der weichen Kinderhaut gleichen **Gesicht aus Gummi.**

Die unzerstörbare Bemalung nach eignem Verfahren.

Die vorbildliche Kinderkleidung nach eignen Entwürfen.

Der leichte, unzerbrechliche Gelenkkörper zum Stehen und Sitzen.

The Strasser Doll

combines three advantages:

Greatest artistic beauty, true to nature to the utmost extent, most substantial workmanship.

The characteristics of the Strasser Dolls are:

The unbreakable head, made to turn (German patent applied for), with **the washable face,** with soft skin like a child's, **of rubber.**

The indestructible painting by our own special process.

The ideal children's clothing to our own designs.

The light, unbreakable jointed body, made to stand or sit.

La muñeca de Strasser

combina tres ventajas:

Suprema belleza artística, grandísima natura, solidísima fabricación.

Característicos de las muñecas de Strasser:

La infrangible cabeza girable (Privilegio de invención presentado en Alemania) con la cara semejante a la piel blanda de niños, **la cual** puede ser lavada, **fabricada de caucho.**

La pintura indestructible ejecutada según un propio proceso.

Il vestido prototípico para niños según propios proyectos.

El ligero cuerpo articular infrangible para estar derecho y para estar sentado.

155/Maria **155**/Gerda

Nr. **155**/Maria. Grösse 60 cm, Gewicht ca. 800 g, in einfachster bis elegantester Ausführung.

„ **155**. Size 60 cm, weight about 800 g, in simplest up to the most elegant styles.

„ **155**. Tamaño 60 cm. Peso cerca de 800 g. Ejecución sencillísima y elegantísima.

Nr. **155**/Gerda. Grösse 45 cm, Gewicht ca. 500 g, volkstümliche Ausführung (links) und elegante Ausführung (rechts). Weitere Modelle laut Spezialkatalog.

„ **155**. Size 45 cm, weight about 500 g, popular style (left) and elegant style (right). Further models as per special catalogue.

„ **155**. Tamaño 45 cm. peso cerca de 500 g. Ejecución popular (a la izquierda) y ejecución elegante (a la derecha). Modelos ulteriores según el catálogo especial.

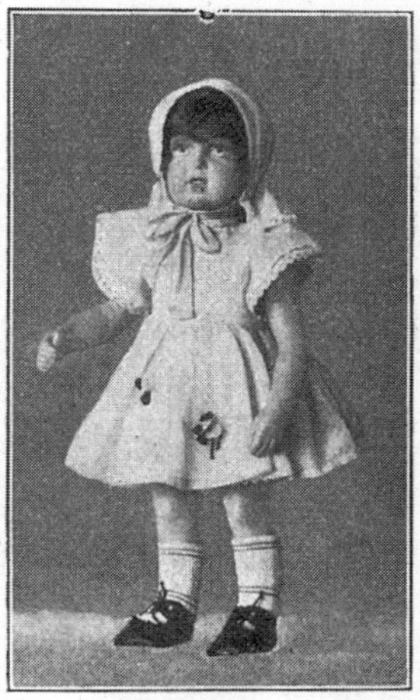

155/Gerda

2 Ausführungen
2 Styles
2 Ejecuciones

Nr. **155** „Die Volkspuppe". Künstlerische Volkstrachten. Größe 45×60 cm laut Spezialkatalog.

„ **155**. "The National Doll". Artistic national costumes. Sizes 45 and 60 cm, as per spezial catalogue.

„ **155**."La muñeca del pueblo". Trajes populares artísticos. Tamaño 45 y 60 cm según el catálogo especial.

155/ Die Volkspuppe
155/ The National Doll
155/ La muñeca del pueblo

Strasser-Baby **155**/Hansl. Lebensgroß, 55 cm, ca. 800 g, mit Mamastimme.

Strasser doll **155**/Hansl. Life size, 55 cm tall, calling "Mama".

Muñeca de Strasser Baby **155** / Hansl. De grandeza natural con voz de la mamá, cerca de 800 g.

Nr. **155**/Babs, kleines Baby, 30 cm, ca. 300 g, mit Mamastimme.

„ **155**. Little baby, 30 cm tall, about 300 g, calling Mama.

„ **155**. Bebe (niño) pequeño, 30 cm, cerca de 300 g, con voz de la mamá.

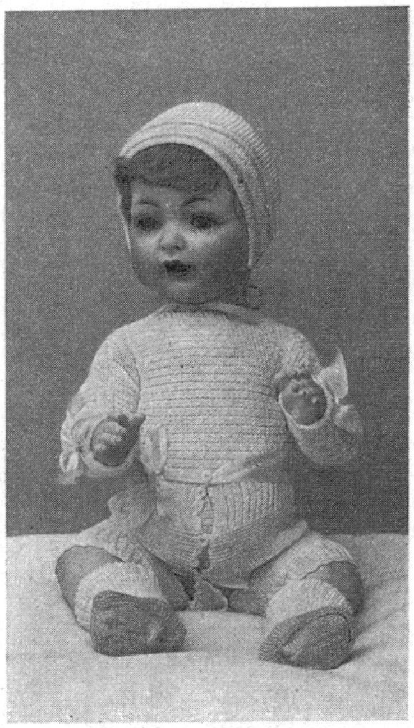

246/1501, Kleid **246**/501

246/1502

Feinste Babys und Puppen.
Finest Babies and Dolls.
Bebés y muñecas finísimas.

Maße und Preise der kompletten Serien befinden sich in separater Preisliste.
Measures and prices of the complete series are in separate price list.
Proporciones y precios de las series completas están en la lista de precios separata.

246/1502

246/8 **246**/17

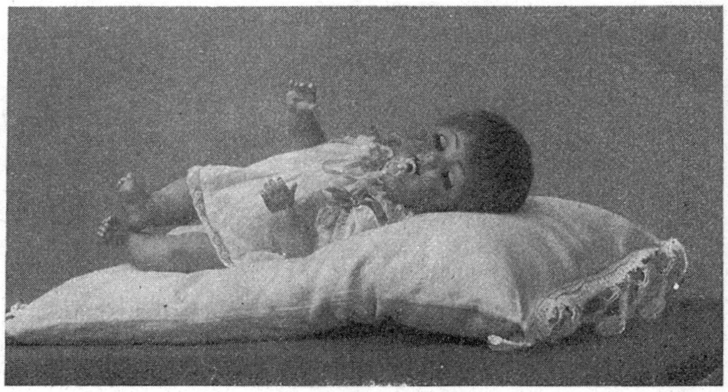

246/1502

246/1810/J und M

246/501/F

246/2002/P

246/2002/F

246/501/P

246/501/K

246/2001/M

246/1801/P **246**/1802/P **246**/1801/K

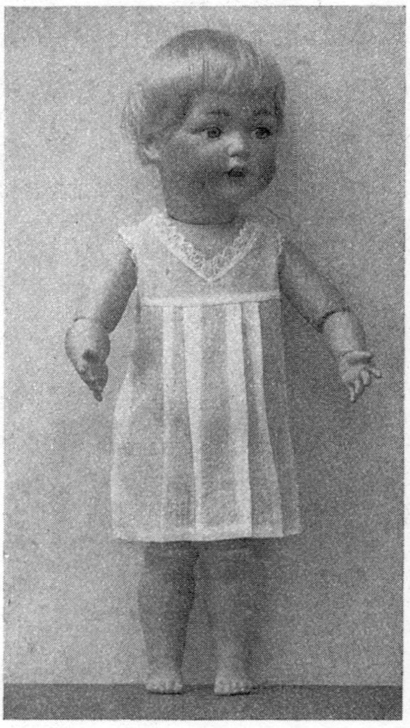

246/2002/K

THE "ULLA" DOLL

THE DELIGHT OF EVERY CHILD THAT LOVES A DOLL

Very finest workmanship
charming gay-coloured silk clothes
Graceful and elegant
With eyes to close, and movable limbs

DIE „ULLA"-PUPPE

DER LIEBLING JEDER PUPPENMUTTER

Allerfeinste Verarbeitung - Entzückende farbenfrohe Seidenkleider - Graziös und elegant - Mit Schlafaugen und beweglichen Gliedern

LA MUÑECA "ULLA"

LA FAVORITA DE TODA MADRE DE MUÑECA

Ejecución finísima; marvillosos vestidos de seda de colores magníficos, graciosos y elegantes
Con ojos móvibles y con miembros móvibles

374/21

GES. GESCH. ULLA PUPPE

380/19

322/26

371/21

375/23

190/11

182/11

57/131/19

57/144/21

57/152/19

57/162/21

57/193/21

57/201/19

57/202/21

57/225/21

57/229/21

57/231/19

57/237/19

57/245/19

57/248/21

57/259/21

57/270/19

57/283/21

57/287/19

57/290/21

57/316/21

57/319/21

57/320/21

57/321/21

57/322/19

57/323/21

57/324/21

57/327/21

57/330/23

57/331/23

57/332/23

57/336/21

57/337/23

57/338/23

57/339/23

57/344/21

57/345/19

57/346/21

Puppenausstattungen, in hochmoderner Ausführung und geschmackvoller Aufmachung.
Doll Outfits, executed in the latest styles and beautifully got up.
Ajuares de muñecas en ejecución modernísima y encajonadas muy gustosamente.

83/48

Nr. **83**/48 **Ostereier,** gefüllt und garniert mit Püppchen und Miniaturspielzeug.
Easter eggs, filled and furnished with little dolls and miniature toys.
Huevos de pascua llenados y guarnecidos de muñecas pequeñas y juguete en miniatura.

83/8005

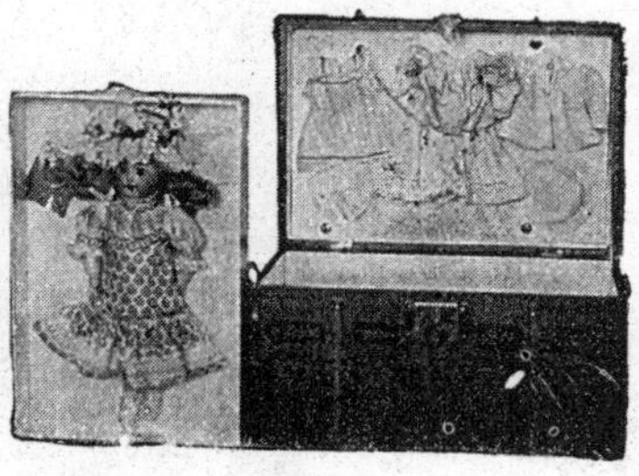

83/56–57

83/8060

83/63

83/8413

Nr. **83**/8005/1 — 4 **Badehaus** aus Holz, garniert mit Porzellan-Schwimmer und Badeausstattung.
Bathing house, of wood, furnished and equipped with porcelain swimmer and bathing appurtenances.
Baño de madera, guarnecido de un flotador de porcelana y teniendo ajuares de baño.

„ **83**/8060/1 — 6 **Strandkörbe,** reich garniert.
Baskets for the sands, richly fitted out.
Cestos de playa para bañar en la mar, guarnecidos copiosamente.

„ **83**/8060/1 — 3 **Strandkörbe,** mit Porzellan-Schwimmer.
Baskets for the sands, with porcelain swimmer.
Cestos de playa con flotador de porcelana.

„ **83**/8060/4 — 6 **Strandkörbe,** mit Celluloid-Stehbaby.
Baskets for the sands, with celluloid baby, standing up.
Cestos de playa, con bebe (niño pequeño) de celuloide en pie derecho.

„ **83**/56 — 57 **Koffer,** garniert mit Puppen und Puppenausstattung.
Trunk, fitted with dolls and dolls' equipments.
Baúl, llenado de muñecas y de ajuares de muñecas.

„ **83**/57 dito, in billiger Ausführung. — Cheaper style. — En ejecución barata.

„ **83**/56 dito, in ff. Ausführung. — Finest get up. — En ejecución finísima.

„ **83**/63/1 — 4 und „ **83** 63/58 — 60 **Schrankkoffer,** garniert mit Puppen und Puppengarderobe.
Cupboard trunk, furnished with dolls and dolls' things.
Baúl en forma de un armario llenado de muñecas y de ajuares de muñecas.

„ **83**/8413/0 — 4 **Puppenschaukel,** elegant garniert mit Puppe.
Dolls swing, elegantly fitted with doll.
Mecedero para muñecas, guarnecido de manera elegante de una muñeca.

83/8411

83/8409

83/8412

83/8410

Nr. **83**/8409/0—6 **Puppenklappstuhl** mit Puppe und Puppengarderobe.
Dolls folding chair, with doll and dolls' things.
Silla plegable para muñecas con muñeca y ropa para muñecas.

„ **83**/8412/0—4 **Schaukelstuhl mit Puppe,** elegant garniert.
Dolls rocking chair, with doll, elegantly fitted out.
Sillón para mecerse con muñeca guarnecida de manera elegante.

„ **83**/8411/0—4 **Puppenschrank aus Holz,** weiß lackiert, garniert mit Puppe und Garderobe.
Dolls wardrobe, of wood, varnished in white, fitted with doll and dolls' things.
Armario para muñecas de madera, embarnizada en blanco, guarnecido de muñeca y ropa.

Nr. **83**/8402 dito, mit Spiegel in ff. Ausführung, mit Kugelgelenk-Stehbaby
ditto, with looking-glass in finest style, with ball-jointed baby, to stand.
idem, con espejo, en ejecución finísima, con baby (niño pequeño) con coyuntura esférica, en pie derecho.

„ **83**/8410/0—5 **Laufgitter aus Holz,** weiß lackiert, mit Baby.
Sliding rail, of wood, varnished in white, with baby.
Rejada cuadrada corredera de madera, embarnizada en blanco, con bebe.

„ **83**/8494 Wie Nr. 83/8411, mit Stoff bezogen, 42×27×14½ cm.
As 83/8411, covered with cloth.
Tal que el No. 83/8411, pero revestido de estofa.

Puppenausstattungen in hochmoderner Ausführung und geschmackvoller Aufmachung.
Doll outfits, executed in the latest styles and beautifully got up.
Ajuares de muñecas en ejecución modernísima y encajonadas muy gustosamente.

83/8499/1—2

83/8408/1—2

83/8404/1—4

83/50/71

83/8420/00—5

83/50/26, 41, 58

83/50/67, 60, 59

83/43/14, 15, 8, 9, 10, 13

Nr. **83**/8499/1—2 **Wickelkommoden** mit Badeeinrichtung, garniert mit Zelluloid-Baby, Wäsche und Toiletteartikel.

Chest of drawers with swaddling clothes, with bath equipment, furnished with celluloid baby, baby linen and toilet articles.

Cómodas con envolturas, con utensilios para bañar, guarnecidas de bebes (niños pequeños) de celuloide, ropa blanca y artículos de tocador.

„ **83**/8408/1 **Ständer** zum Klappen, mit Kongreßstickerei, mit einem Beutel, Höhe 39 cm.

Stands to fold up, with congress embroidery, with one bag, height 39 cm.

Pilar plegable con bordado de congreso, con una bolsa, altura 39 cm.

„ **83**/8408/2 **Ständer** zum Klappen, mit Kongreßstickerei, mit zwei Beuteln, Höhe 60 cm.

Stands to fold up, with congress embroidery, with two bags, height 60 cm.

Pilar plegable con bordado de congreso, con dos bolsas, altura 60 cm.

„ **83**/8404/1—4 **Himmelbetten** aus Metall, weiß lackiert, garniert mit Puppe.

Canopy beds of metal, lacquered white, fitted with doll.

Camas entoldadas de metal, embarnizadas en blanco, guarnecidas con muñecas.

„ **83**/50/71 **Nähständer,** Korbgeflecht, gefüllt, Höhe 61½ cm.

Sewing stand, wickerwork, filled, height 61½ cm.

Pilar para costuras, cesto de zarzo llenado, altura 61½ cm.

Nr. **83**/8420/00—5 **Holzwiege,** weiß lackiert, garniert mit Baby im Bett und Puppenartikel.

Wooden cradle, white varnished, with baby in bed and doll toys.

Cuna de madera, embarnizada en blanco, guarnizada con un bebe en su cama y de artículos para muñecas.

„ **83**/50/26 u. 41 **Babykorb,** reich garniert, mit Baby.

Baby's basket, richly decorated, with baby.

Cesto para bebes, guarnecido copiosament, con bebe.

„ **83**/50/58 **Babykorb,** wie oben, in Herzform.

Baby's basket, as above, heart shaped.

Cesto para bebes, tal que aquello arriba, pero en forma de un corazón.

„ **83**/67/50 **Arbeitskorb** mit angefangenen Stickereien, rund, m. Deckel.

Work basket with embroidery half done, round, with lid.

Tabaque con bordados comenzados, redondo con cubierta.

„ **83**/43/14, 15, 8, 9, 10, 13: **Kartons. mit Inhalt zur Puppenschneiderei** mit ff. Steifgelenkpuppen in feiner Ausführung, mit Klappdeckel.

Cardboard boxes containing articles for doll's tailoring, with dolls with rigid joints in good style, with lid.

Cajitas de cartón con contenido para sastrería para muñecas, con muñecas con coyunturas tiesas en fina ejecución, con cubierta plegable.

„ **83**/12 wie oben, mit Nähmaschine
as above, with sewing machine
tales que arriba, con máquina de coser.

„ **83**/50/59 **Henkelkörbe. — Baskets with handles. — Cestos con asas.**

„ **83**/50/60 **Korbschalen. — Basket dishes. — Fuentes revestidas de mimbres.**

Puppenaustattungen in hochmoderner Ausführung und geschmackvoller Aufmachung.
Doll Outfits executed in the latest styles and beautifully got up.
Ajuares de muñecas en ejecución modernísima y encajonadas muy gustosamente.

83/I—VIII

83/40/317, 318, 433

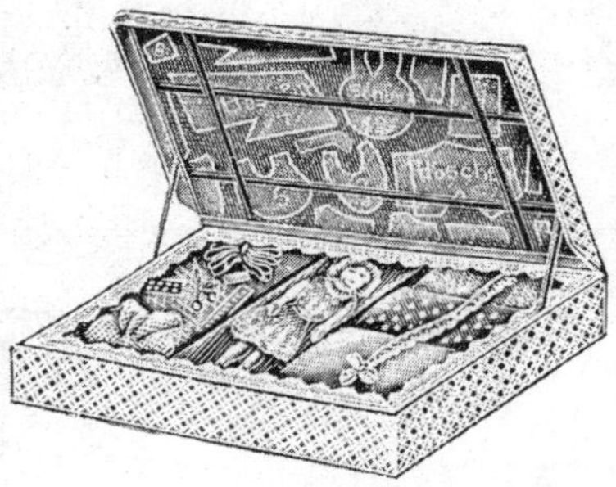

83/43/1—7

83/42/37

83/42/52

Nr. **83**/42/52, 53, 54, 55 **Puppenausstattung** in Kartons, in billiger Ausführung.
Dolls equipment in cardboard box, cheap style.
Muñecas guarnecidas, en cajitas de cartón en ejecución barata.

„ **83**/56, 57, 71: Mit Klappdeckel und ff. Steifgelenkpuppe.
With lid to lift and close and finest doll with rigid limbs.
Con cubierto plegable y muñeca finísima con cojuntura tiesa.

„ **83**/37/1, 42, 58, 41, 61, 60, 62, 63, 67, 68: wie **83**/42/52 bis 57 und 71 in diversen Preislagen und feinerer Aufmachung.
As **83**/42/52—57 and 71 at various prices and in better styles.
Tales que **83**/42/52—57 y 71 a diferentes precios y en encajonada más fina.

83/42/1

Nr. **83**/42/1, 5, 3, 24, 36, 30, 51, 31, 65, 46, 69 **Babyausstattung** in Kartons, reich gefüllt, in allen Preislagen.
Baby equipment in cardboard boxes, richly fitted out, at all prices.
Bebes guarnecidos en cajitas de cartón llenados copiosamente a todos precios.

„ **83**/40/470/1 3, 5, 8 **Stickkästen** auf weißem Kanevas. Kreuzstickerei, ff. Ausführung mit Perlgarn.
Embroidery caskets covered with white canvas. Cross embroidery, in finest style, with pearl thread.
Cajas para bordados sobre canvas blanco. Bordado en cruz, ejecución finísima con hilado para perlas.

„ **83**/40/405/1, **83**/40/473/2, 4, **83**/40/382/5 und **83**/40/477/7, 18 **Stickkästen** auf weißem oder creme Kongreß, Kreuzstickerei mit Perlgarn.
Embroidery caskets covered with white or cream congress cloth. Cross embroidery, with pearl thread.
Cajas para bordados sobre estofa de congreso de color blanco o crema. Bordado en cruz con hilado para perlas.

„ **83**/40/450/4, **83**/40/451/5, **83**/40/398/7, **83**/40/453/8 **Stickkästen** auf weißem Tidostoff, Kreuzstickerei mit Perlgarn.
Embroidery caskets covered with Tido cloth. Cross embroidery, with pearl thread.
Cajas para bordados sobre estofa "Tido" blanco. Bordado con hilado para perlas.

„ **83**/40/407/5, 7, 8 **Stickkästen** auf gestreiftem Mull, Kreuzstickerei, zugeschnitten auf Puppenkleidungsstücke mit Perlgarn.
Embroidery caskets covered with striped mull. Cross embroidery, models for dolls things, with pearl tread.
Cajas para bordados sobre organdí rayado. Bordado en cruz cortado para vestidos de muñecas con hilado para perlas.

„ **83**/40/450/4, 5, 7, 8 **Stickkästen** auf gelbem Satin mit leichten Stickarbeiten mit Perlgarn.
Embroidery caskets covered with yellow satin, with easy embroidery work, with pearl thread.
Cajas para bordados sobre raso amarillo con bordadura fáciles con hilado para perlas.

„ **83**/40/349/1, **83**/40/350/2, **83**/40/450/3 **Stickkästen** auf weißem Leinen, Kreuzstickerei. Inhalt: Tablettdeckchen, Deckchen und Läufer.
Embroidery caskets covered with withe linen. Cross embroidery. Contents: little cloths for trays, little covers, and oblong pieces to lay across.
Cajas para bordados sobre lienzo blanco. Bordado en cruz. Contenido: Pequeña cubierta de batea, cubiertas pequeñas y alfombras de escalera.

„ **83**/40/450/4, 5, 7, 8 **Stickkästen** wie oben, mit Stickrahmen.
Embroidery caskets as above, with embroidery frame.
Cajas para bordados las mismas que tales de arriba con bastidor.

„ **83**/40/465/1, **83**/410/2, **83**/465/3, **83**/417/4, **83**/465/5, **83**/416/7, **83**/465/7 **Stickkästen** auf weißem Leinen, leichte Stickarbeiten, wie oben.
Embroidery caskets covered with white linen, easy embroidery work, as above.
Cajas para bordados sobre lienzo blanco, bordaduras fáciles, las mismas que tales de arriba.

Nr. **83**/I—VIII **Stickkästen** in allen Größen, Ausführungen und Preislagen.
Boxes of Embroideries in all sizes, styles and at all prices.
Cajas de bordados en todos tamaños, todas ejecuciones y a todos precios.

„ **83**/I auf weißem Leinen (Deckchen, Läufer, Tablettdeckchen), Kreuzstickerei mit Perlgarn.
on white linen (little Tablecloths, Strips, Tray covers). Cross embroidery, with pearl yarn.
sobre lencería blanca (cubiertas pequeñas, alfombras de escalera, pequeñas cubiertas de batea). Bordado con puntos en cruz, hilado para perlas.

„ **83**/II wie I, mit leichten Stickarbeiten.
as I, with light embroidery.
tales que I, con bordados fáciles.

„ **83**/III wie II, auf gelbem Satin.
as II, on yellow satin.
tales que II, sobre raso satinado amarillo.

„ **83**/IV auf gestreiftem Mull (zugeschnittene Puppenkleidchen), Kreuzstickerei mit Perlgarn.
on striped mull (dolls dresses cut out), Cross embroidery, with pearl yarn.
sobre organdí alistado (vestidos cortados para muñecas). Bordado con puntos en cruz con hilado para perlas.

„ **83**/V auf weißen oder creme Kongreßstoffen (praktische Gebrauchsgegenstände). Kreuzstickerei mit Perlgarn.
on white or cream congress stuffs (articles of practical use), Cross embroidery, with pearl yarn.
sobre estofas de congreso blancas ó de color de crema (prácticos objetos de uso). Bordado con puntos en cruz con hilado para perlas.

„ **83**/VI auf weißem Kanevasstoff, Kreuzstickerei mit Wollfäden.
on white canvas, Cross embroidery with woolen yarn.
sobre estofa de canvas blanca. Bordado con puntos en cruz con hilos de lana.

„ **83**/VII auf weißem Kanevasstoff, in ff. Ausführung mit Perlgarn.
on white canvas, in finest style with pearl yarn.
sobre estofa de canvass blanca, en ejecución finísima con hilado para perlas.

„ **83**/VIII auf weißem Tidostoff, Kreuzstickerei mit Perlgarn.
on white Tido, Cross embroidery, with pearl yarn.
sobre estofa "Tido" blanco. Bordado con puntos en cruz con hilado para perlas.

„ **83**/40/317, 318, 433 **Stickkasten** mit Klappdeckel mit rundem Stickrahmen in feiner Ausführung.
Embroidery box with fastened lid and round embroidery frame, in finest execution.
Caja para bordados con cubierta plegable con bastidor de bordar redondo en fina ejecución.

„ **83**/43/1—7 **Puppenschneiderei. — Dolls tailoring. — Artículos de sastreria para muñecas.**

„ **83**/43/1—4 Billigere Ausführung. — Cheaper styles. — Ejecución más barata.

„ **83**/43/5—7 Größere Ausführung mit Klappdeckel. — Larger specimens with folding lid. — Ejecución más grande con cubierta plegable.

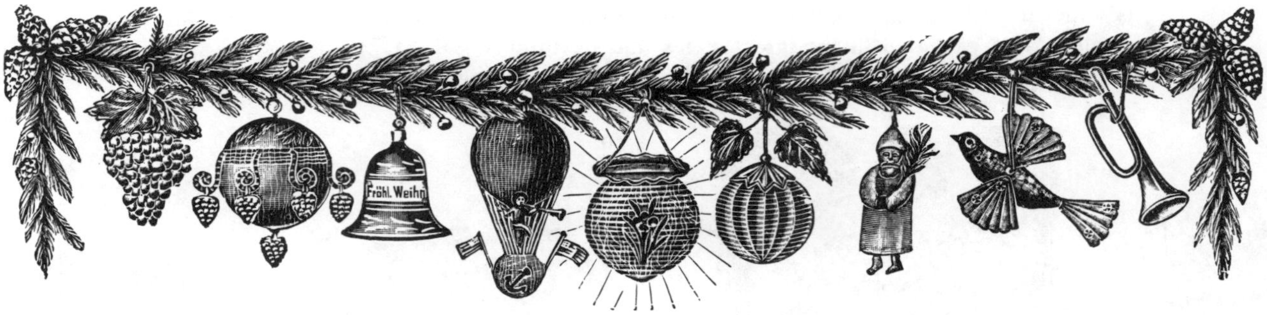

Lametta-Verzierungen. — Tinsel ornaments. — Adornos en lametta.

48/80 31

48/80/60

48/80/71

48/80/114

48/80/87

48/5976B

Lametta-Girlanden. — Lametta garlands. — Guirnaldas en lametta.

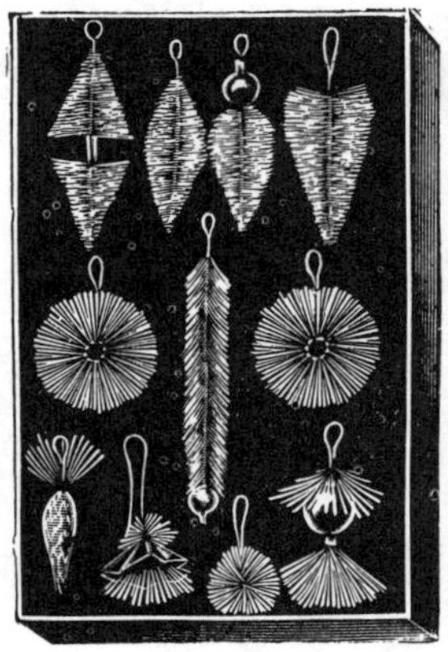

48/275/1112

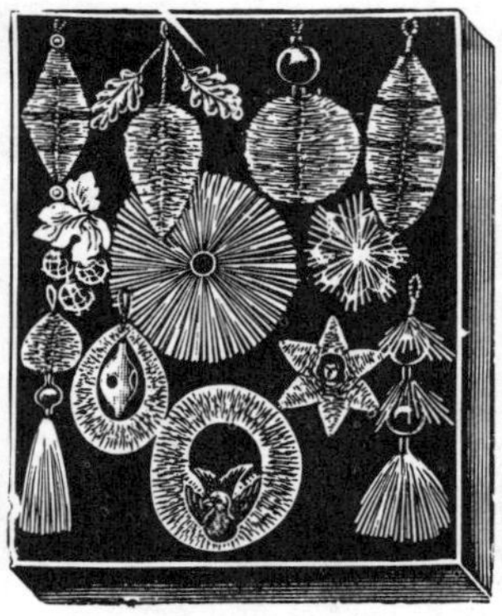

48/275/1113

48/275/485

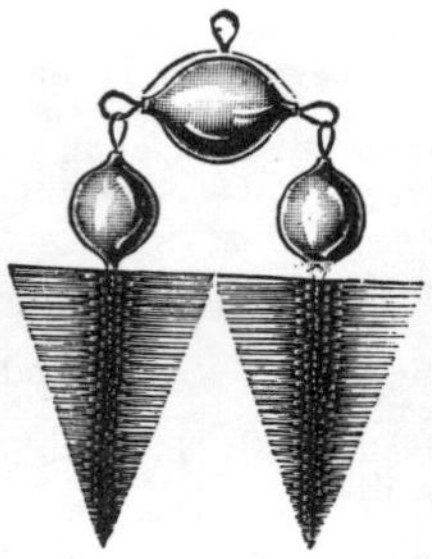

48/275/1034

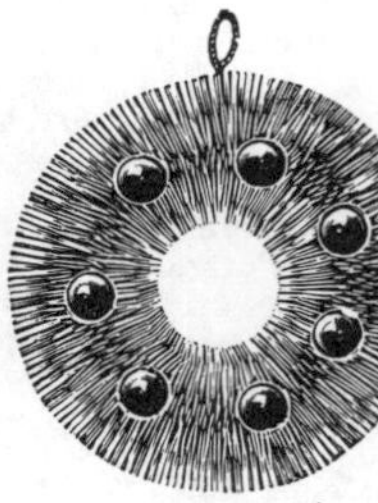

48/275/319

48/275/400

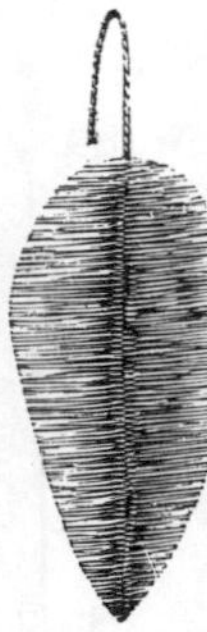

48/275/137

48/L 119

48/275/1074

48/275/527

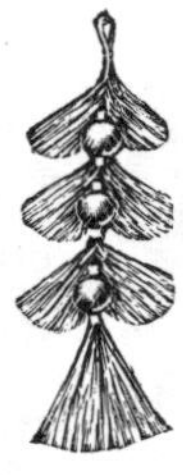

48/275 316

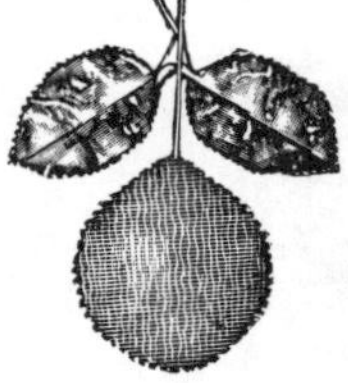

48/275/24

48/275/136

48/275/104

48/275/101

48/275/151

48/L 115

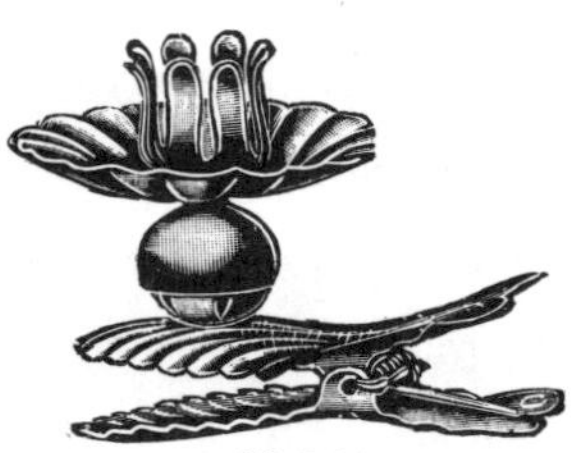

48/L 24

Lichthalter. — Candle holders. Candeleros.

48/K 111/5

Kartons mit 12 Figuren. — Cardboard boxes of 12 figures. 12 figuras en cajitas de cartón.

48/3054/3

48/3039/15½

Weihnachtsbäume. — Christmas trees. Árboles de navidad.

48/11

Christbaumschmuck. Christmas tree ornaments. Adornos para el arbol de navidad.

48/31/36

48/27/20

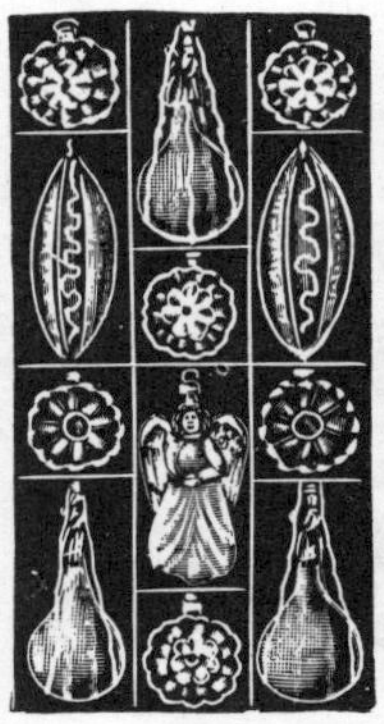

48/29/144

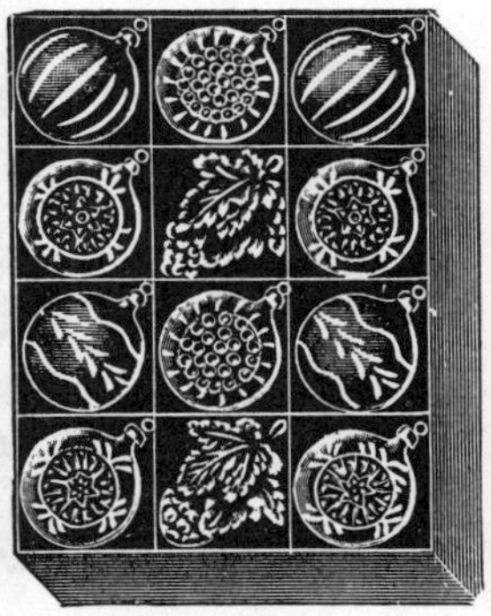

48/16/36

48/21/41

48/9/31

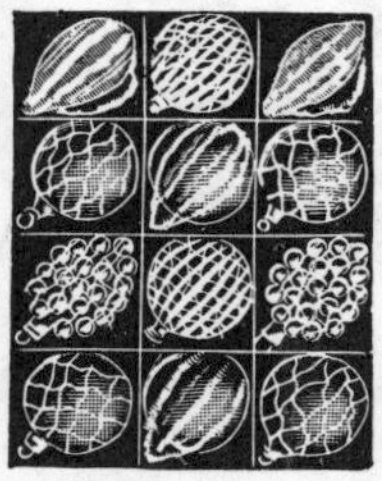

48/8/17

48/250/237

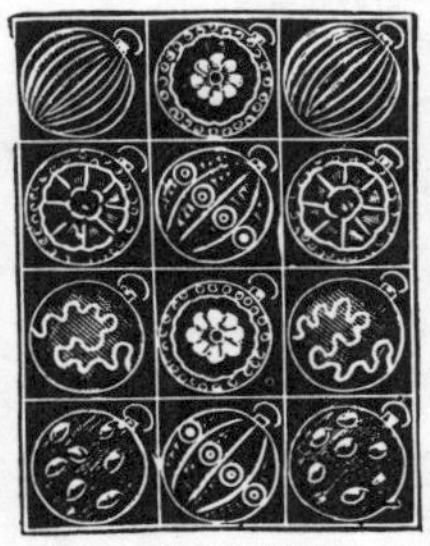

48/12/6

48/R. 5

48/V. 67

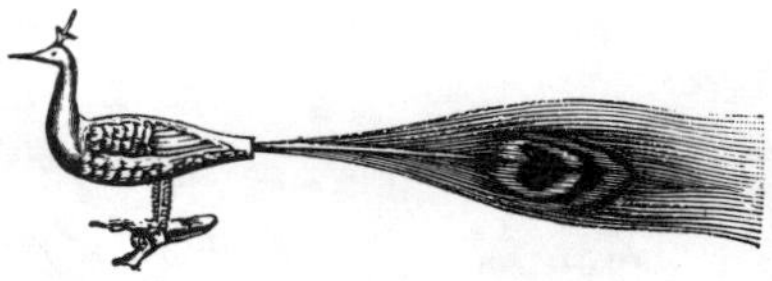

48/V. 247

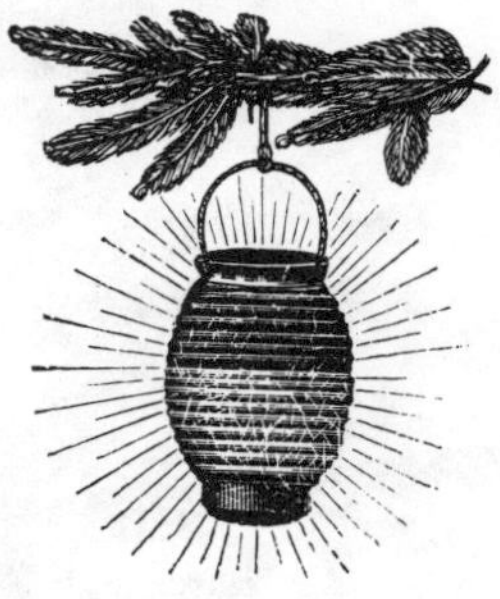

48/100/33

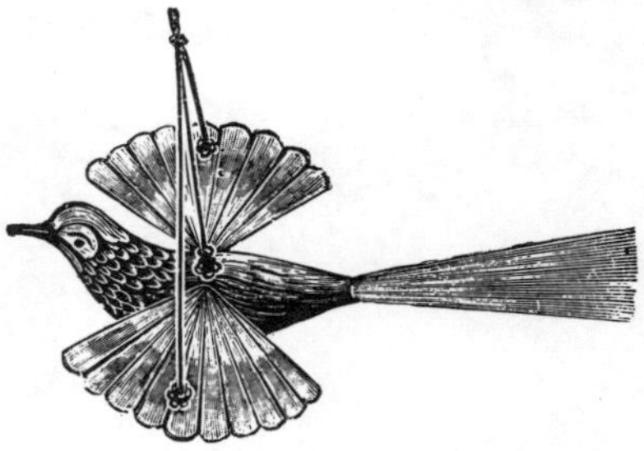

48/V. 188

48/S. 432

48/S. 225

48/S. 300

48/450/2830

48/W. 172

48/Sp. 564

48/Sp. 345

48/Sp. 15

48/Sp. 288

48 600/6

48/400/532

48/200/173

48/E. 84

48 Fg. 32

48/Fg. 142

48/Sp. 347

48/Sp. 602

48/125/1 sort.

48/Fig. 121

48/T. 3

48/T. 67

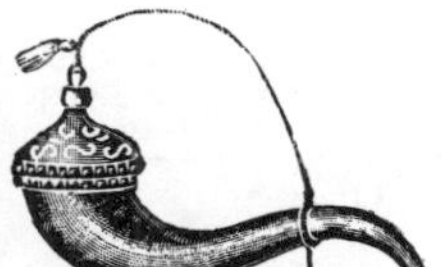

48/Fig. 568

48/Fig. 90

48/150/58

Fruchtkörbe. — Fruit baskets. Cestillos brillantes.

48/F. 409

48/F. 403

48/F. 218

Man verlange Spezial-Katalog Nr. 48.
Please apply special-catalogue Nr. 48.
Sirvase Vd. demandar catálogo especial No. 48.

48/P. 3

Künstliche Christbäume. Artificial christmas trees. Arboles de navidad artificiales.

Erstklassige Qualität. First class quality. Calidad superior.

86/4005

86/4007

86/4009

86/4011

86/4013

86/4015

86/4034

86/4026

86/4019

Mit Lichthaltern und roten Beeren, in weiß lackierten Holztöpfen, zusammenlegbar.

With candleholders and red berries, in white varnished wooden pots, folded up in cartoons.

Con porto-bujías y bayas rojas, en postes de madera barnizados blancos, legados en cartón.

	Höhe mit Topf Height incl. pot Altura total	Lichthalter Candleholders Porto-bujías		Packung Packing Contenido	
Nr. **86**/4001	14 cm	—		3	Dtz. im Karton doz. in cardboard box doc. en cajita de cartón
„ **86**/4002	16 „	—		3	
„ **86**/4003	22 „	3	kleine — small pequeños	3	
„ **86**/4005	30 „	4		2	
„ **86**/4007	40 „	5		2	
„ **86**/4009	45 „	7		2	
„ **86**/4011	53 „	7		1	
„ **86**/4013	60 „	11		1/2	
„ **86**/4015	65 „	5	große — large grandes	1/2	
„ **86**/4017	75 „	8		1/2	
„ **86**/4019	85 „	14		1/2	
„ **86**/4021	95 „	15		1/3	

	Höhe mit Topf Height incl. pot Altura total	Lichthalter Candleholders Porto-bujías	Packung Packing Contenido	
Nr. **86**/4022	100 cm	16	1/3	Dtz. im Karton doz. in cardboard box doc. en cajita de cartón
„ **86**/4023	105 „	16	1/3	
„ **86**/4024	112 „	16	1/3	
„ **86**/4026	130 „	19	1/12	
„ **86**/4028	150 „	22	1/12	
„ **86**/4030	170 „	28	1/12	
„ **86**/4032	190 „	31	1/12	
„ **86**/4034	210 „	34	1/12	
„ **86**/4036	250 „	41	1/12	
„ **86**/4038	300 „	56	1/12	
„ **86**/4040	400 „	88	1/12	

Beschneite Spitzbäumchen, mit rotlackiertem Holztopf.
Frosted trees, pointed shape, with red varnished wooden pots.
Arbolitos, forma puntiaguda, cubiertos de nievez con postes de madera barnizados rojos.

	Höhe mit Topf Height incl. pot Altura total	Packung Packing Contenido	
Nr. **86**/5001	8 cm	1	Dtz. im Karton doz. in cardboard box doc. en cajita de cartón
„ **86**/5002	10 „	1	
„ **86**/5003	12½ „	1	
„ **86**/5004	15 „	1	
„ **86**/5005	24 „	½	
„ **86**/5007	26 „	½	
„ **86**/5008	34 „	⅓	
„ **86**/5009	42 „	⅓	

86/5001

86/5002

86/5003

86/5004

86/5007

86/5008

Miniatur-Christbäume mit imitierten Kerzen u. rotlackiert. Holztöpfen, zusammenlegbar.
Miniature x-mas trees with imitated candles and red varnished wooden pots, folded up in cardboard box.
Arboles de Navidad miniaturas con bujías imitadas y portes de madera barnizados rojos, legadas en cajita de cartón.

Rauhreif-Bäume
Hoar-frosted x-mas trees
Arboles de navidad escarchados

Geschmückte Weihnachtsbäume
Trimmed x-mas trees
Arboles de navidad con adornos

mit Kerzen und roten Beeren, auf Schachteln zum Füllen, zusammenlegbar.
with candles and red berries, on cardboard box to be filled, folded up.
con bujías y bayas rojas, sobre cajitas para llenar, legados en cajita de cartón.

	Höhe mit Schachtel Height incl. box Altura total	Kerzen Candles Bujías	Packung Packing Contenido	
Nr. **86**/5101	28 cm	4	1/12	Dtz. im Karton doz. in cardboard box doc. en cajita de cartón
„ **86**/5102	37 „	5	1/12	
„ **86**/5103	56 „	9	1/12	
„ **86**/5201	33 „	5	1/12	
„ **86**/5202	42 „	6	1/12	
„ **86**/5203	56 „	9	1/12	

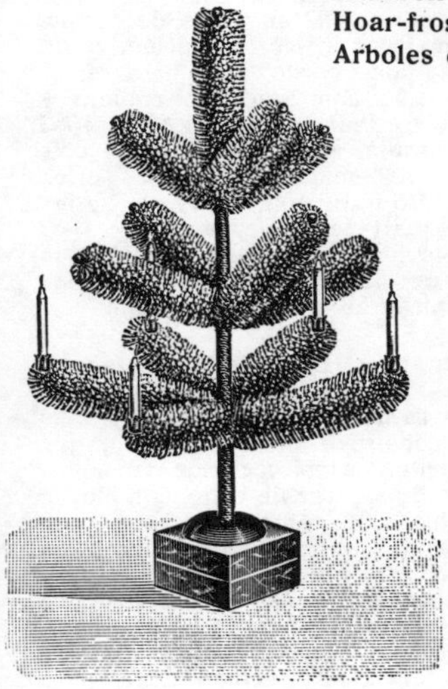
86/5102

Immortellen-Bäumchen, mit Blumen in sortierten Farben oder großen roten Beeren, mit Porzellankübelchen, zusammenlegbar.
Decoration trees, with flowers of assorted patterns or red large berries, with china pot, folded up in cardboard box.
Arbolitos de decoración, con flores de color assurtido ó bayas rojas grandes, con poste de porcelana, legados en cajita de carton.

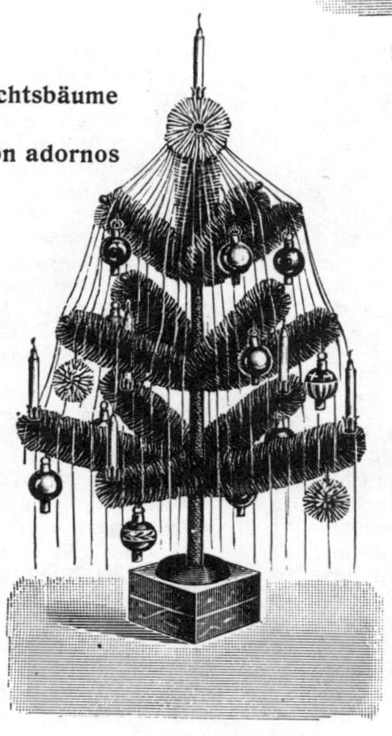
86/5202

86/5304

86/5305

	Höhe mit Topf Height incl. pot Altura total	Packung Packing Contenido	
Nr. **86**/5301	10½ cm	1	Dtz. i. Karton doz. in cardboard box doc. en cajita de cartón
„ **86**/5302	13½ „	1	
„ **86**/5303	18 „	1	
„ **86**/5304	21½ „	1	
„ **86**/5305	27½ „	½	
„ **86**/5307	33 „	½	

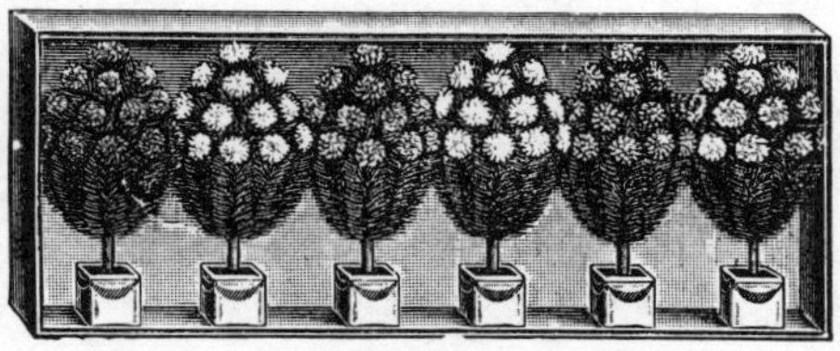
Original Packung. — Packing. — Caja original.
86/5504

86/5504

86/5504 B

86/5505

86/5506

	Höhe mit Topf Height incl. pot Altura total	Blumen oder Beeren Flowers or berries Flores ó bayas	
Nr. **86**/5504	14 cm	20	B= Beeren Berries Bayas
„ **86**/5504 B	14 „	20 B	
„ **86**/5505	16 „	33	

	Höhe mit Topf Height incl. pot Altura total	Blumen oder Beeren Flowers or berries Flores ó bayas	
Nr. **86**/5505 B	16 cm	33 B	B= Beeren Berries Bayas
„ **86**/5506	19 „	46	
„ **86**/5506 B	19 „	46 B	

Farbige beschneite Tannenzapfen mit farbigen Glasperlen.
Colored frosted cones with colored glass beads.
Piñas coloradas, cubiertas de nieve y con perlas coloradas de vidrio.

Christbaumschmuck. — X-mas tree ornaments. — Adornos para arboles de Navidad.

86/5603

86/5605

86/5608

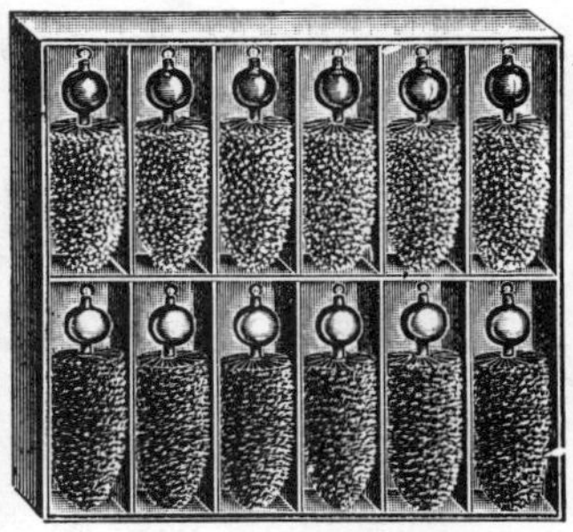
86/5602

Farbige beschneite Kränze, ½ Dutzend rot und grün sortiert im Karton.
Colored frosted wreath, ½ doz. to a cardboard box, red and green assorted.
Coronas coloradas, cubiertas de nieve, ½ doc. en cajita de cartón, rojas y verdes assurtidas.

	Äußerer Durchmesser Outer diameter Diámetro exterior	Mit farbigen With colored Con colorados
Nr. **86**/5603	10 cm	Glasperlen. Glass beads. Perlas de vidrio.
„ **86**/5604	10 cm	Glasherzen. Glass hearts. Corazónitos de vidrio.
„ **86**/5605	12 cm	Glasglocken. Glass bells. Campanitas de vidrio.
„ **86**/5606	12 cm	St. Nikolaus. Sta. Claus. San Nicolas.
„ **86**/5607	12 cm	Glasherzen. Glass hearts. Corazónitos de vidrio.

	Äußerer Durchmesser Outer diameter Diámetro exterior	Mit farbigen With colored Con colorados
Nr. **86**/5608	13½ cm	St. Nikolaus. Sta. Claus. San Nicolas.
„ **86**/5609	13½ cm	Glasglocken. Glass bells. Campanitas de vidrio.
„ **86**/5610	17	Glasglocken. Glass bells. Campanitas de vidrio.
„ **86**/5611	20	Glasglocken. Glass bells. Campanitas de vidrio.

	Ganze Länge Total length Larga total	Packung Packing Contenido
Nr. **86**/5601	9 cm	1 Dtz. rot u. grün sort. i. Karton 1 doz. to a cardboard box, red and green ass. 1 doc. en cajita de cart., piñas rojas y verdes assurtidas.
„ **86**/5602	12 „	

Sortiment 50.

Beschreibung der Abbildungen I bis IX.

Tafel I, II und III: Möbelgarnituren in allen Ausführungen: Wohnzimmer, Salons, Speisezimmer, Herrenzimmer, Küchen, Schule, Kontor, Billardzimmer; aus Eichenholz hell und dunkel, poliertes Holz in verschiedenen Farben, weiß Ahornholz roh usw. Stühle, Sessel und Sofas mit schönen Stoffen bezogen und gepolstert.

Tafel IV: Möbelgarnituren wie oben, ferner einzelne Möbel: Serie 98 in Eiche, Serie 404 in Buche, Serie 156 Küchenmöbel Ahorn, Serie 160 Küchenmöbel weißlackiert, Serie 201 Küchengeräte Ahorn, Wiegen 196 weißlackiert.

Tafel V: Leierkästen mit Schweizer Musikwerken: Kästen Hartholz hell, dunkel und mahagonifarbig mattiert. Metallophone: Serie 1000 ohne Karton, Serie 1002 in Pappkarton, Serie 1006 in besserem Pappkarton, Serie 1018 in Holzrandkasten und Serie 1008 in Holzrandkasten mit halben Tönen. Pianos: Serien 1050, 1063 und 1087 lithographiert, Serien 1057, 1058, 1059, 1061, 1067, 1071, 1099 Eiche lackiert, Serien 1059½, 1063 und 1076 weißlackiert, Serien 1059¾ und 1063¾ schwarzlackiert, Serie 1062 weiß- oder schwarzlackiert. Holzbaukästen 3200/1 bis /6 in Pappkarton, alle übrigen in Holzkasten.

Tafel VI: Serien 18 und 19 Würfel aus Holz. Serie 21 Halmasteine aus Holz. Serie 24 und 25 Damensteine Holz. Nr. 425 Lehruhr als Baukasten, richtiggehend, Anweisungen in mehreren Sprachen. Nr. 2000 Reiseschach mit Einsteckfiguren aus Holz. Nr. 2001 wie 2000, aber mit Galalith-Figuren. Serie 2003 Damenbrett, Pappspielfläche, Rückseite Mühle. Serie 2004 Damenbrett ganz Holz, Rückseite Mühle. 2037 Damenbrett, wie 2004, aber Spielflächen poliert. Serie 2039½ Damenbrett wie 2037, aber mit Eichenrand, innen Papier. Serie 2039 Damenbrett wie 2039½, jedoch innen Tuch. Serie 2013 Schachbrett, Holz, ohne Mühle. Serie 2020 Schachbrett, Holz, mit Mühle. Serie 2021 Schachbrett wie 2013, aber Spielfläche poliert. Serie 2023 Schachbrett wie 2020, jedoch Spielflächen poliert. Serie 2014 Schachbrett wie 2021, jedoch mit Eicherand, mattiert. Serie 2015 Schachbrett wie 2023, jedoch mit Eicherand mattiert. Nr. 2041½/12—17 Schachfiguren, franz. Form, gewachst, in Holzkästen. Nr. 2041½/22—/26 Schachfiguren, Stauntonform, gewachst, in Holzkästen. Nr. 2041½/32—/36 Schachfiguren, Stauntonform, lackpoliert, in Holzkästen. Serie 2079 Tivolis, grüne Lithographie. Serie 2149 Tivolis, grün poliert. Serie 2154 Tivolis mit grünem Tuch. Serie 2160 Tivolis, bunte Lithographie. Serie 2080 Dominos. Serie 2138 Lottos. Serie 2140 Blockkubus. Serie 2141 Pyramydenkubus. Nr. 3300/1—/9 Roulettes, gute Ausführung. Nr. 3300/10—/11 Spielplan, Papier und Wachstuch. Nr. 3500 mechan. Würfelspiel.

Tafel VII: Serien 195 und 196 weißlackierte Baby-Puppenmöbel in bester Ausführung. Serie 912 und 937 Puppenstuben und -Küchen in bester Ausführung. Nr. 3003—3009/2 Kaufläden. Nr. 3020—3033/3 Pferdeställe. Nr. 3040—3048 Festungen. Serie 3060 Kegel in Karton. Serie 3061 lackierte Kegel in Karton. Serie 3062 polierte Kegel in Karton. Serie 3090 Waschgarnituren.

Tafel VIII: Serie 202 Miniatur-Spielwaren einzeln und in Aufmachungen. No. 401—3 Pickhühner. Serie 3052 Sandmühlen. Serie 3053 Gitterwiegen. Serien 3054, 3055, 3056 und 3130 Miniatur-Spielwaren in Karton. Serie 3120 Wackelenten. Serie 3400—3412 Altäre. Serie 3800 Wetterhäuser.

Tafel IX: Serien I—X und 200—225 zweiseitig gut lackierte Holzfiguren mit festen Füßen in Karton. Serien 4000—4040 Hartmasse-Figuren, einzeln. Serien 4050—4087 Hartmasse-Figuren in Karton.

Die Fabrik des Sortiments 50 sendet auf Wunsch gern den reichhaltigen und ausführlichen Hauptkatalog zu.

Arrangement 50.

Description of the pictures I to IX.

Page I, II and III: Dolls furniture in boxes of every kind, drawing- and sitting rooms, library- and dining-rooms, kitchens, schools, office- and billiard-rooms; of oakwood light and dark colour, polished wood in different colours, natural maple-wood, etc. Chairs, seats and sofas with nice satin, silk or velvet coverings.

Page IV: Dolls furniture in boxes, as previously mentioned and single furniture: series 98 oakwood, series 404 beechwood, series 156 kitchen-furniture maple, series 160 kitchen-furniture white varnished, series 201 kitchen-utensils maple, cradles series 196 white varnished.

Page V: Barrel-organs with Swiss mechanism, boxes oakwood, light or dark or mahogany, colour varnished. Dulcimers series 1000 without boxes, series 1002 in cardboard boxes, series 1006 in better cardboard boxes, series 1018 in boxes with wooden frame, and series 1008 in boxes with wooden frame and half tones. Pianos: Series 1050, 1063 and 1087 lithographed, series 1057, 1058, 1059, 1061, 1067, 1071, 1099 oakwood varnished, series 1059½, 1063 and 1076 white-varnished, series 1059¾ and 1063¾ black-varnished, series 1062 white- or black-varnished, on demand. Boxes of wooden bricks 3200/1—/6 in cardboard boxes, all others in wooden boxes.

Page VI: Series 18 and 19 wooden dice. Series 21 wooden-Halmamen. Series 24 and 25 wooden draughts. Nr. 425 Building Clock in a box, correctly going, English instructions. No. 2000 Chessboard for travel with wooden men. Nr. 2001 like 2000, buth with Galalith-men. Series 2003 Draughtboards, cardboard games with reverse-game. Series 2004 Draughtboard entirely wood, with reverse game. Series 2037, like 2004, but polished games. Series 2039½ Draugthboard like 2037 but with oakwood frame, paper inside. Series 2039 Draugthboard like 2039½, but cloth inside. Serie 2013 Chessboard entirely of wood without reverse game. Series 2020 Chessboard entirely wood with reverse game. Series 2021 Draugthboard like 2013, but polished game. Serie 2023 Chessboard like 2020, but with polished games. Series 2014 Chessboard like 2021, but with oakwood frame. Series 2015 Chessboard like 2023, but with oakwood frame. Nr. 2041½/12—/17 Chessmen, French form, waxed, in wooden boxes. Nr. 2041½/22—/26 Chessmen Stauntonform, waxed, in wooden boxes. Nr. 2041½/32—/36 Chessmen, Stauntonform, polish-varnished, in wooden boxes. Series 2079, Bagatelle boards, green lithographed. Series 2149 Bagatelle boards, green polished. Series 2154 Bagatelle boards, with green cloth. Series 2160 Bagatelle boards, coloured lithographed. Series 2080 Domino games. Series 2138 Lotto games. Series 2140 Blockcubes. Series 2141 Pyramid-cubes. Nr. 3300/1—9 Roulettes, first-class finish. Nr. 3300/10—/11 Playing boards, paper and oilcloth. Nr. 3500 mechanical Dice-game.

Page VII: Series 195 and 196 first-class white-enamelled furniture. Series 912 and 937 Dolls houses and kitchens, best make. Nr. 3003—3009/2 Shops. Nr. 3020—3033/3 Stables. Nr. 3040—3048 Fortresses. Series 3060 Skittles in boxes. Series 3061 Varnished skittles in boxes. Series 3062 Polished skittles in boxes. Series 3090 Sets of washing utensils.

Page VIII: Series 202 Miniature-toys single and arrangements. Nr. 401—3 Pecking hens. Series 3052 Sandmills. Series 3053 Folding cradles. Series 3054, 3055, 3056 and 3130 Miniature-toys in boxes. Series 3120 Waddling ducks. Series 3400—3412 Altars. Series 3800 Weather-boxes.

Page IX: Series I—X and 200—225 finely enamelled wooden figures with strong feet in boxes. Series 4000—4040 Plastic-figures, single. Series 4050—4087 Plastic-figures in boxes.

The factory of arrangement 50 will be glad to send its sample and detailed general catalogue.

Surtido 50.

Descripción para las pinturas I hasta IX.

Página I, II y III: Muebles para muñecas en cajas, de toda clase, muebles de cuartos ordinarios, salones, comedores, librerías, cocinas, escuelas, despachos, salas de billar; de madera de encina clara y oscura, de madera pulida en varios colores, de madera de arce natural, etc.; sillas, sillones y sofás cubiertas de satén, seda ó felpa de bonitos colores.

Página IV: Muebles para muñecas en cajas, como por arriba, y mueblos sueltos, como: serie 98 madera de encina, serie 404 haya, serie 156 cocina arce, serie 160 cocina barnizada blanca, serie 201 utensilios de cocina arce, cunas serie 196 barnizadas blancas.

Página V: Organillos con bueno mechanismo suizo, cajas de madera de encina barnizada clara, oscura ó color de caoba. Metalófonos serie 1000 sin cajas, serie 1002 en cajas de cartón, serie 1006 en mejores cajas de cartón, serie 1018 en cajas con borde de madera, y serie 1008 en cajas con borde de madera y con medios tonos. Pianos: Series 1050, 1063 y 1087 con litografía, series 1057, 1058, 1059, 1061, 1067, 1071, 1099 madera de encina, series 1059½, 1063 y 1076 barnizadas blancas, series 1059¾ y 1063¾ barnizadas negras, serie 1062 barnizada blanca ó negra, á deseo. Cajas de construcciones de madera 3200/1—/6 en cajas de cartón, las otras en cajas de madera.

Página VI: Series 18 y 19 dados de madera. Serie 21 peones de Halma de madera. Series 24 y 25 peones de damas de madera. Nr. 425 Reloj que se construye por los niños y que anda correctamente, con instrucciones españolas. No. 2000 Tabero de ajedrez de viaje, con piezas de madera. No. 2001 como 2000, pero con piezas de Galalith. Serie 2003 Tableros de damas, juego de cartón, juego especial al revés. Serie 2004 Tablero de damas enteramente de madera, juego especial al revés. Serie 2037, como 2004, pero con juegos pulidos. Serie 2039½ Tablero de ajedrez como 2037, pero con borde de madera de encina, papel por dentro. Serie 2039 Tablero de damas como 2039½, pero pano por dentro. Serie 2013 Tablero de ajedrez enteramente de madera, sin juego al revés. Serie 2020 Tablero de ajedrez enteramente de madera con juego al revés. Serie 2021 como 2013, pero con juego pulido. Serie 2023 Tablero de ajedrez como 2020, pero con juegos pulidos. Serie 2014 Tablero de ajedrez como 2021, pero con borde de madera de encina. Serie 2015 Tablero de ajedrez como 2023, pero con borde de madera de encina. No. 2041½/12—/17 Piezas de ajedrez, forma francesa, impregnadas de cera, en cajas de madera. No. 2041½/22—/26 Piezas de ajedrez, forma Staunton, impregnadas de cera, en cajas de madera. No. 2041½/32—/36 Piezas de ajedrez, forma Staunton, pulidas-barnizadas, en cajas de madera. Serie 2079 Juegos de Tivoli con litografía verde. Serie 2149 Juegos de Tivoli pulidos verde. Serie 2154 Juegos de Tivoli con paño verde. Serie 2160 Juegos de Tivoli con litografía abigarrada. Serie 2080 Juegos de Domino. Serie 2138 Juegos de Lotto. Serie 4140 Juegos de cubos. Serie 2141 Juegos de cubos. No. 3300/1—/9 Ruletas de mejora hechura. No. 3300/10—/11 Planos de ruleta, papel y encerado. No. 3500 Juego mechan. de dados.

Página VII: Serie 195 y 196 muebles esmaltadas finamente blancas. Series 912 y 937 Casas y cocinas para muñecas, mejora hechura. No. 3003—3009/2 Tiendas. No. 3020—3033/3 Caballerizas. No. 3040—3048 Fortalezas. Serie 3060 Juegos de bolos en cajas. Serie 3061 Juegos barnizados de bolos en cajas. Serie 3062 Juegos pulidos de bolos en cajas. Serie 3090 Utensilios de lavandera.

Página VIII: Serie 202 Juguetes de miniatura sueltos y garnituras. No. 401—3 Gallinas picoteantes. Serie 3052 molinos de arena. Serie 3053 Cunas plegantes. Series 3054, 3055, 3056 y 3130 Juguetes de miniatura en cajas. Serie 3120 Patos. Serie 3400—3412 Altares. Serie 3800 casitas-barometros.

Página IX: Series I—X y 200—225 figuras de madera, esmaltadas finamente, con piés sólidos, en cajas. Series 4000—4040 Figuras plásticas, sueltas. Series 4050—4087 Figuras plásticas en cajas.

La fábrica del surtido 50 enviará con gusto su amplio y especificado catálogo general á deseo.

Sortiment 50 — Arrangement 50 — Surtido 50

1/8 natürl. Größe (size, grandeur, tamaño)

554/18 · 589/12 · 590/2 · 731/57 · 731/75 · 730/2 · 731/81

731/13 · 727/17 · 733/2 · 737/12 · 713/3 · 731/84 · 552/1

737/13 · 733/4 · 729/5 · 731/87 · 731/79 · 729/12

737/14 · 733/6 · 731/80 · 584 · 730/9

737/15 · 731/40 · 527/1 · 527/2 · 638/3½

752/3 · 543/1 · 543/2 · 526/2 · 526/3 · 541/1

552/5 · 527/5 · 543/5 · 731/96 · 577/20

542/3½ · 553/1 · 526/5 · 542/3¾ · 577/25

575/2 · 750/2 · 754/2 · 591/2 · 591/4

Sortiment 50 — Arrangement 50 — Surtido 50

$^1/_8$ natürl. Größe (size, grandeur, tamaño)

577/13½

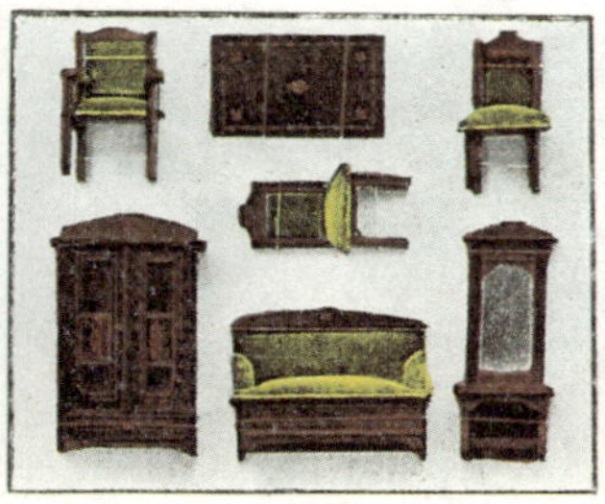

591/3

656/1½

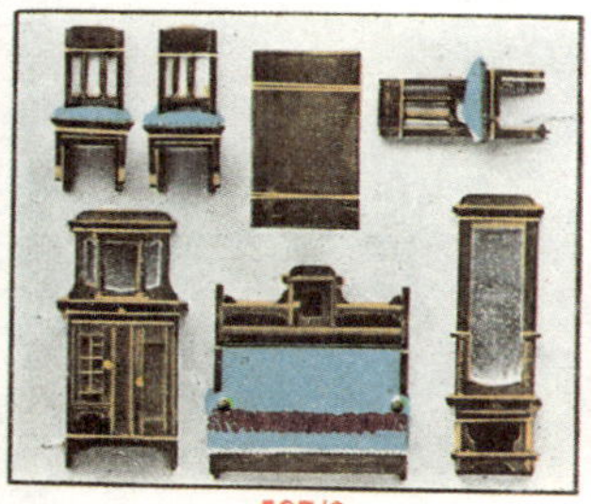

597/2

577/2½

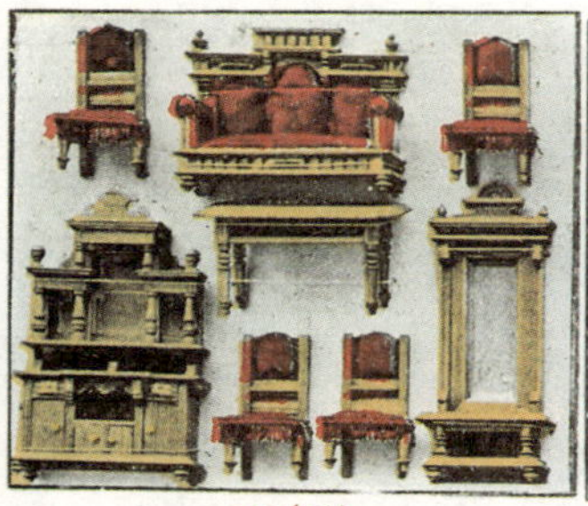

651/4¾

591/6

592/1

746/3

757/2

591/8

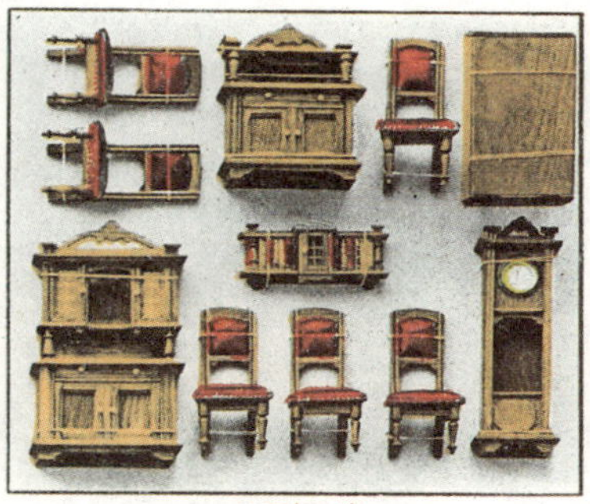

577/14½

529/2

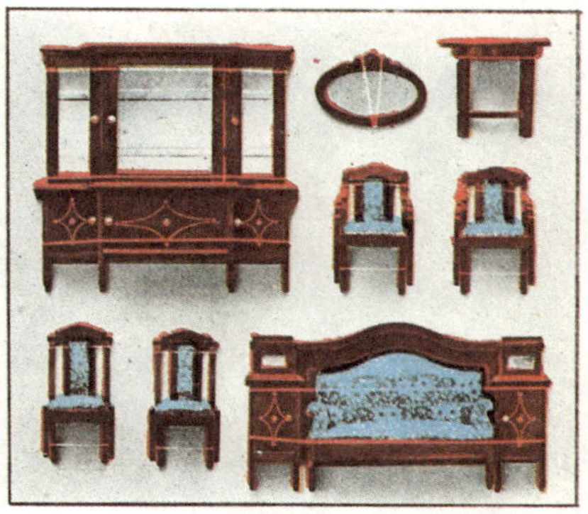

595/5

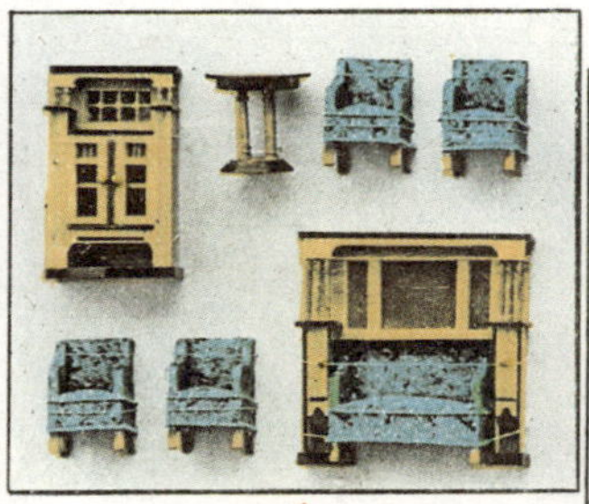

588/4

746/4

587/4

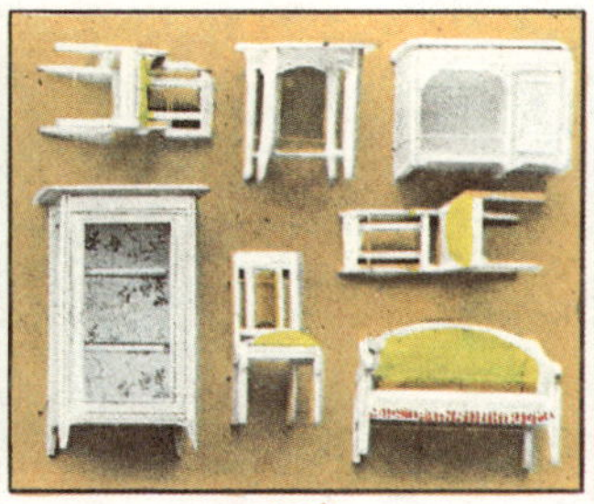

578/3

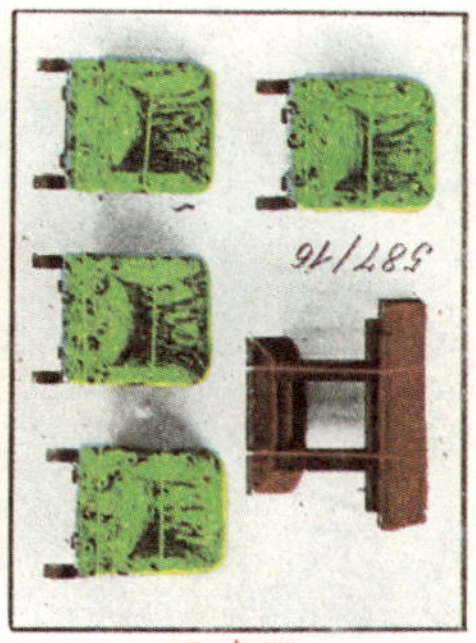

587/16

577/24

595/1

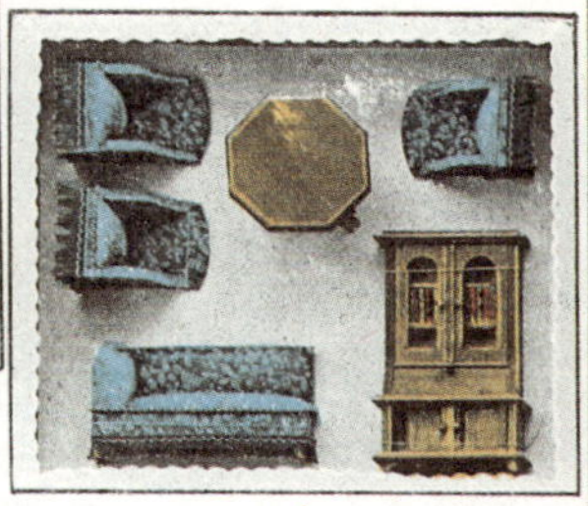

577/21

595/3

565/1

596/2

760

566/6

Sortiment 50 — Arrangement 50 — Surtido 50

1/5 natürl. Größe (size, grandeur, tamaño)

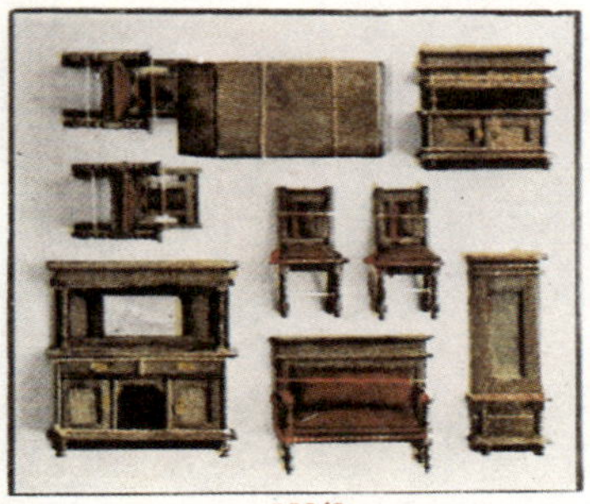
592/3

586/7

586/4

758/2

592/6

592/5

565/4½ gold

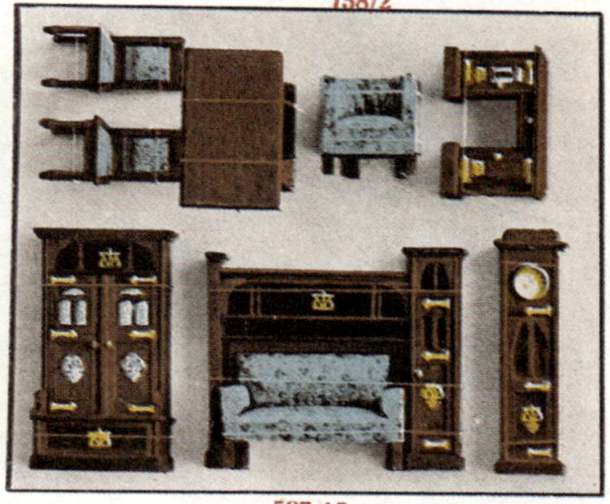
587/15

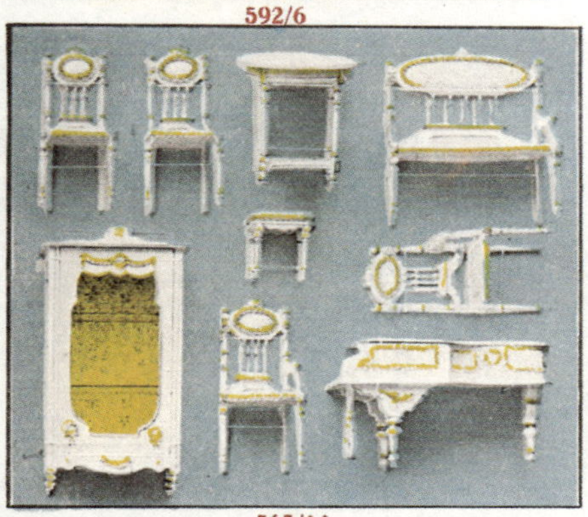
565/14

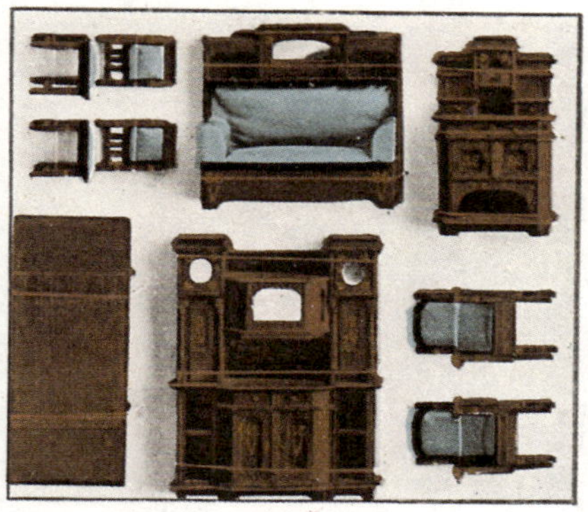
564/2

595/9

592/12

755/2

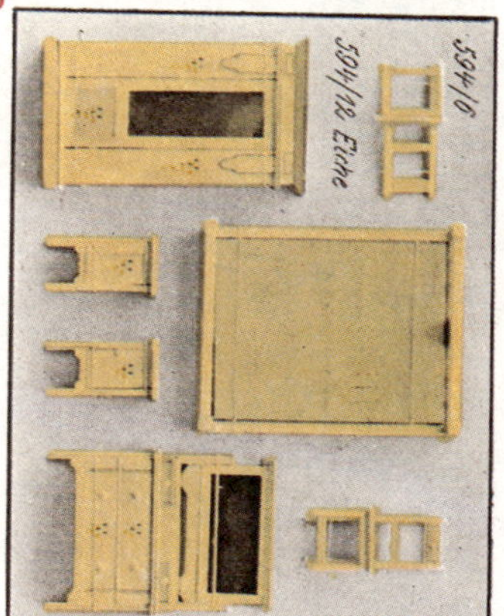

594/6 594/12 Eiche

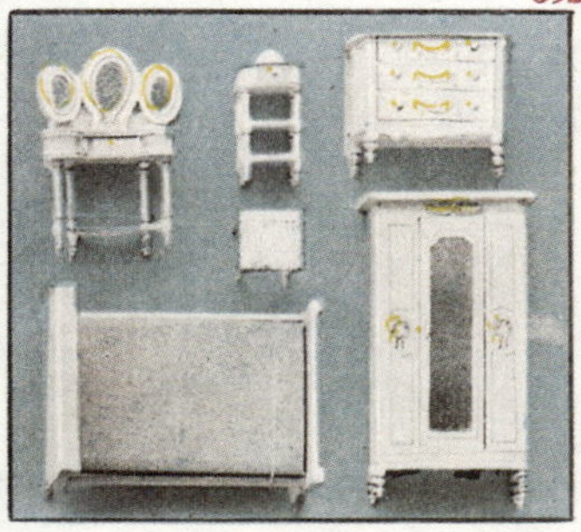
568/1

582/1

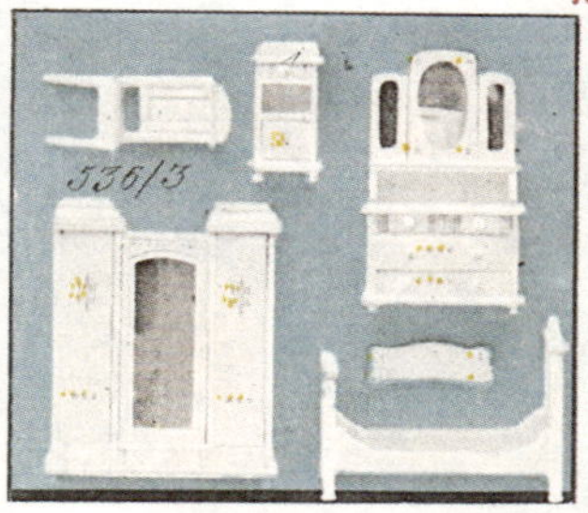

536/3

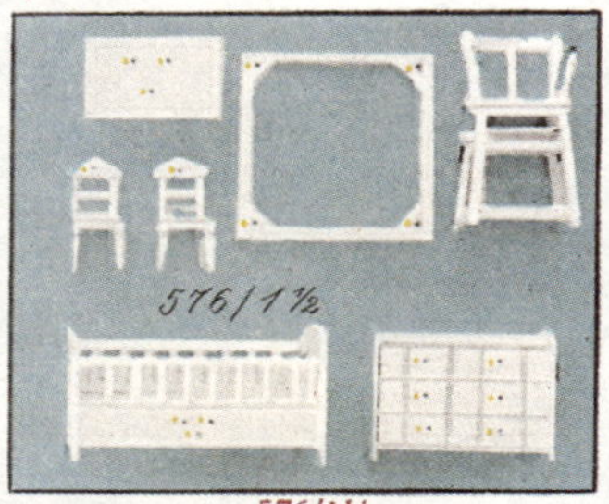

576/1½

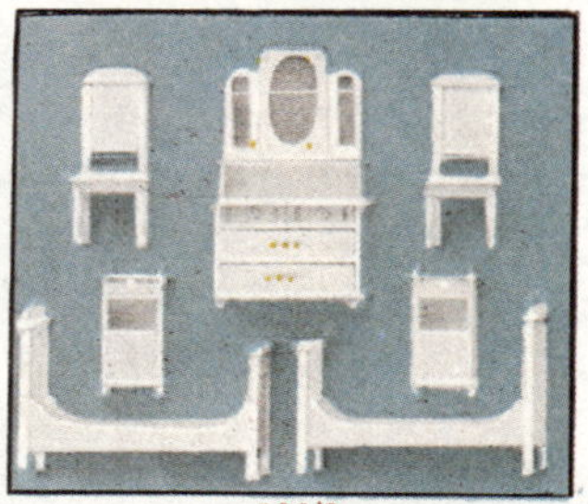
536/2

581/1

594/9 Eiche 594/3 weiß

526/10

577/15½

633/1

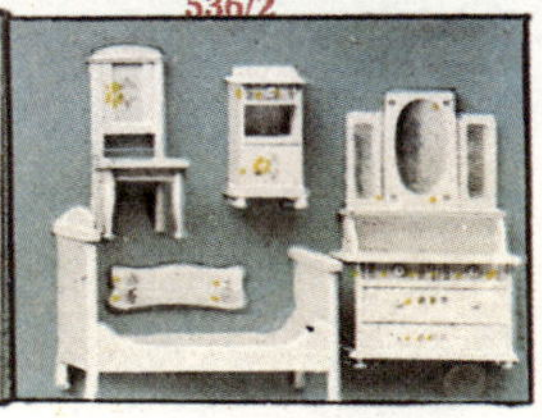
536/1

Sortiment 50 — Arrangement 50 — Surtido 50

$^1/_8$ natürl. Größe (size, grandeur, tamaño)

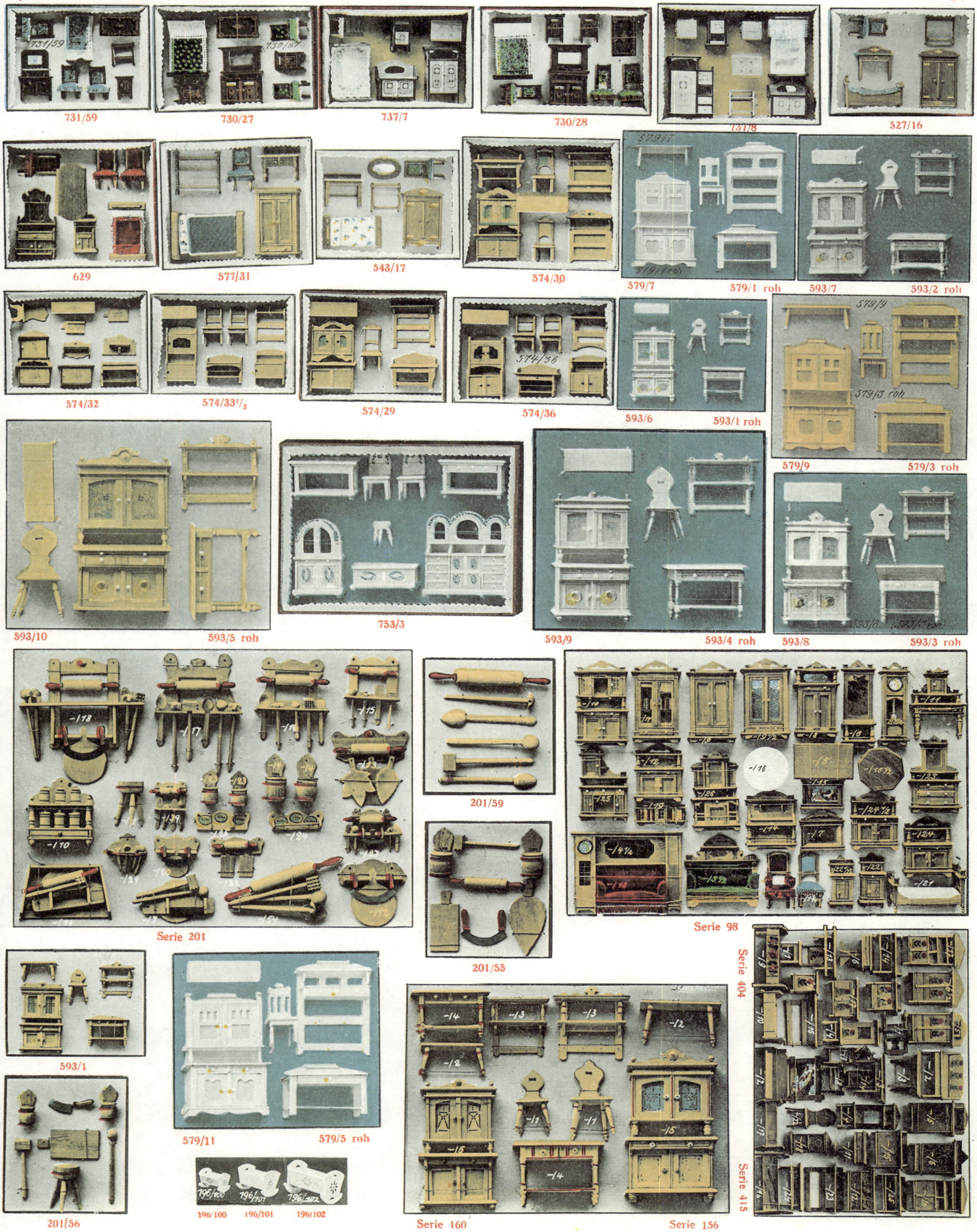

731/59 730/27 737/7 730/28 731/8 527/16

629 577/31 543/17 574/30 579/7 579/1 roh 593/7 593/2 roh

574/32 574/33½ 574/29 574/36 593/6 593/1 roh 579/9 579/3 roh

593/10 593/5 roh 753/3 593/9 593/4 roh 593/8 593/3 roh

Serie 201 201/59 201/55 Serie 98

593/1 579/11 579/5 roh Serie 404 Serie 415

201/56 196/100 196/101 196/102 Serie 160 Serie 156

Sortiment 50 — Arrangement 50 — Surtido 50

1/10 natürl. Größe (size, grandeur, tamaño) V

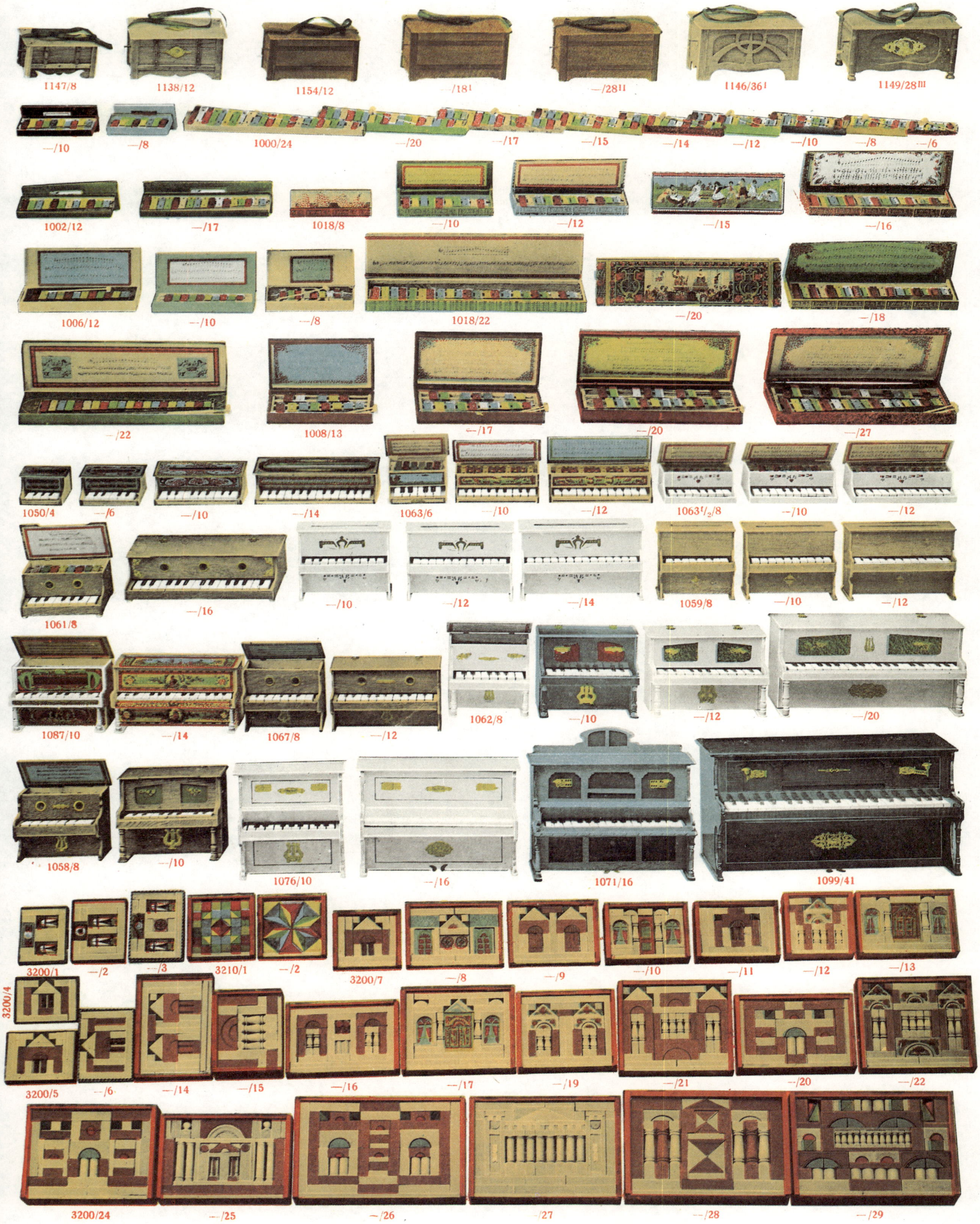

Sortiment 50 — Arrangement 50 — Surtido 50

1/8 natürl. Größe (size, grandeur, tamaño)

Sortiment 50 — Arrangement 50 — Surtido 50

$^{1}/_{8}$ natürl. Größe (size, grandeur, tamaño)

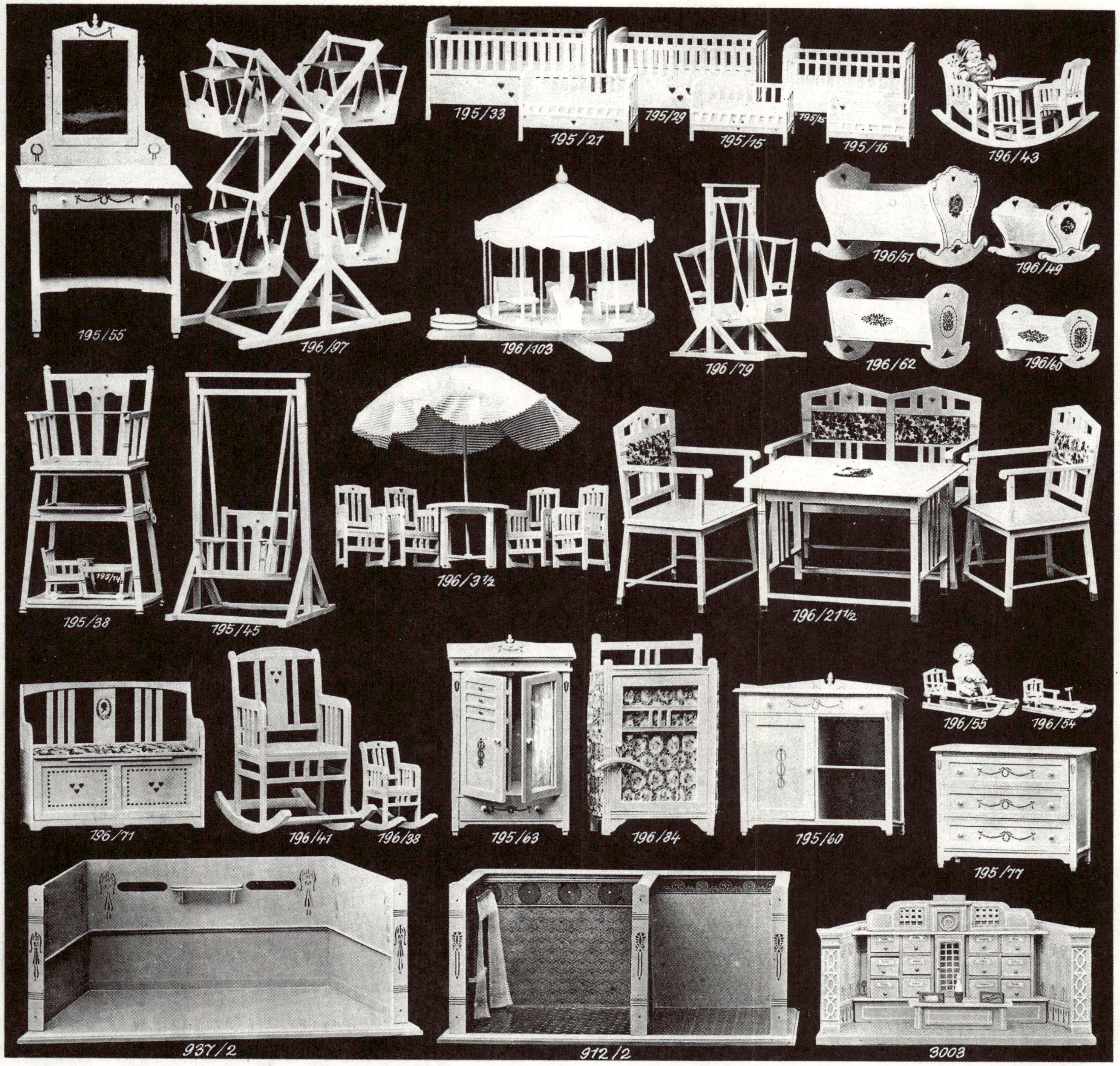

3021

3022/2

3033/1

3043

3009/1½

3090/1

3090/2

3090/3

3090/4

3060/7

—/8

—/9

$^{1}/_{9}$ natürl. Größe

Sortiment 50 — Arrangement 50 — Surtido 50

$^1/_5$ natürl. Größe (size, grandeur, tamaño)

$^1/_9$ natürl. Größe (size, grandeur, tamaño), Altäre, (altars, autels, altares) $^1/_{11}$.

Sortiment 50 — Arrangement 50 — Surtido 50

1/6 natürl. Größe, (size, grandeur, tamaño)

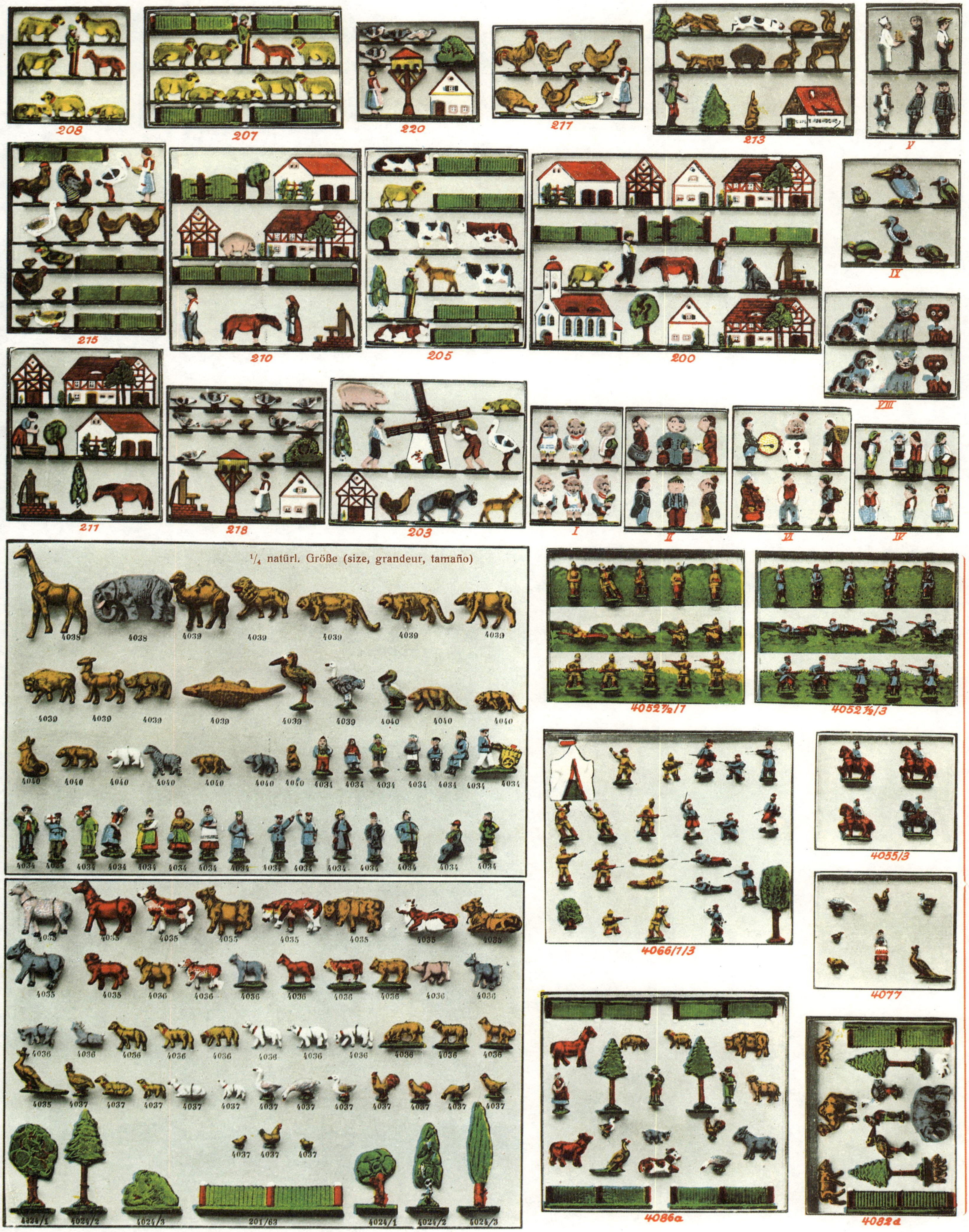

1/4 natürl. Größe (size, grandeur, tamaño)

1/8 natürl. Größe (size, grandeur, tamaño)

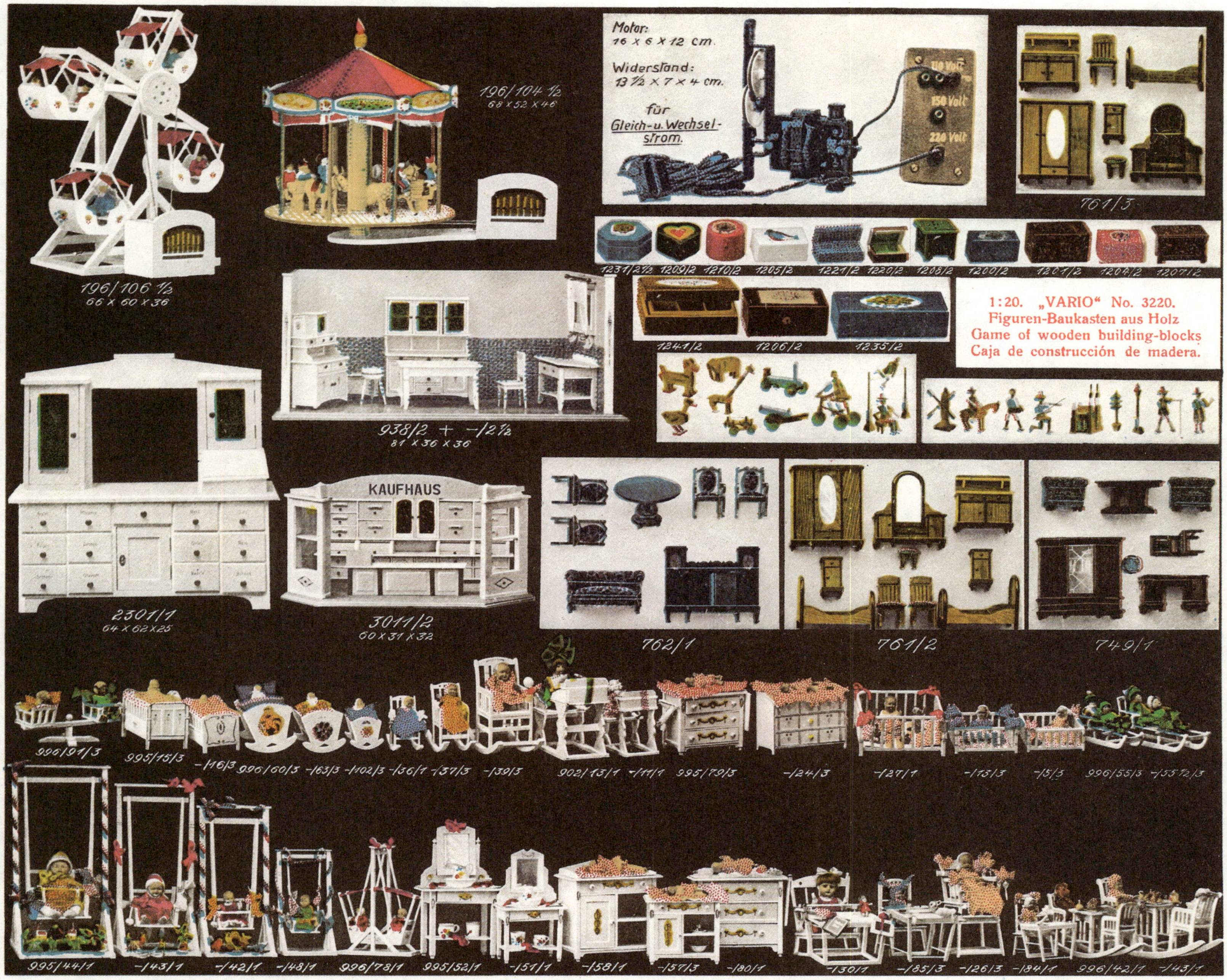

601/11

601/10

601/1

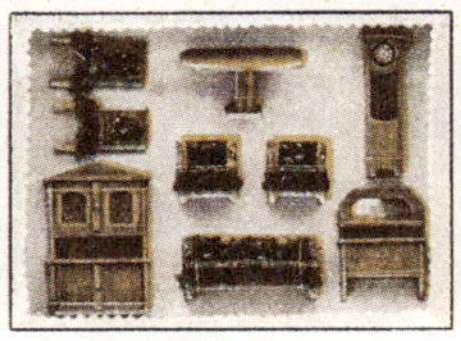
601/2

601/5

601/6

761/1

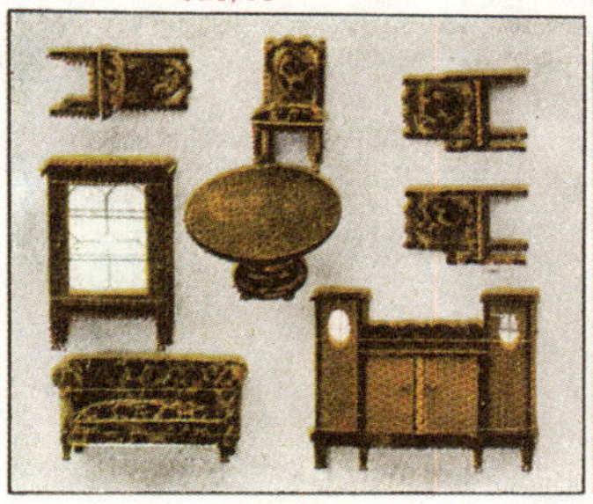
748/4

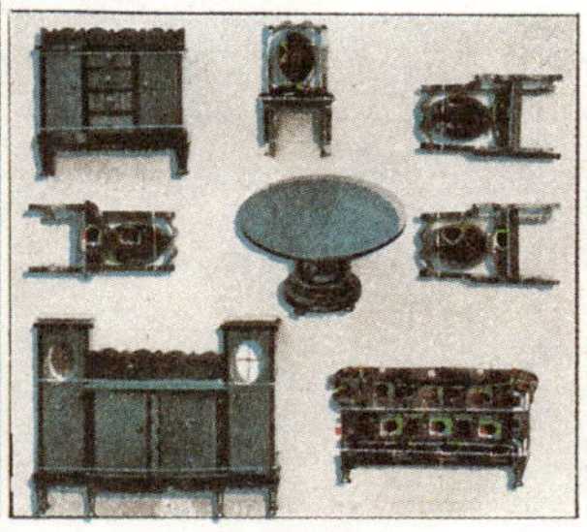
762/2

748/3

749/2

761/2

Serie 235

1088/34

749/4

Monkey Brand

Bengalische Zündhölzer, Wunderkerzen, Feuerwerkssortimente.
Bengal matches, electric sparklers, caps assorted fireworks.
Bujías maravillosas, fósforos bengalies, surtidos pirotec nicos.

Monkey Brand

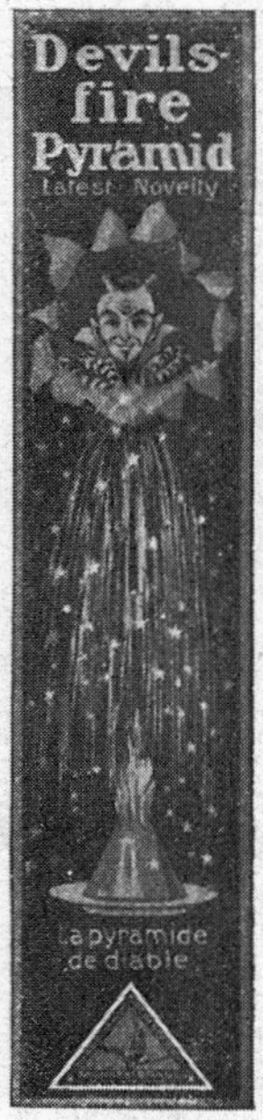

110/200

110/201

Monkey Brand

110/2

110/24

110/14

110/16

110/8

Kompletter Katalog Nr. 138 steht auf Wunsch zur Verfügung.
Complete catalogue Nr. 138 sent at request.
Un catálogo No. 138 está a la disposición del cliente.

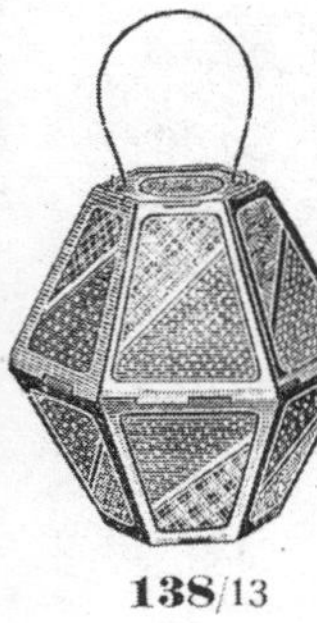

138/13

Gelatine-Klapplaternen.
Klischee 14 zeigt die Laterne zusammengefaltet.
Klischee 13 zeigt dieselbe fertig zum Gebrauch,
in den Größen von 8 bis 28 cm.

Gelatine folding lanterns.
Klische 14 shows the lantern folded.
Klische 13 shows the lantern ready for use.
Sizes from 8 to 28 cm.

Linternas plegables de gelatina.
Clase 14 mostra la linterna en estado plegable.
Clase 13 la misma en estado pronto al servicio,
en los tamaños de 8 hasta 28 cm.

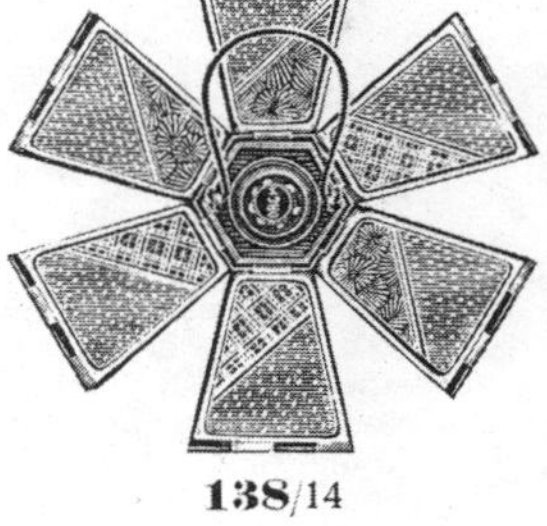

138/14

Knallbonbons in Sortimenten. — Crackers in assortments. — Confites fulminantes en surtidos.

Inhalt: Verschiedene Scherzgegenstände. Contents: various comic articles. Contenido: Diferentes artículos de burla.

107/1

107/7

107/24

107/12

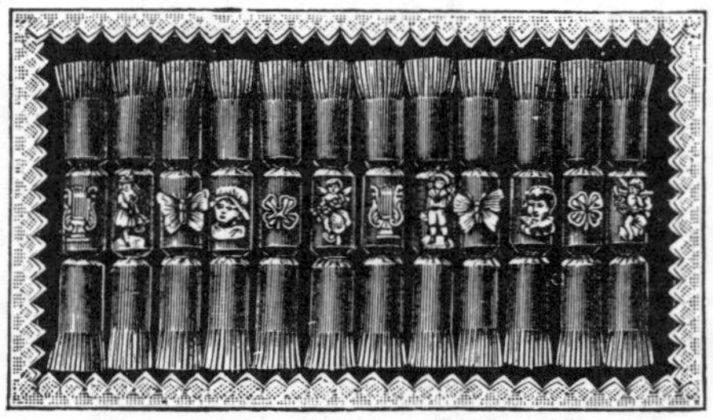

107/11

107/9

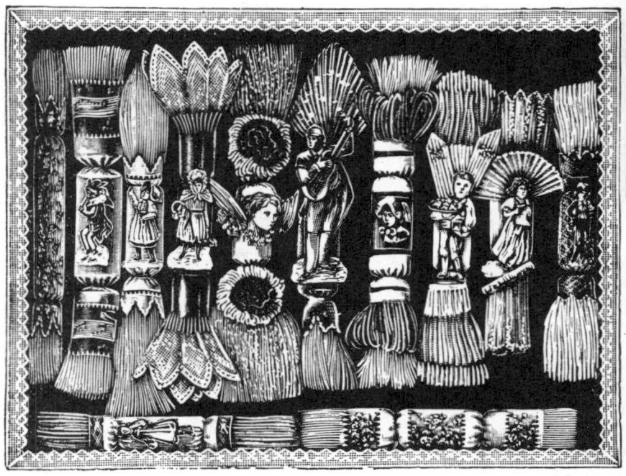

107/18

107/10

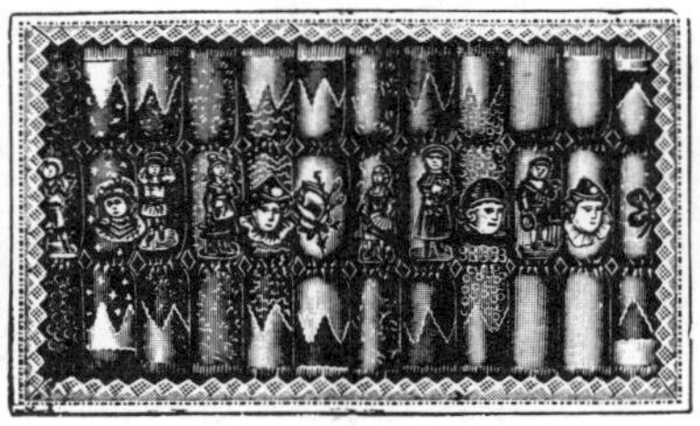

107/8

107/13

Tafeldekorationen aus Knallbonbons zusammengestellt. — Table decorations composed of crackers. Decoraciones para la mesa compuestas de confites fulminantes.

Inhalt: Verschiedene Scherzgegenstände. Contents: various comic articles. Contenido: Diferentes artículos de burla.

107/4479

107/4493

107/4712

107/5346

Obige Abbildungen einiger gangbarer Sortimente und Tafeldekorationen zeigen nur eine ganz geringe Auswahl meiner Kollektion, die aus vielen Hunderten von Nummern in allen Preislagen besteht. Man verlange daher bei größerem Bedarf bemusterte Anstellung möglichst in Originalverpackungen.

The above drawings of a few of the most saleable assortments and table decorations show but a verry small selection from my collection, which consists of many hundreds of numbers at all prices. In case of considerable quantities being required, quotations accompanied by samples should therefore be applied for, and as far as possible in original packages.

Las ilustraciones de algunos surtidos en voga y algunas decorationes para la mesa no mostran que un escogimiento muy pequeño de mi colección compuesta de muchos centenares de números a diferentes precios. Por consiguente, sírvase Vd. demandar ofertas con muestras, si posible, en empaques originales, si se trata de un consumo de consideración.

Kopfbedeckungen aus Papier für Herren. — Paper head coverings for gentlemen. — Tocados (sombreros) de papel para señores.

107/125 **107**/388 **107**/406 **107**/393 **107**/394 **107**/492 **107**/506 **107**/635

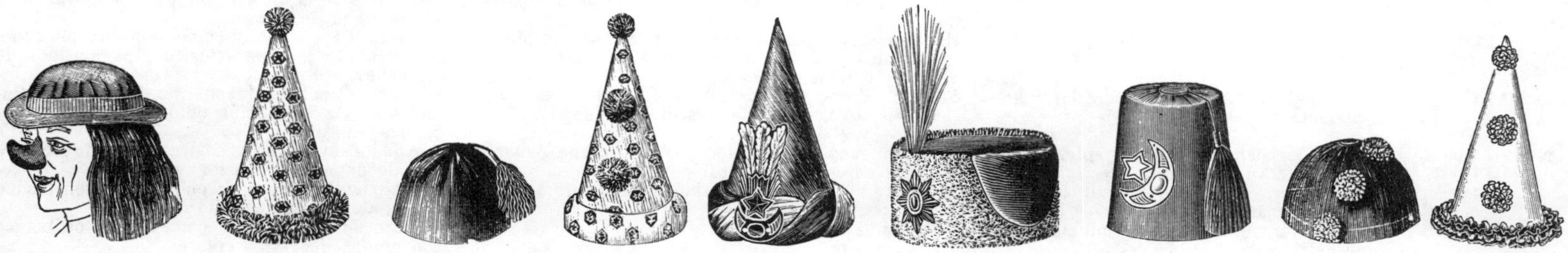

107/650 **107**/682 **107**/683 **107**/687 **107**/716 **107**/764 **107**/788 **107**/804 **107**/852

107/856 **107**/859 **107**/874 **107**/877 **107**/878 **107**/888 **107**/889 **107**/903

Kopfbedeckungen aus Papier für Damen. — Paper head coverings for ladies. — Tocados de papel para señoras.

107/0485 **107**/0580 **107**/0688 **107**/0710 **107**/0797 **107**/0814 **107**/0825

107/0846 **107**/0850 **107**/0858

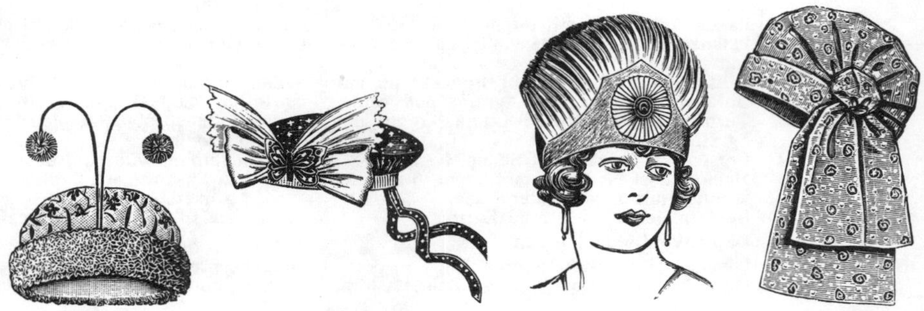

107/0879 **107**/0897 **107**/0887 **107**/0845

107/0880 **107**/0890 **107**/0902 **107**/0906

Nur eine kleine Auswahl meiner Kollektion. Man verlange daher bei größerem Bedarf bemusterte Anstellung möglichst in Originalpackungen.

Only a small selection from my collection. In case of considerable quantities being required, quotations accompanied by samples should therefore be applied for, and as far as possible in original packages.

Solamente un surtido pequeño de mi colección. Por consiguiente, sírvase Vd. demandar ofertas con muestras, si posible, en empaques originales, si se trata de un consumo de consideración.

Nr.	Herrenkopfbedeckungen in Papier.	Birds heads for ladies and gentlemen.	Tocados de papel para señores. (Composituras de cabeza.)
Sort. **141**/A	Vogelköpfe, Kreppapier, nicht gefiedert, in Phantasiefarben sortiert.	Assortment A. Crepe paper, not feathered, assorted in fancy colours.	Surtido A. Cabezas de aves, papel de crespón, no emplumadas, surtidas en colores fantásticos.
„ **141**/B	Vogelköpfe, Kreppapier, gefiedert, in Phantasiefarben sortiert.	Assortment B. Crepe paper, feathered, assorted in fancy colours.	Surtido B. Cabezas de aves, papel de crespón, emplumadas, surtidas en colores fantásticos.
„ **141**/C	Vogelköpfe, Kreppapier, gefiedert, in Phantasiefarben sortiert, hochfeine Ausführung.	Assortment C. Crepe paper, feathered, assorted in fancy colours, stylish execution.	Surtido C. Cabezas de aves, papel de crespón, emplumadas, surtidas en colores fantásticos, ejecución finísima.
Hahn **141**/A	Kreppapier, nicht gefiedert, ähnl. Abbildung der Vogelkopfsortimente.	Cock A. Crepe paper, not feathered, similar to illustration of the assortments of birds heads.	Gallo A. Papel de crespón, no emplumado. Semejante a la ilustración de los surtidos de las cabezas de aves.
„ **141**/B	Kreppapier, gefiedert, ähnl. Abbildung der Vogelkopfsortimente.	Cock B. Crepe paper, feathered, similar to illustration of the assortments of birds heads.	Gallo B. Papel de crespón, no emplumado. Semejante a la ilustración de los surtidos de las cabezas de aves.
Henne **141**/A	Kreppapier, nicht gefiedert, ähnl. Abbildung der Vogelkopfsortimente.	Hen A. Crepe paper, not feathered, similar to illustration of the assortments of birds heads.	Gallina A. Papel de crespón, no emplumado. Semejante a la ilustración de los surtidos de las cabezas de aves.
„ **141**/B	Kreppapier, gefiedert, ähnl. Abbildung der Vogelkopfsortimente.	Hen B. Crepe paper, feathered, similar to illustration of the assortments of birds heads.	Gallina B. Papel de crespón, no emplumado. Semejante a la ilustración de los surtidos de las cabezas de aves.
Storch **141**/B	Kreppapier, gefiedert, ähnl. Abbildung der Vogelkopfsortimente.	Stork B. Crepe paper, feathered, similar to illustration of the assortments of birds heads.	CigüeñaB. Papel de crespón, no emplumado. Semejante a la ilustración de los surtidos de las cabezas de aves.
Nr. **141**/9017	Jockeimütze, mehrfarbig, Kreppapier.	Jockey's cap, in variegated coloured crepe paper.	Gorra de jockey de varios colores, papel de crespón.
„ **141**/9027	Expreßmütze von Karton.	Express cap, of cardboard.	Gorra de expreso de ca tón.
„ **141**/9055	Clowntrichter, weiß Karton, mit farbigem Papierpelzbesatz.	Clown's pyramid hat, white cardboard with coloured tuft.	Sombrero en forma de un embudo, cartón blanco con atados de varios colores.
„ **141**/9206	Clowntrichter, weiß Karton, mit farbigem Papierpelzbesatz.	The same, but simpler.	Sombrero en forma de un embudo, cartón blanco con atados de varios colores.
„ **141**/9203	Clowntrichter, Pergamin, m. Papierpelzbesatz.	The same in colours, parchment paper, with paper fur trimming.	Sombrero en forma de un embudo, pergamino, con guarnición de papel semejante a piel.
„ **141**/9204	Clowntrichter, Karton, mit Papierpelzbesatz.	The same, cardboard, with paper fur trimming.	Sombrero en forma de un embudo, cartón, con guarnición de papel semejante a piel.
„ **141**/86/I	Zylinder, grau Karton, steif, gerade Form.	Top hat, grey cardboard, stiff, straight shape.	Cilindro, gris, cartón, tieso, forma recta.
„ **141**/86/II	Zylinder, weiß Karton, steif, gerade Form.	Top hat, white cardboard, stiff, straight shape.	Cilindro, blanco, cartón, tieso, forma recta.
„ **141**/86/III	Zylinder, schwarz Karton, steif, gerade Form.	Top hat, black cardboard, stiff, straight shape.	Cilindro, negro, cartón, tieso, forma recta.
„ **141**/86/bt	Zylinder, farbig Karton, sort., steif, gerade Form.	Top hat, coloured cardboard, stiff, assorted, straight shape.	Cilindro de varios colores, cartón, surtido, tieso, forma recta.
„ **141**/86/M	Zylinder, farbig Karton, sort., steif, gerade Form, mit Notenband.	Top hat, coloured cardboard, stiff, straight shape, with ribbon with notes on it.	Cilindro de varios colores, cartón, surtido, con cinta de nota.
„ **141**/331e	Mephistokappe.	Mephistopheles cap.	Caperuza mefistofélica.
„ **141**/334	Mephistohut.	Mephistopheles hat.	Sombrero mefistofélico.
„ **141**/1296	Schottisches Barett.	Scotch bonnet.	Birreta escosesa.
„ **141**/9207	Schottisches Barett, Netzkopf.	Scotch bonnet.	Birreta escosesa.
„ **141**/3001	Krone von Goldkarton.	Crown of gilt cardboard.	Corona de cartón dorado.
„ **141**/3002	Krone von Goldkarton, mit farbigen Edelsteinen.	Crown of gilt cardboard, with coloured jewels.	Corona de cartón dorado con piedras preciosas de varios colores.
„ **141**/3009	Teufelskrone von Goldkarton.	Devil's crown in gilt cardboard.	Corona diabólica de cartón dorado.
„ **141**/3031	Chinesenmütze.	Chinese cap.	Gorra chinesca.
zu „ **141**/3031	Schirme Sch/23, Chinesenschirme, 70 cm Durchmesser, 80 cm lang, 10teilig.	Shades Sch/23, chinese shade, 70 cm diam., 80 cm long, 10 segments.	Parasoles Sch/23 parasoles chinescos, diámetro de 70 cm, largura de 80 cm, 10 divisiones.
„ **141**/3044/cli	Spitzer Turban.	Pointed turban.	Turbante agudo.
„ **141**/3048	Runder Turban, mit Quaste.	Round turban, with tassel.	Turbante redondo con borla.
„ **141**/3082	Rokoko-Dreispitz, fein in Seidenpapier, mit Spitzen besetzt.	Rococo three-corner hat, fine make, in silk paper, trimmed with lace.	Fino sombrero tricorne en estilo "Rococo", de papel de seda, guarnecido de encajes.
„ **141**/3086	Rokoko-Dreispitz, mit Zopfperücke, mit Spitzen besetzt.	Rococo three-corner hat, with pigtail wig, in silk paper, trimmed with lace.	Fino sombrero tricorne en estilo "Rococo", con peluca de trenzas de pelo.
„ **141**/3014	Bauernmütze, mit Papier- und Pelzbesatz.	Peasant's hat, trimmed with paper and fur.	Gorra para campesinos guarnecida de papel semejante a piel.
„ **141**/7020/B	Ballonmütze, schwarz und farbig (niedriger als die Abbildungen).	Balloon cap, black and coloured (lower than in illustration).	Gorra globulosa negra con varios colores (más baja que la ilustración).
„ **141**/7048/A	Liliputzylinder, in Farben sort., 10 cm hoch.	Liliput top hat, assorted colours, 10 cm high.	Cilindro lilipuciano surtido en colores, altura de 10 cm.
„ **114**/7048/K	Liliputclowntrichter, in Farben sortiert.	Clown's pyramid hat, assorted, liliput size.	Sombrero en forma de un embudo, lilipuciano surtido en colores.
„ **141**/7048/F	Liliputstrohhut, gelb Karton.	Liliput straw hat, yellow cardboard.	Liliputiano sombrero de paja, cartón amarillo.
Sort. **141**/7048	12 verschiedene Liliputhütchen im Karton.	12 different liliput hats in a cardboard box.	12 diferentes sombreros lilipucianos en una cajita de cartón.
Nr. **141**/9011	Fez v. Kreppap., rot, m. festem Boden u. Quaste.	Fez, red crepe paper, strong top, with tassel.	Fez de papel de crespón en rojo, con fondo firme y borla
„ **141**/9033	Balkanfürst.	Balkan prince.	Príncipe del balcano.
„ **141**/9040	Sportmütze, weiß, Seidenpapier mit Blende.	Sporting cap, white silk paper, with peak.	Gorra de deporte, blanca, de papel de seda, con blenda.
„ **141**/9041	Rokoko-Dreispitz, hochfein, weiß und farbig Karton, mit buntem Besatz und Stutz.	Rococo three-cornered hat, finest make, white and coloured cardboard, with coloured trimming and bush.	Sombrero tricorne en estilo "Rococo", finísimo, blanco, en cajita de cartón, de varios colores, con guarnición y tronchado de varios colores.
„ **141**/9049	Balkanfürst, weiß, mit rotem Kopf.	Balkan prince, white with red head.	Príncipe del balcano, blanco, con cabeza roja.
„ **141**/9104/N	Flaches, rundes Hütchen mit Papierperücke und Nase.	Flat round little hat, with paper wig and nose.	Pequeño sombrero plano y redondo, con peluca de papel y nariz.
„ **141**/9108	Indischer Turban, hochfein Bronzekrepp, mit Golddamastpapier, mit Agraffe und Stutz.	Indian turban, very elegant, bronzed crepe paper, with gilt damask paper, with clasp and bush.	Turbante indio finísimo, crespón de color debronce, con papel de damasco dorado, con agrafa y tronchado.
„ **141**/9110	Turban, hochfein, weiß Damastkrepp, mit Agraffe u d Stutz.	Turban, finest style, white damask crepe, with clasp and bush.	Turbante finísimo, blanco, crespón de damasco, con agrafa y tronchado.
„ **141**/9179	Persischer Turban, mit Sonne, hochfein.	Persian turban, with sun, best style.	Turbante pérsico, con sol, finísimo.
„ **141**/9208/13	Humoristisches Mützensortiment, 6 versch., sämtlich mit anhängender Nase.	Comic cap assortment, 6 different designs, all with nose affixed.	Surtido de gorras humorísticas, 6 diferentes, todas con narizes adherentes.
„ **141**/12206	Biedermeierzylinder, grau Karton.	„Biedermeier" top hat, grey cardboard.	Cilindro(sombrero)en el estilo alemán "Biedermeier".
	Damenkopfbedeckungen.	**For Ladies.**	**Tocados de papel para señoras.**
Nr. **141**/1004	Diadem, Goldkarton, geprägt.	Diadem, pressed gold cardboard.	Diadema, cartón dorado, grabado.
„ **141**/1100	Diadem, Goldkarton, geprägt, Lamettastern.	Diadem, gold cardboard, pressed, with tin foil star.	Diadema, cartón dorado, grabado, con estrella de filos de plata.
„ **141**/1260	Pierrette, weiß, mit Rüsche und Schleifchen.	Pierrette, withe, with frilling and little bows.	Pierrette, blanca, con gorguera y cintas pequeñas.
„ **141**/1308	Pierrette, bunt gemustert, Kreppapier.	Pierrette, in variegated coloured crepe paper.	Pierrette, en vestido de varios color., papel de crespón.
„ **141**/1342	Italienische Fischerin.	Italian fisherwoman, in variegated colour. crepe paper.	Pescadora italiana.
„ **141**/4003	Blumenkopfbedeckungen, Chrysanthemen.	Chrysanthemum head-dress.	Tocador(compostura de cabeza) de flores, crisántemo.
„ **141**/9172	Wie 4507, großer runder Hut, weiß, mit farbig schattierter Pleureuse.	Large round hat, white with coloured shaded pleureuse.	Tal que 4507: Sombrero redondo de gran tamaño, blanco con pumaje, de colores de varias tintas.
„ **141**/9046/D	Wie 8015, Rodelmütze, mit Papierpelz besetzt.	Sleigh caps, trimmed with paper fur.	Tal que 8015: Gorra para el trineo de montaña guarnecida del papel semejante a piel.
„ **141**/9136	Wie 8033, Diadem mit schattiertem Stutz und Perlenschnüren.	Diadem, with shaded bush and pearl strings.	Tal que 8033: Diadema con tronchado matizado, con hilos de perlas.
„ **141**/9186	Wie 8034, Kopfreifen, mit 2 goldenen Flügeln.	Head band, with two gold wings.	Tal que 8034: Anillo al rededor de la cabeza con 2 alas doradas.
„ **141**/8055	Balkanfürstin.	Balkan princess.	Princesa del balcano.
„ **141**/8058	Turban mit Pleureuse, hochfein, in farbig Kreppapier, mit beglimmerter Agraffe.	Turban, with pleureuse, stylish, in coloured crepe paper, with glittering clasp.	Turbante con plumaje, finísimo, en papel de crespón de varios colores con agrafa de mica.
„ **141**/8082	Orientalischer Haarreif mit Gehängen, Goldkarton, mit Glimmern verziert.	Oriental hair band, with suspensions, of gilt cardboard, ornamented with mica.	Anillo de cabellos oriental con pendientes, cartón dorado guarnecido de mica.

Karneval- und Scherzartikel. — Carnival and jest articles. — Artículos de carnaval y de chanza.

141/3031 · **141**/Vogel-ABC · **141**/9032 · **141**/12206

141/8034 · **141**/9045 D · **141**/1100 · **141**/9049 · **141**/8055 · **141**/9033 · **141**/9005 · **141**/18

141/331 e · **141**/86 · **141**/334 · **141**/Sort. 9208—13 · **141**/7020 b · **141**/3082 · **141**/7048 a

141/3086 · **141**/1296 · **141**/9151 · **141**/8015 · **141**/9040 · **141**/9017 · **141**/4507 · **141**/7048/K

141/9011 · **141**/55 · **141**/9179 · **141**/9104 N · **141**/3114 · **141**/Storch B · **141**/2275

141/9148 · **141**/7048/S · **141**/9107/9108 · **141**/9109/9110 · **141**/3044/gli · **141**/9041 · **141**/9106

141/3001 · **141**/3009 · **141**/3048 · **141**/9194 · **141**/9140 · **141**/27

Nr.	Deutsch	English	Español
Nr. **141**/9003	Haarreif mit Rosen.	Hair band, with roses.	Anillo de cabellos con rosas.
„ **141**/9005	Gitterdiadem mit 2 Seitenblumen, beglimmert.	Lattice diadem, with two flowers at sides, glittering.	Diadema enrejada con 2 flores a los lados, con mica.
„ **141**/9032	Biedermeierhut, Geldkarton, mit Kreppkopf.	„Biedermeier" hat of yellow cardboard, with crepe crown.	Sombrero en el estilo alemán "Biedermeier", cartón amarillo, con cabeza de crespón.
„ **141**/9038	Schmetterlingsfühl., Stirnreif., hochf., m. Glim.	Butterflys antennae head band, very stylish, with mica.	Anillo al rededor de la frente, finísimo, con mica.
„ **141**/9045/D	Turban, hochfein, weiß beglimmert, mit Stutz.	Turban, finest style, white, mica-dusted, with bush.	Turbante finísimo, blanco, con mica, con tronchado.
„ **141**/9048	Japanischer Goldhaarreif mit Chrysanthemen.	Japanese gold hair band, with chrysanthemum.	Anillo dorado de cabellos japonés, con crisántemo.
„ **141**/9051	Turban, hochfein, weiß beglimmert, mit Stutz.	Turban of white crepe paper, with glittering clasp and bush.	Turbante blanco, papel de crespón, con agrafa de pampanaje y tronchado.
„ **141**/9052/E	Runder Promenadenhut, weiß Kreppapier, mit zartfarbiger Garnierung.	Round promenade hat, white crepe paper, with delicate coloured trimming.	Sombrero de paseo durante el remar, blanco, papel de crespón, con guarnición de colores de tintas delicadas.
„ **141**/9057	Dreispitz in Bronzedamastpapier, mit Quasten.	There corner hat in bronzed damask paper, with tassels.	Sombrero tricorne en papel de damasco de color de bronce, con borlas.
„ **141**/9059	Runder Hut mit geflochtenem Kreppapier.	Round hat, with plaited bronzed crepe paper.	Sombrero redondo con papel de crespón de color de bronce, acolchado.
„ **141**/9060	Runder Hut, blau Kreppapier, mit gelber Verschnürung.	Round hat, blue crepe paper, with yellow lacing.	Sombrero redondo con papel de crespón azul, con cordeles amarillos.
„ **141**/9077	Runder Hut, Kreppapier, mit Kreppsrosettenkranz.	Round hat, crepe paper, garlanded with crepe roses.	Sombrero redondo, papel de crespón, con corona de rosetas de crespón.
„ **141**/09106	Rotkäppchen, Kopfputz mit 2 Schleifen.	Little red riding hood, head-dress with two bows.	Caperuza roja, tocado con 2 colas.
„ **141**/09107	Indischer Turban, hochfein Bronzekrepp, mit Golddamastpapier, mit Agraffe und Stutz.	Indian turban, very fine bronzed crepe paper, with gold damask paper with clasp and bush.	Turbante indio, finísimo, crespón de color de bronce, con papel de demasco dorado, con agrafa y tronchado.
„ **141**/09109	Turban, hochfein, weiß Damastkrepp, mit Agraffe und Stutz.	Turban, elegant, white damask crepe with clasp and bush.	Turbante finísimo, blanco, crespón de damasco, con agrafa y tronchado.
„ **141**/9113	Kopfputz mit geblümtem Kreppapier und 2 langen Schleifen.	Head-dress, with flowered crepe paper and two long bows.	Tocado con papel de crespón afigurado, con 2 colas largas.
„ **141**/9114	Barett v. Kreppapier, m. Pelzrand u. Schleifen.	Barret of crepe paper, edged with fur and with bow.	Birreta de papel de crespón, con borde de pieles y cola.
„ **141**/9135	Römischer Kopfputz v. Kreppapier, m. Stutz.	Roman head-dress, of crepe paper, with bush.	Tocado romano de papel de crespón, con tronchado.
„ **141**/9149	Runder Hut, geflochtener Kopf von Kreppapier, mit aufgeschlagenem Rand.	Round hat, plaited crepe crown, with brim turned up.	Sombrero redondo, cabeza trenzada de papel de crespón, con borde desdoblado.
„ **141**/9151	Runder Hut von Kreppapier, hochfein, lila mit grün garniert.	Round hat, of crepe paper, stylish, lilac and green trimming.	Sombrero redondo, de papel de crespón, finísimo, guarnecido en lila, con verde.
„ **141**/9171	Marienkäfer, Doguefasson.	Ladybird, dogue fashion.	Coccinela (coquita de San Anton [Dogue]).
„ **141**/9172	Runder Hut, weiß Kreppapier, mit schattierter Pleureuse.	Round hat, white crepe paper, with shaded pleureuse feather.	Sombrero redondo, blanco, papel de crespón con plumaje de colores de varias tintas.
„ **141**/9177	Geflechthut, grau grün Kreppapier, mit grüner Pleureuse.	Plaited hat, grey and green crepe paper, green pleureuse.	Sombrero trenzado de papel de crespón gris verdoso con plumaje verde.
„ **141**/9189	Kopfbedeckung „Flamme", hochfein Kreppapier, beglimmert.	Head-dress „Flame" very stylish, crepe paper glittering.	Tocado (compostura de la cabeza) „Flama" ("Flamme"), finísimo, papel de crespón, con mica.
„ **141**/9194	Colombine mit Netzkopf.	Columbine, with net head covering.	Colombine con cabeza con redecilla.
„ **141**/9195	Pirette mit Federstutz.	Pierrette, with feather bush.	Pierrette con tronchado de plumas.
„ **141**/9199	Turban, zartfarbig Kreppapier, mit Blumenagraffe und seitlichem Schweif.	Turban of delicate coloured crepe paper, with flower-clasp and side bow.	Colores delicados, papel de crespón, con agrafa de flores y cola lateral.
„ **141**/10002	Pfauenkopfreifen, Kreppapier, hochfein beglimmert.	Pea cock's head hoop of crepe paper, glistening highly.	Anillo de cabeza de plumas de pavo de papel de crespón, finísimo, con mica.
„ **141**/10001	Pfauenkopfrf., Kreppap., hochf. beglim. (klein.).	As above, but smaller.	La mismo, pero más pequeño.
„ **141**/10003	Fasanenkopfreifen, Kreppapier, hochfein beglimmert.	Pheasant's head hoop of crepe paper, glistening highly.	Anillo de cabeza de plumas de faisán de papel de crespón, finísimo, con mica.
„ **141**/10004	Truthahnkopfreifen, Kreppapier, hochfein beglimmert.	Turkey cock's head hoop of crepe paper, glistening highly.	Anillo de cabeza de plumas de pavo, de papel de crespón, finísimo, con mica.
„ **141**/10005	Kopfreifen mit Spiralen, hochfein beglimmert.	Hoop foor head, with spirals of crepe paper, glistening highly.	Anillo de cabeza con espirales, papel de crespón, finísimo, con mica.
„ **141**/10006	Fantastischer Kopfreifen, Kreppapier, hochfein beglimmert, mit Perlbehang.	Fancy hoop for head of crepe paper, glistening highly, with pearl trimming.	Anillo de cabeza fantástico, papel de crespón, finísimo, con mica, con colgadura de perlas.
„ **141**/10007	Fantastischer Kopfreifen, Kreppapier, Zweispitzform mit Pleureusen, fein schattiert und beglimmert.	Fancy hoop for head of crepe paper, double painted, with pleureuses, finely shaded and glittering.	Anillo de cabeza fantástico, papel de crespón, en forma de un sombrero bicorne, con plumaje de colores de tintas delicadas, con mica.
„ **141**/10008	Blumenkopfputz mit großem Schmetterling, hochfein beglimmert.	Flower head-dress, with large butterfly, glittering finely.	Tocado de flores con mariposa grande, finísimo, con mica.
„ **141**/9164	Schmetterlingskopfbedeckung.	Butterfly head-dress, glittering finely.	Tocado con mariposas, finísimo, con mica.
„ **141**/10011	Schmetterlingskopfputz, Kreppapier, hochfein beglimmert.	Butterfly head decoration, glittering finely.	Tocado con mariposas, finísimo, con mica.

Charakterkopfbedeckungen von Kreppapier, fein bemalt. / **Character head dresses** of crepe paper, finely painted. / **Tocados de cáracter.** de papel de crespón, pintados finamente.

Nr.	Deutsch	English	Español
„ **141**/T 23	Messengerboy.	Messenger boy.	Messenger Boy (expreso).
„ **141**/T 26	Holländerin.	Dutchwoman.	Holandesa.
„ **141**/T 27	Chinese.	Chinaman.	Chino.
„ **141**/T 28	Teufel.	Devil.	Diablo.

Charakterkopfmasken, hochfein bemalt, von starkem Kreppapier, mit Hinterkopf, Ersatz für Stofftrikotmasken. / **Character head masks** of strong crepe paper, finely painted, with backs. (Substitute for tricot mask.) / **Tocados de carácter** de grueso papel de crespón, pintados, con cogote.

Nr.	Deutsch	English	Español
„ **141**/T 53	Hexe mit Spitzhut und Perücke.	Witch, with pointed hat and wig.	Bruja con sombrero puntiagudo y peluca.
„ **141**/T 54	Hexe ohne Spitzhut mit Perücke.	Witch, without pointed hat, with wig.	Bruja sin sombrero puntiagudo y con peluca.
„ **141**/T 55	Teufel.	Devil.	Diablo.
„ **141**/T 56	Chinese.	Chinaman.	Chino.
„ **141**/T 58	Türke.	Turk.	Turco.
„ **141**/T 59	Schiffer.	Seaman.	Barquero.
„ **141**/T 60	Großmutter mit Hut.	Granny, in bonnet.	Abuela con sombrero.
„ **141**/T 61	Vagabund.	Vagabond.	Vagabundo.
„ **141**/T 72	Biedermeier mit Zylinder und Vatermörder.	„Biedermeier", with tall hat and gladstone collar.	"Biedermaier" (Figura de un alemán antiguo) con sombrero en forma de un cilindro y altísimo cabezón de camisa (Vatermoerder).

Charaktermasken ohne Hinterkopf, Kreppapier, fein bemalt, mit Schnur zum Umbinden. / **Character masks** of crepe paper, finely painted, without back, with string to tie on. / **Máscaras de carácter** sin cogote, papel de crespón, pintadas finamente, con cordee para fijarlas.

Nr.	Deutsch	English	Español
Sort. **141**/T 101/6	6 verschiedene humoristische Gesichter mit Haarpelz besetzt.	Six different comic faces, with furry hair.	6 diferentes caras humorísticas guarnecidas de pieles de pelo.
„ **141**/T 121/26	6 verschiedene humoristische Gesichter mit Haarpelz besetzt, einfache Ausführung.	Six different comical faces, as above, but more simple.	6 diferentes caras humorísticas guarnecidas de pieles de pelo, pero más sencillas.
Nr. **141**/T 131	Alter Mann.	Old man.	Anciano.
„ **141**/T 132	Ein Mann mit Schnurrbart.	Man with moustache.	Hombre con bigote.
„ **141**/T 133	Clown mit Feder auf der Nase.	Clown with feather on his nose.	Bufón (clown) con pluma sobre la nariz.

Tieraufsatzköpfe, hochfein, in starkem Kreppapier, fein gemalt, zusammenlegbar / **Animal heads** to be worn. Finely got up, of strong crepe paper, painted, to fold up. / **Cabezas de animales** para poner encima, finísimas, en grueso papel de crespón, pintadas finamente, plegables.

Nr.	Deutsch	English	Español
Nr. **141**/T 151	Frosch.	Frog.	Rana.
„ **141**/T 152	Hase.	Hare.	Liebre.
„ **141**/T 153	Bär.	Bear.	Oso.
„ **141**/T 154	Katze.	Cat.	Gato.
„ **141**/T 155	Hahn.	Cock.	Gallo.
„ **141**/T 156	Maus.	Mouse.	Rato.

Karneval- und Scherzartikel. — Carnival and jest articles. — Artículos de carnaval y de chanza.

141/10003 **141**/10006 **141**/9189 **141**/10007 **141**/1

141/10011 **141**/10004 **141**/10008 **141**/9149 **141**/9171

141/10005 **141**/9172 **141**/9077 **141**/9199 **141**/9059 **141**/9177

141/9003 **141**/8033 **141**/8055 **141**/9114 **141**/3004 **141**/9135 **141**/1342

141/9051 **141**/8058 **141**/8082 **141**/4003 **141**/9057 **141**/1308

141/9048 **141**/9052

141/1260 **141**/9038 **141**/9113 **141**/9195 **141**/9060 **141**/1004

Tierverkleidungen.

hochfein, in starkem Kreppapier, gefiedert, fein gemalt.

Nr. **141**/131 K Küken.
„ **141**/132 K Henne.
„ **141**/133 K Hahn.

Zwergtheaterfiguren.

Die vorführende Person steht hinter einem Tisch und nur der Oberkörper wird kostümiert. Die auf den Tisch gestützten Arme sind die Beine des Zwergtirolers, während die Arme künstlich angebracht sind. Die Wirkung ist eine unbeschreiblich komische, man denke sich auf dem winzigen kostümierten Körper den normalen großen Kopf eines Menschen. Und dieser Kopf spricht, lacht und singt! Wirklich eine Vortragnummer von allergrößtem Effekt. Man beachte, daß die vordere Seite des Tisches, auf welchem der Vortrag erfolgt, verhängt wird.

Nr. **141**/Z/K 1 Charlie Chaplin.
„ **141**/Z/K 2 Uncle Sam.
„ **141**/Z/K 3 Jockei.
„ **141**/Z/K 4 Gigerl.
„ **141**/Z/K 5 Maurer.
„ **141**/Z/K 6 Jude.
„ **141**/Z/K 7 Gigerldame.
„ **141**/Z/K 8 Karikatur 1.
„ **141**/Z/K 9 Karikatur 2.
„ **141**/Z/K 10 Clown.
„ **141**/Z/K 11 Boxer.

Seidenpapierkostüme.

Für kleine Überraschungen gut geeignet. Von doppeltem Seidenpapier. Nähte mit Stoffstreifen besetzt, so daß die Kostüme wirklich benutzt werden können. Dieselben sind reichlich Normalgröße und passen den meisten Personen. Extraanfertigung nach besonderen Maßen ist bei diesen Sachen nicht möglich.

Nr. **141**/1 Chinese.
„ **141**/101 Chinesin.
„ **141**/2 Zigeuner.
„ **141**/102 Zigeunerin.
„ **141**/3 Pierrot.
„ **141**/103 Pierrette.
„ **141**/4 Türke.
„ **141**/104 Türkin.
„ **141**/5 Matrose.
„ **141**/105 Matrosin.
„ **141**/6 Tiroler.
„ **141**/106 Tirolerin.
„ **141**/8 Russe.
„ **141**/108 Russin.
„ **141**/9 Teufel.
„ **141**/109 Teufelin.
„ **141**/10 Gigerl.
„ **141**/110 Gigerlin.
„ **141**/11 Japaner.
„ **141**/111 Japanerin.
„ **141**/15 Schornsteinfeger.
„ **141**/115 Schornsteinfegerin.
„ **141**/16 Rokokoherr.
„ **141**/116 Rokokodame.
„ **141**/18 Domino.
„ **141**/118 Baby.
„ **141**/20 Ungar.
„ **141**/120 Ungarin.
„ **141**/52 Frack.
„ **141**/151 Hahn mit imitierten Federn, fein schattiert.

Kreppapierkostüme,

schön dem Körper sich anpassend.

Nr. **141**/ 10 c Gigerl.
„ **141**/110 c Gigerldame.
„ **141**/ 11 c Japaner.
„ **141**/111 c Japanerin.
„ **141**/ 12 c Italienischer Fischer.
„ **141**/112 c Italienische Fischerin.
„ **141**/ 20 c Ungar.
„ **141**/120 c Ungarin.
„ **141**/122 c Italienische Fischerin.
„ **141**/ 23 c Teufel.

Knallbonbons.

Nr. **141**/5011 Herzen, bunt verziert, Inhalt Scherzartikel.
„ **141**/5014 Nüsse natürlicher Größe, Inhalt Scherzartikel.
„ **141**/5051 Ostereier, bunt verziert, Inhalt Scherzartikel.
„ **141**/5054 Glücksschwein, Inhalt Mützen.
„ **141**/5505 Kleine Hummer, 11 cm lang, Inhalt Scherzartikel.
„ **141**/5507 Stern, 7 cm Durchmesser, Inhalt Scherzartikel.
„ **141**/5508 Doppelstern, 7 cm Durchmesser, Inhalt Scherzartikel.
„ **141**/5512 Schmetterling, fein schattiert, Inhalt Scherzartikel.
„ **141**/5516 Maikäfer, Inhalt Scherzartikel.
„ **141**/5525 Rose, Inhalt Mützen.

Animal costumes

Finely got up, of strong crepe paper, feathered, finely painted.

Chicken.
Hen.
Cock.

Dwarf stage figures.

The one working the figures stands behind a table, the upper part of his body only being in costume. His arms, resting on the table form the legs of the dwarf tyrolese, whose arms are fixed on separately. The effect is indescribably comical: one need but imagine the microscopically small costumed body surmounted by normally sized head of a man. And that head speaks, laughs and sings. It is really a performance that is superlatively effective.

Charlie Chaplin.
Uncle Sam.
Jockey.
Dandy.
Mason.
Jew.
Lady dandy.
Caricature 1.
Caricature 2.
Clown.
Boxer.

Silk paper costumes.

Excellently adapted for surprises and jokes. Of double silk paper. The seams are strengthened by cloth strips, so that the costumes can really be used. These are all full normal size and so fit most people. It is not possible to make these costumes to measure.

Chinese man.
Chinese woman.
Gipsy.
Gipsy woman.
Pierrot.
Pierrette.
Turk.
Turkish woman.
Mariner.
Female mariner.
Tyrolese man.
Tyrolese woman.
Russian.
Russian woman.
Devil.
Female devil.
Dandy, male.
Dandy, female.
Japanese, male.
Japanese, female.
Sweep, male.
Sweep, female.
Man in Rococo costume.
Woman in rococo costume.
Domino.
Baby.
Hungarian, male.
Hungarian, female.
Dress suit.
Cock, with finely shaded imitation feathers.

Crepe paper costumes

fitting nicely to the body.

Gentleman dandy.
Lady dandy.
Japanese gentleman.
Japanese lady.
Italian fisherman.
Italian fisherwoman.
Hungarian man.
Hungarian woman.
Italian fisherwoman.
Devil.

Crackers.

Hearts, decorated in various colours. Contents comic objects.
Nuts, natural size. Contents comic objects.
Easter Eggs, ernamented in various colours. Contents comic objects.
Lucky pig. Contents: caps.
Small lobsters, 11 cm long. Contents: comic objects.
Star, 7 cm diam. Contents: comic objects.
Double Star, 7 cm long. Contents: comic objects.
Butterfly, beautifully shaded. Contents: comic objects.
Cockchafer. Contents: comic objects.
Rose. Contents: caps.

Disfraces en animales,

finísimos, en grueso papel de crespón, pintados finamente, con plumas.

Polluelos.
Gallina.
Gallo.

Figuras para un teatro pigmeo.

La persona produciendo las figuras está derecho detrás de una mesa, y solamente su busto está disfrazado. Los brazos apoyados sobre la mesa son las piernas del tirolés pigmeo. El efecto es indecibilmente cómico. Se debe imaginarse que la cabeza de tamaño normal de un hombre reposa sobre el pequeñitísimo cuerpo disfrazado. ¡Y este cuerpo está hablando, reyendo y cantando! — en verdad una representación del grandísimo efecto. Sírvase Vd. observar que el frente de la mesa, sobre la cual se efectua la representación, está cubrido de cualquier objeto.

Charly Chaplin.
Uncle Sam.
Jockey.
Caballero remilgándoso y haciendo el don arrogante.
Alcañil.
Judío.
Señora remilgándose y haciendo el dama arrogante.
Caricatura I.
Caricatura II.
Bufones (clowns).
Boxeador.

Trajes de papel de seda

Muy apropiados a maravillas de menor importancia. De papel de seda doble. Costuras guarnecidas de listas de estofa, de modo que se puede emplear en verdad estos trajes, los cuales tienen un tamaño abundantemente normal y se acomodan a las demás personas. No se puede confeccionar estos trajes según med das particulares.

Chino.
China.
Gitano.
Gitana.
Pierrot.
Pierrette.
Turco.
Turca.
Marinero.
Marinera.
Tirolés.
Tirolesa.
Ruso.
Rusa.
Diablo.
Diabla.
Caballero remilgándose y haciendo el con arrogante.
Señora remilgándose y haciendo la dama arrogante.
Japonés.
Japonesa.
Deshollinador.
Deshollinadora.
Señor vestido en estilo "Rococo".
Señora vestida en estilo "Rococo".
Dominó.
Bebé (niño pequeño).
Húngaro.
Húngara.
Frac.
Gallo con plumas imitadas, en colores de varias tintas.

Trajes de papel de crespón

proporcionándose muy bien al cuerpo.

Caballero remilgándose y haciendo el don arrogante.
Señora remilgándose y haciendo la dama arrogante.
Japonés.
Japonesa.
Pescador italiano.
Pescadora italiana.
Húngaro.
Húngara.
Pescadora italiana.
Diablo.

Confites fulminantes.

Corazones decorados en varios colores. Contenido: Artículos de burla.
Nueces en tamaño natural. Contenido: Artículos de burla.
Huevos de Pascua decorados de varios colores. Contenido: Artículos de burla.
Puerco de fortuna. Contenido: Gorras.
Pequeña langosta marina, 11 cm de largo. Contenido: Artículos de burla.
Estrella, diámetro de 7 cm. Contenido: Artículos de burla.
Estrella doble, diámetro de 7 cm. Contenido: Artículos de burla.
Mariposa de tintas finas. Contenido: Artículos de burla.
Melolonte. Contenido: Artículos de burla.
Rosa. Contenido: Gorras.

Karneval- und Scherzartikel.
Carnival and jest articles.
Artículos de carnaval y de chanza.

Masken. — Masks. Máscaras.

141/T 27

141/T/59

141/T/121—126

141/T/121—126

141/T/121—126

141/T/121—126

141/T/151

141/T/132

141/T/53

141/T/28

141/T/133

141/T/72

141/T/23

141/T/58

141/T/60

141/T/61

Papierkostüme. — Paper costumes. — Trajes de papel.

Zwergtheater.

141/151

141/52

141/132/K **141**/131/K

141/133/K

141/109 9 **141**/105 5 **141**/10 110

141/8 108 **141**/119 **141**/104 4 **141**/11 111

141/15 115 **141**/20 120 **141**/18 **141**/102 2

141/116/R **141**/16/R

141/6 106 **141**/1 101 **141**/118 **141**/3 103

Knallbonbons. — Crackers. — Confites fulminantes.

141/5054

141/5051

141/5011

141/5525

141/5014

141/5512

141/5507/8

141/5807

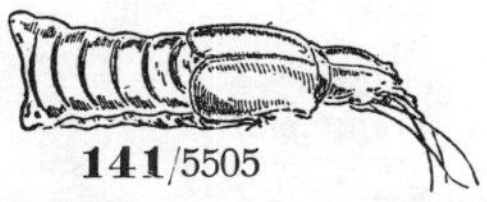
141/5505

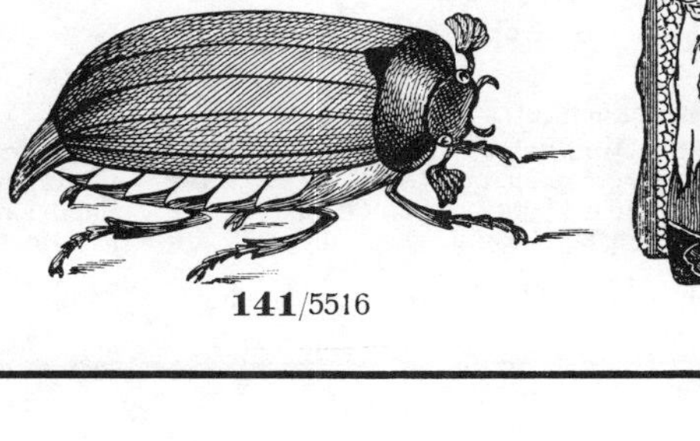
141/5516

141/5812

Nr.	Deutsch	English	Español
Nr. **141**/5807	Puppen mit Kreppapierkleidchen, Inhalt Scherzartikel.	Dolls, with crepe paper cloths. Caps. Contents comic objects.	Muñecas con vestido pequeño de papel de crespón. Contenido: Artículo de burla.
„ **141**/5812	Figuren, Inhalt Scherzartikel.	Figures. Contents comic objects.	Figuras. Contenido: Artículo de burla.
	Der größte Teil dieses Sortiments ist auch mit Mützeneinlagen lieferbar. Man verlange Musterkollektion gegen Berechnung.	The greater part of this assortment can also be supplied with caps inside the articles, extra per gross. Sample assortment sent and charged for.	Se puede entregar los demás artículos de este surtido también con gorras y inclusas. Sírvase Vd. pedir un muestrario contra pago.
	Fächer.	**Fans.**	**Abanicos.**
Nr. **141**/2	Figurenfächer, 28 cm lang, 5teilig sortiert.	Figure fans, 28 cm long, 5 segments, assorted.	Abanicos con figuras, 28 cm de largo, 5 divisiones.
„ **141**/4	Kreppfächer, 22 cm lang, 8teilig, einfarbig.	Crepe fans, 22 cm long, 8 segments, plain colours.	Abanicos de crespón, 22 cm de largo, 8 divisiones, de un solo color.
„ **141**/25	Imitierter Japanfächer, 10teilig.	Imitation japanese fans, 10 segments.	Abanicos japoneses de 10 divisiones
„ **141**/27	Kreppfächer, einfarbig, mit Malerei und beglimmert.	Crepe fans, plain colours, with painted subjects, glittering surface.	Abanicos de crespón de un solo color, con pintura y con mica.
„ **141**/28	Kreppfächer, schwarz, m. Aufschrift i. Glimmer.	Crepe fans, black, with inscription that glitters.	Abanicos de crespón, negros con inscripción en mica.
„ **141**/33	Klappfächer, Papier, mit Glücksschwein.	Folding fans, with lucky pigs represented on them, of paper.	Abanicos plegables de papel, con puercos de fortuna sobre.
„ **141**/42	Klappfächer, Papier, mit lachenden und weinenden Gesichtern.	Folding fans, laughing and crying faces, of paper.	Abanicos plegables de papel con caras reyendo y llorando sobre.
„ **141**/66	Klappfächer, Papier, mit Fantasiemuster, 6teilig.	Folding fans, fancy designs, 6 segments of paper.	Abanicos plegables de papel con muestras fantásticas, 6 divisiones.
„ **141**/68	Klappfächer, Papier, mit Libellenmuster, 6teilig.	Folding fans, dragon fly pattern, 6 segments, of paper.	Abanicos plegables de papel con muestra de libélulas, 6 divisiones.
„ **141**/69 A	Blattfächer, Papier, mit Pfau, hochfein Kreppapier, beglimmert.	Leaf fans of paper crepe, peacock, glittering, very elegant get up.	Abanico de hojas de papel, pavo, finísimo papel de crespón, con mica.
„ **141**/70	Klappfächer, Papier, mit Pfau, hochfein Kreppapier, beglimmert.	Folding fans of paper crepe, peacock, glittering, very elegant get up.	Abanico plegable de papel, pavo, finísimo papel de crespón, con mica.
„ **141**/71	Klappfächer, Papier, mit Truthahn, hochfein Kreppapier, beglimmert.	Folding fans of paper crepe, turkey cock, glittering, very elegant get up.	Abanico plegable, pavo de papel, finísimo papel de crespón, con mica.
„ **141**/73	Klappfächer, Papier, mit Federfächerimitation.	Folding fans of paper, imitating feathers.	Abanico plegable, abanico de plumas de papel imitadas.
„ **141**/74	Blattfächer, Papier, mit Rose und Kreppprüsche.	Leaf fans of paper, with rose and crepe frilling.	Abanico de hojas de papel, con rosa y gorguera de crespón.
„ **141**/75	Blattfächer, Papier, mit Kleeblütengarnierung.	Leaf fans of crepe paper, with clover blossom trimming.	Abanico de hojas de papel de crespón, guarnecido de flores de trébol.
	Schirme.	**Shades.**	**Parasoles y paraguas.**
Nr. **141**/Sch/7	Fransenschirm, hochfein, verschiedenfarbig sortiert, mit geformtem Griff, 8teilig, 70 cm Durchmesser, 80 cm lang.	Shade with fringe, in various colours, assorted, shaped handle, elegant, 70 cm diam., 80 cm long, 8 sections.	Parasol con franjas, finísimo, de varios colores, surtido, con mango torneado, 8 divisiones, diámetro de 70 cm, 80 cm de largo.
„ **141**/Sch/19	Wie Sch/7, dieselbe Ausführung, nur weiß.	As Sch/7, white only.	La misma ejecución, pero blanco.
„ **141**/Sch/19B	T Wie Sch/7, dieselbe Ausf., einfarbig sortiert.	As Sch/7, assorted in plain colours.	La misma ejecución, de un solo color, surtido.
„ **141**/Sch/9	Weiß, mit Rokokosilhouetten, 70 cm Durchmesser, 80 cm lang.	White, with Rococo silhouettes, 70 cm diam., 80 cm long.	Blanco con siluetas de „Rococo" sobre, diámetro de 70 cm, 80 cm de largo.
„ **141**/Sch/12	Fransenschirm, einfarbig, ungefüttert, 70 cm Durchmesser, 80 cm lang.	Fringed Shade, without lining, plain colors, 70 cm diam., 80 cm long.	Parasol con franjas de un solo color, no forrado, diámetro de 70 cm 80 cm de largo.
„ **141**/Sch/12 a A	Wie Sch/12, 55 cm Durchmesser, 70 cm lang.	As Sch/12, 55 cm diam. 70 cm long.	La misma ejecución, diámetro de 55 cm, 70 cm de largo.
„ **141**/Sch/30	Rüschenschirm, reich gepufft, hochfein, mit Griff, 8teilig, 70 cm Durchmesser, 80 cm lang.	Shade, with frill, well puffed out, verry elegant, handled, 8 sections, 70 cm diam., 80 cm long.	Parasol de orla de faldones, con muchos pufos, finísimo, con mango, 8 divisiones, diámetro de 70 cm, 80 cm de largo.
„ **141**/Sch/33	Clownschirm, originell, 25 cm Durchmesser, 90 cm lang, 6teilig.	Clown Shade, very original, 25 cm diam., 90 cm diam. 6 sections.	Parasol (paraguas) para un clown (bufon) cómico, diámetro de 25 cm, 90 cm de largo, 6 divisiones.
„ **141**/Sch/36	Karnevalschirm, 8teilig, 60 cm Durchmesser, 80 cm lang, in verschiedenfarbigen Feldern und humoristischen Maskenbildern.	Carnival Shade, 8 sections, 60 cm diam., 80 cm long, panels of various colours and comic mask designs.	Parasol de carnaval, 8 divisiones, diámetro de 60 cm, 80 cm de largo, con particiones de varios colores y pinturas humorísticas de máscaras.
„ **141**/Sch/102	Zartfarb. Kreppapier, m. Rosenk., hocheleg., Riesenschirm auf bes. fest. Gestell, gearb. m. Griff u. Drahtschl., 80 cm Durchm., 95 cm lang.	Giant shade, on particularly strong frame, handled, sling for carrying, 80 cm diam., 95 cm long.	Parasol gigantesco montado sobre un cuadro extraordinariamente rubusto con puño y lazo para llevar, diámetro de 80 cm, 95 cm de largo.
	Scherzartikel.	**Comic articles.**	**Artículos de burla (artículos chistosos).**
Nr. **141**/B/1	Brillen, Bronzekarton, geprägt, mit Drahtbügeln.	Spectacles, pressed, of bronzed cardboard, with wire frame.	Anteojos, cartón bronzeado, grabados, con arquito de alambre.
„ **141**/B/2	Wie B/1, mit Kartonnasen.	Spectacles, pressed, of bronzed cardboard, with wire frame and cardboard nose.	Anteojos, cartón bronzeado, grabados, con arquito de alambre y nariz de carton.
„ **141**/B/3	Große runde Schildkrötenbrillenform, geprägt, ohne Gläser.	Large tortoise shell spectacle frame, pressed, without glasses.	Anteojos grandes redondos en forma de una tortuga, sin vidrios.
„ **141**/B/4	Wie B/3, stärkere Ausführung.	The same, but stronger make.	Anteojos grandes, pero más robustos.
„ **141**/B/5	Wie B/3, mit Gelatinegläsern.	The same, with gelatine glasses.	Anteojos grandes redondos en forma de con vidrios de gelatina.
„ **141**/M/1	Vorbindemasken, farbige Kartons, ohne Behang, mit Schnur zum Binden.	Masks, to tie on, coloured cardboard, without lower part, with string.	Máscaras para atar por delante, cartón de varios colores, sin colgadura, con cordel para ligar.
„ **141**/M/2	Wie M/1, mit Behang von Kreppapier.	Masks, to tie on, coloured cardboard, with crepe lower part.	La misma con colgadura de papel de crespón.
„ **141**/M/1 Z	Wie M/1, zweifarbig, ohne Behang.	Masks, to tie on, in two colours, without lower part.	La misma sin colgadura.
„ **141**/M/2 Z	Wie M/1, mit Behang, zweifarbig.	Masks, to tie on, in two colours, with lower part.	La misma con colgadura.
„ **141**/M/7	Wie M/1, schmale Lupenform, ohne Behang, schwarz glänzend.	Masks, to tie on, covering eyes only, without lower part, black shiny, cardboard.	Máscaras para atar en forma de una lente estrecha, sin colgadura, cartón en color negro lustrado.
„ **141**/N/3	Nase von Pappe, kaschiert, humoristische Formen, Karton mit Wachs anzukleben.	Pasteboard nose, stiffened, comic shapes, for fastening on with wax.	Nariz de cartón, cubrida, formas humorísticas para fijar con cera.
„ **141**/N/4	Nase von Pappe, kaschiert, humor. Formen, Karton, m. Wachs anzukleben, m. bunt. Feder.	Pasteboard nose, stiffened, comic shapes, with coloured feather.	Nariz de cartón, cubrida, formas humorísticas para fijar con cera con anteojos y bigote.
„ **141**/N/5	Nase von Pappe, kaschiert, humorist. Formen, Kart. m. Wachs anzukl., m. Brille u. Schnurrb.	Pasteboard nose, stiffened, comic shapes, with spectacles and hair moustache.	Nariz de cartón, cubrida formas humorísticas para fijar con cera con anteojos grandes redondos y barba de pelo.
„ **141**/12205	Scherzkragen mit Krawatte (Vatermörder).	Humorous collar, with cravat (Huge Gladstone collar).	Cabezon de camiso be burla con corbata (cabezón altísimo en estilo alemán llamado("Vatermoerder")
„ **141**/12207	Schuhspitze mit hervorstehenden Zehen.	Boot tips, with protruding toes.	Puntas de zapatos con dedos del pie saliendo afuera.
„ **141**/12208	Wackelohren, auf die Ohren zu setzen und durch Ziehen in Bewegung zu bringen.	Wag-ears. Placed over the ears, on being pulled they wag.	Orejas meneándose para meterlas sobre las orejas y para mover tirárdolas.
„ **141**/12209/A	Raffkehände von Kreppapier, reichlich mit imitierten Ringen besetzt	Mr. Newrich's hands, crepe paper, profusely decorated with imitation rings.	Manos de un ladron de papel de crespón, guarnecidas abundantemente con anillos imitados.
„ **141**/12209/B	Teufelshände von Kreppapier.	Devil's hands, of crepe paper; painted claws.	Manos diaból. de pap. de crespón, con garras pintadas.
„ **141**/12209/B	Totenhände von Kreppapier, mit aufgemaltem Handskelett.	Dead man's hands of crepe paper; painted bones and joints.	Manos de un muerto de papel de crespón, con esqueleto de la mano pintado sobre.
„ **141**/12210	Negerhände aus Kreppapier, schwarz.	Negro's hands of crepe paper; black.	Manos de un negro de papel de crespón, negras.
	Ansteckartikel.	**Articles to pin on.**	**Artículos de atacar.**
Nr. **141**/242	Bretzel mit Wurstzipfel, mit Nadel.	Cracknel, with sausage end and pin to fasten on.	Rosquilla con el caba de una salchicha con alfiler.
„ **141**/6206	Champagnerpfropfen mit Nadel.	Champagnecork, with sausage end and pin to fasten on	Corcho de champaña con alfiler.
„ **141**/6212	Würstchen, 10 cm lang, mit Schleife und Nadel.	Small sausage, 10 cm long, with looped ribbon and pin.	Salchichas pequeñas, 10 cm de largo, con lazo y alfiler.
„ **141**/6224	Plastisch geprägte Ratte, ca. 9 cm groß, mit Nadel.	Plastic stamped rat.	Plancha con plástica impresión en realce, tamaño cerca de 9 cm, con alfiler.
„ **141**/4558	Würstelschnur mit humoristischem Anhänger	Sausage string, with a comical figure hanging to it.	Cordel para salchichas con colgadura humorística.

Karneval- und Scherzartikel. — Carnival and jest articles. — Artículos de carnaval y de chanza.

141/25

141/71

141/70

141/27

141/33

141/73

141/69 a

141/74

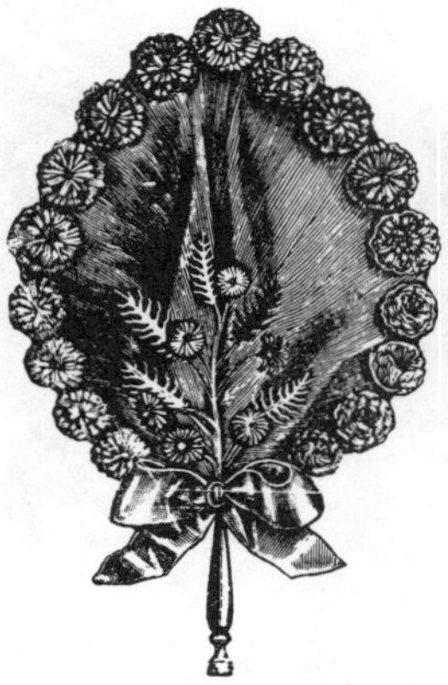
141/75

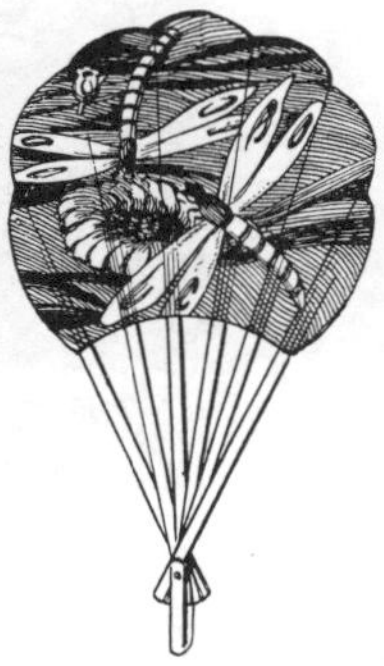
141/68

141/66

141/2

141/4

141/28

141/42

Schirme. Umbrellas. Parasoles.

141/Sch/7

141/Sch/36

141/Sch/9

141/Sch/30

141/Sch/102

141/6206

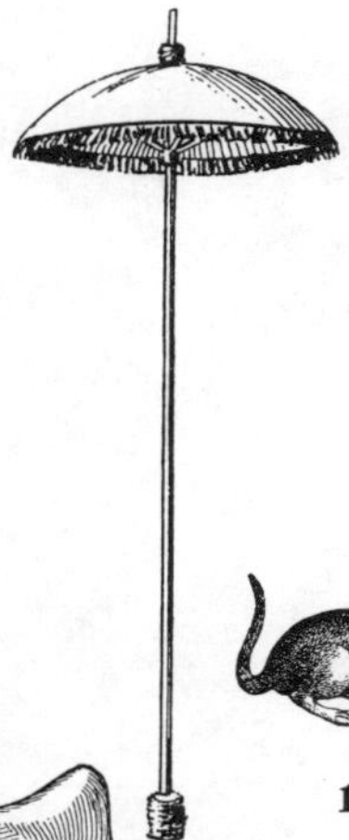
141/Sch/33

141/Sch/72

Scherzartikel. — Jest articles. Artículos de chanza.

141/N/3

141/N/4

141/6224

141/12205

141/6212

141/N/5

141/12207

141/242

141/B/1

141/B/3

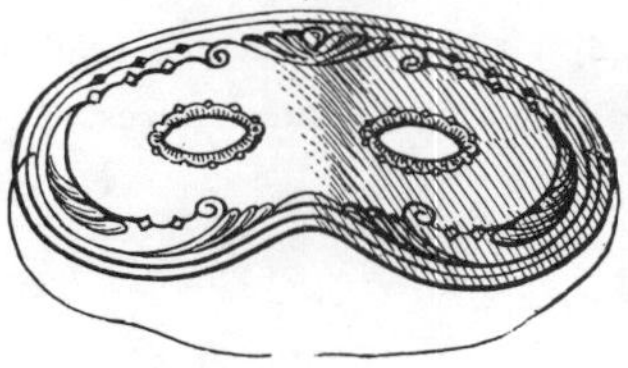
141/M/1

141/12209

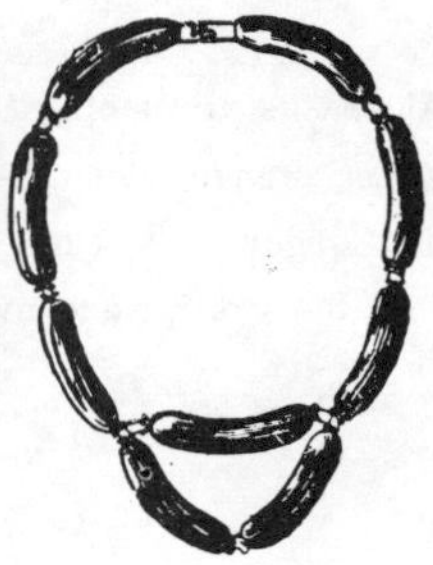
141/4558

Domino-Visiere und Phantasie-Masken aus Samt, Seide und Stoff. — Dominoes and fancy masks of velvet, silk and cloth.

Viseras para dominós y máscaras de fantasía de terciopelo, seda y estofa.

87/F. 1

87/F. 4

87/F. 9

87/F. 10

87/F. 13

87/F. 2

87/F. 5

87/F. 8

87/F. 12

87/F. 14

87/F. 3

87/F. 6

87/F. 7

87/F. 11

87/F. 15

87/F. 16

Alle Masken werden geliefert in schwarz, rot, rosa, grün, gelb, weiß, lila, hellgrün, orange, violett. — Die Behänge sind ca. 14 cm lang, sind aber auch länger zu haben. — Bei Bedarf wolle man Spezialkatalog unter Angabe der Nr. 87, evtl. auch der Form-Nr. mit den neuesten Preisen verlangen.

All masks are supplied in black, red, green, pink, yellow, white, lilac, light green, orange, violet. — The flaps are about 14 cm long, but can also be had longer. — In case of need please apply for special catalogue, stating the No. 87, and eventually the shape No., with the latest prices.

Se entregará todas las máscaras en negro, rojo, en color de rosa, en verde, blanco, lila, verde claro, en color de naranja, en color de violeta. — Las colgaduras tienen una largura de 14 cm más o menos, pero se puede entregarlas tambien más largas. — Cuando Vd. tiene necesidad de estos géneros, sírvase demandar el catálogo especial con los últimos precios indicando el No. 87, eventualmente también el No. de la forma.

74/—

74/40 **74**/16

74/581

74/453

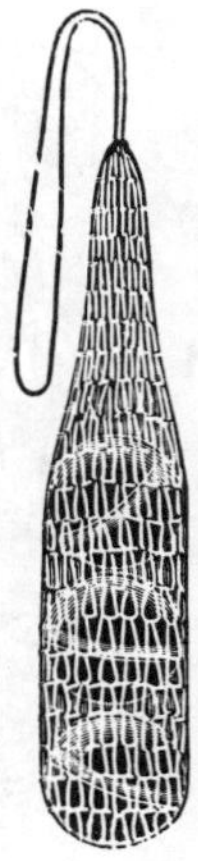

74/108

74/601

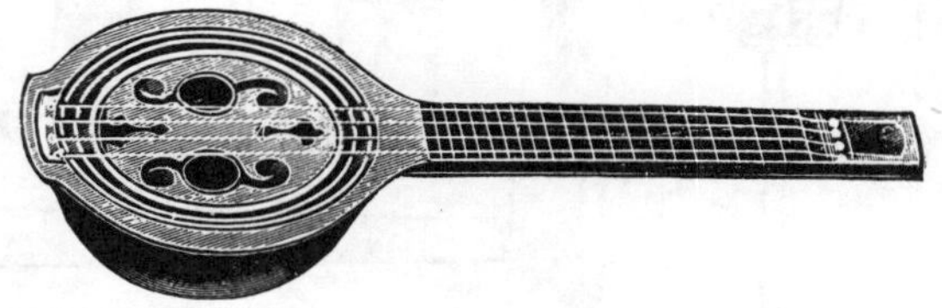

74/300

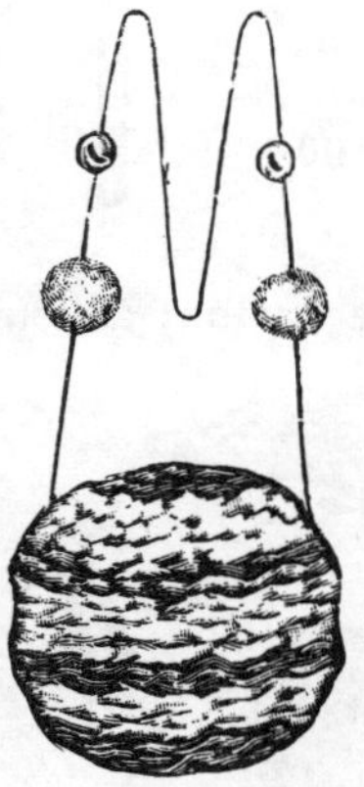

74/82/4

74/748

74/735

74/659

Nr. **74**/— **Globusball** mit Filzüberzug, 2farbig bedruckter Globus, mil Schwamm gefüllt, vollwertiger Ersatz für Gummibälle, in den Größen von 6, 6½, 7, 8, 9, 10, 12, 14, 16 cm Durchmesser.
Globe-ball with felt-covering, printed with two colours, ball filled with sponge, being full substitute for India rubber balls, in the sizes 6, 6½, 7, 8, 9, 10, 12, 14, 16 cm diametre.
Pelota globo, con guarnición de fieltro, con impresión de 2 colores. La pelota tiene esponja á dentro. Sustitución válida por las pelotas de caucho, en los tamaños 6, 6½, 7, 8, 9, 10, 12, 14, 16 cm de diámetro.

„ **74**/40 **Garnball** mit Holzwolle gefüllt, in den Größen 3, 4, 4½, 5, 5½, 6, 6½, 7, 7½, 8, 9, 10, 12, 14, 16 cm Durchmesser, mit und ohne Gummifaden, je nach Wunsch.
Yarn-ball of wood shavings, made in sizes 3, 4, 4½, 5, 5½, 6, 6½, 7, 7½, 8, 9, 10, 12, 14, 16 cm diametre, with and without rubber string, according to requirements.
Pelota con guarnición de hilado, con tundizno leñoso, en los tamaños 3, 4, 4½, 5, 5½, 6, 6½, 7, 7½, 8, 9, 10, 12, 14, 16 cm de diámetro, con y sin hilo elástico, según deseo.

„ **74**/16 **Ball,** aus Pappe geprägt, mit buntem Baumwollüberzug, in den Größen von 4, 5, 6, 6½, 7, 8, 9, 10, 14 cm Durchmesser, mit und ohne Gummi lieferbar.
Ball, stamped of cardboard, with fancy-coloured cotton coating, in the sizes 4, 5, 6, 6½, 7, 8, 9, 10, 14 cm diametre. Can be supplied with and without rubber string.
Pelota, estampada de cartón, con cubierta multicolor de algodón, en los tamaños 4, 5, 6, 6½, 7, 8, 9, 10, 14 cm de diámetro. Se la provée con y sin hilo elástico.

„ **74**/581
„ **74**/453 **Pappbälle** mit Vier- und Sechsfarbendruck in diversen Dekors in den Größen von 5, 6, 6½, 9 und 10 cm Durchmesser. Sämtliche Bälle mit und ohne Gummifaden.
Card-board balls with 4- and 6-colour printing, of different ornaments, in the sizes of 5, 6, 6½, 9 and 10 cm diametre. All balls with and without rubber strings.
Pelotas de cartón con impresión de 4 y 6 colores, de differentes adornos, en los tamaños 5, 6, 6½, 9 y 10 cm de diámetros. Todas las pelotas con ó sin hilo de caucho.

„ **74**/108 **Netzball,** 3 Stück 3 cm Bälle im Netz.
Net-ball, the net containing 3 balls of 3 cm each.
Pelota en red, 3 pelotas de 3 cm en red.

„ **74**/300 **Mandoline,** mit Saiten bespannt, zum Spielen für Kinder, in 4 Größen.
Mandolin, fully fitted with strings, to play for children, 4 sizes.
Mandolina, completo con cuerdas, juguete para niños 4 tamaños.

Nr. 74/300/1	23 cm	Durchmesser / Diametre / Diámetro
„ 74/300/2	25 „	
„ 74/300/3	35 „	
„ 74/300/4	50 „	

„ **74**/601 **Puppenballschlotter** mit diversen Zelluloidköpfen.
Shaky head with different celluloid heads.
Sonajero de muñeca con cabecica de celuloide.

Nr. 74/601/6	6 cm	Durchmesser — Diametre
„ 74/601/6½	6½ „	Diámetro

„ **74**/82/4 **Harmonikaball** mit buntem Fantasiestoffüberzug.
Accordeon-ball with multicoloured fancy-cloth coating.
Pelota de armónica con cubierta de fantasia.

„ **74**/748 **Stehauf,** aus Pappe geprägt, mit Zelluloidkopf.
"Get up", of stamped cardboard, with celluloid head.
"Ponte en pié", fabricado de cartón, con cabeza de celuloide.

Nr. 74/748/5	5 cm	Durchmesser / Diametre / Diámetro
„ 74/748/6	6 „	
„ 74/748/6½	6½ „	
„ 74/748/9	9 „	

„ **74**/735 **Körbchen** zum Füllen, in 3 Größen, aus Pappe, bunt verziert.
Little basket for filling up, 3 sizes, of cardboard, fancy-coloured and adorned.
Canastilla para guarnecer, en 3 tamaños, de cartón, con adornos de colores.

„ **74**/759 **Osterei,** aus Pappe geprägt, in 6 Größen, 5, 6, 6½, 7, 9, 16, 20 cm, diverse Dessins, mit Spitze und guter prima Ausführung, lasiert.
Easter-egg of stamped cardboard, 6 sizes, 5, 6, 6½, 7, 9, 16, 20 cm, different designs, with pointed end, and of good, first class style, polished.
Huevo de pascua, fabricado de cartón, 6 tamaños, 5, 6, 6½, 7, 9, 16, 20 cm, diversos dibujos, con punta y de ejecución superior, embarnizada.

Holzspielwaren-Massenartikel. Wooden toys; bulk articles. Juguetes de madera; artículos fabricados en masa.

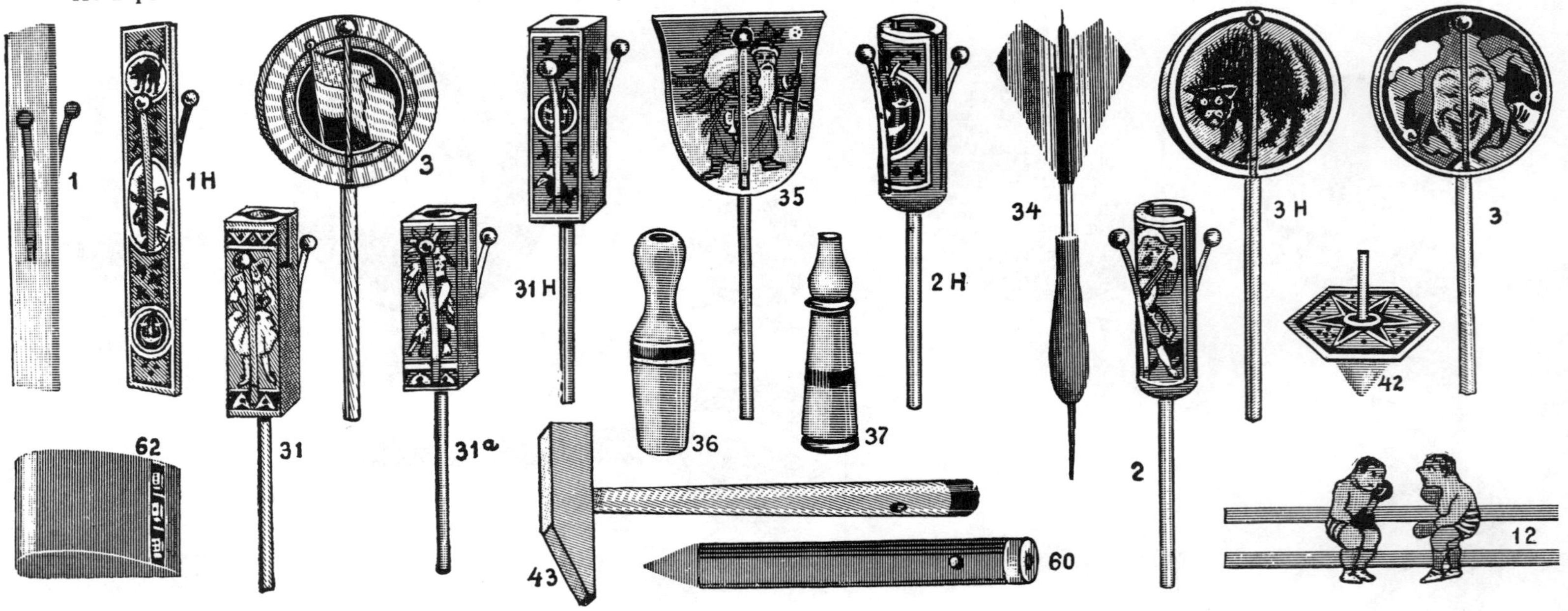

Pappspielwaren-Massenartikel. Cardboard toys; bulk articles. Juguetes de cartón; artículos fabricados en masa.

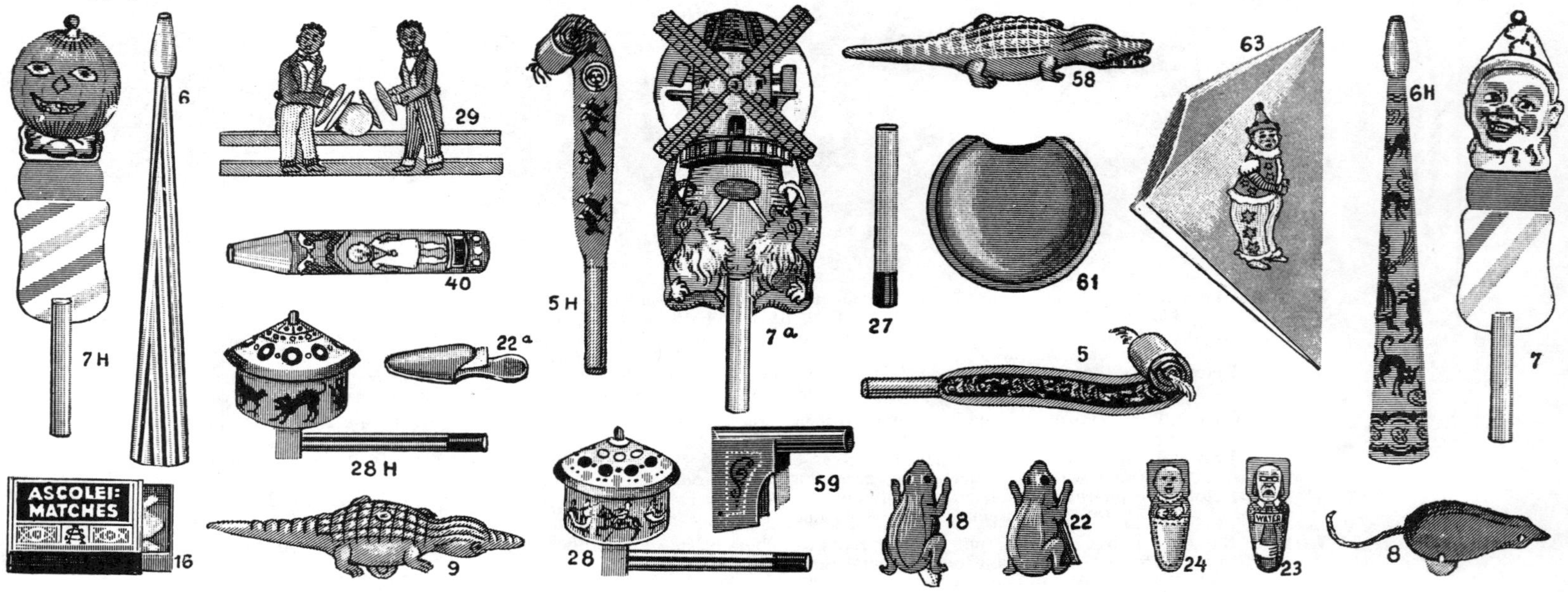

Karneval-, Reklame-, Zugabe-, Radau-, Scherz- und Jux-Artikel. Carnival-, advertising-, gift-, noisy-, jest-, fun-articles. Artículos de carnaval, de reclamo, de adehala, artículos haciendo ruido, artículos jocosos y artículos de chanza.

Bei Auftragserteilung ist die Kollektionsnummer 61 vor die Artikelnummer zu setzen. — When placing an order the coll. Nr. 61 must be stated before the Nr. of the article. — Dandola órden es indispensable meter la collección No. 61 ante el número del artículo.

Kinderfahrzeuge und Schaukeln. — Childrens' vehicles and swings. — Vehículos y columpios para niños.

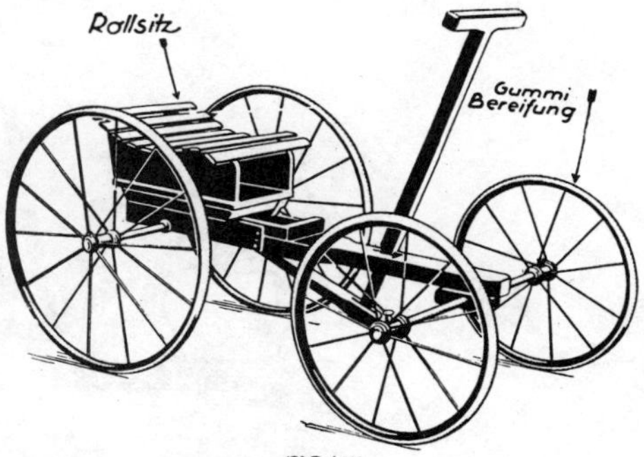

79/45

Nr. **79**/45 **Kindersportfahrzeug „Gig“,** mit *Rollsitz* und Gummibereifung in Größen 65, 70 und 75 cm.

Größe 65 cm Nettogewicht 6,8 kg
„ 70 „ „ 6,9 „
„ 75 „ „ 7 „

Childrens' sporting vehicle "Gig", with *roller seat* and rubber tyres, in the sizes 65, 70 and 75 cm.

Size 65 cm Net weight 6,8 kg
„ 70 „ „ „ 6,9 „
„ 75 „ „ „ 7 „

Vehículo de deporte para niños llamado "Gig" *con asiento para rodar* y bandaje de caucho, en los tamaños 65 70 y 75 cm.

Tamaño 65 cm Peso neto 6,8 kg
„ 70 „ „ „ 6,9 „
„ 75 „ „ „ 7 „

79/46

Nr. **79**/46 **Kindersportfahrzeug „Auto“,** mit *Rollsitz* und Gummibereifung, in Größen 80, 90 und 100 cm.

Größe 80 cm Nettogewicht 9,5 kg
„ 90 „ „ 10 „
„ 100 „ „ 10,5 „

Childrens' sporting vehicle "Auto", with *roller seat* and rubber tyres, in sizes 80, 90 and 100 cm.

Size 80 cm Net weight 9,5 kg
„ 90 „ „ „ 10 „
„ 100 „ „ „ 10,5 „

Vehículo de deporte para niños llamado "Auto" *con asiento para rodar* y bandaje de caucho, en los tamaños 80, 90 y 100 cm.

Tamaño 80 cm Peso neto 9,5 kg
„ 90 „ „ „ 10 „
„ 100 „ „ „ 10,5 „

79/52

Nr. **79**/52 **Bär,** zum Fahren oder Schaukeln, 41 cm hoch, 52 cm lang Nettogewicht 3,2 kg.

Bear, to drive or as rocker, height 41 cm, length 52 cm, net weight 3,2 kg.

Oso, sobre ruedas o para mecerse, 41 cm de altura, 52 cm de largo, peso neto 3,2 kg.

79/50

Nr. **79**/50 **Elefant,** zum Fahren oder Schaukeln, 43 cm hoch, 55 cm lang, Nettogewicht 3,2 kg.

Elephant, to drive or as rocker, height 43 cm, length 55 cm, net weight 3,2 kg.

Elefante, sobre ruedas o para mecerse, 43 cm de altura, 55 cm de largo, peso neto 3,2 kg.

79/51

Nr. **79**/51 **Pferd,** zum Fahren oder Schaukeln, 55 cm hoch, 55 cm lang, Nettogewicht 3,2 kg.

Horse, to drive or as rocker, height 55 cm, length 55 cm, net weight 3,2 kg.

Caballo, sobre ruedas o para mecerse, 55 cm de altura, 55 cm de largo, peso neto 3,2 kg.

79/53

Nr. **79**/53 **Eisbär,** zum Fahren oder Schaukeln, 41 cm hoch, 52 cm lang, Nettogewicht 3,2 kg.

Polar bear, to drive or as rocker, height 41 cm, length 52 cm, net weight 3,2 kg.

Oso blanco, sobre ruedas o para mecerse, 41 cm de altura, 52 cm de largo, peso neto 3,2 kg.

Kinderfahrzeuge und Schaukeln. — Children's vehicles and swings. — Vehículos y columpios para niños.

79/47 a

79/49

79/47 b

Nr. **79**/47 a **Traber mit Elefant,** Gummibereifung, 90 cm lang, 44 cm hoch. Nettogewicht 6,3 kg.
Trotting machine with elephant, rubber tyres, 90 cm long, 44 cm high. Net weight 6,3 kg.
Jinete trotando con elefante, bandaje de caucho, 90 cm de largo, 44 cm de alto. Peso neto 6,3 kg.

Nr. **79**/49 **Schwanen-Schaukel**

in Größen	1	2	3
	20 cm	27 cm	35 cm hoch
	75 cm	85 cm	85 cm lang
Nettogewicht	3 kg	3,2 kg	3,5 kg

Swan rocker,

in sizes	1	2	3
	20 cm	27 cm	35 cm high
	75 cm	85 cm	85 cm long
Net weight	3 kg	3,2 kg	3,5 kg

Mecero de cisne

en tamaños	1	2	3
	20 cm	27 cm	35 cm alto
	75 cm	85 cm	85 cm largo
Peso neto	3 kg	3,2 kg	3,5 kg

Nr. **79**/47 b **Traber mit Pferd,** Gummibereifung, 100 cm lang, 57 cm hoch. Nettogewicht 6,3 kg.
Trotting machine with horse, rubber tyres. 100 cm long, 57 cm high. Net weight 6,3 kg.
Jinete trotando con caballo, bandaje de caucho, 100 cm de largo, 57 cm de alto. Peso neto 6,3 kg.

Nr. **79**/47 c **Traber mit Maultier,** Gummibereifung, 105 cm lang, 53 cm hoch. Nettogewicht 6,3 kg.
Trotting machine with mule, rubber tyres, 105 cm long, 53 cm high. Net weight 6,3 kg.
Jinete trotando con mulo, bandaje de caucho, 105 cm de largo, 53 cm de alto. Peso neto 6,3 kg.

79/54

79/55

79/62

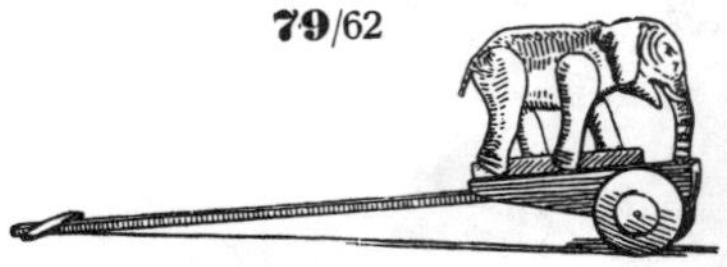

79/63

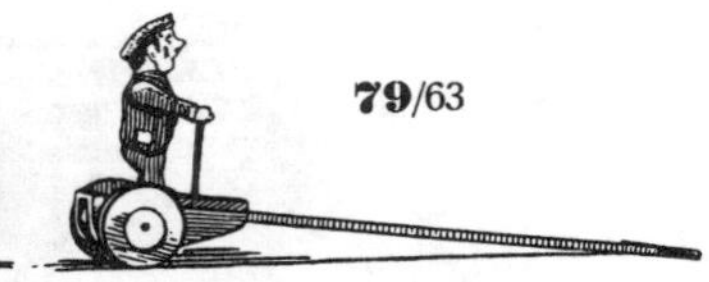

79/56 a

79/57

79/56 b

79/58—61

Nr. **79**/54 **Sandwagen,** abkippbar, **mit Elefant** (beweglicher Rüssel) und beweglicher Figur, Elefant zum Ausspannen, 55 cm lang, 24 cm hoch. Nettogewicht 1,7 kg.
Sand wagon, to tip up, **with elephant** (movable trunk) and movable figure, to unharness, 55 cm long, 24 cm high. Net weight 1,7 kg.
Carro para transportar arena, para voltear, **con elefante** (trompa móvil), elefante para quitarlo, 55 cm de largo, 24 cm de alto. Peso neto 1,7 kg.

„ **79**/55 **Sandwagen,** abkippbar, **mit Pferd** und beweglicher Figur, Pferd zum Ausspannen, 55 cm lang, 21 cm hoch. Nettogewicht 1,6 kg.
Sand wagon, to tip up, **with horse** and movable figure, horse to unharness, 55 cm long, 21 cm high. Net weight 1,6 kg.
Carro para transportar arena, para voltear, **con caballo,** y figura móvil, caballo para quitarlo, 55 cm de largo, 21 cm de alto. Peso neto 1,6 kg.

„ **79**/56 a **Auto, zerlegbar** in 9 Teile, 35 cm lang, 18 cm hoch. Nettogewicht 2,5 kg. Dasselbe mit Holzkasten 4,9 kg.
Motor car, to take to pieces, in 9 parts, 35 cm long, 18 cm high. Net weight 2,5 kg Ditto with wooden case 4,9 kg.
Automóvil, desmontable en 9 partes, 35 cm de largo, 18 cm de alto. Peso neto 2,5 kg. El mismo con caja de madera peso neto 4,9 kg.

„ **79**/57 **Sandwagen,** mit beweglicher Figur, 83 cm lang, 27 cm hoch. Nettogewicht 1 kg.
Sand wagon, with movable figure. 83 cm long, 27 cm high. Net weight 1 kg.
Carro para transportar arena, con figura móvil, 83 cm de largo, 27 cm de alto. Peso neto 1 kg.

Nr. **79**/56 b **Auto,** mit Plan, **zerlegbar** in 15 Teile, 35 cm lang, 23 cm hoch. Nettogewicht 2,550 kg. Dasselbe mit Holzkasten, Nettogewicht 4,950 kg.
Motor car, with plan, to take to pieces, in 15 parts, 35 cm long, 23 cm high. Net weight 2,550 kg. Ditto with wooden case, net weight 4,950 kg.
Automóvil con toldo, **desmontable** en 15 partes, 35 cm de largo, 23 cm de alto. Peso neto 2,550 kg. El mismo con caja de madera, peso neto 4,950 kg.

„ **79**/58—61 **Spielwagen** zum Ziehen, mit 2 beweglichen Figuren, 25 cm hoch, 35 cm lang. Nettogewicht 700 g.
Play cart, to pull, with 2 movable figures, 25 cm high, 35 cm long. Net weight 700 g.
Coche de juego para tirar, con 2 figuras móviles, 25 cm de alto, 35 cm de largo. Peso neto 700 g.

„ **79**/62 **Elefant,** mit beweglichem Rüssel, 75 cm lang, 24 cm hoch. Nettogewicht 750 g.
Elephant, with movable trunk, 75 cm long, 24 cm high. Net weight 750 g.
Elefante, con trompa móvil, 75 cm de largo, 24 cm de alto. Peso neto 750 g.

„ **79**/63 **Stempler,** Figur beweglich, mit Deichsel, 26 cm hoch, 82 cm lang. Nettogewicht 550 g.
Stempler, with movable figure, with pole, 26 cm high, 82 cm long. Net weight 550 g.
Estampillador, figura móvil, con timón (lanza de coche), 26 cm de alto, 82 cm de largo. Peso neto 550 g.

Sortiment **500**/465/4

Sortiment **500**/465 3

Sortiment **500**/466

Nr.		Packung / Packing / Empaque		Länge / Length / Largura	Breite / Breadth / Anchura	Höhe / Height / Altura
Nr. **500**/465/4	**Gespanne,** sortiert / **Teams of animals,** assorted / **Tiros de caballos,** surtidos	½ Dtz.	sortiert / assorted / surtidos	48 cm	15 cm	16 cm
„ **500**/465/3	do.	do. ½ „	do.	do. 40 „	do. 12 „	do. 14 „
„ **500**/466	do.	do. 1 „	do.	do. 35 „	do. 10 „	do. 12 „

Nr. **500**/103

Schafquietschen. — Sheep speakers. — Ovejas chillando.

L. 24 cm. — P. 2 Dtz.

Nr. **500**/101, 102

Schafgespann. — Team of sheep. — Tiro de ovejas.

Nr. **500**/101 L. 12 cm
B. 5 „
H. 6 „
P. 2 Dtz.

„ **500**/102 L. 16 cm
B. 6 „
H. 9 „
P. 2 Dtz.

500/103 **500**/99 **500**/96 **500**/97 **500**/98 **500**/102 **500**/101

Nr.				L.	B.	H.	P.
Nr. **500**/96	**Schafe auf Brett.**	**— Sheep on a board.**	**— Ovejas sobre una tabla.**	L. 10 cm	B. 4 cm	H. 11 cm	P. 2 Dtz.
„ **500**/97	do.	do.	do.	L. 10 „	B. 4 „	H. 11 „	P. 2 „
„ **500**/98	do.	do.	do.	L. 8 „	B. 3 „	H. 7 „	P. 2 „
„ **500**/99	do.	do.	do.	L. 11 „	B. 4 „	H. 12 „	P. 2 „

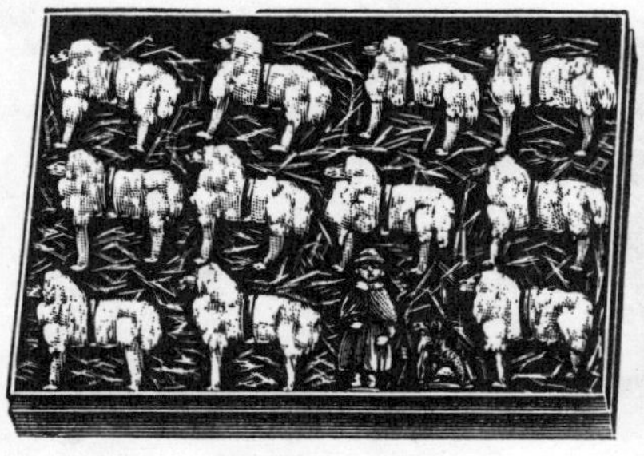

500/104/3

500/104/2

500/104/1

Nr. **500**/104/1, 2, 3 **Schafweiden. — Sheep pastures. — Pastos de ovejas.** Inhalt — Containing — Contenido: ½ Dtz.

Nr. **500**/104/1 L. 16 cm, B. 15 cm. Nr. **500**/104/2 L. 18 cm, B. 18 cm. Nr. **500**/104/3 L. 24 cm, B. 18 cm.

L. = Länge / Length / Largura

B. = Breite / Breadth / Anchura

H. = Höhe / Height / Altura

P. = Packung / Packing / Empaque

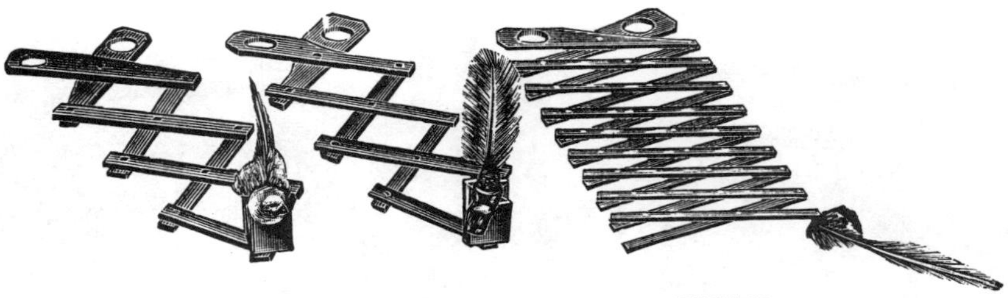

500/829 **500**/827 **500**/752

Scheren. — Scissors. — Tijeras.

Nr. **500**/829	mit Vogel, quietschend, Länge ausgestreckt	40 cm	P. 1/3 grs.
	with cryring bird, Full length	40 „	
	con ave chillando, Largura extendida	40 „	
„ **500**/827	mit Indianer, quietschend / with squeaking indian / con indiano chillando — do.	40 „	P. 1/3 „
„ **500**/752	mit Feder, with spring, con pluma. do.	80 „	P. 1/2 „

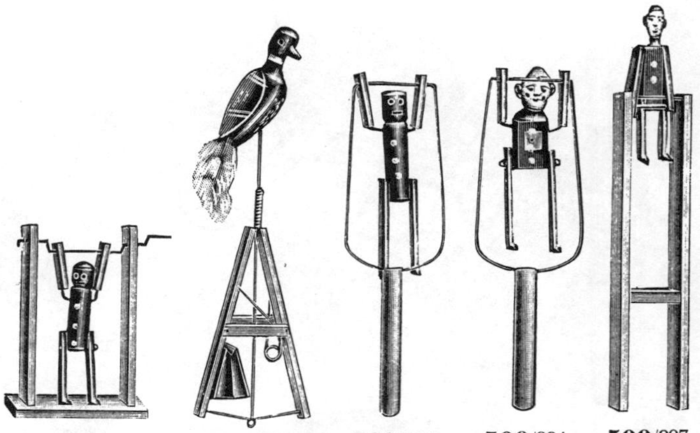

500/828 **500**/826 **500**/831 **500**/824 **500**/297

		L.	B.
Nr. **500**/828	**Reckturner** **Gymnast** **Gimnasta** sobre la barra alta	14	3 cm
„ **500**/826	**Drehorgel** mit Quietschstimme **Barrel organ,** with squeaking noise **Organo** de mano con voz chillando	30	5 „
„ **500**/831	**Schwingturner** **Swinging gymnastic** **Gimnasta** elevandose en el aire	26	8 „
„ **500**/824	**Schwingturner,** mit Quietschstimme **Swinging gymnast,** with squeaking voice **Gimnasta** elevandose en el aire, con voz chillando.	30	8 „
„ **500**/297	**Reckturner** **Gymnast** **Gimnasta** sobre la barra alta	27	5 „

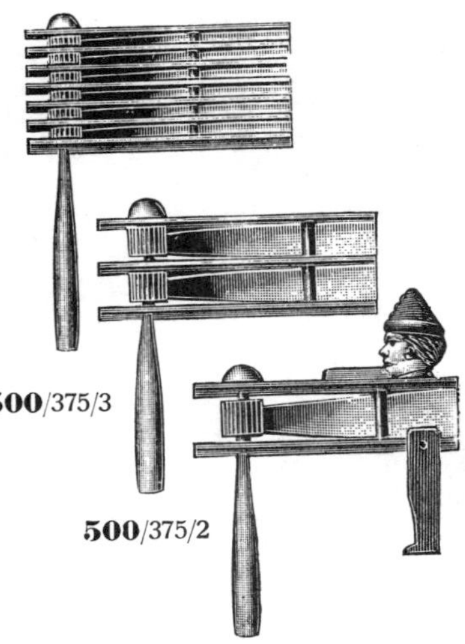

500/375/3

500/375/2

500/825

Knarren. — Rattles. — Matracas.

	P.	L.	B.	Räder, wheels, ruedas
Nr. **500**/375/3	1/6 grs.	14	8 cm	6
„ **500**/375/2	1/6 „	15	6 „	2
„ **500**/375/1	1/6 „	15	5 „	4
„ **500**/825	1/6 „	15	5 „	1

Nr. **500**/967/1 Wachstuch Oilcloth Encerada

„ **500**/967/2 Leder Leather Cuero

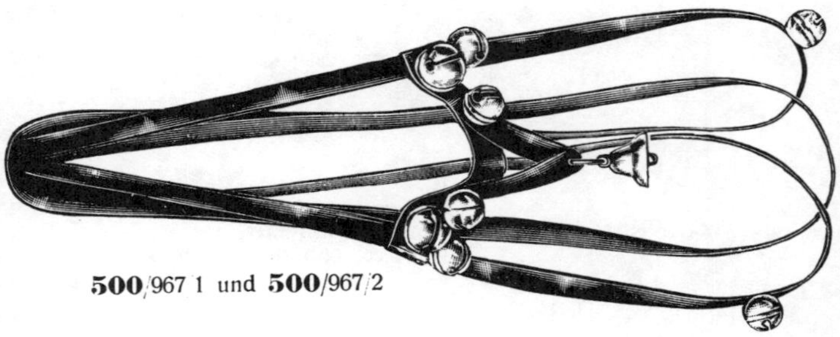

500/967 1 und **500**/967/2

Pferdeleinen. — Horses' Reins. — Cuerdas para caballos.

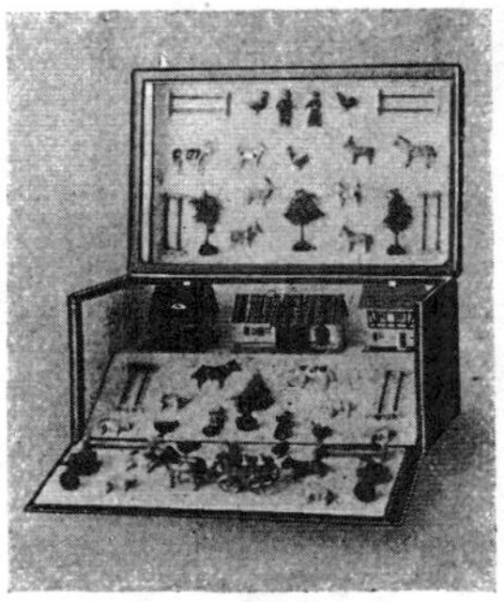

500/321

500/212 2 **500**/212 1 **500**/212 0

Turner. — Gymnast. — Gimnasta.

	L.	B.	H.	P.
Nr. **500**/212/2	20 cm	7 cm	25 cm	1 Dtz.
„ **500**/212/1	16 „	5 „	17 „	1 „
„ **500**/212/0	11 „	3 „	9 „	1 „

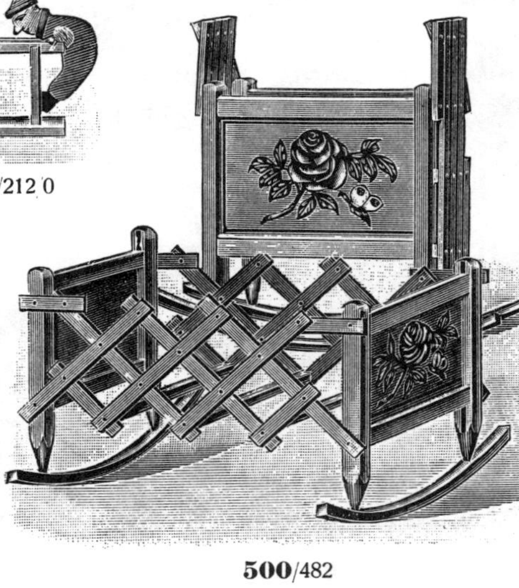

500/482

500/132/2

500/132/1

Puppenkoffer. — Dolls boxes. — Baulas para muñeca.

Nr. **500**/321/1	Größe, Size, Tamaño	16×10×8 cm
„ **500**/321/2	„ „ „	18×11×11 „
„ **500**/321/3	„ „ „	21×16×12 „
„ **500**/321/4	„ „ „	23×14×16 „
„ **500**/321/5	„ „ „	24×15×14 „
„ **500**/321/6	„ „ „	30×19×18 „

Klappwiegen.

Folding Cradles. — Cunas plegables.

	L.	B.	H.
Nr. **500**/482/1	24 cm	12 cm	12 cm
„ **500**/482/2	28 „	14 „	14 „
„ **500**/482/3	35 „	18 „	17 „
„ **500**/482/4	45 „	22 „	22 „

Möbel. — Furniture. — Muebles.

	L.	B.	H.
Nr. **500**/132/1	10	8	4 cm
„ **500**/132/2	16	16	8 „

L. = Länge, Length, Largura
B. = Breite, Breadth, Anchura
H. = Höhe, Height, Altura
P. = Packung, Packing, Contenido.

500/519

500/521/4

500/521/1

500/521/2

500/521/3

500/522

Zeichentafeln.
Drawing slates.
Tablas para dibujar.

Nr.	**500**/519/1	L. 14 cm	B. 12 cm
„	**500**/519/2	„ 17 „	„ 15 „
„	**500**/519/3	„ 23 „	„ 18 „
„	**500**/519/4	„ 28 „	„ 23 „

L. = Länge. — Length. — Largura.
B. = Breite. — Breadth. — Anchura.

Pyramiden. — Pyramids. — Pirámides.

Nr.	**500**/521/1	L.B.H.	7 cm	P. 2 Dtz.
„	**500**/521/2	„	8 „	„ 1 „
„	**500**/521/3	„	9 „	„ 1 „
„	**500**/521/4	„	10 „	„ 1 „
„	**500**/522	„	9 „	„ 1 „

Nr. **500**/222 A B C

H. = Höhe. — Height. — Altura.
P. = Packung. — Packing. — Contenido.

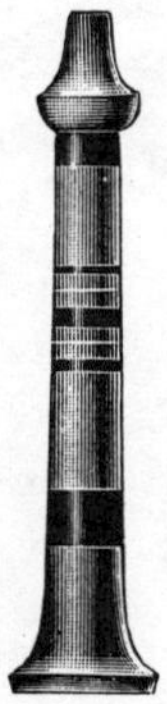

500/376/2 **500**/377

500/135
Gloria-Mosaik. — Gloria mosaic work.
Mosaico de gloria.

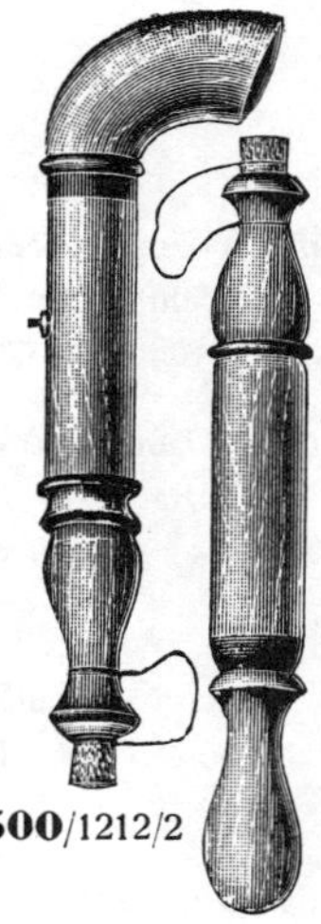

500/1212/2

500/1212/1

Nr. **500**/376/2
Kuckucksflöte. — Cuckoo Flute.
Flauta de cúculo.
L. 12 cm P. 2 Dtz.

Nr. **500**/377
Holztrompete. — Wooden trumpet.
Trompeta de madera.
L. 22 cm P. 2 Dtz.

Nr. **500**/1212
Pistolen. — Pistols. — Pistolas.

Nr. **500**/1212/1	L. 25 cm	P. 2 Dtz.
„ **500**/1212/2	„ 26 „	„ 1 „

Nr. **500**/91 A **Gummibälle,** grau und bunt,
Rubber balls, grey and coloured.
Pelotas de goma, grisas y abigarradas.

In den Größen — In the sizes — En tamaños:
1 1/4, 1 1/2, 1 3/4, 2, 2 1/4, 2 1/2, 2 3/4, 3, 3 1/4, 3 1/2, 3 3/4, 4, 4 1/2, 5, 5 1/2, 6″

Nr. **500**/91 B **Emaillierte Tennisbälle.**
Enamelled tennis balls.
Pelotas de tennis, esmaltadas.

In den Größen — In the sizes — En tamaños:
2, 2 1/4, 2 7/16, 2 1/2″

Flugzeug-Modelle, Baukasten und Flugspielwaren.
Air craft models, air craft toys, and box with parts for building them.
Modelos de máquinas voladoras, cajas de construcción para construir máquinas voladoras y juegos con modelos de máquinas voladoras.

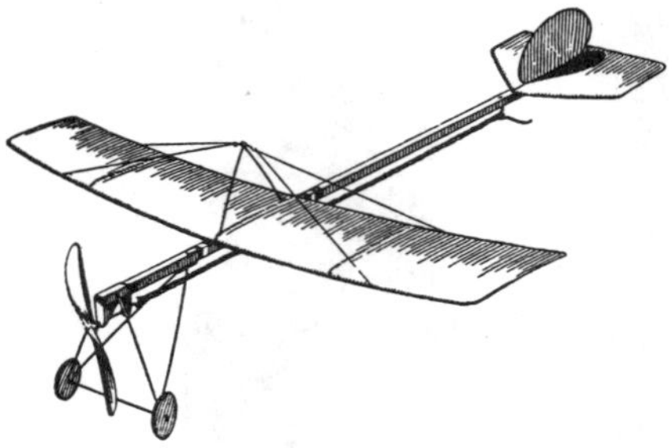

128/2

Nr. **128**/1 **Pfeil-Eindecker.** Flächen aus Stahldraht mit bestem Batist überzogen. Größe 42×40 cm. Gewicht 52 g.

Dart Single Decker. Surfaces made of steel wire covered with the best batiste. Size 42×40 cm. Weight 52 g.

Monoplano "Flecha". Planos de alambre de acero revestidos de la mejor batista. Tamaño 42×40 cm. Peso 52 gramos.

„ **128**/2 **Möve-Eindecker.** Schöner stabiler Stabflieger. Größe 48×53 cm. Gewicht 70 g.

Sea gull Single Decker. Fine stable flier, on rod. Size 48×53 cm. Weight 70 g.

Monoplano "Laro". Tamaño 48×53 cm. Peso 70 gramos.

„ **128**/3 **Taube-Eindecker.** Ganz neuartige Konstruktion. Größe 55×54 cm. Gewicht 100 g.

Pigeon Single Decker. Entirely novel construction. Size 55×54 cm. Weight 100 g.

Monoplano "Paloma". Construcción modernísima. Tamaño 55×54 cm. Peso 100 gramos.

128/3

„ **128**/4 **Parasol-Eindecker.** Hochgesetzte Tragfläche und eingelegter Sperrholzrumpf. Größe 60×62 cm. Gewicht 115 g.

Parasol Single Decker. Supporting plane placed high and wooden body built in. Size 60×62 cm. Weight 115 g.

Monoplano "Parasol". Plano de sustentación arreglada en posición alta y casco de travesaño insertado. Tamaño 60×62 cm. Peso 115 gramos.

„ **128**/6 **Sportflieger.** Dieser Apparat ist äußerst leicht gebaut und genügt auch den verwöhntesten Ansprüchen. Flugstrecken bis zu 100 m Weite. Größe 66×70 cm. Gewicht 165 g.

Sporting Single Decker. Of extremely light build, answering to the most exacting demands. Will fly up to 100 meters. Size 66×70 cm. Weight 165 g.

Aparato volador de deporte. La construcción de este aparato es extraordinariamente ligera; él cumple también con las grandísimas pretensiones. Campo de aviación hasta un alcance de 100 metros más o menos. Tamaño 66×70 cm. Peso 165 gramos.

Nr. **128**/5 **Fokker-Doppeldecker** (wie Abbildung). Ganz neuartige Konstruktion, Sperrholzrumpf, Stahldrahtflächen mit imprägniertem Seidenbatist überzogen. Schöner stabiler Flug. Größe 60×63 cm. Gewicht 135 g.

Fokker Double Decker (as illustration). Entirely novel construction; body of timber ends; surfaces of steel wire, with covering of impregnated silk batiste. Fine steady flight. Size 60×63 cm. Weight 135 g.

Biplano "Fokker" (véase la ilustración). Construcción modernísima. Planos de alambre de acero revestidos de batista de seda impregnada. Hermosa volada estable. Tamaño 60×63 cm. Peso 135 gramos.

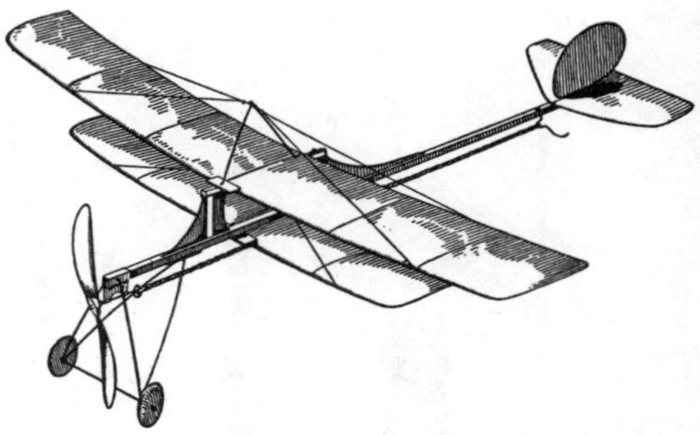

128/5

Nr. **128**/7 **Rumpf-Eindecker.** Die Schwierigkeit, Rumpfkonstruktion mit gutem Flug zu verbinden, ist in diesem schön gebauten Apparat vollkommen gelöst. Rumpfkonstruktion aus Sperrholz mit imprägniertem Seidenbatist, Flächen Stahldraht mit Bambusstreben, Überzug imprägnierter Seidenbatist. Größe 66×66 cm. Gewicht 180 g.

Single Decker, with body. The problem of constructing an aeroplane that has a body, so as to obtain a good flight, has been solved in this beautifully built model. The body is of wooden pieces covered with impregnated silk batiste, the surfaces being of steel wire with bamboo struts and covered with impr. silk batiste. Size 66×66 cm. Weight 180 g.

Monoplano con casco. Este aparato construido tan bien ha vencido absolutamente la dificultad de combinar la construcción de un buen casco con una buena volada. Construcción del casco de travesaño con batista de seda impregnada, planos de alambre de acero con tirantes de bambú, cubierta de batista de seda impregnada. Tamaño 66×66 cm. Peso 180 gramos.

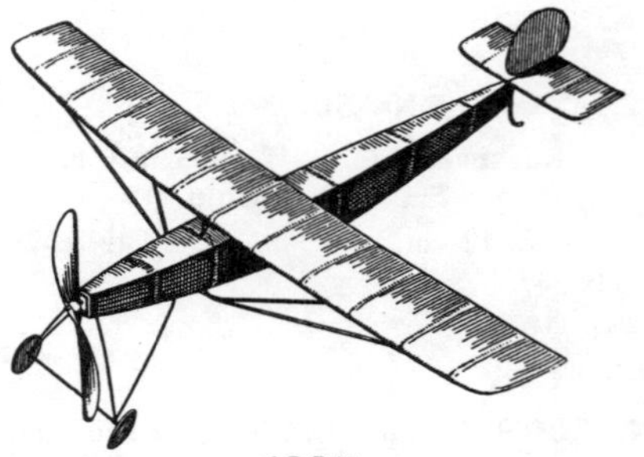

128/7

Flugzeug-Baukasten.

Mit unserem Baukasten lassen sich wirklich gutfliegende Flugzeug-Modelle herstellen, da es immer die Modelle sind, die wir fertigmontiert verkaufen. Hier ist den Knaben die Möglichkeit geboten, selbst zu montieren, ohne befürchten zu müssen, keinen Erfolg zu haben.

Nr. **128**/1 **Pfeil-Eindecker-Baukasten.** Größe 47×18×3 cm. Gewicht 335 g.

„ **128**/3 **Taube-Eindecker-Baukasten.** Größe 55×21×3,5 cm. Gewicht 360 g.

„ **128**/4 **Parasol-Eindecker-Baukasten.** Größe 65×25×4 cm. Gewicht 540 g.

„ **128**/5 **Fokker-Doppeldecker-Baukasten.** Größe 63×24×4 cm. Gewicht 360 g.

„ **128**/12 **Sturmvogel-**(Federflieger)**Baukasten.** (Großer Massenartikel.) Enthält Material für 2 Stück Federflieger (ein Eindecker und ein Doppeldecker). Größe 33×11×2,5 cm. Gewicht 100 g.

Box, with parts for building aeroplanes.

Really good models of air-craft that fly well can be constructed by the help of our box of parts, these being always the very ones we ourselves use in our finished models. With these parts, a boy can build his own aeroplane, with the certainty of getting it to fly well.

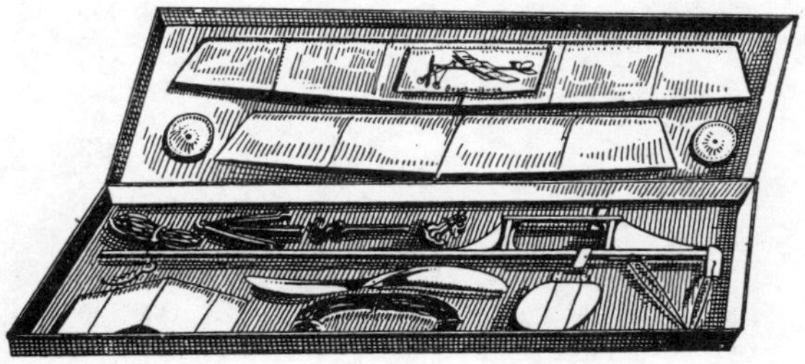

Caja de construcción para construir modelos de aparatos voladores.

Por medio de nuestra caja de construcción se puede construir modelos de aparatos voladores volando en efecto muy bien, porque estos son siempre modelos enteramente montados que vendemos. En este caso, los muchachos tienen la posibilidad de montar el aparato sin ayuda de otra persona y sin temer que sus esfuerzos queden ineficaces.

Nr. **128**/1 **Dart Single Decker Building Box.** Size 47×18×3 cm. Weight 335 g.

„ **128**/3 **Pigeon Single Decker Building Box.** Size 55×21×3,5 cm. Weight 360 g.

„ **128**/4 **Parasol Single Decker Building Box.** Size 65×25×4 cm. Weigth 540 g.

„ **128**/5 **Fokker Double Decker Building Box.** Size 63×24×4 cm. Weight 360 g.

„ **128**/12 **Stormy Petrel** (feather aeroplane) **Building Box.** Size 33×11×2,5 cm. Weight 100 g. Very popular; sells in quantities. Each box contains material for building 2 feather aeroplanes (1 single and 1 double decker).

No. **128**/1 **Cajas para construir monoplanos "Flecha".** Tamaño 47×18×3 cm. Peso 335 gramos.

„ **128**/3 **Caja para construir monoplanos "Paloma".** Tamaño 55×21×3,5 cm. Peso 360 gramos.

„ **128**/4 **Caja para construir monoplanos "Parasol".** Tamaño 65×25×4 cm. Peso 540 gramos.

„ **128**/5 **Caja para construir biplanos "Fokker".** Tamaño 63×24×4 cm. Peso 360 gramos.

„ **128**/12 **Caja de construcción "Procelaria"** (volador volando por medio de plumas). (Artículo fabricado en masa.) La caja contiene el material necesario para 2 voladores volando por medio de plumas (1 monoplano y 1 biplano). Tamaño 33×11×2,5 cm. Peso 100 gramos.

Flugspiele.

Flugmodelle mit Flächen aus Vogelfedern, leicht und auch im Zimmer fliegend. Großer Massenartikel, dabei beste Qualitätsarbeit und bis 50 m Flugweite.

Nr. **128**/10 Modell **Sturmvogel-Doppeldecker.**
„ **128**/11 Modell **Sturmvogel-Eindecker.**

Münchener Künstler-Schmetterlinge, künstlerisch bemalt.

Der neue Luftkreisel **Höllenrad,** schönstes Flugspiel für die Jugend. Flughöhe bis 40 m hoch.

Flying machine games.

These consist of models of flying machines made with birds' feathers, very light, and can fly about in rooms. Splendid seller and at the same of the best workmanship, flight up to 50 m.

Nr. **128**/10 **Stormy Petrel Double Decker.**
„ **128**/11 **Stormy Petrel Single Decker.**

Munich Artistic Butterflies, artistically painted.

Air top, a novelty **"Wheel of Hades"** a splendid game for the young. Flight up to 40 m high.

Juegos con aparatos voladores.

Modelos de aparatos voladores con planos de plumas de aves, ligeros y volando también en el cuarto. Gran artículo fabricado en masa, pero la mejor obra de primera calidad, alcance de la volada hasta 50 metros.

No. **128**/10 Modelo: **Biplano "Procelaria".**
„ **128**/11 Modelo: **Monoplano "Procelaria".**

Mariposas artísticas de Munich. Pintadas artísticamente.

La nueva peonza de aire **"Rueda del Inferno",** hermosísimo juego de volada para jovenes. Altura de la volada hasta 40 metros.

128/10

Nr. **128**/10 **Sturmvogel Doppeldecker.** Das neueste und interessanteste Flugspielzeug. Ohne jede Konkurrenz.

Nr. **128**/10 **Stormy Petrel Double Decker.** The latest and most diverting toy aeroplane. Defies all competition.

Nr. **128**/10 **Biplano "Procelaria".** El juguete de volada modernísimo y más interesante. Sin concurrencia alguna.

Inhalts-Verzeichnis.

Index.

Contenido.

Broschek & Co., Buchdruckerei und Tiefdruckanstalt, Hamburg.

Vorwort.

Die gute Aufnahme, die der von uns Anfang 1924 herausgegebene

UNIVERSAL-SPIELWAREN-KATALOG

überall gefunden hat, veranlaßt uns, nunmehr den vorliegenden Nachtrag zu obigem Katalog herauszugeben.

Sie finden in dem Nachtrag in der Hauptsache die Neuheiten veröffentlicht, die die in dem Hauptkatalog bereits vertretenen Hersteller seitdem herausgebracht haben. Außerdem finden Sie aber eine

GROSSE ANZAHL WEITERER GANGBARER SPIELWAREN,

die im Hauptkatalog noch nicht vertreten waren, und empfehlen wir daher diesen Nachtrag Ihrer vollsten Aufmerksamkeit.

Soweit es sich um Nachträge handelt zu den Veröffentlichungen im Hauptkatalog, finden Sie auf der betr. Seite den Hinweis auf die entsprechende Seite im Hauptkatalog, und bitten wir Sie, bei Aufmachung Ihrer werten Aufträge neben diesem Nachtragskatalog auch stets den Hauptkatalog freundlichst mit zur Hand zu nehmen.

In der Hoffnung, daß auch das vorliegende Werk Sie zu weiteren größeren Bestellungen veranlassen wird, weisen wir auf die gleichfalls erschienene neue Preisliste hin, die zusammengefaßt die Preise für alle Artikel im Haupt- und im Nachtragskatalog enthält.

Bei Aufmachung Ihrer werten Aufträge empfehlen wir aufs neue, nach Möglichkeit von den mit der gleichen Vornummer bezeichneten Artikeln so viel zu bestellen, daß solche eine seemäßige Kiste ergeben.

Abweichungen in der Ausführung und Packung vorbehalten!

Preface.

The good reception, our

UNIVERSAL TOY-CATALOGUE

published by us early in 1924, has met with everywhere, engages us now to bring out the present supplement to the above catalogue.

You will find in the supplement principally the novelties, manufactured since then by those manufacturers who are already represented in the original catalogue. Besides, however, you will meet with a

GREAT NUMBER OF OTHER CURRENT TOYS

the makers of which were not yet represented in the principal catalogue, and therefore we beg to recommend this supplement to your closest attention.

As far as it concerns supplements to the publications in the principal catalogue, you will find on the respective page the reference to the corresponding page in the principal catalogue, and we shall thank you to consult anyhow also the latter, when making up your valued orders after the supplement.

Trusting that the present work may also induce you to favour us with your further important orders, we beg to refer to the new price-list published on this occasion and which contains the prices for all articles represented in the principal catalogue and in the supplement combined.

When making up your valued orders, we beg to recommend again, to possibly order of the articles designated with the same fore-number, a quantity sufficient to complete a seaworthy case.

Subject to alterations in finish and packing!

Prefacio.

La buena recepción que nuestro

CATÁLOGO UNIVERSAL DE JUGUETES

publicado por nosotros en el principio de 1924, ha encontrado en toda parte, nos lleva ahora á publicar también el presente suplemento al catálogo arriba citado.

Vd. encontrará en el suplemento principalmente las novedades, hechas desde entónces por aquellos fabricantes que ya se hallan representados en el catálogo original. Pero, fuera de eso, Vd. descubrirá

GRAN NÚMERO DE OTROS JUGUETES CORRIENTES

cuyos fabricantes no estaban todavía enumerados en el catálogo principal y es por esta razón que recomendamos este suplemento á su mayor atención.

Según se trata de suplementos á las publicaciones en el catálogo principal, Vd. hallará en la repcetiva página la referencia á la página correspondiente del catálogo principal, y rogamos consulte siempre también el catálogo principal cuando hiciere sus apreciables pedidos por el suplemento.

En la espera que la presente obra también le dé motivo á Vd. para honrarnos con sus pedidos importantes, nos referimos á la lista de precios publicada simultáneamente, la cual contiene, combinados, los precios de todos los artículos del catálogo principal y del suplemento.

Cuando haga Vd. sus apreciables pedidos, recomendamos de nuevo de mandar venir, posiblemente, de los artículos designados del mismo ante-número una cantidad suficiente, para completar una caja marítima.

Se reservan alteraciones en ejecución y empaque.

Mechanische Blechspielwaren. — Mechanical tin toys. — Juguetes de lata con mecanismo.

127/25
9 × 18 cm
P = 1/12 Dtz.

127/45
22 × 7 cm
P = 1/12 Dtz.

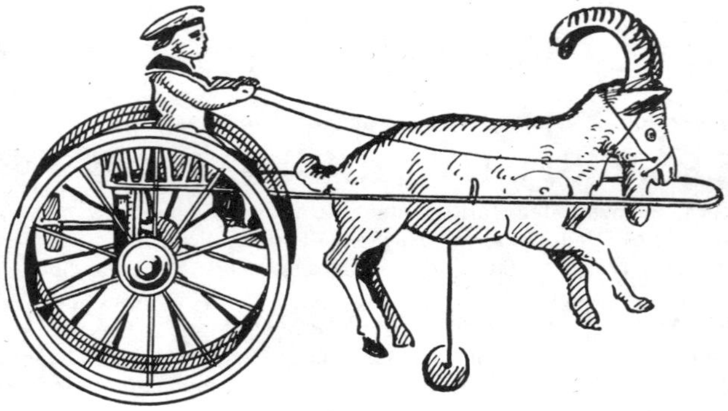

127/1935
28 × 15 cm. — P = 1/12 Dtz.

127/50/3
8 × 14 1/2 cm
P = 1/12 Dtz.

127/21
11 × 16 cm. — P = 1/12 Dtz.

127/2939

127/2939
11 × 10 cm
P = 1/2 Dtz.

127/50/1

127/50/1
29 × 12 cm
P = 1/12 Dtz.

127/110

127/110
18 × 11 cm
P = 1/12 Dtz.

127/340/2

127/340/2
28 × 9 cm
P = 1/12 Dtz.

127/702/2
12 1/2 × 12 cm. — P = 1/12 Dtz.

127/2000/6

127/2000/5
10 × 9 cm. — P = 1/2 Dtz.
6 Tiere sortiert.
6 animals assorted.
6 animales surtidos.

127/20
12 × 16 1/2 cm. — P = 1/12 Dtz.

127/640
18 × 12 cm — P = 1/12 Dtz.

127/313/6
18 × 16 1/2 cm. — P = 1/12 Dtz.

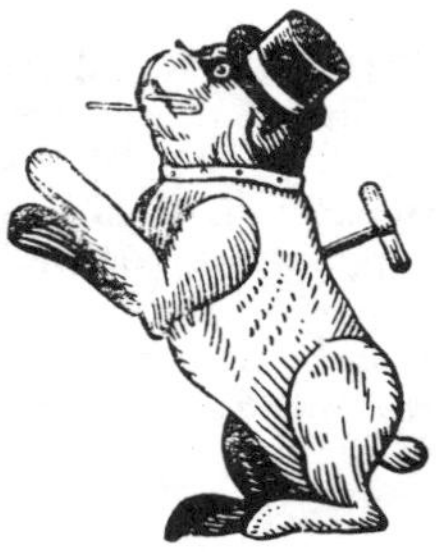

127/100
11 × 16 cm. — P = 1/12 Dtz.

127/345/1
17 × 11 cm. — P = 1/2 Dtz.

127/1020/1
17 × 18 cm. — P = 1/12 Dtz.

127/19
12 × 16 1/2 cm. — P = 1/12 Dtz.

Dtz. = Dutzend — Dozen — Docena. P = Packung — Packing — Contenido.

Mechanische Artikel. — Mechanical toys. — Juguetes con mecanismo.

134/1998/3

134/2071/5

134/1998/2

134/8004 Länge / Length / Longitud = 24 cm
134/8006 Länge / Length / Longitud = 30½ cm
134/8007 Länge / Length / Longitud = 33½ cm

134/1587/5

134/8040 Länge / Length / Longitud = 15 cm
134/8042 Länge / Length / Longitud = 20 cm
134/8044 Länge / Length / Longitud = 24 cm

134/7019

134/7087 Länge / Length / Longitud = 21 cm

134/7018

134/8013 Länge / Length / Longitud = 22½ cm

134/1584/10

134/8074 Länge / Length / Longitud = 25 cm

134/8055 Länge / Length / Longitud = 26½ cm
134/8056 Länge / Length / Longitud = 29 cm
134/8057 Länge / Length / Longitud = 34 cm

134/1591

134/8026 Länge / Length / Longitud = 33 cm
134/8027 Länge / Length / Longitud = 37½ cm

Mechanische Artikel. — Mechanical toys. — Juguetes con mecanismo.

134/7073

134/7071

134/7072

134/7070

134/7074

134/2500

134/7075

134/7107

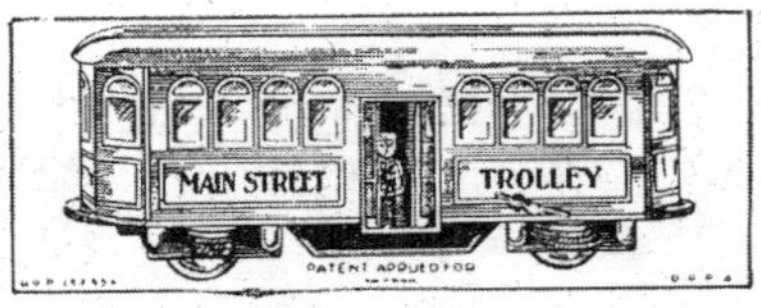

134/7106

134/7104

134/2615

134/7105

134/1966

134/1965/1

134/7101

134/1475

134/7108

134/1698/1

Russische Schaukeln, runde Karussells und Schwinger-Karussells.
Russian wheels, merry-go-rounds and swing-merry-go-rounds.
Columpios rusos, carrusels redondos y carrusels con volante.

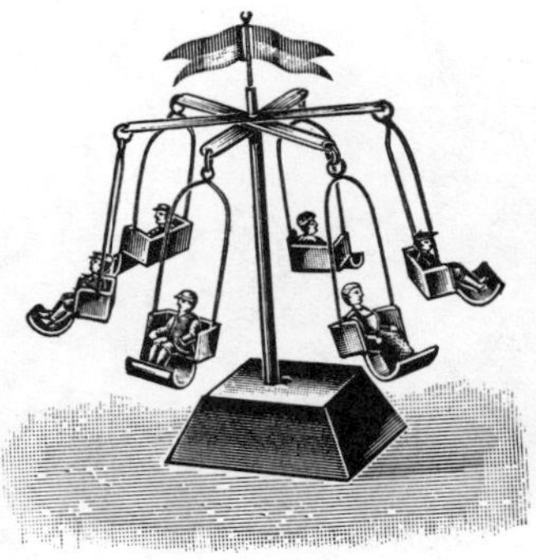

122/421

Höhe / Height / Altura 19 cm.

122/503

122/506

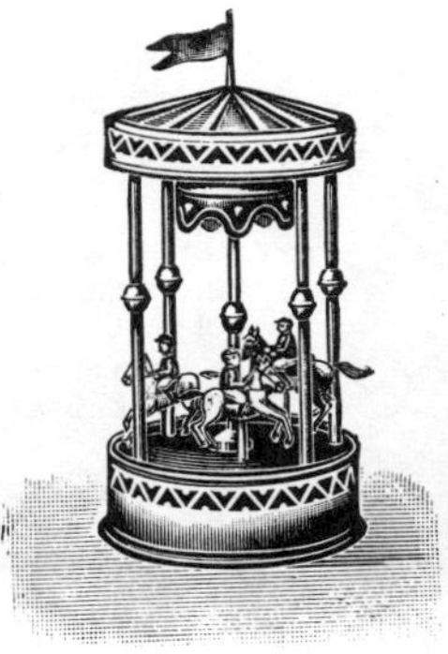

122/507

122/509

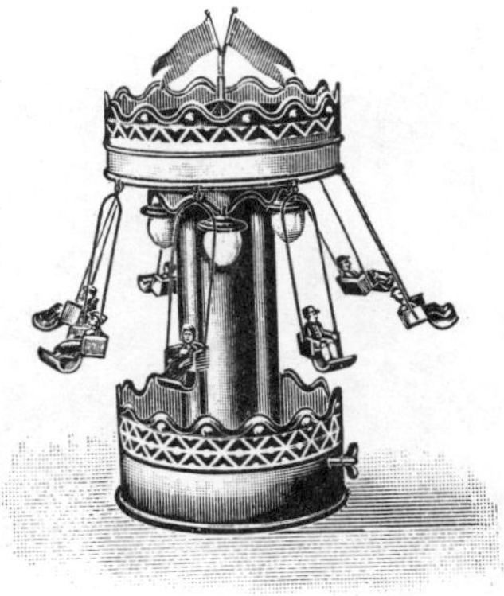

122/767

$^1/_7$ der natürlichen Größe. — $^1/_7$ of natural size. — $^1/_7$ del tamaño natural.

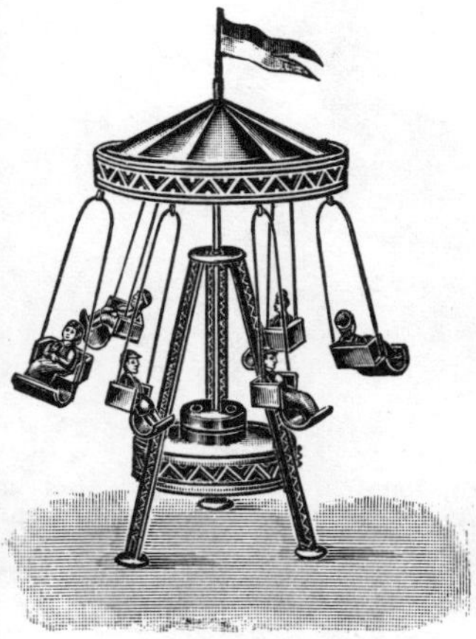

122/764

122/745

122/747

122/512

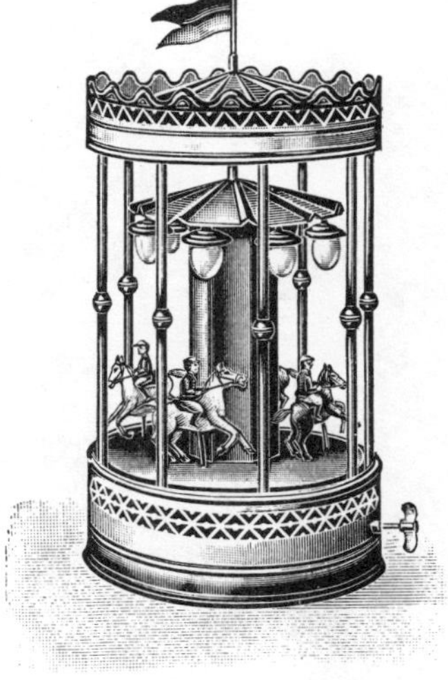

122/612

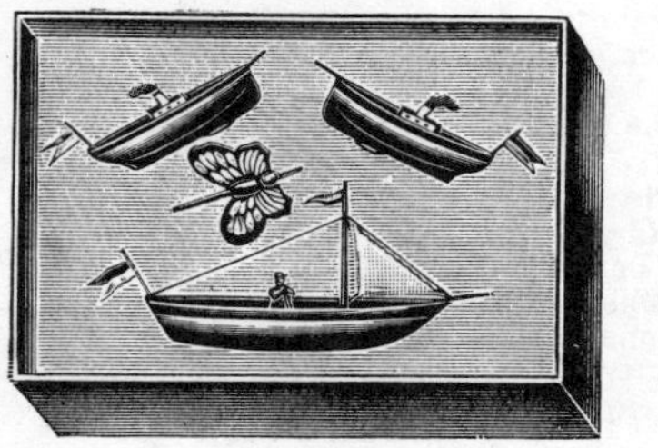

2059/1

2059/4

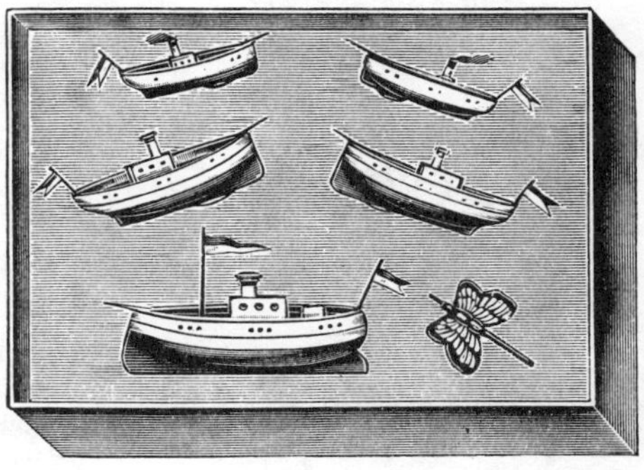

2059/2

2059/5

Magnet-Spiele.
Magnetic toys.
Juguetes magnéticos.

2059/3

Please note also the publication on page 39 of the principal catalogue.
Llamamos también su atención á la publicación en la página 39 del catálogo principal.

Mechanisch-plastische Blechspielwaren. — Mechanical plastic tin toys. — Juguetes mecánicos plásticos.

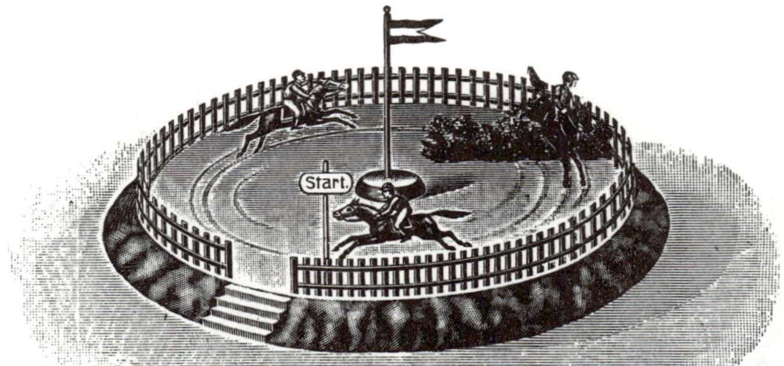

2005/42

2005/42

Pferderennen, mit Uhrwerk.
Race, with clockwork.
Corrida de caballos, con cuerda.

2005/33

Die beiden Motorradrenner fahren um den Felsen und überholen sich dabei gegenseitig.
Both moto-cyclists ride round the rock, overtaking one another mutually.
Ambos moto-ciclistas corren al rededor de la peña, tomando alternativamente la delantera.

2005/33

2005/23

Clown auf Clown vorwärts laufend.
Clown on Clown running forward.
Arlequin sobre arlequin corriendo adelante.
Höhe / Height / Altura 13 cm.
Länge / Length / Largura 15 cm.

2005/32

Pudel, schwimmend, bewegt sich mittels Uhrwerks im Wasser vorwärts.
Swimming poodle, moving forward in the water by clockwork.
Perro de agua, nadando se mueve adelante en el agua mediante mecanismo.

2005/22

Schütze, kniet und steht auf, dabei im Kreise fahrend. — Shooter, kneels and rises while turning round in circle. — Tirador arrodilla y levántase mientras hace giros.

2005/24

Länge / Length / Largura 16 cm.
Höhe / Height / Altura 14 cm.

2005/41

Länge / Length / Largura und / and / y Höhe / Height / Altura 14 cm.

2005/1

Länge / Length / Largura 18 cm.
Höhe / Height / Altura 12 cm.

2005/40

Vogel sitzt auf einem Ast am Baumstamm und singt, während er sich auf und ab bewegt. Das Werk wird durch Anziehen der Aufzugsschnur in Gang gesetzt.
Bird sitting on the bough of a tree and sings, moving up and down. The work is put into motion by pulling at the string.
Pájaro sentado sobre la rama de un árbol y canta, moviendo para cima y para bajo. El mecanismo es puesto en movimiento tirándose de la cuerda.
Länge / Length / Largura 15 cm.
Höhe / Height / Altura 15 cm.

2005/40

2005/43

Länge, Length, Largura } 17 cm.
Höhe, Height, Altura } 14 cm.

2005/44

Länge / Length / Largura 22 cm.
Höhe / Height / Altura 12 cm.

2005/24 Taube mit Stimme und beweglichem Kopf, laufend.
Pigeon with voice and movable head, running.
Paloma con voz y cabeza movible, corriendo.

2005/41 Hahn mit Stimme und Flügeln, laufend.
Cock with voice and wings, running.
Gallo con voz y alas, corriendo.

2005/43 Henne mit Stimme und beweglichen Flügeln, laufend.
Hen with voice and movable wings, running.
Gallina con voz y alas movibles, corriendo.

2005/44 Ente mit 2 Jungen, ohne Stimme.
Duck with 2 ducklings, without voice.
Pata con 2 pollos, sin voz.

2005/1 Wackelente mit Stimme, ahmt beim Laufen die Wackelbewegung einer lebenden Ente nach.
Waddle-Duck with voice, imitates while running the waddling of a live duck.
Pata tambaleando con voz, imitando al correr el andar tambaleante de una pata viva.

2005/26 Vogelbauer, japanisch, mit Stimme. Vogel im Bauer singt und bewegt sich dabei auf- und abwärts.
Japanese Bird's cage, with voice. The bird in the cage singing, while moving up- and downward.
Jaula japonés con pájaro. El pájaro en la jaula canta, moviéndose con eso para cima y para bajo.

2005/26

Länge / Length / Largura 15 cm.
Höhe / Height / Altura 20 cm.

Beachten Sie auch die Veröffentlichung auf Seite 39 des Hauptkataloges.

Please note also the publication on page 39 of the principal catalogue.
Llamamos también su atención á la publicación en la página 39 del catálogo principal.

Eisenbahnen mit Regulator-Uhrwerk, auf Schienen, mit Bremse, Spurweite 35 mm, hochfeine Ausführung, rot überzogene Kartons.
Railways with regulator-clockwork, on rails, with brake, gauge 35 mm, superfine finish, read-lined cardboxes.
Ferrocarriles con mecanismo de regulador, sobre railes, con freno, con anchura de via de 35 mm, ejecución muy elegante, cajitas de cartón forradas de encarnado.

2005/46

Vor- und rückwärts laufend. Lokomotive und Wagen, Länge 17 cm.
Locomotive-engine and carriages, 17 cm long, running forward and backward.
Locomotora y carros, 17 cm de largo, corriendo adelante y atrás.

2005/45 — mit 1 Wagen und 6 runden Schienen. with 1 carriage and 6 round rails. con 1 carro y 6 railes redondos.

2005/46 — mit 2 Wagen und 6 runden Schienen. with 2 carriages and 6 round rails. con 2 carros y 6 railes redondos.

2005/47 — mit 3 Wagen und 6 runden und 2 geraden Schienen. with 3 carriages and 6 round and 2 straight rails. con 3 carros y 6 railes redondos y 2 derechos.

Eisenbahn-Sortiment. — Railway-assortment. — Surtido de ferrocarril.

2005/48

Lokomotive, Tender, 3 Wagen, 12 runde Schienen mit Kreuzung, Signalglocke, Wärterhaus, Übergang, Tunnel und Brücke.

Locomotive-engine, tender, 3 carriages, 12 round rails with crossing, signalbell, watchman's house, viaduct, tunnel and bridge.

Locomotora, tender, 3 carros, 12 railes redondos con cruzamiento, campana de señal, casa de caminero viaducto, túnel y puente.

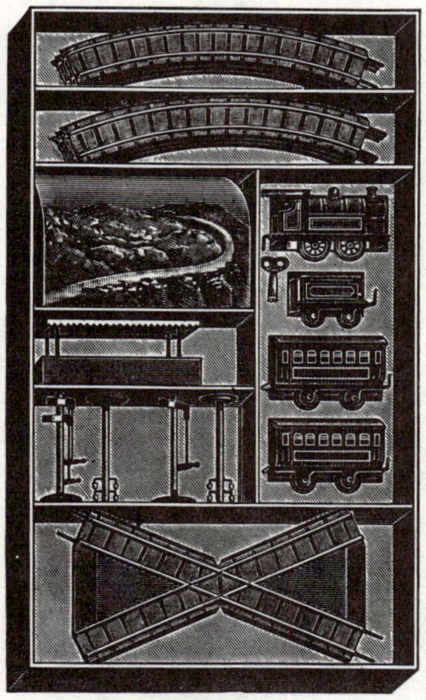

2005/49

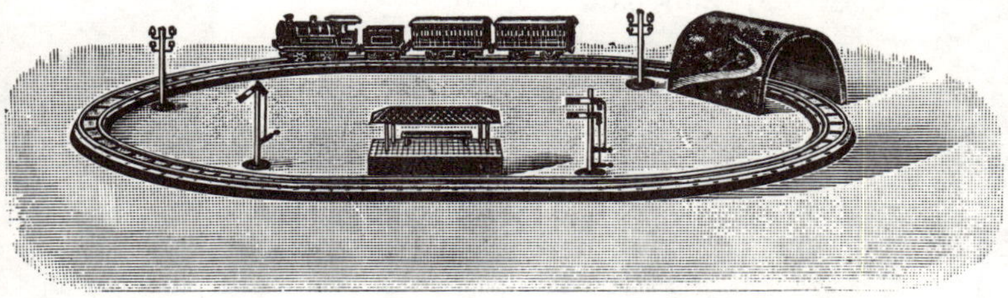

2005/50

Lokomotive, Tender, 2 Wagen, 8 runde, 2 gerade Schienen, Tunnel, Halle, 2 Signale, 2 Telegraphen.

Locomotive-engine, tender, 2 carriages, 8 round rails, 2 straight rails, tunnel, hall, 2 signals, 2 telegraphs.

Locomotora, tender, 2 carros, 8 railes derechos, túnel, portal, 2 señales, 2 telégrafos.

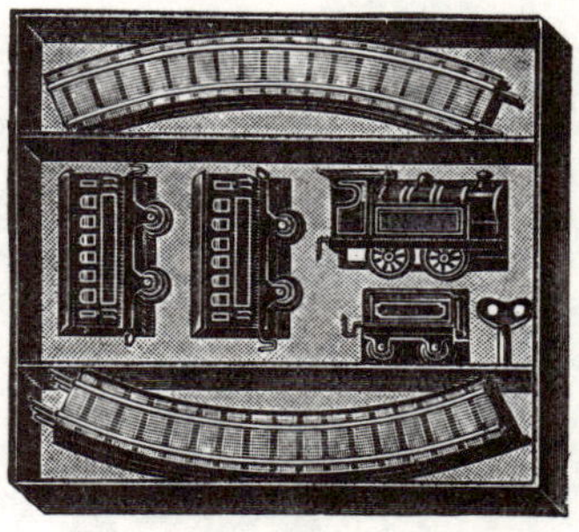

2005/30

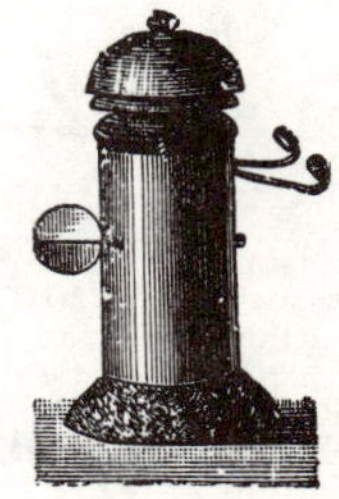

Höhe / Height / Altura $11^1/_2$ cm.

2005/51

2005/52

Gespann mit Uhrwerk.
Team of horse with clockwork.
Junta de caballos con mecanismo.

2005/53

Bahnwärterhaus.
Watchman's house.
Casa de caminero.

Höhe / Height / Altura
$22^1/_2$ cm.

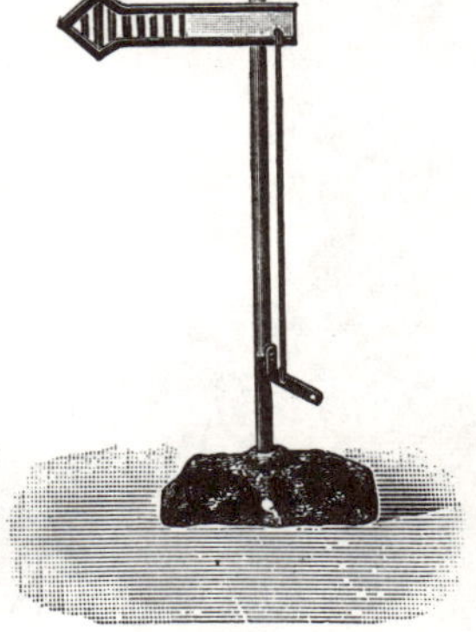

2005/54

Signal.
Signal.
Señal.

Höhe / Height / Altura
23 cm.

2005/55

Bahnhof. — Railway-station.
Estación de ferrocarril.

Höhe / Height / Altura 23 cm.
Länge / Length / Largura 24 cm.

Beachten Sie auch die Veröffentlichung auf Seite 39 des Hauptkataloges.

Please note also the publication on page 51 of the principal catalogue
Llamamos también su atención á la publicación en la página 51 del catálogo principal.

Billige Blechspielwaren mit und ohne Uhrwerk. — Cheap tin toys with and without clockwork. — Juguetes baratos con y sin mecanismo.

2007/13 Ohne Uhrwerk / Without clockwork / Sin mecanismo.
P = 4 Dtz., doz., doc. $14^1/_2 \times 4$ cm.

2007/12 Ohne Uhrwerk / Without clockwork / Sin mecanismo.
P = 4 Dtz., doz., doc. $14^1/_2 \times 5$ cm.

2007/11
Ohne Werk.
Without clockwork.
Sin mecanismo.
P = 4 Dtz., doz., doc.

2007/11 W
Mit Werk.
With clockwork.
Con mecanismo.
P = 2 Dtz., doz., doc.
11 × 5 cm.

2007/10
Ohne Werk.
Without clockwork.
Sin mecanismo.
P = 4 Dtz., doz., doc.

2007/10 W
Mit Werk.
With clockwork.
Con mecanismo.
P = 2 Dtz., doz., doc.
11 × 7 cm.

2007/18/0
Einfarbig, o. Werk.
One-coloured, without clockwork.
Unicolor, sin mecanismo.
P=4 Dtz., doz., doc.

2007/18
Ohne Werk.
Without clockwork.
Sin mecanismo.
P=4 Dtz., doz., doc.

2007/18 W
Mit Werk.
With clockwork.
Con mecanismo.
P=2 Dtz., doz., doc.
$12 \times 4^1/_2$ cm.

2007/20
Ohne Werk.
Without clockwork.
Sin mecanismo.
P=4 Dtz., doz., doc.

2007/20 W
Mit Werk.
With clockwork.
Con mecanismo.
P=2 Dtz., doz., doc.
$11^1/_2 \times 5$ cm.

2007/16/0
Einfarbig, o Werk.
One-coloured, without clockwork.
Unicolor, sin mecanismo.
P=4 Dtz., doz., doc.

2007/16
Ohne Werk.
Without clockwork.
Sin mecanismo.
P=4 Dtz., doz., doc.

2007/16 W
Mit Werk.
With clockwork.
Con mecanismo.
P=2 Dtz., doz., doc.
12 × 5 cm.

2007/19
Ohne Werk.
Without clockwork.
Sin mecanismo.
P=4 Dtz., doz., doc.

2007/19 W
Mit Werk.
With clockwork.
Con mecanismo.
P=2 Dtz., doz., doc.
$11^1/_2 \times 4^1/_2$ cm.

Sortiment / Assortment / Surtido } **2007**/A- **2007**/13, **2007**/12, **2007**/11, **2007**/10, **2007**/18/0, **2007**/20, **2007**/16/0, **2007**/19.
P = 4 Dtz., doz., doc.

Sortiment / Assortment / Surtido } **2007**/B- **2007**/11 W, **2007**/10 W, **2007**/18 W, **2007**/20 W, **2007**/16 W, **2007**/19 W.
P = 2 Dtz., doz., doc.

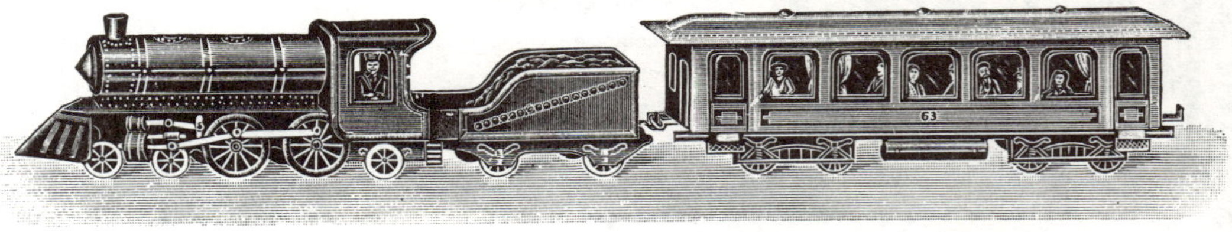

2007/21 Ohne Uhrwerk. Without clockwork. Sin mecanismo.
P=2 Dtz., doz., doc.

2007/21 W Mit Uhrwerk. With clockwork. Con mecanismo. $31 \times 4^1/_2$ cm.
P=1 Dtz., doz., doc.

2007/23 Ohne Uhrwerk / Without clockwork / Sin mecanismo.
2007/23 W Mit Uhrwerk / With clockwork / Con mecanismo.
P=2 Dtz., doz., doc. 10×11 cm.

2007/15 Mit Uhrwerk.
With clockwork.
Con mecanismo.
P = $^1/_{12}$ Dtz., doz., doc.
21 × 18 cm.

2007/14 Mit Uhrwerk.
With clockwork.
Con mecanismo.
P = $^1/_{12}$ Dtz., doz., doc.
21 × 18 × 11 cm.

2007/22 Ohne Uhrwerk / Without clockwork / Sin mecanismo.
2007/22 W Mit Uhrwerk / With clockwork / Con mecanismo.
P=2 Dtz., doz., doc. 10 × 12 cm.

P=Packung — Packing — Contenido.

Beachten Sie auch die Veröffentlichung auf Seite 51 des Hauptkataloges.

Please note also the publication on page 27 and 28 of the principal catalogue.
Llamamos también su atención á la publicación en la página 27 y 28 del catálogo principal.

2007/9 P=2 Dtz. / doz. / doc. $9^1/_2 \times 9^1/_2 \times 3^1/_2$ cm.

2007/9 Ohne Uhrwerk.
Without clockwork.
Sin mecanismo.

2007/17 Mit Uhrwerk.
With clockwork.
Con mecanismo.

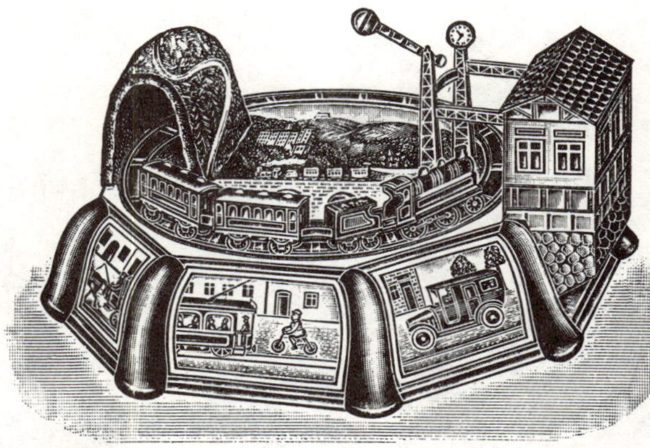

2007/17 P = $^1/_{12}$ Dtz. / doz. / doc. $13 \times 13 \times 7^1/_2$ cm.

Trompeten. — Trumpets. — Trompetas.

2023/10	17	$\times 5^1/_2$ cm.
2023/11	21	$\times 5^1/_2$ „
2023/12	30	$\times 6$ „
2023/13	$31^1/_2$	$\times 6$ „

2023/12

Bunte Kaleidoskope. — Coloured Kaleidoscopes. — Caleidoscopos pintados.

2023/1	$9^1/_2 \times 2^1/_2$	cm
2023/2	12×3	„
2023/3	$13^1/_2 \times 3^1/_2$	„
2023/4	$16 \times 3^1/_2$	„
2023/5	$13^1/_2 \times 4^1/_2$	„
2023/6	$16^1/_2 \times 4^1/_2$	„
2023/7	$20^1/_2 \times 4^1/_2$	„
2023/8	$16 \times 6^1/_2$	„
2023/9	21×7	„

2023/3

2023/4

112/56 EW
Eisenbahn mit Uhrwerk,
$^1/_2$ natürliche Größe.

Railway with clockwork,
$^1/_2$ of nat. size.

Ferrocarril con cuerda,
$^1/_2$ del tamaño natural.

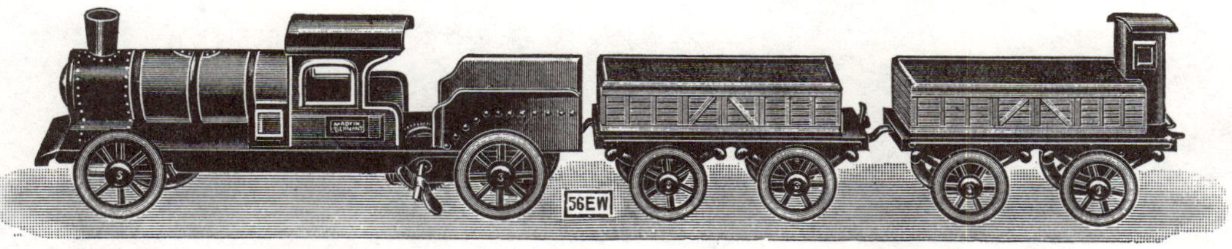

112/56 EW P=$^1/_{12}$ Dtz. / doz. / doc. **112**/56 EZ

112/56 EZ
Eisenbahn ohne Uhrwerk,
$^1/_2$ natürliche Größe.

Railway without clockwork,
$^1/_2$ of nat. size.

Ferrocarril sin cuerda,
$^1/_2$ del tamaño natural.

112/58/1	P=2 Dtz. / doz. / doc.
112/58/1 W	P=1 Dtz. / doz. / doc.
112/33	P=2 Dtz. / doz. / doc.
112/33 W	P=1 Dtz. / doz. / doc.

Of Coll. **112** orders under
\$ 5.— = £ 1.-.- net can not be delivered.
De Coll. **112** no se entregar al
menos de \$ 5.— = £ 1.-.- net.

112/58/1 Ohne Uhrwerk.
Without clockwork.
Sin cuerda.

112/58/1 W Mit Uhrwerk.
With clockwork.
Con cuerda.

$^1/_2$ natürliche Größe. — $^1/_2$ of nat. size.
$^1/_2$ del tamaño natural.

112/33 Ohne Uhrwerk.
Without clockwork.
Sin cuerda.

112/33 W Mit Uhrwerk.
With clockwork.
Con cuerda.

$^2/_3$ natürliche Größe. — $^2/_3$ of nat. size.
$^2/_3$ del tamaño natural.

Sortiment
Assortment
Surtido
} **112**/S 5 = **112**/68, **112**/54, **112**/57, **112**/58, **112**/59, **112**/56, **112**/51

The No. **112**/68, **112**/54, **112**/57, **112**/58, **112**/59, **112**/56, **112**/51 without clockwork are supplied individually.

Los No. **112**/68, **112**/54, **112**/57, **112**/58, **112**/59, **112**/56, **112**/51 sin cuerda se suministran solo.

P=2 Dtz./doz./doc.

$^1/_4$ natürliche Größe. — $^1/_4$ of nat. size.
$^1/_4$ del tamaño natural.

112/S 5
Ohne Uhrwerk.
Without clockwork.
Sin cuerda.

Sortiment.
Assortment.
Surtido.

112/S 5 W
Mit Uhrwerk.
With clockwork.
Con cuerda.

Sortiment
Assortment
Surtido
} **112**/S 5 W = **112**/54 W, **112**/57 W, **112**/58 W, **112**/59 W, **112**/56 W, **112**/51 W,

The No. **112**/54 W, **112**/57 W, **112**/58 W, **112**/59 W, **112**/56 W, **112**/51 W with clockwork are supplied individually.

Los No. **112**/54 W, **112**/57 W, **112**/58 W, **112**/59 W, **112**/56 W, **112**/51 W con cuerda se suministran solo.

P=1 Dtz./doz./doc.

$^1/_4$ natürliche Größe. — $^1/_4$ of nat. cize.
$^1/_4$ del tamaño natural.

P = Packung / Packing / Contenido.

Beachten Sie auch die Veröffentlichung auf Seite 27 und 28 des Hauptkataloges.

Mechanische Blechspielwaren. — Mechanical toys. — Juguetes mecánicos.

2010/67

Länge / Length / Largo	Höhe / Height / Altura	Breite / Breadth / Ancho
16 cm	20 cm	16 cm

Karussell mit 4 reitenden Figuren und guter Musik. Originelle Bewegung des Karusselldrehers am Turm.
Roundabout with 4 riding figures and good music. Peculiar movement of the roundabout-driver at the tower.
Torneo con 4 figuras montadas y buena música. Movimiento singular del empujador de torneo á la torre.

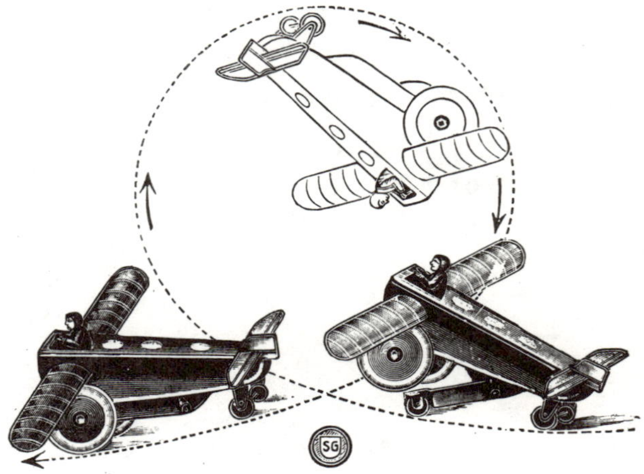

2010/90

Länge / Length / Largo	Höhe / Height / Altura	Breite / Breadth / Ancho
17 cm	10 cm	18 cm

Flugzeug, auf dem Boden laufend und Sturzflüge ausführend, mit Uhrwerk.
Aeroplane, running on the floor and executing somersaults, with clockwork.
Aeroplano, corriendo sobre el suelo y ejecutando volteretas, con mecanismo.

2010/88

Länge / Length / Largo	Höhe / Height / Altura	Breite / Breadth / Ancho
23 cm	24 cm	23 cm

Ausführung wie 2010/67, größer.
Finish like 2010/67, but larger.
Ejecución como 2010/67, pero más grande.

2010/81

Länge / Length / Largo	Höhe / Height / Altura	Breite / Breadth / Ancho
19 cm	$8^1/_2$ cm	19 cm

Aeroplan, an der Schnur fliegend, mit befestigten und zusammenklappbaren Propellern, mit Federwerk.
Aeroplane, flying on a string, with fastened and folding propellers, with clockwork.
Aeroplano, volando sobre una cuerda, con propulsores fijados y plegables, con mecanismo.

2010/85

Länge / Length / Largo	Höhe / Height / Altura	Breite / Breadth / Ancho
25 cm	8 cm	5 cm

Zeppelin-Luftschiff mit Uhrwerk, an der Schnur fliegend.
Zeppelin-Airship, with clockwork, flying on a string.
Zeppelin-máquina aerostática, con mecanismo, volando sobre una cuerda.

2010/91

Länge/Length/Largo $15^1/_2$ cm. Höhe/Height/Altura 9 cm. Breite/Breadth/Ancho 8 cm.

Salto-Clown, überschlagend, mit sehr gutem Uhrwerk.
Clown, throwing a somersault, with very good clockwork.
Arlequin, dando volteretas, con muy buen mecanismo.

Länge/Length/Largo 8 cm
Höhe/Height/Altura 18 cm
Breite/Breadth/Ancho 8cm

2010/71

Rollclown auf Kugel, mit Uhrwerk. Beim Rollen der Kugel dreht sich der Clown um seine eigene Achse. Durch die auf und ab balancierende Bewegung des Clowns wird ein fortwährender Zickzacklauf der Kugel hervorgerufen.
Rolling clown on ball with clockwork. When the ball is rolling, the clown turns round his own axle. By the balancing up and down of the clown the ball will perform a continuous zig-zag run.
Arlequin rodando sobre bola, con mecanismo. Rodando la bola el arlequin gira al rededor de su propio eje. Por el movimiento de balance arriba y abajo es causada una corrida continua de la bola en zigzag.

2010/70

Länge / Length / Largo	Höhe / Height / Altura	Breite / Breadth / Ancho
21 cm	26 cm	12 cm

Klappernde Windmühle in farbenprächtiger Ausführung. Bewegliche Windflügel. Ein bestausgeführtes Federwerk läßt den Müller durch Öffnen des Dachfensters von Zeit zu Zeit erscheinen und verschwinden.
Clapping windmill in richly coloured execution. Moveable sails. A finely finished springwork makes the miller appear and disappear from time to time by opening the roof window.
Molino a viento con taravilla, en ejecución de colores espléndidos. Con alas movibles. Un mecanismo de la mejor construcción hace aparecer y desaparecer al molinero en ciertos intervalos, abriéndose la buharda.

Länge / Length / Largo 16 cm
Höhe / Height / Altura 9 cm
Breite / Breadth / Ancho 9 cm

2010/73

Automobil-Coupé, neuestes Modell, mit aufklappbarem Rücksitz, Chauffeur, Vollräder mit Ballon-Reifen-Imitation, mit Federwerk.
Automobile-coupé, latest type, with folding back-seat, chauffeur, full wheels with balloon-tyre-imitation, with spring-work.
Automóvil-coupé, último modelo con asiento de fondo plegable, chauffeur, ruedas macizas con imitación de neumáticos-balón, con mecanismo.

Länge/Length/Largo 16 cm
Höhe/Height/Altura 6 cm
Breite/Breadth/Ancho 9 cm

2010/72

Rennauto, im Kreis und geradeaus fahrend, mit Federwerk.
Racing motor-car, with circular or straight forward motion, with spring-work.
Automóvil de corridas, con movimiento circular y adelante, con resorte.

Beachten Sie auch die Veröffentlichung auf Seite 41—45 des Hauptkataloges.

Please note also the publication on page 41—45 of the principal catalogue.
Llamamos también su atención á la publicación en la página 41—45 del catálogo principal.

2010/52	Länge / Length / Largura	32 cm	Höhe / Height / Altura	15 cm	Breite / Breadth / Anchura	13 cm
2010/53	„	36 cm	„	20 cm	„	17 cm

Limousine, hochfein in weißer Farbe ausgeführt, Gummibereifung, erstklassiges Uhrwerk mit Absteller.
Limousine, superfine finish in white colour, rubber-tyres, first class clockwork with throw-out-device.
Limousine, elegante ejecución de color blanco, neus, mecanismo de primera clase, con interruptor.

2010/89
Tractor "Fordson"

Länge / Length / Largura 15 cm
Höhe / Height / Altura $9^1/_2$ cm
Breite / Breadth / Anchura 9 cm

2010/87
Tractor

Länge / Length / Largura 21 cm
Höhe / Height / Altura 13 cm
Breite / Breadth / Anchura 13 cm

Tractor „Fordson" mit 3 Anhängern, Frachtwagen, Kultivator und Rechen.
Tractor "Fordson" with 3 coupling cars, freight-car, cultivator and rake.
Tractor "Fordson" con 3 carros acoplados, carro de flete, cultivador y rastrillo.

2010/86

Länge / Length / Largura 57 cm
Höhe / Height / Altura $9^1/_2$ cm
Breite / Breadth / Anchura $10^1/_2$ cm

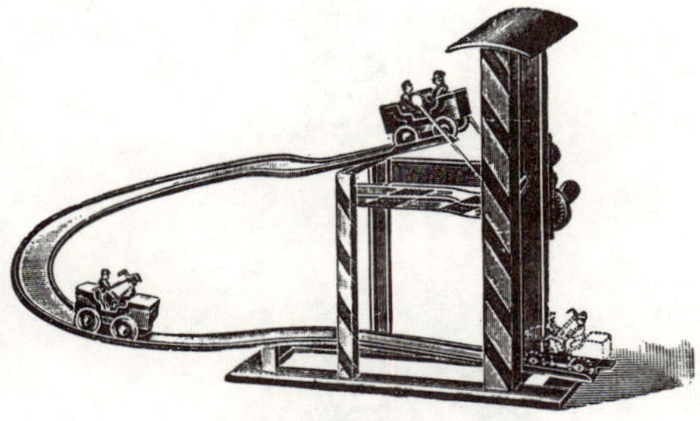

2032/5

Länge / Length / Largura 33 cm
Höhe / Height / Altura 20 cm
Breite / Breadth / Anchura 17,5 cm

Schleifenbahn mit 2 Wagen.
Looping the loop with 2 carriages.
Looping the loop con 2 carros.

2032/6

Länge / Length / Largura $23^1/_2$ cm
Höhe / Height / Altura 12 cm
Breite / Breadth / Anchura 10 cm

Rutschbahn mit 2 Wagen.
Slide with 2 carriages.
Deslizadero ó montaña rusa con 2 carros.

2032/7

Länge / Length / Largura 25 cm
Höhe / Height / Altura $22^1/_2$ cm
Breite / Breadth / Anchura $8^1/_2$ cm

Bub und schreiende Katze mit Ball spielend.
Boy and mewing cat playing with ball.
Niño y gato maullando jugando con pelota.

2032/2

Länge / Length / Largura 15 cm
Höhe / Height / Altura 17 cm
Breite / Breadth / Anchura 8 cm

Laufender Mann mit selbsthebenden Beinen.
Running man with self-lifting legs.
Hombre corriendo con piernas automáticas.

2032/4

Länge / Length / Largura 16 cm
Höhe / Height / Altura 14 cm
Breite / Breadth / Anchura 6 cm

Segelboot auf Rädern, im Kreis und geradeaus fahrend.
Sailing boat on wheels, moving round about and straight forward.
Velero sobre ruedas, moviéndose circularmente y adelante.

2032/1

Kinderwagen mit schreiendem Baby.
Bassinet with crying baby.
Coche de niños con bebé gritando.

Länge / Length / Largura 17 cm
Höhe / Height / Altura 14 cm
Breite / Breadth / Anchura 6 cm

2032/3

Ruderboot, schaukelnd.
Rowing-boat, rocking.
Bote de remos, balanceando.

Länge / Length / Largura 15 cm
Höhe / Height / Altura 10 cm
Breite / Breadth / Anchura $6^1/_2$ cm

Beachten Sie auch die Veröffentlichung auf Seite 41—45 des Hauptkataloges.

Please note also the publication on page 52 and 53 of the principal catalogue.
Llamamos también su atención á la publicación en la página 52 y 53 del catálogo principal.

Uhrwerkeisenbahnen, solide Ausführung, Werk mit Regulator und Bremse. — Clockwork railways, solid make, work with regulator and brake.
Ferrocarriles con mecanismo, ejecución sólida, mecanismo con regulador y freno.

Spurweite / Gauge / Anchura de la via **0** = 35 mm = $1^1/_4$ inch. **I** = 48 mm = $1^3/_4$ inch.

2012/120 Lokomotive, Tender, 1 Wagen, 4 runde, 2 gerade Schienen, Spur 0.
Locomotive-engine, tender, 1 carriage, 4 round, 2 straight rails, gauge 0.
Locomotora, tender 1 carro, 4 railes redondos y 2 derechos, via 0.

2012/121 Lokomotive, Tender, 2 Wagen, 4 runde, 2 gerade Schienen Spur 0.
Locomotive-engine, tender, 2 carriages, 4 round, 2 straight rails, gauge 0.
Locomotora, tender, 2 carros redondos y 2 derechos, via 0.

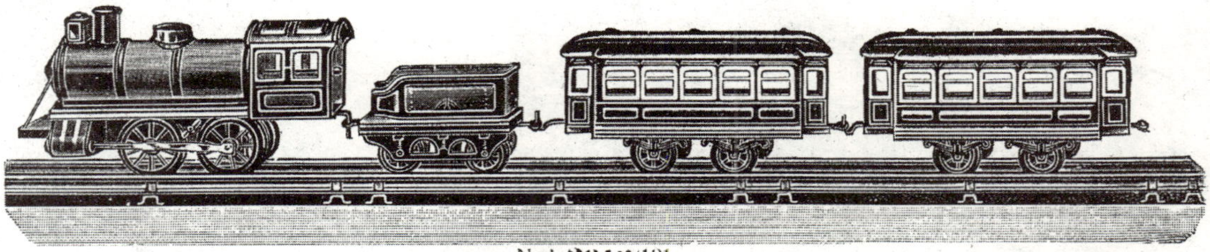

No. **2012**/121

2012/122 Lokomotive, Tender, 1 Wagen, 4 runde weiße Schienen, mit Bremse.
Locomotive-engine, tender, 1 carriage, 4 round white rails, with brake.
Locomotora, tender, 1 carro, 4 railes redondos blancos, con freno.

2012/123 Wie **2012**/122, mit 2 Wagen.
Like **2012**/122, with 2 carriages.
Como **2012**/122, con 2 carros.

No. **2012**/123

Überraschungszüge.
What's a matter-trains. — Trenes ¿qué pasa?

2012/64 Spurweite / Gauge / Anchura de la via 0.
Nach einer kurzen Fahrt hält der Zug, der Lokomotivführer schaut heraus, um nach dem Verkehrshindernis zu suchen. Nach einer Weile geht er wieder zurück, und der Zug fährt weiter.
After a short passage the train stops, the conductor looks out, to seek the cause of obstruction. After a while he retires again and the train proceeds.
Depués de un corto trayecto el tren pára, el conductor mira afuera, para examinar la causa del estorbo. Pasado un trecho él se retira y el tren continúa su viaje.

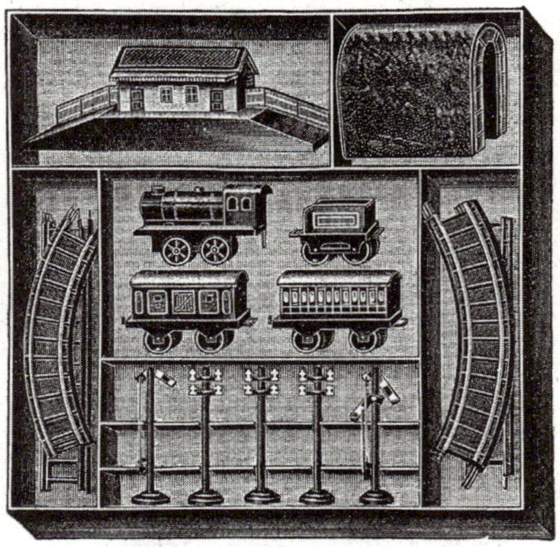

2012/124
Größe des Kartons / Size of the box / Tamaño de la cajita: 34 × 36,5 cm

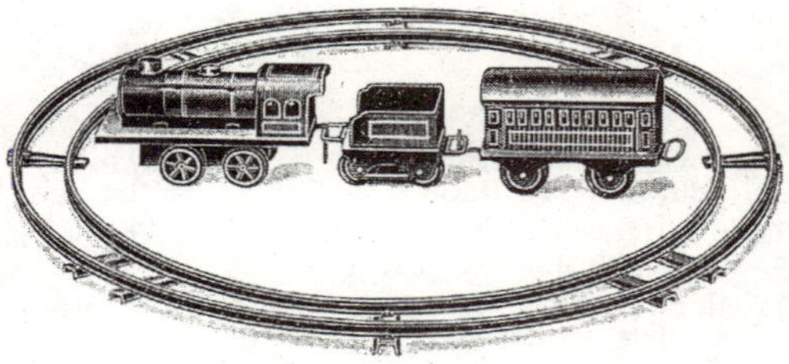

2012/87
Mit 1 Wagen.
With 1 carriage.
Con 1 carro.

2012/88
Mit 2 Wagen.
With 2 carriages.
Con 2 carros.

2012/78
Offenes Automobil, 24 cm lang, vor- und rückwärts laufend, mit Bremse, Kühler, Laternen vernickelt.
Open motor-car, 24 cm long, running forward and backward, with brake, cooler and lanterns nickeled.
Automóvil, abierto, 24 cm de largo, corriendo a delante y atrás, con freno, refrigerador y linternas niquelados.

No. **2012**/126
Höhe / Height / Altura
27 cm

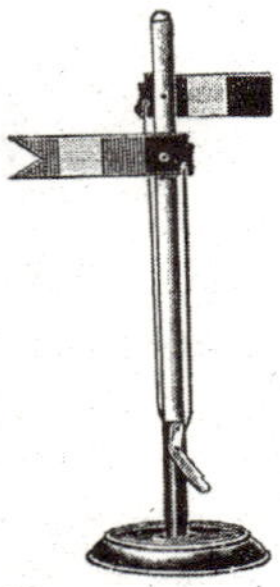

No. **2012**/127
Höhe / Height / Altura
24 cm

2012/55
Höhe / Height / Altura = $23^1/_2$ cm

2012/125
Mit echten Gummirädern.
With real, rubber-tyres.
Con neumáticos verdaderos.

No. **2012**/128

No. **2012**/128
Offenes Automobil in ff. Ausführung, mit Reserverad und Figur, 17 cm lang.
Open motor-car in very fine finish, with spare wheel and figure, 17 cm long.
Automóvil, abierto, primorosamente acabado, con rueda de repuesto y figura, 17 cm de largo.

No. **2012**/76
Limousine mit Reserverad und Figur, ff. Ausführung.
Limousine with spare-wheel and figure, very fine finish.
Limousine con rueda de repuesto y figura, ejecución extrafina.

Länge / Length / Largura 20 cm.

No. **2012**/76

Beachten Sie auch die Veröffentlichung auf Seite 52 und 53 des Hauptkataloges.

Please note also the publication on page 26 of the principal catalogue.
Llamamos también su atención á la publicación en la página 26 del catálogo principal.

Mechanische Artikel. — Mechanical toys. — Juguetes con mecanismo.

2014/29 P = 1/3 Dtz., doz., doc.

2014/27 P = 1/3 Dtz., doz., doc.

2014/26 P = 1/3 Dtz., doz., doc.

1/3 der natürlichen Größe. — 1/3 of natural size. — 1/3 del tamaño natural.

2014/31 P = 1/3 Dtz., doz., doc.

2014/24 P = 1/3 Dtz., doz., doc.

2014/19 P = 1/3 Dtz., doz., doc.

1/3 der natürlichen Größe. — 1/3 of natural size. — 1/3 del tamaño natural.

2014/18 P = 1/3 Dtz., doz., doc.

2014/32 P=1/3 Dtz., doz., doc.

2014/16 P=1/3 Dtz., doz., doc.

2014/17 P = 1/3 Dtz., doz., doc.

1/3 der natürlichen Größe. — 1/3 of natural size. — 1/3 del tamaño natural.

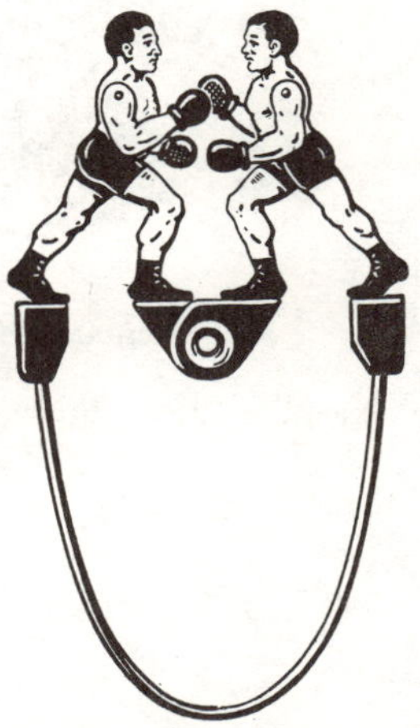

2014/20

Ohne Uhrwerk — without clockwork — sin cuerda.

P = 6 Dtz., doz., doc.

2/3 natürliche Größe.
2/3 of natural size.
2/3 del tamaño natural.

2014/7

P = 1 Dtz., doz., doc.
Ohne Uhrwerk — without clockwork — sin cuerda.
1/3 natürliche Größe — 1/3 of natural size — 1/3 del tamaño natural.

2014/34

2014/33

Sortiment / Assortment / Surtido **2014**/33
- Garage, ohne Feder.
- Rennauto a, ohne Figur.
- Omnibus c.
- Garage, without spring.
- Racing car a, without figur.
- Omnibus c.
- Garage, sin mecanismo.
- Automóvil de carreras, sin figura.
- Omnibus c.

Sortiment / Assortment / Surtido **2014**/34
- Garage, mit Feder, zum Hinausstoßen der Automobile.
- Rennauto a, mit Figur.
- Lastauto b. Omnibus c.
- Garage, with spring, to push out the automobiles.
- Racing car a, with figur.
- Motor lorry b. Omnibus c.
- Garage, con mecanismo, de echar fuera los automóviles.
- Automóvil de carreras a, con figura.
- Automóvil para cargas b. Omnibus c.

Miniatur-Straßenbahn.
Miniature tramway.
Tranvía en miniatura.

Länge / Length / Largura 28 cm
Breite / Breadth / Anchura 22 cm
Höhe / Height / Altura 9 1/2 cm

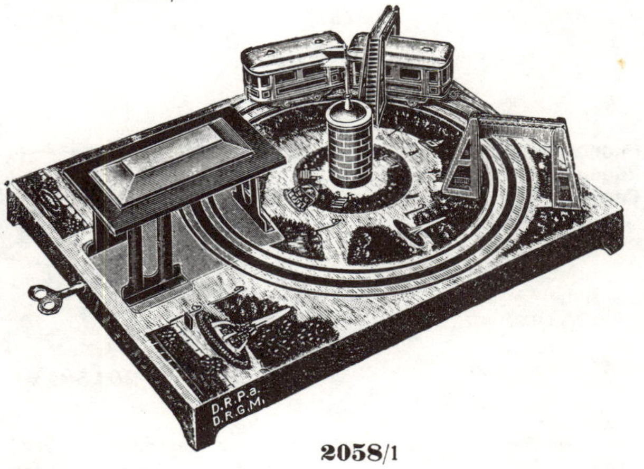

2058/1

P = Packung / Packing / Contenido.

Beachten Sie auch die Veröffentlichung auf Seite 26 des Hauptkataloges.

Please note also the publication on page 34—36 of the principal catalogue.
Llamamos también su atención á la publicación en la página 34—36 del catálogo principal.

Mechanische Blechspielwaren. — Mechanical tin toys. — Juguetes de lata con mecanismo.

**Henne mit 2 Küken. — Hen with 2 chickens.
Gallina con 2 pollitos.**

Länge = 14 cm, Breite = 5 cm, Höhe = 10 cm, P = $^{1}/_{2}$ Dtz., doz., doc.

2015/55'∗

Länge = $14^{1}/_{2}$ cm, Breite = $14^{1}/_{2}$ cm, Höhe = 11 cm, P = $^{1}/_{12}$ Dtz., doz., doc.

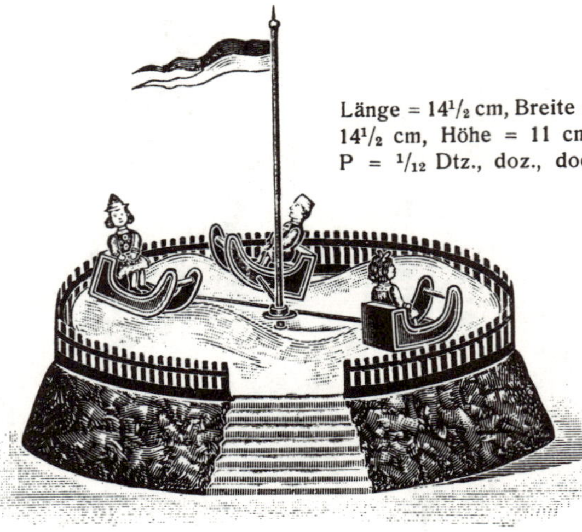

2015/56 ∗

Rutschbahn. — Slide. — Deslizadero.

Länge = 24 cm, Breite = 10 cm, Höhe = 15 cm, P = $^{1}/_{12}$ Dtz., doz., doc

2015/57 ∗

2015/47 ∗

**Schleuderbahn „The Wip". — Swinging career "The Wip".
Carrera lanzadora "The Wip".**

Länge = 22 cm, Breite = $21^{1}/_{2}$ cm, Höhe = $7^{1}/_{2}$ cm, P = $^{1}/_{12}$ Dtz., doz., doc.

2015/58 ○

**Henne mit Küken. — Hen with chicken.
Gallina con pollito.**

Länge = $19^{1}/_{2}$ cm, Breite = $5^{1}/_{2}$ cm, Höhe = 9 cm, P = $^{1}/_{12}$ Dtz., doz., doc.

Zirkus. — Circus. — Circo.

Länge = $16^{1}/_{2}$ cm, Breite = $9^{1}/_{2}$ cm, Höhe = 15 cm, P = $^{1}/_{12}$ Dtz., doz., doc.

2015/59 ∗

**Ente mit Frosch.
Duck with frog.
Pato con rana.**

Länge = 23 cm, Breite = $5^{1}/_{2}$ cm, Höhe = 13 cm. P = $^{1}/_{12}$ Dtz., doz., doc.

2015/60 ∗

**Pudelwagen mit Pferd.
Poodle car with horse.
Carro de perro de agua con caballo.**

Länge = 19 cm, Breite = 5 cm, Höhe = 8 cm, P = $^{1}/_{2}$ Dtz., doz., doc.

2015/49 ∗

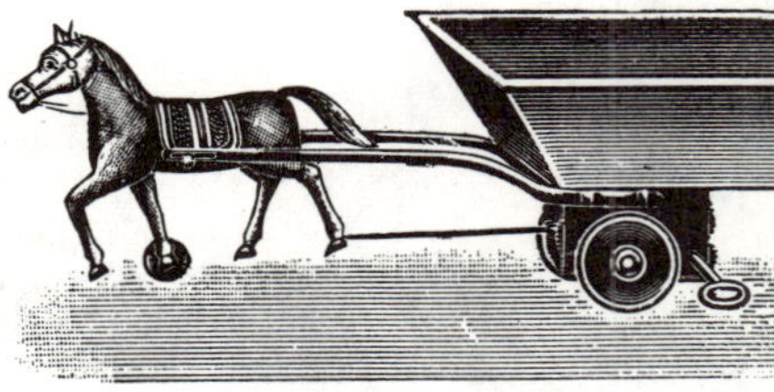

2015/65 ○

Wagen mit beweglichem Pferd. — Car with moveable horse. — Carro con caballo movible.

Länge = 24 cm, Breite = $7^{1}/_{2}$ cm, Höhe = 8 cm, P = $^{1}/_{2}$ Dtz., doz., doc.

∗ = Mit Uhrwerk / with clockwork / con mecanismo de reloj. ○ = Mit Spiralfeder / with spiral spring / con espiral. P = Packung — Packing — Contenido.
Länge = Length — Largura. Breite = Breadth — Anchura. Höhe = Height — Altura

Beachten Sie auch die Veröffentlichung auf Seite 34—36 des Hauptkataloges.

Please note also the publication on page 34—36 of the principal catalogue.
Llamamos también su atención á la publicación en la página 34—36 del catálogo principal.

Mechanische Blechspielwaren. — Mechanical tin toys. — Juguetes de lata con mecanismo.

Feuerwehrauto mit Dampfkessel und Glocke. — Fire-brigade motor-car with boiler and bell. — Automóvil á bomberos con caldera y campana.

2015/41 ○
Länge = 25 cm, Breite = $9^{1}/_{2}$ cm, Höhe = 15 cm, P = $^{1}/_{12}$ Dtz., doz., doc.

2015/61 ○
Länge = 21 cm, Breite = $8^{1}/_{2}$ cm, Höhe = 7 cm, P = $^{1}/_{12}$ Dtz., doz., doc.

Negerwagen mit Uhrwerk. Nigger-cart. — Carro de negro.
Länge = 17 cm, Breite = 6 cm, Höhe = $10^{1}/_{2}$ cm, P = $^{1}/_{2}$ Dtz., doz., doc.

2015/50 ∗

Feuerwehrauto mit Leiter und Glocke.
Fire-brigade motor car with ladder and bell.
Automóvil á bomberos con escala y campana.

Länge = 28 cm,
Breite = $9^{1}/_{2}$ cm,
Höhe = 18 cm,
P = $^{1}/_{12}$ Dtz., doz., doc.

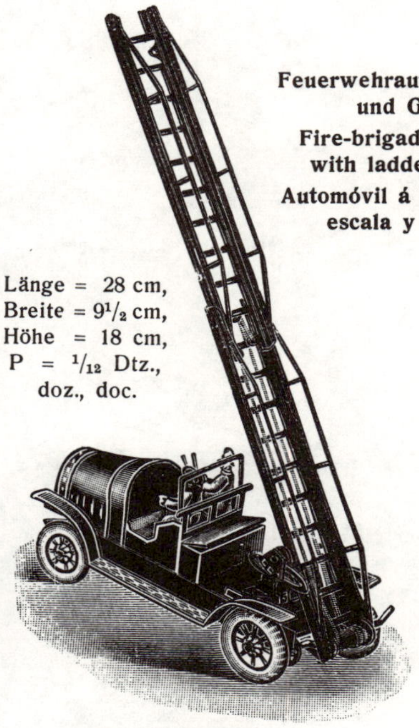

2015/40 ○

Fäßchen mit Neger. — Barrel with nigger. Barril con negro.

2015/46 ∗
Länge = $18^{1}/_{2}$ cm, Breite = 8 cm, Höhe = 7 cm, P = $^{1}/_{12}$ Dtz., doz., doc.

Zeppelin. — Zeppelin-airship. Zeppelin máquina aerostática.

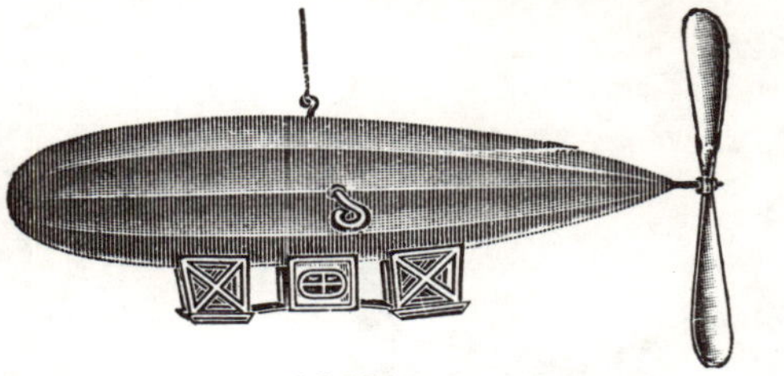

2015/43 ∗
Länge = 19 cm, Breite = $3^{1}/_{2}$ cm, Höhe = $5^{1}/_{2}$ cm, P = $^{1}/_{2}$ Dtz., doz., doc.

Ohne Uhrwerk. — Without mechanic. — Sin mecanismo.

2015/45
Länge = 7 cm,
Breite = 6 cm,
Höhe = $1^{1}/_{2}$ cm,
P = 3 Dtz., doz., doc.

Pistole, schwarz lackiert, mit Gummipfeil auf Bärenkarte, in Kartons verpackt.
Pistol, black varnished, with rubber dart on bear's cart.
Pistola, barnizada negro, con flecha de goma sobre tarjeta con oso.

2015/62
Kartengröße / Size of card / Tamaño de tarjeta } $18^{1}/_{2} \times 13$ cm
P = 1 Dtz., doz., doz.

Wie 2015/62, aber auf Indianerkarte. — Same as 2015/62 but on Indian's card. — La mismo que 2015/62, mas sobre tarjeta con indio.

2015/63
Kartengröße / Size of card / Tamaño de tarjeta } 30 × 14 cm
P = 1 Dtz., doz., doc.

2015/64
Kartongröße / Size of hand-box / Tamaño de la cajita de cartón } $20^{1}/_{2} \times 19^{1}/_{2} \times 2^{1}/_{4}$ cm
P = $^{1}/_{12}$ Dtz., doz., doc.

∗ = Mit Uhrwerk / with clockwork / con mecanismo de reloj. ○ = Mit Spiralfeder / with spiral spring / con espiral. P = Packung — Packing — Contenido.
Länge = Length — Largura. Breite = Breadth — Anchura. Höhe = Height — Altura.

Beachten Sie auch die Veröffentlichung auf Seite 34—36 des Hauptkataloges.

Mechanische Artikel. — Mechanical toys. — Juguetes con mecanismo.

2057/8 31×14 cm. P = 1/2 Dtz., doz., doc.

2057/9 15,8×29 cm. P = 1/12 Dtz.

2057/11 25×21 cm. P = 1/2 Dtz., doz., doc.

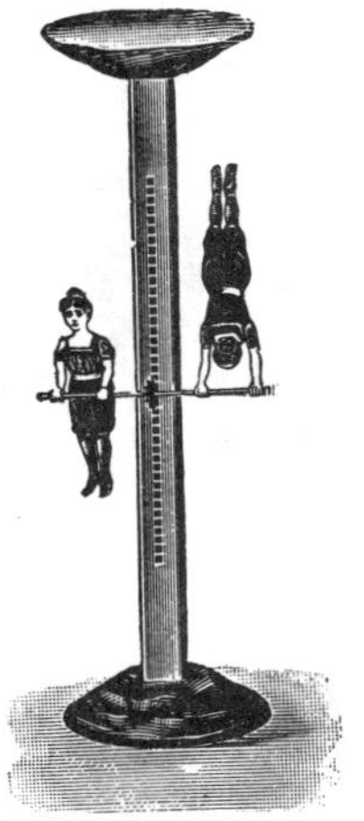

2057/12 8 ×27 cm.
P = 1 Dtz., doz., doc.

Ohne Uhrwerk. — Without clockwork,
Sin cuerda.

2057/13 4,2×14,5 cm.
P = 1 Dtz., doz., doc.

2057/14 13×7,5 cm.
P = 1 Dtz., doz., doc.

2057/15 12,5×9 cm.
P = 1 Dtz., doz., doc.

2057/16 13,5×9,5 cm.
P = 1 Dtz., doz., doc.

2057/17 11,2×9 cm.
P = 1 Dtz., doz., doc.

P = Packung — Packing — Contenido.

2057/21 14×9,5 cm. P=1Dtz.,doz.,doc. **2057**/19 14×8 cm. P=1Dtz.,doz.,doc.
Ohne Uhrwerk. — Without mechanic. — Sin mecanismo.

2057/10 22,5×14,5 cm. P = 1/2 Dtz.,doz.,doc.

2057/22 18×13,4 cm. P=1/2Dtz.,doz.,doc.

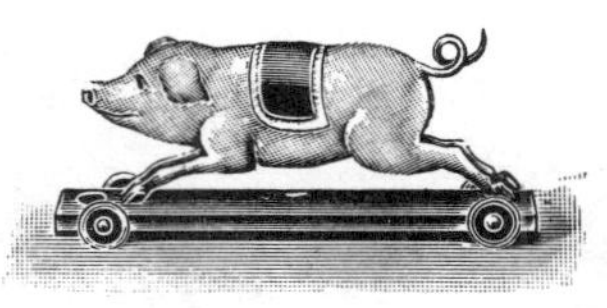

2057/18 14×7 cm. P=1Dtz.,doz.,doc.

2057/20 14×8,5 cm. P=1Dtz.,doz.,doc.

Aluminium-Spielwaren. — Puppenbestecke auf Karton.

Diese Bestecke sind auf farbige Karten aufgenäht und werden 1/2-Gros-weise im Karton verpackt geliefert. (Auch auf Wunsch 1/12 Gros in Papierpackung.) Die Größe der Bestecke No. **163**/10, 14, 20 und 22 = 9 1/2 cm.

Aluminium Toys. — Small forks, knives and spoons on cards.

These forks, knives and spoons are sewed on fancy cards and supplied packed in cardboard boxes containing 1/2 gross each. If desired they will also be supplied 1/12 gross packed in paper. Size of the forks, knives and spoons No. **163**/10, 14, 20 and 22 = 9 1/2 cm.

Juguetes de Aluminio. — Cubiertos de mesa sobre tarjetas.

Estos cubiertos de mesa son cosidos sobre tarjetas abigarradas y se suministran embalados en cajitas de cartón conteniendo 1/2 gruesa cada una. Cuando se desea pueden ser servidos también 1/12 gruesa envolvido en papel. Tamaño de los cubiertos No. **163**/10, 14, 20 y 22 = 9 1/2 cm.

163/10
7×11 cm.

163/20
9×12 cm.

163/14
7×11 cm.

163/22
9×12 cm.

Kartengröße ca. / Size of the cards abt. / Tamaño de las tarjetas unos:
No. **163**/10 und **163**/14 = 7×11 cm.
No. **163**/20 und **163**/22 = 9×12 cm.

Please note also the publication on page 18 of the principal catalogue.
Llamamos también su atención á la publicación en la página 18 del catálogo principal.

Billige Blechspielwaren ohne Uhrwerk. — Cheap tin toys without clockwork. — Juguetes baratos de lata sin mecanismo de reloj.

2018/625 P = 2 Dtz., doz., doc.

2018/980/3 P = 2 Dtz., doz., doc.

2018/626 P = 2 Dtz., doz., doc.

2018/627 P = 2 Dtz., doz., doc.

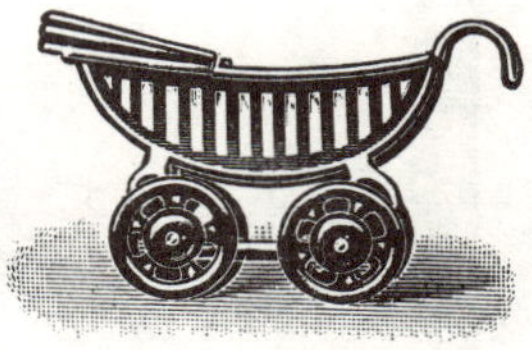

2018/624 P=2Dtz.,doz.,doc.

2018/623 P = 2 Dtz., doz., doc.

2018/304 P = 2 Dtz., doz., doc.

2018/305 P = 2 Dtz., doz., doc.

2018/306 P = 2 Dtz., doz., doc.

2018/615 P = 2 Dtz., doz., doc.

2018/944 P = 2 Dtz., doz., doc.

2018/622/1 P = 2 Dtz., doz., doc.
2018/622 auf Rädern — on wheels sobre ruedas.

2018/618 P = 2 Dtz., doz., doc.

2018/616 P = 2 Dtz., doz., doc.

2018/619 P = 2 Dtz., doz., doc.

2018/628 P = 2 Dtz., doz., doc.

2018/567 P=2Dtz.,doz.,doc.

Mit Uhrwerk.
With clockwork.
Con mecanismo.

2018/616 W
2018/618 W
2018/619 W
2018/620 W
2018/621 W

2018/592/1 P = 1 Dtz., doz., doc.

2018/620 P = 1 Dtz., doz., doc.

2018/621 P = 1 Dtz., doz., doc.

2018/629 P = 1 Dtz., doz., doc.

½ natürliche Größe. — ½ of natural size. — ½ del tamaño natural.

P = Packung / Packing / Contenido.

Beachten Sie auch die Veröffentlichung auf Seite 18 des Hauptkataloges.

Please note also the publication on page 2 and 3 of the principal catalogue.
Llamamos también su atención á la publicación en la página 2 y 3 del catálogo principal.

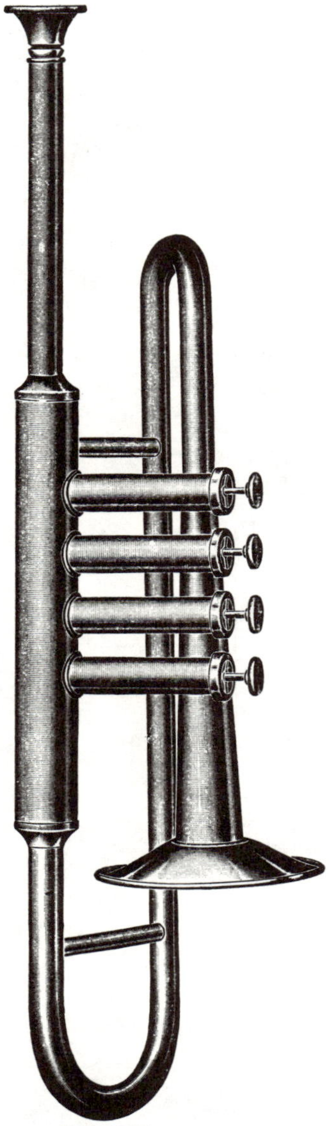

36/1905/4

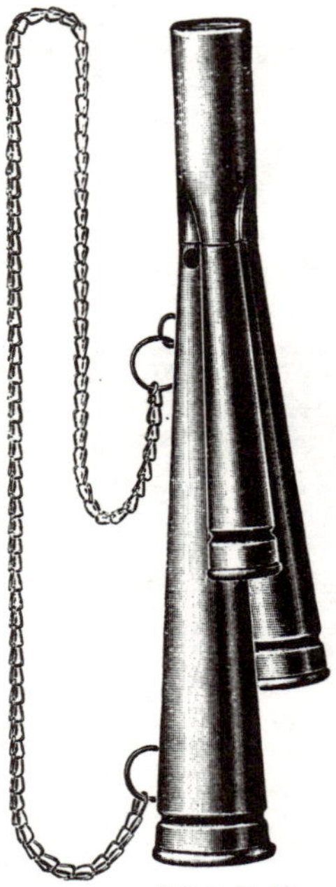

36/1721 K

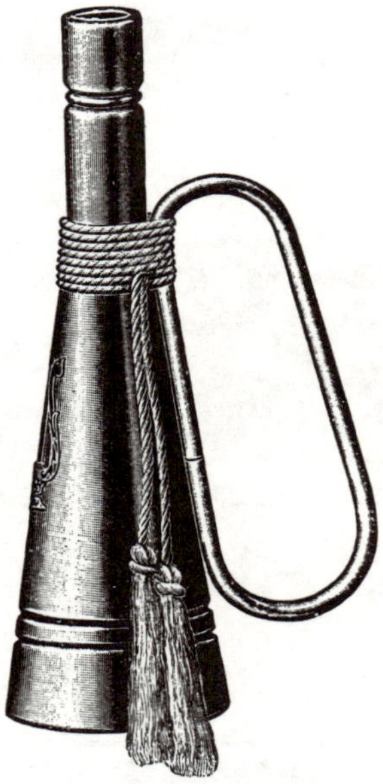

36/1898

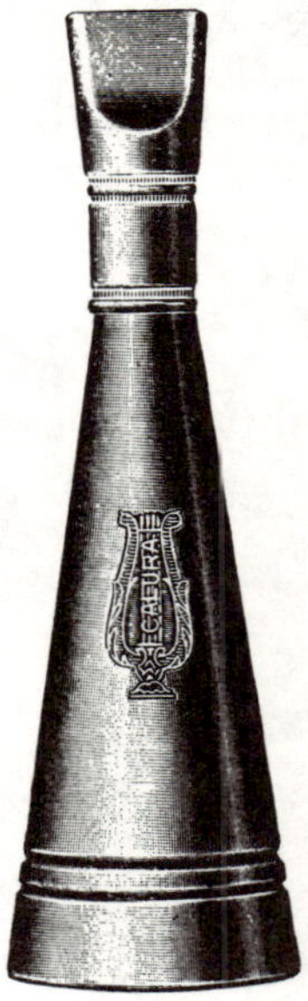

36/1896 o. R.

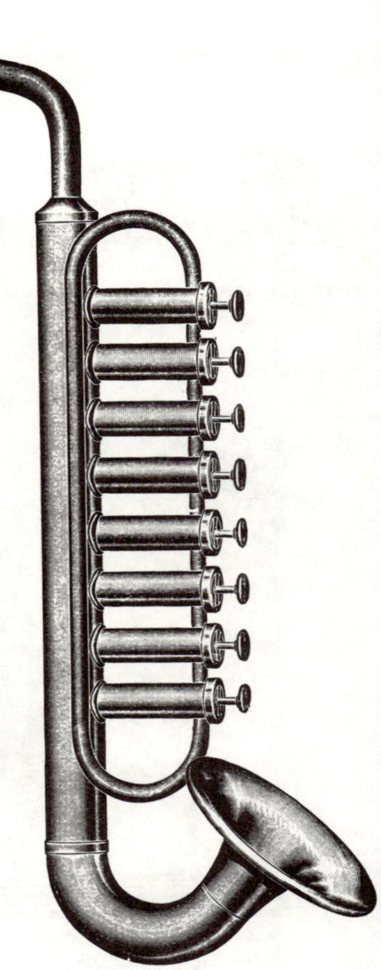

36/1909/8

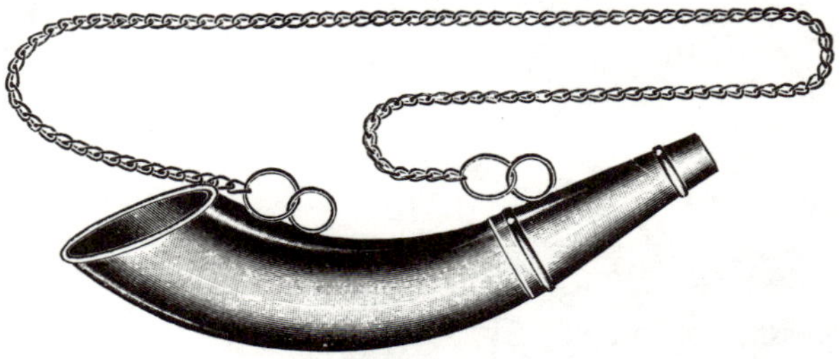

36/1907 K

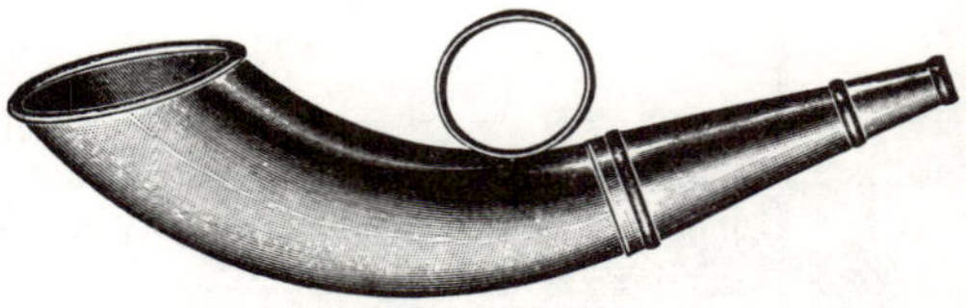

36/1907

No. **36**/1905/4 **Posaune** aus Nickelblech, mit feststehenden Rohren.
Trombone of nickelplate, with fast tubes.
Sacabuche de hoja de niquel, con tubos fijos.

Die Posaunen werden auch mit 6 und 8 Tönen geliefert.
The trombones are also supplied with 6 and 8 tones.
Los sacabuches son también suministrados con 6 y 8 tonos.

No. **36**/1721 K **Dreiklanghupe** mit 40 cm langer Kette.
Three-toned horn with chain of 40 cm length.
Cuerno de tres tonos con cadena de 40 cm de largo.

No. **36**/1898 **Hupen-Trompete,** 2 tönig, mit farbiger Quaste.
Signal-trumpet, double-toned, with coloured tassel.
Trompeta de señal, de tono doble, con borla de color.

No. **36**/1896 o. R. **Sirenenhupe** aus Nickelzink, besonders laut tönend.
Siren of nickelzinc, of specially loud tone.
Sirena de niquel-zinco, de voz muy alta.

No. **36**/1909/8 **Saxophon** aus Nickelblech, 8 tönig.
Saxophone of nickelplate, 8 tones.
Saxofone de hoja de niquel, 8 tonos

Der Artikel wird auch mit 4 und 6 Tönen geliefert.
The article is also supplied with 4 and 6 tones.
El artículo es también suministrado con 4 y 6 tonos.

No. **36**/1909 1/2 Derselbe Artikel in Weißblech, ohne Bügel.
The same article in tin-plate, without bow.
El mismo artículo en hojalata, sin arco.

No. **36**/1907 **Jagdhupe,** 2 tönig, aus Nickelblech.
Bugle, 2 tones, of nickelplate.
Corneta de monte, 2 tonos, de hoja de niquel.

No. **36**/1907 K **Jagdhupe,** 2tönig, aus Nickelblech, mit Kette
Bugle, 2 tones, of nickelplate, with chain.
Corneta de monte, 2 tonos, de hoja de niquel, con cadena.

1/2 natürl. Größe. 1/2 of nat. size. 1/2 del tamaño natural.

Beachten Sie auch die Veröffentlichung auf Seite 2 und 3 des Hauptkataloges.

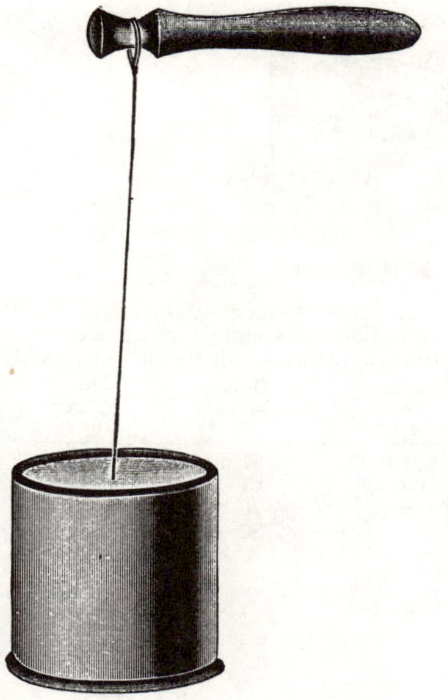

36/1707

36/1737

36/1845 $^1/_2$

36/1643

36/1767

36/1704

36/1682

36/1056

36/1603

36/607 o. R.

36/1885/1

36/1885/18 S.

36/1885/19

36/1886

36/1891/4

No. **36**/1707 — **Waldteufel** (Lärmartikel) aus lackiertem Blech.
Rattle (noisy article) of varnished tinplate.
Matraca (artículo ruidoso) de hojalata barnizada.

No. **36**/1737 — **Hupe** aus lackiertem Blech, mit Hahnenstimme.
Signal-horn of varnished tinplate, with cock's voice.
Cuerno de señal de hojalata barnizada, con voz de gallo.

No. **36**/1845 $^1/_2$ — **Sirenenpfeife** aus Weißblech.
Siren-whistle of tinplate.
Silbato de sirena, de hojalata.

No. **36**/1643 — **Sirenenpfeife** aus Nickelzink.
Siren-whistle of nickelzinc.
Silbato de sirena, de zinc niquelado.

No. **36**/1767 — **Trillerpfeife,** vernickelt.
Trill-whistle, nickeled
Silbato de trino, niquelado.

No. **36**/1704 — **Dreiklangpfeife** aus Weißblech.
Three-tone-whistle of tinplate.
Silbato de tres tonos, de hojalata.

No. **36**/1682 — **Kugel-Trillerpfeife** aus Weißblech.
Spherical trill-whistle of tinplate.
Silbato de trino esférico, de hojalata.

No. **36**/1056 — **Hexenkugel** mit Watte- oder Zelluloid-Ball.
Hag's globe with wadding- or celluloid-ball.
Globo de bruja con pelota de celoloide o algodón.

No. **36**/1603 — **Fanfare** (Singschalmei) aus Aluminium.
Fanfare (Singing shawm) of aluminium.
Fanfarra (zampoña de canto) de aluminio.

No. **36**/607 o. R. — **Sirenenhupe** aus Nickelzink.
Siren-horn of nickelzinc.
Corneta de sirena, de zinc niquelado.

No. **36**/1886 — **Sirenenhupe** aus Nickelzink (einfach).
Siren-horn of nickelzinc (plain).
Corneta de sirena, de zinc niquelado (simple).

No. **36**/1885/1 — **Trillerpfeife** aus Galalith (Kunsthorn), schwarz.
Trill-whistle of galalithe (artificial horn), black.
Silbato de trino, de galalite (cuerno artificial), negro.

No. **36**/1885/18 S — **Trillerpfeife** aus farbigem Galalith, mit Schnur.
Trill-whistle of coloured galalithe, with cord.
Silbato de trino, de galalite colorado, con cuerda.

No. **36**/1885/19 — **Feuerwehr-Pfeife** mit Loch, aus farbigem Galalith.
Fire-brigade's whistle with hole, of coloured galalithe.
Silbato de bombero con agujero, de galalite colorado.

No. **36**/1891/4 — **Zweiklangflöte** (Zauberflöte), schwarz lackiert, mit Goldverzierung.
Double flute (magic flute), black varnished, with gold adornments.
Flauta doble (flauta mágica), barnizada negro, con adornos de oro.

$^1/_2$ natürl. Größe. $^1/_2$ of nat. size. $^1/_2$ del tamaño natural.

Please note also the publication on page 4—13 of the principal catalogue.
Llamamos también su atención á la publicación en la página 4—13 del catálogo principal.

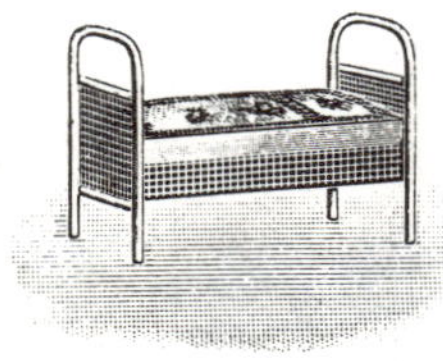

139/811/2

139/1005/14

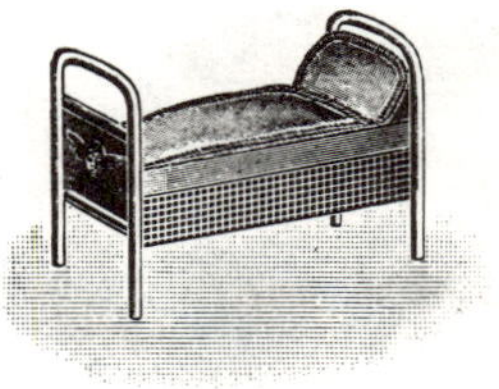

139/1001/14

Betten, weiß lackiert, garniert.
Beds, varnished white, garnished.
Camas, embarnizadas de color blanco, con guarnición.

	Länge Length Largura	Breite Breadth Anchura	Höhe Height Altura
No. **139**/811/1	120 mm	70 mm	100 mm
„ **139**/811/2	135 „	75 „	105 „
„ **139**/811/3	160 „	85 „	110 „
„ **139**/811/4	185 „	95 „	120 „
„ **139**/811/5	215 „	105 „	130 „

Betten, leer, Goldblech.
Beds, without fittings, plate of gold.
Camas, vacías, de chapa de oro.

	Länge Length Largura	Breite Breadth Anchura	Höhe Height Altura
No. **139**/1005/11	92 mm	57 mm	75 mm
„ **139**/1005/12	108 „	61 „	85 „
„ **139**/1005/13	118 „	70 „	100 „
„ **139**/1005/14	132 „	80 „	103 „

Betten, goldbronziert, mit hochfeiner Seidenbatistgarnitur.
Beds, gold-bronzed, with superfine silk-cambric garniture.
Camas, bronceadas oro, con elegante guarnición de batista de seda.

	Länge Length Largura	Breite Breadth Anchura	Höhe Height Altura
No. **139**/1001/11	92 mm	57 mm	75 mm
„ **139**/1001/12	108 „	61 „	85 „
„ **139**/1001/13	118 „	70 „	100 „
„ **139**/1001/14	132 „	80 „	103 „

139/812/4

Betten, weiß lackiert, garniert mit Himmel (Höhe ohne Himmel gemessen).
Beds, varnished white, garnished with tester (height measured without tester).
Camas, embarnizadas de color blanco, con cielo y guarnición (altura sin cielo).

	Länge Length Largura	Breite Breadth Anchura	Höhe Height Altura
No. **139**/812/1	120 mm	70 mm	100 mm
„ **139**/812/2	135 „	75 „	105 „
„ **139**/812/3	160 „	85 „	110 „
„ **139**/812/4	185 „	95 „	120 „
„ **139**/812/5	215 „	105 „	130 „

139/815/3

Betten, goldbronziert, mit hochfeiner Seidenbatistgarnitur, mit Himmel (Höhe ohne Himmel gemessen).
Beds, gold-bronzed, with superfine silk-cambric garniture, with tester (height measured without tester).
Camas, bronceadas oro, con elegante guarnición de batista de seda, con cielo (altura medida sin cielo).

	Länge Length Largura	Breite Breadth Anchura	Höhe Height Altura
No. **139**/815/0	110 mm	63 mm	95 mm
„ **139**/815/1	130 „	70 „	110 „
„ **139**/815/2	150 „	85 „	130 „
„ **139**/815/3	170 „	95 „	145 „
„ **139**/815/4	200 „	105 „	155 „
„ **139**/815/5	220 „	117 „	175 „
„ **139**/815/6	240 „	130 „	205 „

139/814/2

139/1002/12

Betten, goldbronziert mit hochfeiner Seidenbatistgarnitur.
Beds, gold-bronzed, with superfine silk-cambric garniture.
Camas, bronceadas oro, con elegante guarnición de batista de seda.

	Länge Length Largura	Breite Breadth Anchura	Höhe Height Altura
No. **139**/814/0	110 mm	63 mm	95 mm
„ **139**/814/1	130 „	70 „	110 „
„ **139**/814/2	150 „	85 „	130 „
„ **139**/814/3	170 „	95 „	145 „
„ **139**/814/4	200 „	105 „	155 „
„ **139**/814/5	220 „	117 „	175 „
„ **139**/814/6	240 „	130 „	205 „

Betten, goldbronziert, mit hochfeiner Seidenbatistgarnitur, mit Himmel (Höhe ohne Himmel gemessen)
Beds, gold-bronzed, with superfine silk-cambric garniture, with tester (hight measured without tester).
Camas, bronceadas oro, con elegante guarnición de batista de seda, con cielo (altura medida sin cielo).

	Länge Length Largura	Breite Breadth Anchura	Höhe Height Altura
No. **139**/1002/11	92 mm	57 mm	75 mm
„ **139**/1002/12	108 „	61 „	85 „
„ **139**/1002/13	118 „	70 „	100 „
„ **139**/1002/14	132 „	80 „	103 „

Brunnen, hochfein lackiert, mit Eimer.
Fountains, superfine varnished, with pail.
Pozos, elegantemente embarnizados, con balde.

	Bodendurchmesser Diameter of bottom Diámetro del fondo	Höhe Height Altura
No. **139**/91/4	80 mm	180 mm
„ **139**/91/5	90 „	200 „
„ **139**/91/6	100 „	220 „
„ **139**/91/7	110 „	235 „
„ **139**/91/8	130 „	255 „

139/91/6

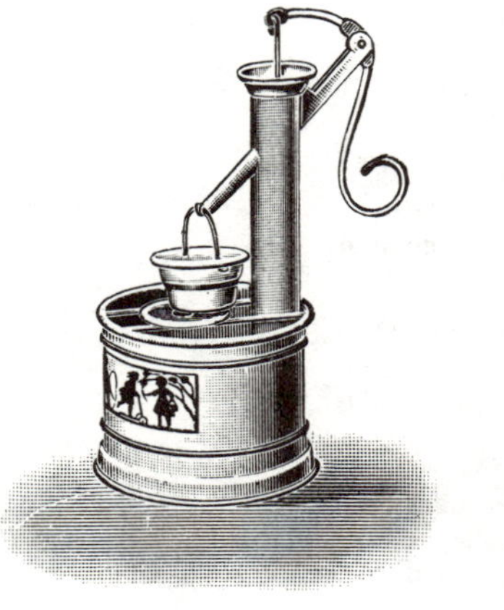

139/92/7

Brunnen, weiß lackiert, mit Bildern.
Fountains, white varnished, with pictures.
Pozos, embarnizados de color blanco, con estampas.

	Bodendurchmesser Diameter of bottom Diámetro del fondo	Höhe Height Altura
No. **139**/92/4	80 mm	180 mm
„ **139**/92/5	90 „	200 „
„ **139**/92/6	100 „	220 „
„ **139**/92/7	110 „	235 „
„ **139**/92/8	130 „	255 „

Beachten Sie auch die Veröffentlichung auf Seite 4—13 des Hauptkataloges.

Please note also the publication on page 4—13 of the principal catalogue.
Llamamos también su atención á la publicación en la página 4—13 del catálogo principal.

Puppengarnituren
in Kartons aufgenäht, in einfacher Ausführung.
Dolls' sets
in cardboard boxes sewed on, in simple finish.
Juegos de muñecas
fijadas en cajas de cartón, tipos sencillos.

No. **139**/800/1 Sp. Kartongröße 210×180×60 mm, mit Badewanne, Puppenwagen, Bett.
Size of cardboard boxes 210×180×60 mm, with bathing-tub, dolls' car, bed.
Tamaño de las cajitas 210×180×60 mm, con bañera, coche para muñeca y cama.

No. **139**/800/2 Sp. Kartongröße 280×240×60 mm, mit Badewanne, Puppenwagen, Bett, Waschtisch.
Size of cardboard boxes 280×240×60 mm, with bathing-tub, dolls' car, bed, washstand.
Tamaño de las cajitas 280×240×60 mm, con bañera, coche para muñeca, cama y lavatorio.

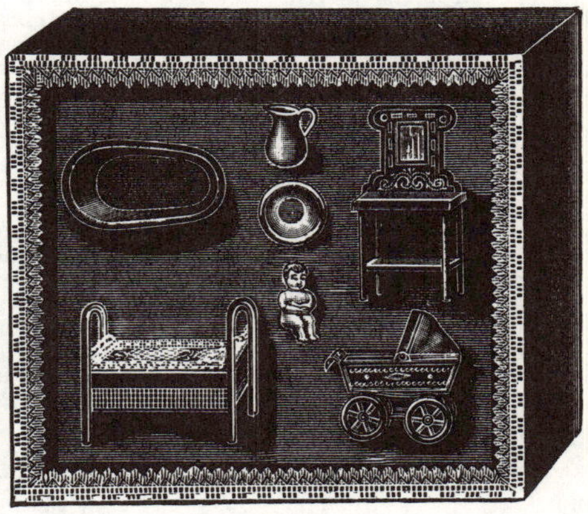

139/800/2 Sp

Puppengarnituren
in hochfein lackierter Ausführung.
Dolls' sets
in superfine varnished finish.
Juegos de muñecas
elegantemente embarnizadas.

No. **139**/801/2½. Kartongröße 305×270×60 mm, mit Badewanne, Puppenwagen, Bett, Waschtisch.
Size of cardboard boxes 305×270×60 mm, with bathing-tub, dolls' car, bed, washstand.
Tamaño de las cajitas 305×270×60 mm, con bañera, coche para muñeca, cama y lavatorio.

139/845/1

Puppenwagen in hochfein lackierter Ausführung, mit Seidendach und Spitzen. — **Dolls' cars** in superfine varnished finish, with silk shade and lace. — **Coches para muñecas,** elegantemente embarnizados, con cubierta de seda y encajes.

No.	Kastenlänge / Length of chest / Largura de caja	Kastenbreite / Breadth of chest / Anchura de caja	Gesamthöhe (ohne Dach) / Total height (without shade) / Altura total (sin cubierta)
No. **139**/845/1	110 mm	56 mm	100 mm
„ **139**/845/2	130 „	65 „	110 „
„ **139**/845/3	150 „	80 „	125 „
„ **139**/845/4	165 „	75 „	150 „
„ **139**/845/5	190 „	80 „	175 „

139/709/2

Waschtische, weiß lackiert, mit Spiegel und Krug.

Washstands, varnished white, with looking-glass and jug.

Lavatorios, embarnizados blanco, con espejo y vaso.

No.		Schüsseldurchmesser / Diameter of vessel / Diámetro del vaso	Höhe / Height / Altura
No. **139**/709/1		63 mm	140 mm
„ **139**/709/2		75 „	155 „
„ **139**/709/3	mit Eimer / with pail / con cubo	80 „	175 „

139/846/2

Puppenwagen, fein lackiert, mit beweglichem Dach. — **Dolls' cars,** finely varnished, with moveable shade. — **Coches para muñecas,** finamente embarnizados, con cubierta movible.

No.	Kastenlänge / Length of chest / Largura de caja	Kastenbreite / Breadth of chest / Anchura de caja	Gesamthöhe (ohne Dach) / Total height (without shade) / Altura total (sin cubierta)
No. **139**/846/1	110 mm	55 mm	100 mm
„ **139**/846/2	130 „	65 „	110 „
„ **139**/846/3	150 „	80 „	125 „

Laufreifen mit lackierten, massiven Doppelrädern, vernickelten Stahlglocken, Pappsteckenpferd.

Rollers with varnished, solid double wheels, nickeled steel bells, cock horse of pastework.

Rodadores con ruedas dobles, macizas, embarnizadas, campanillas de acero niquelado y caballito de cartón.

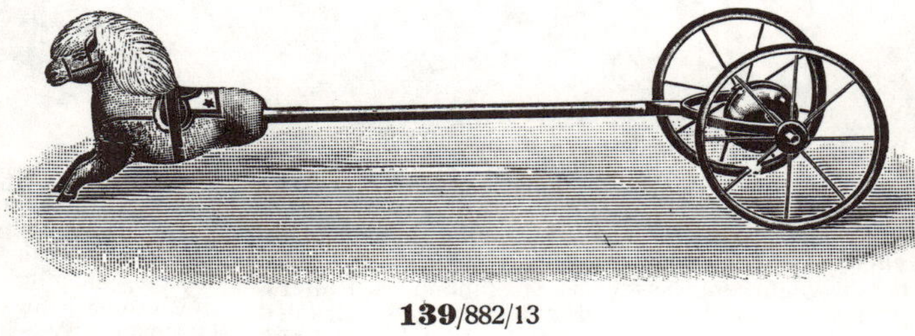

139/882/13

No.	Raddurchmesser / Diameter of wheel / Diámetro de rueda	Glockendurchmesser / Diameter of bell / Diámetro de campanilla
139/882/13	130 mm	50 mm
139/882/14	140 „	55 „
139/882/16	160 „	60 „
139/882/17	170 „	65 „
139/882/19	190 „	70 „
139/882/21	210 „	75 „
139/882/24	240 „	80 „

Roller, bespannt, mit lackierten massiven Patenträdern, vernickelten Stahlglocken, mit ausspannbaren, hochfeinst ausgeführten Hunden (Jagdhunden und Bulldoggen), D. R. G. M.

Rollers, with team, with varnished solid patented wheels, nickeled bells, with superfine executed dogs, to be unharnessed (sporting dog and bulldog), D. R. G. M. (protected by German law).

Rodadores, uñidos, con ruedas macizas patentadas embarnizadas, campanillas de acero niquelado y perros (perros de caza y dogos) de primera calidad, quitables del vehículo, D. R. G. M. (protegido por ley alemana).

139/938/17

No.	Raddurchmesser / Diameter of wheel / Diámetro de rueda	Glockendurchmesser / Diameter of bell / Diámetro de campanilla	Länge / Length / Largura
No. **139**/938/13	130 mm	50 mm	300 mm
„ **139**/938/14	140 „	55 „	310 „
„ **139**/938/16	160 „	60 „	370 „
„ **139**/938/17	170 „	65 „	400 „
„ **139**/938/19	190 „	70 „	430 „
„ **139**/938/21	210 „	75 „	460 „
„ **139**/938/24	240 „	80 „	500 „

Beachten Sie auch die Veröffentlichung auf Seite 4—13 des Hauptkataloges.

Please note also the publication on page 4—13 of the principal catalogue.
Llamamos también su atención á la publicación en la página 4—13 del catálogo principal.

139/939/14

Roller, bespannt, mit lackierten massiven Patenträdern, vernickelten Stahlglocken, mit ausspannbaren, hochfeinst ausgeführten Katzen. D. R. G. M. — **Rollers,** with team, with varnished solid patent wheels, nickeled steel bells, with superfine executed cats, to be unharnessed. Protected by German law. — **Rodadores,** uñidos, con ruedas macizas patentadas embarnizadas, campanilla de acero niquelado, y gatas de ejecución finísima, quitables del vehículo. Protegido por ley alemana.

	Raddurchmesser	Glockendurchmesser	Länge
No. **139**/939/14	140 mm	55 mm	310 mm
„ **139**/939/17	170 „	65 „	400 „
„ **139**/939/21	210 „	75 „	460 „
„ **139**/939/24	240 „	80 „	500 „

139/945/16

Roller, bespannt, mit lackierten massiven Patenträdern, vernickelten Stahlglocken, mit hochfein ausgeführten Plüschpferden. — **Rollers,** with team, with solid varnished patent wheels, nickeled steel bells, with superfinely accomplished plush-horses. — **Rodadores,** uñidos, con ruedas patentadas macizas, embarnizadas, campanillas de acero niquelado, con caballitos de felpa, elegantemente acabados.

	Raddurchmesser	Glockendurchmesser	Länge
No. **139**/945/10½	105 mm	45 mm	240 mm
„ **139**/945/12	120 „	50 „	260 „
„ **139**/945/13	130 „	50 „	280 „
„ **139**/945/14	140 „	55 „	320 „
„ **139**/945/16	160 „	60 „	330 „
„ **139**/945/17	170 „	65 „	380 „
„ **139**/945/19	190 „	70 „	400 „
„ **139**/945/21	210 „	75 „	440 „
„ **139**/945/24	240 „	80 „	550 „

Roller, bespannt, mit lackierten massiven Patenträdern, vernickelten Stahlglocken, mit hochfein ausgeführten Hasen. — **Rollers,** with team, with solid varnished patent wheels, nickeled steel bells, with superfinely accomplished hares. — **Rodadores,** uñidos, con ruedas patentadas macizas, embarnizadas, campanillas de acero niquelado, con liebres elegantemente acabados.

139/946/14

	Raddurchmesser	Glockendurchmesser	Länge
No. **139**/946/12	120 mm	50 mm	255 mm
„ **139**/946/13	130 „	50 „	270 „
„ **139**/946/14	140 „	55 „	305 „
„ **139**/946/16	160 „	60 „	320 „
„ **139**/946/17	170 „	65 „	360 „
„ **139**/946/19	190 „	70 „	400 „
„ **139**/947/8	80 „	35 „	200 „
„ **139**/947/9	90 „	40 „	210 „
„ **139**/947/10½	105 „	45 „	235 „
„ **139**/947/12	120 „	50 „	260 „
„ **139**/947/13	130 „	50 „	285 „
„ **139**/947/14	140 „	55 „	325 „
„ **139**/947/16	160 „	60 „	360 „
„ **139**/947/17	170 „	65 „	390 „
„ **139**/947/19	190 „	70 „	410 „
„ **139**/947/21	210 „	75 „	460 „

139/947/14

Roller, bespannt, mit lackierten massiven Patenträdern, vernickelten Stahlglocken, best ausgeführten Nickeseln. D. R. G. M. — **Rollers,** with team, with varnished solid patented wheels, nickeled steel bells, finest executed donkeys, nodding. Protected by German law. — **Rodadores,** uñidos, con ruedas patentadas macizas, embarnizadas, y asno con cabeza móvil (cabecéa). Protegido por ley alemana.

Roller, bespannt, mit lackierten massiven Patenträdern, vernickelten Stahlglocken, mit best ausgeführten Nickelefanten. D. R. G. M. — **Rollers,** with team, with solid varnished patent wheels, nickeled steel bells, with bestly accomplished elephants, nodding. Protected by German law. — **Rodadores,** uñidos, con ruedas patentadas macizas, embarnizadas, campanillas de acero niquelado y elefantes con cabeza móvil (cabecéa). Proteg. por ley alemana.

139/948/16

139/949/21

Roller, bespannt, mil lackierten massiven Patenträdern, vernickelten Stahlglocken, mit hochfein ausgeführtem Elefanten mit beweglichem Rüssel und Zugstimme. — **Rollers,** with team, with varnished solid patent wheels, nickeled steel bells, with superfinely accomplished elefants with moveable trunk and drawing voice. — **Rodadores,** uñidos, con ruedas patentadas macizas, embarnizadas, campanillas de acero niquelado, con elefantes elegantemente acabados con trompa movible y voz de tirante.

139/950/16

Roller, bespannt, mit lackierten massiven Patenträdern, vernickelten Stahlglocken, mit ausspannbaren, hochfein ausgeführten Bernhardinerhunden. D.R.G.M. — **Rollers,** with team, with varnished solid patent wheels, nickeled steel bells, with highly finished St. Bernhard-dogs, to be unharnessed. Protected by German law. — **Rodadores,** uñidos, con ruedas patentadas macizas, embarnizadas, campanillas de acero niquelado, con perros de San Bernardo elegantemente acabados, quitables del vehículo. Protegido por ley alemana.

Roller, bespannt, mit lackierten massiven Patenträdern, vernickelten Stahlglocken, mit ausspannbaren, hochfein ausgeführten Plüschschäferhunden. D. R. G. M. — **Rollers,** with team, with varnished solid patent wheels, nickeled steel bells, with highly finished plush shepherd-dogs, to be unharnessed. Protected by German Law. — **Rodadores,** uñidos, con ruedas patentadas macizas, embarnizadas, campanilla de acero niquelado, con mastines de felpa elegantemente acabados, quitables del vehículo. Protegido por ley alemana.

139/951/19

	Raddurchmesser	Glockendurchmesser	Länge
No. **139**/948/8	80 mm	35 mm	210 mm
„ **139**/948/12	120 „	50 „	290 „
„ **139**/948/16	160 „	60 „	400 „
„ **139**/948/17	170 „	65 „	440 „
„ **139**/948/19	190 „	70 „	490 „
„ **139**/949/21	210 „	75 „	480 „
„ **139**/949/24	240 „	80 „	590 „
„ **139**/950/14	140 „	55 „	310 „
„ **139**/950/16	160 „	60 „	370 „
„ **139**/950/19	190 „	70 „	430 „
„ **139**/950/21	210 „	75 „	470 „
„ **139**/951/16	160 „	60 „	360 „
„ **139**/951/17	170 „	65 „	400 „
„ **139**/951/19	190 „	70 „	440 „
„ **139**/951/21	210 „	75 „	480 „
„ **139**/951/24	240 „	80 „	560 „

Raddurchmesser
Diameter of wheel
Diámetro de rueda

Glockendurchmesser
Diameter of bell
Diámetro de campanilla

Länge
Length
Largura

Beachten Sie auch die Veröffentlichung auf Seite 4—13 des Hauptkataloges.

Please note also the publication on page 4—13 of the principal catalogue.
Llamamos también su atención á la publicación en la página 4—13 del catálogo principal.

139/952/14

Roller, bespannt, mit lackierten massiven Patenträdern, mit ausspannbaren, gut ausgeführten Elefanten. D. R. G. M.
Rollers, with team, with varnished solid patent wheels, with well finished elefants, to be unharnessed. Protected by German Law.
Rodadores uñidos, con ruedas patentadas, macizas, embarnizadas, con elefantes bien acabadas, quitables del vehículo. Protegido por ley alemana.

	Raddurchmesser Diameter of wheel Diámetro de rueda	Glockendurchmesser Diameter of bell Diámetro de campanilla	Länge Length Largura
No. **139**/952/8	80 mm	35 mm	185 mm
„ **139**/952/12	120 „	50 „	260 „
„ **139**/952/13	130 „	50 „	310 „
„ **139**/952/14	140 „	55 „	340 „
„ **139**/952/16	160 „	60 „	380 „
„ **139**/952/17	170 „	65 „	410 „
„ **139**/952/19	190 „	70 „	460 „
„ **139**/952/21	210 „	75 „	520 „
„ **139**/952/24	240 „	80 „	560 „

139/964/3

Fahrroller mit Nickelböden und massiven lackierten Rädern.
Driving rollers with nickel bottoms and solid varnished wheels.
Rodadores con fondos de niquel y ruedas macizas embarnizadas.

	Raddurchmesser Diameter of wheel Diámetro de rueda	Glockendurchmesser Diameter of bell Diámetro de campanilla
No. **139**/964/3	75 mm	50, 55 mm
mit 2 Büscheln	with two aigrettes	con dos arramilletanos
„ **139**/965/3	90 mm	55, 60, 65 mm
mit 3 Büscheln	with three aigrettes	con tres arramilletados

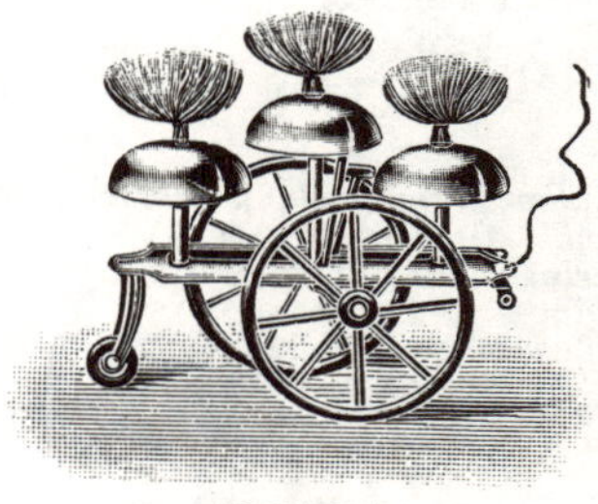

139/965/3

Fahrroller mit Nickelböden und massiven lackierten Rädern, mit ausspannbaren, sortierten Filzpferden und Eseln.

Driving rollers with nickel bottoms and solid varnished wheels, with assorted horses and donkeys of felt, to be unharnessed.

Rodadores con fondos de niquel y ruedas macizas embarnizadas, caballos y asnos de felpa, surtidos, quitables del vehículo.

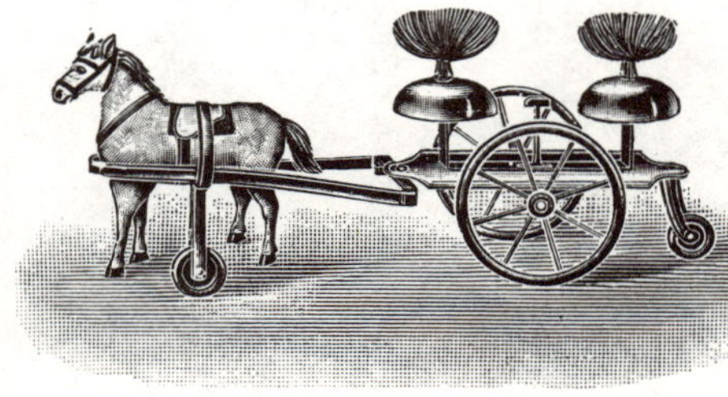

139/966/1

	Raddurchmesser Diameter of wheel Diámetro de rueda	Glockendurchmesser Diameter of bell Diámetro de campanilla
139/966/1	75 mm	50, 55 mm
mit 2 Büscheln	with two aigrettes	con dos arramilletados
139/967/1	90 mm	55, 60, 65 mm
mit 3 Büscheln	with three aigrettes	con tres arramilletados

Fahrroller mit Nickelböden und massiven, lackierten Rädern, mit ausspannbaren braunen Plüschbären.

Driving rollers with nickel bottoms and solid varnished wheels, with brown plush-bears to be unharnessed.

Rodadores con fondos de niquel, ruedas macizas embarnizadas y osos brunos de felpa, quitables del vehículo.

139/967/2

	Raddurchmesser Diameter of wheel Diámetro de rueda	Glockendurchmesser Diameter of bell Diámetro de campanilla
139/966/2	75 mm	50, 55 mm
mit 2 Büscheln	with two aigrettes	con dos arramilletados
139/967/2	90 mm	50, 60, 65 mm
mit 3 Büscheln	with three aigrettes	con tres arramilletados

139/74/6

Eimer in hochfeiner lackierter Ausführung, mit festem Boden, Drahthenkel mit Holzgriff und 2 Goldstreifen.
Pails in superfine varnished finish, with fixed bottom, with wire ring, with wooden handle and 2 gold stripes.
Cubos de primera clase, elegantemente embarnizados, con fondo fijo, asidero de alambre con empuñadura de madera y 2 rayas de oro.

	Durchmesser Diameter Diámetro	Höhe Height Altura
No. **139**/74/4	105 mm	110 mm
„ **139**/74/5	118 „	125 „
„ **139**/74/6	135 „	145 „
„ **139**/74/7	145 „	155 „
„ **139**/74/8	165 „	180 „

Eimer in hochfein weiß lackierter Ausführung, mit Bildern, hohem festen Boden, Drahthenkel mit Holzgriff und 2 Goldstreifen.
Pails in superfine white varnished finish, with pictures, high fixed bottom, wire ring with wooden handle and 2 gold stripes.
Cubos de primera clase, embarnizadas de color blanco, con estampas, fondo alto fijo, asidero de alambre con empuñadura de madera y 2 rayas de oro.

	Durchmesser Diameter Diámetro	Höhe Height Altura
No. **139**/75/4	105 mm	110 mm
„ **139**/75/5	118 „	125 „
„ **139**/75/6	135 „	145 „
„ **139**/75/7	145 „	155 „
„ **139**/75/8	165 „	180 „

139/75/7

Beachten Sie auch die Veröffentlichung auf Seite 4—13 des Hauptkataloges.

Gießkannen, einfach lackiert, sortierte Farben, mit 2 Goldstreifen.

Watering cans, simply varnished, assorted colours, with 2 gold stripes.

Regaderas, sencillamente embarnizadas, en diferentes colores, con 2 rayas de oro.

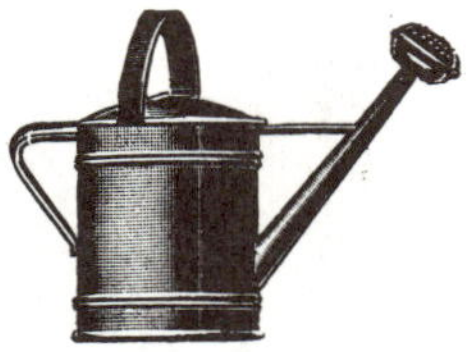

139/81/3

No.		Durchmesser Diameter Diámetro	Höhe Height Altura
No. **139**/81/1	(alte, old, viejo No. **139**/54/0)	60 mm	80 mm
„ **139**/81/2		70 „	82 „
„ **139**/81/3	(„ „ „ „ **139**/55/1)	80 „	90 „
„ **139**/81/4	(„ „ „ „ **139**/55/4)	80 „	125 „
„ **139**/81/5		90 „	125 „
„ **139**/81/6	(„ „ „ „ **139**/56/1)	105 „	125 „
„ **139**/81/7		125 „	175 „
„ **139**/82/2		70 „	82 „
„ **139**/82/3	(„ „ „ „ **139**/55/3)	80 „	90 „
„ **139**/82/4	(„ „ „ „ **139**/55/6)	80 „	125 „
„ **139**/82/5	(„ „ „ „ **139**/56/3)	90 „	125 „
„ **139**/82/6		105 „	125 „
„ **139**/82/7		125 „	175 „

Gießkannen, weiß lackiert, mit 2 Bildern und 2 Goldstreifen.

Watering cans, white varnished, with 2 pictures and 2 gold stripes.

Regaderas, embarnizadas de color blanco, con 2 estampas y 2 rayas de oro.

139/82/5

Gießkannen, in hochfein lackierter Ausführung, mit hohem festen Boden und 2 Goldstreifen.

Watering cans, in superfine varnished finish, with high fixed bottom, with 2 gold stripes.

Regaderas, elegantemente embarnizadas de color blanco, fondo alto fijo y 2 rayas de oro.

139/84/5

No.	Oberer Durchmesser Upper diameter Diámetro superior	Höhe Height Altura
No. **139**/84/2	70 mm	95 mm
„ **139**/84/3	80 „	100 „
„ **139**/84/4	80 „	135 „
„ **139**/84/5	90 „	135 „
„ **139**/84/6	105 „	135 „
„ **139**/84/7	125 „	180 „
„ **139**/85/2	70 „	95 „
„ **139**/85/3	80 „	100 „
„ **139**/85/4	80 „	135 „
„ **139**/85/5	90 „	135 „
„ **139**/85/6	105 „	135 „
„ **139**/85/7	125 „	180 „

Gießkannen, in hochfein lackierter, weißer Ausführung, mit 2 Bildern hohem festen Boden und 2 Goldstreifen.

Watering cans, in superfine white varnished finish, with 2 pictures, high fixed bottom and 2 gold stripes.

Regaderas, elegantemente embarnizadas de color blanco, con 2 estampas, fondo alto fijo y 2 rayas de oro.

139/85/6

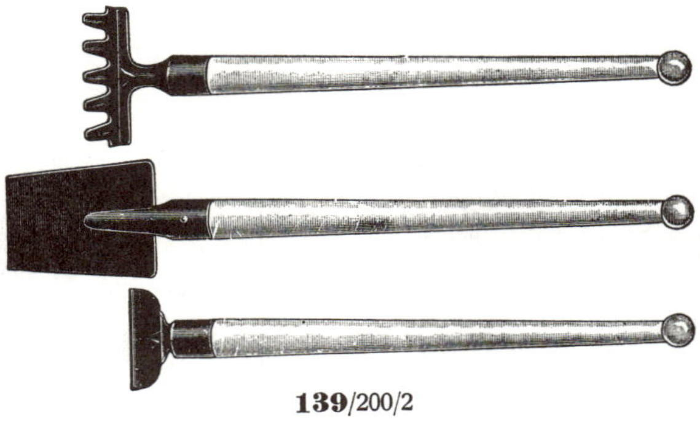

139/200/2

Gartengeräte, bestehend aus: Rechen, Spaten, Hacke, schwarz lackiert, mit gebeizten gedrehten Holzstielen.

Gardening tools, consisting of: rakes, spades, axe, black varnished and stained turned wooden handle.

Utensilios de jardín, compuestos de: rastrillo, pala y azada, embarnizados negro con mangos de madera torneados y macerados.

No.	Länge Length Largura
No. **139**/200/1	ca. 290 mm
„ **139**/200/2	„ 330 „

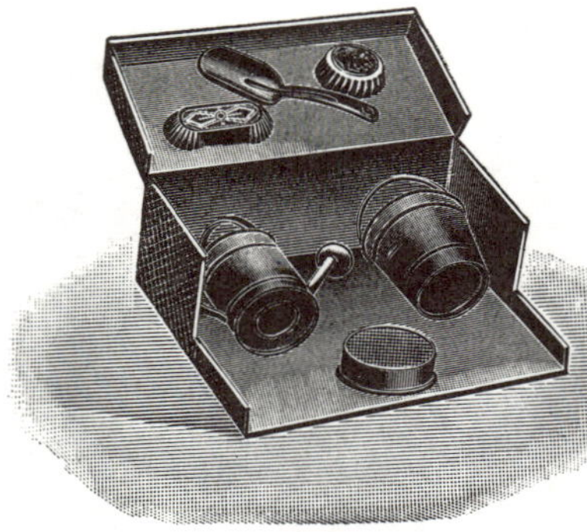

139/600/1

No.	Kartonbreite Breadth of box Anchura de cajita	Kartonlänge Length of box Largura de cajita	Höhe Height Altura	Teile Parts Partes
No. **139**/600/1	250 mm	120 mm	90 mm	6
„ **139**/600/2	300 „	160 „	110 „	7
„ **139**/600/3	350 „	180 „	130 „	8
„ **139**/600/4	400 „	200 „	135 „	8
„ **139**/602/2	300 „	160 „	115 „	6
„ **139**/602/3	350 „	200 „	130 „	7
„ **139**/602/4	400 „	200 „	135 „	7

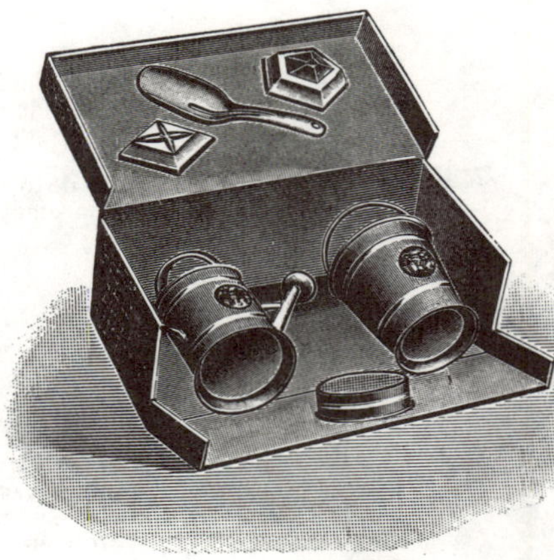

139/602/2

Sandgarnituren (D. R. G. M.) in ges. gesch. Packung, bestehend aus: Eimer, Gießkanne, Sieb, Schaufel und diversen Formen in hochfein lackierter Ausführung, Karton mit Bild.

Sand sets, package protected by German law, consisting of: pail, watering can, sieve, shovel and different forms, in well varnished finish, pasteboard box with picture.

Equipos para la playa (D. R. G. M.) en caja de cartón patentada. Se compone de cubo, regadera, cedazo, pala y diversos moldes, todo el equipo bien ejecutado y embarnizado, caja de cartón con estampa.

Sandgarnituren (D. R. R. M.) in ges. gesch. Packung, bestehend aus: Eimer, Gießkanne, Sieb, Schaufel und diversen Formen in hochfein lackierter Ausführung, Karton mit Bild.

Sand sets, package protected by German law, consisting of: pail, watering can, sieve, shovel and different forms in superfine varnished finish, pasteboard box with picture.

Equipos para la playa (D. R. G. M.) en caja de cartón patentada, consistiendo de: cubo, regadera, cedazo, pala y diversos moldes, elegantemente embarnizados, caja de cartón con estampa.

Please note also the publication on page 4—13 of the principal catalogue.
Llamamos también su atención á la publicación en la página 4—13 del catálogo principal.

Sandsiebe, rund, in hochfein lackierter, weißer Ausführung, mit Bildern und modernen Formen.
Sandsieves, round, in superfine white varnished finish, with pictures and modern forms.
Cedazos para arena, redondos, elegantemente embarnizados de color blanco, con estampas y moldes modernos.

Sandsiebe, rund, in hochfein lackierter, weißer Ausführung, mit Bildern, fein lackierten Formen, wie Fische, Taucher, Schiffe usw.
Sandsieves, round, in superfine white varnished finish, with pictures, well varnished forms, such as fishes, divers, ships, a. s. o.
Cedazos para arena, redondos, elegantemente embarnizados de color blanco, con estampas y moldes, finamente ejecutados representando: peces, buzos, buques etc.

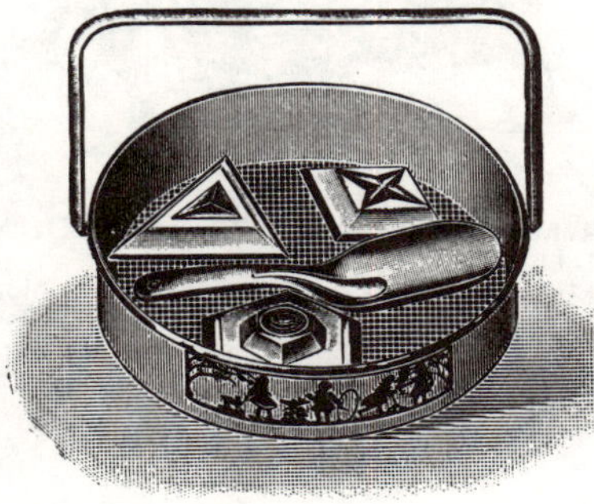

139/613/2

	Siebdurchmesser Diameter of sieve Diámetro del cedazo			
No. **139**/613/1	170 mm	3 teilig,	parts,	partes.
„ **139**/613/2	210 „	4 „	„	„
„ **139**/613/3	240 „	5 „	„	„
„ **139**/614/1	170 „	3 „	„	„
„ **139**/614/2	210 „	4 „	„	„
„ **139**/614/3	240 „	5 „	„	„

139/614/3

Sandspiele, in Spitzenkartons, mit hochfein lackierten Formen, wie Fische, Taucher usw., sowie Holzboote mit Figur, Kartons mit Bild.
Sand toys, in ornamented pasteboard boxes, with superfine varnished forms, such as fishes, divers, a. s. o., and also with wooden boats with figure, pasteboard boxes with picture.
Juegos para la playa, en cajas de cartón ornamentales, con moldes elegantemente embarnizados, representando: peces, buzos etc. barquillas de madera con figura, cajas de cartón con estampa.

139/637/1

	Kartonlänge Length of box Largura de cajita	Kartonbreite Breadth of box Anchura de cajita			
No. **139**/637/1	275 mm	220 mm	5 teilig,	parts,	partes.
„ **139**/637/2	320 „	225 „	6 „	„	„
„ **139**/637/3	320 „	275 „	7 „	„	„
„ **139**/637/4	335 „	310 „	8 „	„	„
„ **139**/637/5	360 „	360 „	9 „	„	„
„ **139**/637/6 *	485 „	360 „	11 „	„	„

* inkl. Eimer und Gießkanne.
* inclusive pail and watering can.
* inclusive cubo y regadera.

Sandspiele, in Kartons, in ges. geschützt. Packung, mit hochfein lackierten Formen, Einlage mit Figur, Karton mit Bild D. R. G. M.
Sand toys, in pasteboard boxes, package protected by German law, with superfine varnished forms, inside with figure, pasteboard box with picture D. R. G. M.
Juegos para la playa, en cajas de cartón patentadas, con moldes elegantemente embarnizados, por dentro con figura, caja de cartón con estampa D. R. G. M.

Sandspiele, in Spitzenkartons, mit hochfein lackierten modernen Formen, Karton mit Bild.
Sand toys, in ornamented pasteboard boxes, with superfine varnished modern forms, pasteboard box with picture.
Juegos para la playa, en cajas de cartón ornamentales, con moldes modernos elegantemente embarnizados, caja de cartón con estampa.

139/638/1

	Kartonlänge Length of box Largura de cajita	Kartonbreite Breadth of box Anchura de cajita			
No. **139**/638/1	320 mm	255 mm	7 teilig,	parts,	partes.
„ **139**/638/2	450 „	355 „	9 „	„	„
„ **139**/639/1	260 „	190 „	4 „	„	„
„ **139**/639/2	275 „	200 „	5 „	„	„
„ **139**/639/3	305 „	220 „	6 „	„	„
„ **139**/639/4	320 „	280 „	7 „	„	„
„ **139**/639/6 *	410 „	300 „	10 „	„	„

* inkl. Eimer und Gießkanne.
* inclusive pail and watering can.
* inclusive cubo y regadera.

139/639/3

Beachten Sie auch die Veröffentlichung auf Seite 4—13 des Hauptkataloges.

Please note also the publication on page 14 and 15 of the principal catalogue.
Llamamos también su atención á la publicación en la página 14 y 15 del catálogo principal.

11/560/4

schwarz lackiert, Weißblech-Türen, Füße mit Bronzestrich.
black varnished, tinplate-doors, feet with bronze edging.
barnizado negro, hojalata puertas, pies con rayas de bronce.

No.	Länge / Length / Largura	Breite / Breadth / Anchura	Höhe / Height / Altura	Geschirr / Pots and pans / Ajuar de la cocina	Packung / Packing / Contenido
No. **11**/560/0	11,8	8	7,5 cm	2 Stck. pc. pz.	1/2 Dtz. Doz. Doc.
„ **11**/560/1	13	8,5	8 „	2 „ „ „	1/2 „ „ „
„ **11**/560/2	14	9,5	8 „	3 „ „ „	1/2 „ „ „
„ **11**/560/3	17	11	9,5 „	3 „ „ „	1/3 „ „ „
„ **11**/560/4	19,5	12	10,5 „	4 „ „ „	1/3 „ „ „
„ **11**/560/5	22	14	10,5 „	4 „ „ „	1/3 „ „ „
„ **11**/560/6	24	15,5	10,5 „	4 „ „ „	1/4 „ „ „
„ **11**/560/7	25,5	16	11,5 „	5 „ „ „	1/4 „ „ „
„ **11**/560/8	28,5	17,5	12,5 „	5 „ „ „	1/12 „ „ „
„ **11**/670/1½	17	11	9 „	4 „ „ „	1/3 „ „ „
„ **11**/670/2	18	12,5	10,5 „	4 „ „ „	1/3 „ „ „
„ **11**/670/2½	19,5	12	10,5 „	5 „ „ „	1/3 „ „ „
„ **11**/670/2¾	20	13	11 „	5 „ „ „	1/4 „ „ „
„ **11**/675/1	21	15	12,5 „	3 „ „ „	1/12 „ „ „
„ **11**/675/2	23,5	16	13,5 „	3 „ „ „	1/12 „ „ „
„ **11**/675/3	25	18	14 „	4 „ „ „	1/12 „ „ „
„ **11**/675/4	27,5	19	14 „	4 „ „ „	1/12 „ „ „
„ **11**/2021/1	23	14,5	13 „	3 „ „ „	1/12 „ „ „
„ **11**/2021/2	24,5	15,5	14 „	3 „ „ „	1/12 „ „ „
„ **11**/2021/3	27,5	17,5	17 „	4 „ „ „	1/12 „ „ „
„ **11**/2021/4	32,5	20	17 „	4 „ „ „	1/12 „ „ „

11/670/2¾

schwarz lackiert, mit Weißblech-Decke stumpfe Töpfe.
black varnished, with tinplate-cover, blunt pots.
barnizado negro, con cubierta de hojalata, pucheros botos.

11/359/9

Blechhausrat, teils stumpf, teils scharf, Weißblech mit Holzteilen, in roten Glacékartons.
Household utensils of tinplate, partly blunt, partly sharp, tinplate with wooden parts, in red glossy hand-boxes.
Utensilios de casa de hojalata, en parte botos, en parte agudos hojalata con partes de madera, en cajitas de cartón rojo brillante.

11/675/3

aus starkem Schwarzblech, Stahlblechdecke mit massiver runder Stange und Schiebelampen.
of strong sheet-iron, steelplate-cover with massive round railing and sliding lamps.
de fuerte palastro negro, cubierta de chapa de acero con barra de resguardo maciza redonda y lámparas de corredera.

11/2021/3

aus starkem Schwarzblech mit polierter Stahlplatte, schrägen Füßen, Nickelgeschirr, Schiebelampe, Ia runder Herdstange, ff. Qualität.
of strong sheet-iron with polished steel-plate, oblique feet, nickel-tray, sliding lamp, first class round railing, extra-fine quality.
de fuerte palastro negro, con cubierta de acero pulido, pies oblícuos, vasos de niquel, lámpara de corredera, barra de resguardo de primera clase, cualidad extrafina.

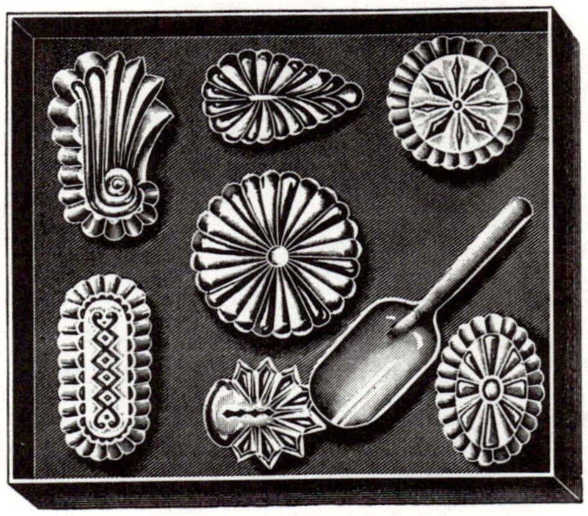

11/830/4

Sandformen, weiß lackiert und abgetönt, eingenäht in roten Glacékartons mit weißer Einlage.
Sand-forms, white varnished and toned down, sewed in red glossy hand-boxes with white lining.
Moldes a jugar con arena, barnizados blanco y con colores neutrales, cosidos en cajitas de cartón rojo brillante con forro blanco.

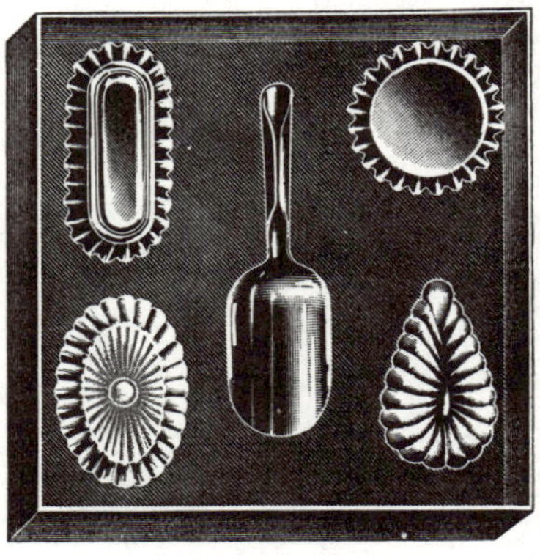

11/840/4

Sandformen, bunt, eingenäht in Kartons.
Sand-forms, gay coloured, sewed in hand-boxes.
Moldes a jugar con arena, multicolores, cosidos en cajitas de cartón.

No.	Kartonlänge / Cardboard length / Largura de cajita	Inhalt / Contents / Contenido	Packung / Packing / Empaque
No. **11**/830/ 1	21,5 cm	5 Stck. pc. pz.	1/4 Dtz. doz. doc.
„ **11**/830/ 2	26,5 „	6 „ „ „	1/4 „ „ „
„ **11**/830/ 3	30,5 „	7 „ „ „	1/4 „ „ „
„ **11**/830/ 4	33 „	8 „ „ „	1/4 „ „ „
„ **11**/830/ 5	35 „	9 „ „ „	1/4 „ „ „
„ **11**/840/ 1	20,5 „	3 „ „ „	1/2 „ „ „
„ **11**/840/ 2	20,5 „	3 „ „ „	1/2 „ „ „
„ **11**/840/ 3	22 „	4 „ „ „	1/2 „ „ „
„ **11**/840/ 4	25,5 „	5 „ „ „	1/2 „ „ „
„ **11**/846	20 „	3 „ „ „	1/2 „ „ „
„ **11**/845	17,5 „	3 „ „ „	1/2 „ „ „
„ **11**/359/ 4	18 „	10 „ „ „	1 „ „ „
„ **11**/359/ 5	20,1 „	11 „ „ „	1/2 „ „ „
„ **11**/359/ 6	21,8 „	13 „ „ „	1/2 „ „ „
„ **11**/359/ 7	22,5 „	15 „ „ „	1/2 „ „ „
„ **11**/359/ 8	24,5 „	16 „ „ „	1/2 „ „ „
„ **11**/359/ 9	27,5 „	18 „ „ „	1/2 „ „ „
„ **11**/359/10	31,5 „	21 „ „ „	1/4 „ „ „
„ **11**/359/11	35 „	23 „ „ „	1/4 „ „ „
„ **11**/359/12	38,5 „	26 „ „ „	1/4 „ „ „

11/846

Sandformen, bunt, eingenäht in Kartons.
Sand-forms, gay coloured, sewed in hand-boxes.
Moldes a jugar con arena, multicolores, cosidos en cajitas de cartón.

Beachten Sie auch die Veröffentlichung auf Seite 14 und 15 des Hauptkataloges.

Please note also the publication on page 77 of the principal catalogue.
Llamamos también su atención á la publicación en la página 77 del catálogo principal.

Blechtrompeten. — Metal-plate trumpets. — Trompetas de hojalata.

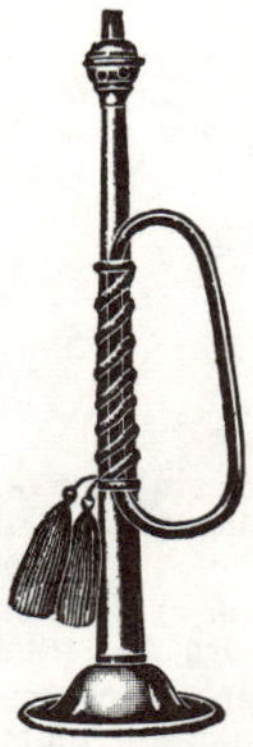
80/510

80/525

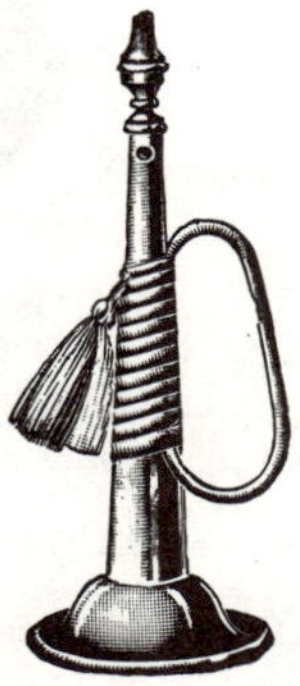
80/615

80/750

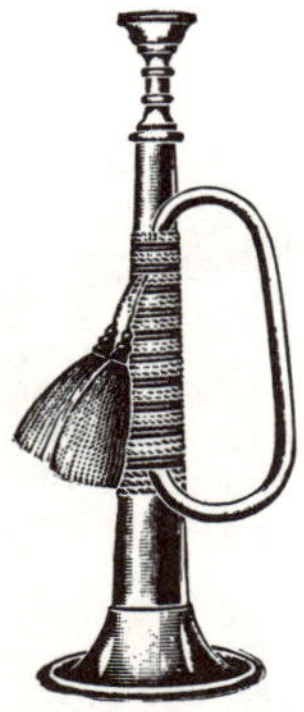
80/770

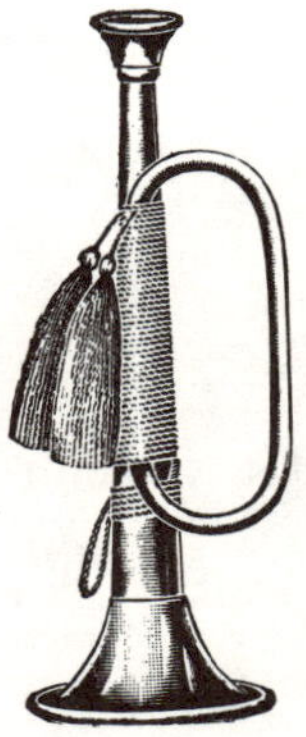
80/205

Mit lackiertem Trichter und einfacher Chenillenumwicklung.
Varnished funnel, simple chenille wrapping.
Con embudo barnizado y envolvimiento sencillo de chenilla.

Größe/Size	**80**/510	**80**/511	**80**/512
Tamaño	24	27	31 cm

Mit poliertem Trichter, Baumwollquaste, Chenillen- und Bortenumwicklung.
With polished funnel, cotton tassel, chenille and border wrapping.
Con embudo pulido, borla de algodón, envolvimiento de chenilla y galón.

Größe/Size	**80**/525	**80**/526	**80**/527	**80**/528
Tamaño	29	31½	36	40½ cm

Mit poliertem Trichter, Chenillenschnüre und Goldumwicklung, Umhangschnur und Seidenquaste.
With polished funnel, chenille string and gold wrapping, hanging string and silk tassel.
Con embudo pulido, cuerdas chenilla y envolvimiento de oro, cuerda de colgar y borla de seda.

Größe/Size	**80**/610	**80**/611	**80**/612	**80**/613	**80**/614	**80**/615
Tamaño	20	22	26½	31	32½	40 cm

Mit poliertem Trichter, beste Ausführung, in Anbindung mit Seidenband und Seidenquaste.
With polished funnel, best work, with binding with silk ribbon and silk tassel.
Con embudo pulido, trabajo mejor a union con cinta de seda y borla de seda.

Größe/Size	**80**/750	**80**/751	**80**/752	**80**/753	**80**/754	**80**/755
Tamaño	22	23½	27	31	36	40 cm

Mit poliertem Trichter, Anbindung in Grün mit Gold, Umhangschnur mit Seidenquaste.
With polished funnel, binding in green and gold, hanging string and silk tassel.
Embudo pulido, en union en verde, cuerda de colcar y borla de seda.

Größe/Size	**80**/770	**80**/771	**80**/772	**80**/773
Tamaño	21	26	31	35½ cm

Mit poliertem Trichter, Anbindung in Rot, mit gleichfarbiger Vollquaste.
With polished tube, red cord and woolen banderol of same colour.
Embudo lustrado, con cordel rojo y borla de lana del mismo color.

Größe/Size	**80**/205	**80**/206	**80**/207
Tamaño	22½	28	31 cm

Hörner. — Corns. — Cuernos.

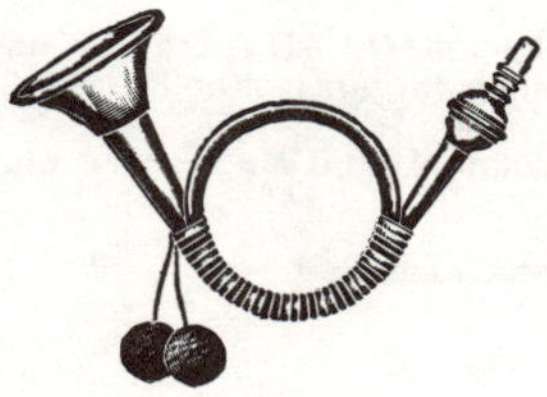
80/824

80/760

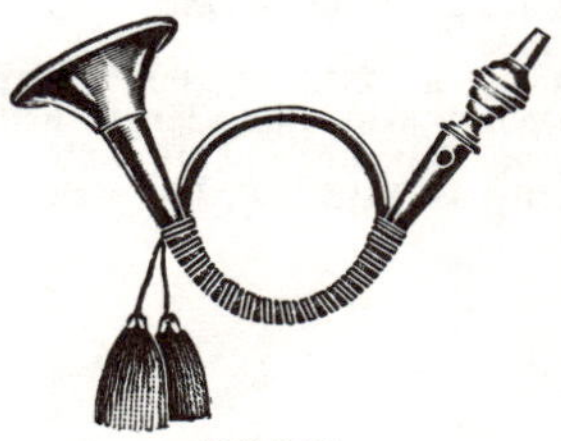
80/816

Blecheimer mit Lithographie.
Tin pail with lithography.
Cubo de lata con litografia.

80/101	5	× 5½	× 6	cm
80/111	4⅓	× 6	× 6½	„
80/121	5½	× 7	× 7½	„
80/131	6	× 8	× 8½	„
80/141	7	× 10	× 10	„
80/151	8½	× 12	× 12	„
80/161	9	× 13	× 13	„

80/111

Mit poliertem Trichter, Beinmundstück, Chenillen- und Goldumwicklung, mit Seidenquaste.
With polished funnel, bone bit, chenille and gold wrapping with silk tassel.
Embudo pulido, boca de hueso, envolvimiento de chenilla y oro con borla de seda.

Größe/Size	**80**/824	**80**/825	**80**/826	**80**/827
Tamaño	18	20	25	29 cm

Mit poliertem Trichter, beste Ausführung, in Umwicklung mit Seidenband und Seidenquaste.
With polished funnel, finest work, wrapped with silk ribben and silk tassel.
Embudo pulido, trabajo mejor, envolvimiento de cinta de seda y borla.

Größe/Size	**80**/760	**80**/761	**80**/762
Tamaño	26	30	32 cm

Mit poliertem Trichter, Chenillenschnur-Umwicklung, mit Baumwollquaste.
With polished funnel, chenille string wrapping with cotton tassel.
Embudo pulido, chenilla y envolvimiento de cuerda con borla de algodón.

Größe/Size	**80**/812	**80**/813	**80**/814	**80**/815	**80**/816
Tamaño	23	26	28	32	35 cm

Blechschlottern mit Blechmundstück und Stimme. — Tin rattles with metal-plate mouthpiece and voice. — Sonajeras de chapa, con boca de chapa y voz.

82/21

82/62

82/115

82/156

Durchmesser/Diameter Diámetro	**82**/8	**82**/3	**82**/5	**82**/15	**82**/14	**82**/21	**82**/23	**82**/25	**82**/30	**82**/61
	2,5	2,8	3,2	3,5	3,5	4	4	4	4	4,5 cm
Länge/Length Largura	9	9,5	10	10	10	12	12	12	12	13 cm

Durchmesser/Diameter Diámetro	**82**/62	**82**/63	**82**/64	**82**/114	**82**/115	**82**/116	**82**/117	**82**/156	**82**/157	**82**/158
	4,5	4,5	4,5	5,3	5,3	5,3	5,3	6	6	6 cm
Länge/Length Largura	13	13	13	13,5	13,5	13,5	13,5	14	14	14 cm

82/408

Glockenschlotter aus Blech. Bell rattle of tin. Sonajera de campanilla de chapa.

	82/403	**82**/406	**82**/408	**82**/410
Durchmesser Diameter Diámetro	4,5	5	6	7 cm
Länge/Length Largura	11	11,5	12	12 cm

¼ der natürlichen Größe. — ¼ of nat. size. — ¼ del tamaño natural.

82/310

Blechtrompeten mit Porzellanmundstück. Metal-plate trumpets with porcelain mouth-piece. Trompetas de chapa con boca de porcelana.

Länge/Length Largura	**82**/308	**82**/307	**82**/310	**82**/304	**82**/306	**82**/309
	14	19	23	12,5	17	19 cm

Die No. **82**/304, **82**/306, und **82**/309 sind mit Blechmundstück.
The No. **82**/304, **82**/306 and **82**/309 are with tin mouth-piece.
Los No. **82**/304, **82**/306 y **82**/309 tienen boca de chapa.

Glockentrompeten mit Holzmundstück.
Bell trumpets with wooden mouth-piece.
Trompetas de campanillas con boca de madera.

Länge/Length Largura	**82**/450	**82**/451	**82**/452
	20	24	30 cm
Glocken ø/Bell ø Campanillas ø	6	7	7 cm

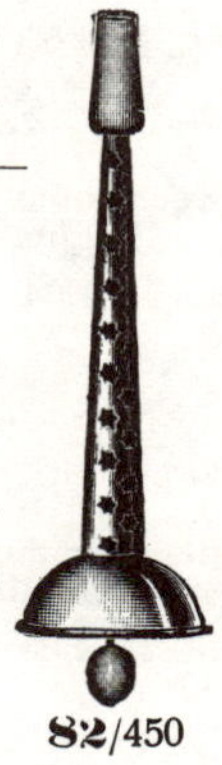
82/450

Beachten Sie auch die Veröffentlichung auf Seite 77 des Hauptkataloges.

Please note also the publication on page 74 and 75 of the principal catalogue.
Llamamos también su atención á la publicación en la página 74 y 75 del catálogo principal.

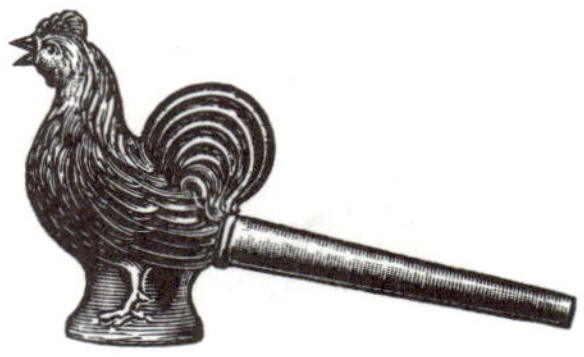

103/17 ass

103/20 ass

Schreihähne No. **103**/17 ass, **ohne Federn,** in Farben sortiert, Länge ca. 9 cm, Höhe ca. 5 cm.
„ No. **103**/18 ass, genau wie **103**/17 ass, aber **mit Federn.**
„ No. **103**/19 ass, genau wie **103**/20 ass, aber **ohne Federn.**
„ No. **103**/20 ass, **mit Federn,** in Farben sortiert, Länge ca. 11 cm, Höhe ca. 7 cm.

Crowing-cocks No. **103**/17 ass, **without feathers,** assorted in colours, length abt. 9 cm, height abt. 5 cm.
„ No. **103**/18 ass, exactly as **103**/17 ass, but **with feathers.**
„ No. **103**/19 ass, exactly as **103**/20 ass, but **without feathers.**
„ No. **103**/20 ass, **with feathers,** assorted in colours, length abt. 11 cm, height abt. 7 cm.

Gallos, cantando No. **103**/17ass, **sin plumas,** surtidos en colores, largura cª 9 cm, altura cª 5 cm.
„ No. **103**/18 ass, exactamente como **103**/17 ass, pero **con plumas.**
„ No. **103**/19 ass, exactamente como **103**/20 ass, mas **sin plumas.**
„ No. **103**/20 ass, **con plumas,** surtidos en colores, largura cª 11 cm, altura cª 7 cm.

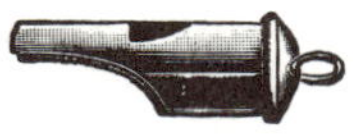

103/6 W & N

103/7 W & N

103/8WR, **103**/8NR, **103**/9W

Trillerpfeifen:
103/6W Weißblech, mit Ring, Länge ca. 4½ cm mit Ring.
103/6N Nickelblech „ „ „ „ „ „ „
103/7W Weißblech „ „ „ „ 7 cm „ „
103/7N Nickelblech „ „ „ „ „ „ „

Triller-Schneckenpfeifen:
103/8W Weißblech, **ohne Ring,** Länge ca. 3½ cm, Durchmesser ca. 2 cm.
103/8WR genau wie **103**/8W, aber **mit Ring.**
103/8N Nickelblech, **ohne Ring,** Länge ca. 3½ cm, Durchmesser ca. 2 cm.
103/8NR genau wie **103**/8N, aber **mit Ring.**
103/9W **Weißblech,** mit Ring, Länge mit Ring ca. 4½ cm, Durchmesser ca. 2½ cm.
103/9N genau wie **103**/9W, aber **Nickelblech.**

Trill-whistles:
103/6W tin-plate, with ring, length abt. 4½ cm incl. ring.
103/6N nickel-plate „ „ „ „ „ „ „
103/7W tin-plate „ „ „ „ 7 cm „ „
103/7N nickel-plate „ „ „ „ „ „ „

Trill Helical-whistles:
103/8W tin-plate, **without ring,** length abt. 3½ cm, diameter abt. 2 cm.
103/8WR exactly as **103**/8W, but **with ring.**
103/8N nickel-plate, **without ring,** length abt. 3½ cm, diameter abt. 2 cm.
103/8NR exactly as **103**/8N, but **with ring.**
103/9W **tin-plate,** with ring, length with ring abt. 4½ cm, diameter abt. 2½ cm.
103/9N exactly as **103**/9W, but **nickel-plate.**

Silbatos de trinar:
103/6W hojalata, con anillo, largura cª 4½ cm incl. anillo.
103/6N niquel „ „ „ „ „ „ „
103/7W hojalata „ „ „ „ 7 cm „ „
103/7N niquel „ „ „ „ „ „ „

Silbatos de trinar, helizoidales:
103/8W hojalata, **sin anillo,** largura cª 3½ cm, diámetro cª 2 cm.
103/8WR exactamente como **103**/8W, mas **con anillo.**
103/8N niquel, **sin anillo,** largura cª 3½ cm, diámetro cª 2 cm.
103/8NR exactamente como **103**/8N, pero **con anillo.**
103/9W **hojalata,** con anillo, largura incl. anillo cª 4½ cm, diámetro cª 2½ cm.
103/9N exactamente como **103**/9W, pero en **niquel.**

103/40

103/65

Flöten:
Nr. **103**/40 **Weißblech,** Länge ca. 21 cm.
„ **103**/55 „ „ „ 24 „ dünn.
„ **103**/60 „ „ „ 24 „ stark.
„ **103**/80 „ „ „ 27 „
„ **103**/105 „ „ „ 29 „
„ **103**/140 „ „ „ 32 „

Flöten:
Nr. **103**/50 **Nickelblech,** Länge ca. 21 cm.
„ **103**/65 „ „ „ 24 „ dünn.
„ **103**/70 „ „ „ 24 „ stark.
„ **103**/90 „ „ „ 27 „
„ **103**/115 „ „ „ 29 „
„ **103**/150 „ „ „ 32 „

Flutes:
Nr. **103**/40 **tin-plate,** length abt. 21 cm.
„ **103**/55 „ „ „ 24 „ thin.
„ **103**/60 „ „ „ 24 „ strong.
„ **103**/80 „ „ „ 27 „
„ **103**/105 „ „ „ 29 „
„ **103**/140 „ „ „ 32 „

Flutes:
Nr. **103**/50 **nickel-plate,** length abt. 21 cm.
„ **103**/65 „ „ „ 24 „ thin.
„ **103**/70 „ „ „ 24 „ strong.
„ **103**/90 „ „ „ 27 „
„ **103**/115 „ „ „ 29 „
„ **103**/150 „ „ „ 32 „

Flautas:
Nr. **103**/40 **hojalata,** largura cª 21 cm.
„ **103**/55 „ „ „ 24 „ delgado.
„ **103**/60 „ „ „ 24 „ fuerte.
„ **103**/80 „ „ „ 27 „
„ **103**/105 „ „ „ 29 „
„ **103**/140 „ „ „ 32 „

Flautas:
Nr. **103**/50 **niquel,** largura cª 21 cm.
„ **103**/65 „ „ „ 24 „ delgado.
„ **103**/70 „ „ „ 24 „ fuerte.
„ **103**/90 „ „ „ 27 „
„ **103**/115 „ „ „ 29 „
„ **103**/150 „ „ „ 32 „

103/83/2

103/84/9

103/85

Blechtrompeten, glattes Weißblech, bemalt, **mit Blechmundstück,** ohne Trichter, ohne Griff.

Nr. **103**/83/	1	2
Länge:	ca. 4,7	10 cm

Blechtrompeten, glattes Weißblech, bemalt, **mit Blechmundstück** und Trichter.

No. **103**/84	-/1	-/2	-/3	-/4	-/5	-/6	-/7	-/8	-/9
	ohne Griff		mit Griff						
Länge: ca.	5,5	8,3	7,5	8,8	9,5	10,5	11,2	12,4	13,8 cm
Trichter-durchmesser:	1,8	1,8	2,7	2,7	2,7	3,6	3,6	3,6	3,6 „

Blechtrompeten, glattes Weißblech, bemalt, **mit Porzellanmundstück,** Trichter und Griff.

Nr. **103**/85 Länge: 14,3 cm
Trichter-durchmesser: 3,6 „

Tin-Trumpets, smooth tin-plate, painted, **with tin mouth-piece,** without funnel, without handle.

Nr. **103**/83/	1	2
Length:	abt. 4,7	10 cm

Tin-Trumpets, smooth tin-plate, painted, **with tin mouth-piece,** and funnel.

No. **103**/84	-/1	-/2	-/3	-/4	-/5	-/6	-/7	-/8	-/9
	without handle		with handle						
Length: abt.	5,5	8,3	7,5	8,8	9,5	10,5	11,2	12,4	13,8 cm
Diameter of funnel:	1,8	1,8	2,7	2,7	2,7	3,6	3,6	3,6	3,6 „

Tin-Trumpets, smooth tin-plate, painted, **with "china" mouth-piece,** funnel and handle.

Nr. **103**/85 Length: 14,3 cm
Diameter of funnel: 3,6 „

Trompetas de hojalata lisa, pintada, **con bocal de hojalata,** sin embudo, sin asa.

Nr. **103**/83/	1	2
Largura:	cª 4,7	10 cm

Trompetas de hojalata lisa, pintada, **con bocal de hojalata** y con embudo.

No. **103**/84	-/1	-/2	-/3	-/4	-/5	-/6	-/7	-/8	-/9
	sin asa		con asa						
Largura: cª	5,5	8,3	7,5	8,8	9,5	10,5	11,2	12,4	13,8 cm
Diámetro del embudo:	1,8	1,8	2,7	2,7	2,7	3,6	3,6	3,6	3,6 „

Trompetas de hojalata lisa, pintada, **con bocal de porcelana,** embudo y asa.

Nr. **103**/85 Largura: 14,3 cm
Diámetro del embudo: 3,6 „

Beachten Sie auch die Veröffentlichung auf Seite 74 und 75 des Hauptkataloges.

Please note also the publication on page 74 and 75 of the principal catalogue.
Llamamos también su atención á la publicación en la página 74 y 75 del catálogo principal.

103/86/6

103/87/6

103/88/1, **103**/89/1

Blechtrompeten, gepreßtes, ornamentiertes Weißblech, bemalt, **Blechmundstück,** Trichter, Griff.

Nr. **103**/86		1	2	3	4	5	6	
Länge:	ca.	10,5	12	14,5	17	18,5	21	cm
Trichterdurchmesser:		3,5	3,5	3,7	4,5	4,5	5	„

Blechtrompeten, gepreßtes, ornamentiertes Weißblech, bemalt, **Porzellanmundstück,** Trichter, Griff.

Nr. **103**/87		1	2	3	4	5	6	
Länge:	ca.	14,3	17	19,3	21,8	25,9	29,5	cm
Trichterdurchmesser:		3,7	4,5	5,5	5,7	6	6,5	„

Blechtrompeten, gepreßtes, ornamentiertes Weißblech, bemalt, **Blechknopfmundstück m. Porzellanspitze,** Trichter, Griff.

Nr. **103**/88		1	2	3	4	5	6	
Länge:	ca.	20,5	21,3	23	24	24,5	25,4	cm
Trichterdurchmesser:		6	6,5	6	6,5	6,5	7	„

Blechtrompeten, genau wie Serie **103**/88, aber **Gelbblech,** bemalt.

Nr. **103**/89		1	2	3	4	5	6	
Länge:	ca.	20,5	21,3	23	24	24,5	25,4	cm
Trichterdurchmesser:		6	6,5	6	6,5	6,5	7	„

Tin-Trumpets, of stamped, ornamented tin-plate, painted, **mouth-piece of tin,** with funnel and handle.

Nr. **103**/86		1	2	3	4	5	6	
Length:	abt.	10,5	12	14,5	17	18,5	21	cm
Diameter of funnel:		3,5	3,5	3,7	4,5	4,5	5	„

Tin-Trumpets, of stamped, ornamented tin-plate, painted, **with china mouthpiece,** with funnel and handle.

Nr. **103**/87		1	2	3	4	5	6	
Length:	abt.	14,3	17	19,3	21,8	25,9	29,5	cm
Diameter of funnel:		3,7	4,5	5,5	5,7	6	6,5	„

Tin-Trumpets, of stamped, ornamented tin-plate, painted, **mouthpiece of tin with china top,** with funnel and handle.

Nr. **103**/88		1	2	3	4	5	6	
Length:	abt.	20,5	21,3	23	24	24,5	25,4	cm
Diameter of funnel:		6	6,5	6	6,5	6,5	7	„

Metal-Trumpets, exactly as series **103**/88, but of **yellow** sheet-metal, painted.

Nr. **103**/89		1	2	3	4	5	6	
Length:	abt.	20,5	21,3	23	24	24,5	25,4	cm
Diameter of funnel:		6	6,5	6	6,5	6,5	7	„

Trompetas de hojalata estampada, ornamentada y pintada, bocal de hojalata, con embudo y asa.

Nr. **103**/86		1	2	3	4	5	6	
Largura:	ca	10,5	12	14,5	17	18,5	21	cm
Diámetro del embudo:		3,5	3,5	3,7	4,5	4,5	5	„

Trompetas de hojalata estampada, ornamentada y pintada, con bocal de porcelana, con embudo y asa.

Nr. **103**/87		1	2	3	4	5	6	
Largura:	ca	14,3	17	19,3	21,8	25,9	29,5	cm
Diámetro del embudo:		3,7	4,5	5,5	5,7	6	6,5	„

Trompetas de hojalata estampada, ornamentada y pintada, bocal de hojalata con punta de porcelana, con embudo y asa.

Nr. **103**/88		1	2	3	4	5	6	
Largura:	ca	20,5	21,3	23	24	24,5	25,4	cm
Diámetro del embudo:		6	6,5	6	6,5	6,5	7	„

Trompetas de hojalata, exactamente como la serie **103**/88, mas de metal **amarillo,** pintado.

Nr. **103**/89		1	2	3	4	5	6	
Largura:	ca	20,5	21,3	23	24	24,5	25,4	cm
Diámetro del embudo:		6	6,5	6	6,5	6,5	7	„

103/90/7

103/91/6

Blechtrompeten, Spiralpressung, Weißblech bemalt, **Blechknopfmundstück mit Porzellanspitze,** Trichter, Griff.

Nr. **103**/90		1	2	3	4	5	6	7	
Länge:	ca.	18,5	20,7	23,3	23	24,5	25,2	32,5	cm
Trichterdurchmesser:		5,5	5,8	6	6,5	6,5	7	7	„

Blechtrompeten, Spiralpressung, Ausführung genau wie Serie **103**/90/—, aber **Gelbblech** bemalt:

Nr. **103**/91		1	2	3	4	5	6	7	
Länge:	ca.	18,5	20,7	23,3	23	24,5	25,2	32,5	cm
Trichterdurchmesser:		5,5	5,8	6	6,5	6,5	7	7	„

Tin-Trumpets, spiral-stamped, painted, **with tin-plate mouth-piece and china top,** with funnel and handle.

Nr. **103**/90		1	2	3	4	5	6	7	
Length:	abt.	18,5	20,7	23,3	23	24,5	25,2	32,5	cm
Diameter of funnel:		5,5	5,8	6	6,5	6,5	7	7	„

Metal-Trumpets, spiral-stamped, exactly as series **103** 90, but **yellow sheet-metal,** painted:

Nr. **103**/91		1	2	3	4	5	6	7	
Length:	abt.	18,5	20,7	23,3	23	24,5	25,2	32,5	cm
Diameter of funnel:		5,5	5,8	6	6,5	6,5	7	7	„

Trompetas de hojalata estampada en espiral, y pintada, **con bocal de hojalata y punta de porcelana,** con embudo y asa.

Nr. **103**/90		1	2	3	4	5	6	7	
Largura:	ca	18,5	20,7	23,3	23	24,5	25,2	32,5	cm
Diámetro del embudo:		5,5	5,8	6	6,5	6,5	7	7	„

Trompetas de hojalata estampada en espiral, exactamente como la serie **103**/90, pero de **metal amarillo,** pintado:

Nr. **103**/91		1	2	3	4	5	6	7	
Largura:	ca	18,5	20,7	23,3	23	24,5	25,2	32,5	cm
Diámetro del embudo:		5,5	5,8	6	6,5	6,5	7	7	„

Beachten Sie auch die Veröffentlichung auf Seite 74 und 75 des Hauptkataloges.

Please note also the publication on page 46 and 47 of the principal catalogue.
Llamamos también su atención á la publicación en la página 46 y 47 del catálogo principal.

Mechanische Artikel. — Mechanical toys. — Juguetes con mecanismo.

93/554/3 Länge / Length / Largura $20^{1}/_{2}$ cm.

93/554/2 Länge / Length / Largura 16 cm.

93/555 Länge / Length / Largura $18^{1}/_{2}$ cm

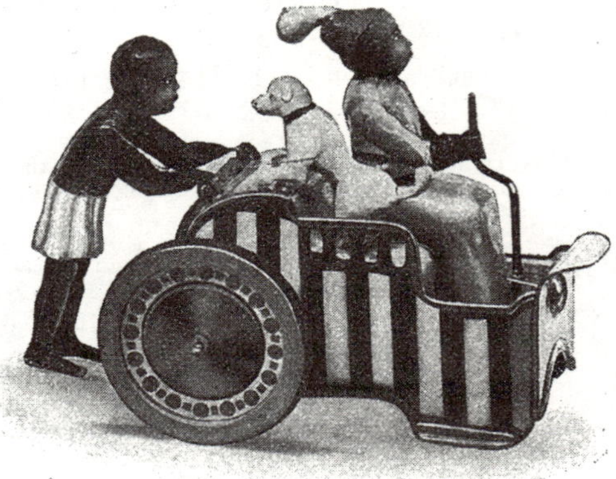

93/552 Länge / Length / Largura 15 cm.

93/551 Länge / Length / Largura $15^{1}/_{2}$ cm.

93/532 Länge / Length / Largura $17^{1}/_{2}$ cm.

93/553 Länge / Length / Largura 18 cm.

93/521 Länge / Length / Largura $16^{1}/_{2}$ cm.

93/500 Länge / Length / Largura $16^{1}/_{2}$ cm.

93/501 Länge / Length / Largura 18 cm.

93/538 Länge / Length / Largura $16^{1}/_{2}$ cm.

93/528 Länge / Length / Largura 31 cm.

Mit Spiralfedern. — With spiral springs. — Con espirales.

93/539 Länge / Length / Largura 18 cm.

Beachten Sie auch die Veröffentlichung auf Seite 46 und 47 des Hauptkataloges.

Please note also the publication on page 46 and 47 of the principal catalogue.
Llamamos también su atención á la publicación en la página 46 y 47 del catálogo principal.

Mechanische Artikel. — Mechanical Toys. — Juguetes con mecanismo.

93/511 Länge / Length / Largura 14 cm.

93/560 Länge / Length / Largura 19½ cm.

93/540 Länge / Length / Largura 19½ cm.

93/561 Länge / Length / Largura 19½ cm

93/530 Länge / Length / Largura 19 cm.

93/546 Länge / Length / Largura 19 cm.

93/545 Länge / Length / Largura 17 cm.

93/547 Länge / Length / Largura 19 cm.

93/519 Länge / Length / Largura 14 cm.

93/542 Länge / Length / Largura 22 cm.

93/507 Länge / Length / Largura 16 cm.

93/526 Länge / Length / Largura 28½ cm.

93/506 Länge / Length / Largura 16 cm.

93/504
Länge / Length / Largura 12½ cm.

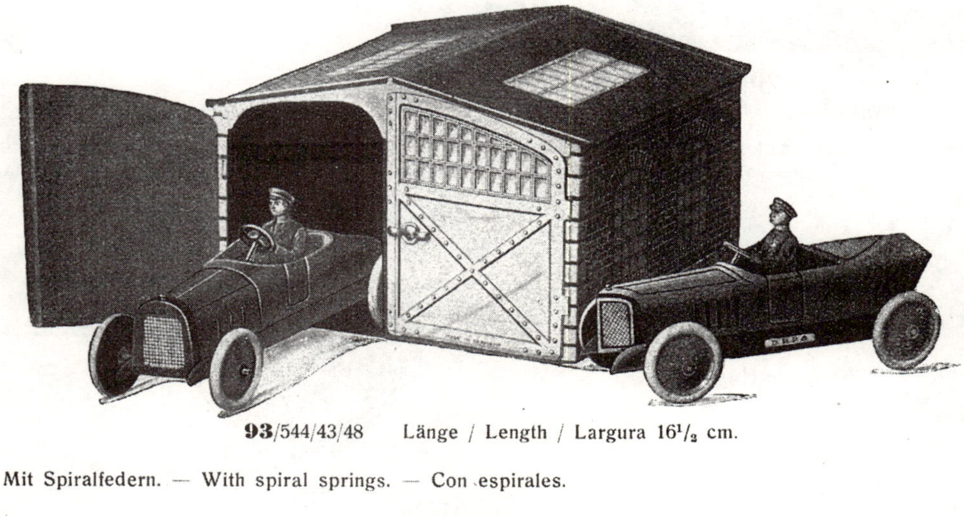

93/544/43/48 Länge / Length / Largura 16½ cm.

Mit Spiralfedern. — With spiral springs. — Con espirales.

Beachten Sie auch die Veröffentlichung auf Seite 46 und 47 des Hauptkataloges.

Please note also the publication on page 50 and 179 of the principal catalogue.
Llamamos también su atención á la publicación en la página 50 y 179 del catálogo principal.

Spielzeug-Nähmaschinen. — Toy sewing-machines. — Máquinas de coser para niños.

26/16

26/16 Für Hand- und Fußbetrieb.
For hand- and foot-drive.
Para movimiento de mano y de pié.

Größe der Maschine 20×14×18 cm. Höhe des Tisches 65 cm, Länge 55 cm, Breite 30 cm. Gewicht der Maschine mit Gestell 12 kg.

Size of the machine 20×14×18 cm. Height of table 65 cm, length 55 cm, width 30 cm. Weight of the machine with frame 12 kg.

Tamaño de la máquina 20×14×18 cm. Altura de la mesa 65 cm, largura 55 cm, anchura 30 cm. Peso de la máquina con armazón 12 kg.

26/25 Länge 25 cm, Breite 18 cm, Höhe 20 cm, Gewicht 3 kg. Eine ausgezeichnete Nähmaschine für alle Arten Hausarbeit. Die Maschine produziert eine vorzügliche Doppelsteppstichnaht. Säumer, Lineal. Schraubenzieher, Ölkanne, 2 Nadeln, 2 Spulen sind der Maschine beigegeben. Praktisches Geschenk für junge Damen.

Length 25 cm, width 18 cm, height 20 cm, weight 3 kg. An excellent sewing-machine for all kinds of homework. The machine produces a superior double quilting stitch seam. Hemmer, rule, screw-driver, oil-can, 2 needles, 2 spools are delivered with machine. Practical present for young ladies.

Largura 25 cm, anchura 18 cm, altura 20 cm, peso 3 kg. Una excelente máquina de coser para toda clase de costura doméstica. La máquina produce una costura excelente de pespunte doble. Orlador, regla, destornillador, aceitera, 2 agujas, 2 husos son suministrados con la máquina. Práctico presente para señoritas.

Doppelsteppstich-Nähmaschine,
Ringschiffchen.
Double quilting stitch sewing-machine,
ring shuttle.
Máquina de coser de pespunte doble.

Kein Spielzeug. — No Toy.
No juguete.

26/25

Messingblech-Spardosen. — Brassplate saving-boxes. — Huchas de hoja de latón.

2044/4

2044/3

2044/2

2044/1

Die Klischees sind $^1/_4$ der natürlichen Größe.
The electroes are $^1/_4$ of natural size.
Los clisés son de $^1/_4$ del tamaño natural.

2044/5

Nickelblech.
Nickelplate.
Hoja de niquel.

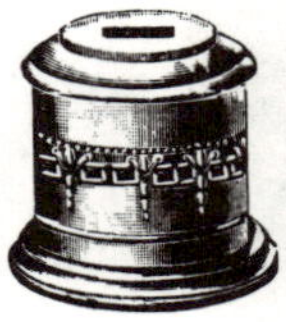

2044/6

Sortiment.
Assortment.
Surtido.

Ozeandampfer mit Kreiselmotor. — Ocean-steamer with turbine-motor. — Vapor transmarino con motor de turbina.

2001/7

Größe / Size / Tamaño $23^1/_2$ cm.

NEUHEIT!

NOVELTY!

¡NOVEDAD!

2001/8

Größe / Size / Tamaño $27^1/_2$ cm.

Die Ozeandampfer mit Kreiselmotor sind in den Größen 18 bis 31 cm lieferbar. — The ocean-steamers with turbine-motor are to be had in sizes from 18 to 31 cm. Los vapores transmarinos con motor de turbina pueden ser suministrados en los tamaños de 18 hasta 31 cm.

Feuersprühender Kreisel.

Fire-casting top.

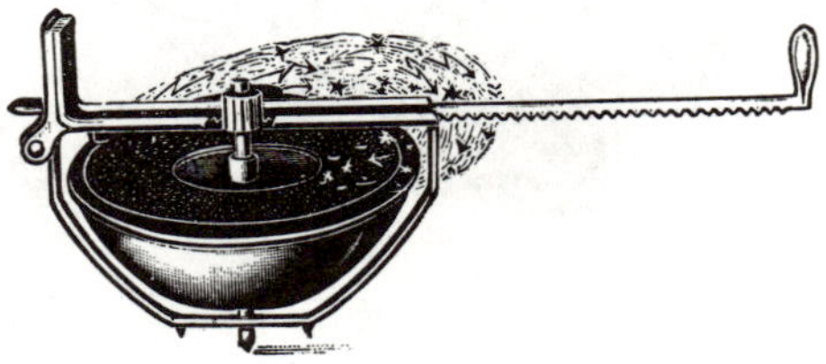

2001/6

Peón hechando fuego.

Beachten Sie auch die Veröffentlichung auf Seite 50 und 179 des Hauptkataloges.

Please note also the publication on page 110—117 of the principal catalogue.
Llamamos también su atención á la publicación en la página 110—117 del catálogo principal.

17/19/5

17/8731/4

17/8731/2

17/90/3

17/1086/1

17/46/2

17/2140/00

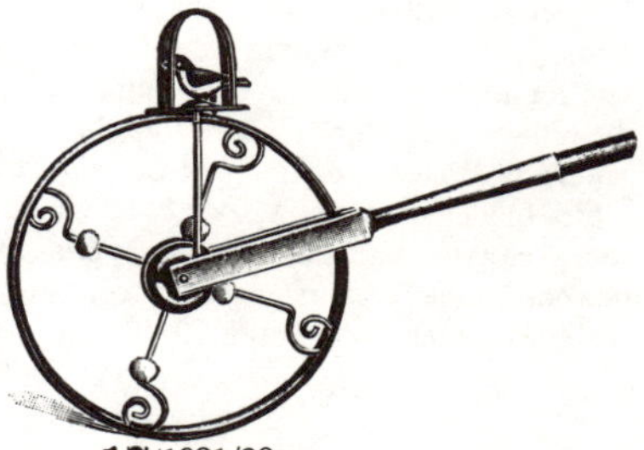
17/1081/00

17/1078/1

17/1415

17/1008

17/141/6

17/1969

17/2024/3

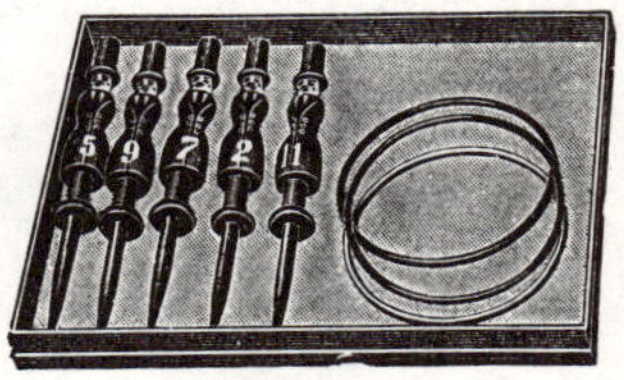
17/2091

17/346

17/51/0

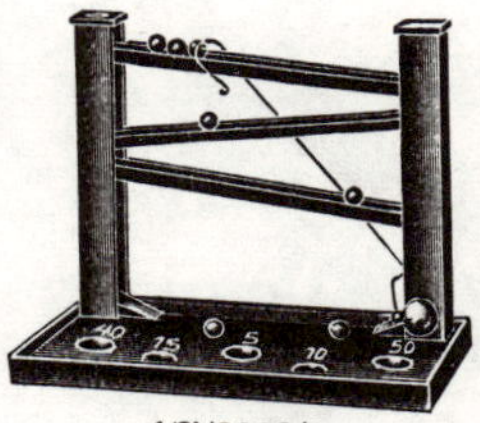
17/3089/1

17/3090/1

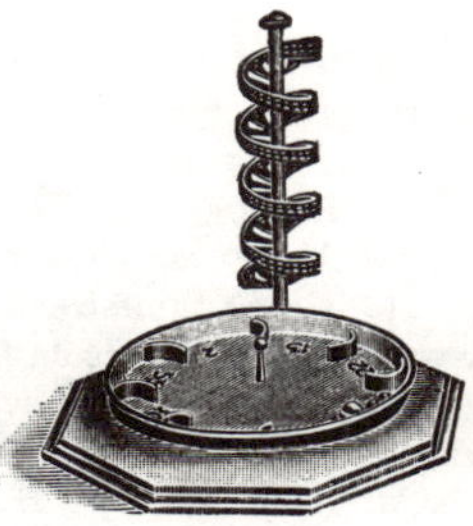
17/107/1

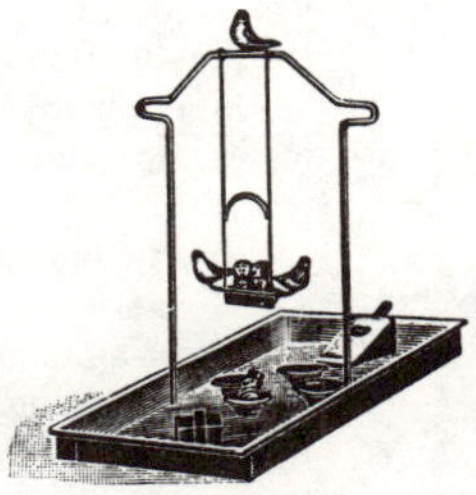
17/2025

17/1092

17/2080

17/2082

17/2079/3

17/2078

17/1090

3

Beachten Sie auch die Veröffentlichung auf Seite 110—117 des Hauptkataloges.

Freifliegende Flugzeugmodelle.

Die Modelle werden durch Gummi- oder Preßluftmotoren angetrieben, und es sind Flugstrecken bis zu 400 m zu erreichen. Jeder einzelne Teil der Modelle ist leicht auswechselbar, und es wird empfohlen, stets einige Ersatzpropeller und Ersatzgummimotoren mit zu bestellen. Alle Apparate sind zusammenlegbar, wodurch engste Verpackung ermöglicht wird. In eine Kiste 120×90×80 cm können verpackt werden: ca. 90 Modelle oder ca. 80 Baukasten. Bruttogewicht einer solchen Kiste ca. 70—95 kg.

Free flying aeroplane-types.

These types are driven by rubber- or compressed air-motors, and flying-stretches of up to 400 meters can be reached at. Each single piece of the types is easily exchangeable, and it is recommended, to ask always for some spare propellers and spare rubber-motors, when ordering an aeroplane. All apparatus are foldable, whereby closest packing will be possible. In a case of abt. 120×90×80 cm there can be packed: abt. 90 types or abt. 80 boxes of construction. Grossweight of such a case abt. 70—95 kg.

Aeroplanos volando libres.

Estos tipos son accionados por motores de goma ó aire comprimido, pudiendo volar espacios hasta 400 metros. Cada pieza singular de los tipos es cambiable sin dificultad, y es recomendable mandar venir con el pedido luego algunos propulsores y motores a goma, de repuesto. Todos los aparatos son plegables, por lo que el empaque será muy reducido. Caben en una caja de ca. 120×90×80 cm: ca. 90 tipos ó ca. 80 cajas de construcción. Peso bruto de una tal caja ca. 70—95 kg.

128/2

Möve-Eindecker, Gewicht 50 g. Die Tragflächen sind verspannt.

Gull-monoplane, weight 50 g. The sails are rigged.

Monoplano "Gaviota", peso 50 g. Las alas están tendidas.

128/100

Liliput-Eindecker, Gewicht 15 g. Bespannung aus Japanpapier.

Liliput-monoplane, weight 15 g. Sails of japan-paper.

Monoplano "Liliput", peso 15 g. Alas de papel japonez.

128/102

Libellen-Eindecker, Gewicht 25 g. Bespannung aus Japanpapier.

Libella-monoplane, weight 25 g. Sails of japan-paper.

Monoplano "Libela", peso 25 g. Alas de papel japonez.

128/1

Pfeil-Eindecker, Gewicht 40 g. Billiger und stabiler Apparat.

Arrow-monoplane, weight 40 g. Cheap and stable apparatus.

Monoplano "Flecha", peso 40 g. Aparato barato y estable.

128/3

Taube-Eindecker, Gewicht 65 g. Ganz neuartige Konstruktion.

Pigeon-monoplane, weight 65g. Quite novel construction.

Monoplano "Paloma", peso 65 g. Construcción del todo nueva.

128/6

Sport-Eindecker, Gewicht 80 g. Besonders leicht gebauter Apparat. Guter Weitstreckenflieger.

Sport-monoplane, weight 80 g. Particularly light construction. Good flyer of wide stretches.

Monoplano "Deporte", peso 80 g. Aparato de construcción particularmente ligera. Buen volador de trechos largos.

128/4

Parasol-Eindecker, Gewicht 80 g. Der Apparat ist mit Stahldraht verspannt.

Parasol-monoplane, weight 80 g. The apparatus is rigged with steel-wire.

Monoplano "Parasol", peso 80 g. El aparato está tendido con alambre de acero.

128/5

Fokker-Doppeldecker, Gewicht 90 g. Neu konstruiert, schöner stabiler Flug.

Fokker-biplane, weight 90 g. Newly constructed, beautiful stable flight.

Biplano "Fokker", peso 90 g. Nuevamente construido, vuelo lindo y estable.

128/7

Rumpf-Eindecker, Gewicht 125 g. Sehr eleganter und gut fliegender Apparat mit stabil gebautem, vollem Rumpf.

Rumpf-monoplane, weight 125 g. Very elegant and well flying apparatus with stably constructed full body.

Monoplano "Rumpf", peso 125 g. Aparato muy elegante de buen vuelo con cuerpo completo de construcción estable.

128/8

Der richtige Start!

The right start!

!El start derecho!

128/9

No. **128**/8 **Rumpf-Doppeldecker.** Gewicht 150 g. Gleicher Apparat wie 128/7 als Doppeldecker.

Rumpf-Biplane, weight 150 g. Same apparatus as 128/7, but biplane.

Biplano "Rumpf", peso 150 g. El mismo aparato con 128/7, pero de biplano.

128/10

No. **128**/9 **Rekord-Modell,** Gewicht 170 g. Prachtvoller Apparat mit Tragflächen, die nach Art der Junkers-Profile gewölbt und doppelseitig bespannt sind.

Record type, weight 170 g. Magnificent apparatus with sails, which are vaulted after the fashion of the Junker's profiles and rigged on both sides.

Tipo „Record", peso 170 g. Aparato magnifico con alas abovedadas al modo de los perfiles de Junker, y tendido en ambos lados.

No. **128**/10 **Motor-Apparat,** Gewicht 500 g. Der Apparat wird angetrieben durch einen neuartigen *3-Zylinder-Preßluft-Motor.* Besonders stabil gearbeitet, mit starker gewölbter Tragfläche. Spannweite 1,20 m.

Motor-apparatus, weight 500 g. The apparatus is driven by a novel *3 cylinder air-compressed motor.* Particularly stable construction with strong vaulted sails, spanning width 1,20 m.

Aparato de motor, peso 500 g. El aparato es impulsado por un *motor de aire comprimido de 3 cilindros,* de construcción moderna. Trabajo muy estable con alas fuertes, abovedadas, envergadura 1,20 m.

Flug-Spiele. — Flying Toys. — Juguetes de vuelo.

128/21

No. **128**/20 **Wolkenkitzler.** Kleiner Segelflieger, der mittels Katapult abgeschossen wird und im Gleitflug wieder zur Erde kommt. Gewicht per Dtz. 600 g.

Sky-tickler. Little sailing-flyer, discharged by a catapult, coming down again in a gliding flight. Weight per doz. 600 g.

Volador a los nubes. Pequeño volador de velar que es impulsado por catapulta, voltando a la tierra en vuelo deslisador. Peso por doc. 600 g.

No. **128**/21 **Paradiesvogel.** Der fliegende Vogel. Große Neuheit. Flugspielzeug aus bunten Federn, genau einem Vogel nachgebildet. Glänzender Reklameartikel. Gewicht per Dtz. 80 g.

Bird of Paradise. The flying bird. Great novelty! Flying toy of gay feathers exactly imitating a bird. Brillant puffing article. Weight per doz. 80 g.

Manucodiata. ¡El pájaro volante! Gran novedad. Juguete de vuelo hecho de plumas multicolores imitando exactamente un pájaro. Artículo brillante de reclamo. Peso por doc. 80 g.

Flugzeug-Baukasten.

In unseren Baukasten ist Konstruktionsmaterial bester Qualität enthalten. Mit diesem Material kann sich jeder Junge an Hand einer genauen Beschreibung wirklich gut fliegende Modelle selbst aufmontieren.

Aeroplane-constructing-boxes.

Our boxes contain the best constructing material for aeroplanes. With this material every boy will be able to erect by himself really well flying types with the aid of an exact description.

Cajas de construcción para aeroplanos.

Nuestras cajas de construcción contienen solamente material de la mejor calidad. Con este material cualquier niño puede montar él mismo tipos de aeroplanos de realmente buen vuelo, con ayuda de una descripción exacta.

128/1 K

Pfeil-Eindecker-Baukasten. Größe 47 × 18 × 3 cm. Gewicht 225 g.
Arrow-monoplane constructing box. Size 47 × 18 × 3 cm. Weight 225 g.
Caja de construcción para monoplano "Flecha". Tamaño 47 × 18 × 3 cm. Peso 225 g.

128/3 K

Taube-Eindecker-Baukasten. Größe 55 × 21 × 3,5 cm. Gewicht 270 g.
Pigeon-monoplane constructing box. Size 55 × 21 × 3,5 cm. Weight 270 g.
Caja de construcción para monoplano "Paloma". Tamaño 55 × 21 × 3,5 cm. Peso 270 g.

Parasol-monoplane constructing-box.
Size 61 × 22 × 3,5 cm. Weight 470 g.

Caja de construcción para monoplano "Parasol".
Tamaño 61 × 22 × 3,5 cm. Peso 470 g.

128/4 K

Parasol-Eindecker-Baukasten. Größe 61 × 22 × 3,5 cm. Gewicht 470 g.

Fokker-biplane constructing box.
Size 61 × 22 × 3,5 cm. Weight 490 g.

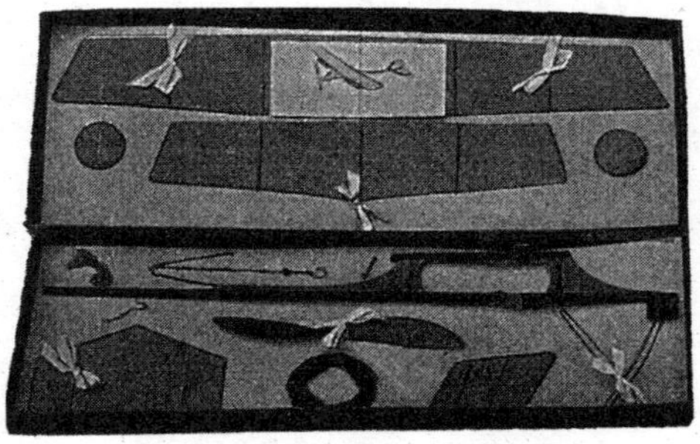

Caja de construcción para biplano "Fokker".
Tamaño 61 × 22 × 3,5 cm. Peso 490 g.

128/5 K

Fokker-Doppeldecker-Baukasten. Größe 61 × 22 × 3,5 cm. Gewicht 490 g.

128/6 K

Ein- und Doppeldecker-Baukasten. Dieser Baukasten enthält 2 Modelle. Größe 61 × 22 × 3,5 cm. Gewicht 490 g.

Monoplane and biplane constructing box. This box contains 2 types. Size 61 × 22 × 3,5 cm. Weight 490 g.

Caja de construcción para monoplano y biplano. Esta caja contiene dos tipos. Tamaño 61 × 22 × 3,5 cm. Peso 490 g.

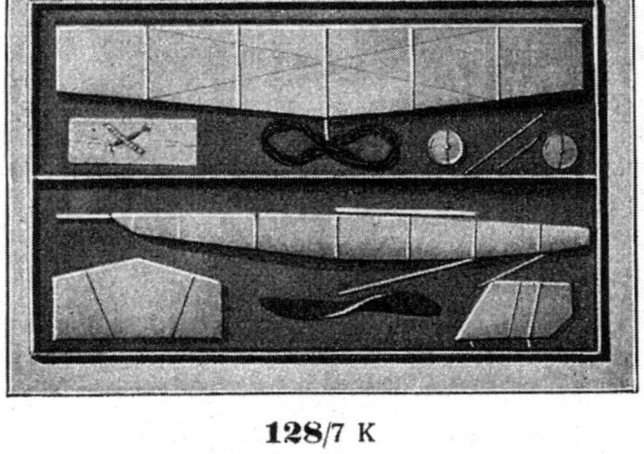

128/7 K

128/7 K

Vollrumpf-Eindecker-Baukasten.
Größe 74 × 23 × 5 cm. Gewicht 680 g.
Full body monoplane constructing box.
Size 74 × 23 × 5 cm. Weight 680 g.
Caja de construcción para monoplano "Vollrumpf".
Tamaño 74 × 23 × 5 cm. Peso 680 g.

10/6001

Schrank. Wardrobe. Armario.
Weiß lackiert. White varnished. Blanco barnizado.

10/6001	3	4	5	6	7	8	9	10
Höhe cm	55	60	70	80	90	100	120	140
Breite „	32	35	40	45	52	58	68	76
Tiefe „	19	20	22	25	27	30	35	40

Neu geborenes Baby.
New born Baby.
Bebé recien-nacido.

10/177/35 cm

10/6011

Kommode. Drawers. Cómoda.
Weiß lackiert. White varnished. Blanco barnizado.

10/6011	3	4	5	6	7	8
Höhe cm	30	35	40	45	50	60
Breite „	39	45	56	62	68	78
Tiefe „	22	26	30	33	35	40

10/2307

Frachtauto mit Anhänger.
Motor-truck.
Camion.

Schaukelstuhl.
Rocking chair.
Mecedora.

Nr. **10**/1010.
Mit Fellkopf.
With skin head.
Con cabeza de piel.

10/1010

Nr. **10**/1010 P.
Mit Plüschkopf.
With plush head.
Con cabeza de felpa.

Nr. **10**/1010 H.
Mit Holzkopf.
With wooden head.
Con cabeza de madera.

Nr. **10**/1010 1/2
Ohne Kopf.
Without head.
Sin cabeza.

10/2311

Puppen-Autos.
Automobiles for dolls.
Automoviles para muñecas.

10/2311
Geöffnet. Open. Abierto.

Menagerie-Auto. — Menagerie motor car. — Casa de fieras.

10/1646 **10**/1647

Kinder-Automobile.
Automobiles for children.
Automóviles para niños.

Nr. **10**/1645 und **10**/1646
Für 1 Kind mittlerer Größe.
For 1 child of middle tallness.
Para 1 niño de altura mediana.

Nr. **10**/1644 und **10**/1647
Für 1 größeres Kind.
For 1 larger child.
Para 1 niño.

10/1644 **10**/1645

Aus Sperrholz und Aluminium.
Of barred wood and aluminium.
De chapa de madera y aluminio.

Dieselben Autos mit Gummirädern. Same automobiles with rubber-tyres. Los mismos con ruedas de goma.

10/1646 Gi.,	**10**/1647 Gi.,	**10**/1644 Gi.,	**10**/1645 Gi.
ca. 115	130	115	95 cm.

Haußers Elastolin-Soldaten in allen Stellungen und Nationen.

88/0/640 u. 640 — 88/0/12 88/2/12 88/3/12 — 88/0/642 u. 642

88/0/41/6 u. 88/41/6

88/76/17

88/0/48/12 u. 88/48/12

88/24/12

88/0/644 u. 88/644

88/0/500/13 u. 88/500/13

88/0/44/8 u. 88/44/8

Nr.	„Elastolin"-Soldaten in allen Stellungen und Nationen. 6½ und 10½ cm hoch.	"Elastolin" Soldiers in all positions and of all nations. 2⅝" and 4⅛" high.	Soldados de "Elastolin" en variadas posiciones y de todas las naciones. 6½ y 10½ cm altura.
88/0/12 u. 2/12	Soldaten im Schritt.	Soldiers marching.	Soldados en marcha.
88/3/12	Engl. und dän. Garde im Schritt.	English and danish guards marching.	Guardia inglesa y danesa en marcha.
88/0/47 u. 47	Trommler, Pfeifer und Hornisten.	Drummers, pipers and bugles.	Tambores, pifanos y cornetas.
88/0/41/6 u. 41/6	1 Hauptmann zu Pferd, 5 Mann im Schritt, 1 Offizier.	1 captain on horseback, 5 men marching, 1 officer.	1 capitán á caballo, 5 hombres en marcha, 1 oficial.
88/0/48 u. 48	Musiker im Schritt.	Musicians marching.	Músicos en marcha.
88/0/49 u. 49	Fahnenträger im Schritt.	Colour-bearer marching.	Abanderado en marcha.
88/0/640 u. 640	Soldat, mit dem Gewehrkolben schlagend.	Men striking with gunbutt.	Soldado combatiendo á culatazos.
88/0/641 u. 641	Infanterie, fechtend.	Infantry fighting.	Infantería combatiendo.
88/0/642 u. 642	Hornist im Sturm.	Bugler storming.	Corneta asaltando.
88/0/644 u. 644	Fahnenträger im Sturm.	Colour-bearer storming.	Abanderado asaltando.
88/0/401 u. 401	Kavallerie zu Pferd.	Cavalry with horse marching.	Caballería, montada en marcha.
88/0/500/13 u. 500/13	9 Mann im Schritt, 4 Reiter zu Pferd.	9 men marching, 4 men on horseback.	9 infantes, 4 ginetes.
88/24/12	10 Mann, 2 Offiziere, Fahne und Schilderhaus.	10 men, 2 officers, 1 colour-bearer, 1 sentry-box of cardboard.	10 hombres, 2 oficiales, 1 abanderado, 1 garita de cartón.
88/0/44/8 u. 44/8	1 Hauptmann, Fahne, 2 Spielleute, 7 Mann, 1 Offizier.	1 captain, colour, 2 musicians, 7 men, 1 officer.	1 capitán, abanderado, 2 músicos, 7 hombres, 1 oficial.
88/44/32	1 Hauptmann, Fahne, 5 Spielleute, 32 Mann, 1 Offizier.	1 captain, colour, 5 musicians, 32 men incl. officer.	1 capitán, abanderado, 5 músicos, 32 hombres incl. oficial.
88/0/48/12 u. 48/12	1 Musikmeister, 11 Musiker.	1 bandmaster, 11 musicians.	1 maestro de banda, 11 músicos.
88/76/17	Parade-Aufmachung. 1 Hauptmann, Fahne, 6 Mann, 2 Offiziere, 7 Musiker.	Infantry Parade-Combinations, 1 captain, 1 colour-bearer, 6 men, 2 officers, 7 musicians.	Infantería en combinaciones de parada, 1 capitán, 1 abanderado, 6 hombres, 2 oficiales, 7 músicos.
88/79/44	1 Hauptmann, Fahne, 15 Mann, 2 Offiziere, 16 Musiker und 9 Kavalleristen.	1 captain, 1 colour-bearer, 15 men, 2 officers, 16 musicians and 9 men on horseback.	1 capitán, 1 abanderado, 15 hombres, 2 oficiales, 16 músicos y 9 ginetes.
88/0/403/6 u. 403/6	6 Reiter zu Pferd im Schritt.	6 men on horseback marching.	6 ginetes en marcha.
88/1/445/6	6 Musiker zu Pferd.	6 musicians on horseback.	6 músicos a caballo.
88/700/4	Erbsenkanone mit Protze, 4 Pferde, 4 Kanoniere.	Pea-canon with carriage, 4 horses, 4 men.	Cañon para garbanzos, con avantrén, 4 caballos, 4 artilleros.
88/709/2	Erbsenkanone mit Amorces, 2 Pferde, 3 Kanoniere.	Pea-canon for caps with carriage, 2 horses, 3 men.	Cañon para garbanzos y fulminantes, con avantrén, 2 caballos, 3 artilleros.
88/716/2	Amorces-Kanone Ia, 1 Fahrer, 2 Pferde, 2 Kanoniere.	Canon for caps Ia, 2 horses, 1 horseman, 2 gunners.	Cañon para fulminantes Ia cal., 2 caballos, 1 ginete, 2 artilleros.

Nr.	Lehr-, Gesellschafts- und Beschäftigungsspiele aus Pappe in allen Sprachen und Preislagen.	Indoor cardboard Games and Kindergarten Pastimes of every description made in all languages and prices.	Juegos de sociedad y de ocupación de cartón, de todos precios é idiomas.
88/116/2—3	Robinson Crusoe (Würfelspiel).	Robinson Crusoe (dice-game).	Robinson Crusoe (juego de dados).

Sortiment umfaßt über 1000 Nummern in Spielen. — Assortment contains over 1000 different games. — Surtido conteniendo mas de 1000 juegos diferentes.

88/15016

88/15120

88/15130

88/51126

88/15124

88/15174

88/1802

Feine Holzspielwaren. — First class wooden toys, handpainted. — Juguetes finos de madera.

88/15016 Raubtierhaus, 3 teilig, kompl. mit Tieren, 47×20×31 cm.	Big Cage for beast of prey, complete with animals, 18 1/2×8 1/8×12 1/4".	Gran jaula con fieras, 47×20×31 cm.
88/15100 Schafhaus mit Strohdach, Umzäung., Baum und Tieren 50×30×33 cm.	Sheep-fold with straw-roof, fences, tree, compl. with animals, 19 3/4×11 7/8×13".	Aprisco con techo de paja, cercado, árbol y corderos, 50×30×33 cm.
88/15113 Stall für Geflügel und Schweine, mit Tieren, 26×15×20 cm.	Poultry- and pig-stable, compl. with animals, 10 1/4×5 7/8×7 7/8".	Establo para aves y puercos, con animales, 26×15×20 cm.
88/15114 Stallung für Schafe, Esel und Ziegen, 38×19 1/2×15 1/2 cm.	Sheepfarm with goat and donkey-stable, compl. with animals, 15×7 5/8×6 1/8".	Establo para corderos, asnos y cabras, con animales, 38×19 1/2×15 1/2 cm
88/15117 Geflügelhof mit Hühner-, Gänse-, Schweine- und Taubenhaus, 43×33 1/2×33 1/2 cm.	Poultry yard with geese and pig-stable and dove cot, compl. with animals, 16 7/8×13 1/4×13 1/4".	Corral de aves, con gallinas, gansos, puercos y palomar, 43×33 1/2×33 1/2 cm.
88/15118 Kleintierfarm mit Kuh-, Geflügel-, Schweine- und Ziegenstall, 42×42×19 1/2 cm.	Countryfarm with cow, poultry, pig- and goat-stable, compl. with animals, 16 1/2×16 1/2×7 5/8".	Finca con establos para ganado, aves, puercos y cabras, 42×42×19 1/2 cm.
88/15120 Bauernhof mit Wohnhaus, Stallgebäude mit Einfahrt, 62×60×26 cm.	Large estate with mansion and extensive stabling and gate-way, complete with animals, 24 3/8×23 5/8×10 1/4".	Granja con casa de habitación, establos y puerta cochera, 62×60×26 cm.
88/15124 Bauernhof, umzäunt, mit Wohnhaus, Stall, Brunnen, 56×33×25 cm.	Countryfarm surrounded with dwelling-house, extensive stabling and fountain, compl. with animals, 22×13×9 7/8".	Granja cercada, con casa de habitación, establo y pozo 56×33×25 cm.
88/15126 Bauernhof mit Mauern und Tor, Wohnhaus, Stall, Wagenstand, 56×56×26 cm.	Large estate with mansion, stabling, coach-house, surrounded by wall and gate-way, compl. with animals, 22×22×10 1/4".	Granja con muralla y puerta cochera, casa de habitación, establo y cochera, 56×56×26 cm.
88/15130 Kleintierfarm mit Mauer und Tor, Geflügel-, Gänse- und Schweinestall, 62×37×29 cm.	Countryfarm with poultry- and goose-stable, sty, wall and gate-way, compl. with animals, 24 3/8×14 5/8×11 1/2".	Finca con muralla y puerta cochera, gallinero y establos para gansos y puercos, 62×37×29 cm.
88/15174 Geflügelstall mit Umzäunung und Tieren, 27×21×17 cm.	Poultry-stable with enclosure, complete with animals, 10 5/8×8 1/4×6 2/3".	Establo de aves, cercado, con animales, 27×21×17 cm.
88/15178 Schweinestall mit Umzäunung und Tieren, 29×22×12 cm.	Sty with enclosure, compl. with animals, 11 1/2×8 2/3×4 3/4".	Establo de puercos, cercado, con animales, 29×22×12 cm.
88/15180 Kuh- und Pferdestall mit Umzäunung und Tieren, 29×22×16 cm.	Cow-and horse-stable with enclosure, compl. with animals, 11 1/2×8 2/3×6 1/3".	Establo de vacas y caballos, cercado, con animales, 29×22×16 cm.
88/15182 Stall mit Wohnung und Umzäunung und Tieren, 34×26×17 cm.	Dwelling-house with stable and enclosure, compl. with animals, 13 3/8×10 1/4×6 2/3".	Establo con habitación, cercado, con animales, 34×26×17 cm.
88/1802 Zugpferd, Größen 13, 14, 17, 22, 26 u. 31 cm lang.	Draught-horse, sizes 5 1/8, 5 1/2, 6 2/3, 8 2/3, 10 1/4 and 12 1/4" long.	Caballo de tiro, tamaños 13, 14, 17, 22, 26 y 31 cm de largo.
88/1818 Sandkarren mit Pferd, Größen 38, 44 und 48 cm lang.	Sandcart with horse, sizes 15, 17 3/8 and 18 7/8" long.	Volquete para arena, con caballo, tamaños 38, 44 y 48 cm de largo.
88/1824/0 1/2 Expreßwagen mit 2 Pferden, 41 cm lang.	Express-waggon with 2 horses, 16 1/8" long.	Camión expreso, con 2 caballos, 41 cm de largo.
88/1840/2 1/2 Bierwagen mit 2 Pferden, 70 cm lang.	Brewery-waggon with 2 horses, 27 1/2" long.	Carro de cerveceria, con 2 caballos, 70 cm de largo.
88/1850/2 1/2 Langholzwagen mit 2 Pferden, 72 cm lang.	Timber-truck with 2 horses. 28 3/8" long.	Carro de maderos, con 2 caballos, 72 cm de largo.
88/1860/2 1/2 Möbelwagen mit 2 Pferden, 61 cm lang.	Furniture-man with 2 horses, 24" long.	Furgón de muebles, con 2 caballos, 61 cm de largo.

Please note also the publication on page 197—199 of the principal catalogue.
Llamamos también su atención á la publicación en la página 197—199 del catálogo principal.

Schutzmarke.
Trade mark.
Marca depositada.

„TIPPLE-TOPPLE-TIERE"

Maché-Tiere und Holzspielwaren. Maché-animals and wooden-toys.
Animales de Maché y juguetes de madera.

Schutzmarke.
Trade mark.
Marca depositada.

32/5383/4, 6, 9, 10, 12, 16, 20
Haustiersortiment.
Assortment of domestic animals.
Surtido de animales domésticos.

32/5185/6, 7, 9, 12, 16, 20, 24, 28, 33
Haustiersortiment.
Assortment of domestic animals.
Surtido de animales domésticos.

32/5397/6, 9, 12, 16, 20
Jagdtier-Sortiment.
Assortment of hunting animals.
Surtido de animales de caza.

32/17024
Schafstall.
Sheep-stable.
Aprisco.

32/17012
Pferdestall.
Horse-stable.
Caballeriza.

32/17036
Bauernhof.
Farm.
Granja de aldeanos.

32/17018
Stall mit Schuppen.
Stable with carriage-remise.
Establo con cochera.

32/16322
Felsenmenagerie.
Rocky-menagery.
Casa de fieras en la roca.

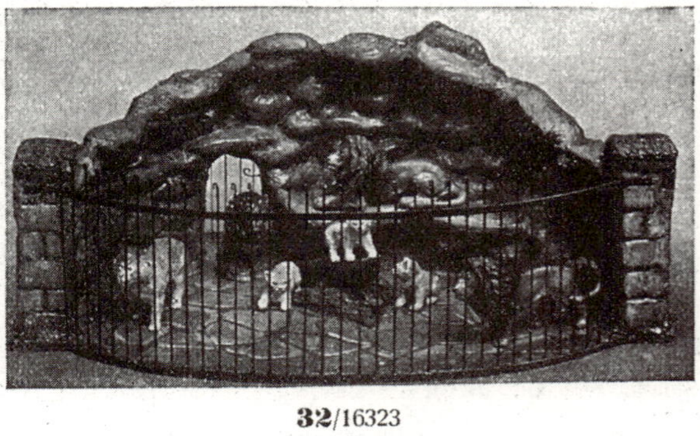

32/16323
Löwenschlucht.
Lion pit.
Jaula de leones.

Beachten Sie auch die Veröffentlichung auf Seite 197—199 des Hauptkataloges.

Please note also the publication on page 185—188 of the principal catalogue.
Llamamos también su atención a la publicación en la página 185—188 del catálogo principal.

STEIFF

SPIELWAREN

Schutzmarke — Knopf im Ohr

Neuheiten 1925/26

Steiff-Spiel- und -Reittiere aus Filz, Plüsch oder Samt sind weich gestopft und unzerbrechlich. Bestes Rohmaterial, jahrzehntelange Erfahrungen und ständige Verbesserungen sind die Grundlagen für die weltberühmte Qualität der Steiff-Spielwaren.

Alle Tiere haben eine Stimme; -,2 automatische Zug- oder Brummstimme, bei Puppen Mamastimme; -,1 Druckbalgstimme.

Abbildungen 1/8 nat. Größe.

28/9/5317w

No. **28**/10
Schimpanse. — Chimpanzee. Chimpancé.
Mohairplüsch, weiß.
Fine plush, white.
Felpa mohair, blanco.
No. 28/9/5307—5317 w (7—17 cm).

28/12 Teddybu 5320

28/12
Teddy
Besonders weich und leicht, mit Kapokfüllung. — Stuffed with kapok. — Rellenado de kapok.
No. 28/12/5317,1K—28/12/5335/,1K (25—50 cm),
Rosa, gelb. — Pink, yellow. — Rosa, amarillo.
No. 28/12/5323,1K—28/12/5330,1K (33—44 cm).
Mit farbiger Filzweste. — With waistcoat. — Con chaleco.
No. 28/12/Teddybu 5315—5322 (22—32 cm).

28/12 Tali Teddy 5307

Teddy und Schimpanse als Talisman f. Radfahrer.
Teddy and Chimp. as mascot.
Teddy y Chimp. para velocipedistas.
No. 28/12 Tali Teddy 5307
No. 28/9 Tali Chimp. 5307

No. **28**/12
Zottelbär. - Shaggy Bear. Oso vêlloso.
Langh. Mohairplüsch, braun meliert.
Longhair fine plush, brown.
Pelo largo felpa mohair, marron.
No. 28/12/1323,01—28/12/1329,01 (23—29 cm).

28/22/7317

No. **28**/22
Ente. — Duck. — Pato.
Mohairplüsch, mehrfarbig.
Fine plush, coloured.
Felpa mohair, multicolore.
No. 28/22/7314—7322 (14—22 cm).

28/36/3317,1

No. **28**/36
Hase. — Hare. — Liebre.
Mohairplüsch, braun meliert.
Fine plush, brown.
Felpa mohair, marron.
No. 28/36/3317,1—3322,1.

No. **28**/26
Foxterrier, Mohair, weiß, white, blanco.
No. 28/26/6307,0—6314,0.

28/26/6314,0

28/49/7314

No. **28**/49
Mops. — Pug dog. — Perro Mops.
Mohair, blond, weiß. — Lightbr., white. — Rubio, blanco.
Nr. 28/49/7314.

TOYS

Trade Mark — Button in Ear

Novelties 1925/26

Steiff-Toys have always been leading and famed for their natural and beautiful shapes and their wonderful, world famed quality. Skilled workmanship only can produce such unequalled toys. They are soft stuffed and unbreakable. The very best raw-material being used.

Each animal with voice; -,2 automatic animal voice, in regard to dolls "mama"-voice; -,1 "cuddle-me" animal voice.

Electros 1/8 nat. size.

28/68

28/68/1335,01k

Molly
Langhaarig. Mohairplüsch, weiß, braun.
White, brown
Blanco, marron.
68/1317,0K—1335,01 K.
68/3317—3380,1 K.

28/69/3322,1

28/69
Flock
Langh. Mohairplüsch, weiß, blond.
Longh. fine plush, white, lightbr.
Pelo largo felpa mohair, blanco, rubio.
No. 28/69/1317,0K—1335,01K
3317—3330,1

28/71/3328,1

28/71
Zotty
Mohair, weiß. — White. — Blanco.
No. 28/71/3328,1 (28 cm).

28/44
Katze. — Cat. — Gato.
Mohairplüsch, rot od. grau gestr.
Fine plush, red or grey striped.
No. 28/44/1317,01—1322,01 (17—22 cm).
Karikatur, Mohair, weiß. — White. — Blanco.
No. 28/44/6317—6322,1 (17—22 cm).

28/44/6322,1

28/44/1322,01

28/48

Löwe. — Lion. — León.
Mohairplüsch, hellbraun.
Fine plush, lightbrown.
Felpa mohair, rubio.
No. 28/48/1328—1350,2 (28—50 cm).

28/48/1335,2

JUGUETES

Marca de Fábrica — Botón en la oreja

Novedad 1925/26

Los juguetes Steiff son rellenos e irrompibles. Para la fabricación de estos juguetes se emplean unicamente materias primas de primera calidad. Su confección está confiada a obreros de gran pericia en este trabajo.

Todos los animales tienen voz; -,2 voz automática, en muñecas voz de mamá; -,1 voz de fuelle.

28/56/5632

28/56
Pferdeleine. — Reins. Ronzal.
Leder. — Leather. — Cuero.
No. 28/56/5625—28/56/7056 G

28/81
Flinko
Schimpanse, braun oder weiß.
Brown or white.
Marron ó blanco.

28/81/Flinko 322
Roly-Droly.
Holzwagen mit Plüschtieren. — Wood-cart with plush animals. — Carro de madera con animales de felpa.
No. 28/81/1012—28/81/3536.

28/136/5815,8

28/136
Lenkfahrzeuge mit Vierradlenkung.
Steering wheel toys with 4 wheel-steering.
Carretas sobre 4 ruedas dirigibles.
Holz, farbig lackiert.
Wood, painted.
Madera pintada.
No. 28/136/4813,8 (Auto).
No. 28/136/5815,8 (Aeroplan)
No. 28/136/6815,8 (Tram).
Ohne Puppe. — Without doll. — Sin muñeca.

28/81/1112

28/138
Kindersporträder. Children sporting articles. Patines para niños.
No. 28/138/Rennro 7878.
Holzrad mit Eisenreif.
Wood wheels with iron tyre.
Ruedas de madera con aro de hierro.

28/81/322

No. 28/138/Rennrogi 7882.
Scheibenräder mit Gummi.
With rubber tyre.
Ruedas con goma.

No. 28/138/Rennrolo 7886.
Große Ausführung mit Gummireif
Large model, with rubber tyre.
Modelo mayor con goma.

No. 28/138/Juniorad 5932.
Juniorad 5940.
Metalldreirad.
Iron tricycle.
Triciclo metálico.

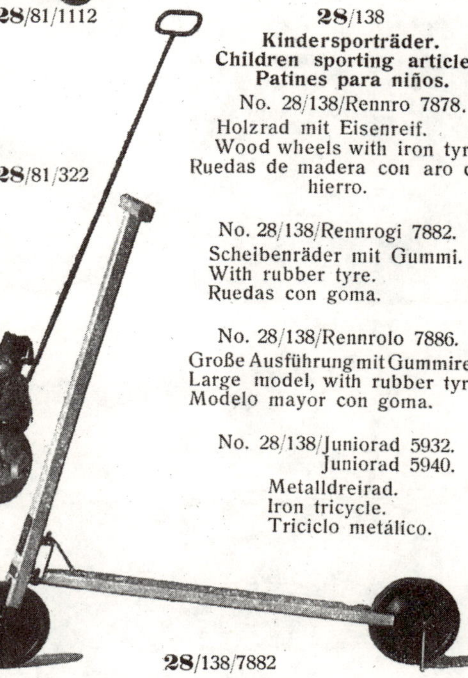

28/138/7882

Alle hier nicht abgebildeten Artikel finden Sie in der Preisliste aufgeführt. — All articles, not shown here, you will find in the corresponding price list.
Todos los artículos no ilustrados aqui son contenidos en la lista de precios.

Beachten Sie auch die Veröffentlichung auf Seite 185—188 des Hauptkataloges.

Please note also the publication on page 54—61 of the principal catalogue.
Llamamos también su atención á la publicación en la página 54—61 del catálogo principal.

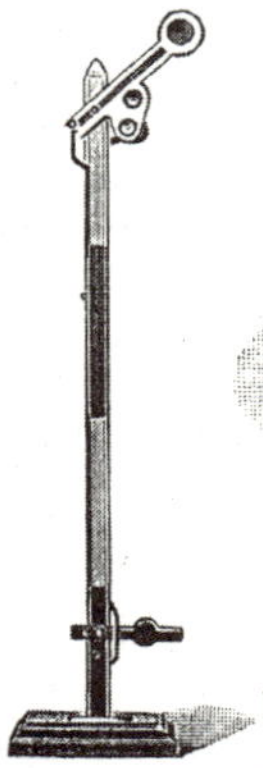
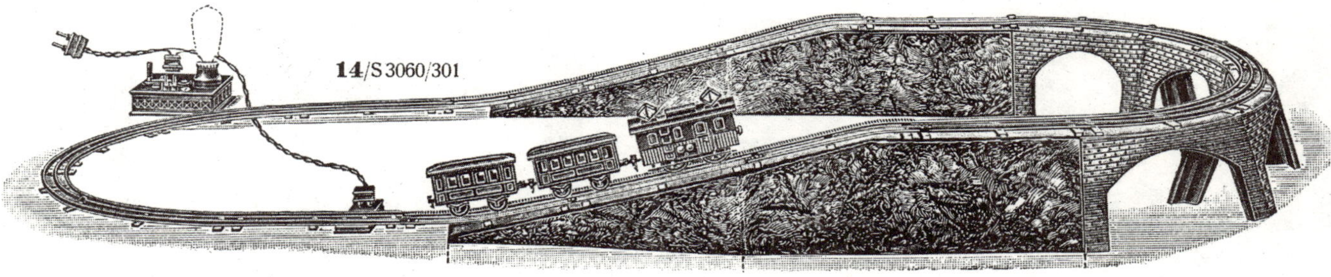

14/S 3060/301

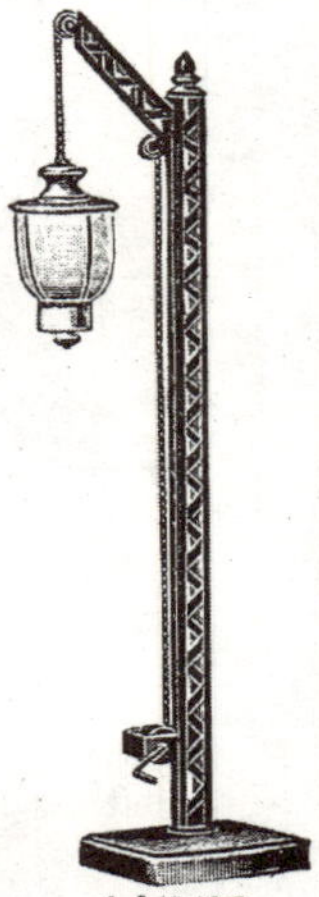

14/2337

14/2153

14/2000 F

14/3070/72 G

14/2437

14/2257

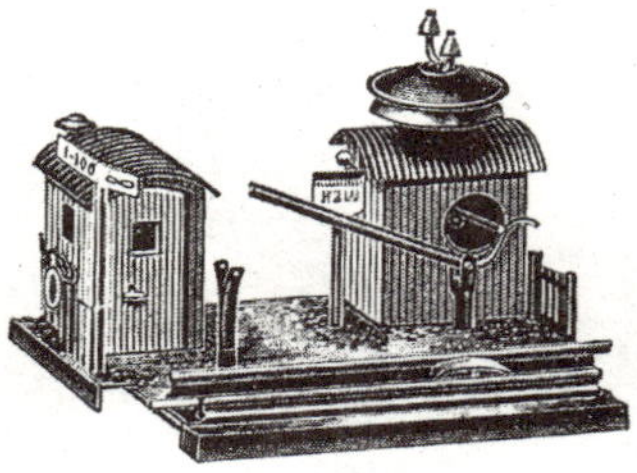

14/2183

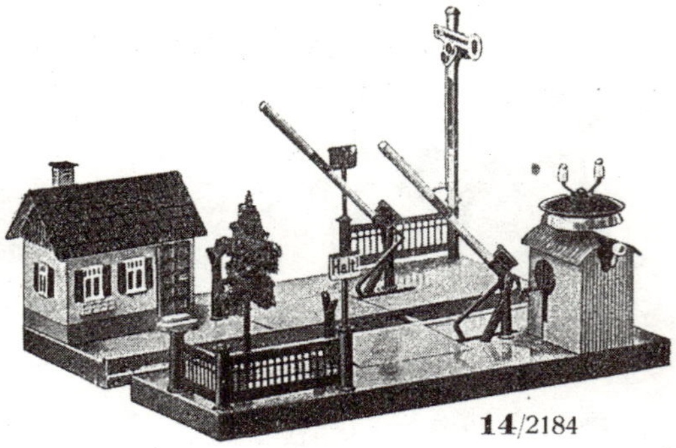

14/2184

14/2536

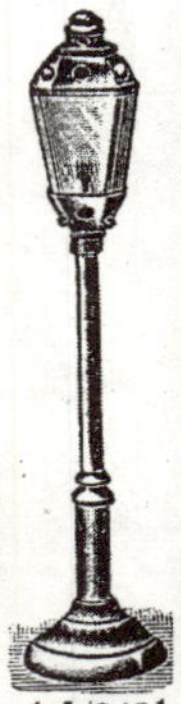

14/2421

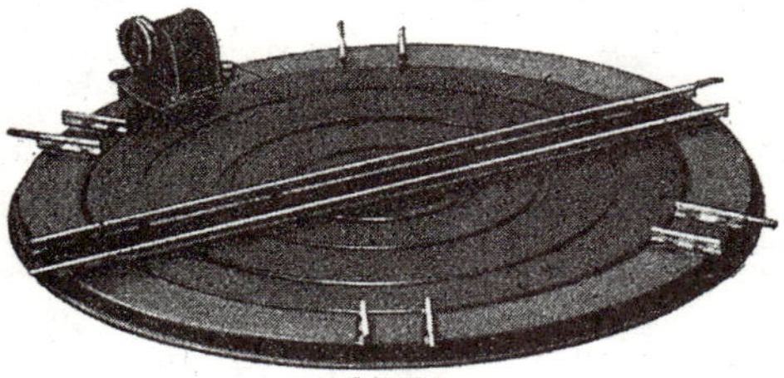

14/2128

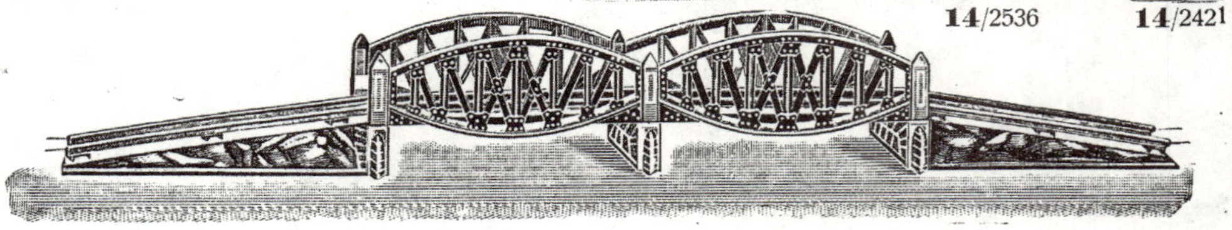

14/2503

14/9062 G

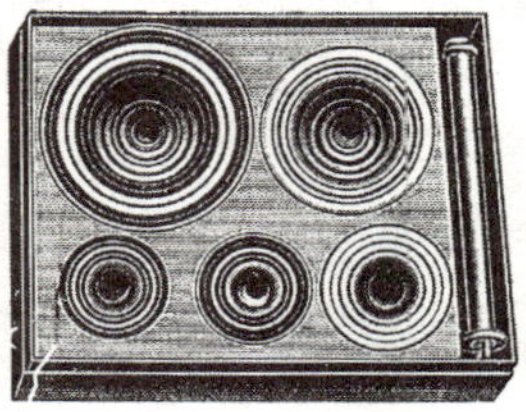

14/9059 G/302

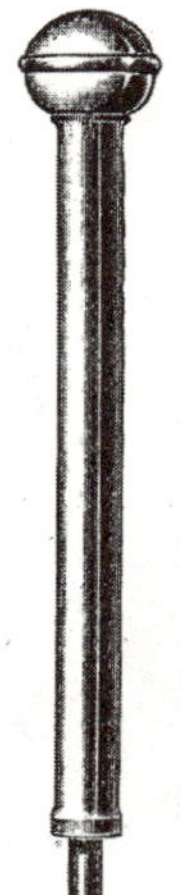
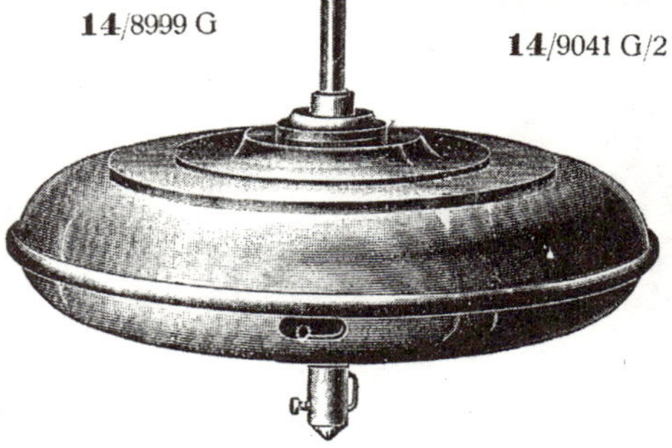

14/8999 G

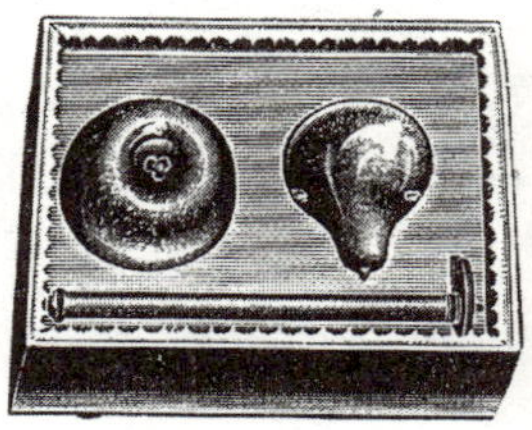

14/9041 G/2

14/9061 G/3

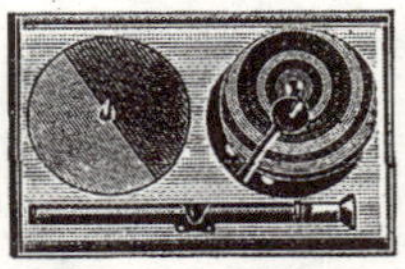

14/9066 G

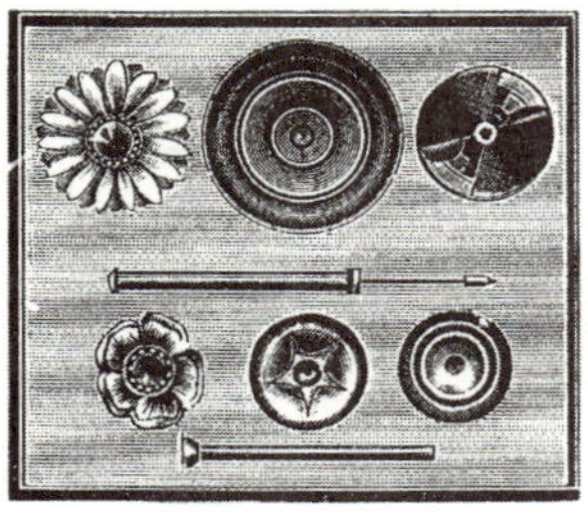

14/8999 G/98

14/8998 G

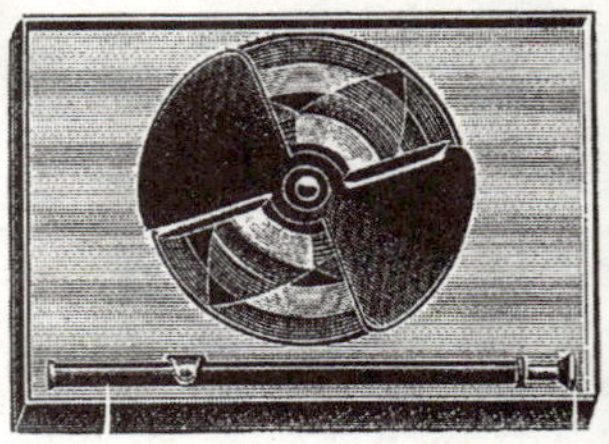

14/9063/G

14/EL 9614

14/EL 9613

14/EL 9615 N

Beachten Sie auch die Veröffentlichung auf Seite 54—61 des Hauptkataloges.

Please note also the publication on page 54—61 of the principal catalogue.
Llamamos también su atención á la publicación en la página 54—61 del catálogo principal.

No.	Eisenbahn-Zubehör.	Railway-Accessories.	Accesorios de Ferrocarril.
14/2000 F	Bahnhof mit seitlichem Schutzdach, durchbrochene Fenster, Bahnsteiggeländer usw. Größe 33,5×13,5×23,5 cm.	Railway Station with covered platform, barrier with sliding doors, fine stamping and japanning etc. Size $13\frac{1}{4}\times5\frac{1}{4}\times8\frac{1}{2}$ in.	Estación de ferrocarril, con plataforma lateral cubierta, ventanas, barrera etc. Tamaño 33,5×13,5×23,5 cm.
14/2128	Drehscheibe mit Handkurbel, automatischer Verriegelung und Auslösetaster. Kräftige Konstruktion, Handlackierung.	Turntable, workable by crank, automatic check. Natural finish, strong make, hand-japanned.	Placa giratorio, con manivela, cierre automático y botón de desembrague. Construcción fuerte, barnizado manual.
14/2128/0	Drehschiene 22 cm, Durchm. 29 cm.	diameter $8\frac{3}{4}$ in., overall 12 in.	Rail 22 cm, diámetro 29 cm.
14/CE 2128/0	„ 33,5 „ „ 43 „	„ $13\frac{1}{2}$ „ „ 17 „	„ 33,5 „ „ 43 „
14/2128/1	„ 33,5 „ „ 43 „	„ $13\frac{1}{2}$ „ „ 17 „	„ 33,5 „ „ 43 „
14/H 2128/1	„ 54 „ „ 66 „	„ 20 „ „ $26\frac{1}{2}$ „	„ 54 „ „ 66 „
	Sämtliche mit der Zusatzbezeichnung El, z. B. El 2128/0, auch für elektrische Bahnen.	The above all to be had for electric railways also.	Todos accesorios con la designación suplementar El, p. e. El 2128/0 se suministran también para ferrocarriles eléctricos.
14/2153	Wärterhaus, mit Umzäunung und Türe zum Öffnen, Dach und Fenster geprägt, fein bemalt. 15×10,5×10 cm.	Guard's House, fence, crossing gate, door to open, stamped roof and window, nicely japanned. $6\times4\frac{1}{4}\times4$ in.	Casa de caminero, con palizada y puerta a abrirse, techo y ventanas estampados, finamente pintados. 15×10,5×10 cm.
14/2183	Bahnübergang, Wellblechhaus, Läutebude, Bahnschranke. Läutewerk mit Kurbelaufzug. Automatischer Betrieb durch vorbeifahrenden Zug. Für alle Spurweiten, mit Mittelschiene für elektr. Bahnen. 19,5×15,5×12,5 cm.	Railway Barrier with guard's house and signal box. Barrier and bell worked automatically by passing train. Suitable for all gauges. With insulated rail for electric railways. Size $8\times6\frac{1}{4}\times5$ in.	Barrera de ferrocarril, casa de hoja ondulada, gabinete de sonar, barrera. Aparato de señales con manivela. Servicio automático por tren en trayecto. Para todas anchuras de vía, con carril aislado para ferrocarriles eléctricos. 19,5×15,5×12,5 cm.
14/2184	Bahnübergang, Wärterhaus, Läutebude, Signal, Schranke usw. Automatischer Betrieb von Schranke und Signalglocke durch vorbeifahrenden Zug. Mittelstrangschiene für elektrische Betrieb. Feine Handlackierung. 32 cm lang.	Railway Barrier, Guard's house, signal box, movable signal arm, barrier etc. Barrier and signal bell worked automatically by passing train. With insulated rails for electric railways. Beautifully japanned. 13 in. long.	Barrera de ferrocarril, casa de caminero, gabinete de sonar, señal, barrera etc. Servicio automático de la barrera y campana de señales por tren cuando pasa. Carril aislado para servicio eléctrico. Fino barnizado manual. 32 cm de largo.
14/2257	Läutewerk mit Uhrwerk, Glocke vernickelt, 10,5 cm hoch.	Signal Bell with clockwork and nickelled bell. Height 4 in.	Aparato de señales con mecanismo; campana nickelada, 10,5 cm de alto.
14/2337	Hauptsignal, verstellbar.	Signal Arm, strong hand lever.	Señal principal de brazo, graduable.
14/2337/0	Spur 0, 19 cm hoch.	Gauge 0, height $7\frac{1}{2}$ in.	Vía 0, 19 cm de alto.
14/2337/1	„ 1, 28 „ „	„ 1, „ 11 „	„ 1, 28 „ „ „
14/2421	Straßenlaterne für Ölbeleuchtung. Brenner mit Docht, solide Ausführung. 20 cm hoch.	Lamp, on post and iron base, to light with oil, very solid make. Heigth 8 in.	Farol para alumbrado a olio, con mecha, sólido trabajo, 20 cm de alto.
14/2437	Bogenlampe für Ölbeleuchtung, Kettenaufzug, massive Eisenkonstruktion. 44 cm hoch.	Arc Lamp, imitation iron girder post, crank hoisting, solid construction. Height $17\frac{1}{2}$ in.	Lámpara de arco, para alumbrado a olio, elevación por cadena, construcción de hierro macizo. 44 cm de alto.
14/2503	Eisenbahnbrücke. Bogenbrücke, hübsch geprägte Eisenkonstruktion, zerlegbar, mit Schienen.	Railway Bridge, tinned iron plate, imitation girder construction, detachable, fine finish and japanning.	Puente de ferrocarril, de arcos, construcción de hierro bonitamente estampado, desmontable, con carriles.
14/2503/0	Spur 0, 1 Bogen, 79 cm lang.	Gauge 0, 1 arch, length 31 in.	Vía 0, 1 arco, 79 cm de largo.
14/2503/1	„ 1, 2 „ 105 „ „	„ 1, 2 arches, „ 41 „	„ 1, 2 arcos, 105 „ „ „
14/El 2503/0	wie oben, für elektr. Bahnen.	As above, for electric railways.	Como supra, para ferrocarril eléctrico.
14/El 2503/1	„ „ „ „ „	„ „ „ „ „	„ „ „ „ „
14/2536	Tunnel, kräftiges Holzgestell mit Pappeüberzug, durch plastisch aufgetragene Masse verstärkt, hübsches Modell.	Tunnel, plastic model, artistically finished on stout wooden frame, solid construction.	Túnel, armazón fuerte de madera cubierto de cartón, reforzado por masa plástica, modelo lindo.
14/2536/0	27 cm lang.	Gauge 0, length $10\frac{1}{2}$ in.	27 cm de largo.
14/2536/1	38 „ „	„ 0, „ 15 „	38 „ „ „
14/S 3060/301	Elektrische Zahnradbahnanlage in Spurweite 35 mm, für 110—250 Volt. Kräftiges Holzgestell, für Landschaft und Viadukt, hübsch bemalt, Steinimitation. Ausstattung: Elektrische Zahnradlokomotive, nur vorwärts fahrend, 2 Wagen, 8 Zahnradschienen, 8 runde Schienen, 1 gerade und 1 Anschlußschiene. Lampenwiderstand, Schraubstöpsel, Anschlußkabel mit Stecker und Muffen. Länge der Anlage 220 cm.	Electric mountain-railway, gauge 0, for 110—250 volts. Strong wooden frame for landscape and viaduct, nicely painted brickwork-imitation. Locomotive fitted with rack climbing gear and one headlight, two carriages, lamp-resistance, cords, plugs and adaptor; 8 rack rails, 8 curved rails, 1 straight and 1 connecting-rail. Length of lay-out 81×34 in.	Instalación de ferrocarril eléctrico a cremallera, vía 35 mm, para 110—250 voltios. Fuerte armazón de madera, para paisaje y viaducto, lindamente pintado. imitación de mazoneria. Equipo: Locomotora eléctrica de cremallera, con movimiento adelante, 2 carros, 8 railes a cremallera, 8 railes redondos, 1 rail derecho y 1 rail de conexión. Resistencia de lámparas, contacto tornillo, cable de conexión con contactos y manguitos. Largura de la instalación 220 cm.
14/3070/72 G	Elektrische Straßenbahn, in Spurweite 35 mm, für 110—250 Volt. Triebwagen mit Stirnlampe, Innenbeleuchtung mit Steckanschluß für die Beleuchtung des Anhängewagens, Schiebetüren, Zelluloidfenster, imitierte Oberleitung. Länge des einzelnen Wagens, 20 cm. Die Garnitur besteht aus 1 Triebwagen, 1 Anhängewagen, 8 runden, 3 geraden Schienen, 1 Auschlußschiene, Widerstand, Anschlußstöpsel, Anschlußkabel, Wagenbeleuchtung mit Verbindungsdraht.	Electric tramway, gauge 0, for 110-250 volts. Driving car with headlamp, interior lighting with plug-contact for lighting the coupled car. Sliding doors, celluloid-windows, imitated overheadline. Length of the single car 8 in. The set consists of 1 driving car, 1 coupled car, 8 curved, 3 straight rails, 1 connecting rail, resistance, contact-plug, connection-cable, car-lighting and connecting wire.	Tren eléctrico, 35 mm de vía, para 110—250 voltios. Carro impulsor con lámpara frontal, alumbrado interior con conexión por contacto para el alumbrado del carro acoplado. Puertas corredizas, ventanas de celuloid, conducto aereo imitado. Largura de cada carro: 20 cm. El juego consta de 1 carro impulsor, 1 carro acoplado, 8 railes redondos, 3 derechos y 1 rail de conexión, resistencia, contactos, cable de conexión alumbrado de carro con alambre de conexión.

No.	Ausstattung	Equipment	Equipo	Kartongröße / Size of box Tamaño de la cajita de cartón cm	inch. / pulg.
	Kreiselspiele.	**Spinning Tops.**	**Juegos a la peonza.**		
14/8998 G	Garnitur mit 1 Tonkreisel.	Set of 1 Tuning Top.	Juego con 1 peón sonador.	15 ×9,5	6×4
	Choralkreisel mit fest verbundenem Antriebstock und automat. Akkordwechsel.	**Choral Tops with fixed driving stem changing the tune automatically.**	**Peón de coreada con varilla fija de impulsión y cambio automático de aco de.**		
14/8999 G/9	Garnitur mit 1 Choralkreisel von 9 cm Durchmesser und 2 Akkorden.	Set of 1 Choral Top of $3\frac{1}{2}$ in. diameter and 2 chords.	Juego con 1 peón de coreada de 9 cm de diámetro y 2 acordes.	17×10	$6\frac{3}{4}\times4$
14/8999 G/12	Garnitur mit 1 Choralkreisel von 12 cm Durchmesser und 2 Akkorden.	Set of 1 Choral Top of $4\frac{3}{4}$ in. diameter and 2 chords.	Juego con 1 peón de coreada de 12 cm de diámetro y 2 acordes.	20×13	8×5
14/8999 G/15	Garnitur mit 1 Choralkreisel von 15 cm Durchmesser und 3 Akkorden.	Set of 1 Choral Top of 6 in. diameter and 3 chords.	Juego con 1 peón de coreada de 15 cm de diámetro y 3 acordes.	22×16	$8\frac{1}{2}\times5\frac{1}{4}$
14/8999 G/98	Garnitur mit 1 Choralkreisel 8999 G/12 und 1 Farbkreisel, 1 Tellerkreisel, 3 Blumenkreiseln.	Set of 1 Choral Top 8999 G/12 and 1 colour top, 1 plate top, 3 flower tops.	Juego con 1 peón de coreada 8999/G12 y 1 peón de colores, 1 peón de plato. 3 peones de flores.	24×21	$9\frac{1}{2}\times8\frac{1}{4}$
14/9041 G/1	Garnitur mit 1 Früchtekreisel.	Set of 1 Fruit Top.	Juego con 1 peón de frutas.	18×11	$7\times4\frac{1}{2}$
14/9041 G/2	„ „ 2 „	„ „ 2 „ „	„ „ 2 peones de frutas.	18×15	7×6
14/9041 G/4	„ „ 4 „	„ „ 3 „ „	„ „ 4 „ „ „	19×18	$7\frac{1}{2}\times7$
14/9059 G/301	Garnitur mit 4 verschiedenen Tellerkreiseln.	Set of 4 different Plate Tops.	„ „ 4 „ diferentes de plato.	17,5×15	7×6
14/9059 G/302	Garnitur mit 5 verschiedenen Tellerkreiseln.	„ „ 5 „ „ „	„ „ 5 „ „ „ „	19×17,5	$7\frac{1}{2}\times7$
14/9061 G/1	Garnitur mit 1 Tellerkreisel.	Set of 1 Plate Top.	„ „ 1 peon de plato.	14×13	$5\frac{1}{2}\times5$
14/9061 G/2	„ „ 2 „	„ „ 2 „ „	„ „ 2 peones de plato.	21×13	8×5
14/9061 G/3	„ „ 3 „	„ „ 3 „ „	„ „ 3 „ „ „	33×16,5	$13\times6\frac{1}{2}$
14/9062 G	Garnitur mit 1 Quellkreisel.	Set of 1 Fountain Top.	„ „ 1 peón de fuente.	15×15	6×6
14/9063 G	Garnitur mit 1 Spektrumkreisel und 4 Farbscheiben.	Set of 1 Spectrum Top and 4 coloured discs.	„ „ 1 „ „ espectro con 4 discos colorados.	21,5×15	$8\frac{1}{2}\times6$
14/9066 G	Garnitur 1 Farbenkreisel und 6 Farbenscheiben.	Set of 1 Kaleidoscopic Top and 6 coloured discs.	Juego con 1 peón de colores y 6 discos colorados.	15×9,5	6×4
	Kinderkochherde mit elektrischer Beheizung.	**Children's Cooking Stoves for electric heating:**	**Fogones para niñas con calentamiento eléctrico.**		
	Zum direkten Anschluß an die Lichtleitungen von 110—250 Volt. Anschlußmaterial wird jedem Herd beigegeben. Bei Bestellung Voltzahl angeben.	For direct connection to main lines 110—250 volts. With cable and plug for connection. With order state voltage.	Para conexión directa a la luz eléctrica de 110—250 voltios. Cada fogón va acompañado de material de conexión. Indicar el voltaje con el pedido.	Größe / Size / Tamaño cm	inch. / pulg.
14/El 9613/3	3 Geschirre aus Weißblech, verzinnt, 1 Drehschalter.	3 tinplate pots and 1 switch.	3 pucheros de hojalata, estañada, 1 comutador.	25×17,5×14	$9\frac{7}{8}\times6\frac{7}{8}\times5\frac{1}{2}$
14/El 9614/3 **14**/El 9614/4	4 Geschirre aus Weißblech, verzinnt, 2 Drehschalter, Bratofen mit Backblech.	4 tinplate pots and 2 switches, oven with baking tin.	4 pucheros de hojalata estañada, 2 comutadores, asadero con placa de cocer pan.	31×23×14 34×26×16	$12\frac{1}{4}\times9\times5\frac{1}{2}$ $13\frac{3}{8}\times10\frac{1}{4}\times6\frac{1}{4}$
14/El 9614/N3 **14**/El 9614/N4	Wie El 9614, aber mit Nickelgeschirren und Nickelschutzstange.	4 nickelplated pots, nickelplated front rail, oven with baking tin.	Como El 9614, pero con pucheros de niquel y con riel protector de niquel.	31×23×14 34×26×16	$12\frac{1}{4}\times9\times5\frac{1}{2}$ $13\frac{3}{8}\times10\frac{1}{4}\times6\frac{1}{4}$
14/El 9615/4 **14**/El 9615/5	4 Weißblechgeschirre und 1 Messingteekessel, Bratofen mit Backblech, 3 Drehschalter.	4 tinplate pots, oven with baking tin, 3 switches, 1 brass tea kettle.	4 pucheros de hojalata y 1 tetera, asador con placa de hacer pan, 3 comutadores.	37×27×18 43,5×33×27	$14\frac{1}{2}\times10\frac{1}{2}\times7\frac{1}{2}$ $17\frac{1}{8}\times13\times10\frac{5}{8}$
14/El 9615/N4	Wie El 9615/4, aber mit Nickelgeschirren und Nickelschutzstange.	4 nickelplated pots and 1 tea kettle, oven with baking tin, nickelplated front rail, 3 switches.	Como El 9615/4, pero con pucheros de niquel y riel protector de niquel.	37×27×18	$14\frac{1}{2}\times10\frac{1}{2}\times7\frac{1}{2}$

Beachten Sie auch die Veröffentlichung auf Seite 54—61 des Hauptkataloges.

Please note also the publication on page 193—196 of the principal catalogue.
Llamamos también su atención á la publicación en la página 193—196 del catálogo principal.

Zelluloidpuppen. — Celluloid dolls. — Muñecas de celuloide. Kollektion No. 60. — Collection No. 60. — Colección No. 60.

Serie Kowenko-Spezial mit Patent-Drehkopf und bemalter Bekleidung; alle Modelle ca. 15—16½ cm groß. No. **60**/30 ca. 12 cm groß. — Series „Kowenko Special" with patent turning head and painted dress; all types abt. 15—16½ cm high, No. **60**/30 abt. 12 cm high. — Serie „Kowenko Especial" con cabeza patente movible y vestido pintado, todos modelos ca. 15—16½ cm de alto. No. **60**/30 ca. 12 cm de alto.

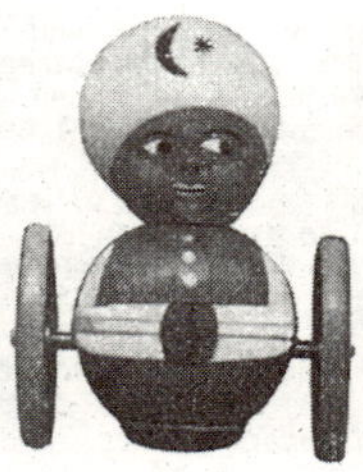

60/286
Roller / Rollers Rodadores

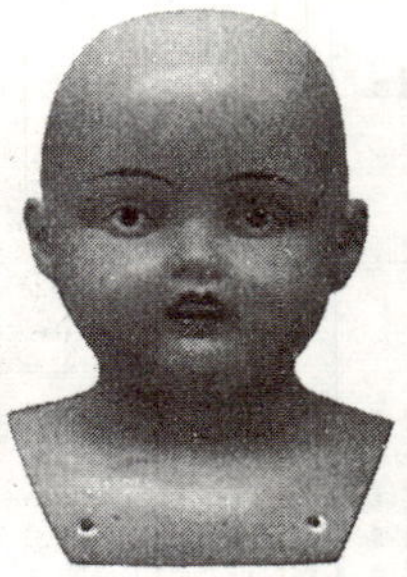

Serie „Perückenköpfe" Brustblattköpfe mit abgeschrägtem Hinterkopf für Frisur. Series "Periwig-heads", Breastplate-heads with bevelled hindhead for hair dress. Serie "cabezas a peluca", cabezas sobre tronco, con nuca oblicuada para el peinado. 11 Größen / Sizes / Tamaños, 8—18 cm.

60/14/2 **60**/14/3 **60**/16 **60**/17 **60**/30
„Kowenko-Spezial" in fleischfarbig, schwarz oder braun, mit Phantasiebekleidung.
"Kowenko Special" in flesh-colour, black or brown, with fancy-dress.
"Kowenko Especial" en color de carne, negro o castaño, con vestido de fantasía.

Hutwackler m. beweg. Zylinder. Hat-waggler with moveable high, hat. / Bamboleador de sombrero sombrero de copa alta movible.

Pupsi B mit beweglichem Zylinder. Pupsi B with moveable high hat. Pupsi B con sombrero alto movible.

60/C — sortiert / assorted / surtido — **60**/C
Cowboy und Girl, mulattenfarbig.
Cowboy and Girl, mulatto coloured.
Vaquero y muchacha, color de mulato.

60/T — sortiert / assorted / surtido — **60**/T
Türkenpaar mit Seidenkostüm, mulattenfarbig.
Pair of Turks with silk costume, mulatto coloured.
Par de Turcos con vestido de seda, color de mulato.

60/W — sortiert / assorted / surtido — **60**/W
Wolltürkenpaar, neger- oder mulattenfarbig.
Pair of woollen Turks, negro or mulatto coloured.
Par de Turcos de lana, color de negro o mulato.

60/H **60**/H
Holländerpaar, sortiert, mit Wollhaaren.
Pair of Hollanders, assorted, with woollen hair.
Par de holandéses, surtidos con pelo de lana.

60/D
Mädchen mit Schleife u. Spitzenröckchen.
Girl with bow and lace frock.
Muchacha con lazo y saya de encajes.

60/1/3 gekl.
Mädchen im Trikotkleidchen.
Girl, tricot dressed.
Muchacha en vestido de tricot.

Pupsi, Wolle.
Pupsi, wool dressed.
Pupsi, vestido de lana.

Pupsi, Seide.
Pupsi, silk dressed.
Pupsi, vestido de seda.

Beachten Sie auch die Veröffentlichung auf Seite 193—196 des Hauptkataloges.

Please note also the publication on page 193—196 of the principal catalogue.
Llamamos también su atención á la publicación en la página 193—196 del catálogo principal.

Zelluloid-Ball-, Schleifen- und Phantasie-Rassel. — Celluloid ball-, bow- and fancy rattles. — Sonajeros de celuloide de pelota, de lazo y de fantasía.

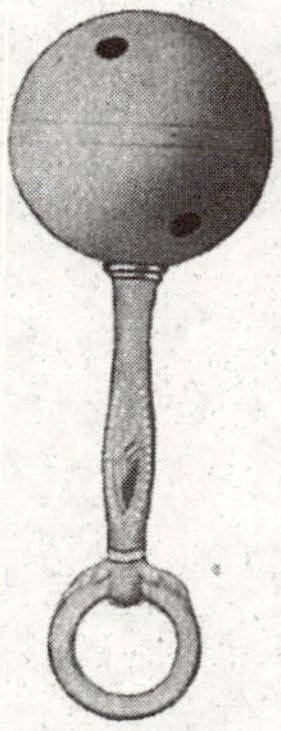
60/9/400/6
60/9/600/6*

60/15/311/$5^{1}/_{2}$

60/D 20/311/$5^{1}/_{2}$

60/9/305/$5^{1}/_{2}$
60/9/505/$5^{1}/_{2}$*

60/6/307/$5^{1}/_{2}$
60/6/507/$5^{1}/_{2}$*

60/7/304/6
60/7/304/6*

60/9/306/6
60/9/506/6*

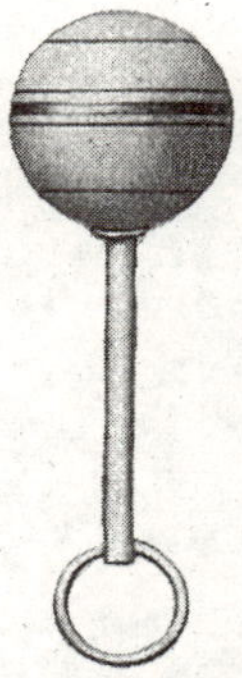
60/16/315/6

60/4999
Verp. $^{1}/_{2}$ Dtz.

60/10/911/7
Extra stark.
Extra strong.
Extra fuerte.

60/21/305/7
60/21/505/7*

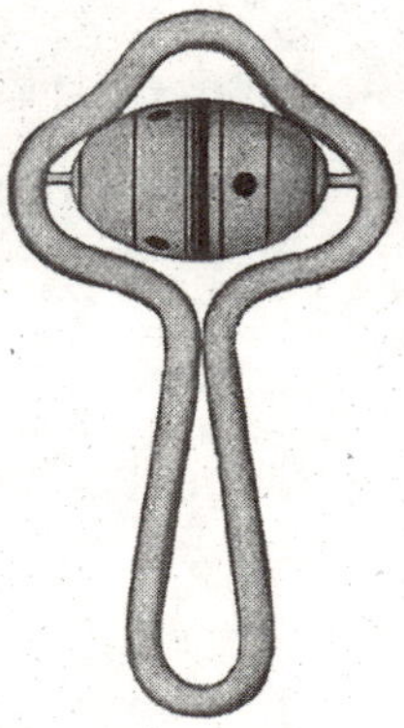
60/26/301 Ei
60/26/301 Ei*

Transparent-Rassel.
Transparent rattle.
Sonajeros transparente.

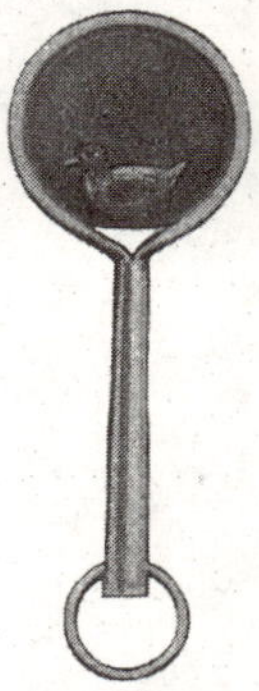
60/2956

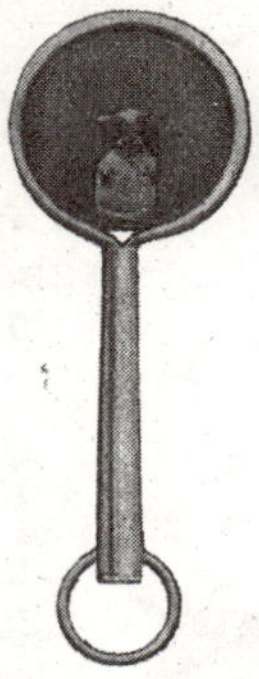
60/2958

Quietschrassel.
Squeaking rattle.
Sonajero gruñidor.

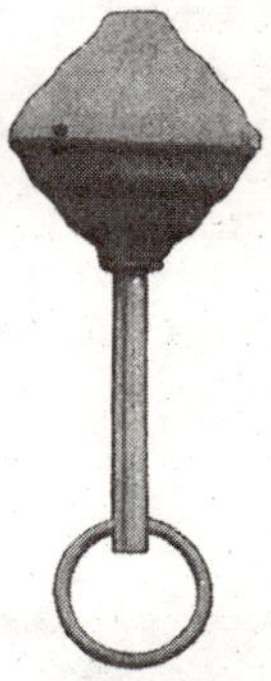
60/3336

60/4927

* Extra starke Qualität.
Especially strong quality.
Calidad extra fuerte.

Wasserspielball mit und ohne Wasser, lieferbar in 8 Größen, von ca. 5—10 cm Durchmesser.
Water-playing ball, suppliable with or without water, in 8 sizes from abt. 5—10 cm diameter.
Pelota de jugar con agua, a suministrarse con o sin agua, en 8 tamaños de ca. 5—10 cm de diámetro.

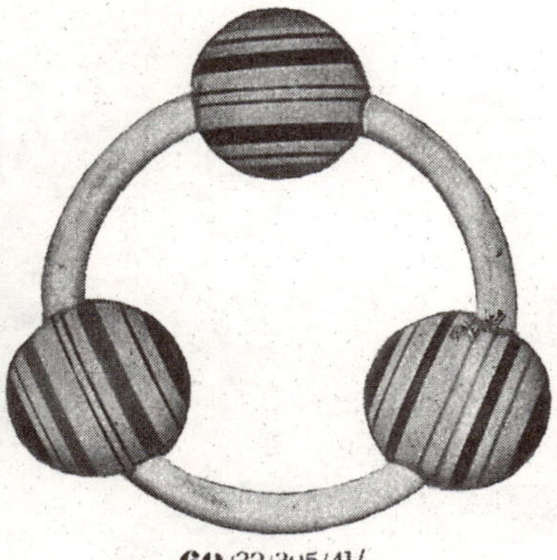
60/32/305/$4^{1}/_{2}$
60/32/505/$4^{1}/_{2}$*

60/5453
13 cm

60/5452
16 cm

äußerer Ringdurchmesser / outward diameter of ring
diámetro exterior del anillo.

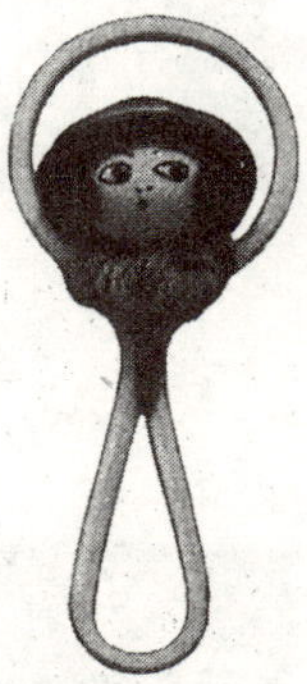
60/3340

Stehauf. — Stand up. — Dominguillo.

60/6495

60/6497 bemalt
primed / imprimado.
60/6498 ausgemalt
painted / pintado.

60/6499

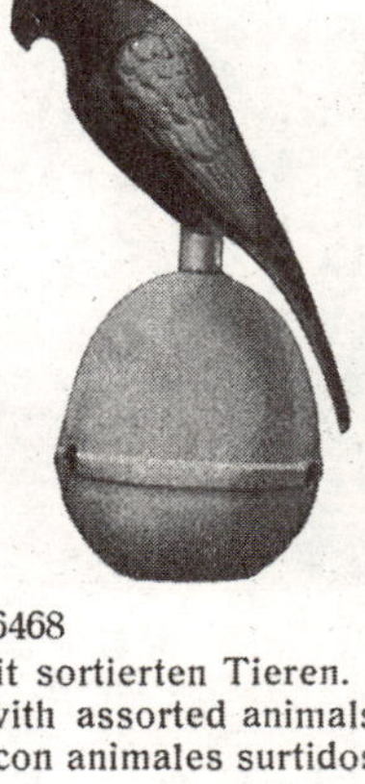
60/6468
Quietsch-Stehauf, mit sortierten Tieren.
Squeaking stand up, with assorted animals.
Dominguillo gruñidor, con animales surtidos.

Vogelpfeifen.
Birds calls.
Silbatos de pájaro.

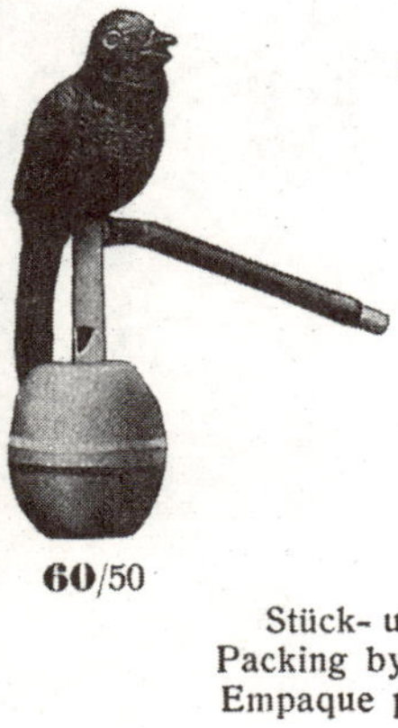
60/50

60/52

Stück- und Dutzend-Packung.
Packing by the piece or by dozen.
Empaque por pieza o por docena.

Beachten Sie auch die Veröffentlichung auf Seite 193—196 des Hauptkataloges.

123/771/14

1/6 nat. Größe. 1/6 of nat. size. 1/6 del tamaño natural.

123/771/11	**123**/771/12	**123**/771/13
25×14×16 cm	31×19×23 cm	34×24×29 cm
123/771/14	**123**/771/15	**123**/771/16
49×29×35 cm	70×42×50 cm	84×50×60 cm

123/763/10

1/9 nat. Größe. 1/9 of nat. size. 1/9 del tamaño natural.
35 teilig. 35 parts. 35 partes.

123/15/0
1/7 nat. Größe
1/7 of nat. size.
1/7 del tamaño natural.

	Höhe der größten stehenden Figur. Size of the tallest standing figure. Tamaño de la figura más grande.	Teile parts partes
123/10/0	5 cm	8
123/11/0	6,5 „	8
123/12/0	8 „	10
123/13/0	10 „	11
123/14/0	12 „	12
123/15/0	14 „	12
123/16/0	17 „	13
123/17/0	20 „	14
123/2 B	7 „	12
123/3 B	9,5 „	12
123/3½ B	10,5 „	12
123/4 B	12,3 „	12
123/5 B	15 „	12
123/6 B	16,5 „	12
123/7 B	18,5 „	12
123/8 B	21 „	12
123/9 B	25,4 „	12
123/10 B	31,5 „	12
123/737/3	—	5
123/737/3½	—	6
123/737/4	—	7
123/737/5	—	8
123/737/6	—	11
123/737/7	—	12
123/737/8	—	12
123/168/5	—	12

Bessere Qualität.
Much better quality.
Calidad mejor.

123/6 B
1/6 natürl. Größe.
1/6 of nat. size.
1/6 del tamaño natural.

123/168/5
1/6 natürl. Größe.
1/6 of nat. size.
1/6 del tamaño natural.

123/170/3
1/6 natürl. Größe.
1/6 of nat. size.
1/6 del tamaño natural.

123/737/8
1/4 natürl. Größe.
1/4 of nat. size.
1/4 del tamaño natural.

123/170/1	3½ cm
123/170/2	5½ — 6 cm
123/170/3	10 — 12 „

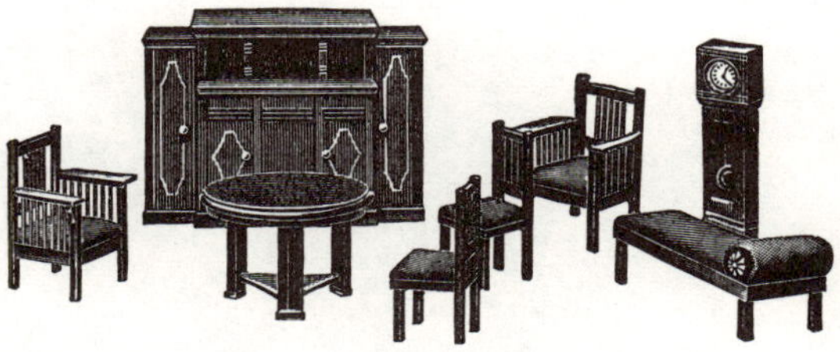

39/385

Herrenzimmer, rot oder braun, enthaltend: 1 Chaiselongue, 1 modernen dreiteiligen Bücherschrank oder Büfett, 1 runden Tisch, 4 Stühle, 1 Standuhr.
Gentlemen's room, red or brown, containing: 1 chaiselongue, 1 modern threepart bookcase or sideboard, 1 round table, 4 chairs, 1 grandfather's clock.
Salón para señores, rojo ó pardo, conteniendo: 1 camillo para descansar (chaiselongue) 1 armario moderno para libros compuesto de tres partes ó bufete, 1 mesa redonda, 4 sillas 1 gran reloj vertical sobre pies.

39/391

Speisezimmer, braun, enthaltend: 1 runden Tisch, 2 Armsessel, 2 Stühle, 1 modernes Büfett, 1 Uhr.
Dining room, brown, containing: 1 round table, 2 easy arm chairs, 2 chairs, 1 modern sideboard, 1 clock.
Comedor, pardo, conteniendo: 1 mesa redonda, 2 sillas de brazos, 2 sillas, 1 bufete (buffet) moderno, 1 reloj.

39/417 b

Speisezimmer, imitiert geschnitzt, havannafarben gebeizt, mit grünem Samt bezogen, antike Form, enthaltend: Büfett, ovalen Auszugtisch, 4 Stühle, 2 Armsessel, Schreibtisch.
Dining room, imitated sculptured, corroded in Havana colour, spreaded over with green velvet in an antique style, containing sideboard, an oval drawing-table, 4 chairs, 2 arm chairs, writing-table.
Comedor de color de habana con una guarnición de terciopelo verde à la moda antigua, conteniendo bufete, mesa oval elástica, 4 sillas, 2 sillas de brazo, escritorio.

39/425 b

Schlafzimmer, engl. Stil, havannafarben oder mahagoni enthaltend: 1 Bett, 2 Stühle, 1 Waschtisch, 1 Spiegelkommode.
Bedroom, English style, havana-coloured, or mahogany, containing 1 bed, 2 chairs, 1 washing-table, 1 chest of drawers with mirror.
Dormitorio estilo inglés, color de habana ó de caoba, constando de 1 cama, 2 sillas, 1 lavabo, 1 cómoda con espejo.

39/426 B

39/405 b

"Wokra" Baukasten zum Bauen von Stadthäusern und Wolkenkratzern.
"Wokra" box of bricks for building town houses and sky scrapers.
"Wokra" caja de construcción para construir casas de ciudad y casas altas á la americana (sky scrapers).

39/405 a
Kleine Ausgabe / Small size / Tamaño pequeño — 257 × 195 mm.

39/405 b
Mittlere Ausgabe / Middle size / Tamaño mediano — 352 × 212 mm.

39/405 c
Große Ausgabe / Large size / Tamaño grande — 415 × 300 mm.

39/405 c

Musikdosen. — Music-boxes. — Cajas de música.

39/303 a U

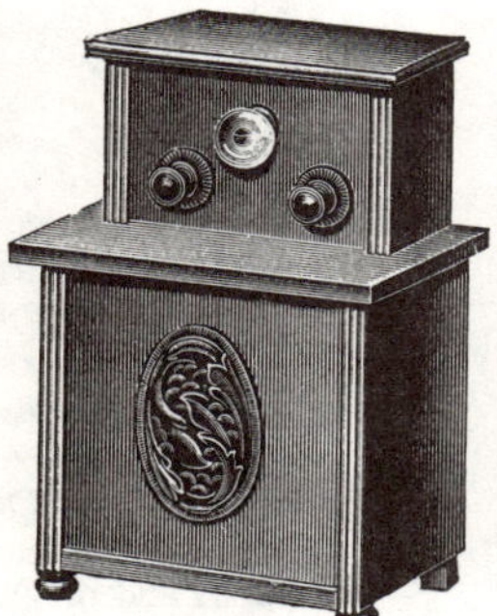

№412
39/412

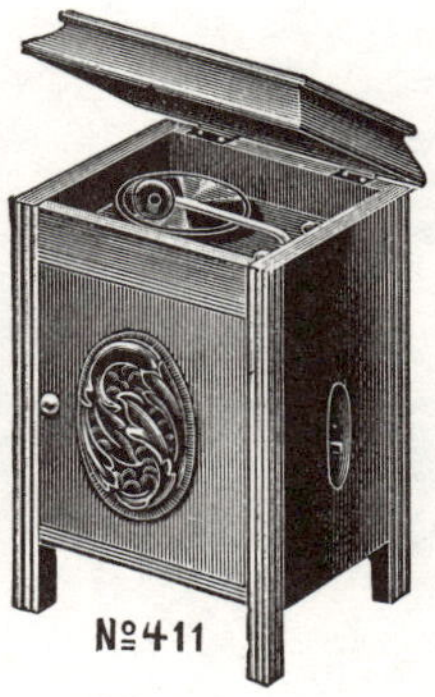

39/411

39/303 a U **Flügel. — Grand piano. — Piano de cola.** 10 cm.

39/412 **Radio** mit elektrischer Einrichtung.
Broadcast with electrical outfit.
Radio con instalación eléctrica. 14 cm.

39/411 **Grammophon** mit sich drehender Platte.
Grammophone with turning record.
Gramofone con placa giratoria. 12 cm.

39/303 U **Klavier,** schwarz.
Piano, black.
Piano, negro. 15 cm.

39/303 a U, **39**/412, **39**/411 und **39**/303 U
werden mit Schweizer Musikwerk geliefert.
are supplied with Swiss automatic music-work.
se suministran con caja de música suiza.

39/303 U

39/386 a

Eisenbahn-D-Zug (Lokomotive und 3 Wagen), Länge 70 cm.
D-Train (engine and 3 waggons), length 70 cm.
D-Ferrocarril (locomotora y 3 wagones), largura 70 cm.

39/282/10

Miniatur-Holzeisenbahn, fein lackiert.
Miniatur wooden railway, finely varnished.
Ferrocarril en miniatura, de madera finamente barnizada.

39/426 B **Wohnzimmer,** englischer Stil, havannafarben oder mahagoni, enthaltend: 1 Büfett, 1 viereckigen Tisch, 4 Stühle, 1 Schreibtisch.
Drawing-room, English style, havana-coloured or mahogany, containing, 1 buffet, 1 square table, 4 chairs, 1 secretary.
Sala de visitas, estilo inglés, color de habana ó de caoba, constando de 1 bufete, 1 meza cuadrada, 4 sillas, 1 secretaria.

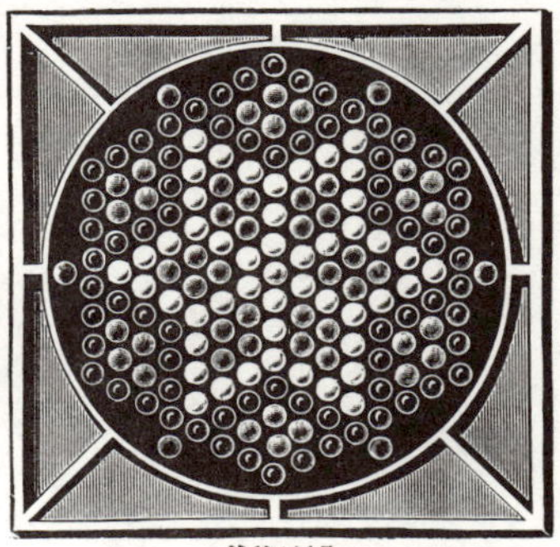

39/415

Kugel-Mosaik, 4 Farben.
Ball-Mosaic, 4 colours.
Mosaico de bolas, 4 colores.

39/415 a Größere Ausgabe. Larger outfit. Tamaño mayor.

39/415 b Mit 6 Farben. With 6 colours. Con 6 colores.

Please note also the publication on page 224 of the principal catalogue.
Llamamos también su atención á la publicación en la página 224 del catálogo principal.

Tafel X

Neuheiten. **50**/196/104$^1/_2$ Reitschule mit Motor. **50**/196/106$^1/_2$ Luftrad mit Motor, Motor mit Widerstand allein. Serie Einzelmöbel: **50**/235 besonders feine, große Eichenmöbel. Serie **50**/601/1—6 neue eichene Wohn- und Schlafzimmergarnituren. Serie **50**/601/10—11 neue weißlackierte Küchengarnituren. Serie **50**/748 neue Salongarnituren, Kirschbaum. Serie **50**/749 (Einzelmöbel **50**/230) moderne gezapfte und gefugte Eichenmöbelgarnituren. Serie **50**/761 moderne Schlafzimmergarnituren, Esche. Serie **50**/762 neue Salongarnituren, taubenblau. **50**/938/2 getäfelte Küche, leer. **50**/938/2$^1/_2$ dito, mit Einrichtung (Einzelmöbel neue Serie **50**/223). Serie **50**/902, **50**/995 und **50**/996 gefällig garnierte, weiß lackierte Babypuppenmöbel. **50**/1088/34 Flügel mit Sessel. **50**/1200—**50**/1235 neue Sparbüchsen und Kästchen. **50**/2301 Verkaufsstand. Serie **50**/3011 Kaufläden. No. **50**/3220 „Vario" Figuren-Baukasten (Holz u. Aluminium), in gefälligem Kasten, mit Vorlagen.

Page X

Novelties. **50**/196/104$^1/_2$ Roundabout with motor. **50**/196/106$^1/_2$ Wheelswing with motor, Motor with resistance. Series **50**/235 highly-finished oakwood single furniture. Series **50**/601/1—6 new oakwood drawing- and bedroom sets. Series **50**/601/10—11 new white varnished kitchen-furniture sets. Series **50**/748 modern sittingroom sets, cherrywood. Series **50**/749 (single furniture **50**/230) new oakwood furniture sets, with tenons and rabbets. Series **50**/761 modern bedroom sets, ashwood. Series **50**/762 modern sittingroom sets, doveblue. **50**/938/2 kitchen, boarded. **50**/938/2$^1/_2$ ditto, with furniture (new single furniture **50**/223). Series **50**/902, **50**/995 and **50**/996 doll's baby-furniture, fitted with dolls and doll's equipments. **50**/1088/34 grandpiano with stool. **50**/1200—**50**/1235 new money- and other boxes. **50**/2301 stalls. Series **50**/3011 shops. No. **50**/3220 "Vario" new box of building-blocks, with aluminium pegs, and designs.

Página X

Novedades. **50**/196/104$^1/_2$ Carrusel con motor. **50**/196/106$^1/_2$ Columbio de rueda con motor, Motor con resistencia suelto. Serie **50**/235 muebles de encina grandes y muy finos, sueltos. Serie **50**/601/1—6 nuevos muebles de encina, cuartos y alcobas, en cajas. Serie **50**/601/10—11 nuevos muebles decocina, barnizados blancos, en cajas. Serie **50**/748 nuevos muebles de salón de cerezo, en cajas. Serie **50**/749 modernos muebles de encina, con clavijas y encajes, en cajas (sueltos serie **50**/230). Serie **50**/761 modernos muebles de alcoba de fresno, en cajas. Serie **50**/762 modernos muebles de salón, color azul, en cajas. **50**/938/2 cocina entarimada, vacía. **50**/938/2$^1/_2$ idem, con muebles (sueltos serie **50**/223). Series **50**/902, **50**/995 y **50**/996 muebles de muñecas barnizados blancos guarnecidos de muñecas y equipos. **50**/1088/34 piano de cola con silla. **50**/1200—**50**/1235 alcancías y cajitas de madera. **50**/2301 tienda. Serie **50**/3011 tienda. No. **50**/3220 "Vario" caja de construcciones de madera, con clavijas de aluminio y con dibujos.

Beachten Sie auch die Veröffentlichung auf Seite 224 des HauptKataloges.

Puppenstubenpuppen Porzellan - Celluloid - Nanking. Reichhaltige unübertreffliche Auswahl in billigen Sortimenten, sowie reizenden und aparten Einzelmustern.

Miniature dressed dolls china - celluloid - nanking beautiful unequalled collection in cheap assortments also charming and choice models.

Muñecas para casa de muñeca porcelana-celuloide-nanquin rica selección inexcedible en surtidos baratos, asi como de dibujos sueltos encantores y esquisitos.

15/26001 sort. **15**/26007 s. **15**/26012 s. **15**/26047

15/26072 **15**/26080 **15**/26069 **15**/26070 **15**/26082 **15**/26097 s. **15**/26018 s.

15/26077 **15**/26073 **15**/26076 **15**/26074 **15**/26025 **15**/26064 **15**/26027 s. **15**/26158 **15**/26157 **15**/26156

15/26036 **15**/26038 **15**/26045 **15**/26178 **15**/26033 **15**/26034 **15**/26106

15/26085 **15**/26086 **15**/26087 **15**/26089 **15**/26088 **15**/26090 **15**/26044 **15**/26043 **15**/26108

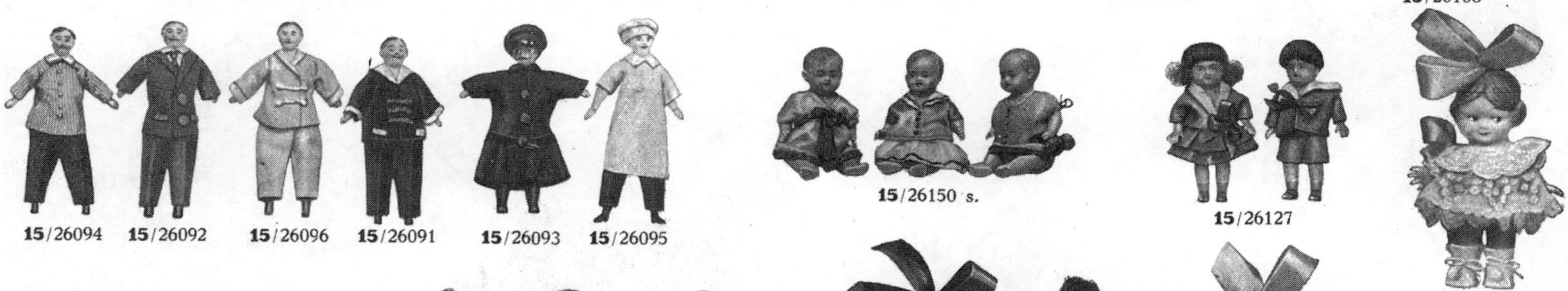

15/26094 **15**/26092 **15**/26096 **15**/26091 **15**/26093 **15**/26095 **15**/26150 s. **15**/26127 **15**/26179

15/26173 **15**/26175 **15**/26177 **15**/26174 **15**/26176 **15**/26183 **15**/26181 **15**/26182

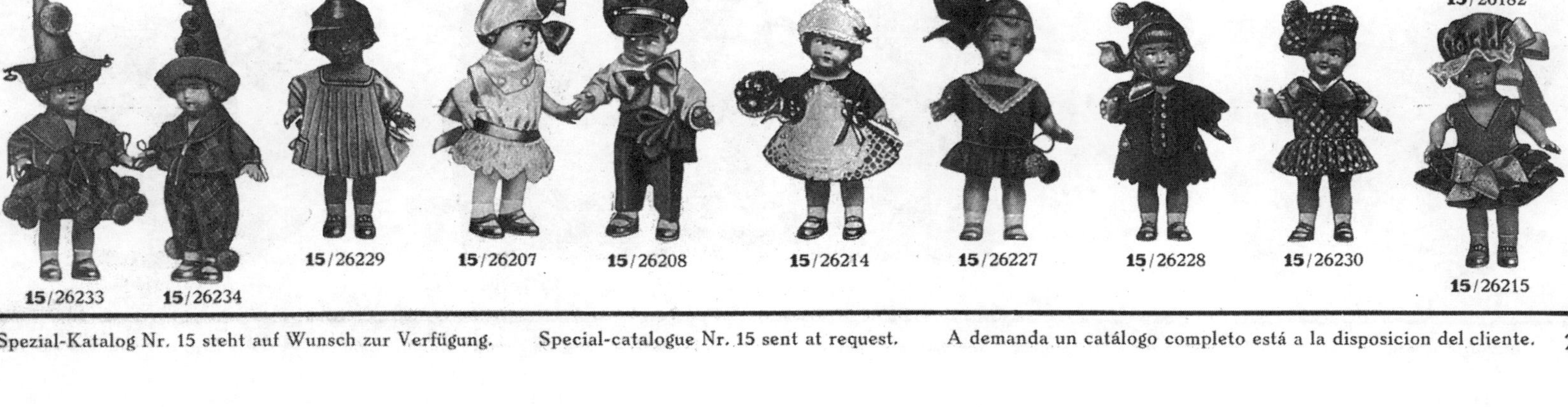

15/26233 **15**/26234 **15**/26229 **15**/26207 **15**/26208 **15**/26214 **15**/26227 **15**/26228 **15**/26230 **15**/26215

Sortiment 15 — Arrangement 15 — Surtido 15

Gestopfte Tiere aller Art, Fahrfiguren ohne Uhrwerk, Wiegengehänge.

Stuffed animals of every description, automechanical driving figures, toys on elastic for perambulators.

Animales estopados de toda especie figuras andantes sin mecanismo, juguetes de suspensorio elastico.

15/26700

15/26718

15/26739

15/26739

15/26733

15/26732

15/26739

15/26736

15/26735

15/26738

15/26854

15/26867

15/26745

15/26730

15/26747 **15**/26748

15/26865

15/26723

15/26811

15/26744

15/26731

15/26808

15/26807

15/26813

15/26734

15/26794 →

15/26796 **15**/26792 **15**/26794

15/26746

 Spezial-Katalog Nr. 15 steht auf Wunsch zur Verfügung. Special-catalogue Nr. 15 sent at request. A demanda un catálogo completo está a la disposicion del cliente.

Gestopfte Tiere aller Art,
Fahrfiguren ohne Uhrwerk,
Wiegengehänge.

Stuffed animals of every description,
automechanical driving figures,
toys on elastic for perambulators.

Animales estopados de toda especie
figuras andantes sín mecanismo,
juguetes de suspensorio elastico.

15/26714

15/26810

15/26713

15/26725

15/26728

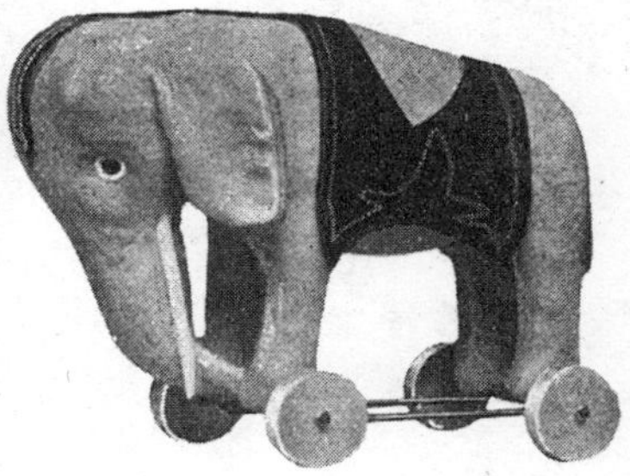
15/26724

15/26814

15/26863

15/26850

15/26861

15/26859

15/26707

15/26803

15/26800

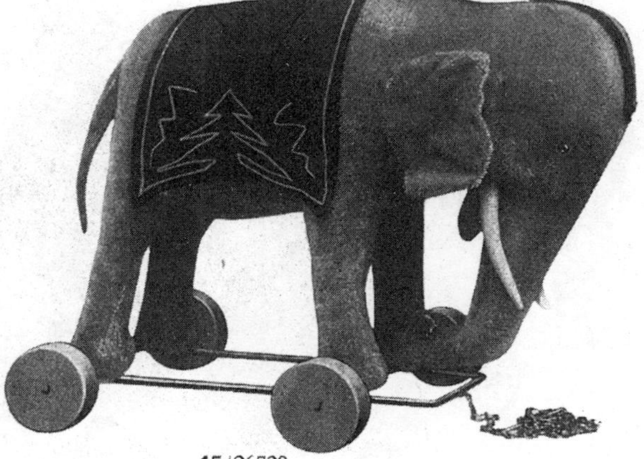
15/26729

15/26720

15/26812

15/26804

15/26816

15/26726

Spezial-Katalog Nr. 15 steht auf Wunsch zur Verfügung. Special-catalogue Nr. 15 sent at request. A demanda un catálogo completo está a la disposicion del cliente.

Sortiment 15   Arrangement 15   Surtido 15

Unzerbrechliche gekleidete Stoffpuppen mit Celluloidkopf. Vom billigsten Stapel-Artikel bis zur feinsten Gelenkpuppe.

Unbreakable dressed cloth dolls with celluloid head. Cheap chain-store articles as well as finest joint dolls.

Infrangibles muñecas vestidas de cuerpos zurvidos, con cabeza de celuloide, baratas y finísimas muñecas.

15/26400 M   **15**/26401   **15**/26404   **15**/26406   **15**/26408   **15**/26409   **15**/26414

15/26412   **15**/26413   **15**/26420   **15**/26416   **15**/26418   **15**/26453   **15**/26452   **15**/26449

15/26467   **15**/26466   **15**/26469   **15**/26485   **15**/26484   **15**/26499   **15**/26486

15/26476   **15**/26475   **15**/26478   **15**/26504   **15**/26505   **15**/26479   **15**/26494   **15**/26495

15/26488   **15**/26492   **15**/26496   **15**/26501   **15**/26500   **15**/26503

 Spezial-Katalog Nr. 15 steht auf Wunsch zur Verfügung. Special-catalogue Nr. 15 sent at request. A demanda un catálogo completo está a la disposicion del cliente.

Please note also the publication on page 192d of the principal catalogue.
Llamamos también su atención á la publicación en la página 192d del catálogo principal.

2/6259 35 cm (14 inches)
Bewegl. Maul und Augen.
Moving mouth and eyes.
Boca y ojos movibles.

2/7403/1 68 cm (24 inches)
2/7403/2 80 cm (32 inches)
2/7403/3 95 cm (38 inches)
Bewegl. Kopf und Augen.
Moving head and eyes.
Cabeza y ojos movibles.

2/6253 90 cm (36 inches)
Bewegl. Arm und Augen.
Moving arm and eyes.
Brazo y ojos movibles.

2/6258 40 cm (16 inches)
Bewegl. Augen.
Moving eyes.
Ojos movibles.

2/6263 38 cm (15 inches) 50 cm (20 inches)
Bewegl. Maul und Augen. Bewegl. Augen.
Moving mouth and eyes. Moving eyes.
Boca y ojos movibles. Ojos movibles.

2/7030 160 cm (65 inches)
Bewegl. Kopf und Maul.
Moving head and mouth.
Cabeza y boca movibles.

2/6257 74 cm (30 inches)
Pferd, bewegl. Ohren, Figur bewegl. Augen.
Horse, moving ears, figure, moving eyes.
Caballo, orejas movibles, figura, ojos movibles.

2/6748 55×50 cm (22×20 inches).
Schaukelnd.
Swinging.
Bamboleando.

2/6702 51 cm (20 inches)
Bewegl. Köpfe.
Moving heads.
Cabezas movibles.

Sämtliche Uhrwerke gehen mehrere Stunden. All clockwork pieces run for several hours. Todos los resortes andan varias horas.

Beachten Sie auch die Veröffentlichung auf Seite 192d des Hauptkataloges.

SCHUCO

Marke Schuco Fabrik-Marke Trade Mark

Patent. Plüsch- und Filzspielwaren. — Patent-Toys of Plush and Felt — Patent-Juguetes de Felpa y de Fieltro.

Die „SCHUCO"-Fabrikate haben sich — durch mehrfache In- und Auslandspatente vor Nachahmung geschützt — in allen Kulturstaaten der Welt Eingang verschafft. Die Vorzüge und charakteristischen Merkmale der in der Spielwarenindustrie mit Recht eine eigene Sparte einnehmenden „SCHUCO"-Artikel sind:

1. Sinnreicher, aber dennoch einfacher Mechanismus.
2. Solide, formvollendete Ausführung.
3. Verwendung nur erstklassigen Materials.

Die SCHUCO-Patent-Kopfbewegung tritt durch bloßes Bewegen des Schwanzes in Tätigkeit und zaubert die drolligsten Effekte hervor. In naturgetreuer Weise hebt und senkt „SCHUCO" den Kopf, guckt rechts und links und rundum. „SCHUCO" ist das lebendige Spielzeug, das sich nicht nur bei den Kindern, sondern auch bei den Damen großer Beliebtheit erfreut.

Die gleichen Eigenschaften, welche die großen SCHUCO-Tiere als Qualitätsspielwaren in höchster Vollendung auszeichnen, sind auch die Kennzeichen der Miniatur-Patent-Tiere **„PICCOLO"**, bei denen jedoch infolge ihrer Kleinheit die saubere, gleichmäßige Ausführung noch mehr in Erscheinung tritt. Welch ein außerordentlich begehrter Artikel **„PICCOLO"** in seinen verschiedenen Variationen ist, dafür spricht die Tatsache, daß davon nachweislich mehr als eine Million innerhalb eines Jahres verkauft wurden.

Neuheiten 1926: Piccolo-Bären und -Affen in kleinster **9 cm** Ausführung, — Für Damentaschen mit Parfümflakon; zum Anstecken; als Scherzartikel m. Spritzball.

Latest Novelties 1926: Piccolo: Bears and Monkeys of smallest shape about **9 cm.** With Scentbottle for Ladie's bags; for pinning; with squirt-ball as joking-article.

Novedades 1926: Osos y monos piccolo en la ejecución más chico ó sea **9 cm.** Para bolsas señora con flacón para perfume; para prender; artículo de broma con goma para echar perfume.

108/4/40

The "SCHUCO"-Manufactures — protected against imitation by various home and foreign patents — have conquered the Toy-Market all over the world. They form a line for themselves and the superiority and particular characters are:

1. Ingenious, but nevertheless simple and handy mechanism.
2. Trustworthy, naturally accomplished execution and finish.
3. Consumption of first class materials.

The SCHUCO-Patent Head-Movement is practiced by the mere sliding of the tail up and down, right and left, thus producing the queerest display. In true imitation to nature SCHUCO raises and lowers its head, looks to the right and left and round about and therefore SCHUCO is claimed the living toy, which is preferred not only by Children but even by Ladies.

Just the same particularities of the big SCHUCO-Animals are the characteristic marks of the Miniature-Patent-Animals **"PICCOLO"**, the small shape of PICCOLO showing the exact execution even more distinctly. The stated sale of more than one Million pieces during one year proves in which high measure the Article **"PICCOLO"** in its varieties is preferred.

Las manufacturas „SCHUCO" — protegido contra imitación por diferentes patentes del pais y del extranjero — estan vendiendose en todas partes del mundo. Las ventajas y las señales características de los artículos "SCHUCO" que forman con razón en la industria de juguetes una parte especial son:

1. El ingenioso y sencillo mecanismo.
2. La sólida y buena ejecución.
3. El empleo de materiales de primera clase.

Moviendo solamente la cola se pone en función el movimiento de la cabeza del patente SCHUCO que da entonces efectos chistosos. En una manera natural sube y baja el "SCHUCO" la cabeza, mirando á la derecha, á la izquierda y por todas partes. "SCHUCO" es el juguete vivo que alegra ni solo á los niños sino también á las señoras.

Las mismas cualidades por las cuales se distinguen los animales grandes "SCHUCO" como juguetes de perfección más completa son también los caracteres de los patentados animales en miniatura **"PICCOLO"** en los cuales en consecuencia de su pequeñez aparece aún, más la ejecución límpia y exacta. Que el **"PICCOLO"** en sus diferentes variaciones es un artículo de una demanda extraordinaria lo prueba el caso que fueron vendidos dentro de un año más de un millón de piezas.

108/6/50

Schimpanse. / Chimpanzee. Chimpancé.

108/5/28	-/36	-/40	-/50	-/70	-/100
s = 28	36	40	50	70	100 cm

Mohairplüsch, braun oder weiß, auf Wunsch mit Brille. — Mohairplush, brown or white, on demand with spectacles. — Felpa mohair, marron ó blanca, deseandolo con anteojos.

108/6/30	-/40	-/45	-/55
s = 30	40	45	55 cm

Mit Brille, langhaariger Mohairplüsch, gold, weiß oder braun. — **With spectacles,** longpile Mohairplush, gold, white or brown. — **Con anteojos,** pelo largo felpa mohair de color de oro ó blanco ó marron

108/2/24 A
s = 24 cm
Affe. / Monkey. Mono.

108/2/24 B
s = 24 cm
Bär. / Bear. Oso.

Mit Plüschkopf, gekleidet. With plush-head, dressed. Vestido, con cabeza de felpa.

Bär. / Bear. / Oso.

108/9/24	-/28	-/32	-/35	-/40
s = 24	28	32	35	40 cm

108/9/45	-/50	-/55	-/60	-/70	-/80
s = 45	50	55	60	70	80 cm

Mohairplüsch, gold oder weiß. — Mohairplush, gold or white. — Felpa mohair de color de oro ó blanco.

108/10/24	-/28	-/32	-/35	-/40
s = 24	28	32	35	40 cm

108/10/45	-/50	-/55	-/60	-/70	-/80
s = 45	50	55	60	70	80 cm

Langhaariger Mohairplüsch, gold oder weiß. — Longpile Mohairplush, gold or white. — Pelo largo felpa mohair de color oro ó blanco.

108/10/40

Neu! „FUNKELAUGEN" Neu!

Novelty! SPARKLING-EYES OJOS BRILLANTES Novedad!

108/3/38 108/2/32

Affen. / Monkeys. / Monos.

108/2/32
s = 32 cm
Mit Plüschkopf, gekleidet.
With plush-head, dressed.
Vestido, con cabeza de felpa.

108/3/38
s = 38 cm
Feine Ausführung.
Best finish.
Ejecución fina.

Fuchs. / Fox. / Zorro.

108/168/24	-/28	-/32	-/35
s = 24	28	32	35 cm

Mit Brille, auf Wunsch mit Funkelaugen; Mohairplüsch, fuchsfarbig. — **With spectacles,** on demand with Sparkling-Eyes; Mohairplush fox-coloured. — **Con anteojos,** deseandolo con ojos brillantes; felpa mohair roja.

Die meisten „SCHUCO"-Fabrikate können auf Wunsch mit **Funkelaugen** und **Brillen** geliefert werden. Die kleineren und mittleren Tiere sind mit **Druckstimme**, die größeren mit **automatischer Brummstimme**, die größeren Fahrtiere mit **Zugstimme** ausgestattet.

108/168/35 108/68

Fuchs. / Fox. / Zorro.

108/68	68/0
s = 18 cm	15 cm

Sitzend, auf Wunsch mit Funkelaugen und Brille; Mohairplüsch, fuchsfarbig. — **Sitting,** on demand with Sparkling-Eyes and spectacles; Mohairplush fox-coloured. — **Sentado,** deseandolo con ojos brillantes y anteojos; felpa mohair roja.

Most of the "SCHUCO"-Products can — on demand — be supplied with **Sparkling-Eyes,** and with **spectacles.** The animals of smaller and medium size are furnished with **press voice,** the larger ones with **automatic growling voice,** the larger Roller-Animals with **draw voice.**

108/149/35

Katze. / Cat. / Gato.

108/149/24	-/28	-/32	-/35
s = 24	28	32	35 cm

Mit Funkelaugen, auf Wunsch mit Brille; langhaarig. Mohairplüsch, weiß, grau oder schwarz. — **With Sparkling-Eyes,** on demand with spectacles; longpile Mohairplush, white, grey or black. — **Con ojos brillantes,** deseandolo con anteojos; pelo largo felpa mohair, blanca, gris ó negra.

La mayoria de los artículos "SCHUCO" pueden ser fornecidos deseandolo con **ojos brillantes** y con **anteojos.** Los animales pequeños y medianos son hechos con **voz de presión,** los grandes con **voz gruñidora automática** y los para accarear con **voz tirante.**

s = Höhe stehend. — Size standing. — Derecho.

Please note also the publication on page 190 of the principal catalogue.
Llamamos también su atención á la publicación en la página 190 del catálogo principal.

„SCHUCO"-Fahrtiere mit SCHUCO-Patent-Kopfbewegung.
"SCHUCO"-Roller-Animals with SCHUCO-Patent-Movement of Head.
Animales "SCHUCO" sobre ruedas con movimiento patentado de la cabeza.

Doppelt geschweißte Fahrgestelle, Holzräder mit Metallager.
Double welded frames, Wooden wheels with metal bearings.
Marcos con soldadura doble, Ruedas de madera con cojinetes de metal.

108/7/40

108/7/40
Messenger-Bär.
Bear-Messenger.
Oso mensajero.

108/7/28	-/40	-/70
s = 28		70 cm

Mit Plüschkopf, gekleidet. / With plush-head, dressed. / Vestido, con cabeza de felpa.

Messenger-Affe.
Monkey-Messenger / Mono mensajero.

108/4/28	-/40	-/70
s = 28	40	70 cm

108/23 A/1

108/23 A/1
Bi - Ba - Bo
Messenger-Affe. Mit Plüschkopf, gekleidet; auf Wunsch mit Stimme.
Monkey-Messenger. With plush-head, dressed; on demand with voice.
Mono mensajero. Vestido, con cabeza de felpa; deseandolo con voz.

Höhe / Height / Altura 21 cm

Bernhardinerhunde. — St. Bernard-Dogs. — Perros Bernardinos.

108/39/35	-/43	-/50	-/60	-/70
s = 35	43	50	60	70 cm

Langhaariger Mohairplüsch, weiß, braun. — Longpile Mohairplush, white and brown. — Pelo largo felpa mohair blanca y marron.

108/148/30
Papagei, Mohairplüsch, bunt. — **Parrot,** Mohairplush coloured. — **Papagayo,** felpa mohair de varios colores.
Höhe / Height / Altura 30 cm

„ACROBATO"
Turnt langanhaltend! Working continually! Hace gimnasia durante largo tiempo!

108/270
Messenger - Affe mit Plüschkopf, gekleidet.
Monkey-Messenger with plush-head, dressed.
Mono mensajero vestido, con cabeza de felpa.

sitzend / sitting sentado 21 cm

108/270

108/11/11 G s = 12 cm
„PICCOLO" - Bär mit Füllfläschchen und Korkverschluß. — **"PICCOLO" - Bear** with filling-bottle and cork-stopper. — **Oso "PICCOLO"** con frasco de vidrio y tapón de corcho.

108/11/11 H

„PICCOLO"-Bär / Bear / Oso.
Mit Wiegengehänge. — With cradle hanging. — Con colgantes de cuna.
s = 12 cm

108/28/80 Elefant. — Elephant. — Elefante.

108/22/19	-/22	-/28	-/35	-/43	-/50	-/60	-/80
s = 19	22	28	35	43	50	60	80 cm

Filz, grau. / Felt, grey. / Fieltro, gris.

108/28/19	-/22	-/28	-/35	-/43	-/50	-/60	-80
s = 19	22	28	35	43	50	60	80 cm

Mohairplüsch, grau / Mohairplush, grey / Felpa mohair, gris.

Fahrbär. - Bear on wheels. - Oso sobre ruedas.

108/18/17	-/22	-/28	-/35	-/43	-/50	-/60	-/80
s = 17	22	28	35	43	50	60	80 cm

Mohairplüsch, braun / Mohairplush, brown
Felpa mohair, marron.

108/15/11 H

„PICCOLO"-Chimpanzee / Chimpancé.
Mit Wiegengehänge. — With cradle hanging. Con colgantes de cuna.
s = 12 cm

108/15/11 P
„PICCOLO"-Schimpanse mit Parfümflacon.
"PICCOLO"-Chimpanzee with scent-bottle.
Chimpancé "PICCOLO" con frasco de perfume.
s = 12 cm

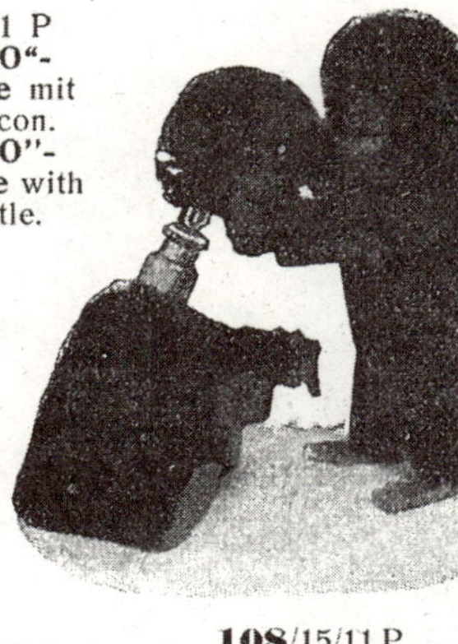

108/15/11 P

PICCOLO

Neuheit! — Novelty! — Novedad!
Spezialität! — Speciality! — Especialidad!
Feinster Mohairplüsch! — Finest Mohairplush!
Felpa mohair de primera calidad!

108/111/11

108/111/11
Bär, gold.
Bear, gold.
Oso, de color de oro.
s = 12 cm

108/115/11
Schimpanse, braun.
Chimpanzee brown.
Chimpancé, marron.
s = 12 cm

108/115/11
als Purzelfigur.
as Tumbler.
dando volteretas.

PICCOLO

Artikel mit SCHUCO-Patent-Kopfbewegung und Brille. — **"PICCOLO"**-Articles with SCHUCO-Patent-Movement of Head and with spectacles. — Artículos **"PICCOLO"** con movimiento patentado de la cabeza y anteojos.

108/30/14

108/30/14
s = 13 cm.
Seidenpinscher, mit Funkelaugen, langhaariger Mohairplüsch, weiß-braun. — **Lap-dog,** with Sparkling-Eyes, longpile Mohairplush white and brown. — **Perro grifón,** con ojos brillantes, pelo largo felpa mohair, blanca y marron.

108/30/14 G dito mit Füllfläschchen — ditto with filling - bottle — idem con frasco de vidrio.
108/30/14 P dito mit Parfümflacon — ditto with scent-bottle — idem con frasco de perfume.
108/130/14 dito mit SCHUCO-Patent-Kopfbewegung — ditto with SCHUCO-Patent-Movement of Head — idem con movimiento patentado de la cabeza.

„PICCOLO"

Uhrwerk bei falschem Aufziehen nicht überdrehbar!
The clockwork cannot be overwound, if wound up the wrong way!
El mecanismo de reloj no se puede danar, siquiera dando cuerda en sentido contrario!

108/73 Bär, gold. / **Bear,** gold. / **Oso,** de color de oro. — s = 12 cm.
108/71 Schimpanse, braun. / **Chimpanzee,** brown. / **Chimpancé,** marron. — s = 12 cm.
108/74 Hase, beige. / **Hare,** natural. / **Liebre,** beige. — s = 14 cm.

„PICCOLO"-Familie in buntem Karton mit Gelatine-Deckel. — **"PICCOLO"-Family** in coloured cardboard-box with gelatine-cover. **Familia de "PICCOLOS"** en caja de fantasia con tapa de gelatina.
Sortiment A. / Set A. / Surtido A.
3 Figuren / 3 pieces / 3 piezas
108/15/11, 108/11/11, 108/15/11.

s = Höhe stehend — Size standing — derecho.

Beachten Sie auch die Veröffentlichung auf Seite 190 des Hauptkataloges.

Please note also the publication on page 207 of the principal catalogue.
Llamamos también su atención á la publicación en la página 207 del catálogo principal.

CITO-BALL

zum Selbstaufblasen.

The Cito-Ball for Self-Filling with wind.

La Pelota Cito llenándola uno mismo de aire.

Aus bestem Gummi hergestellt, daher sehr haltbar. Hygienisch einwandfrei. Sicherer und einfacher Verschluß. Federleicht, zum Spiel im Zimmer geeignet. Billiger als jeder andere Spielball.

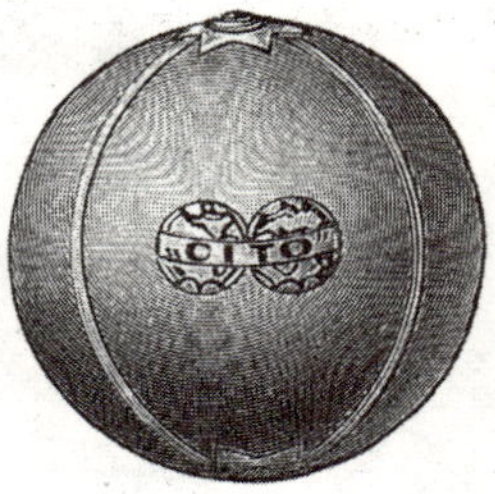

Made of first-class India Rubber. Hygienic. Easily and securely fastened. As light as a feather. Can be used in the parlour. Cheaper than any other playing-ball.

Fabricada de la mejor goma, por lo tanto muy durable. En cuanto á la higiene sin objeción alguna. Con cierre seguro y sencillo. Liviana como una pluma, se presta para jugar en el salón. Más barata que cualquier otra pelota de jugar.

Zusammengelegt in der Tasche zu tragen. — Can be folded and carried in your pocket. — Se puede llevar plegada en el bolsillo.

Ball aufblasen, mit dem Stöpsel verschließen, den Stöpsel in das Innere des Balles versenken, und der Ball ist spielfertig.

Directions: To make the Ball ready for use, blow it up, close it with stopper and press the stopper firmly into the ball. Any child can do it in a minute's time.

Llénese de viento y ciérrese con el tapón, introduciéndolo y la pelota queda lista para el juego.

Der beliebte und billigste Spielball für groß und klein. — The most popular and the cheapest ball for adults as well as for children. La pelota de jugar más apreciada y más barata para niños y adultos.

	164/1	**164**/2	**164**/3	**164**/4	**164**/5	**164**/6	**164**/7	**164**/8	**164**/9	**164**/10	
Durchmesser / Diameter / Diámetro	13	15	17	19	21	23	25	27	29	30	cm.
Umfang / Circumference / Circuito	41	47	53	60	66	72	79	85	91	94	cm.

Bunte Gummipuppen. — Dolls of coloured India rubber. — Muñecas de goma de muchos colores.

133/1001

133/1002

133/1003

133/1004

133/1006

133/1007

133/1008

133/113

133/114

133/115

Beachten Sie auch die Veröffentlichung auf Seite 207 des Hauptkataloges.

Please note also the publication on page 181 and 182 of the principal catalogue.
Llamamos también su atención á la publicación en la página 181 y 182 del catálogo principal.

Holzspielwaren mit und ohne Stimme. — Wooden Toys with and without voice. — Juguetes de madera con y sin voz.

Durchschnittlich
More or less
Uno con otro
Länge / Length / Largura 26 cm
Höhe / Height / Altura 20 cm

Serie **109**/6
P = 1/6 Dtz., Doz., Doc.

Durchschnittlich
More or less
Uno con otro
Höhe / Height / Altura 30 cm

Serie **109**/12
P = 1/6 Dtz., Doz., Doc.

Durchschnittlich
More or less
Uno con otro
Länge / Length / Largura 30 cm
Höhe / Height / Altura 19 cm

Serie **109**/19
P = 1/6 Dtz., Doz., Doc.

109/6, **109**/12 und 19 in mindestens 6 Tieren und Figuren sortiert. — Assorted lowest in 6 animals and figures. — Surtido al menos en 6 animales y figuras.

109/12 und 19 mit beweglichen Augen. — With moving eyes. — Con ojos movibles.

Durchschnittlich
More or less
Uno con otro
Länge / Length / Largura 24 cm
Höhe / Height / Altura 17 cm

Serie **109**/8
P = 1/6 Dtz., Doz., Doc.

Durchschnittlich — More or less — Uno con otro

Länge / Length / Largura 14 cm

Höhe / Height / Altura 8 cm

Serie **109**/1
P = 1 Dtz., Doz., Doc.

Durchschnittlich
More or less
Uno con otro
Länge / Length / Largura 24 cm
Höhe / Height / Altura 17 cm

Serie **109**/35
P = 1/6 Dtz., Doz., Doc.

109/8, **109**/1 und 35 in mindestens 6 Tieren sortiert. — Assorted lowest in 6 animals. — Surtido al menos en 6 animales.

	Länge Length Largura	Höhe Height Altura	Packung Packing Contenido
No. **109**/16/1	20 cm	10 cm	1 Dtz., Doz., Doc.
„ **109**/16/2	24 „	11 „	½ „ „ „
„ **109**/16/3	26 „	12 „	½ „ „ „

Serie **109**/16

Musikkissen.
Musical cushions.
Cojines de música.

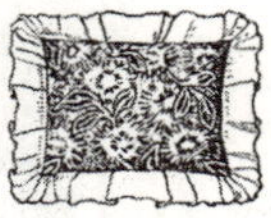

Serie **109**/41

No. **109**/41/1	Größe, size, tamaño	24 × 24 cm
„ **109**/41/1½	„ „ „	27 × 30 „
„ **109**/41/2	„ „ „	33 × 36 „
„ **109**/41/2½	„ „ „	37 × 42 „
„ **109**/41/3	„ „ „	43 × 48 „
„ **109**/41/4	„ „ „	49 × 54 „

Puppe aus gestopftem Körper mit Pappkopf und Frisur, ohne Stimme, in 24 verschiedenen Dessins.

Doll stuffed body with cardboard head and wig, without voice, in 24 different designs.

Muñeca de cuerpo zurcido con cabeza de papel y peluca, sin voz, en 24 diversos intenciones.

Größe
Size
Tamaño
33 cm

Serie **109**/107/33

Neu geborenes Baby.
New born Baby.
Bebé recien-nacido.

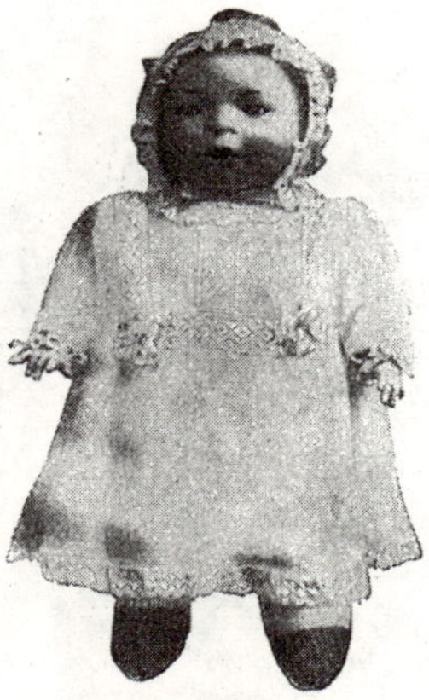

Größen
28 cm — 42 cm
Sizes
28 cm — 42 cm
Tamaños
28 cm — 42 cm

Serie **109**/106/32

P = Packung — Packing — Contenido.

1/5 der natürlichen Größe. — 1/5 of natural size. — 1/5 del tamaño natural.

Beachten Sie auch die Veröffentlichung auf Seite 181 und 182 des Hauptkataloges.

165/800

165/200

165/825

165/140

165/549

165/121

165/225

165/125

165/700

165/120

165/450

165/325

165/300

165/925

165/900

165/620

165/950

165/400

165/570

165/425

165/640

165/554

165/650

165/775

165/850

165/553

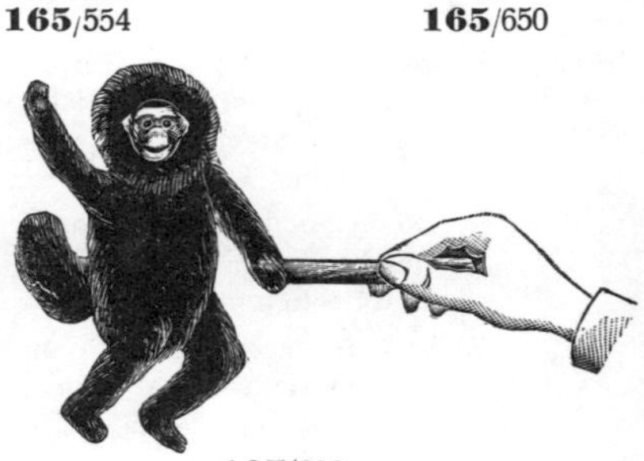
165/630

165/250

165/875

165/552

Please nota also the publication on page 137 and 138 of the principal cataiogue.
Llamamos también su atención á la publicación en la página 137 y 138 del catálogo principal.

Bewegliche Fahrfiguren, künstlerisch ausgeführt. — Movable figures artistically accomplished. — Figuras móviles, artisticamente ejecutadas.

136/AL 48

136/AL 9/1

136/AL 8/1

136/B 301/BF

Marionetten.
Marionettes.
Marionetas.

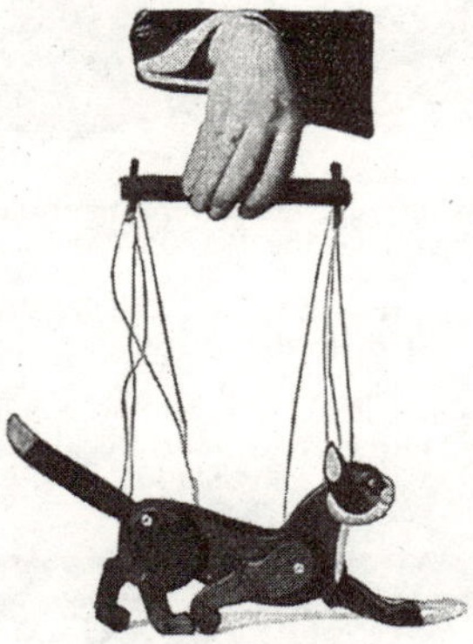

136/K A M 36

136/A M 8/1

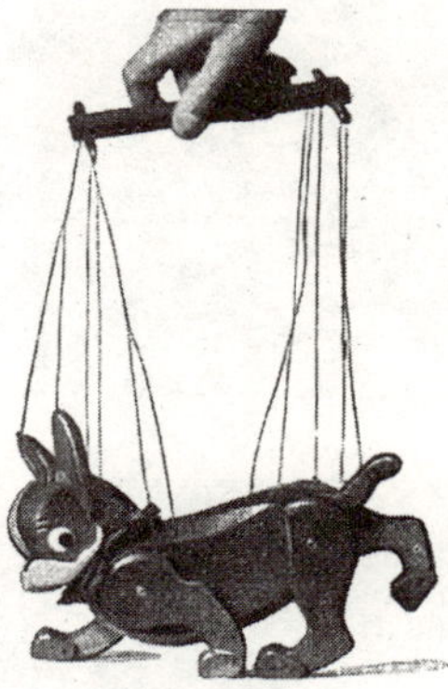

136/A M 21

136/A M 9

ZOO

Gruppen,
zusammengestellt aus Pferd **136**/A 1.
Kartongröße = Modellgröße,
zusammengelegt 45 × 15 × 8 cm.

Folgende Figuren können geliefert werden: Bär, Affe, Elefant mit Mohr, Löwe, Panther, Stierkampf (4teilig), Bulli, Katze, Eichhorn, Zwerg, Esel, Clown, Stier, Hase, Nashorn, Ziegenbock, Kamel mit Treiber, Giraffe, Gnu, Dackel, Nilpferd, Antilope, Zebra, Schaf, Reh, Fuchs, Leopard, Schwein, Bauer und Wolf.

Groups,
composed of horse **136**/A 1.
Size of card-box = size of model,
folded 45 × 15 × 8 cm.

The following figures can be supplied: bear, monkey, elephant with moor, lion, panther, bull-fight (4 parts), bully, cat, squirrel, dwarf, donkey, clown, bull, hare, rhinoceros, buck, camel with driver, giraffe, gnu, badger-dog, hippopotamus, antilope, zebra, sheep, roe, fox, leopard, pig, peasant and wolf.

Grupos,
compuestos de caballo **136**/A 1.
Tamaño de la cajita = tamaño del modelo,
doblado 45 × 15 × 8 cm.

Las figuras siguientes pueden ser suministradas: Oso, mono, elefante con moro, león, pantera, toréo (4 partes), bulli, gato, ardilla, enano, asno, arlequin, toro, liebre, rinoceronte, cabrito, camelo con arriero, jirafa, gnu, perillo raposero, hipopótamo, antilopa, zebra, oveja, corzo, zorra, leopardo, puerco, labrador y lobo.

Das Zoo-Schaukelpferd, laufend und lenkbar.
The Zoo-rocking-horse, running and guidable.
El caballo de mecer del zoo, corriendo y gobernable.

	Höhe Height Altura	Länge Length Largura	Breite Breadth Ancho	
136/I	76	152	38	cm
136/II	64	134	36	cm
136/III	55	116	34	cm

Beachten Sie auch die Veröffentlichung auf Seite 137 und 138 des Hauptkataloges.

119/1020

Puppenhäuser in erstklassiger Ausführung, vollständig eingerichtet, außen feinst bemalt, innen modern tapeziert, Türen und Fenster zum Öffnen. Größe II: 113×85×47 cm, mit Treppen und abnehmbarem Dachgarten, samt Einrichtung.
Dolls' houses, in first class finish, completely fitted up, outward finely painted, inward fashionably wall-papered, doors and windows to be opened. Size II: 113×85×47 cm, with staircases and dismountable roof-garden, with outfit.
Casas de muñecas, muy bien acabadas, completamente amueblada, de fuera finamente pintadas, de dentro modernamente entapizadas, puertas y ventanillas para abrirse. Tamaño II: 113×85×47 cm, con escalas, y jardín de techo desmontable, con mueblaje completo.

119/280

Puppenwohnungen in feinster Ausführung, leer oder eingerichtet, größtenteils zerlegbar, Türen und Fenster zum Öffnen. Größe II: 89×79×35 cm, 3seitig spielbar, mit 5 Räumen samt Einrichtung.
Dolls' dwellings in finest finish, empty or outfitted, the greater part dismountable, doors and windows to de opened. Size II: 89×79×35 cm, to be played from 3 sides, 5 rooms, outfitted.
Habitaciones de muñecas, finamente acabadas, vacíos o amuebladas, la mayor parte desmontables, puertas y ventanillas para abrirse. Tamaño II: 89×79×35 cm, á jugarse desde 3 lados, con 5 cuartos amueblados.

119/310

Puppenwohnungen in feinster Ausführung, leer oder eingerichtet, größtenteils zerlegbar, Türen und Fenster zum Öffnen. Größe III: 170×50×41 cm, zerlegbar, mit echtem, eingelegtem Parkettboden, samt Einrichtung.

Dolls' dwellings, in finest finish, empty or outfitted, the greater part dismountable, doors and windows to be opened. Size III: 170×50×41 cm, dismountable, with genuine inlaid floor, with outfit.

Habitaciones de muñecas, finamente acabados, vacíos o amuebladas, la mayor parte desmontables, puertas y ventanillas para abrirse. Tamaño III: 170×50×41 cm, desmontable, con verdadero suelo de parquete, con mueblaje.

119/600

Puppengarten, Größe II: 85×65 cm, mit Marmorbrunnen, Möbeln und Schaukel, hübsch angelegt.
Dolls' garden, Size II: 85×65 cm, with marble-fountain, furniture and swing, well arranged.
Jardín de muñecas, Tamaño II: 85×65 cm, con fuente de mármol, mueblaje y columpio.

119/K H 150 D

Speisezimmer, Größe II: 10teilig, eiche dunkel gebeizt, samt Bildern und Zubehör.
Dining-room, Size II: 10 pieces, ebonized oak, with pictures and accessories.
Sala de comer, Tamaño II: 10 piezas, roble ebanizado, con estampas y accesorios.

119/510

Puppenküchen, 1- und 2teilig, zerlegbar, in feinster Ausführung, Türen und Fenster zum Öffnen, mit Wasserleitung. Größe IV: 115×55×50 cm, zerlegbar, mit Erkerfenster zum Öffnen, samt Wasserleitung und kompletter weißlackierter Einrichtung.
Dolls' kitchens, 1 and 2 parts, dismountable, in finest finish, doors and windows to be opened, with aqueduct. Size IV: 115×55×50 cm, dismountable, with bow-window to be opened, with aqueduct and complete white varnished outfit.
Cocinas de muñecas, 1 y 2 partes, desmontables, finamente acabadas, puertas y ventanillas á abrirse, con aqueducto. Tamaño IV: 115×55×50 cm, desmontable, con ventanilla de balcón á abrirse, con aqueducto y mueblaje completo, barnizado blanco.

119/K H 150 D

119/K H 511

Schlafzimmer, Größe III: 8teilig, naturlackiert, Hochglanz, samt Bildern und Zubehör.
Bed-room, Size III: 8 pieces, natural varnished, high lustre, with pictures and accessories.
Dormitorio, Tamaño III: 8 piezas, barnizado natural, con estampas y accesorios.

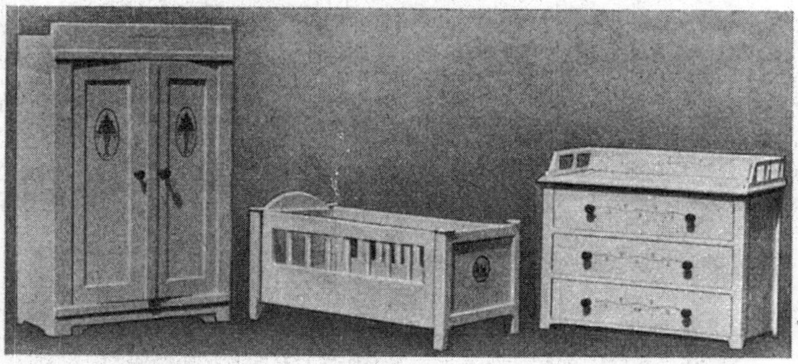

119/10/6 **119**/10/7 **119**/10/2

Möbel für große Puppen in feinster weißer Emaillelackierung. — **Furnitures for tall dolls** in finest white enamel varnish. — **Muebles para muñecas grandes,** finamente barnizados blanco con barniz de esmalte.
119/10/2 Schrank für Kleider und Wäsche / Press for clothes and linen / Guardaropa para vestidos y ropa blanca — Größe 58×34×17 cm
119/10/6 Kommode / Chest of drawers / Cómoda — Größe 40×35×22 cm.
119/10/7 Bettstelle, zerlegbar / Bed-stead, dismountable / Cama, desmontable — Größe 46×23×23 cm.

119/83

Grammophon m. Schweiz. Musikwerk / **Grammophone** with Swiss music work / **Gramofone** con caja de música suiza. Größe 12×10×7 cm.

119/KH 71/w

Küche, Größe III, 8teilig, weiß lackiert, samt Wasserleitung. **Kitchen,** Size III, 8 pieces, white varnished, with aqueduct. **Cocina**, tamaño III, 8 piezas, barnizada blanca, con aqueducto.

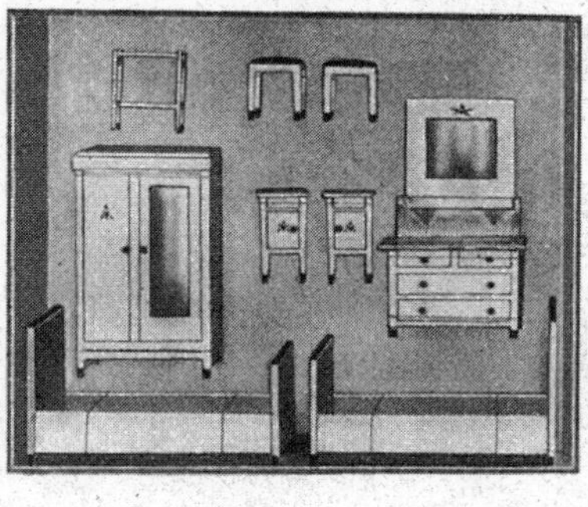

119/Bb 50 w

Schlafzimmer, Größe II, 8 teilig, buche natur oder weiß lackiert. — **Bedchamber,** size II, 8 pieces, natural beech or white varnished. — **Cuarto de dormier,** tamaño II, 8 piezas, haya natural o barnizado blanco.

119/7 f

Klubgarnitur, Größe II, 4teilig, aus Kunstleder oder Kunstlederpapier. **Club furniture set,** size II, 4 pieces, of artificial leather or leather-paper. — **Juego de muebles para club,** tamaño II, 4 piezas, de cuero artificial o de papel imitando cuero.

119/Bi 170 b

Biedermeier-Zimmer, Größe II, 12 teilig, feinst lackiert, mit Plüschpolsterung. — **Biedermeier** (old fashioned) **room,** size II, 12 parts, finely varnished, with plush upholstering. — **Cuarto Biedermeier** (moda antigua), tamaño II, 12 partes, finamente barnizado, acolchado de polucia.

119/Ha 100

Herrenzimmer, Größe II, 8 teilig, eiche schwarz mattiert. — **Gents' room,** size II, 8 pieces, dead varnished oak. — **Cuarto de fumar,** tamaño II, 8 piezas, roble barnizado mate.

119/a

119/c **119**/g

119/f **119**/h

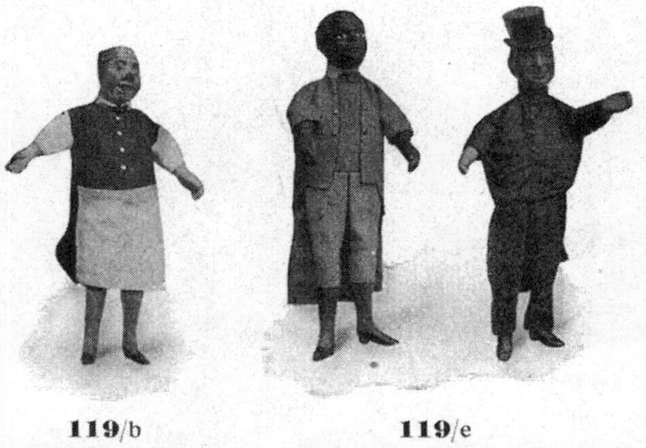

119/b **119**/e

119/d

119/251

Kasperl-Figuren, 40—45 cm hoch, mit gepreßten Holzmasseköpfen oder geschnitzten Holzköpfen, sehr solide, feinst bemalt und gekleidet, viele Modelle.

Größe = Size — Tamaño.

Kasperl-Theater, zusammenlegbar, feinst bemalt und lackiert, samt Hintergrund und Rollvorhang. — **Punch and Judy show,** to be folded, finely decorated and varnished, with background and roller-curtain. — **Teatro de arlequín,** plegable, finamente decorado y barnizado, con fondo y cortina rodante. Größe 190×105×45 cm.

Punch and Judy figures, 40—45 cm high, with pressed wood-pulp heads, or sculptured heads, most solid, finely painted and dressed, many types. — **Figuras de arlequín,** 40—45 cm de alto, con cabezas prensadas de pulpa de madera, o cabezas esculpidas, muy sólidas, finamente pintadas y vestidas, muchos tipos.

Please note also the publication on page 134 of the principal catalogue.
Llamamos también su atención á la publicación en la página 134 del catálogo principal.

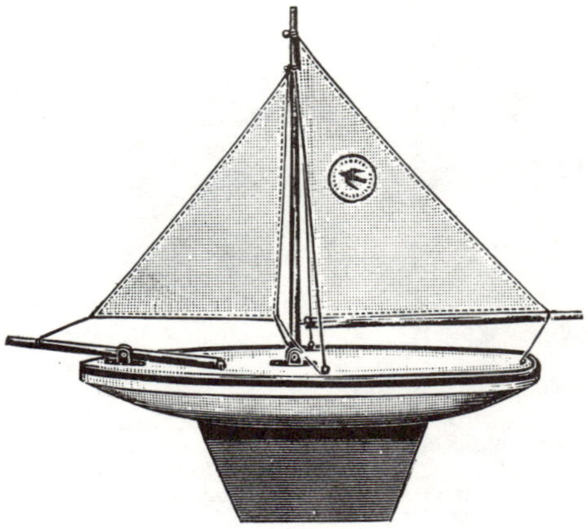

118/785

Segeljacht, garantiert segelnd, mit Fadenstellung sowie umlegbarer Takelage, sehr gut geeignet für Export, da Mastenbruch ausgeschlossen ist. (Größe 18—46 cm)

Sailing yacht, sailing guarranteed, with thread-adjustment, and shifting tackle, very well adapted for exportation, because breaking of mast is excluded. (Sizes 18—46 cm)

Yate de vela, velejando con garantía, con ajuste de hilos, y cordaje cambiable, muy bien apropiado para la exportación, porque no puede haber quebraduras de palos. (Tamaños 18—46cm)

118/707

Segelschiff mit 2 Masten, mit Verdeck und Matrosen. (Größe 25—35 cm)
Sailer with 2 masts, with deck and sailors. (Sizes 25—35 cm)
Buque de vela con 2 palos, con cubierta y marineros. (Tamaños 25—35 cm)

118/180

Kutter mit Strickleitern, feine Ausführung, guter Segler. (Größe 25—120 cm)
Cutter with rope-ladder, fine finish, good sailer. (Sizes 25—120 cm)
Cúter con escala de cuerdas, finamente acabado, buen velero. (Tamaños 25—120 cm)

118/710

Shamrock mit Drahtgalerie. (Größe 18—50 cm)
Shamrock with wire-gallery. (Sizes 18—50 cm)
Shamrock (yate) con galería de alambre. (Tamaños 18—50 cm)

118/740

Dreimastschoner. (Größe 25—40 cm)
Three-masted schooner. (Sizes 25—40 cm)
Goleta de tres palos. (Tamaños 25—40 cm)

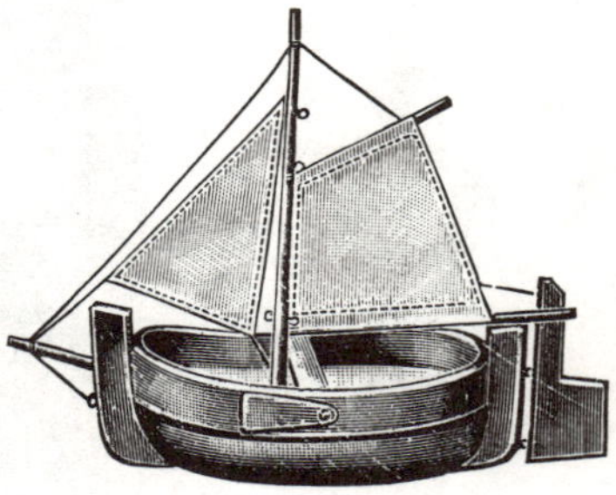

118/611

Holländerboot (Ewer), guter Segler. (Größe 9—50 cm)
Dutch boat (wherry), good sailer. (Sizes 9—50 cm)
Navío holandés (lanchón), buen velador. (Tamaños 9—50 cm)

Beachten Sie auch die Veröffentlichung auf Seite 134 des Hauptkataloges.

Saba-Figuren.
76/1001 **76**/1002—1145
Kugelgelenkfiguren aus Metall, vollkommen unzerbrechlich. Die beweglichsten Figuren der Welt. Verlangen Sie Spezialliste über die große Auswahl verschiedener Typen.

Saba-Figures.
76/1001 **76**/1002—1145
Articulate figures of metal, absolutely unbreakable. The most moveable figures of the world. Please ask for special list of the great choice in different types.

Figuras "Saba".
76/1001 **76**/1002—1145
Figuras articuladas de metal, absolutamente inquebrantables. Las figuras más movibles del mundo. Pidan lista especial de la gran selección en tipos diferentes.

SABA-FIGUREN

Saba-Figures. — Figuras "Saba".

Saba-Figuren.
ungekleidet **76**/1001
gekleidet **76**/1002—1145
144 Typen, sortiert.

Saba-Figures.
undressed **76**/1001
dressed **76**/1002—1145
144 Types, assorted.

Figuras "Saba".
sin vestidos **76**/1001
con vestidos **76**/1002—1145
144 diferentes tipos.

TRADE MARK

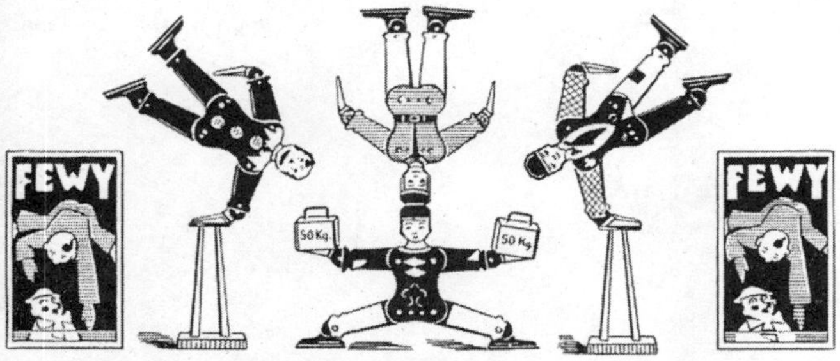

76/1504 **Fewy-Akrobaten:** Billiger, beliebter Massenartikel.
Fewy-Acrobats: Cheap, favourite wholesale-article.
Acrobatos "Fewy": Artícolo barato y apreciado para la venta en grueso.

76/1501 **Puck:** Unsere letzte Neuheit in Massenartikeln. Überschlägt sich selbständig.

Puck: Our latest novelty in wholesale-articles. Throwing a somersault.

Puck: Nuestra última novedad en artícolos al por mayor. Dando salto-mortal.

76/84 **Tramway:** Aus Holz und Blech, fein lackiert.

Tramway: Of wood and tinplate, finely varnished.

Ferrocarril: De madera y hojalata, finamente barnizado.

76/1601 **76**/1602

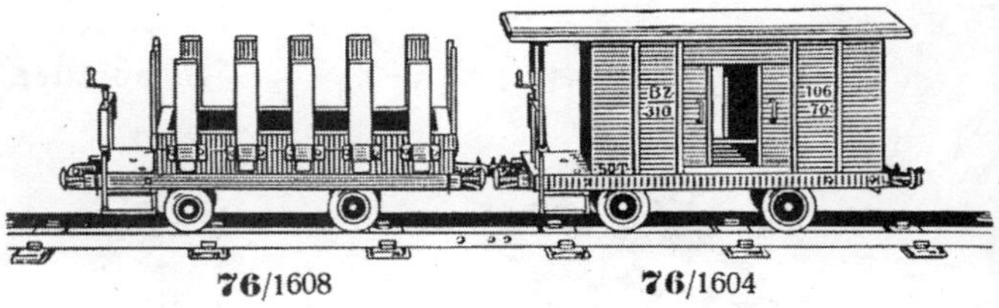

76/1608 **76**/1604

76/1606 **76**/1607

76/1601—1622 **Garteneisenbahn:** Aus massiv Eisen in Verbindung mit Holz konstruiert. Mit starkem Uhrwerk, eisernen Schienen, richtig federnden Puffern, richtig funktionierenden Handbremsen. Jeder Wagen mit Lenkachsen. Fein lackiert.

Garden-Railway: Constructed of massive iron in connection with wood. With strong winding up-mechanism, iron rails, rightly elastic buffers, rightly working handbrakes. Every car with leading axles. Finely varnished.

Ferrocarril de jardin: Construido de hierro macizo en conexión con madera. Con fuerte resorte, railes de hierro, verdaderos para-choques elásticos, verdaderos frenos á mano, funccionando. Cada carro con ejes de guia. Finamente barnizado.

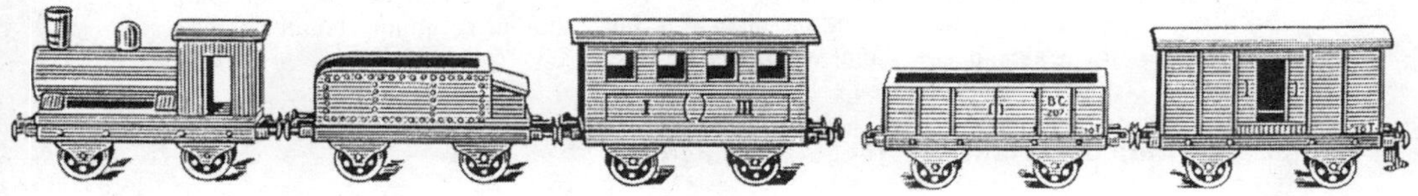

76/1651/1652 **Eisenbahn** wie **76**/1601—1622, jedoch ohne Uhrwerk, Bremsen und Schienen. Solider Bodenroller.

Railway, same as **76**/1601—1622, but without winding up-mechanism, brakes and rails. Solid groundroller.

Ferrocarril, lo mismo como **76**/1601—1622, pero sin resorte, frenos y railes. Sólido rodador de suelo.

76/1661 **Eisenbahn** aus massiv Holz in Verbindung mit Blech, ohne Uhrwerk, mit Treppen und Lenkachsen.

Railway of massive wood in connection with tinplate, without clockwork, with staircases and leading axles.

Ferrocarril de madera maciza en conexión con hojalata, sin resorte, con escaleras y ejes de guia.

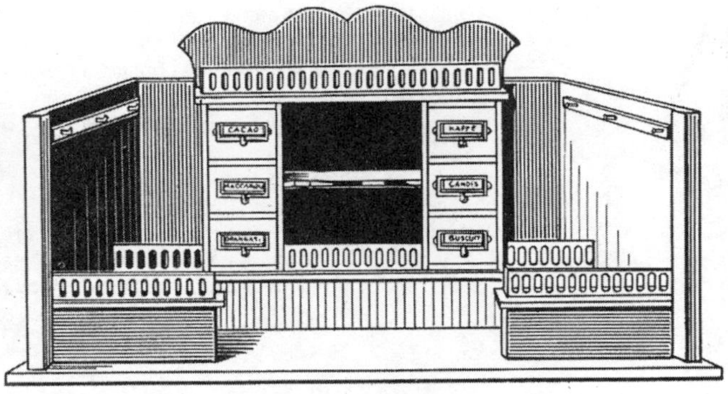

76/43 **Kaufladen** in erstklassiger Ausführung und Lackierung. Verlangen Sie Spezialliste.

Shop in first-class finish and varnishing. Please ask for special list.

Tienda en ejecución de primera clase y finamente barnizada. Pidan la lista especial.

Please note also the publication on page 94—96 of the principal catalogue.
Llamamos también su atención á la publicación en la página 94—96 del catálogo principal.

Schachspiele. — Chessmen. — Ajedreces.

89/931

89/931 a, 89/931 d — Holz / Wood / Madera

89/931 AB, 89/931 DB — Buchsholz / Box wood / Buo

Ausführung Finish Ejecución		Größe Size Tamaño	Höhe Height Altura ca. mm des Königs of king del rey	des Bauern of pawn del peón
89/931 a	matt, schwarz-weiß, in weißen Schiebekasten	0	50	26
	black and white, soft wood sliding boxes	1	58	30
	negro y blanco, cajitas de abeto	2	65	32
89/931 d	matt, gelb-schwarz, in polierten Klappkasten	3	73	36
	yellow and black, boxes polished	4	80	38
	amarillo y negro, cajitas pulidas finas	5	90	50
89/931 AB	matt, schwarz-weiß, in weißen Schiebekasten	0	55	25
	black and white, soft wood sliding boxes	1	65	30
	negro y blanco, cajitas de abeto	2	70	35
89/931 DB	poliert, schwarz-weiß, in polierten Klappkasten	3	75	37
	varnished, black and white, boxes polished	4	85	40
	barnizado, blanco y negro, cajitas pulidas finas	5	90	47

Reiseschach. — Travelling Chess. — Ajedrez de viaje.

89/4596/1
89/4596/2

	Ausführung Finish Ejecución	Größe des geschlossenen Kastens Size of the closed Box Tamaño de la cajita cerrada cm
89/4596/1	Mit Stauntonfiguren aus Bein, extra starke Zapfen. With Staunton bone men, extra thick pegged men. Con figuras de hueso Staunton.	$16^1/_2 \times 8^3/_4 \times 4$
89/4596/2	Derselbe Artikel größer. The same in larger. Más grande.	$20 \times 12^1/_2 \times 4$

Reisehalma. — Travelling halma game. — Halma de viaje.

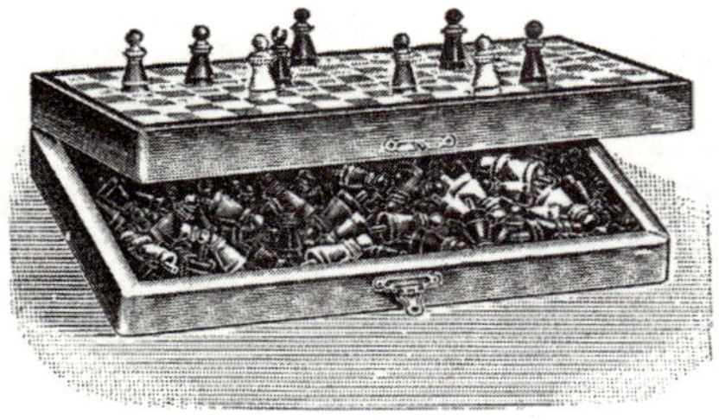

89/4322/1
89/4322/2

89/4322/1	Beinfiguren zum Einstecken With bone pegged men. Con figuras de hueso.	$16^1/_2 \times 8^1/_2 \times 3^1/_2$
89/4322/2	Galalithfiguren zum Aufstellen. With galalith men, flat bottom. Con figuras de galalith.	$21^1/_2 \times 10^1/_2 \times 3^1/_4$

Dambretter. — Draughtboards. — Juegos de damas.

89/110/B, 89/111, 89/113E, 89/113ET, 89/114

Größe Size Tamaño	
1	22 cm
2	27 „
3	32 „
4	37 „
5	41 „

	Ausführung — Finish — Ejecución
89/110 B	Fourniert, inkl. Steine, lith. Puffplan. Unpolished, with men. No pulido, con peones.
89/111	Halbfein, lith. Puffplan, inkl. Steine. Polished board, with men. Cuadros pulidos, con peones.
89/113 E	Eiche gezinkt, poliert, Papierpuff inkl. Steine. Oakwood polished, with men. Roble pulido, con peones.
89/113 ET	Eiche gezinkt, poliert, Tuchpuff, inkl. Steine. Oakwood polished, cloth backgammon. Roble pulido, con peones, con paño.
89/114	ff. Dambretter **ohne** Steine, echt Nußbaum eingelegt, gezinkt, Tuchpuff. Draughtboards without men, real nut, clothbackgammon, inlaid borders. Castaño con paño, extra fino.

Flohspiel. — Tiddledy Winks. — Juego de pulga.

89/4443

89/4454/4 Für 4 Spieler, mit Galalithmarken.
For 4 players, with galalith counters.
Para 4 jugadores, fichas de galalith.

89/4454/6 Dasselbe für 6 Spieler.
The same for 6 players.
Para 6 jugadores.

89/4443 Mit ausgefrästem runden Holzbrett, für 6 Personen.
Woodboards with holes, for 6 players.
Tabla de madera redonda, para 6 jugadores.

89/4454/4, 89/4454/6

Beachten Sie auch die Veröffentlichung auf Seite 94—96 des Hauptkataloges.

Please note also the publication on page 94—96 of the principal catalogue.
Llamamos también su atención á la publicación en la página 94—96 del catálogo principal.

Spielmagazine. — Compendiums of Games. — Combinación de Juegos.

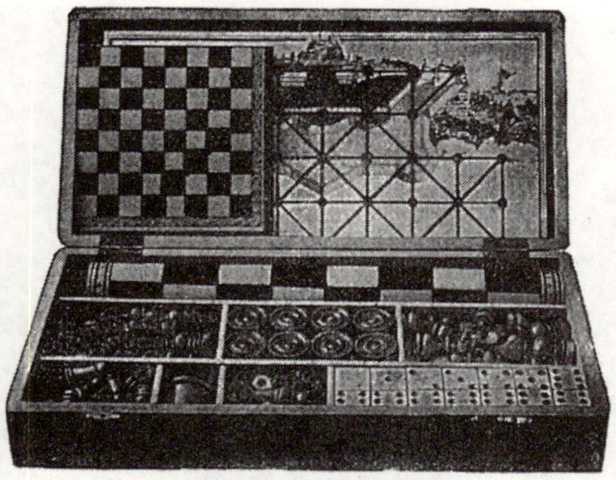

89/4349/1, 89/4349/2

89/4582, 89/4582 gr.

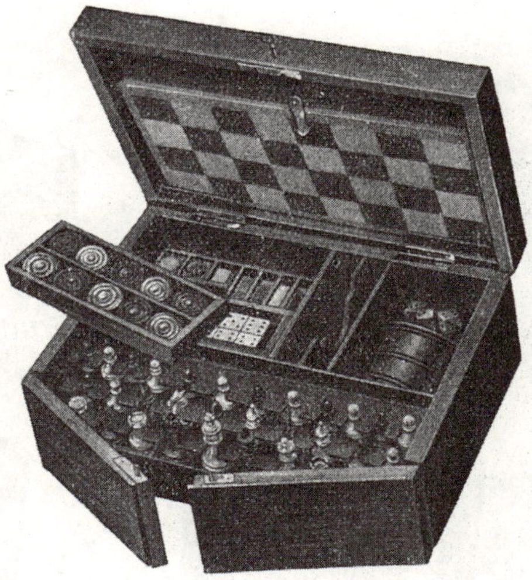

89/4673

89/3914

No. 89/4673 Nußbaum-Kasten, poliert, mit zusammenklappbarem Schach- und Mühlebrett, Bein-Stauntonschach, Domino Galalith mit Holzunterlage, Trolit-Damsteine, 1 Satz Spielmarken in eingerichtetem Holzkästchen, Lederwürfelbecher mit 3 Würfeln.

Box nuttree, with folding Chess- and Millboard, Staunton Bone-Chess, Trolit-Draughtsmen, Domino, 1 Set Counters, Leather Dice-cup with 3 Dice.

Caja nogal, cont.: Ajedrez Staunton Hueso, Tablero, Domino, Peones de Damas Trolit, 1 guarnición de Fichas, Corneta de cuero con 3 Dados de marfil vegetal. 28¼ × 10 × 13 cm.

No. 89/4349/1 Erlenholzkasten, fein poliert. Inhalt: Schachfiguren, Damsteine und Schachplan.
Alder wood polished, contents: Chess- and Draughtsmen, Chessboard.
Aliso pulido, conteniendo: Ajedrez, Peones de Damas y tablero. 35 × 12 × 5 cm.

No. 89/4349/2 Derselbe Kasten, jedoch größer, Inhalt 7 Spiele: Schachfiguren, Damsteine, Schachplan, Celluloid-Domino, Halmaspiel, Belagerungsspiel, Mühle, Holzwürfelbecher.
The same line but larger, containing besides: Celluloid-Domino, Halma, Fortress-Millgame and Dice-cup.
La misma caja, más grande, contenido ulterior: Domino-celluloid, Juego de Halma, Juego de Asalto, de Molino, de Corneta de Dados. 35 × 17 × 5½ cm.

No. 89/4582 Derselbe Kasten, Inhalt: Holz-Stauntonschach, Damsteine, Reisedomino, Pappschachbrett mit Mühle.
The same line, containing: Wood Staunton-Chess, Draughtsmen and Domino, Chess- and Millboard combined.
La misma caja, cont.: Ajedrez Staunton, Peones de Damas, Domino y tablero de Ajedrez y Molino. 25¾ × 13½ × 4¼ cm.

No. 89/4582 gr. Derselbe Artikel, ohne Domino, größer.
The same line, larger, without Domino.
La misma caja, más grande, sin Domino. 29 × 15¾ × 5¼ cm.

No. 89/3914 Kasten, Mahagoni poliert, mit Henkeln, mit eingelegtem Nußbaumklappschachbrett- und Mühlebrett, Flügeltüren Inhalt 7 Spiele: poliertes Staunton-Buchschach mit Tuchunterlage, feines Domino, polierte Buchsdamsteine, gefütterter Lederwürfelbecher mit Würfeln, 1 Satz Pokerwürfel, Mühle, 1 Satz Bostonmarken.
Box with handles, Mahagoni varnished, best Chess- and Millboard, containing 7 Games: Staunton Chess, varnished boxwood, Domino, varnished boxwood Draughtsmen, clothed Leather Dice-cup with Dice, 1 Set Pokerdice, 1 Set Counters, Mille Game.
Caja de caoba barnizada, con mangos niquelados. Conteniendo 7 Juegos: Ajedrez, barnizado Staunton con paño, Domino, Peones de Damas barnizados, Corneta con paño con Dados, 1 guarnición de Dados para el Juego de Poker, 1 guarnición de Fichas, Molino. 35 × 25 × 19 cm.

89/4639

Pokerkasten. — Poker Case. — Caja Poker.

Holzkasten, Eiche gedämpft, mit herausnehmbarem Einsatz, Unterteil leer,
Box oakwood with Tray.
Cajita roble.

Stück pieces piezas	Durchmesser Diameter Diámetro	Farbe colour color	Größe des Kastens Size of box Tamaño de caja
200	30 mm rd	5	
40	20 × 40 „	weiß, white, blanco	22 × 17 × 7 cm
40	18 × 28 „	rosa, pink, rosado	
20	20 × 30 „	grün green, verde	

Beachten Sie auch die Veröffentlichung auf Seite 94—96 des Hauptkataloges.

Nähkasten. Sewing-desk. Neceser de costura.

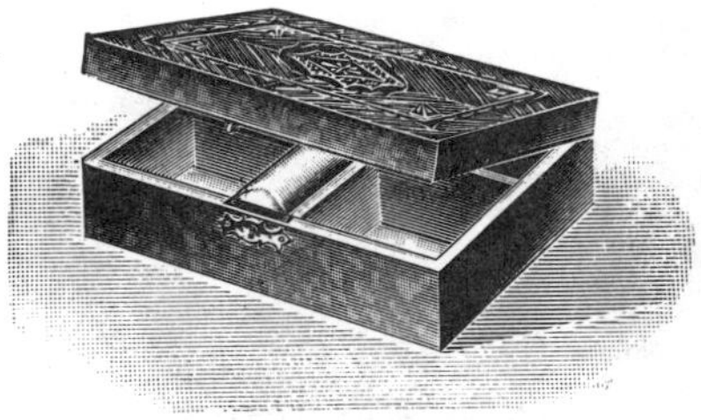

51/6/110. Pulido, con cojín, juego de 3 piezas, con espejo. 21×14×6¹/₂ cm.

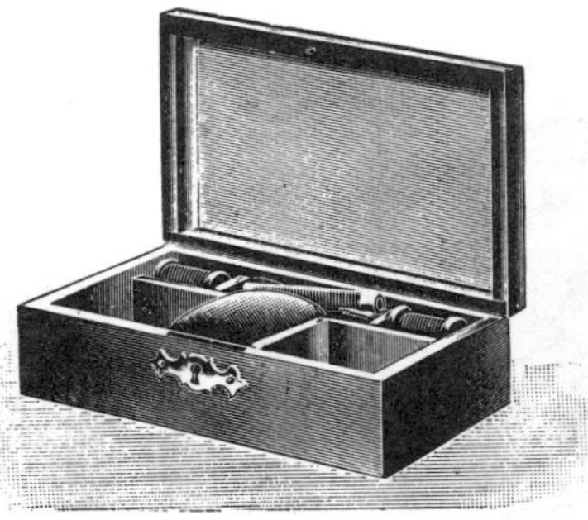

51/7/170. Pulido, con cojín y lleno de hilos. 15¹/₂×10×5¹/₂ cm.

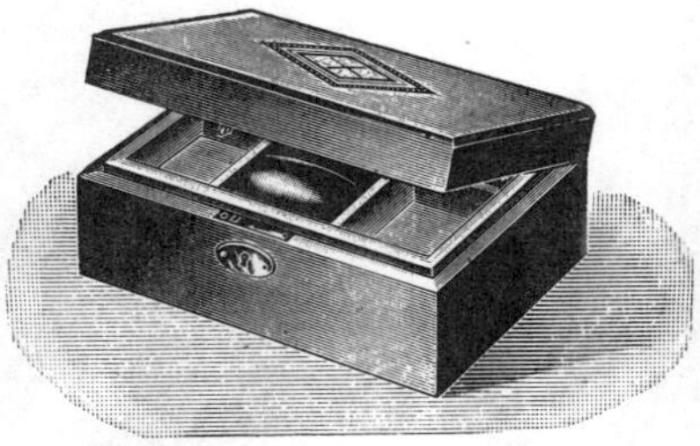

51/8/233. Pulido, con compartimiento de encaje. 20×14×9 cm.

51/8/218. Pulido á manera de roble, con asa y compartimiento de encaje. 20¹/₂×14×8 cm.

51/6/171/1a. Forrado de cuero artificial imitado. 21×15×8¹/₂ cm.

51/8/222/2F. Pulido, con compartimiento de encaje y lleno de hilos. 24×16×9 cm.

51/7/250. Forrado de cuero artificial. 24×17¹/₂×10¹/₂ cm.

51/12/51. Caja para navajas de afeitar pulida, de madera dura. 21¹/₂×17×6 cm.

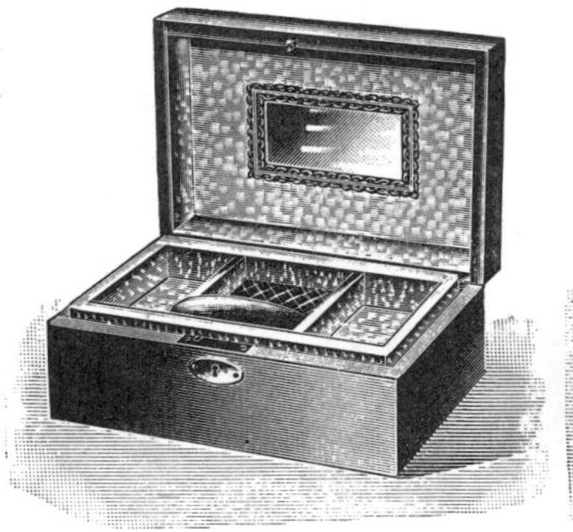

51/8/222. Pulido, con compartimiento de encaje. 20×14×9 cm.

51/6/190/2F. Pulido, con lleno de hilos fino. 24×16×9 cm.

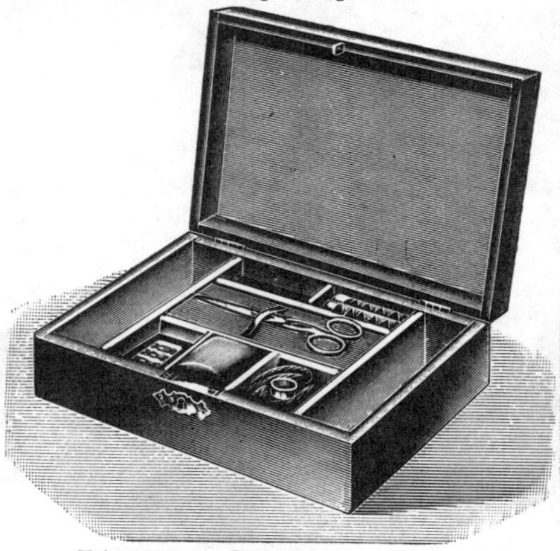

51/6/300/1. Pulido, con estampa de mosaico. 24¹/₂×17×7¹/₂ cm.

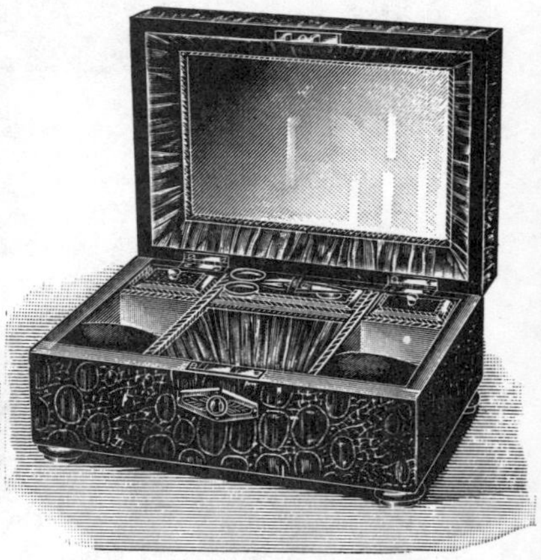

51/6/250. Forrado de cuera artificial imitado fino. 24×17¹/₂×10¹/₂ cm.

51/1/50. Loto en caja de cartón, forrada. 20¹/₂×12¹/₂×6 cm.

51/1/232. Loto en caja de corrediza bruta. 18×11¹/₂×5 cm.

51/305. Loto en caja de corrediza pulida, con inscripción de oro. 19×12¹/₂×4,8 cm.

51/301. Loto en caja pulida de corrediza. 19¹/₂×12×5 cm.

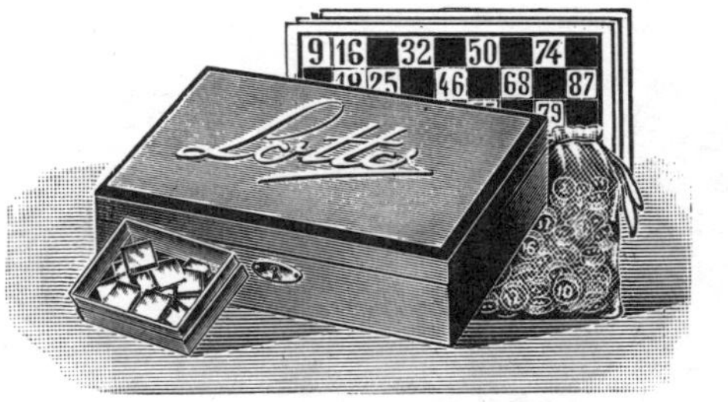

51/1/210/1. Caja de cerradura forrada de papel de roble. 20¹/₂×13×6 cm.

51/830. Caja de cerrar, pulida. 20×12¹/₂×8 cm.

Please note also the publication on page 177 and 178 of the principal catalogue.
Llamamos también su atención á la publicación en la página 177 y 178 del catálogo principal.

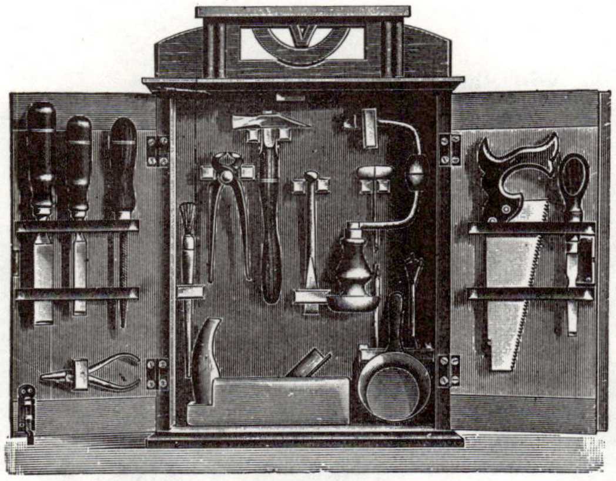

64/152/8
$47 \times 34\frac{1}{2} \times 12$ cm, ca. 5,3 kg.
16 Werkzeuge — 16 tools — 16 herramientas
64/152/9 $60 \times 40 \times 14$ cm, ca. 7,9 kg.
19 Stück — 19 tools — 19 piezas.

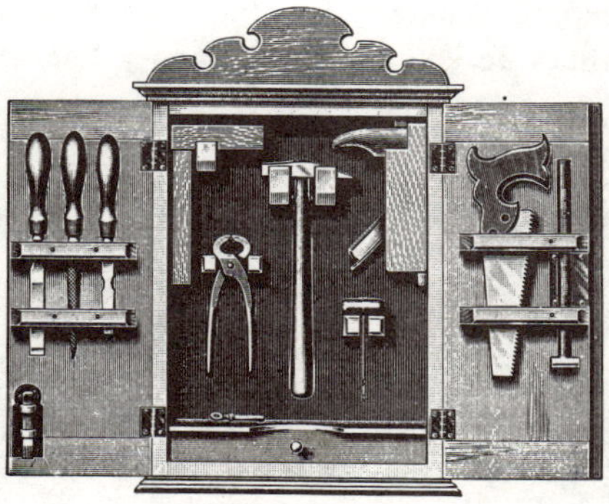

64/152/$11\frac{1}{2}$
$38 \times 28 \times 10$ cm, ca. 2,7 kg.
10 Werkzeuge — 10 tools — 10 herramientas.
64/152/$10\frac{1}{2}$ $45 \times 30 \times 9$ cm, ca. 3,15 kg.
12 Stück — 12 tools — 12 piezas.

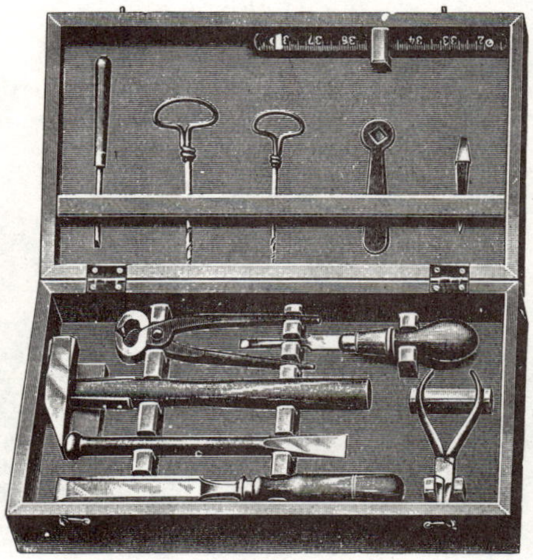

64/151/12
$37 \times 21 \times 8$ cm, ca. 2,4 kg. 11 Stück — 11 tools — 11 piezas.
64/151/3 $38 \times 22 \times 8$ cm, ca. 2,3 kg. 6 Stück—6 tools—6 piezas.

64/160/2
$30 \times 28 \times 7$ cm, ca. 1,75 kg.
10 Stück — 10 tools — 10 piezas.

64/160/1
$33\frac{1}{2} \times 33\frac{1}{2} \times 8$ cm, ca. 2,3 kg.
12 Stck.—12 tools—12 piez.
64/160/3
$28 \times 23 \times 7$ cm. ca. 1,3 kg.
6 Stck. — 6 tools — 6 piez.
64/160/4
$28 \times 18 \times 7$ cm, ca. 1,2 kg.
4 Stck. — 4 tools — 4 piez.

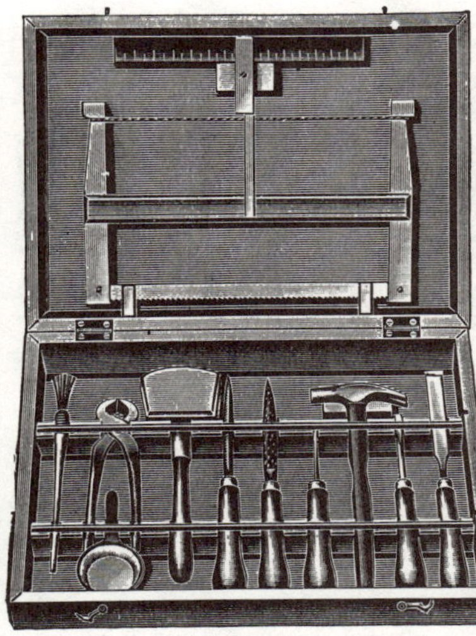

64/168/1
$37 \times 27 \times 7\frac{1}{2}$ cm, ca. 2,5 kg.
12 Stück — 12 tools — 12 piezas.

64/168/2
$30 \times 22 \times 7\frac{1}{2}$ cm, 1,6 kg.
10 Stck.—10 tools—10 piez.
64/168/3
$28 \times 17 \times 7\frac{1}{2}$ cm, 1,4 kg.
8 Stck. — 8 tools — 8 piez.
64/167/2
$31 \times 28 \times 6$ cm, 1,6 kg.
9 Stck. — 9 tools — 9 piez.
64/167/1
$38\frac{1}{2} \times 28 \times 6\frac{1}{2}$ cm, 2 kg.
12 Stck.—12 tools—12 piez.

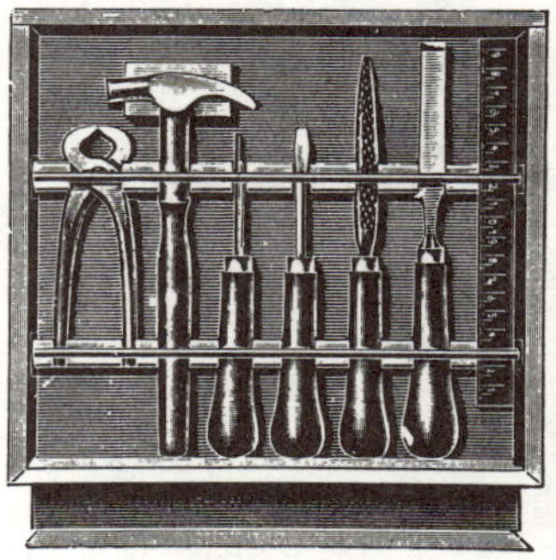

64/167/3
$27 \times 25 \times 6$ cm, ca. 1,25 kg.
7 Stück — 7 tools — 7 piezas.

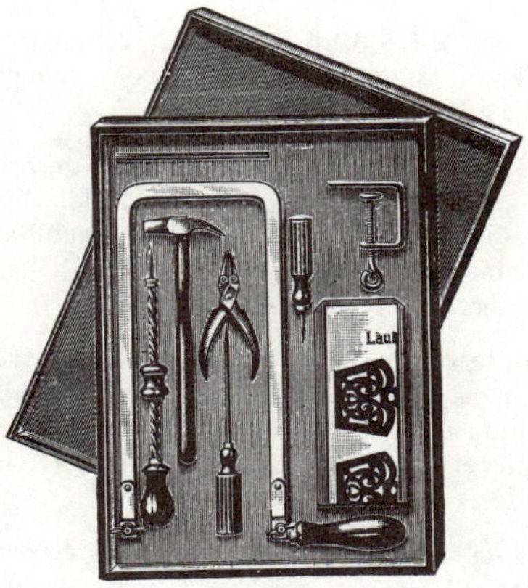

64/345
$40 \times 30 \times 4$ cm, 1,2 kg.
10 Stück — 10 tools — 10 piezas.

64/114 E/21
$31 \times 28 \times 6$ cm,
ca. 1,75 kg.
10 Stück—10 tools
10 piezas.

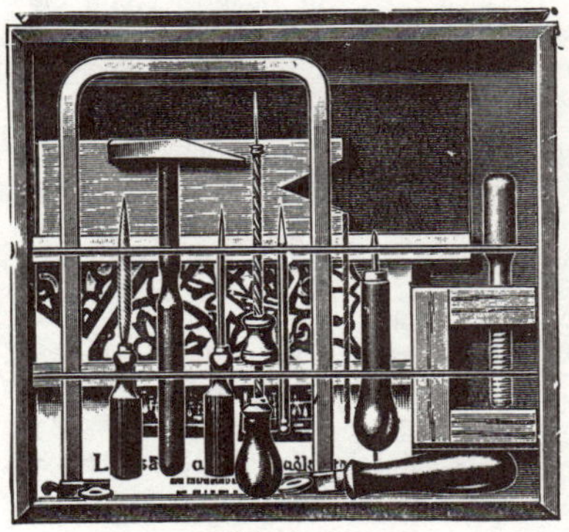

64/114 E/20
$33 \times 31 \times 6$ cm, ca. 1,75 kg.
12 Stück — 12 tools — 12 piezas.

64/114 E/22
$27 \times 25 \times 6$ cm,
ca. 1,3 kg.
9 Stück—9 tools
9 piezas.

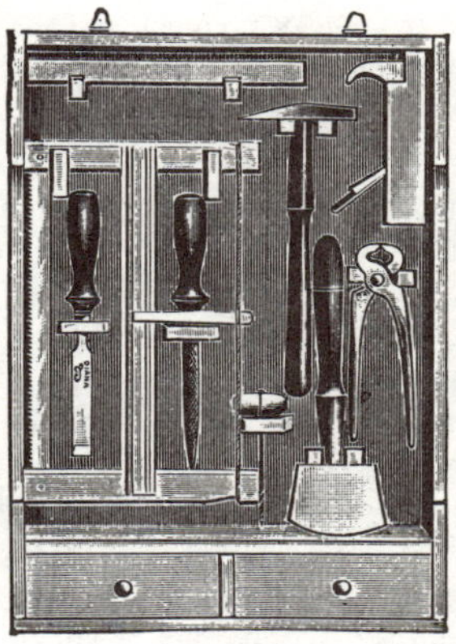

64/160 D
$45 \times 31 \times 6$ cm, 2,5 kg.
9 Stück — 9 tools — 9 piezas.

64/113 A
Dasselbe als Laubsägebrett.
The same with instruments for fret-saw work.
La misma tabla con instrumentos de marquetería.
10 Stück
10 pieces
10 piezas

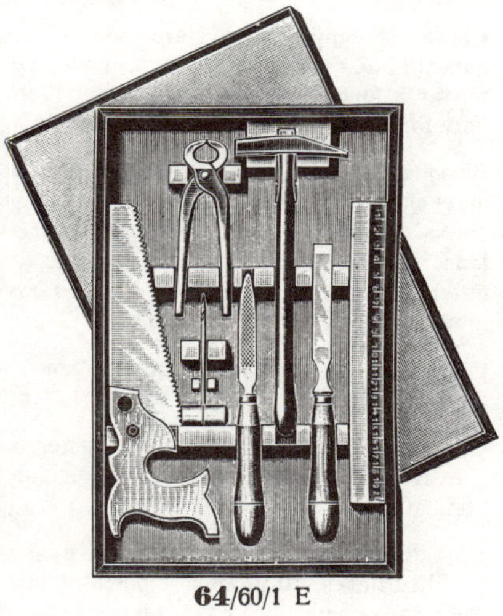

64/60/1 E
$32 \times 20\frac{1}{2} \times 3$ cm, ca. 0,7 kg.
7 Stück — 7 tools — 7 piezas.

64/60/2 E
$27 \times 18\frac{1}{2} \times 3$ cm,
ca. 0,55 kg.
5 Stück — 5 tools
5 piezas.
64/60/3 E
$24 \times 14\frac{1}{2} \times 3$ cm,
ca. 0,4 kg.
4 Stück — 4 tools
4 piezas.

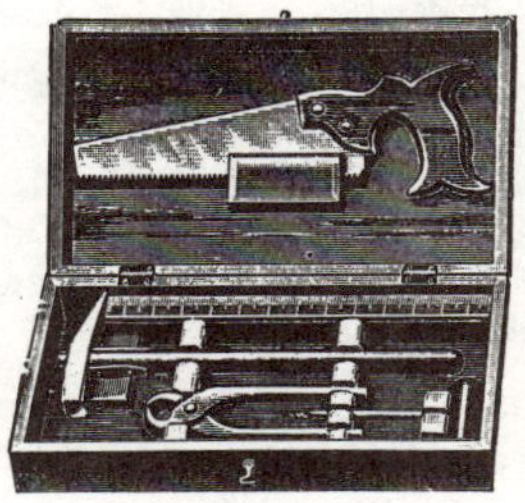

64/163/3
$24 \times 14 \times 4\frac{1}{2}$ cm, 0,7 kg.
5 Stück — 5 tools — 5 piezas.
64/163/2
$27 \times 18 \times 4\frac{1}{2}$ cm, 0,85 kg.
7 Stück — 7 tools — 7 piezas.
64/163/1
$32 \times 21 \times 4\frac{1}{2}$ cm, 1 kg.
8 Stück — 8 tools — 8 piezas.

64/59/1
$39\frac{1}{2} \times 28\frac{1}{2} \times 3\frac{1}{2}$ cm,
ca. 1,55 kg.
13 Stück — 13 tools
13 piezas.
64/59/3
$27\frac{1}{2} \times 17 \times 3\frac{1}{2}$ cm,
ca. 0,75 kg.
5 Stück — 5 tools
5 piezas.
64/59/4
$25 \times 14\frac{1}{2} \times 3\frac{1}{2}$ cm,
ca. 0,5 kg.
4 Stück — 4 tools
4 piezas.

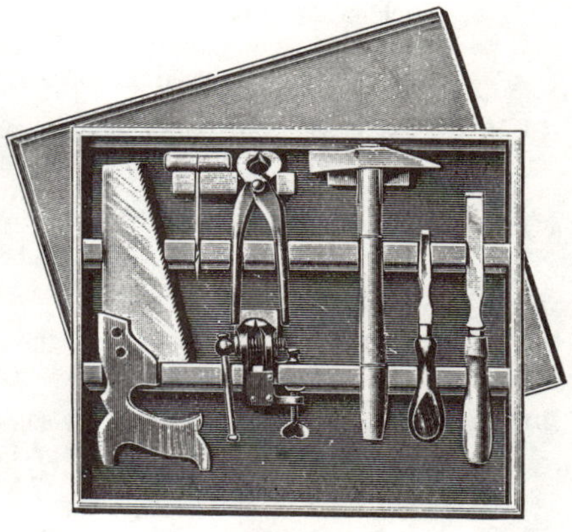

64/59/2
$32 \times 28\frac{1}{2} \times 3\frac{1}{2}$ cm, ca. 1,1 kg.
7 Stück — 7 tools — 7 piezas.

Beachten Sie auch die Veröffentlichung auf Seite 177 und 178 des Hauptkataloges.

Please note also the publication on page 150 and 151 of the principal catalogue.
Llamamos también su atención á la publicación en la página 150 y 151 del catálogo principal.

Farbkasten für Kinder und Schulen. — Paintboxes for Children and Schools.
Cajitas de colores para Niños y Escuelas.

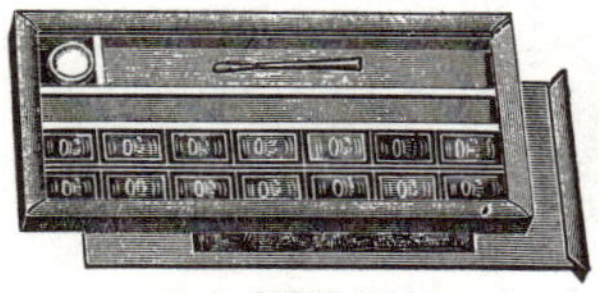

24/402/14

24/309

24/307

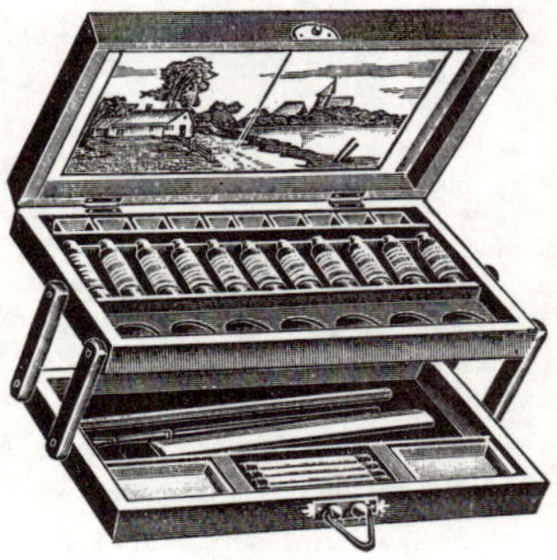

24/240

24/302

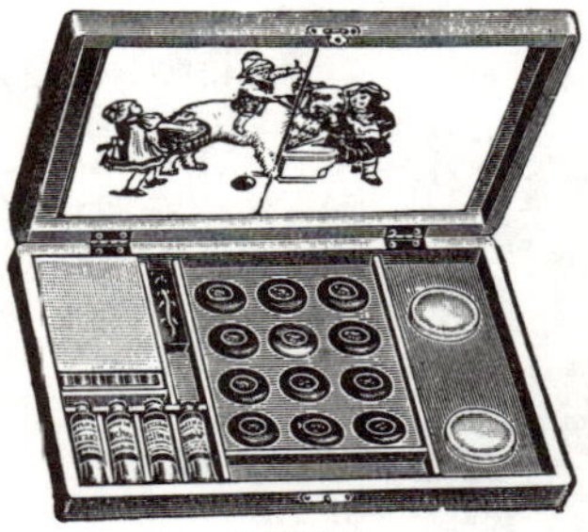

24/306

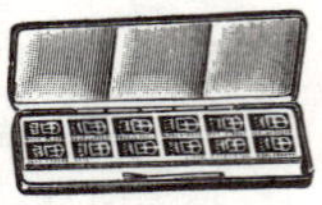

24/520

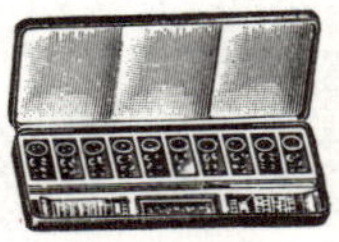

24/500/13

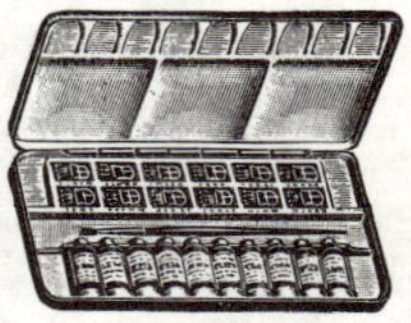

24/523

24/402/14 Kasten mit rot gebeiztem Rand, Deckel mit Chromobild, 14 Farben, 1 Näpfchen und 1 Pinsel, Größe 20×9,3×1,5 cm.

24/430/18 wie **24**/402/14, mit 18 Farben, Sepia und Tusche, 2 Näpfchen und 1 Pinsel, Größe 22×11,5×1,5 cm.

24/427/24 wie **24**/430/18, jedoch mit 24 Farben, Bild, 2 Näpfchen und 1 Pinsel, Größe 23,5×13×1,5 cm.

24/309 Kasten aus Erle, hellmatt, mit Druckverschluß, Deckel mit Mattglaseinlage nebst Zeichenvorlage, 12 Farben, 4 Näpfchen, 1 Stielpinsel, Größe 20,5×11,5×3,5 cm.

24/302 Kasten aus Erle, hellmatt, mit Druckverschluß, Deckel abgerundet, 16 Farben, 1 Sepia, 1 chines. Tusche, 2 Porzellannäpfchen, 1 Pinsel mit Stiel, Größe 20,2×16×3 cm.

24/306 Kasten aus Erle, hellmatt, mit Druckverschluß, 12 Knopffarben, 4 Tuben, 1 Sepia, 1 Etuis mit Pastellkreide, 1 chines. Tusche, 2 Porzellannäpfchen, 1 Pinsel, Größe 23×16,8×3 cm.

24/307 Kasten aus Erle, hellmatt, mit Hakenverschluß, 20 Farben, 2 Tuben, 1 Radiergummi, 1 großer Goldrandnapf, 2 kleine Goldrandnäpfe, 1 Stielpinsel, Größe 25,3×20,8×3 cm.

24/240 Feiner hell mattierter Scherenkasten aus Erlenholz mit Oberteil: 11 Tuben, 10 Porzellan-Schälchen, 7 Farben; Unterteil: 2 Porzellan-Paletten, 1 Kästchen Ölkreide, 1 Zwinge aus Messing, 1 Radiergummi, 3 Pinsel mit Stiel, Größe 23×14,5×5,5 cm.

24/520 Fein schwarz lackierter Blechkasten mit 12 Farben, 1 Pinsel, Größe 16×7×1,5 cm.

24/500/13 Fein schwarz lackierter Blechkasten mit 10 Farben, 2 Tuben und 1 Tusche, 1 Pinsel, 1 Vorschrift, Größe 16,5×7,5×1,5 cm.

24/523 Fein schwarz lackierter Blechkasten mit 12 Farben, 10 Tuben, 1 Stielpinsel, 1 Instruktion, Größe 19,5×11×1,5 cm.

24/402/14 Box with red stained rim, lid with coloured-picture, 14 colours, 1 saucer and 1 ink-brush, size 20×9,3×1,5 cm.

24/430/18 Same as **24**/402/14, with 18 colours, sepia and china ink, 2 saucers and 1 ink brush, size 22×11,5×1,5 cm.

24/427/24 Same as **24**/430/18, but with 24 colours, picture, 2 saucers and 1 ink brush, size 23,5×13×1,5 cm.

24/309 Box of alder wood, light dull, with spring lock, lid with opaque inlaid glass with drawing copy, 12 colours, 4 saucers, 1 brush with handle, size 20,5×11,5×3,5 cm.

24/302 Box of alder wood, light dull, with spring lock, lid rounded, 16 colours, 1 sepia and 1 china ink, 2 porcelain dishes, 1 brush with handle, size 20,2×16×3 cm.

24/306 Box of alder wood, light dull, with spring lock, 12 colours, 4 tubes, 1 sepia, 1 china ink, 1 case with pastel crayon, 2 porcelain dishes, 1 brush, size 23×16,8×3 cm.

24/307 Box of alder wood, light dull, with hook closure, 20 colours, 1 India rubber, 2 tubes, 3 porcelain dishes with gold rim, 1 brush with handle, size 25,3×20,8×3 cm.

24/240 Finely matted folding box with upper part of alder wood, 11 tubes, 10 porcelain dishes, 7 colours, 2 porcelain palettes, 1 box with crayon, 1 holder of brass, 1 India rubber, 3 brushes with handle, size 23×14,5×5,5 cm.

24/520 Finely black japanned tin-box with 12 colours, 1 brush, size 16×7×1,5 cm.

24/500/13 Finely black japanned tin-box with 10 colours, 2 tubes, 1 china ink, 1 brush, 1 instruction, size 16,5×7,5×1,5 cm.

24/523 Finely black japanned tin-box with 12 colours, 10 tubes, 1 brush with handle, 1 instruction, size 19,5×11×1,5 cm.

24/402/14 Caja con borde pintado rojo, tapa con dibujo colorado, 14 colores, 1 escudilla y 1 pincel, tamaño 20×9,3×1,5 cm.

24/430/18 Como **24**/402/14, con 18 colores, sepia y tinta de la china, 2 escudillas y 1 pincel, tamaño 22×11,5×1,5 cm.

24/427/24 Como **24**/430/18, pero con 24 colores, dibujo, 2 escudillas y 1 pincel, tamaño 23,5×13×1,5 cm.

24/309 Cajita de chopo mate claro, cierre de presión, tapa con vidrio opaco embutido, con modelo de dibujo, 12 colores, 4 escudillas, 1 pincel con mango, tamaño 20,5×11,5×3,5 cm.

24/302 Cajita de chopo mate claro, cierre de presión, tapa redondeada, 16 colores, 1 sepia, 1 tinta de china, 2 conchitas de porcelana, 1 pincel con mango, tamaño 20,2×16×3 cm.

24/306 Cajita de chopo mate claro, cierre de presión, 12 colores, 4 tubos, 1 sepia, 1 tinta de china, 1 estuche con greda de pastel, 2 conchitas de porcelana, 1 pincel con mango, tamaño 23×16,8×3 cm.

24/307 Cajita de chopo mate claro, cierre con ganchito, 20 colores, 2 tubos, 1 goma para borrar, 3 conchitas de porcelana con filete dorado, 1 pincel, tamaño 25,3×20,8×3 cm.

24/240 Hermosa caja de tijera de chopo de tono mate claro con 11 tubitos, 7 colores, 10 conchitas de porcelana, 2 paletas de porcelana, 1 cajita de greda blanca, 1 birola de latón, 1 goma para borrar, 3 pinceles con mango, tamaño 23×14,5×5,5 cm.

24/520 Caja de lata finamente barnizada, con 12 colores, 1 pincel, tamaño 16×7×1,5 cm.

24/500/13 Caja de lata barnizada finamente de negro, con 10 colores, 1 pincel, 1 instrucción, tamaño 16,5×7,5×1,5 cm.

24/523 Caja de lata barnizada finamente de negro, con 12 colores, 10 tubitos, 1 pincel, 1 instrucción, tamaño 19,5×11×1,5 cm.

Beachten Sie auch die Veröffentlichung auf Seite 150 und 151 des Hauptkataloges.

Musikdosen. — Musical-boxes. — Cajas de música.

54/403

	Durchmesser Diameter Diámetro	Höhe Height Altura
54/402	$9\frac{1}{4}$ cm	$9\frac{1}{2}$ cm
54/403	$10\frac{1}{2}$ cm	$9\frac{1}{2}$ cm
54/404	$12\frac{1}{2}$ cm	10 cm

Mit Werken nach Schweizer Art, feine, solide Ausführung, ganz aus Nickel.
With works after the Swiss manner, fine solid performance, wholly of nickel.
Cajas de música con máquina a la manera suiza, ejecución elegante y sólida, enteramente de niquel.

54/21

	Durchmesser Diameter Diámetro	Höhe Height Altura
54/21	$7\frac{1}{2}$ cm	$8\frac{1}{2}$ cm
54/23	$7\frac{1}{2}$ cm	12 cm
54/24	$8\frac{1}{2}$ cm	13 cm

Mit lithographiertem Blech und vernickelter Kuppel.
With litographed tinplate and nickeled dome.
Con hojalata litografiada y cúpola niquelada.

54/24

Qualität wie 54/21.
Quality like 54/21.
Calidad como 54/21.

Laufräder mit Musik.
Rollers with music.
Rodadores con música.

54/102

	Durchmesser Diameter Diámetro	Länge Length Largura
54/102	$12\frac{1}{4}$ cm	55 cm
54/103	$13\frac{1}{2}$ cm	60 cm

Hochfeine, tadellose Ausführung, weiß lackiert, mit lebhaften Farben bespritzt.
Superfine faultless performance, white varnished, spotted with vivid colours.
Muy finos, ejecución excelente, barnizados blanco, salpicados de colores vivos.

Centrifugal Wunder-Kreisel.
Centrifugal magic-top.
Peón mágico centrifugal.

	Durchmesser Diameter Diámetro	Höhe mit Turm Height with tower Altura con torre
54/18	$6\frac{1}{4}$ cm	$8\frac{3}{4}$ cm
$54/18\frac{1}{2}$	12 cm	$15\frac{1}{4}$ cm

54/18

Experimentier-Kreisel, Präzision und tadellose Funktion.
Experimental-top, precision and blameless function.
Peón de experimentar, precisión y funccionamiento excelente.

Musik- und Choralkreisel.
Music- and choral top.
Música y péon de coro.

	Durchmesser Diameter Diámetro	Höhe Height Altura
54/146	$12\frac{3}{4}$ cm	$17\frac{1}{4}$ cm
54/159	$13\frac{1}{4}$ cm	$19\frac{3}{4}$ cm
54/160	14 cm	$22\frac{1}{4}$ cm

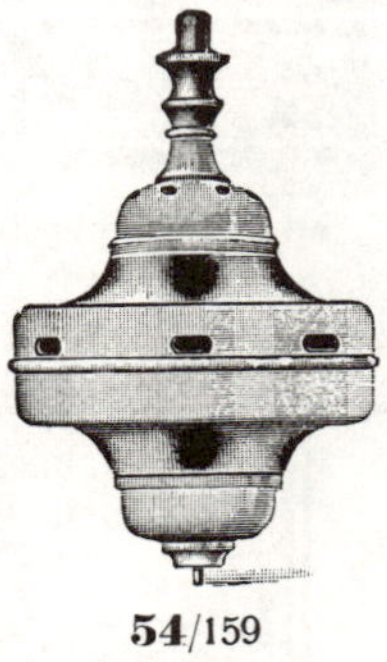

54/159

Hochfeine, tadellose Ausführung, weiß lackiert, mit lebhaften Farben bespritzt.
Superfine, blameless performance, white varnished, spotted with vivid colours.
Muy fino, ejecución excelente, barnizado blanco salpicado de colores vivos.

12/VIII/1	170 × 110 × 70 mm
12/VIII/2	192 × 133 × 80 mm
12/VIII/3	215 × 157 × 90 mm
12/VIII/4	237 × 185 × 102 mm
12/VIII/5	259 × 213 × 113 mm

12/VIII/1—5 259 × 213 × 113 mm.

Weichholz-Nähkasten im Satz, Seiten und Deckel naturpoliert, mit verschiedenen Abzügen.
Sewing-boxes of soft wood in set, sides and lid in natural polish, with different pictures.
Cajas de costura de madera tierna en juego, lados y tapa pulidos al natural, con diferentes estampas.

12/221/1—3 143 × 98 × 61 mm.

Rot gebeizter Sparkasten mit Schloß und mit Aufleimbild aus Weichholz im Satz.
Red stained, saving-boxes with lock and picture glued on.
Huchas económicas maceradas de color encarnado, con cerradura y con estampa encolada encima, de madera tierna en juego.

12/221/1	107 × 58 × 36 mm
12/221/2	123 × 77 × 49 mm
12/221/3	143 × 98 × 61 mm
12/967/1	106 × 50 × 33 mm
12/967/2	126 × 68 × 46 mm
12/967/3	149 × 91 × 58 mm
12/967/4	169 × 112 × 69 mm

12/967/1—4 169 × 112 × 69 mm.

Satz Sparkasten, Hartholz mit Nickelstreifen und Schlitz, Deckel poliert.
Set saving-boxes, hardwood with nickel strip and slot, polished lid.
Juego huchas económicas de madera dura con rayas de niquel y hendidura, tapa pulida.

	12/31 l	12/691	12/124	12/221/1—3	12/967/1—4	12/VIII/1—5
Quantum / quantity / cantidad	50 Dtz., doz., doc.	5 Gross	20 Gross	5 Gross Satz gross set / gross juego	$1\frac{1}{2}$ Gross Satz gross set / gross juego	5 Dtz. / doz. set / doc. juego
Bruttogewicht / gross weight / peso	100 kg	100 kg	175 kg	220 kg	150 kg	130 kg
Kistenmaße / measure of case Dimensión de una caja	95 × 52 × 76 cm	86 × 64 × 78 cm	123 × 78 × 93 cm	127 × 78 × 78 cm	92 × 54 × 73 cm	116 × 54 × 67 cm

12/124 Weichholz-Sparkasten mit Aufschrift, Deckel poliert, 105 × 63 × 36 mm.
Saving-boxes of soft wood with inscription, polished lid, 105 × 63 × 36 mm.
Huchas económicas de madera tierna con inscripción, tapa pulida, 105 × 63 × 36 mm.

12/31 l Hartholz-Sparkasten mit Aufschrift, 4 Spangen, lackiert in gelb, 118 × 70 × 57 mm.
Saving-boxes of hardwood with inscription, 4 clasps, yellow varnished, 118 × 70 × 57 mm.
Huchas económicas de madera dura con inscripción, 4 hebillas, barnizadas amarillo, 118 × 70 × 57 mm.

12/691 Hartholz-Sparkasten, Seiten nußbaum gebeizt, Deckel naturpoliert, mit schwarz-rotem Lackrand, 4 Spangen, 123 × 74 × 53 mm.
Saving-boxes of hardwood, sides walnut-stained, lid natural varnished with black-red varnished rim, 4 clasps, 123 × 74 × 53 mm.
Huchas de madera dura, lados macerados color de nogal, tapa pulida al natural con borde barnizado en negro-encarnado, 4 hebillas, 123 × 74 × 53 mm.

Please note also the publication on page 161—166 of the principal catalogue.
Llamamos también su atención á la publicación en la página 161—166 del catálogo principal.

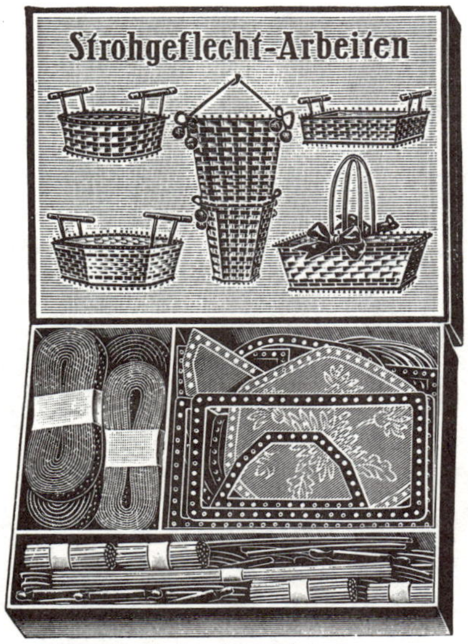

29/3136 Strohgeflecht-Arbeiten.
Straw basket worker.
Labores entretejidas de paja.

29/3183
Körbchen-Arbeiten mit Bastband, 4 Rollen.
Little basket plaiter.
Pequeña cestera.

29/3182
Körbchen-Arbeiten m. Bastband, 3 Rollen.
Little basket plaiter.
Pequeña cestera.

29/3282
Perlkörbchen-Arbeiten.
New Bead Basket Work.
Cestitos de Perlas.

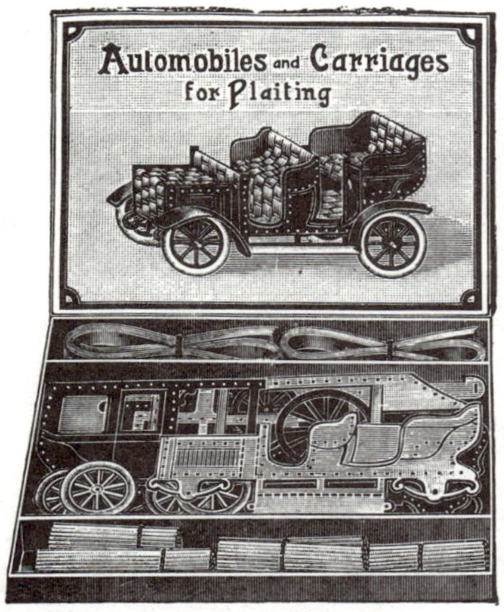

29/3258 Automobile u. Wagen zum Flechten.
Automobiles and carriages for plaiting.
Automóviles y carruajes para trenzar.

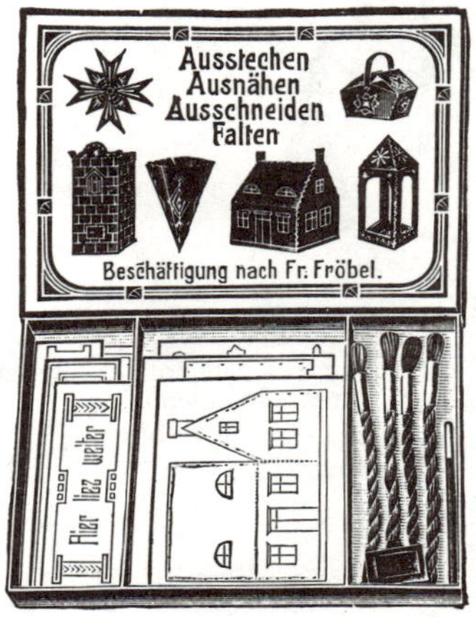

29/3234
Ausstechen, Ausnähen, Ausschneiden.
Pricking, Embroidering, cutting, folding.
Picar, bordar, recortar etc.

29/3315
Holzperlen-Arbeiten.
Wooden bead work.
Labores de perlas de madera.

29/1568
Kleine Gärtnerin.
Little gardener.
Pequeña jardinera.

29/3336 Bunte Bilder.
Coloured motives.
Imagenes de color.

29/1775 Klapphäuser.
Little house builder.
Casas plegables.

29/3330
Wandschmuck-Ausnähen.
Embroidery Work, Wall decoration.
Trabajos de coser decoraciones y adornos para las paredes.

29/3342
Bildersticken.
Perforated cards for embroidering.
Estampas de color.

29/1768 ABC-Lesespiel.
Spelling Game.
Juego de lectura.

29/2268 Zitterspiel.
Spillikins.
Juego de palitos.

Beachten Sie auch die Veröffentlichung auf Seite 161—166 des Hauptkataloges.

Please note also the publication on page 161—166 of the principal catalogue.
Llamamos también su atención á la publicación en la página 161—166 del catálogo principal.

29/2355 Fuchsjagd.
Tally-Ho.
Caza a la zorra.

29/2353 Fuchsjagd.
Tally-Ho.
Caza a la zorra.

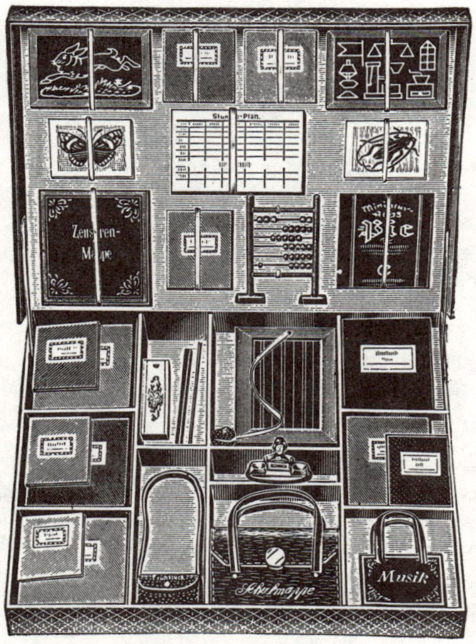

29/1772 Puppenschule.
Dolls' School.
Escuela de muñecas.

29/2332 Die Ringe des Maharadscha.
The rings of the Maharadscha.
Las sortijas del Maharadjá.

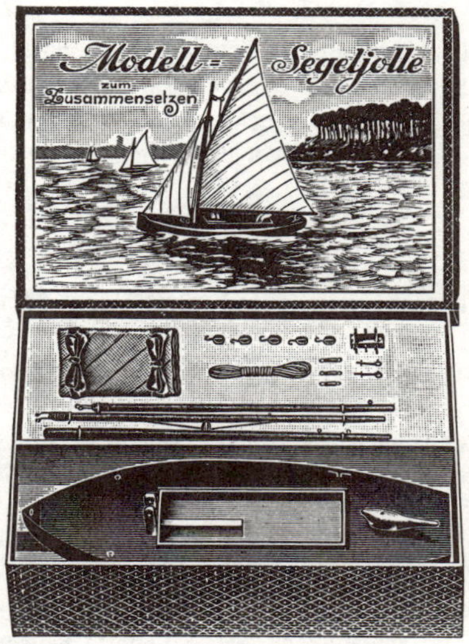

29/1777 Modell-Segeljolle.
Model sailing yacht.
Yates modelos.

29/1757 Das Windrad.
The wind-wheel.
Rueda de viento.

29/2087 Jedes an seinen Ort.
Everything in its proper place.
Cada cosa en su sitio.

29/2317 Lustige Möbel-Versteigerung.
Amusing furniture auction sale.
La alegre almoneda de muebles.

29/1566 Die Festung.
The fortress.
La fortaleza.

29/1576 Tierschnitzer.
Wood animal carving.
Escultor de animales.

Beachten Sie auch die Veröffentlichung auf Seite 161—166 des Hauptkataloges.

Please note also the publication on page 79—86 of the principal catalogue.
Llamamos también su atención á la publicación en la página 79—86 del catálogo principal.

Kinder-Klappwagen. — Children's folding cars. — Coches plegables para niños.

23/2400
Gewicht — Weight — Peso 11 kg

23/2401
Gewicht — Weight — Peso 11,8 kg

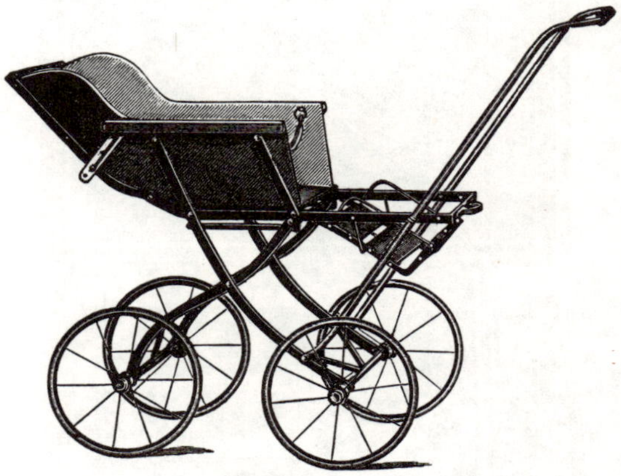

23/2401 S
Gewicht — Weight — Peso 12,5 kg

No. **23**/2400, 2401, 2401 S Mit Gummirädern, Nickelschieber, Holz gebeizt, Metallteile emailliert.
With rubber wheels, nickel-plated pusher, wood stained, metal parts enamelled.
Con ruedas de caucho, empujadora niquelada, las piezas de madera trabajadas con mordiente, las piezas de metál esmaltados.

23/2480
Gewicht — Weight — Peso 13 kg

No. **23**/2480

Tangent-Gummiräder, Nickelschieber, doppelter Ledertuchausschlag, federndes Gestell.

Rubber wheels, nickel-plated pusher, double leather cloth lining, elastical frame.

Con ruedas de caucho, empujadora niquelada, con doble guarnición de tela encerada, armadura elástica.

No. **23**/2478

Riemenfedergestell, Tangent-Gummiräder, Nickelschieber, doppelter Ledertuchausschlag.

Chassis with leather strap springs, rubber wheels, nickel-plated pusher, double leather cloth lining.

Bastidor con correas de suspensión de resorte, con ruedas de caucho, empujadora niquelada, con doble guarnición de tela encerada.

23/2478
Gewicht — Weight — Peso 18 kg

23/5100
Gewicht — Weight — Peso 27 kg

Kinderwagen. — Perambulator. — Coche para niños.

Gewölbte Seitenteile, Riemen-Hängefedergestell, Tangenträder, Porzellangriff, Ledertuchpolsternug, gefüttertes Stahlbügelverdeck, tiefe englische Form, verdeckter Fußkasten.

Arched side walls, suspension spring frames with leather strap, tangent wheels, porcelain handle, frontsides upholstered in pipes, lined and reversible hood with steel frame work, English form i. e. very deep, with invisible footwell.

Con piezas laterales encorvadas, con armadura de resortes de suspensión con correas, ruedas tangenciales, con mango de porcelana, aforrada de tela encerada, la cubierta aforrada y con varillas de acero, forma honda inglesa, caja para los pies encubierta.

Beachten Sie auch die Veröffentlichung auf Seite 79—86 des Hauptkataloges.

Please note also the publication on page 79—86 of the principal catalogue.
Llamamos también su atención á la publicación en la página 79—86 del catálogo principal.

Zierliche Kinderwagen. — Elegant Perambulators. — Elegantes Coches para niños.

23/6300 K
Gewicht — Weight — Peso 18 kg

23/6501 K
Gewicht — Weight — Peso 19 kg

23/2575 L
Gewicht — Weight — Peso 20 kg

No. **23**/6300 K/6501 K Rohrkorb, bei No. **23**/6300 K gelb lackiert, Ledertuchausschlag, Gummiräder, Porzellangriff, Stahlbügelverdeck, Mullvorhänge.

Reed body, with No. **23**/6300 K yellow varnished, leather cloth lining, rubber-tyres, porcelain handle, steel bow hood, detachable muslin curtains.

Con cesta de caña, con No. **23**/6300 K cesta barnizada en amarillo, con guarnición de tela encerada, aros de caucho, con mango de porcelana, con cubierta que tiene refuerzos por varillas de acero, con cortinas de muselina.

No. **23**/2575 L Rundrohrkorb, Riemen-Hängefedergestell, Tangenträder, Porzellangriff, Ledertuchausschlag, gefüttertes Stahlbügelverdeck, Spitzenbehang.

Body made of white bleached Indian round reed, suspension spring frame with leather strap, tangent wheels, porcelain handle, leather cloth lining, lined steel bow hood, lace trimmings.

Cesta de junco de Indias redondo y blanqueado, con armadura de resortes con correas, con ruedas tangenciales, con mango de porcelana, con cubierta aforrada que tiene refuerzos por varillas de acero, guarnición con encajes.

23/2579 L
Gewicht — Weight — Peso 22 kg

23/6601 L
Gewicht — Weight — Peso 23 kg

23/6607
Gewicht — Weight — Peso 24 kg

No. **23**/2579 L/6601/L Gewölbte Seitenteile, Riemen-Hängefedergestell, Tangenträder, Porzellangriff, Ledertuchausschlag, gefüttertes Stahlbügelverdeck, Spitzenbehang.

Arched side walls, suspension spring frames with leather strap, tangent wheels, porcelain handle, leather cloth lining, steel bow hood, lace trimmings.

Con piezas laterales encorvadas, con armadura de resortes con correas, con ruedas tangenciales, con mango de porcelana, con guarnición de tela encerada, con cubierta aforrada que tiene refuerzos por varillas de acero, guarnición con encajes.

No. **23**/6607 Gewölbte Seitenteile, Riemen-Hängefedergestell, Tangenträder, Porzellangriff, Ledertuchpolsterung, gefüttertes Stahlbügelverdeck ohne Garnierung, Fußkasten verdeckt.

Arched side walls, suspension spring frames with leather strap, tangent wheels, porcelain handle, leather cloth lining, lined hood without ornaments, covered foot well.

Con piezas laterales encorvadas, con armadura de resortes con correas, con ruedas tangenciales, con mango de porcelana, con forro de tela encerada, con cubierta aforrada sin guarnición, con caja no visible para los pies.

Beachten Sie auch die Veröffentlichung auf Seite 79—86 des Hauptkataloges.

Please note also the publication on page 79—86 of the principal catalogue.
Llamamos también su atención á la publicación en la página 79—86 del catálogo principal.

Puppenwagen.
Dolls' Perambulators. — Coches para muñecas.

23/1714

No. **23**/1714 Eisenräder, Stoffvorhang.
Iron wheels, cloth curtains.
Con ruedas de hierro, con cortinas de tela.

A	B	C	
45	50	55	cm Länge, length, de largo
2,6	3,2	3,6	kg Gewicht, weight, de peso

23/1715

No. **23**/1715 Eisenräder, Stoffausschlag, Stoffvorhang.
Iron wheels, cloth lining, cloth curtains.
Con ruedas de hierro, con guarnición de tela, con cortinas de tela.

A	B	C	
45	50	55	cm Länge, length, de largo
3,2	4,3	4,8	kg Gewicht, weight, de peso

Ausstattungen der nachfolgenden Puppenwagen:
Equipment of the following dolls' perambulators:
Confección de los siguientes coches para muñeca:

Ausstattung IV: Federgestell, Metallräder, Nickelschieber, Stoffausschlag, Stoffvorhänge.

Equipment IV: Elastic chassis, metal wheels, nickel-plated pusher, cotton linings, cotton curtains.

Confección IV: Armadura elastica, ruedas de metal, empujadora niquelada, con forro de tela, cortinas de tela.

Ausstattung V: Federgestell, Gummiräder, Porzellangriff, Ledertuchausschlag, Stahlbügelverdeck, Spitzenbehang.

Equipment V: Elastic chassis, rubber tyres, porcelain handle, leather cloth linings, hood with steel framework, lace trimmings.

Confección V: Bastidor elastica, ruedas con caucho, mango de porcelana, forro de encerado, capota con varillas de acero, guarnición con encaje.

Ausstattung VI: Riemengestell, sonst wie Ausstattung V.

Equipment VI: Chassis with leather strap springs, other items same as equipment V.

Confección VI: Cuadro con correas de suspensión con resorte, otrosí como confección V.

23/2728 IV u. V

No. **23**/2728

B	C	D	
50	55	60	cm Länge, length, de largo
4,3	5	5,5	kg Gewicht, weight, de peso

23/2735 IV u. V

No. **23**/2735

B	C	
50	55	cm Länge, length, de largo
4,3	5	kg Gewicht, weight, de peso

23/2743 VI

No. **23**/2743 Rohrkorb, farbig verziert.
Body of cane, with colored decorations.
Coche de caña, con adornos de color.

C	D	
55	60	cm Länge, length, de largo
5	5,5	kg Gewicht, weight, de peso

23/2749 VI

No. **23**/2749 Rohrkorb.
Body of cane.
Coche de caña.

D	D½	
60	65	cm Länge, length, de largo
5,5	6,5	kg Gewicht, weight, de peso

23/2396 V

No. **23**/2396

C	D	
55	60	cm Länge, length, de largo
5	5,5	kg Gewicht, weight, de peso

23/2313 V

No. **23**/2313

C	D	D½	
55	60	65	cm Länge, length, de largo
5	5,5	6,5	kg Gewicht, weight, de peso

23/2352 VI

No. **23**/2352

C	D	
55	60	cm Länge, length, de largo
5	5,5	kg Gewicht, weight, de peso

23/2760

No. **23**/2760 Seitenteile gewölbt, Riemen-Hängefedergestell, Tangenträder, Porzellangriff, Ledertuchausschlag, gefüttertes Stahlbügelklappverdeck, verdeckter Fußkasten.
Arched side-walls, suspension spring frames with leather strap, tangent wheels, porcelain handle, leather cloth lining, lined hood without ornaments, covered foot well.
Con piezas laterales encorvadas, con armadura de resortes con correas, ruedas tangenciales, con mango de porcelana, con guarnición de tela encerada, con cubierta aforrada sin guarnición, con caja encubierta para los pies.

D	D½	
60	65	cm Länge, length, de largo
10	11	kg Gewicht, weight, de peso

Beachten Sie auch die Veröffentlichung auf Seite 79—86 des Hauptkataloges.

Please note also the publication on page 79—86 of the principal catalogue.
Llamamos también su atención á la publicación en la página 79—86 del catálogo principal.

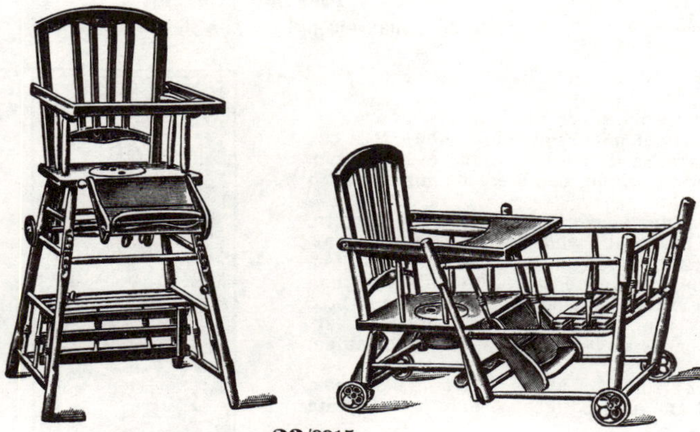

23/3215

Kinderstuhl aus Hartholz, hell lackiert, mit Klosett.
Chair for children of hard wood, light varnished, with privy.
Silla para niños, hecha de madera dura, embarnizada en color claro, con bacin.

Verstellbar als hoher Kinderstuhl für 1 Kind, als niederer fahrbarer Stuhl für 2 Kinder, als Zimmerwagen für 1 Kind zum Liegen. Vernickelte Gummiräder. Gewicht 8,5 kg.

Adjustable, can be used as high chair for 1 child, as low chair for 2 children (can be wheeled about), as perambulator (for indoor use) and at the same time as couch for 1 child. Nickel plated rubber wheels. Weight 8,5 kg.

Transmutable en silla alta para 1 niño, en silla baja sobre ruedas para dos niños, en coche casero como cama para 1 niño. Ruedas niqueladas con goma. Peso 8,5 kg.

Schnelläufer. — Flyers (scooters). — Trotinetas.

23/948½
Gewicht — Weight
Peso 1,85 kg.

Räder — Wheels — Ruedas 12 cm.

23/947
Gewicht — Weight
Peso 2,2 kg.

Räder — Wheels — Ruedas 20 cm.
Mit Rollenlager. — Roll bearing case.
Con cojinetes de rodillos.

23/946
Gewicht — Weight
Peso 2,5 kg.

Räder — Wheels — Ruedas 15 cm.
Mit Rollenlager. — Roll bearing case.
Con cojinete de rodillos.

Straßenrenner.
Racers.
Cicletas de carreras.

23/967 E
Kleine Sitzstellung. — Short position.
Posición corta.

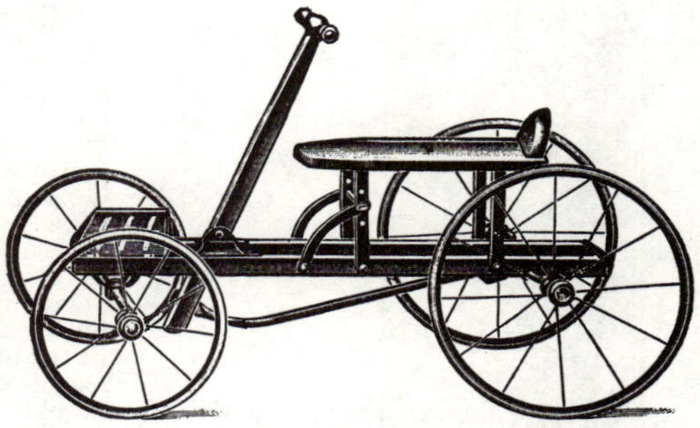

23/967 E
Mittlere Sitzstellung. — Medium position.
Posición media.

No. **23**/927 E Vollständig zusammenlegbar, braucht nicht zerlegt zu werden.

Can be completely folded, it is, therefore, not necessary, to take this racer to pieces when exporting same.

Enteramente plegable, no necesita ser desmontada.

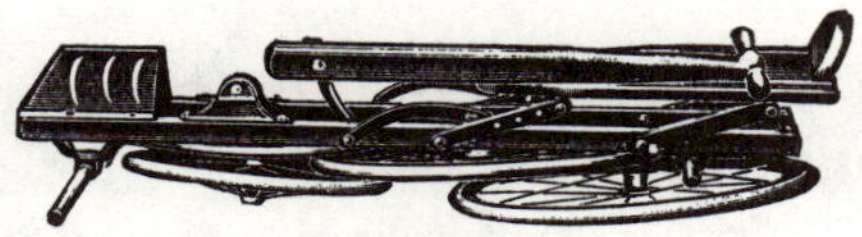

23/967 E
Vollständig zusammengelegt. — Folded.
Plegada.

Gestell ganz aus Metall, 3fach verstellbar für jedes Alter, Kurbelantrieb. Gewicht 6 kg.

Chassis made entirely of metal, adjustable in 3 different positions suitable for children of any age, to be set agoing by means of cranks. Weight 6 kg.

Bastidor enteramente de metal, reglable en 3 posiciones y pues aplicable para niños de varios talles, impulsión por manivela. Peso 6 kg.

23/967 E
Weite Sitzstellung. — Long position.
Posición larga.

23/965

No. **23**/965 Gestell ganz aus Metall, Kurbelantrieb, für Knaben von 3—6 Jahren. Gewicht 6,9 kg.

Chassis made entirely of metal, to be set agoing by means of cranks, suitable for boys of 3—6 years. Weight 6,9 kg.

Bastidor enteramente de metal, impulsión por manivela, para niños de 3—6 años. Peso 6,9 kg.

Beachten Sie auch die Veröffentlichung auf Seite 79—86 des Hauptkataloges.

Eureka-Gewehre und -Pistolen.
Gefahrloser Schießsport mit Gummipfeil.

Eureka-guns and -pistols.
Dangerless shooting sport with rubber-arrow.

Fusiles y Pistolas "Eureka".
Deporte de armas sin peligro con flecha de goma.

43/200

43/201

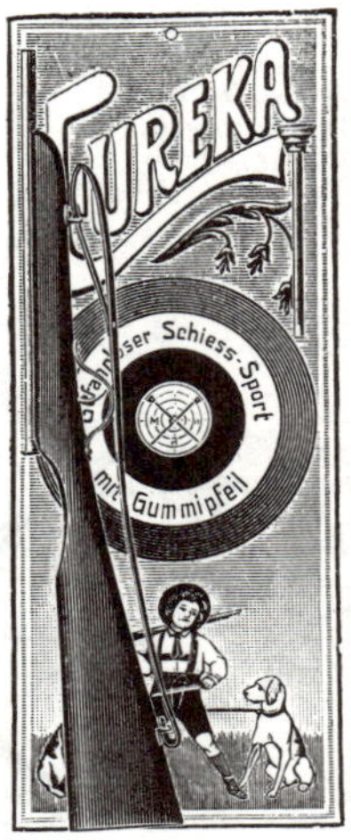

43/222

No. **43**/200 Eureka-Pistole aus Stahlblech, schwarz brüniert, mit 1 Pfeil auf Scheibe 17 × 24 cm.
Eureka-pistol of steel-plate, black burnished, with 1 arrow on target 17 × 24 cm.
Pistola Eureka de hoja de acero, bruñida negro, con 1 flecha sobre blanco 17 × 24 cm.

No. **43**/201 Eureka-Pistole mit lackiertem Holzschaft und vernickeltem Lauf, mit 1 Pfeil auf Scheibe 17 × 24 cm.
Eureka-pistol with varnished wood-stock and nickeled barrel, with 1 arrow on target 17 × 24 cm.
Pistola Eureka con culata de madera barnizada y cañon niquelado, con 1 flecha sobre blanco 17 × 24 cm.

No. **43**/202 Eureka-Pistole, wie 200, mit 1 Pfeil auf Scheibe 17 × 24 cm, das Ganze in elegantem Überkarton.
Eureka-pistol, same as 200, with 1 arrow on target 17 × 24 cm, the whole in elegant hand-box.
Pistola Eureka, como 200, con 1 flecha sobre el blanco 17 × 24 cm, todo en elegante cajita de cartón.

No. **43**/203 Eureka-Pistole, wie 201, mit 1 Pfeil auf Scheibe 17 × 24 cm, das Ganze in elegantem Überkarton.
Eureka-pistol, same as 201, with 1 arrow on target 17 × 24 cm, the whole in elegant hand-box.
Pistola Eureka, como 201, con 1 flecha sobre el blanco 17 × 24 cm, todo en elegante cajita de cartón.

No. **43**/204 Eureka-Pistole, wie 200, jedoch auf Scheibe 24 × 34 cm, mit 2 Pfeilen, das Ganze in elegantem Überkarton.
Eureka-pistol, same as 200, but on target 24 × 34 cm, with 2 arrows, the whole in elegant hand-box.
Pistola Eureka, como 200, pero sobre blanco 24 × 34 cm, con 2 flechas, todo en elegante cajita de cartón.

No. **43**/205 Eureka-Pistole, wie 201, mit 2 Pfeilen auf Scheibe 24 × 34 cm, sowie mit Gürtel und Pistolentasche, das Ganze in elegantem Überkarton.
Eureka-pistol, same as 201, with 2 arrows on target 24 × 34 cm, as well as with belt and pistol-bag, the whole in elegant hand-box.
Pistola Eureka, como 201, con 2 flechas sobre blanco de 24 × 34 cm, así como con cintura y bolsa de pistola, todo en elegante cajita de cartón.

No. **43**/220 Eureka-Gewehr aus kräftigem Stahlblech mit hübsch lackiertem Schaft, 1 Pfeil auf Scheibe 17 × 24 cm.
Eureka-gun, of strong steel-plate with nicely varnished stock, 1 arrow on target 17 × 24 cm.
Fusil Eureka, de fuerte hoja de acero, con culata lindamente barnizada, 1 flecha sobre blanco de 17 × 24 cm.

No. **43**/221 Eureka-Gewehr, wie 220, mit 1 Pfeil auf Scheibe 15 × 59 cm.
Eureka-gun, same as 220, with 1 arrow on target 15 × 59 cm.
Fusil Eureka, como 220, con 1 flecha sobre blanco de 15 × 59 cm.

No. **43**/222 Eureka-Gewehr, wie 220, mit Ledertragriemen und 1 Pfeil auf Scheibe 19 × 59 cm.
Eureka-gun, same as 220, with leather-strap and 1 arrow on target 19 × 59 cm.
Fusil Eureka, como 220, con porta-fusil de cuero y 1 flecha sobre blanco de 19 × 59 cm.

No. **43**/223 Eureka-Gewehr größer und stärker als 220, mit vernickeltem Lauf und hübsch lackiertem Schaft, mit Ledertragriemen und 2 Pfeilen auf Scheibe 20 × 70 cm.
Eureka-gun, larger and stronger than 220, with nickeled barrel and nicely varnished stock, with leather strap and 2 arrows on target 20 × 70 cm.
Fusil Eureka, mayor y más fuerte que 220, con cañon niquelado y culata lindamente barnizada, con porta-fusil de cuero y 2 flechas sobre blanco 20 × 70 cm.

No. **43**/224 Eureka-Gewehr, wie 223, mit Ledertragriemen und Gürtel, 2 Pfeilen auf Scheibe 20 × 70 cm.
Eureka-gun, same as 223, with leather-strap and belt, 2 arrows on target 20 × 70 cm.
Fusil Eureka, como 223, con porta-fusil de cuero, y cintura, 2 flechas sobre blanco 20 × 70 cm.

No. **43**/225 Eureka-Gewehr mit vernickeltem Lauf und hübscher, vernickelter Schloßgarnitur, lackiertem Holzschaft und Ledertragriemen und 2 Pfeilen auf Scheibe 20 × 70 cm.
Eureka-gun with nickeled barrel and nice, nickeled lock-furniture, varnished wooden stock and leather-strap and 2 arrows on target 20 × 70 cm.
Fusil Eureka con cañon niquelado y bonita guarnición de rastrillo niquelada, culata de madera barnizada, y porta-fusil de cuero y 2 flechas sobre blanco 20 × 70 cm.

No. **43**/226 Eureka-Gewehr, wie 225, in solidem Tuchfutteral, mit Lederbesatz und Tragriemen, mit 2 Pfeilen und Scheibe 24 × 34 cm.
Eureka-gun, same as 225, in solid cloth-casing, trimmed with leather, and strap, with 2 arrows and target 24 × 34 cm.
Fusil Eureka, como 225, en sólido estuche de paño, guarnecido con cuero, y porta-fusil, con 2 flechas y blanco 24 × 34 cm.

No. **43**/230 Großes, sehr schönes Eureka-Gewehr mit vernickeltem Stahlblechlauf und hübsch lackiertem Schaft, sehr kräftig und solide konstruiert, mit Ledertragriemen und 2 Pfeilen auf eleganter Scheibe 28 × 80 cm.
Eureka-gun, big and very beautiful with nickeled steelplate-barrel and nicely varnished stock, of very strong and solid construction, with leather-strap and 2 arrows on elegant target 28 × 80 cm.
Fusil Eureka, grande y muy lindo, con cañon de hoja de acero niquelada y culata lindamente barnizada, de construcción muy fuerte y sólida, con porta-fusil de cuero y 2 flechas sobre blanco elegante 28 × 80 cm.

No. **43**/231 Eureka-Gewehr, wie 230, in solidem Tuchfutteral mit Lederbesatz und Tragriemen, mit 2 Pfeilen auf eleganter Scheibe 28 × 80 cm.
Eureka-gun, same as 230, in solid cloth-casing, trimmed with leather, and strap, with 2 arrows on elegant target 28 × 80 cm.
Fusil Eureka, como 230, en sólido estuche de paño guarnecido de cuero, y con porta-fusil, con 2 flechas sobre blanco elegante 28 × 80 cm.

43/225

43/230

Eureka-Pfeile, für Pistolen und Gewehre passend. — Eureka-arrows, fit for pistols and guns. — Flechas Eureka adecuadas á pistolas y fusiles.

Hervorragende Neuheit!
Prominent novelty!
Novedad prominente!

Jugendmodell bester, solidester Konstruktion!
Youths' type, of best, solid construction!
Tipo para niños, de la mejor y más sólida construcción!

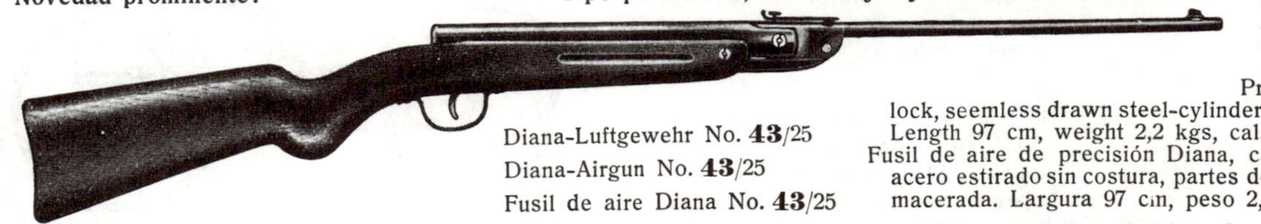

Diana-Luftgewehr No. **43**/25
Diana-Airgun No. **43**/25
Fusil de aire Diana No. **43**/25

No. **43**/25 Präzisions-Diana-Luftgewehr, massiver Stahllauf, automatischer Verschluß, nahtlos gezogener Stahlzylinder; Metallteile brüniert, Buchenholzschaft hübsch mattiert. Länge 97 cm, Gewicht 2,2 kg, Kal. 4,5 mm, mit glattem oder gezogenem Lauf.
Precision-Diana-airgun, massive steel-barrel, automatic lock, seemless drawn steel-cylinder; metal-parts browned, beechen-stock, nicely deadened. Length 97 cm, weight 2,2 kgs, cal. 4,5 mm, with smooth or rifled barrel.
Fusil de aire de precisión Diana, cañon de acero macizo, cierre automático, cilindro de acero estirado sin costura, partes de metal bruñidas, culata de madera de haya, lindamente macerada. Largura 97 cm, peso 2,2 kgs, cal. 4,5 mm, con cañon liso ó acanalado.

Präzisions-Diana-Luftpistole.

Die Diana-Luftpistole ist dank ihrer äußerst handlichen, gefälligen Form, ihrer einfachen Handhabung, ihrer guten Schußleistung und wegen der geringen Munitionskosten eine ganz vorzügliche Übungspistole. Die Pistole ist sehr solide konstruiert, ganz aus kräftigem Stahlblech hergestellt und tiefschwarz brüniert. Der Lauf der Pistole ist mit feinen Drallzügen versehen.

Jede Pistole ist in einem starken Karton verpackt, dem eine Gebrauchsanweisung sowie Spannschlüssel und 200 Diabolo-Kugeln beiliegen. Gewicht 550 g, fertig verpackt 770 g. Preis mit gezogenem Lauf.

Precision Diana air-pistol.

The Diana air-pistol is, thanks to its handy, agreeable form, its simple handling, its good shooting capacity and for the 'small cost of ammunition, a very excellent exercising pistol. It is very solidly constructed, wholly made of strong steel plate, and dark-black burnished. The barrel of the pistol is fitted with fine rifles.

Every pistol is packed in a strong hand-box, containing also instruction for use and spanning key and 200 Diabolo-balls. Weight 550 g, packed 770 g. Price with rifled barrel.

Pistola Diana, de aire, de precisión

La pistola de aire Diana, gracias á su forma manejable y agradable, á su simple manejo, á su buena capacidad de tirar y por causa de sus pequeños gastos de munición, es una pistola excelente de ejercicio. La pistola es de construcción muy sólida, hecha enteramente de fuerte hoja de acero y bruñida de color negro oscuro. El cañon de la pistola está finamente acanalado.

Cada pistola está empaquetada en una fuerte cajita de cartón, que aún contiene una instrucción de uso, y llave de dar cuerda y 200 balas Diabolo. Peso 550 g, con embalaje 770 gr. Precio con cañon acanalado.

Diana-Luftpistole.
Diana air-pistol.
Pistola de aire Diana.

Kindersäbel. — Toy Swords. — Sables.

Sämtliche Säbel werden gebogen oder gerade geliefert.
All numbers will be delivered with straight or curved blades.
Todos los sables se suministran o derechos o corvos.

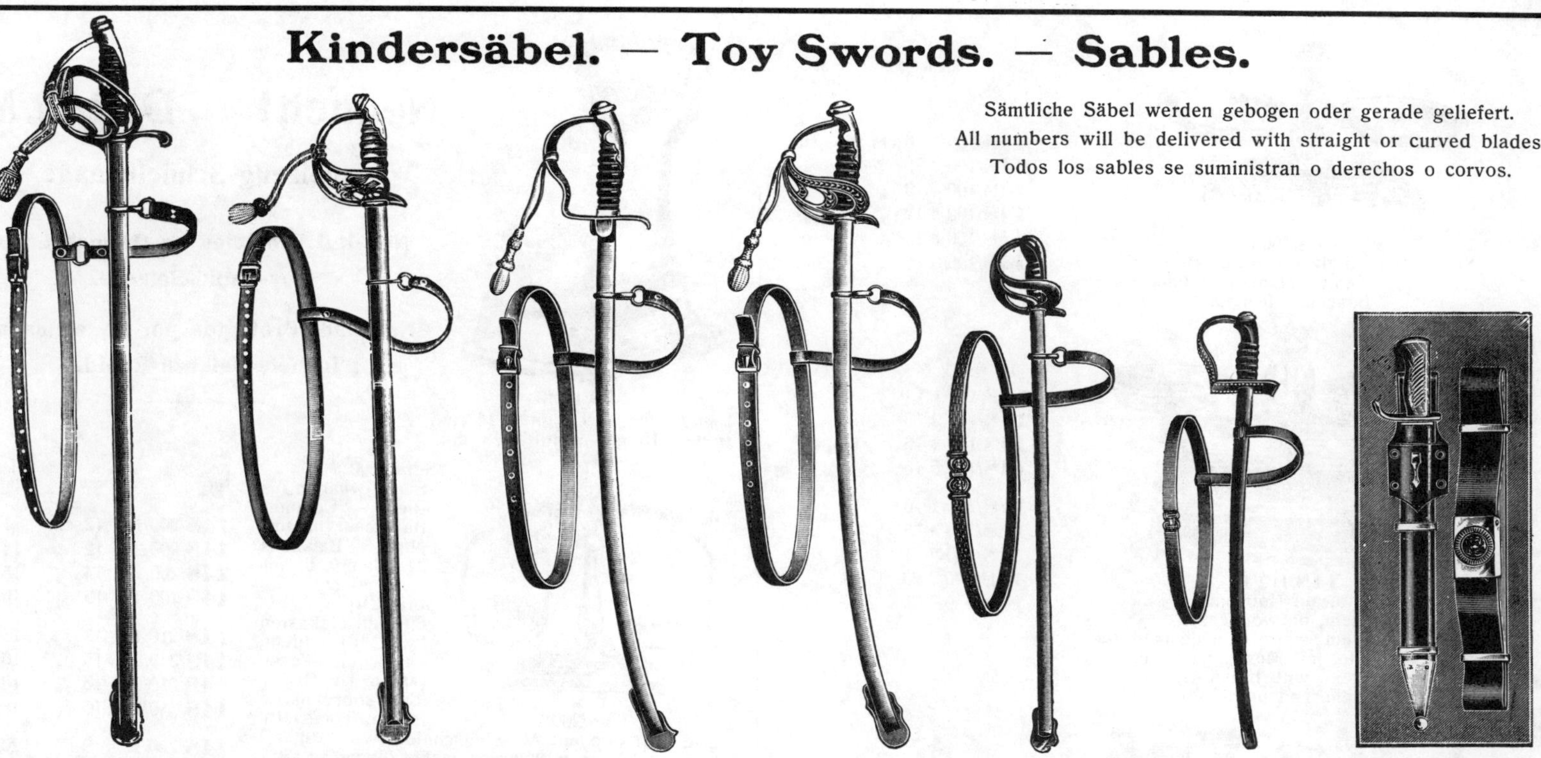

Serie A | Serie B | Serie C | Serie D | Serie E | Serie F | Bajonett

No.	Länge Length Largura cm	Ausführung	Beschreibung	Finish	Description	Ejecución	Descripción
			Serie A. Säbel mit Spangenkörben.		**Series A. Swords with buckle-hilts.**		**Serie A. Sables con guarnición de hebilla.**
152/526	55	mittlere	Korb vernickelt, Wachstuchkoppel ohne Portepee.	average	hilt nickeled, oilcloth-belt without tassel.	mediana	guarnición niquelada, cinturón de tela encerada, sin dragona.
152/528	65	„	dito.	„	ditto.	„	idem.
152/540	55	solide	Korb vernickelt, Lederkoppel mit Portepee.	solid	hilt nickeled, leather-belt with tassel.	sólida	guarnición niquelada, cinturón de cuero, con dragona.
152/538	65	„	dito.	„	ditto.	„	idem.
152/754	71	beste	Klinge, Scheide und Korb vernickelt, Lederkoppel mit Portepee.	best	blade, sheath and hilt nickeled, leather-belt with tassel.	la mejor	hoja, vaina y guarnición niqueladas, cinturón de cuero, con dragona.
152/756	80	„	dito.	„	ditto.	„	idem.
			Serie B. Säbel mit Adlerkörben.		**Series B. Swords with eagle-hilts.**		**Serie B. Sables con guarnición de águila.**
152/528/1	65	mittlere	Korb vermessingt, Wachstuchkoppel ohne Portepee.	average	hilt brassed, oilcloth-belt without tassel.	mediana	guarnición de latón, cinturón de tela encerada, sin dragona.
152/531	65	solide	Korb vermessingt, Lederkoppel mit Portepee.	solid	hilt brassed, leather-belt with tassel.	sólida	guarnición de latón, cinturón de cuero, con dragona.
152/755/1	70	beste	Korb vermessingt, Klinge und Scheide vernickelt, Lederkoppel mit Portepee.	best	hilt brassed, blade and sheath nickeled, leather-belt with tassel.	la mejor	guarnición de latón, hoja y vaina niqueladas, cinturón de cuero, con dragona.
152/758	80	„	dito, Korb jedoch vernickelt.	„	ditto, but with nickeled hilt.	„	idem, mas con guarnición niquelada.
			Serie C. Säbel mit Bügel.		**Series C. Swords with bow-hilts.**		**Serie C. Sables con guarnición de arco.**
152/525	54	mittlere	Bügel vernickelt, Wachstuchkoppel ohne Portepee.	average	hilts nickeled, oilcloth-belt without tassel.	mediana	guarnición niquelada, cinturón de tela encerada, sin dragona.
152/527	65	„	dito.	„	ditto.	„	idem.
152/529	65	solide	Bügel vernickelt, Lederkoppel und Portepee.	solid	hilts nickeled, leather-belt and tassel.	sólida	guarnición niquelada, cinturón de cuero, con dragona.
152/753	71	beste	Bügel, Klinge und Scheide vernickelt, Lederkoppel mit Portepee.	best	hilt, blade and sheath nickeled, leather-belt with tassel.	la mejor	guarnición, hoja y vaina niqueladas, cinturón de cuero, con dragona.
			Serie D. Säbel mit breiten Schuppenkörben.		**Series D. Swords with broad scale-hilts.**		**Serie D. Sables con guarnición larga de carillera.**
152/522	65	mittlere	Korb vernickelt, Wachstuchkoppel ohne Portepee.	average	hilt nickeled, oilcloth-belt without tassel.	mediana	guarnición niquelada, cinturón de tela encerada, sin dragona.
152/533	54	gute	Korb vernickelt, Wachstuchkoppel ohne Portepee.	good	hilt nickeled, oilcloth-belt without tassel.	buena	guarnición niquelada, cinturón de tela encerada, sin dragona.
152/530	65	„	dito.	„	ditto.	„	idem.
152/752	65	solide	Korb und Scheide vernickelt, Lederkoppel und Portepee.	solid	hilt and sheath nickeled, leather-belt and tassel.	sólida	guarnición y vaina niqueladas, cinturón de cuero, con dragona.
			Serie E. Säbel mit Blechkörben.		**Series E. Swords with tinplate-hilts.**		**Serie E. Sables con guarnición de hojalata.**
152/502	46	billigste bis bessere Ausführungen.	diverse Ausführungen und Preislagen.	cheapest to better finish	various outfit and price-ranges.	las más baratas hasta medianas	varias ejecuciones y precios.
152/507	55						
152/513	55						
152/621	65						
152/515	65						
152/620	65						
152/514	54						
152/516	63						
152/520	65						
			Serie F. Säbel mit Blechbügel.		**Series F. Swords with tinplate bow-hilts.**		**Serie F. Sables con guarnición simple de hojalata.**
152/500	46	billigste	bis bessere Ausführungen	cheapest to better finish		las más baratas hasta medianas	
152/506	55						
152/509	55						
152/609	65						
			Bajonette.		**Bayonets.**		**Bayonetas.**
152/60	33	billigste		cheapest		la más baratas	
152/61	33	einfache	Wachstuchkoppel.	simple	oilcloth-belt.	simple	cinturón de tela encerada.
152/62	33	bessere	dito.	better	ditto.	mejor	idem.
152/63	33	bessere	Lederkoppel.	better	leather-belt.	mejor	cinturón de cuero.
152/64	33	solide	dito.	solid	ditto.	sólida	idem.
152/65	37	beste	vernickelt, und Lederkoppel.	best	nickeled, and leather-belt.	la mejor	niquelada, con cinturón de cuero.

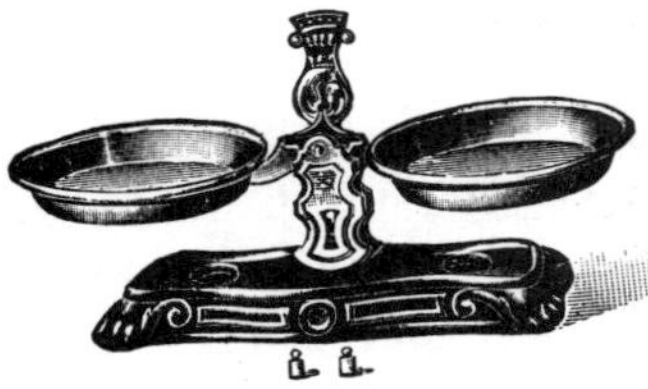

148/100/6

Serie 100: Tafelwaagen aus Blech.
Table-Balances of tin-plate.
Básculas de hojalata.

No. No. No.	Länge Length Longitud	Höhe Height Altura
148/100/1	6 cm	$3^1/_2$ cm
148/100/3	8 „	4 „
148/100/4	9 „	4 „
148/100/5	12 „	7 „
148/100/6	$13^1/_2$ „	7 „
148/100/8	16 „	8 „

148/110/4

Serie 110: dito, auf Holzkasten.
idem, on woodcase.
idem, sobre caja de madera.

Serie 120: dito, mit Messingschalen.
idem, with brass scales.
idem, con platillos de latón.

148/110/1	$13^1/_2$cm	9 cm
148/110/3	16 „	10 „
148 110/4	16 „	11 „
148/110/5	16 „	11 „
148/120/1	16 „	11 „
148/120/3	18 „	11 „
148/120/5	21 „	11 „
148/120/7	23 „	11 „
148/120/9	25 „	13 „

148/130/5

Serie 130: dito, auf Ladentisch.
idem, with counter.
idem, con mostrador.

148/130/1	16 cm	13 cm
148/130/3	18 „	14 „
148/130/5	23 „	15 „
148/130/6	24 „	16 „

148/160/4

Serie 160 Ganz Metall, weiß lackiert.
idem, all metal, white lacquered.
idem, todo de metal, barnizado blanco.

148/160/0	13 cm	7 cm
148/160/1	17 „	8 „
148/160/2	18 „	8 „
148/160/4	21 „	9 „
148/160/7	24 „	9 „
148/160/8	25 „	9 „
148/160/9	25 „	10 „

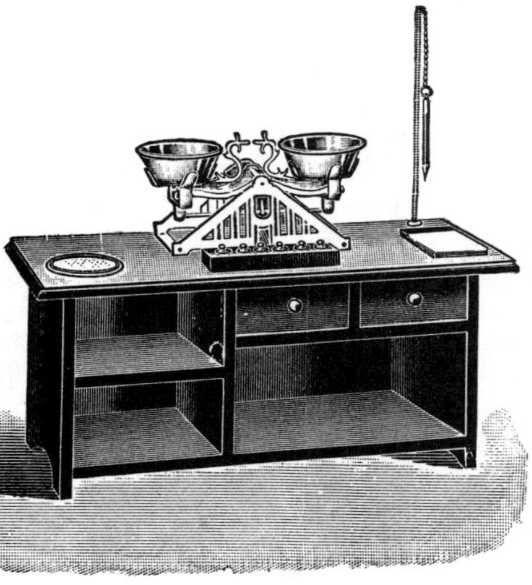

148/180/2

Serie 180: Ladentisch mit Ausstattung.
idem, counter with fittings.
idem, mostrador con guarnición.

148/180/0	23 cm	18 cm
148/180/1	26 „	20 „
148/180/2	35 „	23 „
148/180/3	40 „	26 „

Neuheit! D.R.G.M.

Spielzeug-Schnellwaage

Novelty! Protected by German Law.
Toy-Rapid-Balance.

Novedad! Protegida por ley alemana.
Juguete-Balanza Rápida.

148/190/2

Länge / Length / Longitud 14 cm.
Höhe / Height / Altura 18 cm.

148/200/1

Serie 200: Säulenwaagen aus Blech. — Column-Balances, of tin-plate. — Balanzas de columna, de hojalata.

Serie 210: dito auf Holzkasten (wie 110). — Idem, on wood-case (same as 110).— Idem, sobre caja de madera (como 110).

Serie 220: dito mit Messingschalen (wie 120).
idem, with brass-scales (same as 120).
idem, con platillos de latón (como 120).

No. No. No.	Länge Length Longitud	Höhe Height Altura
148/200/1	12 cm	11 cm
148/200/2	12 „	14 „
148/200/3	14 „	15 „
148/200/4	15 „	16 „
148/210/1	12 „	15 „
148/210/3	15 „	16 „
148/210/5	16 „	18 „
148/210/6	16 „	18 „
148/220/1	16 „	20 „
148/220/3	19 „	22 „
148/220/5	20 „	24 „
148/220/6	22 „	27 „
148/220/8	24 „	30 „

148/230/5

Serie 230: dito auf Ladentisch.
idem, on counter.
idem, sobre mostrador.

148/230/1	18 cm	22 cm
148/230/3	20 „	27 „
148/230/5	23 „	30 „
148/230/6	24 „	33 „

148/240/4

Serie 240: in Messingausführung.
idem, of brass.
idem, de latón.

148/240/0	15 cm	15 cm
148/240/1	15 „	18 „
148/240/2	18 „	19 „
148/240/4	20 „	22 „
148/240/6	24 „	28 „
148/240/8	26 „	30 „

Jedes Stück im Karton mit Gewichten. — Every piece in cardboard-box, with weights. — Cada pieza en cajita de cartón, con pesos.
Kleine Änderungen vorbehalten. — Subject to slight alterations. — Sujeto á pequeñas alteraciones.

Please note also the publication on page 71 of the principal catalogue.
Llamamos también su atención á la publicación en la página 71 del catálogo principal.

Laterna magica. Magic lanterns. Linternas mágicas.

2006/10

Dieser Apparat ist aus starkem feinen schwarz lackierten S. M. Blech gefertigt, auf massiven Metallfuß montiert und ist mit Flachbrenner-Petroleumlampe mit Glaszylinder, 2 Glasbildern 3 cm und 1 Objektiv 26 mm Durchmesser ausgestattet.

This apparatus is made of strong, finely black-varnished S. M. tinplate, mounted on massive metal-base, and fitted with flatburner-petrol-lamp with glass-cylinder, 2 glass-pictures 3 cm and 1 object-glass of 26 mm Ø.

Este aparato está hecho de fuerte hojalata S. M. finamente barnizado negro, montado sobre base macizo de metal y provisto de lámpara de petróleo con mechero llano y tubo de vidrio, 2 dibujos de vidrio de 3 cm y 1 objetivo de 26 mm diámetro.

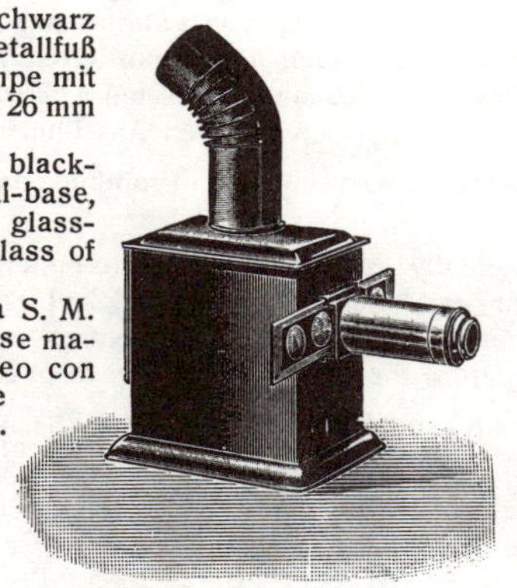

2006/10 $10^1/_2 \times 11 \times 6$ cm

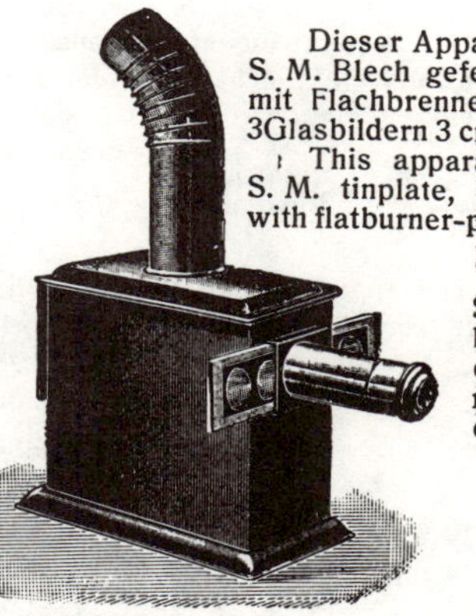

2006/6 $12 \times 6^1/_2 \times 13$ cm

2006/6

Dieser Apparat ist aus starkem feinen schwarz lackierten S. M. Blech gefertigt, auf massiven Metallfuß montiert und ist mit Flachbrenner-Petroleumlampe mit Glaszylinder, Reflektor, 3 Glasbildern 3 cm und 1 Objektiv 26 mm Durchmesser ausgestattet.

This apparatus is made of strong, finely blackvarnished S. M. tinplate, mounted on massive metal-base and fitted with flatburner-petrol-lamp with glass-cylinder, reflector, 3 glass-pictures of 3 cm and 1 object-glass of 26 mm Ø.

Este aparato está hecho de fuerte hojalata S. M., finamente barnizado negro, montado sobre base macizo de metal y provisto de lámpara de petróleo con mechero llano y tubo de vidrio, reflector, 3 dibujos de vidrio de 3 cm y 1 objetivo de 26 mm de diámetro.

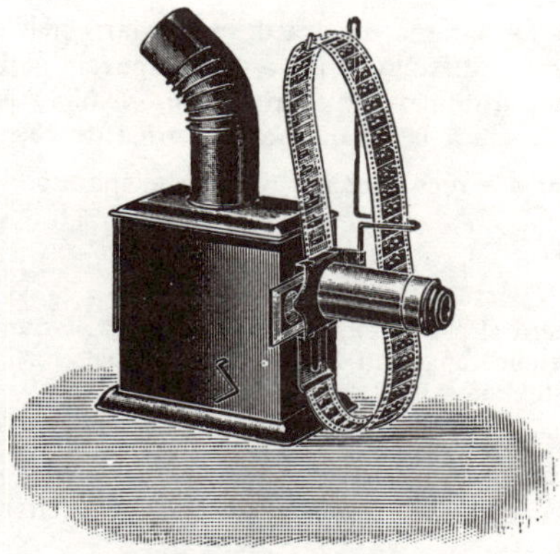

2006/11 10,5×6,5×11,5 cm

2006/12 15×10×21,5 cm

Kinematograph
gleichzeitig auch Laterna magica.

Cinematograph
at the same time magic lantern.

Cinematógrafo
al mismo tiempo linterna mágica.

2006/11.

Dieser Apparat ist aus starkem feinen schwarz lackierten S. M. Blech gefertigt, mit gutem Mechanismus auf soliden Metallfuß montiert und ist mit Filmstange, Filmhalter, Flachbrenner-Petroleumlampe mit Glaszylinder, 1 Film, ca. 56 cm lang, 1 Glasbild, 3 cm breit, und einem Objektiv, 26 mm Durchmesser, ausgestattet.

This apparatus is made of strong, finely blackvarnished S. M. tinplate, mounted with good mechanism on solid metal-base and is fitted with film-rod, film-holder, flatburner-petrol-lamp with glass-cylinder, 1 film abt 56 cm long, 1 glass-picture 3 cm wide and one object-glass of 26 mm Ø.

Este aparato está hecho de fuerte hojalata S. M. finamente barnizada de negro, montado con buen mecanismo sobre sólida base de metal y provisto de barra de filmo, porta-filmo, lámpara de petróleo con mechero llano y tubo de vidrio, 1 filmo ca. 56 cm de largo, 1 dibujo de vidrio de 3 cm de ancho y de 1 objetivo de 26 mm diámetro.

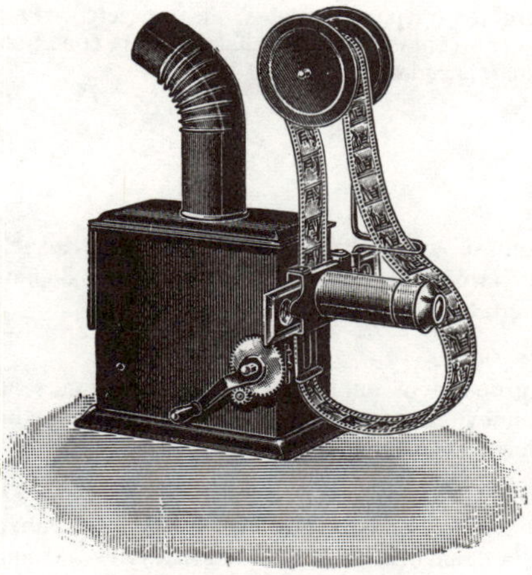

2006/1 12×6,5×13 cm

2006/1.

Dieser Apparat ist aus starkem feinen schwarz lackierten S. M. Blech gefertigt, mit gutem Mechanismus auf soliden Metallfuß montiert und ist mit Filmstange mit Rolle, Filmhalter, Flachbrenner-Petroleumlampe mit Glaszylinder, 1 Film, ca. 56 cm lang, 3 Glasbildern. 3 cm breit, und einem Objektiv, 26 mm Durchmesser, ausgestattet.

This apparatus is made of strong, finely blackvarnished S. M. tinplate, mounted with good mechanism on solid metal-base and is fitted with film-rod with roller, film-holder, flatburner-petrol-lamp with glass-cylinder, 1 film abt. 56 cm long, 3 glass-pictures 3 cm wide, and one object-glass of 26 mm Ø.

Este aparato está hecho de fuerte hojalata S. M. finamente barnizada de negro, montado con buen mecanismo sobre sólida base de metal y provisto de barra de filmo con rollos, porta-filmo, lámpara de petróleo con mechero llano y tubo de vidrio, 1 filmo ca. 56 cm de largo, 3 dibujos de vidrio de 3 cm de ancho y un objetivo de 26 mm de diámetro.

2006/12.

Dieser Apparat ist aus starkem feinen schwarz lackierten S. M. Blech gefertigt, mit gutem Mechanismus auf massiven Metallfuß montiert und ist mit Duplexbrenner-Petroleumlampe mit Glaszylinder, Reflektor, Schwungscheibe, Verschwinder, verstellbarer Filmstange mit Rolle, 2 Filmen, je 112 cm lang, 12 Glasbildern, $4^1/_2$ cm und 1 Objektiv, 40 mm Durchmesser, ausgestattet. Optik besteht aus 3 sauber geschliffenen Linsen.

This apparatus is made of strong, finely blackvarnished S. M. tinplate, mounted with good mechanism on massive metal-base and is fitted with duplex-burner-petrol-lamp with glass-cylinder, reflector, fly-disc, vanisher, adjustable film-rod with roller, 2 films each 112 cm long, 12 glass-pictures of $4^1/_2$ cm and one object-glass of 40 mm Ø. The optic consists of 3 accurately ground lenses.

Este aparato está hecho de fuerte hojalata S. M. finamente barnizada de negro, montado con buen mecanismo sobre base macizo de metal, y provisto de lámpara de petróleo con mechero duplex y tubo de vidrio, reflector, disco volante, desvanecedor, barra de filmo graduable con rollo, 2 filmos de 112 cm de largo cada uno, 12 dibujos de vidrio de $4^1/_2$ cm y 1 objetivo de 40 mm diámetro. La óptica consta de 3 lentes cuidadosamente pulidas.

2006/13 13×8,5×16 cm

2006/8

2006/8

Mit elektrischer Beleuchtung, ca. 2 m Kupferlitze, Nickelaufsatz, Litzenklemmer, stabiler Messingfassung und Schraubstöpsel.

With electric lighting, abt. 2 m copper-cable, nickel head-piece, binders, stable brass-socket and screw-plug.

Con alumbrado eléctrico, ca. 2 m cuerda de cobre, pieza superior de niquel, borna, guarnición estable de latón y contacto de tornillo.

2006/13.

Dieser Apparat ist aus starkem feinen schwarz lackierten S. M. Blech gefertigt, mit gutem Mechanismus auf massiven Metallfuß montiert und ist mit Flachbrenner-Petroleumlampe mit Glaszylinder, Reflektor, Schwungscheibe, Verschwinder, verstellbarer Filmstange mit Rolle, 1 Film ca. 112 cm lang, 3 Glasbildern, $3^1/_2$ cm und 1 Objektiv, 30 mm Durchmesser, ausgestattet. Optik besteht aus 3 sauber geschliffenen Linsen.

This apparatus is made of strong, finely blackvarnished S. M. tinplate, mounted with good mechanism on massive metal-base and is fitted with flatburner petrol-lamp with glass-cylinder, reflector, fly-disc, vanisher, adjustable film-rod with roller, 1 film abt. 112 cm long, 3 glass-pictures $3^1/_2$ cm and 1 object-glass of 30 mm Ø. The optic consists of 3 accurately ground lenses.

Este aparato está hecho de fuerte hojalata S. M. finamente barnizada de negro, montado con buen mecanismo sobre base macizo de metal y provisto de lámpara de petróleo con mechero llano y tubo de vidrio, de reflector, disco volante, desvanecedor, barra de filmo graduable con rollo, 1 filmo ca. 112 cm de largo, 3 dibujos de vidrio de $3^1/_2$ cm y 1 objetivo de 30 mm diámetro. La óptica consta de 3 lentes cuidadosamente pulidas.

Schleifenbahn
ist 29 cm lang, 21 cm hoch und 9 cm breit.

Looping the loop
is 29 cm long, 21 cm high and 9 cm wide.

Looping the loop
tiene 29 cm de largo, 21 cm de alto and 9 cm de ancho.

2006/9

Beachten Sie auch die Veröffentlichung auf Seite 71 des Hauptkataloges.

Please note also the publication on page 63—69 of the principal catalogue.
Llamamos también su atención á la publicación en la página 63—69 del catálogo principal.

Kinematograph, zugleich als Laterna magica verwendbar, elektrisch. — Kinetograph, also applicable as magic lantern, electrical. — Cinematógrafo, también aplicable como linterna mágiça, eléçtrico.

2000/233 E

Der Apparat eignet sich auch vorzüglich zur Vorführung von Laterna-magica-Bildern jeder Art (4 cm). Die Beleuchtung erfolgt elektrisch, ein Widerstand ist bei diesem Modell nicht erforderlich. Die Filmrolle ist für Filme bis zu 50 m Länge eingerichtet. Größe des Apparates ca. 350×150×460 mm. Preis mit 6 Glasbildern, 4 cm, einem 25-m-Theaterfilm, Kontakt und Kabel (ohne Birne) zum direkten Anschluß an jede Hausleitung.

Besonders ist für diesen Apparat die Osram-Nitra-Projektionslampe (etwa 100 Watt) zu empfehlen.

The apparatus can also be utilized excellently for presenting magic lantern-pictures of every kind (4 cm). The lighting is electric, a resistance is not necessary with this apparatus. The film-roll is arranged for films of 50 m long. Size of the apparatus about 350×150×460 mm. Price with 6 glass-pictures 4 cm; a theatre-film of 25 m, contact and cable (without glow-lamp) for direct connection to every house-conduction.

The Osram-Nitra projection-lamp (about 100 watt) may be specially recommended for this apparatus.

El aparato puede también ser excelentemente utilizado para apresentar dibujos de linterna mágica de cualquier especie (4 cm). El alumbrado es eléctrico, no es necesaria una resistencia con este aparato. El rollo de filmo está dispuesto para filmos de 50 m de largo. Tamaño del aparato ca. 350×150×460 mm. Precio con 6 dibujos en vidrio 4 cm, un filmo de teatro de 25 m, contacto y cable (sin lámpara incandescente) para conexión directa á la conducción eléctrica de casa.

La lámpara de proyección Osram-Nitra (ca. 100 watios) puede ser especialmente recomendada para este aparato.

2000/154/0 E

Postkarten-Projektions-Apparat. Etwa 1/6 natürl. Größe.
Dieser Apparat eignet sich zur Projektion von undurchsichtigen Bildern (Postkarten, Zeichnungen usw.) Ausgestattet mit vorzüglicher Optik und Einrichtung für elektrische Beleuchtung, mit Kontakt und Kabel, fertig zum Anschluß. Birne wird nicht mitgeliefert.

Postcard-projection-apparatus. About 1/6 nat. size.
This apparatus is appropriate for the projection of not transparent pictures (postcards, designs, etc.). Fitted with excellent optic and arrangement for electric lighting, with contact and cable, ready for connection. Glow-lamp is not supplied.

Aparato de proyectar tarjetas postales. Ca. 1/6 tamaño natural.
Este aparato está apropiado á la proyección de dibujos no transparentes (tarjetas postales, diseños, etc.). Provisto con excelente óptica y dispositivo para alumbrado eléctrico, con contacto y cable, lista para la conexión. Lámpara incandescente no es suministrada.

2000/362/2 **Dampfmaschine** wie **2000**/362/1.
Größe etwa 175×110×260 mm, mit Sicherheitsventil, Dampfpfeife und Wasserablaßschraube.

2000/362/2 **Steam-engine** same as **2000**/362/1.
Size about 175×110×260 mm, with safety-valve, steam-whistle and wateroutlet-screw.

2000/362/2 **Máquina de vapor,** lo mismo que **2000**/362/1.
Tamaño ca. 175×110×260 mm, con válvula de seguridad, silbato de vapor y tornillo de purga.

2000/362/1

2000/362/3 **Dampfmaschine** wie **2000**/362/2, jedoch mit Kesselhausanbau für den Kamin. Größe etwa 210×120×300 mm, mit Sicherheitsventil, Dampfpfeife und Wasserablaßschraube.

2000/362/3 **Steam-engine** same as **2000**/362/2, with annex to boiler-house for the chimney. Size about 210×120×300 mm, with safety-valve, steam-whistle and wateroutlet-screw.

2000/362/3 **Máquina de vapor,** lo mismo que **2000**/362/2, con anexo á la casa de caldera para la chimenéa. Tamaño ca. 210×120×300 mm, con válvula de seguridad, silbato de vapor y tornillo de purga.

2000/362/1 **Dampfmaschine**
mit Doppelschwungrädern, in Lokomobilform, mit stahlblau patiniertem Messingkessel auf starkem Metallsockel. Größe etwa 150×95×230 mm, mit Sicherheitsventil, Dampfpfeife und Wasserablaßschraube.

2000/362/1 **Steam-engine**
with double fly-wheels, in portable form, with steel-blue patina-overlaid brass-boiler on strong metal-base. Size about 150×95×230 mm, with safety-valve, steam-whistle and wateroutlet-screw.

2000/362/1 **Máquina de vapor**
con dobles volantes, de tipo portátil, con caldera de latón patinado color azul-acero sobre fuerte base de metal. Tamaño ca. 150×95×230 mm, con válvula de seguridad, silbato de vapor y tornillo de purga.

2000/350 **Dampfmaschine**
mit Sicherheitsventil, Dampfpfeife, Wasserfüllschraube.
Größe der Maschine etwa 185×185×270 mm.

2000/350 **Steam-engine**
with safety-valve, steam-whistle, waterfilling screw.
Size of the machine 185×185×270 mm.

2000/350 **Máquina de vapor**
con válvula de seguridad, silbato de vapor, tornillo de carga.
Tamaño de la máquina 185×185×270 mm.

2000/350

2000/356 **Dampfmaschine** mit Manometer, Dampfpfeife, Gewichtsventil, Wasserfüllschraube, Wasserablaßschraube, Wasserstandsanzeiger. Größe der Maschine etwa 235×235×365 mm.

2000/356 **Steam-engine** with manometer, steam-whistle, weighted valve, waterfilling screw, wateroutlet-screw, water-gauge. Size of engine about 235×235×365 mm.

2000/356 **Máquina de vapor,** con manómetro, silbato de vapor, válvula de contrapeso, tornillo de purga, tornillo de carga, indicador de nivel de agua. Tamaño de la máquina ca. 235×235×365 mm.

2000/356

Beachten Sie auch die Veröffentlichung auf Seite 63—69 des Hauptkataloges.

Please note also the publication on page 63—69 of the principal catalogue.
Llamamos también su atención á la publicación en la página 63—69 del catálogo principal.

2000/385

2000/385 Dampfmaschine
mit feststehendem, doppeltwirkendem Dampfzylinder, Regulator, Wasserfüllschraube, Dampfpfeife, Dampfdom, Gewichts-Sicherheitsventil, Manometer, Wasserstandsanzeiger, Wasserablaß und Selbstöler zur leichten Ölzuführung für den Dampfzylinder. Größe etwa 305×305×445 mm. Ohne Kesselspeisepumpe.

2000/385 Steam-engine
with fixed double-acting steam-cylinder, governor, waterfilling screw, steam-whistle, steam-dome, weighted safety-valve, manometer, water-gauge, water-outlet, and self-acting oiler to facilitate the lubrication of the steam-cylinder. Size about 305×305×445 mm. Without boiler feed-pump.

2000/385 Máquina de vapor
con cilindro fijo de doble efecto, regulador, tornillo de carga, silbato de vapor, domo de vapor, válvula de seguridad de contrapeso, manómetro, indicador de nivel de agua, tornillo de purga y lubrificador automático para facilitar la lubrificación del cilindro. Tamaño ca. 305×305×445 mm. Sin bomba alimentadora de la caldera.

2000/370

2000/370 Modell-Dampfmaschine
mit 2 feststehenden Messing-Dampfzylindern, vor- und rückwärts laufend, ohne Umsteuerung. Armaturen aus Messing, fein vernickelt, mit Sicherheitsventil, Dampfpfeife, Wasserablaßschraube, Wasserstandsanzeiger und Selbstöler zur leichten Ölzuführung für die Dampfzylinder. Größe etwa 330×250×410 mm.

2000/370 Model-Steam-engine
with 2 fixed brass steam-cylinders, forward- and backward-run, without reversing gear. Brass fittings, finely nickeled, with safety-valve, steam-whistle, wateroutlet-screw, water-gauge and self-acting oiler to facilitate the lubrication of steam-cylinders. Size about 330×250×410 mm.

2000/370 Máquina de vapor modelo, con 2 cilindros de vapor fijos, de latón, marcha adelante y atrás, sin dispositivo para cambio de marcha. Accesorios de latón, finamente niquelados, con válvula de seguridad, silbato de vapor, tornillo de purga, indicador de nivel de agua, y lubrificador automático para facilitar el engrase de los cilindros de vapor. Tamaño ca. 330×250×410 mm.

Modelle. — Models. — Modelos.

2000/652/1

2000/652/1 enthaltend:
1 Windmotor,
1 Kreissäge,
1 Schleifstein und
1 Transmission.

2000/652/1 containing
1 wind-wheel,
1 circular saw,
1 grindstone and
1 transmission.

2000/652/1 conteniendo
1 motor de viento,
1 sierra circular,
1 piedra de amolar,
1 transmisión.

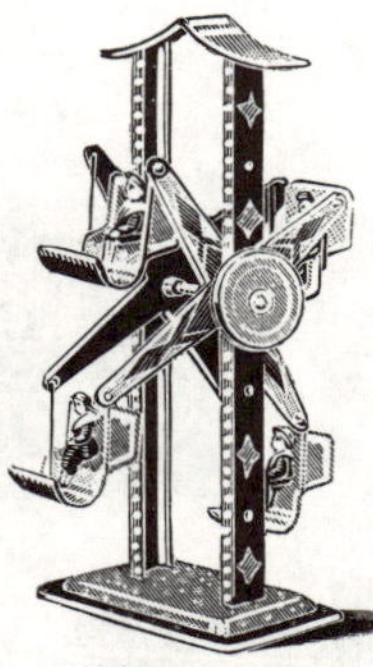

2000/455/3

2000/455/3 Russische Schaukel mit 4 Sitzen. 125×130×235 mm.

2000/455/3 Swing-boat with 4 seats. 125×130×235 mm.

2000/455/3 Columpio ruso con 4 asientos. 125×130×235 mm.

2000/450/2 Fontäne mit Windkessel, aus starkem Zinkblech; gleichmäßiges Springen. Durchmesser ca. 215 mm. Höhe 140 mm.

2000/450/2 Fountain with air-chamber, of strong zinc-plate; uniform jets. Diameter about 215 mm. Height 140 mm.

2000/450/2 Fuente con cámara de ar, de hoja de zinc muy fuerte; chorros uniformes. Diámetro ca. 215 mm. Altura 140 mm.

2000/450/2

2000/446/2 Mechanische Werkstatt
mit Kreissäge, Schleifstein und Bohrmaschine, etwa 350 mm lang.

2000/446/2 Mechanical workshop
with circular saw, grindstone and boring-machine, about 350 mm long.

2000/446/2 Taller mecanico
con sierra circular, piedra de afilar y máquina perforadora, ca. 350 mm de largo.

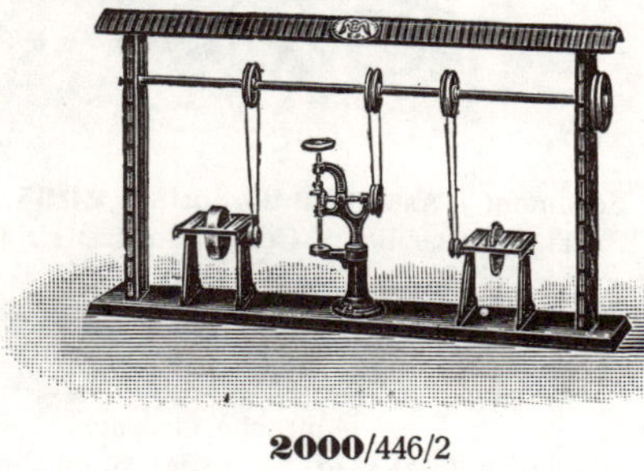

2000/446/2

2000/676 Bergbahn mit Abstellvorrichtung. Mit Uhrwerk. 500×90×250 mm.

2000/676 Mountain-railway with stopping-device. With clockwork. 500×90×250 mm.

2000/676 Ferrocarril de montaña con dispositivo de parar. Con mecanismo. 500×90×250 mm.

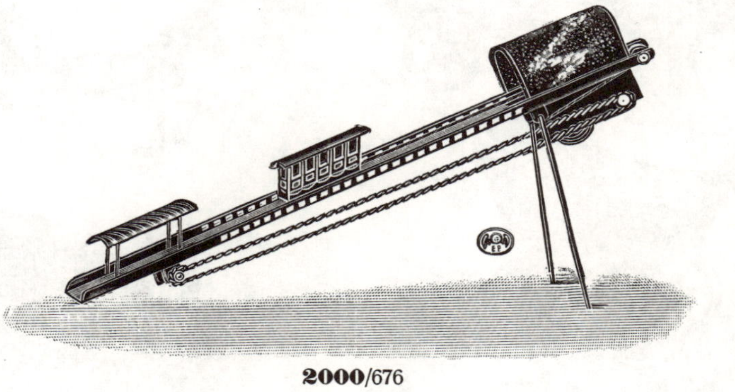

2000/676

Beachten Sie auch die Veröffentlichung auf Seite 63—69 des Hauptkataloges.

Blechspielwaren ohne Uhrwerk — Tin Toys without clockwork — Juguetes de lata sin cuerda

Sortiment — Assortment Surtido — **2061**/1
Packung — Packing — Contenido 3 Dtz., doz., doc.

1 Kiste
1 case } = 50 Gross.
1 caja

wie **2061**/11
like **2061**/11
como **2061**/11

aber mit Wagen
but with carriages
pero con carros

2061/6	2
2061/7	3
2061/8	4
2061/9	5
2061/10	6
2061/11	7
2061/12	8
2061/13	9
2061/14	10

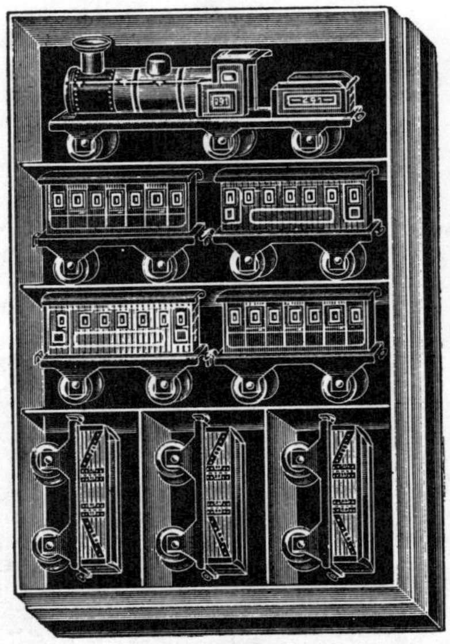

2061/11
ohne Uhrwerk — without clock work — sin cuerda
mit 7 Wagen
with 7 carriages
con 7 carros.

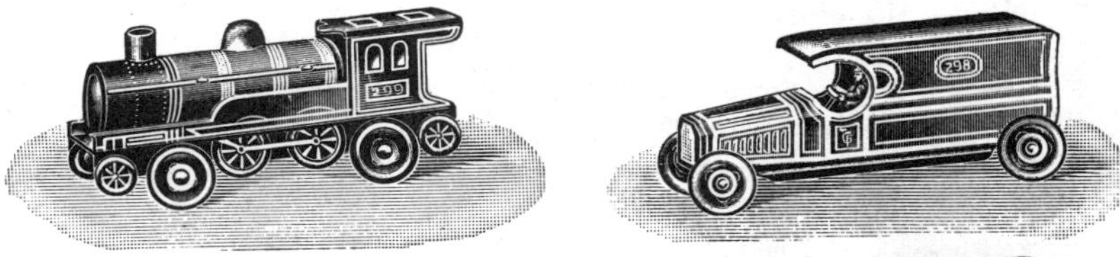

Sortiment / Assortment / Surtido **2061**/2
Packung / Packing / Contenido 2 Dtz., doz., doc.

1 Kiste
1 case } = 25 Gross.
1 caja

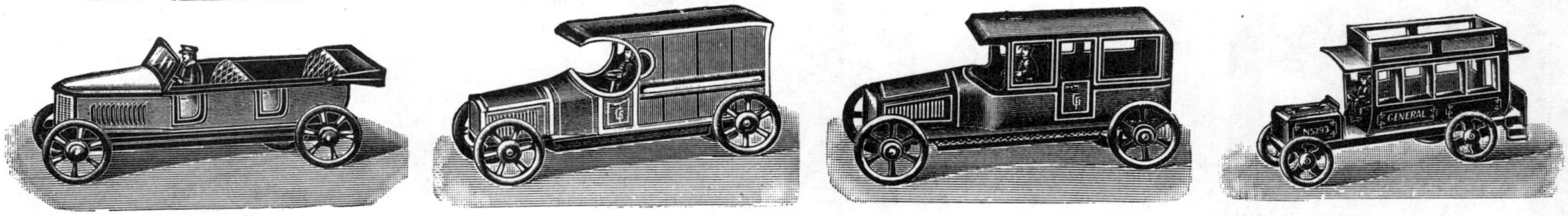

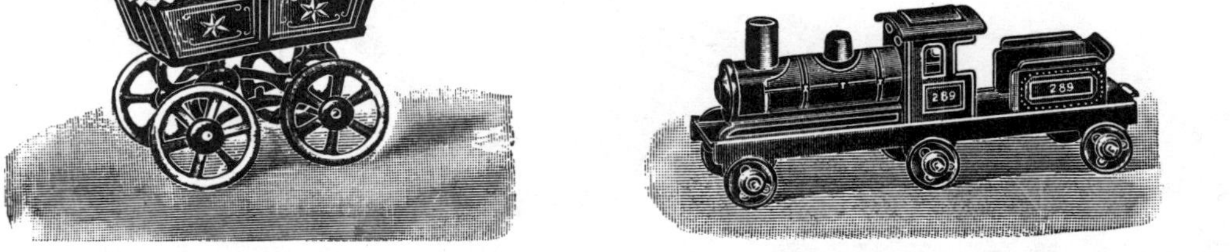

Sortiment / Assortment / Surtido **2061**/3
Packung / Packing / Contenido 2 Dtz., doz., doc.

1 Kiste
1 case } = 25 Gross.
1 caja

$^1/_2$ natürliche Grösse.
$^1/_2$ of natural size. — $^1/_2$ del tamaño natural.

Blechspielwaren ohne Uhrwerk. — Tin toys without clockwork. — Juguetes de lata sin cuerda.

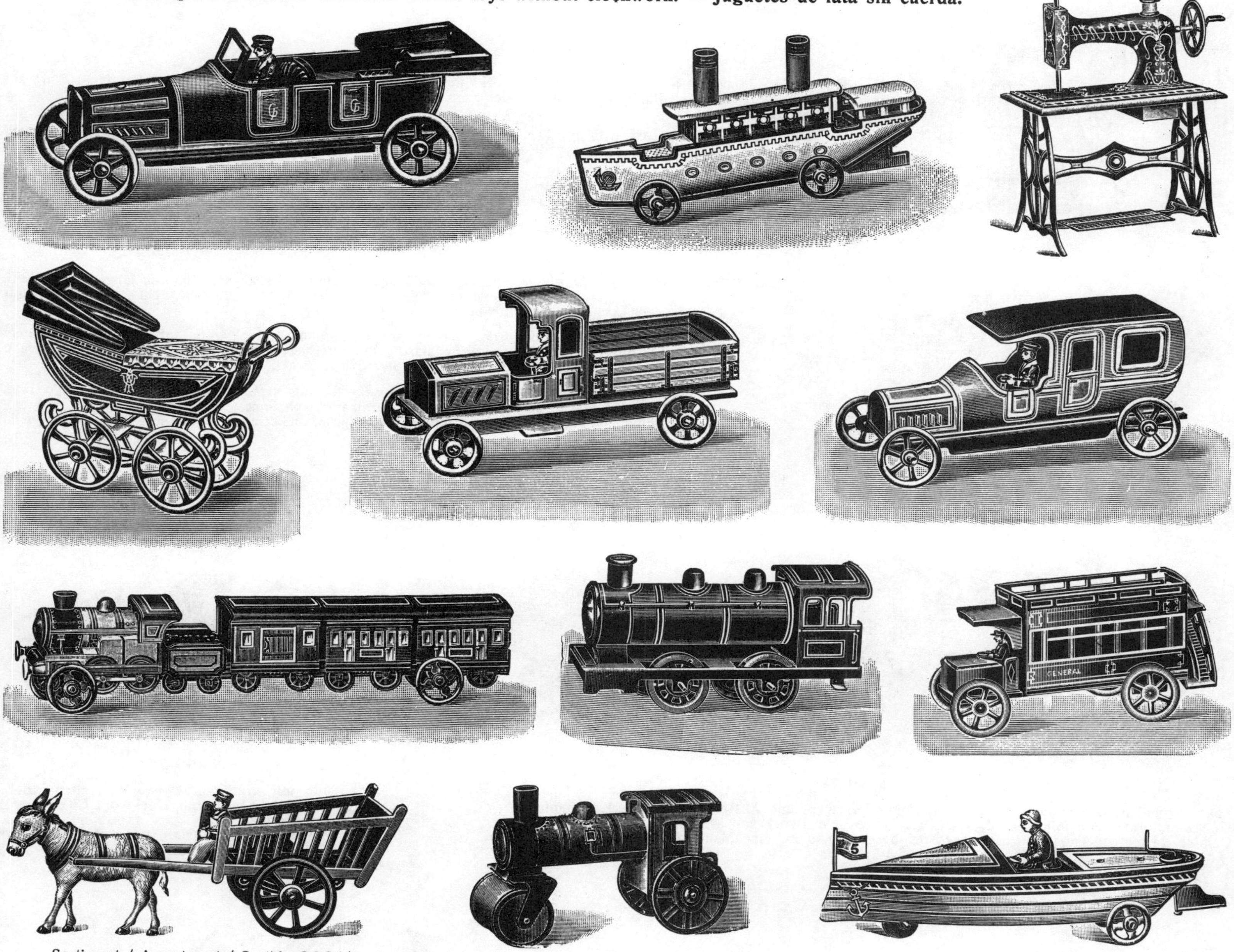

Sortiment / Assortment / Surtido **2061**/4 Packung / Packing / Contenido: 2 Dtz. / dozen / docena. 1 Kiste / 1 case / 1 caja = 20 Gross.

Mit Uhrwerk. — With clockwork. — Con cuerda.

Sortiment / Assortment / Surtido **2061**/5 Packung / Packing / Contenido: 1 Dtz. / dozen / docena. 1 Kiste / 1 case / 1 caja = 10 Gross.

$^{1}/_{2}$ natürliche Grösse. — $^{1}/_{2}$ of natural size. — $^{1}/_{2}$ del tamaño natural.

Please note also the publication on page 63—69 of the principal catalogue.
Llamamos también su atención á la publicación en la página 63—69 del catálogo principal.

2000/751

2000/751 Transport-Karren mit gutem Uhrwerk, mit Figur und 2 Kisten Ladung, etwa 110 mm lang, fährt auf kleinem Platze selbsttätig in den verschiedensten Richtungen.

Transporting-cart with good clockwork, with figure and 2 cases load, about 110 mm long, moves automatically in sundry directions in a small place.

Carro de transporte con buen mecanismo, con figura y 2 cajas de carga, ca. 110 mm de largo, mueve automáticamente en diversas direcciones sobre un pequeño espacio.

2000/752

2000/752 Lastauto mit kräftigem, langsam und lange laufendem Werk, etwa 150 mm lang, fein lackiert, mit Figur, biegt während der Fahrt mehrmals automatisch nach rechts, wobei die Figur den Arm in dieser Richtung ausstreckt.

Goods-motorcar, with strong, slowly and long running clockwork, abt. 150 mm long, finely lacquered, with figure, turns, during the ride, several times automatically to the right, while the figure extends the arm toward that direction.

Camión de mercancías, con mecanismo fuerte, que trabaja lentamente y por longo rato, ca. 150 mm de largo, finamente embarnizado, con figura, tornando, durante el trayecto, diversas veces automáticamente a la derecha, mientras la figura levanta el brazo en la misma dirección.

2000/762/2

Lastauto und Anhänger aus Metall, mit kräftigem Uhrwerk und Abstellvorrichtung. Kettenantrieb.
Goods-motorcar with follower, of metal, with strong clockwork and stopping device.
Camión de mercancías, con carro anexo de metal, con fuerte mecanismo y con dispositivo de parar.

2000/759

Lastauto mit kräftigem Uhrwerk. Kettenantrieb.
Goods-motorcar with strong clockwork. Chain-drive.
Camión de mercancías con fuerte mecanismo. Accionado por cadena.

Orchestrion. — Orchestrion. — Orquestrión.

2028/1	12×12×17 cm
2028/2	13×13×19 cm
2028/3	18×11×13 cm
2028/4	13×13×19½ cm
2028/5	17×11×10½ cm

Neuheit!
Novelty!
Novedad!

Mit Uhrwerk.
With mechanic.
Con mecanismo.

2014/35

Packung / Packing / Contenido: ½ Dtz., doz., doc.

2028/5

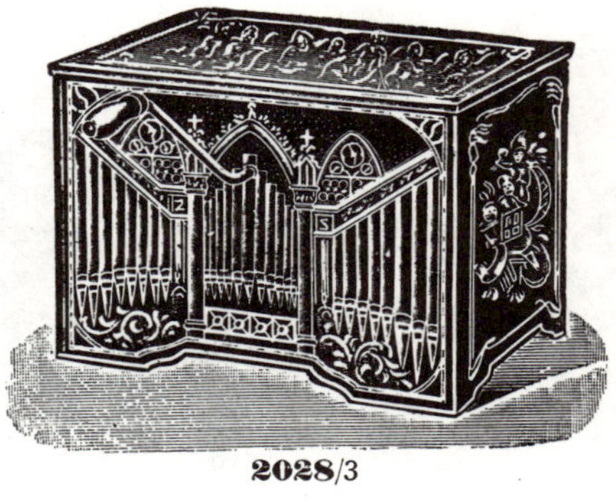

2028/3

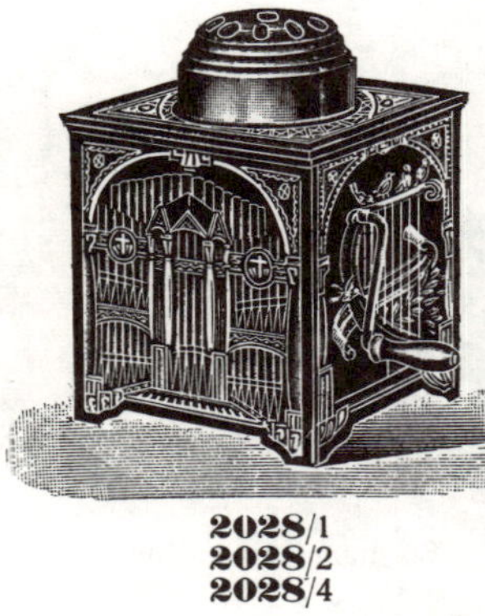

2028/1
2028/2
2028/4

Beachten Sie auch die Veröffentlichung auf Seite 63—69 des Hauptkataloges.

Please note also the publication on page 176 of the principal catalogue.
Llamamos también su atención á la publicación en la página 176 del catálogo principal.

Gekleidete mechanische Spielwaren. — Dressed mechanical toys. — Juguetes con mecanismo forrados de tela.

Purzelnde Figuren. — Tumbling figures. — Figuras dando vueltas.

25/364

Schusterjunge als Purzelfigur.
Shoemakers-boy as tumbling-figur.
Aprendiz de zapatero, dando vueltas.
25 × 13 cm.

25/365

Indischer Gaukler als Purzelfigur.
Indian Juggler as tumbling figure.
Mágico índico dando vueltas.
25 × 13 cm.

25/350 – 351

Max und Moritz als Purzelfiguren.
Max and Moritz tumbling figures.
Max y Moritz, dando vueltas.
25 × 13 cm.

25/349

Gekleideter Affe als Purzelfigur.
Dressed Monkey as tumbling figure.
Mono vestido, dando vueltas.
25 × 13 cm.

25/329 L

Lamm, einen Leiterwagen ziehend.
Lamb, pulling a car.
Cordero tirando un coche de laderas.
11 × 25 cm.

25/164

Bärenführer und Bär, tanzend.
Bear-leader and bear, dancing.
Domador de osos y oso, bailando.
19 × 14 cm.

25/329 Z

Ziege, einen Leiterwagen ziehend.
Goat, pulling a car.
Cabra tirando un carro de laderas.
11 × 25 cm.

25/323

Knabe, Ski laufend.
Boy skieing.
Muchacho de Sky, andando.
25 × 22 cm.

25/234

Eskimo auf Hundeschlitten.
Esquimo on sleigh with dog.
Ésquimo en trinéo con perro.
15 × 29 cm.

25/162

Knabe auf Rodelschlitten.
Boy on sleigh.
Muchacho en trinéo.
15 × 16 cm.

25/213

Amme, Sportwagen fahrend.
Nurse pushing a mail-cart.
Nodriza con coche de niños.
20 × 25 cm.

25/358

3 Häschen, Ringelreihen tanzend.
3 Rabbitdolls,dancingRing around roses.
3 Liebrecitos jugando y bailando.
17 × 15 cm

25/209

Hase, einen Wagen mit Osterei ziehend.
Rabbit pulling a car with egg.
Liebre tirando un coche con huevo.
16 × 25 cm.

25/262

Gekleideter Hase, mit Rückenkorb, natürlich laufend.
Rabbit doll, dressed, with basket on back, walking naturally.
Liebre vestida con cesta de cuestas, andando naturalmente.
23 × 10 cm.

25/239

Hasenpaar, tanzend.
Rabbits, dressed as boy and girl, dancing.
Par de liebres, bailando.
16 × 11 cm.

25/321

Gekleideter Hase, einen Karren schiebend.
Rabbit doll pushing a post-car.
Liebre vestida, empujando un coche.
22 × 21 cm.

25/264

Hasenpaar, tanzend.
Rabbits, dressed as boy and girl, dancing.
Par de liebres, bailando.
23 × 15 cm.

Sämtliche Figuren sind gekleidet und mit prima Uhrwerk versehen. — All the figures are dressed and have 1st class clockworks.
Todas las figures son vestidas y tienen cuerdas muy buenas.

Beachten Sie auch die Veröffentlichung auf Seite 176 des Hauptkataloges.

Please note also the publication on page 176 of the principal catalogue.
Llamamos también su atención á la publicación en la página 176 del catálogo principal.

Gekleidete mechanische Spielwaren. — Dressed mechanical toys. — Juguetes con mecanismo forrados de tela.

25/366

Purzelclown (mit Schlüssel aufzuziehen).
Tumbling-clown (wind up by key).
Payazo dando voltetas (dar cuerda por llave).
17×8 cm.

25/368

Purzel-Max(mitSchlüssel aufzuziehen).
Tumbling-Max (wind up by key).
Max dando vueltas (dar cuerda por llave).
17×8 cm.

25/369

Purzel-Moritz (mit Schlüssel aufzuziehen).
Tumbling-Moritz (wind up by key).
Moritz dando vueltas (dar cuerda por llave).
17×8 cm.

Natürlich laufende Figuren. — Naturally walking figures. — Figuras andandas naturalmente.

25/342

Clown, natürlich laufend.
Clown, walking naturally.
Payazo, andando naturalmente.
24×10 cm.

25/348

Gekleideter Affe, natürl. laufend.
Dressed monkey, walking nat.
Mono vestido, andando nat.
24×10 cm.

25/346

Neger-Clown, natürlich laufend.
Nigger-clown, walking naturally.
Negrito, andando naturalmente.
24×10 cm.

25/356

Indisches Mädchen, laufend.
Indian girl, walking.
Muchacha indica, corriento.
24×10 cm.

25/357

Indischer Gaukler, laufend.
Indian juggler, walking.
Mágico índico, corriento.
24×10 cm.

25/355

Cow-Boy, laufend.
Cow-Boy, walking.
Vaquero, corriento.
24×10 cm

25/319

Weihnachtsmann mit Christbaum, natürlich laufend.
Santa-Claus with Xmas tree, walking naturally.
El Viejo de Navidad, con árbol, andando naturalmente.
25×10 cm.

25/340 W

Matrose, natürlich laufend.
Sailor, walking naturally.
Marinero, andando naturalmente.
23×10 cm.

25/367

Knabe auf Trittroller.
Boy on scooter
Muchacho sobre rodador.
18×12 cm.

25/352

Purzelclown.
Clown, tumbling.
Clown, dando vueltas.
25×13 cm.

25/252

Knabe auf Selbstfahrer, beweglich.
Boy on handcar, moveable.
Muchacho en automóvil, movible.
15×15 cm.

Sämtliche Figuren sind gekleidet und mit prima Uhrwerk versehen. — All the figures are dressed and have 1st class clockwork.
Todas las figuras son vestidas y tienen cuerdas muy buénas.

Beachten Sie auch die Veröffentlichung auf Seite 176 des HauptKataloges.

Mechanische Artikel. — Mechanical toys. — Juguetes con mecanismo.

2009/290 P = 1/2 Dtz., doz., doc. 12×6×12 cm

2009/240 P = 1/12 Dtz., doz., doc. 22×9×13 cm

2009/287 P = 1/12 Dtz., doz., doc. 7 × 7 × 20 cm

2009/286 P = 1/12 Dtz., doz., doc.

2009/305 P = 2 Dtz., doz., doc.

Ohne Uhrwerk — Without clockwork — Sin mecanismo.

2009/279 P = 1 Dtz., doz., doc.

P = Packung — Packing — Contenido.

Please note also the publication on page 19—25 of the principal catalogue.
Llamamos también su atención á la publicación en la página 19—25 del catálogo principal.

Blechspielwaren mit und ohne Uhrwerk. — Tin toys with and without clockwork. — Juguetes de lata con y sin mecanismo.

2009/297W P=1/12 Dtz., doz., doc.
Mit Uhrwerk / With clockwork / Con mecanismo.

2009/298 P=2 Dtz., doz., doc.
Mit Uhrwerk / With clockwork / Con mecanismo.

2009/299

2009/300
Ohne Uhrwerk / Without clockwork / Sin mecanismo.
2009/300 W
Mit Uhrwerk / With clockwork / Con mecanismo.
P=2 Dtz., doz., doc.

2009/301 P=1/12 Dtz., doz., doc.
Mit Uhrwerk With clockwork Con mecanismo.

2009/302 P=1 Dtz., doz., doc.
Mit Uhrwerk / With clockwork / Con mecanismo.

2009/303
Ohne Uhrwerk / Without clockwork / Sin mecanismo.
2009/303W
Mit Uhrwerk. With clockwork Con mecanismo.
P=2 Dtz., doz., doc.

2009/304 P=4 Dtz., doz., doc.

P = Packung / Packing / Contenido.

Beachten Sie auch die Veröffentlichung auf Seite 19—25 des Hauptkataloges.

Uhrwerkeisenbahnen. — Railways with clockwork. — Ferrocarriles con mecanismo.

2009/292

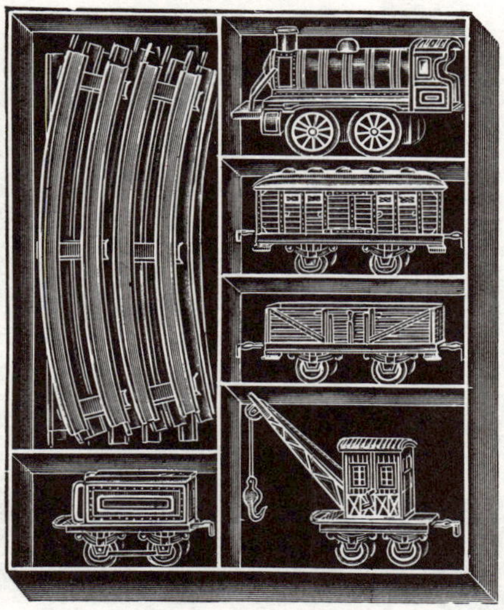

2009/293

2009/294

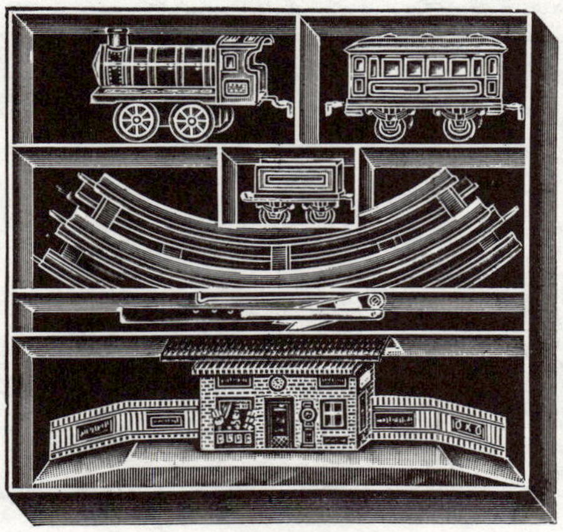

2009/295

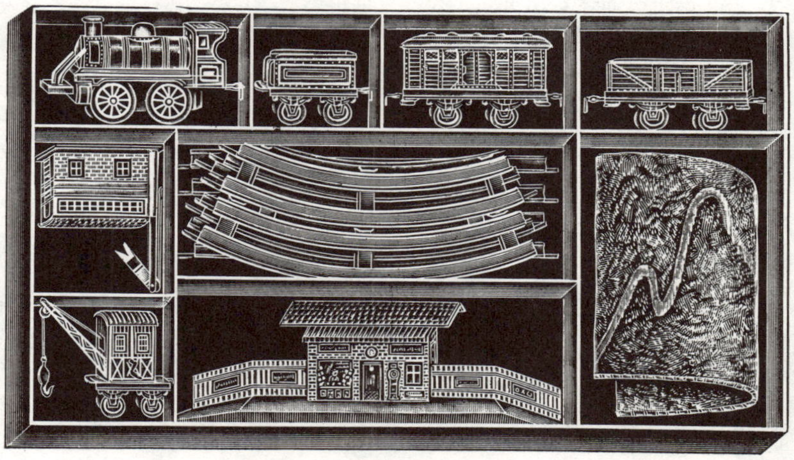

2009/296

Mechanische Spielwaren. — Mechanical tin toys. — Juguetes con mecanismo.

111/314 21½ × 14 cm P = 1/12 Dtz.

111/465 17 × 14 cm P = 1/12 Dtz.

111/811 13 × 13 cm P = 1/2 Dtz.

111/872 15½ × 15 cm P = 1/2 Dtz.
111/872/1 15½ × 15 cm P = 1/12 Dtz.

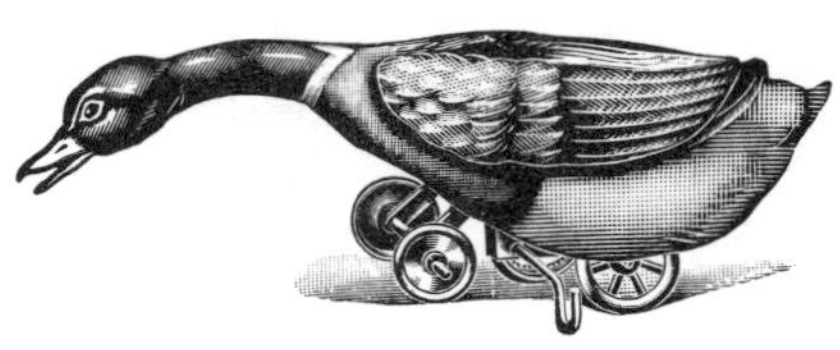

111/875 24 × 8 cm P = 1/2 Dtz.
111/875/1 24 × 8 cm P = 1/12 Dtz.

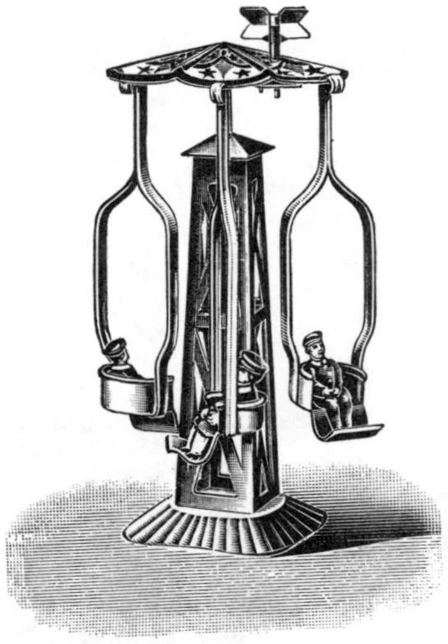

111/835/3 26½ × 10 cm P = 1/12 Dtz.
111/835/3m with music / con música
111/835/2m with music / con música but only with 2 trapezes / solo con 2 trapecios
111/835/2 with 2 trapezes without music / con 2 trapecios sin música.

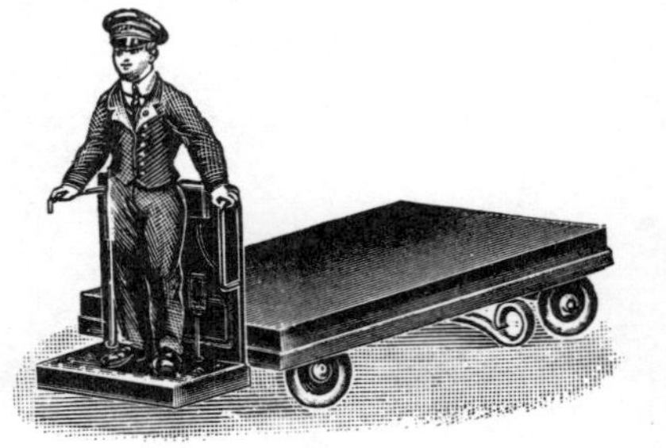

111/890
16 × 11 cm
P = 1/2 Dtz.

111/890/0
ohne Uhrwerk
without clockwork
sin mecanismo
16 × 11 cm
P = 1/2 Dtz.

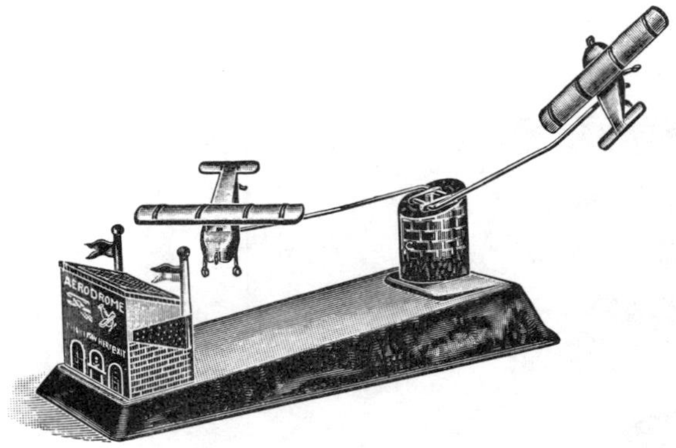

111/894 22½ × 10 cm P = 1/12 Dtz.
111/893 mit 1 Flieger / with 1 Aeroplane / con 1 aeroplano.
22½ × 10 cm P = 1/12 Dtz.

111/892
16 × 11 cm
P = 1/2 Dtz.

111/892/0
ohne Uhrwerk
without clockwork
sin mecanismo
16 × 11 cm
P = 1/2 Dtz.

111/651T 24½ × 9 cm P = 1/12 Dtz.
111/652T 31 × 11 cm P = 1/12 Dtz.

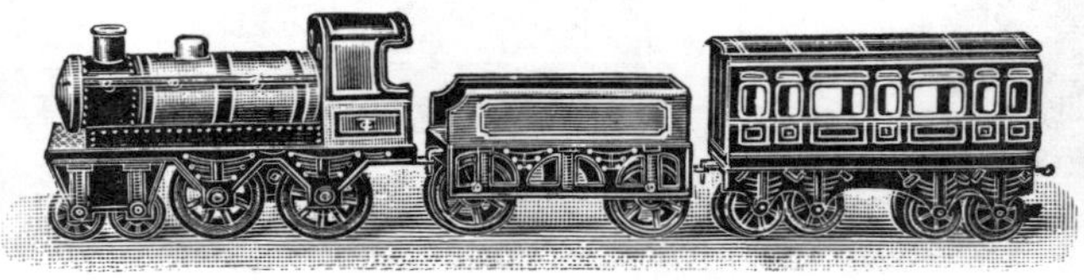

111/652T/1 49 × 11 cm P = 1/12 Dtz.
111/654T/1 53½ × 11 cm P = 1/12 Dtz.

111/654T 34 × 11 cm P = 1/12 Dtz.

Sämtliche Lokomotiven sind auch mit Kuhfang lieferbar.
All engines may be delivered also with cowcatchers.
Todas las locomotoras se suministran también con cogedor de vacas.

111/658T 52½ × 14 cm P = 1/12 Dtz.
111/656T 40 × 14 cm P = 1/12 Dtz.

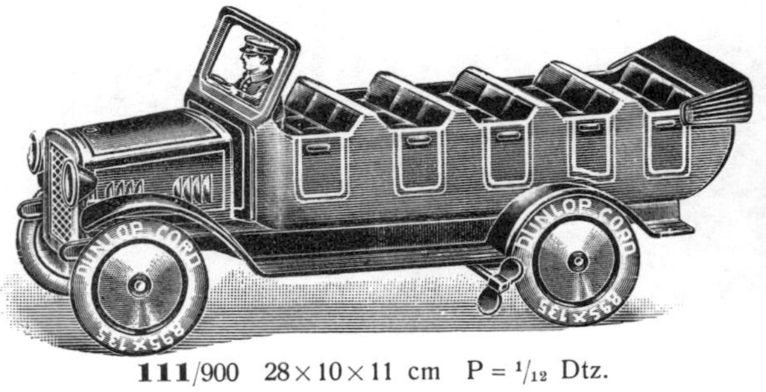

111/900 28 × 10 × 11 cm P = 1/12 Dtz.

111/850/1 18 × 6 cm P = 1/2 Dtz.
111/850/1/0 without chauffeur / sin mecánico.

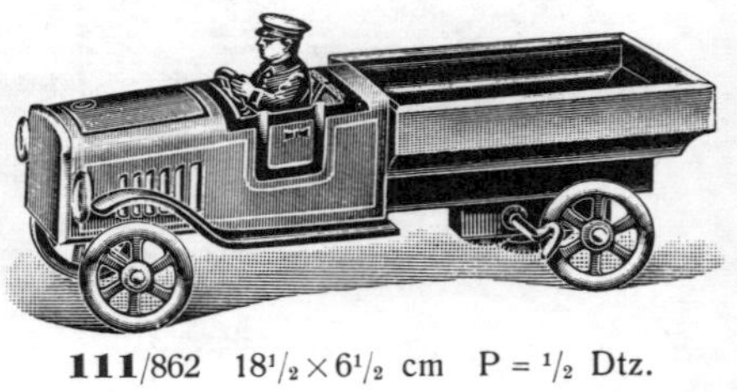

111/862 18½ × 6½ cm P = 1/2 Dtz.

P = Packung — Packing — Contenido. Dtz. = dozen — docena.

111/850 18×6 cm P=$^{1}/_{2}$ Dtz., doz., doc.
111/851 26×9 cm P=$^{1}/_{12}$ Dtz., doz., doc.
111/856 30×11 cm P=$^{1}/_{12}$ Dtz., doz., doc.

111/901 28×10×12 cm P=$^{1}/_{12}$ Dtz., doz., doc.

111/850/1 18×6 cm P=$^{1}/_{2}$ Dtz., doz., doc.
111/854 26×10 cm P=$^{1}/_{12}$ Dtz., doz., doc.
111/857 30×11 cm P=$^{1}/_{12}$ Dtz., doz., doc.

111/912 24$^{1}/_{2}$×10×15 cm P=$^{1}/_{12}$ Dtz., doz., doc.

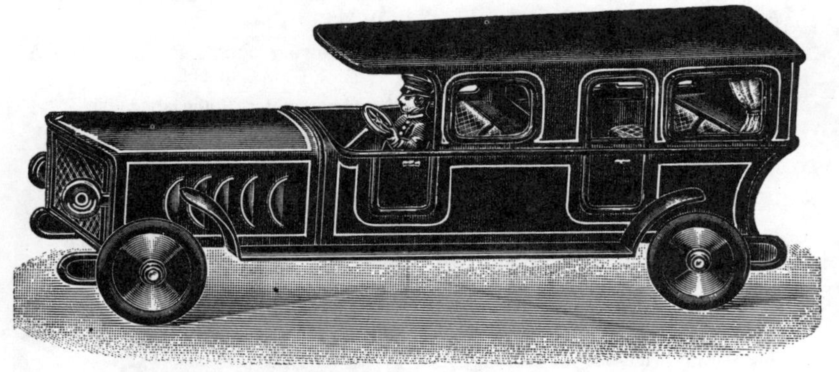

111/855 26×10 cm P=$^{1}/_{12}$ Dtz., doz., doc.
111/858 30×11 cm P=$^{1}/_{12}$ Dtz., doz., doc.

111/910 24$^{1}/_{2}$×10×12$^{1}/_{2}$ cm. P=$^{1}/_{12}$ Dtz., doz., doc.

111/911 24$^{1}/_{2}$×10×12$^{1}/_{2}$ cm P=$^{1}/_{12}$ Dtz., doz., doc.

111/860 wie **111**/855, aber Sanitätsauto.
111/860 like **111**/855, but Ambulance.
111/860 como **111**/855, pero Automóvil de sanidad.

111/861 wie **111**/858, aber Sanitätsauto.
111/861 like **111**/858, but Ambulance.
111/861 como **111**/858, pero Automóvil de sanidad.

111/920 Leiter einfach.
Ladder single.
Escalera simple.
25×8×11 cm. P=$^{1}/_{3}$ Dtz., doz., doc.

111/921 Leiter doppelt.
Ladder double.
Escalera doble.
25×8×11 cm. P=$^{1}/_{12}$ Dtz., doz., doc.

111/921/4 P=$^{1}/_{3}$ Dtz., doz., doc.

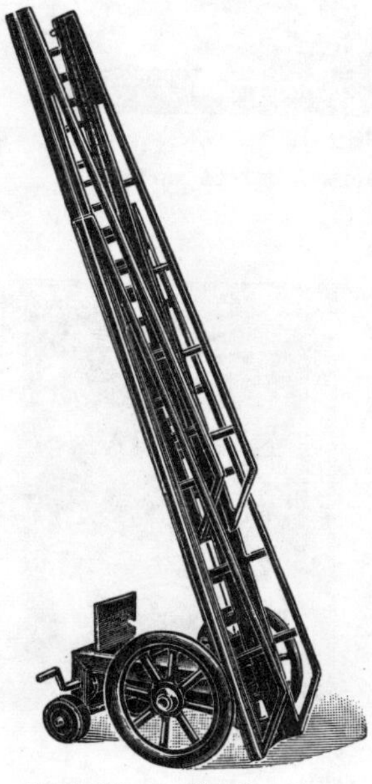

111/921 25×8×11 cm
P=$^{1}/_{12}$ Dtz., doz., doc.

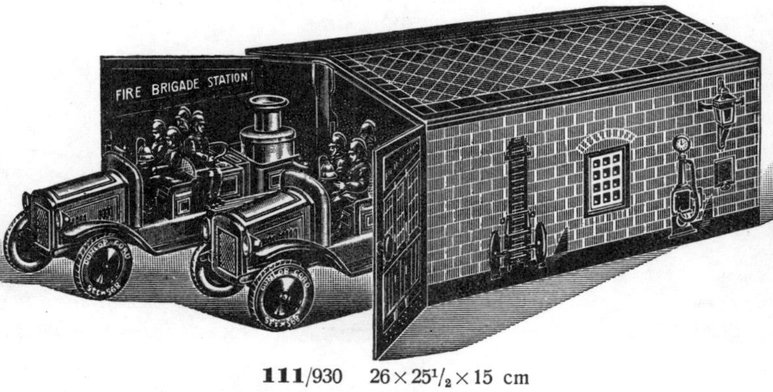

111/930 26×25$^{1}/_{2}$×15 cm
Fire Brigade Station.
Depósito de la brigada de incendios con carruaje de bomberos y escalera de incendios.

P = Packung — Packing — Contenido.

Please note also the publication on page 62 and 206 of the principal catalogue.
Llamamos también su atención á la publicación en la página 62 y 206 del catálogo principal.

Schiffe mit Uhrwerk. — Steamers with mechanic. — Vapores con mecanismo.

Novelty!
Pleasure-steamer with promenading movable passengers.
German Patent.

116/1807
Vergnügungsdampfer mit promenierenden, sich bewegenden Passagieren D. R. G. M. No. 934 329.

Novidad!
Vapor de recréo con pasajeros móviles de paséo.
Patente alemana.

116/1420
Raddampfer. / Paddle steamer.
Buque de vapor con ruedas.

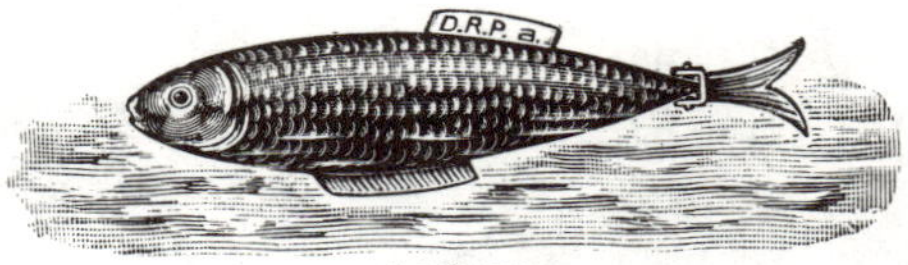

116/200
Fisch schwimmt natürlich durch Bewegung der Schwanzflosse.
Fish swimming naturally by moving its tail-fin.
Pez nadando como natural por el movimiento de la aleta de cola.

116/751
Passagierdampfer. / Passenger steamer.
Vapor de pasajeros.

116/600
Paddel-Boot. / Paddle boat. / Barco de paddles.
D. R. G. M. No. 933 025.
116/600 schwimmt durch Paddelbewegung
swims by paddling
nadando por movimiento de palas

116/700
Ruderboot. / Rowing boat. / Barco de remos.
D. R. G. M. No. 909 212.
116/700 schwimmt durch Ruderbewegung
swims by Rowing-movement
nadando por movimiento de remos

116/501
Rennboot. / Racing boat. / Barco de corridas.

116/1610
Wasserfahrstuhl. / Water-rolling-chair.
Sillón ambulante sobre agua.

Maße und Preise der **kompletten Serien** sowie einiger weiteren Typen befinden sich in separater Preisliste.

Measures and prices of the **complete series,** also some other types are in separate price-list.

Dimensiones y precios de las **series completas,** aún algunas otras barcas estan en la lista de precios separada.

116/1712
Sortiment. / Boat sets. / Barcos surtidos.

Puppengarnitur. — Dolls sets. — Guarniciones para muñecas.

Koll. **59** Coll. **59** Coll. **59**

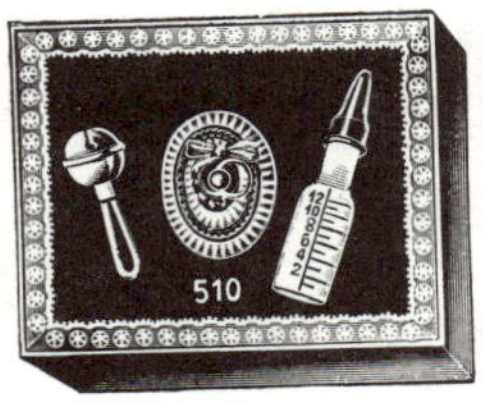

59/510

59/510/1

59/510/2

59/510/3

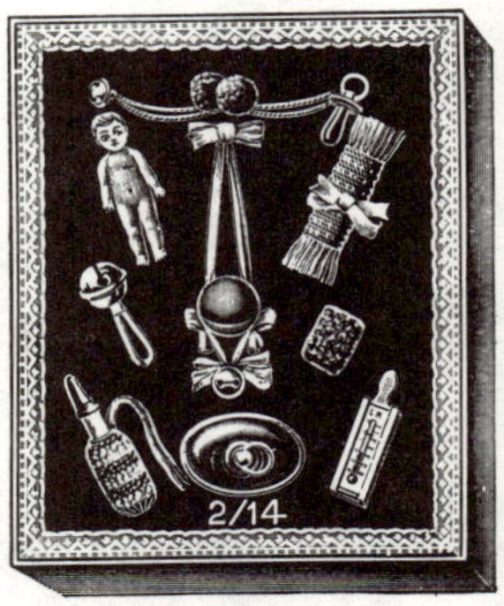

59/2/14

Bei Auftragserteilung ist die am Kopfe angeführte Kollektionsnummer **59** unbedingt vor die jeweilige Artikelnummer zu setzen.
When placing an order the coll. No. **59** specified at the head hereof should anyhow be stated before the No. of the individual article in question.
Dando la órden, es indispensable meter el no de colección No. **59** indicado arriba ante el número del respectivo artículo en questión.

Beachten Sie auch die Veröffentlichung auf Seite 62 und 206 des Hauptkataloges.

Lokomotive in feiner Ausführung, mit Pfeife. — Locomotive in fine finish, with whistle. — Locomotora finamente acabada, con silbato. — **134**/1059/1=24 cm, **134**/1059/2=33 cm, **134**/1059/3=37 cm.

134/1055 3 Lokomotive mit Uhrwerk. — Locomotive with clockwork. — Locomotora con mecanismo. — **134**/1055 4 dieselbe mit Pfeife. — The same with whistle. — La misma con silbato.

134/1057 1—6 Lokomotiven in allen Größen und Preislagen, mit Uhrwerk. — Locomotives of all sizes and prices, with clockwork. — Locomotoras de todos tamaños y precios, con mecanismo.

134/1056/1 Lokomotive mit Uhrwerk, 26 cm. — Locomotive with clockwork, 26 cm. — Locomotora con mecanismo, 26 cm. **134**/1056/2 dieselbe mit Glocke. — The same with bell. La misma con campanilla.

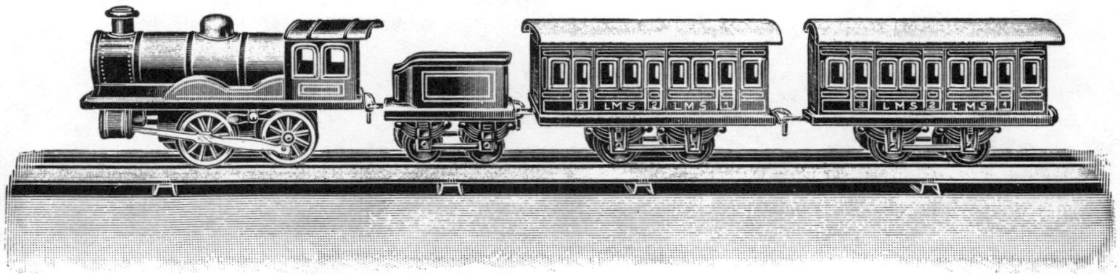

134/4065 2 Uhrwerk-Eisenbahn, Lokomotive mit Zylinderbewegung, Tender, 2 Wagen, vorwärtsfahrend, mit Bremse, Aufmachung in solidem Karton. — Clockwork-railway, locomotive with cylinder-movement, tender, 2 cars, moving forward, with brake, outfit in solid card-box. — Ferrocarril con mecanismo, locomotora con movimiento de los cilindros, tender, 2 coches, andando adelante, con freno, guarnecido en sólido cartón.

134/1051 Tanklokomotive, zeitweise stehenbleibend und nach Flaggenwechsel weiterfahrend. — Tank-locomotive, stopping from time to time, and going on after change of flag. — Locomotora con estanque, parando de vez en cuando, y procediendo después de haber cambiado la bandera.

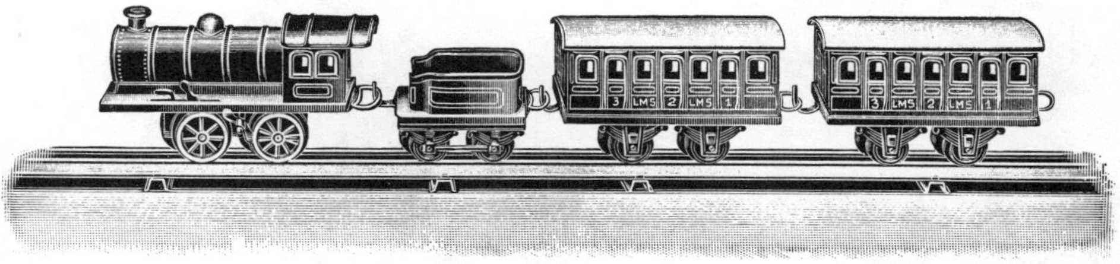

134/4045 2 Uhrwerk-Eisenbahn, Lokomotive mit Bremse, Tender, 2 Wagen, vorwärtsfahrend, in rotem Karton. — Clockwork-railway, locomotive with brake, tender, 2 cars, going forward, in red card-box. — Ferrocarril con mecanismo, locomotora con freno, tender, 2 coches, andando adelante, en cartón rojo.

134/200 L Tanklokomotive. — Tank-locomotive Locomotora con estanque.

134/4020/1 Uhrwerk-Eisenbahn, Lokomotive mit Bremse, Tender, 1 Wagen, 4 runde Schienen. — Clockwork-railway, locomotive with brake, tender, 1 car, 4 round rails. — Ferrocarril con mecanismo, locomotora con freno, tender, 1 coche, 4 railes redondos.

134/240 Kohlenwagen. — Coal-van. Carro de carbón.

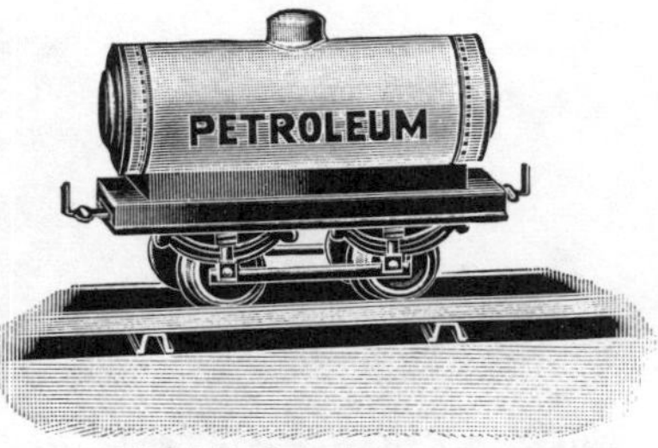

134/241 Petroleumwagen. Petroleum-car. — Carro de petróleo.

134/243 Gaswagen. Gas-car. — Carro para gas.

134/244 Kippwagen. dump-car. — Carro de vuelco.

134/245 Güterwagen. Goods-waggon. — Wagón de mercancías.

134/200/4 Güterzugbahn auf Schienen, neue Tanklokomotive. Feine Packung. Goods-train on rails, new tank-locomotive. Fine packing. Tren de mercancías sobre railes, nueva locomotora con estanque. Fino empaque.

Please note also the publication on page 50 of the principal catalogue.
Llamamos también su atención á la publicación en la página 50 del catálogo principal.

Blechspielwaren mit und ohne Uhrwerk. — Tin toys with and without clockwork. — Juguetes con y sin mecanismo.

2016/57 $9\times3^{1}/_{2}\times6$ cm

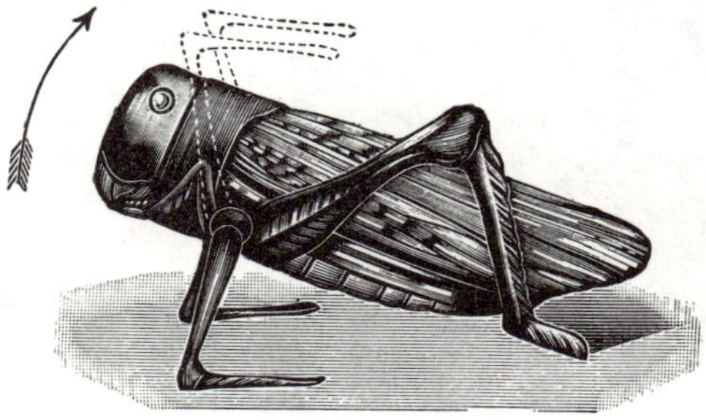

2016/55, $18{,}5\times10\times8{,}5$ cm, mit Uhrwerk
with clockwork / con mecanismo

2016/54 $27\times9^{1}/_{2}\times3$ cm

2016/58 $10\times6\times3$ cm
2016/58 W mit Uhrwerk
with clockwork / con mecanismo

2016/60 $20\times6^{1}/_{2}\times5$ cm

2016/61 $17\times3^{1}/_{2}\times2^{1}/_{2}$ cm

2016/59 $11\times5^{1}/_{2}\times5$ cm
2016/59 W mit Uhrwerk
with clockwork / con mecanismo

2016/56

2016/42

	Length of box Largura del cajita	Breadth of box Ancho del cajita
2016/42	43	20 cm
2016/56	29	12 cm
2016/62	34	24 cm

2016/62

2060/2

Ohne Werk Without clockwork Sin cuerda	Kartongröße Size of box Tamaño de cajita
2060/1	$24^{1}/_{2}\times7\times5$ cm
2060/2	$17^{1}/_{2}\times12\times5$ cm
2060/3	$22^{1}/_{2}\times12^{1}/_{2}\times5$ cm
2060/4	$18\times18\times5^{1}/_{2}$ cm
2060/5	$30\times8\times6$ cm
2060/6	$22^{1}/_{2}\times15\times6$ cm
2060/7	$28^{1}/_{2}\times15\times6$ cm
2060/8	$22^{1}/_{2}\times22^{1}/_{2}\times6$ cm

Mit Uhrwerk With clockwork Con cuerda	Kartongröße Size of box Tamaño de cajita
2060/5 W	$30\times8\times6$ cm
2060/6 W	$22^{1}/_{2}\times15\times6$ cm
2060/7 W	$28^{1}/_{2}\times15\times6$ cm
2060/8 W	$22^{1}/_{2}\times22^{1}/_{2}\times6$ cm

	Länge / Length Largura	Höhe / Height Altura
2060/9	26	13 cm
2060/10	38	20 cm
2060/11	38	8 cm

2060/9
2060/10

2060/8 **2060**/8 W

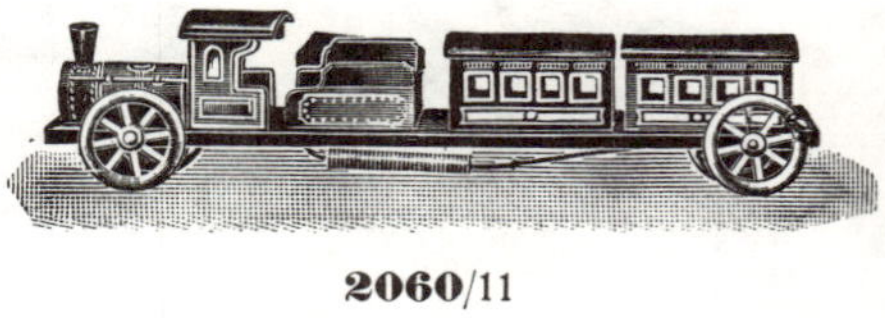

2060/11

Beachten Sie auch die Veröffentlichung auf Seite 50 des Hauptkataloges.

Füll-Artikel. — Filling articles. — Artículos de llenar.

105 × 38 × 59 mm.

100 × 28 × 51 mm.

100 × 48 × 52 mm.

86 × 34 × 50 mm.

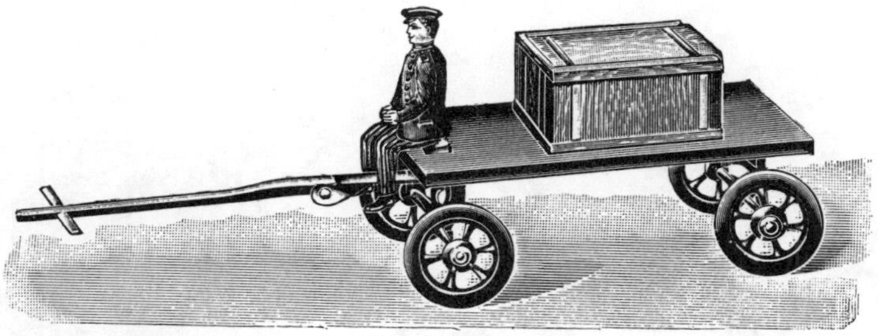

135 × 33 × 54 mm.

65 × 32 × 63 mm.

Sortiment / Assortment / Surtido **2035**/4

Packung / Packing / Contenido: 2 Dtz. / dozen / docena.

2049/3 Packung / Packing / Contenido: 1 Dtz. / dozen / docena.
Länge / Length / Largura 25 cm. Breite / Breadth / Anchura 5 cm.

2049/1
Packung / Packing / Contenido: $^1/_3$ Dtz. / dozen / docena.
Länge / Length / Largura 24 cm.
Breite / Breadth / Anchura 5 cm.

2007/24 9×9×4 cm.

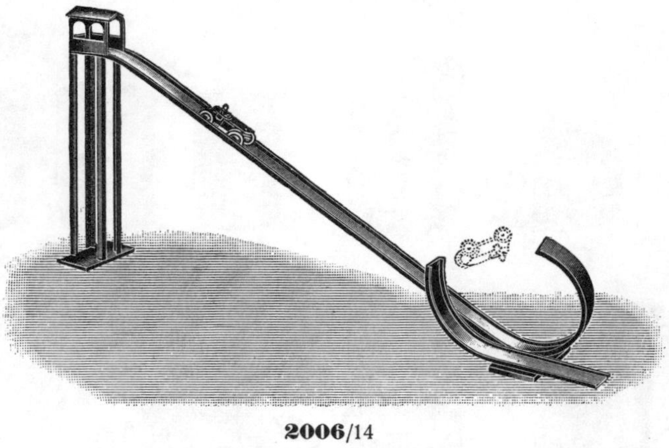

2006/14
$^1/_9$ natürlicher Größe.
$^1/_9$ of natural size.
$^1/_9$ del tamaño natural.
Länge / Length / Largura 72 cm.
Breite / Breadth / Anchura 9 cm.
Höhe / Height / Altura . . 31 cm.

2007/25 mit Uhrwerk / with clockwork / con mecanismo. 27×19×8$^1/_2$ cm.

Metallschlottern mit bunter oder Nickelkugel. — Metall-rattles with vary-coloured or nickel-ball.
Sonajeras de metal con bola variegada ó de niquel.

5/4 5/5 5/6 5/11/Ia 5/17 5/2 5/4/I 5/8 5/3 5/7 5/9 5/18

Weißblech.
Tinplate.
Hojalata.

Nickelschlotter.
Nickel-rattle.
Sonajera de niquel.

Echt versilbert oder vergoldet.
Genuine silver-plated or gold-plated.
Genuinamente plateado ò dorado.

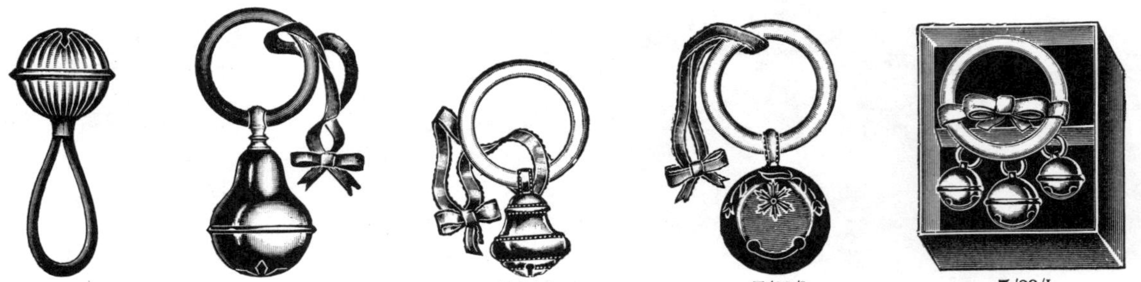

5/1 5/15 5/21/Ia 5/22/Ia 5/23/I

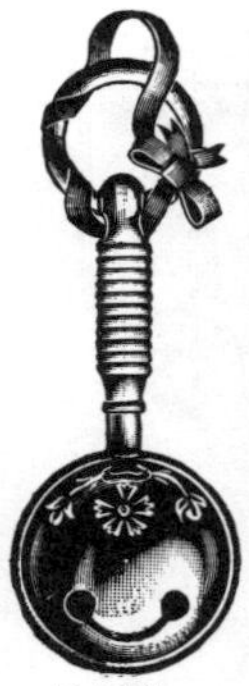

5/12/Ia

5/20/Ia

Vernickelt. — Nickeled. — Niquelado.

5/31 5/34 5/32

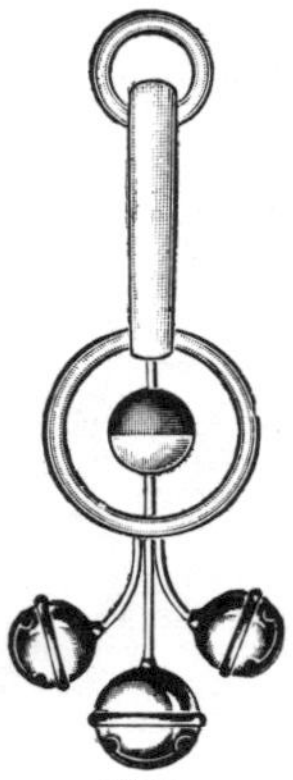

5/30

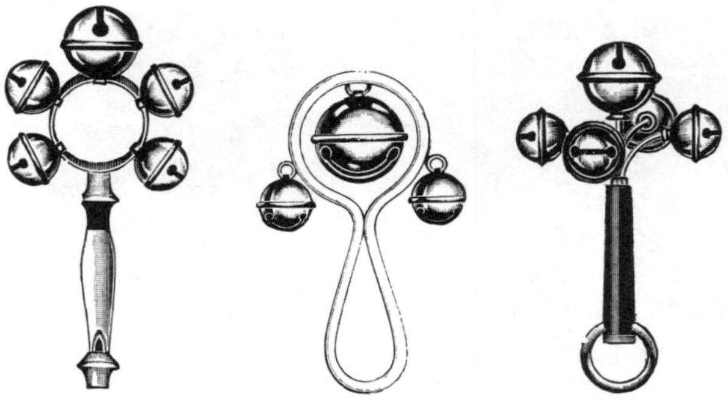

5/27 5/25 5/28

Nickelhupe.
Nickel horn.
Cuerno de niquel.

5/44

Zelluloid-Schlottern und Trompeten. — Celluloid-rattles and trumpets.
Sonajeras de celluloide y trompetas.

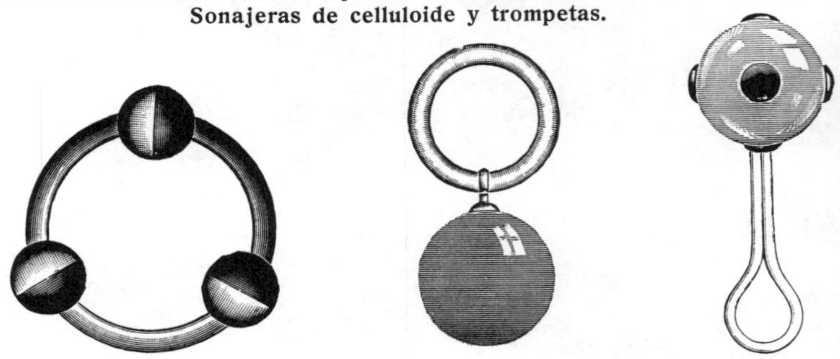

5/43 5/42 5/40

Satzbecher aus Nickel oder Aluminium. — Set-goblets of nickel or aluminium.
Copas en juego de niquel ó aluminio.

5/54 5/55

5/53

Kartendose mit Spielteller.
Card-box with playing-plate.
Caja para naipes con plato.

5/52

Sauger aus rotem oder transparentem Gummi.
Suckers of red or transparent rubber.
Chupadores de goma roja ó transparente.

Kindersauger.
Children's suckers.
Chupadores para niños.

5/49/25

Ringdurchmesser — Diameter of ring Diámetro del anillo	
5/49/25	25 mm
5/49/35	35 mm
5/49/45	45 mm

5/41 5/48 5/45

Die Ulla-Puppe

57/399/W21

57/520/26

57/464/26

57/406/W21

57/524/21

57/521/W21

57/522/23

57/187/9 57/248/9 57/417/9 57/418/9 57/423/9 57/424/9 57/425/9 57/482/9 57/484/9 57/485/9 57/514/9 57/515/9

57/193/11 57/196/11 57/214/11 57/216/11 57/231/11 57/237/11 57/297/11 57/382/11 57/383/11 57/426/11 57/429/11 57/483/11

57/348/12 57/415/12 57/444/12 57/446/12 57/453/12 57/458/12 57/490/12 57/491/12 57/492/12 57/493/12

57/362/15 57/371/15 57/385/15 57/386/15 57/422/15 57/436/15 57/437/15 57/455/15

57/382/19 57/415/19 57/444/19 57/502/19 57/511/19 57/513/19 57/514/19

57/362/21 57/372/21 57/404/21 57/409/21 57/440/21 57/441/21 57/446/21

57/449/21 57/459/21 57/499/21 57/500/21 57/505/21 57/509/21 57/525/21

57/389/23 57/461/23 57/462/23 57/498/23 57/511/26 57/519/26

Ormond-Puppen — Ormond-dolls — Muñecas Ormond

Celluloid-Puppen in Kunstseiden Pomponkleidung

Celluloid dolls in artificial silk pompon clothes — **Muñecas de celuloide** con vestidos de seda artificial

Pirouette: 156/1555 b — 156/1555 a — 156/1556 a — 156/1556 a — 156/1555 a

Porzellan-Puppen

Porcelain dolls

Muñecas de porcelana

156/1557 **Pipa** — 156/1558 **Pirola** — 156/1558 **Pirola** — 156/1558 **Pirola** — 156/1557 **Pipa**

Porzellan	**Celluloid**	**Porzellan**
Porcelain — Porcelana	Celluloid — Celuloide	Porcelain — Porcelana

156/1560 **Piasta** — 156/1561 **Pimonta** — 156/1559 **Pitty**

Musikball	**Musikdrehpuppe**	**Quietschpuppe**	**Stehauf** mit Celluloid-Puppe
Musical balls	Gyrating musical dolls	Squeaking dolls	Tumblers with doll
Pelota con música	Muñeca giratoria con música	Muñeca chillona	Dominguillo con muñeca de celuloide

156/1622 — 156/1662 — 156/1661 — 156/1621 — 156/1621

Spielpuppe	Wiegengehänge	Stabharlekin	Stehauf	Spielpuppe
Dolls	Dolls for cradles	Clown on stick	Tumblers	Dolls
Muñecas para jugar	Colgante para cunas	Arlequín con varilla	Dominguillo	Muñecas para jugar

156/1580 156/1665 156/1660 156/1620/II 156/1580 156/1280/II

Kasperle-Puppen mit handkunstgeschnitztem Holzkopf (Fortsetzung Tafel III)

Dolls for Punch and Judy shows with artistically hand carved heads (Continuation of page III)

Muñecas de títeres con cabeza de madera labrada a mano artísticamente (Continuación pág III)

156/1200 156/1201 156/1202 156/1205 156/1211 156/1209 156/1214

Bi-Ba-Bo-Puppen mit Maché-Kopf (zum Aufstreifen über die Hand)

Bi-Ba-Boo-Dolls with papier maché heads (for slipping over the hand)

Muñecas Bi-Ba-Bo con cabeza de pasta de maché (para ponerlo por encima de la mano)

156/1400 156/1401 156/1402 156/1403 156/1404 156/1405 156/1406 156/1407 156/1408 156/1409

Handarbeitskästen — Needle and thread cases — Cajas de labores de mano

156/1703 **(Vesta)** 156/1700 **(Simplex)** 156/1702 **(Optima)** 156/1703 **(Vesta)**

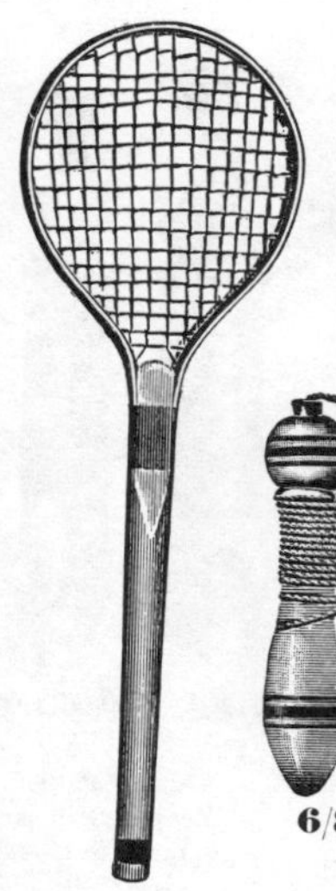

6/32/5

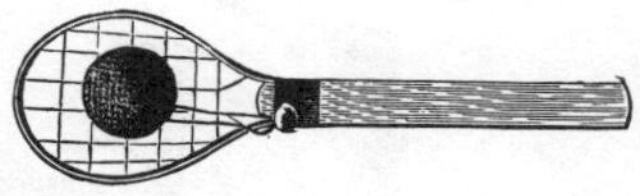

6/55/1

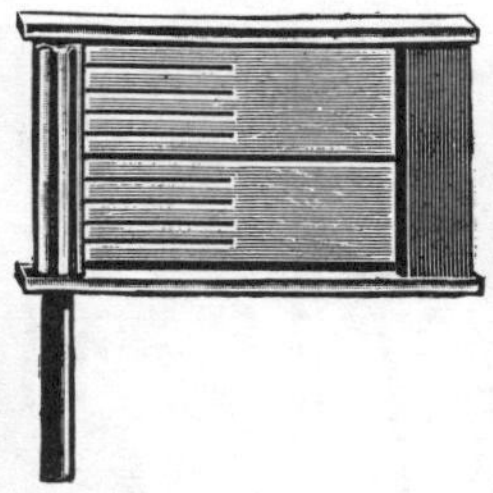

6/111/3

6/157/3

6/165/4

6/89/3

6/81/1

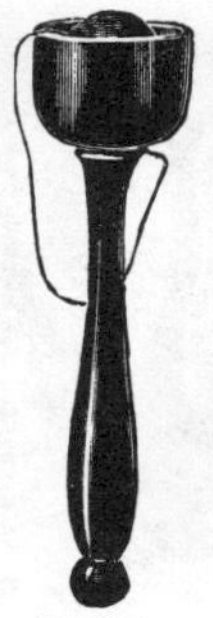

6/76/1

6/137½/2

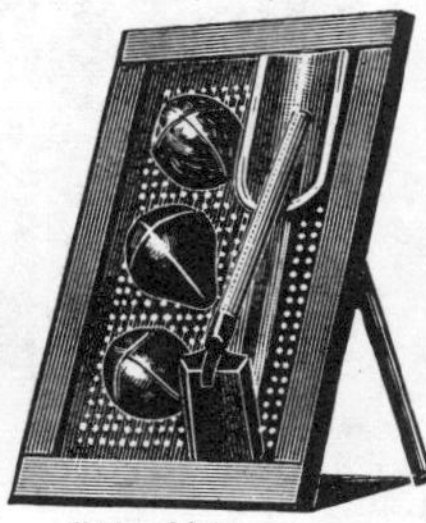

6/146¾/1

6/151/5

6/216/1

6/217/3

	Länge / Length Largura	
6/32/5	48	cm
6/32/7	49	„
6/32/8	56	„
6/55/1	29	„
6/55/2	29	„
6/55/3	31	„
6/55/4	34	„
6/55/5	37	„
6/55/6	40	„
6/76/½	15	„
6/76/1	19	„
6/76/2	25	„
6/81/1	20	„
6/81/2	23	„
6/81/3	26½	„
6/89/1	11½	„
6/89/2	14	„
6/89/3	14	„
6/111/½	15	„
6/111/1	18	„
6/111/3	18	„
6/111/3½	24	„
6/111/4	30	„

6/32/5 Rakette mit Blechrahmen, Hanfbindfadenbezug und rundem Stiel.
Rackets, metal rims, hemp strings and round handles.
Raquetas

6/55/1 Rakette mit Ball und Gummifaden.
Rackets with knitted ball and India rubber.
Raquetas, con pelota, con cordón de goma.

6/76/1 Fangbecher, rot gefärbt, mit Holzkugel.
Cup and ball, red stained.
Cubilete para coger la bola de madera.

6/81/1 Fangbecher, fein lackiert, mit farbigen Reifen.
Cup and ball, white varnished, with coloured rings.
Cubilete blanco, pintado de cercos, de color.

6/89/3 Sprungschnüre, 5 mm starke Hanfschnur von 2 m Länge.
Skipping ropes with turned hemp cord of 5 mm strength and 2 m length.
Cuerda para los volatines, largo 2 m, cuerda de cáñamo de diámetro 5 mm.

6/111/3 Bretter-Ratschen, Hartholz, mit einem Rad.
Wooden rattles, with one, strong wheel.
Matraca.

6/137½/2 Sandspiel-Garnituren, als Sandsieb mit Sandformen und Schaufel.
Sand-toy-set, tin basket, perforated, filled with moulds.
Surtido de moldes en canastillo de hojalata, entera barnizada al azul, con fondo como criba, moldes al colores naturales de madera y de hojalata.

6/146¾ Sandspielgarnituren.
Sand screens.
Juegos con arena.

6/151/5 Blechpferde, lackiert, Sattel gemalt.
Tin horses, varnished, saddel painted.
Caballos de hojalata.

6/157/3 Blechschaukelpferde.
Tin rocking-horses.
Caballos de hojalata sobre columpio de hojalata.

6/165/4 Leiterwagen mit Blechpferd.
Hay cart, red, with tin horse.
Carro de laderas con caballo de hojalata.

6/216/1 Champagnerflasche mit Drehdose.
Champagne bottles with music box.
Botellas champañas con organillos.

6/217/3 Harlekins mit Drehdose.
Clown with music box.
Arlequinos con organillos.

6/137½/0	Ø12½	cm
6/137/1	Ø16	„
6/137/2	Ø20	„

	Länge / Length Largura	
6/146¾/1	22	cm
6/146¾/2	26	„
6/146¾/3	30	„
6/151/1	10	„
6/151/3	12	„
6/151/4	15	„
6/151/5	16	„
6/151/6	21	„
6/157/3	13½	„
6/157/4	16	„
6/157/5	18	„
6/165/2	16½	„
6/165/3	19	„
6/165/4	19	„
6/165/5	21½	„
6/165/6	23	„
6/216/1	14	„
6/216/3	19	„
6/216/4	21	„
6/217/1	14½	„
6/217/3	17½	„
6/217/4	21	„

6/221/1

6/196/2

6/197/2

6/215FB/4/6

6/206½/3

6/206/6

6/221/3

6/186/5

	Länge / Length Largura		Töne Tones Tonos
6/186/1	17	cm	
6/186/2	20	„	
6/186/3	21	„	
6/186/4	21	„	
6/186/5	24	„	
6/196/1	Ø 5	cm	3
6/196/2	Ø 5	„	4
6/197/1	Ø 6½	„	4
6/197/2	Ø 6½	„	6
	Länge / Length Largura		
6/206½/3	9	cm	3
6/206/4	16	„	4
6/206/6	16	„	6
	Höhe / Height Altura		
6/215FB/1/6	5	cm	6
6/215FB/2/6	5½	„	6
6/215FB/3/6	6	„	6
6/215FB/4/6	7½	„	6
6/221/1	8½	„	4
6/221/2	8½	„	6
6/221/3	8½	„	6
6/221/4	8½	„	8
6/221/5	12	„	8
6/221/6	12	„	10
6/221/7	12	„	15
6/221/8	12	„	20

6/186/5 Musikwagen.
Musical vans.
Carro con música.

6/196/2 Drehdosen, rund, aus Blech.
Tin music boxes, round.
Organillos de hojalata.

6/197/2 Drehdosen, rund, aus Blech, mit Bild.
Tin music boxes, round, with pictures.
Organillo como el precedente.

6/206½/3 Hühnerställe mit pickendem Huhn, mit Drehdose.
Picking Chicken in cage with music box.

6/206/6 Hühnerställe, 2 pickende Hühner, mit Drehdose.
Picking Chicken, 2 birds, in cage with music box.

6/215FB/4/6 Drehdosen aus lackiertem Blech, mit beweglicher Figur.
Jack in music box.

6/221 Drehorgeln aus Pappe, ganz mit feinen Bildern bezogen.
Square music boxes of card board, with fine pictures.
Organillos con imágenes finos.

6/227/2

6/228/1

6/229/6

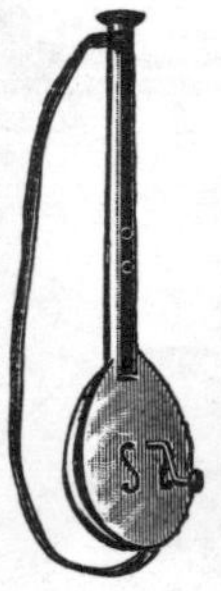

6/232/2

6/233/1

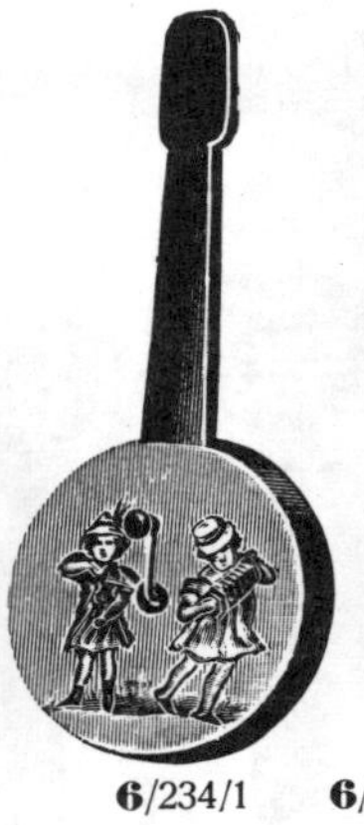

6/234/1

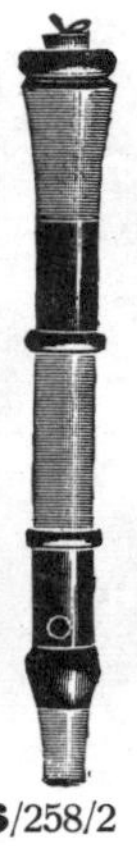

6/258/2

6/262/1

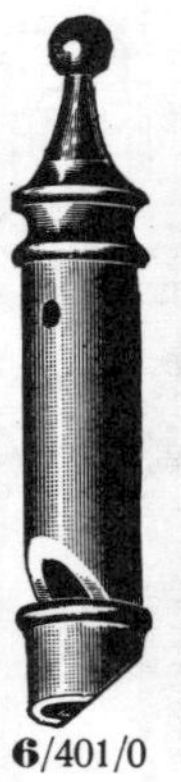

6/401/0

6/403/0

	Höhe Height Altura cm	Töne Tones Tonos
6/227/1	10	4
6/227/2	13	4
6/227/3	13	6
6/227/4	15	6
6/228/1	18	6
6/228/3	18	10
6/228/4	18	15
6/229/1	10	3
6/229/2	13	4
6/229/3	13	6
6/229/4	17	6
6/229/5	17	8
6/229/6	21	8
6/229/7	21	10
6/229/8	21	15
6/229/9	$32^{1}/_{2}$	15

	Länge Length Largura cm	Saiten Strings Cuerdas
6/232/1	18	3
6/232/2	$23^{1}/_{2}$	3
6/232/3	$23^{1}/_{2}$	4
6/233/1	25	4
6/233/2	$26^{1}/_{2}$	6
6/233/3	$36^{1}/_{2}$	10
6/233/4	50	15
6/234/1	24	4
6/234/2	38	6
6/234/3	38	10
6/234/4	45	15
6/258/$^{1}/_{2}$	24	1
6/258/$1^{1}/_{2}$	34	1
6/258/2	29	1
6/258/6	37	1
6/262/1	$19^{1}/_{2}$	—
6/262/2	24	—
6/262/3	29	—
6/262/4	34	—

6/227/2 Drehorgeln aus Pappe in Pianoform.
Pianos of card board with music box and picture.
Organillo forma de piano con imágen.

6/228/1 Drehorgeln aus Blech, mit Drehdose.
Tin piano varnished, with music box and picture.
Organillos, forma de piano, de hojalata, con imágen bello.

6/229/6 Kindertheater mit Drehdose, mit feinen Bildern bezogen und wechselnden Bildern.
Punch and Judy show, with music box and moving pictures.
Teatro con organillo con imágenes, á mudar durante la música.

6/232/2 Mandolinen, Nickel, mit Drehdose, Hals mit Trompete und Schnur.
Nickel Mandolins, neck with trumpet, body with music box.
Mandolina de hojalata con organillo, mango con clarin.

6/233/1 Gitarren mit Drehdose, Körper aus Pappe, rot lackiert, mit Lithographie und Holzhals.
Guitars of card board, varnished, with music box and lithograph picture.
Guitarras con organillos de carton, barnizadas, con imágen, mango de madera.

6/234/1 Banjos, gleiche Qualität wie **6**/233/1.
Banjos, same quality as **6**/233/1.
Banjos, misma cualidad como **6**/233/1.

6/258/2 Knallbüchsen in Flötenform, Mundstück mit Trompeten-Stimme, Selbstlader.
Pop guns, flute shape, with trumpet voice, selfloading.
Cerbatana, forma de flauta, con clarín.

6/262/1 Knallbüchsen, Selbstlader, Hammer mit rot poliertem Griff und schwarzem Kopf.
Pop guns, hammers, selfloading.
Cerbatana, forma de martillo.

6/267/0 Knallbüchsen, Selbstlader, mit gebogenem Griff.
6/267/6 Pop guns, selfloading, round handle.
Cerbatana.

6/270/5 Knallbüchsen, Selbstlader, blau, weiß und rot lackiert, mit Harmonikastimmen.
Musical pop guns, selfloading, blue, white and red varnished.
Cerbatanas, barnizadas al azul, blanco, rojo, con cintas de niquel y armónica.

6/329/$^{1}/_{3}$ Mandolinen mit Stahlsaiten bezogen, lackierter Blechkörper und Holzhals.
Mandolins with wire strings, tin body, varnished, wooden neck.
Mandolines de hojalata, mango de madera.

6/332/2/4 Mandolinen mit Pappkörper, fein lackiert.
Mandolin with card board body, fine painted.
Mandolinas de cartón, mango de madera, bueno acordadas.

6/333 NB/4 Gitarren, lackierter Pappkörper, Deckel mit Bild, Holzhals.
Guitars, with card board body, varnished, top with pictures.
Guitarras de cartón, mango de madera.

6/334/4 Banjos, lackierter Pappkörper, Deckel mit Bild, Holzhals.
Banjos with card board body, varnished, top with pictures.
Banjos de cartón, mango de madera.

6/336/2 Banjos, Körper aus Eisenblech, aus einem Stück gezogen, Holzhals, gelb und rot lackiert.
Banjos, same make as **6**/334/4, but tin body, drawn from one piece, red and yellow varnished.
Banjos de hojalata entera, barnizados rojos y amarillos, bueno acordados.

6/339/4 Zithern aus Eisenblech, mit Holzeinlagen, braun lackiert und Bild, mit Notenblatt.
Tin Zithers, with wooden frame inside, brown varnished and picture.
Citaras con cuerdas de acero, de hojalata, con tripas de madera, imágen en abertura de rezonadero, bueno acordadas, con libro de música.

6/341 B/8 Bilderzithern in Stückkartons.
Wooden Zithers with fine Tirolian picture, each in a box.
Citara como, precedente con bello imágen, cada una en cartón.

6/362/$^{1}/_{16}$ Blechviolinen, fein lackiert und gemalt wie richtige Violinen, mit Holzhals, Bogen mit Pferdehaaren, mit echten Darmsaiten und Kolophonium, in Stückkartons.
TinViolins, fine varnished and painted, stripped as good violins, wooden neck, bow with horse hair, cat-gut strings, rosin packed each in a box.
Violines de hojalata, bueno acordados, con mango de madera, arco con crines y colofonia, con verdaderas cuerdas de tripa, cada una en caja.

6/401/0 Trillerpfeife aus Holz, naturpoliert, mit bunten Reifen bemalt.
Wooden whistle, turned, white polished, with coloured rings.
Chifletes de gorjeo, de madera.

6/403/0 Kuckucksflöte, aus Holz, naturpoliert, mit bunten Reifen bemalt.
Cuckoo flute of wood, turned, white polished, with coloured rings.
Flautas con voz del cúculo, de madera, en color natural.

	Länge Length Largura cm	Saiten Strings Cuerdas
6/267/3/0	25	—
6/267/0	28	—
6/267/2	31	—
6/267/6	33	—
6/270/5	26	2
6/270/6	26	3
6/270/7	29	4
6/329/1/3	23	—
6/329/3/4	$23^{1}/_{2}$	—
6/329/4/4	33	—
6/332/2/4	33	—
6/332/4/6	38	—
6/332/5/8	46	—
6/333 NB/4	36	—
6/334/4	37	—
6/334/6	43	—
6/334/8	47	—
6/336/1	33	4
6/336/2	40	4
6/336/3	45	4
6/339/1	22	6
6/339/$2^{1}/_{2}$	22	8
6/339/3	28	8
6/339/4	28	10
6/339/5	31	12
6/341 B/8	28	—
6/341 B/10	32	—
6/341 B/12	34	—
6/341 B/15	39	—
6/352/$^{1}/_{20}$	24	—
6/352/$^{1}/_{16}$	$28^{1}/_{2}$	—
6/352/$^{1}/_{10}$	32	—
6/352/$^{1}/_{8}$	$36^{1}/_{2}$	—
6/352/$^{1}/_{4}$	$42^{1}/_{2}$	—
6/352/$^{1}/_{2}$	49	—
6/401/0	13	—
6/403/0	13	—

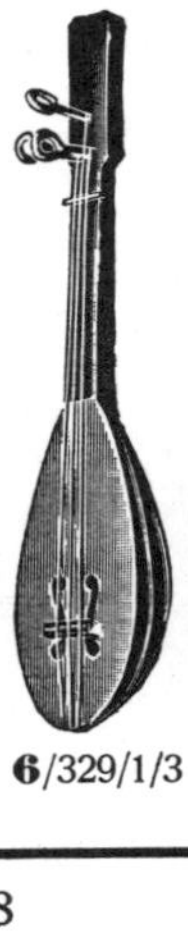

6/329/1/3

6/332/2/4

6/333NB/4

6/334/4

6/336/2

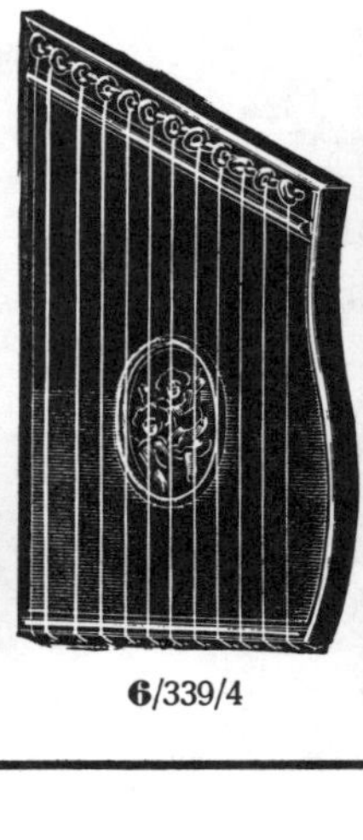

6/339/4

6/341 B/8

6/270/5

6/352/$^{1}/_{16}$

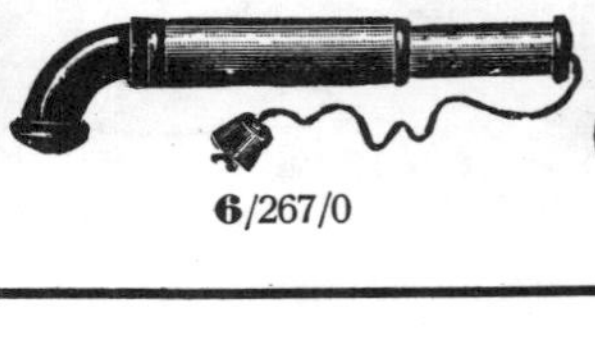

6/267/0

6/267/6

6/406/2

6/451/1

6/408/2

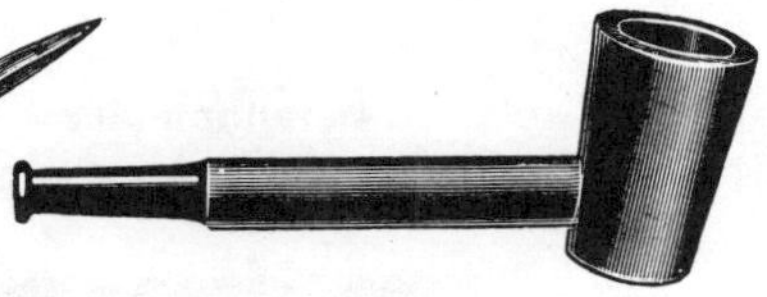

6/454/0

6/406/1

6/416/3

6/412/9

6/428$^{1}/_{2}$

6/503/1

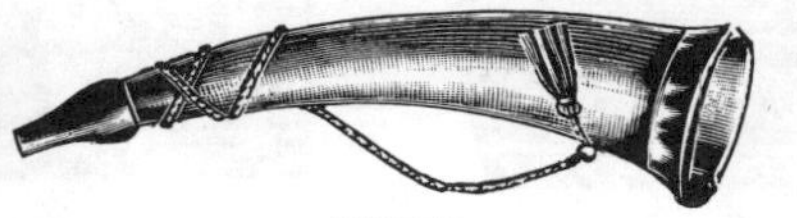

6/583/3

6/510/3

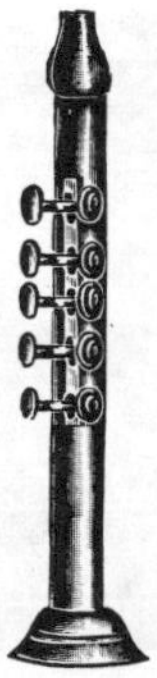

6/648/5

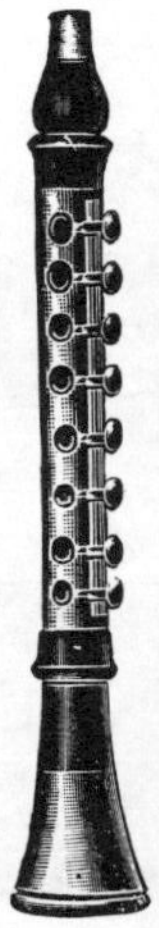

6/653$^{1}/_{2}$/8

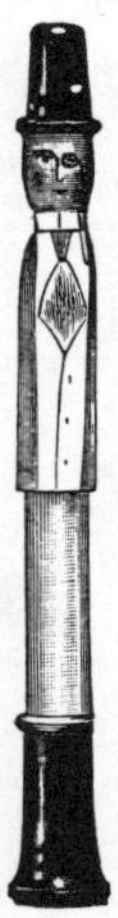

6/476/4

	Höhe / Height Altura (cm)	
6/406/1	14	
6/406/2	8	
	Länge / Length Largura (cm)	
6/408/2	17	
	Höhe / Height Altura (cm)	Töne Tones Tonos
6/412/1	14	3
6/412/2	14	4
6/412/3	14	6
6/412/4	16	4
6/412/5	16	6
6/412/6	18	6
6/412/7	18	8
6/412/8	18	10
6/412/9	18	14
6/412/10	21	14
6/416/0	6	—
6/416/1	8	—
6/416/2	11	—
6/416/3	12	—
6/428$^{1}/_{2}$	8	—
6/451/1	$8^{1}/_{2}$	—
6/451/5	11	—
	Länge / Length Largura (cm)	
6/454/0	9	
6/454/2	$13^{1}/_{2}$	
6/476/2/0	15	
6/476/0	18	
6/476/1	23	
6/476/2	26	
6/476/3	29	
6/476/4	36	
6/476/5	43	
6/503/1	10	
6/510/0	12	
6/510/1	13	
6/510/2	$14^{1}/_{2}$	
6/510/3	22	
6/583/1	16	
6/583/2	19	
6/583/3	24	
6/583/4	27	

	Länge / Length Largura (cm)
6/583/5	30
6/648/3	21
6/648/4	21
6/648/5	$23^{1}/_{2}$
6/648/6	27
6/653$^{1}/_{2}$/4	26
6/653$^{1}/_{2}$/5	28
6/653$^{1}/_{2}$/6	29
6/653$^{1}/_{2}$/8	37
6/660 B/8	
6/661/4	27
6/661/5	30
6/661/6	32
6/662 EB/8	42
6/664$^{1}/_{2}$/4	22
6/667 M/3	22
6/667 M/4	25
6/667 M/5	27
6/667 M/6	31
6/681/2	15
6/681/3	20
6/681/4	25
6/682/4	25
6/682/6	27
6/682/8	30
6/729$^{1}/_{2}$/3	$14^{1}/_{2}$
6/729$^{1}/_{2}$/4	17
6/729$^{1}/_{2}$/5	19
6/729$^{1}/_{2}$/6	21
6/729$^{1}/_{2}$/8	24
6/731/3	$20^{1}/_{2}$
6/731/4	23
6/731/5	26
6/738 TB/4	29
6/738 TB/6	34
6/738 TB/8	38
6/750$^{1}/_{2}$/3	20
6/750$^{1}/_{2}$/4	23
6/750$^{1}/_{2}$/5	28
6/750$^{1}/_{2}$/6	32
6/750$^{1}/_{2}$/8	38
6/783/4	$17 \times 8^{1}/_{2}$
6/783/6	$17 \times 8^{1}/_{2}$
6/783/8	$21 \times 11^{1}/_{2}$

6/406/1 Tin cock, painted, with cock crow. Gallos de hojalata, con voz de gallos.

6/406/2 Tin bird, painted, on green wooden stand, with trumpet voice. Pájaros de hojalata en colores naturales, con voz de clarin.

6/408/2 Bird on polished wooden branch, fine painted, with Cuckoo whistle. Pájaro sobre ramo de madera bruñida, con chiflete.

6/412/9 Bird in cage, movable, with music box.

6/416/3 Champagne bottle, red stained, labeled "Champagne", with trumpet voice. Botella de champaña con ton, barnizada negra.

6/428$^{1}/_{2}$ Wooden Teat, varnished, with trumpet voice. Chupadores de niños de madera con ton.

6/451/1 Musical wooden cigars, brown stained. Cigarros de madera con ton.

6/454/0 Musical pipes, red stained, with black mouth-piece. Pipas cortas para fumar, bruñidas rojas, con estrangul, negro, ton de clarin.

6/476/4 Wooden trumpets with painted figures, strong trumpet voice. Trompetas de madera con figuritas, ton sonoro.

6/503/1 Wooden trumpets, red stained, with handle. Trompetas de madera, con mango, bruñidas rojas.

6/510/3 Wooden posthorns, blue, white and red varnished, with trumpet voice. Cornetas de postillon, de madera, barnizadas, azul, blanca y roja, con ton de clarin.

6/583/3 Tin horns (imitation cow-horns), fine varnished, wooden mouth piece, double note and tassel.

6/648/5 Metal Clarionets, with blacked polished wooden mouth piece and spring keys of best quality.

6/653$^{1}/_{2}$/8 Wooden Clarionets, blue, white and red varnished, with spring keys. Clarinetas, barnizados, azul, blancos, rojos, lenguettas, de hojalata blanca.

6/661/5 Saxaphones of wood, silver bronzed, with good spring keys.

6/662 EB/8 Saxaphones of wood, silver bronzed, with nickel bell, with good spring keys, tuned in tremolo in fine red box.

6/664$^{1}/_{2}$/4 Wooden Saxaphones, black varnished, metal mouth piece.

6/667 M/3 Saxaphones, all brass.

6/681/2 Wooden cornets, fine white and red varnished, with tin keys. Clarin de madera, barnizado fino blanco y rojo, con lengüettas.

6/682/8 like **6**/681/2 — como **6**/681/2.

6/729$^{1}/_{2}$/8 Cornets a Piston in tin. Cornetas a Pistones de hojalata blanca.

6/731/4 Cornets a Piston, nickel. Cornetas a Pistones de lata de niquel.

6/738 TB/4 Cornets a Piston, brass, fine polished, tuned in tremolo.

6/750$^{1}/_{2}$/8 Nickel-Trombones. Sacabuches a tirar de lata de niquel.

6/781 A/3 Accordions for children, with patent bellow, 2 card board tops with fancy paper. Accordeones para niños, con papel de colores.

6/782 B/4 Accordions for children, with patent bellow, 2 wooden frames, with card board tops and fancy paper. Accordeones para niños, marco de madera.

6/783/8 Accordions for children, with patent bellow, 2 wooden frames, 2 card board tops with fancy paper. Accordeones para niños, 2 marcos de madera, 1 lengüetta de bajo.

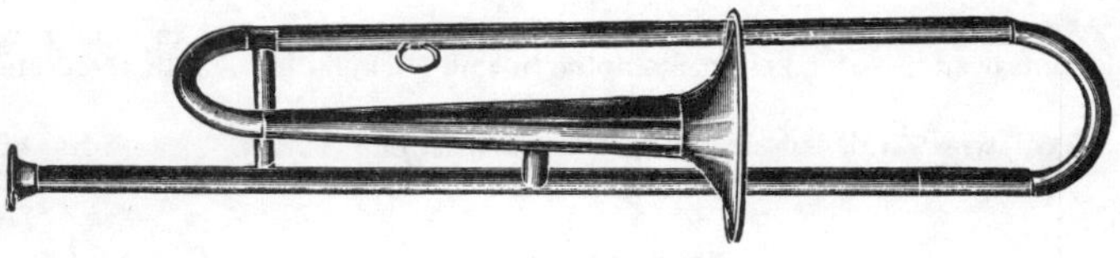

6/750$^{1}/_{2}$/8

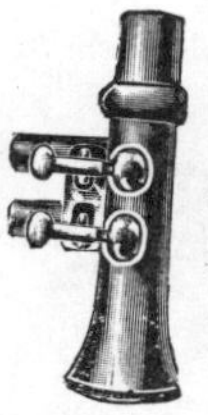

6/681/2

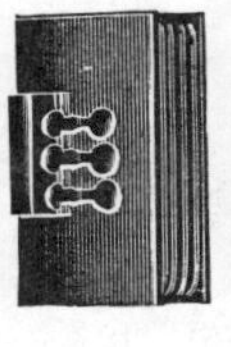

6/781 A/3
$11^{1}/_{2} \times 4^{1}/_{2}$ cm

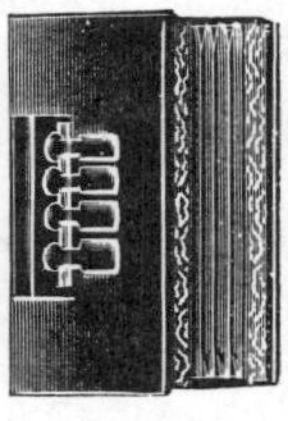

6/782 B/4
$14^{1}/_{2} \times 9^{1}/_{2}$ cm

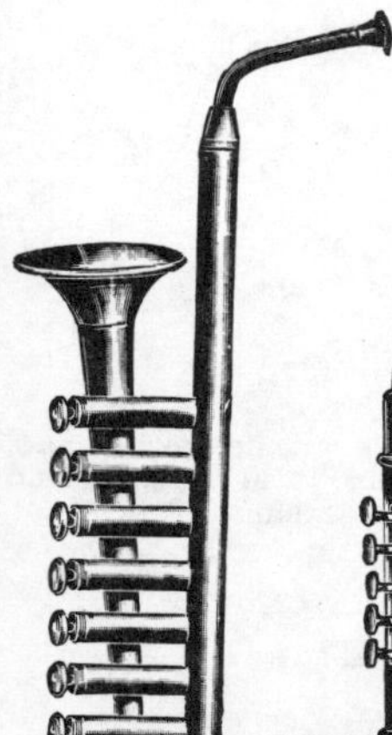

6/660 B/8

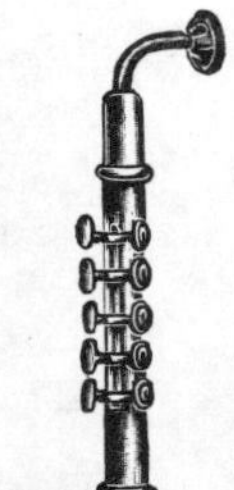

6/661/5

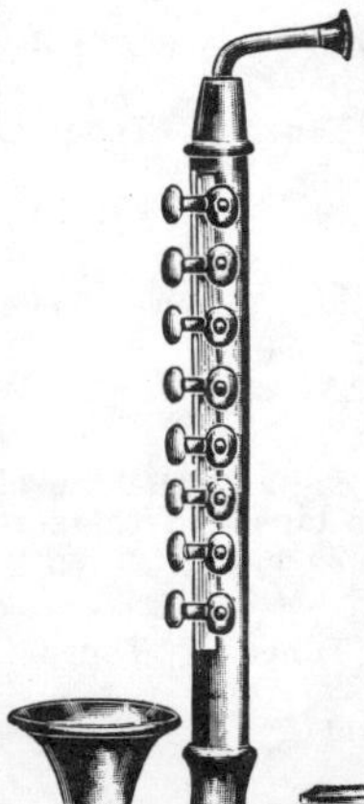

6/662 EB/8

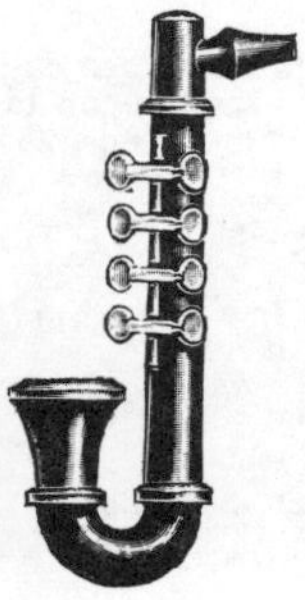

6/664$^{1}/_{2}$/4

6/667 M/3

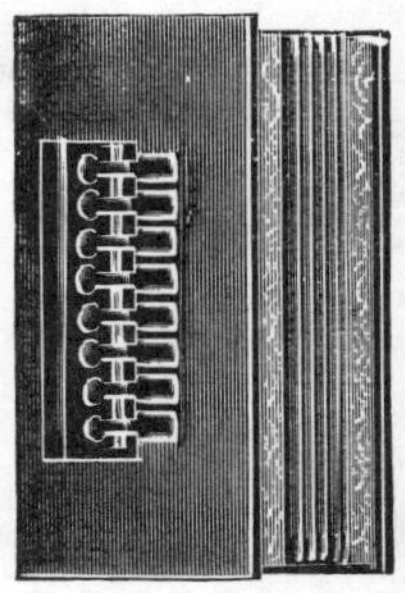

6/783/8

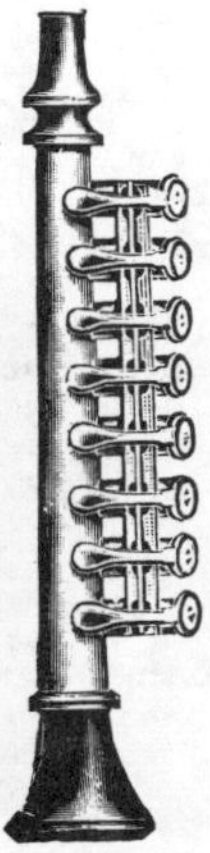

6/682/8

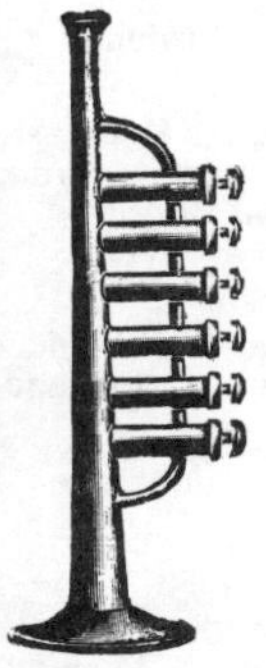

6/729$^{1}/_{2}$/8

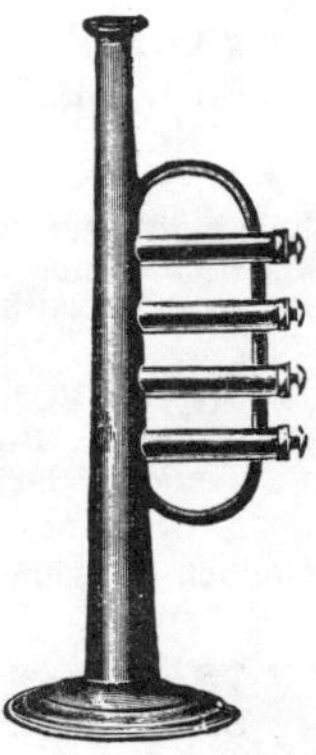

6/731/4

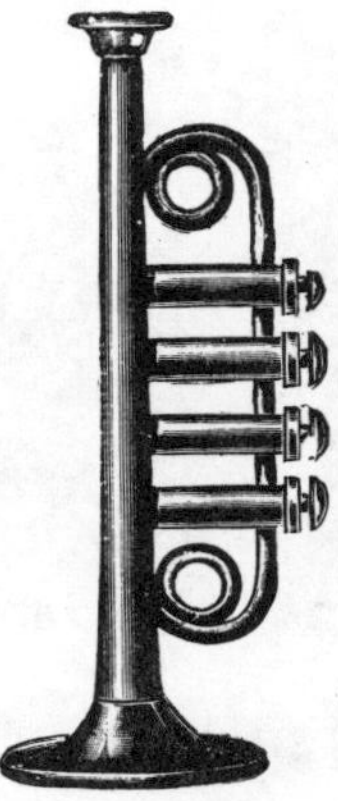

6/738 TB/4

Please note also the publication on page 157—159 of the principal catalogue.
Llamamos también su atención á la publicación en la página 157—159 del catálogo principal.

Metallophone. — Metallophones. — Metalófonos.

75/1

75/4 A

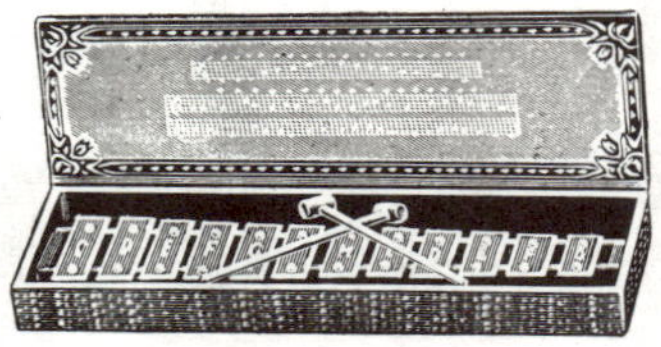

75/4 B

75/5

75/6

75/7

75/1 offen, auf 3 cm hohem lithogr. Holzsteg, mit 16 mm breiten bronzierten Stahlplatten.
open, on lithogr. wooden bridge 3 cm high, with bronzed steel-plates, 16 mm wide.
abierto, sobre puente de madera litogr. de 3 cm de alto, con placas de acero bronceadas de 16 mm de ancho.

75/2 wie **75**/1, aber auf 4 cm hohem lithogr. Holzsteg, mit 18 mm breiten bronzierten Stahlplatten.
same as **75**/1, but on lithogr. wooden bridge of 4 cm height, with bronzed steel-plates of 18 mm width.
como **75**/1, pero sobre puente de madera litogr. de 4 cm de alto, con placas de acero bronceadas de 18 mm de ancho.

75/4 A in 3,5 cm hohem lithogr. Holzkarton, mit 16 mm breiten bronzierten Stahlplatten.
in lithogr. wooden box of 3,5 cm height, with bronzed steel-plates of 16 mm width.
en cajita de madera litogr. de 3,5 cm de alto, con placas de acero bronceadas de 16 mm de ancho.

75/4 B in 3 cm hohem lithogr. Holzkarton mit Klappdeckel (Buchform), 19 mm breiten bronziert. Stahlplatten.
in lithogr. wooden box with raising-lid (book-shape), bronzed steel-plates of 19 mm width.
en cajita de madera litogr. con tapa de levantar (forma de libro), placas de acero bronceadas de 19 mm de ancho.

75/4 C in 3 cm hohem Glanzkarton, mit 16 mm breiten vernickelten Stahlplatten.
in lustre card-box of 3 cm height, with nickeled steel-plates of 16 mm width.
en cajitas de cartón de lustro de 3 cm de alto, con placas de acero niquelado de 16 mm de ancho.

75/4 D wie **75**/4 C, aber mit 20 mm breiten vernickelten Stahlplatten.
same as **75**/4 C, but with nickeled steel-plates of 20 mm width.
como **75**/4 C, pero con placas de acero niquelado de 20 mm de ancho.

75/4 A	-/8	-/10	-/12	-/14	-/15	-/16	-/18	-/20	-/22	Tönen / Tones / T onos
Breite / Breadth / Ancho	20,5	25	31	34	36,5	38,5	43	46,5	51	cm
Tiefe / Depth / Profundo	5,5	9,5	10,5	10,5	10,5	11	11	11	12,5	cm

75/4 B	-/8	-/10	-/12	-/14	-/15	-/16	-/18	-/20	Tönen / Tones / Tonos
Breite / Breadth / Ancho	26,5	30,5	34,5	38,5	40,5	43,5	48,5	52,5	cm
Tiefe / Depth / Profundo	10,5	11	11,5	12'5	12,5	13,5	13,5	14,5	cm

75/4 C	-/8	-/10	-/12	-/14	-/15	-/16	-/18	-/20	Tönen / Tones / Tonos
Breite / Breadth / Ancho	8,5	9	10,5	10,5	10,5	10,5	11,5	11,5	cm
Tiefe / Depth / Profundo	20	24	29,5	33,5	36	38,5	42,5	45,5	cm

75/4 D	-/8	-/10	-/12	-/14	-/15	-/16	-/18	-/20	Tönen / Tones / Tonos
Breite / Breadth / Ancho	22	28,5	33,5	36,5	38	40,5	44,5	47	cm
Tiefe / Depth / Profundo	9,5	10,5	10,5	10,5	10,5	10,5	11	11	cm

75/5 in 4 cm hohem lithogr. Holzkarton mit Haken, 24 mm breiten bronzierten Stahlplatten und Nickelstiften.
in lithogr. wood-box of 4 cm height with hook, with bronzed steel-plates of 24 mm width, and nickel-pins.
en cajita de madera litogr. de 4 cm de alto con gancho, con placas de acero bronceado de 24 mm de ancho y clavijas de niquel.

75/5 a wie **75**/5, jedoch mit ganzen und halben Tönen.
same as **75**/5, but with whole- and half-tones.
como **75**/5, pero con tonos enteros y medios.

75/5	-/8	-/10	-/12	-/14	-/15	-/16	-/18	-/20	Tönen / Tones / Tonos
Breite / Breadth / Ancho	27	33	37	41	44	46	53	57	cm
Tiefe / Depth / Profundo	11	12	13	13	13,5	14	15	15	cm

75/5 A	-/8 and/y 5	-/9 and/y 6	-/10 and/y 7	-/12 and/y 8	-/15 and/y 10	-/18 and/y 12	-/22 and/y 15	Tönen / Tones / Tonos
Breite / Breadth / Ancho	29	35	35	41	49	57	67	cm
Tiefe / Depth / Profundo	18	20	20	20	20	22,5	22,5	cm

75/6 in 4 cm hohem lithogr. Holzkasten mit Haken, 20 mm breiten vernickelten Stahlplatten und Nickelstiften.
in lithogr. wooden box of 4 cm height with hook, with nickeled steel-plates of 20 mm width, and nickel-pins.
en cajita de madera litogr. de 4 cm de alto con gancho, con placas de acero niquelado de 20 mm de ancho y clavijas de niquel.

75/6a wie **75**/6, jedoch mit ganzen und halben Tönen.
same as **75**/6, but with whole- and half-tones.
como **75**/6, pero con tonos enteros y medios.

75/6	-/8	-/10	-/12	-/14	-/15	-/16	-/18	-/20	Tönen / Tones / Tonos
Breite / Breadth / Ancho	27	33	37	41	44	46	53	57	cm
Tiefe / Depth / Profundo	11	12	13	13	13,5	14	15	15	cm

75/6 A	-/8 and/y 5	-/9 and/y 6	-/10 and/y 7	-/12 and/y 8	-/15 and/y 10	-/18 and/y 12	-/22 and/y 15	Tönen / Tones / Tonos
Breite / Breadth / Ancho	29	35	35	41	49	57	67	cm
Tiefe / Depth / Profundo	18	20	20	20	20	22,5	22,5	cm

75/7 in 6 cm hohem ff. lithographierten Holzkasten, mit Scharnierdeckel 23 mm breiten, vernickelten Stahlplatten und Nickelstiften.
in superfine lithogr. wooden case of 6 cm height with hinged lid, nickeled steel-plates of 23 mm width, and nickel-pins.
en cajita de madera, elegante litogr., de 4 cm de alto, con tapa con charneras, placas de acero niquelado de 23 mm de ancho, y clavijas de niquel.

75/7	-/8	-/10	-/12	-/14	-/15	-/16	-/18	-/20	Tönen / Tones / Tonos
Breite / Breadth / Ancho	33	33	44	49	51	53	57	64	cm
Tiefe / Depth / Profundo	12	13	14	14	15	15	15	16	cm

75/7a wie **75**/7, jedoch mit ganzen und halben Tönen.
same as **75**/7, but with whole- and half-tones.
como **75**/7, pero con tonos enteros y medios.

75/7 a	-/8 and/y 5	-/9 and/y 6	-/10 and/y 7	-/12 and/y 8	-/15 and/y 10	-/18 and/y 12	-/22 and/y 15	Tönen / Tones / Tonos
Breite / Breadth / Ancho	32	35	38	45	53	56,5	66	cm
Tiefe / Depth / Profundo	18	19	20	20	21	24	24	cm

Beachten Sie auch die Veröffentlichung auf Seite 157—159 des Hauptkataloges.

Please note also the publication on page 157—159 of the principal catalogue.
Llamamos también su atención á la publicación en la página 157—159 del catálogo principal.

75/171 **Flügel,** mit Nickelplatten, Tastenverdeck, weiß lackiert mit Gold abgesetzt.

Grand-piano, with nickel-plates, covered keys, white japanned set off with gold.

Piano de cola, con placas de niquel, teclado cubierto, embarnizado blanco con decoración de oro

mit — with — con	10,	12,	16 Tönen/Tones/Tonos.
Breite — Breadth — Ancho	30	34,5	44 cm
Höhe — Height — Altura	22,5	22,5	22,5 cm
Tiefe — Depth — Fondo	45,5	47	51 cm

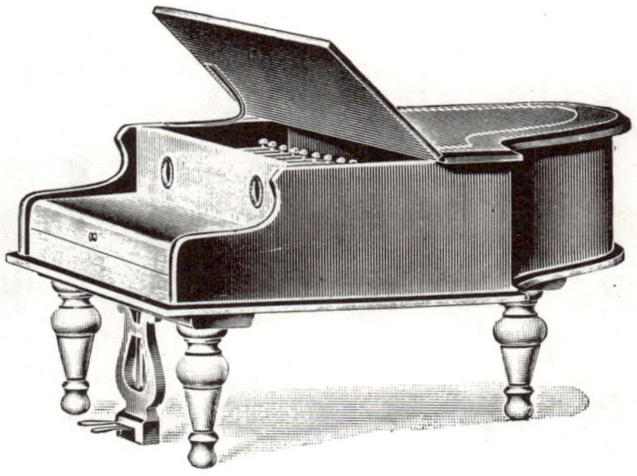

75/171

75/172 wie **75**/171, jedoch mit ganzen und halben Tönen.

same as **75**/171, but with whole- and half-tones.

como **75**/171, pero con tonos enteros y medios

mit — with — con	12 and y 8	16 and y 11	Tönen Tones Tonos.
Breite — Breadth — Ancho	36	45,5	cm
Höhe — Height — Altura	27	27	cm
Tiefe — Depth — Fondo	58	71	cm

75/182 **Zitherpiano,** aus Eiche

Zither-piano, of oak

Piano de cítara, de roble

75/182

mit — with — con	12,	16,	20 Tönen/Tones/Tonos
Breite — Breadth — Ancho	34,5	45	55 cm
Tiefe — Depth — Fondo	21,5	22,5	25 cm
Höhe — Height — Altura	36	40,5	57 cm

Drehorgeln. — Barrel-organs. — Realejos.

75/357

75/361

75/357 in bunter Lithographie, mit Schweizer Musikwerk, 1 lange Arie spielend mit 36 Stimmen. Breite 26,5 cm, Tiefe 14 cm, Höhe 14,5 cm.

in many-coloured litography, with Swiss musicwork, playing 1 long air with 36 notes. Width 26,5 cm, depth 14 cm, height 14,5 cm.

en litografía variegada, con caja de música suiza, tocando 1 aria larga con 36 tonos. Ancho 26,5 cm, fondo 14 cm, alto 14,5 cm.

75/359 aus Eichenholz, mit gleichem Musikwerk. Breite 29,5 cm, Tiefe 15,5 cm, Höhe 13 cm.

of oak-wood, with equal musicwork. Width 29,5 cm, depth 15,5 cm, height 13 cm.

de madera de roble, con igual caja de música. Ancho 29,5 cm, fondo 15,5 cm, alto 13 cm.

75/359

75/360 aus Eichenholz, mit gleichem Musikwerk, jedoch 2 lange Arien spielend. Breite 34 cm, Tiefe 17 cm, Höhe 18,5 cm.

of oak-wood, with equal musicwork, but playing 2 long airs. Width 34 cm, depth 17 cm, height 18,5 cm.

de madera de roble, igual caja de música, mas tocando 2 largas arias. Ancho 34 cm, fondo 17 cm, alto 18,5 cm.

75/372

75/361 Drehorgel in Pianoform, aus Eichenholz, mit Schweizer Musikwerk, 1 lange Arie spielend mit 36 Stimmen. Breite 21 cm, Tiefe 11,5 cm, Höhe 20 cm.

barrel-organ, piano-shaped, of oak-wood, with Swiss musicwork, playing 1 long air with 36 notes. Width 21 cm, depth 11,5 cm, height 20 cm.

Realejo, forma de piano, de madera de roble, con caja de música suiza, tocando 1 larga aria con 36 tonos. Ancho 21 cm, fondo 11,5 cm, alto 20 cm.

75/372 Drehorgel in Pianoform, aus Eichenholz, mit Schweizer Musikwerk und auswechselbaren Notenscheiben. Breite 24 cm, Tiefe 10,5 cm Höhe 25 cm.

barrel-organ, piano-shaped, of oak-wood, with Swiss musicwork and exchangeable note-plates. Width 24 cm, depth 10,5 cm, height 25 cm.

Realejo, forma de piano, de madera de roble, con caja de música suiza y placas de música cambiables. Ancho 24 cm, fondo 10,5 cm, alto 25 cm.

75/360

75/373 Drehorgel aus Eichenholz, mit Schweizer Musikwerk und auswechselbaren Notenscheiben. Breite 38 cm, Tiefe 17,5 cm, Höhe 22 cm.

barrel-organ of oak-wood, with Swiss musicwork and exchangeable note-plates. Width 38 cm, depth 17,5 cm, height 22 cm.

Realejo de madera de roble, con caja de música suiza y placas de música cambiables. Ancho 38 cm, fondo 17,5 cm, alto 22 cm.

75/373

Beachten Sie auch die Veröffentlichung auf Seite 157 159 des Hauptkataloges.

Please note also the publication on page 216 a — 216 d of the principal catalogue.
Llamamos también su atención á la publicación en la página 216 a — 216 d del catálogo principal.

ULLA BLEIBT ULLA

DIE ULLA-PUPPE ist das beliebte Spielkind jeder Puppenmutter.

DIE ULLA-PUPPE ist farbenfroh, geschmackvoll und eigenartig gekleidet; als Material sind teils seidene, teils kunstseidene Bänder verwandt.

DIE ULLA-PUPPE in 9 und 11 Zentimeter ist auf eine feine Porzellanpuppe mit Glasaugen, mit beweglichen Armen und Beinen, gekleidet.

DIE ULLA-PUPPE in 12, 15, 19, 21, 23 und 26 Zentimeter ist eine Ia. Steifgelenkpuppe mit feinem Porzellankopf, mit Schlafaugen und solider Mohairfrisur; Kopf, Arme und Beine sind beweglich.

DIE ULLA-PUPPE wird in 9 und 11 Zentimeter zu 6 Stück in weißem Spitzenkarton geliefert, alle anderen Größen in kunstgewerblichem Einzelkarton.

ULLA REMAINS ULLA

THE ULLA-DOLL is the favourite play-child of every doll's mother.

THE ULLA-DOLL is dressed in gay colours, tasteful and peculiar; as material partly silk ribbons, partly artificial silk ribbons have been used.

THE ULLA-DOLL of 9 and 11 centimetres is dressed on a fine porcelain-doll with glass-eyes, with movable arms and legs.

THE ULLA-DOLL of 12, 15, 19, 21, 23 and 26 centimetres is a first class stiff-jointed doll with fine porcelain-head, with eyes to be closed and solid mohair-wig; head, arms and legs are articulate.

THE ULLA-DOLL of 9 and 11 centimetres is packed by sixes in white lace-trimmed card-boxes, all other sizes singly in artistic card-boxes.

ULLA QUEDA ULLA

LA MUÑECA ‚ULLA' es la hija favorita de cada madrecita de muñecas.

LA MUÑECA ‚ULLA' está vestida de colores vivos, con gusto y con particularidad; como material se emplean por parte cintas de seda, por parte cintas de seda artificial.

LA MUÑECA ‚ULLA' de 9 y 11 centímetros está vestida sobre un cuerpo de porcelana fina con ojos de vidrio, con brazos y piernas movibles.

LA MUÑECA ‚ULLA' de 12, 15, 19, 21, 23 y 26 centímetros ès una muñeca de primera clase de articulación rígida con fina cabeza de porcelana, con ojos cerradizos y peinado sólido de mohair; cabeza, brazos y piernas son movibles.

LA MUÑECA ‚ULLA' de 9 y 11 centímetros está empaquetada por seis piezas en una cajita de cartón, guarnecida con encajes; todos los otros tamaños están una por una en una cajita artística de cartón.

*

Beachten Sie auch die Veröffentlichung auf Seite 216 a — 216 d des Hauptkataloges.

Tafel I. Table I. Tabla I.

Nr.	Deutsch	English	Español
	„Ormond"-Pirouette in Original-Kunstseiden-Pomponkleidung, beweglich. D. R. G. M. 881 387.	**"Ormond"-Pirouette in original tufty dress of artificial silk**, moveable. D. R. G. M. 881 387.	**Pirueta "Ormond", vestido original de seda artifical con pompones**, movible. D. R. G. M. 881 387.
156/1555a	Celluloid-Puppe, 11 cm, stehend. P=1 Dtz.	Celluloid-doll, 11 cm, standing. P=1 doz.	Muñeca de celuloid, 11 cm, de pié. P=1 doc.
156/1555b	Celluloid-Puppe, 11 cm, stehend. $P=\frac{1}{12}$ Dtz. Luxuskarton.	Celluloid-doll, 11 cm, standing. $P=\frac{1}{12}$ doz., fancy cardbox.	Muñeca de celuloid, 11 cm, de pié. $P=\frac{1}{12}$ doc., cajita de lujo.
156/1556a	Celluloid-Puppe, $9\frac{1}{2}$ cm, sitzend. P=1 Dtz.	Celluloid-doll, $9\frac{1}{2}$ cm, seated. P=1 doz.	Muñeca de celuloid, $9\frac{1}{2}$ cm, sentada. P=1 doc.
156/1556b	Celluloid-Puppe, $9\frac{1}{2}$ cm, sitzend. $P=\frac{1}{12}$ Dtz. Luxuskarton.	Celluloid-doll, $9\frac{1}{2}$ cm, seated. $P=\frac{1}{12}$ doz., fancy cardbox.	Muñeca de celuloid, $9\frac{1}{2}$ cm, sentada. $P=\frac{1}{12}$ doc., cajita de lujo.
156/1556a/II	Celluloid-Puppe, $9\frac{1}{2}$ cm, sitzend. P=1 Dtz. (Keine Abbildung.)	Celluloid-doll, $9\frac{1}{2}$ cm, seated. P=1 doz. (no picture).	Muñeca de celuloid, $9\frac{1}{2}$ cm, sentada. P=1 doc. (sin dibujo).
156/1557a	„Pipa" Porzellan-Puppe, $10\frac{1}{2}$ cm, stehend, $P=\frac{1}{2}$ Dtz.	"Pipa" porcelain-doll, $10\frac{1}{2}$ cm, standing. $P=\frac{1}{2}$ dz.	„Pipa", muñeca de porcelana, $10\frac{1}{2}$ cm, de pié. $P=\frac{1}{2}$ doc.
156/1557b	„Pipa" Porzellan-Puppe, $10\frac{1}{2}$ cm, stehend. $P=\frac{1}{12}$ Dtz., Luxuskarton.	"Pipa" porcelain-doll, 10¹/ cm, standing. $P=\frac{1}{12}$ dz., fancy cardbox.	„Pipa", muñeca de porcelana, $10\frac{1}{2}$ cm, de pié. $P=\frac{1}{12}$ doc., cajita de lujo.
156/1558a	„Pirola" Porzellan-Puppe, 14 cm, sitzend und stehend. $P=\frac{1}{2}$ Dtz.	"Pirola" porcelain-doll, 14 cm, seated and standing. $P=\frac{1}{2}$ doz.	„Pirola", muñeca de porcelana, 14 cm, de pié y sentada. $P=\frac{1}{2}$ doc.
156/1558b	„Pirola" Porzellan-Puppe, 14 cm, sitzend und stehend. $P=\frac{1}{12}$ Dtz., Luxuskarton.	"Pirola" porcelain-doll, 14 cm, seated and standing. $P=\frac{1}{12}$ doz., fancy cardbox.	„Pirola", muñeca de porcelana, 14 cm, de pié y sentada. $P=\frac{1}{12}$ doc., cajita de lujo.
156/1558a/II	„Pirola" Porzellan-Puppe, 12 cm, sitzend und stehend. $P=\frac{1}{2}$ Dtz. (Keine Abbildung.)	"Pirola" porcelain-doll, 12 cm, seated and standing. $P=\frac{1}{2}$ doz. (no picture).	„Pirola", muñeca de porcelana, 12 cm, de pié y sentada. $P=\frac{1}{2}$ doc. (sin dibujo).
156/1558b/II	„Pirola" Porzellan-Puppe, 12 cm, sitzend und stehend. $P=\frac{1}{12}$ Dtz., Luxuskart. (Keine Abb.)	"Pirola" porcelain-doll, 12 cm, seated and standing. $P=\frac{1}{12}$ doz., fancy cardbox (no picture).	„Pirola", muñeca de porcelana, 12 cm, de pié y sentada. $P=\frac{1}{12}$ doc., cajita de lujo (sin dibujo).
156/1559	„Pitty" Porzellan-Puppe in kunstseidener Häkelkleidung, $8\frac{1}{2}$ cm, stehend. $P=\frac{1}{2}$ Dtz.	"Pitty" porcelain-doll in crochet artificial silk-dress, $8\frac{1}{2}$ cm, standing. $P=\frac{1}{2}$ doz.	„Pitty", muñeca de porcelana, vestido de seda artificial en crochet, $8\frac{1}{2}$ cm, de pié. $P=\frac{1}{2}$ doc.
156/1560	„Piasta" Porzellan-Puppe mit kunstseidenem Pomponkopfputz, 11 cm, stehend. $P=\frac{1}{4}$ Dtz.	"Piasta" porcelain-doll with tufty head-dress of artificial silk, 11 cm, standing. $P=\frac{1}{4}$ doz.	„Piasta", muñeca de porcelana, adorno de cabeza de seda artificial con pompom, 11 cm, de pié. $P=\frac{1}{4}$ doc.
156/1561	„Pimonta" Celluloid-Puppe, 12 cm, sitzend. $P=\frac{1}{2}$ Dtz.	"Pimonta" celluloid-doll, 12 cm, seated. $P=\frac{1}{2}$ doz.	„Pimonta", muñeca de celuloid, 12 cm, sentada. $P=\frac{1}{2}$ doc.
156/1622	Musikball mit Seidenband, Wollball, mit Schweizer Musikwerk, zum Drücken, „1 Arie", 12 cm Ø. $P=\frac{1}{12}$ Dtz.	Musical balls with silk-riband, wool-ball, with Swiss music-work for pressing down, "1 air", 12 cm Ø. $P=\frac{1}{12}$ doz.	Pelota con música, con cinta de seda, pelota de lana, con mecanismo de música suizo a empujar, „1 ária", 12 cm ø. $P=\frac{1}{12}$ doc.
156/1662	Schwenkpuppe in prima Wollkleidung, mit Celluloid-Kopf, 35 cm, und Schweizer Musikwerk, „1 Arie", $P=\frac{1}{4}$ Dtz.	Swinging doll in 1st class wool dress with celluloid head, 35 cm, and Swiss music-work, „1 air", $P=\frac{1}{4}$ doz.	Muñeca de voltear, vestida de lana de Iª clase, con cabeza de celuloid, 35 cm, y mecanismo de música suizo, „1 ária". $P=\frac{1}{4}$ doc.
156/1661	Stabharlekin m. Stimme, Porzellankopf, 30 cm. $P=\frac{1}{2}$ Dtz.	Stick-harlequin with voice, porcelain-head, 30 cm. $P=\frac{1}{2}$ doz.	Arlequin sobre palo, con voz, cabeza de porcelana, 30 cm. $P=\frac{1}{2}$ doc.
156/1621	Stehauf-Figur mit bunter Wolle umhäkelt und Celluloid-Baby, garniert, hochfeine Ausführung, 16 cm. $P=\frac{1}{2}$ Dtz.	Rise-up figure, crocheted round with colored wood, and celluloid baby, trimmed, extra-fine finish, 16 cm. $P=\frac{1}{2}$ doz.	Dominguillo vestido de crochet de lana multicolor, y bebé guarnecido, ejecución muy fina, 16 cm. $P=\frac{1}{2}$ doc.

Tafel II. Table II. Tabla II.

Nr.	Deutsch	English	Español
156/1580	Harlekin, weichgestopft, Celluloid-Kopf, 38 cm. $P=\frac{1}{3}$ Dtz.	Harlequin, soft stuffed, celluloid-head, 38 cm. $P=\frac{1}{3}$ dz.	Arlequin, estopado fofo, cabeza de celuloid, 38 cm. $P=\frac{1}{3}$ doc.
156/1665	Wiegengehänge mit Seidenband, Filzkleid und Celluloid-Kopf, 28 cm. $P=\frac{1}{2}$ Dtz.	Elastic-suspension with silk riband, felt-dress and celluloid head, 28 cm. $P=\frac{1}{2}$ dz.	Colgadura elástica, con cinta de seda, vestido de fieltro y cabeza de celuloid, 28 cm. $P=\frac{1}{2}$ doc.
156/1660	Stabharlekin, weichgestopft, Celluloid-Kopf, Glockenbehang, 38 cm. $P=\frac{1}{3}$ Dtz.	Stick-harlequin, soft stuffed, celluloid-head, bell-trimmed, 38 cm. $P=\frac{1}{3}$ dz.	Arlequin sobre palo, estopado fofo, cabeza de celuloid, guarnecido de campanillas, 38 cm. $P=\frac{1}{3}$ doc.
156/1620/I	Stehauf-Figur in Filzkleid, Celluloid-Kopf, 13 cm. P=1 Dtz.	Rise-up figure in felt-dress, celluloid head, 13 cm. P=1 dz.	Dominguillo, vestido de fieltro, cabeza de celuloid, 13 cm. P=1 doc.
156/1620/II	Stehauf-Figur in Filzkleid, Celluloid-Kopf, 17 cm. P=1 Dtz.	Rise-up figure in felt-dress, celluloid head, 17 cm. P=1 dz.	Dominguillo, vestido de fieltro, cabeza de celuloid, 17 cm. P=1 doc.
	Kasperle-Theater zusammenlegbar, mit auswechselbaren Kulissen.	**Punch- and Judy-Theater, pliable, with interchangeable scenes.**	**Teatro de polichinelo, plegable, con bastidores cambiables.**
156/1280/I	In Pappe, bunt bemalt, 90×60 cm. (Keine Abbildung.)	Of cardboard, gaily painted, 90×60 cm. (No picture.)	De pasta, pintado variegado, 90×60 cm (sin dibujo).
156/1280/II	115×70 cm.	115×70 cm.	115× 70 cm
156/1280/III	140×80 cm. (Keine Abbildung.)	140×80 cm. (No picture.)	140× 80 cm (sin dibujo).
156/1280/IV	170×100 cm. (Keine Abbildung.)	170×100 cm. (No picture.)	170×100 cm (sin dibujo).
	Kasperle-Puppen aus buntem Filz, mit Schuhen, Stoffhänden und -beinen.	**Punch and Judy Puppets of colored felt, with shoes, cloth-hands and -legs.**	**Muñecos para teatro de polichinelo de fieltro variegado, con piés, manos de paño y piernas de idem.**
	Kopf: handkunstgeschnitzt Holz, schwer.	Head: artistically carved in wood, heavy.	Cabeza: artisticamente esculpida en madera, pesado.
156/1200	Kasper	Punch	Polichinelo
156/1201	Polizist	Policeman	Policía
156/1202	Teufel	Devil	Diablo
156/1205	Hexe	Witch	Bruja
156/1209	Junger Mann	Young man	Joven
156/1211	Räuber	Robber	Salteador
156/1214	Gerichtsherr	Judge	Juez
	(alle) 42 cm.	(all) 42 cm	(todos) 42 cm.
	Fortsetzung von Tafel III.	Continued from Table III	Continuado de tabla III.
	Bi—Ba—Bo-Puppen.	**Bi—Ba—Bo-Dolls.**	**Muñecos Bi—Ba—Bo.**
	Bewegliche Filzpuppen zum Aufstreifen über die Hand, ohne Beine, farbige Filzbekleidung.	moveable felt-dolls for pulling over the hand, without legs, colored felt-dress.	Muñecos de fieltro, movibles, para ser tirados sobre la mano, sin piernas, vestido variegado de fieltro.
	Kopf: Maché, mittelschwer.	Head: Maché, medium weight.	Cabeza: papel maché, peso medio.
156/1400	Max	Max	Max
156/1401	Moritz	Moritz	Moritz
156/1402	Münchner Kindl	Munich Kindl	Munich kindl
156/1403	Schielerjunge	Squinting boy	Niño bizco
156/1404	Schielermädchen	Squinting girl	Niña bizca
156/1405	Bajazzo	Jester	Gracioso
156/1406	Tiroler	Tyrolese	Tirolés
156/1407	Mops	Pug-dog	Perrillo
156/1408	Harlekin	Harlequin	Arlequin
156/1409	Bauer	Clown.	Bufón
	(alle) 21 cm.	(all) 21 cm	(todos) 21 cm.

Tafel III. Table III. Tabla III.

Beschäftigungsarbeiten „Ormond", Handarbeitskasten nach Fröbelart.

156/1700	„Simplex", Stern- und Blattstickerei.	P=$^1/_{12}$ Dtz.
156/1701	„Media", lustige Tier- u. Groteskfiguren. (Keine Abbildung.)	P=$^1/_{12}$ Dtz.
156/1702	„Optima", praktische Geschenkartikel.	P=$^1/_{12}$ Dtz.
156/1703	„Vesta", Puppenschneiderei.	P=$^1/_{12}$ Dtz.
156/1704	„Trousseau", Puppenausstattung. (Keine Abbildung.)	P = $^1/_{12}$ Dtz.

Kasperle-Puppen aus buntem Filz, mit Schuhen, Stoffhänden und -beinen.

Kopf aus Holz, handkunstgeschnitzt, schwer.

156/1203	Handelsmann	42 cm.
156/1204	Tod	
156/1206	Junge Frau	
156/1207	Mädchen	
156/1208	Alter Mann	
156/1210	Studio	
156/1212	König	
156/1213	Königin	
156/1215	Max	
156/1216	Moritz	
156/1217	Vagabund	
156/1218	Großmutter	
156/1219	Mohr	(Keine Abbildung.)
156/1220	Clown	(Keine Abbildung.)

Kopf aus Holz, maschinell hergestellt, mittelschwer.

156/1150	Kasper	Größe I=30 cm. Größe II=36 cm. Größe III=42 cm.
156/1151	Polizist	
156/1152	Teufel	
156/1153	Handelsmann	
156/1154	Tod	
156/1155	Alte Frau	
156/1156	Junge Frau	
156/1157	Mädchen	
156/1158	Alter Mann	
156/1159	Junger Mann	
156/1160	Studio	
156/1161	Junge	
156/1162	König	
156/1163	Königin	
156/1164	Pastor	
156/1165	Mohr	
156/1166	Räuber	
156/1167	Tünnes	

156/1195/I	Ungeheuer (Krokodil), 32 cm. (Keine Abbildung.)
156/1195/II	Ungeheuer (Krokodil), 39 cm.
156/1195/III	Ungeheuer (Krokodil), 44 cm. (Keine Abbildung.)

Kopf aus Papp-Präparat, leicht.

156/1100	Kasper	30 cm.
156/1101	Polizist	
156/1102	Teufel	
156/1103	Handelsmann	
156/1104	Tod	
156/1105	Alte Frau	
156/1106	Mädchen	
156/1107	Junge	
156/1108	Mohr	
156/1109	Clown	
156/1110	Max	
156/1111	Moritz	
156/1112	Affe	
156/1113	Harlekin	

Bi—Ba—Bo-Puppen.

Bewegliche Filzpuppen zum Aufstreifen über die Hand, ohne Beine, unzerbrechlich, farbige Filzbekleidung.

Kopf aus Papp-Präparat, leicht.

156/1300	Clown	21 cm.
156/1301	Mädchen	
156/1302	Max	
156/1303	Moritz	
156/1304	Mohr	
156/1305	Teufel	
156/1306	Tod	
156/1307	Harlekin	
156/1308	Kasper	
156/1309	Polizist	
156/1310	Handelsmann	
156/1311	Alte Frau	
156/1312	Affe	
156/1313	Baby	

156/1295	Kasperle-Textbücher. (Keine Abbildung.)	
156/1298/I	Galgen, Säbel, Pritsche, 28 cm.	(Keine Abbildung.)
156/1298/II	32 cm.	
156/1298/III	36 cm.	

Pastime Plays "Ormond", working-box after Froebel's manner.

"Simplex", embroidering of stars and leaves. P=$^1/_{12}$ doz.

"Media", jolly animals'- and grotesque-figures. P=$^1/_{12}$ doz. (no picture).

"Optima", practical present-articles. P=$^1/_{12}$ doz.

"Vesta", dolls' tailoring. P=$^1/_{12}$ doz.

"Trousseau", dolls' dowry. P=$^1/_{12}$ doz. (no picture).

Punch and Judy Puppets of colored felt, with shoes, cloth-hands and -legs,

head carved artistically in wood, heavy.

Tradesman	42 cm.
Death	
Young woman	
Girl	
Old man	
Student	
King	
Queen	
Max	
Moritz	
Loafer	
Grandam	
Moor	(No picture.)
Harlequin	(No picture.)

Head of wood, mechanical make, medium weight.

Punch	Size I=30 cm. Size II=36 cm. Size III=42 cm.
Policeman	
Devil	
Tradesman	
Death	
Old woman	
Young woman	
Lass	
Old man	
Young man	
Student	
Boy	
King	
Queen	
Parson	
Moor	
Robber	
Buffoon	

Monster (crocodile), 32 cm (no picture).
Monster (crocodile), 39 cm.
Monster (crocodile), 44 cm (no picture).

Head of paste-preparation, light.

Punch	30 cm.
Policeman	
Devil	
Tradesman	
Death	
Old woman	
Lass	
Boy	
Moor	
Buffoon	
Max	
Moritz	
Monkey	
Harlequin	

Bi—Ba—Bo-Dolls.

Moveable felt-dolls for pulling over the hand, without legs, unbreakable, colored felt-dress.

Head of paste preparation, light.

Buffoon	21 cm.
Lass	
Max	
Moritz	
Moor	
Devil	
Death	
Harlequin	
Punch	
Policeman	
Tradesman	
Old woman	
Monkey	
Baby	

Punch text-books (no picture).

Gallows, sabre, club, 28 cm.	(No picture.)
32 cm.	
36 cm.	

Juegos de pasatiempo „Ormond", cajitas de ocupación según Froebel.

„Simplex", para bordar estrellas y hojas. P=$^1/_{12}$ doc.

„Media", alegres figuras de animales y grotescos. P=$^1/_{12}$ doc. (sin dibujo).

„Optima", artículos prácticos para presentes. P=$^1/_{12}$ doc.

„Vesta", modista de muñecas. P=$^1/_{12}$ doc.

„Trousseau", dotación de muñeca. P=$^1/_{12}$ doc. (sin dibujo).

Muñecos para teatro de polichinelo de fieltro variegado, con sapatos, manos y piernas de paño

cabeza artisticamente esculpida en madera, pesado.

Mercader	42 cm.
Muerte	
Mujer vieja	
Muchacha	
Anciano	
Estudiante	
Rey	
Reina	
Max	
Moritz	
Vagabundo	
Abuela	
Moro	(Sin dibujo.)
Arlequin	(Sin dibujo.)

Cabeza de madera, hechos mecánicamente, peso mediano.

Polichinelo	tamaño I=30 cm. tamaño II=36 cm. tamaño III=42 cm.
Policía	
Diablo	
Mercader	
Muerte	
Mujer vieja	
Mujer nueva	
Muchacha	
Hombre viejo	
Mozo	
Estudiante	
Muchacho	
Rey	
Reina	
Padre	
Moro	
Salteador	
Bufón	

Mónstruo (cocodrilo), 32 cm (sin dibujo).
Mónstruo (cocodrilo), 39 cm.
Mónstruo (cocodrilo), 44 cm (sin dibujo).

Cabeza de preparado de pasta, ligero.

Polichinelo	30 cm.
Policía	
Diablo	
Mercader	
Muerte	
Mujer vieja	
Muchacha	
Muchacho	
Moro	
Bufón	
Max	
Moritz	
Mono	
Arlequin	

Muñecos Bi—Ba—Bo.

Muñecos de fieltro, movibles, para tirar sobre la mano, sin piernas, inquebrantables, vestido de fieltro variegado.

Cabeza de preparado de pasta, ligero.

Bufón	21 cm.
Muchacha	
Max	
Moritz	
Moro	
Diablo	
Muerte	
Arlequin	
Polichinelo	
Policía	
Mercader	
Mujer vieja	
Mono	
Bebé	

Libretos para teatro de polichinelo (sin dibujo).

Horca, sable, espadón, 28 cm.	(Sin dibujo.)
32 cm.	
36 cm.	

Kinderservice aus Steingut. — Children's set of crockery — Servicio para niños, de loza.

106/1 31×27×7,4 cm

106/2 31×27×7,4 cm

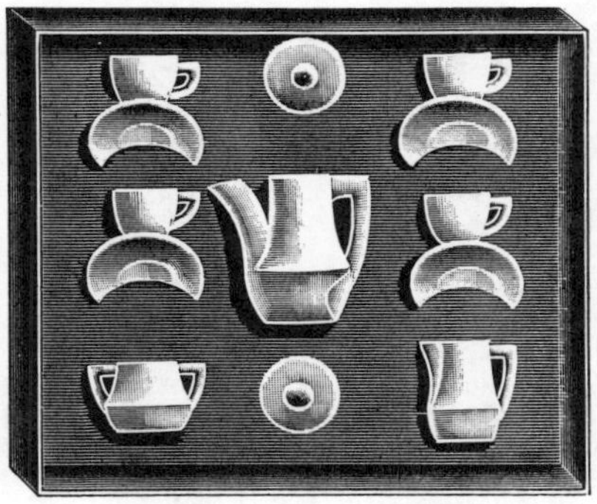

106/3/4 31×27×6,5 cm

106/3/6 31×27×6,5 cm

106/4 31×27×7,4 cm

106/5 31×27×6,5 cm

106/6 31×27×7,4 cm

106/7 31×27×6,5 cm

106/8 31×27×6,5 cm

106/9 21,5×19×6,5 cm

106/10 21,5×19×6,5 cm

106/11 21,5×19×6,5 cm

106/1 **106**/2 **106**/3/4 **106**/3/6 **106**/4 **106**/5
106/6 **106**/7 **106**/8 **106**/9 **106**/10 **106**/11 } braun glasiert / brown glazed / vidriado bruno.

106/1 C **106**/2 C usw., türkisblaulicht / turquoise light-blue / turquesa azul claro.

D rosa / pink / rosa.
H grün / green / verde.
L hellgelb / light yellow / amarillo claro.
O erbsengrün / pea-green / verde-guisante.
E lichtblau / light blue / azul claro.
J gelb feurig / yellow-fiery / armarillo fogoso.
M türkisblaugrün feurig / turquoise-blue-green fiery / turquesa-azul verde fogoso.
P rot / red / encarnado.

Please note also the publication on page 118 of the principal catalogue.
Llamamos también su atención á la publicación en la página 118 del catálogo principal.

69/648 P=1 dtz.
Länge/Length/Largura
12 cm

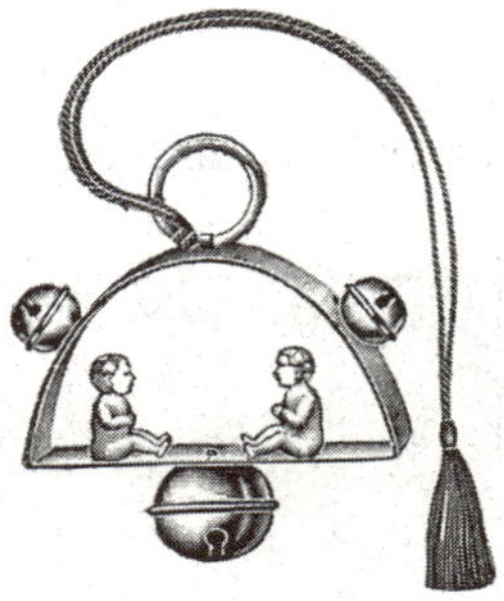

69/650 P=1 dtz.
Länge/Length/Largura
11 cm

648 Gehänge, Zelluloidpuppe auf Schaukel, 1 große Messingglocke, 4 kl. vermess. Glocken m. Quasten.
Elastic hanging, celluloid-doll on swing, 1 big brass-bell, 4 small brass-plated bells with tassels.
Colgadura elástica, muñeca de celuloide sobre columpio, 1 campana de latón, 4 campanillas de latón chapeado con borlas.

650 Gehänge, 2 schaukelnde Zelluloidpuppen, 1 große Messingglocke, 2 kl. vermess. Glocken m. Quasten.
Elastic hanging, 2 rocking celluloid-dolls, 1 big brass-bell, 2 small brass-plated bells with tassels.
Colgadura elástica, 2 muñecas de celuloide columpiándose, 1 campana de latón, 2 campanillas de latón chapeado con borlas.

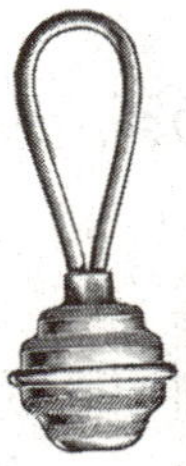

69/962
Länge
Length
Largura
10 cm

69/710
Höhe
Height
Altura
8 cm

69/302
Breite
Breadth
Anchura
5 cm

962 Aluminiumschlotter mit lackiertem Rohrstiel.
Aluminium-rattle with lacquered cane-handle.
Sonajera de aluminio con mango de caña barnizado.

710 Tischglocke, Stahlblech vernickelt, schwarz lack. Holzgriff.
Dinner-bell, steel-plate nickeled, black lacquered wooden handle.
Campanilla de mesa, lata de acero niquelada, mango de madera barnizado negro.

711 Wie 710, in Weißblechausführung.
Same as 710, but of tinplate.
Como 710, pero de hojalata blanca.

302 Taschenkino, sortierte Bilder.
Pocket-cinema, assorted pictures.
Cinema de bolsillo, dibujos surtidos.

69/1000
5 cm

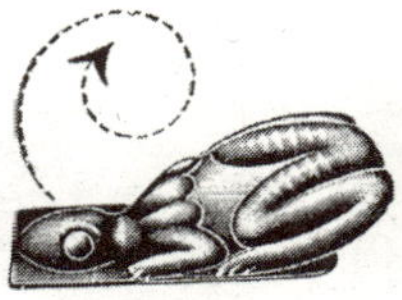

69/301
Länge
Length
Largura
$4^1/_2$ cm
P=1 Grs.

69/101
Länge
Length
Largura
18 cm
P=1 Grs.

1000 Holzpfeife, bunt lackiert.
Wooden whistle, lacquered many-coloured.
Silbato de madera, barnizado variegado.

301 „Cri-Cri"-Frosch, hüpfend, aus dekoriertem Schwarzblech.
"Cri Cri"-frog, leaping, of decorated black plate.
Rana "Cri Cri" saltando, de hojalata negra decorada.

101 Kinder-Uhrenarmband aus Zelluloid.
Childrens' watch-bracelet of celluloid.
Brazalete de reloj para niños, de celuloide.

69/200 Weißblech. Tinplate. Hojalata.
69/215 Stahlblech vernickelt. Steelplate nickeled. Lata de acero niquelada.
69/220 Vermessingt. Brass-plated. Latón chapeado.
69/225 Rein Messing. Pure brass. Latón puro.

Weißblech	**69**/200/5	-/4	-/3	-/2	-/1	-/0
Stahlblech, vern.	**69**/215/5	-/4	-/3	-/2	-/1	-/0
Vermessingt	**69**/220/5	-/4	-/3	-/2	-/1	-/0
Rein Messing	**69**/225/5	-/4	-/3	-/2	-/1	-/0

Die Schellen werden mit eingestanzter Patentöse geliefert. Sämtliche Schellen können auch auf Wunsch mit Zacken zum Umbiegen oder mit Loch zum Befestigen mit Ösen zum gleichen Preis geliefert werden.
The bells are supplied with stamped patent eyes. All bells can also be had, on desire, with tooths for bending or with hole for fastening with eyelets, at same price.
Las campanillas son suministradas con ojetes patente estampados. Todas campanillas pueden tambien ser suministradas con dientes para doblar ó con agujero para la sujeción con ojetes, al mismo precio.

Peitschen-Sortimente.
Whip Assortments.
Azotamientos en surtidos.

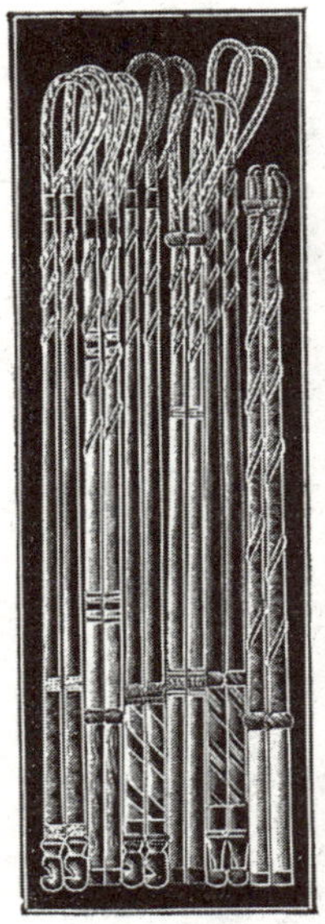

Sortiment **2026**/97
Assortment **2026**/97
Surtido **2026**/97
Länge/Length/Largura
65—75 cm

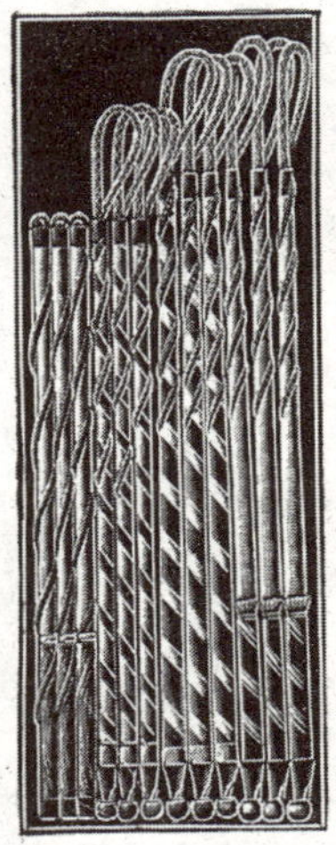

Sortiment **2026**/96
Assortment **2026**/96
Surtido **2026**/96
Länge/Length/Largura
50—65 cm

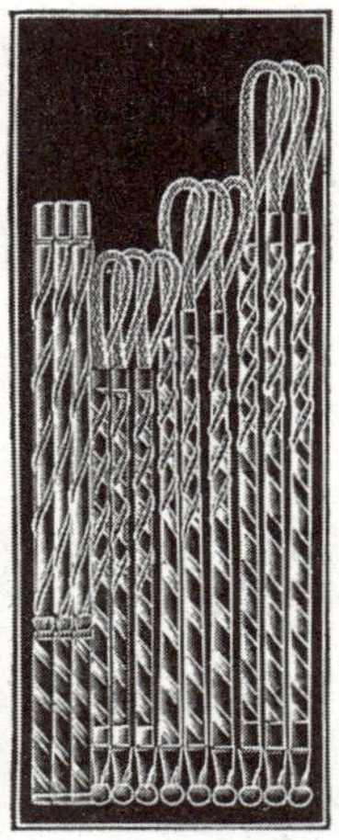

Sortiment **2026**/95
Assortment **2026**/95
Surtido **2026**/95
Länge/Length/Largura
45—60 cm

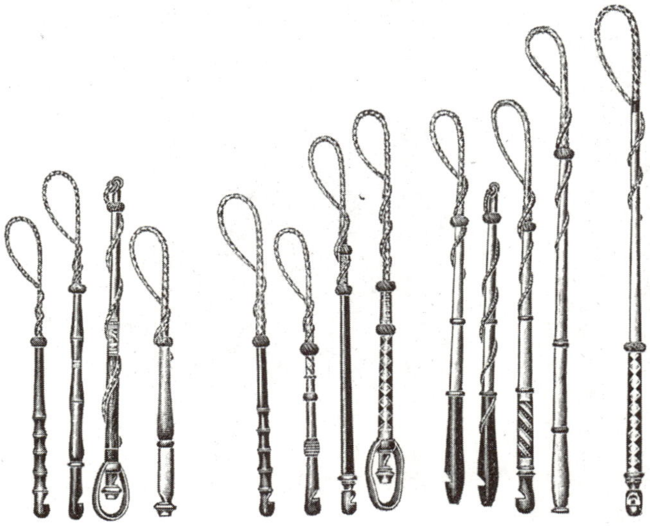

2026/26 48 „
2026/28 55 „
2026/98 50 „
2026/99 45 cm
2026/100 50 „
2026/101 45 „
2026/102 60 „
2026/103 60 cm
2026/104 60 „
2026/35 48 „
2026/36 60 „
2026/105 70 cm
2026/50 80 cm

Schmetterlingsnetze.
One who catches butterflies. — Red para coger insectos aéreos y acuáticos.

	Gesamtlänge Total Length Toda Largura	Netzdurchmesser Diameter of the net Diámetro de la Red
2031/1	120 cm	14 cm
2031/2	122 „	16 „
2031/3	128 „	16 „
2031/4	130 „	18 „
2031/5	136 „	20 „
2031/6	136 „	20 „
2031/7	140 „	22 „

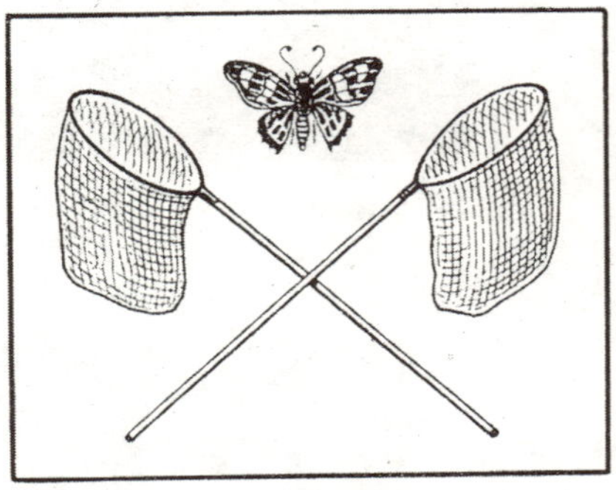

2031/1

500/3127

Billige Babys und Puppen.
Cheap Babies and dolls.
Bebés y muñecas barátos.

500/3127 25—60 cm.
500/701 18—50 cm.

500/701

Beachten Sie auch die Veröffentlichung auf Seite 118 des Hauptkataloges.

Stoff-Zügel. — Stuff-bridle. — Brida de tecido.

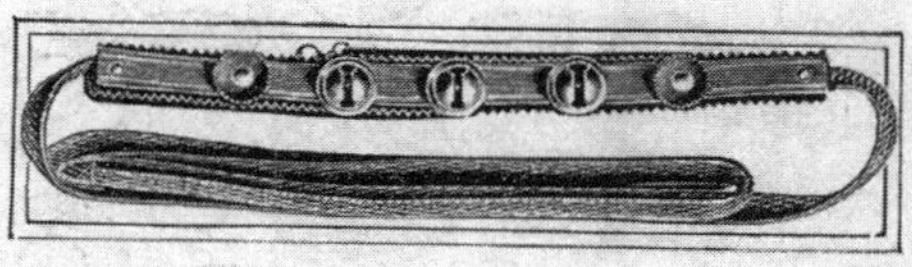

2043/1

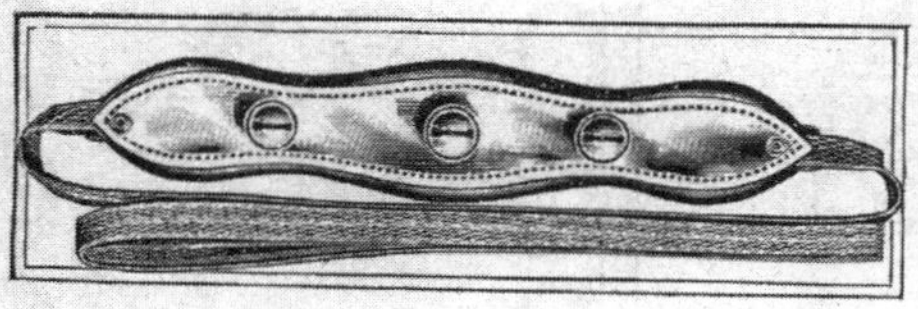

2043/14

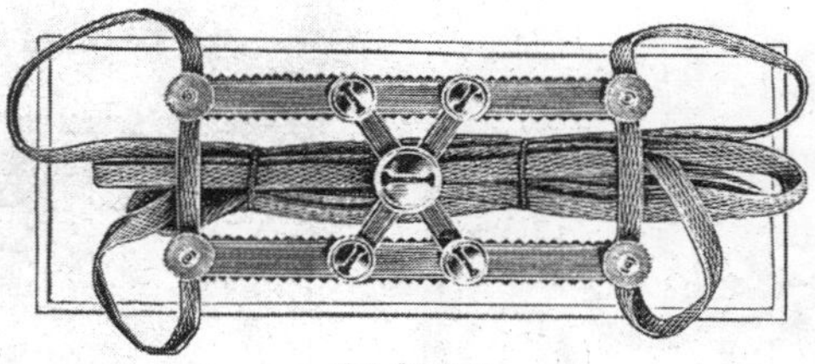

2043/15

Leder-Zügel. — Leather-bridle. — Brida de cuero.

2043/16

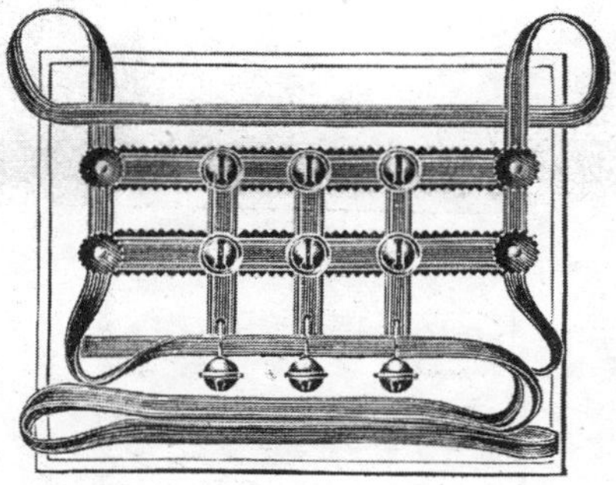

2043/18

Arm-Zügel.
Arm-bridle.
Brida de brazo.

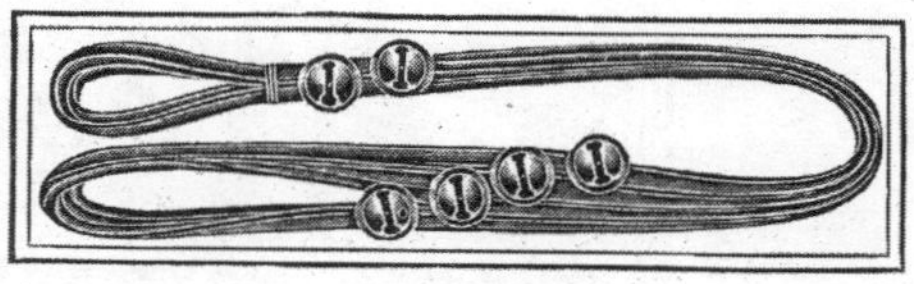

2043/19

2043/17

Schaffner-Garnituren. — Conductors-outfits. — Equipos de conductor.

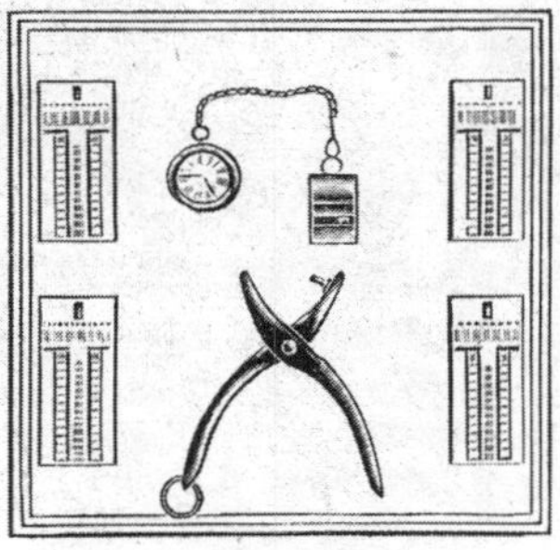

2043/13

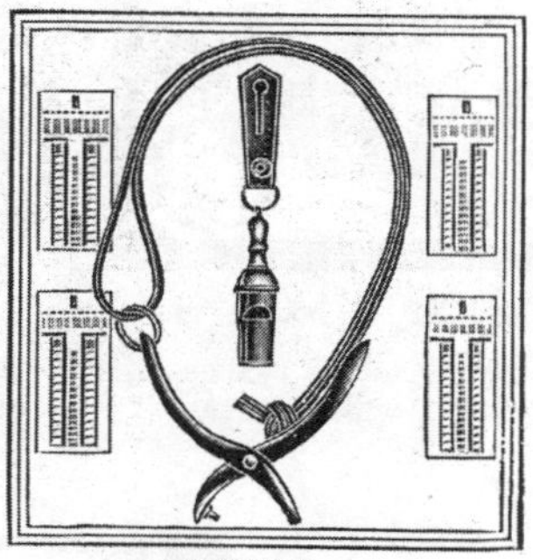

2043/9

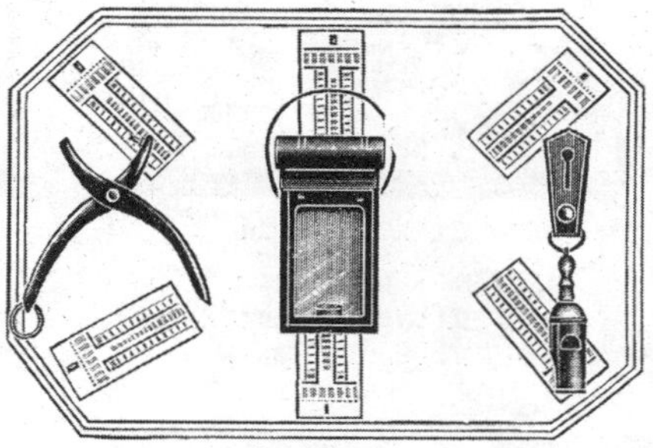

2043/11

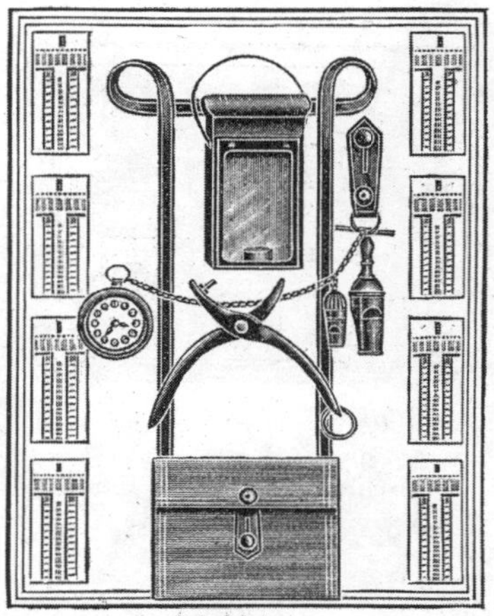

2043/12

1/5 natürliche Größe. — 1/5 of natural size. — 1/5 del tamaño natural.

Glasmärbel. — Glass-marbles. — Bolas de vidrio.

94/00 12/13 mm — **94**/0 14/15 mm — **94**/1 17/18 mm

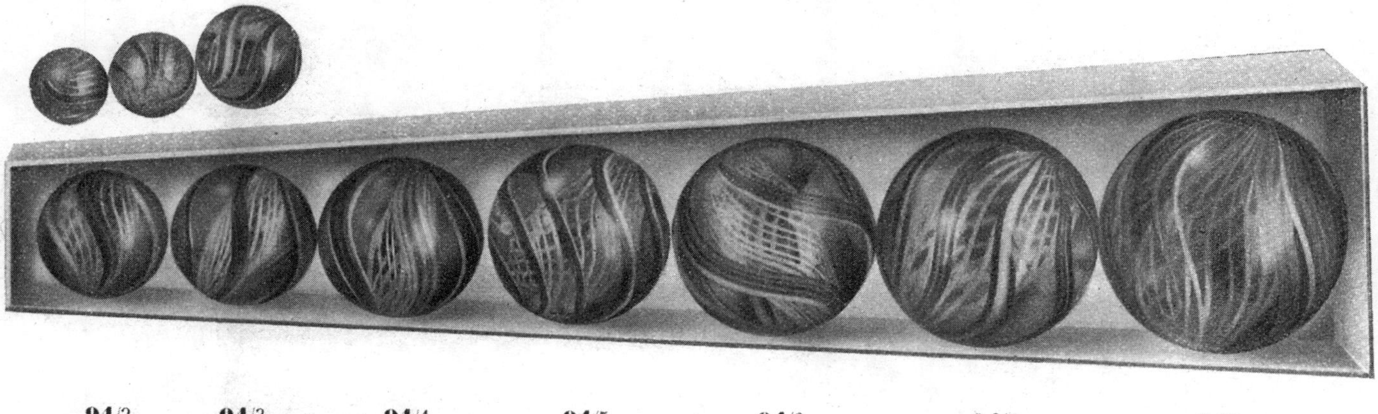

94/2 20/21 mm — **94**/3 23/24 mm — **94**/4 26/27 mm — **94**/5 29/30 mm — **94**/6 32/33 mm — **94**/7 36/37 mm — **94**/8 40/41 mm

Porzellan-Kinderservice. — Children's set of porcelain. — Servicio de porcelana para niños.

9/650/372 22,7 × 16,4 cm

9/651/372 mit 3 Tassen.
9/652/372 with 4 Cups.
9/670/372 con 6 Jícaras.

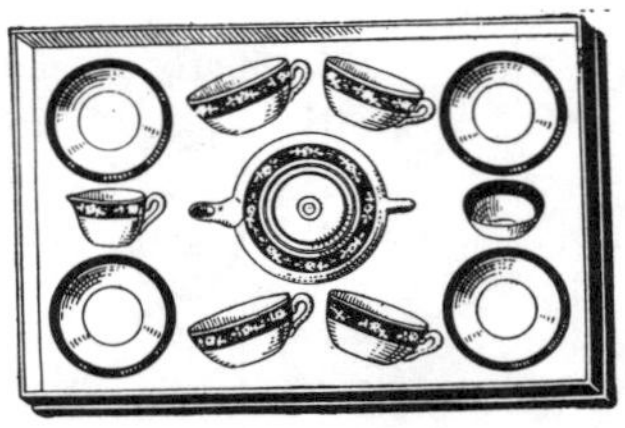

9/673/387 28 × 18,5 cm

9/672/387 mit 2 Tassen.
9/674/387 with 6 Cups.

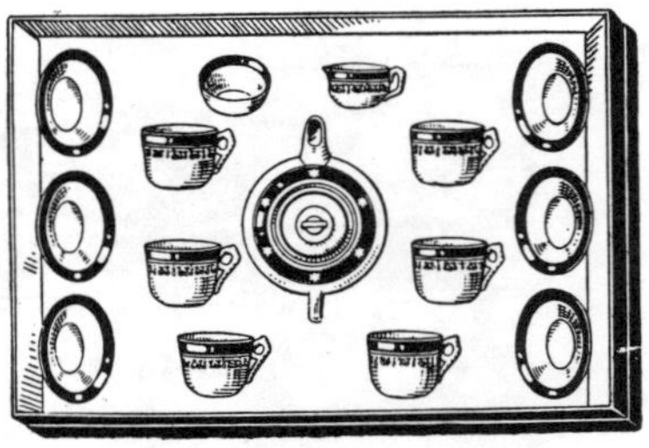

9/686/408 31 × 22 cm

9/683/408 with 2 Cups.
9/684/408 con 3 Jícaras.
9/685/408 con 4 Jícaras.

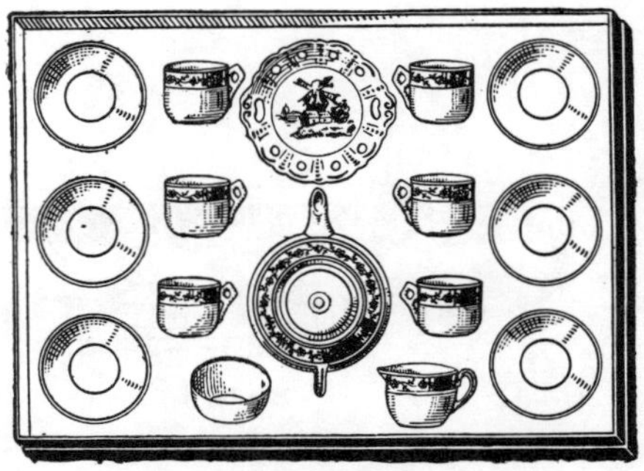

9/665/973 36,5 × 28,2 cm

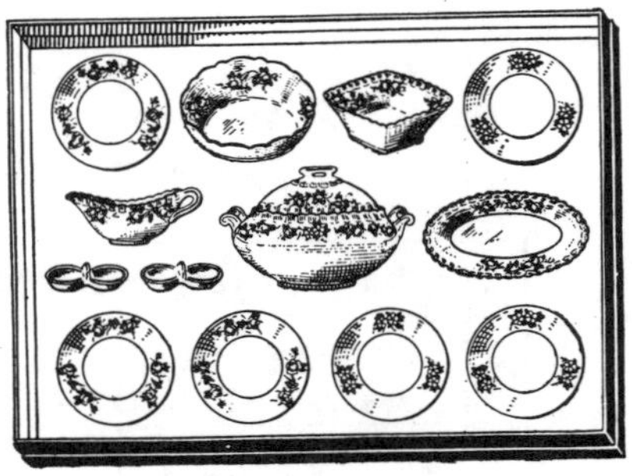

9/S 12/902 35 × 25 cm

9/S 2/0/373 21 × 15 cm

In allen Größen und Preislagen lieferbar.
Suppliable in all sizes and prices.
Suministrables en todos tamaños y precios.

9/576/336 32,5 × 28 cm

9/572/336 mit 2 Tassen.
9/573/336 with 3 Cups.
9/574/336 con 4 Jícaras.

9/570/331 26,5 × 20 cm

9/568/331 mit 2 Tassen.
9/569/331 with 3 Cups.
9/575/331 con 6 Jícaras.

9/638/971 24,5 × 16 cm

9/639/971 mit 3 Tassen.
9/640/971 with 4 Cups.
9/641/971 con 6 Jícaras.

9/445/242 18,5 × 15 cm

9/465/242 mit 6 Tassen.
9/464/242 with 4 Cups.

9/634/970 28,5 × 22 cm

9/632/970 mit 2 Tassen.
9/633/970 with 3 Cups.
9/635/970 con 6 Jícaras.

9/230/11 16 × 13 cm

9/W 100/3 14 × 12 cm

9/230/37 16 × 13 cm

Nestei aus Porzellan.
Nest-egg of porcelain.
Nidal de porcelana.

9/Nestei
6 cm

9/208/126/544
4,1 cm

9/208/31½/499
4,6 cm

9/205/62/296
6,2 cm

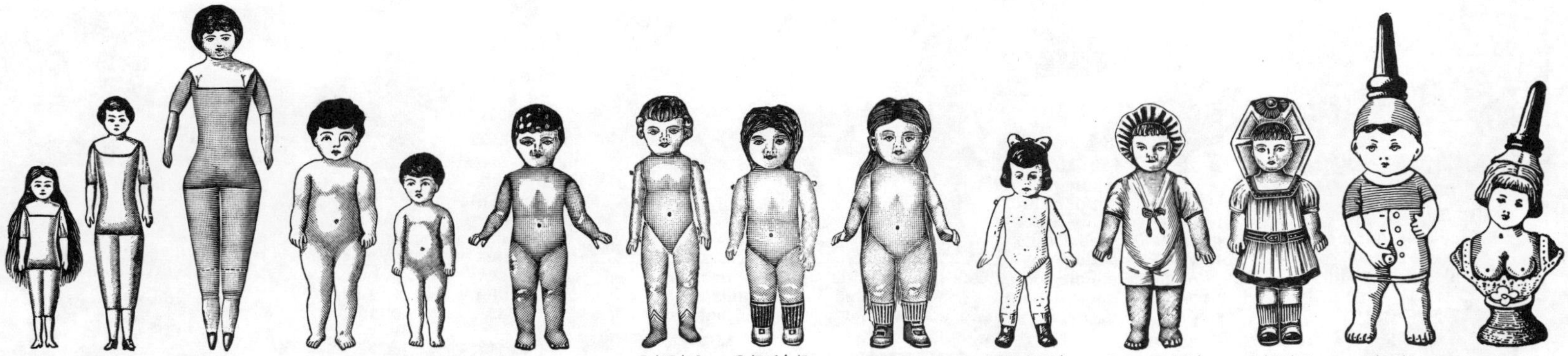

9/63 Z/12 9/63 G/16 9/63 G/27 9/26/9 9/26/12 9/28/10 9/29/10 9/35½/9 9/35½/15 9/51/10½ 9/225/4/7½ 9/30/10 9/39/41 9/38/1

9/63 Z/ 9	9 cm	9/63 G 9	9 cm	9/26/2½	2½cm	9/28/ 4½	4½ cm	9/29/ 5	5 cm	9/225/4/ 6½	6½ cm
9/63 Z/12	12 cm	9/63 G12	12 cm	9/26/3	3 cm	9/28/ 5½	5½ cm	9/29/ 7	7 cm	9/225/4/ 7½	7½ cm
9/63 Z/14	14 cm	9/63 G14	14 cm	9/26/4	4 cm	9/28/ 6½	6½ cm	9/29/ 9	9 cm	9/225/4/ 9	9 cm
9/63 Z/16	16 cm	9/63 G16	16 cm	9/26/5	5 cm	9/28/ 7½	7½ cm	9/29/10	10 cm	9/225/4/10	10 cm
9/63 Z/18	18 cm	9/63 G18	18 cm	9/26/6	6 cm	9/28/ 8	8 cm	9/29/11	11 cm	9/30/ 7	7 cm
9/63 Z/20	20 cm	9/63 G20	20 cm	9/26/7	7 cm	9/28/ 8½	8½ cm	9/35/½ 7	7 cm	9/30/ 8	8 cm
9/63 Z/22	22 cm	9/63 G22	22 cm	9/26/8	8 cm	9/28/ 9	9 cm	9/35/½ 9	9 cm	9/30/10	10 cm
9/63 Z/24	24 cm	9/63 G24	24 cm	9/26/9	9 cm	9/28/10½	10½ cm	9/35/½10	10 cm	9/39/41	8½ cm
9/63 Z/27	27 cm	9/63 G27	27 cm	9/26/10	10 cm	9/28/13	13 cm	9/35/½11	11 cm	9/38/ 1	7 cm
9/63 Z/30	30 cm	9/63 G30	30 cm	9/26/11	11 cm	9/28/14	14 cm	9/35/½12	12 cm		
9/63 Z/32	32 cm	9/63 G32	32 cm	9/26/12	12 cm	9/28/15	15 cm	9/35/½13	13 cm		
				9/26/13	13 cm	9/28/16½	16½ cm				
				9/26/14	14 cm	9/28/18	18 cm				
				9/26/15	15 cm	9/28/19	19 cm				
				9/26/17	17 cm						
				9/26/20	20 cm						

9/180 9/601/2 9/600 9/400 9/B95/27 9/0717/2 9/0716/2

9/180 7 cm 9/601/2 9 cm 9/600 10 cm 9/400 11 cm 9/B95/27 27 cm 9/0717/2 12 cm 9/0716/2 9 cm

In allen Größen und Preislagen lieferbar.
Suppliable in all sizes and prices.
Suministrables en todos tamaños y precios.

9/5485/1 9/5480/31 9/5466/3 9/5422/4 9/5418/2 9/5481/16 9/T/7/2 9/St 2

9/5485/1 5 cm 9/5480/31 7½ cm 9/5466/3 6½ cm 9/5422/4 9 cm 9/5418/2 10½ cm 9/5481/16 9 cm
9/T/7/2 12 cm 9/St 2 10 × 13 cm

34/2/60/34
40 × 28½ × 7½ cm
Karton-Ausstattung.
Box-trousseau.
Guarnición en cajita.

34/4/14/30
Gestopfte Samtpuppe. / Soft Velvet Doll. / Muñeca de terciopelo, estopada.

34/2/301/21
Ia. gekleidete Steifgelenkpuppe. / Stiff jointed dressed Doll. / Elegantemente vestido, juntura rígida.

34/2/359/28 34/2/359/39 34/2/366/35
Gekleidete Modepuppen, einfaches Gelenk.
Single jointed Vogue Dolls, dressed.
Muñecas a la moda, vestidas, juntura sencilla.

34/2/242/21
Ia. gekleidete Steifgelenkpuppe. / Stiff jointed dressed Doll. / Elegantemente vestido, juntura rígida.

34/4/10/50
Gestopfte Samtpuppe. / Soft Velvet Doll. / Muñeca de terciopelo, estopada.

34/2/61/10
40 × 28½ × 7½ cm
Nähkasten.
Sewing-box.
Neceser de costura.

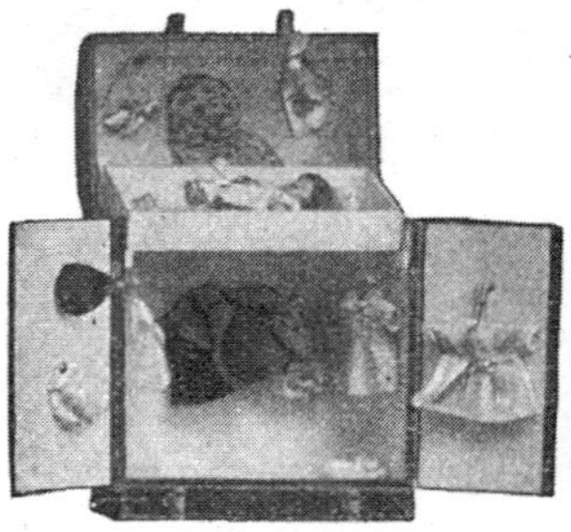

34/2/25/3 N
23 × 15 × 31½ cm
Schrankkoffer mit Puppenausstattung.
Wardrobe trunk, fitted.
Cofre-armadio con guarnición de muñeca.

34/2/21/2 x
33 × 16 × 9 cm
Flachkoffer, garniert.
Doll trunk, fitted.
Baúl llano, guarnecido.

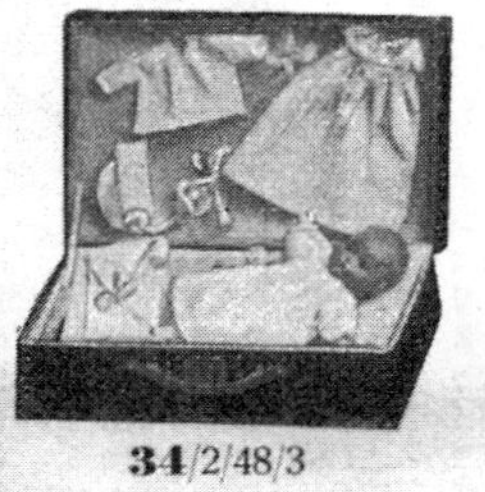

34/2/48/3
30 × 19 × 9½ cm
Handtasche mit Baby-Ausstattung.
Cabin Doll trunk, fitted.
Bolsa manual con guarnición de bebé.

34/2/24/7 G
24½ × 16½ × 16½ cm
Koffer mit Baby-Garnitur.
Trunk with Baby-outfit.
Cofre con guarnición de bebé.

34/2/21/3 N
40 × 19 × 11½ cm
Flachkoffer, garniert.
Doll trunk, fitted.
Baúl llano, guarnecido.

34/2/24/8 N
31½ × 21 × 18½ cm
Reisekoffer-Ausstattung
Doll trunk outfit.
Guarnición de maleta de viaje.

34/2/129/E/2
31½ × 21 × 16½ cm
Korb mit Puppen-Ausstattung.
Basket with Doll outfit.
Cesta con guarnición de muñeca.

34/2/123/2 G
23 × 23 × 13 cm
Korb mit Baby-Ausstattung.
Baby basket, fitted.
Cesta con guarnición de bebé.

34/2/18/2
17 × 18½ × 34 cm
Schrankkoffer-Ausstattung.
Wardrobetrunk, fitted.
Cofre-armadio con guarnición.

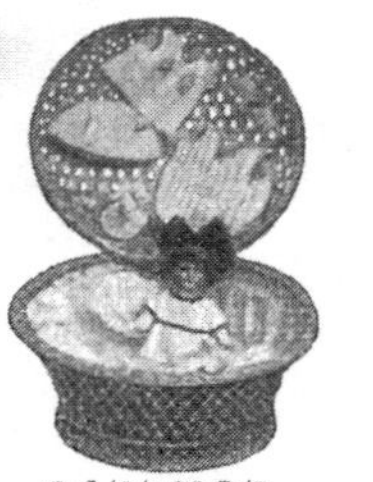

34/2/129C/2
23 × 23 × 13 cm
Korb m. Puppen-Ausstattung.
Basket with Doll outfit.
Cesta con guarnición de muñeca.

34/2/131/3 G
30 × 22 × 34 cm
Korbständer m. Baby-Ausstattung.
Baby basket outfit.
Estante de cesta con guarnición de bebé.

34/2/21/2/0 N	21 × 12 × 6½ cm
34/2/21/0 N	24 × 13 × 7 „
34/2/21/1 N	27 × 14 × 8 „
34/2/21/2 N	33 × 16 × 9 „
34/2/21/3 N	40 × 19 × 11½ „
34/2/21/4 N	45 × 20 × 13 „
34/2/21/2/0 X	21 × 12 × 6½ „
34/2/21/0 X	24 × 13 × 7 „
34/2/21/1 X	27 × 14 × 8 „
34/2/21/2 X	33 × 16 × 9 „
34/2/24/4 N	17½ × 11 × 10½ „

34/2/24/5 N	20 × 13 × 12 cm
34/2/24/6 N	22½ × 14½ × 14 „
34/2/24/7 N	24½ × 16½ × 16½ „
34/2/24/8 N	31½ × 21 × 18½ „
34/2/24/9 N	36 × 22½ × 20 „
34/2/24/10 N	39 × 25 × 22½ „
34/2/25/0 N	15½ × 10 × 20 „
34/2/25/1 N	17 × 12 × 24 „
34/2/25/2 N	20 × 14 × 28 „
34/2/25/3 N	23 × 15 × 31½ „
34/2/25/4 N	26 × 17 × 36½ „
34/2/25/5 N	30 × 18 × 39 „
34/2/25/6 N	33 × 21 × 45 „
34/2/48/1	20 × 13 × 6½ „
34/2/48/2	25 × 16 × 8 „
34/2/48/3	30 × 19 × 9½ „
34/2/48/4	35 × 22 × 10½ „
34/2/123/1 G	21 × 21 × 10½ „
34/2/123/2 G	23 × 23 × 13 „
34/2/123/3 G	25 × 25 × 13½ „
34/2/123/4 G	27 × 27 × 14½ „
34/2/127/1	31 × 20 × 10 „

34/2/127/2	37 × 24 × 11 cm
34/2/127/3	43 × 28 × 13 „
34/2/128/1	31 × 20 × 10 „
34/2/128/2	37 × 24 × 11 „
34/2/128/3	43 × 28 × 13 „
34/2/129 C/1	21 × 21 × 10½ „
34/2/129 C/2	23 × 23 × 13 „
34/2/129 C/3	25 × 25 × 13½ „

34/2/129 C/4	27 × 27 × 14½ cm
34/2/129 E/1	29 × 19 × 15 „
34/2/129 E/2	31½ × 21 × 16½ „
34/2/129 W/1	30 × 25 × 8 „
34/2/129 W/2	36 × 29 × 8 „
34/2/129 W/3	39 × 32 × 9 „
34/2/131/1 G	22 × 15 × 24 „
34/2/131/2 G	25 × 18 × 30 „
34/2/131/3 G	30 × 22 × 34 „
34/2/146/1	28 × 15 × 21½ „
34/2/146/2	40 × 20 × 32 „
34/2/146/3	53 × 24 × 41 „
34/2/146/4	69 × 31 × 51 „

34/2/129 W 3 39 × 32 × 9 cm
Baby-Korbausstattung.
Baby Basket outfit.
Guarnición de cesta para bebé.

34/2/130 G 30 × 23 × 58 cm
Korb mit Baby-Ausstattung.
Baby basket outfit.
Cesta con guarnición de bebé.

34/2/128/2 37 × 24 × 11 cm
Korb mit Baby-Ausstattung.
Baby basket outfit.
Cesta con guarnición de bebé.

34/2/127/2 37 × 24 × 11 cm.
Korbausstattung mit Puppe.
Basket trousseau.
Guarnición de cesta con muñeca.

34/2/146/3 53 × 24 × 41 cm
Korbschrank mit Baby-Ausstattung.
Baby basket trousseau.
Cesta-armadio con guarnición de bebé.

27/I C 100 Size — Tamaño 43 cm.

Käthe Kruse-Puppen

Werkstätte der Käthe Kruse-Puppen.

Alle Käthe-Kruse-Puppen sind einschließlich des Kopfes ganz aus Stoff gefertigt und, bis auf wenige Maschinennähte, reine Handarbeit. Sie sind waschbar, weich und unzerbrechlich, und ihr Sinn ist: Erziehung zur Mütterlichkeit. Die Herstellung steht unter ständiger persönlicher Leitung von Frau Käthe Kruse.

Modell I: 43 cm hoch, ist die bisher am weitesten bekanntgewordene Käthe-Kruse-Puppe. Das Material ist imprägnierter Nessel, nach Original-Schnitt in Formen genäht, mit Rehhaaren gestopft. — Abbildung auch umseitig.

Modell II: das Schlenkerchen, ist 33 cm hoch. Es weist eine ganz neue Herstellungsart auf (D. R. P. und U. St. L. P.) Der Körper wird über einem biegsamen Gestell aus Watte und Binden gewickelt (modelliert) und mit Trikot überzogen. So läßt es kein Gelenk mehr sehen und ist die einzige Puppe, die auch nackt schön ist. Mit vollendet erreichter Natürlichkeit schmiegt sie sich in den Arm des Kindes. Abbildung siehe nächstes Blatt.

Diese beiden Puppenarten sind im Hemdchen oder Höschen sowie gekleidet in vier verschiedenen Preisserien, A, B, C und D, zu beziehen.

Modell V: nach derselben Methode wie Schlenkerchen hergestellt ist das lebensgroße neugeborene Baby. Es ist zu haben mit schlafendem Köpfchen (**27**/V s) und in natürlichem Gewicht des Neugeborenen (5 Pfund), so besonders für den Unterricht in Säuglingspflege geeignet, oder unbeschwert (ca. 2 Pfund schwer), mit offenen Augen (**27**/V w) als Spielpuppe. Beide Puppen eignen sich auch hervorragend als Schaupuppen für die Baby-Abteilung und können auf Wunsch größer, d. i. etwa 4 Wochen alt, geliefert werden (**27**/VI s resp. **27**/VI w) Siehe buntes Bild in Körbchen, nächstes Blatt.

Qualität, Arbeitsart und Wirkung der Käthe-Kruse-Puppen sind mit keinem andern Industrie-Erzeugnis zu vergleichen. Denn im bewußten Gegensatz zu andern Erscheinungen, die alle lediglich „hübsch aussehen" wollen, wenden sich die Käthe-Kruse-Puppen an das Gefühl. — Zieht man nebenbei noch ihre Haltbarkeit in Betracht, so sind die Preise niedrig zu nennen.

Hüten Sie sich vor den zahllosen Nachahmungen, besonders der Käthe-Kruse-Puppe I. — Jede Käthe-Kruse-Puppe trägt auf der linken Fußsohle das obige Faksimile und am Handgelenk die Schutzmarke. Auch die geschmackvollen Originalkartons tragen den Namen Käthe Kruse.

Studio of the Käthe-Kruse-Dolls.

All Käthe-Kruse-dolls are made entirely of woven stuff, including the heads and, save some few machinal seams, are purely hand-made. They are washable, soft and unbreakable and they signify: Education to motherliness. The manufacture is under the permanent personal control of Mrs. Käthe Kruse.

Type I: 43 cm high is the Käthe-Kruse-doll of the hitherto widest publicity. The material consists of impregnated nettle, sewed to forms after the original cut and stuffed with roe's hair. See also illustration overleaf.

Type II: The Little Dangler is 33 cm high. It shows a quite novel kind of make (German Patent and U. St. L. P.). The body is modelled of wadding and bandages wound around a flexible frame, and covered with tricot. So it will show no joint anymore, being the only doll, which will also be beautiful, when naked. It will cling to the child's arm with a perfectly reached naturalness. Illustration see overleaf.

These two types of dolls are supplied in shirt or trowsers, as well as fully dressed, in four different price-series, A, B, C and D.

*Type V: manufactured after the same method as the little Dangler, is the full-sized new-born baby. It may be had with sleeping head (**27**/V s) and in the natural weight of the new-born (5 pounds), and will then be specially adapted to teaching of infants' fostering, or unburdened (weighing abt. 2 pounds) with open eyes (**27**/V w) as a playing doll. Both dolls are also eminently appropriate as show-dolls for a Baby-Department, and on desire may be supplied taller, viz. 4 weeks old (**27**/VI s and **27**/VI w resp.). See coloured picture in basket, overleaf.*

Quality, mode of confection and effect of the Käthe-Kruse-Dolls must not be compared with any other industrial product. For in intentional contradiction with other products, which all pretend to "look nice", the Käthe-Kruse-Dolls apply to the feeling. Considering moreover their durability, prices must be called low.

Beware of the innumerous imitations, particularly of the Käthe-Kruse-Doll I. Every Käthe-Kruse-Doll shows the above facsimile on the left sole, and the trade-mark on the wrist. Also the tasteful original card-boxes are marked with the name of Käthe Kruse.

Taller de las Muñecas Käthe Kruse.

Todas las muñecas Käthe Kruse son hechas enteramente de paño, inclusive las cabezas, y, salvo algunas pocas costuras por máquina, son puro trabajo manual. Son lavables, muelles é inquebrantables y su sentido es: Educación para la maternalidad. La fabricación está bajo la dirección permanente y personal de la Sra. Käthe Kruse.

Modelo I: 43 cm de alto, es la muñeca Käthe Kruse de la mayor publicidad hasta ahora. El material consiste de ortiga impregnada, cosido para formas según el corte original y estopado con pelo de corzo. Véase también el grabado al otro lado.

Modelo II: El Bambaleador, tiene 33 cm de alto. Muestra un modo todo nuevo de fabricación (patente alemana y norte-americana). El cuerpo está modelado de algodón en rama y bandas arrolladas al rededor de una armadura flexible, y cubierto de tricot. Así ya no presentará ninguna articulación, siendo la única muñeca, que aún será linda, cuando desnuda. Se coserá con el brazo de la niña con una naturalidad perfectamente alcanzada. Véase el grabado al otro lado.

Estos dos tipos de muñecas se suministran vestidas con camisita ó calzones, así como completamente vestidas, en cuatro diferentes series de precio, A, B, C y D.

Modelo V: fabricado según el mismo método que el Bambaleador representa al bebé recien-nacido en tamaño natural. Puede ser suministrada con cabeza durmiendo (**27**/V s) y en el peso natural del recien-nacido (5 libras), adaptándose entonces especialmente al ensino del mantenemiento de mamantes, ó descargada (pesando ca 2 libras) con los ojos abiertos (**27**/V w), sirviendo de muñeca para niñas. Ambas muñecas están también eminentemente propias para muñecas de muestra en un departamento de bebés, y a petición pueden ser hechas mayores, a saber de 4 semanas de edad. (**27**/VI s y **27**/VI w resp.) Véase el grabado de colores en cesta, a la página siguiente.

La cualidad, el modo de confección y el efecto de las muñecas Käthe Kruse no pueden ser comparados con cualquier otro producto industrial. Pues en contradicción intencional de otros productos, que todos pretienden de "ser lindos", las muñecas Käthe Kruse se dirigen al sentimiento. Considerando, fuera de eso, su durabilidad, los precios deben ser llamados bajos.

Cuidado con las imitaciones sin número, particularmente de la muñeca Käthe Kruse I. Cada muñeca Käthe Kruse lleva el facsímile arriba en la suela del pié izquierdo y la marca registrada en la muñeca de la mano. También las elegantes cajitas de cartón llevan el nombre de Käthe Kruse.

Please note also the publication on page 210 and 211 of the principal catalogue.
Llamamos también su atención á la publicación en la página 210 y 211 del catálogo principal.

Modell I, 43 cm.

27/I B 119 **27**/I B 120
Size — Tamaño 43 cm

27/I A 117 **27**/I C 123
Size — Tamaño 43 cm

27/I C 125
Size — Tamaño 43 cm

27/I C 39
Size — Tamaño 43 cm

27/I D 124
Size — Tamaño 43 cm

Sämtliche Puppen ohne Zutaten. — All the dolls without garnishing. — Todas las muñecas sin avíos.

27/I C 122
Size — Tamaño 43 cm

27/I D 121
Size — Tamaño 43 cm

27/I B 118
Size — Tamaño 43 cm

27/I C 126
Size — Tamaño 43 cm

Beachten Sie auch die Veröffentlichung auf Seite 210 und 211 des Hauptkataloges.

Please note also the publication on page 210 and 211 of the principal catalogue.
Llamamos también su atención á la publicación en la página 210 y 211 del catálogo principal.

Modell II 33 cm

27/II C 13
Size / Tamaño 33 cm.

27/II A 1
Size / Tamaño 33 cm.

27/II B 10
Size / Tamaño 33 cm.

27/II B 8
Size / Tamaño 33 cm.

Sämtliche Puppen ohne Zutaten. — All the dolls without garnishing. — Todas las muñecas sin avíos.

27/II C 14

27/II C 4

27/II C 15

Modell V 50 cm

27/V s

Mit ständig schlafendem Köpfchen, nicht mit beweglichen Augen.

With permanent sleeping head, not with movable eyes.

Con cabeza permanentemente durmiendo, no con ojos movibles.

27/V s A

27/V w

Mit ständig offenen Augen, nicht mit Schlafaugen.

With permanent open eyes, not with closing eyes.

Con los ojos permanentes abiertos, no con ojos cerradizos.

Beachten Sie auch die Veröffentlichung auf Seite 210 und 211 des HauptKataloges.

Bella-Dolls
The most exquisite

Muñecas "Bella"
Lo más exquisito

„Bella"-Puppen
Das Exquisiteste

Diese modernsten Gliederpuppen und Babys mit Schelmenaugen und Gummihändchen zeichnen sich durch einzigartige Eleganz aus.
Jede Puppe ist ein Modell und ein Schmuckstück für jedes Schaufenster.

These most modern joint-dolls and babies with roguish eyes and rubber-hands distinguish themselves by their unique elegance.
Every doll is a model and a piece of display for every show-window.

Estas muñecas articuladas muy modernas y bebés con ojos de pícaro y manitas de goma se distinguen por una elegancia única.
Cada muñeca es un modelo y una pieza de adorno para todo escaparate.

137/700/31/106

137/600/30/167

137/400/53/146

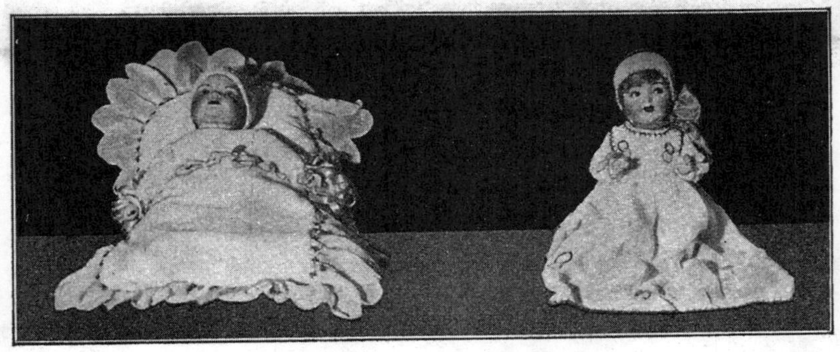

137/20/1 **137**/700/36/43

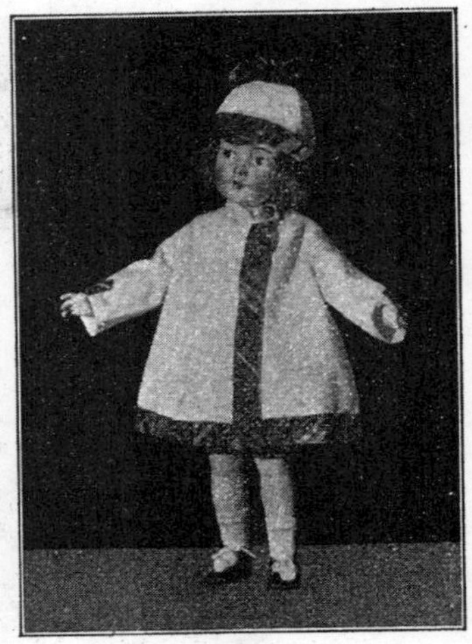

137/400/53/149

137/400/46/15 **137**/400/46/20 **137**/300/46/173 **137**/400/46/115

137/400/53/170 **137**/400/53/171 **137**/400/53/92. **137**/400/53/142 Lo **137**/400/53/14

137/400/62/145 **137**/400/62/133 **137**/400/62/100 **137**/400/62/143

137/400/70/142

137/400/70/119

137/400/53/21

137/400/80/159

137/400/70/147

137/400/70/18

Please note also the publication on page 216 of the principal catalogue.
Llamamos también su atención á la publicación en la página 216 del catálogo principal.

46/4136 L Schelm

Feinste Babys und Puppen.

Finest Babies and Dolls.

Bebés y muñecas finísimas.

46/4136 BC Schelm

46/1599 Mulatte

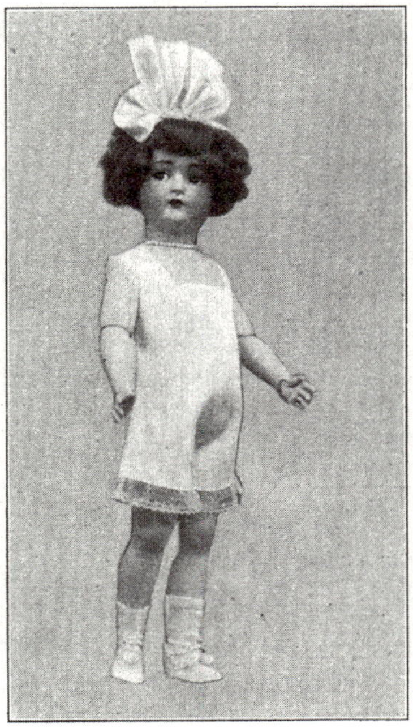

46/3136 BC Schelm

Maße und Preise der kompletten Serien befinden sich in separater Preisliste.

Measures and prices of the complete series are in separate price list.

Proporciones y precios de las series completas están en la lista de precios separata.

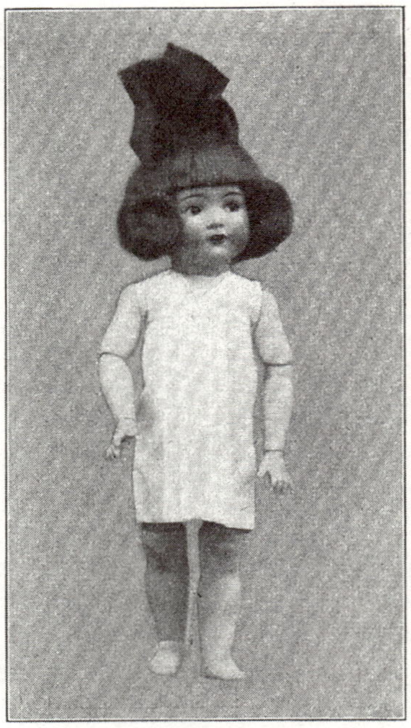

46/2094 P Schelm

Beachten Sie auch die Veröffentlichung auf Seite 216 des Hauptkataloges.

Please note also the publication on page 215 of the principal catalogue.
Llamamos también su atención á la publicación en la página 215 del catáloge principal.

155/M 8

155/G 9

STRASSER-PUPPEN

sind jedes Stück ein Kunstwerk, hergestellt aus weichem, elastischem Material, von größter Naturwahrheit, mit individuellem Geschmack gekleidet und ausgestattet.

STRASSER-PUPPEN

vereinigen die künstlerischen Ziele des modernen Kunstgewerbes mit den technischen Erfahrungen der Jahrhunderte alten Puppen-Industrie Deutschlands.

STRASSER-DOLLS

are piece by piece a work of art, made of soft, elastic material, true to nature and dressed and got up with characteristic taste.

STRASSER-DOLLS

unite the artistical aims of modern applied art with the technical experiences of the Doll Industrie existing centuries already in Germany.

LAS MUÑECAS STRASSER

son, cada una, obras de arte, confeccionadas de material blando y elástico, de la más perfecta naturalidad, vestidas y pertrechadas con gusto personal.

LAS MUÑECAS STRASSER

son el producto de los fines artísticos del arte aplicado moderno y de las experiencias técnicas de la industria alemana de muñecas que data de siglos atras.

155/Buby

155/Plumsi

Beachten Sie auch die Veröffentlichung auf Seite 215 des Hauptkataloges

Please note also the publication on page 184 of the principal catalogue.
Llamamos también su atención á la publicación en la página 184 del catálogo principal.

Serie **37**/12 B

Neugeborene Babies in amerikanischem Steckkissen, Porzellan-Charakterkopf mit offenem Mund, beweglicher Zunge und Gummisauger, der in den offenen Mund eingesteckt werden kann, Schlafaugen, selbsttätiger Weinstimme.
Artikel gesetzlich geschützt!

Newborn babies in american carrying-pillow, porcelain character-head with open mouth, movable tongue and rubber-sucker, which may be put into the open mouth, with sleeping-eyes, and self-acting weeping-voice.
Article protected by law!

Bebés recien nacidos en cojinito americano, cabeza-carácter de porcelana con boca abierta, lengua movible y chupador de goma que puede ser metido en la boca abierta, con ojos de dormir y voz de lloro automática.
Artículo protegido por ley!

Serie **37**/14 B

Neugeborene Babies in feinem Batiststeckkissen, Porzellan-Charakterkopf mit offenem Mund, beweglicher Zunge und Gummisauger, der in den offenen Mund eingesteckt werden kann, Schlafaugen und selbsttätiger Weinstimme.
Artikel gesetzlich geschützt!

Newborn babies in fine cambric carrying-pillow, porcelain character-head with open mouth, movable tongue and rubber-sucker, which may be put into the open mouth, with sleeping eyes and self-acting weeping-voice.
Article protected by law!

Bebés recien nacidos en fino cojinito de cambray, cabeza-carácter de porcelana con boca abierta, lengua movible y chupador de goma que puede ser metido en la boca abierta, con ojos de dormir y voz de lloro automática.
Artículo protegido por ley!

Serie **37**/10 N

Neugeborene Babies, Neger, mit Pappkopf, gemalten Augen und selbsttätiger Weinstimme.

Newborn babies, negro, with pasteboard-head, painted eyes, self-acting weeping-voice.

Bebés recien nacidos, negros, con cabeza de cartón, ojos pintados, voz de lloro automática.

Serie **37**/10 D

Neugeborene Babies mit feinem Seidenbatist-Tragkleid, Porzellan-Charakterkopf, Doppelgesicht, drehbar, auf der einen Seite weinend, auf der andern Seite lachend, mit offenem Mund, beweglicher Zunge und Gummisauger, der in den offenen Mund eingesteckt werden kann, Schlafaugen, selbsttätiger Weinstimme.
Artikel gesetzlich geschützt.

Newborn babies with fine silk cambric long clothes, porcelain character-head, double face, turnable, one side laughing, the other side weeping, with open mouth, movable tongue and rubber-sucker, which may be put into the open mouth, with sleeping eyes, and selfacting weeping voice.
Article protected by law!

Bebés recien nacidos, con vestido de llevar en brazos, de fino cambray de seda, cabeza-carácter de porcelana, cara doble, girable, de un lado llorando, del otro lado riéndose, con boca abierta, lengua movible y chupador de goma, que puede ser metido en la boca abierta, con ojos de dormir, y voz de lloro automática.
Artículo protegido por ley!

Serie **37**/15 B

Neugeborene Babies mit farbigem, fein ausgeführtem Umschlagschal, Porzellan-Charakterkopf mit offenem Mund, beweglicher Zunge und Gummisauger, der in den offenen Mund eingesteckt werden kann, Schlafaugen, selbsttätiger Weinstimme.
Artikel gesetzlich geschützt.

Serie **37**/15 B

Newborn babies with coloured finely finished wrapping-shawl, porcelain character-head with open mouth, movable tongue and rubber-sucker, which may be put into the open mouth, sleeping-eyes, and self-acting weeping-voice.
Article protected by law!

Bebés recien nacidos con chal de envolver, de colores, finamente ejecutado, cabeza-carácter de porcelana con boca abierta. lengua movible y chupador de goma, que puede ser metida en la boca abierta, con ojos de dormir y voz de lloro automática.
Artículo protegido por ley.

Serie **37**/10 B

Neugeborene Babies mit besserem Seidenbatisttragkleid und Unterkleid, Porzellan-Charakterkopf mit offenem Mund, beweglicher Zunge und Gummisauger, der in den offenen Mund eingesteckt werden kann, Schlafaugen, selbsttätiger Weinstimme.
Artikel gesetzlich geschützt!

Newborn babies with better silk cambric long clothes and underfrock, porcelain character-head with open mouth, movable tongue and rubber-sucker, which may be put into the open mouth, with sleeping-eyes and self-acting weeping-voice.
Article protected by law!

Bebés recien nacidos con vestido de llevar en brazos, de cambray de seda con saya, cabeza-carácter de porcelana con boca abierta, lengua movible y chupador de goma, que puede ser metida en la boca abierta, con ojos de dormir y voz de lloro automática.
Artículo protegido por ley!

Serie **37**/7 B

Neugeborene Babies mit einfachem Batistkleid, Porzellan-Charakterkopf mit offenem Mund, beweglicher Zunge und Gummisauger, der in den offenen Mund eingesteckt werden kann, Schlafaugen und selbsttätiger Weinstimme.
Artikel gesetzlich geschützt!

Newborn babies with simple cambric-dress, porcelain character-head with open mouth, movable tongue and rubber-sucker, which may be put into the open mouth, with sleeping eyes and self-acting weeping-voice.
Article protected by law!

Bebés recien nacidos con vestido sencillo de cambray, cabeza-carácter de porcelana con boca abierta, lengua movible y chupador de goma, que puede ser metido en la boca abierta, con ojos de dormir y voz de lloro automática.
Artículo protegido por ley!

Puppen: Friedel, Betty, Käthe usw.
Feingekleidete, haargestopfte Künstlerpuppen mit Zelluloid-Charakterkopf, Gelenkarmen und -händen, unzerbrechlich und sehr leicht.

Dolls: Friedel, Betty, Käthe, etc.
Finely dressed, hair-stuffed artistic dolls with character-head of celluloid, articulate arms and hands, unbreakable and very light.

Muñecas: Friedel, Betty, Käthe, etc.
Muñecas artísticas finamente vestidas y estapados de pelo, con cabeza-carácter, brazos y manos artículados, infrangibles y muy ligeras.

Serie **37**/310

Stoffpuppen mit bunten Filzkleidern, weich gestopft, mit gemaltem Pappkopf und Mohairfrisur, unzerbrechlich und sehr leicht.

Stuff-dolls with vary-coloured felt-dresses, soft-stuffed, with painted pasteboard-head, mohair wig, unbreakable, and very light.

Muñecas de estofo con vestidos de fieltro variegado, blandamente estopadas, con cabeza de cartón pintada, con peluca de mohair, infrangibles y muy ligeras.

Beachten Sie auch die Veröffentlichung auf Seite 184 des HauptKataloges.

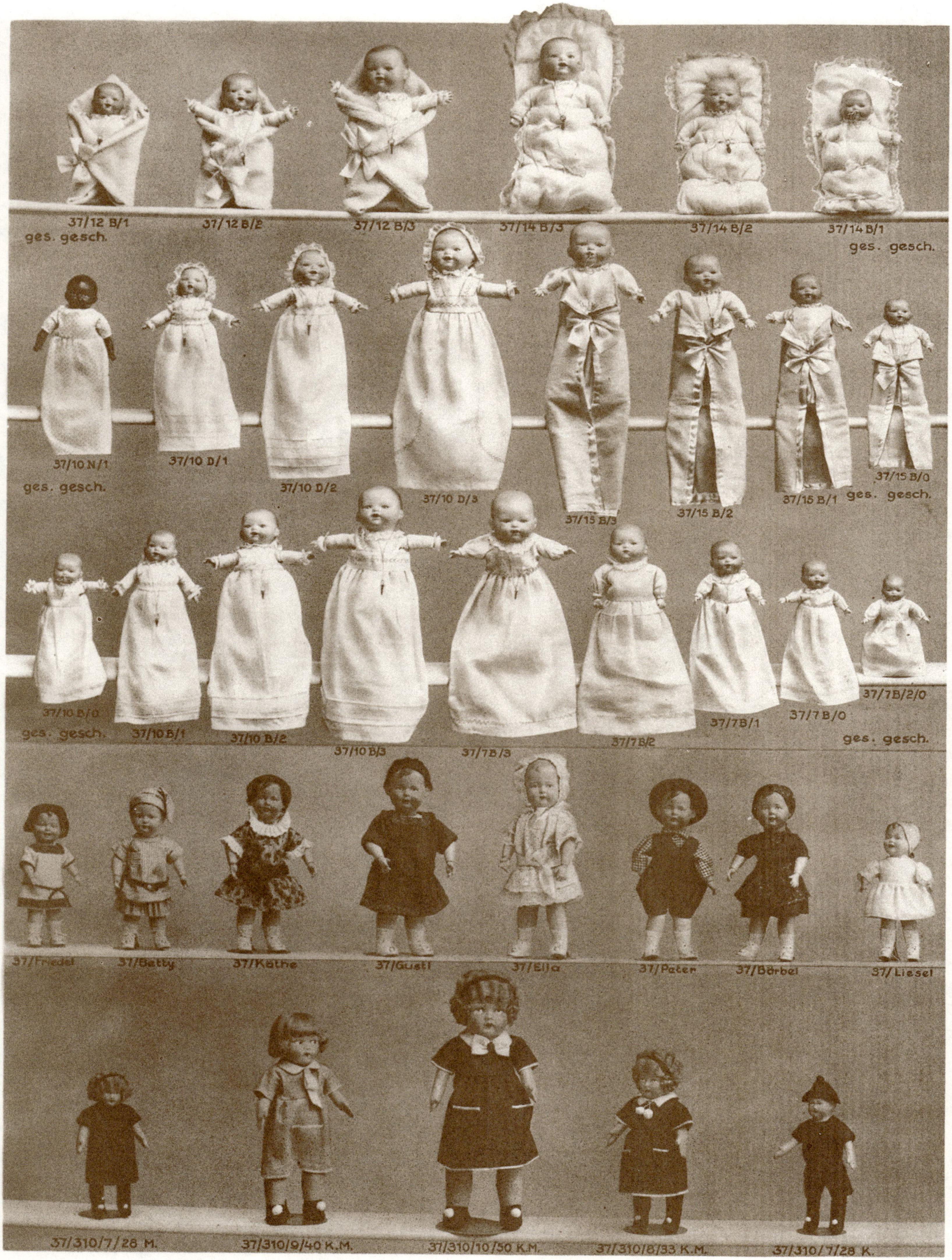
37/12 B/1
ges. gesch.
37/12 B/2
37/12 B/3
37/14 B/3
37/14 B/2
37/14 B/1
ges. gesch.
37/10 N/1
ges. gesch.
37/10 D/1
37/10 D/2
37/10 D/3
37/15 B/3
37/15 B/2
37/15 B/1
37/15 B/0
ges. gesch.
37/10 B/0
ges. gesch.
37/10 B/1
37/10 B/2
37/10 B/3
37/7 B/3
37/7 B/2
37/7 B/1
37/7 B/0
37/7 B/2/0
ges. gesch.
37/Friedel
37/Betty
37/Käthe
37/Gustl
37/Ella
37/Peter
37/Bärbel
37/Liesel
37/310/7/28 M.
37/310/9/40 K.M.
37/310/10/50 K.M.
37/310/8/33 K.M.
37/310/7/28 K.

95/1/36

Beste Waltershäuser Spezial - Vollgelenk-Puppen mit Porzellankopf, Schlafaugen und Wimpern, echter Mohair - Lockenperücke mit Seidenschleife, im Hemd mit Ausputz, Schuhen und Strümpfen, jedes Stück im Karton verpackt.

★

"The finest special-doll on the market". Finest Waltershäuser special full-jointed doll with biscuit head, moving eyes with eyelashes, sewed curley mohair-wig with silk bow, shirt with lace, silk ribbon, open worked stockings, cloth shoes, each doll in a strong box.

★

Muñecas especiales de Waltershausen, de la. calidad, plenamente articuladas, con cabeza de porcelana, ojos con pestañas de dormir, peluca genuina de bucles, de mohair con lazo de seda, en camisa con cintas, zapatos y medias, cada pieza en cajita de cartón.

★

95/1/65

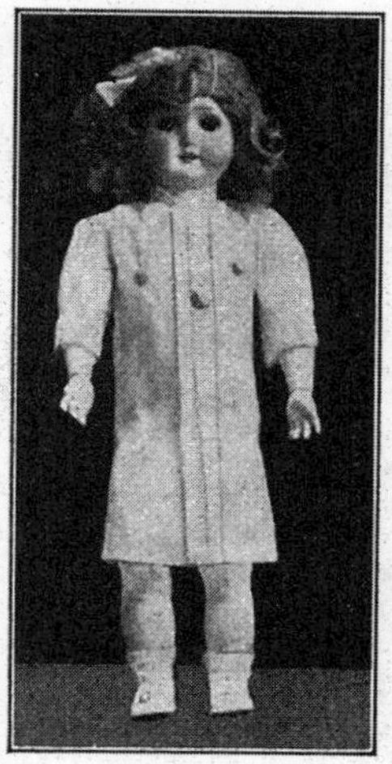

95/1/45

95/1/32	32 cm
95/1/36	36 cm
95/1/38	38 cm
95/1/40	40 cm
95/1/42	42 cm
95/1/45	45 cm
95/1/47	47 cm
95/1/50	50 cm
95/1/52	52 cm
95/1/55	55 cm
95/1/58	58 cm
95/1/60	60 cm
95/1/63	63 cm
95/1/65	65 cm
95/1/68	68 cm
95/1/70	70 cm
95/1/72	72 cm
95/1/75	75 cm
95/1/78	78 cm
95/1/85	85 cm
95/1/100	100 cm

95/1/55

95/1/75

131/103 S/21 cm **131**/101 S/21 cm

131/751 S/28 cm

131/129 S/34 cm

131/1117 S/34 cm

131/131 S/36 cm

131/1047/ S/50 cm

131/137 S/40 cm

131/133 S/36 cm

131/132 S/36 cm

Steifgelenkpuppen mit Schlafaugen, sortiert gekleidet.

Stiff jointed Dolls with moving eyes, assorted dressed.

Muñecas de articulación rígida con ojos de dormir, vestidos surtidos.

120/135 Sicora
Ia. Filzbekleidung

Sico — die preisgekrönte Wunderpuppe, patentamtlich geschützt, mit der selbsttätigen verstellbaren Laufvorrichtung. Ohne Feder, nicht zum Aufziehen.

Sicora — die neuen Wunderpuppen und Teddys, welche laufen und den Kopf dabei nach rechts und links drehen, patentamtlich geschützt. Ohne Feder, nicht zum Aufziehen.

Sico- und Sicora-Puppen sind weich gestopft und unzerbrechlich, haben vorzügliche Mama-Dauerstimme. Frisuren sind zum Abnehmen eingerichtet. Mit dem ges. geschützten Laufschuh laufen die Puppen auf dem glattesten Linoleum oder Parkett. Herstellung in 42 cm und 52 cm.

Sico — the prize-crowned wonder-doll, protected by patent, with the self-acting, adjustable walking-contrivance.

Sicora — the modern wonder-dolls and teddies, which walk while moving their head to the right and left, protected by patent.

Sico- und Sicora-dolls are soft-stuffed and unbreakable, have an excellent lasting voice. Wigs can be taken off. By means of the running-shoe, protected by law, the dolls are walking on the smoothest linoleum or inlaid floor. Make in 42 cm and 52 cm.

Sico — la muñeca premiada miraculosa, protegida por patente, con el dispositivo automático, graduable de andar.

Sicora — las muñecas y teddis modernos, miraculosos, que andan mientras mueven la cabeza a la derecha e izquierda, protegidos por patente.

Las muñecas Sico y Sicora estan de relleno fofo y inquebrantables, y tienen una voz excelente y duradora. La peluca puede ser quitada. Mediante el sapato andador protegido por ley, las muñecas andan sobre el linóleo ó tablado embutido más lisos. Hechas en tamaños de 42 cm y 52 cm.

120/122 Sico
Ia. Sammetbekleidung

Please note also the publication on page 209 and 214 of the principal catalogue.
Llamamos también su atención á la publicación en la página 209 y 214 del catálogo principal.

Puppen
aus gestopften Körpern und Zelluloidkopf, gemaltem Haar und Augen, deshalb unzerbrechlich. Größe 28—50 cm.

Dolls
stuffed body and celluloid head, painted hair and eyes, and consequently unbreakable. Sizes 28—50 cm.

Muñecas
de cuerpos estopados, con cabeza de celuloide, cabellos y ojos pintados, por consiguiente infrangibles. Tamaño 28—50 cm.

149/1/V 28 cm
149/1/IV 32 „
149/1/III 37 „
149/1/II 42 „
149/1/I 50 „

Mit Schlafaugen / With sleeping eyes
Con ojos para dormir
149/2/V 28 cm
149/2/IV 32 „
149/2/III 37 „
149/2/II 42 cm
149/2/I 50 „

149/3/V 28 cm
149/3/IV 32 „
149/3/III 38 „

149/4/V 28 cm
149/4/IV 32 „
149/4/III 38 „

Sämtliche Puppen werden zu gleichen Preisen in Filz-, Seide-, Samt- oder Strickkleidung geliefert.
All dolls are supplied at equal prices in felt-, silk-, velvet- or knitting-dresses.
Todas las muñecas se suministran a precios iguales, indiferente que sean los vestidos de fieltro, de seda, de terciopelo ó de punto de media.

Muk- und Lisa-Puppen

sind abwaschbar, beweglich und unzerbrechlich. Bei guter Qualität günstige Preise. Der Balg der Puppen besteht aus Satin und ist mit Scherwolle gestopft. Die Kleider sind ebenfalls aus Satin.

Muk- and Lisa-Dolls

are washable, articulate and unbreakable. Although good quality, yet favorable prices. The body of the dolls is made of satin and stuffed with fleece. The dresses are likewise of satin.

153/19/1 **153**/19/2
Größe / Size / Tamaño 39 cm.

Las Muñecas Muk y Lisa

son lavables, articuladas e inquebrantables. A pesar de buena calidad los precios son favorables. El cuerpo de las muñecas está hecho de raso y estopado de lana. Los vestidos son igualmente de raso.

Beachten Sie auch die Veröffentlichung auf Seite 209 und 214 des Hauptkataloges.

Mama-Laufpuppen

mit wirklich lauten und gutgehenden Patent-Mamastimmen. Prima Ausführung. Mit unzerbrechlichem Kopf und Beinen, fein bemalt, mit Holzwolle gestopfter Körper. Sehr vorteilhafter Exportartikel nach allen Ländern.

Mama-doll, walking,

with a really good patent mama-voice. First quality. Head and legs unbreakable, nicely painted, body filled with wood-wool. Very favourable article of export to all countries.

Muñeca pudiendo marchar y decir mamá.

Se he dado privilegio de invención a la voz. Primera ejecución. Cabeza y piernas infrangibles y bien pintadas. Cuerpo henchido con lana de leña. Artículo de exportación muy importante para todos los países.

13/1064/52

13/1064/52 Mama-Laufpuppe, Mädchen mit Satinbluse, buntfarbigem Rock und Haube, durchbrochenen Strümpfen und Wachstuchschuhen gekleidet.

Mama-doll, walking, girl in blouse of satin, frock and lady's cap of many colours. Pierced stockings and shoes of oil cloth.

Mama-muñeca, marchante en blusa de satén, falda y gorro en varios colores, medias de filigrana zapatos en hule.

13/1085/52

13/1085/52 Junge, mit Spielschürze gekleidet, mit bunten Hosen, Jacke, durchbrochenen Strümpfen und Wachstuchschuhen.

Boy dressed with apron for playing, breeches of many colours, pierced stockings and shoes of oil cloth.

Muchacho, vestido de delantal, calzón en varios colores, medias de filigrana, zapatos en hule.

13/1082/52

13/1082/52 Mädchen in sehr hübschem, weißem Matrosenkleid mit blauem Kragen, Schleife und Matrosenmütze, durchbrochenen Strümpfen und Wachstuchschuhen.

Girl in a very nice white sailor's dress, blue collar, sailor's knot and cap, pierced stockings and shoes of oil cloth.

Muchacha en traje marino blanco con cuello, undó, gorro azules, medias de filigrana, zapatos en hule.

13/1083/52

13/1083/52 in derselben Ausführung wie **13**/1082/52, nur als Junge gekleidet.

Boy dressed same as **13**/1082/52.

Muchacho en la misma ejecución como **13**/1082/52.

13/1072/52 Mädchen in hellem Kleid mit buntem Stoff garniert. Haube in gleicher Ausführung. Durchbrochene Strümpfe und Wachstuchschuhe. Diese Nummer wird besonders gern gekauft.

Girl, dress light colours and trimmed with many-coloured stuff. Cap of the same kind. Pierced stockings and shoes of oil cloth. People are fond of buying this doll.

Muchacha, traje claro, guarnecido de estofa en varios colores, medias de filigrana y zapatos en hule. Este número se compra de preferencia.

13/1072/52

13/1062/52 Junge in buntem Stoff, alle Farben sortiert, in Spielhose gekleidet. Durchbrochene Strümpfe und Wachstuchschuhe.
Spezialschlagerpuppe, diese Nummer ist die vorteilhafteste, billigste Spezialausführung.

Boy in many-coloured stuff, all colours assorted, breeches for playing. Pierced stockings and shoes of oil cloth.
Doll of first quality and very cheap.

Muchacho en estofa varia, vestido de calzón de juego, medias de filigrana, zapatos en hule.
Este número es la ejecución más ventajosa y barata.

13/1062/52

Photographische Abbildungen vom ganzen Sortiment Mama-Laufpuppen sind vorrätig, und bitte höflichst, von Interessenten anzufordern.
Please ask for faithful photographs of mama-walking-dolls.
Exija V. fotografias de todos surtidos de mamá-muñecas.

Please note also the publication on page 222 and 223 of the principal catalogue.
Llamamos también su atención á la publicación en la página 222 y 223 del catálogo principal.

Neuheiten! Novelties! Novedades!

Künstliche Christbäume mit Musik
(Schweizer Werk), extra voll und dicht,, mit großen roten Beeren.

Christmas trees with musical boxes
(Swiss works), extra full and thick, with large red berries.

Arboles de Navidad con caja de música
(mecanismo suizo), muchas ramas muy compactas y bayas rojas grandes.

86/6515

Höhe — height — altura 120 cm

1 Weihnachtslied — 1 Christmast carol
1 cantico de Navidad.

86/6520

Höhe — height — altura 160 cm

2 Weihnachtslieder — 2 Christmas carols
2 canticos de Navidad.

86/6525

Höhe — height — altura 210 cm

2 Weihnachtslieder — 2 Christmas carols — 2 canticos de Navidad.

Weihnachts-Dekorationsleuchter, beschneit.
Christmas Candlestands, frosted.
Candelabros de Navidad, escarchados.

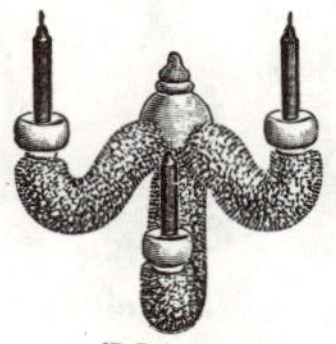

86/6102

86/5903

86/5905

86/5906

	Höhe incl. Kerze Height incl. candle Altura con bujía	Packung Packing Contenido	
No. **86**/5903	16 cm	1	Dtz.
„ **86**/5905	23 „	1	im Karton
„ **86**/5906	27 „	1/2	doz. in box
„ **86**/6102		1/3	doc.en cartón

* = in 3 Teile zerlegbar, to be cut in 3 sections, a descomponer en 3 partes.

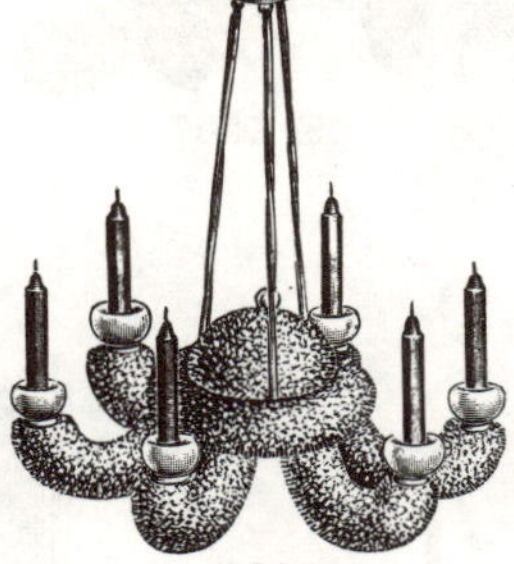

86/6204

86/6306

	Durchmesser Diameter Diámetro	Kerzen Candles Bujías	Packung Packing Contenido	
No. **86**/6202	30 cm	6	1/12	
„ **86**/6204	37 „	6	1/12	
„ **86**/6206	45 „	8	1/12	Dtz.
„ **86**/6302*	30 „	7	1/12	im Karton
„ **86**/6304*	37 „	7	1/12	doz. in box
„ **86**/6306*	46 „	9	1/12	doc.en cartón
„ **86**/6403	31 „	5	1/3	
„ **86**/6405	37 „	5	1/3	

Dekorationssterne, beschneit, rot und grün sortiert.
Christmas stars, frosted, red and green assorted.
Estrellas de decoración, escarchadas, rojas y verdes assurtidas.

86/6606

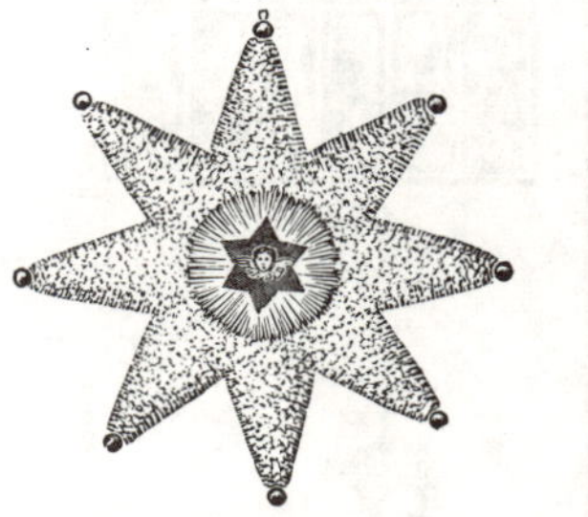

86/6707

	Durchmesser Diameter Diámetro	Zacken Points Puntas	Packung Packing Contenido	
No. **86**/6601	13 cm	5	1/2	
„ **86**/6602	19 „	5	1/2	
„ **86**/6603	23 „	5	1/2	Dtz.
„ **86**/6604	28 „	5	1/3	im Karton
„ **86**/6605	33 „	5	1/12	doz. in
„ **86**/6606	38 „	5	1/12	cardboard
„ **86**/6702	18 „	6	1/2	box
„ **86**/6703	$22^1/_2$ „	6	1/2	doc. en cajita
„ **86**/6704	26 „	6	1/3	de cartón
„ **86**/6705	33 „	6	1/12	
„ **86**/6707	38 „	8	1/12	
„ **86**/6708	47 „	8	1/12	
„ **86**/6711	88 „	8	1/12	

Beachten Sie auch die Veröffentlichung auf Seite 222 und 223 des HauptKataloges.

Please note also the publication on page 220 and 221 of the principal catalogue.
Llamamos también su atención á la publicación en la página 220 y 221 del catálogo principal.

48/14/83 **48**/18/81 **48**/40/122 **48**/22/188 **48**/21/42

48/38/43 **48**/400/420 **48**/400/494 **48**/400/404 **48**/400/401 **48**/400/343 **48**/400/351

48/200/15 **48**/Fig.352 **48**/Fig.28 **48**/Fig. 662 **48**/Fig. 683 **48**/Fig. 390 **48**/Fig. 200 **48**/Fig. 515 **48**/V 294

48/V 211 **48**/V 148 **48**/V 147 **48**/V 114 **48**/Sp 591 **48**/7151 **48**/100/100 **48**/100/130 **48**/125/17 **48**/Gel. 13

48/Sp 388 **48**/Sp 656 **48**/Sp 355 **48**/Sp 768 **48**/Sp 349/2 **48**/Sp 346

48/Sp 639 **48**/Sp 124 **48**/Sp 600 **48**/Sp 436 **48**/Sp 350 **48**/Sp 339

Beachten Sie auch die Veröffentlichung auf Seite 220 und 221 des Hauptkataloges.

Please note also the publication on page 220 and 221 of the principal catalogue.
Llamamos también su atención á la publicación en la página 220 y 221 del catálogo principal.

48/S 501

48/S 507

48/S 462

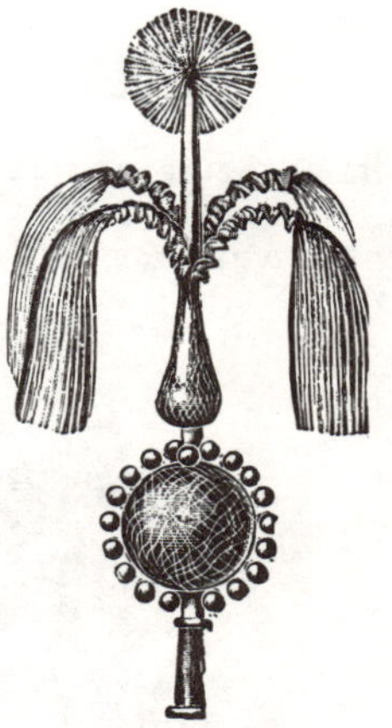
48/S 446

48/275/1104

48/300/111

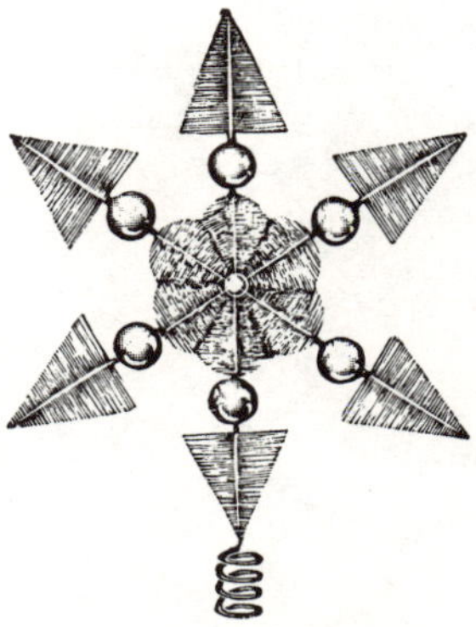
48/275/518

48/275/1133

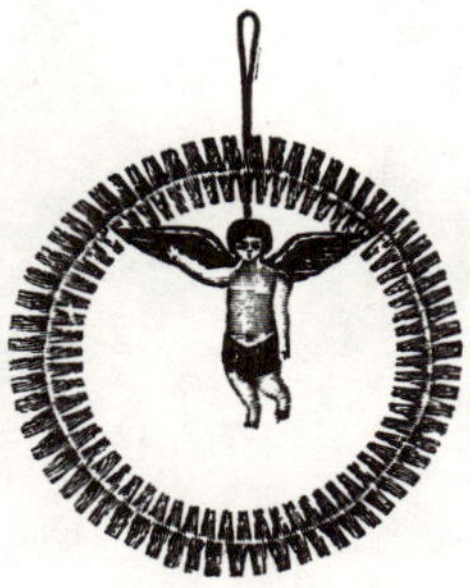
48/275/1128

48/275/380

48/275/502

48/275/1110

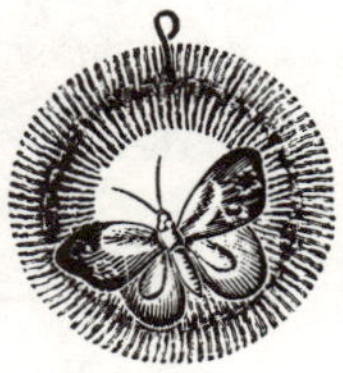
48/275/371

48/275/1043

48/275/435

48/450/2739

48/450/412

48/450/431

48/450/399

48/450/411

48/450/2680

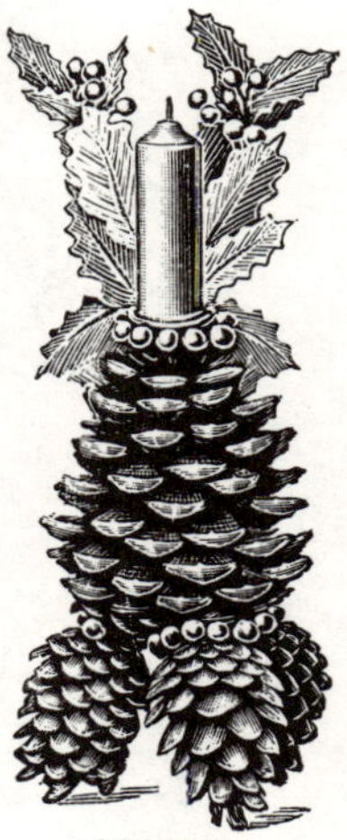
48/125/25

48/80/99

48/125/39

48/80/30

48/80/81

48/125/34

48/997/446

48/997/429

48/997/243

48/F 407

48/997/572

Beachten Sie auch die Veröffentlichung auf Seite 220 und 221 des Hauptkataloges.

Please note also the publication on page 236 of the principal catalogue.
Llamamos también su atención á la publicación en la página 236 del catálogo principal.

Domino-Visiere und Phantasie-Masken aus Samt, Seide und Stoff. — Dominoes and fancy masks of velvet, silk and cloth.

Viseras para dominós y máscaras de fantasía de terciopelo, seda y estofa.

87/80, 82, 83.

87/32, 33, 136, 145.

87/261

87/75, 76, 77, 78.

87/2, 12, 22, 27, 47, 52, 55, 57, 59, 91, 96, 97, 102, 105, 112, 117, 122, 132, 136, 142, 146, 152.

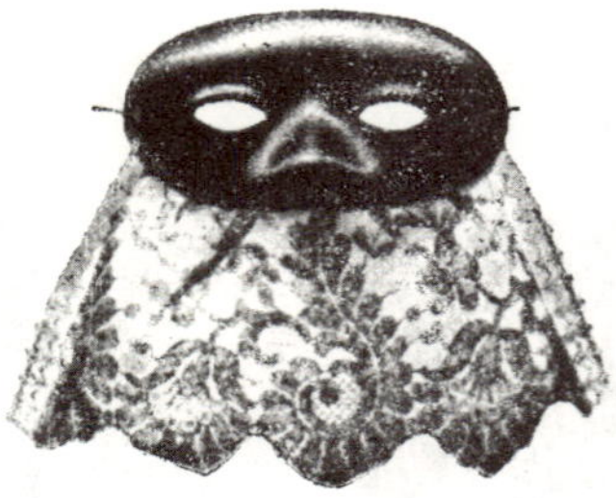

87/3, 13, 48, 53, 56, 92, 106, 113, 118.

87/2, 12, 22, 27, 32, 33, 47, 52, 55, 57, 91, 96, 97, 102, 105, 112, 117, 122, 132, 136, 142, 146, 152.

spitziger Behang.

87/249

87/235, 237, 239, 241.

87/71, 72, 73, 74.

87/5, 16, 25, 36, 37, 44, 50, 58, 60, 94, 100, 115, 125, 134, 138, 144, 154, 158.

87/61, 62, 63, 64.

87/287, 297, 281, 283, 285, 288, 289, 291, 293, 295, 299, 301, 311, 313, 315, 317, 319, 321, 323, 325, 327, 331, 333, 335.

87/1, 11, 21, 26, 31, 41, 46, 51, 54, 121, 131, 135, 141, 151, 155.

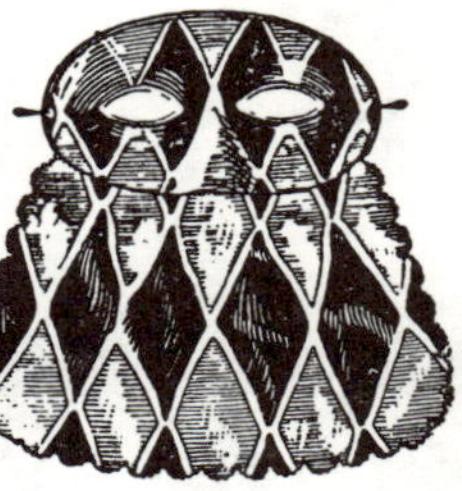

87/250

87/201

87/4, 15, 24, 43, 93, 99, 114, 124, 133, 153, 157.

87/202, 203, 204.

Alle Masken werden geliefert in schwarz, rot, rosa, hellblau, mittelblau, grün, gelb, weiß, lila, hellgrün, orange, violett. — Die Behänge sind ca. 14 cm lang, sind aber auch länger zu haben. — Bei Bedarf wolle man Spezialkatalog unter Angabe der No. 87, eventuell auch der Form-No., mit den neuesten Preisen verlangen.

All masks are supplied in black, red, green, pink, yellow, white, lilac, light green, orange, violet. — The flaps are about 14 cm long, but can also be had longer. — In case of need please apply for special catalogue, stating the No. 87, and eventually the shape No., with the latest prices.

Se entregará todas las máscaras en negro, rojo, en color de rosa, en verde, blanco, lila, verde claro, en color de naranja, en color de violeta. — Las colgaduras tienen una largura de 14 cm más o menos, pero se puede entregarlas también más largas. — Cuando Vd. tiene necesidad de estos géneros, sírvase demandar el catálogo especial con los últimos precios indicando el No. 87, eventualmente también el No. de la forma.

Beachten Sie auch die Veröffentlichung auf Seite 236 des Hauptkataloges.

Please note also the publication on page 236 of the principal catalogue.
Llamamos también su atención á la publicación en la página 236 del catálogo principal.

87/1 Extrafeine Atlas-Dominos für Damen, ohne Behang.
Extrafine satin-dominoes for ladies, without flaps.
Dominós de raso, extrafinos, para señoras, sin colgadura.

87/2 Extrafeine Atlas-Dominos für Damen, mit feinem Atlasbehang.
Extrafine satin-dominoes for ladies, with fine satin-flaps.
Dominós de raso, extrafinos, para señoras, con colgadura fina de raso.

87/3 Extrafeine Atlas-Dominos für Damen, mit prima Spitzenbehang.
Extrafine satin-domineoes for ladies, with first class lace-flaps.
Dominós de raso, extrafinos, para señoras, con colgadura de encaje, de Ia.

87/4 Extrafeine Atlas-Dominos für Herren, ohne Behang.
Extrafine satin-dominoes for gentlemen, without flaps.
Dominós de raso, extrafinos, para hombres, sin colgadura.

87/5 Extrafeine Atlas-Dominos für Herren, mit feinem Atlasbehang.
Extrafine satin-dominoes for gentlemen, with fine satin-flaps.
Dominós de raso, extrafinos, para hombres, con fina colgadura de raso.

87/11 Ia. Atlas-Dominos für Damen, ohne Behang.
1st class satin-dominoes for ladies, without flaps.
Dominós de raso Ia, para señoras, sin colgadura.

87/12 Ia. Atlas-Dominos für Damen, mit Atlasbehang.
1st class satin-dominoes for ladies, with satin-flaps.
Dominós de raso, Ia, para señoras, con colgadura de raso.

87/13 Atlas-Dominos für Damen, mit Ia. Spitzenbehang.
1st class satin-dominoes for ladies, with Ia. lace-flaps.
Dominós de raso, Ia, para señoras, con colgadura de encajes, de Ia.

87/15 Ia. Atlas-Dominos für Herren, ohne Behang.
1st class satin-dominoes for gents, without flaps.
Dominós de raso, Ia, para hombres, sin colgadura.

87/16 Ia. Atlas-Dominos für Herren, mit Atlasbehang.
1st class satin-dominoes for gents, with satin-flaps.
Dominós de raso, Ia, para hombres, con colgadura de raso.

87/21 IIa. Atlas-Dominos für Damen, ohne Behang.
2nd class satin dominoes for ladies, without flaps.
Dominós de raso, IIa, para señoras, sin colgadura.

87/22 IIa. Atlas-Dominos für Damen, mit Atlasbehang.
2nd class satin dominoes for ladies, with satin-flaps.
Dominós de raso, IIa, para señoras, con colgadura de raso.

87/24 IIa. Atlas-Dominos für Herren, ohne Behang.
2nd class satin dominoes for gents, without flaps.
Dominós de raso, IIa, para hombres, sin colgadura.

87/25 IIa. Atlas-Dominos für Herren, mit Atlasbehang.
2nd class satin dominoes for gents, with satin-flaps.
Dominós de raso, IIa, para hombres, con colgadura de raso.

87/26 IIa. Atlas-Dominos für Damen, neue Form, ohne Behang.
2nd class satin dominoes for ladies, new shape, without flaps.
Dominós de raso, IIa, para señoras, nueva forma, sin colgadura.

87/27 IIa. Atlas-Dominos für Damen, neue Form, mit Behang.
2nd class satin dominoes for ladies, new shape, with flaps.
Dominós de raso, IIa, para señoras, nueva forma, con colgadura.

87/31 IIIa. Atlas-Loup für Damen, kleine Form, ohne Behang.
3rd class satin-small size for ladies, without flaps.
Raso IIIa, tamaño pequeño, para señoras, sin colgadura.

87/32 IIIa. Atlas-Loup für Damen, kleine Form, mit 12 cm langem Behang.
3rd class satin-small size for ladies, with flaps of 12 cm long.
Raso IIIa, tamaño pequeño, para señoras, con colgadura de 12 cm de largo.

87/33 IIIa. Atlas-Loup für Damen, mit 14 cm langem Behang.
3rd class satin-small size for ladies, with flaps, 14 cm long.
Raso IIIa, tamaño pequeño para señoras, con colgadura de 14 cm de largo.

87/36 IIIa. Atlas für Herren, kleinere Form, mit 12 cm langem Atlasbehang.
3rd satin for gents, small size, with satin-flaps, 12 cm long.
Raso IIIa. para hombres, tamaño pequeño, con colgadura de raso, 12 cm de largo.

87/37 IIIa. Atlas für Herren, kleinere Form, mit 14 cm langem Atlasbehang.
3rd satin for gents, small size, with satin-flaps, 14 cm long.
Raso IIIa para hombres, tamaño pequeño, con colgadura de raso, 14 cm de largo.

87/41 Zweifarbige Atlas-Dominos für Damen, ohne Behang.
Two-coloured satin dominoes for ladies, without flaps.
Dominós de raso bi-color, para señoras, sin colgadura.

87/43 Zweifarbige Atlas-Dominos für Herren, ohne Behang.
Two-coloured satin dominoes for gents, without flaps.
Dominós de raso bi-color, para hombres, sin colgadura.

87/44 Zweifarbige Atlas-Dominos für Herren, mit zweifarbigem Atlasbehang.
Two-coloured satin dominoes for gents, with two-coloured satin flaps.
Dominós de raso bi-color, para hombres, con colgadura de raso bi-color.

87/46 Extrafeine Atlas-Dominos für Damen, mit Seidenfutter, ohne Behang.
Extrafine satin dominoes for ladies, with silk-lining, without flaps.
Dominós extrafinos de raso, para señoras, forrados de seda, sin colgadura.

87/47 Extrafeine Atlas-Dominos für Damen, mit Seidenfutter und mit feinem Atlasbehang.
Extrafine satin dominoes for ladies, with silk-lining and with fine satin-flaps.
Dominós extrafinos de raso, para señoras, forrados de seda y con colgadura de raso fino.

87/48 Extrafeine Atlas-Dominos für Damen, mit Seidenfutter und Ia. Spitzenbehang.
Extrafine satin dominoes for ladies, with silk-lining and first class lace-flaps.
Dominós extrafinos de raso, para señoras, forrados de seda y colgadura de encajas, Ia.

87/50 Extrafeine Atlas-Dominos für Herren, mit Seidenfutter u. feinem Atlasbehang.
Extrafine satin dominoes for gents, with silk-lining and fine satin-flaps.
Dominós extrafinos de raso, para hombres, forrados de seda y con colgadura de raso fino.

87/51 Extrafeine Atlas-Loup, neue Form, für Damen, mit Seidenfutter ohne Behang.
Extrafine satin small-size, new shape, for ladies, with silk-lining without flaps.
Raso extrafino, tamaño pequeño, nueva forma, para señoras, forrados de seda, sin colgadura.

87/52 Extrafeine Atlas-Loup, neue Form, für Damen, mit Seidenfutter und extrafeinem Spitzenbehang.
Extrafine satin small-size, new shape, for ladies, with silk-lining and fine satin-flaps.
Raso extrafino, tamaño pequeño, nueva forma, para señoras, forrados de seda y con colgadura de raso fino.

87/53 Extrafeine Atlas-Loup, neue Form, für Damen, mit Seidenfutter und extrafeinem Spitzenbehang.
Extrafine satin small-size, new shape, for ladies, with silk-lining and extrafine lace-flaps.
Raso extrafino, tamaño pequeño, nueva forma, para señoras, forrados de seda y con colgadura extrafina de encajes.

87/54 Extrafeine Atlas-Loup, neue Form, mit Shirtingfutter, für Damen, ohne Behang.
Extrafine satin small-size, new shape, with shirting-lining, for ladies, without flaps.
Raso extrafino, tamaño pequeño, nueva forma, para señoras, con forro de cambray, sin colgadura.

87/55 Extrafeine Atlas-Loup, neue Form, für Damen, mit Shirtingfutter und prima Spitzenbehang.
Extrafine satin small-size, new shape, for ladies, with shirting-lining and first class lace-flaps.
Raso extrafino, tamaño pequeño, nueva forma, para señoras, con forro de cambray y colgadura de raso Ia.

87/56 Extrafeine Atlas-Loup, neue Form, für Damen, mit Shirtingfutter und prima Spitzenbehang.
Extrafine satin small-size, new shape for ladies, with shirting-lining and first class lace-flaps.
Raso extrafino, tamaño pequeño, nueva forma, para señoras, con forro de cambray y colgadura de encajes de Ia.

87/57 Extrafeine Atlas-Dominos für Damen, mit extrafeinem 15 cm langen Behang.
Extrafine satin dominoes for ladies, with extrafine flaps, 15 cm long.
Dominós de raso extrafino, para señoras, con colgadura extrafina de 15 cm de largo.

87/58 Extrafeine Atlas-Dominos für Herren, mit extra feinem 15 cm langen Behang.
Extrafine satin dominoes for gents, with extrafine flaps, 15 cm long.
Dominós de raso extrafino, para hombres, con colgadura extrafina de 15 cm de largo.

87/59 Extrafeine Atlas-Dominos für Damen, mit Seidenfutter und extra langem 15-cm-Behang.
Extrafine satin dominoes for ladies, with silk-lining and extra long flaps, 15 cm long.
Dominós extrafinos de raso, para señoras, con forro de seda y colgadura extra larga de 15 cm.

87/60 Extrafeine Atlas-Dominos für Herren, mit Seidenfutter und extra langem 15-cm-Behang.
Extrafine satin dominoes for gents, with silk-lining and extra long flaps of 15 cm.
Dominós extrafinos de raso, para hombres, con forro de seda y colgadura extra larga de 15 cm.

Folies. Follies. Folías.

Domino-ähnliche Halbmasken für Damen, werden nur ohne Behang getragen.
Domino-like half-masks for ladies, are used only without flaps.
Medias máscaras a la dominó, para señoras, se usan solamente sin colgadura.

87/61 Prima Seiden-Atlas-Folie.
First class silk-satin folly.
Folías de raso de seda, de Ia.

87/62 Prima Seiden-Atlas-Folie, zweifarbig.
First class silk-satin folly, two-coloured.
Folías de raso de seda, de Ia, bi-color.

87/63 Percal-Folie.
Percale-folly.
Folía de percal.

87/64 Ia. Satinet-Folie.
First class satinet folly.
Folía de satineta, Ia.

Halbmasken und Hohlaugen. — Half-masks and hollow eyes.
Medias máscaras y ojos huecos.

87/71 Atlas-Stirn-Halbmasken mit beweglichem Kinn, Schnurr- und Kinnbart.
Satin forehead-halfmasks with movable chin, mustache and pointed beard.
Medias máscaras de frente, de raso, con barba movible, bigotes y barbilla.

87/72 Atlas-Stirn-Halbmasken, zweifarbig, mit beweglichem Kinn, Schnurr- und Kinnbart.
Satin forehead-halfmasks, two-coloured, with movable chin, mustache, and pointed beard.
Medias máscaras de frente, de raso, bi-color, con barba movible, bigotes y barbilla.

87/73 Satinet-Stirn-Halbmasken mit Kinn und Bart.
Satinet forehead-halfmasks with chin and beard.
Medias máscaras de frente, de satineta, con barba y bigotes.

87/74 Patent-Satinet-Stirn-Halbmasken mit Kinn und Bart.
Patent satinet forehead-halfmasks with chin and beard.
Medias máscaras de frente, patentadas, de satineta, con barba y bigotes.

87/75 Atlas-Stirn-Halbmasken mit Kotelettbart, ohne Kinn.
Satin forehead-halfmasks with whiskers, without chin.
Medias máscaras de frente, de raso, con suizas, sin barba.

87/76 Satinet-Stirn-Halbmasken mit Kotelettbart, ohne Kinn.
Satinet forehead-halfmasks with whiskers, without chin.
Medias máscaras de frente, de satineta, con suizas, sin barba.

87/77 Patent-Satinet-Stirn-Halbmasken mit Kotelettbart, ohne Kinn.
Patent satinet forehead-halfmasks with whiskers, without chin.
Medias máscaras de frente, patentadas, de satineta, con suizas, sin barba.

87/78 Atlas-Stirn-Halbmasken, zweifarbig, mit Kotelettbart, ohne Kinn.
Satin forehead-halfmasks, two-coloured, with whiskers, without chin.
Medias máscaras de frente, de raso, bi-color, con suizas, sin barba.

87/80 Patent-Satinet-Nasen mit Hohlaugen und Haarbesatz, mit Kinn.
Patent satinet noses with hollow eyes and hair-trimming, with chin.
Narices patentadas de satineta con ojos huecos, guarnecidas de pelo, con barba.

87/82 Atlas-Nasen mit Hohlaugen und Haarbesatz und beweglichem Kinn.
Satin noses with hollow eyes and hair-trimming and movable chin.
Narices de raso con ojos huecos, y guarnición de pelo, y barba movible.

87/83 Atlas-Nasen mit Hohlaugen u. Haarbesatz, zweifarbig, m. beweglichem Kinn.
Satin noses with hollow eyes and hair-trimming, two-coloured, with movable chin.
Narices de raso con ojos huecos y guarnición de pelo, bi-color, con barba movible.

Samt-Dominos werden in allen Farben geliefert.
Velvet Dominoes are supplied in all colours.
Dominós de terciopelo se suministran en todos los colores.

87/91 Prima Samt-Dominos für Damen, mit Ia. Atlasbehang.
First class velvet dominoes for ladies, with first class satin-flaps.
Dominós de terciopelo, Ia, para señoras, con colgadura de raso, de Ia.

87/92 Prima Samt-Dominos für Damen, mit prima Seidenspitzenbehang.
First class velvet dominoes for ladies, with first class silklace-flaps.
Dominós de terciopelo, Ia, para señoras, con colgadura de raso de seda, de Ia.

Beachten Sie auch die Veröffentlichung auf Seite 236 des Hauptkataloges.

87/93 Prima Samt-Dominos für Herren, ohne Behang.
First class velvet dominoes for gents, without flaps.
Dominós de terciopelo, Iª, para hombres, sin colgadura.

87/94 Prima Samt-Dominos für Herren, mit Ia. Atlasbehang.
First class velvet dominoes for gents, with first class satin-flaps.
Dominós de terciopelo, Iª, para hombres, con colgadura de raso, de Iª.

87/96 IIa. Samt-Dominos für Damen, mit Satinet-Behang.
IInd velvet dominoes for ladies, with satinet-flaps.
Dominós de terciopelo IIª, para señoras, con colgadura de satineta.

87/97 IIa. Samt-Dominos für Damen, mit IIa. Atlasbehang.
IInd velvet dominoes for ladies, with IInd satin-flaps.
Dominós de terciopelo IIª, para señoras, con colgadura de raso de IIª.

87/100 IIa. Samt-Dominos für Herren, mit IIa. Atlasbehang.
IInd velvet dominoes for gents, with IInd satin-flaps.
Dominós de terciopelo de IIª, para hombres, con colgadura de raso de IIª.

87/102 IIa. Samt-Loup für Damen, mit Satinetbehang.
IInd velvet small-size for ladies, with satinet-flaps.
Terciopelo de IIª, tamaño pequeño, para señoras, con colgadura de satineta.

87/105 Extrafeine Samt-Loup für Damen, mit Shirtingfutter und Ia. Atlasbehang.
Extrafine velvet small-size for ladies, with shirting-lining and first class satin-flaps.
Terciopelo extrafino, tamaño pequeño, para señoras, con forro de cambray y colgadura de raso de Iª.

87/106 Extrafeine Samt-Loup für Damen, mit Shirtingfutter und Ia. Spitzenbehang.
Extrafine velvet small-size for ladies, with shirting-lining and first class lace-flaps.
Terciopelo extrafino, tamaño pequeño, para señoras, con forro de cambray y colgadura de encajes de Iª.

87/112 Extrafeine Samt-Dominos für Damen, innen weiß Atlasfutter, mit feinem Atlasbehang.
Extrafine velvet dominoes for ladies, within white satin lining, with fine satin-flaps.
Dominós extrafinos de terciopelo, para señoras, dentro forro de raso blanco, con colgadura de raso fino.

87/113 Extrafeine Samt-Dominos für Damen, innen weiß Atlasfutter, mit hochfeinem Seidenspitzenbehang.
Extrafine velvet dominoes for ladies, within white satin lining, with very fine silk lace-flaps.
Dominós extrafinos de terciopelo, para señoras, por dentro forro de raso blanco, con colgadura de encajes de seda finísima.

87/114 Extrafeine Samt-Dominos für Herren, innen weiß Atlasfutter, ohne Behang.
Extrafine velvet dominoes for gents, within white satin lining, without flaps.
Dominós de terciopelo extrafinos, para hombres, por dentro forro de raso blanco, sin colgadura.

87/115 Extrafeine Samt-Dominos für Herren, innen weiß Atlasfutter, mit feinem Atlasbehang.
Extrafine velvet dominoes for gents, within white satin lining, with fine satin-flaps.
Dominós de terciopelo extrafinos, para hombres, por dentro forro de raso blanco, con colgadura de raso fino.

87/117 Extrafeine Samt-Loup für Damen, innen weiß Atlasfutter, mit Ia. Atlasbehang.
Extrafine velvet small-size for ladies, within white satin lining, with first class satin-flaps.
Terciopelo extrafino, tamaño pequeño, para señoras, por dentro forro de raso blanco, con colgadura de raso de Iª.

87/118 Extrafeine Samt-Loup für Damen, innen weiß Atlasfutter, mit Ia. Spitzenbehang.
Extrafine velvet small-size for ladies, within white satin lining, with first class lace-flaps.
Terciopelo extrafino, tamaño pequeño, para señoras, por dentro forro de raso blanco, con colgadura de encajes de Iª.

Extrafeine Seiden-Satinet-Dominos. — Extrafine silk-satinet Dominoes. — Dominós de satineta de seda, extrafinos.

87/121 Ia. Satinet-Dominos für Damen, ohne Behang.
First class satinet dominoes for ladies, without flaps.
Dominós de satineta Iª, para señoras, sin colgadura.

87/122 Ia. Satinet-Dominos für Damen, mit Behang.
First class satinet dominoes for ladies, with flaps.
Dominós de satineta Iª, para señoras, con colgadura.

87/124 Ia. Satinet-Dominos für Herren, ohne Behang.
First class satinet dominoes for gents, without flaps.
Dominós de satineta Iª, para hombres, sin colgadura.

87/125 Ia. Satinet-Dominos für Herren, mit Behang.
First class satinet dominoes for gents, with flaps.
Dominós de satineta Iª, para hombres, con colgadura.

Percal-Dominos. — Percale Dominoes. — Dominós de Percal.

87/131 Percal-Dominos für Damen, ohne Behang.
Percale dominoes for ladies, without flaps.
Dominós de percal, para señoras, sin colgadura.

87/132 Percal-Dominos für Damen, mit Behang.
Percale dominoes for ladies, with flaps.
Dominós de percal, para señoras, con colgadura.

87/133 Percal-Dominos für Herren, ohne Behang.
Percale dominoes for gents, without flaps.
Dominós de percal, para hombres, sin colgadura.

87/134 Percal-Dominos für Herren, mit Behang.
Percale dominoes for gents, with flaps.
Dominós de percal, para hombres, con colgadura.

87/135 Percal-Domino-Loup für Damen, kleine Form, ohne Behang.
Percale dominoes small-size for ladies, without flaps.
Dominós de percal, tamaño pequeño, para señoras, sin colgadura.

87/136 Percal-Domino-Loup für Damen, kleine Form, mit Behang.
Percale dominoes small-size for ladies, with flaps.
Dominó de percal, tamaño pequeño, para señoras, con colgadura.

87/138 Percal-Domino für Herren, kleinere Form, mit Behang.
Percale dominoes small-size for gents, with flaps.
Dominó de percal, tamaño pequeño, para hombres, con colgadura.

87/141 Patent-Satinet-Dominos für Damen, auf Gaze, ohne Behang.
Patent satinet dominoes for ladies, on gauze, without flaps.
Dominós de satineta, patente, para señoras, sobre gasa, sin colgadura.

87/142 Patent-Satinet-Dominos für Damen, auf Gaze, mit Behang.
Patent satinet dominoes for ladies, on gauze, with flaps.
Dominós de satineta, patente, para señoras, sobre gasa, con colgadura.

87/144 Patent-Satinet-Dominos für Herren, auf Gaze, kleinere Form, mit Behang.
Patent satinet dominoes for gents, on gauze, small-size, with flaps.
Dominós de satineta, patente, para hombres, sobre gasa, tamaño pequeño, con colgadura.

87/145 Patent-Satinet-Loup für Damen, auf Gaze, kleine Form, ohne Behang.
Patent satinet small-size for ladies, on gauze, without flaps.
Satineta patente, tamaño pequeño, para señoras, sobre gasa, sin colgadura.

87/146 Patent-Satinet-Loup für Damen, auf Gaze, kleine Form, mit Behang.
Patent satinet small-size for ladies, on gauze, with flaps.
Satineta patente, tamaño pequeño, para señoras, sobre gasa, con colgadura.

Patent-Satinet-Dominos. — Patent Satinet Dominoes. — Dominós patente de satineta.

87/151 Ia. Patent-Satinet-Dominos für Damen, ohne Behang.
First class patent satinet dominoes for ladies, without flaps.
Dominós patente de satineta Iª, para señoras, sin colgadura.

87/152 Ia. Patent-Satinet-Dominos für Damen, mit Behang.
First class patent satinet dominoes for ladies, with flaps.
Dominós patente de satineta Iª, para señoras, con colgadura.

87/153 Ia. Patent-Satinet-Dominos für Herren, ohne Behang.
First class patent satinet dominoes for gents, without flaps.
Dominós patente de satineta Iª, para hombres, sin colgadura.

87/154 Ia. Patent-Satinet-Dominos für Herren, mit Behang.
First class patent satinet dominoes for gents, with flaps.
Dominós patente de satineta Iª, para hombres, con colgadura.

87/155 Ia. Patent-Satinet-Dominos für Damen, zweifarbig, ohne Behang.
First class patent satinet dominoes for ladies, two-coloured, without flaps.
Dominós patente de satineta Iª, para señoras, bi-color, sin colgadura.

87/157 Patent-Satinet-Dominos für Herren, zweifarbig, ohne Behang.
Patent satinet dominoes for gents, two-coloured, without flaps.
Dominós patente de satineta para hombres, bi-color, sin colgadura.

87/158 Patent-Satinet-Dominos für Herren, zweifarbig, mit Behang.
Patent satinet dominoes for gents, two-coloured, with flaps.
Dominós patente de satineta para hombres, bi-color, con colgadura.

Neue Fantasie-Masken. Spitzen-Masken. — New Fancy-Masks. Lace-Masks. — Nuevas máscaras de fantasía. Máscaras de encajes.

87/201 Ia. Ia. Spitzen-Dominos mit Flitter in Figuren benäht, alle Farben.
First class lace-dominoes with tinsel in figures sewed on, all colours.
Dominós de encajes de Iª Iª, cosidos con lentejuelas en figuras, todos colores.

87/203 Payett-Brille auf Seidenfutter, mit Seidenspitzen, alle Farben.
Payett spectacles on silk-lining, with silk-lace, all colours.
Anteojos de payeta sobre forro de seda, con encajes de seda, todos colores.

87/204 Payett-Brille auf Seidenfutter, mit kleiner Rüsche, alle Farben.
Payett spectacles, on silk-lining, with small ruche, all colours.
Anteojos de payeta sobre forro de seda, con rizado estrecho, todos colores

Atlas-Damen (garniert). — Satin ladies (trimmed). — Raso para Señoras (guarnecido).

87/236 Extrafeine Atlas-Damen, herzförmig geschnitten, mit Samtblumen und Perlen und feinem Atlasbehang, alle Farben.
Extrafine satin ladies, cut heart-shaped, with velvet-flowers and pearls and fine satin flaps, all colours.
Raso extrafino para señoras, corte cordiforme, con flores de terciopelo y perlas y colgadura de raso fino, todos colores.

87/237 Extrafeine Atlas-Damen, herzförmig geschnitten, mit Samtblumen und Perlen, ohne Behang, alle Farben.
Extrafine satin ladies, cut heart-shaped, with velvet-flowers and pearls, without flaps, all colours.
Raso extrafino para señoras, corte cordiforme, con flores de terciopelo y perlas, sin colgadura, todos colores.

87/239 Extrafeine Atlas-Damen, herzförmig geschnitten, mit gouffrierter Rüsche, alle Farben.
Extrafine satin ladies, cut heart-shaped, with goffered ruche, all colours.
Raso extrafino para señoras, corte cordiforme, con rizado estampado, todos colores.

87/241 Extrafeine Atlas-Damen, herzförmig geschnitten, mit feinem Flitterschlung, alle Farben.
Extrafine satin ladies, cut heart-shaped, with fine tinsel, all colours.
Raso extrafino para señoras, corte cordiforme, con lentejuelas finas, todos colores.

87/249 Domino-Visiere, aus Atlas, kariert, für Clowns, in 8 verschiedenen Farben, ohne Behang.
Domino-visors of satin, chequered, for clowns, in 8 different colours, without flaps.
Viseras de dominó, de raso, de ajedrez para payazos, en 8 diferentes colores, sin colgadura.

87/250 Domino-Visiere, aus Atlas, kariert, für Clowns, in 8 verschiedenen Farben, mit Behang.
Domino-visors of satin, chequered, for clowns, in 8 different colours, with flaps.
Viseras de dominó, de raso, de ajedrez para payazos, en 8 diferentes colores, con colgadura.

87/261 IIa. Samt-Loup mit dreieckigem Spitzenbehang und mit Fransen garniert, nur schwarz.
IInd velvet small-size with triangular lace-flaps and trimmed with fringes, only black.
Terciopelo IIª, tamaño pequeño, con colgadura triangular de encajes y guarnecido de franjas, solamente negro.

Samt-Brillen (garniert). — Velvet-Spectacles (trimmed). Anteojos de terciopelo (guarnecidos).

87/281 Ia. Ia. Samt-Brille auf Seidenfutter, mit Flitter und Perlen benäht und plissierter Rüsche, nur schwarz.
First class velvet spectacles on silk-lining, with tinsel and pearls sewed on and plaited ruche, only black.
Anteojos de terciopelo de Iª Iª, sobre forro de seda, guarnecidos con lentejuelas y perlas y con rizado de pliegues, solo negro.

87/283 Ia. Ia. Samt-Brille auf Seidenfutter, mit Seidenfransen, nur schwarz.
First class velvet spectacles on silk-lining, with silk fringes, only black.
Anteojos de terciopelo Iª Iª, sobre forro de seda, franjas de seda, solamente negro.

87/285 Ia. Ia. Samt-Brille auf Seidenfutter, mit plissierter Rüsche, nur schwarz.
First class velvet spectacles on silk lining, with plaited ruche, only black.
Anteojos de terciopelo Iª Iª, sobre forro de seda, con rizado de pliegues, solamente negro.

Please note also the publication on page 120 and 236 of the principal catalogue.
Llamamos también su atención á la publicación en la página 120 y 236 del catálogo principal.

87/287 Ia. Ia. Samtbrille auf Seidenfutter, mit Payett-Borte und Seidenspitzen, nur schwarz.
First class velvet spectacles on silk lining, with payett rim and silk-lace, only black.
Anteojos de terciopelo Iª Iª, sobre forro de seda, con orla de payeta y encajes de seda, solamente negro.

87/288 Ia. Ia. Samt-Brille auf Seide, mit schmaler Rüsche, nur schwarz.
First class velvet spectacles on silk, with small ruche, black only.
Anteojos de terciopelo Iª Iª sobre seda, con rizado estrecho, solamente negro.

87/289 Prima Samt-Brille auf Weißzeugfutter, mit Seidenfransen, nur schwarz.
First class velvet spectacles on linen lining, with silk fringes, black only.
Anteojos de terciopelo Iª, sobre forro de lienzo y con franjas de seda, solamente negro.

87/291 Ia. Samt-Brille auf Weißzeug, mit plissierter Rüsche, nur schwarz.
First class velvet spectacles on linen, with plaited ruche, black only.
Anteojos de terciopelo Iª, sobre lienzo, con rizado de pliegues, solamente negro.

87/293 Ia. Samt-Brille auf Weißzeug, mit gouffrierter Rüsche, nur schwarz.
Ist velvet spectacles on linen, with goffered ruche, black only.
Anteojos de terciopelo Iª, sobre lienzo, con rizado estampado, solamente negro.

87/295 IIa. Samt-Brille auf Weißzeug, mit plissierter Rüsche, nur schwarz.
IInd class velvet spectacles on linen, with plaited ruche, black only.
Anteojos de terciopelo IIª, sobre lienzo, con rizado de pliegues, solamente negro.

87/297 IIa. Samt-Brille mit Payettborte und Seidenspitzen garniert, nur schwarz.
IInd velvet spectacles with payett rim and trimmed with silk lace, black only.
Anteojos de terciopelo IIª, con orla de payeta y encajes de seda, solamente negro.

87/299 IIa. Samt-Brille auf Weißzeug, mit gouffrierter Rüsche, nur schwarz.
IInd velvet spectacles on linen, with goffered ruche, black only.
Anteojos de terciopelo IIª, sobre lienzo, con rizado estampado, solamente negro.

87/301 IIa. Samt-Brille mit Payettborte und kleiner Rüsche, nur schwarz.
IInd velvet spectacles with payett rim and small ruche, black only.
Anteojos de terciopelo IIª, con orla de payeta y rizado pequeño, solamente negro.

Atlas-Brillen (garniert). — Satin spectacles (trimmed). — Anteojos de raso (guarnecidos).

87/311 Extrafeine Atlas-Brille auf Seide, mit Flitter und Perlen benäht und Seidenfransen, nur schwarz.
Extrafine satin spectacles on silk, trimmed with tinsel and pearls and silk fringes, black only.
Anteojos de razo extrafino sobre seda, guarnecidos con lentejuelas y perlas, y con franjas de seda, solamente negro.

87/313 Extrafeine Atlas-Brille auf Seide, mit Flitter und Perlen benäht und breiter plissierter Rüsche, nur schwarz.
Extrafine satin spectacles on silk, trimmed with tinsel and pearls and with broad plaited ruche, black only.
Anteojos de raso extrafino sobre seda, guarnecidos de lentejuelas y perlas, y con rizado ancho de pliegues, solamente negro.

87/215 Extrafeine Atlas-Brille auf Seide, mit breiter plissierter Rüsche, nur schwarz.
Extrafine satin spectacles on silk, with broad, plaited ruche, black only.
Anteojos de raso extrafino sobre seda, con rizado ancho de pliegues, solamente negro.

87/317 Extrafeine Atlas-Brille auf Weißzeug, mit Flitter nnd Perlen benäht und breiter plissierter Rüsche, nur schwarz.
Extrafine satin spectacles on linen, trimmed with tinsel and pearls and with broad, plaited ruche, black only.
Anteojos de raso extrafino sobre lienzo, guarnecidos de lentejuelas y perlas y con rizado ancho de pliegues, solamente negro.

87/319 Extrafeine Atlas-Brille auf Seide, mit schmaler Rüsche, alle Farben.
Extrafine satin spectacles on silk, with narrow ruche, all colours.
Anteojos de raso extrafino sobre seda, con rizado estrecho, todos colores.

87/321 Extrafeine Atlas-Brille auf Weißzeug, mit breiter plissierter Rüsche, nur schwarz.
Extrafine satin spectacles on linen, with broad, plaited ruche, black only.
Anteojos de raso extrafino sobre lienzo, con rizado ancho de pliegues, solamente negro.

87/323 Extrafeine Atlas-Brille auf Weißzeug, mit Seidenfransen, nur schwarz.
Extrafine satin spectacles on linen, with silk fringes, black only.
Anteojos de raso extrafino sobre lienzo, con franjas de seda, solamente negro.

87/325 Extrafeine Atlas-Brille auf Weißzeug, mit Flitter und Perlen benäht und schmaler Rüsche, alle Farben.
Extrafine satin spectacles, on linen, trimmed with tinsel and pearls and with narrow ruche, all colours.
Anteojos de raso extrafino sobre lienzo, guarnecidos de lentejuelas y perlas y con rizado estrecho, todos colores.

87/327 Extrafeine Atlas-Brille auf Weißzeug, mit gouffrierter Rüsche, alle Farben.
Extrafine satin spectacles on linen, with goffered ruche, all colours.
Anteojos de raso extrafino sobre lienzo, con rizado estampado, todos colores.

87/331 IIa. Atlas-Brille mit Bauernbändchen auf Weißzeug, alle Farben.
IInd satin spectacles with clown-ribands, on linen, all colours.
Anteojos de raso IIª, con lazos de paisano sobre lienzo, todos colores.

87/333 IIa. Atlas-Brille auf Weißzeug, mit schmaler Rüsche, alle Farben.
IInd satin spectacles on linen, with narrow ruche, all colours.
Anteojos de raso IIª, sobre lienzo, con rizado estrecho, todos colores.

87/335 Satinet-Brille mit schmaler Rüsche, alle Farben.
Satinet spectacles with narrow ruche, all colours.
Anteojos de satineta, con rizado estrecho, todos colores.

Bessere Kinder- und Schülertrommeln.
Better children's and schoolboys' drums.
Tambores para niños y escolares, de calidad superior.

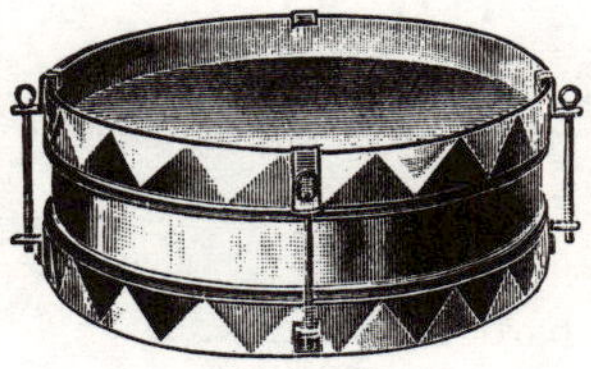

16/10 S

Mit Schrauben, 2 Seiten Fell, Blechkessel, gemalte Reifen.

With screws, both sides skin, tin-case, painted rims.

Con tornillos, ambos lados de piel, cercos pintados.

	Durchmesser Diameter Diámetro
16/10 S/20	20 cm
16/10 S/22	22 „
16/10 S/24	24 „
16/10 S/26	26 „
16/10 S/28	28 „
16/10 S/30	30 „
16/10 S/32	32 „

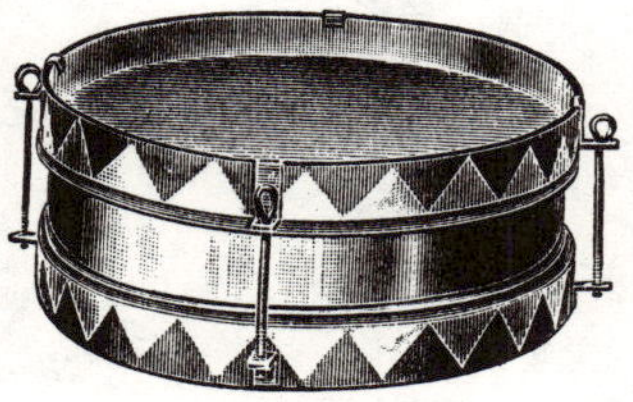

16/150

Mit Schrauben, Nickelkessel, 2 Seiten Fell, gemalte Reifen.

With screws, nickel-case, both sides skin, painted rims.

Con tornillos, caja de niquel, ambos lados de piel, cercos pintados.

	Durchmesser Diameter Diámetro
16/150/20	20 cm
16/150/22	22 „
16/150/24	24 „
16/150/26	26 „
16/150/28	28 „
16/150/30	30 „
16/150/32	32 „

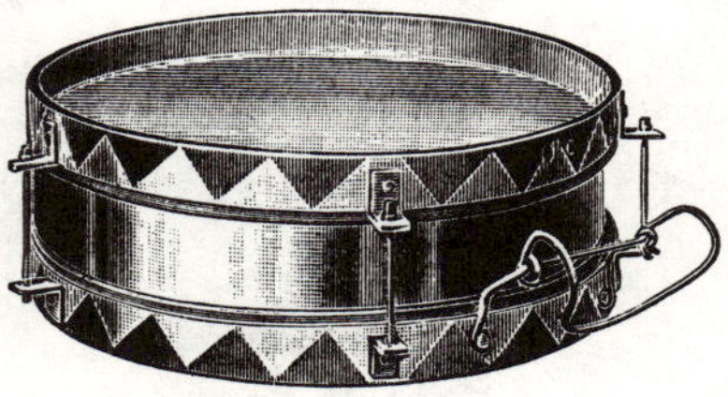

16/350

Mit Quadratkopfschrauben, angenietete Winkel, Kniebügel, Adler, Schlüssel, Nickelkessel, 2 Seiten Fell.

With square head-screws, soldered angles, knee-bow, eagle, key, nickel-case, both sides skin.

Con tornillos de cabeza cuadrada, ángulos soldados, arco para rodilla, águia, llave, caja de niquel, ambos lados de piel.

	Durchmesser Diameter Diámetro
16/350/20	20 cm
16/350/22	22 „
16/350/24	24 „
16/350/26	26 „
16/350/28	28 „
16/350/30	30 „
16/350/32	32 „

Beachten Sie auch die Veröffentlichung auf Seite 120 und 236 des Hauptkataloges.

Drahtmasken.
Wire masks.
Caretas de alambre.

121/72

121/75

Kindermasken.
Children's masks.
Caretas para niños.

121/100

121/100/1

121/101/15

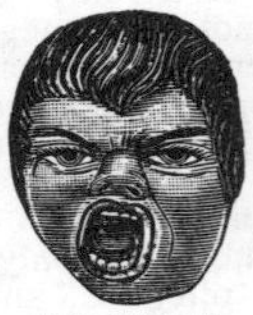
121/112/1

121/112/3

Kartonmasken.
Paper masks.
Caretas de cartón.

121/121

121/131

Charaktermasken.
Charakters.
Carácteres.

121/137

Clowns.
Clowns.
Payasos.

121/207/5

Nationen.
Nations.
Naciones.

121/226

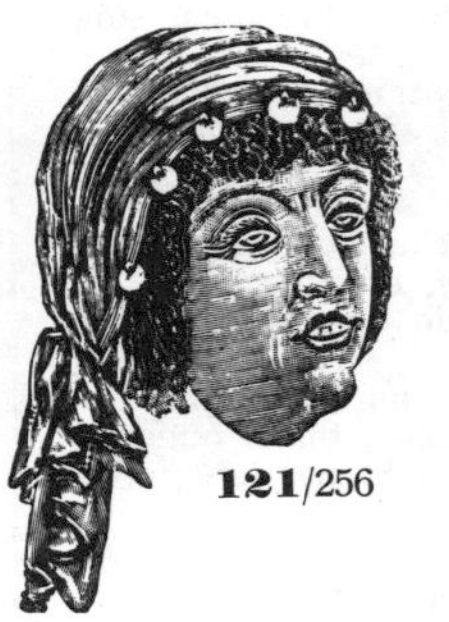
121/256

Teufel.
Devils.
Diablos.

121/265

Knecht Ruprecht.
Father Christmas.
Eremitaños.

121/167/2

Karikaturen.
Caricatures.
Caricaturas.

121/299

121/316a

Charaktermasken.
Charakters.
Carácteres.

121/372

Babymasken.
Babies.
Niños.

121/389

Bummler.
Tramps.
Vagabundos.

121/448/1

121/431/1

Halbmasken
Halfmasks.
Caretas medias.

121/933

121/1048/2

Nasen. — Noses. — Narices.

121/846

121/857 T

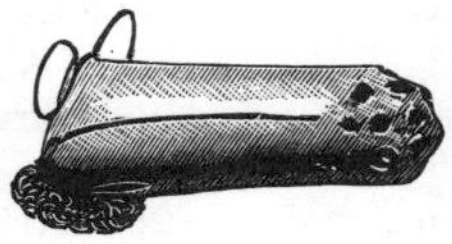
121/827 m

121/864/1

121/878/1

Trikotmasken.
Stockinet masks.
Caretas de tricot.

121/1180/5

Große Aufsetzköpfe.
Large heads.
Cabezas tamaño grande.

121/1302/22

Bärte.
Beards.
Barbas.

121/1202/1

Perücken. — Wigs. — Pelucas.

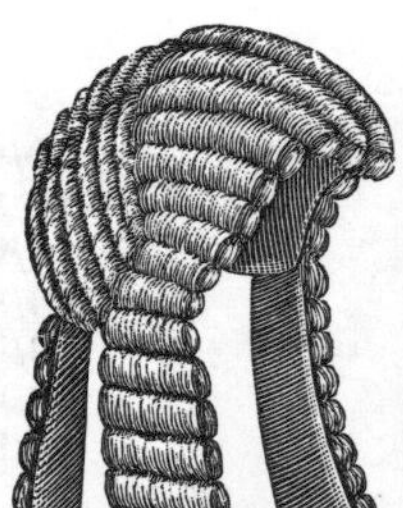
121/1233

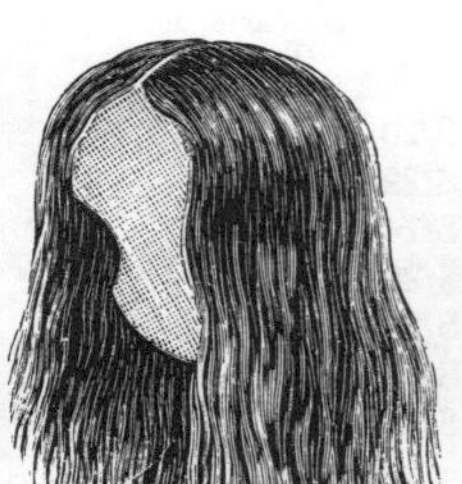
121/1261/6

121/1262/7

Please note also the publication on page 226 and 227 of the principal catalogue.
Llamamos también su atención á la publicación en la página 226 y 227 del catálogo principal.

Kopfbedeckungen aus Papier für Herren. — Paper head coverings for gentlemen. — Tocados de papel para señores.

107/911

107/986

107/974

107/922

107/970

107/948

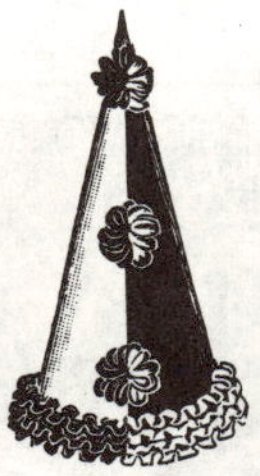
107/945

107/953

107/947

107/952

107/964

107/931

107/780

107/975

107/489

107/949

107/923

107/904

107/924

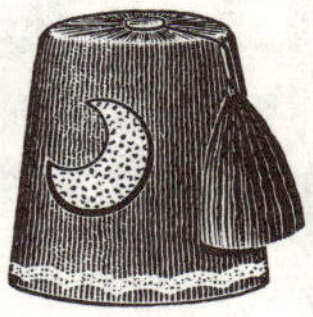
107/973

Kopfbedeckungen aus Papier für Damen.
Paper head coverings for ladies. — Tocados de papel para señoras.

107/0614

107/0985

107/0929

107/0930

107/0978

107/0972

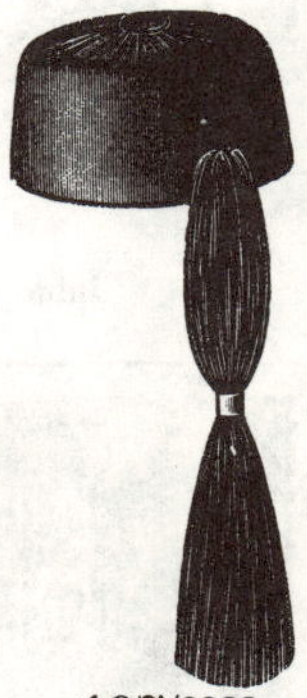
107/0982

107/0969

107/0796

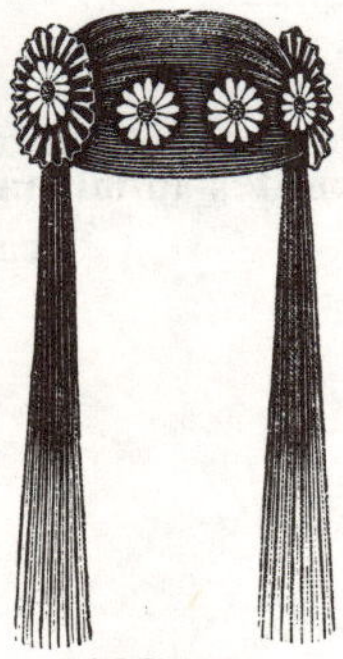
107/0976

107/0977

107/0636

107/0997

107/0968

107/0966

107/0951

107/0971

107/0946

Beachten Sie auch die Veröffentlichung auf Seite 226 und 227 des Hauptkataloges.

Please note also the publication on page 226 and 227 of the principal catalogue.
Llamamos también su atención á la publicación en la página 226 y 227 del catálogo principal.

Knallbonbons in Sortimenten. — Crackers in assortments. — Confites fulminantes en surtidos.

Inhalt: Verschiedene Scherzgegenstände. Contents: Various comic articles. Contenido: Diferentes artículos de burla.

107/15

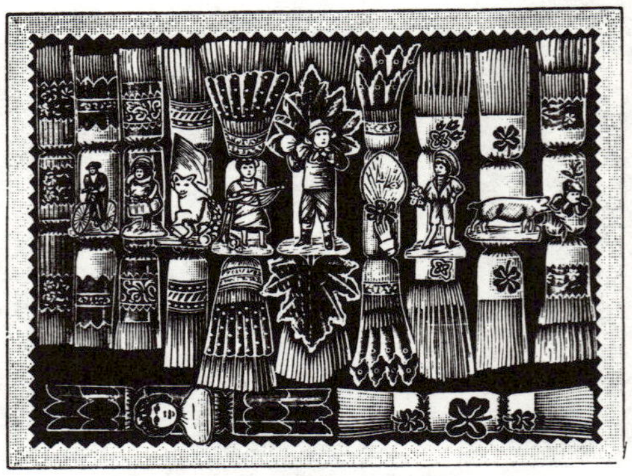

107/21

107/30

107/14

107/5

107/16

Knallbonbons in Sortimenten. — Crackers in assortments. — Confites fulminantes en surtidos.

Inhalt: Kopfbedeckungen. Contents: Head coverings. Contenido: Sombreros.

107/1000

107/1200

107/1500

Tafeldekorationen aus Knallbonbons zusammengestellt. — Table decorations composed of crackers. Decoraciones para la mesa compuestas de confites fulminantes.

Inhalt: Verschiedene Scherzgegenstände. Contents: Various comic articles. Contenido: Diferentes artículos de burla.

107/5398

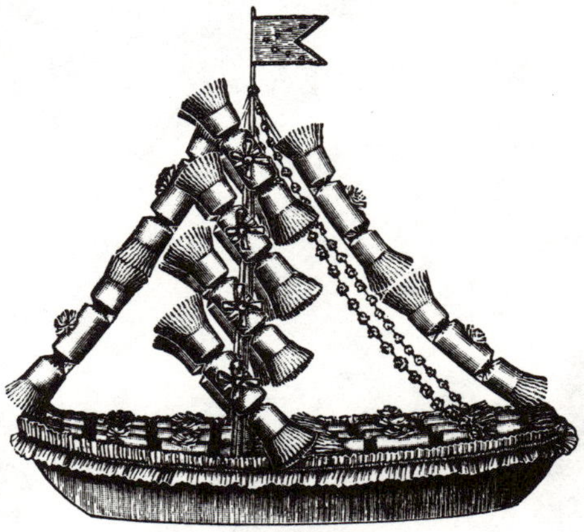

107/5462

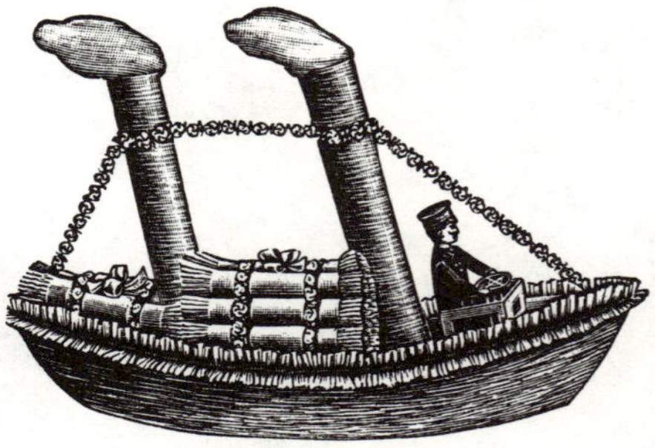

107/5463

Obige Abbildungen einiger gangbarer Sortimente und Tafeldekorationen zeigen nur eine ganz geringe Auswahl meiner Kollektion, die aus vielen Hunderten von Nummern in allen Preislagen besteht. Man verlange daher bei größerem Bedarf bemusterte Anstellung möglichst in Originalverpackungen.

The above drawings of a few of the most saleable assortments and table decorations show but a very small selection of my collection, which consists of many hundreds of numbers at all prices. In case of considerable quantities being required, quotations accompanied by samples should therefore be applied for, and as far as possible in original packages.

Las ilustraciones de algunos surtidos en voga y algunas decoraciones para la mesa no mostran una selección muy pequeña de mi colección compuesta de muchos centenares de números a diferentes precios. Por consiguiente, sírvase Vd. demandar ofertas con muestras, si posible, en empaques originales, si se trata de una cantidad de consideración.

Beachten Sie auch die Veröffentlichung auf Seite 226 und 227 des HauptKataloges.

Inhalts-Verzeichnis

Index

Contenido

Broschek & Co., Buchdruckerei und Tiefdruckanstalt, Hamburg.

Commentary

Play and life form an entity — magically interlaced.
The games take on the colorful tones of reality, a phenomenon
with the dazzling magic of fantasy.

Klaus Mann (1906–1949).

Preface

Sample book and catalog The sample books which emerged during the first half of the 19th century, and were especially representative of Thuringia and the Erzgebirge, served to promote market research by agents and the development of a profitable toy industry. Indeed, the pictorial presentation of toys for sales promotion purposes quickly became a much handier and more easily transportable replacement of the heavy toy sample cases. Significantly, such illustrated forms could be extended at will and their inclusions, true to both scale and detail, provided an impression of the multiplicity of high-grade craftmanship in toy manufacture. The earlier sample sheets, it should be noted, were not only a means of attracting potential clients but at the same time guidelines for manufacturers (mainly home industry toy makers in the Erzgebirge) whose social conditions were totally inadequate in the wake of rigorous exploitation. The agents exerted a direct influence on the design of toys by passing on clients' wishes verbally or as drawings. Moreover, as older and out-of-print literature, including warehouse and other catalogs, became accessible as new editions to researchers and collectors, in particular after 1965 and in the early 1970s in England and the USA, folklorists were already delving into the toy sample books in the hands of museums. Karl-Ewald Fritzsch (1894–1974), son of a maker of toy arks from the Erzgebirge, pupil and close collaborator of Adolf Spamer (1883–1953), has since 1958 furnished a whole number of studies which, utilizing the example of toy sample books from the Erzgebirge, convincingly testify to their rich cultural history. Hans-Peter His, a Swiss collector (1896–1974), whose items form the veritable foundation of the magical Riehen toy collection near Basle, drew attention at an early date to the need to analyze these pictorial sources; similarly Otto Keil, for many years the distinguished director of the Spielzeugmuseum Sonneberg. However, all these activities initially ignored those toys featured in the warehouse catalogs. Main attraction were the lithographed and painted sample books, often characterized as a unicum, which introduced ranges to clients.

Little is as yet known about the sample book designers. What was their social background? Did they work simultaneously for several agents? How were they regarded by the toy makers? Just a few names have been handed down as signatures, for instance the engravers F. Scharrer and A. Kolb from Nuremberg. Entries in Thuringian toy sample books indicate that owners of agencies also worked as designers. Apparently in the Erzgebirge as well as in other toy centers the design instructors of the vocational schools set up during the second half of the 19th century to "upgrade" the industry had also submitted one or the other draft. There are many aspects still crying out for an answer in this social context.

Changes in printing technology are, indeed, remarkable. During the first half of the 19th century lithography gained in importance as a duplication process, alongside the drawn and painted, intaglio printed, copper and hand-colored plates. However, the individual drawing soon became the favorite method because of the almost yearly sample changes and the customer's interest in true-to-life replicas. But these factually correct "working drawings" only assume an artistic parameter after having been treated by accomplished folklorists. Since the turn of this century sample books have been completely replaced by printed lists of goods and catalogs which, however, had already existed earlier. Photography superseded drawings.

The toy sample books of Waldkirchen, presented between 1840 and 1850 by the toy agent C. H. Oehme, are not only the oldest such works featuring solely toy motifs but equally the most antiquated sample books in the Erzgebirge as a whole. Thanks to fortunate finds and the initiative of Edition Leipzig Publishers the author in 1977 was able to present true to origin and with copious notes the Waldkirchen Toy Sample Book of 1850, and in 1979 the Sonneberg Toy Sample Book of 1831. For Nuremberg Christa Pieske in 1979 published an omnibus volume *Schönes Spielzeug aus alten Musterbüchern* (Beautiful toys from old sample books). Still more recently Brunhild Meyfarth released as an inventory a thorough study of all toy sample books, sheets and cards in the Sonneberg Museum.

The analysis of the toy sample books confirms that their extensive wealth of forms is not merely a regionally restricted achievement but, in principle, simultaneously the ideal basis of manufacturing processes in all German toy making areas. Indeed, the toy makers often took up specific motifs — provided by agents and manufacturers — which, however, they subsequently modified and probably also improved by means of their own innovations. On the other hand, special features of home production were equally encountered in the diversity of forms in other areas. In fact, these sample books are nowadays gems of exceptional cultural-historical value. They are, as reliable facsimile editions, vastly superior to the colorful illustrated volumes, whose scientific texts often confuse the reader who, in searching for exact information, frequently overlooks the much more modestly presented studies filled to the brim with essential, valid data. The same applies to the quickly prepared collector guidelines, the speculative character and minimal scientific findings of which merely reflect prevailing market trends in the toy sector, moreover with historical adornments which, thus, often pander to a "nostalgia" oriented art market.

It is not necessary to repeat what the author has previously summarized in the cited commentaries (1977, 1979) regarding the degree of investigation into toy sample books and their function for manufacturers, trade and customers.

Following the appearance as reprints of the first major mail-order catalogs (i.e., *Montgomery Ward & Co., Chicago 1895*; *Army & Navy Co-operative Society, London 1907*; *Illustrierter Hauptkatalog 1912* and *Illustrierter Hauptkatalog 2, 1926* by August Stukenbrok, Einbeck; *Warenhaus A. Wertheim 1903/04*), there came in direct sequence in recent years reprints of catalogs of well-known firms generally associated with mechanical toys. As far as German toy manufacturers are concerned, attention is drawn, amongst others, to reprints of the *Märklin-Kataloge* (1975 et seq.), to the series *Die anderen Nürnberger* (1973 et seq.) as well as the catalogs of the Bing Bros., Jean Schoenner, Georges Carette and Ernst Plank. Usually the introduction also briefly covers company history. However, we are also enraptured by such basic works as Marianne and Jürgen Cieslik's *Blechspielzeug-Patente* (1977, 1979) and reprints of historic company commemorative publications such as the *Familienbuch der Schildkrötpuppen* (1980), *Silbernes Jubiläum einer Puppenfabrik — 25 Jahre Kämmer & Reinhardt, Waltershausen 1886–1911* (1978) and *Steiff 1880–1980 — Geschichte und Gegenwart einer Marke* (1980) and the highly informative *VEDES-Kataloge*. On the occasion of the 100th jubilee of Europe's most tradition-steeped toy retailing organization, the Franz-Carl-Weber group in Zurich, and the justifiably "unconventional jubilee script" which appeared in 1981 entitled *Homo ludens. Buch zum Film* draws attention to the exceptional historic significance of the company's catalogs handed down (and archived!) alongside exemplary reproductions: "Whatever the toy trade had offered during the last 100 years, the range appeared virtually in full in Franz Carl Weber's catalogs. In this context, therefore, the various editions of the *Büchlein vom Spielzeug* are far more than a mere 'enumeration of goods' but virtually a cultural-political document. Indeed, the range changes year by year, reflecting mankind's advance in both science and technology: When Franz Carl Weber opened up his first toy shop in Zurich Europe had entered the *Gründerjahre* characterized by rapid growth and increasing human mobility; FCW outlets faced a growing demand for model railways. And, as the up-and-coming film industry gained substantial ground during the 1920s, FCW catalogs were featuring the good old magic lantern technologically which extended into a cinematography. Moreover, hot on the heels of the first thousand cars in the country FCW was always quick to show the latest model as a clockwork toy. These examples can be continued at will. Furthermore, Franz Carl Weber's toy catalogs are meticulous copies of Swiss everyday commercial art whilst the covers, particularly over the last few decades, were designed by foremost artists. Moreover, they perceived how to make visual in a challenging manner the subject of playing and toys: in this respect, too, Franz Carl Weber's toy booklets in their entirety make up an expertly illustrated contemporary document."

Historical toy sample books are also contemporary documents vividly augmenting our authentic knowledge, recording both everyday and festive styles and changes, illustrating social features and processes such as advances in science and technology as well as, in the final analysis, reflecting the class structure of society. During times where catalogs extolled coachmen's uniforms, room fountains, coffee cups with monarchical portraits and "always yours" assurances there was always something newer, more fashionable and advantageous than a few years earlier. Indeed, catalogs are in themselves reflections of a relatively short period and reliable sources of everyday realities. The encyclopaedic volume *Sammlungen zur Alltags- und Industriekultur. Ein Standortverzeichnis* (1983), testifies, for the collections in the Federal Republic of Germany alone, to the value of a systematic classification of older catalogs and other omnibus books for cultural-historical research.

Moreover, the pronounced development of rail and postal links in the second half of the 19th century led to much more mail-order business as a new, intensified form of customer services — a particularly beneficial practice for traders in rural areas thus now able to order by post from catalogs. In fact, the catalogs could increasingly present illustrated production programs and, from about 1860 onwards, gradually displaced the sample books. In this manner a great many toys which mail-order businesses obtained directly from industry were sold, for instance in the USA (by, amongst others, the Marshall Field mail-order company which, around 1900, was offering a well-illustrated catalog), and in the British Empire (in particular by A. W. Gamage Ltd. with main offices in Holborn/London), where a Christmas catalog with a great many pictures appeared annually and was sent to English colonial officials all over the world. Similarly also in Germany, for example, by the first German mail-order stores, Stukenbrok in Einbeck, established around 1890, which marketed a considerable selection of tin toys from Bing. One of the earliest special toy catalogs is G. Söhlke's *Illustrierter Catalog und Preiscourant von Kinder-Spiel-Waaren* (1858).

However, catalogs for consumers, nowadays quite customary, only came to stay from about 1920 onwards. Earlier catalogs had been conceived essentially as information sources for traders; their list prices pertained solely to conditions of delivery for dealers and were not actual selling prices (usually some 30 to 35 percent higher). Prior to 1920 information for buyers featured mainly simple brochures or summarized mini-catalogs containing but a selection of offered items. Only the mail-order firms generally released complete stock details. Special lists in which discontinued models from stock are marketed at reduced prices are a particular type of catalog. A great number of such inventories featuring export models not normally available to home buyers and generally, therefore, also missing in home market catalogs, were issued, in particular by Märklin, during the 1920s and 1930s.

Let us consider at this juncture the history of mail-order business. As far as the toy trade is concerned the mail-order company of the Nuremberg fancy goods trader and agent Georg Hieronimus Bestelmeier (1764–1829) — undoubtedly one of the best-known personalities in toy history — has, since 1792/93, been releasing regularly the first illustrated catalogs, *Magazine*, as well as *Verzeichnisse* (lists without illustrations setting out and describing a category of goods). Interestingly, the 1798 *Verzeichnis* which only includes toys contains some 8000 items despite the omission of dolls, dolls' kitchens and playthings. Thanks to his far-sighted business acumen Bestelmeier, notwithstanding vehement objections and many years of opposition from craftsmen, above all the joiners, managed to obtain both a license for a furniture section and to start a wallpaper manufactory (1823) in his company. Then, in 1826, Bestelmeier entrusted his business "Manufaktur- und Galanteriekommission" to his son, Johann Martin Christoph (1796–1854), who directed operations until his death. The city's register of traders indicates no successor.

Georg Hieronimus Bestelmeier, resident in Nuremberg, Lorenzer Seite Nr. 7, died on 2 February 1829 and is lauded thus in the city chronicles: "As a trader he zealously sought the greatest conceivable perfection in his local manufacturing activities. His new and tastefully constructed dwelling house (the former Barfüsserkirche) which, during the visit of the deceased Czar Alexander of Russia, was deemed best suited for his reception, the museum built under his direction, equally his commendable instructions as a committee member of the Dutzendteich shareholders are commensurate proof of his indefatigable activities.

Backed by voluntary, sometimes extremely scanty contributions, he started on the layout and planting of the paths and footways in front of the Spittler and Neuenthor and soon had the pleasure of witnessing the flourishing progress of his work. His fellow citizens gratefully revere the name of a man who lives on as one of the initial founders of the considerably expanded gardens on the fringes of the city."[1] Moreover, the catalogs which appeared around 1800 must have been in great demand for several reprints were soon necessary.[2] The new, improved edition of his 1803 *Magazin*, subdivided into eight sections (the seventh section is dated 1801), together with a systematic index, similarly features an extensive introduction by Bestelmeier which simultaneously indicates his pedagogical ambitions and praises the skills of the Nuremburg craftsmen — although he also marketed articles of outside manufacturers — but, in particular, characterizes an economically minded trader.[3]

The breakdown of the *Magazin* into twelve fields also testifies to Bestelmeier as a businessman with a special eye on all scientific and technological advances within the overall framework of the industrial revolution: 1. Architectural and horticultural skills for young enthusiasts. 2. Toys and useful things for boys and girls. 3. Entertaining and educational games for children and adults. 4. Astronomy, gnomonics and meteorology. 5. Electricity. 6. Geometry and arithmetic. 7. Hydraulics and hydrostatics. 8. Magnetism. 9. Mechanics. 10. Optics. 11. Music. 12. Economy, technology and luxuries.

Each article is numbered and briefly described. The pictorial section is based on this numerical classification. The ingenious businessman directs his offer first and foremost to educators and teachers. However, toys in the narrower sense are only a portion of the listed objects. Moreover, the opinions of toy researchers vary as regards the quantitative share, for many items are borderline cases. A recent, convincing analysis of the 1803 edition maintains that 612 of the 1111 numbered and illustrated *Magazin* positions are, in fact, toys.[4] Bestelmeier's magazines are catalogs, it should be noted, offering toys and implements from all manufacturing spheres of rural wood crafts. The items in point are not merely toys and parlor games but equally envisaged for schools and technical wings with physical teaching aids, for bourgeois dwellings with household goods, jewelry and decorative objects.[5] In later issues these items predominate still more. Illustrations from the *Magazin* soon appear in the Nuremberg and Sonneberg catalogs and, later still, also in the Erzgebirge sample books.

In 1852 J. G. Kohl notes in conjunction with his visit to Bestelmeier's mail-order business: "In Nuremberg I was given a most unusual document by a tradesman, namely a catalog detailing all varieties of children's toys marketed by his company. This catalog is the most complex goods register I have ever seen. It comprises almost as many item numbers as characters in the Chinese alphabet, about 12,000. As a warehouse for toys must, of necessity, be a veritable microcosm in which every existing thing and being has its place in miniature, it thus becomes clear that of all traders in the world the toy merchant is required to cope with the most extensive range of goods; all the same, what surprised me most was how well and efficiently this sector of trade has been organized in recent years.

Each kind of animal, wild and domestic, cattle, sheep, has its own catalog number. The same applies to people —, each army... the Bavarian, Austrian, Prussian army. All these thousands of items were similarly available at special prices in ordinary or precious materials in smaller or larger sizes. Alongside each number appeared a brief description of the article, indeed everything was so arranged that a shopkeeper elsewhere need only tell the Nuremberg wholesaler the required catalog number in order to obtain the very article young folk in his little rural centre are especially interested in."[6]

Bestelmeier's engraver, G. Roth, seems not to have sought an overall artistic effect. The geometrical and organic forms are accurately drawn with sound perspective. However, as each engraving of 16 × 19 cm is often filled with twenty, thirty or more representations, positioned irregularly, figures are sometimes difficult to recognize.

Indeed, in our context it is by no means accidental that a digression into the life work of Georg Hieronimus Bestelmeier, based extensively on the activities of Wenzel, Hessler and Fritzsch, as well as documentary material from the Nuremberg municipal and Regional Church archives[7], features prior to the notes: Bestelmeier's *Magazin* contained the first valid cross-section of an entire epoch of toy ranges — our universal toy catalog is the last of this type.

The reprinted catalog now presented — corresponding to contemporary research results — is, slightly more than one hundred years after Bestelmeier's *Magazinen*, the last complete edition on the German toy industry — restricted timewise to the ranges of the 1920s, — now available as a reference book for a scientific penetration of the cultural history of toys in the first decades of the 20th century, for toy collectors, folklorists, educationists, toy designers and antique dealers. It had originally been intended for exports and provided, in a detailed manner, extensive information regarding the then program of the German toy industry. In its day the catalog was considered an epochal achievement, an aid to boosting companies' turnover alongside enriching to a marked extent the world reputation of the responsible and esteemed trading company releasing this universal toy sample book.

German toy production between the Post-World-War I period of the Inflation and the World Economic Recession of 1929

During the two decades prior to the First World War German toy exports rose immeasurably and yielded high profit rates. This, then, was a period of dynamic economic growth which, conversely, exerted virtually no influence whatsoever on living standards of either toy workers in factories or in home industry. Toy exports, moreover, doubled, attaining the following figures in thousands of marks: 1900: 53,441; 1905: 68,400; 1910: 86,128; 1913: 103,385. The situation even seemed exceptionally favorable at the beginning of 1914, notwithstanding the fact that the market was already fluctuating because of international events (revolution in Mexico, unrest in various Central and South American states, tension amongst the major European powers). Main clients were the American and English markets which, in 1913, themselves accounted for 55 percent of all exports, followed by South America and France.

In contrast, toy imports before the war appeared modest indeed and, in 1913, constituted but a $^{1}/_{88}$th part of foreign sales. The principal importers were Austria/Hungary, Great Britain and France.

In comparison with 1913, however, by 1920 toy exports had dwindled by some 18 percent; main clients were Great Britain, the USA, the Netherlands and South America.

As the First World War began colossal stocks were in the warehouses — the outbreak of war coinciding timewise with the commencement of the main export period — the threads of world trade were severed coupled with higher import duties on German toys, import prohibitions by various states, uncertainties in transportation and other problems, also precipitating social unrest: factories closed down, or cut-back operations, a rapid growth in unemployment which, however, by the end of 1915 had been more or less adjusted amongst the male labor force through the compulsory military service stipulations whilst there remained a surplus of female labor.

The outbreak of the First World War also heralded a reorientation of the German toy industry to war production. This proved relatively easy for the metal toy manufacturers. Thus, for example, the assets of the *Nürnberger Metall- und Lackierwarenfabrik* Bing. Bros. A. G., originally established in 1866 as a wholesale outlet, rose from 500,000 marks in 1914 to 3.7 million marks in 1916 and the astronomical figure of 14.5 million marks by 1918! Smaller enterprises with restricted capital resources were simply unable to keep pace. The switch-over in Thuringia and the Erzgebirge was hampered through a lack of machines, minimal capital and local fragmentation of home-based industry. Instead, workshops and factories in the Erzgebirge were now manufacturing foundation planks, wire winding devices, wooden rings for shells, hand-grenade handles and soles for wooden shoes whilst those in Sonneberg were turning out ammunition holders and parts of uniforms.

As the war continued the toy industry encountered tremendous difficulties stemming from the growing shortage of auxiliary and raw materials (sheet-metal, stamping powder, glue, tin, fabrics, spirit) and imposed rationing.

After the war and in the wake of the November Revolution toy workers—often in alliance with the German Woodworkers Association and the Association of Factory Workers—struggled to retain the social and political rights they had gained.

The conditions of workers during the Weimar Republic were characterized on the one hand by significantly improved social policies and shorter working hours coupled, conversely, with a general worsening of workers' circumstances as a result of devaluation (1918–1923), a relatively high level of unemployment between 1924 and 1929, rationing (1924–1932), and then exceptionally high unemployment (1930–1932). The suppression of the Kapp *Putsch* in March 1920 and the general strike of 12 million workers and employees finally precipitated, in 1923, a crisis which spotlighted the growing capacity of the workers and was a response to the declining living standards of the people.

Coining such phrases as "patriotic duty," the major toy makers' associations, during the initial post-war years, sought to ginger up industry and trade. An appeal in the *Deutsche Spielwaren-Zeitung* in 1920 emphasizes: "Alarm! The German toy industry faces ruin and, thus, our children's world great losses in *joie de vivre*. Toy prices are nowadays so high that only extremely rich parents are still able to purchase good toys, which are, in the first instance teaching and occupational aids for their offspring. The same applies to sports equipment and playthings for young people. Consequently, clubs and communities, too, will also no longer be in a position to acquire sufficient sports gear. The results will include cutbacks in essential youth welfare and in the education of the up-and-coming generation through games and sports. We do not wish, at this juncture, to examine the causes of this dismal trend. The boundless price increases of raw materials, present wage levels and business costs are contributory factors. Moreover, the goods themselves are frequently so out of proportion to cost that both purchasers and sellers must often be wondering how the said prices are calculated. Buyers nowadays are solely those circles who simply don't know to handle their so easily earned money. This was corroborated by last Easter's sales. Needless to say, the very marked decrease in toy purchases is also exerting an adverse effect on the toy industry which, in turn, has home market users from whom the best suggestions are forthcoming as its most consistent clients. The trade is both powerless and helpless in the face of this development. Only industry can assist and it remains the patriotic duty and task of all involved to find ways and means of warding off these consequences. Therefore, we are raising our voices in warning. For the sake of the German child and the young generation and, finally, also in the interests of the toy industry, help and ensure that the German toy trade does not perish.

Vedes, Vereinigung Deutscher Spielwarenhändler e.G.m.b.H., Berlin
Deutscher Spielwarenverband e.V., Abteilung Handelsgruppe, Sonneberg
Spielwarenhändlerverband e.G.m.b.H., Berlin
Verband Berliner Spielwaren-Spezialgeschäfte E.V., Berlin
Vereinigung Dresdner Spielwarenhändler, E.V., Dresden
Vereinigung der Grosshändler der Kurz-, Galanterie- und Spielwarenbranche Deutschlands E.V., Berlin
Nord und Süd. Einkaufsgenossenschaft m.b.H., Berlin
Nürnberger Bund, E.G.m.b.H., Nuremberg
Verband deutscher Waren- und Kaufhäuser E.V., Berlin
Verband Deutscher Sportgeschäfte, E.V., Berlin."

A report published by the Chamber of Trade and Commerce in Sonneberg in 1921 has this to say about the situation in the doll industry: "... Great difficulties exist in obtaining raw and auxiliary materials for the doll industry. It proved virtually impossible to procure textiles through regular, recurring purchases with the result that the industry found itself mainly dependent on random buying. Generally speaking, only foreign, in particular English cottonware, was processed. The anticipated substantial price cuts in March and April 1920 failed to materialize. In fact, toward the end of last year the market for cotton goods evidenced a marked rising tendency with the overall price level higher than during the March period, and leather (white tanned sheep's leather), unobtainable as the year opened, now again being offered. However, prices are about twentyfold the peacetime levels. Silk, for instance, has become so expensive that it has more or less disappeared from the doll industry. During the first months of the year the industry was particularly badly affected by the scarcity of porcelain heads. Moreover, although demand dwindled, supplies of such heads remained inadequate during the summer months. The shortage of dolls' heads was even accentuated by quite substantial exports of this article ...

... As the crisis in the doll industry dawned, considerable orders for dolls' heads were withdrawn. Nonetheless, not even the most pressing demands could be met. The coal shortage here also ruled out the required increase in production. Indeed, greater manufacturing costs, the result, above all, of wood firing, price increases of Bohemian kaolin and wage demands led, as 1920 opened, to considerable price mark-ups of finished goods. The porcelain manufactories themselves only handled deliveries abroad to a limited extent so that the traditional supplies by home industry could be upheld at all costs. The demand of non-German countries is very considerable and, under the present conditions, could hardly be met at all. Business expectations for the year are generally assessed as favorable as large orders are expected from America."

Stefan Zweig described the German inflation as "bedlam in colossal proportions." And, indeed: "In the history of mankind currency never and nowhere recorded such staggering fits and starts as in 1923 in Germany. As prices rose feverishly, a shoe-lace all of a sudden cost more than had a shoe a few days earlier, and was even more expensive than thousands of pairs of luxury footwear a week previously. Beggars became multi-millionaires yet remained hungry in front of the meagre dripping and horse sausage window-dressing. Workers heaved their weekly earnings, which had formerly fitted into a narrow packet, back home in rucksacks and laundry baskets and, if they didn't spend everything at once, were hardly able to pay for as much coal as the bank-notes weighed. Indeed, prices often doubled within hours. The amount needed in the morning for a pound of meat would hardly suffice for a crust in the evening. Savings which officials' wives had put aside assiduously for decades would now barely do for a tramway ticket. The bank-note presses, unremittingly fed by three hundred paper-works operating to full capacity, delivered million and billion denomination bills day and night which, hardly had the ink dried, were again valueless and could only be retained as a short-term currency by overprints with still more noughts.

Mid-1923 witnessed more than five million unemployed. Poverty and hunger were spreading apace whilst industrial output, at 47 percent of the 1913 figure was at its lowest level since the end of the war.

The share of the Nuremberg-Fürth area volume of production was 32 percent of the total German toy industry output in 1927, followed by Sonneberg, including the Coburg district with 26.6 percent and the Erzgebirge accounting for 7.4 percent. The remaining production was mainly in Berlin-Brandenburg, Württemberg and northern Thuringia. Strikingly, the Nuremberg-Fürth district was to the fore with 32 percent although it only employed 22 percent of all German toy workers, as opposed to the 31.2 percent in the Sonneberg-Coburg area. The reasons for the higher labor productivity were the greater utilization of machinery through rationalization, the adaptation of metal processing and precision mechanical production technologies, the specific nature of articles (tin toys!) and a greater concentration of capital by manufacturers. As the world economic crisis struck Germany late in 1929, causing unemployment to spiral to over eight million by 1932, exports declined sharply and the struggle against competition, aggravated by differing customs' regulations, became more intense still and dealt a blow to the predominance of the German toy industry.

Investigations undertaken by the Enquete Commission revealed that German toy industry output rose from 135 million marks in 1913 to some 200 million marks by 1927 alongside a simultaneous increase in world figures from 250 to 650 million marks over the same period. However, in this conjunction, the influence of the higher price level must bé heeded.

Following the 1923 inflation there was a growing tendency to eliminate wholesalers. Moreover, the latter were so weakened that they had become unable to lend support to manufacturers by absorbing articles in good time and with prompt payments. In this connexion attention is drawn to VEDES, founded in 1904, which established a purchasing outlet in Nuremberg in 1917, another one in 1919 in Kupferhammer-Grünthal near Olbernhau in the middle of the Erzgebirge toy region, transferred its headquarters from Berlin to Nuremberg in 1926 and, in 1932, set up a further purchasing unit in Sonneberg. In this manner the co-operative of specialist toy retailers — today leading amongst world companies — opened up branches in the key production areas.

The situation in Sonneberg, the principal toy centre in Thuringia, was characteristic of the conditions at that time. Foreign capital, above all the funds of American concerns, was employed to exploit the inflation in Germany; thus, the Sonneberg toy industry handled large orders for attired dolls in order to yield momentous extra profits. The sell-out of Sonneberg toys typified the competition between monopoly groups at home and abroad. Speculative buying-out attained its gravest dimensions in 1922 and 1923 because of a constant dollar rate alongside the falling German mark (1 dollar = 4.2 billion marks). Indeed, a great many Sonneberg companies fell prey to these corrupt business practices and the ever more rapid currency devaluation. On 1 January 1913 the American Woolworth concern inaugurated a buying branch in Sonneberg to handle purchases solely for New York. A special Woolworth-GmbH was set up in Berlin for home sales in so-called uniform price shops. The Sonneberg company established direct links with small and extremely small "manufacturers" and producers. Turnover, above all exports, ran at between 10 and 11 million marks annually over some ten years. There were between 800 and 900 company suppliers of whom 25 percent were independent home-based workers. The small manufacturers were given supplies of materials to compensate for lack of capital. In 1925 the company gathered in almost 25 million dollars.

Further purchasing outlets in Sonneberg, for instance Kresge, Kress, Burgfeldt, Butler Brothers, Louis Wolf and others were able to exert a considerable influence on the toy sector. However, notwithstanding the general economic upsurge, the production volume prior to the First World War was never attained. The reasons are:

1: The lack of own capital, despite foreign capital investment, for the necessary development of the toy industry.
2: Many foreign companies which had supplied Sonneberg traders before the war established their own toy sectors, notably in Japan and the USA.
3: Some Sonneberg manufacturers introduced new articles to their production ranges serving, above all, German armaments and yielding greater profits.

The number of doll-making outlets in Sonneberg, including Neustadt, was 2066 with some 6600 workers in 1927. The production value figure of 10.7 million marks was inclusive of 6.4 million marks worth of exports. However, production declined in the wake of the world recession and by 1937, the last full trading year between the wars, there were only 120 doll manufacturers left. By 1932, unemployment in the overpopulated Sonneberg area had risen to 15,307 — highest level — representing almost half the able-bodied labor force. By comparison: there were 11,019 toy manufacturing outlets with 55,049 workers in the German Reich in 1925; of these 5809 with 21,129 hands still existed in 1933.

Home-based and children's work Home workers' conditions were indeed frightful after the First World War. The *Gewerkschafts-zeitung* notes on 5 May 1925: "Thousands of home workers are still today waging a similar struggle for their very existence to the one portrayed by Gerhart Hauptmann in his *Weavers*. In listing various cases one might be pardoned for ignoring the chipboard box-makers in the Glatz area with hourly earnings of three and four pfennigs for theirs is a petering-out line to which the workers, it should be noted, are just as strongly attached and devoted as to their impoverished homes keeping them in the locality. What remains are countless instances of typical home-worker impoverishment in many localities and trades. Pitiable conditions prevail, above all in Erzgebirge brush and doll furniture manufacture, the toy industry in the Sonneberg district, the tin goods outlets in and near Nuremberg and wicker-working in Upper Franconia.

"The most terrible forms of children's labor are prevalent virtually without exception in the toy industry. Even the smallest, not yet of school age, work day in day out making articles intended to give children pleasure. They have become a scourge for those engaged in their manufacture.

Indeed frequently enough, despite the assistance of the children, hourly rates are a mere seven to twelve pfennigs, for instance for the manufacture of primitive metal toys in the Nuremberg area. The result is that the working day extends well into the night."

The Home Industries' Exhibitions of the Reich (1904, 1906, 1908 and 1925) did, to a certain extent, provide enlightening information on the social position of toy makers and other cottage industry workers. The biggest exposition of all was the one in 1925 in the Exhibition Halls by Lehrter railway station in Berlin. The event was backed by all kinds of trade unions, the Society for Social Reform — with the explicit co-responsibility of the industrial inspection authority and several committees of experts. Max Taut (1884–1967), who was, in 1933, banned from professional activities, handled the architectural side. The event set out as its aim a report back on the Law on Outworkers, proclaimed in 1911, which was also intended to concern itself with health protection and the wages issue. An "objective picture" with vivid examples was promised — "neither a one-sided presentation of poverty nor an equally unilateral display of particularly pleasurable successes." Leading worker representatives referred to "a knife without a blade."

The German toy industry was depicted on a triple-storeyed table thirty-five metres in length which also illustrated the tremendous expansion in home working. A realistic picture was sought after by means of photographs of the social environment of home-industry families and other documents. Each of the exhibition items included cards which, on the basis of a questionnaire action, provided information on work performance, working hours, piece rate, daily working hours, sex and age of the maker, deduction of charges which encumbered the home workers, comparative earnings of factory workers etc. However, one frequently dispensed with such facts in the section so "as not to encourage stores and wholesalers to exert price pressure" or one avoided any reference to working conditions for fear of forfeiting one's employment … thus the whole show was anything but an "objective" that is to say comprehensive reflection of the real situation. The hourly wage levels brought to light by the German Woodworkers Association ranged between twenty-five and fifty pfennigs. The exhibition provided convincing evidence of the immense degree of child labor.

Quite a number of visual artists, among them Theodor Hosemann, Hans Baluschek, Max Liebermann, Heinrich Zille, Bernhard Kretzschmar, Johannes Wüsten, Lea and Hans Grundig produced works championing the poor and deprived in German cottage industry. The destitution of the "golden" twenties, unemployment, hunger, homelessness, illness and death find expression as a painful indictment in the works of Käthe Kollwitz (1867–1945), "I am perfectly happy for my art to pursue goals. I wish to exert an influence in this period where the people are so much perplexed and in need of help" (1922). A whole number of her accusing posters were on show during the 1906 and 1925 Home Industries' Exhibitions.

The story of the Wilhelm Möller firm/John Hess successor
Founded in 1886
Commercial agent for export and home sales · Hamburg

The *Handelshaus*, which published the universal toy catalog marks its one hundredth anniversary in 1986. Moreover, although the size of the company, the number of firms it represents, ranges and countries to which it exports have all been subject to changes, a number of commercial policy factors remained valid. However, the world political currents, the events and processes in German history have not left the firm unscathed.

The documents of the Hess family, which can be traced back to 1640 in Altona, include a report in 1670 of a wife accompanying her husband to the Leipzig Fair. The company founder, John Hess (1864–1918) was apprenticed for several years to the coffee importer, Hugo Fehr. When this firm went bankrupt he was given, as compensation for wages still due, an old pair of scales with upright operation which were subsequently used for many years in his own organization. In 1886, aged twenty-two, he established the John Hess company (with offices in Hamburg, Dammtorstrasse 5–7). Right from the start his firm only handled agencies. (His best clients included Magirius in Ulm who, through Hess, delivered fire-brigade equipment to South America, where fire-brigades had been set up apace during the last decade, and did extremely well). On 1 August 1887 John Hess moved into larger premises in Raboisen 96 and was listed in the trade register on 9 November 1887 (on 21 September 1892 as a general partnership).

In 1889 he took over as representative of the Gramophone firm Ernst Holz, successor, Leipzig and, from 1896 onward followed the first representations in the toy sector, which subsequently became the company's principle field of activities. The first firms included among others Georg Bruchlos, Eisfeld/Thuringia; A. Riedeler, Königsee/Thur.; Michael Seidel, Zirndorf (in sheet metal for India) and Gustav Fischer, Zöblitz/Erzgebirge. The agreement concluded in 1899 for the representation of the firm Märklin Bros. & Cie in Göppingen (which in 1859 commenced the manufacture of metal crockery and stoves for doll's houses and displayed the world's first clockwork railway with variable plug-in track system at the Leipzig Fair in 1891, although the idea itself presumably stemmed from the Ludwig Lutz company, founded in Ellwangen in 1846, which purchased Märklin in 1891) and the agreement around 1900 for the representation of the Margarete Steiff company, which had been making felt animals by hand in Giengen/Brenz since 1880 and finally attained world renown during the "bear years" (the company turned out 974,000 Teddy Bears alone in 1907), were both steps of decisive economic importance for the firm's later years. The progress of the John Hess company was indeed amazing as more and more requests for representation came in. Expansion caused the firm in 1888 to move to new, bigger rooms in Neuer Wall 44; in 1894 once again to Alter Wall 62; and, finally, in 1903 to the largest premises of all in Neuer Wall 64/66. The latter offices were on three floors of two houses and, thus, provided excellent display facilities for a colossal range of items which testified to the company's heyday and established its international reputation. The press reacted most favorably to the exhibition rooms with "electric elevators, broad steps and telephones" in which home customers met once or twice a year to purchase their requirements, in particular, however, the Hamburg and Bremen exporters who handled overseas deliveries (for John Hess did not export himself).

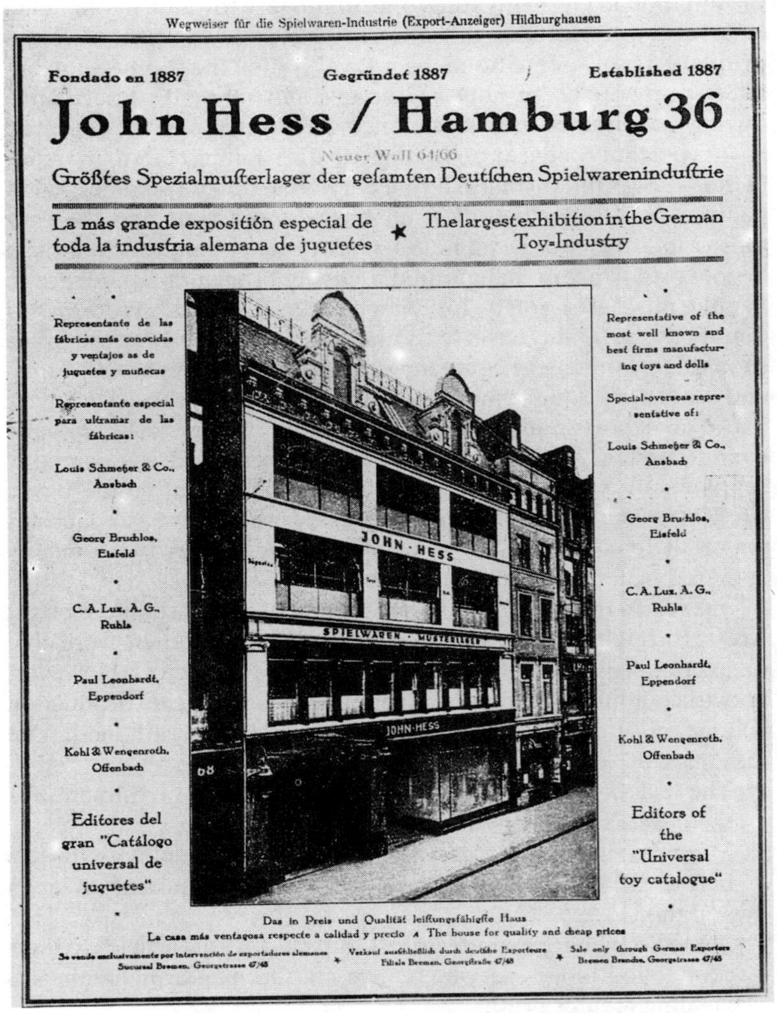

Advertisement by the firm of John Hess in Wegweiser für die Spielwaren-Industrie

The *Hamburger Nachrichten* of 10 May 1903 reports: "A sample display of toys, musical instruments and dolls. The export company John Hess has opened new show-rooms on the first, second and third floors in Neuer Wall 64/66, premises completed last year in accordance with plans drawn up by the architect A. Heidtmann and master-mason F. F. M. Blatt & sons. The rooms are exceptionally practical and comfortably furnished thus enabling exporters to provide their clients from overseas with an overall picture of the initially cited articles, moreover in a manner hitherto impossible during either a world or national display. In Germany, too, the Hess company has taken precisely the kind of initiatives required to attract buyers from far beyond Hamburg's city boundaries."

The economic development of the company made necessary an expansion in staff. In 1891, Nathan Hess, the brother of the firm's founder, who had lived in England for several years, became a partner and in 1892 the company was confirmed as a general partnership. There were twenty persons on the staff when the First World War broke out creating serious economic problems for John Hess and the toy industry as a whole. Furthermore, the war also had a most diverse effect on the family: Richard Hess, the oldest son of Nathan Hess, lost his life in Russia in 1916. Hans, John Hess' son, who had been in the business since 1917 fell as a soldier in 1918 and John Hess himself died on 4 September. The management was subsequently the sole prerogative of Nathan Hess; Rosalie Hess b. Reiss, the widow of John Hess joined the company as partner on 13 December 1918. She resigned as co-partner in 1930. (Cp. entry in the trade register of 15 July 1933). Following clarification in the families concerned, in 1921 resp. 1922 Georg Jonas Nathan Hess, the son of Nathan Hess, and Fritz John Hess, the second son of company's founder became co-partners assuming responsibility for its direction (Cp. entries in the trade register of 29. 7. 1921 and 30. 12. 1922). Notwithstanding the inflation their initiative heralded a new boom: thirty staff members visited offices, show-rooms and stores. They published (1924) the first ever toy sample book envisaged exclusively for exports and which contained, apart from gross charges, weights and dimensions, a description in German, English and Spanish of all articles. This catalog was welcomed as a sensation by the market and consolidated the company's international prestige.

During the early 1920s the firm also appointed commercial travellers who called on clients, whilst qualified teachers of Hamburg and outside commercial schools, as well as students of specialist disciplines, frequented sample rooms and acquired an insight into toy marketing trends.

Differences with the owners of the building in Neuer Wall 64/66 caused the transfer of business operations to the Levante house in Mönkebergstrasse 7. The show-room there, covering 1000 m² and equipped with every conceivable modern contrivance, experts regarded as the best in Germany and, at times, even in the world. A full page advertisement by "the leading company in price and quality" with its main text in English and Spanish, appeared in the *Wegweiser für die Spielwaren-Industrie Export-Anzeiger* in the late 1920s depicting the building in Neuer Wall 64/66 and drawing attention to the publisher of the catalog; the cited company representatives are the firms Louis Schmetzer & Co., Ansbach; Georg Bruchlos, Eisfeld; C. A. Lux, A. G. Ruhla; Kohl and Wengenroth, Offenbach, and Paul Leonhardt, Eppendorf.

From 1930 onward it became increasingly common practice for factories which had developed from former craft workshops to seek their own marketing facilities, a tendency initiated ultimately through the extension of production and the effects of the world economic recession. There was, above all, a stagnation in sales of high grade and commensurately expensive toys and some manufacturers of branded items supplied the sales outlets themselves. Moreover, the expansion of individual makers' ranges led compulsorily to an overlapping of collections with the result that the John Hess company also marketed competing products and, consequently, lost a number of its business partners. This quite naturally prompted a reduction in the variety of items available. Commensurately, the establishment of a branch in Nuremberg in 1935 and a branch office in Fürth (Cp. entry in the trade register of 11 March 1938) close to the productive hinterland of the Nuremberg-Fürth tin toy sector, were important moves to stabilize the company. The John Hess company became a commissioner itself handling, as representative, some of the articles manufactured in Nuremberg and surrounding areas. These activities led to the setting-up of a packing center in the toy trade metropolis where all toys destined for export were packaged in a seaworthy manner. Thus, it was no longer necessary to meet inland freight charges to the Hamburg stores; the company could avail itself of the favorable export freight deliveries to the free port. Furthermore, all Nuremberg enterprises utilizing this opportunity and delivering less through outside channels received a discount allowance.

The Universal Toy Catalog

The publishers, in continuing reprints of former literature on toys, decided to open up for research, toy collectors and museums, equally for the art and antiques trade the two volumes of the catalog existing as an inventory in the Spielzeugmuseum Sonneberg, the more than 4000 representations of which provide a survey of toy ranges during the years immediately following the First World War. Subsequent enquiries to the leading specialist museums in both German states and a great many other European collections revealed that only the Spielzeugmuseum Lydia Bayer in Nuremberg has a second copy which differs slightly in the single volume edition from the Sonneberg set. In addition, Marianne and Jürgen Cieslik (Jülich-Koslar, Federal Republic of Germany) acquired a third issue in 1983. However, neither in their prefaces nor elsewhere do these specimens include any reference whatsoever to the publishers. A response solicited from Broschek & Co., printers still in existence today, provided no further information. Moreover, both the voucher archive of the company and all documents pertaining to orders were destroyed by air raids during World War Two.

Neither was confirmation forthcoming for the initial presumption that our catalog had been a form of export advertising by VEDES, Nuremberg, or another leading exporter in the Nuremberg or Sonneberg area. The fact that the catalog appeared not only in German but also in English and Spanish seems to indicate that it must have stemmed from a company in northern Germany, for Spanish, in conjunction with English and German, made up the most suitable linguistic combination for exports to Latin America and South Africa.

A set of fortunate circumstances led to the establishment of links with Frau Hilde Bormann and Herr Dieter Bormann, Hamburg, who, notwithstanding the fact that their archive with catalogs, price lists and a card-index of agents in 1943 had similarly fallen prey to bombing, still had recourse to old company records showing that John Hess had published the catalog. In addition, we discovered memoranda and company announcements, pictures of business premises, amongst others, in the *Wegweiser für die Spiel-, Galanterie- und Kurzwarenindustrie* (Guide to the toy, fancy goods and smallwares industry) (1918, 1920) and, above all, a whole page advertisement in the *Wegweiser für die Spielwarenindustrie (Export-Anzeiger) Hildburghausen* (Guide to the toy industry (export gazette) Hildburghausen) containing an explicit reference to the publication of the catalog.

Vorwort

zum

UNIVERSAL-SPIELWAREN-KATALOG 1930

Die rege Nachfrage nach meinem Universal-Spielwaren-Katalog hat mich zu dieser Neuausgabe 1930 veranlaßt.

Erteilen Sie Ihre Bestellungen nur noch nach meinem Universal-Spielwaren-Katalog Ausgabe 1928 und Ausgabe 1930, da die älteren Jahrgänge größtenteils überholt und nicht mehr gültig sind.

Die Ausarbeitung des vorliegenden Katalogs ist auf Grund der gemachten Erfahrungen so übersichtlich wie möglich und mit größter Sorgfalt vorgenommen worden und ich bin fest davon überzeugt, daß auch Sie den reich illustrierten Universal-Spielwaren-Katalog 1930 mit Interesse durchsehen und, wie ich hoffe, manche Anregung zu Bestellungen finden werden.

Ich möchte ganz besonders darauf hinweisen, daß sämtliche mit Beleuchtung ausgestatteten oder durch Batterie angetriebenen Artikel ohne Taschenbatterie geliefert werden. Die Preise verstehen sich demnach ohne Taschenbatterie.

Beachten Sie bitte, daß die mit den gleichen fettgedruckten Vornummern versehenen Artikelnummern das Produkt eines Fabrikanten darstellen und daß es bei Erteilung von Aufträgen durchaus in Ihrem Interesse liegt, von den so als zusammengehörend kenntlich gemachten Artikeln nach Möglichkeit so viel zu bestellen, daß sich zumindest eine mittelgroße Kiste ergibt.

In Ihren Bestellungen wollen Sie unbedingt die ganzen Artikelnummern, auch die fettgedruckten Vornummern aufgeben, damit Rückfragen vermieden werden. Am Kopfe einiger Seiten sind Kollektionsnummern vermerkt, die Sie bei Bestellungen von Artikeln dieser Seiten, bei denen die fettgedruckten Vornummern fehlen, mit aufgeben wollen.

Die Preise wollen Sie aus separater Preisliste ersehen, die in der Seiten-Reihenfolge des Katalogs aufgemacht ist, so daß Sie jeden Preis rasch auffinden können.

Geringe Abweichungen in den Größenangaben und das Ersetzen von aus der Fabrikation ausgeschiedenen Artikeln durch ähnliche vorbehalten.

Der Herausgeber

Preface

to the

UNIVERSAL TOY CATALOGUE 1930

The brisk demand for my Universal Toy Catalogue has caused me to publish this *New Edition 1930.*

Please have your orders in future made up but exclusively from my Universal Toy Catalogue *Edition 1928* and *Edition 1930,* because the annual sets of former years have been for the most part superseded, being no more valid.

The elaboration of the present catalogue has been arranged as clearly as possible and with the utmost care, based on my long years' experience, and I am sure that you will be interested in perusing also the richly illustrated Universal Toy Catalogue of 1930, trusting that it may give you many inducements for committing your orders to me.

I should like to mention particularly that all articles fitted with lighting or driven by electric battery are delivered *without pocket battery* and prices consequently are understood without the latter.

Please note that the article numbers provided with the same prefixed numbers in fat type represent the product of *one* manufacturer and that it will be wholly in your own interest to order of such articles marked as belonging together *possibly* so much, that the quantity will give at least a medium sized case.

Please to state in your orders anyhow the whole article numbers, also the prefixed numbers in fat type, in order to avoid any return questions. You will find on top of some pages collection numbers which please indicate when ordering articles of these pages, because the prefixed numbers in fat type have been omitted. Prices kindly see from the separate pricelist, made up in the order of the consecutive page numbers of the catalogue, so that you will be enabled to find any price quickly.

Small deviations from sizes stated in catalogue and the substitution of some articles superseded in manufacture by others similar reserved.

The Editor

Prefacio

al

CATÁLOGO UNIVERSAL DE JUGUETES 1930

La viva demanda por mi Catálogo Universal de Juguetes ha motivado la publicación de esta *Nueva Edición 1930.* Sírvanse Vds., al hacer sus pedidos futuros, de referirse exclusivamente á mi Catálogo Universal de Juguetes Edición 1928 y Edición 1930, porque la mayor parte de los artículos contenidos en los catálogos de años anteriores ha quedado anticuada, no siendo más válidos.

La elaboración del presente catálogo ofrece una clareza cuanto mayor posible en la disposición de los artículos y fué hecha con el mayor cuidado, basado en mi experiencia de largos años, y estoy seguro de que Vds. se interesarán á pasar una vista en el Catálogo Universal de Juguetes 1930, ricamente ilustrado, esperando que Vds. muchas veces se vean motivados á conferirme sus apreciados encargos.

Aprovecho la ocasión para llamar su particular atención sobre el hecho de que todos los artículos provistos de alumbrado ó movidos por batería eléctrica se suministran sin la batería de bolsillo. Los precios se entienden, pues, sin la dicha batería. Fíjense Vds. también en que todos los números de artículos que lleven el mismo número prefijo en cifras gruesas son el producto de un sólo fabricante, y que está absolutamente en el interés de Vds., al conferir sus pedidos, de pedir de los artículos marcados como pertenecientes juntos, en lo posible una cantidad tal que resulte á lo menos una caja de tamaño mediano.

Sírvanse indicar en sus pedidos los números completos de los artículos, también los números prefijos en cifras gruesas, para evitar preguntas en retorno. Hay indicados, á la cabeza de algunas páginas, números de colección, los que quieran indicar en sus pedidos de estos artículos en las dichas páginas, en las que faltan los números prefijos en cifras gruesas.

Sírvanse ver los precios en la lista de precios separada, la cual está hecha de acuerdo con las páginas consecutivas del catálogo, de manera que el pronto encuentro de cualquier precio no ofrecerá dificultad.

Se reservan pequeñas deviaciones en los tamaños indicados en el catálogo, así como el reemplazo de los artículos descontinuados por otros similares.

El Editor

Preface to the 1930 edition of the Universal Toy Catalog

An announcement by "John Hess, Hamburg, Mönkebergstrasse 7" which appeared in the *Deutsches Spielwaren-Adressbuch* (Address book of German toys) of 1938 points out: "Universal toy catalog available on demand." This indicates conclusively that the 1924/1926 catalog must have been followed by further issues over ten years. Indeed, in spring 1983 Frau Dr. Lydia Bayer, director of the Spielzeugmuseum in Nuremberg, managed to obtain a single volume copy of the 1930 catalog during an auction. The preface, once again without reference to a company, indicates that a further edition must have appeared in 1928, too. An announcement in the *Deutsche Spielwarenzeitung* (vol. 1928 p. 28) says, inter alia, about the company: "The decisive purchasing source of all outlets handling toys. Biggest special sample store of the sector, comparable with its 1200 square meters of exhibition space to a small permanent fair." A similarly worded announcement can also be found in vol. 1927, p. 74. The puzzle was resolved in 1983 when Marianne and Jürgen Cieslik managed to acquire a 1928 edition of the universal toy catalog and, at the same time, a copy was found in the Spielzeugmuseum Sonneberg.

Common to the issues of 1924/1926, 1928 and 1930 are:

1: Identical cover presentation and size.

2: The separate price-list referred to is lacking (nor have any remained in the company), similarly the explanation for users and the "significant" preface to the price index.[8] Only the 1928 issue features the price-list with a brief introduction (56 pages). However, it is smaller in size than the illustrated catalog volumes.

3: The article numbers in bold type are preceded by preliminary figures which, respectively, draw attention to the collections of individual manufacturers. In all catalogs an index of names by means of company details, imprints, references to branded items has only been partly included. The manufacturers gave their models catalog numbers in order to facilitate ordering and to rule out errors. This number often appears on the model itself, for example in the case of engines and Märklin carriages. The numerical indication, moreover, was frequently positioned, together with the firm's symbol, on car registrations. Company symbols came to Germany around 1890 as the bulk of production was being exported to England where, at this time, a precise designation of imported goods was required in order to protect home industry. As a result, during the subsequent period many firms had their symbols protected through trade-marks which, in turn, led to the development of branded goods.

4: The volumes (1924, 1926, 1928 and 1930) feature the same preliminary numbers for the various manufacturers (i.e., Hausser-Elastolin 88; Märklin 14; K. Kruse 27; Lehmann (presumably) 20). A list of makers was not included. However, because of bomb damage the company today no longer has an index of clients making possible a precise decoding of the former sound numbering system.

5: The volumes evidence no systematic order according to subject groups and only orient in line with manufacturers' numbers. However, these too do not feature in an ordered sequence (for that reason the 1930 issue has added to it an index listing systematically the "collection numbers" from 2 to 196 and then again from 2000 to 2079 whilst the respective pages with the representations are featured alongside). The numbering from 2 to 2079 features substantial gaps as not all intermediate numbers have been included. This surely corroborates changes in the supplier companies.

6: The 1928 and 1930 issues have the same foreign language sections as earlier volumes.

7: Insertions (some in color) of "exclusively" represented companies (1924/26: 26 pages of colored representations, 1930: 20 colored pages).

8: Imprints or other company references are not featured throughout.

9: Occasional reference to playing age reveals publicity intentions.

10: Details regarding sizes, weight and number of items for each packet.

11: A list of contents of toy forms, the same sequence, however, the catchwords more differentiated than the index of the supplementary volume of 1926.

The following differences emerge in issues:

1: The principal volume 1924 according to the preface of the 1926 supplementary volume has page references where novelties have been included. Pages 1–386, however, have distinct index lists). The 1930 issue, without any explanation in its preface, begins the page numbering with 600 (which corresponds to the list of contents) and ends with page 803. In between is the 1928 volume with pages 400–584.

2: The name of the printer does not appear.

3: The graphical design, nature and size of the representations and the arrangement of pages in the 1928 and 1930 issues differ in many respects from the first issues of 1924 and 1926.
4: The 1930 edition indicates clearly changes in the representing firms.
5: Technological development in production, latest pedagogical findings, ideological influences as well as new requirements of the market cause the 1930 volume to feature ranges, many novelties and, not to be overlooked, a relative extension of military toys. More model cars feature, rubber-operated planes, a great number of prank items ("Pat and Patachon" as novelty!), parlor games, "Cabaso," children's cars etc.

Moreover, applicable to all issues is the following: the reason why only a few issues, commensurate with contemporary research, have been retained probably hinges on the fact that export offers predominated and that, therefore, the bulk of the catalogs went abroad. The inclusion of specific company publicity material in the general issues (Märklin, Steiff, K. Kruse) is renewed confirmation that the publishing company was John Hess for the latter, in part since the end of the 19th century, had been the sole exporting agent for these manufacturers.

History proves that the manufacture of toys has always depended on productive forces and the prevailing conditions of production, contemporary ideas, educational currents and customs, social patterns, artistic style-historical epochs, cultural-political influences and, last but not least, the market-conditioned cycles of industrial-technological preconditions (wood, paper, tin, metal, synthetic materials, the application of lithography, the steam-engine, electricity, electronics etc.).[9] Other relevant factors are those stemming from education and training, advertising and other expectation patterns imbued in children (and parents) by the mass media although, here too, the qualification applies which Walter Benjamin established in a review of the standard work *Kinderspielzeug aus alter Zeit* (Children's toys of former times) by Gröber (1928): "To be sure, one would neither attain reality nor a veritable conception of toys if one sought to explain this solely from the vantage point of the children. A child is not a Robinson, nor are children some sort of segregated community but part of the people and the class from which they originate. Therefore, neither do their toys testify an autonomous, special pattern of life but are rather more a silent sign dialog between child and people. A sign dialog which can be deciphered accurately by means of this work."[10] Seen in such a light toys as objects are " indicators of a social system in all its interrelationships" (Ingeborg Weber-Kellermann).

Rapid changes occur between 1920 and 1930 in the appearance on the market of "novelties" (frequently propagated as market "hits"), a pace, it should be noted, dictated above all by the striving of manufacturers and the trade at large for greater turnover and profits. Thus, the children's "Junios" typewriter with dial instead of type cam (the principle was used until 1960!) has been in vogue since 1920 (Schmidt Bros. company). The cinematograph (Bing company) appears in 1925 as successor to the magic lantern, whose predecessors, is has been proved, had existed since 1700 and, at long last, brings the pictures into motion with spirit lamp, hand-winch and glass optics, although the magic lantern remains a branch hit. The highly decorative, metal humming top, called *Trudelmadame* in Nuremberg, has been rendering tones and sequences of sounds since about 1920. Submarines (already registered as a patent as early as in 1901) boost offers of ships.

The first ever children's gramophones at "super prices" for "well-to-do" families have been on sale as portables (presumably the Bing company) since 1925 together with small records called "Odeonette," a mere 14 cm in diameter (records: the Odeon company). That same year Lehmann in Brandenburg brings onto the market the replica of the elegant vogue cabriolet ("Velleda") of this period along with chauffeur, steering folding seats, and spring-drive. Although limousines were still predominant in 1920 Bing turns out new models accessories such as railway stations. Then, in 1928, there appears a 17 cm high, metal, felt-covered figure of Charlie Chaplin operated by a spring mechanism, able to dance in a similar way to the celluloid dancing model of the colored "Uncle Tom." And, since 1929 Walt Disney's Mickey Mouse (which he created in 1928) has been capturing the hearts of children (presumably the Distler company in 1929, sole distributors VEDES).

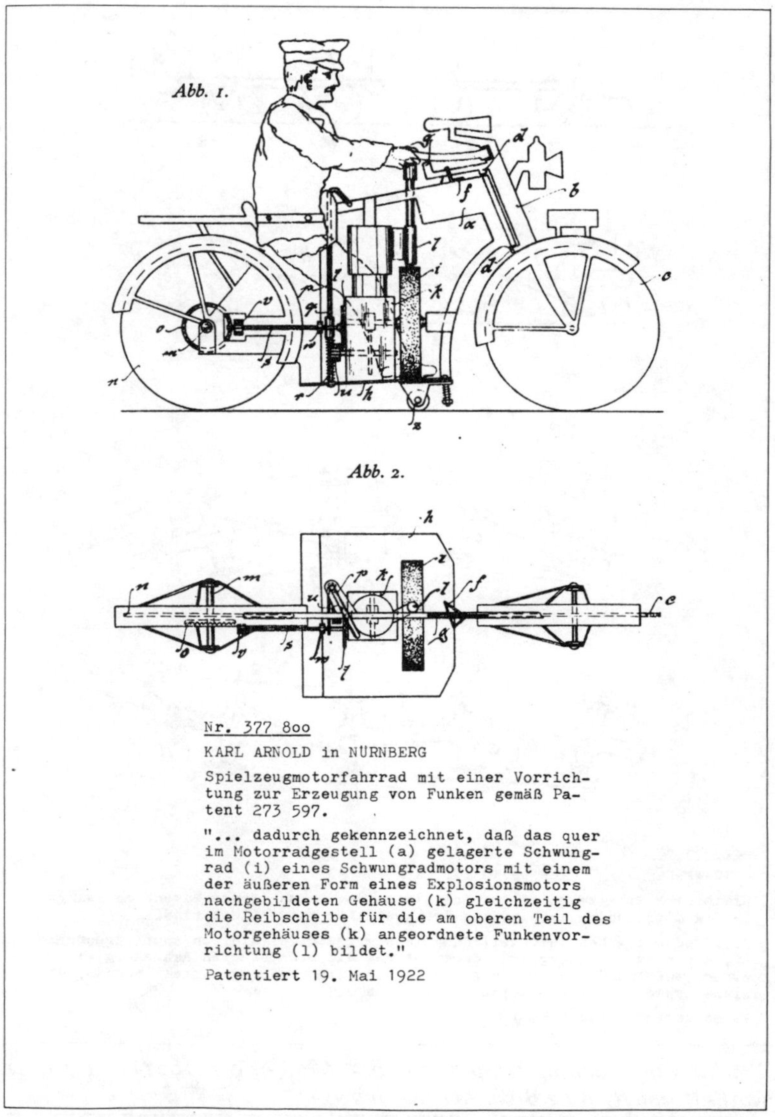

Toy motorcycle with a device for yielding sparks, tin toy patent (No. 377800 of 19.5. 1922) of Karl Arnold in Nuremberg

One of the first female comic strip figures was "Orphan-Annie," featured in the *New York Daily News* in 1924. Notwithstanding a great many difficulties Annie, the courageous, warm-hearted orphan child was able to master her life. She was always accompanied by Sandy, her faithful and intelligent dog. This attractive, always skipping orphan child was brought onto the market as a mechanical tin figure in 1932 by the New York toy maker Louis Marx.

The game "Catch the hat" (1927, Otto Maier, Ravensburg), one assumes, stems from the Indian peoples. "By Night to the Ice" (1929, Hausser) exerted a pronounced magical appeal. It deals with Peary's break-through to the North Pole in 1909. The game of chance "Monopoly" had already been discovered by an American in 1930 although it only appeared on the German toy market after

1945. The "695 E" toy aeroplane (1930, Günthermann), a tin model of the legendary and infamous "Ju 52", became a wonderous attraction in children's rooms, clockwork driven and suspended from the ceiling. Nine years later the originals were hurtling down bombs on the peaceful countryside.

The toy ranges depicted in the catalogs are presented in a somewhat confused manner and only illustrate in a rather all-round way items offered in the 1920s.

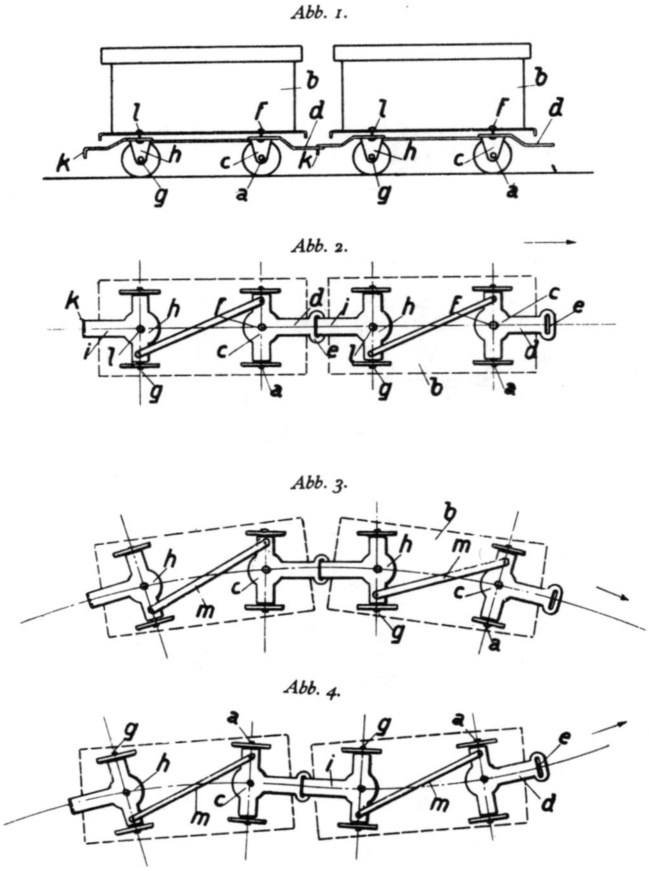

Nr. 356 808

BING-WERKE, vorm. GEBR. BING AG. in NÜRNBERG

Gleisloser Spielzeugzug, bei dem die beiden Achsen jedes Wagens zu zwangläufig miteinander verbundenen Drehgestellen ausgebildet sind.

"... dadurch gekennzeichnet, daß die Drehgestelle (c,h) in Kupplungsorgane (i, k bzw. d, e) übergehen, durch welche die benachbarten Achsen (g,a) zweier aufeinanderfolgender Wagen (b) so miteinander gekuppelt werden, daß diese Achsen parallel zueinander bleiben..."

Patentiert 9. Januar 1921

Trackless toy train, tin toy patent (No. 356808 of 9. 1. 1921) of the Bing works (formerly Bing Bros. AG Nuremberg)

Alongside doll production it appears beyond any shadow of doubt that particular attention was devoted to a wide variety of tin toys extending from the simplest figures to extremely "racy" mechanical models: figures with and without clockwork; vehicles with flywheel and clockwork, the most popular type being fire-brigade conveyances, also contemporary, modern models; steam-engines and dynamo varieties with a great many drive models; ships ranging from modest barges with steam and clockwork drive to the "submersible boat"; model railways with and without clockwork, similarly, electrically driven tramways along with a multitude of accessories (stations etc.); cinematograph and magic lantern; equally unassuming playthings for sand, gardening equipment for children (watering-cans), children's rattles, simple musical instruments, steel pianos, mechanical clockwork gadgets and rotating Swiss musical boxes. The assortment of the manufacturing company E. T. Lehmann (founded in Brandenburg in 1881) is featured in some considerable detail; Märklin has included an exclusive advertising section presenting, amongst other things, building blocks; then we have "Ebo" with cars (Hans Eberl, Nuremberg). One may justifiably assume that all highly productive tin toy firms presented contemporary ranges in the catalog.

The depicted aeroplanes are a sound example of how technology found its reflection in toys: tin model aeroplanes with clockwork, real gliders able to fly (also in building-block system) whilst the 1926 issue also contains models with rubber drive and "compressed-air engines" including double-deckers so that children are able to transform their dreams of flying into reality. The technological dot on the i is a 14 cm "mini" radio with electric mechanism.

It is, moreover, impossible to overlook the great bevy of dolls: babies, mama and rubber dolls, character figures, dressed and naked "artistic dolls" as well as wax decoration models representing the woman's ideal of the 1920s for "elegant residential and business premises" etc. appear on many catalog pages. The following ranges are presented along with firms or trade-marks: Strasser dolls ("Plumpsi"), K. Kruse, "Ormond," Sigora, "Ulla," Casadora dolls able to move their eyes, walk and speak; "Muck" and "Bella," the "most exquisite" doll of all with moving limbs and rubber hands along with a great many more varieties in fashionable wear (the celluloid "Ormond" in silk costumes).

Accessories for dolls feature prominently: vessels made of tin and ceramics, dolls' prams, children's sewing machines, dolls' houses and dolls' rooms, puppet shows and kiosks. There are, in addition, numerous animal figures ranging from simple wooden ones (which can be pulled) to those supplied by M. Steiff and the plush and felt varieties, with moving parts, made by Schuco (founded in Nuremberg in 1912). The extensive range of Margarete Steiff includes not only animals but also other figures and footboard scooters.

Construction sets as developed by Fröbel, stone-structure packs of wood, Fröbel modelling sets, printing shops, all kinds of parlor games including cards, occupational games with diverse subjects serve to stimulate the child's own creativity. A novelty in 1926 was a building set for skyscrapers.

The home industry toy makers of the Erzgebirge attracted particular attention through their manufacture of very simple wooden toys: boats, miniature vehicles and figures, arks (in various designs) filled to the brim with rubber animals, box fillings (for instance, farmsteads) with turned figures and rubber animals and much more.

The horse and cart in various materials and extending from the rocking horse to a children's carriage drawn by real billy-goats still retains its hold.

Children's devices such as scooters, sports cycles, children's furniture sets, for example wooden chairs, as well as perambulators and cars for sitting in (with pedal mechanism) and sports equipment stimulate open air pursuits.

Military playthings are hardly in evidence: Hausser Elastolin markets "soldiers in all postures and of all nations," whilst tin soldiers and a few cannon serve to recall the war. "Eureka" rifles (with rubber darts) and pistols, "Diana" airguns and sports guns with banger corks and warning shots encourage the staging of sports contests. (The 1930 catalog features considerably more military playthings, an indication of the pending rearmament program).

The catalogs also contain a large selection of items which actually transcend the scope of toys proper: artificial Christmas figures with adornments and musical boxes, glass Christmas decorations, boxes of paints and pencils, tools for households and children, fretsaw collections, table decorations, novelties, cotillon and carnival articles ranging from toy-torpedoes to paper hats and caps, conjuring tricks and masks.

Postscript

It was not the intent of these notes to classify all items represented in the catalog according to firms and in chronological order. The absence of lists with the names of manufacturers and numbers for their collections (a numerical list is available for the subsequent 1930 issue, and a price-list for the 1928 volume) moreover, sources have been set out according to pages, however the makers' names are not indicated; the reason for this is the fragmentation of the German toy industry into a very great number of medium, small and microscopic units irrespective of the number of representations and the volume of toys. In addition, the extensive and relevant collectors' literature for individual firms, reference works on company signets and brands (dolls!), reprints of firms' catalogs etc. are a rich source for determining the subject matter of single companies. It was only possible to undertake a thesis-like comparison of the ranges in the 1924 and 1926 issues with those of the 1930 volume for, otherwise, the representations would also have had to be printed, and this would have transcended the permissible scope.

The bibliography only contains a selection of those titles possessing information, assertive historical and general value in terms of toys for the period under consideration. In this respect it augments the bibliography in the 1977 and 1979 reprints of the toy sample books. In processing volumes, I was again helped by a great many specialists. I am particularly indebted to Frau Dr. L. Bayer, director of the Spielzeugmuseum in Nuremberg who rendered exemplary assistance in my efforts to determine the publisher. I am equally grateful to Frau H. Bormann, Herr D. Bormann and Herr K. Bormann (Hamburg) who engaged in so much painstaking spade-work in bringing to light company documents. I must most sincerely thank the following for useful advice, hints and the procurement of material: Herr W. Steinacker (deceased) and Herr H. Schwarzmann, VEDES Nuremberg; Herr Meidenbauer, Nuremberg; Herr E. Riemer, Nuremberg; Frau M. Cieslik and Herr J. Cieslik, Jülich-Koslar; Herr M. Meisenbach, Bamberg; Herr P. Ulmer, Fürth Municipal Archive; the Broschek and Co. printers, Hamburg; Herr W. Schmidt, Spielzeugmuseum Nuremberg and Frau M. Weber-Beck, Spielzeugmuseum Zurich; H. Bilz, director of the Spielzeugmuseum Seiffen, whose untiring efforts yielded a great deal of material for comparisons. Above all, my gratitude is extended to H. Gauss, director of the Spielzeugmuseum Sonneberg who kindly placed at my disposal for reprinting the copy of the catalog in his collection. Last but not least, my thanks are due to Edition Leipzig Publishers whose responsible staff members did so much to ensure meticulous processing. Frau W. Damm and Frau M. Zimmer, Dresden, attended to the technical side.

I dedicate these notes to my deceased parents and parents-in-law who, as workers, were amongst the eight million unemployed (1932) during the years of the World Economic Recession. They were not in a position to enrich their children's early playing years with those toys, whose boundless creativity has been so aptly reflected in our catalog.

Dresden, Summer 1984 *Manfred Bachmann*

Annotations

The numbers in brackets refer to the bibliography.

[1] Municipal Archive in Nuremberg:
Municipal Chronicles, 2 February 1829, p. 115 f.

[2] Karl Ewald Fritzsch drew attention to the difficulties in determining conclusively bibliographical data. Cp. *Sächsische Heimatblätter* 1965, vol. 6, p. 501 f.

[3] Theo Gantner supplied a reprint in 1979. Cp. bibliography 26.

[4] Cp. Hans-Georg Soldat: *Die grossen Kataloge.* 10.7.1983/11.7.1983 (radio transmission, part IV: *Welt im Bild*).

[5] The prices indicate clearly that the toys on offer could only be purchased by the well-to-do strata. The *Landoeconomie im Kleinen*, illustrated by means of more than 40 miniature implements, cost 25 florin (gulden), which corresponded to twenty-five weeks' wages (!) of a miner in the Erzgebirge.

[6] J. G. Kohl [97], p. 45.

[7] Cp. in particular [26], [84] and [187].

[8] Cp. our reprint 1924 (preface).

[9] Recently Theo Gantner also expressly drew attention to this fact. Cp. [71].

[10] Walter Benjamin, [24], p. 65.

Bibliography

1 ANGELETTI, CHARLOTTE: *Geformtes Wachs. Kerzen, Votive, Wachsfiguren.* Munich, 1980.

2 ANKA, GEORGINE/URSULA GAUDER: *Die deutsche Puppenindustrie 1815–1940.* Stuttgart, 1978.

3 *Arbeiter, Kultur und Lebensweise im Königreich Württemberg* (Exhibition companion volume). Tübingen, 1976.

4 ARIÈS, PHILIPPE: *Geschichte der Kindheit.* Munich, 1975.

5 ARNDT, PAUL: *Heimarbeiterelend in Deutschland.* Jena, 1927.

6 ARNDT, PAUL: *Die wirtschaftliche und soziale Bedeutung der Heimarbeit.* Jena, [2] 1932.

7 BACHMANN, MANFRED/CLAUS HANSMANN: *Dolls the wide world over.* New York, 1977.

8 BACHMANN, MANFRED/REINHOLD LANGNER: *Berchtesgadener Volkskunst.* Leipzig 1957.

9 BACHMANN, MANFRED: *Holzspielzeug aus dem Erzgebirge.* Dresden, 1984.

10 BACHMANN, MANFRED: "Zur Geschichte der Seiffener Volkskunst." In: *Abhandlungen und Berichte des Staatlichen Museums für Völkerkunde Dresden*, Vol. 28. Berlin, 1968.

11 BACHMANN, MANFRED: "Zur Entwicklung der erzgebirgischen Holzschnitzerei."
In: *Abhandlungen und Berichte des Staatlichen Museums für Völkerkunde Dresden,* Vol. 22. Berlin, 1963.

12 BACHMANN, MANFRED: *Seiffener Spielzeugschnitzer.* Leipzig, 1956.

13 BACHMANN, MANFRED: "Die Widerspiegelung des Bergbaus in der traditionellen Holzschnitzerei des sächsischen Erzgebirges." In: *Arbeit und Volksleben.* Göttingen, 1967, p. 174 ff.

14 BACHMANN, MANFRED: "Das Zürcher Spielzeugmuseum." In: *du* (art magazine), Basel, 1982, issue 7, p. 4 ff.

15 BAECKER, CARLERNST J./BOTHO G. WAGNER: *Blechspielzeug Eisenbahnen* (Battenberg collectors' catalog). Munich, 1982.

16 BAECKER, CARLERNST J./CHRISTIAN VÄTERLEIN: *Vergessenes Blechspielzeug. Die Anderen Württemberger.* Frankfurt/M., 1982.

17 BAER, ULRICH: *Wörterbuch der Spielpädagogik.* Basel, 1981.

18 BALDET, MARCEL: *Von der Tonfigur zum Bleisoldaten. Die Welt in Miniaturen.* Düsseldorf, 1961.

19 BAYER, LYDIA: *Das Spielzeugmuseum der Stadt Nürnberg.* Nuremberg, 1978.

20 BAYER, LYDIA: "Altes Spielzeug." In: *Kaysers Kunst- und Antiquitätenbuch,* Munich, 1967, vol. III, p. 329 ff.

21 BAYER, LYDIA: "Puppenstube und Dampfmaschine." In: Hermann Glaser (ed.), *Industriekultur in Nürnberg.* Munich, 1980, p. 266 ff.

22 BECHER, UDO: *Als die Züge fahren lernten.* Berlin, 1982.

23 BECHER, UDO/WERNER REICHE: *Bodenläufer, Spielzeug, Supermodell.* Leipzig, 1982.

24 BENJAMIN, WALTER: *Über Kinder, Jugend und Erziehung.* Frankfurt/M., 1969.

25 BERGSCHICKER, HEINZ: *Deutsche Chronik 1933–1945. Ein Zeitbild der faschistischen Diktatur.* Berlin, 1981.

26 BESTELMEIER, GEORG HIERONIMUS: *Magazin von verschiedenen Kunst- und anderen nützlichen Sachen ... 1803.* Edited by Theo Gantner. Zurich, 1979 (Reprint).

27 BIERER, WILLY: *Die hausindustrielle Kinderarbeit im Kreise Sonneberg. Ein Beitrag zur Kritik des Kinderschutzgesetzes.* Tübingen, 1913.

28 BILZ, HELLMUT: *Die gesellschaftliche Stellung und soziale Lage der hausindustriellen Seiffener Spielzeugmacher im 19. und Anfang des 20. Jahrhunderts* (serial publication, issue 2). Seiffen, 1975.

29 BILZ, HELLMUT: *Das Reifendrehhandwerk im Spielwarengebiet Seiffen* (serial publication, issue 3). Seiffen, 1982.

30 BOEHN, MAX VON: *Puppen.* Munich, 1929.

31 BORMANN, HILDE/DIETER BORMANN: *Wilhelm Möller. John Hess Nachfolger. 1886–1961.* (Commemoration volume). Hamburg, 1961.

32 BRAUCH, MARGOT/ALBRECHT BANGERT: *Blechspielzeug. Mechanische Raritäten und ihre Hersteller.* Munich, 1980.

33 BRENTJES, BURCHARD/SIEGFRIED RICHTER/ROLF SONNEMANN: *Geschichte der Technik.* Leipzig, 1978.

34 BRÜTIGAM, HEINZ: *Faschismus an der Macht.* Frankfurt/M., 1982.

35 Catalog: *Spielzeug der bürgerlichen Zeit. Zeugnisse für Kindererziehung und Kinderarbeit.* Marburg, 1973/74.

36 Catalog: *Puppe, Fibel, Schiessgewehr. Das Kind im kaiserlichen Deutschland.* Berlin (West), 1977.

37 Catalog: *Kunst und Technik in den zwanziger Jahren.* Munich, 1980.

38 Catalog: *Die gesellschaftliche Wirklichkeit der Kinder in der bildenden Kunst.* Berlin (West), 1980.

39 Catalog: *Laterna Magica — Vergnügen — Belehrung — Unterhaltung — Der Projektionskünstler Paul Hofmann.* Historisches Museum Frankfurt/M., 1981.

40 Catalog: *Blechspielzeug der Firma E. P. Lehmann.* Kevelaer, 1982.

41 Catalog: *Spiel als Beispiel.* No place, 1982.

42 Catalog: *Spielzeugmuseum Michelstadt.* 1982.

43 Catalog reprint: *Weinheimer Auktionshaus: Ernst Plank, Nürnberg. Ausgabe E. P. 1903.* Weinheim, 1973.

44 Catalog reprint: Levy, Allen: *The great toys of Georges Carette — a trade catalogue for mechanical, optical and electrical teaching material toys first published by Georges Carette in 1911, with Supplement for 1905 and 1934.* London, 1975.

45 Catalog reprint: BAECKER CARLERNST/DIETER HAAS/CLAUDE JEANMAIRE: *Märklin-Technisches Spielzeug im Wandel der Zeit* (series, 12 vols. planned). Frankfurt/M., 1978 ff.

46 Catalog reprints: BAECKER, CARLERNST/DIETER HAAS: *Die anderen Nürnberger — Technisches Spielzeug aus der "guten alten Zeit"* (5 vols.). Frankfurt/M., 1973 ff.

47 Catalog reprints: JEANMAIRE, CLAUDE: *Bing, die Modellbahnen unserer Großväter,* Villingen, 1972.
Gebrüder Bing, die großen Nürnberger. Villingen, 1974.
Märklin — die großen Spurweiten. Villingen, 1969.
Nürnberger Spielzeug — Jean Schoenner. Spielzeugeisenbahnen und Schiffe. Villingen, 1977.

48 CIESLIK, JÜRGEN: *Blechspielzeug.* Munich, 1980.

49 CIESLIK, MARIANNE and JÜRGEN: *Blechspielzeug-Patente.* Vol. 1: *1878–1915.* Bad Honnef/Rhöndorf, 1977.

50 CIESLIK, MARIANNE and JÜRGEN: *Blechspielzeug-Patente.* Vol. 2: *1916–1940.* Jülich-Koslar, 1979.

51 CIESLIK, MARIANNE and JÜRGEN: *Silbernes Jubiläum einer Puppenfabrik. 25 Jahre Kämmer & Reinhardt, Waltershausen.* Bad Honnef/Rhöndorf, 1978 (Reprint of the commemoration volume of 1910).

52 CIESLIK, MARIANNE and JÜRGEN: *Puppenhandbuch.* Bad Honnef/Rhöndorf, 1976–1978.

53 CIESLIK, MARIANNE and JÜRGEN: *Puppen. Europäische Puppen 1800–1930.* Munich, 1979.

54 CIESLIK, MARIANNE and JÜRGEN: *Ein Jahrhundert Blechspielzeug. Ein Jahrhundert E. P. Lehmann.* Munich, 1981.

55 COLEMAN, DOROTHY, ELIZABETH and EVELYN: *The collector's Encyclopedia of dolls.* New York, 1968.

56 CULLF, ROBERT: *The world of Toys.* London, 1969.

57 *Das Waldkirchner Spielzeugmusterbuch. Neu herausgegeben und kommentiert von Manfred Bachmann (Die bibliophilen Taschenbücher Nr. 278).* Dortmund, 1981.

58 DORT, R. VAN/J. OEGEMA: *Handbuch Modell-Dampfmaschinen.* Villingen/Schwenningen, 1979.

59 DROBIK, ERWIN: *Chronik des Trachten-Puppen-Museums Neustadt bei Coburg.* Neustadt, 1980.

60 ESKONIN, D. B.: *Psychologie des Spiels* (Contributions on psychology, vol. 7). Berlin, 1980.

61 ESTELMANN, GEORG: *Die Nürnberger Spielwarenherstellung von den ältesten Zeiten bis zur Gegenwart.* Frankfurt/M., 1926.

62 FRASER, ANTONIA: *Spielzeug.* Oldenburg/Hamburg, 1966.

63 FRENZEL, ROSE-MARIE: *Beim Spiel.* Leipzig, 1977.

64 FRICK, FELIX: *Franz Carl Weber. Wegbereiter zum europäischen Spielwarenfachhandel.* Zurich, 1983.

65 FRIEBE, WOLFGANG: *Building of the World Exhibitions.* Leipzig, 1985.

66 FRITZSCH, KARL-EWALD: "Erzgebirgische Spielzeugmusterbücher." In: *Deutsches Jahrbuch für Volkskunde.* Berlin, 1958, vol. IV, p. 91 ff.

67 FRITZSCH, KARL-EWALD: "Haus, Siedlung und bäuerliche Arbeit im

Spielzeugmodell." In: *Sächsische Heimatblätter*. Dresden, 1968, issue 6, p. 268 ff.
68 Fritzsch, Karl-Ewald: "Die Arche." In: *Sächsische Heimatblätter*. 22/1976, issue 6. p. 250 ff.
69 Fritzsch, Karl-Ewald/Manfred Bachmann: *An illustrated history of toys*. London, 1978.
70 Fugmann, Ernst R.: *Der Sonneberger Wirtschaftsraum*. Halle, 1939.
71 Gantner, Theo/Waltraud Hartmann: *Das Spielzeugbuch*. Frankfurt/M./Innsbruck, 1973.
72 Gantner, Theo: *Die verkleinerte Welt. Abbild — Modell — Spielzeug* (Papers for the press). Basel, 1977.
73 Gantner, Theo: *Truhen und Kästchen* (Catalog). Basel, 1981.
74 Gebhard, Torsten: "Warenmusterkataloge." In: *Bayerisches Jahrbuch für Volkskunde 1972–1975*, Volkach, 1975, p. 213 f.
75 Glaser, Hermann: *Maschinenwelt und Alltagsleben. Industriekultur in Deutschland vom Biedermeier bis zur Weimarer Republik*. Frankfurt/M., 1981.
76 Glaser, Hermann: *Industriekultur in Nürnberg. Eine deutsche Stadt im Maschinenzeitalter*. Munich, 1980.
77 Glonneger, Erwin: *Schöne alte Spiele* (Exhibition companion volume). Ravensburg, 1983.
78 Greilsamer, J./B. Azema: *Catalogue of Model Cars of the World*. London, 1967.
79 Gröber, Karl: *Kinderspielzeug aus alter Zeit*. Berlin, 1927.
80 Gröber, Karl: *Alte Oberammergauer Hauskunst*. Rosenheim, ^{2}1980.
81 Gürge, W.: *Die deutsche Spielwarenindustrie, ihre Entwicklung in der Nachkriegszeit und ihre wirtschaftlichen Beziehungen*. Frankfurt/M., 1924.
82 Hamilton, Ellis: *Model Railways 1838–1939*. London, 1962.
83 Herré, Florence (ed.): *Geschichte der deutschen Frauenbewegung*. Cologne, ^{2}1982.
84 Hessler, August: *Die Entwicklung des Nürnberger Wirtschaftslebens*. Würzburg, 1928.
85 Hillier, Mary: *Automata and Mechanical Toys*. London, 1976.
86 Himmelheber, Georg: *Kleine Möbel. Modell-, Andachts- und Kassettenmöbel vom 13.–20. Jahrhundert*. Munich, 1979.
87 Hinrichsen, Torkild: *Spielzeug* (Battenberg antiques catalog). Munich, 1980.
88 Holme, C. Geoffrey: *Children's toys of yesterday*. New York, 1932.
89 *Homo ludens* (Commemoration volume on the jubilee of the F.-C.-Weber-group). Zurich, 1981.
90 Hoppe, Ruth: *Dokumente zur Geschichte der Lage des arbeitenden Kindes in Deutschland von 1700 bis zur Gegenwart*. Berlin, 1969.
91 Huber, Rudger: *Blechspielzeug. Autos – Motorräder*. (Battenberg-collectors' catalog). Munich, 1982.
92 Kaiser, Wolf/Carlernst Baecker: *Blechspielzeug – Dampfspielzeug* (Battenberg collectors' catalog). Munich, 1983.
93 Kanitz, Otto E.: *Das proletarische Kind in der bürgerlichen Gesellschaft*. Frankfurt/M., 1974.
94 Keil, Otto: "Aus alten Spielzeugmusterbüchern." In: *Gebrauchsgraphik*. Issue 12, 1960, p. 34 ff.
95 Kerler, Christine/Gertrud Rosemann: *Trachtenpuppen aus aller Welt*. Rosenheim, 1980.
96 Könneker, Marie-Luise (ed.): *Kinderschaukel. Ein Lesebuch zur Geschichte der Kindheit in Deutschland*.
Vol. 1: 1745–1860
Vol. 2: 1860–1930.
97 Kohl, J. G.: *Reisen im südöstlichen Deutschland*. 1852.
98 Kruse, Käthe: *Ich und meine Puppen*. Freiburg/B., 1982.
99 Kuczynski, Jürgen: *Studien zur Geschichte der Lage des arbeitenden Kindes in Deutschland von 1700 bis zur Gegenwart*. Berlin, 1968.
100 Kuczynski, Jürgen: *Geschichte des Alltags des deutschen Volkes 1918–1945* (studies 5). Berlin, 1982.
101 Kuczynski, Jürgen: *Darstellung der Lage der Arbeiter in Deutschland von 1917/18 bis 1932/33*. Berlin, 1966.
102 Kulischer, Josef: *Allgemeine Wirtschaftsgeschichte des Mittelalters und der Neuzeit*. (2 vols.). Berlin, 1954.
103 Kutschera, Volker: *Spielzeug. Spiegelbild der Kulturgeschichte*. Salzburg, 1975.
104 Langbein, Werner: *Die wirtschaftliche Organisation der Sonneberger Spielwarenindustrie*. Cologne, 1923.
105 Lebermann, Karl: *Die Konzentration der Bingwerke Nürnberg (Wirtschafts- und Verwaltungsstudien, mit bedingter Berücksichtigung Bayerns)*. Edited by Dr. Georg Schwarz. Leipzig/Erlangen, 1924.
106 Lindenberg, Fritz: *Heimarbeit in der Spielzeugindustrie des oberen Erzgebirges*. Leipzig, 1936.
107 Ludwig-Lazina, S.: *Die Sonneberger Spielwarenindustrie*. Frankfurt/M., 1928.
108 Mara, Wolfgang: *Absatzbedingungen und Absatzgestaltung der deutschen Spielwarenwirtschaft*. Leipzig, 1940.
109 Martin, Paul: *Der standhafte Zinnsoldat. Bunte Welt aus Zinn und Blei*. Stuttgart, 1961.
110 Mausbach, Hans/Barbara Mausbach-Bromberger: *Feinde des Lebens. NS-Verbrechen an Kindern*. Frankfurt/M., 1979.
111 Meyfarth, Brunhild: *Die Sonneberger Spielzeugmacher. Zu den Arbeits- und Lebensbedingungen der Sonneberger Spielzeugmacher Ende des 19. und Anfang des 20. Jahrhunderts*. Sonneberg, 1981.
112 Mieskes, Hans: *Kriegsspielzeug und matriarchalischer Geist*. Bamberg, 1981.
113 Mottek, Hans/Walter Becker/Alfred Schröter: *Wirtschaftsgeschichte Deutschlands. Ein Grundriss* (Vol. III). Berlin, 1975.
114 Moser-Rath, Elfriede (ed.): *Lirum Larum Löffelstiel, wer mischt mit beim Kinderspiel?* Göttingen, 1979.
115 Nussbaum, Manfred: *Wirtschaft und Staat in Deutschland während der Weimarer Republik*. Berlin, 1978.
116 Pätzold, Kurt: "Von der Vertreibung zum Genozid. Zu den Ursachen, Triebkräften und Bedingungen der antijüdischen Politik des faschistischen deutschen Imperialismus." In: *Faschismusforschung Positionen – Probleme – Polemik*. Berlin, 1980, p. 182 ff.
117 Pätzold, Kurt (ed.): *Verfolgung – Vertreibung – Vernichtung. Dokumente des faschistischen Antisemitismus um 1933–1942*. Leipzig, 1983.
118 Petzold, Joachim: *Die Demagogie des Hitlerfaschismus*. Berlin, 1982.
119 Pieske, Christa: *Schönes Spielzeug aus alten Nürnberger Musterbüchern*. Munich, 1979.
120 Pinon, Roger: "Probleme einer europäischen Kinderspielforschung." In: *Hessische Blätter für Volkskunde*. Vol. 58. Giessen, 1967.
121 Polaine, Reggie: *Spielzeugsoldaten*. No. 1: *Die Geschichte von Hausser-Elastolin*. Neustadt near Coburg, no year.
122 Poliakov, Léon/Josef Wulf: *Das Dritte Reich und seine Diener. Dokumente*. Berlin, 1975.
123 Pressland, David: *Die Kunst des Blechspielzeugs*. Zurich, 1976.
124 *Puppen und Spielzeug*. Magazine, edited by Ursula Gander-Bonnet. Stuttgart, 1976 ff.
125 Reder, Gustav: *Mit Uhrwerk, Dampf und Strom*. Düsseldorf, 1970.
126 Reher, Uwe: "Technisches Spielzeug." In: *Volkskunst*. Munich, 1979, issue 4, p. 214 ff.
127 Reher, Uwe: *Eisenbahnspielzeug*. Frankfurt/M./Villingen, 1977.
128 Reible, Karl: *Die deutsche Spielwarenindustrie, ihre Entwicklung und ihr gegenwärtiger Stand*. Giessen, 1925.
129 Remise, Jac/Jean Fondin: *The Golden Age of Toys*. Lausanne, 1967.
130 Retter, Hein: *Spielzeug, Handbuch zur Geschichte und Pädagogik der Spielmittel*. Weinheim/Basel, 1979.
131 Rilke, Rainer Maria/Lotte Pritzel: *Puppen*. Munich, 1922.
132 Röder, Ludwig: *Heimarbeit in der Landwirtschaft*. Jena, 1925.
133 Roer, Hans H.: *Bleisoldaten*. Munich, 1981.
134 Röhrich, Lutz: "Noah und die Arche in der Volkskunst." In: *Volkskunde* (Commemoration volume for Leopold Schmidt). Vienna, 1972, p. 433 ff.
135 Rogers, Carole: *Penny Banks*. New York, 1977.
136 Rosenhaupt, Karl: *Die Nürnberg-Fürther Metallspielwarenindustrie in geschichtlicher und sozialpolitischer Beleuchtung*. Stuttgart, 1907.
137 Rubinstein, Hilde/Lydia Bayer: *Nachdenken über Spielsachen*. Nuremberg, 1973.
138 Rüder, Peter von/Kurt Koszyk: *Dokumente und Materialien zur Kulturgeschichte der deutschen Arbeiterbewegung 1848–1918*. Frankfurt/M., 1979.
139 Ruge, Wolfgang: *Deutschland 1917–1933. Beiträge*. Berlin, 1967.
140 Ruge, Wolfgang: *Weimar – Republik auf Zeit*. Berlin, 1980.
141 Schelling, Walter: *Die sächsisch-erzgebirgische Holzwarenindustrie seit dem Ausbruch des Weltkrieges*. Leipzig, 1935.

142 SCHICKELE, RENÉ: *Das Puppenbuch.* Berlin, 1921.
143 SCHIFFMANN, RENÉ: *Die Welt im Blechspielzeug* (Catalog). Riehen, 1978.
144 SCHMITZ, GERHARD: *Wohnung – Siedlung – Lebensweise. Aus Werken und Briefen von Karl Marx und Friedrich Engels.* Berlin, ²1982.
145 SIMON, M.: *Die thüringische Heimarbeit in der Wirtschaftskrise.* Leipzig, 1937.
146 SÖHLKE, G.: *Illustrierter Catalog und Preis-Courant von Kinder-Spiel-Waaren.* Berlin, 1858.
147 SOMBART, WERNER: "Hausindustrie (Verlagssystem)." In: *Handwörterbuch der Staatswissenschaften.* Jena, 1923, 5th vol., p. 179 ff.
148 *Spielmittel.* Magazine, edited by Werner Nostheide. Bamberg, 1981 ff.
149 STÄBLEIN, RITA: *Altes Holzspielzeug aus Gröden.* Bozen, 1980.
150 STENBOCK-FERMOR, GRAF ALEXANDER: *Deutschland von unten. Reisen durch die proletarische Provinz 1930.* (Reprint). Lucerne/Frankfurt/M., 1980.
151 STEPHAN, ARTUR: *Der Absatz der Erzeugnisse der deutschen Spielwarenindustrie unter besonderer Berücksichtigung der Verhältnisse in der Nachkriegszeit.* Halle, 1924.
152 STORDEUR, ROCHUS: *Spielzeug in Schleusingen.* Sonneberg, 1974.
153 STREISAND, JOACHIM: *Deutsche Geschichte in einem Band.* Berlin, ⁵1980.
154 STURM-GODRAMSTEIN, HEINZ: *Kinderwagen gestern und heute.* Oberursel, no year.
155 SY, MARGARETE: *Die Thüringer Spielwarenindustrie im Kampf um ihre Existenz.* Jena, 1929.
156 Team of authors: *1880–1980 Geschichte und Gegenwart einer Marke.* (Commemoration volume of the Steiff GmbH). Giengen/Brenz, 1980.
157 Team of authors: *1883–1983. 100 Jahre Verlagsarbeit. Otto-Maier-Verlag.* Ravensburg, 1983.
158 Team of authors: *"Das war ein Vorspiel nur ..." Bücherverbrennung Deutschland 1933: Voraussetzungen und Folgen.* Berlin (West), 1983.
159 Team of authors: *50 Jahre im Spiel* (Commemoration volume of the Lego group). Billund, 1982.
160 Team of authors: *Geschichte der Erziehung.* Berlin, 1969.
161 Team of authors: *Die Welt aus Blech. Mechanisches Spielzeug aus zwei Jahrhunderten* (Publication on the exhibition in the Stadtmuseum Munich, 1981). Mainz, 1981.
162 Team of authors: *Handbuch der Wirtschaftsgeschichte.* 2 vols. Berlin, 1981
163 Team of authors: *Juden in Preussen. Ein Kapitel deutscher Geschichte (Die bibliophilen Taschenbücher No. 259/260).* Dortmund, ⁴1983.
164 Team of authors: *Klassenkampf-Tradition-Sozialismus. (Grundriss).* Berlin, 1974.
165 Team of authors: *Naziterror gegen Kinder 1933–1945.* (Catalog). Frankfurt/M., 1981.
166 Team of authors: *Quellen zur Geschichte der Erziehung.* Berlin, 1968.
167 Team of authors: *Sachwörterbuch der Geschichte Deutschlands und der deutschen Arbeiterbewegung.* 2 vols. Berlin, 1969/1970.
168 Team of authors: *Spielzeug.* Leipzig, 1958.
169 Team of authors: *Spielzeug zum Spielen. Beiträge zu Kriterien für gutes Spielzeug.* Berlin, 1980.
170 Team of authors: *Spielzeug gestern und heute.* Sonneberg, 1981.
171 Team of authors: *Sammlung zur Alltags- und Industriekultur. Ein Standortverzeichnis.* Berlin (West), 1983.
172 Team of authors: *Wirtschaftsgeschichte. Ein Leitfaden.* Berlin, 1980.
173 Team of authors: *Zur Geschichte der Arbeitserziehung in Deutschland.* Part 1: *Von den Anfängen bis 1900.* Berlin, 1970.
Part 2: *Von 1900 bis zur Gegenwart.* Berlin, 1971.
174 Team of authors: *Zur Geschichte der Kultur und Lebensweise der werktätigen Klassen und Schichten des deutschen Volkes vom 11. Jahrhundert bis 1945.* Berlin, 1972.
175 Team of authors: *Zwischen Rennsteig und Sonneberg (Werte unserer Heimat.* Vol. 39). Berlin, 1983.
176 *The toy sample book of Sonneberg of 1831.* New ed. with notices by Manfred Bachmann. Leipzig, 1979. (Reprint).
177 *The toy sample book of Waldkirchen.* New ed. with notices by Manfred Bachmann. New York, 1978 (Reprint).
178 Vedes e.G.: *Festschrift 75 Jahre Vereinigung der Spielwaren-Fachgeschäfte e.G. Nürnberg.* Nuremberg, 1979.
179 Vedes e.G.: *Vedes-Ratgeber.* Nuremberg.
180 Vedes GmbH: *Warenkataloge.* Nuremberg.
181 VOGEL, HEINER: *Bilderbogen und Würfelspiel. Volkstümliche Graphik für Kinder und Papierspielzeug von den Anfängen bis ins 19. Jahrhundert.* Leipzig, 1981.
182 VOLK, GUDRUN: *Kinderarbeit in der Spielzeugindustrie des Kreises Sonneberg in der Zeit zwischen der Novemberrevolution und dem Ausbruch des zweiten Weltkrieges und ihre Auswirkungen auf die Lebensweise der Kinder.* Berlin, 1977.
183 WEBER-KELLERMANN, INGEBORG: "Spielzeugbefragung. Überlegungen anlässlich einer Marburger Ausstellung Spielzeug als Indikator eines sozialen Systems." In: *Zeitschrift für Volkskunde,* Stuttgart 1974, vol. 70, part II, pp. 194–209.
184 WEBER-KELLERMANN, INGEBORG: *Die Familie.* Frankfurt/M., 1976.
185 WEBER-KELLERMANN, INGEBORG: *Das Weihnachtsfest. Eine Kultur- und Sozialgeschichte der Weihnachtszeit.* Lucerne/Frankfurt/M., 1978.
186 WEBER-KELLERMANN, INGEBORG: *Die Kindheit.* Frankfurt/M., 1979.
187 WENZEL, GEORG: *Die Geschichte der Nürnberger Spielzeugindustrie.* Erlangen/Nuremberg, 1967.
188 WHITE, GWEN: *European and American Dolls and their marks and patents.* London, 1966.
189 WHITE, GWEN: *Antique Toys and their background.* London, 1971.
190 WHITE, GWEN: *Toys, Dolls, Automata, Marks and Labels.* London/Sydney, 1975.
191 WIEDERHOLZ, H.: *Die Wandlungen in den Absatz- und Erzeugungsbedingungen der deutschen Spielwarenindustrie.* Brandenburg, 1931.
192 WILLMANN, HEINZ: *Geschichte der Arbeiter-Illustrierten Zeitung 1921–1938.* Berlin, 1974.
193 WINKLER, JOHANNES: *Entwicklung und Lage der Holzspielwarenindustrie des sächsischen Erzgebirges in den beiden letzten Jahrzehnten.* Halle–Wittenberg, 1935.
194 WUNDERLICH, FRIEDA: *Die deutsche Heimarbeitsausstellung 1925.* Jena, 1927.
195 WUSSING, HANS (ed.): *Geschichte der Naturwissenschaften.* Leipzig, 1983.

Sources of representations

We express our thanks for the provision of the comparative representations to Lydia Bayer, Nuremberg, Jürgen and Marianne Cieslik, Jülich-Koslar and the Spielzeugmuseum in Sonneberg.

Note: The commentary was shortened by request of Hobby House Press.
The German edition of Edition Leipzig Publishers contains the unabridged version.